ELEVENTH EDITION

Psychology Applied to Modern Life

ADJUSTMENT IN THE 21ST CENTURY

WAYNE WEITEN
University of Nevada, Las Vegas

DANA S. DUNN
Moravian College

ELIZABETH YOST HAMMER
Xavier University of Louisiana

CENGAGE
Learning·

Australia • Brazil • Mexico • Singapore • United Kingdom • United States

Psychology Applied to Modern Life, **Eleventh Edition**
Wayne Weiten, Dana S. Dunn, Elizabeth Yost Hammer

Product Director: Jon-David Hague

Product Manager: Timothy Matray

Content Developer: Trina McManus

Content Coordinator: Paige Leeds

Product Assistant: Nicole Richards

Media Developer: Jasmin Tokatlian

Marketing Manager: Jennifer Levanduski

Content Project Manager: Jennifer Risden

Art Director: Vernon Boes

Manufacturing Planner: Karen Hunt

Rights Acquisitions Specialist: Dean Dauphinais

Production Service and Layout: Joan Keyes, Dovetail
Publishing Services

Photo Researcher: PremediaGlobal

Text Researcher: PremediaGlobal

Copy Editor: Jackie Estrada

Illustrator: Carol Zuber-Mallison; Dovetail Publishing
Services

Text Designer: Liz Harasymczuk

Cover Designer: Irene Morris

Cover Image: *The Psychology of Love* by Jennifer Main

Design Images: Jennifer Main; film reels: Magictorch/
Photographer's Choice RF/Getty Images; sphere with
pictures over a white background: Joel Calheiros/
Shutterstock.com; Row of color books with mobile
phone on white background: Mmaxer/Shutterstock.com

Compositor: Graphic World, Inc.

For product information and technology assistance, contact us at
Cengage Learning Customer & Sales Support, 1-800-354-9706.
For permission to use material from this text or product, submit all
requests online at **www.cengage.com/permissions.**
Further permissions questions can be e-mailed to
permissionrequest@cengage.com.

Library of Congress Control Number: 2013948833

ISBN-13: 978-1-285-45995-0

ISBN-10: 1-285-45995-4

Cengage Learning
200 First Stamford Place, 4th Floor
Stamford, CT 06902
USA

Cengage Learning is a leading provider of customized learning
solutions with office locations around the globe, including Singapore,
the United Kingdom, Australia, Mexico, Brazil, and Japan. Locate your
local office at **www.cengage.com/global.**

Cengage Learning products are represented in Canada by
Nelson Education, Ltd.

To learn more about Cengage Learning Solutions,
visit **www.cengage.com.**

Purchase any of our products at your local college store or at our
preferred online store **www.cengagebrain.com.**

Printed in the United States of America
1 2 3 4 5 6 7 17 16 15 14 13

*To two pillars of stability in this era
of turmoil—my parents*
W.W.

For Sarah
D.S.D.

*To Kristin Habashi Whitlock, one of my
favorite psychology teachers*
E.Y.H.

ABOUT THE AUTHORS

WAYNE WEITEN is a graduate of Bradley University and received his Ph.D. in social psychology from the University of Illinois, Chicago, in 1981. He currently teaches at the University of Nevada, Las Vegas. He has received distinguished teaching awards from Division 2 of the American Psychological Association (APA) and the College of Du-Page, where he taught until 1991. He is a fellow of Divisions 1 and 2 of the American Psychological Association. In 1991, he helped chair the APA National Conference on Enhancing the Quality of Undergraduate Education in Psychology and in 1996–1997 he served as president of the Society for the Teaching of Psychology. In 2006, one of the five national teaching awards given annually by the Society for the Teaching of Psychology was named in his honor. Weiten has conducted research on a wide range of topics, including educational measurement, jury decision making, attribution theory, stress, and cerebral specialization. He is also the author of *Psychology: Themes & Variations* (Wadsworth, 2013) and the creator of *PsykTrek: A Multimedia Introduction to Psychology*.

DANA S. DUNN earned his B.A. in psychology from Carnegie Mellon University and received his Ph.D. in social psychology from the University of Virginia. He is currently professor of psychology and assistant dean for special projects at Moravian College in Bethlehem, PA. A past chair of Moravian's Psychology Department, Dunn is a fellow of Divisions 1, 2, and 22 of the American Psychological Association (APA) and the Association for Psychological Science (APS). Dunn served as the president of the Society for the Teaching of Psychology (APA Division 2) in 2010. A frequent speaker at national and regional disciplinary conferences, Dunn has written numerous articles, chapters, and book reviews concerning his research interests: the teaching of psychology, social psychology, rehabilitation psychology, and educational assessment. He is the author or editor of seventeen books, including *The Practical Researcher* (2013), *Research Methods for Social Psychology* (2013), and *A Short Guide to Writing about Psychology* (2011). Dunn was the 2013 recipient of the American Psychological Foundation's Charles L. Brewer Award for Distinguished Teaching of Psychology.

ELIZABETH YOST HAMMER earned her B.S. in psychology from Troy State University and received her Ph.D. in experimental social psychology from Tulane University. She is currently Kellogg Professor in Teaching in the Psychology Department and director of the Center for the Advancement of Teaching (CAT) at Xavier University of Louisiana in New Orleans. Her work in CAT includes organizing pedagogical workshops and faculty development initiatives. She is a fellow of Division 2 of the American Psychological Association (APA) and is a past president of Psi Chi, the International Honor Society in Psychology. She has served as the treasurer for the Society for the Teaching of Psychology. She is passionate about teaching and has published on collaborative learning, service learning, the application of social psychological theories to the classroom, and mentoring students.

TO THE INSTRUCTOR

Many students enter adjustment courses with great expectations. They've ambled through their local bookstores, and in the "Psychology" section they've seen numerous self-help books that offer highly touted recipes for achieving happiness for a mere $15.95. After paying far more money to enroll in a college course that deals with the same issues as the self-help books, many students expect a revelatory experience. However, the majority of us with professional training in psychology or counseling take a rather dim view of self-help books and the pop psychology they represent. Psychologists tend to see this literature as oversimplified, intellectually dishonest, and opportunistic and often summarily dismiss the pop psychology that so many students have embraced. Instructors try to supplant pop psychology with more sophisticated academic psychology based on current scholarship, which is more complex and less accessible.

In this textbook, we have tried to come to grips with the problem of differing expectations between student and teacher. Our goal has been to produce a comprehensive, serious, research-oriented treatment of the topic of adjustment that also acknowledges the existence of popular psychology and looks critically at its contributions. Our approach involves the following:

- In Chapter 1 we confront the phenomenon of popular self-help books. We take students beneath the seductive surface of such books and analyze some of their typical flaws. Our goal is to make students more critical consumers of this type of literature by encouraging them to focus on substance, not on trendy claims.

- While encouraging a more critical attitude toward self-help books, we do not suggest that all should be dismissed. Instead, we acknowledge that some of them offer authentic insights. With this in mind, we highlight some of the better books in this genre in Recommended Reading boxes sprinkled throughout the text. These recommended books tie in with the adjacent topical coverage and show the student the interface between academic and popular psychology. Additional Recommended Reading boxes can be found in the CourseMate for this text (www.cengagebrain.com).

- We try to provide the student with a better appreciation of the merits of the empirical approach to understanding behavior. This effort to clarify the role of research, which is rare for an adjustment text, appears in the first chapter.

- Recognizing that adjustment students want to leave the course with concrete, personally useful information, we end each chapter with an application section. The Applications are "how to" discussions that address everyday problems students encounter. While they focus on issues that are relevant to the content of the particular chapter, they contain more explicit advice than the text proper.

In summary, we have tried to make this book both challenging and applied. We hope that our approach will help students better appreciate the value and use of scientific psychology.

Philosophy

A certain philosophy is inherent in any systematic treatment of the topic of adjustment. Our philosophy can be summarized as follows:

- We believe that an adjustment text should be a resource book for students. We have tried to design this book so that it encourages and facilitates the pursuit of additional information on adjustment-related topics. It should serve as a point of departure for more learning.

- We believe in theoretical eclecticism. This book will not indoctrinate your students along the lines of any single theoretical orientation. The psychodynamic, behavioral, and humanistic schools of thought are all treated with respect, as are cognitive, biological, cultural, evolutionary, and other perspectives.

- We believe that effective adjustment requires taking charge of one's own life. Throughout the book we try to promote the notion that active coping efforts are generally superior to passivity and complacency.

Changes in the Eleventh Edition

One of the exciting things about psychology is that it is not a stagnant discipline. It continues to progress at what seems a faster and faster pace. A good textbook must evolve with the discipline. Although the professors and students who used the earlier editions of this book did not clamor for change, we have made countless content changes to keep up with new developments in psychology—adding and deleting some topics, condensing and reorganizing others, and updating everything (there are over 1100 new references). A brief overview of some of these changes, listed chapter-by-chapter, can be found on pages viii–xii following this preface.

The most significant change in this edition is the addition of what we call Reel Research, a box feature with a video link to psychological research related to each chapter's content. Using the publisher's vast video collection, we have made connections between studies captured on camera with important concepts in each chapter. The videos discuss relevant research topics, and the Reel Research feature includes a brief description of the study or studies and researchers involved, an explanation of how it relates to the chapter's concepts, and three discussion questions. Instructors can use these questions for class discussion or as homework assignments. Students will be able to access the videos through the CourseMate for this text. Here are some of the Reel Research topics:

- Online Relationships
- Emotions, Cortisol, and Immune Response
- Resilience in Children
- Suspicion and the Minnesota Trust Game
- Sexual Prejudice in America
- Stereotype Threat and Test Performance
- Understanding Addiction

We believe that the topical research included in the Reel Research features will provide students with an engaging introduction to how psychological research related to adjustment issues is conducted.

This new edition also has a new look in terms of the book's design and layout. A new color scheme and graphic design have been created for the chapters. Instructors who know the book will notice that quite a few new figures have been added and that many familiar ones have been updated to resonate with the book's new look. A variety of new, eye-catching photos are also integrated into each chapter, where they are placed to reflect the subject matter reviewed in the text.

As already noted, we incorporated many new research citations into this edition in order to represent the expansion of the psychological literature since the previous edition went to print. At the same time, we were mindful about the problem posed to student readers when they are confronted with too many citations. Thus, at the same time we added new references, we carefully culled many older ones to control the density of citations.

What hasn't changed? The ordering of the chapters in this edition matches the previous one. That said, we write our chapters to be largely self-contained so that you can assign them in virtually any order you like. The *Personal Explorations Workbook* again appears at the back of the text, following the references and indexes. Instructors have the option of having students complete workbook exercises and tear them out (they are printed on perforated paper) for submission as homework. The appendix on the timely issue of sustainability was also retained for this edition. It explains how sustainability depends on changes in individuals' behavior more than any other single factor. It focuses on the cognitive and behavioral processes that tend to impede environmentally responsible behavior, as well as the alterations in behavior that will be necessary to sustain the world's natural resources for future generations.

Writing Style

This book has been written with the student in mind. We have tried to integrate the technical jargon of our discipline into a relatively informal and down-to-earth writing style. We use concrete examples extensively to clarify complex concepts and to help maintain student interest. Although we now have three authors, the original author of this book (Wayne Weiten) continues to do the final rewrite of all sixteen chapters to ensure stylistic consistency.

Features

This text contains a number of features intended to stimulate interest and enhance students' learning. These special features include the aforementioned Reel Research boxes, Applications, Recommended Reading boxes, Learn More Online, Practice Tests, a didactic illustration program, and cartoons.

Applications

The end-of-chapter Applications should be of special interest to most students. They are tied to chapter content in a way that should show students how practical applications emerge out of theory and research. Although some of the material covered in these sections shows up frequently in adjustment texts, much of it is unique. Some of the Applications include the following:

- Understanding Intimate Partner Violence
- Improving Academic Performance
- Understanding Eating Disorders
- Getting Ahead in the Job Game
- Building Self-Esteem
- Enhancing Sexual Relationships
- Boosting Your Own Happiness

Recommended Reading Boxes

Recognizing students' interest in self-help books, we have sifted through hundreds of them to identify some that may be especially useful. These books are featured in boxes that briefly review some of the higher-quality books, several of which were published recently. These Recommended Reading boxes are placed where they are germane to the material being covered in the text. Some of the recommended books are well known, while others are less so. Although we make it clear that we don't endorse every idea in every book, we think they all have something worthwhile to offer. This feature replaces the conventional suggested readings lists that usually appear at the ends of chapters, where they are almost universally ignored by students.

Learn More Online

The Internet is rapidly altering the landscape of modern life, and students clearly need help dealing with the information explosion in cyberspace. To assist them, we recruited web expert Vincent Hevern (Le Moyne College) to evaluate hundreds of psychology- and adjustment-related sites and to come up with some recommendations that appear to provide reasonably accurate, balanced, and empirically sound information. Short descriptions of these recommended Learn

More Online websites are dispersed throughout the chapters, adjacent to related topical coverage. Because URLs change frequently, we have not included them in the book. Insofar as students are interested in visiting these sites, we recommend that they do so through the CourseMate for this text at www.cengagebrain.com. Links to all the recommended websites are maintained there, and the Cengage webmaster periodically updates the URLs. Of course, students can also use search engines such as Google to locate the recommended websites.

Practice Tests

Each chapter ends with a ten-item multiple-choice Practice Test that should give students a fairly realistic assessment of their mastery of that chapter and valuable practice in taking the type of test that many of them will face in the classroom (if the instructor uses the Test Bank). This feature grew out of some research on students' use of textbook pedagogical devices (see Weiten, Guadagno, & Beck, 1996). This research indicated that students pay scant attention to some standard pedagogical devices. When students were grilled to gain a better understanding of this perplexing finding, it quickly became apparent that students are pragmatic about pedagogy. Essentially, their refrain was, "We want study aids that will help us pass the next test." With this mandate in mind, we added the Practice Tests. They should be very realistic, as many of the items came from the Test Banks for previous editions (these items do not appear in the Test Bank for the current edition). Additional practice tests can be found in the CourseMate for this text at www.cengagebrain.com.

Didactic Illustration Program

The illustration program is once again in full color, and as already noted, many new figures have been added along with extensive redrawing of many graphics. Although the illustrations are intended to make the book attractive and to help maintain student interest, they are not merely decorative: They have been carefully selected and crafted for their didactic value to enhance the educational goals of the text.

Cartoons

A little comic relief usually helps keep a student interested, so we've sprinkled numerous cartoons throughout the book. Like the figures, most of these have been chosen to reinforce ideas in the text.

Personal Explorations Workbook

As mentioned earlier, the *Personal Explorations Workbook* can be found in the very back of the text. It contains experiential exercises for each text chapter, designed to help your students achieve personal insights. For each chapter, we have included one Self-Assessment exercise and one Self-Reflection exercise. The self-assessments are psychological tests or scales that students can take and score for themselves. The self-reflections consist of questions intended to help students think about themselves in relation to issues raised in the text. These exercises can be invaluable homework assignments. To facilitate assigning them as homework, we have printed the workbook section on perforated paper, so students can tear out the relevant pages and turn them in. In addition to providing easy-to-use homework assignments, many of these exercises can be used in class to stimulate lively discussion.

Learning Aids

A number of learning aids have been incorporated into the text to help the reader digest the wealth of material:

- The *outline* at the beginning of each chapter provides the student with a preview and overview of what will be covered.
- *Headings* are used extensively to keep material well organized.
- To help alert your students to key points, *learning objectives* are distributed throughout the chapters, after the level-1 headings.
- *Key terms* are identified with **blue italicized boldface** type to indicate that these are important vocabulary items that are part of psychology's technical language.
- An *integrated running glossary* provides an on-the-spot definition of each key term as it is introduced in the text. These formal definitions are printed in **blue boldface** type.
- An *alphabetical glossary* is found in the back of the book, as key terms are usually defined in the integrated running glossary only when they are first introduced.
- *Italics* are used liberally throughout the text to emphasize important points.
- A *chapter review* is found at the end of each chapter. Each review includes a concise but thorough summary of the chapter's key ideas, a list of the key terms that were introduced in the chapter, and a list of important theorists and researchers who were discussed in the chapter.

Supplementary Materials

A complete teaching/learning package has been developed to supplement *Psychology Applied to Modern Life*. These supplementary materials have been carefully coordinated to provide effective support for the text.

Instructor's Manual

The *Instructor's Manual* is available as a convenient aid for your educational endeavors. It provides a thorough overview of each chapter and includes a wealth of suggestions for lecture topics, class demonstrations, exercises, and discussion questions, organized around the content of each chapter in the text.

Test Bank

The *Test Bank,* revised by Joan Thomas-Spiegel of Los Angeles Harbor College, contains an extensive collection of multiple-choice questions for objective tests, all closely tied to the learning objectives found in the text chapters. We're confident that you will find this to be a dependable and usable test bank.

Cengage Learning Testing Powered by Cognero

Cengage Learning Testing Powered by Cognero is a flexible, online system that allows you to author, edit, and manage test bank content from multiple Cengage Learning solutions, create multiple test versions in an instant, and deliver tests from you LMS, your classroom or wherever you want.

CourseMate

Cengage Learning's CourseMate brings course concepts to life with interactive learning, study, and exam preparation tools that support the printed textbook. CourseMate includes an integrated eBook, glossaries, flashcards, quizzes, videos, and more—as well as EngagementTracker, a first-of-its-kind tool that monitors student engagement in the course. The accompanying instructor website, available through login.cengage.com, offers access to password-protected resources such as an electronic version of the instructor's manual, test bank files, and PowerPoint® slides. CourseMate can be bundled with the student text. Contact your Cengage sales representative for information on getting access to CourseMate.

Culture and Modern Life

Culture and Modern Life is a small paperback intended to help your students appreciate how cultural factors moderate psychological processes and how the viewpoint of one's own culture can distort one's interpretation of the behavior of people from other cultures. Written by David Matsumoto (San Francisco State University), a leading authority on cross-cultural psychology, this supplementary book should greatly enhance your students' understanding of how culture can influence adjustment. *Culture and Modern Life* can be ordered shrinkwrapped with the text.

Critical Thinking Exercises

A set of critical thinking exercises can be found in the CourseMate for this text at www.cengagebrain.com. Written by Jeffry Ricker (Scottsdale Community College), these exercises are intended to introduce students to specific critical thinking skills, such as recognizing extraneous variables, sampling bias, and fallacies in reasoning. The exercises also challenge students to apply these skills to adjustment-related topics on a chapter-by-chapter basis.

Highlights of Content Changes in the Eleventh Edition

To help professors who have used this book over many editions, we are providing an overview of the content changes in the current edition. The following list is not exhaustive, but it should alert faculty to most of the major changes in the book.

CHAPTER *1* Adjusting to Modern Life

New discussion of Sherry Turkle's argument that our digital, networked world actually fosters isolation and deficits in intimacy

New example of naturalistic observation research focusing on ethnic differences in sociability and illustrating an innovative, new way to conduct such research

New example of case study research focusing on assessing the effectiveness of a specific therapy (IPT) for bulimic disorders

New example of survey research showing how the amount of time people spend watching TV relates to social class and their health

Revised discussion of the relationship between income and subjective well-being, including a recent study by Kahneman and Deaton (2010)

Revised discussion of age and happiness, including new research reporting a U-shaped relationship between age and subjective well-being

New research linking the depth of participants' daily conversations to their subjective well-being

New research on the link between religiosity and happiness, which appears to be stronger in societies where life circumstances are more difficult and stressful

Revised coverage of personality and happiness featuring new data on how extraversion and neuroticism can color people's evaluations of their experiences

New findings on the importance of study habits to college success

New research on how students' retrieval practice and question generation can enhance mastery of reading assignments

New coverage of how the testing effect (on memory) generalizes to real-world educational settings and new theorizing on why this effect is so potent

CHAPTER *2* Theories of Personality

New data on the relationship between the Big Five traits and socioeconomic class

Revised critique of the five-factor model

Expanded critique of Freudian theory

New research on the ramifications of a repressive coping style

New research on how reaction formation may underlie homophobia

Updated discussion of self-efficacy

New discussion of a proposed revision of Maslow's hierarchy of needs

Condensed coverage of behavioral genetics research on the heritability of personality

New coverage of recent genetic mapping studies of specific genes and personality

New research testing evolutionary analyses of the origins of individual differences in extraversion

New findings on the neuroscience of personality

Revised critique of biological models of personality

Expanded description of those who score high in narcissism

New discussion of the social consequences of narcissism

CHAPTER 3 Stress and Its Effects

New discussion of APA's 2010 "Stress in America" survey results

Additional coverage of work-related pressure, coupled with academic pressure, as a source of stress

New material on poverty-related stress and mental and physical health outcomes

New discussion of the 2010 Hate Crime Statistics related to race

New data from Merz and colleagues demonstrating that stress disrupts memory for socially relevant information, such as people's names

New discussion of Keicolt-Glaser and colleagues' work on stress-induced chronic inflammation as the reason stress causes broad physical health problems

New findings from a 2010 meta-analysis of hardiness studies

New coverage of positive emotional style and enhanced immune response and longevity

Expanded coverage of choking under pressure to include research on attention and personality factors

New material on economic stress and its consequences

New findings from a recent meta-analysis on social support and mortality

CHAPTER 4 Coping Processes

Updated categorization and a new figure of coping techniques reflecting Charles Carver's recommended coping distinctions

New discussion of research on humor in the workplace as a stress reducer

New research on benefit finding as a form of appraisal-focused coping that helps deployed soldiers adjust to the challenges of war

Included discussion of circumstances in which social support is helpful in buffering the effects of stress

New illustrative story of Eva Mozes, who survived life-threatening experimentation at Auschwitz and yet chose to forgive the Nazis

New discussion concerning research examining some potentially negative aspects of forgiveness

Added discussion of how meditation enhances well-being and mental health by increasing positive emotions and favorable reappraisals of negative events

New discussion of how music can reduce stress through relaxation

New section on spirituality as an emotion-focused constructive coping technique

New application section on "Using Time More Effectively"

New discussion of interruptions as a cause of wasted time

Review of innovative research on procrastination on enjoyable tasks

New discussion regarding the importance of clarifying short-term goals as a time management technique

New research-based recommendation to "schedule relaxation time" to enhance time management

CHAPTER 5 Psychology and Physical Health

Updated historical overview of how causes of mortality have changed since the early 20th century

Additional discussion of how lifestyle changes following a heart attack can prevent subsequent cardiac events

New discussion of research indicating that anxiety, not hostility, is apt to be a greater source of heart disease in women

New review of evidence that hostility is not always a precursor to heart disease; rather, it likely serves as a risk factor only to some individuals or exerts an indirect influence

Addition of research emphasizing the fact no solid evidence for a type C or "cancer-prone" personality exists

New discussion of stress headaches as predictors of other health problems

Updated figure linking stress to a variety of chronic diseases

New information on the mortality rates linked to smoking, its discovery in the new world, and how the link between education and predisposition to smoke differs across some nations

Discussion of new finding that neither men nor women have an easier time quitting smoking

Discussion of new data on college students' alcohol consumption

New figure on recognizing drinking problems and alcohol abuse

New discussion of research linking lack of adequate sleep to obesity

New review of reduced mortality rates among people with AIDS as linked to new drugs, healthy lifestyles, and positive attitudes

Addition of material on stable rates indicating lack of adherence to medical regimens

Updated discussion linking cocaine use to cardiovascular problems

CHAPTER 6 The Self

New and expanded definition of the self-concept

Discussion of new research suggesting that competition (or the lack thereof) may be the basis for the better-than-average effect

Introduction of new self-concept research concerning frequency of peer praise in independent versus interdependent cultures

Expanded coverage of behaviors and psychological outlooks linked to high and low self-esteem

New findings highlighting domain-specific self-esteem as behaviorally more predictive than general self-esteem

New example of authoritative parenting as responsible for preventing problem behaviors during adolescence

New figure listing sources of internal and external attributions

New research discussion of alternative perspective explaining self-esteem differences between adolescent boys and girls

New discussion of the source and psychosocial consequences of the spotlight effect

New discussion concerning how the drive for self-verification can lead people to act in ways that confirm their identities

New finding linking downward social comparisons with strong self-protective processes

Additional material on the ubiquity of the self-serving bias and people's inability to recognize its influence in their judgments

New example of basking-in-reflected-glory (BIRG) in a political context

Expanded discussion of self-defeating behaviors as attractive due to their short-term benefits

New discussion of how people's true selves can be revealed when they exert effort to create a favorable impression in the minds of others

CHAPTER 7 Social Thinking and Social Influence

New discussion of email content and tone as a nonverbal cue for person perception

New example of how strangers who look like familiar others we know and like trigger favorable snap judgments

New discussion of a strategy for reducing susceptibility to the confirmation bias

New example of how interpersonal warmth (or the lack thereof) represents a familiar and common source of self-fulfilling prophecy in daily life

New findings indicating that the ubiquity of self-fulfilling prophecy in psychological research may itself be a case of biased expectations

Expanded discussion of research on distinctiveness bias in social categorization

New discussion of a study on how imagining contact with a member of an outgroup can reduce people's propensity to respond using negative stereotypes

New example of religion as a cultural source of the fundamental attribution error

Broadened discussion of defensive attributions and how they can explain people's responses to random positive events

New Recommended Reading on *Whistling Vivaldi* by Claude M. Steele

New example of how trying to control prejudiced thinking can tax self-regulation ability

Additional examples linking the elaboration likelihood model of persuasion to positive health changes

New figure illustrating the continuum of social influence

New discussion of a recent study indicating that mimicking authority figure's actions can promote antisocial obedience

New materials introducing additional factors that can promote the persuasive power of the foot-in-the-door-technique

Additional examples of recent research demonstrating the door-in-the-face-technique of persuasion

New example of the scarcity principle of persuasion in action

CHAPTER 8 Interpersonal Communication

Expanded list of examples for electronically mediated communications

New research indicating that shy or introverted individuals rely on some electronically mediated communication modes more than others do

New research indicating that people reduce their personal space when they expect to interact directly with others, including strangers

New finding revealing that general crowding in commuter settings (e.g., trains) may be less stressful than perceptions of being physically close to and closed in by others

New finding arguing for anxiety as a seventh distinct and recognizable facial expression

New figure showing an anxious facial expression

Reporting of additional evidence that older people have greater difficulty decoding facial expressions than younger people do

New finding that children over age 6 can accurately decode people's mental and emotional states based on eye contact

New evidence demonstrating eye contact as a source of a self-serving bias

Recent consumer research revealing how interpersonal touching reduces liking toward products

New figure illustrating how well experts identify truth or lies

New discussion of deception research revealing that even married people cannot usually determine when a spouse is lying

New research indicating that when self-presentational skills become overtaxed, observers begin to suspect deception is operating

New data on reaction time for responses as an aid for detecting deceptive communications

Extended discussion of research on the consequences of self-esteem's link to self-disclosure in online venues

New discussion of social phobia as undermining self-disclosure and romantic relationship satisfaction

New detailed review of culture's impact on relationship mobility and problems associated with establishing and ending connections with others

Additional new material on communication apprehension as a problematic personality variable and as a cultural factor influencing social life

New suggestions for reducing communication apprehension in public venues

New recommendations for dealing with interpersonal conflict often grounded in family life

New discussion of assertiveness as occurring outside of face-to-face interactions

CHAPTER 9 Friendship and Love

Updated data on the annual number of cosmetic procedures in the United States from American Society for Aesthetic Plastic Surgery

New study cited that examines the effect of proximity on friendship development in a real-life context

New findings from a 2010 Internet survey of over 16,000 participants examining Sternberg's dimensions of love, personality, and relationship length

New discussion of sexual dissatisfaction as a correlate of adult attachment styles

New research showing that insecure people are especially good at reaching out to potential partners, presenting themselves as interesting, and conveying their positive qualities

New 2010 data on causes of relational boredom in dating and married couples

Section on Internet and Close Relationships revised to include subsections on developing close relationships online, building online intimacy, and moving beyond online relationships

New loneliness data from a national survey of individuals ages 57 to 85

CHAPTER *10* Marriage and Intimate Relationships

Expanded cross-cultural coverage on collectivist views on marriage

Added discussion of cross-cultural research on polygamy

New opening quote from a 2012 blogger for the Deciding to Marry section

New discussion of research comparing depressive symptoms of postpartum and adoptive mothers

Inclusion of a discussion of covenant marriages

Highlights the work of the late Judith Wallerstein, with a bulleted summary of her key findings

Inclusion of a new section of research titled Same-Sex Marriage

Revised and updated discussion of intimate partner violence based on the recommendations from the Rape, Abuse, and Incest National Network (RAINN)

Expanded coverage of key considerations regarding consent in intimate relationships

Updated data on rape and sexual assault from the Bureau of Justice Statistics

New discussion of RAINN's three stages of acquaintance rape

CHAPTER *11* Gender and Behavior

Introduction of inconsistency in the use of the terms *sex* and *gender*, suggesting that the distinction has become less meaningful over time

New discussion of a recent meta-analysis of over 200 studies and four national datasets indicating there are no longer gender differences in mathematical performance

New data and a new figure on the shrinking gap between genders on the high end of mathematical ability

Updated statistics on gender differences in violent crime

Added results of a recent meta-analysis on gender differences in sexual attitudes and behaviors

New discussion of gender differences in distortions of body image

New discussion of parental communication as a source of gender-role socialization

Added discussion of a 2010 content analysis of after-school commercials from Nickelodeon, the popular children's television network, revealing that gender stereotypes are common

Update of data on the gender wage gap in weekly earning for various occupational categories

Inclusion of Lakoff's classic model of gender communication and her observations that discrepancies in speaking style are responsible for gender inequalities

Expanded coverage of gender differences in nonverbal communication

CHAPTER *12* Development and Expression of Sexuality

Update of entire chapter with 2010 data from the National Survey of Sexual Health and Behavior (NSSHB), a nationally representative study of the sexual and sexual health–related behaviors of adolescents and adults in the United States

Added discussion of the term *queer* as a preferred term for lesbian, gay, bisexual, and transgendered communities

Updated statistics on sources of information about birth control among teens

Revised and updated summary of gender differences in sexual socialization based on a current review of the literature

Revised and updated Gender Differences in Sexual Socialization section, reflecting recent meta-analytic data from 2010 and 2011 including both individual samples and large national data sets

New discussion of terms *coming out* and *in the closet* with regard to disclosing sexual identity

Updated opinion data on Americans' attitudes toward same-sex marriage

Updated data on racial differences in attitudes toward homosexuality

Updated statistics on gender differences in the experience of orgasm

Updated statistics on the variety of sexual activities practiced by young adult American men and women

Discussion of the debate regarding whether oral sex counts as "having sex"

Added discussion of anal sex

Updated statistics on frequency of sex among married couples

New section on emergency contraception

CHAPTER *13* Careers and Work

New discussion of link between intelligence and job satisfaction

New discussion of why higher education is worth the cost and is of great interest to employers

New career option point emphasizing the importance of mobility

Additional material on postponing retirement due to concerns over the economy

New material on the popularity of job sharing in certain career paths

Updated figure concerning education's impact on income

Updated discussion of average lower compensation for women compared to men

New discussion of on-the-job discrimination as likely to be subtle and covert, not obvious

New evidence that affirmative action is embraced by groups of diverse women and men

New entries in figure illustrating common stressors among younger and older adults

New consideration of job stress as affecting employees whose personal philosophies conflict with company's views

New discussion of burnout as being linked to people-oriented professional positions

New entry in figure on common signs of employee burnout

Added discussion of vacations as having limited impact on employee burnout

New citation of evidence linking unemployment to suicide rates

New and updated material on workaholism as addictive and leading to interpersonal aggression

New figure containing typical questions asked during structured and unstructured interviews

CHAPTER 14 Psychological Disorders

New introductory vignette focusing on contemporary celebrities with obsessive-compulsive disorder

Discussion of psychodiagnosis introducing the concept of comorbidity

Description of the transition from DSM-IV to DSM-5

Explanation that OCD has been given its own category in DSM-5

New data on the most common types of phobic fears

Added discussion of how phobias can be acquired through observation or exposure to fear-inducing information

Added discussion of how agoraphobia was made a separate disorder in DSM-5, rather than just a complication of panic disorder

Explanation that depression and bipolar disorder were given their own categories in DSM-5

Discussion of major depression introducing the concept of anhedonia

New coverage of chronic depression

Expanded discussion of how mood swings tend to be patterned in bipolar disorders

New discussion of hormonal factors that contribute to depressive disorders

Explanation that the four subtypes of schizophrenic disorders were discarded in DSM-5

Updated coverage of neurochemical factors in the etiology of schizophrenia

New research on whether cannabis use may help precipitate schizophrenia in young people who are vulnerable to the disorder

New research linking childhood trauma to vulnerability to schizophrenia

New coverage of autism spectrum disorder, including recent findings on the dramatic increase in its prevalence

New discussion of the etiology of autism, including the autism-vaccination controversy

CHAPTER 15 Psychotherapy

New findings on the extent to which drug therapy has become the dominant mode of treatment for psychological disorders

New data on the demographics of who seeks treatment

New inclusion of marriage and family therapists in coverage of professions providing mental health services

New summary of the core features of modern psychodynamic therapies

In coverage of insight therapies, new section on couples/marital therapy

In coverage of insight therapies, new section on family therapy

New work distinguishing two groups that report recovered memories of abuse that differ in the likelihood of corroboration

New discussion of exposure therapies for anxiety disorders

Coverage of one-session treatment (OST) of phobias

New research on the value of antidepressants in relation to the severity of patients' depression

New findings on how often psychiatrists prescribe multiple medications to patients

Critique of drug therapy, mentioning new theory that in the long run psychiatric drugs may *increase* patients' vulnerability to psychological disorders

New evidence on ethnic disparities in mental health care

New discussion of the need to expand the delivery of clinical services to reduce the number of people who go untreated

New discussion of how therapy can be delivered via videoconferencing and telephone

New coverage of computerized treatments delivered via the Internet

CHAPTER 16 Positive Psychology

New material on the importance of juxtaposing the negative in life with the positive

Discussion of a new model of mental health emphasizing flourishing

A new figure showing a model conceptualizing flourishing

Consideration of the tension between the new positive psychology and established humanistic psychology

Review of new research linking faster thought speed with increased risk taking

Expanded description of the flow experience

New examples indicating when flow is likely to occur

Description of personality characteristics that increase or decrease the likelihood of experiencing flow

Additional examples indicating why mindfulness is beneficial to health and well-being

New discussion of ways that "pastoral breaks" with nature can promote mindfulness

New figure highlighting ways to cultivate resilience

Added section discussing the noncognitive trait known as "grit," which promotes perseverance in the face of challenge

A new figure listing the items found in the Grit Scale

New entries in list of benefits of religious and spiritual behaviors

New discussion of pro-social spending as promoting happiness, including activity suggestions, in the chapter's Application

ACKNOWLEDGMENTS

This book has been an enormous undertaking, and we want to express our gratitude to the innumerable people who have influenced its evolution. To begin with, we must cite the contribution of our students who have taken the adjustment course. It is trite to say that they have been a continuing inspiration—but they have.

We also want to express our appreciation for the time and effort invested by the authors of various ancillary books and materials: Vinny Hevern (Le Moyne College), Bill Addison (Eastern Illinois University), Britain Scott (University of St. Thomas), Susan Koger (Willamette University), Jeffry Ricker (Scottsdale Community College), David Matsumoto (San Francisco State University), Lenore Frigo (Shasta College), Elizabeth Garner (Tallahassee Community College), and Joan Thomas-Spiegel (Los Angeles Harbor College). In spite of tight schedules, they all did commendable work.

The quality of a textbook depends greatly on the quality of the prepublication reviews by psychology professors around the country. The reviewers listed on pages xiv–xv have contributed to the development of this book by providing constructive reviews of various portions of the manuscript in this or earlier editions. We are grateful to all of them.

We would also like to thank Tim Matray, who has served as product manager of this edition. He has done a wonderful job following in the footsteps of Claire Verduin, Eileen Murphy, Edith Beard Brady, Michele Sordi, and Jon-David Hague, to whom we remain indebted. We are also grateful to Jackie Estrada, for an excellent job of copyediting and indexing; Joan Keyes, who performed superbly as our production editor; and Liz Harasymczuk, who created the new design. Others who have made significant contributions to this project include Jennifer Risden (content project manager), Trina McManus (content developer), Paige Leeds (content coordinator), Jennifer Levanduski (marketing manager), Nicole Richards (product assistant), Jasmin Tokatlian (media developer), and Vernon Boes (art director).

In addition, Wayne Weiten would like to thank his wife, Beth Traylor, who has been a steady source of emotional support despite the demands of her medical career, and his son, T. J., who adds a wealth of laughter to his dad's life. Dana Dunn thanks his wife, Sarah, and his children, Jake and Hannah, for their usual support during the writing process. Dana continues to be grateful to Wayne and Elizabeth for their camaraderie as authors and friends. He also appreciates the excellent efforts of the Cengage team who supported his work during preparation of this edition. Elizabeth Yost Hammer would like to thank Elliott Hammer—her partner in work and play—for far too much to list here. She is especially grateful to Marion N. Alejos, Joni C. Banks, Terreca Cato, Jarica D. Garner, Shanti G. Hubbard, and LaShante' Q. Scott for their outstanding research assistance. Finally, she is grateful to Olivia Crum for her invaluable support.

Wayne Weiten
Dana S. Dunn
Elizabeth Yost Hammer

REVIEWERS

David Ackerman
Rhodes College

David W. Alfano
Community College of Rhode Island

Gregg Amore
DeSales University

Jeff Banks
Pepperdine University

David Baskind
Delta College

Marsha K. Beauchamp
Mt. San Antonio College

Robert Biswas-Diener
*Portland State University (USA)/
Centre for Applied Positive
Psychology*

John R. Blakemore
Monterey Peninsula College

Barbara A. Boccaccio
Tunxis Community College

Paul Bowers
Grayson County College

Amara Brook
Santa Clara University

Tamara L. Brown
University of Kentucky

George Bryant
East Texas State University

James F. Calhoun
University of Georgia

Robert Cameron
Fairmont State College

David Campbell
Humboldt State University

Bernardo J. Carducci
Indiana University, Southeast

Richard Cavasina
California University of Pennsylvania

M. K. Clampit
Bentley College

Meg Clark
*California State Polytechnic
University–Pomona*

Stephen S. Coccia
*Orange County Community
College*

William C. Compton
Middle Tennessee State University

Dennis Coon
Santa Barbara City College

Katherine A. Couch
Eastern Oklahoma State College

Tori Crews
American River College

Salvatore Cullari
Lebenon Valley College

Kenneth S. Davidson
Wayne State University

Lugenia Dixon
Bainbridge College

Jean Egan
Asnuntuck Community College

Pamela Elizabeth
University of Rhode Island

Ron Evans
Washburn University

Belinda Evans-Ebio
Wayne County Community College

Richard Furhere
University of Wisconsin–Eau Claire

R. Kirkland Gable
California Lutheran University

Laura Gaudet
Chadron State College

Lee Gills
Georgia College

Chris Goode
Georgia State University

Lawrence Grebstein
University of Rhode Island

Bryan Gros
Louisiana State University

Kristi Hagen
Chippewa Valley Technical College

David Hamilton
Canadore College

Kyle Max Hancock
Utah State University

Barbara Hansen Lemme
College of DuPage

Jerry Harazmus
Western Technical College

Robert Helm
Oklahoma State University

Barbara Herman
Gainesville College

Jeanne L. Higbee
University of Minnesota

Robert Higgins
Central Missouri State University

Clara E. Hill
University of Maryland

Michael Hirt
Kent State University

Fred J. Hitti
Monroe Community College

William M. Hooper
Clayton College and State University

Joseph Horvat
Weber State University

Kathy Howard
Harding University

Teresa A. Hutchens
University of Tennessee–Knoxville

Howard Ingle
Salt Lake Community College

Brian Jensen
Columbia College

Jerry Jensen
*Minneapolis Community & Technical
College*

Walter Jones
College of DuPage

Wayne Joose
Calvin College

Bradley Karlin
Texas A&M University

Margaret Karolyi
University of Akron

Lambros Karris
Husson College

Martha Kuehn
Central Lakes College

Susan Kupisch
Austin Peay State University

Robert Lawyer
Delgado Community College

Jimi Leopold
Tarleton State University

Harold List
*Massachusetts Bay Community
College*

Corliss A. Littlefield
Morgan Community College

Louis A. Martone
Miami Dade Community College

Richard Maslow
San Joaquin Delta College

Sherri McCarthy
Northern Arizona Community College

William T. McReynolds
University of Tampa

Fred Medway
*University of South Carolina–
Columbia*

Fredrick Meeker
California State Polytechnic University–Pomona

Mitchell Metzger
Pennsylvania State University– Shenago Campus

John Moritsugu
Pacific Lutheran University

Jeanne O'Kon
Tallahassee Community College

Gary Oliver
College of DuPage

William Penrod
Middle Tennessee State University

Joseph Philbrick
California State Polytechnic University–Pomona

Barbara M. Powell
Eastern Illinois University

James Prochaska
University of Rhode Island

Megan Benoit Ratcliff
University of Georgia

Bob Riesenberg
Whatcom Community College

Katherine Elaine Royal
Middle Tennessee State University

Joan Royce
Riverside Community College

Joan Rykiel
Ocean County College

John Sample
Slippery Rock University

Thomas K. Savill
Metropolitan State College of Denver

Patricia Sawyer
Middlesex Community College

Carol Schachat
De Anza College

John Schell
Kent State University

Norman R. Schultz
Clemson University

Dale Simmons
Oregon State University

Gail Simpson
Wayne County Community College

Sangeeta Singg
Angelo State University

Valerie Smead
Western Illinois University

Krishna Stilianos
Oakland Community College

Dolores K. Sutter
Tarrant County College– Northeast

Karl Swain
Community College of Southern Nevada

Diane Teske
Penn State Harrisburg

Kenneth L. Thompson
Central Missouri State University

Joanne Viney
University of Illinois Urbana/ Champaign

Davis L. Watson
University of Hawaii

Deborah S. Weber
University of Akron

Clair Wiederholt
Madison Area Technical College

J. Oscar Williams
Diablo Valley College

David Wimer
Pennsylvania State University, University Park

Raymond Wolf
Moraine Park Technical College

Raymond Wolfe
State University of New York at Geneseo

Michael Wolff
Southwestern Oklahoma State University

Madeline E. Wright
Houston Community College

Norbet Yager
Henry Ford Community College

BRIEF CONTENTS

CONTENTS

CHAPTER 1 Adjusting to Modern Life 1

Greg Epperson/Shutterstock.com

Alan Poulson Photography/Shutterstock.com

ollyy/Shutterstock.com

Phil Date/Shutterstock.com

Yuri Arcurs/Shutterstock.com

Jupiterimages/Brand X Pictures/Getty Images

CREATISTA/Shutterstock.com

© bikeriderlondon/Shutterstock.com

© Aleksei Potov/Shutterstock.com

© Zhu difeng/Shutterstock.com

© mangostock/Shutterstock.com

© Stephen Coburn/Shutterstock.com

© erics/Shutterstock.com

© iStockphoto.com/bowdenimages/Mark Bowden

© iStockphoto/David Newton

TO THE STUDENT

In most college courses students spend more time with their textbooks than with their professors. Given this reality, it helps if you like your textbook. Making textbooks likable, however, is a tricky proposition. By its very nature, a textbook must introduce a great many new concepts, ideas, and theories. If it doesn't, it isn't much of a textbook, and instructors won't choose to use it—so you'll never see it anyway. Consequently, we have tried to make this book as likable as possible without compromising the academic content that your instructor demands. Thus, we have tried to make the book lively, informal, engaging, well organized, easy to read, practical, and occasionally humorous. Before you plunge into Chapter 1, let us explain some of the key features that can help you get the most out of the book.

Learning Aids

Mastering the content of this text involves digesting a great deal of information. To facilitate this learning process, we've incorporated a number of instructional aids into the book.

- *Outlines* at the beginning of each chapter provide you with both a preview and an overview of what will be covered. Think of the outlines as road maps, and bear in mind that it's easier to reach a destination if you know where you're going.
- *Headings* are used extensively to keep material well organized.
- To help alert you to key points, *learning objectives* are found throughout the chapters, immediately after the level-1 headings.
- *Key terms* are identified with **blue italicized boldface** type to indicate that these are important vocabulary items that are part of psychology's technical language.
- An *integrated running glossary* provides an on-the-spot definition of each key term as it's introduced in the text. These formal definitions are printed in **blue boldface** type. It is often difficult for students to adapt to the jargon used by scientific disciplines. However, learning this terminology is an essential part of your educational experience. The integrated running glossary is meant to make this learning process as painless as possible.
- An *alphabetical glossary* is provided in the back of the book, as key terms are usually defined in the running glossary only when they are first introduced. If you run into a technical term that was introduced in an earlier chapter and you can't remember its meaning, you can look it up in the alphabetical glossary instead of backtracking to find the place where it first appeared.

- *Italics* are used liberally throughout the book to emphasize important points.
- A *chapter review* near the end of each chapter includes a thorough summary of the chapter and lists key terms and important theorists, with page references. Reading over these review materials can help ensure that you've digested the key points in the chapter.
- Each chapter ends with a ten-item *practice test* that should give you a realistic assessment of your mastery of that chapter and valuable practice taking multiple-choice tests that will probably be representative of what you will see in class (if your instructor uses the test bank designed for this book).

Reel Research

We believe that good textbooks in psychology should both satisfy curiosity and encourage readers to learn more about disciplinary research. To this end, we have added a feature we call Reel Research to the book. Using the publisher's vast video collection, we created Reel Research to make connections between studies captured on camera and important concepts in each chapter. The box includes a brief description of the study or studies and researchers involved, an explanation of how it relates to the chapter's concepts, and three discussion questions. You will be able to access the videos through the CourseMate for this text. Watch the video to learn more about psychological studies and delve even deeper by responding to the discussion questions. For example, Chapter 1's video deals with a topic that ties directly to most readers' experiences: online relationships. Have you ever wondered whether people are more content with face-to-face encounters or those based on instant messaging (IM)? After reading the text and watching the video, you can reflect on the research implications of the work by thinking about the discussion questions.

Recommended Reading Boxes

This text should function as a resource book. To facilitate this goal, particularly interesting self-help books on various topics are highlighted in boxes within the chapters. Each box provides a brief description of the book. We do not agree with everything in these recommended books, but all of them are potentially useful or intriguing. The main purpose of this feature is to introduce you to some of the better self-help books that are available. You can find additional Recommended Readings in the CourseMate for this text at www.cengagebrain.com.

Learn More Online

To help make this book a rich resource guide, we have included Learn More Online boxes, which are recommended websites that can provide you with additional information on adjustment-related topics. The recommended sites were selected by Vincent Hevern, the former Internet editor for the Society for the Teaching of Psychology. Professor Hevern sought out sites that are interesting, that are relevant to adjustment, and that provide accurate, empirically sound information. As with the Recommended Reading boxes, we cannot say that we agree with everything posted on these web pages, but we think they have some real value. The Learn More Online boxes are dispersed throughout the chapters, adjacent to related topical coverage. Because URLs change frequently, we have not included them for the Learn More Online boxes in the book. If you are interested in visiting these sites, we recommend that you do so through the website for this text (available at www.cengagebrain .com). Links to all the recommended websites are maintained there, and the Cengage webmaster periodically updates the URLs. Of course, you can also use a search engine, such as Google, to locate the recommended websites.

Personal Explorations Workbook

The *Personal Explorations Workbook*, which can be found in the very back of the text, contains interesting, thought-provoking experiential exercises for each chapter. These exercises are designed to help you achieve personal insights. The Self-Assessment exercises are psychological tests or scales that you can take, so you can see how you score on various traits discussed in the text. The Self-Reflection exercises consist of questions intended to help you think about issues in your personal life in relation to concepts and ideas discussed in the text. Many students find these exercises to be quite interesting, even fun. Hence, we encourage you to use the *Personal Explorations Workbook*.

A Concluding Note

We sincerely hope that you find this book enjoyable. If you have any comments or advice that might help us improve the next edition, please write to us in care of the publisher, Cengage Learning, 20 Davis Drive, Belmont, CA 94002. There is a form in the back of the book that you can use to provide us with feedback. Finally, let us wish you good luck. We hope you enjoy your course and learn a great deal.

Wayne Weiten
Dana S. Dunn
Elizabeth Yost Hammer

Psychology Applied
to Modern Life

ADJUSTMENT IN THE 21ST CENTURY

CHAPTER 1

Adjusting to Modern Life

© geodigital/Alamy

The immense Boeing 747 lumbers into position to accept its human cargo. The passengers make their way on board. In a tower a few hundred yards away, air traffic controllers diligently monitor radar screens, radio transmissions, and digital readouts of weather information. At the reservation desk in the airport terminal, clerks punch up the appropriate ticket information on their computers and quickly process the steady stream of passengers. Mounted on the wall are video screens displaying up-to-the-minute information on flight arrivals, departures, and delays. Back in the cockpit of the plane, the flight crew calmly scan the complex array of dials, meters, and lights to assess the aircraft's readiness for flight. In a few minutes, the airplane will slice into the cloudy, snow-laden skies above Chicago. In a little over three hours, its passengers will be transported from the piercing cold of a Chicago winter to the balmy beaches of the Bahamas. Another everyday triumph for technology will have taken place.

THE PARADOX OF PROGRESS

LEARNING OBJECTIVES

- Describe three examples of the paradox of progress.
- Explain what is meant by the paradox of progress and how theorists have explained it.

We are the children of technology. We take for granted such impressive feats as transporting 300 people over 1500 miles in a matter of hours. After all, we live in a time of unparalleled progress. Our modern Western society has made extraordinary strides in transportation, energy, communication, agriculture, and medicine. Yet despite our technological advances, social problems and personal difficulties seem more prevalent and more prominent than ever before. This paradox is evident in many aspects of contemporary life, as seen in the following examples.

Point. *Modern technology has provided us with countless time-saving devices.* Automobiles, telephones, vacuum cleaners, dishwashers, photocopiers, and personal computers all save time. Today, cell phones with headsets allow people to talk to friends or colleagues while battling rush hour traffic. In a matter of seconds, a personal computer can perform calculations that would take months if done by hand.

Counterpoint. *Nonetheless, most of us complain about not having enough time.* Our schedules overflow with appointments, commitments, and plans. Surveys suggest that a majority of people subjectively feel they have less and less time for themselves. Part of the problem is that in our modern society, work follows people home. Thus, Peter Whybrow (2005) comments, "Citizens find themselves tethered to their jobs around the clock by the same nomadic tools—cell phones, pagers, wireless email—that were heralded first as instruments of liberation" (p. 158).

To deal with this time crunch, more and more people are cutting back on their sleep as they attempt to juggle work, family, and household responsibilities. Sleep experts assert that American society suffers from an epidemic of sleep deprivation (Walsh, Dement, & Dinges, 2011). Unfortunately, research indicates that chronic sleep loss can have significant negative effects on individuals' daytime functioning, as well as their mental and physical health (Banks & Dinges, 2011).

Point. *The range of life choices available to people in modern societies has increased exponentially in recent decades.* For example, Barry Schwartz (2004) describes how a simple visit to a local supermarket can require a consumer to choose from 285 varieties of cookies, 61 suntan lotions, 150 lipsticks, and 175 salad dressings. Although increased choice is most tangible in the realm of consumer goods and services, Schwartz argues that it also extends into more significant domains of life. Today, people tend to have unprecedented opportunities to make choices about how they will be educated (vastly more flexible college curricula are available, not to mention online delivery systems), how and where they will work (telecommuting presents employees with all sorts of new choices about how to accomplish their work), how their intimate relationships will unfold (people have increased freedom to delay marriage, cohabit, not have children, and so forth), and even how they will look (advances in plastic surgery have made personal appearance a matter of choice).

Barry Schwartz argues that people in modern societies suffer from choice overload. He maintains that the endless choices people are presented with lead them to waste countless hours weighing trivial decisions and ruminating about whether their decisions were optimal.

Counterpoint. *Although increased choice sounds attractive, recent research suggests that an overabundance of choices has unexpected costs.* Studies suggest that when people have too many choices, they experience "choice overload" and struggle with decisions (White & Hoffrage, 2009). Decision dilemmas can deplete mental resources and undermine self-control (Vohs et al., 2008). Furthermore, Schwartz (2004) argues that when decisions become more complex, errors are more likely. And he explains how having more alternatives increases the potential for rumination, postdecision regret, and anticipated regret. Ultimately, he argues, the malaise associated with choice overload undermines individuals' happiness and contributes to depression. Consistent with this analysis, research data suggest that the incidence of depressive disorders has increased over the last 50 years (Hidaka, 2012). Average anxiety levels have also gone up substantially in recent decades (Twenge, 2000, 2011). It is hard to say whether choice overload is the chief culprit underlying these trends, but it is clear that increased freedom of choice has not resulted in enhanced tranquillity or improved mental health.

Point. *Modern technology has gradually provided us with unprecedented control over the world around us.* Advances in agriculture have dramatically increased food production, and biotechnology advocates claim that genetically modified crops will make our food supply more reliable than ever before. Elaborate water supply systems, made up of hundreds of miles of canals, tunnels, and pipelines, along with dams, reservoirs, and pumping stations, permit massive metropolitan areas to grow in inhospitable deserts. Thanks to progress in medicine, doctors can reattach severed limbs, use lasers to correct microscopic defects in the eye, and even replace the human heart.

Counterpoint. *Unfortunately, modern technology has also had a devastating negative impact on our environment.* It has contributed to global warming, destruction of the ozone layer, deforestation, exhaustion of much of the world's fisheries, widespread air and water pollution, and extensive exposure of plants and animals to toxic chemicals. Many experts worry that in a few generations the earth's resources will be too depleted to sustain an adequate quality of life. To most people, these crises sound like technical problems that call for technological answers, but they are also behavioral problems in that they are fueled by overconsumption and waste (Koger & Winter, 2010; see the appendix on sustainability in the back of this book). In North America and Europe, the crucial problem is excessive consumption of the world's natural resources. As Kitzes et al. (2008) put it, "If everyone in the world had an ecological footprint equivalent to that of the typical North American or Western European, global society would overshoot the planet's biocapacity three to five fold" (p. 468).

All these apparent contradictions reflect the same theme: *The technological advances of the past century, impressive though they may be, have not led to perceptible improvement in our collective health and happiness.* Indeed, many social critics argue that the quality of our lives and our sense of personal fulfillment have declined rather than increased. This is the paradox of progress.

What is the cause of this paradox? Many explanations have been offered. Alvin Toffler (1980) attributes our collective alienation and distress to our being overwhelmed by rapidly accelerating cultural change. Robert Kegan (1994) maintains that the mental demands of modern life have become so complex, confusing, and contradictory that most of us are "in over our heads." Tim Kasser (2002) speculates that excessive materialism weakens the social ties that bind us, stokes the fires of insecurity, and undermines our collective sense of well-being. Micki McGee (2005) suggests that modern changes in gender roles, diminished job stability, and other social trends have fostered an obsession with self-improvement that ultimately undermines many individuals' sense of security and satisfaction with their identity. According to McGee, our "makeover culture" nourishes the belief that we can all reinvent ourselves as needed, but this assumption can create tremendous pressures on people that "foster rather than quell their anxieties" (p. 17). Sherry Turkle (2011) asserts that in our modern, digital, socially networked world, we spend more and more time with technology and less and less with each other. Although people pile up huge numbers of "friends" on Facebook, Americans report that they have fewer friends than ever before (Turkle, 2011). The resulting sense of loneliness and isolation just deepens people's dependence on superficial communication in the online world, leaving an increasing number of people suffering from an intimacy deficit.

REEL RESEARCH

Online Relationships

Across the world, people are increasingly interacting in online environments. On average, Americans spend a whopping 120 hours per month online (New Media Trend Watch, 2012). Although technological advances produce many benefits for human interaction, Internet-mediated rather than face-to-face communication has its drawbacks. Melanie Green, a social psychologist from the University of North Carolina explains what she characterizes as "Internet good" versus "Internet bad" and investigates the relationship between human behavior and Internet use in this thought-provoking video.

The purpose of Green's research is to examine how Internet use affects social interaction. In one study, participants complete a survey that includes questions about life satisfaction and Internet use. The results showed some interesting patterns: Participants who use instant messaging (IM) frequently have lower life satisfaction and also report they use the Internet too much and would like to use it less. In another study, participants fill out a mood survey followed by a conversation with another "student"—either face to face or via IM. The dialogue is the same in either environment, controlled by the "student" experimenter, and participants are told that the study measures eye movements. The

findings reveal an interesting paradox, as 64% of the participants felt that the face-to-face conversations were more meaningful than the IM conversations—even though those who interacted with the experimenter over IM were reportedly happier than those who interacted with her face to face.

Watch the *Online Relationships* video to learn more about research on Internet use and social relationships. Delve even deeper by responding to the following discussion questions.

DISCUSSION QUESTIONS

1. How is your daily life affected by the Internet? Record the time you spend in front of a screen—television, cell phone, or computer—for a week and explain why you should or shouldn't change your Internet behavior based on the results.
2. Why would the researcher mislead the participants by placing fake cameras in the room and telling them that the study involved eye-movement measurements?
3. What are some benefits of Internet-based communication? What are some trade-offs?

Whatever the explanation, many theorists, working from varied perspectives, agree that *the basic challenge of modern life has become the search for meaning, a sense of direction, and a personal philosophy* (Dolby, 2005; Emmons, 2003; Sagiv, Roccas, & Hazan, 2004). This search involves struggling with such problems as forming a solid

sense of identity, arriving at a coherent set of values, and developing a clear vision of a future that realistically promises fulfillment. Centuries ago, problems of this kind were probably much simpler. As we'll see in the next section, today it appears that many of us are foundering in a sea of confusion.

THE SEARCH FOR DIRECTION

LEARNING OBJECTIVES

- Provide some examples of people's search for direction.
- Describe some common problems with self-help books and what to look for in quality self-help books.
- Summarize the philosophy underlying this textbook.

We live in a time of unparalleled social and technological mutation. According to a number of social critics, the kaleidoscope of change that we see around us creates feelings of anxiety and uncertainty, which we try to alleviate by searching for a sense of direction. This search, which sometimes goes awry, manifests itself in many ways.

For example, we could discuss how hundreds of thousands of Americans have invested large sums of money to enroll in "self-realization" programs such as Scientology, Silva Mind Control, John Gray's Mars and Venus relationship seminars, and Tony Robbins's Life Mastery seminars. These programs typically promise to provide profound enlightenment and quickly turn one's life around. Many participants claim that the programs have revolutionized their lives. However, most experts characterize such programs as intellectually bankrupt, and book and magazine exposés reveal them as simply lucrative money-making schemes (Behar, 1991; Pressman, 1993). In a particularly scathing analysis of these programs, Steve Salerno (2005) outlines the enormous financial benefits reaped by their inventors, such as Tony Robbins ($80 million in annual income), Dr. Phil ($20 million in annual income), and John Gray ($50,000 per speech). In his critique, Salerno also attacks the hypocrisy and inflated credentials of many leading self-help gurus. For example, he asserts that John Gray's doctorate came from a nonaccredited correspondence college; that Dr. Phil has a history of alleged marital infidelity and that some of his video segments are contrived to a degree that would make Jerry Springer proud; and that Dr. Laura is "a critic of premarital and extramarital sex who's indulged in both" (2005, p. 44). More than anything else, the enormous success of these self-help gurus and self-realization programs demonstrates just how desperate some people are for a sense of direction and purpose in their lives.

For the most part, self-realization programs are harmless scams that appear to give some participants an illusory sense of purpose or a temporary boost in self-confidence. But in some cases they probably lead people down ill-advised pathways that

prove harmful. The ultimate example of the potential for harm unfolded in October 2009 in Sedona, Arizona, where three people died and eighteen others were hospitalized, many with serious injuries, after participating in a "spiritual warrior" retreat that required them to spend hours in a makeshift sweat lodge (Harris & Wagner, 2009). The retreat was run by James Ray, a recently popular self-help guru whose website promises to teach people "how to trigger your Unconscious Mind to automatically increase your level of wealth and fulfillment." Ray, who has written inspirational books and appeared on popular TV talk shows, has built a $9-million-a-year self-help empire. The fifty to sixty people who participated in his ill-fated retreat paid over $9,000 apiece for the privilege. After spending 36 hours fasting in the desert on a "vision quest," they were led into a tarp-covered sweat lodge for an endurance challenge that was supposed to show them that they could gain confidence by conquering physical discomfort (Kraft, 2009).

Unfortunately, the sweat lodge turned out to be poorly ventilated and overheated, so that within an hour people began vomiting, gasping for air, and collapsing. Undaunted, Ray urged his followers to persevere, telling them that the vomiting was good for them and saying, "You have to go through this barrier" (Doughtery, 2009). No one was physically forced to stay (and a few did leave), but Ray was an intimidating presence who strongly exhorted everyone to remain, so they could prove that they were stronger than their bodies. Tragically, he pushed their bodies too far; by the end of the ceremony many of the participants were seriously ill. Yet, according to one account, "At the conclusion, seemingly unaware of the bodies of the unconscious lying around him, Ray emerged triumphantly, witnesses said, pumping his fist because he had passed his own endurance test" (Whelan, 2009).

Some of the aftermath of this event has also proven revealing. Consistent with the assertion that it really is all about the money, Ray provided a *partial* refund to the family of Kirby Brown, a participant who *died* in the sweat lodge (Martinez, 2009). And the reactions of some of Ray's followers after the sweat lodge tragedy have been illuminating. You might think that, after inad-

Sergei Bachlakov/Shutterstock.com

The inside of the tarp-covered sweat lodge in Sedona that proved to be a death trap for three participants in an endurance challenge can be seen here. James Ray, the self-help guru who organized the event, was arrested in February 2010 and was subsequently convicted on three counts of negligent homicide.

AP Photo/Yavapai County Sheriff's Office

vertently but recklessly leading people "over a cliff," Ray might be discredited in the eyes of his followers. But think again. Reporters working on this horrific story had no trouble finding Ray advocates who continued to enthusiastically champion his vision for self-improvement (Kraft, 2009). This unwavering faith in Ray's teachings provides a remarkable testimonial to the persuasive power of the charismatic leaders who promote self-realization programs. Nonetheless, in 2011 an Arizona jury deliberated for less than 12 hours before convicting Ray on three counts of negligent homicide (Riccardi, 2011).

We could also discuss how a number of unorthodox religious groups—commonly called *cults*—have attracted countless converts who voluntarily embrace a life of regimentation, obedience, and zealous ideology. It is difficult to get good data, but one study suggested that more than 2 million young adults are involved with cults in the United States (Robinson, Frye, & Bradley, 1997). Most of these cults flourish in obscurity, unless bizarre incidents—such as the 1997 mass suicide of the Heaven's Gate cult near San Diego—attract public attention. It is widely believed that cults use brainwashing and mind control to seduce lonely outsiders (Richardson & Introvigne, 2001), but in reality converts are a diverse array of normal people who are swayed by ordinary—albeit sophisticated—social influence strategies (Singer, 2003; Zimbardo, 2002). It appears that people join cults because these groups appear to provide simple solutions to complex problems, a sense of purpose and belongingness, and a structured lifestyle that reduces feelings of uncertainty (Coates, 2011; Zimbardo, 1992). According to Hunter (1998), alienation, identity confusion, and weak community ties make some people particularly vulnerable to seduction by cults.

And, if you would like a mundane, everyday example of people's search for direction, you need look no farther than your radio, where you will find that the hottest nationally syndicated personality is "Dr. Laura" Schlessinger,

who doles out advice to millions of listeners. Even though only seven or eight people get through to her during each show, an astonishing 75,000 people call each day to seek her unique brand of blunt, outspoken, judgmental advice. Dr. Laura, who is not a psychologist or psychiatrist (her doctorate is in physiology), analyzes callers' problems in more of a moral than psychological framework. Unlike most therapists, she is confrontational, manifests little

P.J. Heller/ZUMAPRESS/Newscom

There are many manifestations of our search for a sense of direction, including the astonishing popularity of "Dr. Laura."

by TOM TOMORROW

Copyright 2000. Used by permission. tomtomorrow@ix.netcom.com

empathy for her callers, and preaches to her audience about how they ought to lead their lives (Arkowitz & Lilienfeld, 2010). In many instances she is insulting to her callers, models intolerance, and provides questionable advice. In an editorial in *Psychology Today,* Robert Epstein (2001) concluded that "no legitimate mental health professional would ever give the kind of hateful, divisive advice that Schlessinger doles out daily" (p. 5). Yet, the remarkable popularity of her highly prescriptive advice demonstrates once again that many people are eager for guidance and direction.

Learn More Online

Psychological Self-Help

Clinical psychologist and professor Clayton E. Tucker-Ladd spent over 30 years exploring how individuals can help themselves deal with personal issues and problems from a psychological perspective. Here you will find an online twelve-chapter self-help book that he wrote, grounded in up-to-date research, that complements this textbook extremely well.

Note: The URLs (addresses) for the Learn More Online websites can be found on the website for this text (http://www.cengagebrain.com), or you can find them using a search engine such as Google.

Although we might choose to examine any of these examples of people's search for a sense of direction, we will reserve our in-depth analysis for a manifestation of this search that is even more germane to our focus on everyday adjustment: the spectacular success of bestselling "self-help" books.

Self-Help Books

Americans spend roughly $650 million annually on "self-help books" that offer do-it-yourself treatments for common personal problems (Arkowitz & Lilienfeld, 2006). According to a recent report by Marketdata Enterprises, if you include self-help audiotapes, CDs, DVDs, software, Internet sites, lectures, seminars, and life coaching, self-improvement appears to be a $10 billion-a-year industry. This fascination with self-improvement is nothing new. For decades American readers have displayed a voracious appetite for self-help books such as *I'm OK—You're OK* (Harris, 1967), *The Seven Habits of Highly Effective People* (Covey, 1989), *Ageless Body, Timeless Mind* (Chopra, 1993), *Don't Sweat the Small Stuff . . . and It's All Small Stuff* (Carlson, 1997), *The Purpose Driven Life* (Warren, 2002), *The Secret* (Byrne, 2006), *Become a Better You: Seven Keys to Improving Your Life Every Day* (Osteen, 2009), *The Power of Habit: Why We Do What We Do in Life and Business* (Duhigg, 2012), and *You're Stronger Than You Think* (Parrott, 2012).

With their simple recipes for achieving happiness, the authors of these books have generally not been timid about promising to change the quality of the reader's life. Unfortunately, merely reading a book is not likely to turn your life around. If only it were that easy! If only someone could hand you a book that would solve all your problems! If the consumption of these literary narcotics were even remotely as helpful as their publishers claim, we would be a nation of serene, happy, well-adjusted people. It is clear, however, that serenity is not the dominant national mood. Quite the contrary, as already noted, in recent decades the prevalence of anxiety and depression appear to have increased. The multitude of self-help books that crowd bookstore shelves represent just one more symptom of our collective distress and our search for the elusive secret of happiness.

The Value of Self-Help Books

It is somewhat unfair to lump all self-help books together for a critique, because they vary widely in quality (Norcross et al., 2003). Surveys exploring psychotherapists' opinions of self-help books suggest that there are some excellent books that offer authentic insights and sound advice (Starker, 1992). Many therapists encourage their patients to read carefully selected self-help books (Campbell & Smith, 2003). A few books have even been tested in clinical trials with favorable results (Floyd, 2003; Gregory et al., 2004), although the studies have often had methodological weaknesses (Arkowitz & Lilienfeld, 2006). Thus, it would be foolish to dismiss all these books as shallow drivel. In fact, some of the better self-help books are highlighted in the Recommended Reading boxes that appear throughout this text. Unfortunately, however, the gems are easily lost in the mountains of rubbish. A great many self-help books offer little of real value to the reader. Generally, they suffer from four fundamental shortcomings.

First, they are dominated by "psychobabble." The term *psychobabble,* coined by R. D. Rosen (1977), seems appropriate to describe the "hip" but hopelessly vague language used in many of these books. Statements such as "It's beautiful if you're unhappy," "You've got to get in touch with yourself," "You have to be up front," "You gotta be you 'cause you're you," and "You need a real high-energy experience" are typical examples of this language. At best, such terminology is ill-defined; at worst, it is meaingless. Clarity is sacrificed in favor of a jargon that prevents, rather than enhances, effective communication.

A second problem is that self-help books tend to place more emphasis on sales than on scientific soundness. The advice offered in these books is far too rarely based on solid, scientific research (Ellis, 1993; Paul, 2001; Rosen, 1993). Instead, the ideas are frequently based on the authors' intuitive analyses, which may be highly speculative. Even when

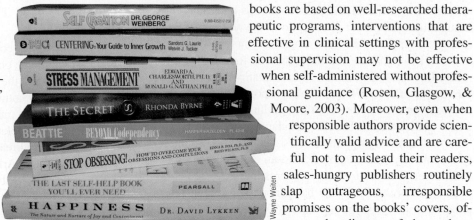

books are based on well-researched therapeutic programs, interventions that are effective in clinical settings with professional supervision may not be effective when self-administered without professional guidance (Rosen, Glasgow, & Moore, 2003). Moreover, even when responsible authors provide scientifically valid advice and are careful not to mislead their readers, sales-hungry publishers routinely slap outrageous, irresponsible promises on the books' covers, often to the dismay of the authors (Rosen et al., 2003).

The third shortcoming is that self-help books don't usually provide explicit directions about how to change your behavior. These books tend to be smoothly written and "touchingly human" in tone. They often strike responsive chords in the reader by aptly describing a common problem that many of us experience. The reader says, "Yes, that's me!" Unfortunately, when the book focuses on how to deal with the problem, it usually provides only a vague distillation of simple common sense, which could be covered in 2 rather than 200 pages. These books often fall back on inspirational cheerleading in the absence of sound, explicit advice.

Fourth, many of these books encourage a remarkably self-centered, narcissistic approach to life (Justman, 2005). **Narcissism is a personality trait marked by an inflated sense of importance, a need for attention and admiration, a sense of entitlement, and a tendency to exploit others.** The term is based on the Greek myth of Narcissus, an attractive young man in search of love who saw himself

Anton Gvozdikov/Shutterstock.com

reflected in water and fell in love with his own image. Although there are plenty of exceptions, the basic message in many self-help books is "Do whatever you feel like doing, and don't worry about the consequences for other people." According to McGee (2005), this mentality began to creep into books in the 1970s, as "bald proposals that one ought to 'look out for #1' or 'win through intimidation' marked a new ruthlessness in the self-help landscape" (p. 50). This "me first" philosophy emphasizes self-admiration, an entitlement to special treatment, and an exploitive approach to interpersonal relationships. Interestingly, research suggests that narcissism levels have increased among recent generations of college students (Twenge & Campbell, 2009; see Chapter 2). It is hard to say how much popular self-help books have fueled this rise, but surely they have contributed (the most widely used measure of narcissism is included in the *Personal Explorations Workbook* in the back of this text).

What to Look for in Self-Help Books

Because self-help books vary so widely in quality, it seems a good idea to provide you with some guidelines about what to look for in seeking genuinely helpful books. The following thoughts give you some criteria for judging books of this type:

1. Clarity in communication is essential. Advice won't do you much good if you can't understand it. Try to avoid drowning in the murky depths of psychobabble.

2. This may sound backward, but look for books that do not promise too much in the way of immediate change. The truly useful books tend to be appropriately cautious in their promises and realistic about the challenge of altering your behavior. As Arkowitz and Lilienfeld (2006, p. 79) put it, "Be wary of books that make promises that they obviously cannot keep, such as curing a phobia in five minutes or fixing a failing marriage in a week."

3. Try to check out the credentials of the author or authors. Book jackets will often exaggerate the expertise of authors, but these days a quick Internet search can often yield more objective biographical information and perhaps some perceptive reviews of the book.

4. Try to select books that mention, at least briefly, the theoretical or research basis for the program they advocate. It is understandable that you may not be interested in a detailed summary of research that supports a particular piece of advice. However, you should be interested in

whether the advice is based on published research, widely accepted theory, anecdotal evidence, clinical interactions with patients, or pure speculation by the author. Books that are based on more than personal anecdotes and speculation should have a list of references in the back (or at the end of each chapter).

5. Look for books that provide detailed, explicit directions about how to alter your behavior. Generally, these directions represent the crucial core of the book. If they are inadequate in detail, you have been shortchanged.

6. More often than not, books that focus on a particular kind of problem, such as overeating, loneliness, or marital difficulties, deliver more than those that promise to cure all of life's problems with a few simple ideas. Books that cover everything are usually superficial and disappointing. Books that devote a great deal of thought to a particular topic tend to be written by authors with genuine expertise on that topic. Such books are more likely to pay off for you.

The Approach of This Textbook

Clearly, in spite of our impressive technological progress, we are a people beset by a great variety of personal problems. Living in our complex, modern society is a formidable challenge. This book is about that challenge. It is about you. It is about life. Specifically, it summarizes the scientific research on human behavior that appears relevant to the challenge of living effectively in contemporary society. It draws primarily, but not exclusively, from the science we call psychology.

This text deals with the same kinds of problems addressed by self-help books, self-realization programs, and popular media "therapists": anxiety, stress, interpersonal relationships, frustration, loneliness, depression, self-control. However, it makes no boldly seductive promises about solving your personal problems, turning your life around, or helping you achieve tranquillity. Such promises simply aren't realistic. Psychologists have long recognized that changing a person's behavior is a difficult challenge, fraught with frustration and failure (Seligman, 1994). Troubled individuals sometimes spend years in therapy without resolving their problems.

This reality does not mean that you should be pessimistic about your potential for personal growth. You most certainly can change your behavior. Moreover, you can often change it on your own without consulting a professional psychologist. We would not be writing this text if we did not believe it could be beneficial to our readers. But it is important that you have realistic expectations. Reading this book will not be a revelatory experience. No mysterious secrets are about to be unveiled. All this book can do is give you some useful information and point you in some potentially beneficial directions. The rest is up to you.

In view of our criticisms of self-realization programs and self-help books, it seems essential that we explicitly lay out the philosophy that underlies the writing of this text. The following statements summarize the assumptions and goals of this book:

1. *This text is based on the premise that accurate knowledge about the principles of psychology can be of value to you in everyday life.* It has been said that knowledge is power. Greater awareness of why people behave as they do should help you in interacting with others as well as in trying to understand yourself.

2. *This text attempts to foster a critical attitude about psychological issues and to enhance your critical thinking skills.* Information is important, but people also need to develop effective strategies for evaluating information. Critical thinking involves subjecting ideas to systematic, skeptical scrutiny. Critical thinkers ask tough questions, such as: What exactly is being asserted? What assumptions underlie this assertion? What evidence or reasoning supports this assertion? Is there contradictory evidence? Are there alternative explanations? Critical thinkers try to avoid emotional reasoning and oversimplification. They also recognize that sometimes they have to tolerate uncertainty. We have already attempted to illustrate the importance of a critical attitude in our evaluation of self-help books, and we'll continue to model critical thinking strategies throughout the text.

3. *This text should open doors.* The coverage in this book is broad; we tackle many topics. Therefore, in some places it may lack the depth or detail that you would like. However, you should think of it as a resource that can introduce you to other books or techniques or therapies, which you can then pursue on your own.

4. *This text assumes that the key to effective adjustment is to take charge of your own life.* If you are dissatisfied with some aspect of your life, it does no good to sit around and mope about it. You have to take an active role in attempting to improve the quality of your life. Doing so may involve learning a new skill or pursuing a particular kind of help. In any case, it is generally best to meet problems head-on rather than trying to avoid them.

Learn More Online

Foundation for Critical Thinking

How can students best develop skills that go beyond merely acquiring information to actively weighing and judging information? The many resources of the Foundation for Critical Thinking at Sonoma State University are directed primarily toward teachers at every level to help them develop their students' critical thinking abilities.

THE PSYCHOLOGY OF ADJUSTMENT

LEARNING OBJECTIVES

- Describe the two key facets of psychology.
- Explain the concept of adjustment.

Now that we have spelled out our approach in writing this text, it is time to turn to the task of introducing you to some basic concepts. In this section, we'll discuss the nature of psychology and the concept of adjustment.

What Is Psychology?

Psychology **is the science that studies behavior and the physiological and mental processes that underlie it, and it is the profession that applies the accumulated knowledge of this science to practical problems.** Psychology leads a complex dual existence as both a *science* and a *profession.* Let's examine the science first. Psychology is an area of scientific study, much like biology or physics. Whereas biology focuses on life processes and physics focuses on matter and energy, psychology focuses on *behavior* and *related mental and physiological processes.*

Behavior **is any overt (observable) response or activity by an organism.** Psychology does *not* confine itself to the study of human behavior. Many psychologists believe that the principles of behavior are much the same for all animals, including humans. As a result, these psychologists often prefer to study animals—mainly because they can exert more control over the factors influencing the animals' behavior.

Psychology is also interested in the mental processes—the thoughts, feelings, and wishes—that accompany behavior. Mental processes are more difficult to study than behavior because they are private and not directly observable. However, they exert critical influence over human behavior, so psychologists have strived to improve their ability to "look inside the mind."

Finally, psychology includes the study of the physiological processes that underlie behavior. Thus, some psychologists try to figure out how bodily processes such as neural impulses, hormonal secretions, and genetic coding regulate behavior.

Practically speaking, all this means that psychologists study a great variety of phenomena. Psychologists are interested in maze running in rats, salivation in dogs, and brain functioning in cats, as well as visual perception in humans, play in children, and social interaction in adults.

As you probably know, psychology is not all pure science. It has a highly practical side, represented by the many psychologists who provide a variety of professional services to the public. Although the profession of psychology is quite prominent today, this aspect of psychology was actually slow to develop. Until the 1950s psychologists were found almost exclusively in the halls of aca-

demia, teaching and doing research. However, the demands of World War II in the 1940s stimulated rapid growth in psychology's first professional specialty: clinical psychology. *Clinical psychology* **is the branch of psychology concerned with the diagnosis and treatment of psychological problems and disorders.** During World War II, a multitude of academic psychologists were pressed into service as clinicians to screen military recruits and treat soldiers suffering from trauma. Many found their clinical work interesting and returned from the war to set up training programs to meet the continued high demand for clinical services. Soon, about half of the new Ph.D.'s in psychology were specializing in clinical work. Psychology had come of age as a profession.

What Is Adjustment?

We have used the term *adjustment* several times without clarifying its exact meaning. The concept of adjustment was originally borrowed from biology. It was modeled after the biological term *adaptation,* which refers to efforts by a species to adjust to changes in its environment. Just as a field mouse has to adapt to an unusually brutal winter, a person has to adjust to changes in circumstances such as a new job, a financial setback, or the loss of a loved one. Thus, *adjustment* **refers to the psychological processes through which people manage or cope with the demands and challenges of everyday life.**

The demands of daily life are diverse, so in studying the process of adjustment we will encounter a broad variety of topics. In our early chapters we discuss general issues, such as how personality affects people's patterns of adjustment, how individuals are affected by stress, and how they use coping strategies to deal with stress. From there we move on to chapters that examine adjustment in an interpersonal context. We discuss topics such as prejudice, persuasion, social conflict, behavior in groups, friendship, love, marriage, divorce, gender roles, career development, and sexuality. Finally, toward the end of the book we discuss how the process of adjustment influences a person's psychological health, look at how psychological disorders can be treated, and delve into the newly developing domain of positive psychology. As you can see, the study of adjustment enters into nearly every corner of people's lives, and we'll be discussing a diverse array of issues. Before we begin considering these topics in earnest, however, we need to take a closer look at psychology's approach to investigating behavior: the scientific method.

THE SCIENTIFIC APPROACH TO BEHAVIOR

LEARNING OBJECTIVES

- Explain the nature of empiricism and the advantages of the scientific approach to behavior.
- Describe the experimental method, distinguishing between independent and dependent variables and between experimental and control groups.
- Distinguish between positive and negative correlation, and explain what the size of a correlation coefficient means.
- Describe three correlational research methods.
- Compare the advantages and disadvantages of experimental versus correlational research.

We all expend a great deal of effort in trying to understand our own behavior as well as the behavior of others. We wonder about any number of behavioral questions: Why am I so anxious when I interact with new people? Why is Sam always trying to be the center of attention at the office? Why does Juanita cheat on her wonderful husband? Are extraverts happier than introverts? Is depression more common during the Christmas holidays? Given that psychologists' principal goal is to explain behavior, how are their efforts different from everyone else's? The key difference is that psychology is a *science*, committed to *empiricism*.

The Commitment to Empiricism

Empiricism is the premise that knowledge should be acquired through observation. When we say that scientific psychology is empirical, we mean that its conclusions are based on systematic observation rather than on reasoning, speculation, traditional beliefs, or common sense. Scientists are not content with having ideas that sound plausible; they must conduct research to *test* their ideas. Whereas our everyday speculations are informal, unsystematic, and highly subjective, scientists' investigations are formal, systematic, and objective.

In these investigations, scientists formulate testable hypotheses, gather data (make observations) relevant to their hypotheses, use statistics to analyze these data, and report their results to the public and other scientists, typically by publishing their findings in a technical journal. The process of publishing scientific studies allows other experts to evaluate and critique new research findings.

Advantages of the Scientific Approach

Science is certainly not the only method that can be used to draw conclusions about behavior. We can also turn to logic, casual observation, and good old-fashioned common sense. Because the scientific method often requires painstaking effort, it seems reasonable to ask: What exactly are the advantages of the empirical approach?

The scientific approach offers two major advantages. The first is its clarity and precision. Commonsense notions about behavior tend to be vague and ambiguous. Consider the old truism "Spare the rod and spoil the child." What does this generalization about childrearing amount to?

How severely should children be punished if parents are not to "spare the rod"? How do parents assess whether a child qualifies as "spoiled"? Such statements can have different meanings to different people. When people disagree about this assertion, it may be because they are talking about entirely different things. In contrast, the empirical approach requires that scientists specify *exactly* what they are talking about when they formulate hypotheses (the ideas they want to test). This clarity and precision enhance communication about important ideas.

The second advantage offered by the scientific approach is its relative intolerance of error. Scientists subject their ideas to empirical tests. They also scrutinize one another's findings with a critical eye. They demand objective data and thorough documentation before they accept ideas. When the findings of two studies conflict, they try to figure out why the studies reached different conclusions, usually by conducting additional research. In contrast, common sense and casual observation often tolerate contradictory generalizations, such as "Opposites attract" and "Birds of a feather flock together." Furthermore, commonsense analyses involve little effort to verify ideas or detect errors, so that many myths about behavior come to be widely believed.

All this is not to say that science has a copyright on truth. However, the scientific approach does tend to yield more accurate and dependable information than casual analyses and armchair speculation. Knowledge of empirical data can thus provide a useful benchmark against which to judge claims and information from other kinds of sources.

Now that we have an overview of how the scientific enterprise works, we can look at some of the specific research methods that psychologists depend on most. The two main types of research methods in psychology are *experimental* and *correlational*. We discuss them separately because an important distinction exists between them.

Experimental Research: Looking for Causes

Does misery love company? This question intrigued social psychologist Stanley Schachter. When people feel anxious, do they want to be left alone, or do they prefer to have others around? Schachter hypothesized that increases in anxiety would cause increases in the desire to be with others, which psychologists call the *need for affiliation*. To test this hypothesis, Schachter (1959) designed a clever experiment. The **experiment is a research method in which the investigator manipulates one (independent) variable under carefully controlled conditions and observes whether any changes occur in a second (dependent) variable as a result.** Psychologists depend on this method more than any other.

Independent and Dependent Variables

An experiment is designed to find out whether changes in one variable (let's call it *x*) cause changes in another variable (let's call it *y*). To put it more concisely, we want to know how *x* affects *y*. In this formulation, we refer to *x* as the independent variable, and we call *y* the dependent variable. **An *independent variable* is a condition or event that an experimenter varies in order to see its impact on another variable.** The independent variable is the variable that the experimenter controls or manipulates. It is hypothesized to have some effect on the dependent variable. The experiment is conducted to verify this effect. **The *dependent variable* is the variable that is thought to be affected by the manipulations of the independent variable.** In psychology studies, the dependent variable is usually a measurement of some aspect of the subjects' behavior.

In Schachter's experiment, *the independent variable was the participants' anxiety level,* which he manipulated in the following way. Subjects assembled in his laboratory were told by a Dr. Zilstein that they would be participating in a study on the physiological effects of electric shock and that they would receive a series of shocks. Half of the participants were warned that the shocks would be very painful. They made up the *high-anxiety* group. The other half of the participants, assigned to the *low-anxiety* group, were told that the shocks would be mild and painless. These procedures were simply intended to evoke different levels of anxiety. In reality, no one was actually shocked at any time. Instead, the experimenter indicated that there would be a delay while he prepared the shock apparatus for use. The participants were asked whether they would prefer to wait alone or in the company of others. *This measure of the subjects' desire to affiliate with others was the dependent variable.*

Experimental and Control Groups

To conduct an experiment, an investigator typically assembles two groups of participants who are treated differently in regard to the independent variable. We call these groups the experimental and control groups. **The *experimental group* consists of the subjects who receive some special treatment in regard to the independent variable. The *control group* consists of similar subjects who do not receive the special treatment given to the experimental group.**

Let's return to the Schachter study to illustrate. In this experiment, the participants in the high-anxiety condition were the experimental group. They received a special treatment designed to create an unusually high level of anxiety. The participants in the low-anxiety condition were the control group.

It is crucial that the experimental and control groups be similar except for the different treatment they receive in regard to the independent variable. This stipulation brings us to the logic that underlies the experimental method. If the two groups are alike in all respects *except for the variation created by the manipulation of the independent variable,* then any differences between the two groups on the dependent variable *must be due to this manipulation of the independent variable.* In this way researchers isolate the effect of the independent variable on the dependent variable. In his experiment, Schachter isolated the impact of anxiety on need for affiliation. What did he find? As predicted, he found that increased anxiety led to increased affiliation. The percentage of people who wanted to wait with others was nearly twice as high in the high-anxiety group as in the low-anxiety group.

The logic of the experimental method rests heavily on the assumption that the experimental and control groups are alike in all important matters except for their different treatment with regard to the independent variable. Any other differences between the two groups cloud the situation and make it difficult to draw solid conclusions about the relationship between the independent variable and the dependent variable. To summarize our discussion of the experimental method, **Figure 1.1** provides an overview of the various elements in an experiment, using Schachter's study as an example.

Advantages and Disadvantages

The experiment is a powerful research method. Its principal advantage is that it allows scientists to draw conclusions about cause-and-effect relationships between variables. Researchers can draw these conclusions about causation because the precise control available in the experiment permits them to isolate the relationship between the independent variable and the dependent variable. No other research method can duplicate this advantage.

For all its power, however, the experimental method has its limitations. One disadvantage is that researchers are often interested in the effects of variables that cannot be manipulated (as independent variables) because of ethical concerns or practical realities. For example, you might want to know whether being brought up in an urban area as opposed to a rural area affects people's values. A true experiment would require you to assign similar families to live in urban and rural areas, which obviously is impossible to do. To explore this question, you would have to use correlational research methods, which we turn to next.

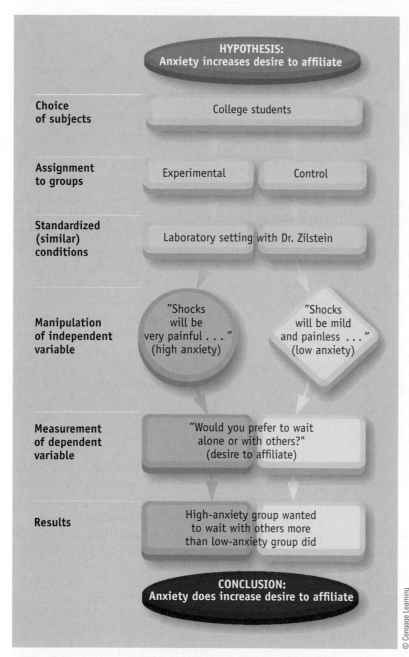

Figure 1.1

The basic elements of an experiment. This diagram provides an overview of the key features of the experimental method, as illustrated by Schachter's study of anxiety and affiliation. The logic of the experiment rests on treating the experimental and control groups alike except for the manipulation of the independent variable.

Learn More Online

Research Methods Tutorials

Bill Trochim's classes in research and program design at Cornell University have assembled tutorial guides for undergraduate and graduate students on more than fifty topics at this subpage (titled Trochim Presentations) of the Web Center for Social Research Methods. Students new to research design may find these tutorials particularly helpful.

Correlational Research: Looking for Links

As we just noted, in some cases psychologists cannot exert experimental control over the variables they want to study. In such situations, all a researcher can do is make systematic observations to see whether a link or association exists between the variables of interest. Such an association is called a correlation. **A *correlation* exists when two variables are related to each other.** The definitive aspect of correlational studies is that the researchers cannot control the variables under study.

Measuring Correlation

The results of correlational research are often summarized with a statistic called the *correlation coefficient*. We'll be referring to this widely used statistic frequently as we discuss studies throughout the remainder of this text. **A *correlation coefficient* is a numerical index of the degree of relationship that exists between two variables.** A correlation coefficient indicates (1) how strongly related two variables are and (2) the direction (positive or negative) of the relationship.

Two kinds of relationships can be described by a correlation. A *positive* correlation indicates that two variables co-vary in the same direction. This means that high scores on variable x are associated with high scores on variable y and that low scores on variable x are associated with low scores on variable y. For example, there is a positive correlation between high school grade point average (GPA) and subsequent college GPA. That is, people who do well in high school tend to do well in college, and those who perform poorly in high school tend to perform poorly in college (see **Figure 1.2** on the next page).

In contrast, a *negative* correlation indicates that two variables co-vary in the opposite direction. This means that people who score high on variable x tend to score low on variable y, whereas those who score low on x tend to score high on y. For example, in most college courses, there is a negative correlation between how often a student is absent and how well the student performs on exams. Students who have a high number of absences tend to earn low exam scores, while students who have a low number of absences tend to get higher exam scores (see **Figure 1.2**).

While the positive or negative sign indicates whether an association is direct or inverse, the *size* of the coefficient indicates the *strength* of the association between two variables. A correlation coefficient can vary between 0 and

Figure 1.2

Positive and negative correlations. Variables are positively correlated if they tend to increase and decrease together and are negatively correlated if one variable tends to increase when the other decreases. Hence, the terms *positive correlation* and *negative correlation* refer to the *direction* of the relationship between two variables.

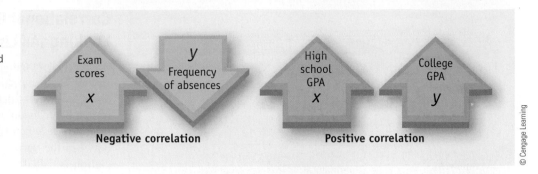

Negative correlation   Positive correlation

© Cengage Learning

+1.00 (if positive) or between 0 and −1.00 (if negative). A coefficient near zero tells us there is no relationship between the variables. The closer the correlation to either −1.00 or +1.00, the stronger the relationship. Thus, a correlation of +.90 represents a stronger tendency for variables to be associated than a correlation of +.40 does (see **Figure 1.3**). Likewise, a correlation of −.75 represents a stronger relationship than a correlation of −.45. Keep in mind that the *strength* of a correlation depends only on the size of the coefficient. The positive or negative sign simply shows whether the correlation is direct or inverse. Therefore, a correlation of −.60 reflects a stronger relationship than a correlation of +.30.

Correlational research methods comprise a number of approaches, including naturalistic observation, case studies, and surveys. Let's examine each of these to see how researchers use them to detect associations between variables.

Naturalistic Observation

In *naturalistic observation* **a researcher engages in careful observation of behavior without intervening directly with the subjects.** This type of research is called *naturalistic* because behavior is allowed to unfold naturally (without interference) in its natural environment— that is, the setting in which it would normally occur. Of course, researchers have to make careful plans to ensure systematic, consistent observations (Angrosino, 2007).

As an example, consider a study by Ramirez-Esparza and colleagues (2009) that examined ethnic differences in sociability using an innovative device called an electronically activated recorder (EAR). The EAR is an unobtrusive, portable audio recorder carried by participants that periodically records their conversations and other ambient sounds as they go about their normal daily activities (Mehl, 2007). Using this clever device, the researchers investigated an interesting paradox—stereotypes suggest that Mexicans are outgoing and sociable, but when asked they rate themselves as less sociable than Americans. The study found, as usual, that Mexican participants rated themselves as less extraverted than American participants rated themselves. But the EAR data on Mexicans' actual daily behavior showed that they were *more* sociable than their American counterparts. The major strength of naturalistic observation is that it allows researchers to study behavior under conditions that are less artificial than in experiments.

Figure 1.3

Interpreting correlation coefficients. The magnitude of a correlation coefficient indicates the strength of the relationship between two variables. The closer a correlation is to either +1.00 or −1.00, the stronger the relationship between the variables. The square of a correlation, which is called the *coefficient of determination,* is an index of a correlation's strength and predictive power. This graph shows how the coefficient of determination and predictive power goes up as the magnitude of a correlation increases.

© Cengage Learning

Case Studies

A *case study* is an in-depth investigation of an individual subject. Psychologists typically assemble case studies in clinical settings where an effort is being made to diagnose and treat some psychological problem. To achieve an understanding of an individual, a clinician may use a variety of procedures, including interviewing the person, interviewing others who know the individual, direct observation, examination of records, and psychological testing. When clinicians assemble a case study for diagnostic purposes, they generally are *not* conducting empirical research. Case study *research* typically involves investigators analyzing a collection or consecutive series of case studies to look for patterns that permit general conclusions.

For example, one study (Arcelus et al., 2009) evaluated the efficacy of a revised version of a treatment called interpersonal psychotherapy (IPT) for people suffering from bulimia (an eating disorder marked by out-of-control overeating followed by self-induced vomiting, fasting, and excessive exercise). Over a two-year period, 59 bulimic patients were treated with IPT at an eating disorders clinic in Great Britain. Case histories were compiled for all the patients, who also took a battery of tests that assessed their eating pathology and other aspects of their psychological functioning. Careful assessments were made of the patients at the midpoint, and at the end of the sixteen-session course of IPT treatment, and three months after treatment was concluded. The results demonstrated that interpersonal therapy can be an effective treatment for bulimic disorders. Case studies are particularly well suited for investigating certain phenomena, especially the roots of psychological disorders and the efficacy of selected therapeutic practices (Fishman, 2007).

Surveys

***Surveys* are structured questionnaires designed to solicit information about specific aspects of participants' behavior.** They are sometimes used to measure dependent variables in experiments, but they are mainly used in correlational research. Surveys are commonly used to gather data on people's attitudes and on aspects of behavior that are difficult to observe directly (marital interactions, for instance). As an example, consider a study that explored the health ramifications of sedentary behavior, in particular the amount of time that people devote to TV and other screen-based entertainment. Stamatakis and colleagues (2009) conducted household interviews with a representative sample of the adult population of Scotland. Almost 8000 participants were interviewed about how many hours per day they devote to television or other screen-based entertainment (including video games and material on computers). The participants also responded to questionnaires about their physical activity, general health, and cardiovascular health, as well as demographic characteristics (income, education, and other indicators of social class). Finally, subjects' height and weight were measured to permit the calculation of their body mass index (BMI), which is a widely used indicator of obesity.

What did the survey data reveal? The data showed a clear association between the amount of time allocated to screen-based entertainment and impaired health. The more people watched TV, the more likely they were to be obese, or to report doctor-diagnosed diabetes or cardiovascular disease, and the less likely they were to report good general health (see **Figure 1.4**). The data also uncovered a rather strong link between social class and time devoted to screen-based entertainment: The people from lower socioeconomic strata spent considerably more time in front of TVs and other screens. The study results underscored the health ramifications of sedentary behavior and demonstrated that lower social class is a key risk factor for elevated sedentary behavior.

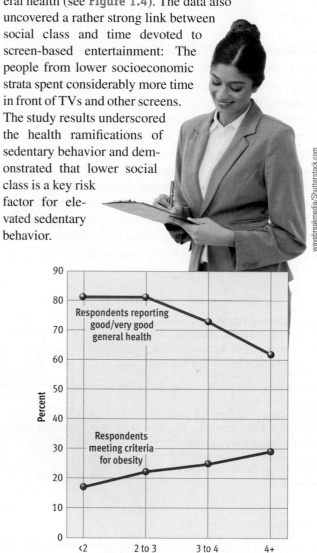

Figure 1.4

TV viewing in relation to health indicators. In the survey by Stamatakis and colleagues (2009), participants provided information about their daily TV viewing habits, answered questions about their physical health, and had their height and weight measured to permit calculation of their body mass index (BMI), which is a standard index of obesity. The blue data line shows the percentage of people who reported being in good or very good general health in relation to TV viewing time. The red data line plots the percentage of participants who met the criteria of obesity in relation to TV watching. Clearly, as TV time increases, general health tends to decline and obesity tends to increase. (Based on Stamatakis et al., 2009)

Advantages and Disadvantages

Correlational research methods give psychologists a way to explore questions that they could not examine with experimental procedures. Consider, for instance, the study on whether the amount of time people spend watching TV relates to their health. Obviously, investigators cannot assign subjects to watch a certain number of hours of TV per day for a decade or two to see if this manipulation affects their health. But the correlational methods used by Stamatakis and colleagues (2009) facilitated the collection of enlightening data on the link between sedentary behavior and health. Thus, *correlational research broadens the scope of phenomena that psychologists can study.*

Unfortunately, correlational methods have one major disadvantage. The investigator does not have the opportunity to control events in a way to isolate cause and effect. *Consequently, correlational research cannot demonstrate conclusively that two variables are causally related.* The crux of the problem is that correlation is no assurance of causation.

When we find that variables x and y are correlated, we can safely conclude only that x and y are related. We do not know *how* x and y are related. We do not know whether x causes y, whether y causes x, or whether both are caused by a third variable. For example, survey studies show a positive correlation between relationship satisfaction and sexual satisfaction (Schwartz & Young, 2009). Although it's clear that good sex and a healthy intimate relationship go hand in hand, it's hard to tell what's causing what. We don't know whether healthy relationships promote good sex or whether good sex promotes healthy relationships. Moreover, we can't rule out the possibility that both are caused by a third variable. Perhaps sexual satisfaction and relationship satisfaction are both caused by compatibility in values. The plausible causal relationships in this case are diagrammed for you in **Figure 1.5**, which illustrates the "third-variable problem" in interpreting correlations. This problem occurs often in correlational research. Indeed, it will surface in the next section, where we review the empirical research on the determinants of happiness.

Figure 1.5

Possible causal relations between correlated variables. When two variables are correlated, there are several possible explanations. It could be that x causes y, that y causes x, or that a third variable, z, causes changes in both x and y. As the correlation between relationship satisfaction and sexual satisfaction illustrates, the correlation itself does not provide the answer. This conundrum is sometimes referred to as the "third-variable problem."

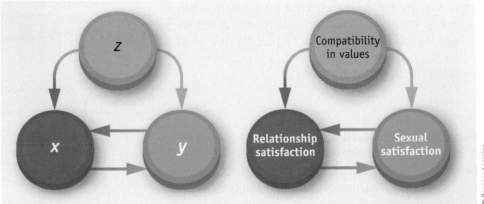

© Cengage Learning

THE ROOTS OF HAPPINESS: AN EMPIRICAL ANALYSIS

LEARNING OBJECTIVES

- Identify the various factors that are surprisingly unrelated to happiness.
- Describe the factors that are somewhat or very important to happiness.
- Summarize conclusions about the determinants of happiness.

What exactly makes a person happy? This question has been the subject of much speculation. Commonsense hypotheses about the roots of happiness abound. For example, you have no doubt heard that money cannot buy happiness. But do you believe it? A television commercial says, "If you've got your health, you've got just about everything." Is health indeed the key? What if you're healthy but poor, unemployed, and lonely? We often hear about the joys of parenthood, the joys of youth, and the joys of the simple, rural life. Are these the factors that promote happiness?

In recent years, social scientists have begun putting these and other hypotheses to empirical test. Quite a number of survey studies have been conducted to explore the determinants of *subjective well-being*—**individuals' personal assessments of their overall happiness or life satisfaction.** The findings of these studies are quite interesting. We review this research because it is central to the topic of adjustment and because it illustrates the value of collecting data and putting ideas to an empirical test. As you will see, many commonsense notions about happiness appear to be inaccurate.

The first of these ideas is the apparently widespread assumption that most people are relatively unhappy. Writers, social scientists, and the general public seem to believe that people around the world are predominantly dissatisfied, yet empirical surveys consistently find that the vast majority of respondents—even those who are poor or disabled—characterize themselves as fairly happy (Diener & Diener, 1996). When people are asked to rate their happiness, only a small minority place themselves below the neutral point on the various scales used (see **Figure 1.6**). When the average subjective well-being of entire nations is computed, based on almost 1000 surveys, the means

cluster toward the positive end of the scale, as shown in **Figure 1.7** (Tov & Diener, 2007). Moreover, these national happiness scores generally have been on the rise since the 1980s (Inglehart et al., 2008). That's not to say that everyone is equally happy. Researchers have found substantial and thought-provoking disparities among people in subjective well-being, which we will analyze momentarily. But the overall picture seems rosier than anticipated.

What Isn't Very Important?

Let us begin our discussion of individual differences in happiness by highlighting those things that turn out to be relatively unimportant determinants of subjective well-being. Quite a number of factors that one might expect to be influential appear to bear little or no relationship to general happiness.

Money. Most people think that if they had more money, they would be happier. There *is* a positive correlation between income and feelings of happiness, but the association is surprisingly weak (Diener & Seligman, 2004). Within specific nations, the correlation between income and happiness tends to fall somewhere between .12 and .20. Obviously, being poor can contribute to unhappiness. Yet it seems once people ascend above a certain level of income, additional wealth does not foster greater happiness. One recent study in the United States estimated that once people exceed an income of around $75,000, little relation is seen between wealth and subjective well-being (Kahneman & Deaton, 2010).

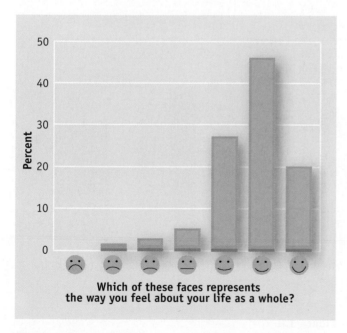

Figure 1.6
Measuring happiness with a nonverbal scale. Researchers have used a variety of methods to estimate the distribution of happiness. For example, in one study in the United States, respondents were asked to examine the seven facial expressions shown and to select the one that "comes closest to expressing how you feel about your life as a whole." As you can see, the vast majority of participants chose happy faces. (Data adapted from Myers, 1992)

Figure 1.7
The subjective well-being of nations. Veenhoven (1993) combined the results of almost 1000 surveys to calculate the average subjective well-being reported by representative samples from forty-three nations. The mean happiness scores clearly pile up at the positive end of the distribution, with only two scores falling below the neutral point of 5. (Data adapted from Diener and Diener, 1996)

Why isn't money a better predictor of happiness? One reason is that a disconnect seems to exist between actual income and how people feel about their financial situation. Recent research (Johnson & Krueger, 2006) suggests that the correlation between actual wealth and people's subjective perceptions of whether they have enough money to meet their needs is surprisingly modest (around .30).

Another problem with money is that in this era of voracious consumption, rising income contributes to escalating material desires (Kasser et al., 2004). People who have lots of nice things tend to want even more. When they cannot afford more, their frustration is likely to undermine their well-being (Norris & Larsen, 2011; Solberg et al., 2002). Thus, complaints about not having enough money are routine even among people who earn hefty six-figure incomes. Interestingly, there is some evidence that people who place an especially strong emphasis on the pursuit of wealth and materialistic goals tend to be somewhat less happy than others (Van Boven, 2005). Perhaps they are so focused on financial success that they derive less satisfaction from other aspects of their lives (Nickerson et al, 2003). Consistent with this view, one study (Kahneman et al., 2006) found that higher income was associated with working longer hours and allocating fewer hours to leisure pursuits (see **Figure 1.8**). The results of another recent study suggested that wealthy people become jaded in a way that undermines their ability to savor positive experiences (Quoidbach et al., 2010).

Age. Age has generally been found to be unrelated to global estimates of happiness (Lykken, 1999; Myers & Diener, 1997). For example, a study of over 7000 adults concluded that levels of happiness did not vary with age (Cooper et al., 2011). That said, some recent studies have found modest-sized links between age and subjective well-being. For instance, a recent Gallup telephone poll of over 340,000 people uncovered a U-shaped relationship between age and happiness (Stone et al., 2010). That is, reports of happiness were relatively high for people in their 20s and 30s, dipped a bit when people were in their 40s and 50s, and climbed steadily for people in their 60s and 70s. Thus, conclusions about the relationship between age and happiness may require some revision, although more research is needed.

Gender. Women are treated for depressive disorders about twice as often as men (Nolen-Hoeksema, 2002), so one might expect that women are less happy on the average. And

Lykken (1999) notes that "men still tend to have better jobs than women do, and get higher pay for the same jobs . . . but they report well-being levels as high as those of men" (p. 181). Thus, surprisingly, research suggests that gender accounts for less than 1% of the variation in people's subjective well-being (Myers, 1992).

Parenthood. Children can be a tremendous source of joy and fulfillment, but they can also be a tremendous source of headaches and hassles. Compared to childless couples, parents worry more and experience more marital problems. Apparently, the good and bad aspects of parenthood balance each other out, because the evidence indicates that people who have children are neither more nor less happy than people without children (Argyle, 2001).

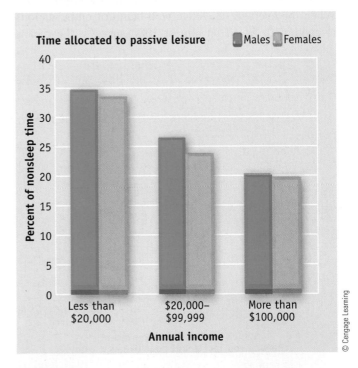

Figure 1.8

Income and leisure. In an influential study of happiness, Nobel laureate Daniel Kahneman and his colleagues (2006) attempted to shed light on why the association between income and subjective well-being is so weak. One of their key findings was that as income goes up, the time devoted to work increases, and hence, the time left for leisure declines. This graph shows the percentage of nonsleep time devoted to passive leisure activities for three levels of income.

Intelligence. Intelligence is a highly valued trait in modern society, but researchers have not found an association between IQ scores and happiness (Diener, Kesebir, & Tov, 2009). Educational attainment also appears to be unrelated to life satisfaction (Ross & Van Willigen, 1997).

Physical attractiveness. Good-looking people enjoy a variety of advantages in comparison to unattractive people. Given that physical attractiveness is an important resource in Western society, we might expect attractive people to be happier than others, but the available data indicate that the correlation between attractiveness and happiness is negligible (Diener, Wolsic, & Fujita, 1995).

What Is Somewhat Important?

Research has identified four facets of life that appear to have a moderate impact on subjective well-being: health, social activity, religious belief, and culture.

Health. Good physical health would seem to be an essential requirement for happiness, but people adapt to health problems. Research reveals that individuals who develop serious, disabling health conditions aren't as unhappy as one might guess (Riis et al., 2005). Good health may not, by itself, produce happiness, because people tend to take good health for granted. Such considerations may help explain why researchers find only a moderate positive correlation (average = .32) between health status and subjective well-being (Argyle, 1999). While health may promote happiness to a moderate degree, happiness may also foster better health, as research has found a positive correlation between happiness and longevity (Veenhoven, 2008).

Social activity. Humans are social animals, and people's interpersonal relations *do* appear to contribute to their happiness. People who are satisfied with their friendship networks and who are socially active report above-average levels of happiness (Diener & Seligman, 2004). And people who score as exceptionally happy tend to report greater satisfaction with their social relations than others (Diener & Seligman, 2002). One recent study that periodically recorded participants' daily conversations found that people who had more deep, substantive conversations were happier than those who mostly engaged in small talk (Mehl et al., 2010). This finding is not all that surprising, in that one would expect that people with richer social networks would have more deep conversations.

Religion. The link between religiosity and subjective well-being is modest, but a number of surveys suggest that people with heartfelt religious convictions are more likely to be happy than people who characterize themselves as nonreligious (Myers, 2008). The association between reli-

gion and happiness appears to be stronger in societies where circumstances are difficult and stressful, and it is weaker in more affluent societies where circumstances are less threatening (Diener, Tay, & Myers, 2011). These findings suggest that religion may help people cope with adversity, and they may shed some light on why many people are leaving organized religions in affluent countries, where overall adversity is low.

Culture. Surveys suggest that there are some moderate differences among nations in mean levels of subjective well-being. These differences correlate with economic development, as the nations with the happiest people tend to be affluent and those with the least happy people tend to be among the poorest (Diener, Kesebir, & Tov, 2009). Although wealth is a weak predictor of subjective well-being *within* cultures, comparisons *between* cultures tend to yield rather strong correlations between nations' wealth and their people's average happiness (Tov & Diener, 2007). How do theorists explain this paradox? They believe that national wealth is a relatively easy-to-measure marker associated with a matrix of cultural conditions that influence happiness. Specifically, they point out that nations' economic development correlates with greater recognition of human rights, greater income equality, greater gender equality, and more democratic governance (Tov & Diener, 2007). So, it may not be affluence per se that is the driving force behind cultural disparities in subjective well-being. Consistent with this analysis, a recent study found that income inequality is associated with reduced happiness (Oishi, Kesebir, & Diener, 2011).

What Is Very Important?

The list of factors that turn out to be very important ingredients of happiness is surprisingly short. Only a few variables are strongly related to overall happiness.

Love, marriage, and relationship satisfaction. Romantic relationships can be stressful, but people consistently rate being in love as one of the most critical ingredients of happiness (Myers, 1999). Furthermore, although people complain a lot about their marriages, the evidence indicates that marital status is a key correlate of happiness. Among both men and women, married people are happier than people who are single or divorced (Myers & Diener, 1995), and this disparity holds around the world in widely different cultures (Diener et al., 2000). And among married people, marital satisfaction predicts personal well-being (Proulx, Helms, & Buehler, 2007). The research in this area generally has used marital status as a crude but easily measured marker of relationship satisfaction. In all likelihood, it is relationship satisfaction that fosters happiness. In other words, one does not have to be married to be

Research on the correlates of happiness suggests that one key ingredient of subjective well-being is a rewarding work life.

Peter Bernik/Shutterstock.com

happy. Relationship satisfaction probably has the same association with happiness in cohabiting heterosexual couples and gay couples. In support of this line of thinking, a recent study found that both married and cohabiting people were happier than those who remained single (Musick & Bumpass, 2012).

Work. Given the way people often complain about their jobs, we might not expect work to be a key source of happiness, but it is. Although less critical than relationship satisfaction, job satisfaction is strongly associated with general happiness (Judge & Klinger, 2008). Studies also show that unemployment has strong negative effects on subjective well-being (Lucas et al., 2004). It is difficult to sort out whether job satisfaction causes happiness or vice versa, but evidence suggests that causation flows both ways.

Genetics and personality. The best predictor of individuals' future happiness is their past happiness (Lucas & Diener, 2008). Some people seem destined to be happy and others unhappy, regardless of their triumphs or setbacks. The limited influence of life events was highlighted in a fascinating study that found only modest differences in overall happiness between recent lottery winners and recent accident victims who became quadriplegics (Brickman, Coates, & Janoff-Bulman, 1978). Investigators were amazed that extremely fortuitous and horrible events like these didn't have a dramatic impact on happiness. Actually, *several* lines of evidence suggest that happiness does not depend on external circumstances—buying a nice house, getting promoted—as much as on internal factors, such as one's outlook on life (Lyubomirsky, Sheldon, & Schkade, 2005).

With this finding in mind, researchers have investigated whether a hereditary basis might exist for variations in happiness. These studies suggest that people's genetic predispositions account for a substantial portion of the variance in happiness, perhaps as much as 50% (Lyubomirsky et al., 2005). How can one's genes influence one's happiness? Presumably, by shaping one's temperament and personality, which are known to be highly heritable. Hence, researchers have begun to look for links between personality

Mark Davidson/Alamy

and subjective well-being, and they have found some relatively strong correlations (Steel, Schmidt, & Schultz, 2008). For example, *extraversion* is one of the better predictors of happiness. People who are outgoing, upbeat, and sociable tend to be happier than others. Another potent predictor is *neuroticism*—the tendency to be anxious, hostile, insecure, and self-conscious. Those who score high in neuroticism tend to be less happy than others. Such personality traits may influence happiness by shaping how people recall and evaluate their personal experiences (Zhang & Howell, 2011). Extraverts tend to look at their lives through rose-tinted glasses, leaning toward positive evaluations with few regrets. Those who are neurotic tend to evaluate their experiences with more of a negative slant.

Conclusions

We must be cautious in drawing inferences about the causes of happiness, because most of the available data are correlational (see **Figure 1.9**). Nonetheless, the empirical evidence suggests that many popular beliefs about the sources of happiness are unfounded. The data also demonstrate that happiness is shaped by a complex constellation of variables. Despite this complexity, however, a number of worthwhile insights about human adjustment can be gleaned from research on the correlates of subjective well-being.

First, research on happiness demonstrates that the determinants of subjective well-being are precisely that: subjective. *Objective realities are not as important as subjective feelings.* In other words, your health, your wealth, your job, and your

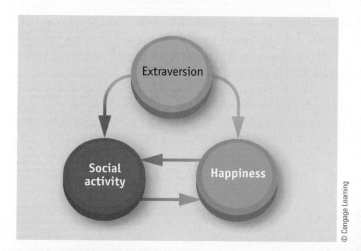

© Cengage Learning

Figure 1.9

Possible causal relations among the correlates of happiness. Although we have considerable data on the correlates of happiness, it is difficult to untangle the possible causal relationships. For example, we know that a moderate positive correlation exists between social activity and happiness, but we can't say for sure whether high social activity causes happiness or whether happiness causes people to be more socially active. Moreover, in light of the finding that a third variable—extraversion—correlates with both variables, we have to consider the possibility that extraversion causes both greater social activity and greater happiness.

age are not as influential as how you *feel* about your health, wealth, job, and age (Schwarz & Strack, 1999).

Second, *when it comes to happiness, everything is relative.* In other words, you evaluate what you have relative to what the people around you have. Thus, people who are wealthy assess what they have by comparing themselves to their wealthy friends and neighbors, and their *relative ranking* is crucial (Boyce, Brown, & Moore, 2010). This is one reason for the surprisingly low correlation between wealth and happiness within specific societies. You might have a lovely home, but if it sits next to a neighbor's palatial mansion, this situation might be a source of more dissatisfaction than happiness.

Third, *research on happiness has shown that people are surprisingly bad at predicting what will make them happy.* We assume that we know what is best for us. But research on **affective forecasting—efforts to predict one's emotional reactions to future events**—suggests otherwise (Gilbert, 2006b; Wilson & Gilbert, 2005). People routinely overestimate the pleasure that they will derive from buying an expensive automobile, taking an exotic vacation, earning an important promotion, moving to a beautiful coastal city, or building their dream home (see the Recommended Reading Box and Chapter 6 for more on affective forecasting). Likewise, people tend to overestimate the misery and regret they will experience if they have a romantic breakup, don't get into the college they want, fail to get a promotion, or develop a serious illness. Thus, the roadmap to happiness is less clearly marked than widely assumed.

Fourth, *research on subjective well-being indicates that people often adapt to their circumstances.* This adaptation effect is one reason that an increase in income doesn't necessarily bring an increase in happiness. Thus, **hedonic adaptation occurs when the mental scale that people use to judge the pleasantness-unpleasantness of their experiences shifts so that their neutral point, or baseline for comparison, is changed** (*hedonic* means related to pleasure). Unfortunately, when people's experiences improve,

RECOMMENDED reading

Stumbling on Happiness
by Daniel Gilbert (HarperCollins, 2006)

Do you think you know what will make you happy? Think again. If you read this book, you won't be nearly so confident about what will provide you with pleasure in the years to come. Daniel Gilbert is a Harvard psychologist who has pioneered research on *affective forecasting*—people's tendency to predict their emotional reactions to future events. This research shows that people tend to be reasonably accurate in anticipating whether events will generate positive or negative emotions, but they are often way off the mark in predicting the intensity and duration of their emotional reactions. Why are people's predictions of their emotional reactions surprisingly inaccurate? A number of factors can contribute. One consideration is that people often assume they will spend a lot of time dwelling on a setback or relishing a triumph, but in reality a variety of other events and concerns will compete for their attention. Another consideration is that most people do not fully appreciate just how effective humans tend to be in rationalizing, discounting, and overlooking their failures and mistakes. People exhibit several cognitive biases that help them insulate themselves from the emotional fallout of life's difficulties, but they do not factor this peculiar "talent" into the picture when making predictions about their emotional reactions to setbacks. In this wide-ranging book, Gilbert ventures far beyond the work on affective forecasting, profiling research on a host of related topics (especially peculiarities in decision making), but the central theme is that people's expectations about what will bring them happiness are surprisingly inaccurate. As you may have already gathered, this is not a self-help book per se, but it makes for fascinating reading that has some important implications for the never-ending pursuit of happiness. Although he describes a great deal of research, Gilbert's writing is so accessible, engaging, and humorous, it never feels like a review of research.

Log on to CourseMate at **www.cengagebrain.com** *for descriptions of other recommended books.*

hedonic adaptation may *sometimes* put them on a *hedonic treadmill*—their baseline moves upward, so that the improvements yield no real benefits (Kahneman, 1999). However, when people have to grapple with major setbacks, hedonic adaptation probably helps protect their mental and physical health. For example, people who are sent to prison and people who develop debilitating diseases are not as unhappy as one might assume, because they adapt to their changed situations and evaluate events from a new perspec-

tive (Frederick & Loewenstein, 1999). That's not to say that hedonic adaptation in the face of life's difficulties is inevitable or complete, but people adapt to setbacks much better than widely assumed (Lucas, 2007).

We turn next to an example of how psychological research can be applied to everyday problems. In our first application section, we will review research evidence related to the challenge of being a successful student.

Application

IMPROVING ACADEMIC PERFORMANCE

LEARNING OBJECTIVES

- List three steps for developing sound study habits.
- Discuss some strategies for improving reading comprehension and getting more out of lectures.
- Describe various study strategies that that can aid memory.

Answer the following "true" or "false."

___ **1.** If you have a professor who delivers chaotic, hard-to-follow lectures, there is little point in attending class.

___ **2.** Cramming the night before an exam is an efficient way to study.

___ **3.** In taking lecture notes, you should try to be a "human tape recorder" (that is, take down everything exactly as said by your professor).

___ **4.** Outlining reading assignments is a waste of time.

As you will soon learn, all of these statements are false. If you answered them all correctly, you may already have acquired the kinds of skills and habits that lead to academic success. If so, however, you are not typical. Today, a huge number of students enter college with remarkably poor study skills and habits—and it's not entirely their fault. The U.S. educational system generally does not provide much in the way of formal instruction on good study techniques. So, in this first Application, we'll start with the basics and try to remedy this deficiency to some extent by sharing some insights that psychology can provide on how to improve your academic performance. We will discuss how to promote better study habits, how to enhance reading efforts, how to get more out of lectures, and how to make your memory more effective.

Developing Sound Study Habits

People tend to assume that academic performance in college is largely determined by students' intelligence or general mental ability. This belief is supported by the fact that college admissions tests (the SAT and ACT), which basically assess general cognitive ability, predict college

grades fairly well (Kobrin et al., 2008). What is far less well known, however, is that measures of study skills, habits, and attitudes also predict college grades pretty well. In a large-scale review of 344 independent samples consisting of over 72,000 students, Crede and Kuncel (2008) reported that aggregate measures of study skills and habits predicted college grades almost as well as admissions tests did, and that they accounted for variability in performance that the admissions tests could not account for. In other words, this massive review of evidence found that study habits are almost as influential as ability in determining college success. The practical meaning of this finding is that most students probably underestimate the importance of their study skills. And while most adults probably cannot increase their mental ability much, their study habits can usually be enhanced considerably.

In any event, the first step toward effective study habits is to face up to the reality that studying usually involves hard work. You don't have to feel guilty if you don't look forward to studying. Most students don't. Once you accept the premise that studying doesn't come naturally, it should

Learn More Online

Sites to Promote Academic Success

This site provides links to a number of other sites that provide advice on a diverse array of study-related topics, such as time management, effective note taking, memory-improvement strategies, and test-taking skills. Developed by Linda Walsh, a psychology professor at the University of Northern Iowa, it is an invaluable resource for students seeking to improve their chances of academic success.

be apparent that you need to set up an organized program to promote adequate study. According to Siebert and Karr (2008), such a program should include the following considerations.

Set up a schedule for studying. Research on the differences between successful and unsuccessful college students suggests that successful students monitor and regulate their use of time more effectively (Allgood et al., 2000). If you wait until the urge to study hits you, you may still be waiting when the exam rolls around. Thus, it is important to allocate definite times to study. Review your time obligations (work, housekeeping, and so on) and figure out in advance when you can study. In allotting certain times to studying, keep in mind that you need to be wide awake and alert. Be realistic, too, about how long you can study at one time before you wear down from fatigue.

Allow time for study breaks; they can revive sagging concentration.

It's important to write down your study schedule (Tracy, 2006). Doing so serves as a reminder and increases your commitment to the schedule. As shown in **Figure 1.10**, you should begin by setting up a general schedule for the quarter or semester. Then, at the beginning of each week, plan the specific assignments that you intend to work on during each study session. This approach should help you avoid cramming for exams at the last minute. Cramming is an ineffective study strategy for most students (Wong, 2012). It will strain your memorization capabilities, can tax your energy level, and may stoke the fires of test anxiety.

In planning your weekly schedule, try to avoid the tendency to put off working on major tasks such as term papers and reports. Time management experts point out that many of us tend to tackle simple, routine tasks first, saving larger tasks for later, when we supposedly will have more time. This common tendency leads many of us to delay working on major assignments until it's too late to do a good job. You can avoid this trap by breaking major assignments into smaller component tasks that you schedule individually.

Find a place to study where you can concentrate. Where you study is also important. The key is to find a place where distractions are likely to be minimal. Most people cannot study effectively while watching TV, listening to loud music, or overhearing conversations. Don't depend on willpower to carry you through these distractions. It's much easier to plan ahead and avoid the distractions altogether.

Reward your studying. One of the reasons it is so difficult to motivate oneself to study regularly is that the payoffs for studying often lie in the distant future. The ultimate reward, a degree, may be years away. Even shorter-term rewards, such as an A in the course, may be weeks or months off. To combat this problem, it helps to give yourself immediate rewards for studying. It is easier to motivate yourself to study if you reward yourself with a tangible payoff, such as a snack, TV show, or phone call to a friend, when you finish. Thus, you should set realistic study goals and then reward yourself when you meet them.

	MON	TUES	WED	THURS	FRI	SAT	SUN
8 A.M.						Work	
9 A.M.	History	Study	History	Study	History	Work	
10 A.M.	Psych	French	Psych	French	Psych	Work	
11 A.M.	Study		Study		Study	Work	
Noon	Math	Study	Math	Study	Math	Work	Study
1 P.M.							Study
2 P.M.	Study	English	Study	English	Study		Study
3 P.M.	Study		Study		Study		Study
4 P.M.							
5 P.M.							
6 P.M.	Work	Study	Work				Study
7 P.M.	Work	Study	Work				Study
8 P.M.	Work	Study	Work				Study
9 P.M.	Work	Study	Work				Study
10 P.M.	Work		Work				

Figure 1.10

Example of an activity schedule. One student's general activity schedule for a semester is shown here. Each week the student fills in the specific assignments to work on during the upcoming study sessions.

ELnur/Shutterstock.com

© Cengage Learning

Improving Your Reading

Much of your study time is spent reading and absorbing information. The keys to improving reading comprehension are to preview reading assignments section by section, work hard to actively process the meaning of the information, strive to identify the key ideas of each paragraph, and carefully review these key ideas after each section. Modern textbooks often contain a variety of learning aids that you can use to improve your reading. If a book provides a chapter outline, chapter summary, or learning objectives, don't ignore them. These study elements can help you recognize the important points in the chapter. A lot of effort and thought go into formulating these and other textbook learning aids. It is wise to take advantage of them.

Another important issue related to textbook reading is whether and how to mark up one's reading assignments. Many students deceive themselves into thinking that they are studying by running a marker through a few sentences here and there in their text. If they do so without thoughtful selectivity, they are simply turning a textbook into a coloring book. This reality probably explains why some professors are skeptical about the value of highlighting textbooks. Nonetheless, research suggests that highlighting textbook material *is* a useful strategy—if students are reasonably effective in focusing on the main ideas in the material and if they subsequently review what they have highlighted (Caverly, Orlando, & Mullen, 2000).

When executed effectively, highlighting can foster active reading, improve reading comprehension, and reduce the amount of material that one has to review later (Van Blerkom, 2012). The key to effective text marking is to identify (and highlight) only the main ideas, key supporting details, and technical terms. Most textbooks are carefully crafted such that every paragraph has a purpose for being there. Try to find the sentence or two that best captures the purpose of each paragraph. Text marking is a delicate balancing act. If you highlight too little of the content, you are not identifying enough of the key ideas. But if you highlight too much of the content, you are not going to succeed in condensing what you have to review to a manageable size.

Other methods can also be used to enhance the effectiveness of your reading. One approach is to read a section of text and then set it aside and try to recall as much of the information as possible; then review the material again and repeat the recall effort. A study of this *retrieval practice* approach found it to be clearly superior to simple repeated study for an equal amount of time and even to elaborate concept-mapping procedures (Karpicke & Blunt, 2011). A related approach is to read a passage and then set it aside and generate questions about the passage, which you then try to an-swer. A study of this strategy found that it yielded greater mastery of material than simply reading and rereading sections of text (Weinstein, McDermott, & Roediger, 2010).

Getting More out of Lectures

Although lectures are sometimes boring and tedious, it is a simple fact that poor class attendance is associated with poor grades. For example, Lindgren (1969) found that absences from class were much more common among "unsuccessful" students (grade average of C− or below) than among "successful" students (grade average of B or above), as shown in **Figure 1.11**. Even when you have an instructor who delivers hard-to-follow lectures from which you learn virtually nothing, it is still important to go to class. If nothing else, you'll get a feel for how the instructor thinks. Doing so can help you anticipate the content of exams and respond in the manner your professor expects.

Fortunately, most lectures are reasonably coherent. Studies indicate that attentive note taking *is* associated with enhanced learning and performance in college classes (Titsworth & Kiewra, 2004). However, research also shows that many students' lecture notes are surprisingly incomplete, with the average student often recording less than 40% of the crucial ideas in a lecture (Armbruster, 2000). Thus, the key to getting more out of lectures is to stay motivated, stay attentive, and expend the effort to make your notes as complete as possible. Books on study skills (Downing, 2011; McWhorter & Sember, 2013) offer a number of suggestions on how to take good-quality lecture notes. These suggestions include:

- *Use active listening procedures.* With active listening, you focus full attention on the speaker. Try to anticipate what's coming and search for deeper meanings. Pay

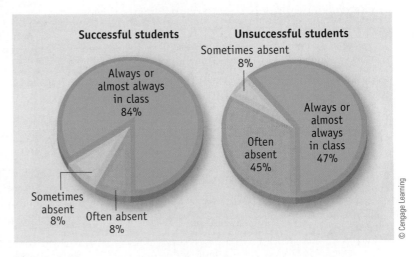

Figure 1.11

Successful and unsuccessful students' class attendance. Lindgren (1969) found that attendance was much better among successful students than unsuccessful students.

attention to nonverbal signals that may serve to further clarify the lecturer's intent or meaning.

- *Prepare for lectures by reading ahead on the scheduled subject in your text.* If you review the text, you have less information to digest that is brand new. This strategy is especially important when course material is complex and difficult.
- *Write down lecturers' thoughts in your own words.* Don't try to be a human tape recorder. Translating the lecture into your own words forces you to organize the ideas in a way that makes sense to you.
- *Look for subtle and not-so-subtle clues about what the instructor considers to be important.* These clues may range from simply repeating main points to saying things like "You'll run into this again."
- *Ask questions during lectures.* Doing so keeps you actively involved and allows you to clarify points you may have misunderstood. Many students are more bashful about asking questions than they should be. They don't realize that most professors welcome questions.

Applying Memory Principles

Scientific investigation of memory processes dates back to 1885, when Hermann Ebbinghaus published a series of insightful studies. Since then, psychologists have discovered a number of principles about memory that are relevant to helping you improve your study skills.

Engage in Adequate Practice

Practice makes perfect, or so you've heard. In reality, practice is not likely to guarantee perfection, but repeatedly reviewing information usually leads to improved retention. Studies show that retention improves with increased rehearsal (Greene, 1992). Evidence suggests that it even pays to overlearn material. ***Overlearning* is continued rehearsal of material after you have first appeared to master it.** In one classic study, after participants mastered a list of nouns (they recited the list without error), Krueger (1929) required them to continue rehearsing for 50% or 100% more trials (repetitions). Measuring retention at intervals of up to 28 days, Krueger found that overlearning led to better recall of the list. Modern studies have also shown that overlearning can enhance performance on an exam that occurs within a week, although the evidence on its long-term benefits (months later) is inconsistent (Rohrer et al., 2005).

Although the benefits of practice are well known, people have a curious tendency to overestimate their knowledge of a topic and how well they will perform on a subsequent memory test of this knowledge (Koriat & Bjork, 2005). After studying material, people also tend to underestimate the value of additional study and practice (Kornell et al., 2011). That's why it is a good idea to informally test yourself on information you think you have mastered before confronting a real test. In addition to checking your mastery, recent research suggests that testing actually enhances retention, a phenomenon dubbed the *testing effect* (Roediger & Butler, 2011). Studies have shown that taking a test on material increases performance on a subsequent test even more than studying for an equal amount of time (see **Figure 1.12**). The favorable effects of testing are enhanced if participants are provided feedback on their test performance (Butler & Roediger, 2008). Moreover, studies have demonstrated that the laboratory findings on the testing effect replicate in real-world educational settings (McDaniel et al., 2011; Roediger et al., 2011). Unfortunately, given the recent nature of this discovery, relatively few students are aware of the value of testing (Karpicke, Butler, & Roediger, 2009).

Why is testing so beneficial? The key appears to be that testing forces students to engage in effortful retrieval of information, which promotes future retention (Roediger et al., 2010). Indeed, even *unsuccessful* retrieval efforts can enhance retention (Kornell, Hays, & Bjork, 2009). In any event, self-testing appears to be an excellent memory tool, which suggests that it would be prudent to take the Practice Tests in this text or additional tests available on the website for the book.

Use Distributed Practice

Let's assume that you are going to study 9 hours for an exam. Is it better to "cram" all of your study into one 9-hour period (massed practice) or distribute it among, say, three 3-hour periods on successive days (distributed practice)? The evidence indicates that retention tends to be greater after distributed practice than massed practice (Kornell et al., 2010; Rohrer & Pashler, 2010). Moreover, a review of over 300 experiments (Cepeda et al., 2006) showed that the longer the retention interval between studying and testing, the bigger the advantage for spaced practice, as shown in **Figure 1.13**. The same review concluded that the longer the retention interval, the longer the optimal "break" between practice trials. When an upcoming test is more than two days away, the optimal interval between practice periods appears to be around 24 hours. The superiority of distributed practice over massed practice provides another reason why cramming is an ill-advised approach to studying for exams.

Organize Information

Retention tends to be greater when information is well organized (Einstein & McDaniel, 2004). Hierarchical organization is particularly helpful when it is applicable. Thus, it may be a good idea to *outline* reading assignments for school. Consistent with this reasoning, there is some empirical evidence that outlining material from textbooks can enhance retention of the material (McDaniel, Waddill, & Shakesby, 1996).

Emphasize Deep Processing

One line of research suggests that how *often* you go over material is less critical than the *depth* of processing that you engage in (Craik & Tulving, 1975). Thus, if you expect to remember what you read, you have to wrestle fully with its meaning (Einstein & McDaniel, 2004). Many students could probably benefit if they spent less time on rote repetition and more on actually paying attention to and analyzing the meaning of their reading assignments. In particular, it is useful to make material *personally* meaningful. When you read your textbooks, try to relate information to your own life and experience. For example, if you're reading in your psychology text about the personality trait of assertiveness, you can think about which people you know who are particularly assertive and why you would characterize them as being that way.

Use Mnemonic Devices

Of course, it's not always easy to make something personally meaningful. When you study chemistry, you may have a hard time relating to polymers at a personal level. This problem has led to the development of many **mnemonic devices, or strategies for enhancing memory,** that are designed to make abstract material more meaningful.

Acrostics and acronyms. *Acrostics* are phrases (or poems) in which the first letter of each word (or line) functions as

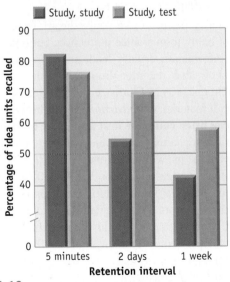

Figure 1.12

The testing effect. In one study by Roediger and Karpicke (2006b), participants studied a brief prose passage for 7 minutes. Then, some of them studied it again for 7 minutes while others took a 7-minute test on the material. In the second phase of the study, subjects took another test on the material after either 5 minutes, 2 days, or 1 week. There wasn't much of a performance gap when subjects were tested over a 5-minute retention interval, but the testing group showed a significant advantage in recall when the retention interval was extended to 2 days or 1 week.

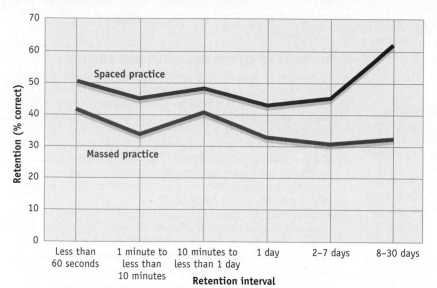

Figure 1.13
Effects of massed versus distributed practice on retention. In a review of over 300 experiments on massed versus distributed practice, Cepeda et al. (2006) examined the importance of the retention interval. As you can see, spaced practice was superior to massed practice at all retention intervals, but the gap widened at longer intervals. These findings suggest that distributed practice is especially advantageous when you need or want to remember material over the long haul. (Based on data from Cepeda et al., 2006)

a cue to help you recall the abstract words that begin with the same letter. For instance, you may remember the order of musical notes with the saying "Every good boy does fine" (or "deserves favor"). A variation on acrostics is the *acronym*—a word formed out of the first letters of a series of words. Students memorizing the order of colors in the light spectrum often store the name "Roy G. Biv" to remember red, orange, yellow, green, blue, indigo, and violet. Acrostics and acronyms that individuals create for themselves can be effective memory tools (Hermann, Raybeck, & Gruneberg, 2002).

Link method. The *link method* involves forming a mental image of items to be remembered in a way that links them together. For instance, suppose you are going to stop at the drugstore on the way home and you need to remember to pick up a news magazine, shaving cream, film, and pens. To remember these items, you might visualize a public figure likely to be in the magazine shaving with a pen while being photographed. Some researchers suggest that the more bizarre the images, the better they will be remembered (Iaccino, 1996).

Method of loci. The *method of loci* involves taking an imaginary walk along a familiar path where you have associated images of items you want to remember with certain locations. The first step is to commit to memory a series of loci, or places along a path. Usually these loci are specific locations in your home or neighborhood. Then envision each thing you want to remember in one of these locations. Try to form distinctive, vivid images. When you need to remember the items, imagine yourself walking along the path. The various loci on your path should serve as retrieval cues for the images that you formed (see **Figure 1.14**). The method of loci assures that items are remembered in their correct order because the order is determined by the sequence of locations along the pathway. Empirical studies have supported the value of this method for memorizing lists (Massen & Vaterrodt-Plünnecke, 2006). One study found that using loci along a pathway from home to work was more effective than a pathway through one's home (Massen et al., 2009).

Figure 1.14
The method of loci. In this example from Bower (1970), a person about to go shopping pairs items to be remembered with familiar places (loci) arranged in a natural sequence: (1) hot dogs/driveway; (2) cat food/garage; (3) tomatoes/front door; (4) bananas/coat closet; (5) whiskey/kitchen sink. As the last panel shows, the shopper recalls the items by mentally touring the loci associated with them.

CHAPTER *1* | Review

KEY IDEAS

THE PARADOX OF PROGRESS

- Although our modern era has seen great technological progress, personal problems have not diminished. In spite of many time-saving devices, people tend to have less free time. The life choices available to people have increased greatly, but evidence suggests that choice overload undermines individuals' happiness.
- Although we have unprecedented control over the world around us, we seem to create as many problems as we solve. Thus, many theorists argue that technological progress has brought new, and possibly more difficult, adjustment problems.

THE SEARCH FOR DIRECTION

- According to many theorists, the basic challenge of modern life has become the search for a sense of direction and meaning. This search has many manifestations, including the appeal of self-realization programs, religious cults, and media "therapists."
- The enormous popularity of self-help books is an interesting manifestation of people's struggle to find a sense of direction. Some self-help books offer worthwhile advice, but most are dominated by psychobabble and are not based on scientific research. Many also lack explicit advice on how to change behavior and some encourage a self-centered, narcissistic approach to interpersonal interactions.
- Although this text deals with many of the same issues as self-realization programs, self-help books, and other types of pop psychology, its philosophy and approach are quite different. This text is based on the premise that accurate knowledge about the principles of psychology can be of value in everyday life.

THE PSYCHOLOGY OF ADJUSTMENT

- Psychology is both a science and a profession that focuses on behavior and related mental and physiological processes. Adjustment is a broad area of study in psychology concerned with how people adapt effectively or ineffectively to the demands and pressures of everyday life.

THE SCIENTIFIC APPROACH TO BEHAVIOR

- The scientific approach to understanding behavior is empirical. Psychologists base their conclusions on formal, systematic, objective tests of their hypotheses, rather than reasoning, speculation, or common sense. The scientific approach is advantageous in that it puts a premium on clarity and has little tolerance for error.
- Experimental research involves manipulating an independent variable to discover its effect on a dependent variable. The experimenter usually does so by comparing experimental and control groups, which must be alike except for the variation created by the manipulation of the independent variable. Experiments permit conclusions about cause-effect relationships between variables, but this method isn't usable for the study of many questions.
- Psychologists conduct correlational research when they are unable to exert control over the variables they want to study. The correlation coefficient is a numerical index of the degree of relationship between two variables. Correlational research methods include naturalistic observation, case studies, and surveys. Correlational research facilitates the investigation of many issues that are not open to experimental study, but it cannot demonstrate that two variables are causally related.

THE ROOTS OF HAPPINESS: AN EMPIRICAL ANALYSIS

- A scientific analysis of happiness reveals that many common-sense notions about the roots of happiness appear to be incorrect, including the notion that most people are unhappy. Factors such as money, age, gender, parenthood, intelligence, and attractiveness are only weakly correlated with subjective well-being.
- Physical health, social relationships, religious faith, and culture appear to have a modest impact on feelings of happiness. The only factors that are clearly and strongly related to happiness are love and marriage, work satisfaction, and personality, which probably reflects the influence of heredity.
- Happiness is a relative concept mediated by people's highly subjective assessments of their lives. Research on affective forecasting shows that people are surprisingly bad at predicting what will make them happy. Individuals adapt to both positive and negative events in their lives, which creates a hedonic treadmill effect.

APPLICATION: IMPROVING ACADEMIC PERFORMANCE

- Evidence suggests that study habits are almost as influential as ability in determining college success. To foster sound study habits, you should devise a written study schedule and reward yourself for following it. You should also try to find places for studying that are relatively free of distractions.
- You should use active reading techniques to select the most important ideas from the material you read. Highlighting textbook material *is* a useful strategy—if you are reasonably effective in focusing on the main ideas in the material and if you subsequently review what you have highlighted. Good note taking can help you get more out of lectures. It's important to use active listening techniques and to record lecturers' ideas in your own words.
- Rehearsal, even when it involves overlearning, facilitates retention. The process of being tested on material seems to enhance retention of that material. Distributed practice and deeper processing tend to improve memory. Evidence also suggests that organization facilitates retention, so outlining reading assignments can be valuable.
- Meaningfulness can be enhanced through the use of mnemonic devices such as acrostics and acronyms. The link method and the method of loci are mnemonic devices that depend on the value of visual imagery.

KEY TERMS

Adjustment p. 10
Affective forecasting p. 21
Behavior p. 10
Case study p. 15
Clinical psychology p. 10
Control group p. 12
Correlation p. 13
Correlation coefficient p. 13
Dependent variable p. 12
Empiricism p. 11
Experiment p. 12
Experimental group p. 12
Hedonic adaptation p. 21
Independent variable p. 12
Mnemonic devices p. 26
Narcissism p. 7
Naturalistic observation p. 14
Overlearning p. 25
Psychology p. 10
Subjective well-being p. 17
Surveys p. 15

CHAPTER 1 | Practice Test

1. Technological advances have not led to perceptible improvement in our collective health and happiness. This statement defines
   a. escape from freedom.
   b. the point/counterpoint phenomenon.
   c. modern society.
   d. the paradox of progress.

2. Barry Schwartz (2004) argues that
   a. life choices have increased dramatically in modern society.
   b. the abundance of life choices has unexpected costs.
   c. an overabundance of choices increases the potential for rumination and postdecision regret.
   d. all of the above are true.

3. Which of the following is *not* offered in the text as a criticism of self-help books?
   a. They are infrequently based on solid research.
   b. Most don't provide explicit directions for changing behavior.
   c. The topics they cover are often quite narrow.
   d. Many are dominated by psychobabble.

4. The adaptation of animals when environments change is similar to _____ in humans.
   a. orientation   c. evolution
   b. assimilation   d. adjustment

5. An experiment is a research method in which the investigator manipulates the _____ variable and observes whether changes occur in a (an) _____ variable as a result.
   a. independent; dependent
   b. control; experimental
   c. experimental; control
   d. dependent; independent

6. A researcher wants to determine whether a certain diet causes children to learn better in school. In this study, the independent variable is
   a. the type of diet.
   b. a measure of learning performance.
   c. the age or grade level of the children.
   d. the intelligence level of the children.

7. A psychologist collected background information about a psychopathic killer, talked to him and people who knew him, and gave him psychological tests. Which research method was she using?
   a. Case study
   b. Naturalistic observation
   c. Survey
   d. Experiment

8. The principal advantage of experimental research is that
   a. it has a scientific basis and is therefore convincing to people.
   b. experiments replicate real-life situations.
   c. an experiment can be designed for any research problem.
   d. it allows the researcher to draw cause-and-effect conclusions.

9. Research has shown that which of the following is moderately correlated with happiness?
   a. Income
   b. Intelligence
   c. Parenthood
   d. Social activity

10. A good reason for taking notes in your own words, rather than verbatim, is that
    a. most lecturers are quite wordy.
    b. "translating" on the spot is good mental exercise.
    c. it reduces the likelihood that you'll later engage in plagiarism.
    d. it forces you to assimilate the information in a way that makes sense to you.

ANSWERS

1. d Pages 1–2
2. d Pages 1–2
3. c Pages 7–9
4. d Page 10
5. a Page 12
6. a Page 12
7. a Page 15
8. d Page 12
9. d Pages 17–19
10. d Page 25

COURSEMATE

Go to **CengageBrain.com** to access Psychology CourseMate, where you will find an interactive eBook, glossaries, flashcards, quizzes, videos, and more.

PERSONAL EXPLORATIONS WORKBOOK

Go to the *Personal Explorations Workbook* in the back of your textbook for exercises that can enhance your self-understanding in relation to issues raised in this chapter.

Exercise 1.1 *Self-Assessment:* Narcissistic Personality Inventory

Exercise 1.2 *Self-Reflection:* What Are Your Study Habits Like?

Theories of Personality

Imagine that you are hurtling upward in an elevator with three other persons when suddenly a power blackout brings the elevator to a halt forty-five stories above the ground. Your companions might adjust to this predicament differently. One might crack jokes to relieve tension. Another might make ominous predictions that "we'll never get out of here." The third might calmly think about how to escape from the elevator. These varied ways of coping with the same stressful situation occur because each person has a different personality. Personality differences significantly influence people's patterns of adjustment. Thus, theories intended to explain personality can contribute to our effort to understand adjustment processes.

In this chapter, we introduce you to various theories that attempt to explain the structure and development of personality. Our review of personality theory will also serve to acquaint you with four major theoretical perspectives in psychology: the psychodynamic, behavioral, humanistic, and biological perspectives. These theoretical approaches are conceptual models that help explain behavior. Familiarity with them will help you understand many of the ideas that you will encounter in this book, as well as in other books about psychology.

THE NATURE OF PERSONALITY

LEARNING OBJECTIVES

- Clarify the meaning of personality and personality traits.
- Describe the five-factor model of personality and relations between the Big Five traits and life outcomes.

To discuss theories of personality effectively, we need to digress momentarily to come up with a definition of personality and to discuss the concept of personality traits.

What Is Personality?

What does it mean if you say that a friend has an optimistic personality? Your statement suggests that the person has a fairly *consistent tendency* to behave in a cheerful, hopeful, enthusiastic way, looking at the bright side of things, across a wide variety of situations. In a similar vein, if you note that a friend has an "outgoing" personality, you mean that she or he consistently behaves in a friendly, open, and extraverted manner in a variety of circumstances. Although no one is entirely consistent in his or her behavior, this quality of *consistency across situations* lies at the core of the concept of personality.

Distinctiveness is also central to the concept of personality. Everyone has traits seen in other people, but each individual has her or his own distinctive *set* of personality traits. Each person is unique. Thus, as illustrated by our elevator scenario, the concept of personality helps explain why people don't all act alike in the same situation.

Lucian Coman/Shutterstock.com

In summary, we use the idea of personality to explain (1) the stability in a person's behavior over time and across situations (consistency) and (2) the behavioral differences among people reacting to the same situation (distinctiveness). We can combine these ideas into the following definition: *personality* **refers to an individual's unique constellation of consistent behavioral traits.** Let's look more closely at the concept of traits.

What Are Personality Traits?

We all make remarks like "Melanie is very *shrewd*" or "Doug is too *timid* to succeed in that job" or "I wish I could be as *self-assured* as Antonio." When we attempt to describe an individual's personality, we usually do so in terms of specific aspects, called traits. A *personality trait* **is a durable disposition to behave in a particular way in a variety of situations.** Adjectives such as *honest, dependable, moody, impulsive, suspicious, anxious, excitable, domineering,* and *friendly* describe dispositions that represent personality traits.

Most trait theories of personality assume that some traits are more basic than others. According to this notion, a small number of fundamental traits determine other, more superficial traits. For example, a person's tendency to be impulsive, restless, irritable, boisterous, and impatient might all derive from a more basic tendency to be excitable.

A number of psychologists have taken on the challenge of identifying the basic traits that form the core of personality. For example, Raymond Cattell (1950, 1966) used the statistical procedure of *factor analysis* to reduce a list of 171 personality traits compiled by Gordon Allport (1937) to just 16 basic dimensions of personality. In *factor analysis, correlations among many variables are analyzed to identify closely related clusters of variables.* If the measurements of a number of variables (in this case, personality traits) correlate highly with one another, the assumption is that a single factor is influencing all of them. Factor analysis is used to identify these hidden factors. Based on his factor analytic work, Cattell concluded that an individual's personality can be described completely by measuring just 16 traits. The 16 crucial traits are listed in **Figure 2.23**, which can be found in the Application, where we discuss a personality test that Cattell designed to assess these traits.

The Five-Factor Model of Personality

In recent years, Robert McCrae and Paul Costa (2003, 2008a) have used factor analysis to arrive at an even simpler, five-factor model of personality. They argue that the vast majority of personality traits derive from just five higher-order traits that have come to be known as the "Big Five": extraversion, neuroticism, openness to experience, agreeableness, and conscientiousness (see **Figure 2.1**). Let's take a closer look at these traits:

1. *Extraversion.* People who score high in extraversion are characterized as outgoing, sociable, upbeat, friendly, assertive, and gregarious. They also have a more positive outlook on life and are motivated to pursue social contact, intimacy, and interdependence (Wilt & Revelle, 2009).

2. *Neuroticism.* People who score high in neuroticism tend to be anxious, hostile, self-conscious, insecure, and vulnerable. Those who score high in neuroticism tend to overreact in response to stress (Mroczek & Almeida, 2004). They also tend to exhibit more impulsiveness and emotional instability than others (Widiger, 2009).

3. *Openness to experience.* Openness is associated with curiosity, flexibility, vivid fantasy, imaginativeness, artistic sensitivity, and unconventional attitudes. People who are high in openness tend to be tolerant of ambiguity and have less need for closure on issues (McCrae & Sutin, 2009).

4. *Agreeableness.* Those who score high in agreeableness tend to be sympathetic, trusting, cooperative, modest, and straightforward. People who score at the opposite end of this personality dimension are characterized as suspicious, antagonistic, and aggressive. Agreeableness is associated with empathy and helping behavior (Graziano & Tobin, 2009). However, it is negatively associated with income, especially among men (Judge, Livingston, & Hurst, 2012).

5. *Conscientiousness.* Conscientious people tend to be diligent, disciplined, well organized, punctual, and dependable. Conscientiousness is associated with strong self-discipline and the ability to regulate oneself effectively (Roberts et al., 2009). Studies have also shown that conscientiousness fosters diligence and dependability in the workplace (Lund et al., 2007).

Recent research suggests that there may be some interesting relations between the Big Five traits and socioeconomic status (SES). In a large-scale study of personality, social class, and mortality, Chapman and colleagues (2010) discovered that the number of people scoring high on specific Big Five traits varies with social class. **Figure 2.2** shows the likelihood of scoring in the top 20% on each of the Big Five traits as a function of SES. As you can see, the probability of being strongly conscientious rises dramatically as social class goes up. The prevalence of high scores on openness and extraversion also increases, although more gradually, as socioeconomic level rises. In contrast, strong agreeableness and neuroticism are less prevalent in the upper classes. The causal relations that might underlie these correlations are currently unclear.

Correlations have also been found between the Big Five traits and quite a variety of important life outcomes. For instance, higher grades (GPA) in both high school and

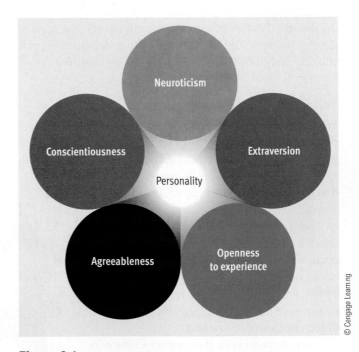

Figure 2.1
The five-factor model of personality. Trait models attempt to break down personality into its basic dimensions. McCrae and Costa (1987, 1997, 2003) maintain that personality can be described adequately with the five higher-order traits identified here, widely known as the Big Five traits.

Source: Trait descriptions from McCrae, R. R., & Costa, P. T. (1986). Clinical assessment can benefit from recent advances in personality psychology. *American Psychologist, 41,* 1001–1003.

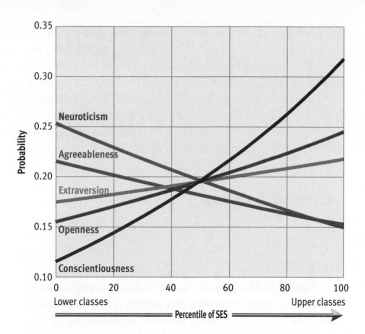

Figure 2.2

The Big Five and social class. In an investigation of how personality and social class jointly relate to health and mortality, Chapman and colleagues (2010) mapped out the association between specific Big Five traits and socioeconomic status (SES). This graph shows the probability that people would score in the top 20% on each Big Five trait for various levels of SES. For example, strong conscientiousness is much more likely to be seen in the higher social classes, which may contribute to the reduced mortality seen in higher classes.

Source: Chapman. B. P., Fiscella, K., Kawachi, I., & Duberstein, P. R. (2010). Personality, socioeconomic status, and all-cause mortality in the United States. *American Journal of Epidemiology, 171*, 83–92. By permission of Oxford University Press.

college are associated with higher conscientiousness, primarily because conscientious students work harder (Noftle & Robins, 2007). Several of the Big Five traits are associated with occupational attainment (career success). Extraversion and conscientiousness are positive predictors of occupational attainment, whereas neuroticism is a negative predictor (Miller Burke & Attridge, 2011; Roberts, Caspi, & Moffitt, 2003). The likelihood of divorce can also be predicted by personality traits, as neuroticism elevates the probability of divorce, whereas agreeableness and conscientiousness reduce it (Roberts et al., 2007). Finally, and perhaps most important, two of the Big Five traits are related to health and mortality over the course of the life span. Neuroticism is associated with an elevated prevalence of virtually all of the major mental disorders, not to mention a number of physical illnesses (Lahey, 2009; Widiger, 2009), whereas conscientiousness is correlated with the experience of less illness and with reduced mortality (Kern & Friedman, 2008). It is not hard to figure out why this is the case, as conscientiousness is inversely related to just about every health-impairing behavior you can think of, including drinking, excessive eating, smoking, drug use, lack of exercise, and various risky practices (Roberts et al., 2009).

McCrae and Costa maintain that personality can be described adequately by measuring the five basic traits they've identified. Their bold claim has been supported in many studies by other researchers, and the five-factor model has become the dominant conception of personality structure in contemporary psychology (John, Naumann, & Soto, 2008). These traits have been characterized as the "latitude and longitude" along which personality should be mapped (Ozer & Reise, 1994, p. 361).

However, some theorists have been critical of the five-factor model. One camp of critics maintain that more than five traits are necessary to account for the bulk of the variation seen in human personality (Boyle, 2008). For example, one article argued that honesty-humility ought to be recognized as a fundamental sixth factor in personality (Lee & Ashton, 2008). Ironically, other theorists have argued for an even simpler three-factor model of personality (De Radd et al., 2010). The debate about how many dimensions are necessary to describe personality is likely to continue for many years to come. As you'll see throughout the chapter, the study of personality is an area in psychology that has a long history of "dueling theories." We'll begin our tour of these theories by examining the influential work of Sigmund Freud and his followers.

PSYCHODYNAMIC PERSPECTIVES

LEARNING OBJECTIVES

- Explain Freud's view of personality structure and the role of conflict and anxiety.
- Identify key defense mechanisms, and outline Freud's view of development.

- Summarize the psychodynamic theories proposed by Jung and Adler.
- Evaluate the strengths and weaknesses of the psychodynamic approach to personality.

Psychodynamic theories **include all the diverse theories descended from the work of Sigmund Freud that focus on unconscious mental forces.** Freud inspired many brilliant scholars who followed in his intellectual footsteps. Some of these followers simply refined and updated Freud's theory. Others veered off in new directions and established independent, albeit related, schools of thought. Today, the psychodynamic umbrella covers a large collection of related theories. In this section, we'll examine Freud's ideas in some detail and then take a brief look at the work of two of his most significant followers, Carl Jung and Alfred Adler.

Freud's Psychoanalytic Theory

National Library of Medicine

Sigmund Freud

Born in 1856, Sigmund Freud grew up in a middle-class Jewish home in Vienna, Austria. He showed an early interest in intellectual pursuits and became an intense, hardworking young man. He dreamed of achieving fame by making an important discovery. His determination was such that in medical school he dissected 400 male eels to prove for the first time that they had testes. His work with eels did not make him famous. However, his later work with people made him one of the most influential and controversial figures of modern times.

Freud was a physician specializing in neurology when he began his medical practice in Vienna near the end of the 19th century. Like other neurologists in his era, he often treated people troubled by nervous problems such as irrational fears, obsessions, and anxieties. Eventually he devoted himself to the treatment of mental disorders using an innovative procedure he developed, called *psychoanalysis,* that required lengthy verbal interactions in which Freud probed deeply into patients' lives. Decades of experience with patients provided much of the inspiration for his theory of personality.

Although Freud's theory gradually gained prominence, most of his contemporaries were uncomfortable with it, for at least three reasons. First, he argued that unconscious forces govern human behavior. This idea was disturbing because it suggested that people are not masters of their own minds. Second, he claimed that childhood experiences strongly determine adult personality. This no-

Peter Aprahamian/Encyclopedia/Corbis

Freud's psychoanalytic theory was based on decades of clinical work. He treated a great many patients in the consulting room pictured here. The room contains numerous artifacts from other cultures—and the original psychoanalytic couch.

tion distressed many, because it suggested that people are not masters of their own destinies. Third, he said that individuals' personalities are shaped by how they cope with their sexual urges. This assertion offended the conservative, Victorian values of his time. Thus, Freud endured a great deal of criticism, condemnation, and outright ridicule, even after his work began to attract more favorable attention. What were these ideas that generated so much controversy?

Structure of Personality

Freud (1901, 1920) divided personality structure into three components: the id, the ego, and the superego. He saw a person's behavior as the outcome of interactions among these three elements.

The *id* is the primitive, instinctive component of personality that operates according to the pleasure principle. Freud referred to the id as the reservoir of psychic energy. By this he meant that the id houses the raw biological urges (to eat, sleep, defecate, copulate, and so on) that energize human behavior. The id operates according to the *pleasure principle,* which demands immediate gratification of its urges. The id engages in *primary process thinking,* which is primitive, illogical, irrational, and fantasy oriented.

The *ego* is the decision-making component of personality that operates according to the reality principle. The ego mediates between the id, with its forceful desires for immediate satisfaction, and the external social world, with its expectations and norms regarding suitable behavior. The ego considers social realities—society's norms, etiquette, rules, and customs—in deciding how to behave. The ego is guided by the *reality principle,* which seeks to delay gratification of the id's urges until appropriate outlets and situations can be found. In short, to stay out of trouble, the ego often works to tame the unbridled desires of the id. As Freud put it, the ego is "like a man on horseback, who has to hold in check the superior strength of the horse" (Freud, 1923, p. 15).

In the long run, the ego wants to maximize gratification, just like the id. However, the ego engages in *secondary process thinking,* which is relatively rational, realistic, and oriented toward problem solving. Thus, the ego strives

Learn More Online

Sigmund Freud Museum, Vienna, Austria

This online museum, in both English and German versions, offers a detailed chronology of Freud's life and explanations of the most important concepts of psychoanalysis. The highlights, though, are the rich audiovisual resources, including online photos, amateur movie clips, and voice recordings of Freud.

to avoid negative consequences from society and its representatives (for example, punishment by parents or teachers) by behaving "properly." It also attempts to achieve long-range goals that sometimes require putting off gratification.

While the ego concerns itself with practical realities, **the *superego* is the moral component of personality that incorporates social standards about what represents right and wrong.** Throughout their lives, but especially during childhood, individuals receive training about what constitutes good and bad behavior. Eventually they internalize many of these social norms, meaning that they truly *accept* certain moral principles, then *they* put pressure on *themselves* to live up to these standards. The superego emerges out of the ego at around 3 to 5 years of age. In some people, the superego can become irrationally demanding in its striving for moral perfection. Such people are plagued by excessive guilt.

According to Freud, the id, ego, and superego are distributed across three levels of awareness. He contrasted the unconscious with the conscious and preconscious (see **Figure 2.3**). **The *conscious* consists of whatever one is aware of at a particular point in time.** For example, at this moment your conscious may include the current train of thought in this text and a dim awareness in the back of your mind that your eyes are getting tired and you're beginning to get hungry. **The *preconscious* contains material just beneath the surface of awareness that can be easily retrieved.** Examples might include your middle name, what you had for supper last night, or an argument you had with a friend yesterday. **The *unconscious* contains thoughts, memories, and desires that are well below the surface of conscious awareness but that nonetheless exert great influence on one's behavior.** Material

that might be found in your unconscious would include a forgotten trauma from childhood or hidden feelings of hostility toward a parent.

Conflict and Defense Mechanisms

Freud assumed that behavior is the outcome of an ongoing series of internal conflicts. Battles among the id, ego, and superego are routine. Why? Because the id wants to gratify its urges immediately, but the norms of civilized society frequently dictate otherwise. For example, your id might feel an urge to clobber a co-worker who constantly irritates you. However, society frowns on such behavior, so your ego would try to hold this urge in check, and you would find yourself in a conflict. You may be experiencing conflict at this very moment. In Freudian terms, your id may be secretly urging you to abandon reading this chapter so you can watch television or go online. Your ego may be weighing this appealing option against your society-induced need to excel in school (or at least pass your courses).

Freud believed that conflicts dominate people's lives. He asserted that individuals career from one conflict to another. The following scenario provides a fanciful illustration of how the three components of personality interact to create constant conflicts.

Imagine your alarm clock ringing obnoxiously as you lurch across the bed to shut it off. It's 7 a.m. and time to get up for your history class. However, your id (operating according to the pleasure principle) urges you to return to the immediate gratification of additional sleep. Your ego (operating according to the reality principle) points out that you really must go to class since you haven't been able to decipher the textbook on your own. Your id (in its typical unrealistic

Figure 2.3

Freud's model of personality structure. Freud theorized that people have three levels of awareness: the conscious, the preconscious, and the unconscious. To dramatize the size of the unconscious, it has often been compared to the portion of an iceberg that lies beneath the water's surface. Freud also divided personality structure into three components—id, ego, and superego—that operate according to different principles and exhibit different modes of thinking. In Freud's model, the id is entirely unconscious, but the ego and superego operate at all three levels of awareness.

Conscious: Contact with outside world

Preconscious: Material just beneath the surface of awareness

Unconscious: Difficult to retrieve material; well below the surface of awareness

Ego Reality principle Secondary process thinking

Superego Moral imperatives

Id Pleasure principle Primary process thinking

© Cengage Learning

fashion) smugly assures you that you will get the A that you need. It suggests lying back to dream about how impressed your roommate will be. Just as you're relaxing, your super-ego jumps into the fray. It tries to make you feel guilty about the tuition your parents paid for the class that you're about to skip. You haven't even gotten out of bed yet—and there is already a pitched battle in your psyche.

Let's say your ego wins the battle. You pull yourself out of bed and head for class. On the way, you pass a donut shop and your id clamors for cinnamon rolls. Your ego reminds you that you're gaining weight and that you are supposed to be on a diet. Your id wins this time. After you've attended your history lecture, your ego reminds you that you need to do some library research for a paper in philosophy. However, your id insists on returning to your apartment to watch some sitcom reruns. It's only midmorning—and already you have been through a series of internal conflicts.

"ALL I WANT FROM THEM IS A SIMPLE MAJORITY ON THINGS."

ScienceCartoonsPlus.com 1999 by Sidney Harris

Freud believed that conflicts centering on sexual and aggressive impulses are especially likely to have far-reaching consequences. Why did he emphasize sex and aggression? Two reasons were prominent in his thinking. First, he thought that sex and aggression are subject to more complex and ambiguous social controls than other basic motives. Thus, people often get inconsistent messages about what's appropriate. Second, he noted that the aggressive and sexual drives are thwarted more regularly than other basic, biological urges. Think about it: If you get hungry or thirsty, you can simply head for a nearby vending machine or a drinking fountain. But when you see an attractive person who inspires lustful urges, you don't normally walk over and propose hooking up in a nearby broom closet. Freud ascribed great importance to these needs because social norms dictate that they're routinely frustrated.

Most psychic conflicts are trivial and are quickly resolved one way or the other. Occasionally, however, a conflict will linger for days, months, and even years, creating internal tension. Indeed, Freud believed that lingering conflicts rooted in childhood experiences cause most personality disturbances. More often than not, these pro-

longed and troublesome conflicts involve sexual and aggressive impulses that society wants to tame. These conflicts are often played out entirely in the unconscious. Although you may not be aware of these unconscious battles, they can produce *anxiety* that slips to the surface of conscious awareness. This anxiety is attributable to your ego worrying about the id getting out of control and doing something terrible.

The arousal of anxiety is a crucial event in Freud's theory of personality functioning (see **Figure 2.4**). Anxiety is distressing, so people try to rid themselves of this unpleasant emotion any way they can. This effort to ward off anxiety often involves the use of defense mechanisms. ***Defense mechanisms* are largely unconscious reactions that protect a person from painful emotions such as anxiety and guilt.** Typically, they are mental maneuvers that work through self-deception. A common example is *rationalization,* **which involves creating false but plausible excuses to justify unacceptable behavior.** You would be rationalizing if, after cheating someone in a business transaction, you tried to reduce your guilt by explaining that "everyone does it."

Figure 2.4
Freud's model of personality dynamics.
According to Freud, unconscious conflicts between the id, ego, and superego sometimes lead to anxiety. This discomfort may lead to the use of defense mechanisms, which may temporarily relieve anxiety.

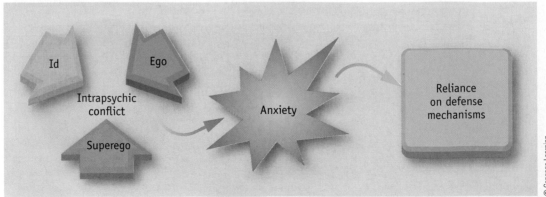

Id — Ego — Superego — Intrapsychic conflict → Anxiety → Reliance on defense mechanisms

© Cengage Learning

Characterized as "the flagship in the psychoanalytic fleet of defense mechanisms" (Paulhus, Fridhandler, & Hayes, 1997, p. 545), *repression* is the most basic and widely used defense mechanism. **Repression involves keeping distressing thoughts and feelings buried in the unconscious.** People tend to repress desires that make them feel guilty, conflicts that make them anxious, and memories that are painful. Repression is "motivated forgetting." If you forget a dental appointment or the name of someone you don't like, repression may be at work.

Self-deception can also be seen in the mechanisms of projection and displacement. **Projection involves attributing one's own thoughts, feelings, or motives to another.** For example, if your lust for a co-worker makes you feel guilty, you might attribute any latent sexual tension between the two of you to the *other person's* desire to seduce you. **Displacement involves diverting emotional feelings (usually anger) from their original source to a substitute target.** If your boss gives you a hard time at work and you come home and slam the door, yell at your dog, and lash out at your spouse, you are displacing your anger onto irrelevant targets. Unfortunately, social constraints often force people to hold back their anger until they end up expressing it toward the people they love the most.

Other prominent defense mechanisms include reaction formation, regression, and identification. **Reaction formation involves behaving in a way that is exactly the opposite of one's true feelings.** Guilt about sexual desires often leads to reaction formation. Freud theorized that many males who ridicule homosexuals are defending against their own latent homosexual impulses. The telltale sign of reaction formation is the exaggerated quality of the opposite behavior (such as trying to be ultra-nice in order to mask feelings of hostility).

Regression involves a reversion to immature patterns of behavior. When anxious about their self-worth, some adults respond with childish boasting and bragging (as opposed to subtle efforts to impress others). For example, a fired executive having difficulty finding a new job might start making ridiculous statements about his incomparable talents and achievements. Such bragging is regressive when it is marked by massive exaggerations that anyone can see through.

Identification involves bolstering self-esteem by forming an imaginary or real alliance with some person or group. For example, youngsters often shore up precarious feelings of self-worth by identifying with rock stars, movie stars, or famous athletes. Adults may join exclusive country clubs or civic organizations with which they identify.

Additional examples of the defense mechanisms we've described can be found in **Figure 2.5**. According to Freud, everyone uses defense mechanisms to some extent. They become problematic only when a person depends on them excessively. The seeds for psychological disorders are sown when defenses lead to wholesale distortion of reality.

Recent decades have brought a revival of interest in research on defense mechanisms. For example, a series of studies have identified a *repressive coping style* and have shown that "repressors" have an impoverished memory for events that are likely to trigger unpleasant emotions and that they avoid negative information regarding themselves (Myers, 2010). Moreover, studies have found a link between repressive coping and poor physical health, including heart disease (Denollet et al., 2008; Myers et al., 2007). In another line of recent research, support has been found for the Freudian hypothesis that reaction formation underlies **homophobia, which involves an intense fear and intolerance of homosexuality** (Weinstein et al., 2012). This research found that people who report that they are

DEFENSE MECHANISMS, WITH EXAMPLES	
Definition	**Example**
Repression involves keeping distressing thoughts and feelings buried in the unconscious.	A traumatized soldier has no recollection of the details of a close brush with death.
Projection involves attributing one's own thoughts, feelings, or motives to another person.	A woman who dislikes her boss thinks she likes her boss but feels that the boss doesn't like her.
Displacement involves diverting emotional feelings (usually anger) from their original source to a substitute target.	After a parental scolding, a young girl takes her anger out on her little brother.
Reaction formation involves behaving in a way that is exactly the opposite of one's true feelings.	A parent who unconsciously resents a child spoils the child with outlandish gifts.
Regression involves a reversion to immature patterns of behavior.	An adult has a temper tantrum when he doesn't get his way.
Rationalization involves the creation of false but plausible excuses to justify unacceptable behavior.	A student watches TV instead of studying, saying that "additional study wouldn't do any good anyway."
Identification involves bolstering self-esteem by forming an imaginary or real alliance with some person or group.	An insecure young man joins a fraternity to boost his self-esteem.

© Cengage Learning

Figure 2.5
Defense mechanisms. According to Freud, people use a variety of defense mechanisms to protect themselves from painful emotions. Definitions of seven commonly used defense mechanisms are shown on the left, along with examples of each on the right.

straight but show an unconscious attraction to the same sex on subtle psychological tests, tend to exhibit elevated hostility toward gays and endorse anti-gay policies. The research suggested that homophobics are threatened by gays because gays remind them of latent homosexual desires within themselves that they find uncomfortable. Thus, they lash out with hostility toward gays to mask their conflicting feelings about homosexuality.

Development: Psychosexual Stages

Freud made the startling assertion that the foundation of an individual's personality is laid down by the tender age of 5! To shed light on the crucial early years, he formulated a stage theory of development that emphasized how young children deal with their immature, but powerful, sexual urges (he used the term "sexual" in a general way to refer to many urges for physical pleasure, not just the urge to copulate). According to Freud, these sexual urges shift in focus as children progress from one stage to another. Indeed, the names for the stages (oral, anal, genital, and so on) are based on where children are focusing their erotic energy at the time. Thus, *psychosexual stages* **are developmental periods with a characteristic sexual focus that leave their mark on adult personality.**

Freud theorized that each psychosexual stage has its own unique developmental challenges or tasks, as outlined in **Figure 2.6**. The way these challenges are handled supposedly shapes personality. The notion of *fixation* plays an important role in this process. *Fixation* **is a failure to move forward from one stage to another as expected.** Essentially, the child's development stalls for a while. Fixation is caused by *excessive gratification* of needs at a particular stage or by *excessive frustration* of those needs. Either way, fixations left over from childhood affect adult

According to Freudian theory, a child's feeding experiences are crucial to later development. Fixation at the oral stage could lead to an overemphasis on, for example, smoking or eating in adulthood.

personality. Generally, fixation leads to an overemphasis on the psychosexual needs that were prominent during the fixated stage.

Freud described a series of five psychosexual stages. Let's examine some of the major features of each stage.

Oral stage. During this stage, which usually encompasses the first year of life, the main source of erotic stimulation is the mouth (in biting, sucking, chewing, and so on). How caretakers handle the child's feeding experiences is supposed to be crucial to subsequent development. Freud attributed considerable importance to the manner in which the child is weaned from the breast or the bottle. According to Freud, fixation at the oral stage could form the basis for obsessive eating or smoking (among many other things) later in life.

Anal stage. In their second year, children supposedly get their erotic pleasure from their bowel movements, through either the expulsion or retention of feces. The crucial event at this time is toilet training, which represents society's first systematic effort to regulate the child's biological urges. Severely punitive toilet training is thought to lead to a variety of possible outcomes. For example, excessive punishment might produce a latent feeling of hostility toward the "trainer," who is usually the mother. This hostility might generalize to women in general.

FREUD'S STAGES OF PSYCHOSEXUAL DEVELOPMENT			
Stage	Approximate ages	Erotic focus	Key tasks and experiences
Oral	0–1	Mouth (sucking, biting)	Weaning (from breast or bottle)
Anal	2–3	Anus (expelling or retaining feces)	Toilet training
Phallic	4–5	Genitals (masturbating)	Identifying with adult role models; coping with Oedipal crisis
Latency	6–12	None (sexually repressed)	Expanding social contacts
Genital	Puberty onward	Genitals (being sexually intimate)	Establishing intimate relationships; contributing to society through working

Figure 2.6

Freud's stages of psychosexual development. Freud theorized that people evolve through the series of psychosexual stages summarized here. The manner in which certain key tasks and experiences are handled during each stage is thought to leave a lasting imprint on one's adult personality.

Another possibility is that heavy reliance on punitive measures might lead to an association between genital concerns and the anxiety that the punishment arouses. This genital anxiety from severe toilet training could evolve into anxiety about sexual activities later in life.

Phallic stage. Near age 4, the genitals become the focus for the child's erotic energy, largely through self-stimulation. During this pivotal stage, the *Oedipal complex* emerges. Little boys develop an erotically tinged preference for their mother. They also feel hostility toward their father, whom they view as a competitor for mom's affection. Little girls develop a special attachment to their father. At about the same time, they learn that their genitals are very different from those of little boys, and they supposedly develop *penis envy*. According to Freud, girls feel hostile toward their mother because they blame her for their anatomical "deficiency." To summarize, in **the *Oedipal complex* children manifest erotically tinged desires for their other-sex parent, accompanied by feelings of hostility toward their same-sex parent.** The name for this syndrome was taken from the Greek myth of Oedipus, who was separated from his parents at birth. Not knowing the identity of his real parents, he inadvertently killed his father and married his mother.

According to Freud, the way parents and children deal with the sexual and aggressive conflicts inherent in the Oedipal complex is of paramount importance. The child has to resolve the dilemma by giving up the sexual longings for the other-sex parent and the hostility toward the same-sex parent. Healthy psychosexual development is supposed to hinge on the resolution of the Oedipal conflict. Why? Because continued hostile relations with the same-sex parent may prevent the child from identifying adequately with that parent. Without such identification, Freudian theory predicts that many aspects of the child's development won't progress as they should.

Latency and genital stages. Freud believed that from age 6 through puberty, the child's sexuality is suppressed—it becomes "latent." Important events during this *latency stage* center on expanding social contacts beyond the family. With the advent of puberty, the child evolves into the *genital stage*. Sexual urges reappear and focus on the genitals once

again. At this point the sexual energy is normally channeled toward peers of the other sex, rather than toward oneself, as in the phallic stage.

In arguing that the early years shape personality, Freud did not mean that personality development comes to an abrupt halt in middle childhood. However, he did believe that the foundation for one's adult personality is solidly entrenched by this time. He maintained that future developments are rooted in early, formative experiences and that significant conflicts in later years are replays of crises from childhood.

In fact, Freud believed that unconscious sexual conflicts rooted in childhood experiences cause most personality disturbances. His steadfast belief in the psychosexual origins of psychological disorders eventually led to bitter theoretical disputes with two of his most brilliant colleagues: Carl Jung and Alfred Adler. They both argued that Freud overemphasized sexuality. Freud summarily rejected their ideas, and the other two theorists felt compelled to go their own ways, developing their own psychodynamic theories of personality.

Jung's Analytical Psychology

Swiss psychiatrist Carl Jung called his new approach *analytical psychology* to differentiate it from Freud's psychoanalytic theory. Like Freud, Jung (1921, 1933) emphasized the unconscious determinants of personality. However, he proposed that the unconscious consists of two layers. The first layer, called the *personal unconscious,* is essentially the same as Freud's version of the unconscious. The personal unconscious houses material from one's life that is not within one's conscious awareness because it has been repressed or forgotten. In addition, Jung theorized the existence of a deeper layer he called the collective unconscious. **The *collective unconscious* is a storehouse of latent memory traces inherited from people's ancestral past that is shared with the entire human race.** Jung called these ancestral memories *archetypes*. They are not memories of actual, personal experiences. Instead, *archetypes* **are emotionally charged images and thought forms that have universal meaning.** These archetypal images and ideas show up frequently in dreams and are often manifested in a culture's use of symbols in art, literature, and religion. Jung felt that an understanding of archetypal symbols

Learn More Online

C. G. Jung, Analytical Psychology, and Culture

Synchronicity, archetypes, collective unconscious, introversion, extraversion—these and many other important concepts arising from analytical psychology and Jung's tremendously influential theorizing are examined at this comprehensive site.

helped him make sense of his patients' dreams. Doing so was of great concern to him because he depended extensively on dream analysis in his treatment of patients.

Jung's unusual ideas about the collective unconscious had little impact on the mainstream of thinking in psychology. Their influence was felt more in other fields, such as anthropology, philosophy, art, and religious studies. However, many of Jung's other ideas *have* been incorporated into the mainstream of psychology. For instance, Jung was the first to describe the personality dimension of extraversion-introversion, which eventually became central to most trait theories of personality.

Adler's Individual Psychology

Alfred Adler was a charter member of Freud's inner circle—the Vienna Psychoanalytic Society. However, he soon began to develop his own theory of personality, which he christened *individual psychology.* Adler (1917, 1927) argued that the foremost human drive is not sexuality, but a *striving for superiority.* He viewed such striving as a universal drive to adapt, improve oneself, and master life's challenges. He noted that young children understandably feel weak and helpless in comparison to more competent older children and adults. These early inferiority feelings supposedly motivate individuals to acquire new skills and develop new talents.

Adler asserted that everyone has to work to overcome some feelings of inferiority. *Compensation* involves efforts to overcome imagined or real inferiorities by developing one's abilities. Adler believed that compensation is entirely normal. However, in some people inferiority feelings can become excessive, resulting in what is widely known today as an *inferiority complex*—exaggerated feelings of weakness and inadequacy. Adler thought that either parental pampering or parental neglect (or actual physical handicaps) could cause an inferiority problem. Thus, he agreed with Freud on the importance of early childhood, although he focused on different aspects of parent-child relations.

Adler explained personality disturbances by noting that an inferiority complex can distort the normal process of striving for superiority (see **Figure 2.7**). He maintained that some people engage in *overcompensation* in order to conceal, even from themselves, their feelings of inferiority. Instead of working to master life's challenges, people with an inferiority complex work to achieve status, gain power over others, and acquire the trappings of success (fancy clothes, impressive cars, or whatever seems important to them). They tend to flaunt their success in an effort to cover up their underlying inferiority complex. The problem is that such people engage in unconscious self-deception, worrying more about *appearances* than *reality.*

Evaluating Psychodynamic Perspectives

The psychodynamic approach has given us a number of far-reaching theories of personality. These theories yielded some bold new insights for their time. Psychodynamic theory and research have demonstrated that (1) unconscious forces can influence behavior, (2) internal conflict often plays a key role in generating psychological distress,

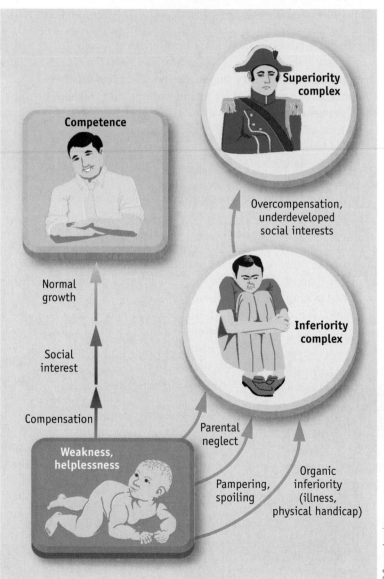

Figure 2.7

Adler's view of personality development. Like Freud, Adler believed that early childhood experiences exert momentous influence over adult personality. However, he focused on children's social interactions rather than on their grappling with their sexuality. According to Adler, the roots of personality disturbances typically lie in excessive parental neglect or pampering, which can lead to overcompensation.

(3) early childhood experiences can exert considerable influence over adult personality, and (4) people do rely on defense mechanisms to reduce their experience of unpleasant emotions (Bornstein, 2003; Porcerelli et al., 2010; Westen, Gabbard, & Ortigo, 2008).

In a more negative vein, psychodynamic formulations have been criticized on several grounds, including the following (Crews, 2006; Kramer, 2006; Torrey, 1992):

1. *Poor testability.* Scientific investigations require testable hypotheses. Psychodynamic ideas have often been too vague to permit a clear scientific test. Concepts such as the superego, the preconscious, and collective unconscious are difficult to measure.

2. *Unrepresentative samples.* Freud's theories were based on an exceptionally narrow sample of upper-class, neurotic, sexually repressed Viennese women who were not even remotely representative of Western European culture, let alone other cultures.

3. *Inadequate evidence.* The empirical evidence on psychodynamic theories has often been characterized as inadequate. The approach depends too much on case studies, in which it is easy for clinicians to see what they expect to see based on their theory. Reexaminations of Freud's own clinical work suggest that he sometimes distorted his patients' case histories to mesh with his theory (Esterson, 2001; Sulloway, 1991) and that a substantial disparity existed between Freud's writings and his actual therapeutic methods (Lynn & Vaillant, 1998). Insofar as researchers have accumulated evidence on psychodynamic theories, it has provided only modest support for the central hypotheses (Westen, Gabbard, & Ortigo, 2008; Wolitzky, 2006).

4. *Sexism.* Many critics have argued that psychodynamic theories harbor a bias against women. Freud believed that females' penis envy made them feel inferior to males. He also thought that females tended to develop weaker superegos and to be more prone to neurosis than males. He dismissed female patients' reports of sexual

Adler's theory has been used to analyze the tragic life of the legendary actress Marilyn Monroe (Ansbacher, 1970). During her childhood, Monroe suffered from parental neglect that left her with acute feelings of inferiority. Her inferiority feelings led her to overcompensate by flaunting her beauty, marrying celebrities (Joe DiMaggio and Arthur Miller), keeping film crews waiting for hours, and seeking the adoration of her fans.

Photononstop/SuperStock

molestation during childhood as mere fantasies. Admittedly, sexism isn't unique to Freudian theories, and the sex bias in modern psychodynamic theories has been reduced considerably. But the psychodynamic approach has generally provided a rather male-centered viewpoint (Lerman, 1986; Person, 1990).

It's easy to ridicule Freud for concepts such as penis envy and to point to ideas that have turned out to be wrong. Remember, though, that Freud, Jung, and Adler began to fashion their theories over a century ago. It is not entirely fair to compare these theories to other models that are only a few decades old. That's like asking the Wright brothers to race a supersonic jet. Freud and his psychodynamic colleagues deserve great credit for breaking new ground. Standing at a distance a century later, we have to be impressed by the extraordinary impact that psychodynamic theory has had on modern thought. No other theoretical perspective in psychology has been as influential, except for the one we turn to next: behaviorism.

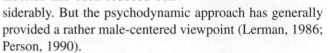

BEHAVIORAL PERSPECTIVES

LEARNING OBJECTIVES

- Describe Pavlov's classical conditioning and its contribution to understanding personality.
- Discuss how Skinner's principles of operant conditioning can be applied to personality development.

- Describe Bandura's social cognitive theory and his concept of self-efficacy.
- Evaluate the strengths and weaknesses of behavioral theories of personality.

***Behaviorism* is a theoretical orientation based on the premise that scientific psychology should study observable behavior.** Behaviorism has been a major school of thought in psychology since 1913, when John B. Watson published an influential article. In it, he argued that psy-

chology should abandon its earlier focus on the mind and mental processes and focus exclusively on overt behavior. He contended that psychology could not study mental processes in a scientific manner, because these processes are private and not accessible to outside observation.

Figure 2.8

A behavioral view of personality. Behaviorists devote little attention to the structure of personality, because it is unobservable. But they implicitly view personality as an individual's collection of response tendencies. A possible hierarchy of response tendencies for a specific stimulus situation is shown here. In the behavioral view, personality is made up of countless response hierarchies for various situations.

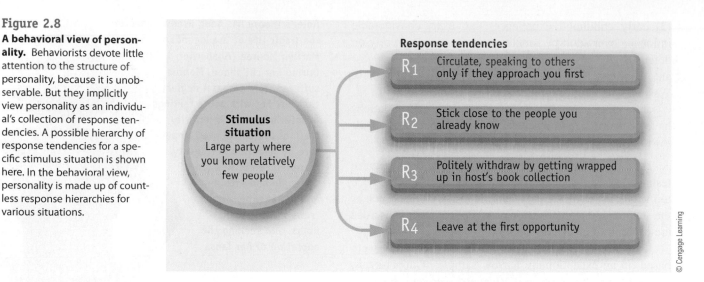

Response tendencies

Stimulus situation
Large party where you know relatively few people

R₁ Circulate, speaking to others only if they approach you first

R₂ Stick close to the people you already know

R₃ Politely withdraw by getting wrapped up in host's book collection

R₄ Leave at the first opportunity

© Cengage Learning

In completely rejecting mental processes as a suitable subject for scientific study, Watson took an extreme position that is no longer dominant among modern behaviorists. Nonetheless, his influence was enormous, as psychology changed its primary focus from the study of the mind to the study of behavior.

The behaviorists have shown little interest in internal personality structures such as Freud's id, ego, and superego, because such structures can't be observed. They prefer to think in terms of "response tendencies," which *can* be observed. Thus, most behaviorists view an individual's personality as a *collection of response tendencies that are tied to various stimulus situations.* A specific situation may be associated with a number of response tendencies that vary in strength, depending on an individual's past experience (see **Figure 2.8**).

Despite their lack of interest in personality structure, behaviorists have focused extensively on personality *development.* They explain development the same way they explain everything else—through learning. Specifically, they focus on how children's response tendencies are shaped through classical conditioning, operant conditioning, and observational learning. Let's look at these processes.

Pavlov's Classical Conditioning

Ivan Pavlov

Bettmann/CORBIS

Do you go weak in the knees when you get a note at work that tells you to go see your boss? Do you get anxious when you're around important people? When you're driving, does your heart skip a beat at the sight of a police car—even when you're driving under the speed limit? If so, you probably acquired these common responses through classical conditioning. *Classical conditioning* **is a type of learning in** which a neutral stimulus acquires the capacity to evoke a response that was originally evoked by another stimulus. This process was first described back in 1903 by Ivan Pavlov, a prominent Russian physiologist who did Nobel Prize–winning research on digestion.

The Conditioned Reflex

Pavlov (1906) was studying digestive processes in dogs when he discovered that the dogs could be trained to salivate in response to the sound of a tone. What was so significant about a dog salivating when a tone was sounded? The key was that the tone started out as a *neutral* stimulus; that is, originally it did not produce the response of salivation (after all, why should it?). However, Pavlov managed to change that by pairing the tone with a stimulus (meat powder) that did produce the salivation response. Through this process, the tone acquired the capacity to trigger the response. What Pavlov had demonstrated was *how learned reflexes are acquired.*

At this point we need to introduce the special vocabulary of classical conditioning (see **Figure 2.9**). In Pavlov's experiment the bond between the meat powder and salivation was a natural association that was not created through conditioning. In unconditioned bonds, **the *unconditioned stimulus (UCS)* is a stimulus that evokes an unconditioned response without previous conditioning. The *unconditioned response (UCR)* is an unlearned reaction to an unconditioned stimulus that occurs without previous conditioning.**

Debra Bardowicks/Getty Images

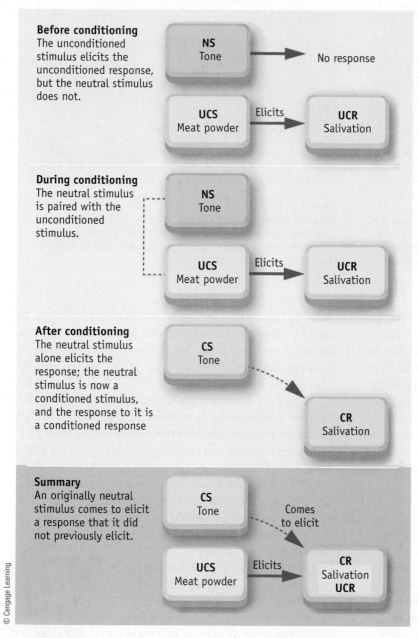

Before conditioning
The unconditioned stimulus elicits the unconditioned response, but the neutral stimulus does not.

NS Tone → No response

UCS Meat powder —Elicits→ UCR Salivation

During conditioning
The neutral stimulus is paired with the unconditioned stimulus.

NS Tone

UCS Meat powder —Elicits→ UCR Salivation

After conditioning
The neutral stimulus alone elicits the response; the neutral stimulus is now a conditioned stimulus, and the response to it is a conditioned response

CS Tone

CR Salivation

Summary
An originally neutral stimulus comes to elicit a response that it did not previously elicit.

CS Tone ⟶ Comes to elicit

UCS Meat powder —Elicits→ CR Salivation UCR

© Cengage Learning

Figure 2.9
The process of classical conditioning. The sequence of events in classical conditioning is outlined here. As we encounter new examples of classical conditioning throughout the book, you will see diagrams like that shown in the fourth panel, which summarizes the process.

In contrast, the link between the tone and salivation was established through conditioning. In conditioned bonds, **the *conditioned stimulus (CS)* is a previously neutral stimulus that has acquired the capacity to evoke a conditioned response through conditioning. The *conditioned response (CR)* is a learned reaction to a conditioned stimulus that occurs because of previous conditioning.** Note that the unconditioned response and conditioned response often involve the same behavior (although there may be subtle differences). In Pavlov's initial demonstration, salivation was an unconditioned response

when evoked by the UCS (meat powder) and a conditioned response when evoked by the CS (the tone). The procedures involved in classical conditioning are outlined in **Figure 2.9**.

Pavlov's discovery came to be called the *conditioned reflex.* Classically conditioned responses are viewed as reflexes because most of them are relatively involuntary. Responses that are a product of classical conditioning are said to be *elicited.* This word is meant to convey the idea that these responses are triggered automatically.

Classical Conditioning in Everyday Life

What is the role of classical conditioning in shaping personality in everyday life? Among other things, it contributes to the acquisition of emotional responses, such as anxieties, fears, and phobias (Antony & McCabe, 2003; Mineka & Zinbarg, 2006). This is a relatively small but important class of responses, as maladaptive emotional reactions underlie many adjustment problems. For example, one middle-aged woman reported being troubled by a bridge phobia so severe that she couldn't drive on interstate highways because of all the viaducts she would have to cross. She was able to pinpoint the source of her phobia. Back in her childhood, whenever her family would drive to visit her grandmother, they had to cross a little-used, rickety, dilapidated bridge out in the countryside. Her father, in a misguided attempt at humor, made a major production out of these crossings. He would stop short of the bridge and carry on about the enormous danger of the crossing. Obviously, he thought the bridge was safe or he wouldn't have driven across it. However, the naive young girl was terrified by her father's scare tactics, and the bridge became a conditioned stimulus eliciting great fear (see **Figure 2.10** on the next page). Unfortunately, the fear spilled over to all bridges, and 40 years later she was still carrying the burden of this phobia. Although a number of processes can cause phobias, it is clear that classical conditioning is responsible for many people's irrational fears.

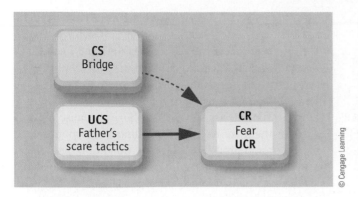

Figure 2.10
Classical conditioning of a phobia. Many emotional responses that would otherwise be puzzling can be explained as a result of classical conditioning. In the case of one woman's bridge phobia, the fear originally elicited by her father's scare tactics became a conditioned response to the stimulus of bridges.

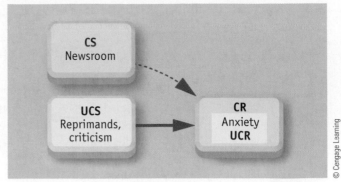

Figure 2.11
Classical conditioning of anxiety. A stimulus (in this case, a newsroom) that is frequently paired with anxiety-arousing events (reprimands and criticism) may come to elicit anxiety by itself, through classical conditioning.

Classical conditioning also appears to account for more realistic and moderate anxiety responses. For example, imagine a news reporter in a high-pressure job where he consistently gets negative feedback about his work from his bosses. The negative comments from his supervisors function as a UCS eliciting anxiety. These reprimands are paired with the noise and sight of the newsroom, so that the newsroom becomes a CS triggering anxiety, even when his supervisors are absent (see **Figure 2.11**). Our poor reporter might even reach a point at which the mere *thought* of the newsroom elicits anxiety when he is elsewhere.

Fortunately, not every frightening experience leaves a conditioned fear in its wake. A variety of factors influence whether a conditioned response is acquired in a particular situation. Furthermore, a newly formed stimulus-response bond does not necessarily last indefinitely. The right circumstances can lead to *extinction*—**the gradual weakening and disappearance of a conditioned response tendency.** What leads to extinction in classical conditioning? It is the consistent presentation of the CS *alone,* without the UCS. For example, when Pavlov consistently presented *only* the tone to a previously conditioned dog, the tone gradually stopped eliciting the response of salivation. How long it takes to extinguish a conditioned response depends on many factors. Foremost among them is the strength of the conditioned bond when extinction begins. Some conditioned responses extinguish quickly, while others are difficult to weaken.

Skinner's Operant Conditioning

Even Pavlov recognized that classical conditioning is not the only form of conditioning. Classical conditioning best explains reflexive responding controlled by stimuli that *precede* the response. However, both animals and humans make many responses that don't fit this description. Consider the response you are engaging in right now—studying. It is definitely not a reflex (life might be easier if it were). The stimuli that govern it (exams and grades) do not precede it. Instead, your studying response is mainly influenced by events that follow it—specifically, its *consequences.*

This kind of learning is called *operant conditioning.* **Operant conditioning is a form of learning in which voluntary responses come to be controlled by their consequences.** Operant conditioning probably governs a larger share of human behavior than classical conditioning, since most human responses are voluntary rather than reflexive. Because they are voluntary, operant responses are said to be *emitted* rather than *elicited.*

The study of operant conditioning was led by B. F. Skinner (1953, 1974, 1990), a Harvard University psychologist who spent most of his career studying simple responses made by laboratory rats and pigeons. The fundamental principle of operant conditioning is uncommonly simple. Skinner demonstrated that *organisms tend to repeat those responses that are followed by favorable consequences, and they tend not to repeat those responses that are followed by neutral or unfavorable consequences.* In Skinner's scheme, favorable, neutral, and unfavorable consequences involve reinforcement, extinction, and punishment, respectively. We'll look at each of these concepts in turn.

B. F. Skinner

The Power of Reinforcement

According to Skinner, reinforcement can occur in two ways, which he called *positive reinforcement* and *negative reinforcement.* **Positive reinforcement occurs when a response is strengthened (increases in frequency) because** it is followed by the arrival of a (presumably) pleasant stimulus. Positive reinforcement is roughly synonymous with the concept of reward. Notice, however, that reinforcement is defined *after the fact,* in terms of its effect on behavior. Why? Because reinforcement is subjective. Something that serves as a reinforcer for one person may not function as a reinforcer for another. For example, peer approval is a potent reinforcer for most people, but not all.

Positive reinforcement motivates much of everyday behavior. You study hard because good grades are likely to follow as a result. You go to work because this behavior produces paychecks. Perhaps you work extra hard in the hope of winning a promotion or a pay raise. In each of these examples, certain responses occur because they have led to positive outcomes in the past.

Positive reinforcement influences personality development in a straightforward way. Responses followed by pleasant outcomes are strengthened and tend to become habitual patterns of behavior. For example, a youngster might clown around in class and gain appreciative comments and smiles from schoolmates. This social approval will probably reinforce clowning-around behavior (see **Figure 2.12**). If such behavior is reinforced with some regularity, it will gradually become an integral element of the youth's personality. Similarly, whether or not a youngster develops traits such as independence, assertiveness, or selfishness depends on whether the child is reinforced for such behaviors by parents and by other influential persons.

Negative reinforcement **occurs when a response is strengthened (increases in frequency) because it is followed by the removal of a (presumably) unpleasant stimulus.** Don't let the word *negative* here confuse you. Negative reinforcement *is* reinforcement. Like positive reinforcement, it strengthens a response. However, this strengthening occurs because the response gets rid of an aversive stimulus. Consider a few examples: You rush home in the winter to get out of the cold. You clean your house to get rid of a mess. Parents give in to their child's begging to halt his whining.

Negative reinforcement plays a major role in the development of avoidance tendencies. As you may have noticed, many people tend to avoid facing up to awkward situations and sticky personal problems. This personality trait typically develops because avoidance behavior gets rid of anxiety and is therefore negatively reinforced. Recall our imaginary newspaper reporter whose work environment (the newsroom) elicits anxiety (as a result of classical conditioning). He might notice that on days when he calls in sick, his anxiety evaporates, so this response is gradually strengthened—through negative reinforcement (shown in **Figure 2.12**). If his avoidance behavior continues to be successful in reducing his anxiety, it might carry over into other areas of his life and become a central aspect of his personality.

Extinction and Punishment

Like the effects of classical conditioning, the effects of operant conditioning may not last forever. In both types of conditioning, *extinction* refers to the gradual weakening and disappearance of a response. In operant conditioning, extinction begins when a previously reinforced response stops producing positive consequences. As extinction progresses, the response typically becomes less and less frequent and eventually disappears.

Thus, the response tendencies that make up one's personality are not necessarily permanent. For example, the youngster who found that his classmates reinforced clowning around in grade school might find that his attempts at comedy earn nothing but indifferent stares in middle school. This termination of reinforcement would probably lead to the gradual extinction of the clowning-around behavior. How quickly an operant response extinguishes depends on many factors in the person's earlier reinforcement history.

Some responses may be weakened by punishment. In Skinner's scheme, *punishment* **occurs when a response is weakened (decreases in frequency) because it is followed by the arrival of a (presumably) unpleasant stimulus.** The concept of punishment in operant conditioning confuses many students on two counts. First, it is often mixed up with negative reinforcement because both involve aversive (unpleasant) stimuli. Please note, however,

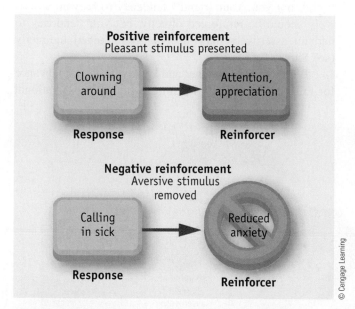

Figure 2.12

Positive and negative reinforcement in operant conditioning. Positive reinforcement occurs when a response is followed by a favorable outcome, so that the response is strengthened. In negative reinforcement, the removal (symbolized here by the "No" sign) of an aversive stimulus serves as a reinforcer. Negative reinforcement produces the same result as positive reinforcement: The person's tendency to emit the reinforced response is strengthened (the response becomes more frequent).

© Cengage Learning

that they are altogether different events with opposite outcomes! In negative reinforcement, a response leads to the *removal* of something aversive, and as a result this response is *strengthened*. In punishment, a response leads to the *arrival* of something aversive, and this response tends to be *weakened*.

The second source of confusion involves the tendency to view punishment only as a disciplinary procedure used by parents, teachers, and other authority figures. In the operant model, punishment occurs whenever a response leads to negative consequences. Defined in this way, the concept goes far beyond actions such as parents spanking children or teachers handing out detentions. For example, if you wear a new outfit and your friends make fun of it and hurt your feelings, your behavior has been punished, and your tendency to wear this clothing will decline. Similarly, if you go to a restaurant and have a horrible meal, in Skinner's terminology your response has led to punishment, and you are unlikely to return.

The impact of punishment on personality development is just the opposite of reinforcement. Generally speaking, those patterns of behavior that lead to punishing (that is, negative) consequences tend to be weakened. For instance, if your impulsive decisions always backfire, your tendency to be impulsive should decline.

According to Skinner, conditioning in humans operates much as it does in the rats and pigeons that he has studied in his laboratory. Hence, he assumes that conditioning strengthens and weakens people's response tendencies "mechanically"—that is, without their conscious participation. Like John Watson (1913) before him, Skinner asserted that we can explain behavior without being concerned about individuals' mental processes.

Skinner's ideas continue to be influential, but his mechanical view of conditioning has not gone unchallenged by other behaviorists. Theorists such as Albert Bandura have developed somewhat different behavioral models in which cognition plays a role. *Cognition* is another name for the thought processes that behaviorists have traditionally shown little interest in.

Bandura's Social Cognitive Theory

Albert Bandura is one of several theorists who have added a cognitive flavor to behaviorism since the 1960s. They take issue with Skinner's view. They point out that humans obviously are conscious, thinking, feeling beings. Moreover, these theorists argue that in neglecting cognitive processes, Skinner ignores the most distinctive and important feature of human behavior. Bandura and like-minded theorists originally called their modified brand of behaviorism *social learning theory*. Today, Bandura refers to his model as *social cognitive theory*.

Albert Bandura

Bandura (1986, 1999b) agrees with the basic thrust of behaviorism in that he believes that personality is largely shaped through learning. However, he contends that conditioning is not a mechanical process in which people are passive participants. Instead, he maintains that individuals actively seek out and process information about their environment in order to maximize their favorable outcomes.

Observational Learning

Bandura's foremost theoretical contribution has been his description of observational learning. *Observational learning* **occurs when an organism's responding is influenced by the observation of others, who are called models.** Bandura does not view observational learning as entirely separate from classical and operant conditioning. Instead, he asserts that both classical and operant conditioning can take place indirectly when one person observes another's conditioning.

To illustrate, suppose you observe a friend behaving assertively with a car salesman. Let's say that his assertiveness is reinforced by the exceptionally good buy he gets on the car. Your own tendency to behave assertively with salespeople might well be strengthened as a result. Notice that the favorable consequence is experienced by your friend, not you. Your friend's tendency to bargain assertively should be reinforced directly, but your tendency to bargain assertively may also be strengthened indirectly (see **Figure 2.13**).

The theories of Skinner and Pavlov make no allowance for this type of indirect learning. After all, observational

Figure 2.13

Observational learning. In observational learning, an observer attends to and stores a mental representation of a model's behavior (for example, assertive bargaining) and its consequences (such as a good deal on a purchase). According to social cognitive theory, many of our characteristic responses are acquired through observation of others' behavior.

Peter Cade/The Image Bank/Getty Images

learning requires that you pay *attention* to your friend's behavior, that you *understand* its consequences, and that you store this *information* in *memory*. Obviously, attention, understanding, information, and memory involve cognition, which behaviorists used to ignore.

As social cognitive theory has been refined, it has become apparent that some role models tend to be more influential than others (Bandura, 1986). Both children and adults tend to imitate people they like or respect more so than people they don't. People are also especially prone to imitate the behavior of those they consider attractive or powerful (such as celebrities). In addition, imitation is more likely when individuals see similarity between the model and themselves. Thus, children imitate same-sex role models somewhat more than other-sex models. Finally, as noted before, people are more likely to copy a model if they see the model's behavior leading to positive outcomes.

Self-Efficacy

Bandura (1993, 1997) believes that *self-efficacy* is a crucial element of personality. **Self-efficacy is one's belief about one's ability to perform behaviors that should lead to expected outcomes.** When a person's self-efficacy is high, he or she feels confident in executing the responses necessary to earn reinforcers. When self-efficacy is low, the individual worries that the necessary responses may be beyond her or his abilities. Perceptions of self-efficacy are subjective and specific to different kinds of tasks. For instance, you might feel extremely confident about your ability to handle difficult social situations but doubtful about your ability to handle academic challenges.

Perceptions of self-efficacy can influence which challenges people tackle and how well they perform. Studies have found that feelings of greater self-efficacy are associated with reduced procrastination (Steel, 2007), greater success in giving up smoking (Schnoll et al., 2011), greater adherence to exercise regimens (Ayotte, Margrett, & Hicks-Patrick, 2010), more-effective weight-loss efforts

(Linde et al., 2006), higher quality of life after a heart attack (Brink et al., 2012), greater physical activity among adolescents (Rutkowski & Connelly, 2012), reduced disability from problems with chronic pain (Hadjistavropoulos et al., 2007), better study habits (Prat-Sala & Redford, 2010), higher levels of academic performance (Weiser & Riggio, 2010), reduced vulnerability to anxiety and depression in childhood (Muris, 2002), less jealousy in romantic relationships (Hu, Zhang, & Li, 2005), reduced vulnerability to posttraumatic stress disorder in the face of severe stress (Hirschel & Schulenberg, 2009), greater success in searching for a new job (Saks, 2006), more proactive customer care by employees in the service industry (Raub & Liao, 2012), and greater resistance to stress (Jex et al., 2001), among many other things.

Evaluating Behavioral Perspectives

Behavioral theories are firmly rooted in empirical research rather than clinical intuition. Pavlov's model has shed light on how conditioning can account for people's sometimes troublesome emotional responses. Skinner's work has demonstrated how personality is shaped by the consequences of behavior. Bandura's social cognitive theory has shown how people's observations mold their characteristic behavior.

Behaviorists, in particular Walter Mischel (1973, 1990), have also provided the most thorough account of why people are only moderately consistent in their behavior. For example, a person who is shy in one context might be quite outgoing in another. Other models of personality largely ignore this inconsistency. The behaviorists have shown that it occurs because people behave in ways they think will lead to reinforcement in the situation at hand. In other words, situational factors are important determinants of behavior. Thus, a major contribution of the behavioral perspective has been its demonstration that personality factors and situational factors jointly and interactively shape behavior (Funder, 2009; Reis & Holmes, 2012).

Of course, each theoretical approach has its shortcomings, and the behavioral approach is no exception. Major lines of

Warren Goldswain/Shutterstock.com

Log on to CourseMate at www.cengagebrain.com **to watch this video.**

Historically, researchers have been interested in the stability of personality as it varies over time and across situations. Rodolfo Mendoza Denton, a psychologist at University of California–Berkeley, studies the stability and variability of personality in relation to emotions in this Reel Research video.

Using *personality signatures*, Denton explains that individuals' behavior varies by situation but is stable across time. When asked how they would respond to a poor grade on a test, students with a more *global* reaction explained that they would feel like a failure, whereas those with a *compartmentalized* reaction focused only on the poor performance. Often, people with a global personality signature experience extremes of emotions, whether their performance is strong or poor. In one study, students are asked to rate their mood on a face scale, then listen to an audiotape that varies by participant. The tape prompts students to recall emotional school-related events, like test performances or social interactions, that have either good or bad outcomes. After listening to the tape, they are given two written prompts and asked to rate their mood again. When a global

prompt is given, students show a larger difference in their mood ratings pre- and post-tape. When an if-then prompt is given, students are better able to regulate their emotions across the study. Using these data, Denton hopes to better understand the relations between personality and the regulation of emotions.

Watch the *Personality, Situations, and Emotion* video to learn more about contemporary personality research. Delve even deeper by responding to the following discussion questions.

DISCUSSION QUESTIONS

1. How would you define *personality signatures* as described by Denton in the video?
2. How are the findings of Denton's research applied to the performance of athletes after a poor or strong performance? To improve performance, how should athletes behave postgame, whether or not the game went well?
3. Do you behave the same way in all situations, or does your behavior differ given the environment? Explain whether you think you use global or if-then reasoning.

---

criticism include the following (Liebert & Liebert, 1998; Pervin & John, 2001):

1. *Dilution of the behavioral approach.* The behaviorists used to be criticized because they neglected cognitive processes, which clearly are important factors in human behavior. The rise of social cognitive theory blunted this criticism. However, social cognitive theory undermines the foundation on which behaviorism was built—the idea that psychologists should study only observable behavior.

Thus, some critics complain that behavioral theories aren't very behavioral anymore.

2. *Overdependence on animal research.* Many principles in behavioral theories were discovered through research on animals. Some critics, especially humanistic theorists, argue that behaviorists depend too much on animal research and that they indiscriminately generalize from the behavior of animals to the behavior of humans.

HUMANISTIC PERSPECTIVES

LEARNING OBJECTIVES

- Describe the forces that gave rise to humanism, and articulate Rogers's views on the self-concept.
- Describe Maslow's hierarchy of needs, and summarize his findings on self-actualizing persons.
- Evaluate the strengths and weaknesses of humanistic theories of personality.

Humanistic theory emerged in the 1950s as something of a backlash against the behavioral and psychodynamic theories (Cassel, 2000; DeCarvalho, 1991). The principal charge hurled at these two models was that they were dehumanizing. Freudian theory was criticized for its belief that primitive, animalistic drives dominate behavior. Behaviorism was criticized for its preoccupation with animal research. Critics argued that both schools view people as helpless pawns controlled by their environment and their past, with little capacity for self-direction. Many of these critics blended into a loose alliance that came to be known as "humanism" because of its exclusive interest in human behavior. *Humanism* **is a theoretical orientation that emphasizes the unique qualities of humans, especially their free will and their potential for personal growth.** Humanistic psychologists do not believe that we can learn anything of significance about the human condition from animal research.

Humanistic theorists, such as Carl Rogers and Abraham Maslow, take an optimistic view of human nature. Humanistic theorists believe that (1) human nature includes an innate drive toward personal growth, (2) individuals have the freedom to chart their courses of action and are not pawns of their environment, and (3) humans are largely conscious and rational beings who are not dominated by unconscious, irrational needs and conflicts. Humanistic theorists also maintain that one's subjective view of the world is more important than objective reality. According to this notion, if you *think* you are homely, or bright, or sociable, that belief will influence your behavior more than the actual realities of how homely, bright, or sociable you are.

Rogers's Person-Centered Theory

Carl Rogers (1951, 1961) was one of the founders of the human potential movement, which emphasizes personal growth through sensitivity training, encounter groups, and other exercises intended to help people get in touch with their true selves. Like Freud, Rogers based his personality theory on his extensive therapeutic interactions with many clients. Because of his emphasis on a person's subjective point of view, Rogers called his approach a *person-centered theory.*

Carl Rogers

The Self and Its Development

Rogers viewed personality structure in terms of just one construct. He called this construct the *self,* although it is more widely known today as the *self-concept.* **A *self-concept* is a collection of beliefs about one's own nature, unique qualities, and typical behavior.** Your self-concept is your mental picture of yourself. It is a collection of self-perceptions. For example, a self-concept might include such beliefs as "I am easygoing" or "I am pretty" or "I am hardworking."

Rogers stressed the subjective nature of the self-concept. Your self-concept may not be entirely consistent with your actual experiences. To put it more bluntly, your self-concept may be inaccurate. Most people are prone to distort their experiences to some extent to promote a relatively favorable self-concept. For example, you may believe that you are quite bright academically, but your grade transcript might suggest otherwise. Rogers used the term *incongruence* **to refer to the disparity between one's self-concept and one's actual experience.** In contrast, if a person's self-concept is reasonably accurate, it is said to be *congruent* with reality. Everyone experiences *some* incongruence; the crucial issue is how much (see **Figure 2.14** on the next page). Rogers maintained that a great deal of incongruence undermines a person's psychological well-being.

In terms of personality development, Rogers was concerned with how childhood experiences promote congruence or incongruence. According to Rogers, everyone has a strong need for affection, love, and acceptance from others. Early in life, parents provide most of this affection. Rogers maintained that some parents make their affection *conditional.* That is, they make it depend on the child's behaving well and living up to expectations. When parental love seems conditional, children often distort and block out of their memory those experiences that make them feel

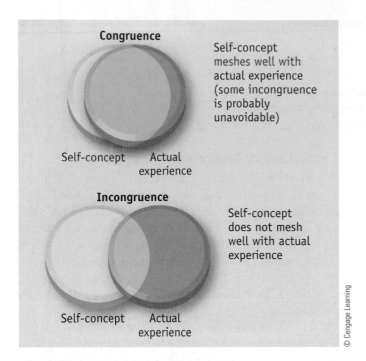

Figure 2.14

Rogers's view of personality structure. In Rogers's model, the self-concept is the only important structural construct. However, Rogers acknowledged that one's self-concept may not jell with the realities of one's actual experience—a condition called incongruence. Different people have varied amounts of incongruence between their self-concept and reality.

"Just remember, son, it doesn't matter whether you win or lose—unless you want Daddy's love."

unworthy of love. At the other end of the spectrum, Rogers asserted that some parents make their affection *unconditional.* Their children have less need to block out unworthy experiences because they have been assured that they are worthy of affection no matter what they do.

Rogers believed that unconditional love from parents fosters congruence and that conditional love fosters incongruence. He further theorized that individuals who grow up believing that affection from others (besides their parents) is conditional go on to distort more and more of their experiences in order to feel worthy of acceptance from a wider and wider array of people, making the incongruence grow.

Anxiety and Defense

According to Rogers, experiences that threaten people's personal views of themselves are the principal cause of troublesome anxiety. The more inaccurate your self-concept, the more likely you are to

LWA/Dann Tardif/Blend Images/Getty Images

have experiences that clash with your self-perceptions. Thus, people with highly incongruent self-concepts are especially likely to be plagued by recurrent anxiety (see **Figure 2.15**). To ward off this anxiety, individuals often behave defensively in an effort to reinterpret their experience so that it appears consistent with their self-concept. Thus, they ignore, deny, and twist reality to protect and perpetuate their self-concept. For example, a young lady who is selfish but unable to face that reality might attribute friends' comments about her selfishness to their jealousy of her good looks.

Rogers's theory can explain defensive behavior and personality disturbances, but he also emphasized the importance of psychological health. Rogers held that psychological health is rooted in a congruent self-concept. In turn, congruence is rooted in a sense of personal worth, which stems from a childhood saturated with unconditional affection from parents and others. These themes are similar to those emphasized by the other major humanistic theorist, Abraham Maslow.

Maslow's Theory of Self-Actualization

Abraham Maslow (1970) was a prominent humanistic theorist who argued that psychology should take a greater interest in the nature of the healthy personality, instead of dwelling on the causes of disorders. "To oversimplify the matter somewhat," he said, "it is as if Freud supplied to us the sick half of psychology and we must now fill it out with the healthy half" (Maslow, 1968, p. 5). Maslow's key contributions were his analysis of how motives

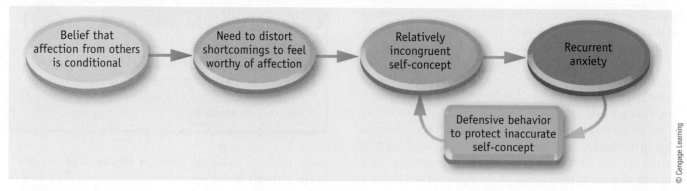

Figure 2.15

Rogers's view of personality development and dynamics. Rogers's theory of development posits that conditional love leads to a need to distort experiences, which fosters an incongruent self-concept. Incongruence makes one prone to recurrent anxiety, which triggers defensive behavior, which fuels more incongruence.

Courtesy Abraham Maslow

Abraham Maslow

are organized hierarchically and his description of the healthy personality.

Hierarchy of Needs

Maslow proposed that human motives are organized into a *hierarchy of needs—a systematic arrangement of needs, according to priority, in which basic needs must be met before less basic needs are aroused.* This hierarchical arrangement is usually portrayed as a pyramid (see **Figure 2.16**). The needs toward the bottom of the pyramid, such as physiological or security needs, are the most basic. Higher levels in the pyramid consist of progressively less basic needs. When a person manages to satisfy a level of needs reasonably well (complete satisfaction is not necessary), *this satisfaction activates needs at the next level.*

Like Rogers, Maslow argued that humans have an innate drive toward personal growth—that is, evolution toward a higher state of being. Thus, he described the needs in the uppermost reaches of his hierarchy as *growth needs.* These include the needs for knowledge, understanding, order, and aesthetic beauty. Foremost among the growth needs is **the *need for self-actualization,* which is the need to fulfill one's potential;** it is the highest need in Maslow's motivational hierarchy. Maslow summarized this concept with a simple statement: "What a man *can* be, he *must* be." According to Maslow, people will be frustrated if they are unable to fully utilize their talents or pursue their true interests. For example, if you have great musical talent but must work as an accountant, or if you have scholarly interests but must work as a sales clerk, your need for self-actualization will be thwarted. Maslow's pyramid has penetrated popular culture to a remarkable degree. For example, Peterson and Park (2010) note that a Google

Need for self-actualization:
Realization of potential

Aesthetic needs:
Order and beauty

Cognitive needs:
Knowledge and understanding

Esteem needs:
Achievement and gaining of recognition

Belongingness and love needs:
Affiliation and acceptance

Safety and security needs:
Long-term survival and stability

Physiological needs:
Hunger, thirst, and so forth

Progression if lower needs are satisfied

Regression if lower needs are not being satisfied

Figure 2.16

Maslow's hierarchy of needs.
According to Maslow, human needs are arranged in a hierarchy, and individuals must satisfy their basic needs first, before progressing to higher needs. In the diagram, higher levels in the pyramid represent progressively less basic needs. People move upward in the hierarchy when lower needs are satisfied reasonably well, but they may regress back to lower levels if basic needs cease to be satisfied.

search located over 766,000 images of Maslow's pyramid on the Internet—a figure that topped the number of images for the *Mona Lisa* and *The Last Supper*!

Recently, almost 70 years after Maslow first proposed his influential pyramid of needs, theorists have proposed a major renovation. Working from an evolutionary perspective, Kenrick and colleagues (2010) argue for a reworking of the upper levels of Maslow's hierarchy. They acknowledge that decades of research and theory provide support for the priority of the first four levels of needs. But they contend that the higher needs in the pyramid are not that fundamental and that they are really pursued in service of esteem needs—that people seek knowledge, beauty, and self-actualization to impress others. After grouping Maslow's higher needs with the esteem needs, Kenrick et al. (2010) fill in the upper levels of their revised hierarchy with needs related to reproductive fitness—that is, passing on one's genes. Specifically, they propose that the top three needs in the pyramid should be the need to find a mate, the need to retain a mate, and the need to successfully parent offspring (see **Figure 2.17**).

It hard to say whether this sweeping revision of Maslow's pyramid will gain traction. Most commentaries thus far acknowledge that Kenrick and his colleagues have compiled some compelling arguments in favor of their renovated pyramid. However, such a radical transformation of an iconic theoretical model is bound to invite second-guessing. For example, critics have argued that the revised hierarchy is no longer uniquely human (Kesebir, Graham, & Oishi, 2010) and that it is premature to dismiss the need for self-actualization (Peterson & Park, 2010).

The Healthy Personality

Because of his interest in self-actualization, Maslow conducted research to analyze the nature of the healthy personality. He called people with exceptionally healthy personalities *self-actualizing persons* because of their commitment to continued personal growth. Maslow identified various traits characteristic of self-actualizing people;

Learn More Online

The Personality Project

William Revelle, director of the graduate program in personality at Northwestern University's Psychology Department, has assembled a directory to many Internet-based resources in the study of personality.

many of these traits are listed in **Figure 2.18**. In brief, Maslow found that self-actualizers are accurately tuned in to reality and that they're at peace with themselves. He found that they're open and spontaneous. They also retain a fresh appreciation of the world around them. Socially, they're sensitive to others' needs and enjoy rewarding interpersonal relations. However, they're not dependent on others for approval or uncomfortable with solitude. They thrive on their work, and they enjoy their sense of humor. Maslow also noted that they have "peak experiences" (profound emotional highs) more often than others. Finally, he found that they strike a nice balance between many polarities in personality. For instance, they can be both childlike and mature, both rational and intuitive, both conforming and rebellious.

Evaluating Humanistic Perspectives

The humanists added a refreshing perspective to the study of personality. Their argument that a person's subjective views may be more important than objective reality has proven compelling. The humanistic approach also deserves credit for making the self-concept an important construct in psychology. Finally, one could argue that the humanists' optimistic, growth, and health-oriented approach laid the foundation for the emergence of the positive psychology movement that is increasingly influential in contemporary psychology (Sheldon & Kasser, 2001b; Taylor, 2001).

Of course, there is a negative side to the balance sheet as well. Critics have identified some weaknesses in the

Figure 2.17

Proposed revision of Maslow's pyramid. According to Kenrick and colleagues (2010), the lower levels of needs in Maslow's hierarchy have been supported by research, but the needs in the upper portion of his pyramid should be replaced. Working from an evolutionary perspective, they argue that humans' highest needs involve motives related to reproductive fitness, as shown here.

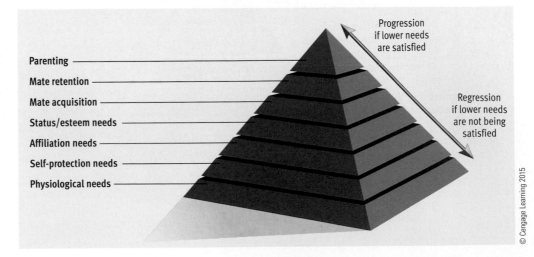

© Cengage Learning 2015

CHARACTERISTICS OF SELF-ACTUALIZING PEOPLE

- Clear, efficient perception of reality and comfortable relations with it
- Spontaneity, simplicity, and naturalness
- Problem centering (having something outside themselves they "must" do as a mission)
- Detachment and need for privacy
- Autonomy, independence of culture and environment
- Continued freshness of appreciation
- Mystical and peak experiences
- Feelings of kinship and identification with the human race
- Strong friendships, but limited in number
- Democratic character structure
- Ethical discrimination between means and ends, between good and evil
- Philosophical, unhostile sense of humor
- Balance between polarities in personality

© Cengage Learning

Figure 2.18

Characteristics of self-actualizing people. Humanistic theorists emphasize psychological health instead of maladjustment. Maslow's sketch of the self-actualizing person provides a provocative picture of the healthy personality.

humanistic approach to personality, including the following (Burger, 2008; P. T. P. Wong, 2006):

1. *Poor testability.* Like psychodynamic theorists, the humanists have been criticized for proposing hypotheses that are difficult to put to a scientific test. Humanistic concepts such as personal growth and self-actualization are difficult to define and measure.

2. *Unrealistic view of human nature.* Critics also charge that the humanists have been overly optimistic in their assumptions about human nature and unrealistic in their descriptions of the healthy personality. For instance, Maslow's self-actualizing people sound *perfect*.

3. *Inadequate evidence.* Humanistic theories are based primarily on discerning but uncontrolled observations in clinical settings. Humanistic psychologists have not compiled a convincing body of research to support their ideas.

BIOLOGICAL PERSPECTIVES

LEARNING OBJECTIVES

- Outline Eysenck's view of personality, and summarize behavioral genetics research on personality.
- Summarize neuroscience and evolutionary research on personality.
- Evaluate the strengths and weaknesses of biological theories of personality.

Could personality be a matter of genetic inheritance? This possibility was largely ignored for many decades of personality research until Hans Eysenck made a case for genetic influence in the 1960s. In this section, we'll discuss Eysenck's theory and look at more recent behavioral genetics research on the heritability of personality. We'll also examine neuroscience and evolutionary perspectives on personality.

Eysenck's Theory

Hans Eysenck was born in Germany but fled to London during the era of Nazi rule. He went on to become one of Britain's most prominent psychologists. According to Eysenck (1967), "Personality is determined to a large extent by a person's genes" (p. 20). How is heredity linked to personality in Eysenck's model? In part, through conditioning concepts borrowed from behavioral theory. Eysenck (1967, 1982, 1991) theorizes that some people can be conditioned more readily than others because of inherited differences in their physiological functioning (specifi-

cally, their level of arousal). These variations in "conditionability" are assumed to influence the personality traits that people acquire through conditioning.

Eysenck views personality structure as a hierarchy of traits. Numerous superficial traits are derived from a smaller number of more basic traits, which are derived from a handful of fundamental higher-order traits, as shown in **Figure 2.19** on the next page. Eysenck has shown a special interest in explaining variations in *extraversion-introversion*, the trait dimension first described years earlier by Carl Jung. He has suggested that introverts tend to have higher levels of physiological arousal than extraverts. This higher arousal purportedly motivates them to avoid social situations that will further elevate their arousal and makes them more easily conditioned than extraverts. According to Eysenck, people who condition easily acquire more conditioned inhibitions than others. These inhibitions, coupled with their relatively high arousal, make them more bashful, tentative, and uneasy in social situations. This social discomfort leads them to turn inward. Hence, they become introverted. Research has provided mixed support for Eysenck's analysis of the roots of

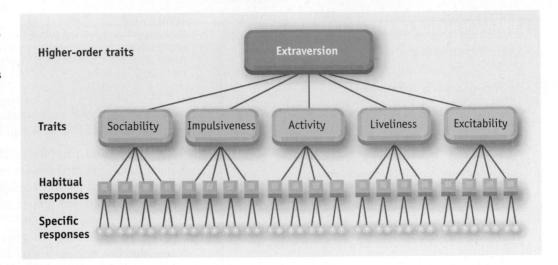

Figure 2.19

Eysenck's model of personality structure. Eysenck describes personality structure as a hierarchy of traits. In this scheme, a few higher-order traits (such as extraversion) determine a host of lower-order traits (such as sociability), which determine one's habitual responses (such as going to lots of parties).

Source: From Eysenck, H. J. (1967). *The biological basis of personality,* p. 36. Springfield, IL: Charles C. Thomas. Courtesy of Charles C. Thomas.

Higher-order traits: Extraversion

Traits: Sociability | Impulsiveness | Activity | Liveliness | Excitability

Habitual responses

Specific responses

---

introversion (de Geus & Neumann, 2008; Stelmack & Rammsayer, 2008). Part of the problem is that the concept of physiological arousal and reactivity has turned out to be much more multifaceted and difficult to measure than Eysenck originally anticipated.

Recent Research in Behavioral Genetics

Recent twin studies have provided impressive support for Eysenck's hypothesis that personality is largely inherited. **In *twin studies* researchers assess hereditary influence by comparing the resemblance of identical twins and fraternal twins on a trait.** The logic underlying this comparison is as follows. *Identical twins* emerge from one egg that splits, so that their genetic makeup is exactly the same (100% overlap). *Fraternal twins* result when two eggs are fertilized simultaneously; their genetic overlap is only 50%. Both types of twins *usually* grow up in the same home, at the same time, exposed to the same relatives, neighbors, peers, teachers, events, and so forth. Thus, both kinds of twins normally develop under similar environmental conditions, but identical twins share more genetic kinship. Hence, if sets of identical twins exhibit more personality resemblance than sets of fraternal twins, this greater similarity is probably attributable to heredity rather than to environment. The results of twin studies can be used to estimate the heritability of personality traits and other characteristics. **A *heritability ratio* is an estimate of the proportion of trait variability in a population that is determined by variations in genetic inheritance.** Heritability can be estimated for any trait. For example, the heritability of height is estimated to be around 80% (Johnson, 2010), whereas the heritability of intelligence appears to be about 50%–70% (Petrill, 2005).

The accumulating evidence from twin studies suggests that heredity exerts considerable influence over many personality traits (Rowe & van den Oord, 2005). For instance, in research on the Big Five personality traits, identical twins have been found to be much more similar than fraternal twins on all five traits (Plomin et al., 2008). Some skeptics still wonder whether identical twins might exhibit more personality resemblance than fraternal twins because they are raised more similarly. In other words, they wonder whether environmental factors (rather than heredity) could be responsible for identical twins' greater similarity. This nagging question can be answered only by studying identical twins who have been reared apart.

Fortunately, an influential twin study at the University of Minnesota provided the necessary data (Tellegen et al., 1988). Most of the twins reared apart were separated quite early in life (median age of 2.5 months) and remained separated for a long time (median period of almost 34 years). The results revealed that identical twins reared apart were substantially more similar in personality than fraternal twins reared together. The heritability estimates for the traits examined ranged from 40% to 58%. Overall, five decades of research on the determinants of the Big Five traits suggests that the heritability of each trait is in the vicinity of 50% (Krueger & Johnson, 2008).

There has been considerable excitement—and controversy—about recent reports linking specific genes to specific personality traits. Recently developed *genetic mapping* techniques are beginning to permit investigators to look for associations between specific genes and aspects of behavior. A number of studies have found a link between a specific gene and measures of extraversion, novelty seeking, and impulsivity, but many failures to replicate this association have also been reported (Canli, 2008; Munafo et al., 2008). In a similar vein, a variety of studies have reported a link between another gene and measures of neuroticism, but many attempts at replication have failed (Canli, 2008; Sen, Burmeister, & Ghosh, 2004). Overall, the evidence suggests that both of these links are genuine, but difficult to replicate consistently because the correlations are very weak (Canli, 2008; Ebstein, 2006). Hence, subtle differences between studies in sampling or the specific personality tests used can lead to inconsistent findings. The ultimate problem, however, is probably that specific personality traits may be influenced by *hundreds* of genes, each of which may have a very small effect that is difficult to detect (Kreuger & Johnson, 2008).

The Neuroscience of Personality

In recent years neuroscientists have begun to explore the relationships between specific personality traits and aspects of brain structure and function. The thinking is that the behavioral regularities that reflect personality traits may have their roots in individual differences in the brain (DeYoung & Gray, 2009). Thus far, research and theory have focused primarily on the Big Five traits. For example, a recent study used MRI technology to look for associations between the Big Five traits and variations in the relative size of specific areas of the brain (DeYoung et al., 2010). The study uncovered some interesting findings. For example, participants' extraversion correlated with the volume of brain regions known to process reward. Variations in neuroticism correlated with the volume of brain areas known to be activated by threat, punishment, and negative emotions. And the size of brain areas thought to regulate planning and voluntary control correlated with subjects' degree of conscientiousness. This line of research is brand new, but the promising initial results suggest that it may be fruitful to explore the neurological bases of personality traits.

The Evolutionary Approach to Personality

In the realm of biological approaches to personality, the most recent development has been the emergence of an evolutionary perspective. Evolutionary psychologists assert that the patterns of behavior seen in a species are products of evolution in the same way that anatomical characteristics are. ***Evolutionary psychology* examines behavioral processes in terms of their adaptive value for members of a species over the course of many generations.** The basic premise of evolutionary psychology is that natural selection favors behaviors that enhance organisms' reproductive success—that is, passing on genes to the next generation. Evolutionary theorists assert that personality has a biological basis because natural selection has favored certain personality traits over the course of human history (Figueredo et al., 2005, 2009). Thus, evolutionary analyses of personality focus on how various traits—and the ability to recognize these traits in others—may have contributed to reproductive fitness in ancestral human populations.

For example, David Buss (1991, 1995) has argued that the Big Five personality traits stand out as important dimensions of personality across a variety of cultures because those traits have had significant adaptive implications. Buss points out that humans have historically depended heavily on groups, which afford protection from predators or enemies, opportunities for sharing food, and a diverse array of other benefits. In the context of these group interactions, people have had to make difficult but crucial judgments about the characteristics of others, asking such questions as: Who will make a good member of my coalition? Who can I depend on when in need? Who will share their resources? Thus, Buss (1995) argues, "Those individuals able to accurately discern and act upon these individual differences likely enjoyed a considerable reproductive advantage" (p. 22). According to Buss, the Big Five emerge as fundamental dimensions of personality because humans have evolved special sensitivity to variations in the ability to bond with others (extraversion), the willingness to cooperate and collaborate (agreeableness), the tendency to be reliable and ethical (conscientiousness), the capacity to be an innovative problem solver (openness to experience), and the ability to handle stress (low neuroticism). In a nutshell, Buss argues that the Big Five reflect the most salient features of others' adaptive behavior over the course of evolutionary history.

Daniel Nettle (2006) takes this line of thinking one step further, asserting that the traits themselves (as opposed to the ability to recognize them in others) are products of evolution that were adaptive in ancestral environments. For example, he discusses how extraversion could have promoted mating success, how neuroticism could have fueled competitiveness and avoidance of dangers, how agreeableness could have fostered the effective building of coalitions, and so forth. Nettle also discusses how each of the Big Five traits may have had adaptive costs. Extraversion, for example, is associated with risky behavior and increased competition with status rivals. Thus, he argues that evolutionary analyses of personality need to weigh the *trade-offs* between the adaptive advantages and disadvantages of the Big Five traits.

One recent article informed by this view hypothesized that variations among people in their level of extraversion may be shaped by their status on two physical traits that would have shaped the reproductive value of extraversion in human ancestral environments (Lukaszewski & Roney, 2011). The authors assert that over the course of human history the reproductive payoffs of extraverted behavior probably were higher (1) for men and women who exhibited greater physical attractiveness and (2) for men who exhibited greater physical strength. They theorize that to some extent indviduals learn to adjust or calibrate their level of extraversion to reflect their level of attractiveness and strength. Thus, they predicted that attractiveness should correlate positively with extraversion in both sexes and that strength should be predictive of extraversion in men, which is what they found in two studies. Thus, in addition to explaining why certain traits are important dimensions of personality, evolutionary analyses may be able to help explain the origins of individual variations on these dimensions.

Evaluating Biological Perspectives

Recent research in behavioral genetics has provided convincing evidence that biological factors help shape personality. Evolutionary theorists have developed thought-provoking hypotheses about how natural selection may have sculpted the basic architecture of personality. Nonetheless, we must take note of some weaknesses in biological approaches to personality:

1. *Problems with estimates of hereditary influence.* Efforts to carve personality into genetic and environmental components with statistics are ultimately artificial. The effects of heredity and environment are twisted together in complicated interactions that can't be separated cleanly (Rutter, 2007). For example, a genetically influenced trait, such as a young child's surly, sour temperament, might evoke a particular style of parenting. In essence then, the child's genes have molded his or her environment. Thus, genetic and environmental influences on personality are not entirely independent, because the environmental circumstances that people are exposed to may be shaped in part by their genes.

2. *Hindsight bias in evolutionary theory.* **Hindsight bias—the common tendency to mold one's interpre-**

tation of the past to fit how events actually turned out— presents thorny problems for evolutionary theorists, who generally work backward from known outcomes to reason out how adaptive pressures in humans' ancestral past may have led to those outcomes (Cornell, 1997). The assertion that the Big Five traits had major adaptive implications over the course of human history seems plausible, but what would have happened if other traits, such as dominance or sensation seeking, had shown up in the Big Five? With the luxury of hindsight, evolutionary theorists surely could have constructed plausible explanations for how these traits promoted reproductive success in the distant past. Thus, some critics have argued that evolutionary explanations are post hoc, speculative accounts contaminated by hindsight bias.

CONTEMPORARY EMPIRICAL APPROACHES TO PERSONALITY

LEARNING OBJECTIVES

- Describe the traits of sensation seeking and narcissism.
- Explain the chief concepts and hypotheses of terror management theory.

So far, our coverage has been devoted to grand, panoramic theories of personality. In this section we'll examine some contemporary empirical approaches that are narrower in scope. In modern personality research programs, investigators typically attempt to describe and measure an important personality trait, shed light on its development, and ascertain its relationship to other traits and behaviors. To get a sense of this kind of research, we'll take a look at research on two traits: *sensation seeking* and *narcissism*. We'll also look at an influential new approach called *terror management theory* that focuses on personality dynamics rather than personality traits.

Sensation Seeking: Life in the Fast Lane

Perhaps you have friends who prefer "life in the fast lane." If so, they're probably high in the personality trait of sensation seeking. **Sensation seeking is a generalized preference for high or low levels of sensory stimulation.** People who are high in sensation seeking prefer a high level of stimulation. They're always looking for new and exhilarating experiences. People who are low in sensation seeking prefer more modest levels of stimulation. They tend to choose tranquillity over excitement. Sensation seeking was first described by Marvin Zuckerman (1979), a biologically oriented theorist influenced by Hans Eysenck's views. Zuckerman (1996, 2008) believes that there is a strong genetic predisposition to high or low sensation seeking.

Sensation-seeking tendencies are measured by Zuckerman's (1984) Sensation Seeking Scale. Sensation seeking is distributed along a continuum, and many people fall in the middle. Factor analyses indicate that the personality trait of sensation seeking consists of four related components (Arnaut, 2006): (1) thrill and adventure seeking, (2) attraction to unusual experiences, (3) lack of inhibitions, and (4) easy susceptibility to boredom.

High sensation seekers' zest for action influences the types of sports and entertainment they find intriguing. In regard to sports they are much more likely to be drawn to high-risk activities such as mountain climbing, sky diving, and hang gliding, whereas low sensation seekers are more likely to get involved in golf, swimming, or baseball (Arnaut, 2006). In the realm of entertainment, high sensation seekers tend to prefer violent movies, horror movies, and fast-paced action-adventure flicks, whereas low sensation seekers are more likely to enjoy musical and romantic movies (Zuckerman, 2006).

According to Zuckerman, incompatibility in sensation seeking places a strain on intimate relationships. He theorizes that persons very high and very low in sensation seeking may have difficulty understanding and relating to each other, not to mention finding mutually enjoyable activities. These considerations may explain why spouses tend to be more similar in sensation seeking than in most other personality traits (Bratko & Butkovic, 2003). One advantage for those who are high in sensation seeking is that they are relatively tolerant of stress—they find many types of potentially stressful events to be less threatening and anxiety arousing than others (Arnaut, 2006).

More than anything else, sensation seeking is associated with elevated risk-taking behavior. High sensation seekers are more likely than others to engage in high-risk sexual practices, such as unprotected sex and sleeping with many partners (Hoyle, Fejfar, & Miller, 2000; Zuckerman, 2007); health-impairing habits, such as smoking (Urbán, 2010), excessive drinking, and recreational drug use (Zuckerman, 2008); reckless driving (Zuckerman, 2009); aggressive behavior (Wilson & Scarpa, 2011); and pathological gambling (Fortune & Goodie, 2010). Thus, high sensation seeking may be more maladaptive than adaptive.

Renewed Interest in Narcissism

As we noted in Chapter 1, **narcissism is a personality trait marked by an inflated sense of importance, a need for attention and admiration, a sense of entitlement, and a tendency to exploit others.** The concept of narcissism was originally popularized over a century ago by pioneering sex researcher Havelock Ellis and by Sigmund Freud (Levy, Ellison, & Reynoso, 2011). Psychoanalytic writings characterized narcissists as having grandiose, but shaky, self-concepts that required extensive defensive manuevers to protect illusory feelings of superiority (Rhodewalt & Peterson, 2009). Of course, these inflated self-concepts were assumed to be rooted in a childhood history of troubled relationships.

The syndrome of narcissism was not widely discussed outside of psychoanalytic circles until 1980 when the American Psychiatric Association published a massive revision of its diagnostic system that describes various psychological disorders (see Chapter 14). The revised diagnostic system included a new condition called *narcissistic personality disorder (NPD)* (Reynolds & Lejuez, 2011). Among other things, the key symptoms of this new disorder included (1) a grandiose sense of importance, (2) preoccupation with fantasies of unlimited power and success, (3) a constant need for attention, (4) difficulty dealing with criticism, (5) a sense of entitlement, and (6) interpersonal exploitiveness. Narcissistic personality disorder is viewed as an extreme, pathological manifestation of narcissism that is seen in perhaps 5%–6% of people (Pulay, Goldstein, & Grant, 2011).

The formal description of NPD inspired some researchers to start investigating lesser, nonpathological manifestations of narcissim in the general population. This research led to the development of scales intended to assess narcissism as a normal personality trait. Of these scales, the Narcissistic Personality Inventory (NPI), developed by Robert Raskin and colleagues (Raskin & Hall, 1979, 1981; Raskin & Terry, 1988), has become the most widely used measure of narcissism (Tamborski & Brown, 2011). The NPI has been used in hundreds of studies. You can see how you score on a variant of this scale in Exercise 1.1 in the *Personal Explorations Workbook* in the back of this text.

These studies have painted an interesting portrait of those who score high in narcissism (Rhodewalt & Peterson, 2009). Narcissists have highly positive but easily threatened self-concepts. Above all else, their behavior is driven by a need to maintain their fragile self-esteem. They are far more interested in making themselves look powerful and successful than they are in forging lasting bonds with others (Campbell & Foster, 2007). They work overtime to impress people with self-aggrandizing descriptions of their accomplishments. As you might guess, in this era of social networking via the Internet, those who are high in narcissism tend to post relatively blatant self-promotional content on Facebook and similar websites (Buffardi, 2011; Carpenter, 2012). Research has also shown that narcissists tend to be more likely than others to cheat on college exams and assignments (Brunell et al., 2011) and that they are prone to unprovoked aggression (Reidy, Foster, & Zeichner, 2010).

The social consequences of narcissism are interesting (Back, Schmukle, & Egloff, 2010). When they first meet people, narcissists are often perceived as charming, self-assured, and even charismatic. Thus, initially, they tend to be well liked. With repeated exposure, however, their constant need for attention, brazen boasting, and sense of entitlement tend to wear thin. Eventually, they tend to be viewed as arrogant, self-centered, and unlikable. Interestingly, recent research has shown that narcissists have some awareness of the fact that they make favorable first impressions that deteriorate over time (Carlson, Vazire, & Oltmanns, 2011).

Based on a variety of social trends, Jean Twenge and colleagues (2008) suspected that narcissism might be increasing in recent generations. To test this hypothesis they gathered data from eighty-five studies dating back to the 1980s in which American college students had been given the NPI. Their analysis revealed that NPI scores have been rising, going from a mean of about 15.5 in the 1980s to almost 17.5 in 2005–2006. This finding was replicated in a recent study that extended the trend through 2009 (Twenge & Foster, 2010).

In a discussion of the possible ramifications of this trend, Twenge and Campbell (2009) have argued that rising narcissism has fueled an obsessive concern in young people about being physically attractive, leading to unhealthy dieting, overuse of cosmetic surgery, and steroid-fueled body building. They also assert that narcissists' "me-first" attitude has led to increased materialism and overconsumption of the earth's resources, contributing to the current environmental crisis and economic meltdown. They also discuss how the "look at me" mentality seen on Internet sites such as Facebook and Google+ reflects the increase in narcissism in contemporary society.

Terror Management Theory

Terror management theory emerged as an influential perspective in the 1990s. Although the theory borrows from Freudian and evolutionary formulations, it provides its own unique analysis of the human condition. Developed by Sheldon Solomon, Jeff Greenberg, and Tom Pyszczynski (1991, 2004b), this fresh perspective is currently generating a huge volume of research.

One of the chief goals of terror management theory is to explain why people need self-esteem. Unlike other animals, humans have evolved complex cognitive abilities that permit self-awareness and contemplation of the future. These cognitive capacities make humans keenly aware that life can be snuffed out at any time. The collision between humans' self-preservation instinct and their awareness of the inevitability of death creates the potential for experiencing anxiety, alarm, and terror when people think about their mortality (see **Figure 2.20**).

How do humans deal with this potential for terror? According to terror management theory, "What saves us is culture. Cultures provide ways to view the world—worldviews—that 'solve' the existential crisis engendered by the awareness of death" (Pyszczynski, Solomon, & Greenberg, 2003b, p. 16). Cultural worldviews diminish anxiety by providing answers to universal questions such as "Why am I here?" and "What is the meaning of life?" Cultures create stories, traditions, and institutions that give their members a sense of being part of an enduring legacy and thus soothe their fear of death.

Where does self-esteem fit into the picture? Self-esteem is viewed as a sense of personal worth that depends on one's confidence in the validity of one's cultural worldview and the belief that one is living up to the standards prescribed by that worldview. Hence, self-esteem helps protect people from the profound anxiety associated with

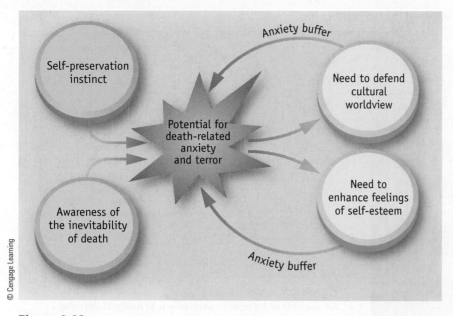

Figure 2.20

Overview of terror management theory. This graphic maps out the relations among the key concepts proposed by terror management theory. The theory asserts that humans' unique awareness of the inevitability of death fosters a need to defend one's cultural world-view and one's self-esteem, which serve to protect one from mortality-related anxiety.

the awareness that they are transient animals destined to die. In other words, self-esteem serves a *terror management* function (refer to **Figure 2.20**).

The notion that self-esteem functions as an *anxiety buffer* has been supported by numerous studies (Pyszczyn-ski et al., 2004; Schmeichel et al., 2009). In many of these experiments, researchers have manipulated what they call *mortality salience* (the degree to which subjects' mortality is prominent in their minds). Typically, mortality salience is temporarily increased by asking participants to briefly think about their own future death. Consistent with the anxiety buffer hypothesis, reminding people of their mortality leads subjects to engage in a variety of behaviors that are likely to bolster their self-esteem, thus reducing anxiety (see Chapter 6 for more on the terror management function of self-esteem).

Increasing mortality salience also leads people to work harder at defending their cultural worldview (Arndt & Vess, 2008; Burke, Martens, & Faucher, 2010). For instance, after briefly pondering their mortality, research participants (1) hand out harsher penalties to moral transgressors, (2) respond more negatively to people who criticize their country, and (3) show more respect for cultural icons, such as a flag. This need to defend one's cultural world-view may even fuel prejudice and aggression (Greenberg et al., 2009). Reminding subjects of their mortality leads to (1) more negative evaluations of people from different religious or ethnic backgrounds, (2) more stereotypic thinking about minority group members, and (3) more aggressive behavior toward people with opposing political views.

Terror management theory yields novel hypotheses regarding many phenomena. For instance, Solomon, Greenberg, and Pyszczynski (2004a) explain excessive materialism in terms of the anxiety-buffering function of self-esteem. Specifically, they argue that "conspicuous possession and consumption are thinly veiled efforts to assert that one is special and therefore more than just an animal fated to die and decay" (p. 134). A similar motive seems to underlie the finding that mortality salience increases the appeal of fame and the admiration of celebrities (Greenberg et al., 2010). A number of studies have even applied terror management theory to the political process. This research suggests that mortality salience increases subjects' preference for "charismatic" candidates who articulate a grand vision that makes people feel like they are part of an important movement of lasting significance (Cohen & Solomon, 2011). Although terror management theory may seem a tad implausible at first glance, the predictions of the theory have been supported in hundreds of experiments (Burke, Martens, & Faucher, 2010).

CULTURE AND PERSONALITY

LEARNING OBJECTIVES

- Discuss whether the five-factor model has any relevance in non-Western cultures.
- Explain how researchers have found both cross-cultural similarities and disparities in personality.

Are there connections between culture and personality? In recent decades psychology has become more interested in culture, sparking a renaissance in culture-personality research (Church, 2010). This research has sought to deter-mine whether Western personality constructs are relevant to other cultures and whether cultural differences can be seen in the strength of specific personality traits. These studies have found both continuity and variability across cultures.

Terror management theory has been applied to a remarkably wide range of phenomena. For example, it has even been used to explain conspicuous consumption.

dean bertoncelj/Shutterstock.com

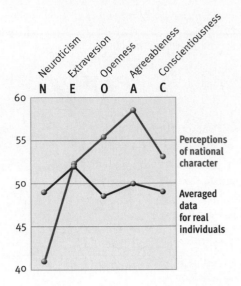

Figure 2.21

An example of inaccurate perceptions of national character. Terracciano et al. (2005) found that perceptions of national character (the prototype or typical personality for a particular culture) are largely inaccurate. The data shown here for one culture—Canadians—illustrate this inaccuracy. Mean scores on the Big Five traits for a sample of real individuals from Canada are graphed in red. Averaged perceptions of national character for Canadians are graphed in blue. The discrepancy between perception and reality is obvious. Terracciano et al. found similar disparities between views of national character and actual trait scores for a majority of the cultues they studied. (Adapted from McCrae & Terracciano, 2005)

For the most part, continuity has been apparent in cross-cultural comparisons of the *trait structure* of personality. When English-language personality scales have been translated and administered in other cultures, the predicted dimensions of personality have emerged from the factor analyses (Chiu, Kim, & Wan, 2008). For example, when scales that tap the Big Five personality traits have been administered and subjected to factor analysis in other cultures, the usual five traits have typically emerged (McCrae & Costa, 2008b). Thus, research tentatively suggests that the basic dimensions of personality trait structure may be universal.

On the other hand, some cross-cultural variability is seen when researchers compare the average trait scores of samples from various cultural groups. For example, in a study comparing fifty-one cultures, McCrae et al. (2005) found that Brazilians scored relatively high in neuroticism, Australians in extraversion, Germans in openness to experience, Czechs in agreeableness, and Malaysians in conscientiousness, to give but a handful of examples. These findings should be viewed as very preliminary, as a variety of methodological problems make it difficult to ensure that samples and scores from different cultures are comparable (Church et al., 2011; Heine,

Buchtel, & Norenzayan, 2008). Nonetheless, the findings suggest that genuine cultural differences may exist in some personality traits. That said, the observed cultural disparities in average trait scores were modest in size.

The availability of the data from the McCrae et al. (2005) study allowed Terracciano et al. (2005) to revisit the concept of *national character*. Terracciano and his colleagues asked subjects from many cultures to describe the *typical* member of *their* culture on rating forms guided by the five-factor model. Generally, subjects displayed substantial agreement on these ratings of what was typical for their culture. The averaged ratings, which served as the measures of each culture's national character, were then correlated with the actual mean trait scores for various cultures compiled in the McCrae et al. (2005) study. The results were definitive: The vast majority of the correlations were extremely low and often even negative. In other words, there was little or no relationship between perceptions of national character and actual trait scores for various cultures (see **Figure 2.21**). People's beliefs about national character, which often fuel cultural prejudices, turned out to be profoundly inaccurate stereotypes (McCrae & Terracciano, 2006).

ASSESSING YOUR PERSONALITY

LEARNING OBJECTIVES

- Explain the concepts of standardization, test norms, reliability, and validity.
- Discuss the value and the limitations of self-report inventories and projective tests.

Answer the following "true" or "false."

_____ **1.** Responses to personality tests are subject to unconscious distortion.

_____ **2.** The results of personality tests are often misunderstood.

_____ **3.** Personality test scores should be interpreted with caution.

_____ **4.** Personality tests may be quite useful in helping people to learn more about themselves.

If you answered "true" to all four questions, you earned a perfect score. Yes, personality tests are subject to distortion. Admittedly, test results are often misunderstood, and they should be interpreted cautiously. In spite of these problems, however, psychological tests can be very useful.

We all engage in efforts to size up our own personality as well as that of others. When you think to yourself that "this salesman is untrustworthy," or when you remark to a friend that "Howard is too timid and submissive," you are making personality assessments. In a sense, then, personality assessment is part of daily life. However, psychological tests provide much more systematic assessments than casual observations do.

The value of psychological tests lies in their ability to help people form a realistic picture of their personal qualities. Thus, we have included a variety of personality tests in the *Personal Explorations Workbook* that can be found in the back of this text. We hope that you may gain some insights by responding to these scales. But it's important to understand the logic and limitations of such tests. To facilitate your use of these and other tests, this Application discusses some of the basics of psychological testing.

Key Concepts in Psychological Testing

A *psychological test* **is a standardized measure of a sample of a person's behavior.** Psychological tests are measurement instruments. They are used to measure abilities, aptitudes, and personality traits.

Note that your responses to a psychological test represent a *sample* of your behavior. This fact should alert you to one of the key limitations of psychological tests: It's always possible that a particular behavior sample is not representative of your characteristic behavior. We all have our bad days. A stomachache, a fight with a friend, a prob-

lem with your car—all might affect your responses to a particular test on a particular day. Because of the limitations of the sampling process, test scores should always be interpreted *cautiously.* Most psychological tests are sound measurement devices, but test results should not be viewed as the "final word" on one's personality and abilities because of the everpresent sampling problem.

Most psychological tests can be placed in one of two broad categories: (1) mental ability tests, and (2) personality tests. *Mental ability tests,* such as intelligence tests, aptitude tests, and achievement tests, often serve as gateways to schooling, training programs, and jobs. *Personality* tests measure various aspects of personality, including motives, interests, values, and attitudes. Many psychologists prefer to call these tests personality *scales,* since the questions do not have right and wrong answers like those on tests of mental abilities.

Standardization and Norms

Both personality scales and tests of mental abilities are *standardized* measures of behavior. **Standardization refers to the uniform procedures used to administer and score a test.** All subjects get the same instructions, the same questions, the same time limits, and so on, so that their scores can be compared meaningfully.

The standardization of a test's scoring system includes the development of test norms. **Test norms provide information about where a score on a psychological test ranks in relation to other scores on that test.** Why do we need test norms? Because in psychological testing, everything is relative. Psychological tests tell you how you score *relative to other people.* They tell you, for instance, that you are average in impulsiveness, or slightly above average in assertiveness, or far below average in anxiety. These interpretations are derived from the test norms.

Reliability and Validity

Any kind of measuring device, whether it's a tire gauge, a stopwatch, or a psychological test, should be reasonably consistent. That is, repeated measurements should yield reasonably similar results. To appreciate the importance of reliability, think about how you would react if a tire pressure gauge gave you several very different readings for the same tire. You would probably conclude that the gauge was broken and toss it into the garbage, because you know that consistency in measurement is essential to accuracy.

***Reliability* refers to the measurement consistency of a test.** A reliable test is one that yields similar results upon repetition (see **Figure 2.22**). Like most other types of measuring devices, psychological tests are not perfectly reliable. They usually do not yield the exact same score when repeated. A certain amount of inconsistency is unavoidable, because human behavior is variable. Personality tests tend to have lower reliability than mental ability tests because daily fluctuations in mood influence how people respond to such tests.

Even if a test is quite reliable, we still need to be concerned about its validity. ***Validity* refers to the ability of a test to measure what it was designed to measure.** If we develop a new test of assertiveness, we have to provide some evidence that it really measures assertiveness. Validity can be demonstrated in a variety of ways. Most of them involve correlating scores on a test with other measures of the same trait, or with related traits.

Self-Report Inventories

The vast majority of personality tests are self-report inventories. ***Self-report inventories* are personality scales that ask individuals to answer a series of questions about their characteristic behavior.** When you respond to a self-report personality scale, you endorse statements as true or false as applied to you, you indicate how often you behave in a particular way, or you rate yourself with respect to certain qualities. For example, on the Minnesota Multiphasic Personality Inventory, people respond "true," "false," or "cannot say" to 567 statements such as the following:

I get a fair deal from most people.
I have the time of my life at parties.
I am glad that I am alive.
Several people are following me everywhere.

The logic underlying this approach is simple: Who knows you better than you do? Who has known you longer? Who has more access to your private feelings?

The entire range of personality traits can be measured with self-report inventories. Some scales measure just one trait dimension, such as the Sensation Seeking Scale (SSS), which you can take in your *Personal Explorations Workbook*. Others simultaneously assess a multitude of traits. The Sixteen Personality Factor Questionnaire (16PF), developed by Raymond Cattell and his colleagues (Cattell, Eber, & Tatsuoka, 1970), is an example of a multitrait inventory. The 16PF is a 187-item scale that measures 16 basic dimensions of personality, called source traits, which are shown in **Figure 2.23**. The current, fifth edition of this test continues to enjoy widespread usage (Cattell & Mead, 2008).

As noted earlier, some theorists believe that only five trait dimensions are required to provide a full description of personality. The five-factor model led to the creation of the NEO Personality Inventory. Developed by Paul Costa and Robert McCrae (1992), the NEO Inventory is designed to measure the Big Five traits: neuroticism, extraversion, openness to experience, agreeableness, and conscientiousness. The NEO Inventory is widely used in research and clinical work, and updated revisions of the scale have been released (Costa & McCrae, 2008).

To appreciate the strengths of self-report inventories, consider how else you might assess your personality. For instance, how assertive are you? You probably have some vague idea, but can you accurately estimate how your assertiveness compares to other people's? To do that, you need a great deal of comparative information about others' usual behavior—information that all of us lack. In contrast, a self-report inventory inquires about your typical behavior in a wide variety of circumstances requiring assertiveness and generates an exact comparison with the typical behavior

Figure 2.22

Test reliability. Subjects' scores on the first administration of an assertiveness test are represented on the left, and their scores on a second administration (a few weeks later) are represented on the right. If subjects obtain similar scores on both administrations, the test measures assertiveness consistently and is said to have high reliability. If subjects get very different scores when they take the assertiveness test a second time, the test is said to have low reliability.

reported by many other respondents for the same circumstances. Thus, self-report inventories are much more thorough and precise than casual observations.

However, these tests are only as accurate as the information that the test takers provide (Ben-Porath, 2003). Deliberate deception can be a problem with these tests (Rees & Metcalfe, 2003), and some people are unconsciously influenced by the social desirability or acceptability of the statements (Kline, 1995). Without realizing it, they endorse only those statements that make them look good. This problem provides another reason why personality test results should always be regarded as suggestive rather than definitive.

Projective Tests

Projective tests, which all take a rather indirect approach to the assessment of personality, are used extensively in clinical work. *Projective tests* **ask people to respond to vague, ambiguous stimuli in ways that may reveal the respondents' needs, feelings, and personality traits.** The Rorschach test, for example, consists of a series of ten inkblots. Respondents are asked to describe what they see in the blots. In the Thematic Apperception Test (TAT), a series of pictures of simple scenes is presented to subjects who are asked to tell stories about what is happening in them and what the characters are feeling. For instance, one TAT card shows a young boy contemplating a violin resting on a table in front of him.

The assumption underlying projective testing is that ambiguous materials can serve as a blank screen onto which people project their concerns, conflicts, and desires. Thus, a competitive person who is shown the TAT card of the boy at the table with the violin might concoct a story

about how the boy is contemplating an upcoming musical competition at which he hopes to excel. The same card shown to a person high in impulsiveness might elicit a story about how the boy is planning to sneak out the door to go dirt-bike riding with friends.

Proponents of projective tests assert that the tests have two unique strengths. First, they are not transparent to subjects. That is, the subject doesn't know how the test provides information to the tester. Hence, it may be difficult for people to engage in intentional deception (Groth-Marnat, 1997). Second, the indirect approach used in these tests may make them especially sensitive to unconscious, latent features of personality.

Unfortunately, the scientific evidence on projective measures is unimpressive (Garb, Florio, & Grove, 1998; Hunsley, Lee, & Wood, 2003). In a thorough review of the relevant research, Lilienfeld, Wood, and Garb (2000) conclude that projective tests tend to be plagued by inconsistent scoring, low reliability, inadequate test norms, cultural bias, and poor validity estimates. They also assert that, contrary to advocates' claims, projective tests are susceptible to some types of intentional deception (primarily, faking poor mental health). Based on their analysis, Lilienfeld and his colleagues argue that projective tests should be referred to as projective "techniques" or "instruments" rather than tests because "most of these techniques as used in daily clinical practice do not fulfill the traditional criteria for psychological tests" (p. 29). In spite of these problems, projective tests continue to be used by many clinicians. Although the questionable scientific status of these techniques is a very real problem, their continued popularity suggests that they yield subjective information that many clinicians find useful (Viglione & Rivera, 2003).

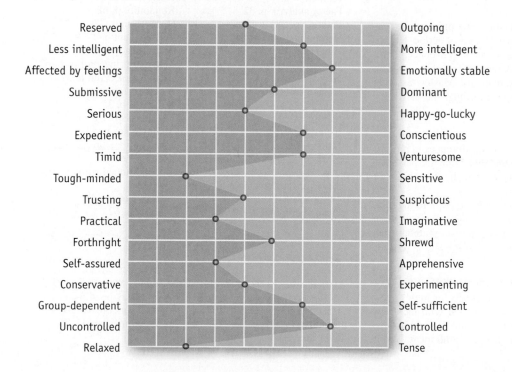

Figure 2.23

The Sixteen Personality Factor Questionnaire (16PF). Cattell's 16PF is designed to assess sixteen basic dimensions of personality. The pairs of traits listed across from each other in the figure define the sixteen factors measured by this self-report inventory. The profile shown is the average profile seen among a group of airline pilots who took the test.

Source: Adapted from Cattell, R. B. (1973, July). Personality pinned down. *Psychology Today,* 40–46. Reprinted by permission of Psychology Today Magazine. Copyright © 1973 Sussex Publishers, Inc.

CHAPTER 2 | Review

KEY IDEAS

THE NATURE OF PERSONALITY

- The concept of personality explains the consistency in individuals' behavior over time and situations while also explaining their distinctiveness. Personality traits are dispositions to behave in certain ways.
- Some theorists suggest that the complexity of personality can be reduced to just five basic traits: extraversion, neuroticism, openness to experience, agreeableness, and conscientiousness. The Big Five traits predict important life outcomes, such as grades, occupational attainment, divorce, health, and mortality.

PSYCHODYNAMIC PERSPECTIVES

- Freud's psychoanalytic theory emphasizes the importance of the unconscious. Freud described personality structure in terms of three components (id, ego, and superego), operating at three levels of awareness, that are involved in internal conflicts, which generate anxiety.
- According to Freud, people often ward off anxiety and other unpleasant emotions with defense mechanisms, which work through self-deception. He described five psychosexual stages that children undergo in their personality development.
- Jung's analytical psychology stresses the importance of the collective unconscious. Adler's individual psychology emphasizes how people strive for superiority to compensate for feelings of inferiority.

BEHAVIORAL PERSPECTIVES

- Behavioral theories view personality as a collection of response tendencies shaped through learning. Pavlov's classical conditioning can explain how people acquire emotional responses.
- Skinner's model of operant conditioning shows how consequences such as reinforcement, extinction, and punishment shape behavior. Bandura's social cognitive theory shows how people can be conditioned indirectly through observation. He views self-efficacy as an especially important personality trait.

HUMANISTIC PERSPECTIVES

- Humanistic theories take an optimistic view of people's conscious, rational ability to chart their own courses of action. Rogers maintained that incongruence between one's self-concept and reality creates anxiety and leads to defensive behavior. Maslow theorized that needs are arranged hierarchically. Maslow asserted that psychological health depends on fulfilling the need for self-actualization.

BIOLOGICAL PERSPECTIVES

- Eysenck argued that inherited individual differences in physiological functioning affect conditioning and thus influence personality. Behavioral genetics research suggests that the heritability of each of the Big Five traits is around 50%.
- In recent years neuroscientists have begun to explore the relationships between specific personality traits and aspects of brain structure and function. Evolutionary psychologists maintain that natural selection has favored the emergence of the Big Five traits as crucial dimensions of personality.

CONTEMPORARY EMPIRICAL APPROACHES TO PERSONALITY

- Sensation seeking is a generalized preference for high or low levels of sensory stimulation, which is associated with increased risk-taking behavior. Narcissism is a trait marked by an inflated sense of self, need for attention, and a sense of entitlement. Levels of narcissism have been increasing in recent generations. Terror management theory proposes that self-esteem and faith in a cultural worldview shield people from the profound anxiety associated with their mortality.

CULTURE AND PERSONALITY

- Research suggests that the basic trait structure of personality may be much the same across cultures, as the Big Five traits usually emerge in cross-cultural studies. People's perceptions of national character appear to be remarkably inaccurate.

APPLICATION: ASSESSING YOUR PERSONALITY

- Psychological tests are standardized measures of behavior. Psychological tests should produce consistent results upon retesting, a quality called reliability. Validity refers to the degree to which a test measures what it was designed to measure.
- Self-report inventories, such as the 16PF and NEO Personality Inventory, ask respondents to describe themselves. Projective tests, such as the Rorschach and TAT, assume that people's responses to ambiguous stimuli reveal something about their personality.

KEY TERMS

Archetypes p. 39
Behaviorism p. 41
Classical conditioning p. 42
Collective unconscious p. 39
Compensation p. 40
Conditioned response (CR) p. 43
Conditioned stimulus (CS) p. 43
Conscious p. 35
Defense mechanisms p. 36
Displacement p. 37
Ego p. 34
Evolutionary psychology p. 55
Extinction p. 44
Factor analysis p. 32
Fixation p. 38
Heritability ratio p. 54
Hierarchy of needs p. 51
Hindsight bias p. 56
Homophobia p. 37
Humanism p. 49
Id p. 34
Identification p. 37
Incongruence p. 49
Narcissism p. 57
Need for self-actualization p. 51
Negative reinforcement p. 45
Observational learning p. 46
Oedipal complex p. 39

Operant conditioning p. 44
Personality p. 31
Personality trait p. 31
Positive reinforcement pp. 44–45
Preconscious p. 35
Projection p. 37
Projective tests p. 63
Psychodynamic theories p. 33
Psychological test p. 61
Psychosexual stages p. 38
Punishment p. 45
Rationalization p. 36
Reaction formation p. 37
Regression p. 37
Reliability p. 62
Repression p. 37
Self-concept p. 49
Self-efficacy p. 47
Self-report inventories p. 62
Sensation seeking p. 57
Standardization p. 61
Superego p. 35
Test norms p. 61
Twin studies p. 54
Unconditioned response (UCR) p. 42
Unconditioned stimulus (UCS) p. 42
Unconscious p. 35
Validity p. 62

KEY PEOPLE

Alfred Adler p. 40
Albert Bandura pp. 46–47
Hans Eysenck pp. 53–54
Sigmund Freud pp. 33–39
Carl Jung pp. 39–40

Abraham Maslow pp. 50–52
Ivan Pavlov pp. 42–44
Carl Rogers pp. 49–50
B. F. Skinner pp. 44–46

64   CHAPTER 2

CHAPTER 2 | Practice Test

1. Which of the following is *not* included in McCrae and Costa's five-factor model of personality?
   a. Neuroticism
   b. Extraversion
   c. Conscientiousness
   d. Authoritarianism

2. You're feeling guilty after your third bowl of ice cream. You tell yourself it's all right because yesterday you skipped lunch. Which defense mechanism is at work?
   a. Conceptualization
   b. Displacement
   c. Rationalization
   d. Identification

3. According to Adler, _____ is a universal drive to adapt, improve oneself, and master life's challenges.
   a. compensation
   b. striving for superiority
   c. avoiding inferiority
   d. social interest

4. The strengthening of a response tendency by virtue of the fact that the response leads to the removal of an unpleasant stimulus is
   a. positive reinforcement.
   b. negative reinforcement.
   c. primary reinforcement.
   d. punishment.

5. Self-efficacy is
   a. the ability to fulfill one's potential.
   b. one's belief about one's ability to perform behaviors that should lead to expected outcomes.
   c. a durable disposition to behave in a particular way in a variety of situations.
   d. a collection of beliefs about one's nature, unique qualities, and typical behavior.

6. According to Rogers, disparity between one's self-concept and actual experience is referred to as
   a. a delusional system.
   b. dissonance.
   c. conflict.
   d. incongruence.

7. According to Maslow, which of the following is *not* characteristic of self-actualizing persons?
   a. Accurate perception of reality
   b. Being open and spontaneous
   c. Being uncomfortable with solitude
   d. Sensitivity to others' needs

8. If identical twins exhibit more personality resemblance than fraternal twins, it's probably due mostly to
   a. similar treatment from parents.
   b. their greater genetic overlap.
   c. their strong identification with each other.
   d. others' expectations that they should be similar.

9. Research on terror management theory has shown that increased mortality salience leads to all of the following except
   a. increased striving for self-esteem.
   b. more stereotypic thinking about minorities.
   c. a preference for charismatic political candidates.
   d. reduced respect for cultural icons.

10. In psychological testing, consistency of results over repeated measurements refers to
    a. standardization.
    b. validity.
    c. statistical significance.
    d. reliability.

ANSWERS

1. d Page 32
2. c Pages 36–37
3. b Page 40
4. b Page 45
5. b Page 47
6. d Pages 49–50
7. c Pages 52–53
8. b Page 54
9. d Pages 58–59
10. d Pages 61–62

COURSEMATE

Go to **CengageBrain.com** to access Psychology CourseMate, where you will find an interactive eBook, glossaries, flashcards, quizzes, videos, and more.

PERSONAL EXPLORATIONS WORKBOOK

Go to the *Personal Explorations Workbook* in the back of your textbook for exercises that can enhance your self-understanding in relation to issues raised in this chapter.

Exercise 2.1 *Self-Assessment:* Sensation Seeking Scale

Exercise 2.2 *Self-Reflection:* Who Are You?

Stress and Its Effects

© Dmitriy Shironosov/Shutterstock

You're in your car headed home from school. Traffic is barely moving. You groan as the radio reports that the traffic jam is only going to get worse. Another motorist's car nearly hits you trying to cut into your lane. Your pulse quickens as you shout insults at the driver, who cannot even hear you. Your stomach knots up as you think about the term paper that you have to work on tonight. If you don't finish the paper soon, you won't be able to find any time to study for your math test, not to mention your biology quiz. Suddenly you remember that you promised the person you're dating that the two of you would get together tonight. There's no way. Another fight looms on the horizon. Your classmate asks how you feel about the tuition increase the college announced yesterday. You've been trying not to think about it. You're already in debt. Your parents are bugging you about changing schools, but you don't want to leave your friends. Your heartbeat quickens as you contemplate the debate you'll have to wage with your parents. You feel wired with tension as you realize that the stress in your life never seems to let up.

As this example shows, many circumstances can create stress in people's lives. Stress comes in all sorts of packages: large and small, pretty and ugly, simple and complex. All too often, the package is a surprise. In this chapter, we analyze the nature of stress, outline the major sources of stress, and discuss how people respond to stressful events at several levels. We also discuss some factor that influence one's tolerance for stress.

In a sense, stress is what a course on adjustment is all about. Recall from Chapter 1 that adjustment essentially deals with how people manage to cope with various demands and pressures. These demands and pressures represent the core of stressful experience. Thus, the central theme in a course such as this is: How do people adjust to stress, and how might they adjust more effectively?

THE NATURE OF STRESS

Over the years, the term *stress* has been used in different ways by different theorists. Some have viewed stress as a *stimulus* event that presents difficult demands (a divorce, for instance), while others have viewed stress as the *response* of physiological arousal elicited by a troublesome event. Many contemporary researchers view stress as neither a stimulus nor a response alone, but rather as a special stimulus-response transaction in which one feels threatened or experiences loss or harm (Contrada, 2011). Hence, we will define **stress as any circumstances that threaten or are perceived to threaten one's well-being and thereby tax one's coping abilities.** The threat may be to one's immediate physical safety, long-range security, self-esteem, reputation, or peace of mind. Stress is a complex concept—so let's dig a little deeper.

Stress Is an Everyday Event

Stress is a part of everyday life. So much so that the term *stress* has become part of our colloquial speech. It is a noun (*We have stress*). It is an adjective (*He has a stressful job*). It is an adverb (*She acts stressed*). And it is a verb (*Writing a paper stresses me*). Indeed, a poll by the American Psychological Association (2010) shows that, for many of us, stress levels are high and are on the rise. One-third of Americans surveyed reported "living with extreme stress," and nearly half believed that their stress had "increased over the past 5 years." It seems that being "stressed out" has become a hallmark of modern life.

Undeniably, stress is associated with overwhelming, traumatic crises such as bombings, floods, earthquakes, and nuclear accidents. Studies conducted in the aftermath of such traumas typically find elevated rates of psychological problems and physical illness in the affected communities (Dougall & Swanson, 2011). However, these infrequent events represent the tip of the iceberg. Many everyday events, such as waiting in line, having car trouble, misplacing your keys, and staring at bills you can't pay, are also stressful. Of course, major and minor stressors are not entirely independent. A major stressful event, such as going through a divorce, can trigger a cascade of minor stressors,

BABY BLUES

such as looking for an attorney, taking on new household responsibilities, and so forth.

You might guess that minor stressors would produce minor effects, but that isn't necessarily true. Research shows that routine hassles may have significant negative effects on a person's mental and physical health (Almeida, 2005). In fact, according to the national APA (2010) survey, daily problems concerning money, work, and the economy were the top three reported causes of stress (see **Figure 3.1**.

Why would minor hassles be related to mental health? Many theorists believe that stressful events can have a *cumulative* or *additive* impact (Seta, Seta, & McElroy, 2002). In other words, stress can add up. Routine stresses at home, at school, and at work might be fairly benign individually, but collectively they can create great strain. Whatever the reason, it is evident that daily hassles make important contributions to psychological distress (Serido, Almeida, & Wethington, 2004).

Not everyone becomes overwhelmed by stress from daily hassles. As we'll see later in this chapter, certain personal characteristics such as resilience and optimism can buffer the distressing effects of daily hassles. Research indicates that hassles that evoke strong negative emotions are the ones most related to stress (McIntyre, Korn, & Matsuo, 2008). And perceiving a situation as threatening elicits negative emotions (Schneider, 2008). Therefore, individual perceptions are important in how people experience stress.

Stress Lies in the Eye of the Beholder

The experience of feeling threatened depends on what events you notice and how you choose to interpret or *appraise* them. Appraisals account for many of the individual differences in reactions to potential stressors (Folkman, 2011). Events that are stressful for one person may be routine for another. For example, many people find flying

Figure 3.1

Reported causes of stress.
In 2010, the American Psychological Association conducted a national survey on stress in America. The majority of respondents reported moderate to high stress, and almost half said that their stress had increased in the past 5 years. This graph shows the percentage of respondents reporting various causes of their stress. Note that economic issues dominate the top spots.

Source: Adapted from the American Psychological Association (2010). *Stress In America findings.* Washington, DC: APA.

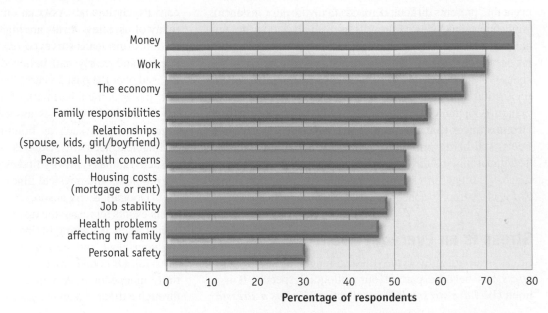

in an airplane somewhat stressful, but frequent fliers may not even raise an eyebrow. Some people enjoy the excitement of going out on a date with someone new; others find the uncertainty terrifying.

In discussing appraisals of stress, Richard Lazarus and Susan Folkman (1984) distinguish between primary and secondary appraisal (see **Figure 3.2**). *Primary appraisal* **is an initial evaluation of whether an event is (1) irrelevant to you, (2) relevant but not threatening, or (3) stressful.** When you view an event as stressful, you are likely to make a *secondary appraisal,* **which is an evaluation of your coping resources and options for dealing with the stress.** For instance, your primary appraisal would determine whether you saw an upcoming job interview as stressful. Your secondary appraisal would determine how stressful the interview appeared, in light of your ability to deal with the event.

Richard Lazarus

It should come as no surprise that people's appraisals of stressful events alter the impact of the events themselves. Research has demonstrated that negative interpretations of events are often associated with increased distress surrounding these events. In fact, when studying a sample of children after the September 11, 2001 terrorist attacks, Lengua and her colleagues (2006) found that children's appraisals of the event predicted their stress symptoms as much as factors such as their coping styles or pre-attack stress loads.

People are rarely objective in their appraisals of potentially stressful events. A classic study of hospitalized patients awaiting surgery showed only a slight correlation between the objective seriousness of a person's upcoming surgery and the amount of fear the person experienced (Janis, 1958). Clearly, some people are more prone to negative interpretations of life's difficulties than others are. Research shows that anxious, neurotic people are more likely to make threat appraisals as well as to report more negative emotions related to stress than people with less anxiety (Schneider et al., 2012). Thus, stress lies in the eye

(actually, the mind) of the beholder, and people's appraisals of stressful events are highly subjective.

Stress May Be Embedded in the Environment

Although the perception of stress is a highly personal matter, many kinds of stress come from the environmental circumstances that individuals share with others. *Ambient stress* **consists of chronic environmental conditions that, although not urgent, are negatively valued and place adaptive demands on people.** Features of the environment such as excessive noise, traffic, and pollution can threaten well-being and leave their mark on mental and physical health. For example, investigators found an association between chronic exposure to high levels of noise and elevated blood pressure among children attending school near Los Angeles International Airport (Cohen et al., 1980). Similarly, studies of children living near Munich International Airport (Evans, Hygge, & Bullinger, 1995) found elevated stress hormones, reading and memory deficits, and poor task persistence in samples of schoolchildren.

Crowding is a major source of environmental stress. Even temporary experiences of crowding, such as being packed into a passenger train for a crowded commute, can be stressful (Evans & Wener, 2007). However, most of the research on crowding has focused on the effects of residential density. Generally, studies suggest an association between high density and increased physiological arousal, psychological distress, and social withdrawal (Evans & Stecker, 2004). Siddiqui and Pandey (2003) found crowding to be one of the most critical stressors for urban residents in Northern India, indicating that this is an important issue that goes well beyond Western cities.

Psychologists have also explored the repercussions of living in areas that are at risk for disaster. For instance, studies suggest that people who live near nuclear power plants, hazardous waste sites, waste incinerators, or polluting industrial facilities experience higher levels of distress (Lima, 2004). Similarly, residents in areas prone to earth-

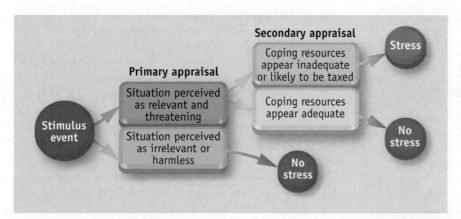

Figure 3.2
Primary and secondary appraisal of stress.
Primary appraisal is an initial evaluation of whether an event is (1) irrelevant to you, (2) relevant but not threatening, or (3) stressful. When you view an event as stressful, you are likely to make a *secondary appraisal,* which is an evaluation of your coping resources and options for dealing with the stress. (Based on Lazarus & Folkman, 1994)

Stress can be caused by environmental circumstances such as pollution, excessive noise, crowding, traffic jams, and urban decay.

quakes or hurricanes may experience increased stress (Dougall & Baum, 2000).

Noise and crowding are not the only environmental factors related to stress. There is considerable evidence that exposure to community violence, whether as a victim or as a witness, is associated with anxiety, depression, anger, and aggression among urban youth (Margolin & Gordis, 2004). Although it's clear that exposure to violence and emotional distress are linked, researchers are still exploring the mechanisms underlying this connection. One such mechanism is the stress associated with the experience of community violence (Overstreet, 2000). Children who report recent exposure to traumatic events show increased stress hormones (Bevans, Cerbone, & Overstreet, 2008).

Finally, investigators have examined poverty as a source of environmental stress. Children from lower-income homes tend to have higher levels of stress hormones than their higher-income peers (Blair et al., 2011). Poverty-related stress takes its toll on both mental and physical health (Chandola & Marmot, 2011). Studies suggest that some of the link between poverty and poorer adjustment

Learn More Online

American Psychological Association: Stress

The American Psychological Association is the largest professional organization for psychologists. This website presents up-to-date coverage of stress research, including recent press releases and psychological research in the news. It also provides a peek into stress research currently being published.

can be explained by perceived social class discrimination (Fuller-Rowell, Evans, & Ong, 2012).

Stress Is Influenced by Culture

Although certain types of events (such as the loss of a loved one) are probably viewed as stressful in virtually all human societies, cultures vary greatly in the predominant forms of stress their people experience. Obviously, the challenges of daily living encountered in modern, Western cities like Montreal or Philadelphia are quite different from the day-to-day difficulties experienced in indigenous societies in Africa or South America. Indeed, culture sets the context in which people experience and appraise stress. In some cases, a specific cultural group may be exposed to pervasive stress that is unique to that group. For example, the ethnic cleansing of Albanians in Kosovo in 1999 and the devastating and widespread destruction from the tsunami in Indonesia and regions of Southeast Asia in 2004 were extraordinary forms of stress distinctive to these societies. Our discussion of stress largely focuses on the types of stressors confronted in contemporary, Western society, but you should be aware that life in Western society is not necessarily representative of life around the world.

Moreover, even within the modern, Western world, disparities can be found in the constellation of stressors experienced by specific cultural groups. Social scientists have explored the effects of ethnicity-related sources of stress experienced by African Americans, Hispanic Americans, Asian Americans, and other minority groups, and they have documented that racial discrimination negatively affects the mental health and well-being for targets of racism (Brondolo et al., 2011). Further, exposure to racism through social exclusion, stigmatization, and harassment affects appraisals of stressful events. Extreme forms of racism still exist. Of all hate crime incidents reported for 2010, 48.2% were motivated by race, and the majority of those were anti-black (see **Figure 3.3**).

Although overt racial discrimination in America has declined in recent decades, covert expressions of ethnic prejudice continue to be commonplace (Dovidio & Gaertner, 1999). Everyday discrimination can take many forms, including verbal insults (ethnic slurs), negative evaluations, avoidance, denial of equal treatment, and threats of aggression. Feldman-Barrett and Swim (1998) emphasize that these acts of discrimination are often subtle and am-

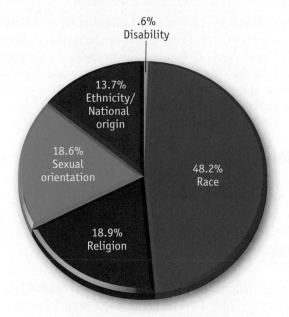

Figure 3.3

Motivations behind hate crimes. Social scientists have explored the effects of ethnicity-related sources of stress experienced by African Americans, Latin Americans, Asian Americans, and other minority groups. Exposure to racism through social exclusion, stigmatization, and harassment affects appraisals of stressful events. However, extreme forms of racism still exist. Of all hate crime incidents reported for 2010, 48.2% were motivated by race, and the majority of those were anti-black.

Source: Adapted from Federal Bureau of Investigation (2011). *Hate crime statistics, 2010.* http://www.fbi.gov/about-us/cjis/ucr/hate-crime/2010/narratives/hate-crime-2010-victims

biguous (e.g., "The clerk seemed to be ignoring me"). Hence, minority group members may experience stress not only from explicit discrimination but also from the subjective perception of discrimination in ambiguous situations (Williams & Mohammed, 2007). In one study, black participants showed cognitive impairment following ambiguous (but not blatant) prejudice, apparently as a result of grappling with the uncertainty (Salvatore & Shelton, 2007). Such perceived discrimination has been linked to greater psychological distress, higher levels of depression, and decreased well-being for a variety of minority groups, including sexual minorities (Lewis et al., 2006; Moradi & Risco, 2006; Swim, Johnston, & Pearson, 2009).

For immigrants, **acculturation, or changing to adapt to a new culture,** is a major source of stress related to reduced well-being. Indeed, acculturation stress is associated with depression and anxiety (Revollo et al., 2011). Studies show that the discrepancy between what individuals *expect* before immigrating and what they actually *experience* once they do immigrate is related to the amount of acculturation stress they report (Negy, Schwartz, & Reig-Ferrer, 2009). Schwartz and colleagues (2010) note that how one is received into the new culture (for instance, with scorn or displeasure) also relates to acculturation stress levels. The extra layers of stress experienced by minority group members clearly take their toll, but scientists are still exploring the degree to which ethnicity-related stress may have detrimental effects on individuals' mental and physical health.

MAJOR SOURCES OF STRESS

LEARNING OBJECTIVES

- Distinguish between acute, chronic, and anticipatory stressors.
- Describe frustration, internal conflict, life changes, and pressure as sources of stress in modern life.

An enormous variety of events can be stressful for one person or another. To achieve a better understanding of stress, theorists have tried to analyze the nature of stressful events and divide them into subtypes. One sensible distinction involves differentiating between *acute stressors* and *chronic stressors*. **Acute stressors are threatening events that have a relatively short duration and a clear endpoint.** Examples would include having a difficult encounter with a belligerent drunk, waiting for the results of a medical test, or having your home threatened by severe flooding. **Chronic stressors are threatening events that have a relatively long duration and no readily apparent time limit.** Examples would include persistent financial strains produced by huge credit card debts, ongoing pressures from a hostile boss at work, or the demands of caring for a sick family member over a period of years. Of course,

this distinction is far from perfect. It is hard to decide where to draw the line between a short-lived versus lengthy stressor, and even brief stressors can have long-lasting effects.

Robert Sapolsky, a leading authority on stress, points out another type of stressor that is unique to humans. **Anticipatory stressors are upcoming or future events that are perceived to be threatening.** That is, we anticipate the impact of the event even though it has not happened yet. We may worry about breakups that never occur, bad grades we never receive, or hurricanes that never make landfall. The problem with anticipatory stress is that it can

Robert Sapolsky

affect us psychologically and physically just as strongly as actual stressors do (Sapolsky, 2004). However we classify them (acute, chronic, or anticipatory), stressors come from all aspects of our lives. Let's take a look at four major sources of stress: frustration, conflict, change, and pressure. As you read about each of them, you'll surely recognize some familiar adversaries.

Frustration

"It has been very frustrating to watch the rapid deterioration of my parents' relationship. Over the last year or two they have argued constantly and have refused to seek any professional help. I have tried to talk to them, but they kind of shut me and my brother out of their problem. I feel very helpless and sometimes even very angry, not at them, but at the whole situation."

This scenario illustrates frustration. As psychologists use the term, *frustration* **occurs in any situation in which the pursuit of some goal is thwarted.** In essence, you experience frustration when you want something and you can't have it. Everyone has to deal with frustration virtually every day. Long daily commutes, traffic jams, and annoying drivers, for instance, are routine sources of frustration that can produce negative moods and increase levels of stress (Wener & Evans, 2011). Such frustration often leads to aggression; even artificially induced frustration in a laboratory setting can lead to increased aggression from participants (Verona & Curtin, 2006). Some frustrations, such as *failures* and *losses,* can be sources of significant stress. Fortunately, most frustrations are brief and insignificant. You may be quite upset when you go to the autoshop to pick up your car and find that it hasn't been fixed as promised. However, a few days later you'll probably have your precious car back, and all will be forgotten.

More often than not, frustration appears to be the culprit at work when people feel troubled by environmental stress (Graig, 1993). Excessive noise, heat, pollution, and crowding are most likely stressful because they frustrate the desire for quiet, a comfortable

Alan Poulson Photography/Shutterstock.com

body temperature, clean air, and adequate privacy. Frustration also plays a role in the aggressive behaviors associated with "road rage" (Jovanović, Stanojević, & Stanojević, 2011). Further, frustration in the workplace often results in burnout (Lewandowski, 2003), a specific effect of stress that we will discuss later in this chapter.

Internal Conflict

"Should I or shouldn't I? I became engaged at Christmas. My fiancé surprised me with a ring. I knew if I refused the ring he would be terribly hurt and our relationship would suffer. However, I don't really know whether or not I want to marry him. On the other hand, I don't want to lose him either."

Like frustration, internal conflict is an unavoidable feature of everyday life. That perplexing question "Should I or shouldn't I?" comes up countless times on a daily basis. *Internal conflict* **occurs when two or more incompatible motivations or behavioral impulses compete for expression.** As we discussed in Chapter 2, Sigmund Freud proposed over a century ago that internal conflicts generate considerable psychological distress. This link between conflict and distress was measured with precision in studies by Laura King and Robert Emmons (1990, 1991). They used an elaborate questionnaire to assess the overall amount of internal conflict experienced by subjects. They found higher levels of conflict to be associated with higher levels of psychological distress.

Conflicts come in three types, which were originally described by Kurt Lewin (1935) and investigated extensively by Neal Miller (1944, 1959). These types—approach-approach, avoidance-avoidance, and approach-avoidance—are diagrammed in **Figure 3.4**.

Courtesy Neal Miller

Neal Miller

In an *approach-approach conflict* **a choice must be made between two attractive goals.** The problem, of course, is that you can choose just one of the two goals. For example, you have a free afternoon; should you play tennis or go to the movies? You're out for a meal; do you want to order the pizza or the spaghetti? You can't afford both: should you buy the blue sweater or the gray jacket? Among the three kinds of conflict, the approach-approach type tends to be the least stressful. People don't usually stagger out of restaurants, exhausted by the stress of choosing which of several appealing entrees to eat. In approach-approach conflicts you typically have a reasonably happy ending, whichever way you decide to go. Nonetheless, approach-approach conflicts centering on important issues may sometimes be troublesome. If you are torn between two appealing college majors or two attractive job

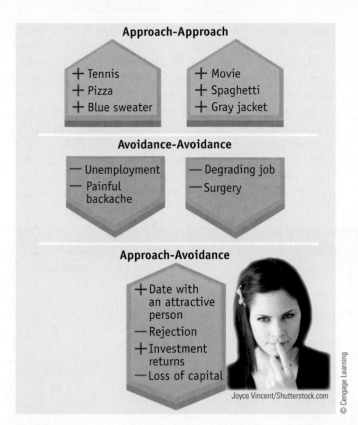

Approach-Approach

+ Tennis
+ Pizza
+ Blue sweater

+ Movie
+ Spaghetti
+ Gray jacket

Avoidance-Avoidance

— Unemployment
— Painful backache

— Degrading job
— Surgery

Approach-Avoidance

+ Date with an attractive person
— Rejection
+ Investment returns
— Loss of capital

Joyce Vincent/Shutterstock.com

© Cengage Learning

Figure 3.4

Types of conflict. Psychologists have identified three basic types of conflict. In approach-approach and avoidance-avoidance conflicts, the person is torn between two goals. In an approach-avoidance conflict only one goal is under consideration, but it has both positive and negative aspects.

offers, you may find the decision-making process quite stressful.

In **an *avoidance-avoidance conflict* a choice must be made between two unattractive goals.** Forced to choose between two repelling alternatives, you are, as the expression goes, "caught between a rock and a hard place." For example, let's say you have painful backaches. Should you submit to surgery that you dread, or should you continue to live with the pain? Or you might need to decide between

staying in an unsatisfying relationship or being alone. Obviously, avoidance-avoidance conflicts are most unpleasant and highly stressful. Typically, people keep delaying their decision as long as possible, hoping that they will somehow be able to escape the conflict situation. For example, you might delay surgery in the hope that your backaches will disappear on their own.

In **an *approach-avoidance conflict* a choice must be made about whether to pursue a single goal that has both attractive and unattractive aspects.** For instance, imagine that you're offered a job promotion that will mean a large increase in pay. The catch is that you will have to move to a city that you hate. Approach-avoidance conflicts are common, and they can be highly stressful. Any time you have to take a risk to pursue some desirable outcome, you are likely to find yourself in an approach-avoidance conflict. Should you risk rejection by asking out that attractive person in class? Should you risk your savings by investing in a new business that could fail? Approach-avoidance conflicts often produce *vacillation*. That is, people go back and forth, beset by indecision that can create stress. Fortunately we are equipped to focus on the positive aspects of our decision once it has been made (Brehm, 1956).

Change

"After graduation, I landed my dream job and moved to another state. For the first time, I am living alone, far away from my friends and family. My biggest stress is getting used to my new life. Everything is different. I am learning how to do my new job, trying to make friends, and navigating my way around my new city. I love my job and my new location, but I am having difficulties dealing with all these changes at once."

Life changes may represent a key type of stress. *Life changes* **are any noticeable alterations in one's living circumstances that require readjustment.** Research on life change began when Thomas Holmes, Richard Rahe, and their colleagues set out to explore the relation between

BLONDIE

stressful life events and physical illness (Holmes & Rahe, 1967; Rahe & Arthur, 1978). They interviewed thousands of tuberculosis patients to find out what kinds of events preceded the onset of their disease. Surprisingly, the frequently cited events were not uniformly negative. The list included plenty of aversive events, as expected, but patients also mentioned many seemingly positive events, such as getting married, having a baby, or getting promoted.

Why would positive events, such as moving to a nicer home, produce stress? According to Holmes and Rahe, it is because they produce *change*. Their thesis is that disruptions of daily routines are stressful. According to their theory, changes in personal relationships, changes at work, changes in finances, and so forth can be stressful even when the changes are welcomed.

Based on this analysis, Holmes and Rahe (1967) developed the Social Readjustment Rating Scale (SRRS) to measure life change as a form of stress. The scale assigns numerical values to forty-three major life events that are supposed to reflect the magnitude of the readjustment required by each change (see **Figure 3.5**). Respondents are

SOCIAL READJUSTMENT RATING SCALE

Life event	Mean value	Life event	Mean value
Death of a spouse	100	Son or daughter leaving home	29
Divorce	73	Trouble with in-laws	29
Marital separation	65	Outstanding personal achievement	28
Jail term	63	Spouse begins or stops work	26
Death of close family member	63	Begin or end school	26
Personal injury or illness	53	Change in living conditions	25
Marriage	50	Revision of personal habits	24
Fired at work	47	Trouble with boss	23
Marital reconciliation	45	Change in work hours or conditions	20
Retirement	45	Change in residence	20
Change in health of family member	44	Change in school	20
Pregnancy	40	Change in recreation	19
Sex difficulties	39	Change in church activities	19
Gain of a new family member	39	Change in social activities	18
Business readjustment	39	Loan for lesser purchase (car, TV, etc.)	17
Change in financial state	38	Change in sleeping habits	16
Death of a close friend	37	Change in number of family get-togethers	15
Change to a different line of work	36	Change in eating habits	15
Change in number of arguments with spouse	35	Vacation	13
Mortgage or loan for major purchase	31	Christmas	12
Foreclosure of mortgage or loan	30	Minor violations of the law	11
Change in responsibilities at work	29		

Figure 3.5

Social Readjustment Rating Scale (SRRS). Devised by Holmes and Rahe (1967), this scale is designed to measure the change-related stress in one's life. The numbers on the right are supposed to reflect the average amount of stress (readjustment) produced by each event. Respondents check off the events they experienced recently and add up the associated numbers to arrive at their stress scores.

Source: Adapted from Holmes, T. H., & Rahe, R. H. (1967). The Social Readjustment Rating Scale. *Journal of Psychosomatic Research, 11*(12), 213–218. Copyright © 1967 with permission from Elsevier Science Publishing Co.

asked to indicate how often they experienced any of these forty-three events during a certain time period (typically, the past year). The person then adds up the numbers associated with each event checked. The total is an index of the amount of change-related stress the person has recently experienced.

The SRRS and similar scales have been used in thousands of studies by researchers all over the world. Overall, these studies have shown that people with higher scores on the SRRS tend to be more vulnerable to many kinds of physical illness—and many types of psychological problems as well (Scully, Tosi, & Banning, 2000). However, experts have criticized this research, citing problems with the methods used and raising questions about the meaning of the findings (Anderson, Wethington, & Kamarck, 2011). These experts have argued that the SRRS does not measure *change* exclusively. The list of life changes on the SRRS is dominated by events that are clearly negative or undesirable (death of a spouse, marital separation, and so on). These negative events probably generate great frustration. So even though the scale contains some positive events, it could be that frustration (generated by negative events), rather than change, creates most of the stress assessed by the scale. Indeed, when researchers asked participants to indicate the desirability of the events on the scale, they found that life change is *not* the crucial dimension measured by the SRRS and that in fact undesirable or negative life events cause much of the stress tapped by the scale (McLean & Link, 1994; Turner & Wheaton, 1995).

Should we discard the notion that change is stressful? Not entirely. More research is needed, but it is quite plausible that change constitutes a major type of stress in people's lives. However, we have little reason to believe that change is *inherently* or *inevitably stressful*. Some life changes may be quite challenging, while others may be quite benign.

Pressure

"My father questioned me at dinner about some things I did not want to talk about. I know he doesn't want to hear my answers, at least not the truth. My father told me when I was little that I was his favorite because I was 'pretty near perfect' and I've spent my life trying to keep that up, even though it's obviously not true. Recently, he has begun to realize this and it's made our relationship very strained and painful."

At one time or another, most of us have probably remarked that we were "under pressure." What does that expression mean? ***Pressure* involves expectations or demands that one behave in a certain way.** Pressure can be divided into two subtypes: the pressure to *perform* and the pressure to *conform*. You are under pressure to perform when you are expected to execute tasks and responsibilities quickly, efficiently, and successfully. For example, salespeople are usually under pressure to move lots of merchandise. Professors at research institutions are often under pressure to publish in prestigious journals. Comedians are under pressure to get laughs. Pressures to conform to others' expectations are also common. Businessmen are expected to wear suits and ties. Suburban homeowners are expected to keep their lawns manicured. Teenagers are expected to adhere to their parents' values and rules.

Pressure is widely discussed by the general public. Ironically though, the concept of pressure has received scant attention from researchers. However, Weiten (1988, 1998) has devised a scale to measure pressure as a form of life stress. In research with this scale, a strong relationship has been found between pressure and a variety of psychological symptoms and problems. In fact, pressure has turned out to be more strongly related to measures of mental health than the SRRS and other established measures of stress (see **Figure 3.6**).

A recent 15-year study of over 12,000 nurses found that increased pressure at work was related to an increased risk for heart disease (Väänänen, 2010). Participants who reported that their work pressure was much too high were

© Cengage Learning

Figure 3.6

Pressure and psychological symptoms. A comparison of pressure and life change as sources of stress suggests that pressure may be more strongly related to mental health than change is. In one study, Weiten (1988) found a correlation of .59 between scores on the Pressure Inventory (PI) and symptoms of psychological distress. In the same sample, the correlation between SRRS scores and psychological symptoms was only .28.

Pressure comes in two varieties: pressure to perform and pressure to conform. For example, workers on assembly lines are often expected to maintain high productivity with few mistakes (performance pressure), and suburban homeowners are typically expected to maintain well-groomed exteriors (conformity pressure).

almost 50% more likely to develop heart disease than those who experienced normal levels of pressure. Academic pressures, common for students worldwide, are related to increased anxiety and depression and affect student motivation and concentration (Andrews & Hejdenberg, 2007). Research also suggests that stress resulting from academic pressure may actually impede academic performance (Kaplan, Liu, & Kaplan, 2005) and lead to problematic escape behaviors such as drinking (Kieffer, Cronin, & Gawet, 2006).

We tend to think of pressure as something imposed from outside forces. However, students often report that pressure is self-imposed (Hamaideh, 2011). For example, you might sign up for extra classes to get through school

quickly. Or you might actively seek additional leadership positions to impress your family. Self-imposed stress doesn't stop when you complete your education. People frequently put pressure on themselves to rapidly climb the corporate ladder or to be perfect parents. Even the pressure that modern people put on themselves to maintain a proper work-family balance can serve as a source of stress. Individuals who think that failure to meet exceedingly high standards is unacceptable (that is, negative perfectionists) are more prone to fatigue and depression (Dittner, Rimes, & Thorpe, 2011). In sum, because individuals might create stress by embracing unrealistic expectations for themselves, they might have more control over their stress than they realize.

RESPONDING TO STRESS

LEARNING OBJECTIVES

- Summarize research on typical emotional responses (both positive and negative) to stress, and discuss some effects of emotional arousal.
- Describe some physiological responses to stress, including the fight-or-flight response, the general adaptation syndrome, and

the two major pathways along which the brain sends signals to the endocrine system.
- Discuss the concept of coping.

The human response to stress is complex and multidimensional (Segerstrom & O'Connor, 2012). Stress affects people on several levels. Consider again the chapter's opening scenario, in which you're driving home in heavy traffic, thinking about overdue papers, relationship conflicts, tuition increases, and parental pressures. Let's look at some of the reactions we mentioned. When you groan in reaction to the traffic report, you're experiencing an *emotional response* to stress—in this case, annoyance and anger. When your pulse quickens and your stomach knots up, you're exhibiting *physiological responses* to stress. When you shout insults at

another driver, your verbal aggression is a *behavioral response* to the stress at hand. Thus, we can analyze people's reactions to stress at three levels: (1) their emotional responses, (2) their physiological responses, and (3) their behavioral responses. **Figure 3.7** depicts these three levels.

Emotional Responses

Emotion is an elusive concept. Psychologists debate how to define emotion, and many conflicting theories purport to explain people's feelings. However, everybody has had

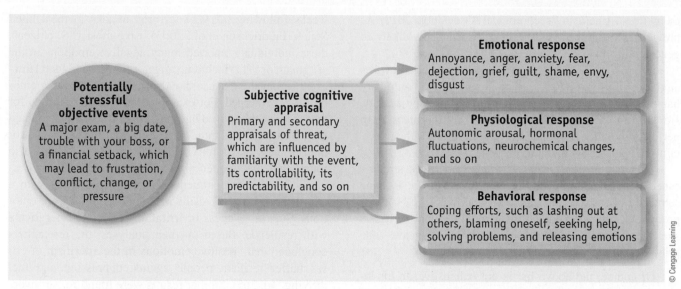

Figure 3.7

The multidimensional response to stress. A potentially stressful event, such as a major exam, will elicit a subjective, cognitive appraisal of how threatening the event is. If the event is viewed with alarm, the stress may trigger emotional, physiological, and behavioral reactions. The human response to stress is multidimensional.

extensive personal experience with emotions. Everyone has a good idea of what it means to be anxious, elated, gloomy, jealous, disgusted, excited, guilty, or nervous. So rather than pursue the technical debates about emotion, we'll rely on your familiarity with the concept and simply note that *emotions* **are powerful, largely uncontrollable feelings, accompanied by physiological changes.** When people are under stress, they often react emotionally. More often than not, stress tends to elicit unpleasant emotions. In studying one of the most severe disasters of modern times, the Indian Ocean tsunami of 2004, researchers found that almost 84% of survivors showed signs of severe emotional distress, including depression and anxiety (Souza et al., 2007). Emotional responses to stress seem to transcend

time and culture. For instance, a historical researcher, examining texts from 2100–2000 B.C., found evidence that core negative emotional reactions to trauma have not really changed over the millennia (Ben-Ezra, 2004).

Negative Emotions

There are no simple one-to-one connections between certain *types* of stressful events and particular emotions, but researchers *have* uncovered some strong links between specific *cognitive reactions to stress* and specific emotions (Lazarus, 2006). For example, self-blame tends to lead to guilt, helplessness to sadness, and so forth. Although stressful events can evoke many negative emotions, some are certainly more likely than others. According to Richard Lazarus (1993), common negative emotional responses to stress include the following:

● *Annoyance, anger, and rage.* Stress often produces feelings of anger ranging in intensity from mild annoyance to uncontrollable rage. In fact, in a national survey, respondents reported irritability or anger as the most frequent symptom of

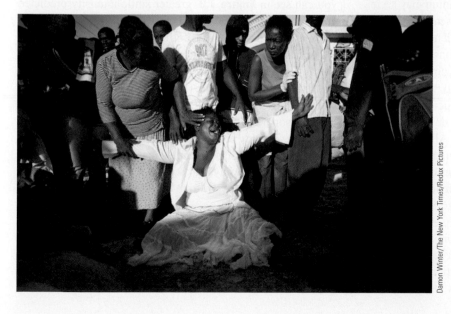

The huge earthquake in Haiti in January of 2010 produced overwhelming trauma for countless people. Individuals experiencing severe stress have emotional, physiological, and behavioral reactions. Emotional responses to extreme stress (such as grief, anxiety, and fear) appear to transcend culture.

their stress (American Psychological Association, 2010). As previously mentioned, frustration is particularly likely to generate anger.

- *Apprehension, anxiety, and fear.* Stress often evokes anxiety and fear. As we saw in Chapter 2, Freudian theory has long recognized the link between conflict and anxiety. However, anxiety can also be elicited by the pressure to perform, the threat of impending frustration, or the uncertainty associated with change.

- *Dejection, sadness, and grief.* Sometimes stress—especially frustration—simply brings one down. Routine setbacks, such as traffic tickets and poor grades, often produce feelings of dejection. More profound setbacks, such as deaths and divorces, typically leave one grief-stricken.

Of course, the above list is not exhaustive. In his insightful analyses of stress-emotion relations, Richard Lazarus (1991, 1993) mentions five other negative emotions that often figure prominently in reactions to stress: guilt, shame, envy, jealousy, and disgust. In the short term, these reactions are to be expected in response to stressful events. Experiencing such emotions does not mean that you are weak or that you are "losing it." For most people these reactions usually dissipate over time. If negative reactions such as these persist indefinitely and interfere with one's social, occupational, or family functioning, a diagnosis of *posttraumatic stress disorder* may be applicable (see pages 86–87). If your reactions to a traumatic event are especially severe, persistent, and debilitating, it may be wise to seek professional help.

Positive Emotions

Investigators have tended to focus heavily on the connection between stress and negative emotions. However, research shows that positive emotions also occur during periods of stress (Finan, Zautra, & Wershba, 2011; Folkman, 2008). This finding may seem counterintuitive, but researchers have found that people experience a diverse array of pleasant emotions even while enduring the most dire of circumstances. For instance, Susan Folkman and her colleagues (1997) conducted a 5-year study of coping patterns in 253 caregiving partners of men with AIDS. Surprisingly, over the course of the study the caregivers reported experiencing positive emotions about as often as they experienced negative ones—except during the time immediately surrounding the death of their partners.

Susan Folkman

Courtesy Susan Folkman

Similar findings have been observed in some other studies of serious stress that made an effort to look for positive emotions. One study examined participants' emotional functioning early in 2001 and then again in the weeks following the 9/11 terrorist attacks in the United States (Fredrickson et al., 2003). Like most U.S. citizens, these individuals reported many negative emotions in the aftermath of 9/11, including anger, sadness, and fear. However, within this "dense cloud of anguish," positive emotions also emerged. For example, people felt gratitude for the safety of their loved ones, many took stock and counted their blessings, and quite a few reported renewed love for their friends and family. Fredrickson et al. (2003) also found that the frequency of pleasant emotions (such as happiness and contentment) correlated positively with a measure of subjects' resilience, whereas unpleasant emotions (such as sadness or irritation) correlated negatively with resilience. Based on their analyses, the researchers concluded that "positive emotions in the aftermath of crises buffer resilient people against depression and fuel thriving" (p. 365). Similar results were found for survivors of the 2001 El Salvador earthquake (Vazquez et al., 2005). Thus, contrary to common sense, positive emotions do *not* vanish during times of severe stress. Moreover, these emotions appear to play a key role in helping people bounce back from the negative emotions associated with stress (Zautra & Reich, 2011).

One particularly interesting finding has been that a positive emotional style is associated with an enhanced immune response (Cohen & Pressman, 2006). Positive emotions also appear to be protective against heart disease (Davidson, Mostofsky, & Whang, 2010). These effects probably contribute to the recently discovered association between positive emotions and longevity (Ong, 2010; Xu & Roberts, 2010). Yes, people who report experiencing a high level of positive emotions appear to live longer than others! One recent study exploring this association looked at photos of major league baseball players taken from the Baseball Register for 1952. The intensity of the players' smiles was used as a crude index of their tendency to experience positive emotions, which was then related to how long they lived. As you can see in **Figure 3.8**, greater smile intensity predicted greater longevity (Abel & Kruger, 2010).

Simply put, positive emotions can contribute to building social, intellectual, and physical resources that can be helpful in dealing with stress and allow one to experience flourishing mental health (Fredrickson & Losada, 2005). In fact, the benefits of positive emotions are so strong that Fredrickson (2006) argues that people should "cultivate positive emotions in themselves and in those around them as means to achieving psychological growth and improved psychological and physical well-being over time" (p. 85). Chapter 16 discusses positive emotions in more detail.

Effects of Emotional Arousal

Emotional responses are a natural and normal part of life. Even unpleasant emotions serve important purposes. Like physical pain, painful emotions can serve as warnings that

Figure 3.8

Positive emotions and longevity. To look at the relation between positive emotions and longevity, Abel and Kruger (2010) used the intensity of baseball players' smiles in photographs as a rough indicator of their characteristic emotional tone. All the photos in the *Baseball Register* for 1952 were reviewed and classified as showing no smile, a partial smile, or a big smile. Then the age of death was determined for the players (except the 46 who were still alive in 2009). As you can see, greater smile intensity was associated with living longer.

one needs to take action. However, strong emotional arousal can also hamper efforts to cope with stress. For example, research has found that high emotional arousal can sometimes interfere with attention and memory retrieval and can impair judgment and decision making (Janis, 1993).

The well-known problem of *test anxiety* illustrates how emotional arousal can hurt performance. Often students who score poorly on an exam will nonetheless insist that they know the material. Many of them are probably telling the truth. Researchers have found a negative correlation between test-related anxiety and exam performance. That is, students who display high test anxiety tend to score low on exams (Bin Kassim, Hanafi, & Hancock, 2008). Test anxiety can interfere with test taking in several ways, but one critical consideration appears to be the disruption of attention to the test. Many test-anxious students waste too much time worrying about how they're doing and wondering whether others are having similar problems. In addition, there is evidence that test anxiety may deplete one's capacity for self-control, increasing the likelihood of poor performance (Oaten & Cheng, 2005). In other words, once distracted, test-anxious students might not have the self-control to get themselves back on course. This tendency is related to a concept called *ego depletion* that we will discuss in Chapter 6.

Although emotional arousal may hurt coping efforts, this isn't *necessarily* the case. The *inverted-U hypothesis* predicts that task performance should improve with increased emotional arousal—up to a point, after which further increases in arousal become disruptive and performance deteriorates (Mandler, 1993). This idea is referred to as the inverted-U hypothesis because plotting performance as a function of arousal results in graphs that approximate an upside-down U (see **Figure 3.9**). In these graphs, the level of arousal at which performance peaks is characterized as the *optimal level of arousal* for a task.

This optimal level of arousal appears to depend in part on the complexity of the task at hand. The conventional

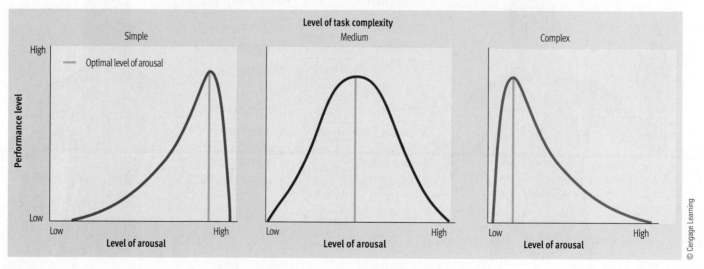

Figure 3.9

Arousal and performance. Graphs of the relationship between emotional arousal and task performance tend to resemble an inverted U, as increased arousal is associated with improved performance up to a point, after which higher arousal leads to poorer performance. The optimal level of arousal for a task depends on the complexity of the task. On complex tasks, a relatively low level of arousal tends to be optimal. On simple tasks, however, performance may peak at a much higher level of arousal.

wisdom is that *as tasks become more complex, the optimal level of arousal (for peak performance) tends to decrease.* This relationship is depicted in **Figure 3.9**. As you can see, a fairly high level of arousal should be optimal on simple tasks (such as driving 8 hours to help a friend in a crisis). However, performance should peak at a lower level of arousal on complex tasks (such as making a major decision in which you have to weigh many factors).

The research evidence on the inverted-U hypothesis is inconsistent and subject to varied interpretations. The original formulation of this hypothesis was more related to animal learning than to human performance in stressful situations (Hancock & Ganey, 2003). Hence, it may be risky to generalize this principle to the complexities of everyday coping efforts. However, scientists argue that the theory should be refined rather than discarded (Landers, 2007).

Physiological Responses

As we have seen, stress frequently elicits strong emotional responses. These responses also bring about important physiological changes. Test anxiety, for example, is associated with elevations in blood pressure (Conley & Lehman, 2012). Even in cases of moderate stress, you may notice that your heart has started beating faster, you have begun to breathe harder, and you are perspiring more than usual. How does all this (and much more) happen? Let's see.

The "Fight-or-Flight" Response

Even though he did not refer to it as stress, Walter Cannon (1929, 1932) was a pioneer in stress research with his work on the fight-or-flight response. **The *fight-or-flight response* is a physiological reaction to threat that mobilizes an organism for attacking (fight) or fleeing (flight) an enemy.** For instance, you see a threatening figure and your heart rate increases, blood pressure rises, respiration increases, digestion slows—all things that prepare you to act and that are evolutionarily advantageous (Sapolsky, 2004). These responses occur in the body's autonomic nervous system. **The *autonomic nervous system (ANS)* is made up of the nerves that connect to the heart, blood vessels, smooth muscles, and glands.** As its name hints, the autonomic nervous system is somewhat *autonomous.* That is, it controls involuntary, visceral functions that people don't normally think about, such as heart rate, digestion, and perspiration.

The autonomic nervous system can be broken into two divisions (see **Figure 3.10**). The *parasympathetic division* of the ANS generally conserves bodily resources. For instance, it slows heart rate and promotes digestion to help the body save and store energy. The fight-or-flight response is mediated by the *sympathetic division* of the autonomic nervous system, which mobilizes bodily resources for emergencies. In one experiment, Cannon studied the fight-or-flight response in cats by confronting them with dogs. Among other things, he noticed an immediate acceleration

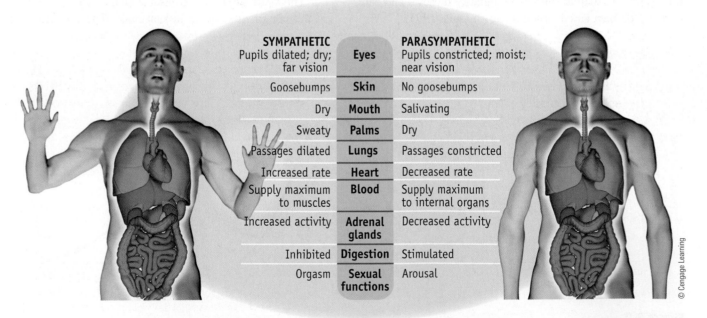

SYMPATHETIC		PARASYMPATHETIC
Pupils dilated; dry; far vision	**Eyes**	Pupils constricted; moist; near vision
Goosebumps	**Skin**	No goosebumps
Dry	**Mouth**	Salivating
Sweaty	**Palms**	Dry
Passages dilated	**Lungs**	Passages constricted
Increased rate	**Heart**	Decreased rate
Supply maximum to muscles	**Blood**	Supply maximum to internal organs
Increased activity	**Adrenal glands**	Decreased activity
Inhibited	**Digestion**	Stimulated
Orgasm	**Sexual functions**	Arousal

© Cengage Learning

Figure 3.10

The autonomic nervous system (ANS). The ANS is composed of the nerves that connect to the heart, blood vessels, smooth muscles, and glands. The ANS is subdivided into the *sympathetic division,* which mobilizes bodily resources in times of need, and the *parasympathetic division,* which conserves bodily resources. Some of the key functions controlled by each division of the ANS are summarized in the center of the diagram.

in the cats' breathing and heart rate and a reduction in digestive processes.

Shelley Taylor and her colleagues (Taylor & Master, 2011) have questioned whether the fight-or-flight model applies equally well to both males and females. They note that in most species females have more responsibility for the care of young offspring than males do. Using an evolutionary perspective, they argue that this disparity may make fighting and fleeing less adaptive for females, as both responses may endanger offspring and thus reduce the likelihood of an animal passing on its genes. Taylor and colleagues maintain that evolutionary processes have fostered more of a "tend and befriend" response to stress in females. According to this analysis, in reacting to stress females allocate more effort to the care of offspring and to seeking help and support. Consistent with this theory, David and Lyons-Ruth (2005) found gender differences in how infants respond to threat. Specifically, when frightened, female infants showed more approach behaviors toward their mothers than male infants did. Taylor (2011a) speculates that the hormone oxytocin signals the need for affiliation in females in times of social distress. More research is needed to evaluate this provocative analysis. Even though they hypothesize some gender differences in responses to stress, Taylor and her colleagues are quick to note that the "basic neuroendocrine core of stress responses" is largely the same for males and females.

Our physiological responses to stress are part of the fight-or-flight syndrome seen in many species. In a sense, this automatic reaction is a leftover from our evolutionary past. It is clearly an adaptive response for many animals, as the threat of predators often requires a swift response of fighting or fleeing (picture the gazelle escaping from the lion on the Discovery Channel). Likewise, the fight-or-flight response was probably adaptive among ancestral humans who routinely had to deal with acute stressors involving threats to their physical safety. But in our modern world, the fight-or-flight response may be less adaptive for human functioning than it was thousands of generations ago. Most modern stressors cannot be handled simply through fight or flight. Work pressures, marital problems, and financial difficulties require far more complex responses. Moreover, these chronic (and anticipatory) stressors often continue for lengthy periods of time, so that the fight-or-flight response leaves one in a state of enduring physiological arousal. Concern about the effects of prolonged physical arousal was first voiced by Hans Selye, a Canadian scientist who conducted extensive research on stress.

The General Adaptation Syndrome

The concept of stress was popularized in both scientific and lay circles by Hans Selye (1936, 1956, 1982). Although born in Vienna, Selye spent his entire professional career at McGill University in Montreal, Canada. Beginning in the 1930s, Selye exposed laboratory animals to a diverse array of unpleasant stimuli (heat, cold, pain, mild shock, restraint, and so on). The patterns of physiological arousal he observed in the animals were largely the same, regardless of which unpleasant stimulus elicited them. Thus, Selye concluded that stress reactions are *nonspecific*. In other words, they do not vary according to the specific type of circumstances encountered. Initially, Selye wasn't sure what to call this nonspecific response to a variety of noxious agents. In the 1940s, he decided to call it *stress,* and his influential writings gradually helped make the word part of our everyday vocabulary (Cooper & Dewe, 2004).

To capture the general pattern all species exhibit when responding to stress, Selye (1956, 1974) formulated a seminal theory called the general adaptation syndrome (see **Figure 3.11** on the next page). **The *general adaptation syndrome* is a model of the body's stress response, consisting of three stages: alarm, resistance, and exhaustion.** In the first stage of the general adaptation syndrome, an *alarm reaction* occurs when an organism recognizes the existence of a threat (whether a lion, a big deadline, or a mugger). Physiological arousal increases as the body musters its resources to combat the challenge. Selye's alarm reaction is essentially the fight-or-flight response originally described by Cannon.

Hans Selye

However, Selye took his investigation of stress a couple of steps further by exposing laboratory animals to *prolonged stress,* similar to the chronic stress often endured by humans. If stress continues, the organism may progress to the second phase of the general adaptation syndrome, called the *stage of resistance.* During this phase, physiological changes stabilize as coping efforts get under way. Typically, physiological arousal continues to be higher than normal, although it may level off somewhat as the organism becomes accustomed to the threat.

If the stress continues over a substantial period of time, the organism may enter the third stage, called the

Learn More Online

The American Institute of Stress

The American Institute of Stress is a nonprofit organization established in 1978 at the request of stress pioneer Hans Selye. Its Board of Trustees reads like a who's who of stress researchers. The resources available online are a bit limited, as one has to send for the information packets published by the institute. But the site contains an interesting tribute to Selye.

Figure 3.11
The general adaptation syndrome. According to Selye, the physiological response to stress can be broken into three phases. During the first phase, the body mobilizes its resources for resistance after a brief initial shock. In the second phase, resistance levels off and eventually begins to decline. If the third phase of the general adaptation syndrome is reached, resistance is depleted, leading to health problems and exhaustion.

stage of exhaustion. According to Selye, the body's resources for fighting stress are limited. If the stress cannot be overcome, the body's resources may be depleted, and physiological arousal will decrease. Eventually, the individual may collapse from exhaustion. During this phase, the organism's resistance declines. This reduced resistance may lead to what Selye called "diseases of adaptation," such as cardiovascular disease or high blood pressure.

Selye's theory and research forged a link between stress and physical illness. He showed how prolonged physiological arousal that is meant to be adaptive could lead to diseases. His theory has been criticized because it ignores individual differences in the appraisal of stress (Lazarus & Folkman, 1984), and his belief that stress reactions are nonspecific remains the subject of debate (Kemeny, 2003). However, his model provided guidance for generations of researchers who worked out the details of how stress reverberates throughout the body. Let's look at some of those details.

Brain-Body Pathways

When you experience stress, your brain sends signals to **the *endocrine system*, which consists of glands that secrete chemicals called hormones into the bloodstream.** These signals travel through the endocrine system along two major pathways. The *hypothalamus,* a small structure near the base of the brain, appears to initiate action along both pathways.

The first pathway (shown in blue on the right in **Figure 3.12**) is routed through the autonomic nervous system. The hypothalamus activates the sympathetic division of the ANS. A key part of this activation involves stimulating the central part of the *adrenal glands* (the adrenal medulla) to release large amounts of *catecholamines* into the bloodstream. These hormones radiate throughout the body,

producing many important physiological changes. The net result of catecholamine elevation is that the body is mobilized for action. Heart rate and blood flow increase, pumping more blood to the brain and muscles. Respiration and oxygen consumption speed up, facilitating alertness. Digestive processes are inhibited to conserve energy. The pupils of the eyes dilate, increasing visual sensitivity.

The second pathway (shown in purple on the left in **Figure 3.12**) involves more direct communication between the brain and the endocrine system. The hypothalamus sends signals to the so-called master gland of the endocrine system, the *pituitary gland.* The pituitary secretes a hormone (ACTH) that stimulates the outer part of the adrenal glands (the adrenal cortex) to release another important set of hormones—*corticosteroids.* These hormones play an important role in the response to stress. They stimulate the release of chemicals that help increase your energy and

Figure 3.12
Brain-body pathways in stress. In times of stress, the brain sends signals along two pathways. The pathway through the autonomic nervous system (shown in blue on the right) controls the release of catecholamine hormones that help mobilize the body for action. The pathway through the pituitary gland and the endocrine system (shown in purple on the left) controls the release of corticosteroid hormones that increase energy and ward off tissue inflammation.

REEL RESEARCH

Emotions, Cortisol, and Immune Response

Log on to CourseMate at www.cengagebrain.com **to watch this video.**

The link between stress and health is well established. The body releases cortisol in response to stress, stimulating anti-inflammatory pathways and providing added energy to face fight-or-flight events. However, prolonged exposure to high levels of cortisol may have damaging effects on physical health. Cortisol is one of the measures that Sheldon Cohen, professor of health psychology at Carnegie Mellon University, and Cuneyt Alper, physician from University of Pittsburgh Medical Center, use in the studies discussed in this Reel Research video.

Each study demonstrates the relationship between emotional factors, such as loneliness or sociability, and physiological health. In one demonstration, researchers administer a flu virus and participants are sequestered and tested daily over a six-day period. Another study looks at the relationship between sociability and development of the common cold. In a study of loneliness, Cohen and Alper measure the body's ability to create antibodies before and after a flu shot. First, participants provide psychological information, including their relationships with others. For two weeks, participants electronically rate their emotional state a number of times throughout the day and are asked to chew a cotton ball to store their saliva, which is used later to measure cortisol in their bodies. Researchers also draw blood to test participants' antibody levels during the first and fourth month of the study. The results of this study indicate that participants who rated lowest in loneliness produce the most antibodies, while those highest in loneliness produce the least antibodies.

Watch the video to learn more about these studies and the stress that emotions—like loneliness—can have on physical health. Delve even deeper by responding to the following discussion questions.

DISCUSSION QUESTIONS

1. The video presents several studies. Describe the various measures researchers used in the studies to determine participants' emotional and physical health.
2. Based on the research findings, how are sociability and the likelihood of developing a cold related?
3. Why do researchers measure cortisol in studies of stress? What other chemicals released by the body demonstrate that the body is reacting to stress?

---

help inhibit tissue inflammation in case of injury. *Cortisol* is a type of corticosteroid that is often used as a physiological indicator of stress in humans (Lundberg, 2011). In fact, many of the studies discussed in this chapter used cortisol as a measure of subjects' response to stress.

Stress can also produce other physiological changes that we are just beginning to understand. The most critical changes occur in the immune system. Your immune system provides you with resistance to infections. However, evidence indicates that stress can suppress certain aspects of the multifaceted immune response, reducing its overall effectiveness in repelling invasions by infectious agents (Dhabhar, 2011). The exact mechanisms underlying immune suppression are complicated, but it appears likely that both sets of stress hormones (catecholamines and corticosteroids) contribute (Dantzer & Mormede, 1995).

Contemporary research implicates stress-induced *chronic inflammation,* a risk factor for disease, as an indicator of an immune system that is chronically activated (Gouin et al., 2012). Paradoxically, this state of high alert weakens the ability of the immune system to fend off illness over the long run. In any case, it is becoming clear that physiological responses to stress extend into every corner of the body. Moreover, some of these responses may persist long after a stressful event has ended. As you will see, these physiological reactions can have an impact on both mental and physical health.

Behavioral Responses

Although people respond to stress at several levels, their behavior is a crucial dimension of these reactions. Emotional and physiological responses to stress—which are often undesirable—tend to be largely automatic. However, dealing effectively with stress at the behavioral level may shut down these potentially harmful emotional and physiological reactions.

Most behavioral responses to stress involve coping. *Coping* **refers to active efforts to master, reduce, or tolerate the demands created by stress.** Notice that this definition is neutral as to whether coping efforts are healthy or maladaptive. The popular use of the term often implies that coping is inherently healthy. When we say that someone "coped with her problems," we imply that she handled them effectively. In reality, coping responses may be either healthy or unhealthy. For example, if you were flunking a history course at midterm, you might cope with this stress by (1) increasing your study efforts, (2) seeking help from a tutor, (3) blaming your professor for your poor grade, or (4) giving up on the class. Clearly, the first two coping responses would more likely lead to a positive outcome than the second two would.

People cope with stress in a variety of ways. Coping efforts can be directed at reducing the perceived threat of a stressor, diminishing negative emotions brought on by stress, or addressing the problem directly (Carver, 2011). Because of the complexity and importance of coping processes, we devote all of the next chapter to ways of coping. At this point, it is sufficient to note that coping strategies help determine whether stress has any positive or negative effects on an individual. In the next section, you'll see what some of those effects can be as we discuss the possible outcomes of people's struggles with stress.

RECOMMENDED reading

Why Zebras Don't Get Ulcers: The Acclaimed Guide to Stress, Stress-Related Diseases, and Coping

by Robert M. Sapolsky (W. H. Freeman, 2004)

This book provides a superb, wide-ranging discussion of the nature and effects of stress. The author is a neuroscientist at Stanford University whose research focuses on such issues as the relationship between stress and the cellular and molecular events underlying neural decay in the hippocampal area of the brain. That is not the type of résumé you would normally associate with lively, witty discourse, but the book is written with flair and humor. Sapolsky's basic thesis is that the physiological response to stress is a remnant of evolution that is no longer adaptive for the majority of stressful situations that humans face. He outlines in detail how neuroendocrine responses to stress can cause or worsen a host of physical and psychological afflictions, including cardiovascular disease, ulcers, colitis, diarrhea, infectious diseases, and depression.

Sapolsky does an excellent job of making complicated research understandable. Although opinionated, his overviews of research are scientifically sound and thoroughly documented in notes at the back of the book. This is not a coping manual, yet it is probably the most insightful and interesting dissection of the stress response available today and is highly worthwhile reading.

Log on to CourseMate at **www.cengagebrain.com** *for descriptions of other recommended books.*

THE POTENTIAL EFFECTS OF STRESS

LEARNING OBJECTIVES

- Explain the influence of stress on task performance, cognitive functioning, and burnout.
- Assess the potential impact of stress on psychological and physical health.
- Articulate three ways in which stress might lead to beneficial effects.

People struggle with stressors every day, most of which come and go without leaving any enduring imprint. However, when stress is severe or when demands pile up, stress may have long-lasting effects, often called "adaptational outcomes." Although stress can have beneficial effects, research has focused mainly on negative outcomes, so you'll find our coverage slanted in that direction. Note that we will discuss *reducing* the effects of stress (that is, coping) in the next chapter.

Impaired Task Performance

Stress often takes its toll on the ability to perform effectively on a task. For instance, Roy Baumeister (1984) theorized that pressure to perform often makes people self-conscious and that this elevated self-consciousness disrupts their attention, thereby interfering with performance. He theorizes that attention may be distorted in two ways. First, elevated self-consciousness may divert attention from the demands of the task, creating a distraction. Second, on well-learned tasks that should be executed almost automatically, the self-conscious person may focus *too* much attention on the task. Thus, the person thinks too much about what he or she is doing.

Baumeister (1984) found support for his theory in a series of laboratory experiments in which he manipulated the pressure to perform on a simple perceptual-motor task. He found that many people tend to "choke" under pressure (Butler & Baumeister, 1998; Wallace, Baumeister, & Vohs, 2005). His theory also garnered some support in a pair of studies of the past performance of professional sports teams in championship contests (Baumeister, 1995; Baumeister & Steinhilber, 1984). These findings were particularly impressive in that gifted professional athletes are probably less likely to choke under pressure than virtually any other sample one might assemble. Laboratory research on "normal" individuals suggests that choking under pressure is fairly common (Butler & Baumeister, 1998).

Recent studies suggest that Baumeister was on the right track in looking to *attention* to explain how stress impairs task performance. According to Beilock (2010), choking under pressure tends to occur when worries about performance distract attention from the task at hand and use up one's limited cognitive resources. Consistent with this analysis, one study found that chronic stress (preparing for difficult and important medical board exams) undermined participants' performance on a task requiring attention shifts (Liston, McEwen, & Casey, 2009). Moreover, using fMRI brain scans, the investigators were able to pinpoint diminished activity in the prefrontal cortex as the underlying basis for participants' impaired attentional control. Fortunately, these effects were short-lived. One month after the medical board exams, when participants' stress levels were back to normal, their attention was unimpaired.

It appears that personality might play role in one's tendency to choke under pressure. In a study of experienced basketball players, researchers found that athletes with a greater fear of negative evaluation showed more choking and more anxiety in high-pressure situations than those with less of that fear (Mesagno, Harvey, & Janelle, 2012).

Disruption of Cognitive Functioning

The effects of stress on task performance often result from disruptions in thinking or in cognitive functioning. In a study of stress and decision making, Keinan (1987) measured participants' attention under stressful and nonstressful conditions and found that stress disrupted two specific aspects of attention. First, it increased participants' tendency to jump to a conclusion too quickly without considering all their options. Second, it increased their tendency to do an unsystematic, poorly organized review of their available options. Brandes et al. (2002) examined trauma survivors within days of their experience and found that those with severe stress levels had poorer attention levels than those with few distress symptoms. Brandes speculates that poor attention might play an important role in shaping one's memory for a traumatic event.

Indeed, studies suggest that stress can have detrimental effects on certain aspects of memory functioning (Shors, 2004). In order to affect memory, stressors do not have to be major; even minor day-to-day or anticipatory stressors can have a negative impact (Lindau, Almkvist, & Mohammed, 2007). Evidence suggests that stress can reduce the efficiency of the "working memory" system that allows people to juggle information on the spot (Markman & Worthy, 2006). Thus, under stressful situations, people may not be able to process, manipulate, or integrate new information as effectively as normal.

Additionally, Merz and colleagues (2010) demonstrated that stress disrupts memory for socially relevant information (for instance, names). These researchers found that exposure to a stressful situation in a laboratory (giving an impromptu public speech) caused an increase in production of cortisol, a more negative mood, and a reduction in social memory. Though more research is needed, this study suggests that stress hormones might play a role in the recall of certain memories.

Ironically, simply being in a situation where you need cognitive resources the most (studying for a final exam, traveling in a foreign country) can produce this resource-sapping stress effect. Researchers note, however, that stress has a complicated relationship with memory in that short-term, mild-to-moderate stressors can actually enhance memory, especially for emotional aspects of events (Sapolosky, 2004).

Burnout

Burnout is an overused buzzword that means different things to different people. Nonetheless, a few researchers have described burnout in a systematic way that has facilitated scientific study of the phenomenon (Maslach & Leiter, 1997, 2007). **Burnout is a syndrome involving physical and emotional exhaustion, cynicism, and a lowered sense of self-efficacy that is attributable to work-related stress.** Exhaustion, which is central to burnout, includes chronic fatigue, weakness, and low energy. Cynicism is manifested in highly negative attitudes toward oneself, one's work, and life in general. Reduced self-efficacy involves declining feelings of competence at work that give way to feelings of hopelessness and helplessness.

What causes burnout? According to Maslach and Leiter (2007), "Burnout is a cumulative stress reaction to ongoing occupational stressors" (p. 368). The conventional wisdom is that burnout occurs because of some flaw or weakness within the person, but Christina Maslach (2003) asserts that "the research case is much stronger for the contrasting argument that burnout is more a function of the situation than of the person" (p. 191). Factors in the workplace that appear to promote burnout include work overload, interpersonal conflicts at work, lack of control over responsibilities and outcomes, and inadequate recognition for one's work (see **Figure 3.13**). Physical conditions such as noise, light, and temperature can also contribute to workplace stress, as can night and rotating shift work (Lundberg, 2007; Sulsky & Smith, 2007). As you might expect, burnout is associated with increased absenteeism and reduced productivity, as well as increased vulnerability to a variety of health problems (Maslach & Leiter, 2007). Decades of research have shown that burnout is found all over the world in a wide variety of cultures (Schaufeli, Leiter, & Maslach, 2009).

Psychological Problems and Disorders

On the basis of clinical impressions, psychologists have long suspected that chronic stress might contribute to many types of psychological problems and mental disorders. Since the late 1960s, advances in the measurement of stress have allowed researchers to verify these suspicions in empirical studies. In the domain of common psychological problems, studies indicate that stress may contribute to poor academic performance (Akgun & Ciarrochi, 2003), insomnia and other sleep disturbances (Akerstedt, Kecklund, & Axelsson, 2007), sexual difficulties (Slowinski, 2007), and substance abuse (Grunberg, Berger, & Hamilton, 2011). Beyond these everyday problems, research reveals that stress often contributes to the onset of full-fledged psychological disorders, including depression (Gutman & Nemeroff, 2011), schizophrenia (McGlashan & Hoffman, 2000), anxiety disorders (Falsetti & Ballenger, 1998), and eating disorders (Loth et al., 2008).

Recall that daily hassles can be a huge source of stress for individuals. For instance, as the repercussions of the worldwide recession continue to unfold, unemployment remains at historically high levels in many nations, economic growth has given way to economic stagnation in most countries, and economic instability continues to be a major concern around the world. These factors create stress that takes a psychological toll. A study of people going through foreclosure found that 29% were burdened by medical bills they could not afford, 58% had to skip meals due to a lack of money, 47% suffered from minor to major depression, and a substantial portion had increased their smoking or drinking since their foreclosure (Pollack & Lynch, 2009). A more recent study found a causal link between unemployment and the onset of mental health problems, especially anxiety and depression (McLaughlin et al., 2012). Indeed, studies have found an association between unemployment and elevated suicide rates (Classen & Dunn, 2012); one study estimated that suicide rates are four times higher among those suffering through long-term unemployment (Maki & Martikainen, 2012).

In addition to daily stressors, some individuals are exposed to extremely stressful, traumatic incidents that can

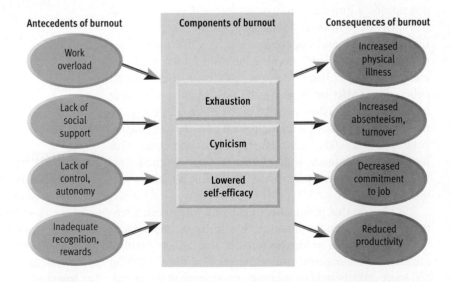

Figure 3.13

The antecedents, components, and consequences of burnout. Christina Maslach and Michael Leiter have developed a systematic model of burnout that specifies its antecedents, components, and consequences. The antecedents on the left in the diagram are the stressful features of the work environment that cause burnout. The burnout syndrome itself consists of the three components shown in the center of the diagram. Some of the unfortunate results of burnout are listed on the right. (Based on Maslach & Leiter, 2007) leave a lasting imprint on their psychological functioning. *Posttraumatic stress disorder (PTSD)* **involves enduring psychological disturbance attributed to the experience of a major traumatic event.** Researchers began to appreciate the frequency and severity of posttraumatic stress disorder after the Vietnam war ended in 1975 and a great many psychologically scarred veterans returned home. These veterans displayed a diverse array of psychological problems and symptoms that in many cases lingered much longer than expected. Studies suggest that nearly a half million Vietnam veterans were still suffering from PTSD over a decade after the end of the war (Schlenger et al., 1992). PTSD did not become an official psychological diagnosis until 1980, and since that time researchers have studied the disorder extensively to better understand the long-term impact of exposure to trauma. Currently, PTSD is being examined in military returnees from the Afghanistan and Iraq wars. Similar to Vietnam veterans, these U.S. troops show elevated rates of PTSD upon returning home, especially those individuals deployed more than once (Munsey, 2008a).

Although PTSD is widely associated with the experiences of veterans, it is seen in response to other cases of traumatic stress as well. It is frequently seen after a rape, a serious automobile accident, a robbery or assault, or the

witnessing of someone's death. PTSD is also common in the wake of major disasters, such as floods, hurricanes, earthquakes, fires, and so forth. Exposure to traumatic events such as the 9/11 terrorists attacks is also associated with PTSD, even several years later (Neria, DiGrande, & Adams, 2011). Research suggests that approximately 9% of people have suffered from PTSD at some point in their lives, and it is twice as common in women as men (Feeny, Stines, & Foa, 2007). PTSD is seen in children as well as adults, and children's symptoms often show up in their play or drawings (La Greca, 2007). In some instances, PTSD does not surface until many months or years after a person's exposure to severe stress (Holen, 2007).

What are the symptoms of posttraumatic stress disorder? Common symptoms include reexperiencing the traumatic event in the form of nightmares and flashbacks, emotional numbing, alienation, problems in social relations, and elevated arousal, anxiety, and guilt. PTSD is also associated with an elevated risk for substance abuse, depression, and anxiety disorders, as well as a great variety of physical health problems (Yehuda & Wong, 2007). The frequency and severity of posttraumatic symptoms usually decline gradually over time, but in some cases the symptoms never completely disappear.

Although PTSD is fairly common in the wake of traumatic events, the vast majority of people who experience such events do *not* develop PTSD. Thus, a current focus of research is to determine what factors make certain people more (or less) susceptible than others to the ravages of severe stress. According to McKeever and Huff (2003), this vulnerability probably depends on complex interactions among a number of biological and environmental factors. One key predictor that emerged in a recent review of the relevant research is the *intensity of one's reaction at the time of the traumatic event* (Ozer et al., 2003). Individuals who have especially intense emotional reactions during or immediately after the traumatic event go on to show elevated vulnerability to PTSD. Vulnerability seems to be greatest among people whose reactions are so intense that they report *dissociative experiences* (such as a sense that things are not real, that time is stretching out, or that one is watching oneself in a movie).

STR/AFP/Getty Images

Physical Illness

Stress can also have an impact on one's physical health. The idea that stress can contribute to physical ailments is not entirely new. Evidence that stress can cause physical illness began to accumulate back in the 1930s. By the 1950s, the concept of psychosomatic disease was widely accepted. **Psychosomatic diseases were defined as genuine physical ailments thought to be caused in part by stress and other psychological factors.** The classic psychosomatic illnesses were high blood pressure, peptic ulcers, asthma, skin disorders such as eczema and hives, and migraine and tension headaches. Please note, these diseases were not regarded as *imagined* physical ailments. The term *psychosomatic* has often been misused to refer to physical ailments that are "all in one's head," but that is an entirely different syndrome (see Chapter 14). Rather, psychosomatic diseases were viewed as authentic organic maladies that were heavily stress related.

Since the 1970s, the concept of psychosomatic disease has gradually fallen into disuse because research has shown that stress can contribute to the development of a diverse array of other diseases previously believed to be purely physiological in origin. Although there is room for debate on some specific diseases, stress may influence the onset and course of heart disease, stroke, gastrointestinal disorders, tuberculosis, multiple sclerosis, arthritis, diabetes, leukemia, cancer, various types of infectious disease, and probably many other types of illnesses. Thus, it has become apparent that there is nothing unique about the psychosomatic diseases that require a special category. Chapter 5 goes into greater detail, but suffice it to say that modern evidence continues to demonstrate that the classic psychosomatic diseases are influenced by stress, but so are numerous other diseases (Bekkouche et al., 2011; Dougall & Swanson, 2011).

Of course, stress is only one of many factors that may contribute to the development of physical illness. Some of the physical effects of stress might be exacerbated by the risky behaviors people are more likely to engage in when stressed (Friedman & Silver, 2007). For example, stress appears to be related to increases in substance abuse, including problematic drinking and cigarette smoking (Grunberg et al., 2011). Obviously, these behaviors come with their own health hazards. Add stress to the mix and the person becomes even more vulnerable to disease and illness.

Positive Effects

The effects of stress are not entirely negative. Recent years have brought increased interest in positive aspects of the stress process, including favorable outcomes that follow in the wake of stress. To some extent, the new focus on the possible benefits of stress reflects a new emphasis on "positive psychology." Some influential theorists have argued that the field of psychology has historically devoted too much attention to pathology, weakness, damage, and how to heal suffering (Seligman, 2003a). This approach has yielded valuable insights and progress, but it has also resulted in an unfortunate neglect of the forces that make life worth living. The positive psychology movement seeks to shift the field's focus away from negative experiences. This movement is so relevant that we devote all of Chapter 16 to it. For now, know that advocates of positive psychology argue for increased research on well-being, contentment, hope, courage, perseverance, nurturance, tolerance, and other human strengths and virtues (Peterson & Seligman, 2004). One of these strengths is resilience in the face of stress. The beneficial effects of stress may prove more difficult to pinpoint than the harmful effects because they may be subtler. However, there appear to be at least three ways in which stress can have positive effects.

First, stress can promote positive psychological change, or what Tedeschi and Calhoun (1996) call *posttraumatic growth*. Experiences of posttraumatic growth are now well documented, and it appears that this phenomenon is evident in people facing a variety of stressful circumstances, including bereavement, cancer, sexual assault, and combat (Tedeschi & Calhoun, 2004). Stressful events sometimes force people to develop new skills, reevaluate priorities, learn new insights, and acquire new strengths. In other words, the adaptation process initiated by stress may lead to personal changes for the better. For example, a breakup with a boyfriend or a girlfriend may lead individuals to change aspects of their behavior that they find unsatisfactory.

Second, stressful events help satisfy the need for stimulation and challenge. Studies suggest that most people prefer an intermediate level of stimulation and challenge in their lives (Sutherland, 2000). Although we think of stress in terms of stimulus overload, underload can be stressful as well (Goldberger, 1993). Thus, most people would experience a suffocating level of boredom if they lived a stress-free existence. In a sense, then, stress fulfills a basic need of the human organism.

Third, today's stress can inoculate and psychologically prepare individuals so that they are less affected by tomorrow's stress. Some studies suggest that exposure to stress can increase stress tolerance—as long as the stress isn't overwhelming (Meichenbaum, 1993). Further, dealing with some adversity provides an opportunity to develop coping skills that can decrease distress when new stressors arise. That is, it can build "mental toughness" (Seery, 2011). Thus, a woman who has previously endured business setbacks may be much better prepared than most people to deal with a bank foreclosure on her home. In light of the negative effects that stress can have, improved stress tolerance is a desirable goal. We'll look next at the factors that influence the ability to tolerate stress.

FACTORS INFLUENCING STRESS TOLERANCE

● Explain how social support, hardiness, and optimism moderate the impact of stress.

Some people seem to be able to withstand the ravages of stress better than others. Why? Because a number of *moderator variables* can soften the impact of stress on physical and mental health. To shed light on differences in how well people tolerate stress, we'll look at a number of key moderator variables, including social support, hardiness, and optimism. As you'll see, these factors influence people's emotional, physical, and behavioral responses to stress. These complexities are diagrammed in **Figure 3.14**, which builds on **Figure 3.7** to provide a more complete overview of the factors involved in individual reactions to stress.

Social Support

Friends may be good for your health! This startling conclusion emerges from studies on social support as a moderator of stress. *Social support* **refers to various types of aid and succor provided by members of one's social networks.** Over the last two decades, a vast body of literature has found evidence that social support is favorably related to physical health (Taylor, 2007). For example, Jemmott and Magloire (1988) examined the effect of social support on immune response in a group of students going through the stress of final exams. They found that students who

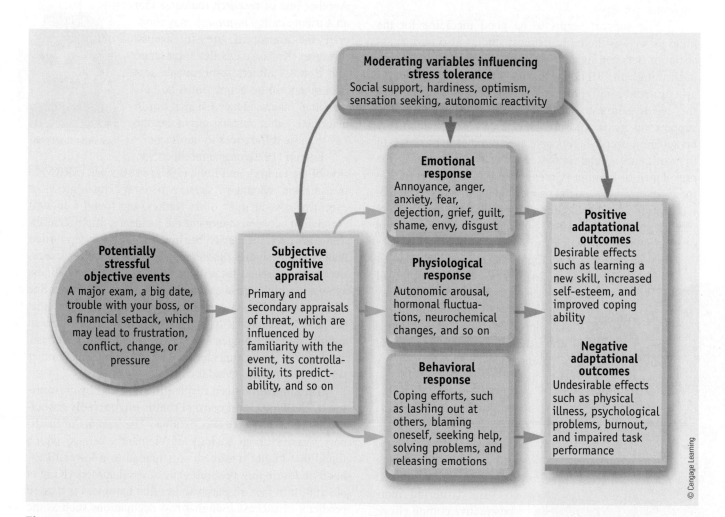

Figure 3.14

Overview of the stress process. This diagram builds on **Figure 3.7** (the multidimensional response to stress) to provide a more complete overview of the factors involved in stress. This diagram adds the potential effects of stress (seen on the far right) by listing some of the positive and negative adaptational outcomes that may result from stress. It also completes the picture by showing moderating variables (seen at the top) that can influence the effects of stress (including some variables not covered in the chapter).

reported stronger social support had higher levels of an antibody that plays a key role in warding off respiratory infections. Positive correlations between high social support and greater immune functioning have been observed in quite a number of studies with diverse samples (Kennedy, 2007; Uchino, Cacioppo, & Kiecolt-Glaser, 1996).

The favorable effects of social support are even strong enough to have an impact on participants' life expectancy! A recent meta-analysis of the results of 148 studies reported that solid social support increased people's odds of survival by roughly 50% (Holt-Lunstad, Smith, & Layton, 2010). The strength of the impact of social support on life expectancy was surprising. To put this finding in perspective, the researchers compared the effect of social support on life expectancy to other established risk factors. They note that the negative effect of inadequate social support is greater than the negative effects of being obese, not exercising, drinking excessively, and smoking (up to fifteen cigarettes per day).

Social support seems to be good medicine for the mind as well as the body, as most studies also find an association between social support and mental health (Uchino & Birmingham, 2011). It appears that social support serves as a protective buffer during times of high stress, reducing the negative impact of stressful events—and that social support has its own positive effects on health, which may be apparent even when people aren't under great stress. In the workplace, social support has been shown to reduce the prevalence of burnout (Greenglass, 2007). With regard to more severe stress, social support appears to be a key factor in reducing the likelihood of PTSD among Vietnam veterans (King et al., 1998) and increasing the likelihood of posttraumatic growth (Prati & Pietrantoni, 2009).

The mechanisms underlying the connection between social support and wellness have been the subject of considerable debate. A variety of factors may be at work. Among other things, social support could promote wellness by making appraisals of stressful events more benign, dampening the intensity of physiological reactions to stress, reducing health-impairing behaviors such as smoking and drinking, encouraging preventive behaviors such as regular exercise and medical checkups, and fostering more constructive coping efforts (Taylor, 2007).

Research suggests that *providing* social support to others can also have both psychological benefits (less depression and perceived

David Young-Wolff/PhotoEdit

stress) and physical benefits (lower blood pressure) (Brown et al., 2003; Piferi & Lawler, 2006). One study found that the personality trait of sociability (being friendly and agreeable), which certainly helps people build supportive social networks, is independently associated with reduced susceptibility to infectious disease (Cohen et al., 2003). Thus, it appears that there are many aspects of social support that have some bearing on individuals' wellness.

Although the benefits outweigh the costs, social support networks have their drawbacks (conflict role strain, additional responsibilities, dependency). Further, support that is thought to be disingenuous or inappropriate can be counterproductive and decrease one's well-being (Rook, August, & Sorkin, 2011). This is a research area that bears watching in the near future.

Hardiness

Courtesy Suzanne C. Ouellette

Suzanne Ouellette

Another line of research indicates that an attribute called *hardiness* may moderate the impact of stressful events. Suzanne (Kobasa) Ouellette reasoned that if stress affects some people less than others, some people must be *hardier* than others. Hence, she set out to determine what factors might be the key to these differences in hardiness.

Kobasa (1979) used a modified version of the Holmes and Rahe (1967) stress scale (SRRS) to measure the amount of stress experienced by a group of executives. As in most other studies, she found a modest correlation between stress and the incidence of physical illness. However, she carried her investigation one step further than previous studies. She compared the high-stress executives who exhibited the expected high incidence of illness against the high-stress executives who stayed healthy. She administered a battery of psychological tests and found that the hardier executives "were more committed, felt more in control, and had bigger appetites for challenge" (Kobasa, 1984, p. 70). These traits have also shown up in many other studies of hardiness (Maddi, 2007).

Thus, **hardiness is a disposition marked by commitment, challenge, and control that is purportedly associated with strong stress resistance.** The benefits of hardiness showed up in a study of Vietnam veterans, which found that higher hardiness was related to a lower likelihood of developing posttraumatic stress disorders (King et al., 1998). In fact, research shows that hardiness is a good predictor of success in high-stress occupations such as the military (Bartone et al., 2008).

Hardiness may reduce the effects of stress by altering appraisals or fostering more active coping. In an analysis of 180 studies, Eschleman and colleagues (2010) found that hardiness was positively related to personality factors (such as optimism) that protect one against stress and negatively related to personality factors (neuroticism) that make stress worse. Based on their findings, these researchers argue that "hardiness is one of the best dispositional predictors of well-being" (p. 303). Fortunately, it appears that hardiness can be learned, and it often comes from strong social support and encouragement from those around us (Maddi, 2007).

Optimism

Everyone knows someone whose glass is always half full, who sees the world through rose-colored glasses, who is an optimist. *Optimism* **is a general tendency to expect good outcomes.** Pioneering research in this area by Michael Scheier and Charles Carver (1985) found a correlation between optimism and relatively good physical health in a sample of college students. In studies that focused on surgical patients, optimism was found to be associated with a faster recovery and better postsurgery adjustment (Scheier et al., 1989; Shelby et al., 2008). More than 20 years of research has consistently shown that optimism is associated with better mental and physical health (Scheier & Carver, 2007).

In a related line of research, Christopher Peterson and Martin Seligman have studied how people explain bad events (personal setbacks, mishaps, disappointments, and such). These researchers identified a *pessimistic explanatory style,* in which people tend to blame setbacks on their own personal shortcomings, versus an *optimistic explanatory style,* which leads people to attribute setbacks to temporary situational factors. In two retrospective studies of people born many decades ago, they found an association between this optimistic explanatory style and relatively good health (Peterson, Seligman, & Vaillant, 1988) and increased longevity (Peterson et al., 1998). Many other studies have linked the optimistic explanatory style to positive outcomes, including superior physical health,

higher achievement in a variety of areas, and higher marital satisfaction (Peterson & Steen, 2009) (see Chapter 6 for more on the ramifications of an optimistic versus pessimistic explanatory style).

Why does optimism promote a variety of desirable outcomes? Above all else, research suggests that optimists cope with stress in more adaptive ways than pessimists (Carver, Scheier, & Segerstrom, 2010). Optimists are more likely to engage in action-oriented, problem-focused, carefully planned coping and are more willing than pessimists to seek social support. By comparison, pessimists are more likely to deal with stress by avoiding it, giving up, or engaging in denial. In a study of college students, a pessimistic explanatory style was linked to more thoughts of suicide following a traumatic event (Hirsch et al., 2009). We will be discussing specific types of coping styles in the next chapter.

Even with all these benefits, psychologists debate whether or not optimism is always beneficial. What about times when a rosy outlook is inaccurate and unrealistic? Does it really benefit an employee to be optimistic about that promotion if there isn't much chance she'll get it? Additionally, being optimistic can lead to risky behaviors if one holds an "it-can't-happen-to-me" attitude. Research shows that women with an optimistic bias toward their risk for breast cancer are less likely to go in for screening (Clarke at al., 2000). And optimistic smokers are more like to endorse myths such as "All lung cancer is cured" and "There is no risk of lung cancer if you only smoke for a few years" (Dillard et al., 2006). One study found that the usefulness of optimism might depend on the type of stressful experience. That is, it is beneficial in the face of mild stress, but not when the stress is more severe (O'Mara, McNulty, & Karney, 2011). Gillham and Reivich (2007) argue that, when it comes to optimism, what is most adaptive is some sort of middle ground where one displays "optimism that is closely tied to the strength of wisdom" (p. 320).

Application

REDUCING STRESS THROUGH SELF-CONTROL

LEARNING OBJECTIVES

- Explain how behavior modification can be used to improve self-control.
- Summarize the five steps in the process of self-modification.

Answer the following "yes" or "no."

____ **1.** Do you have a hard time passing up food, even when you're not hungry?

____ **2.** Do you wish you studied more often?

____ **3.** Would you like to cut down on your smoking or drinking?

____ **4.** Do you experience difficulty in getting yourself to exercise regularly?

____ **5.** Do you wish you had more willpower?

It is clear that a sense of control is important to one's appraisal and experience of stress. If you answered "yes" to any of the above questions, you have struggled with the challenge of self-control. Self-control—or rather a lack of it—underlies many of the stressors that people struggle with in everyday life. Think back to the sources of stress. Many of them can be reduced through self-control. For instance, one can start exercising to reduce the *frustration* of poor fitness, or stop procrastinating to reduce *pressure* in a course. This Application discusses how you can use the techniques of behavior modification to improve your self-control.

***Behavior modification* is a systematic approach to changing behavior through the application of the principles of conditioning.** Advocates of behavior modification assume that behavior is a product of learning, conditioning, and environmental control. They further assume that *what is learned can be unlearned*. Thus, they set out to "recondition" people to produce more-desirable patterns of behavior. The technology of behavior modification has been applied with great success in schools, businesses, hospitals, factories, child-care facilities, prisons, and mental health centers (Goodall, 1972; Kazdin, 2001; Rachman, 1992). Behavior modification techniques have been used to treat a variety of issues, including attention disorders and childhood obesity (Berry et al., 2004; Pelham, 2001).

Behavior modification techniques have proven particularly valuable in efforts to improve self-control. Our discussion will borrow liberally from an excellent book on self-modification by David Watson and Roland Tharp (2007). We will discuss five steps in the process of self-modification, which are outlined in **Figure 3.15**.

Specifying Your Target Behavior

The first step in a self-modification program is to specify the target behavior(s) that you want to change. Behavior modification can only be applied to a clearly defined response, yet many people have difficulty pinpointing the behavior they hope to alter. They tend to describe their problems in terms of unobservable personality *traits* rather than overt behaviors. For example, asked what behavior he would like to change, a man might say, "I'm too irritable." That may be true, but it is of little help in designing a self-modification program. To identify target responses, you need to think about past behavior or closely observe future behavior and list specific *examples* of responses that lead to the trait description. For instance, the man who regards himself as "too irritable" might identify two overly frequent responses, such as arguing with his wife and snapping at his children. These are specific behaviors for which he could design a self-modification program.

Gathering Baseline Data

The second step in behavior modification is to gather baseline data. You need to systematically observe your target behavior for a period of time (usually a week or two) be-

Figure 3.15

Steps in a self-modification program. This flowchart provides an overview of the steps necessary to execute a self-modification program.

fore you work out the details of your program. In gathering your baseline data, you need to monitor three things.

First, you need to determine the initial response level of your target behavior. After all, you can't tell whether your program is working effectively unless you have a baseline for comparison. In most cases, you would simply keep track of how often the target response occurs in a certain time interval. Thus, you might count the daily frequency of snapping at your children, smoking cigarettes, or biting your fingernails. If studying is your target behavior, you will probably monitor hours of study. If you want to modify your eating, you will probably keep track of how many calories you consume. Whatever the unit of measurement, *it is crucial to gather accurate data*. You should keep permanent written records, preferably in the form of a chart or graph (see **Figure 3.16**).

Second, you need to monitor the antecedents of your target behavior. ***Antecedents* are events that typically precede the target response.** Often these events play a major role in evoking your target behavior. For example, if your target is overeating, you might discover that the bulk of your overeating occurs late in the evening while you watch TV. If you can pinpoint this kind of antecedent-response connection, you may be able to design your program to circumvent or break the link.

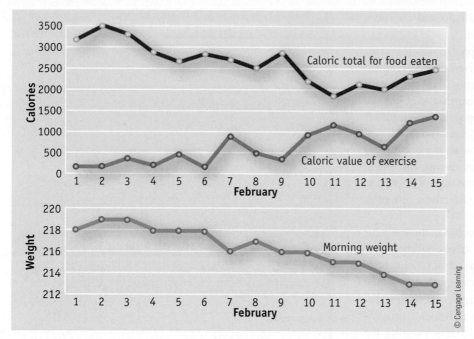

Figure 3.16

Example of recordkeeping in a self-modification program for losing weight. Graphic records are ideal for tracking progress in behavior modification efforts.

every time, as most behavior is maintained by intermittent reinforcement.

Designing Your Program

Once you have selected a target behavior and gathered adequate baseline data, it is time to plan your intervention program. Generally speaking, your program will be designed to either increase or decrease the frequency of a target response.

Increasing Response Strength

Efforts to increase the frequency of a target response depend largely on the use of positive reinforcement. In other words, you reward yourself for behaving properly. Although the basic strategy is quite simple, doing it skillfully involves a number of considerations.

Selecting a reinforcer. To use positive reinforcement, you need to find a reward that will be effective for you. Reinforcement is subjective—what is reinforcing for one person may not be reinforcing for another. **Figure 3.17** lists questions you can ask yourself to help you determine your

Third, you need to monitor the typical consequences of your target behavior. Try to identify the reinforcers that are maintaining an undesirable target behavior or the unfavorable outcomes that are suppressing a desirable target behavior. In trying to identify reinforcers, remember that avoidance behavior is usually maintained by negative reinforcement (see Chapter 2). That is, the payoff for avoidance is usually the removal of something aversive, such as anxiety or a threat to self-esteem. You should also take into account the fact that a response may not be reinforced

WHAT ARE YOUR REINFORCERS?	
1. What will be the rewards of achieving your goal?	12. What would be a nice present to receive?
2. What kind of praise do you like to receive, from yourself and others?	13. What kinds of things are important to you?
3. What kinds of things do you like to have?	14. What would you buy if you had an extra $20? $50? $100?
4. What are your major interests?	15. On what do you spend your money each week?
5. What are your hobbies?	16. What behaviors do you perform every day? (Don't overlook the obvious or commonplace.)
6. What people do you like to be with?	17. Are there any behaviors you usually perform instead of the target behavior?
7. What do you like to do with those people?	
8. What do you do for fun?	18. What would you hate to lose?
9. What do you do to relax?	19. Of the things you do every day, which would you hate to give up?
10. What do you do to get away from it all?	20. What are your favorite daydreams and fantasies?
11. What makes you feel good?	21. What are the most relaxing scenes you can imagine?

Figure 3.17

Selecting a reinforcer. The questions listed here may help you to identify your personal reinforcers.

Source: Adapted from Watson, D. L., & Tharp, R. G. (1993). *Self-directed behavior: Self-modification for personal adjustment*. Belmont, CA: Wadsworth. Reprinted by permission.

personal reinforcers. Be sure to be realistic and choose a reinforcer that is really available to you.

You don't have to come up with spectacular new reinforcers that you've never experienced before. *You can use reinforcers that you are already getting.* However, you have to restructure the contingencies so that you get the reward only if you behave appropriately. For example, if you normally watch your favorite television show on Thursday nights, you might make this viewing contingent on studying a certain number of hours during the week. Making yourself earn rewards that you've taken for granted is often a useful strategy in a self-modification program.

Arranging the contingencies. Once you have chosen your reinforcer, you have to set up reinforcement contingencies. These contingencies will describe the exact behavioral goals that must be met and the reinforcement that may then be awarded. For example, in a program to increase exercise, you might make spending $40 on clothes (the reinforcer) contingent on having jogged 15 miles during the week (the target behavior).

Try to set behavioral goals that are both challenging and realistic. You want your goals to be challenging so that they lead to improvement in your behavior. However, setting unrealistically high goals—a common mistake in self-modification—often leads to unnecessary discouragement.

You also need to be concerned about handing out too much reinforcement. If reinforcement is too easy to get, you may become *satiated*, and the reinforcer may lose its motivational power. One way to avoid the satiation problem is to put yourself on a token economy. **A *token economy* is a system for doling out symbolic reinforcers that are exchanged later for a variety of genuine reinforcers.** Thus, you might develop a point system for exercise behavior, accumulating points that can be spent on clothes, movies, restaurant meals, and so forth. You can also use a token economy to reinforce a variety of related target behaviors, as opposed to a single, specific response. The token economy in **Figure 3.18**, for instance, is set up to strengthen three different, though related, responses (jogging, tennis, and sit-ups).

Shaping. In some cases, you may want to reinforce a target response that you are not currently capable of making, such as speaking in front of a large group or jogging 10 miles a day. This situation calls for *shaping,* **which is accomplished by reinforcing closer and closer approximations of the desired response.** Thus, you might start jogging 2 miles a day and add a half-mile each week until you reach your goal. In shaping your behavior, you should set up a schedule spelling out how and when your target behaviors and reinforcement contingencies should change. Generally, it is a good idea to move forward gradually.

RESPONSES EARNING TOKENS		
Response	**Amount**	**Number of tokens**
Jogging	1/2 mile	4
Jogging	1 mile	8
Jogging	2 miles	16
Tennis	1 hour	4
Tennis	2 hours	8
Sit-ups	25	1
Sit-ups	50	2

REDEMPTION VALUE OF TOKENS	
Reinforcer	**Tokens required**
Download an album of your choice	30
Go to movie	50
Go to nice restaurant	100
Take special weekend trip	500

© Cengage Learning

Figure 3.18

Example of a token economy to reinforce exercise. This token economy was set up to strengthen three types of exercise behavior. The person can exchange tokens for four types of reinforcers.

Decreasing Response Strength

Let's turn now to the challenge of reducing the frequency of an undesirable response. You can go about this task in a number of ways. Your principal options are reinforcement, control of antecedents, and punishment.

Reinforcement. Reinforcers can be used in an indirect way to decrease the frequency of a response. This may sound paradoxical, since you have learned that reinforcement strengthens a response. The trick lies in how you define the target behavior. For example, in the case of overeating you might define your target behavior as eating more than 1800 calories a day (a response that you want to decrease) or, alternatively as eating less than 1800 calories a day (a response that you want to increase). If you choose the latter definition, you can reinforce yourself whenever you eat less than 1800 calories in a day which ultimately decreases your overeating.

Control of antecedents. A worthwhile strategy for decreasing the occurrence of an undesirable response may be to identify its antecedents and avoid exposure to them. This strategy is especially useful when you are trying to decrease the frequency of a consummatory response, such as smoking or eating. In the case of overeating, for instance, the easiest way to resist temptation is to avoid having to face it. Thus, you might stay away from favorite restaurants, minimize time spent in your kitchen, shop for groceries just after eating (when willpower is higher), and avoid purchasing favorite foods.

Punishment. The strategy of decreasing unwanted behavior by punishing yourself for that behavior is an obvious option that people tend to overuse. The biggest problem with punishment in a self-modification effort is the difficulty in following through and punishing oneself. If you're going to use punishment, keep two guidelines in mind. First, do not use punishment alone. Use it in conjunction with positive reinforcement. If you set up a program in which you can earn only negative consequences, you probably won't stick to it. Second, use a relatively mild punishment so that you will actually be able to administer it to yourself. Nurnberger and Zimmerman (1970) developed a creative method of self-punishment. They had subjects write out a check to an organization they hated (for instance, the campaign of a political candidate they despised). The check was held by a third party who mailed it if subjects failed to meet their behavioral goals. Such a punishment is relatively harmless, but it can serve as a strong source of motivation.

Executing and Evaluating Your Program

Once you have designed your program, the next step is to put it to work by enforcing the contingencies that you have carefully planned. During this period, you need to continue to accurately record the frequency of your target behavior so you can evaluate your progress. The success of your program depends on your not "cheating." The most common form of cheating is to reward yourself when you have not actually earned it.

You can do two things to increase the likelihood that you will comply with your program. One is to make up a *behavioral contract*—a written agreement outlining a promise to adhere to the contingencies of a behavior modification program (see **Figure 3.19**). The formality of signing such a contract in front of friends or family seems to make many people take their program more seriously. You can further reduce the likelihood of cheating by having someone other than yourself administer the reinforcers and punishments.

Behavior modification programs often require some fine-tuning, so don't be surprised if you need to make a few adjustments. Several flaws are especially common in designing self-modification programs. Among those you should look out for are (1) depending on a weak reinforcer, (2) permitting lengthy delays between appropriate behavior and delivery of reinforcers, and (3) trying to do too much too quickly by setting unrealistic goals. Often, a small revision or two can turn a failing program around and make it a success.

Ending Your Program

Ending your program involves setting terminal goals such as reaching a certain weight, studying with a certain regularity, or going without cigarettes for a certain length of time. Often, it is a good idea to phase out your program by planning a gradual reduction in the frequency or potency of your reinforcement for appropriate behavior.

If your program is successful, it may fade away without a conscious decision on your part. Often, new, improved patterns of behavior such as eating right, exercising, or studying diligently become self-maintaining. Whether or not you end your program intentionally, you should always be prepared to reinstitute the program if you find yourself slipping back to your old patterns of behavior. Ironically, it can be the very stress we are trying to reduce that drives use back into old, unhealthy habits.

I, _____ , do hereby agree to initiate my self-change strategy as of (date) _____ and to continue it for a minimum period of _____ weeks—that is, until (date) _____ .

My specific self-change strategy is to

_____

_____

I will do my best to execute this strategy to my utmost ability and to evaluate its effectiveness only after it has been honestly tried for the specified period of time.

Optional Self-Reward Clause: For every _____ day(s) that I successfully comply with my self-change contract, I will reward myself with _____

_____

In addition, at the end of my minimum period of personal experimentation, I will reward myself for having persisted in my self-change efforts. My reward at that time will be

_____

I hereby request that the witnesses who have signed below support me in my self-change efforts and encourage my compliance with the specifics of this contract. Their cooperation and encouragement throughout the project will be appreciated.

Signed _____

Date _____

Witness:

Witness:

© Cengage Learning

Figure 3.19

A behavioral contract. Behavior modification experts recommend the use of a formal, written contract similar to that shown here to increase commitment to one's self-modification program.

CHAPTER 3 | Review

KEY IDEAS

THE NATURE OF STRESS

● Stress involves transactions with the environment that are perceived to be threatening and that tax one's coping abilities. Stress is a common, everyday event, and even routine hassles can be problematic. To a large degree, stress lies in the eye of the beholder. According to Lazarus and Folkman, primary appraisal determines whether events appear threatening, while secondary appraisal assesses whether one has the resources to cope with challenges. How one appraises an event can alter the impact of the event.

● Some of the stress that people experience comes from their environment. Examples of environmental stimuli that can be stressful include excessive noise, crowding, urban decay, and community violence. Stress can vary with culture. Within Western culture, ethnicity and discrimination can be a source of stress in a variety of ways. Adapting to a new culture can also cause stress.

MAJOR SOURCES OF STRESS

● Stress can be acute, chronic, or anticipatory. Major sources of stress include frustration, conflict, change, and pressure. Frustration occurs when an obstacle prevents one from attaining some goal. There are three principal types of internal conflict: approach-approach, avoidance-avoidance, and approach-avoidance.

● A large number of studies with the SRRS suggest that change is stressful. Although that may be true, it is now clear that the SRRS is a measure of general stress rather than just change-related stress. Pressure (to perform and to conform) also appears to be stressful. Often this pressure is self-imposed.

RESPONDING TO STRESS

● Emotional reactions to stress typically involve anger, fear, or sadness. However, people also experience positive emotions while under stress, and these positive emotions promote well-being. Emotional arousal may interfere with task performance. As tasks get more complex, the optimal level of arousal declines.

● Physiological arousal in response to stress was originally called the fight-or-flight response by Cannon. Taylor has proposed an alternative response ("tend and befriend") that might be more applicable to females. Selye's general adaptation syndrome describes three stages in the physiological reaction to stress: alarm, resistance, and exhaustion. Diseases of adaptation may appear during the stage of exhaustion.

● In response to stress, the brain sends signals along two major pathways to the endocrine system. Actions along these paths release two sets of hormones into the bloodstream, catecholamines and corticosteroids. Stress can also lead to suppression of the immune response.

● Behavioral responses to stress involve coping, which may be healthy or maladaptive. If people cope effectively with stress, they can short-circuit potentially harmful emotional and physical responses.

THE POTENTIAL EFFECTS OF STRESS

● Common negative effects of stress include impaired task performance, disruption of attention and other cognitive processes, and pervasive emotional exhaustion known as burnout. Other effects include a host of everyday psychological problems, full-fledged psychological disorders including posttraumatic stress disorder, and varied types of damage to physical health.

● However, stress can also have positive effects. Stress fulfills a basic human need for challenge and can lead to personal growth and self-improvement. Stress can also have an inoculation effect, preparing us for the next stressful event.

FACTORS INFLUENCING STRESS TOLERANCE

● People differ in how much stress they can tolerate without experiencing ill effects. A person's social support can be a key consideration in buffering the effects of stress. The personality factors associated with hardiness—commitment, challenge, and control—may increase stress tolerance. People high in optimism also have advantages in coping with stress, although unrealistic optimism can be problematic.

APPLICATION: REDUCING STRESS THROUGH SELF-CONTROL

● In behavior modification, the principles of learning are used to change behavior directly. Behavior modification techniques can be used to increase one's self-control. The first step in self-modification is to specify the overt target behavior to be increased or decreased.

● The second step is to gather baseline data about the initial rate of the target response and identify any typical antecedents and consequences associated with the behavior. The third step is to design a program. If you are trying to increase the strength of a response, you'll depend on positive reinforcement. A number of strategies can be used to decrease the strength of a response, including reinforcement (indirectly), control of antecedents, and punishment.

● The fourth step is to execute and evaluate the program. Self-modification programs often require some fine-tuning. The final step is to determine how and when you will phase out your program

KEY TERMS

Acculturation p. 71
Acute stressors p. 71
Ambient stressors p. 69
Antecedents p. 92
Anticipatory stress p. 71
Approach-approach conflict p. 72
Approach-avoidance conflict p. 73
Autonomic nervous system (ANS) p. 80
Avoidance-avoidance conflict p. 73
Behavior contract p. 95
Behavioral modification p.92
Burnout p. 85
Chronic stressors pp. 71
Coping p. 84
Emotions p. 77
Endocrine system p. 82
Fight-or-flight response p. 80
Frustration p. 72
General adaptation syndrome p. 81
Hardiness p. 90
Internal conflict p. 72
Life changes p. 73
Optimism p. 91
Posttraumatic stress disorder (PTSD) pp. 86–87
Pressure p. 75
Primary appraisal p. 69
Psychosomatic diseases p. 88
Secondary appraisal p. 69
Shaping p. 94
Social support p. 89
Stress p. 67
Token economy p. 94

KEY PEOPLE

Susan Folkman p. 78
Thomas Holmes and Richard Rahe pp. 73–74
Richard Lazarus p. 69
Neal Miller p. 72
Suzanne (Kobasa) Ouellette p. 90
Robert Sapolsky pp. 71–72, 84
Hans Selye pp. 81–82
Shelley Taylor p. 81

1. Secondary appraisal refers to
   a. second thoughts about what to do in a stressful situation.
   b. second thoughts about whether an event is genuinely threatening.
   c. initial evaluation of an event's relevance, threat, and stressfulness.
   d. evaluation of coping resources and options for dealing with a stressful event.

2. Don just completed writing a 10-page report. When he tried to save it, the computer crashed and he lost all his work. What type of stress is Don most likely experiencing?
   a. frustration
   b. conflict
   c. life change
   d. pressure

3. Betty is having a hard time deciding whether she should buy a coat. On the one hand, it is a name brand coat on sale for a great price. On the other hand, it is an ugly mold-green color. Betty is experiencing what type of conflict?
   a. approach-approach
   b. avoidance-avoidance
   c. approach-avoidance
   d. life change

4. The optimal level of arousal for a task appears to depend in part on
   a. one's position on the optimism/pessimism scale.
   b. how much physiological change an event stimulates.
   c. the complexity of the task at hand.
   d. how imminent a stressful event is.

5. The fight-or-flight response is mediated by the
   a. sympathetic division of the autonomic nervous system.
   b. sympathetic division of the endocrine system.
   c. parasympathetic division of the autonomic nervous system.
   d. parasympathetic division of the endocrine system.

6. Selye exposed lab animals to various stressors and found that
   a. each type of stress caused a particular physiological response.
   b. each type of animal responded to stress differently.
   c. patterns of physiological arousal were similar, regardless of the type of stress.
   d. patterns of physiological arousal were different, even when stressors were similar.

7. Stress can _____ the functioning of the immune system.
   a. stimulate
   b. destroy
   c. suppress
   d. enhance

8. Salvador works as an art director at an advertising agency. His boss overloads him with responsibility but never gives him any credit for all his hard work. He feels worn down, disillusioned, and helpless at work. Salvador is probably experiencing
   a. an alarm reaction.
   b. burnout.
   c. posttraumatic stress disorder.
   d. a psychosomatic disorder.

9. Joan has a personal disposition marked by commitment, challenge, and control. She appears to be stress tolerant. This disposition is referred to as
   a. hardiness.
   b. optimism.
   c. courage.
   d. conscientiousness.

10. A system providing for symbolic reinforcers is called a(n)
    a. extinction system.
    b. token economy.
    c. endocrine system.
    d. symbolic reinforcement system.

ANSWERS

1. d Page 69	6. c Page 81
2. a Page 72	7. c Page 83
3. c Page 73	8. b Pages 85–86
4. c Pages 79–80	9. a Page 90
5. a Page 80	10. b Page 94

COURSEMATE

Go to **CengageBrain.com** to access Psychology CourseMate, where you will find an interactive eBook, glossaries, flashcards, quizzes, videos, and more.

PERSONAL EXPLORATIONS WORKBOOK

Go to the *Personal Explorations Workbook* in the back of your textbook for exercises that can enhance your self-understanding in relation to issues raised in this chapter.

Exercise 3.1 *Self-Assessment:* The Life Experience Survey (LES)

Exercise 3.2 *Self-Reflection:* Stress—How Do You Control It?

CHAPTER 4

Coping Processes

BlueMoon Stock/Alamy

"I have begun to believe that I have intellectually and emotionally outgrown my husband. However, I'm not really sure what this means or what I should do. Maybe this feeling is normal and I should ignore it and continue my present relationship. This seems to be the safest route. Maybe I should seek a lover while continuing with my husband. Then again, maybe I should start anew and hope for a beautiful ending with or without a better mate."

The woman quoted above is in the throes of a thorny conflict. Although it is hard to tell just how much emotional turmoil she is experiencing, it's clear that she is under substantial stress. What should she do? Is it psychologically healthy to remain in an emotionally hollow marriage? Is having an affair a reasonable way to cope with this unfortunate situation? Should she just strike out on her own and let the chips fall where they

may? These questions have no simple answers. As you'll soon see, decisions about how to cope with life's difficulties can be incredibly complex.

In the previous chapter we discussed the nature of stress and its effects. We learned that stress can be a challenging, exciting stimulus to personal growth. However, we also saw that stress can prove damaging to people's psychological and physical health because it often triggers physiological responses that may be harmful. Controlling the effects of stress depends on the behavioral responses people make to stressful situations. Thus, a person's mental and physical health depends, in part, on his or her ability to *cope* effectively with stress (Taylor & Stanton, 2007).

This chapter focuses on how people manage stress. We begin with a general discussion of the concept of coping. Then we review some common coping patterns that tend to have relatively little value. After discussing these ill-advised coping techniques, we offer an overview of what it means to engage in healthier, "constructive" coping. The remainder of the chapter expands on the specifics of constructive coping. In the application, we discuss how to cope with one of the most common stressors: lack of time. We hope our discussion provides you with some new ideas about how to deal with the stresses of modern life.

ZINQ Stock/Shutterstock.com

THE CONCEPT OF COPING

LEARNING OBJECTIVES

- Describe the variety of coping strategies that people use.
- Understand why it is beneficial to use a variety of coping strategies and how these strategies differ in their adaptive value.

In Chapter 3, you learned that **coping refers to efforts to master, reduce, or tolerate the demands created by stress.** Let's take a closer look at this concept and discuss some general points about coping.

People cope with stress in many ways. A number of researchers have attempted to identify and classify the coping techniques that people use in dealing with stress. Their work reveals quite a variety of strategies; in fact, one review of the literature found over 400 distinct coping techniques (Skinner et al., 2003). To simplify things, Carver suggests that we consider four important distinctions or

groupings (Carver & Connor-Smith, 2010), which are listed in **Figure 4.1** on the next page. Thus, in grappling with stress, people select their coping tactics from a large and varied menu of options.

It is most adaptive to use a variety of coping strategies. Even with a large menu of tactics to choose from, most people come to rely on some coping strategies more than others. However, Cheng (2001, 2003) has argued that flexibility is more desirable than consistently relying on the same strategy. The ability to use multiple strategies (called *coping flexibility*) has been related to enhanced

TYPES OF COPING STRATEGIES	
Coping distinction/grouping	**Example**
Problem-focused vs. emotion-focused coping	Problem-focused: I save money in anticipation of layoffs. Emotion-focus: I engage in self-soothing relaxation exercises to handle the stress brought about by layoffs.
Engagement vs. disengagement coping	Engagement: I work on finding a new place to live after the looming divorce. Disengagement: I refuse to believe that the divorce is happening.
Meaning-focused coping	Losing my house and possessions in a fire reminded me of what is truly important in life—my family and friends.
Proactive coping	I know that this confrontation with my friend is going to be challenging, so I'm going to make sure I have my thoughts organized before I bring up our issues.

Figure 4.1

Classifying coping strategies. There are literally hundreds of coping techniques. Carver and Connor-Smith (2010) point to four important distinctions or groupings of coping strategies that have proved to be meaningful. The groupings are listed here, along with a representative example from each category. As with other distinctions, there is significant overlap among the categories. As you can see, people use quite a variety of coping strategies.

Source: From Carver, C. S., & Connor-Smith, J. (2010). Personality and coping. *Annual Review of Psychology, 61,* 679-704.

psychological health and reduced depression, anxiety, and distress (Kato, 2012). Flexible copers can differentiate among stressful events in terms of controllability and impact, which is important information to know when choosing a coping strategy (Cheng & Cheung, 2005). Indeed, the ability to select a particular coping tactic to deal with a

specific adversity helps people avoid becoming hindered by a problematic strategy (Carbonell, Reinherz, & Beardslee, 2005). Although everyone has an individual style of coping with life's difficulties, this need for flexibility may explain why people's coping methods show only moderate stability across varied situations (Schwartz et al., 1999).

Coping strategies vary in their adaptive value. In everyday terms, when we say that someone "coped with her problems," we imply that she handled them effectively. In reality, however, not all strategies are created equal. Coping processes range from the helpful to the counterproductive. For example, coping with the disappointment of not getting a good grade by plotting to sabotage your professor's computer would clearly be a problematic way of coping. Hence, we distinguish between coping patterns that tend to be helpful and those that tend to be maladaptive. In general, the use of maladaptive strategies is associated with poorer psychological adjustment, whereas adaptive strategies are related to enhanced well-being (Aldo, Nolen-Hoeksema, & Schweizer, 2010). Bear in mind, however, that our generalizations about the adaptive value of various coping strategies are based on trends or tendencies identified by researchers. Unlike what many self-help books and talk show hosts would have you believe, no coping strategy can guarantee a successful outcome. Furthermore, the adaptive value of a coping technique depends on the exact nature of the situation. As you'll see in the next section, even ill-advised coping strategies may have adaptive value in some instances.

COMMON COPING PATTERNS OF LIMITED VALUE

LEARNING OBJECTIVES

- Analyze the adaptive value of giving up as a response to stress.
- Describe the adaptive value of aggression as a response to stress, including the research on media violence as catharsis.
- Evaluate the adaptive value of indulging yourself as a response to stress.

- Discuss the adaptive value of self-blame as a response to stress.
- Evaluate the adaptive value of defense mechanisms, including recent work on healthy illusions.

"Recently, after an engagement of 22 months, my fiancée told me that she was in love with someone else and that we were through. I've been a wreck ever since. I can't study

because I keep thinking about her. I think constantly about what I did wrong in the relationship and why I wasn't good enough for her. Getting drunk is the only way I can get her off my mind. Lately, I've been getting plastered about five or six nights a week. My grades are really hurting, but I'm not sure that I care."

This young man is going through a difficult time and does not appear to be handling it well. He's blaming himself for the breakup with his fiancée. He's turning to alcohol to dull the pain that he feels, and it sounds like he may be giving up on school. These coping responses aren't particularly unusual in such situations, but they're only going to make his problems worse.

In this section, we'll examine some relatively common coping patterns that tend to be less than optimal. Specifically, we'll discuss giving up, aggression, self-indulgence, self-blame, and defense mechanisms. Some of these coping tactics may be helpful in certain circumstances, but more often than not, they are counterproductive.

Giving Up

When confronted with stress, people sometimes simply give up and withdraw from the battle. This response of apathy and inaction tends to be associated with the emotional reactions of sadness and dejection. Martin Seligman (1974, 1992) has developed a model of this giving-up syndrome that sheds light on its causes. In Seligman's original research, animals were subjected to electric shocks they could not escape. The animals were then given an opportunity to learn a response that would allow them to escape the shock. However, many of the animals became so apathetic and listless that they didn't even try to learn the escape response. When researchers made similar manipulations with *human* subjects using inescapable noise (rather than shock) as the stressor, they observed parallel results (Hiroto & Seligman, 1975). This syndrome is referred to as learned helplessness. **Learned helplessness is passive behavior produced by exposure to unavoidable aversive events.** Unfortunately, this tendency to give up may be transferred to situations in which one is not really helpless. Hence, some people routinely respond to stress with fatalism and resignation, passively accepting setbacks that might be dealt with effectively. In adolescents, learned helplessness is associated with disengagement in academics and an increase in depression (Maatta, Nurmi, & Stattin, 2007). Interestingly, Evans and Stecker (2004) argue that environmental stressors, such as excessive noise, crowding, and traffic (see Chapter 3), often produce a syndrome that resembles learned helplessness.

Seligman originally viewed learned helplessness as a product of conditioning. However, research with human participants has led Seligman and his colleagues to revise their theory. Their current model proposes that people's *cognitive interpretation* of aversive events determines whether they develop learned helplessness. Specifically, helplessness seems to occur when individuals come to believe that events are beyond their control. This belief is particularly likely to emerge in people who exhibit a pessimistic explanatory style. As discussed in Chapter 3, such people tend to attribute setbacks to personal inadequacies instead of situational factors. This explanatory style is associated with poorer physical health and increased depression and anxiety (Wise & Rosqvist, 2006).

Overall, giving up is not a highly regarded method of coping. Carver and his colleagues (1989, 1993) have studied this coping strategy, which they refer to as *behavioral disengagement,* and found that it is associated with increased rather than decreased distress. A study of college students after the September 11 terrorist attacks supports this assertion, finding that behavioral disengagement was associated with increased anxiety shortly after the attack, even for those indirectly affected (Liverant, Hofmann, & Litz, 2004).

However, giving up could be adaptive in some instances. For example, if you are thrown into a job that you are not equipped to handle, it might be better to quit rather than face constant pressure and diminishing self-esteem. Studies show that people who are better able to disengage from unattainable goals report better health and exhibit lower levels of a key stress hormone (Wrosch, 2011; Worsch et al., 2007). People in our competitive culture tend to disparage the concept of "giving up." Thus, the researchers note that it might be better to characterize this coping tactic as "goal adjustment." Regardless, there is something to be said for recognizing one's limitations, avoiding unrealistic goals, and minimizing self-imposed stress.

Acting Aggressively

A young man, age 17, cautiously edged his car into traffic on the Corona Expressway in Los Angeles. His slow speed apparently irritated the men in a pickup truck behind him. Unfortunately, he angered the wrong men—they shot him to death. During that same weekend there were six other roadside shootings in the Los Angeles area, all of them triggered by minor incidents or "fender benders." Frustrated motorists are attacking each other more and more frequently, especially on the overburdened highways of Los Angeles.

Such tragic incidents of highway violence—so-called "road rage"—exemplify maladaptive ways in which drivers cope with the stress, anxiety, and hostility experienced while driving. These incidents have unfortunately become common enough that some professionals are calling for road rage to become an official psychiatric diagnosis (Ayar, 2006). Road rage vividly illustrates that people often respond to stressful events by acting aggressively. **Aggression is any behavior intended to hurt someone, either physically or verbally.** Snarls, curses, and insults are much more common than shootings or fistfights, but aggression of any kind can be problematic.

© iStockphoto.com/Mac99

As you learned in Chapter 3, frustration is a major source of stress. Many years ago, a team of psychologists (Dollard et al., 1939) proposed the *frustration-aggression hypothesis,* which held that aggression is always due to frustration. Decades of research eventually showed that there isn't an inevitable link between frustration and aggression, but this research also supported the basic idea that frustration *does* frequently elicit aggression (Berkowitz, 1989).

People often lash out aggressively at others who had nothing to do with their frustration, especially when they can't vent their anger at the real source of their frustration. Thus, you'll probably suppress your anger rather than lash out verbally at a police officer who gives you a speeding ticket. Twenty minutes later, however, you might be downright brutal in rebuking a waiter who is slow in serving your lunch. As we discussed in Chapter 2, Sigmund Freud noticed this diversion of anger to a substitute target long ago; he called it *displacement*. Unfortunately, research suggests that when someone is provoked, displaced aggression is a common response (Hoobler & Brass, 2006). In fact, displaced aggression is a contributing factor to road rage (Sansone & Sansone, 2010).

Aggressive responses to frustration are more likely if the person ruminates about being provoked and if he or she has a depleted capacity for self-control (Denson, DeWall, & Finkel, 2012). Alcohol also plays a role (Denson et al., 2008). Feelings of security and anonymity in one's personal space also influence aggressive tendencies. For instance, aggressive driving behaviors are more common among those who report a territorial attachment to their cars and those who feel anonymous or detached in their cars because of locked doors or tinted windows (Conkle & West, 2008; Szlemko et al., 2008).

Freud theorized that behaving aggressively could get pent-up emotion out of one's system and thus be adaptive. He coined the term *catharsis* **to refer to this release of emotional tension.** The Freudian notion that it is a good idea to vent anger has become widely disseminated and accepted in modern society. Books, magazines, and self-appointed experts routinely advise that it is healthy to "blow off steam" and thereby release and reduce anger. However, experimental research generally has *not* supported the catharsis hypothesis. Indeed, most studies find just the opposite: *Behaving in an aggressive manner tends to fuel more anger and aggression* (Lohr et al., 2007).

Conventional wisdom holds that viewing violent media or playing violent video games can be cathartic—that watching a murder on a TV show or fighting a fictional character in a game can release pent-up anger and hostility. However, the research evidence strongly suggests that this is simply not true (Anderson et al., 2010). Craig Anderson and Brad Bushman (2001) conducted a groundbreaking review of the research on violent video games and found that playing these games was related to increased aggression, physiological arousal, and aggressive thoughts and to decreased prosocial behavior. In fact, they found that the relationship between media violence and aggressive behavior was almost as strong as the relationship between smoking and cancer (Bushman & Anderson, 2001; see **Figure 4.2**). Exposure to media violence not only desensitizes people to violent acts, it also encourages aggressive self-views and automatic aggressive responses (Bartholow, Bushman, & Sestir, 2006),

Photo: © Wassel du Plooy/Shutterstock.com

Figure 4.2

Comparison of the relationship between media violence and aggression to other correlations. Many studies have found a correlation between exposure to media violence and aggression. However, some critics have argued that the correlation is too weak to have any practical significance in the real world. In a rebuttal of this criticism, Bushman and Anderson (2001) note that the average correlation in studies of media violence and aggression is .31. They argue that this association is almost as strong as the correlation between smoking and the probability of developing lung cancer, which is viewed as relevant to real-world issues and notably stronger than a variety of other correlations shown here that are assumed to have practical importance.

Source: Adapted from Bushman, B. J., & Anderson, C. A. (2001). Media violence and the American public. *American Psychologist, 56*(6-7), 477–489. (Figure 2). Copyright © 2001 American Psychological Association. Reprinted by permission of the publisher and authors.

and increases feelings of hostility (Arriaga et al., 2006a). Further, it increases one's perception of hostile intent on the part of others in ambiguous situations (Hasan, Bègue, & Bushman, 2012).

Experimental studies using a variety of violent media, diverse laboratory conditions, and many kinds of participants continue to find convergent evidence that video games and other forms of violent media do not provide cathartic effects; rather, they increase aggressive tendencies (Bushman & Huesmann, 2012). Today we have sophisticated equipment to study the activity of the brain (for example, functional magnetic resonance imaging). Preliminary research using brain-imaging procedures indicates that although people are aware that video game violence is fantasy, the brain reacts as if it is real. Thus, "engaging in virtual violence could impact neural systems in a manner comparable with engaging in actual violence" (Carnagey, Anderson, & Bartholow, 2007, p. 181).

Is there an up side to anger and aggression? Some argue that feeling anger can be beneficial when one is about to engage in a confrontational task (Tamir, 2009). However, as a coping strategy, acting aggressively has little value. Carol Tavris (1982, 1989) points out that aggressive behavior usually backfires because it elicits aggressive responses from others that generate more anger. She asserts, "Aggressive catharses are almost impossible to find in continuing relationships because parents, children, spouses, and bosses usually feel obliged to aggress back at you" (1982, p. 131). In fact, the interpersonal conflicts that often emerge from aggressive behavior actually induce additional stress.

Indulging Yourself

Stress sometimes leads to reduced impulse control, or *self-indulgence*. For instance, after an exceptionally stressful day, some people head for their kitchen, a grocery store, or a restaurant in pursuit of something sweet. Others cope with stress by making a beeline for the nearest shopping mall for a spending spree. Still others respond to stress by indulging in inju-

dicious patterns of drinking, smoking, gambling, and drug use.

Moos and Billings (1982) identified *developing alternative rewards* as a common response to stress. It makes sense that when things are going poorly in one area of your life, you may try to compensate by pursuing substitute forms of satisfaction. Thus, it is not surprising that there is evidence of stress-induced eating (O'Connor & Conner, 2011), smoking (McClernon & Gilbert, 2007), gambling (Wood & Griffiths, 2007), and alcohol and drug use (Grunberg, Berger, & Hamilton, 2011). In fact, psychologists speculate that the general relationship between stress and poor physical health might be attributable in part to these unhealthy behaviors (Carver, 2011).

A more recent manifestation of this coping strategy is the tendency to immerse oneself in the online world of the Internet. Kimberly Young (2009) has described a syndrome called **Internet addiction, which consists of spending an inordinate amount of time on the Internet and an inability to control online use**. People who exhibit this syndrome tend to feel anxious, depressed, or empty when they are not online. Their Internet use is so excessive, it begins to interfere with their functioning at work, at school, or at home, leading victims to start concealing the extent of their dependence on the Internet. Some people exhibit pathological Internet use for one particular purpose, such as online sex or online gaming, whereas others exhibit a general, global pattern of Internet addiction (Davis, 2001). Estimates of the prevalence of Internet addiction, which range from 1.5% to 8.2% of the population, vary considerably because the criteria of this new syndrome are still evolving (Weinstein & Lejoyeux, 2010); however, the syndrome does *not* appear to be rare. Research suggests that Internet addiction is not limited to shy,

CATHY

Experts disagree about whether excessive Internet use should be characterized as an addiction, but the inability to control online use appears to be an increasingly common syndrome.

male computer whizzes, as one might expect (Young, 1998). Nor is it a strictly Western phenomenon; rates appear to be higher in China than in the United States (Zhang, Amos, & McDowell, 2008). Internet addiction is associated with increased depression among youth and adults (Morrison & Gore, 2010). Although not all psychologists agree about whether excessive Internet surfing should be classified as an *addiction* (Czincz & Hechanova, 2009; Pies, 2009), it is clear that this coping strategy can result in a disruption of time, ultimately increasing one's stress levels (Chou, Condron, & Belland, 2005).

There is nothing inherently maladaptive about indulging oneself as a way of coping with life's stresses. If a hot fudge sundae, some new clothes, or chatting online can calm your nerves after a major setback, who can argue? In fact, connecting with online social support has been shown to reduce stress and anxiety (Leung, 2007). However, if a person consistently responds to stress with excessive self-indulgence, obvious problems are likely to develop. Stress-induced eating is typically unhealthy (one rarely craves broccoli or grapefruit after a hard day) and may result in poor nutrition or obesity. Excesses in drinking and drug use may endanger one's health and affect work or relationship quality. Additionally, these indulgences can cause emotional ambivalence, as immediate pleasure gives way to regret, guilt, or embarrassment (Ramanathan & Williams, 2007). Given the risks associated with self-indulgence, it has marginal adaptive value.

Blaming Yourself

In a postgame interview after a tough defeat, a prominent football coach was brutally critical of himself. He said that he had been outcoached, that he had made poor decisions, and that his game plan was faulty. He almost eagerly assumed all the blame for the loss himself. In reality, he had taken some reasonable risks that didn't go his way and had

suffered the effects of poor execution by his players. Looking at it objectively, the loss was attributable to the collective failures of fifty or so players and coaches. However, the coach's unrealistically negative self-evaluation was a fairly typical response to frustration. When confronted by stress (especially frustration and pressure), people often become highly self-critical.

The tendency to engage in "negative self-talk" in response to stress has been noted by a number of influential theorists. As we will discuss in greater detail later in this chapter, Albert Ellis (1973, 1987) calls this phenomenon "catastrophic thinking" and focuses on how it is rooted in irrational assumptions. Aaron Beck (1976, 1987) analyzes negative self-talk into specific tendencies. Among other things, he asserts that people often (1) unreasonably attribute their failures to personal shortcomings, (2) focus on negative feedback from others while ignoring favorable feedback, and (3) make unduly pessimistic projections about the future. Thus, if you performed poorly on an exam, you might respond to this stress by blaming it on your woeful stupidity, dismissing a classmate's comment that the test was unfair, and hysterically predicting that you will flunk out of school.

According to Ellis, catastrophic thinking causes, aggravates, and perpetuates emotional reactions to stress that are often problematic. Along even more serious lines, researchers have found that self-blame is associated with increased distress and depression for individuals who have experienced traumas such as sexual assault, war, and natural disasters (DePrince, Chu, & Pineda, 2011; Kraaij & Garnefski, 2006). For victims of sexual assault specifically, self-blame is associated with heightened PTSD symptoms and greater feelings of shame (Ullman et al., 2007; Vidal & Petrak, 2007). Likewise, blaming oneself is related to increased depression and anxiety for those dealing with serious health issues (Hill et al., 2011; Kraaij, Garnefski, & Vlietstra, 2008). Although being realistic and recognizing one's weaknesses has value, especially when one is engaging in problem solving, Ellis and Beck agree that self-blame as a coping strategy can be enormously counterproductive. We cover Ellis's advice on more constructive thinking later in this chapter, and we discuss Beck's recommendations for more effective coping in our chapter on psychotherapy (Chapter 15).

Using Defensive Coping

Defensive coping is a common response to stress. We noted in Chapter 2 that the concept of defense mechanisms was originally developed by Sigmund Freud. Though rooted in the psychoanalytic tradition, this concept has gained acceptance from psychologists of most persuasions. Building on Freud's initial insights, modern psychologists have broadened the scope of the concept and added to Freud's list of defense mechanisms.

The Nature of Defense Mechanisms

Defense mechanisms are largely unconscious reactions that protect a person from unpleasant emotions such as anxiety and guilt. A number of coping strategies fit this definition. For example, Laughlin (1979) lists 49 different defenses. In our discussion of Freud's theory in Chapter 2, we described seven common defenses. **Figure 4.3** introduces another five defenses that people use with some regularity. Although widely discussed in the popular press, defense mechanisms are often misunderstood. We will use a question-answer format to elaborate on the nature of defense mechanisms in the hopes of clearing up any misconceptions.

What do defense mechanisms defend against? Above all else, defense mechanisms shield the individual from the *emotional discomfort* elicited by stress. Their main purpose is to ward off unwelcome emotions or to reduce their intensity. Foremost among the emotions guarded against is anxiety. People are especially defensive when the anxiety is the result of some threat to their self-esteem. They also use defenses to prevent dangerous feelings of anger from exploding into acts of aggression. Guilt and dejection are two other emotions that people often try to evade through defensive maneuvers.

How do they work? Defense mechanisms work through *self-deception*. They accomplish their goals by distorting reality so it does not appear so threatening (Aldwin, 2007). Let's say you're doing poorly in school and are in danger of flunking out. Initially, you might use *denial* to block awareness of the possibility that you could fail. This tactic might temporarily fend off feelings of anxiety. If it becomes difficult to deny the obvious, you might resort to *fantasy*, daydreaming about how you will salvage adequate grades by getting spectacular scores on the upcoming final exams, when the objective fact is that you are hopelessly behind in your studies. Thus, defense mechanisms work their magic by bending reality in self-serving ways (Bowins, 2004).

COMMON DEFENSE MECHANISMS

Defense mechanism	Example
Denial. Refusal to acknowledge or face up to unpleasant realities in one's life.	A student allows her family to plan a trip to her graduation even though she is failing a class required for graduation.
Fantasy. Fulfilling conscious or unconscious wishes and impulses in one's imagination.	An unpopular man imagines that he has an extensive network of outgoing and popular friends.
Intellectualization. Dealing with difficulties by looking at them in a detached, abstract way, thus suppressing one's emotional reactions.	A man who has just been diagnosed with a terminal illness attempts to learn everything there is to know about the disease and the minute details of medical treatment.
Undoing. Attempting to counteract feelings of guilt through acts of atonement.	A daughter who feels guilty about insulting her mother compliments her mother's appearance after each insult.
Overcompensation. Making up for real or imagined deficiencies by focusing on, or exaggerating, desirable characteristics.	A transfer student who has not made any new friends focuses on excelling in her classes.

Figure 4.3

Additional defense mechanisms. Like the seven defense mechanisms described in the discussion of Freudian theory in Chapter 2 (see **Figure 2.5**), these five defenses are frequently used in people's efforts to cope with stress.

Are they conscious or unconscious? Mainstream Freudian theory originally assumed that defenses operate entirely at an unconscious level. However, the concept of defense mechanisms has been broadened to include maneuvers that people may have some awareness of. Thus, defense mechanisms operate at varying levels of awareness and can be conscious or unconscious (Kramer, 2010).

Are they normal? Definitely. Most people use defense mechanisms on a fairly regular basis (Thobaben, 2005).

Calvin and Hobbes

They are entirely normal patterns of coping. The notion that only neurotic people use defense mechanisms is inaccurate.

Can Defense Mechanisms Ever Be Healthy?

This is a critical and complicated question. More often than not, the answer is no. In fact, defensive coping has been linked to increased negative emotions, depression, and suicide risk (Hovanesian, Isakov, & Cervellione, 2009; Steiner et al., 2007). In general, defense mechanisms are poor ways of coping, for a number of reasons. First, defensive coping is an avoidance strategy, and avoidance rarely provides a genuine solution to problems. In fact, Holahan and his colleagues (2005) found that avoidance coping is associated with increased chronic and acute life stressors as well as increased depressive symptoms. Second, defenses such as denial, fantasy, and projection represent "wishful thinking," which is likely to accomplish little. In a study of how students coped with the stress of taking the Medical College Admissions Test (MCAT), Bolger (1990) found that those who engaged in a lot of wishful thinking experienced greater increases in anxiety than other students as the exam approached. Third, a defensive coping style has been related to poor health, in part because it often leads people to delay facing up to their problems (Weinberger, 1990). For example, if you were to block out obvious warning signs of cancer or diabetes and failed to obtain needed medical care, your defensive behavior could be fatal. Although illusions may protect one from anxiety in the short term, they can create serious problems in the long term.

Shelley Taylor

Most theorists used to regard accurate contact with reality as the hallmark of sound mental health. However, Shelley Taylor and Jonathon Brown (1988, 1994) have reviewed several lines of evidence suggesting that defensive "illusions" may be adaptive for mental health and well-being. For example, they note that "normal" (that is, nondepressed) people tend to have overly favorable self-images. In contrast, depressed people exhibit less favorable—but more realistic—self-concepts. Also, "normal" participants overestimate the degree to which they control chance events. In comparison, depressed participants are less prone to this illusion of control. Finally, "normal" individuals are more likely than their depressed counterparts to display unrealistic optimism in making projections about the future.

A variety of other studies have also provided support for the hypothesis that positive illusions promote well-being and positive health outcomes (Taylor, 2011b). For example, studies of individuals diagnosed with AIDS show that those with unrealistically optimistic expectations of the likely course of their disease actually experience a less rapid course of illness (Reed et al., 1999). In a laboratory study, Taylor et al. (2003) found that participants who tended to exhibit positive illusions showed lower cardiovascular responses to stress, quicker cardiovascular recovery from stress, and lower levels of a key stress hormone. Further, a study of retirees found that those who held an exaggerated youthful bias reported higher self-esteem, better perceived health, and less boredom than those who held an accurate perception of their age (Gana, Alaphilippe, & Bailly, 2004).

As you might guess, critics have expressed considerable skepticism about the idea that illusions are adaptive. For example, Colvin and Block (1994) make an eloquent case for the traditional view that accuracy and realism are healthy. Moreover, they report data showing that overly favorable self-ratings are correlated with maladaptive personality traits (Colvin, Block, & Funder, 1995). One possible resolution to this debate is Roy Baumeister's (1989) theory that it's all a matter of degree and that there is an "optimal margin of illusion." According to Baumeister, extreme self-deception is maladaptive, but small illusions may often be beneficial.

THE NATURE OF CONSTRUCTIVE COPING

LEARNING OBJECTIVES

- Describe the nature of constructive coping.
- Distinguish among the three categories of constructive coping.

Our discussion thus far has focused on coping strategies that tend to be less than ideal. Of course, people also exhibit many healthy strategies for dealing with stress. We will use the term *constructive coping* **to refer to efforts to deal with stressful events that are judged to be relatively healthful.** Keep in mind that even the healthiest coping responses may turn out to be ineffective in some cases. Thus, the concept of constructive coping is simply meant to convey a healthy, positive connotation, without promising success.

What makes a coping strategy constructive? Frankly, in labeling certain coping responses constructive or healthy, psychologists are making value judgments. It's a gray area in which opinions will vary to some extent. Nonetheless, some consensus emerges from the burgeoning research on coping and stress management. Key themes in this literature include the following (Kleinke, 2007):

1. Constructive coping involves confronting problems directly. It is task relevant and action oriented. It involves a conscious effort to rationally evaluate your options in an effort to solve your problems.

2. Constructive coping takes effort. Using such strategies to reduce stress is an active process that involves planning.

3. Constructive coping is based on reasonably realistic appraisals of your stress and coping resources. A little self-deception may sometimes be adaptive, but excessive self-deception and highly unrealistic negative thinking are not.

4. Constructive coping involves learning to recognize and manage potentially disruptive emotional reactions to stress.

5. Constructive coping involves learning to exert some control over potentially harmful or destructive habitual behaviors. It requires the acquisition of some behavioral self-control.

These points should give you a general idea of what we mean by constructive coping. They will guide our discourse in the remainder of this chapter as we discuss how to cope more effectively with stress. To organize our discussion, we will use a classification scheme proposed by Moos and Billings (1982) to divide constructive coping techniques into three broad categories: *appraisal-focused coping* (aimed at changing one's interpretation of stressful events), *problem-focused coping* (aimed at altering the stressful situation itself), and *emotion-focused coping* (aimed at managing potential emotional distress). **Figure 4.4** shows common coping strategies that fall under each category. It is important to note that many strategies could fall under more than one category. For instance, one could seek social support in order to talk through and come to an understanding of a problem (appraisal-focused), to get practical help (problem-focused), or to gain emotional support (emotion-focused). Further, these categories are not mutually exclusive (Carver, 2011). For example, tackling a problem head-on can reduce unwanted negative emotions.

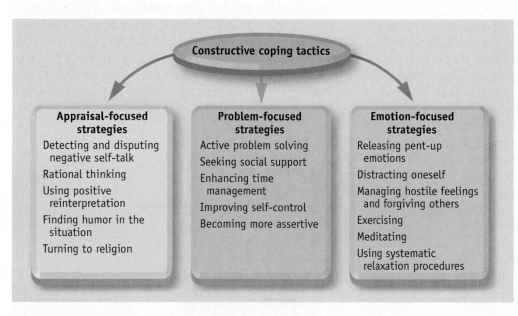

Figure 4.4

Overview of constructive coping tactics. Coping tactics can be organized in several ways, but we will use the classification scheme shown here, which consists of three categories: appraisal-focused strategies, problem-focused strategies, and emotion-focused strategies. The list of coping tactics in each category is not exhaustive. Most, but not all, of the listed strategies are discussed in our coverage of constructive coping.

APPRAISAL-FOCUSED CONSTRUCTIVE COPING

LEARNING OBJECTIVES

- Explain rational thinking as an appraisal-focused coping strategy by using Ellis's theory of catastrophic thinking.
- Discuss the merits of humor in coping with stress, including the research on different types of humor.

- Assess positive reinterpretation and benefit finding as appraisal-focused coping strategies.

As we've seen, the experience of stress depends on how one interprets or appraises threatening events. People often underestimate the importance of the appraisal phase in the stress process. They fail to appreciate the highly subjective feelings that color the perception of threat to one's well-

being. In fact, a useful way to deal with stress is to alter your appraisal of threatening events. In this section, we'll examine Albert Ellis's ideas about reappraisal and discuss the value of using humor and positive reinterpretation to cope with stress.

Ellis's Rational Thinking

Albert Ellis

Courtesy Albert Ellis Institute

Albert Ellis (1977, 1985, 1996, 2001b) was a prominent and influential theorist who died in 2007 at the age of 93. He believed that people could short-circuit their emotional reactions to stress by altering their appraisals of stressful events. Ellis's insights about stress appraisal are the foundation for his widely used system of therapy (Ellis & Ellis, 2011). His *rational-emotive behavior therapy* **is an approach to therapy that focuses on altering clients' patterns of irrational thinking to reduce maladaptive emotions and behavior.**

Ellis maintained that *you feel the way you think*. He argued that problematic emotional reactions are caused by negative self-talk, which, as we mentioned earlier, he called catastrophic thinking. *Catastrophic thinking* **involves unrealistic appraisals of stress that exaggerate the magnitude of one's problems.** Ellis used a simple A-B-C sequence to explain his ideas (see **Figure 4.5**):

A. *Activating event.* The A in Ellis's system stands for the activating event that produces the stress. The activating event may be any potentially stressful transaction. Examples might include a car accident, the cancellation of a date, a delay while waiting in line at the bank, or a failure to get a promotion you were expecting.

B. *Belief system.* B stands for your belief about the event, which represents your appraisal of the stress. According to Ellis, people often view minor setbacks as disasters, engaging in catastrophic thinking: "How awful this is. I can't stand it!" "Things never turn out fairly for me." "I'll be in this line forever." "I'll never get promoted."

C. *Consequence.* C stands for the consequence of your negative thinking. When your appraisals of stressful events are highly negative, the consequence tends to be emotional distress. Thus, you feel angry, outraged, anxious, panic stricken, disgusted, or dejected.

Ellis asserts that most people do not understand the importance of phase B in this three-stage sequence. They unwittingly believe that the activating event (A) *causes* the consequent emotional turmoil (C). However, Ellis maintains that A does *not* cause C. It only appears to do so. Instead, Ellis asserts that B causes C. Emotional distress is actually caused by one's catastrophic thinking in appraising stressful events.

According to Ellis, it is common for people to turn inconvenience into disaster and make "mountains out of molehills." For instance, imagine that someone stands you up on a date you were eagerly looking forward to. You might think, "Oh, this is terrible. I'm going to have another boring weekend. People always mistreat me. I'll never find anyone to fall in love with. I must be an ugly, worthless person." Ellis would argue that such thoughts are irrational. He would point out that it does not follow logically from being stood up that you (1) must have a lousy weekend, (2) will never fall in love, or (3) are a worthless person. Thinking this way does nothing but increase distress. Indeed, research indicates that the tendency toward catastrophic thinking is a risk factor for developing posttraumatic stress disorder (see Chapter 3) (Bryant & Guthrie, 2005). As a result, the United States Army offers a 10-day training course that teaches officers to recognize Ellis's ABC sequence in order to increase resilience (Reivich, Seligman, & McBride, 2011).

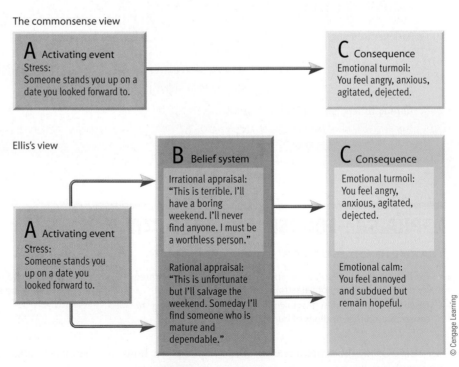

Figure 4.5

Albert Ellis's A-B-C model of emotional reactions. Most people are likely to attribute their negative emotional reactions (C) directly to stressful events (A). However, Ellis argues that emotional reactions are really caused by the way individuals think about these events (B).

© Cengage Learning

The Roots of Catastrophic Thinking

Ellis theorized that unrealistic appraisals of stress are derived from the irrational assumptions people hold. He maintained that if you scrutinize your catastrophic thinking, you will find that your reasoning is based on an unreasonable premise, such as "I must have approval from everyone" or "I must perform well in all endeavors." These faulty assumptions, which most people hold unconsciously, generate catastrophic thinking and emotional turmoil. To facilitate emotional self-control, it is important to learn to spot irrational assumptions and the unhealthy patterns of thought they generate. Here are four particularly common irrational assumptions:

1. *I must have love and affection from certain people.* Everyone wants to be liked and loved. There is nothing wrong with that. However, many people foolishly believe that they should be liked by everyone they come into contact with. If you stop to think about it, that's clearly unrealistic. Once individuals fall in love, they tend to believe that their future happiness depends absolutely on the continuation of that one, special relationship. They believe that if their current love relationship were to end, they would never again be able to achieve a comparable one. This is an unrealistic view of the future. Such views make the person anxious during a relationship and severely depressed if it comes to an end.

2. *I must perform well in all endeavors.* We live in a highly competitive society. We are taught that victory brings happiness. Consequently, we feel that we must always win. For example, many athletes are never satisfied unless they perform at their best level. However, by definition, their best level is not their typical level, and they set themselves up for inevitable frustration.

3. *Other people should always behave competently and be considerate of me.* People are often angered by others' stupidity and selfishness. For example, you may become outraged when a mechanic fails to fix your car properly or when a salesperson treats you rudely. It would be nice if others were always competent and considerate, but you know better—they are not! Yet many people go through life unrealistically expecting others' efficiency and kindness in every situation.

4. *Events should always go the way I like.* Some people simply won't tolerate any kind of setback. They assume that things should always go their way. For example, some commuters become tense and angry each time they get stuck in rush-hour traffic. They seem to believe that they are entitled to coast home easily every day, even though they know that rush hour is rarely a breeze. Such expectations are clearly unrealistic and doomed to be violated. Yet few people recognize the obvious irrationality of the assumption that underlies their anger unless it is pointed out to them.

Reducing Catastrophic Thinking

How can you reduce your unrealistic appraisals of stress? Ellis asserts that you must learn (1) how to detect catastrophic thinking and (2) how to dispute the irrational assumptions that cause it. Detection involves acquiring the ability to spot unrealistic pessimism and wild exaggeration in your thinking. Examine your self-talk closely. Ask yourself why you're getting upset. Force yourself to verbalize your concerns, covertly or out loud. Look for key words that often show up in catastrophic thinking, such as *should, ought, always, never,* and *must.*

Disputing your irrational assumptions requires subjecting your entire reasoning process to scrutiny. Try to root out the source of your conclusions, the assumptions that are deriving them. Most people are unaware of their assumptions. Once these thoughts are unearthed, their irrationality may be quite obvious. If your assumptions seem reasonable, ask yourself whether your conclusions follow logically. Try to replace your catastrophic thinking with more low-key rational analyses. Such strategies should help you to redefine stressful situations in ways that are less threatening. Challenging one's assumptions isn't the only appraisal-based coping strategy; another way to defuse such situations is to turn to humor.

Humor as a Stress Reducer

In the aftermath of Superstorm Sandy on the East Coast in late 2012, singer Aimee Mann performed a tongue-in-cheek song called "Sandy" (to the tune of Barry Manilow's "Mandy"). In a New Orleans suburb following Hurricane Katrina, a flooded, grimy Chevrolet pickup parked outside a shattered two-story house had a shiny new sign: "For Sale. Like New. Runs Great." Obviously, disasters don't destroy people's sense of humor. When the going gets tough, finding some humor in the situation is not uncommon and is usually beneficial.

Empirical evidence showing that humor moderates the impact of stress has been accumulating over the last 25 years (Lefcourt, 2005). For instance, in one influential study, Martin and Lefcourt (1983) found that a good sense of humor functioned as a buffer to lessen the negative impact of stress on mood. Some of their results are presented in **Figure 4.6** on the next page, which shows how mood disturbance increased as stress went up in two groups of participants—those who were high or low in their use of humor. Notice how high-humor participants were less affected by stress than their low-humor counterparts were. More recently, humor has been linked to increases in self-efficacy, positive mood, and optimism, and with decreases in stress, depression, and anxiety (Crawford & Caltabiano, 2011).

Humor can also reduce workplace stress. In a recent review of forty-nine studies, researchers found that employees who used humor at work showed enhanced

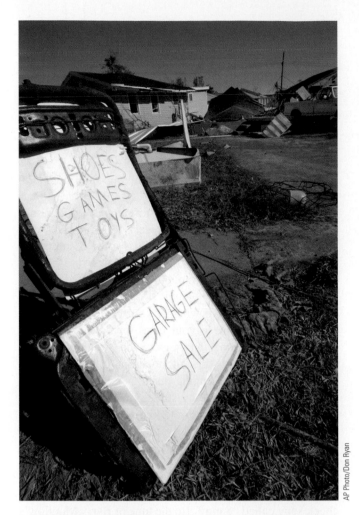

People often turn to humor to help themselves cope during difficult times, as this photo taken in the aftermath of Hurricane Katrina in New Orleans illustrates. Research suggests that humor can help reduce the negative impact of stressful events.

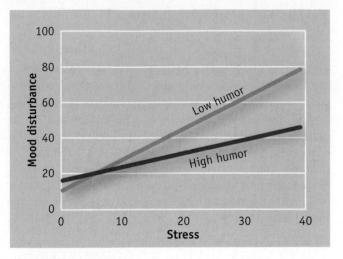

Figure 4.6

Humor and coping. Martin and Lefcourt (1983) related stress to mood disturbance in subjects who were either high or low in their use of humor. Increased stress led to smaller increases in mood disturbance in the high-humor group, suggesting that humor has some value in efforts to cope with stress.

Source: Adapted from Martin, R. A., & Lefcourt, H. M. (1983). Sense of humor as a moderator of the relation between stressors and moods. *Journal of Personality and Social Psychology, 45* (6), 1313–1324. Copyright © 1983 by the American Psychological Association. Adapted by permission.

performance, satisfaction, and health, as well as decreased burnout and stress. Having a supervisor who uses humor is related to enhanced work performance and satisfaction, as well as higher worker satisfaction with the supervisor (Mesmer-Magnus, Glew, & Viswesvaran, 2012). This research demonstrates that one way a good sense of humor relates to good physical and mental health is by buffering the negative effects of workplace stress.

It appears that some types of humor are more effective than others in reducing stress. Chen and Martin (2007) found that humor that is affiliative (used to engage or amuse others) or self-enhancing (maintaining a humorous perspective in the face of adversity) is related to better mental health. In contrast, coping through humor that is self-defeating (used at one's own expense) or aggressive (criticizing or ridiculing others) is related to poorer mental health. Likewise, using a lot of self-defeating humor and

very little self-enhancing or affiliative humor is associated with increased depression (Frewen et al., 2008).

How does humor help reduce the effects of stress and promote wellness? Several explanations have been proposed (see **Figure 4.7**). One possibility is that humor affects *appraisals* of stressful events. Jokes can help people put a less-threatening spin on their trials and tribulations. Kuiper, Martin, and Olinger (1993) demonstrated that students who used coping humor were able to appraise a stressful exam as a positive challenge, which in turn lowered their perceived stress levels.

Another possibility is that humor increases the experience of *positive emotions*. In a study of laughter in the workplace, participants who practiced laughing 15 minutes a day for 3 weeks showed significant increases in positive emotions, even 90 days after the study was over (Beckman, Regier, & Young, 2007). As we discussed in Chapter 3, positive emotions can help people bounce back from stressful events (Tugade, 2011). A study comparing types of constructive coping found that strategies that increased positive emotions were most strongly associated with well-being (Shiota, 2006).

Yet another hypothesis is that a good sense of humor buffers the effects of stress by facilitating positive social interactions, which promote social support (Martin, 2002). In a study of Vietnam prisoners of war, Henman (2001) found that using humor to build connections "contributed to the survival and resilience of these men" (p. 83).

Figure 4.7

Possible explanations for the link between humor and wellness. Research suggests that a good sense of humor buffers the effects of stress and promotes wellness. Four hypothesized explanations for the link between humor and wellness are outlined in the middle column of this diagram. As you can see, humor may have a variety of beneficial effects

off the mark.com   by Mark Parisi

I CAN DEAL WITH IT... I'VE BEEN EATEN BY A SNAKE, BUT I'LL JUST GO ON WITH MY LIFE... I'M OKAY!

LEWIS TESTS THE LIMITS OF POSITIVE THINKING.

Finally, Lefcourt and colleagues (1995) argue that high-humor people may benefit from not taking themselves as seriously as low-humor people do. As they put it, "If persons do not regard themselves too seriously and do not have an inflated sense of self-importance, then defeats, embarrassments, and even tragedies should have less pervasive emotional consequences for them" (p. 375). Thus, humor is a rather versatile coping strategy that may have many benefits.

Positive Reinterpretation

When you are feeling overwhelmed by life's difficulties, you might try the commonsense strategy of recognizing that "things could be worse." No matter how terrible your problems seem, you probably know someone who has even bigger troubles. That is not to say that you should derive satisfaction from others' misfortune, but rather that comparing your own plight with others' even tougher struggles can help you put your problems in perspective. Research suggests that this strategy of making positive comparisons with others is a common coping mechanism that can result in improved mood and self-esteem (Wills & Sandy, 2001). Moreover, this strategy does not depend on knowing others who are clearly worse off. You can simply imagine yourself in a similar situation with an even worse outcome (example: two broken legs after a horseback-riding accident instead of just one). One healthy aspect of

positive reinterpretation is that it can facilitate calming reappraisals of stress without the necessity of distorting reality. Over time this perspective can decrease the stress of the situation (Aldwin, 2007).

Another way to engage in positive reinterpretation is to search for something good in a bad experience. Distressing though they may be, many setbacks have positive elements. After experiencing divorces, illnesses, layoffs, and the like, many people remark that, "I came out of the experience better than I went in," or "I grew as a person." Studies of victims of natural disasters, heart attacks, and bereavement have found an association between this type of *benefit finding* under duress and relatively sound psychological and physical health (Lechner, Tennen & Affleck, 2009; Nolen-Hoeksema & Davis, 2005). Researchers have begun to examine benefit finding as a form of appraisal-focused coping that may help soldiers adjust to the challenges of combat (Wood et al., 2012). Indeed, Wood and colleagues (2011) tested almost 2000 soldiers who were deployed to Iraq and learned that benefit finding was related to lower levels of PTSD and depression.

Of course, the positive aspects of a traumatic experience or a personal setback may be easy to see after the stressful event is behind you. The challenge is to recognize these positive aspects while you are still struggling with the event, so that it becomes less stressful.

Log on to CourseMate at www.cengagebrain.com to watch this video.

© Cengage Learning 2015

© Cengage Learning 2015

Annette Rutues is a single mother of three who is battling cancer and homelessness. She is an exceptional example of how recognizing positive aspects in life can help one overcome adversity and foster resilience. In this Reel Research video, Ann Masten, developmental psychologist at the University of Minnesota, conducts experiments with Annette's 11-year-old son, Andrew, and explains how she measures resilience.

The purpose of Masten's research is to determine *resilience,* a person's ability to recover and often prosper following some consequential life event. To determine resilience, Masten measures both adversity experienced and success in overcoming adversity. Even though the Rutues family is in a particularly difficult situation, the children thrive socially and academically because they have a protective, competent, and attentive parent to guide them. Both of Annette's older children participate in extracurricular activities, like sports and playing the saxophone, while maintaining strong GPAs. Using the Rutues family as an example of resilience, Masten and her researchers conducted an array of interactive experiments

with Andrew. His actions demonstrate resilience through an ability to adapt, be attentive, and follow instructions—all aspects of effortful control. Masten credits much of Andrew's success to the quality of parenting Annette gives her children. In her research, Masten found that resilience is predictive of overall life adjustment and academic performance.

Watch the *Resilience in Children* video to learn more about Masten's research. Delve even deeper by responding to the following discussion questions.

DISCUSSION QUESTIONS

1. What qualities does Andrew possess that are essential to overcoming adversity? How might these qualities apply to academic performance?

2. Summarize the tasks the experimenter and Andrew conducted in the demonstration. What other tasks would you create to study effortful control?

3. What protective factors does Masten describe as important for parents and caregivers to provide in any situation?

PROBLEM-FOCUSED CONSTRUCTIVE COPING

LEARNING OBJECTIVES

- List and describe four steps in systematic problem solving.
- Discuss the adaptive value of seeking help as a coping strategy.

- Describe how people's time orientation might influence their time management.

Problem-focused coping includes efforts to remedy or conquer the stress-producing problem itself. This type of coping is associated with positive outcomes such as emotional

growth in times of stress (Karlsen, Dybdahl, & Vitterso, 2006). In this section, we'll discuss systematic problem solving, the importance of seeking help, and time management.

Using Systematic Problem Solving

In dealing with life's problems, the most obvious (and often most effective) course of action is to tackle them head on. In fact, problem solving has been linked to better psychological adjustment, lower levels of depression, reduced alcohol use, and fewer health complaints (Heppner & Lee, 2005). Obviously, people vary in their problem-solving skills. However, evidence suggests that these skills can be enhanced through training (Heppner & Lee, 2005). With this thought in mind, we will sketch a general outline of how to engage in more systematic problem solving. The plan described here is a synthesis of observations by various experts, especially Mahoney (1979), Miller (1978), and Chang and Kelly (1993).

Clarify the Problem

You can't tackle a problem if you're not sure what it is. Therefore, the first step in any systematic problem-solving effort is to clarify the nature of the problem. Sometimes the problem will be all too obvious. At other times the source of trouble may be quite difficult to pin down. In any case, you need to arrive at a specific concrete definition of your problem.

Two common tendencies typically hinder people's efforts to get a clear picture of their problems. First, people often describe their problems in vague generalities ("My life isn't going anywhere" or "I never have enough time"). Second, they tend to focus too much on negative feelings, thereby confusing the consequences of problems ("I'm so depressed all the time" or "I'm so nervous I can't concentrate") with the problems themselves ("I don't have any friends at my new school" or "I have taken on more responsibilities that I can realistically handle").

Generate Alternative Courses of Action

The second step in systematic problem solving is to generate alternative courses of action. Notice that we did not call these alternative *solutions*. Many problems do not have a readily available solution that will completely resolve the situation. If you think in terms of searching for complete solutions, you may prevent yourself from considering many worthwhile courses of action. Instead, it is more realistic to search for alternatives that may produce some kind of improvement in your situation.

Besides avoiding the tendency to insist on solutions, you need to avoid the temptation to go with the first alternative that comes to mind. Many people are a little trigger-happy. They thoughtlessly try to follow through on the first response that occurs to them. Various lines of evidence suggest that it is wiser to engage in brainstorming about a problem. **Brainstorming is generating as many ideas as possible while withholding criticism and evaluation.** In other words, you generate alternatives without paying any attention to their practicality. This approach facilitates creative expression of ideas and can lead to more alternative courses of action to choose from.

Evaluate Your Alternatives and Select a Course of Action

Once you generate as many alternatives as you can, you need to start evaluating the possibilities. There are no simple criteria for judging the relative merits of your alternatives. However, you will probably want to address three general issues. First, ask yourself whether each alternative is realistic. In other words, what is the probability that you can successfully execute the intended course of action? Try to think of any obstacles you may have failed to anticipate. In making this assessment, it is important to try to avoid both foolish optimism and unnecessary pessimism.

Second, consider any costs or risks associated with each alternative. Sometimes the "solution" to a problem can be worse than the problem itself. Assuming you can successfully implement your intended course of action, what are the possible negative consequences? Third, compare the desirability of the probable outcomes of each alternative. In making your decision, you have to ask yourself, "What is important to me? Which outcomes do I value the most?" Through careful evaluation, you can select the best course of action.

Take Action While Maintaining Flexibility

You can plan your course of action as thoughtfully and intentionally as possible, but no plan works if you don't follow through and implement it. In so doing, try to maintain flexibility. Do not get locked into a particular plan. Few choices are truly irreversible. You need to monitor results closely and be willing to revise your strategy.

In evaluating your course of action, try to avoid the simplistic success/failure dichotomy. You should look for improvement of any kind. If your plan doesn't work out too well, consider whether it was undermined by any circumstances that you could not have anticipated. Finally, remember that you can learn from your failures. Even if things did not work out, you may now have new information that will facilitate a new attack on the problem.

Learn More Online

Mind Tools

This site offers practical techniques to help people deal with the world more efficiently and effectively. It houses useful information on several of the topics discussed in this chapter, including stress management, time management, and effective problem solving.

Seeking Help

In Chapter 3, we saw that social support is a powerful force that helps buffer the deleterious effects of stress and has positive effects of its own (Taylor, 2011a; Uchino & Birmingham, 2011). In trying to tackle problems directly, it pays to keep in mind the value of seeking aid from friends, family, co-workers, and neighbors. So far, we have discussed social support as if it were a stable, external resource available to different people in varying degrees. In reality, social support fluctuates over time and evolves out of one's interactions with others. Some people have more support than others because they have personal characteristics that attract more support or because they make more effort to seek support.

Juanmonino/E+/Getty Images

Although the benefits of social support on mental and physical health are well documented, there are instances when the presence of friends or family is not experienced as supportive. Taylor (2011a) notes that friends can sometimes increase physiological reactivity to stress and increase evaluation apprehension. Further, there might be instances where social support networks are intrusive or give poor advice or when the help offered doesn't match the need. Finally, merely having to ask for help might undermine one's sense of self, thus increasing one's stress.

Interestingly, cultural factors, often overlooked by researchers, seem to play an important role in what individuals see as problems and how they solve them. This is especially true with regard to who seeks social support (Taylor, 2011b). Taylor and colleagues (2004) found that Asians and Asian Americans are less likely to seek social support in times of stress than European Americans are. When examined closely, this difference appears to be rooted in cultural concerns about relationships. That is, individuals from cultures high in collectivism (discussed in Chapter 6) don't want to risk straining relationships or disrupting group harmony by calling on others for help in times of stress (Kim et al., 2006). When using social support for coping, Asian Americans tend to benefit more from support that does not involve disclosure of personal distress—that is, support that doesn't emotionally burden the other person (Kim, Sherman, & Taylor, 2008). Of course, broad *similarities* exist in how people from different cultures react to stress. For example, individuals from both collectivistic and individualistic cultures view receiving comfort as an effective coping strategy. There appear to be cultural differences, however, in actively *seeking* that help (Mortenson, 2006). Given that social support is such an important resource, researchers will no doubt continue to examine it within a cultural context.

Improving Time Management

Talk to the average person and you will discover that many of the stressors of modern life result from a lack of time. Individuals vary in their time perspectives. Some people are *future oriented*, able to see the consequences of immediate behavior for future goals, whereas others are *present oriented*, focused on immediate events and not worried about consequences. These orientations influence how people manage their time and meet their time-related commitments. Future-oriented individuals, for example, are less likely to procrastinate and are more reliable in meeting their commitments (Harber, Zimbardo, & Boyd, 2003). Regardless of orientation, most people could benefit from more effectively managing their time. Because it is such a crucial coping strategy, we devote the entire application at the end of this chapter to time management.

EMOTION-FOCUSED CONSTRUCTIVE COPING

LEARNING OBJECTIVES

- Clarify the nature and value of emotional intelligence.
- Analyze the adaptive value of expressing emotions.
- Discuss the importance of managing hostility and forgiving others' transgressions.
- Understand how exercise can foster improved emotional functioning.
- Summarize the evidence on the effects of meditation and relaxation.

Let's be realistic: There are going to be occasions when appraisal-focused coping and problem-focused coping are not successful in warding off emotional turmoil. Some problems are too serious to be whittled down much by reappraisal, and others simply can't be "solved." Moreover, even well-executed coping strategies may take time to work before emotional tensions begin to subside. Because evidence suggests that it is helpful to recognize and control one's emotions when dealing with stress (Stanton, 2011), we will discuss a variety of coping abilities and strategies that relate mainly to the regulation of emotions.

Enhancing Emotional Intelligence

According to some theorists, *emotional intelligence* is the key to being resilient in the face of stress. The concept of emotional intelligence was originally formulated by Peter Salovey and John Mayer (1990). **Emotional intelligence consists of the ability to perceive and express emotion, use emotions to facilitate thought, understand and reason with emotion, and regulate emotion.** Emotional intelligence includes four essential components (Mayer, Salovey, & Caruso, 2008). First, people need to be able to accurately perceive emotions in themselves and in others and to have the ability to express their own emotions effectively. Second, people need to be aware of how their emotions shape their thinking, decision making, and coping with stress. Third, people need to be able to understand and analyze their emotions, which may often be complex and contradictory. Fourth, people need to be able to regulate their emotions so that they can dampen negative emotions and make effective use of positive ones.

Researchers have developed several tests to measure the concept of emotional intelligence. The test that has the strongest empirical foundation is the Mayer-Salovey-Caruso Emotional Intelligence Test (2002). The authors have strived to make this test a performance-based measure of the ability to deal effectively with emotions rather than a measure of personality or temperament. Results suggest that they have made considerable progress toward this goal, as evidenced by the scale's ability to predict intelligent management of emotions in real-world situations (Mayer et al., 2001). It has been found to reliably predict the quality of individuals' social interactions (Lopes et al., 2004), leadership effectiveness (Antoniou & Cooper, 2005), and mental and physical health (Martins, Ramalho, & Morin, 2010; Schutte et al., 2007).

Emotional intelligence has been explored in relation to coping. Pashang and Singh (2008) found that those high in emotional intelligence were more likely to use problem-solving strategies to deal with anxiety, whereas those with lower levels used more distraction and denial. Low emotional intelligence has also been linked to increased worry and avoidance (Matthews et al., 2006). At work, low emotional intelligence is related to increased burnout (Xie, 2011). Because this construct appears to be important for general well-being, investigators are exploring ways to cultivate emotional intelligence in classrooms, workplaces, and counseling settings. One study found that positive emotional expression can lead to an increase in emotional intelligence (Wing, Schutte, & Byrne, 2006). That leads us to our next topic.

Expressing Emotions

Try as you might to redefine or resolve stressful situations, you no doubt will still go through times when you feel wired with stress-induced tension. When this happens, there's merit in the commonsense notion that you should try to release the emotions welling up inside. Why? Because the physiological arousal that accompanies emotions can become problematic. For example, research suggests that people who inhibit the expression of anger and other emotions are somewhat more likely than other people to have elevated blood pressure (Jorgensen et al., 1996). Moreover, research suggests that efforts to actively sup-

RECOMMENDED reading

Emotional Intelligence: Why It Can Matter More Than IQ

by Daniel Goleman (Bantam Books, 2006)

It's great to see a book like this make the bestseller lists. It is a serious, scholarly, yet readable analysis of how emotional functioning is important in everyday life. Daniel Goleman is a psychologist and journalist who writes about the behavioral sciences for the *New York Times*. In this book, he synthesizes the research of many investigators as he argues that emotional intelligence may be more important to success than high IQ. The concept of emotional intelligence, as originally developed by Peter Salovey and John Mayer (1990), languished in relative obscurity until Goleman's book attracted attention. He views emotional intelligence more broadly than Salovey and Mayer, who focused primarily on people's ability to access, monitor, and express their own emotions and to interpret and understand others' emotions. Goleman includes all of these ingredients but adds social poise and skill, strong motivation and persistence, and some desirable personality traits, such as optimism and conscientiousness.

One can argue that Goleman's concept of emotional intelligence is too much of a hodgepodge of traits to be measureable or meaningful, but his broad view yields a wide-ranging book that discusses innumerable examples of how social finesse and emotional sensitivity can foster career success, marital satisfaction, and physical and mental health. In the course of this analysis, Goleman discusses research on a diverse array of topics in an exceptionally lucid manner. More recently, Goleman has applied this theory to the area of leadership in *Leadership: The Power of Emotional Intelligence* (2011).

Log on to CourseMate at www.cengagebrain.com *for descriptions of other recommended books.*

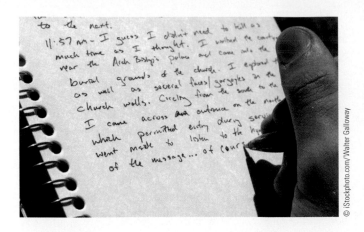

Managing Hostility and Forgiving Others

In 1944, when Eva Mozes was 10 years old, she and her twin sister were subjected to life-threatening experimentation at the Auschwitz concentration camp in Poland during World War II. She and her twin survived, although their parents and older sisters did not. In adulthood, she did something almost unimaginable: she forgave the Nazis, stating that forgiveness gave her "back the power" she lost as a victim (Pope, 2012). One might ask: Why did she choose this route? How did she manage to overcome the anger and hostility related to her early experiences? In fact, researchers have shown that Eva made a good choice, and we'll discuss why.

Scientists have compiled quite a bit of evidence that hostility is bad for you. It is related to increased risk for heart attacks and other types of illness (see Chapter 5). So how can individuals effectively regulate negative emotions that include anger and hostility? The goal of hostility management is not merely to suppress the overt expression of hostility that may continue to seethe beneath the surface, but to actually reduce the frequency and intensity of one's hostile feelings. The first step toward this goal is to learn to quickly recognize one's anger. A variety of strategies can be used to decrease hostility, including positive reinterpretation of annoying events, distraction, and the kind of rational self-talk advocated by Albert Ellis. Efforts to increase empathy and tolerance can also contribute to hostility management, as can forgiveness, which

press emotions result in increased stress and autonomic arousal (Butler et al., 2003; Gross, 2001). A meta-analysis that included over 6,500 participants found that coping by repressing negative feelings is related to increase cardiovascular diseases, especially hypertension (Mund & Mitte, 2012). Please note that such findings do not mean you should act aggressively (a coping strategy of limited value discussed earlier in this chapter). Instead, our focus here is on appropriate, healthy expression of emotions.

James Pennebaker and his colleagues have shown that emotional expression through writing about traumatic events can have beneficial effects (Baddeley & Pennebaker, 2011). For example, in one study of college students, half the subjects were asked to write three essays about their difficulties in adjusting to college. The other half wrote three essays about superficial topics. The participants who wrote about their personal problems and traumas enjoyed better health in the following months than the other subjects did (Pennebaker, Colder, & Sharp, 1990). Additionally, emotional disclosure, or "opening up," is associated with improved mood, more positive self-perceptions, fewer visits to physicians, and enhanced immune functioning (Niederhoffer & Pennebaker, 2005; Smyth & Pennebaker, 2001). It has even been linked to improved academic performance for college students (Lumley & Provenzano, 2003). Smyth and Pennebaker (1999) assert that "when people put their emotional upheavals into words, their physical and mental health seems to improve markedly." They conclude that "the act of disclosure itself is a powerful therapeutic agent" (p. 70).

The research on emotional disclosure indicates that both writing and talking about important personal issues can be beneficial (Smyth, Pennebaker, & Arigo, 2012). Thus, if you can find a good listener, it may be wise to let your secret fears, misgivings, and suspicions spill out in a candid conversation. Of course, confiding in others about one's problems can be awkward and difficult. Therein lies the beauty and appeal of the writing approach, which can be kept private. **Figure 4.8** summarizes some guidelines for writing about personal issues and trauma that should make this coping strategy more effective.

INSTRUCTIONS FOR WRITING ABOUT PERSONAL EXPERIENCES

- Plan to spend 20 minutes or so writing each day.

- Try to write for three consecutive days or more.

- Write about your very deepest thoughts and feelings about any stressful or emotionally disturbing experiences going on in your life at the moment, or traumatic events from the past.

- You may want to discuss how your topic is related to your relationships with others, such as parents, friends, or intimate others.

- You may want to analyze how your topic relates to who you are now or who you would like to be.

- Write spontaneously, you do not need to worry about spelling or grammar.

- Keep in mind that you are only writing for yourself; this is a private endeavor.

Figure 4.8

Using writing about emotional experiences as a coping strategy. Many studies have shown that writing about traumatic experiences and sensitive issues can have beneficial effects on mental and physical health. These guidelines can help you to use this coping strategy. (Based on Gortner, Rude, & Pennebaker, 2006) has become the focus of a contemporary line of research in psychology.

People tend to experience hostility and other negative emotions when they feel "wronged"—that is, when they believe that the actions of another person were harmful, immoral, or unjust. People's natural inclination is either to seek revenge or to avoid further contact with the offender (McCullough & Witvliet, 2005). Although there is debate among researchers about the exact definition, *forgiveness* **involves counteracting the natural tendencies to seek vengeance or avoid an offender, thereby releasing this person from further liability for his or her transgression.** Research suggests that forgiving is an effective emotion-focused coping strategy that is associated with better adjustment and well-being (Worthington, Soth-McNett, & Moreno, 2007). For example, in one study of divorced or permanently separated women, the extent to which the women had forgiven their former husbands was positively related to several measures of well-being and was inversely related to measures of anxiety and depression (McCullough, 2001). In another study, when participants were instructed to think actively about a grudge they had nursed and to think about forgiving it, the forgiving thoughts were associated with more positive emotions and reduced physiological arousal (Witvliet, Ludwig, & Vander Laan, 2001). Forgiveness not only decreases one's own psychological distress, it also increases one's empathy and positive regard for the offending person (Riek & Mania, 2012; Williamson & Gonzales, 2007).

In contrast, research shows that vengefulness is correlated with more rumination and negative emotion and with lower levels of life satisfaction (McCullough et al., 2001). Further, researchers have identified certain personality characteristics such as narcissistic entitlement as barriers to forgiveness (Exline et al., 2004). Interestingly, researchers are beginning to explore some of the potential negative aspects of forgiveness (McNulty, 2011). For instance, could forgiveness relieve an offender of his guilt to the extent that he is more likely to offend again? Although there is more work to be done in this area, findings to date suggest that it may be healthy for people to learn to forgive others more readily.

Exercising

There are numerous benefits to physical activity, both preventative and therapeutic. In Chapter 5 you will learn about the effects of exercise on health, so here we will limit our discussion to exercise as an emotion-focused coping strategy. Physical exercise is a healthy way to deal with overwhelming emotions related to stress (Edenfield & Blumenthal, 2011). In fact, one study found that people who participated in a 2-month program of regular exercise showed an increase in emotional control and a decrease in emotional distress (Oaten & Cheng, 2006). Even 20-minute sessions of regular aerobic exercise can lead to improved psychological health (Rendi et al., 2008). Exercise is an ideal coping strategy because it provides multiple coping-related benefits: an outlet for frustration, a distraction from the stressor, and benefits to physical and psychological health (Sapolsky, 2004). Regular exercise is related to decreases in depression, anxiety, and hostility, as well as increases in self-esteem and energy (Puetz, O'Connor, & Dishman, 2006; Spencer, 1990). Likewise, psychiatric patients showed significant increases in psychological well-being after an 8- to 12-week voluntary exercise intervention (Tetlie et al., 2008).

Of course, these findings must be interpreted with caution. Although it appears likely that exercise increases quality of life, it could be that those with a higher quality of life are more likely to exercise (de Geus & Stubbe, 2007). Even with this caveat, however, exercise is an effective coping strategy. In fact, psychologists are starting to wonder why more mental health professionals don't recommend it more often (Walsh, 2011).

Sapolosky (2004) asserts that to get maximal benefits from physical exercise, you should consider three rules.

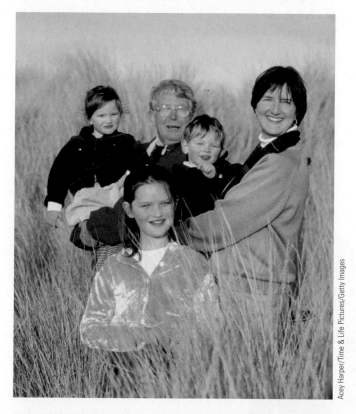

In September 1994, Reg and Maggie Green were vacationing in Italy when their 7-year-old son, Nicholas, was shot and killed during a highway robbery. In an act of forgiveness that stunned Europe, the Greens chose to donate their son's organs, which went to seven Italians. The Greens, shown here 5 years after the incident, have weathered their horrific loss better than most, perhaps in part because of their willingness to forgive.

Acey Harper/Time & Life Pictures/Getty Images

First, you should *want* to exercise. Forcing yourself to do something you don't want to do, even if that something is good for you, can be stressful in and of itself. Second, you should engage in aerobic exercise (such as jogging, swimming, or bicycling) because most of the positive effects come from this type of exercise. Third, you should exercise on a regular basis. Of course, regular exercise requires discipline and self-control. One of the main predictors of exercise maintenance is self-efficacy, a belief that you can do it (Sullum, Clark, & King, 2000). If you are not currently as physically active as you would like, perhaps you could use the self-modification techniques covered in the Application section at the end of Chapter 3 to improve your exercise habits. Advice on devising an effective exercise program can also be found in Chapter 5.

As with other types of exercise, there is mounting evidence that yoga has psychological benefits (Novotney, 2009). Yoga is a specific kind of exercise that typically includes meditation and relaxation, issues we consider next.

Using Meditation and Relaxation

Recent years have seen an increased interest in meditation as a method for regulating negative emotions caused by stress. *Meditation* **refers to a family of mental exercises in which a conscious attempt is made to focus attention in a nonanalytical way** There are many approaches to meditation. In the United States, the most widely practiced approaches are those associated with yoga, Zen, transcendental meditation (TM), and mindfulness. Relaxation is one of the benefits of meditation, although meditation isn't the only way to achieve relaxation.

Advocates of meditation claim that it can improve learning, energy level, work productivity, physical health, mental health, and general happiness, while reducing tension and anxiety caused by stress (Shapiro, Schwartz, & Santerre, 2005). These are not exactly humble claims. Let's examine the scientific evidence on meditation.

What are the immediate *physical* effects of going into a meditative state? Most studies find decreases in participants' heart rate, respiration rate, oxygen consumption, and carbon dioxide elimination (Whitehouse, Orne, & Orne, 2007). Meditation has also been linked to improvements in blood pressure (Barnes, Treiber, & Davis, 2001). Taken together, these physical changes suggest that meditation can lead to a potentially beneficial physiological state characterized by relaxation and suppression of arousal (Travis, 2001).

What about the long-term *psychological* benefits that have been claimed for meditation? Research suggests that meditation may have some value in reducing the effects of stress (Walsh, 2011). In particular, regular meditation is associated with lower levels of some stress hormones (Infante et al., 2001). Research also suggests that meditative exercises can improve mental health by reducing anxiety and depression (Hofmann et al., 2010). Other studies report that meditation may have beneficial effects on self-esteem (Emavardhana & Tori, 1997), mood and one's sense of control (Easterlin & Cardena, 1999), happiness (Smith, Compton, & West, 1995), and overall well-being (Reibel et al., 2001). Waelde and colleagues (2008) studied a meditation intervention in mental health workers in New Orleans following Hurricane Katrina. Their participants attended a 4-hour meditation workshop that included instructions on guided practice, breathing, mantra repetition, and letting go of intrusive thoughts. Then they practiced meditation at home 6 days a week for 8 weeks. The results showed that the meditation intervention led to reductions in PTSD symptoms and anxiety, and these improvements were positively correlated with the amount of daily meditation practiced.

Researchers are just beginning to explore how meditation works to enhance well-being (see Chapter 16). It appears that the effects of meditation might be due in part to the increase in positive emotions brought on by meditative techniques (Garland et al., 2010). In fact, Garland and colleagues (2011) suggest that meditation and positive reappraisal of negative events mutually support each other, creating an "upward spiral" of mental health.

At first glance these results are impressive, but they need to be viewed with some caution. Critics wonder whether placebo effects, sampling bias, and other methodological problems may contribute to some of the reported benefits of meditation (Sedlmeier et al., 2012; Shapiro et al., 2005). In addition, at least some of these beneficial effects may be just as attainable through other mental focusing procedures, such as systematic relaxation (Shapiro, 1984; Walsh, 2011).

Indeed, ample evidence suggests that relaxation procedures can soothe emotional turmoil and reduce stress-induced physiological arousal (Smyth et al., 2001). And a recent controlled experiment comparing meditation and relaxation found that they decreased distress and increased positive moods equally well (Jain et al., 2007). There are a number of worthwhile approaches to achieving beneficial relaxation. For example, relaxation can be achieved by listening to soothing music. However, its stress reducing properties depend on the type of music. One study found that college

ollyy/Shutterstock.com

"I'm learning how to relax, doctor —
but I want to relax *better* and *faster!*
I want to be on the cutting edge of relaxation!"

students who listened to classical or self-selected relaxing music experienced a greater increase in relaxation, fewer negative emotions, and less psychological arousal in response to stress than those who listened to heavy metal music (Labbé et al., 2007) (see **Figure 4.9**). Let's discuss another approach to relaxation that is so simple that virtually anyone can learn to use it.

After studying various approaches to meditation, Herbert Benson, a Harvard Medical School cardiologist, con-

Figure 4.9

Change in relaxation as a function of music genre. Studies show that relaxation can be achieved by listening to soothing music. Labbé and colleagues (2007) found that college students who listened to classical or self-selected relaxing music experienced a greater increase in relaxation than those who listened to heavy metal music.

Source: From Benson, H., & Klipper, M. Z. (1975, 1988). *The relaxation response.* New York: Morrow.

cluded that elaborate religious rituals and beliefs are not necessary for someone to profit from meditation. He also concluded that what makes meditation beneficial is the relaxation it induces. After "demystifying" meditation, Benson (1975) set out to devise a simple, nonreligious procedure that could provide similar benefits. He calls his procedure the "relaxation response." To practice this response, you should sit comfortably with closed eyes and relaxed muscles. Breathe in through your nose and as you breath out say the word "one" to yourself. Continue for 10 to 20 minutes. For full benefit, the response should be practiced daily. According to Benson, four factors are critical to effective practice of the relaxation response:

1. *A quiet environment.* It is easiest to induce a relaxation response in a distraction-free environment. After you become skilled at the relaxation response, you may be able to accomplish it in a crowded subway. Initially, however, you should practice it in a quiet, calm place.

2. *A mental device.* To shift attention inward and keep it there, you need to focus it on a constant stimulus, such as a sound or word that you recite over and over. You may also choose to gaze fixedly at a bland object, such as a vase. Whatever the case, you need to focus your attention on something.

3. *A passive attitude.* It is important not to get upset when your attention strays to distracting thoughts. You must realize that such distractions are inevitable. Whenever your mind wanders from your focus, calmly redirect attention to your mental device.

4. *A comfortable position.* Reasonable body comfort is essential in order to avoid a major source of potential distraction. Simply sitting up straight works well for most people. Some people can practice the relaxation response lying down, but for most people such a position is too conducive to sleep.

Spirituality

Experts estimate that approximately 90% of people around the globe identify with a religion or spiritual practice (Koenig, 2004). People generally report that religious beliefs bring a sense of comfort in times of stress. Harold Koenig (2010), a medical doctor and leading researcher in the field, argues that spirituality is a means of coping with stress. Often linked with adaptive coping techniques such as social support, reappraisals, forgiveness, and meditation, spiritual practices are related to every part of the coping process (Pargament, 2011). Like other strategies, spirituality can be viewed as appraisal, problem, or emotion focused, depending on the goal. Regardless of its goal,

Koenig and his colleagues have found spiritual involvement to be linked to better physical and mental health.

Specifically, spirituality has been linked to lowered suicide rates, reduced substance abuse, lowered anxiety, and greater optimism. Physically, spirituality is associated with enhanced immune functioning, lower blood pressure, reduced heart disease, and better general health behaviors (Koenig, 2004). Evidence further suggests that religiosity is related to self-control, an important characteristic for both physical and mental health. In an innovative study, Rounding and colleagues (2012) found that psychology students who were primed to think about religion showed more self-control on a subsequent task than those who were not (see **Figure 4.10**).

Researchers note that the relationship between spirituality and well-being is more complex that it might appear (for a related discussion, see Chapter 16), in that it can be counterproductive as a stress reducer in some instances. Religious involvement that focuses on punishment or guilt (as opposed to positive themes of love and forgiveness) tends to be detrimental to mental health (Walsh, 2011). Further, struggling with one's spiritual beliefs can induce stress (Pargament, 2011). Still, the evidence for the positive effects of spirituality are so strong that researchers recommend that psychologists and physicians alike take into account the "spiritual histories" of their patients when planning therapeutic treatment (Koenig, 2004).

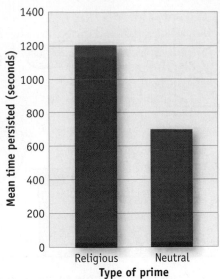

Photo by Robin Lin © CURE Media Group

Harold Koenig

Figure 4.10

Self-control as a function of religious priming. Evidence suggests that spirituality is related to self-control, an important characteristic for coping with stress. Rounding and colleagues (2012) assessed self-control by measuring how long participants persisted in an impossible task, in this case solving impossible puzzles. The researchers found that psychology students who were primed to think about religion showed more self-control on the task than did those who received a neutral prime.

Source: Rounding, K., Lee, A., Jacobson, J. A., & Ji, L. (2012). Religion replenishes self-control. *Psychological Science, 23*(6), 635–642.

Now that we have looked at numerous constructive coping tactics, in the following Application we turn to one of the most common sources of stress—poor time management—and examine ways to use time more effectively.

Application

USING TIME MORE EFFECTIVELY

LEARNING OBJECTIVES

- Explain five common causes of wasted time.
- Identify the causes and consequences of procrastination.
- Summarize advice on managing time effectively.

Answer the following "yes" or "no."

_____ **1.** Do you constantly feel that you have too much to do and too little time in which to do it?

_____ **2.** Do you feel overwhelmed by your responsibilities at work, at school, and at home?

_____ **3.** Do you feel like you're always rushing around, trying to meet an impossible schedule?

_____ **4.** Do you often procrastinate on school or work assignments?

_____ **5.** Do you often jump around from one task to another?

If you answered yes to the majority of these questions, you're struggling with time pressure, a huge source of stress in modern life. You can estimate how well you manage time by responding to the brief questionnaire in **Figure 4.11**. If the results suggest that your time is out of your control, you may be able to make your life less stressful by learning sound time-management strategies.

R. Alec Mackenzie (1997), a prominent time-management researcher, points out that time is a nonrenewable resource. It can't be stockpiled like money, food, or other precious resources. You can't turn back the clock.

Alexander Santander/Shutterstock.com

HOW WELL DO YOU MANAGE YOUR TIME?

Listed below are ten statements that reflect generally accepted principles of good time management. Answer these items by circling the response most characteristic of how you perform your job. Please be honest. No one will know your answers except you.

1. Each day I set aside a small amount of time for planning and thinking about my job.
   0. Almost never 1. Sometimes 2. Often 3. Almost always

2. I set specific, written goals and put deadlines on them.
   0. Almost never 1. Sometimes 2. Often 3. Almost always

3. I make a daily "to do list," arrange items in order of importance, and try to get the important items done as soon as possible.
   0. Almost never 1. Sometimes 2. Often 3. Almost always

4. I am aware of the 80/20 rule and use it in doing my job. (The 80/20 rule states that 80 percent of your effectiveness will generally come from achieving only 20 percent of your goals.)
   0. Almost never 1. Sometimes 2. Often 3. Almost always

5. I keep a loose schedule to allow for crises and the unexpected.
   0. Almost never 1. Sometimes 2. Often 3. Almost always

6. I delegate everything I can to others.
   0. Almost never 1. Sometimes 2. Often 3. Almost always

7. I try to handle each piece of paper only once.
   0. Almost never 1. Sometimes 2. Often 3. Almost always

8. I eat a light lunch so I don't get sleepy in the afternoon.
   0. Almost never 1. Sometimes 2. Often 3. Almost always

9. I make an active effort to keep common interruptions (visitors, meetings, telephone calls) from continually disrupting my work day.
   0. Almost never 1. Sometimes 2. Often 3. Almost always

10. I am able to say no to others' requests for my time that would prevent my completing important tasks.
    0. Almost never 1. Sometimes 2. Often 3. Almost always

To get your score, give yourself

3 points for each "almost always"
2 points for each "often"
1 point for each "sometimes"
0 points for each "almost never"

Add up your points to get your total score.

If you scored

0–15   Better give some thought to managing your time.
15–20   You're doing OK, but there's room for improvement.
20–25   Very good.
25–30   You cheated!

Figure 4.11

Assessing your time management. The brief questionnaire shown here is designed to evaluate the quality of one's time management. Although it is geared more for working adults than college students, it should allow you to get a rough handle on how well you manage your time.

Source: From Le Boeuf, M. (1980, February). Managing time means managing yourself. *Business Horizons Magazine*, p. 45. Copyright © by the Foundation for the School of Business at Indiana University. Used with permission.

Furthermore, everyone, whether rich or poor, gets an equal share of time—24 hours per day, 7 days a week. Although time is our most equitably distributed resource, some people spend it much more wisely than others. Let's look at some of the ways in which people let time slip through their fingers without accomplishing much.

The Causes of Wasted Time

When people complain about "wasted time," they're usually upset because they haven't accomplished what they really wanted to do with their time. Wasted time is time devoted to unnecessary, unimportant, or unenjoyable activities. There are many reasons people waste time on such activities.

Inability to set or stick to priorities. Time consultant Alan Lakein (1996) emphasizes that it's often tempting to deal with routine, trivial tasks ahead of larger and more difficult tasks. Thus, students (or professors for that matter) working on a major paper often check Facebook, fold the laundry, or reorganize their desk instead of concentrating on the paper. Why? Routine tasks are easy, and working on them allows people to rationalize their avoidance of more important tasks. Unfortunately, many of us spend too much time on trivial pursuits, leaving our more important tasks undone.

Inability to say no. Other people are constantly making demands on our time. They want us to exchange gossip in the hallway, go out to dinner on Friday night, cover their hours at work, help with a project, listen to their sales pitch on the phone, join a committee, or coach Little League. Clearly, we can't do everything that everyone wants us to. However, some people just can't say no to others' requests for their time. Such people end up fulfilling others' priorities instead of their own. Thus, McDougle (1987) concludes, "Perhaps the most successful way to prevent yourself from wasting time is by saying *no*" (p. 112).

Inability to delegate responsibility. Some tasks should be delegated to others—assistants, subordinates, fellow committee members, partners, spouses, children, and so on. However, many people have difficulty delegating work. Barriers to delegation include unwillingness to give up any control, lack of confidence in subordinates, fear of being disliked, the need to feel needed, and the attitude that "I can do it better myself" (Mitchell, 1987). The problem, of course, is that people who can't delegate waste a lot of time on trivial work or others' work.

Inability to throw things away. Some people are pack rats who can't throw anything into the wastebasket. Their desks are cluttered with piles of mail, newspapers, magazines, reports, and books. Their filing cabinets overflow with old class notes or ancient memos. At home, their kitchen drawers bulge with rarely used utensils and their closets bulge with old clothes that are never worn. Pack rats lose time looking for things that have disappeared among all the chaos and end up reshuffling the same paper, rereading the same mail, resorting the same files, and so on. According to Mackenzie (1997), they would be better off if they made more use of their wastebaskets.

Blend Images/Shutterstock.com

Inability to avoid interruptions. Our lives are full of interruptions. Friends stop by when we are studying, coworkers want to chat while we are working under deadlines, and family emergencies arise whether we have time to deal with them or not. In addition, phone calls, texts, and emails can interrupt our workflow. As a result, people must protect blocks of uninterrupted time to accomplish their goals. Turning off your phone and shutting your door can go along way toward protecting your time. Of course, researchers suggest allowing for flexibility for unexpected events as you set your schedule (Pandey et al., 2011).

Inability to accept anything less than perfection. To maximize the use of one's time, one should avoid perfectionism (Pandey et al., 2011). High standards are admirable, but some people have difficulty finishing projects because they expect their work to be flawless. They can't let go. They dwell on minor problems and keep making microscopic changes in their papers, projects, and proposals. They are caught in what Emanuel (1987) calls the "paralysis of perfection." They end up spinning their wheels, redoing the same work over and over instead of moving on to the next task. Perfectionism can be troublesome in many ways. For example, it is associated with increased fatigue (Dittner, Rimes, & Thorpe, 2011). In a review of the literature on perfectionism, Leonard and Harvey (2008) report that it has been linked to depression, anxiety, job stress, substance abuse, eating disorders, interpersonal conflict, and procrastination, which we turn to next.

The Problem of Procrastination

Procrastination **is the tendency to delay tackling tasks until the last minute.** Almost everyone procrastinates on occasion. For example, 70%–90% of college students procrastinate before beginning academic assignments (Knaus, 2000). However, research suggests that about 20% of adults are chronic procrastinators (Ferrari, 2001). Not just a U.S. phenomenon, this trend appears to apply to a number of cultures (Ferrari et al., 2007). Procrastination is more likely when people have to work on aversive tasks or when they are worried about their performance being evaluated (Milgram, Marshevsky, & Sadeh, 1995; Senecal, Lavoie, & Koestner, 1997).

Interestingly, research demonstrates that procrastinators put off enjoyable tasks as well. For instance, one study found that, contrary to commonsense predictions, people procrastinated in redeeming gift certificates that had longer deadlines more than those with shorter deadlines, and thus were less likely to redeem them (Shu & Gneezy, 2010) (see **Figure 4.12**). These researchers also showed that in vacation destination cities, people with unlimited time windows (such as residents) delay visiting desired landmarks.

Figure 4.12

Gift card redemption rates as a function of deadline length.
Research demonstrates that procrastinators will put off enjoyable as well as aversive tasks. For instance, Shu and Gneezy (2010) found that people procrastinated more in redeeming gift certificates that had longer deadlines than they did with shorter deadlines, and thus were less likely to redeem them.

Source: From Shu, S. B., & Gneezy, A. (2010). Procrastination of enjoyable experiences. *Journal of Marketing Research, 47*(5), 933–944.

Why do people procrastinate? In a recent review of the literature Steel (2007) found that procrastination was strongly related to low self-efficacy, low conscientiousness, lack of self-control, poor organization, low achievement motivation, and high distractibility. The type of irrational thinking described by Albert Ellis seems to foster procrastination (Bridges & Roig, 1997), as does a strong fear of failure (Chow, 2011) and excessive perfectionism (Flett, Hewitt, & Martin, 1995; Rice, Richardson, & Clark, 2012).

Other factors besides personality can affect procrastination. Schraw and colleagues (2007) identified six general principles related to academic procrastination, including these three:

1. *Desire to minimize time on a task.* As you know, the modern student is busy—studying, working, socializing, and maintaining a personal life. Time is at a premium. Sometimes delaying as much academic work as possible seems to be a way to safeguard some personal time. As one student reported, "The truth is, I just don't have time *not* to procrastinate. If I did everything the way it could be done, I wouldn't have a life" (Schraw et al., 2007, p. 21).

2. *Desire to optimize efficiency.* Procrastination can be viewed as allowing one to be optimally efficient, concentrating academic work into focused time frames. Students reported that being pressed for time means that there is less opportunity for busywork, boredom, or false starts.

3. *Close proximity to reward.* Students often procrastinate because they are rewarded for it. By putting off academic work until the last minute, students not only get more immediate feedback (the grade), but they also get a sudden release of stress. In this way, procrastination is similar to other thrill-seeking behaviors.

Although these principles seem reasonable and many people rationalize their delaying tactics by claiming that "I work best under pressure" (Ferrari, 1992; Lay, 1995), the empirical evidence suggests otherwise. Studies show that procrastination tends to have a negative impact on the quality of task performance (Ferrari, Johnson, & McCown, 1995). In fact, Britton and Tesser (1991) found that time management was a better predictor of college GPA than SAT scores! Procrastinators may often underestimate how much time will be required to complete a task effectively, or they experience unforeseen delays and then run out of time because they didn't allow any "cushion." Another consideration is that waiting until the last minute may make a task more stressful—and while the release of this built-up stress might be exciting, performance often declines under conditions of high stress (as we saw in Chapter 3). Moreover, work quality may not be the only thing that suffers when people procrastinate. Studies indicate that as a deadline looms, procrastinators tend to experience elevated anxiety and increased health problems (Tice & Baumeister, 1997).

People who struggle with procrastination often impose deadlines and penalties on themselves. This practice can be helpful, but self-imposed deadlines are not as effective as externally imposed ones. Let's discuss some effective ways to manage your time.

Time-Management Techniques

What's the key to better time management? Most people assume that it's increased *efficiency*—that is, learning to perform tasks more quickly. Improved efficiency may help a little, but time-management experts maintain that efficiency is overrated. They emphasize that the key to better time management is increased *effectiveness*—that is, learning to allocate time to your most important tasks. This distinction is captured by a widely quoted slogan in the time-management literature: "Efficiency is doing the job right, while effectiveness is doing the right job." Here are some suggestions for using your time more effectively (based on Lakein, 1996; Mackenzie, 1997; Morgenstern, 2000):

1. *Monitor your use of time.* The first step toward better time management is to monitor your use of time to see where it all goes. Doing so requires keeping a written record of your activities, similar to that shown in **Figure 4.13** on the next page. At the end of each week, you should analyze how your time was allocated. Based on your personal roles and responsibilities, create categories of time use such as studying, child care, housework, commuting, working at the office, working at home, going online, spending time with friends, eating, and sleeping. For each day, add up the hours devoted to each category. Record this information on a summary sheet like that in **Figure 4.14** on page 125. Two weeks of recordkeeping should allow you to draw some conclusions about where your time goes. Your records will help you make informed decisions about reallocating your time. When you begin your time-management program, these records will also give you a baseline for comparison, so that you can see whether your program is working.

2. *Clarify your goals.* You can't wisely allocate your time unless you decide what you want to accomplish. Some people lack goals to guide their time, while others have so many goals it is impossible to meet them all. For short-term goals (such as finishing a term paper or completing a house project) set smaller priorities that will lead to the desired outcome, and stick to them. Be sure they are realistic. For longer-term goals, Lakein (1996) suggests that you ask yourself, "What are my lifetime goals?" Write down all the goals you can think of, even relatively frivolous things like going deep-sea fishing or becoming a wine

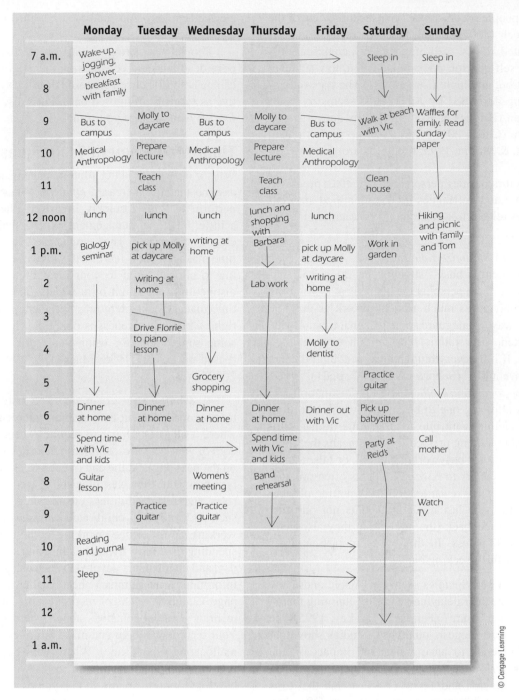

	Monday	Tuesday	Wednesday	Thursday	Friday	Saturday	Sunday
7 a.m.	Wake-up, jogging, shower, breakfast with family					Sleep in	Sleep in
8							
9	Bus to campus	Molly to daycare	Bus to campus	Molly to daycare	Bus to campus	Walk at beach with Vic	Waffles for family. Read Sunday paper
10	Medical Anthropology	Prepare lecture	Medical Anthropology	Prepare lecture	Medical Anthropology		
11		Teach class		Teach class		Clean house	
12 noon	lunch	lunch	lunch	lunch and shopping with Barbara	lunch		Hiking and picnic with family and Tom
1 p.m.	Biology seminar	pick up Molly at daycare	writing at home		pick up Molly at daycare	Work in garden	
2		writing at home		Lab work	writing at home		
3		Drive Florrie to piano lesson					
4					Molly to dentist		
5			Grocery shopping			Practice guitar	
6	Dinner at home	Dinner at home	Dinner at home	Dinner at home	Dinner out with Vic	Pick up babysitter	
7	Spend time with Vic and kids			Spend time with Vic and kids		Party at Reid's	Call mother
8	Guitar lesson		Women's meeting	Band rehearsal			
9		Practice guitar	Practice guitar				Watch TV
10	Reading and journal						
11	Sleep						
12							
1 a.m.							

Figure 4.13

Example of a time log. Experts recommend keeping a detailed record of how you use your time if you are to improve your time management. This example shows the kind of recordkeeping that should be done.

© Cengage Learning

expert. Some of your goals will be in conflict. For instance, you can't become a vice president at your company in Wichita and still move to the West Coast. Thus, the tough part comes next. You have to wrestle with your goal conflicts. Figure out which goals are most important to you, and order them in terms of priority. These priorities should guide you as you plan your activities on a daily, weekly, and monthly basis.

3. *Plan your activities using a schedule.* People resist planning because it takes time, but in the long run planning saves time. Thorough planning is essential to effective time management. At the beginning of each week, you should

TIME USE SUMMARY FORM									
Activity	**Mon.**	**Tues.**	**Wed.**	**Thurs.**	**Fri.**	**Sat.**	**Sun.**	**Total**	**%**
1. Sleeping	8	6	8	6	8	7	9	52	31
2. Eating	2	2	3	2	3	2	3	17	10
3. Commuting	2	2	2	2	2	0	0	10	6
4. Housework	0	1	0	3	0	0	2	6	4
5. In class	4	2	4	2	4	0	0	16	9
6. Part-time job	0	5	0	5	0	3	0	13	8
7. Studying	3	2	4	2	0	4	5	20	12
8. Relaxing	5	4	3	2	7	8	5	34	20
9.									
10.									

© Cengage Learning

Figure 4.14

Time use summary. To analyze where your time goes, you need to review your time log and create a weekly time use summary, like the one shown here. The exact categories to be listed on the left depend on your circumstances and responsibilities.

make a list of short-term goals. This list should be translated into daily "to do" lists of planned activities. To avoid the tendency to put off larger projects, break them into smaller, manageable components, and set deadlines for completing the components. Your planned activities should be allocated to various time slots on a written schedule. Schedule your most important activities into the time periods when you tend to be most energetic and productive.

4. *Protect your prime time.* The best-laid plans can quickly go awry because of interruptions. There isn't any foolproof way to eliminate interruptions, but you may be able to shift most of them into certain time slots while protecting your most productive time. Reply to emails, texts, and phone messages at scheduled times, perhaps once in the morning and once in the later afternoon. The trick is to announce to your family, friends, and co-workers that you're blocking off certain periods of "quiet time" when visitors and phone calls will be turned away. Of course, you also have to block off periods of "available time" when you're ready to deal with everyone's problems.

5. *Increase your efficiency.* Although efficiency is not the key to better time management, it's not irrelevant. Time-management experts do offer some suggestions for improving efficiency, including the following (Klassen, 1987; Schilit, 1987):

- *Handle paper once.* When e-mails, letters, reports, and such cross your desk, they should not be stashed away to be read again and again before you deal with them. Most paperwork can and should be dealt with immediately.

- *Tackle one task at a time.* Jumping from one problem to another is inefficient. As much as possible, stick with a task until it's done. In scheduling your activities, try to allow enough time to complete tasks.

- *Group similar tasks together.* It's a good idea to bunch up small tasks that are similar. This strategy is useful when you're paying bills, replying to e-mails, returning phone calls, and so forth.

- *Make use of your downtime.* Most of us endure a lot of "downtime," waiting in doctors' offices, sitting in needless meetings, or riding on buses and trains. In many of these situations, you may be able to get some of your easier work done—if you think ahead and bring it along.

- *Build in some time to relax.* Everyone needs time to recharge his or her batteries. Taking time to relax and engage in healthy, enjoyable activities can help individuals be more effective when work time rolls around.

It's not an easy skill to learn, but in today's face-paced world, time management is crucial. By following the tips provided here and getting your tasks under control, you can avoid stress down the road.

CHAPTER 4 | Review

KEY IDEAS

THE CONCEPT OF COPING

• Coping involves behavioral efforts to master, reduce, or tolerate the demands created by stress. People cope with stress in many ways, and flexibility is important when choosing a strategy. Coping strategies vary in their adaptive value.

COMMON COPING PATTERNS OF LIMITED VALUE

• Giving up, possibly best understood in terms of learned helplessness, is a common coping pattern that tends to be of limited value. Another is engaging in aggressive behavior. Frequently caused by frustration, aggression tends to be counterproductive because it often creates new sources of stress.

• Indulging oneself is a common coping strategy that is not inherently unhealthy, but it is frequently taken to excess and thus becomes maladaptive. Internet addiction is a relatively new form of self-indulgence. Blaming yourself with negative self-talk can be quite counterproductive.

• Defensive coping is common and may involve any of a number of defense mechanisms. However, the adaptive value of defensive coping tends to be less than optimal. Although some illusions may be healthful, extreme forms of self-deception are maladaptive.

THE NATURE OF CONSTRUCTIVE COPING

• Constructive coping involves efforts to deal with stress that are judged as relatively healthful. Constructive coping is action oriented, effortful, and realistic. It involves managing emotions and self-control.

APPRAISAL-FOCUSED CONSTRUCTIVE COPING

• Appraisal-focused constructive coping depends on altering appraisals of threatening events. Ellis maintains that catastrophic thinking causes problematic emotional reactions. He asserts that catastrophic thinking can be reduced by digging out the irrational assumptions that cause it.

• Evidence indicates that the use of humor can reduce the negative effects of stress through a variety of mechanisms. Positive reinterpretation and benefit finding are also valuable strategies for dealing with some types of stress.

PROBLEM-FOCUSED CONSTRUCTIVE COPING

• Systematic problem solving can be facilitated by following a four-step process: (1) clarify the problem, (2) generate alternative courses of action, (3) evaluate your alternatives and select a course of action, and (4) take action while maintaining flexibility.

• A problem-focused coping tactic with potential value is seeking social support. There appear to be cultural differences regarding who seeks social support. Improving time management can also aid problem-focused coping.

EMOTION-FOCUSED CONSTRUCTIVE COPING

• Emotional intelligence may help people to be more resilient in the face of stress. Inhibition of emotions appears to be associated with increased health problems. Thus, it appears that appropriate emotional expression is adaptive.

• Research suggests that it is wise for people to learn how to manage their feelings of hostility. New evidence also suggests that forgiving people for their offenses is healthier than nursing grudges.

• Exercise is a healthy way to deal with emotional distress. Physical activity provides an outlet for frustration, can distract one from the stress, and is related to improved physical and mental health.

• Meditation can be helpful in soothing emotional turmoil. Meditation is associated with lower levels of stress hormones, improved mental health, and other indicators of wellness. Relaxation procedures, such as listening to soothing music or Benson's relaxation response, can be effective in reducing troublesome emotional arousal.

• Spiritual practices are related to every part of the coping process. Spirituality is related to better physical and mental health outcomes. This relationship is complex in that religious involvement can increase stress under some circumstances.

APPLICATION: USING TIME MORE EFFECTIVELY

• There are many causes of wasted time, including the inability to stick with priorities, to say no, to delegate, to throw things away, to avoid interruption, and to accept anything less that perfection. Procrastination tends to have a negative impact on the quality of work, so it is helpful to avoid this common tendency.

• Effective time management doesn't depend on increased efficiency so much as on setting priorities and allocating time wisely. Engaging in sound time-management techniques can reduce time-related stress.

KEY TERMS

Aggression p. 101	Forgiveness p. 117
Brainstorming p. 113	Internet addiction p. 103
Catastrophic thinking p. 108	Learned helplessness p. 101
Catharsis p. 102	Meditation p. 118
Constructive coping p. 106	Procrastination p. 122
Coping p. 99	Rational-emotive behavior
Defense mechanisms p. 105	therapy p. 108
Emotional intelligence p. 115	

KEY PEOPLE

Herbert Benson p. 119	James Pennebaker p. 116
Albert Ellis p. 108	Martin Seligman p. 101
Sigmund Freud pp. 104–105	Shelley Taylor p. 106
Harold Koenig pp. 119–120	

1. Which of the following assertions is supported by re-search on the cathartic effects of media violence?
   a. Playing violent video games is related to increased aggression.
   b. Playing violent video games releases pent-up hostility.
   c. Playing violent video games is related to increased prosocial behavior.
   d. Playing violent video games decreases physiological arousal

2. Richard feels sure that he failed his calculus exam and that he will have to retake the course. He is very upset. When he gets home, he orders a jumbo-size pizza and drinks two six-packs of beer. Richard's behavior illustrates which of the following coping strategies?
   a. Catastrophic thinking
   b. Defensive coping
   c. Self-indulgence
   d. Positive reinterpretation

3. Defense mechanisms involve the use of _____ to guard against negative _____.
   a. self-deception, behaviors
   b. self-deception, emotions
   c. self-denial, behaviors
   d. self-denial, emotions

4. When studying defensive illusions, Taylor and Brown found that "normal" people's self-images tend to be _____; depressed people's tend to be _____.
   a. accurate, inaccurate
   b. less favorable, more favorable
   c. overly favorable, more realistic
   d. more realistic, overly favorable

5. According to Albert Ellis, people's emotional reactions to life events result mainly from
   a. their arousal level at the time.
   b. their beliefs about events.
   c. congruence between events and expectations.
   d. the consequences following events.

6. Brainstorming is associated with which of the following appraisal-focused coping strategies?
   a. Systematic problem solving
   b. Catastrophic thinking
   c. Positive reinterpretation
   d. Self-enhancing humor

7. Wanda works at a software firm. Today her boss unfairly blamed her for the fact that a new program is way behind schedule. The unjustified public criticism really had an impact on Wanda. Later that evening, she went for a long run to get her anger under control. Wanda is engaging in which category of coping?
   a. Self-focused coping
   b. Appraisal-focused coping
   c. Problem-focused coping
   d. Emotion-focused coping

8. Research by James Pennebaker and his colleagues suggests that wellness is promoted by
   a. depending on more mature defense mechanisms.
   b. strong self-criticism.
   c. writing about one's traumatic experiences.
   d. inhibiting the expression of anger.

9. Which of the following is an emotion-focused coping strategy that provides an outlet for frustration, a distraction from the stressor, and benefits to physical and psychological health?
   a. Systematic problem solving
   b. Defensive coping
   c. Benefit finding
   d. Exercise

10. Which of the following is *not* listed in your text as a cause of wasted time?
    a. Inability to set priorities
    b. Inability to work diligently
    c. Inability to delegate responsibility
    d. Inability to throw things away

ANSWERS

1. a Page 102	6. a Page 113
2. c Page 103	7. d Pages 114–115
3. b Page 105	8. c Page 116
4. c Page 106	9. d Pages 117–118
5. b Page 108	10. b Pages 121–122

COURSEMATE

Go to **CengageBrain.com** to access Psychology CourseMate, where you will find an interactive eBook, glossaries, flashcards, quizzes, videos, and more.

PERSONAL EXPLORATIONS WORKBOOK

Go to the *Personal Explorations Workbook* in the back of your textbook for exercises that can enhance your self-understanding in relation to issues raised in this chapter.

Exercise 4.1 *Self-Assessment:* Barnes-Vulcano Rationality Test

Exercise 4.2 *Self-Reflection:* Analyzing Coping Strategie

Psychology and Physical Health

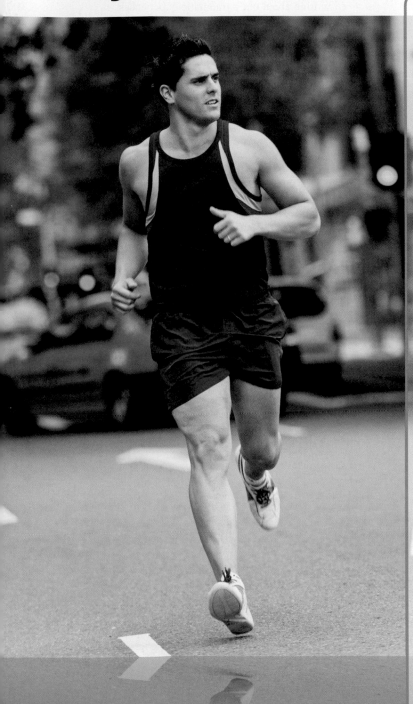

Janet is a fairly typical student. She carries a full course load, works a part-time job, and plans to pursue a challenging career in nursing. She hopes to work in a hospital for a few years before enrolling in graduate school. Right now, however, her life is regulated by work: homework, her job, and more school-related work in the wards of the teaching hospital where she learns the science and practice of nursing. In a typical semester, Janet feels under control for the first few weeks, but then her work piles up: tests, papers, reading, appointments, labs, and so on. She feels anxious and stressed. Instead of getting eight full hours of sleep, she often gets by with much less. Fast food becomes a familiar and necessary comfort—she doesn't have time to prepare, let alone eat, healthy and well-balanced meals. Her regular exercise routine often gives way to other time commitments; she can't jog or get to the gym as much as she'd like. On the rare occasion she does take a break, it tends to involve watching television, catching up with friends on Facebook, or texting with her boyfriend, who attends another school. By the end of the term, she is anxious, stressed, tired, and run down. In fact, she usually celebrates the end of the semester by getting sick and ending up in bed for a few days instead of having relaxing times with her friends and family. And then this unfortunate cycle repeats itself the next semester.

Are you at all like Janet? How often do you become ill in a typical semester? Do you begin strong and healthy but feel worn out and frayed by the end? If you are like many students, your lifestyle has a close connection to your health and well-being. In the past few decades, research has demonstrated quite clearly that health is affected by social and psychological factors as well as biological ones. In other words, health is affected not just by germs or viruses but also by the behavioral choices people make and the lives they lead.

Consider how the leading causes of mortality have changed from the start of the twentieth century to the early twenty-first century. In the United States in 1900, for example, cancer caused 3.7% of the recorded deaths, whereas in 2005 cancer led to 22.8% of recorded deaths (Kung et al., 2008). Over the same time period, heart disease rose from 6.2% to 26.6%. How do we explain the dramatic increases? Certainly, our life span has increased (in 1900, life expectancy was 47.3 years and today it is over 77; U.S. Bureau of the Census, 1975, 2007), but that alone is not a sufficient explanation for the greater incidence of cancer and heart disease.

More than any other time in history, people's health is likely to be compromised by such *chronic diseases—* conditions that develop across many years—rather than by *contagious diseases,* those caused by specific infectious agents (such as measles, pneumonia, or tuberculosis). Moreover, lifestyle and stress play a much larger role in the development of chronic diseases than they do in contagious diseases. Today, the three leading chronic diseases (heart disease, cancer, and stroke) account for almost 60% of all deaths in the United States, and these mortality statistics reveal only the tip of the health iceberg. Psychological and social factors also contribute to many other, less serious maladies, such as headaches, insomnia, backaches, skin disorders, asthma, and ulcers.

In light of these trends, it is not surprising that the way we think about illness is changing. Traditionally, illness has been thought of as a purely biological phenomenon produced by an infectious agent or some internal physical breakdown in the body (Papas, Belar, & Rozensky, 2004). However, the shifting patterns of disease and new findings relating stress to physical illness have rocked the foundation of the traditional biological model. In its place a new model has gradually emerged (Leventhal, Musumeci, & Leventhal, 2006). The **biopsychosocial model holds that physical illness is caused by a complex interaction of biological, psychological, and sociocultural factors.** This model does not suggest that biological factors are unimportant. Rather, it simply asserts that biological factors operate in a psychosocial context that can also be highly influential. Medical and psychological professionals who adhere to the bio-psychosocial model also focus on other factors, in-cluding cultural values (Landrine & Klonoff, 2001), that can affect the ways individuals think about and deal with chronic illness, especially where interac-tions with health care providers and adherence to treatments are concerned (Fava & Sonino, 2008; Sperry, 2006). **Figure 5.1** illustrates how the three factors in the biospsychosocial model affect one an-other and, in turn, health.

The growing recognition that psychological factors influence physical health led to the develop-ment of a new specialty within psychology (Fried-man & Adler, 2007). **Health psychology is concerned with how psychosocial factors relate to the promo-tion and maintenance of health and with the cau-sation, prevention, and treatment of illness.** This specialty is relatively young, having emerged in the late 1970s (Baum, Perry, & Tarbell, 2004). In this chapter we focus on the rapidly growing domain of health psychology (Belar, 2008). The chapter's first section analyzes the link between stress and illness. The second section examines common health-impairing habits, such as smoking and overeating. The third section discusses how people's reactions to illness can affect their health. The Application expands on one particular type of health-impairing habit: the use of recreational drugs.

Figure 5.1

The biopsychosocial model. The biopsychosocial model assumes that health is not just attributable to biological processes. According to this increasingly influential view, one's physical health depends on interactions between bio-logical factors, psychological factors, and social system factors. Some key fac-tors in each category are depicted here.

Learn More Online

healthfinder

Through the U.S. Department of Health and Human Ser-vices, the government has opened an ambitious online gateway to consumer-oriented information about health in all its aspects. Annotated descriptions are available for all resources identified in no-cost searches of this database.

STRESS, PERSONALITY, AND ILLNESS

LEARNING OBJECTIVES

- Describe the Type A personality and its link to hostility and heart disease.
- Summarize evidence relating emotional reactions and depres-sion to heart disease.

- Discuss the evidence linking stress to cancer, various diseases, and immune functioning.
- Evaluate the strength of the relationship between stress and illness.

What does it mean to say that personality can affect well-ness? A guiding assumption is that a person's characteris-tic demeanor can influence his or her physical health

(Friedman & Martin, 2011; Kern & Friedman, 2011a). As noted in Chapter 2, *personality* is made up of the unique grouping of behavioral traits that a person exhibits consistently across situations. Thus, an individual who is chronically grumpy, often hostile toward others, and routinely frustrated is more likely to develop an illness and perhaps even to die earlier than someone who is emotionally open, is routinely warm and friendly toward others, and leads a balanced life (Friedman, 2007). Of course, the link between personality and disease is somewhat more complex, but nonetheless real (Kern & Friedman, 2011b). We begin with a look at heart disease, far and away the leading cause of death in North America.

Personality, Emotions, and Heart Disease

As noted earlier, heart disease accounts for nearly 27% of the deaths in the United States every year. *Coronary heart disease results from a reduction in blood flow through the coronary arteries, which supply the heart with blood.* This type of heart disease causes about 90% of heart-related deaths. Atherosclerosis is the principal cause of coronary disease (Giannoglou et al., 2008). *Atherosclerosis is a gradual narrowing of the coronary arteries,* usually caused by a buildup of fatty deposits and other debris on the inner walls (see **Figure 5.2**). Atherosclerosis progresses slowly over many years. Narrowed coronary arteries may eventually lead to situations in which the heart is temporarily deprived of adequate blood flow, causing a condition known as *myocardial ischemia.* This ischemia may be accompanied by brief chest pain, called *angina,* as well as shortness of breath. If a coronary artery is blocked completely (by a blood clot, for instance), the abrupt interruption of blood flow can produce a full-fledged heart attack, or *myocardial infarction.* Established risk factors for coronary disease include smoking, diabetes, high cholesterol levels, and high blood pressure (Greenland et al., 2003; Khot et al., 2003). Smoking and diabetes are somewhat stronger risk factors for women than for men (Stoney, 2003).

Figure 5.2
Atherosclerosis. Atherosclerosis, a narrowing of the coronary arteries, is the principal cause of coronary disease. **(a)** A normal artery. **(b)** Fatty deposits, cholesterol, and cellular debris on the walls of the artery have narrowed the path for blood flow. **(c)** Advanced atherosclerosis. In this situation, a blood clot might suddenly block the flow of blood through the artery.

Cholesterol, fatty deposits, and cellular debris

(a) (b) (c)

© Cengage Learning

Contrary to public perception, cardiovascular diseases—those related to the heart and blood vessels—kill women just as much as men (Liewer et al., 2008) but these diseases tend to emerge in women about 10 years later than in men (Stoney, 2003). Interestingly, when women reach menopause—usually around age 50—they have a higher risk of heart disease than men (Mattar et al., 2008).

Recently, attention has shifted to the possibility that inflammation may contribute to atherosclerosis and elevated coronary risk (Pilote et al., 2007). Evidence is mounting that the swelling and reddening of arteries in the heart plays a key role in the initiation and progression of atherosclerosis, as well as the acute complications that trigger heart attacks (Abi-Saleh et al., 2008; Libby, Ridker, & Maseri, 2002). The presence of stress and depression, too, can be related to inflammation (Miller & Blackwell, 2006). Fortunately, researchers have found a marker— levels of C-reactive protein (CRP) in the blood—that may help physicians estimate individuals' coronary risk more accurately than was previously possible (Ridker, 2001). CRP levels are also predictive of the development of hypertension (high blood pressure), suggesting that it may be part of an inflammatory syndrome (Sesso et al., 2003).

There is some good news, as many heart patients successfully undergo cardiac rehabilitation. Such treatment often involves intervention by psychologists, who work with cardiac patients to change their lifestyle (diet, exercise, stress-related habits) to minimize risk factors that can lead to subsequent heart attacks. As we will see, however, overcoming the predispositions of personality can be a challenge.

Hostility and Coronary Risk

In the 1960s and 1970s a pair of cardiologists, Meyer Friedman and Ray Rosenman (1974; Rosenman et al., 1975), were investigating the causes of coronary disease. Originally, they were interested in the usual factors thought to produce a high risk of heart attack: smoking, obesity, physical inactivity, and so forth. Although they found these factors to be important, they eventually recognized that a piece of the puzzle was missing. Many people who smoked constantly, got little exercise, and were severely overweight still managed to avoid the ravages of heart disease. Meanwhile, others who seemed to be in much better shape with regard to these risk factors experienced the misfortune of a heart attack. What was their explanation for these perplexing findings? Stress! Specifically, they identified an apparent connection between coronary risk and a pattern of behavior they called the *Type A personality*, which involves self-imposed stress and intense reactions to stress (Allan, 2011).

Friedman and Rosenman divided people into two basic types (Friedman, 1996; Rosenman, 1993). The *Type A personality includes three elements: (1) a strong competitive orientation, (2) impatience and time urgency,* and (3) anger and hostility. In contrast, **the *Type B personality* is marked by relatively relaxed, patient, easygoing, amicable behavior.** Type A's are ambitious, hard-driving perfectionists who are exceedingly time conscious. They routinely try to do several things at once. They fidget frantically over the briefest delays, are concerned with numbers, and often focus on the acquisition of material objects. They tend to be highly competitive, achievement-oriented workaholics who drive themselves with many deadlines. They are easily aggravated and get angry quickly. In contrast, Type B's are less hurried, less competitive, and less easily angered than Type A's, and there is some evidence that Type B's engage in more preventive and less risky behaviors when facing stress (Korotkov et al., 2011).

Decades of research uncovered a tantalizingly modest correlation between Type A behavior and increased coronary risk. More often than not, studies found an association between Type A personality and an elevated incidence of heart disease, but the findings were not as strong or as consistent as expected (Smith & Gallo, 2001). However, in recent years, researchers have found a stronger link between personality and coronary risk by focusing on a specific component of the Type A personality: anger and hostility (Myrtek, 2007; Rozanski, Blumenthal, & Kaplan, 1999). *Hostility* **refers to a persistent negative attitude marked by cynical, mistrusting thoughts, feelings of anger, and overtly aggressive actions.** In fact, an early researcher interested in hostility argued that individuals who use anger as a response for dealing with interpersonal problems were at an elevated risk for heart disease (Williams, 1989). For example, in one study of almost 13,000 men and women who had no prior history of heart disease, investigators found an elevated incidence of heart attacks among participants who exhibited an angry temperament (Williams et al., 2000). The participants, who were followed for a median period of 4.5 years, were classified as being low (37.1%), moderate (55.2%), or high (7.7%) in anger. Among those with normal blood pressure, the high-anger subjects experienced almost three times as many coronary events as the low-anger subjects (see **Figure 5.3**). In another study, CT scans were used to look for signs of atherosclerosis in a sample of 374 men and women whose cynical or pessimistic hostility had been assessed a decade earlier when they were 18 to 30 years old (Iribarren et al., 2000). Participants with above-average hostility scores were twice as likely to exhibit atherosclerosis as participants with below-average hostility scores.

Many other studies have also found an association between hostility and various aspects of cardiovascular disease (Eaker et al., 2004; Nelson, Franks, & Brose, 2005), including CRP levels (Suarez, 2004). Thus, recent research trends suggest that hostility may be the crucial toxic element that accounts for the correlation between Type A behavior and heart disease. Interestingly, there is some evidence that hostility plays a greater role in cardiovascular risk for blacks than for whites (Cooper & Waldstein, 2004).

Other research points to an intriguing gender difference concerning hostility and its link to heart disease. As already acknowledged, as a personality variable, hostility predicts cardiovascular disease in men (Consedine, Magai, & Chin, 2004). What about in women? At least one study suggests that anxiety, or one's predisposition to worry, may be a stronger predictor of heart disease in women than hostility (Consedine et al., 2004).

Why are anger and hostility associated with coronary risk? There are several reasons. First, let's be clear about some distinctions between these two responses. Anger is an unpleasant emotion that is accompanied by physiological arousal, whereas hostility involves a social component—a negative attitude and often reaction toward others (Suls & Bunde, 2005). People cannot avoid experiencing anger in their lives, however, which means it may be less of a risk factor in the development of heart disease. The manner in which individuals deal with their anger, though, may be quite consequential, creating a link to hostility toward others. Research has uncovered a number of possible explanations linking anger and hostility (see **Figure 5.4**). First, anger-prone individuals appear to exhibit greater physiological reactivity than those lower in hostility (Smith & Gallo, 1999). The frequent ups and downs in heart rate

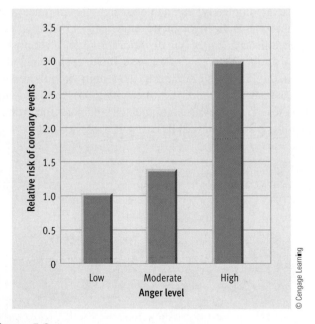

Figure 5.3

Anger and coronary risk. Working with a large sample of healthy men and women who were followed for a median of 4.5 years, Williams et al. (2000) found an association between trait anger and the likelihood of a coronary event. Among subjects who manifested normal blood pressure at the beginning of the study, a moderate anger level was associated with a 36% increase in coronary attacks, and a high level of anger nearly tripled participants' risk for coronary disease.

Figure 5.4
Mechanisms that may link hostility and anger to heart disease. Explanations for the apparent link between cynical hostility and heart disease are many and varied. Four widely discussed possibilities are summarized in the middle column of this diagram.

and blood pressure may create wear and tear in their cardiovascular systems. Such reactivity is especially high among African Americans (Merritt et al., 2004; Suarez et al., 2004). One explanation for this finding is emotional reactions to experiences of discrimination (Clark, 2003; Lepore et al., 2006).

Second, hostile people probably create additional stress for themselves (Smith, 2006; Smith, Glazer, & Ruiz, 2004). For example, their quick anger may provoke many arguments and conflicts with others, including friends and family members. Consistent with this line of thinking, Smith and colleagues (1988) found that subjects high in hostility reported more hassles, more negative life events, more marital conflict, and more work-related stress than subjects who were lower in hostility.

Third, thanks to their antagonistic ways of relating to others, hostile individuals tend to have less social support than others (Chen, Gilligan, & Coups, 2005; Smith, 2003). Women who perceive little or no social support at home or at work are at greater risk for mortality resulting from a heart attack than other women (Kawachi et al., 1994). Living alone following a cardiac event actually increases a person's risk for a subsequent heart attack. Williams (1996), for example, found that single people or those who had no close friend to share private thoughts and concerns with were three times more likely to die in a 5-year period after their original heart attack than those who had either a spouse or a close friend.

Fourth, perhaps because of their cynicism, people high in anger and hostility seem to exhibit a higher prevalence of poor health habits that may contribute to the development of cardiovascular disease. For example, people high in hostility are more likely to smoke, drink alcohol and coffee, and be overweight than others (Everson et al.,

1997; Siegler et al., 1992). One reason this matters is that physical fitness mediates cardiac reactivity: People who stay in good physical shape have lower reactivity than those in poor shape (Wright et al., 2007).

Finally, keep in mind that hostility does not always lead to the development of cardiovascular problems. One large-population project did not find any overall effect for hostility and the onset of heart disease (Surtees et al., 2005). This result does not mean that hostility is not a good predictor—ample evidence we already examined indicates that it can be. Instead, hostility may be a decided risk factor for some people but not others, just as it may exert its influence on promoting heart disease through some other pathway. Perhaps, for example, some people do not express their hostility directly to others but nonetheless experience it. Such suppressed emotion still takes its toll (Pennebaker, 2002).

Emotional Reactions and Heart Disease

Although work on personality risk factors has dominated research on how psychological functioning contributes to heart disease, recent studies suggest that emotional reactions may also be critical. *One line of research has supported the hypothesis that transient mental stress and the resulting emotions can tax the heart.* Laboratory experiments with cardiology patients have shown that brief periods of mental stress can trigger acute symptoms of heart disease, such as myocardial ischemia and angina (Gottdiener et al., 1994).

Related research considers the impact of holding back or suppressing emotions, particularly anger. Ironically, perhaps, keeping negative emotions to oneself is potentially more harmful than expressing anger toward others

Research suggests that excessive anger and hostility are associated with an increased risk for various types of heart disease.

(Jorgensen & Kolodziej, 2007). A related form of suppressed emotion is *rumination*—engaging in repetitive and negative thinking about some event. Going over and over the incident heightens negative feelings as well as depression (Hogan & Linden, 2004). Over time, this relentless mental "stewing" can become a negative coping strategy that actually increases people's risk for cardiac problems. Learning to recognize one's impending emotional state, such as feeling angry, but then expressing the emotion as calmly and rationally as possible may be a healthier response (Siegman, 1994),

Depression and Heart Disease

Another line of research has recently implicated depression as a major risk factor for heart disease (Dornelas, 2008; Glassman, Maj, & Sartorius, 2011). *Depressive disorders,* which are characterized by persistent feelings of sadness and despair, are a fairly common form of psychological disorder (see Chapter 14). Over the years, many studies have found elevated rates of depression among patients suffering from heart disease, but most theorists have explained this correlation by asserting that being diagnosed with heart disease makes people depressed. Indeed, depression is the most common psychological reaction to having a heart attack (Artham, Lavie, & Milani, 2008). However, studies conducted in the last decade or so have suggested that the causal relation may also flow in the opposite direction—*that the emotional dysfunction of depression may cause heart disease* (Brown et al., 2011; Goldston & Baillie, 2008). For example, Pratt and colleagues (1996) examined a large sample of people 13 years after they were screened for depression. They found that participants who had been depressed at the time of the original study were four times more likely than others to experience a heart attack during the intervening 13 years.

Because the participants' depressive disorders preceded their heart attacks, one cannot argue that their heart disease caused their depression. In some supporting research, damage to the arteries of the heart has been found among depressed teens (Tomfohr, Martin, & Miller, 2008).

Overall, studies have found that depression roughly doubles one's chances of developing heart disease (Lett et al., 2004; Rudisch & Nemeroff, 2003). Moreover, depression also appears to influence how heart disease progresses, as it is associated with a worse prognosis among cardiology patients (Glassman et al., 2003), including increased mortality rates within 6 months of the first cardiac episode (Blumenthal, 2008). Although the new emphasis is on how depression contributes to heart disease, experts caution that the relationship between the two conditions is surely bidirectional and that heart disease also increases vulnerability to depression (Sayers, 2004).

Stress and Cancer

If one single word can strike terror into most people's hearts, it is probably *cancer.* We think of cancer as a human disease, but other animals and even plants can develop cancers. People generally view cancer as the most sinister, tragic, frightening, and unbearable of diseases. In reality, cancer is actually a *collection* of over 200 related diseases that vary in their characteristics and amenability to treatment (Nezu et al., 2003). *Cancer* **refers to malignant cell growth, which may occur in many organ systems in the body.** The core problem in cancer is that cells begin to reproduce in a rapid, disorganized fashion. As this reproduction process lurches out of control, the teeming new cells clump together to form tumors. If this wild growth continues unabated, the spreading tumors cause tissue damage and begin to interfere with normal functioning in the affected organ systems.

It is widely believed by the general public that stress and personality play major roles in the development of cancer (McKenna et al., 1999), and researchers have considered the links between stressful circumstances and traits (Johansen, 2010). Some psychologists searched for evidence for the so-called Type C or "cancer-prone personality" but failed to find any link between disposition and the development of the disease (Temoshok, 2004). In fact, the research linking psychological factors to the *onset* of cancer is extremely weak. For example, one prospective study of twins found that extraversion and neuroticism (two of the Big Five personality traits; see Chapter 2) were unrelated to increased risk of cancer (Hansen et al., 2005). However, a few retrospective studies found evidence that high stress precedes the development of cancer (Cohen, Kunkel, & Levenson, 1998; Katz & Epstein, 2005). More recently, a careful meta-analysis of 165 independent studies revealed unequivocally that stress-related psychosocial variables are associated with cancer (Chida et al., 2008). The study demonstrated that stress predicted higher rates of the disease in initially healthy populations, lower survival rates among individuals diagnosed with cancer, and higher cancer mortality in general. Of course, stress can also encourage people to engage in unhealthy behaviors that can increase the disease's progress (Carlson et al., 2007; Temoshok, 2004). Note that these results are suggestive but by no means definitive. Stress is related to but not necessarily causally linked to cancer; thus, the debate continues (Baum, Trevino, & Dougall, 2011; Tez & Tez, 2008).

Although efforts to link psychological factors to the onset of cancer have produced equivocal findings, more convincing evidence has shown that stress and personality influence the *course* of the disease. The onset of cancer frequently sets off a chain reaction of stressful events (Andersen, Golden-Kreutz, & DiLillo, 2001), and people display different responses as they try to adjust to the disease and its consequences (Helgeson, Snyder, & Seltman, 2004). Patients typically have to grapple with fear of the unknown; difficult and aversive treatment regimens; nausea, fatigue, and other treatment side effects; interruptions in intimate relationships; career disruptions; job discrimination; and financial worries. Moreover, depression can become a problem among cancer patients during active treatment (Reich, Lesur, & Perdrizet-Chevallier, 2008). Such stressors may often contribute to the progress of the disease, perhaps by impairing certain aspects of immune system functioning (Andersen, Kiecolt-Glaser, & Glaser, 1994). The impact of all this stress may depend in part on one's personality. Research suggests that mortality rates are somewhat higher among patients who respond with depression, repressive coping, and other negative emotions (Friedman, 1991). In contrast, prospects appear to be better for patients who can maintain their emotional stability and enthusiasm.

Stress and Other Diseases

The development of questionnaires to measure life stress has allowed researchers to look for correlations between stress and a variety of diseases. On one end of the spectrum, consider headaches, a common problem or "everyday disease" but one that can sometimes point to more serious health conditions. So-called tension headaches, marked by muscle rigidity in the region of the head and neck, are what people most frequently experience. Stress is characterized as the one of the leading causes of headaches (Deniz et al., 2004). Among infectious diseases, stress has been clearly implicated in development of the common cold (Cohen, 2005). The typical research paradigm is to intentionally inoculate healthy volunteers with cold viruses, keep them under quarantine (in separate hotel rooms), and then observe who does or does not come down with a cold. The finding? People reporting higher levels of

stress are more likely to become ill. Interestingly, people who are social and agreeable are at lower risk of getting a cold after exposure to a virus (Cohen et al., 2003).

Figure 5.5 provides a longer list of health problems that have been linked to stress, including several chronic diseases. Many of these stress-illness connections are based on tentative or inconsistent findings, but the sheer length and diversity of the list is remarkable. Why should stress increase the risk for so many kinds of illness? A partial answer may lie in immune functioning.

HEALTH PROBLEMS THAT MAY BE LINKED TO STRESS	
Health Problem	**Representative evidence**
Common cold	Mohren et al. (2005)
Ulcers	Levenstein (2002)
Asthma	Chen & Miller (2007)
Migraine headaches	Maki et al. (2007)
Premenstrual distress	Stanton et al. (2002)
Vaginal infections	Williams & Deffenbacher (1983)
Herpes virus	Ashcraft & Bonneau (2008)
Skin disorders	Magnavita et al. (2011)
Rheumatoid arthritis	Motivala et al. (2008)
Chronic back pain	Preuper et al. (2011)
Diabetes	Faulenbach et al. (2011)
Complications of pregnancy	Dunkel-Schetter et al. (2001)
Hyperthyroidism	Yang, Liu, & Zang (2000)
Hemophilia	Buxton et al. (1981)
Stroke	Tsutsumi, Kayaba, & Ishikawa (2011)
Appendicitis	Schietroma et al. (2012)
Multiple sclerosis	Riise et al. (2011)
Periodontal disease	Reners & Brecx (2007)
Hypertension	O'Callahan, Andrews, & Krantz (2003)
Cancer	Holland & Lewis (1993)
Coronary heart disease	Orth-Gomer et al. (2000)
AIDS	Perez, Cruess, & Kalichman (2010)
Inflammatory bowel disease	Kuroki et al. (2011)
Epileptic seizures	Sawyer & Escayg (2010)

© Cengage Learning

Figure 5.5

Stress and health problems. The onset or progress of the health problems listed here *may* be affected by stress. Although the evidence is fragmentary in many instances, it's alarming to see the number and diversity of problems on this list.

Stress and Immune Functioning

The apparent link between stress and many types of illness probably reflects the fact that stress can undermine the body's immune functioning (Dhabhar, 2011). The *immune response* **is the body's defensive reaction to invasion by bacteria, viral agents, or other foreign substances.** The human immune response works to protect the body from many forms of disease. A wealth of studies indicate that experimentally induced stress can impair immune functioning *in animals* (Moynihan & Ader, 1996). That is, stressors such as crowding, shock, food restriction, and restraint reduce various aspects of immune reactivity in laboratory animals (Chiappelli & Hodgson, 2000). Of course, stress can affect animal immune function in natural settings, as well (Nelson & Demas, 2004).

Studies by Janice Kiecolt-Glaser and her colleagues have also related stress to suppressed immune activity *in humans* (Kiecolt-Glaser, 2009; Kiecolt-Glaser & Glaser, 1995). In one study, medical students provided researchers with blood samples so that their immune response could be assessed at various points (Kiecolt-Glaser et al., 1984). The students provided the baseline sample a month before final exams and contributed the "high-stress" sample on the first day of their finals. The subjects also responded to the Social Readjustment Rating Scale (SRRS; see Chapter 3) as a measure of recent stress. Reduced levels of immune activity were found during the extremely stressful finals week. Reduced immune activity was also correlated with higher scores on the SRRS.

Janice Kiecolt-Glaser

Chronic illnesses have a negative impact on immune function (Nelson et al., 2008), and the presence of stress renders people's abilities to deal with these illnesses even worse (Fang et al., 2008). In a thorough review of 30 years of research on stress and immunity, Segerstrom and Miller (2004) concluded that chronic stress can reduce both *cellular immune responses* (which attack intracellular pathogens, such as viruses) and *humoral immune responses* (which attack extracellular pathogens, such as bacteria). They also report that the *duration* of a stressful event is a key factor determining its impact on immune function. Long-lasting stressors, such as caring for a seriously ill spouse or enduring unemployment for months, are associated with greater immune suppression than relatively brief stressors (Cohen et al., 1998).

Underscoring the importance of the link between stress and immune function, a recent study found evidence that chronic stress may produce *premature aging of immune system cells* (Epel et al., 2004). The study revealed that women who were dealing with heavy, long-term stress (caring for a child with a serious, chronic illness, such as

cerebral palsy) had immune system cells that appeared to be a decade older than their chronological age, perhaps shedding light for the first time on why people under severe stress often look old and haggard. Unfortunately, evidence suggests that in the face of stress, people's immune systems do not fight off illness as well when they grow older (Gouin et al., 2012; Graham, Christian, & Kiecolt-Glaser, 2006). To summarize, scientists have assembled impressive evidence that stress can temporarily suppress human immune functioning, which can make people more vulnerable to infectious disease agents.

Conclusions

A wealth of evidence suggests that stress influences physical health. However, virtually all of the relevant research is correlational, so it cannot demonstrate conclusively that stress *causes* illness (Smith & Gallo, 2001; Watson & Pennebaker, 1989). The association between stress and illness could be due to a third variable (see **Figure 5.6**). Perhaps some aspect of personality or some type of physiological predisposition makes people overly prone to interpret events as stressful *and* overly prone to interpret unpleasant physical sensations

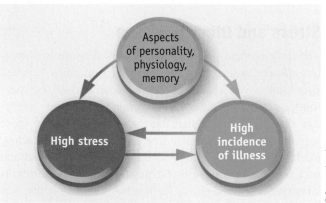

Figure 5.6

The stress/illness correlation. Based on the evidence as a whole, most health psychologists would probably accept the assertion that stress often contributes to the causation of illness. However, some critics argue that the stress-illness correlation could reflect other causal processes. One or more aspects of personality, physiology, or memory might contribute to the correlation between high stress and a high incidence of illness.

as symptoms of illness. Moreover, critics of this research note that many of the studies have used research designs that may have inflated the apparent link between stress and illness (Schwarzer & Schulz, 2003). Alternatively, stress may simply alter health-related behaviors, increasing the incidence of "bad habits"—smoking, eating poorly, drinking alcohol, using illegal drugs, sleeping less—all of which increase people's risk for diseases and disrupt their immunity (Segerstrom & Miller, 2004).

Despite methodological problems favoring inflated correlations, the research in this area consistently indicates that the *strength* of the relationship between stress and health is modest. The correlations typically fall in the .20s and .30s (Cohen, Kessler, & Gordon, 1995). Clearly, stress is not an irresistible force that produces inevitable effects on health. Actually, this fact should come as no surprise. As we saw in Chapter 3, some people handle stress better than others. Furthermore, stress is only one actor on a crowded stage. A complex network of biopsychosocial factors influence health, including genetic endowment, exposure to infectious agents and environmental toxins, and the choices people make in daily life. In the next section we look at some of these factors as we examine health-impairing habits and lifestyles.

HABITS, LIFESTYLES, AND HEALTH

LEARNING OBJECTIVES

- Identify some reasons that people develop health-impairing habits.
- Discuss the health effects of smoking and the challenges of quitting smoking.
- Summarize data on patterns of alcohol use and the health risks and social costs of drinking.
- Discuss obesity's origins and health risks, as well as effective weight-loss and exercise programs.
- Describe AIDS, and summarize evidence on the transmission of the HIV virus.

Some people seem determined to dig an early grave for themselves. They do precisely those things they have been warned are particularly bad for their health. For example, some people drink heavily even though they know they're corroding their liver. Others eat all the wrong foods even though they know they're increasing their risk for a heart attack. Unfortunately, health-impairing habits contribute to

far more deaths than most people realize. In a recent analysis of the causes of death in the United States, Mokdad and colleagues (2004) estimate that unhealthy behaviors are responsible for about half of all deaths each year. The habits that account for the most premature mortality, by far, are smoking and poor diet/physical inactivity (see **Figure 5.7**). Other leading behavioral causes of death

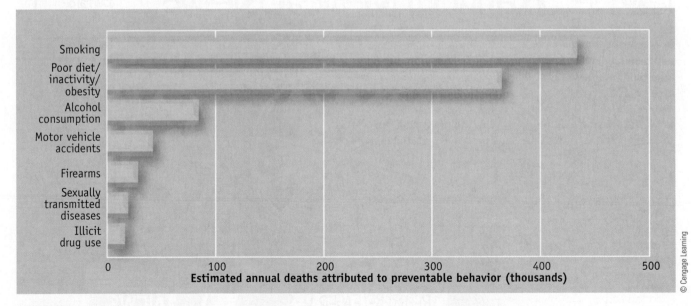

Figure 5.7

Mortality due to health-impairing behaviors. Synthesizing data from many sources, Mokdad and colleagues (2004) estimated the number of annual deaths in the United States attributable to various health-impairing behaviors in an article published in *The Journal of the American Medical Association*. As you can see, their calculations suggest that smoking and obesity are the leading causes of preventable mortality. However, their mortality estimate for obesity has proven controversial and is the subject of some debate (some experts argue that their estimate is too high).

include alcohol consumption, unsafe driving, sexually transmitted diseases, and illicit drug use.

It may seem puzzling that people behave in self-destructive ways. Why do they do it? Several factors are involved. First, many health-impairing habits creep up on people slowly. For instance, drug use may grow imperceptibly over years, or exercise habits may decline ever so gradually. Second, many health-impairing habits involve activities that are quite pleasant at the time. Actions such as eating favorite foods, smoking cigarettes, and getting "high" are potent reinforcing events that are often encouraged, even celebrated, by our culture. Third, the risks associated with most health-impairing habits are related to chronic diseases such as cancer that usually take 10, 20, or 30 years to develop. It is relatively easy to ignore risks that lie in the distant future.

Fourth, it appears that *people have a tendency to underestimate the risks associated with their own health-impairing habits* while viewing the risks associated with others' self-destructive behaviors much more accurately (Weinstein, 2003). In other words, most people are aware of the dangers associated with certain habits, but they often engage in *denial* when it is time to apply this information to themselves. Thus, some people exhibit **unrealistic optimism,** in which they are aware that certain health-related behaviors are dangerous, but they erroneously view those dangers as risks for others rather than

themselves. In effect, they say to themselves "bad things may well happen to other people, but not to me" (Gold, 2008; Sharot, Korn, & Dolan, 2011). Of course, we have already learned that, in general, optimism is a beneficial personality trait (see Chapter 3). However, in the context of taking health risks and engaging in unwise behavior, unrealistic optimism may prevent people from taking appropriate precautions to protect their physical and mental well-being (Waters et al., 2011). One recent study found, for example, that unrealistic optimism was linked with the risk of developing atherosclerosis (Ferrer et al., 2012).

Yet another problem is that people are exposed to a great deal of conflicting information about what's healthy and what isn't. It seems like every week a report in the media claims that yesterday's standard health advice has been contradicted by new research. This apparent inconsistency confuses people and undermines their motivation to pursue healthy habits. Sometimes it seems that health and happiness are more a matter of luck than anything else. In reality, the actions individuals take and the self-control they exercise can matter a great deal.

In this section we discuss how health is affected by smoking, drinking, overeating and obesity, poor nutrition, and lack of exercise. We also look at behavioral factors that relate to AIDS. The health risks of recreational drug use are covered in the Application.

Smoking

Here is a surprising and stark fact: Cigarettes lead to the death of more people each year than suicides, car accidents, homicides, alcohol, illegal drugs, and AIDS combined (American Cancer Society, 2008). And here is another: Smoking is actually the most preventable cause of mortality in the United States.

Why do people smoke? Tobacco smoking, a discovery in the "new world," became popular in the sixteenth century and has been with us ever since (Kluger, 1996). Social factors, such as peer pressure among adolescents (Stewart-Knox et al., 2005) and the influence of advertising (Pierce et al., 2005), are obvious candidates, but some people smoke in order to control their weight (Jenks & Higgs, 2007), and many smokers claim that cigarettes elevate their mood, suppress hunger pangs (which they believe helps them stay thin), and enhance alertness and attention.

Who smokes? The percentage of people who smoke has declined noticeably since the mid-1960s (see **Figure 5.8**). Nonetheless, about 24% of adult men and 18% of adult women in the United States continue to smoke regularly. Smoking among college-aged students has dropped from close to 30% to just under 20% (Harris, Schwartz, & Thompson, 2008). Unfortunately, smoking is all-too-common in many other countries. In the United States, people with higher levels of education are less likely to smoke (Rock et al., 2007; Wetter et al., 2005). One study found that under 8% of individuals with masters or doctorial degrees smoked, compared to over 50% of those with only a General Education Diploma (GED) (Rock et al., 2007). Smoking may be a reasonable predictor of people's occupations. As you might also surmise, income is linked with smoking: Smokers are poorer than nonsmokers (Zagorsky, 2004). Interestingly, these trends are not entirely similar in Europe. For instance, tobacco consumption is associated with higher educational levels among British men and women, as well as Italian men (Giskes et al., 2005).

Health Effects

Accumulating evidence clearly shows that smokers face a much greater risk of premature death than nonsmokers. For example, the average smoker has an estimated life expectancy *13–14 years shorter* than that of a similar nonsmoker (Schmitz & Delaune, 2005). The overall risk is positively correlated with the number of cigarettes smoked and their tar and nicotine content. Despite people's beliefs to the contrary (O'Connor et al., 2007), cigar smoking, which has increased dramatically in recent years, elevates health risks almost as much as cigarette smoking (Baker et al., 2000).

Why are mortality rates higher for smokers? In the first place, tobacco contains around 500 chemicals, and the smoke emanating from it holds another 4000 chemicals (Dube & Green, 1982). At least 60 of the latter are known cancer-causing agents, or carcinogens (American Cancer Society, 2008). Smoking increases the likelihood of developing a surprisingly large range of diseases, as you can see in **Figure 5.9** on the next page (Schmitz & Delaune, 2005; Woloshin, Schwartz, & Welch, 2002). Lung cancer and heart disease kill the largest number of smokers; in fact, smokers are almost twice as likely to succumb to cardiovascular disease as nonsmokers are. Smokers also have an elevated risk for oral, bladder, and kidney cancer, as well as cancers of the larynx, esophagus, and pancreas; for atherosclerosis, hypertension, stroke, and other cardiovascular diseases; and for bronchitis, emphysema, and other pulmonary diseases (U.S. Department of Health and Human Services, 2004).

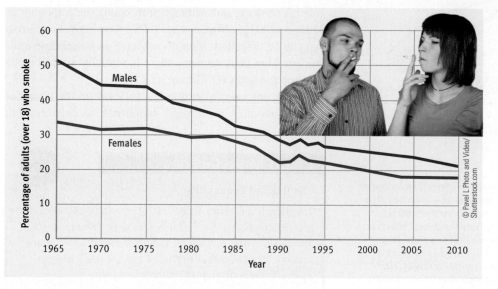

Figure 5.8

The prevalence of smoking in the United States. This graph shows how the percentage of U.S. adults who smoke has declined steadily since the mid-1960s. Although considerable progress has been made, smoking still accounts for about 435,000 premature deaths each year. (Data from Centers for Disease Control)

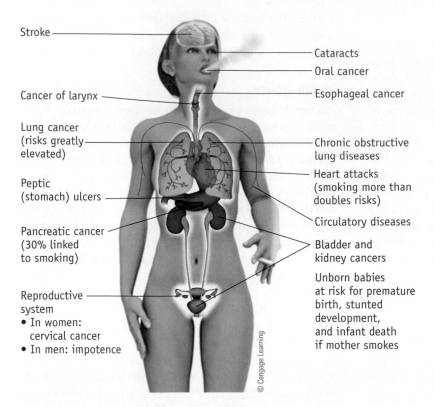

Stroke

Cancer of larynx

Lung cancer
(risks greatly
elevated)

Peptic
(stomach) ulcers

Pancreatic cancer
(30% linked
to smoking)

Reproductive
system
• In women:
cervical cancer
• In men: impotence

Cataracts

Oral cancer

Esophageal cancer

Chronic obstructive
lung diseases

Heart attacks
(smoking more than
doubles risks)

Circulatory diseases

Bladder and
kidney cancers

Unborn babies
at risk for premature
birth, stunted
development,
and infant death
if mother smokes

© Cengage Learning

Figure 5.9

Health risks associated with smoking. This figure provides an overview of the various diseases that are more common among smokers than nonsmokers. As you can see, tobacco elevates one's vulnerability to a remarkably diverse array of diseases, including the three leading causes of death in the modern world: heart attack, cancer, and stroke.

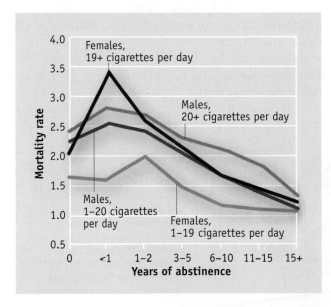

Figure 5.10

Quitting smoking and mortality. Research suggests that various types of health risks associated with smoking decline gradually after people give up tobacco. The data shown here, from the 1990 U.S. Surgeon General's report on smoking, illustrate the overall effects on mortality rates. The mortality rates on the vertical axis show how much death rates are elevated among smokers and ex-smokers in comparison to nonsmokers. For example, a mortality rate of 3.0 would mean that smokers' death rate was triple that of nonsmokers. (Data from U.S. Department of Health and Human Services, 1990)

Most smokers know about the risks associated with tobacco use, but, due to unrealistic optimism, they tend to underestimate the actual risks as applied to themselves (Ayanian & Cleary, 1999; Waltenbaugh & Zagummy, 2004). At the same time, they overestimate the likelihood they can quit smoking when they want to (Weinstein, Slovic, & Gibson, 2004).

Giving Up Smoking

Studies show that if people can give up smoking, their health risks decline reasonably quickly (Kenfield et al., 2008; Williams et al., 2002). Five years after people stop smoking, their health risk is already noticeably lower than that for people who continue to smoke. The health risks for people who give up tobacco continue to decline until they reach a normal level after about 15 years (see **Figure 5.10**). Evidence suggests that 70% of smokers would like to quit, but they are reluctant to give up a major source of pleasure and they worry about craving cigarettes, gaining weight, becoming anxious and irritable, and feeling less able to cope with stress (Grunberg, Faraday, & Rahman, 2001).

Research shows that long-term success rates for efforts to quit smoking are in the vicinity of only 25% (Cohen et al., 1989). Light smokers are somewhat more successful at quitting than heavy smokers (but see Schachter, 1982), as are older smokers compared to younger ones (Ferguson et al., 2005). Discouragingly, people who enroll in formal smoking cessation programs are only slightly more successful than people who try to quit on their own (Swan, Hudman, & Khroyan, 2003). In fact, it is estimated that the vast majority of people who successfully give up smoking quit without professional help (Niaura & Abrams, 2002; Shiffman et al. 2008). And here is one myth that can be dispelled: Men do not have an easier time quitting smoking than women—there is virtually no difference between the sexes (O'Connor, 2012).

In recent years attention has focused on the potential value of *nicotine substitutes*, which can be delivered via

Learn More Online

The QuitNet Community

The Boston University School of Public Health sponsors an online community of individuals who seek to quit smoking and tobacco use. A range of resources, including an online support "community" available 24 hours a day, can help make this behavioral health change a reality.

REEL RESEARCH

Understanding Addiction

© Cengage Learning 2015

© Cengage Learning 2015

Illicit drug use is on the rise. According to a national survey, over 9% of Americans—roughly 23 million people across the country—used illicit drugs in the month prior to the survey (Substance Abuse and Mental Health Services Administration, 2011). Researchers seek to understand addiction to recreational drugs by studying nicotine use. Anthony Caggiula and Ken Perkins, psychologists at University of Pittsburgh, examine the relationship between nicotine and cues and their combined influence on addiction in this Reel Research video.

Using participants who are addicted to nicotine along with another drug as a sample population, Caggiula found that although everyone ranked nicotine as a "low reinforcer," when asked which drug is the hardest to quit they unanimously said nicotine. Even though other drugs, like cocaine or alcohol, are high reinforcers used by the group, nicotine was more difficult to give up.

In another demonstration, Caggiula studies addiction through the behavior of laboratory rats. By learning to press levers in their cage, rats self-administer small doses of different types of drugs—nicotine and cocaine among them. With no other stimuli present, the rat presses the lever to receive cocaine more frequently than nicotine. When a visual cue, a light that turns on and off when the nicotine lever is pressed, is introduced, the rats show a tremendous increase in choosing nicotine over other, more potent drugs. Caggiula

believes that visual cues are enhanced through nicotine use and that the combination is highly reinforcing.

Perkins, in a study with human subjects, shows a smoker playing games on a computer to earn either puffs on a cigarette or dollars. If a lit cigarette is present in the room as the smoker plays games, which vary in complexity, the likelihood that she will choose puffs over dollars raises dramatically.

Watch the *Understanding Addiction* video to learn more about the relationship between visual cues and addiction. Delve even deeper by responding to the following discussion questions.

DISCUSSION QUESTIONS

1. Why is nicotine considered a "low reinforcer"? What type of drug is a "high reinforcer"?

2. Discuss the last study shown in the video involving the smoker and the computer games. How did the smoker's behavior change given the complexity of the game, whether earning puffs or dollars? What did researchers introduce that changed this behavior? Explain your answers.

3. How might you apply the findings in the research discussed in the video to helping a friend quit smoking? What sensory and/or behavioral cues might you predict promote his/her smoking?

gum, pills like Chantix, skin patches, nasal sprays, or inhalers. The rationale for nicotine substitutes is that insofar as nicotine is addictive, using a substitute might be helpful during the period when the person is trying to give up cigarettes. Do these substitutes work? They do help (Stead et al., 2008). Controlled studies have demonstrated that nicotine substitutes increase long-term rates of quitting in comparison to placebos (Stead et al., 2008; Swan, Hudman, & Khroyan, 2003). However, the increases are modest, and the success rates are still discouragingly low.

"There's no shooting—we just make you keep smoking."

Nicotine substitutes are not a magic bullet or a substitute for a firm determination to quit. The various methods of nicotine delivery seem to be roughly equal in effectiveness, but combining a couple of methods appears to increase the chances of quitting successfully (Schmitz & Delaune, 2005).

women reported that they engage in binge drinking with the intention of getting drunk, and 40% of college students report drinking five or more alcoholic drinks at one sitting at least monthly (Johnston et al., 2009). College students who belong to fraternities and sororities consume more alcohol than those who do not belong to these organization (Karam, Kypri, & Salamoun, 2007). Perhaps most telling, college students spend far more money on alcohol ($5.5 billion annually) than they do on their books.

Drinking

Alcohol rivals tobacco as one of the leading causes of health problems in North America. Alcohol encompasses a variety of beverages containing ethyl alcohol, such as beers, wines, and distilled spirits. The concentration of alcohol in these drinks varies from about 4% in most beers up to 40% in 80-proof liquor (or more in higher-proof liquors). Survey data indicate that about half of adults in the United States drink. As **Figure 5.11** shows, per capita consumption of alcohol in the United States declined in the 1980s and 1990s, but this decrease followed decades of steady growth, and alcohol consumption remains relatively high, although certainly not the highest in the world. **Figure 5.12** shows the percentage of adults in the United States who are regular, infrequent, or former drinkers.

Drinking is particularly prevalent on college campuses. When researchers from the Harvard School of Public Health surveyed nearly 11,000 undergraduates at 119 schools, they found that 81% of the students drank (Wechsler et al., 2002). Moreover, 49% of the men and 41% of the

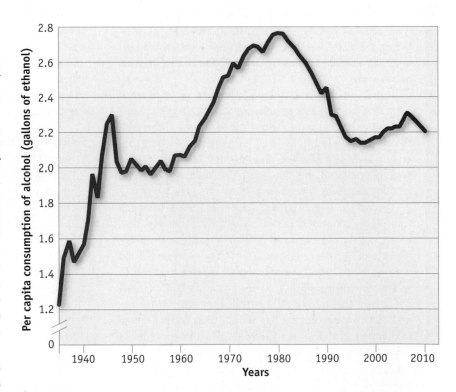

Figure 5.11

Drinking in America. Drinking in the United States, as indexed by per capita consumption (average consumed per person per year) of ethanol in gallons, rose steadily through most of the 20th century, although notable declines occurred during the 1980s and 1990s. (Data from National Institute on Alcohol Abuse and Alcoholism and U.S. Department of Health and Human Services)

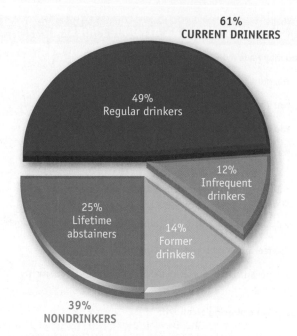

61%
CURRENT DRINKERS

49%
Regular drinkers

12%
Infrequent drinkers

25%
Lifetime abstainers

14%
Former drinkers

39%
NONDRINKERS

Figure 5.12

Types of adult drinkers in the United States. Just over 60% of adults in the United States categorize themselves as current drinkers. About one-quarter of all adults are lifelong abstainers.

Source: Adapted from *Healthy United States, 2007* (Table 68), 2007, by National Center for Health Statistics, Hyattsville, MD: U.S. Government Printing Office.

Why Do People Drink?

The effects of alcohol are influenced by the user's experience, relative size and weight, gender, motivation, and mood, as well as by the presence of food in the stomach, the proof of the beverage, and the rate of drinking. Thus, we see great variability in how alcohol affects different people on different occasions. Nonetheless, the central effect is a "Who cares?" brand of euphoria that temporarily boosts self-esteem as one's problems melt away. Negative emotions such as tension, worry, anxiety, and depression are dulled, and inhibitions may be loosened (Johnson & Ait-Daoud, 2005). Thus, when first-year college students are asked why they drink, they say it's to relax, to feel less tense in social situations, to keep friends company, and to forget their problems. Of course, many other factors are

also at work (Wood, Vinson, & Sher, 2001). Families and peer groups often encourage alcohol use. Drinking is a widely endorsed and encouraged social ritual in our culture. Its central role is readily apparent if you think about all the alcohol consumed at weddings, reunions, sports events, holiday parties, and so forth. Moreover, the alcohol industry spends hundreds of millions of dollars on advertising to convince us that drinking is cool, sexy, sophisticated, and harmless.

Short-Term Risks and Problems

Alcohol has a variety of side effects, including some that can be very problematic. To begin with, we have that infamous source of regret, the "hangover," which may include headaches, dizziness, nausea, and vomiting. In the constellation of alcohol's risks, however, hangovers are downright trivial. For instance, life-threatening overdoses are more common than most people realize. Although it's possible to overdose with alcohol alone, a more common problem is overdosing on combinations of alcohol and sedative or narcotic drugs.

In substantial amounts, alcohol has a decidedly negative effect on intellectual functioning and perceptual-motor coordination. The resulting combination of tainted judgment, slowed reaction time, and reduced coordination can be deadly when people attempt to drive after drinking (Gmel & Rehm, 2003). Depending on one's body weight, it may take only a few drinks for driving to be impaired. It's estimated that alcohol contributes to 40% of all automobile fatalities in the United States (Yi, Chen, & Williams, 2006). Drunk driving is a major social problem and the leading cause of death in young adults. Alcohol is also implicated in many other types of accidents. Victims test positive for alcohol in 38% of fire fatalities, 49% of drownings, and 63% of fatal falls (Smith, Branas, & Miller, 1999).

With their inhibitions released, some drinkers become argumentative and prone to aggression. In the Harvard survey of undergraduates from 119 schools, 29% of the students who did *not* engage in binge drinking reported that they had been insulted or humiliated by a drunken student; 19% had experienced serious arguments; 9% had been pushed, hit, or assaulted; and 19.5% had been the target of unwanted sexual advances (Wechsler et al., 2002). Individuals who have been drinking are more likely than sober people to find themselves in forced sexual experiences, either as the perpetrator or a victim (Testa, Vazile-Tamsen, & Livingston, 2004). Worse yet, alcohol appears to contribute to about 90% of student rapes and 95% of violent crime on campus. In society at large, alcohol is associated with a variety of violent crimes, including murder, assault, child abuse, and intimate partner violence (Foran & O'Leary, 2008), as well as suicide attempts and suicidal ideation (Schaffer, Jeglic, & Stanley, 2008). In fact, alcohol is associated with suicide attempts more than other drugs (Rossow, Grøholt & Wichstrøm, 2005).

Long-Term Health Effects

Alcohol's long-term health risks are mostly (but not exclusively) associated with chronic, heavy consumption of alcohol. Estimates of the number of people at risk vary considerably. According to Schuckit (2000) approximately 5%–10% of American men and women engage in chronic alcohol abuse and another 10% of men and 3%–5% of women probably suffer from *alcohol dependence*, or *alcoholism*. **Alcohol dependence (alcoholism) is a chronic, progressive disorder marked by a growing compulsion to drink and impaired control over drinking that eventually interferes with health and social behavior.** Whether alcoholism is best viewed as a disease or as a self-control problem is the source of considerable debate, but experts have reached a reasonable consensus about the warning signs of a drinking problem and alcohol abuse. These signs include drinking in secret, experiencing "blackouts," drinking to cope with stress or worry, and neglecting responsibilities at home, school, or work, among the other indicators listed in **Figure 5.13**.

Alcoholism and problem drinking are associated with an elevated risk for a wide range of serious health problems, which are summarized in **Figure 5.14** (Mack, Franklin, & Frances, 2003; Moak & Anton, 1999). Although there is some thought-provoking evidence that moderate drinking may reduce one's risk for coronary disease (Klatsky, 2008; Mukamal et al., 2003) and Type 2 diabetes (Hendriks, 2007), it is clear that heavy drinking increases the risk for heart disease, hypertension, and stroke. Excessive drinking is also correlated with an elevated risk for various types of cancer, including oral, stomach, pancreatic, colon, and rectal cancer. Moreover, serious drinking problems can lead to cirrhosis of the liver, malnutrition, pregnancy complications, brain damage, and neurological disorders. Finally, alcoholism can produce severe psychotic states, characterized by delirium, disorientation, and hallucinations.

Overeating

Obesity is a common health problem. The criteria for obesity vary considerably. One simple, intermediate criterion is to classify people as obese if their weight exceeds their ideal body weight by 20%. If this criterion is used, 31% of men and 35% of women in the United States qualify as obese (Brownell & Wadden, 2000), and this problem is projected to persist well into the middle of the twenty-first century (National Center for Health Statistics, 2006). Obesity is an immediate and growing problem: For instance, as recently as the 1980s, only 13% of adult Americans were considered to be obese (Ogden, Carroll, & Flegal, 2008; see also, Corsica & Perry, 2003).

Many experts prefer to assess obesity in terms of *body mass index (BMI)—weight (in kilograms) divided by height (in meters) squared (kg/m²).* This increasingly

---

IDENTIFYING AN ALCOHOL PROBLEM

You may have a drinking problem if:

- You drink in secret.

- You feel worried about your drinking.

- You routinely consume more alcohol than you expected.

- You experience "blackouts" so that you forget what you did or said while drinking.

- You hear concern expressed by family and friends about your drinking.

- You cover up or lie about how often, and how much, you drink.

- You feel ashamed about your drinking.

- You get into arguments with those close to you about your drinking.

You may be abusing alcohol if:

- You frequently consume alcohol to deal with stress or worry.

- You know your drinking is harming your personal relationships, but you continue to drink anyway.

- Your drinking is causing you to neglect your responsibilities at home, at school, or at work.

- Your behavior is illegal and dangerous to others (e.g., you drink and drive).

- You want to stop drinking but you cannot seem to do it.

- You find yourself dropping other activities (e.g., exercise, hobbies, spending time with friends or family) because you need to have a drink.

Figure 5.13

Identifying an alcohol problem. Facing the reality that one has a problem with alcohol is always difficult. Here is a list of signs pointing to a possible drinking problem as well as a list indicating the likely presence of alcohol abuse.

Source: Based on http://www.helpguide.org/mental/alcohol_abuse_alcoholism_signs_effects_treatments.htm; http://www.med.unc.edu/alcohol/prevention/signs.html http://www.webmd.com/mental-health/alcohol-abuse/alcohol-abuse-and-dependence-symptoms

---

used index of weight controls for variations in height. A BMI of 25.0–29.9 is typically regarded as overweight, and a BMI over 30 is considered obese (Björntorp, 2002). If a BMI over 25 is used as the cutoff, almost two-thirds of American adults are struggling with weight problems (Sarwer, Foster, & Wadden, 2004). Moreover, they have plenty of company from their children, as weight problems among children and adolescents have increased 15%–22% in recent decades (West, Harvey-Berino, & Raczynski, 2004).

Obesity is similar to smoking in that it exerts a relatively subtle impact on health that is easy for many people to ignore. Nevertheless, the long-range effects can be quite dangerous; obesity is a significant health problem that

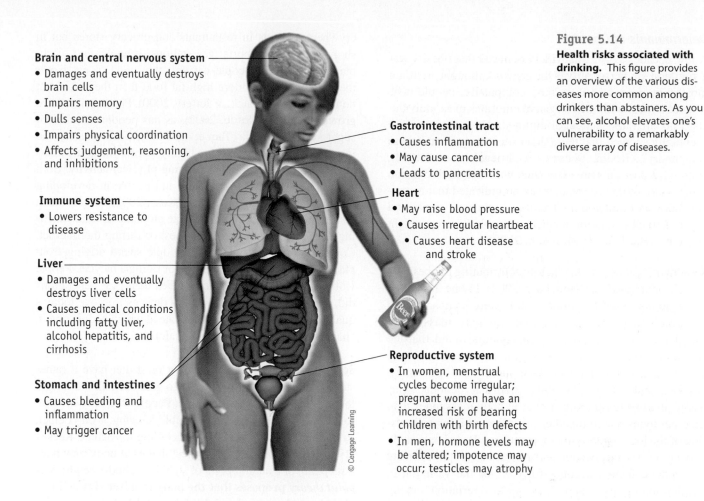

Brain and central nervous system
- Damages and eventually destroys brain cells
- Impairs memory
- Dulls senses
- Impairs physical coordination
- Affects judgement, reasoning, and inhibitions

Immune system
- Lowers resistance to disease

Liver
- Damages and eventually destroys liver cells
- Causes medical conditions including fatty liver, alcohol hepatitis, and cirrhosis

Stomach and intestines
- Causes bleeding and inflammation
- May trigger cancer

Gastrointestinal tract
- Causes inflammation
- May cause cancer
- Leads to pancreatitis

Heart
- May raise blood pressure
- Causes irregular heartbeat
- Causes heart disease and stroke

Reproductive system
- In women, menstrual cycles become irregular; pregnant women have an increased risk of bearing children with birth defects
- In men, hormone levels may be altered; impotence may occur; testicles may atrophy

© Cengage Learning

Figure 5.14
Health risks associated with drinking. This figure provides an overview of the various diseases more common among drinkers than abstainers. As you can see, alcohol elevates one's vulnerability to a remarkably diverse array of diseases.

elevates one's mortality risk (Allison et al., 1999). In fact, obesity is probably responsible for the early deaths of well over a quarter of a million people in North America each year (DeAngelis, 2004). Overweight people are more vulnerable than others to heart disease, diabetes, hypertension, respiratory problems, gallbladder disease, stroke, arthritis, some cancers, muscle and joint pain, and back problems (Manson, Skerrett, & Willet, 2002; Pi-Sunyer, 2002). For example, **Figure 5.15** shows how the prevalence of diabetes, hypertension, coronary disease, and musculoskeletal pain are elevated as BMI increases.

Evolution-oriented researchers have a plausible explanation for the dramatic increase in the prevalence of obesity (Pinel, Assanand, & Lehman, 2000). They point out that over the course of history, most animals and humans have lived in environments in which there was fierce competition for limited, unreliable food resources and starvation was a very real threat. However, in today's modern, industrialized societies, the vast majority of humans live in environments that provide an abundant, reliable supply of tasty, high-calorie food. Most people in such environments tend to overeat in relation to their physiological needs, but because of variations in genetics, metabolism, and other factors only some become overweight.

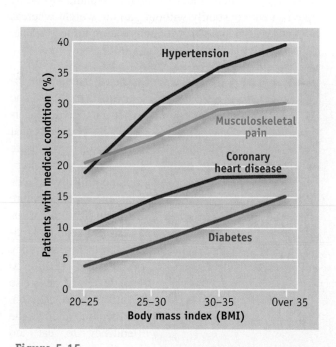

Figure 5.15
Weight and the prevalence of various diseases. This graph shows how obesity, as indexed by BMI, is related to the prevalence of four common types of illness. The prevalence of diabetes, heart disease, muscle pain, and hypertension increases as BMI goes up. Clearly, obesity is a significant health risk. (Data from Brownell & Wadden, 2000)

Determinants of Obesity

A few decades ago it was widely believed that obesity was a function of personality. Obesity was thought to occur mostly in depressed, anxious, compulsive people who overeat to deal with their negative emotions or in individuals who are lazy and undisciplined. However, research eventually showed that there is no such thing as an "obese personality" (Rodin, Schank, & Striegel-Moore, 1989), although some traits are associated with weight fluctuation (Sutin et al., 2011). Instead, research indicated that a complex network of interacting factors—biological, social, and psychological—determine whether people develop weight problems (Berthoud & Morrison, 2008).

Heredity. Chief among the factors contributing to obesity is *genetic predisposition* (Bouchard, 2002). In one influential study, adults raised by foster parents were compared with their biological parents in regard to body mass index (Stunkard et al., 1986). The investigators found that the adoptees resembled their biological parents much more than their adoptive parents. In a subsequent *twin study,* Stunkard and associates (1990) found that identical twins reared apart were far more similar in body mass index than fraternal twins reared together (see Chapter 2 for a discussion of the logic underlying twin studies). Based on a study of over 4000 twins, Allison and colleagues (1994) estimate that genetic factors account for 61% of the variation in weight among men and 73% of the variation among women. These genetic factors probably explain why some people can eat constantly without gaining weight whereas other people grow chubby eating far less (Cope, Fernández, & Allison, 2004).

Justaman/Shutterstock.com

Excessive eating and inadequate exercise. The bottom line for overweight people is that their energy intake from food consumption chronically exceeds their energy expenditure from physical activities and resting metabolic processes. In other words, they eat too much in relation to their level of exercise (Wing & Polley, 2001). In modern America, the tendency to eat too much and to exercise too little is easy to understand (Henderson & Brownell, 2004). Tasty, caloric, high-fat foods are readily available nearly everywhere, not just in restaurants and grocery stores but in shopping malls, airports, gas stations, schools, and workplaces. And when people eat out, they tend to eat larger meals and consume more high-fat food than they would at home (French, Harnack, & Jeffery, 2000). Portion sizes have grown (Young & Nestle, 2002), as has people's desire for sugar-sweetened soda (Tam et al., 2006). Unfortunately, the increased availability of these highly caloric foods in America has been paralleled by declining physical activity. Both Americans (Pereira et al., 2005) and people in developing countries (Finkelstein, Ruhm, & Kosa, 2005) eat too much fast food and then spend inordinate amounts of time watching television, playing video games, or surfing the Internet. Consider, too, how much time people spend driving from place to place rather than walking or riding a bicycle. People work and play less with their bodies than past generations did, and a number of labor-saving devices improve today's quality of life while reducing the rate at which people obtain "natural" exercise that burns off calories.

Set point. People who lose weight on a diet have a rather strong (and depressing) tendency to gain back all the weight they lose. The reverse is also true: People who have to work to put weight on often have trouble keeping it on (Leibel, Rosenbaum, & Hirsch, 1995). According to Richard Keesey (1995), these observations suggest that each body may have a *set point,* or a natural point of stability in body weight. **Set-point theory proposes that the body monitors fat-cell levels to keep them (and weight) fairly stable.** When fat stores slip below a crucial set point, the body supposedly begins to compensate for this change (Keesey, 1993). This compensation apparently leads to increased hunger and decreased metabolism (Horvath, 2005). Studies have raised some doubts about various details of set-point theory, leading some researchers to propose an alternative called *settling-point theory* (Pinel et al., 2000). **Settling-point theory proposes that weight tends to drift around the level at which the constellation of factors that determine food consumption and energy expenditure achieve an equilibrium.** According to this view, weight tends to remain stable as long as there are no durable changes in any of the factors that influence it (e.g., diet, exercise or the lack thereof, stress, sleep). Settling-point theory casts a much wider net than set-point theory, which attributes weight stability to specific physiological processes. Another difference is that set-point theory asserts that an obese person's body will initiate processes that actively defend an excessive weight, whereas settling-point theory suggests that if an obese person makes long-term changes in eating or exercise, that person's settling point will drift downward without active resistance. Thus, settling-point theory is a little more encouraging to those who hope to lose weight.

Lack of adequate sleep. One additional factor is thought to be a cause of obesity: sleep deprivation. Sleep seems to be linked with weight regulation, and insufficient rest has been associated with weight gain. One representative sample study found that persons who get less than 7 hours of sleep per night were more likely to be classified as overweight or obese (Gangwisch et al., 2005). Another study found that this relationship holds true among obese children (Latzer, Tzischinsky, & Roer, 2007). What's the causal culprit? Sleep deprivation appears to alter the hormones involved in regulating appetite, eating, and satiety (Knutson & Van Cauter, 2008). Avoiding weight gain may well be one more reason to make certain you are routinely getting enough sleep each night.

Losing Weight

Whether out of concern about their health or just old-fashioned vanity, an ever-increasing number of people are trying to lose weight. One study found that at any given time, about 21% of men and 39% of women are dieting (Hill, 2002), and a subsequent survey yielded similar percentages by gender (Kruger et al., 2004). Research has provided some good news for those who need to lose weight. Studies have demonstrated that relatively modest weight reductions can significantly diminish many of the health risks associated with obesity. For example, a 10% weight loss is associated with reduced risks for diabetes, cancer, and heart disease (Jeffery et al., 2000). Thus, the traditional objective of obesity treatment—reducing to one's ideal weight—has been replaced by more modest and realistic goals (Sarwer et al., 2004).

While many factors may contribute to obesity, there is only one way to lose weight: Individuals must change their ratio of energy intake (food consumption) to energy output (physical activities). To be quite specific, to lose 1 pound a person needs to burn up 3500 more calories than he or she consumes. Those wanting to shed pounds have three options in trying to change their ratio of energy input to energy output: (1) sharply reduce food consumption, (2) sharply increase exercise output, or (3) simultaneously decrease food intake and step up exercise output in more moderate ways. Dieting alone is unlikely to be sufficient to lose weight and maintain the loss (Jeffery et al., 2004). Virtually all experts recommend the third option. Simply put, exercise is an essential ingredient of an effective weight-loss regimen (Manson et al., 2004). Exercise seems especially important for *maintaining* reduced weight, as it is the single best predictor of long-term weight loss (Curioni & Lourenco, 2005).

Some people opt for surgery to reduce their weight, an increasingly popular choice for weight control (Vetter, Dumon, & Williams, 2011). This option is generally reserved for individuals who are seriously obese or who have other weight problems that warrant drastic action to cause weight loss quickly. One popular form of surgery essentially shrinks the size of the stomach by placing what is

David Sipress/The New Yorker Collection/www.cartoonbank.com

known as a gastric band around it. Another surgical option is a gastric bypass, in which food is rerouted around the bulk of the stomach and a portion of the intestines (Buchwald et al., 2004). Both procedures involve risks and are life altering; patients must usually take food supplements while carefully watching their food consumption for the rest of their lives (Tucker, Szomstein, & Rosenthal, 2007).

Finally, self-modification techniques (see the Chapter 3 Application) can be helpful in achieving gradual weight loss. Indeed, behavior modification procedures represent the cornerstone of most reputable, professional weight-loss programs. Overall, the evidence on weight-loss programs suggests that they are moderately successful in the short term (the first 6 months), but in the long run the vast majority of people regain most of the weight they lost (Jeffery et al., 2000).

Poor Nutrition

Nutrition **is a collection of processes (mainly food consumption) through which an organism utilizes the materials (nutrients) required for survival and growth.** The term also refers to the *study* of these processes. Unfortunately, most of us don't study nutrition very much. Moreover, the cunning mass marketing of nutritionally worthless foods makes maintaining sound nutritional habits more and more difficult.

Nutrition and Health

We are what we eat. Evidence is accumulating that patterns of nutrition influence susceptibility to a variety of diseases and health problems. For example, in a study of over 42,000 women, investigators found an association between a measure of overall diet quality and mortality. Women who reported poorer quality diets had elevated mortality rates (Kant et al., 2000). What are the specific links be-

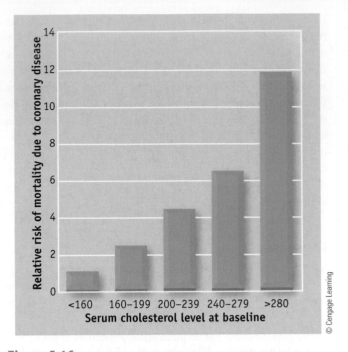

Figure 5.16

The link between cholesterol and coronary risk. In a review of several major studies, Stamler et al. (2000) summarized crucial evidence on the association between cholesterol levels and the prevalence of cardiovascular disease. This graph is based on a sample of over 11,000 men who were 18 to 39 at the beginning of the study (1967–1973) when their serum cholesterol level was measured. The data shown here depict participants' relative risk for coronary heart disease during the ensuing 25 years as a function of their initial cholesterol level.

tween diet and health? In addition to the problems associated with obesity, other possible connections between eating patterns and health include the following:

1. Heavy consumption of foods that elevate serum cholesterol level (eggs, cheeses, butter, shellfish, sausage, and the like) appears to increase the risk of cardiovascular disease (Stamler et al., 2000; see **Figure 5.16**). Eating habits are only one of several factors that influence serum cholesterol level, but they do make an important contribution.

2. Vulnerability to cardiovascular diseases may also be influenced by other dietary factors. For example, low-fiber diets may increase the likelihood of coronary disease (Timm & Slavin, 2008) and high intake of red and processed meats, sweets, potatoes, and refined grains is associated with increased cardiovascular risk (Hu & Willett, 2002). Recent research indicates that the omega-3 fatty acids found in fish and fish oils offer some protection against coronary disease (Din, Newby, & Flapan, 2004).

3. High salt intake is thought to be a contributing factor in the development of hypertension (Havas, Dickinson, & Wilson, 2007), although there is still some debate about its exact role.

4. High caffeine consumption may elevate one's risk for hypertension (James, 2004) and for coronary disease (Happonen, Voutilainen, Salonen, 2004), although the negative effects of caffeine appear relatively modest.

5. High-fat diets have been implicated as possible contributors to cardiovascular disease (Melanson, 2007) and to some forms of cancer, especially prostate cancer (Rose, 1997), colon and rectal cancer (Shike, 1999), and breast cancer (Wynder et al., 1997). Some studies also suggest that high-fiber diets may reduce one's risk for breast cancer, colon cancer, and diabetes (Timm & Slavin, 2008).

Learn More Online

Go Ask Alice!

One of the longest standing and most popular sources of frank information on the web has been *Alice!* from Columbia University's Health Education Program. Geared especially to the needs of undergraduate students, *Alice!* offers direct answers to questions about relationships, sexuality and sexual health, fitness and nutrition, alcohol and drug consumption, emotional health, and general health.

Of course, nutritional habits interact with other factors—genetics, exercise, environment, and so on—to determine whether someone will develop a particular disease. Nonetheless, the examples just described indicate that eating habits can influence physical health.

Nutritional Goals

The most healthful approach to nutrition is to follow well-moderated patterns of food consumption that ensure nutritional adequacy while limiting the intake of certain substances that can be counterproductive. Here are some general guidelines for achieving these goals:

1. *Consume a balanced variety of foods.* Food is made up of a variety of components, six of which are essential to your physical well-being. These six *essential nutrients* are proteins, fats, carbohydrates, vitamins, minerals, and fiber. Proteins, fats, and carbohydrates supply the body with its energy. Vitamins and minerals help release that energy and serve other important functions as well. Fiber provides roughage that facilitates digestion. Educational efforts to promote adequate intake of all essential nutrients have generally suggested that people should be guided by the classic food pyramid published by the U.S. Department of Agriculture (see **Figure 5.17**). Although the food pyramid remains a useful benchmark, it has been subjected to considerable criticism and hotly

debated revisions (Norton, 2004). The principal problem with the food pyramid is its failure to distinguish between different types of fat, different forms of carbohydrates, and different sources of protein (Willett & Stampfer, 2003). For example, the current thinking is that monounsaturated and polyunsaturated fats are healthy, whereas saturated fats should be consumed sparingly. A revised food pie chart, which takes distinctions such as these into consideration, is shown in **Figure 5.18** on the next page.

2. *Avoid excessive consumption of saturated fats, cholesterol, refined-grain carbohydrates, sugar, and salt.* These commodities are all overrepresented in the typical American diet. It is particularly prudent to limit the intake of saturated fats by eating less beef, pork, ham, hot dogs, sausage, lunch meats, whole milk, and fried foods. Consumption of many of these foods should also be limited in order to reduce cholesterol intake, which influences vulnerability to heart disease. In particular, beef, pork, lamb, sausage, cheese, butter, and eggs are high in cholesterol. Refined-grain carbohydrates, such as white bread, pasta, and white rice, are problematic because they increase glucose levels in the blood too quickly. Refined (processed) sugar is believed to be grossly overconsumed. Hence, people should limit their dependence on soft drinks, chocolate, candy, pastries, and high-sugar cereals. Finally, many people should cut down on their salt intake. Doing so may require more than simply ignoring the salt shaker

- Fats (naturally occurring and added)
- Sugars (added)

Fats, oils, and sweets
Use sparingly

Milk, yogurt, and cheese
2–3 servings

Meat, poultry, fish, eggs, dry beans, and nuts
2–3 servings

Vegetable group
3–5 servings

Fruit group
2–4 servings

Breads, cereal, rice, and pasta group
6–11 servings

© Cengage Learning

Figure 5.17
The food guide pyramid.
The food pyramid, endorsed in 1992 by the U.S. Department of Agriculture, is intended to provide a simple and easy guide to nutritionally balanced eating. It identifies key categories of food and makes recommendations about how many daily servings one should have in each category. As your text explains, it has been subjected to considerable criticism.

Figure 5.18

The healthy eating pie chart. As you can see, the revised view of healthy eating encourages people to focus primarily on fruits and vegetables followed by grains, breads, and starches. Meat, poultry, fish, and dairy should be eaten more sparingly. Chocolate and other sugar-based products should be eaten least often, as the treats they are meant to be.

Elena Schweitzer/Shutterstock.com

or passing up the potato chips, since many prepackaged foods are loaded with salt.

3. *Increase consumption of polyunsaturated fats, whole-grain carbohydrates, natural sugars, and foods with fiber.* To substitute polyunsaturated fats for saturated ones, people can eat more fish, chicken, turkey, and veal; trim fat off meats more thoroughly; use skim (nonfat) milk; and switch to vegetable oils that are high in polyunsaturated fats. Healthy carbohydrates include whole-grain foods such as whole wheat bread, oatmeal, and brown rice, which are digested more slowly than refined-grain carbohydrates. Fruits and vegetables tend to provide natural sugars and ample fiber.

Lack of Exercise

A great deal of evidence suggests that there is a link between exercise and health. Research indicates that regular exercise is associated with increased longevity (Lee & Skerrett, 2001). Moreover, you don't have to be a dedicated athlete to benefit from exercise. Even a moderate level of reasonably regular physical activity is associated with lower mortality rates (Richardson et al., 2004; see **Figure 5.19**). Unfortunately, physical fitness appears to be declining in the United States. Only 25% of American

adults get an adequate amount of regular exercise (Dubbert et al., 2004). Why might this be? There are many possible reasons. Just consider, for example, the impact of technology. How much time do children (and many adults) now spend playing video games rather than going outdoors and playing physical games? Video games and other online pursuits may exercise the mind but, as you will see, we need rigorous, regular physical exercise to maintain health and well-being.

Benefits and Risks of Exercise

Exercise is correlated with greater longevity because it promotes a diverse array of specific benefits. First, an appropriate exercise program can enhance cardiovascular fitness and thereby reduce one's susceptibility to cardiovascular problems (Schlicht, Kanning, & Bös, 2007). Fitness is associated with reduced risk for coronary disease, stroke, and hypertension (Blair, Cheng, & Holder, 2001). Second, regular physical activity can contribute to the avoidance of obesity (Hill & Wyatt, 2005; Jakicic & Otto, 2005), reducing one's risk for a variety of obesity-related health problems, including diabetes, respiratory difficulties, arthritis, and back pain. Third, some studies suggest that physical fitness is also associated with a decreased risk for colon cancer and for breast and reproductive cancer in

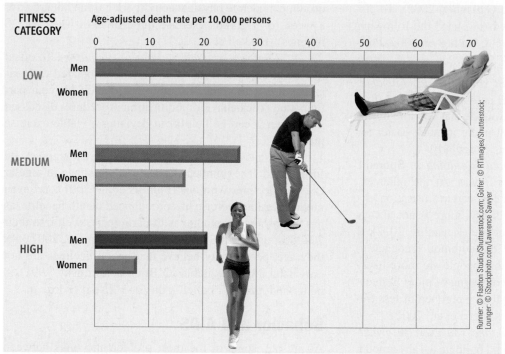

FITNESS CATEGORY

Age-adjusted death rate per 10,000 persons

LOW — Men, Women

MEDIUM — Men, Women

HIGH — Men, Women

Runner: © Flashon Studio/Shutterstock.com; Golfer: © RTimages/Shutterstock; Lounger: © iStockphoto.com/Lawrence Sawyer

© Cengage Learning

Figure 5.19

Physical fitness and mortality. Blair et al. (1989) studied death rates among men and women who exhibited low, medium, or high fitness. Even medium fitness was associated with lower mortality rates in both genders. The investigators note that one could achieve this level of fitness by taking a brisk half-hour walk each day.

women (Thune & Furberg, 2001). The apparent link between exercise and reduced cancer risk has been a pleasant surprise for scientists, who are scrambling to replicate the findings and figure out the physiological mechanisms underlying this association (Rogers et al., 2008). Exercise has even been found to help people who have cancer, including helping to manage the fatigue that accompanies treatments (Cramp & Daniel, 2008).

Fourth, exercise may serve as a buffer that reduces the potentially damaging effects of stress (Plante, Caputo, & Chizmar, 2000). This buffering effect may occur because people high in fitness show less physiological reactivity to stress than those who are less fit. Fifth, exercise may have a favorable impact on mental health, which in turn may have positive effects on physical health. Exercise increases people's happiness (Hyde et al., 2011). Studies have also

found a consistent association between regular exercise over a period of at least 8 weeks and reduced depression (Phillips, Kiernan, & King, 2001), which is important given the evidence that depression is correlated with increased vulnerability to heart disease. Sixth, successful participation in an exercise program can produce desirable personality changes, such as enhanced self-esteem (Ryan, 2008), that may promote physical wellness. Research suggests that fitness training can lead to improvements in one's mood, self-esteem, and work efficiency, as well as reductions in tension and anxiety (Dunn, Trivedi, & O'Neal, 2001; Wipfli, Rethorst, & Landers, 2008).

Devising an Exercise Program

Putting together a good exercise program is difficult for many people. Exercise is time consuming, and if you're out of shape, your initial attempts may be painful, aversive, and discouraging. People who do not get enough exercise cite lack of time, lack of convenience, and lack of enjoy-

Supri Suharjoto/Shutterstock.com

Learn More Online

About.Com: Health

About.com is a commercial endeavor enlisting subject experts to edit topic-specific directories with annotated links and other information resources. More than sixty directories related to topics of health and healthy living—including alcoholism, substance abuse, and smoking cessation—are now available at About.com.

ment as the reasons (Jakicic & Gallagher, 2002). To circumvent these problems, it is wise to heed the following advice (Greenberg, 2002; Jakicic & Gallagher, 2002; Phillips et al., 2001):

1. *Look for an activity that you will find enjoyable.* You have a great many physical activities to choose from (see **Figure 5.20**). Shop around for one that you find intrinsically enjoyable. Doing so will make it much easier for you to follow through and exercise regularly.

2. *Exercise regularly without overdoing it.* Sporadic exercise will not improve your fitness. At the other extreme, an overzealous approach can lead to frustration, not to mention injury. Moderation is key; more is not always better and may be counterproductive (Reynolds, 2012). If you experience injuries, avoid the common tendency to ignore them. One study found that people are more likely to stick to an exercise regimen consisting of more frequent workouts of moderate intensity than a regimen of less frequent but more intense workouts (Perri et al., 2002).

3. *Increase the amount of time you exercise gradually.* Don't rush it. Start slowly and build up, as any amount of exercise is apt to be better than no exercise. For example, healthy people between the ages of 18 and 65 should do some moderate physical activity for half an hour, 5 days a week (or vigorous exercise three times a week for 20 minutes) (Haskell et al., 2007).

4. *Reinforce yourself for your participation.* To offset the inconvenience or pain that may be associated with exercise, it is a good idea to reinforce yourself for your participation. The behavior modification procedures discussed in Chapter 3 can be helpful in devising a viable exercise program.

5. *It's never too late to begin an exercise regimen.* Be forewarned: The number of people who engage in regular exercise declines with age (Phillips et al., 2001). Yet even modest regular exercise has pronounced health benefits, as has been shown in studies with participants well into their 70s, 80s, and 90s (Everett, Kinser, & Ramsey, 2007). As they age, people may believe that health declines are not only natural but inevitable (O'Brien & Vertinsky, 1991). A better and more apt belief is this one: Use it or lose it.

Behavior and AIDS

At present, some of the most problematic links between behavior and health may be those related to AIDS, a pandemic, or worldwide epidemic. AIDS stands for *acquired*

HOW BENEFICIAL IS YOUR FAVORITE SPORT?														
Physical fitness	Jogging	Bicycling	Swimming	Skating (ice or roller)	Handball/ Squash	Skiing (Nordic)	Skiing (Alpine)	Basketball	Tennis	Calisthenics	Walking	Golf	Softball	Bowling
Cardiorespiratory endurance (stamina)	21	19	21	18	19	19	16	19	16	10	13	8	6	5
Muscular endurance	20	18	20	17	18	19	18	17	16	13	14	8	8	5
Muscular strength	17	16	14	15	15	15	15	15	14	16	11	9	7	5
Flexibility	9	9	15	13	16	14	14	13	14	19	7	9	9	7
Balance	17	18	12	20	17	16	21	16	16	15	8	8	7	6
General well-being														
Weight control	21	20	15	17	19	17	15	19	16	12	13	6	7	5
Muscle definition	14	15	14	14	11	12	14	13	13	18	11	6	5	5
Digestion	13	12	13	11	13	12	9	10	12	11	11	7	8	7
Sleep	16	15	16	15	12	15	12	12	11	12	14	6	7	6
Total	**148**	**142**	**140**	**140**	**140**	**139**	**134**	**134**	**128**	**126**	**102**	**67**	**64**	**51**

Figure 5.20

A scorecard on the benefits of fourteen sports and exercises. Here is a summary of how seven experts rated the value of fourteen sports activities (the highest rating possible on any one item was 21). The ratings were based on vigorous participation four times per week.

Source: Adapted from Conrad, C. C. (1976, May). How different sports rate in promoting physical fitness. *Medical Times*, pp. 45. Copyright 1976 by Romaine Pierson Publishers. Reprinted by permission.

immune deficiency syndrome, **a disorder in which the immune system is gradually weakened and eventually disabled by the human immunodeficiency virus (HIV).** Being infected with the HIV virus is *not* equivalent to having AIDS. AIDS is the final stage of the HIV infection process, typically manifested about 7–10 years after the original infection (Carey & Vanable, 2003). With the onset of AIDS, one is left virtually defenseless against a number of opportunistic infectious agents. The symptoms of AIDS vary widely depending on the specific constellation of diseases that one develops (Cunningham & Selwyn, 2005). The worldwide prevalence of this deadly disease continues to increase at an alarming rate, especially in certain regions of Africa (UNAIDS, 2005). And, unfortunately, some people infected with HIV sincerely believe that there is no evidence the virus causes AIDS (Kalichman, Eaton, & Cherry, 2010).

Prior to 1996–1997, the average length of survival for people after the onset of the AIDS syndrome was about 18 to 24 months. Encouraging advances in the treatment of AIDS with drug regimens referred to as *highly active antiretroviral therapy* hold out promise for substantially longer survival (Anthony & Bell, 2008; Hammer et al., 2006). Medical experts are concerned that the general public has gotten the impression that these treatments have transformed AIDS from a fatal disease to a manageable one, which is a premature conclusion. HIV strains are evolving, and many have developed resistance to the currently available antiretroviral drugs (Trachtenberg & Sande, 2002). Moreover, many patients do not respond well to the new drugs, which often have adverse side effects (Beusterien et al., 2008). Another daunting problem is that these expensive new drugs remain largely unavailable in developing nations, which have not seen progress in treatment. In some African nations the impact of AIDS has reduced life expectancy to levels not seen for hundreds of years. In Botswana, for instance, projections suggest that life expectancy has declined from 66 to 33 years (Carey & Vanable, 2003).

There is some good news in the ongoing battle with the AIDS pandemic, including evidence that blends of antiretroviral drugs are slowing HIV's progression among infected persons and lengthening their life span as a result (UNAIDS, 2008). Longevity is due to early detection of the disease, the aforementioned drug regimens, and behavioral changes that promote health and well-being. Thus, smoking, drinking alcohol, and enjoying illicit drugs are out, while regular exercise, healthy eating, and sufficient rest are helping people with HIV/AIDS live longer (Chou et al., 2004). Having a positive and optimistic attitude is also linked with reduced AIDS mortality rates (Moskowitz, 2003).

Transmission

The HIV virus is transmitted through person-to-person contact involving the exchange of bodily fluids, primarily semen and blood. The two principal modes of transmission in the United States have been sexual contact and the sharing of needles by intravenous (IV) drug users. In the United States, sexual transmission has occurred primarily among gay and bisexual men, but heterosexual transmission has increased in recent years (Centers for Disease Control, 2006). In the world as a whole, infection through heterosexual relations has been more common from the beginning (UNAIDS, 2007). In heterosexual relations, male-to-female transmission is estimated to be about eight times more likely than female-to-male transmission (Ickovics, Thayaparan, & Ethier, 2001). Although the HIV virus can be found in the tears and saliva of infected individuals, the concentrations are low, and there is no evidence that the infection can be spread through casual contact. Even most forms of noncasual contact, including kissing, hugging, and sharing food with infected individuals, appear safe (Kalichman, 1995). Children born to HIV-positive women can also acquire the disease, usually during the birthing process, although breastfeeding can also pass the virus from mother to child (Steinbrook, 2004).

Misconceptions

Misconceptions about AIDS are widespread. Ironically, the people who hold these misconceptions fall into two polarized camps. On the one hand, a great many people have unrealistic fears that AIDS can be readily transmitted through casual contact with infected individuals. These people worry unnecessarily about contracting AIDS from a handshake, a sneeze, or an eating utensil. They tend to be paranoid about interacting with homosexuals, thus fueling discrimination against gays. Some people also believe that it is dangerous to donate blood when, in fact, blood donors are at no risk whatsoever.

On the other hand, many young heterosexuals who are sexually active with a variety of partners foolishly downplay their risk for HIV, naively assuming that they are safe as long as they avoid IV drug use and sexual relations with gay or bisexual men. They greatly underestimate the probability that their sexual partners may have previously used IV drugs or had unprotected sex with an infected individual. They don't understand, for instance, that most bisexual men do not disclose their bisexuality to their female partners (Kalichman et al., 1998). Also, because AIDS is usually accompanied by discernible symptoms, many young people believe that prospective sexual partners who carry the HIV virus will exhibit telltale signs of illness. However, as we have already noted, having AIDS and being infected with HIV are not the same thing, and HIV carriers often remain healthy and symptom-free for many years after they are infected. Indeed, one study screened over 5000 men for HIV and found that 77% of those who tested HIV-positive were previously unaware of their infection (MacKellar et al., 2005).

In sum, many myths about AIDS persist, despite extensive efforts to educate the public about this complex and controversial disease. **Figure 5.21** contains a short quiz to test your knowledge of the facts about AIDS.

Prevention

The behavioral changes that minimize the risk of developing AIDS are fairly straightforward, although making the changes is often easier said than done (Coates & Collins, 1998). In all groups, the more sexual partners a person has, the higher the risk that he or she will be exposed to the HIV virus. Thus, people can reduce their risk by having sexual contacts with fewer partners and by using condoms to control the exchange of semen. It is also important to curtail certain sexual practices (in particular, anal sex) that increase the probability of semen/blood mixing. New cohorts of young people appear to be much less concerned about the risk of HIV infection than the generation that witnessed the original emergence of AIDS (Jaffe, Valdiserri, & De Cock, 2007; Mantell, Stein, & Susser, 2008). In particular, experts are concerned that recent advances in treatment may lead to more casual attitudes about risky sexual practices, a development that would not bode well for public health efforts to slow the spread of AIDS (Kalichman et al., 2007; van Kesteren, Hospers, & Kok, 2007). This false sense of security among young adults may have dire consequences in the long run unless they adopt prevention practices and an attitude of vigilance. Indeed, by the year 2015, fully half of all cases of HIV/AIDS in the United States are projected to be among adults who are 50 and older (Centers for Disease Control, 2006).

AIDS RISK KNOWLEDGE TEST

Answer the following "true" or "false."

T F **1.** The AIDS virus cannot be spread through kissing.

T F **2.** A person can get the AIDS virus by sharing kitchens and bathrooms with someone who has AIDS.

T F **3.** Men can give the AIDS virus to women.

T F **4.** The AIDS virus attacks the body's ability to fight off diseases.

T F **5.** You can get the AIDS virus by someone sneezing, like a cold or the flu.

T F **6.** You can get AIDS by touching a person with AIDS.

T F **7.** Women can give the AIDS virus to men.

T F **8.** A person who got the AIDS virus from shooting up drugs cannot give the virus to someone by having sex.

T F **9.** A pregnant woman can give the AIDS virus to her unborn baby.

T F **10.** Most types of birth control also protect against getting the AIDS virus.

T F **11.** Condoms make Intercourse completely safe.

T F **12.** Oral sex is safe if partners "do not swallow."

T F **13.** A person must have many different sexual partners to be at risk for AIDS.

T F **14.** It is more important to take precautions against AIDS in large cities than in small cities.

T F **15.** A positive result on the AIDS virus antibody test often occurs for people who do not even have the virus.

T F **16.** Only receptive (passive) anal intercourse transmits the AIDS virus.

T F **17.** Donating blood carries no AIDS risk for the donor.

T F **18.** Most people who have the AIDS virus look quite ill.

Answers: 1.T 2.F 3.T 4.T 5.F 6.F 7.T 8.F 9.T 10.F 11.F 12.F 13.F 14.F 15.F 16.F 17.T 18.F

Figure 5.21

A quiz on knowledge of AIDS. Because misconceptions about AIDS abound, it may be wise to take this brief quiz to test your knowledge.

Source: Adapted from Kalichman, S. C. (1995). *Understanding AIDS: A guide for mental health professionals.* Washington, DC: American Psychological Association. Copyright © 1995 by the American Psychological Association. Adapted with permission of the author.

REACTIONS TO ILLNESS

LEARNING OBJECTIVES

- Summarize evidence on patterns of treatment-seeking behavior, including the appeal of the "sick role."
- Identify factors that can undermine doctor-patient communication, and discuss how to improve it.
- Discuss the prevalence of nonadherence to medical advice and its causes.

So far we have emphasized the psychosocial aspects of maintaining health and minimizing the risk of illness. Health is also affected by how individuals respond to physical symptoms and illnesses. Some people engage in denial and ignore early-warning signs of developing diseases. Others engage in active coping efforts to conquer their diseases. In this section, we discuss the decision to seek medical treatment, the sick role, communication with health providers, and compliance with medical advice.

The Decision to Seek Treatment

Have you ever experienced nausea, diarrhea, stiffness, headaches, cramps, chest pains, or sinus problems? Of course you have; everyone experiences some of these problems periodically. However, whether you view these sensations as *symptoms* is a matter of individual interpretation, and the level of symptoms is what prompts people to seek medical advice (Ringström et al., 2007). When two persons experience the same unpleasant sensations, one may shrug them off as a nuisance, while the other may rush to a physician (Leventhal, Cameron, & Leventhal, 2005). Studies suggest that those who are relatively high in anxiety and neuroticism tend to report more symptoms of illness than others do (Feldman et al., 1999; Goodwin & Friedman, 2006). Those who are extremely attentive to bodily sensations and health concerns also report more symptoms than the average person (Barsky, 1988). When feeling ill, women report more symptoms and higher distress than men do (Koopmans & Lamers, 2007).

Variations in the perception of symptoms help explain why people vary so much in their readiness to seek medical treatment (Cameron, Leventhal, & Leventhal, 1993). Generally, people are more likely to seek medical care when their symptoms are unfamiliar, appear to be serious, last longer than expected, or disrupt their work or social activities (Martin et al., 2003). Social class matters, too. Higher socioeconomic groups report having fewer symptoms and better health, but when sickness occurs, members of these groups are more likely to seek medical care than lower-income people are (Grzywacz et al., 2004).

Another key consideration is how friends and family react to the symptoms. Medical consultation is much more likely when friends and family view symptoms as serious and encourage the person to seek medical care, although nagging a person about seeking care can sometimes backfire (Martin et al., 2003). Gender also influences decisions to seek treatment, as women are much more likely than men to utilize medical services (Galdas, Cheater, & Marshall, 2005). Finally, age matters: Young children (age 5 and under) and older adults (late middle age and beyond) are more likely to utilize health services (U.S. Department of Health and Human Services, 1995). These facts should not be surprising, especially in the case of young children, who often experience illnesses and vaccinations and have parents or caregivers who take them for frequent checkups.

The process of seeking medical treatment can be divided into three stages of active, complex problem solving (Martin et al., 2003). First, people have to decide that their physical sensations *are* symptoms—that they are indicative of illness. Second, they have to decide that their apparent illness warrants medical attention. Third, they have to go to the trouble to make the actual arrangements for medical care, which can be complicated and time consuming. The task of checking insurance coverage, finding an appropriate doctor, negotiating an appointment, arranging to get off work or take care of children, and so forth can be a huge series of hassles.

Small wonder then, that the biggest problem in regard to treatment seeking is the tendency of many people to delay the pursuit of needed professional consultation. Delays can be important, because early diagnosis and quick intervention can facilitate more effective treatment of many health problems. Unfortunately, procrastination is the norm even when people are faced with a medical emergency, such as a heart attack (Martin & Leventhal, 2004).

The Sick Role

Although many people tend to delay medical consultations, some people are actually eager to seek medical care. Given this reality, it is not surprising that up to 60% of patients' visits to their primary care physicians appear to have little medical basis (Ellington & Wiebe, 1999). Many of the people who are quick to solicit medical assistance probably have learned that there are potential benefits in adopting the "sick role" (Hamilton, Deemer, & Janata, 2003). For instance, the sick role absolves people from responsibility for their incapacity and can be used to exempt them from many of their normal duties and obligations (Segall, 1997). Fewer demands are placed on sick people, who can often be selective in deciding which demands to ignore. Illness can provide a convenient, face-saving excuse for one's failures (Wolinksky, 1988). Sick people may also find themselves receiving lots of attention (affection, concern, sympathy) from friends and relatives. This positive attention can be rewarding and can encourage the maintenance of symptoms (Walker, Claar, & Garber, 2002).

Of course, there are also some people who refuse to play the sick role under any circumstances. That is, they may well be sick but they are nonetheless determined to continue their normal routines. People who worry that they could lose their job, for example, will go to work even if they are ill (Bloor, 2005). So will people who feel dedicated to their job, as will those who have good rapport with their co-workers (Biron et al., 2006).

Communicating with Health Providers

When people seek help from physicians and other health care providers, many factors can undermine effective communication. A large portion of medical patients leave their doctors' offices not understanding what they have been told and what they are supposed to do (Johnson & Carlson, 2004). This situation is unfortunate, because good communication is a crucial requirement for sound medical decisions, informed choices about treatment, and appropriate follow-through by patients (Buckman, 2002).

There are many barriers to effective provider-patient communication (Beisecker, 1990; DiMatteo, 1997). Economic realities dictate that medical visits usually be quite brief, allowing little time for discussion. Illness and pain are subjective matters that may be difficult to describe. Many providers use too much medical jargon and overestimate their patients' understanding of technical terms. Some providers are uncomfortable being questioned and discourage their patients' information seeking. Patients

Communication between health care providers and patients tends to be far from optimal for a variety of reasons.

who are upset and worried about their illness may simply forget to report some symptoms or to ask questions they meant to ask. Other patients are evasive about their real concerns because they fear a serious diagnosis. Many patients are reluctant to challenge doctors' authority and are too passive in their interactions with providers. Doctors and nurses often believe their explanations are clear; however, patient misunderstanding can be a common phenomenon, one posing particular problems for individuals whose instructions regarding diagnosis, treatment, and medication are complex (Parker, 2000).

Adherence to Medical Advice

Many patients fail to adhere to the instructions they receive from physicians and other health care professionals. Noncompliance with medical advice may occur 30% of the time when short-term treatments are prescribed for acute conditions and 50% of the time when long-term treatments are needed for chronic illness (Johnson & Carlson, 2004). Nonadherence takes many forms. Patients may fail to begin a treatment regimen, may stop the regimen early, may reduce or increase the levels of treatment that were prescribed, or may be inconsistent and unreliable in following treatment procedures (Clifford, Barber, & Horn, 2008). Nonadherence is a major problem that has been linked to increased sickness, treatment failures, and higher mortality (DiMatteo et al., 2002). Moreover, nonadherence wastes expensive medical visits and medications and increases hospital admissions, leading to enormous economic costs. Robin DiMatteo (2004), a leading authority on compliance, speculates that in the United States alone, nonadherence may be a $300 billion a year drain on the health care system. DiMatteo (2004) also points to a sobering statistic: Adherence rates have barely improved over the past 50 years, often because medical practitioners have done little to encourage patients to comply with their recommendations.

Robin DiMatteo

Here are some considerations that influence the likelihood of adherence (Dunbar-Jacob & Schlenk, 2001; Johnson & Carlson, 2004):

1. *Frequently, noncompliance occurs because patients simply forget instructions or fail to understand the instructions as given.* Medical professionals often forget that what seems obvious and simple to them may be obscure and complicated to many of their patients.

2. *Another key factor is how aversive or difficult the treatments are.* If the prescribed regimen is unpleasant, compliance tends to decrease. For example, adherence is reduced when prescribed medications have many severe side effects and when instructions interfere with routine behavior.

3. *If a patient has a negative attitude toward a physician, the probability of noncompliance will increase.* When patients are unhappy with their interactions with the doctor, they're more likely to ignore the medical advice provided. When a working alliance is formed between patient and physician, however, then compliance is likely to occur (Fuertes et al., 2007).

4. *Treatment adherence can be improved when physicians do follow-ups.* Patients are more likely to follow prescribed treatments if their doctors pay attention to them after the diagnosis has been made (Llorca, 2008).

In response to the noncompliance problem, researchers have investigated many methods of increasing patients' adherence to medical advice (Martin et al., 2010). Interventions have included simplifying instructions, providing more rationale for instructions, reducing the complexity of treatment regimens, helping patients with emotional distress that undermines adherence, and training patients in the use of behavior modification strategies. All of these interventions can improve adherence, although their effects tend to be modest (Christensen & Johnson, 2002).

Application

UNDERSTANDING THE EFFECTS OF DRUGS

LEARNING OBJECTIVES

- Explain the concepts of drug tolerance, physical and psychological dependence, and overdose.
- Summarize the main effects and risks of narcotics, sedatives, stimulant drugs, and hallucinogens.
- Outline the main effects and risks of marijuana and ecstasy (MDMA).

Answer the following "true" or "false."
____ **1.** Smoking marijuana can make men impotent and sterile.
____ **2.** Overdoses caused by cocaine are relatively rare.
____ **3.** It is well documented that LSD causes chromosome damage.
____ **4.** Hallucinogens are addictive.
____ **5.** Ecstasy is a relatively harmless drug.

As you will learn in this Application, all of these statements are false. If you answered all of them accurately, you may already be well informed about drugs. If not, you *should* be. Intelligent decisions about drugs require an understanding of their effects and risks.

This Application focuses on the use of drugs for their pleasurable effects, commonly referred to as *drug abuse* or *recreational drug use*. Drug abuse reaches into every corner of our society and is a problematic health-impairing habit. Although small declines appear to have occurred in the overall abuse of drugs in recent years, survey data show that illicit drug use has mostly been increasing since the 1960s (Winick & Norman, 2005). The onset of drug use is typically in adolescence (Swendsen et al., 2012).

Recreational drug use involves personal, moral, political, and legal, as well as occasionally religious, issues that are not matters for science to resolve. However, the more knowledgeable you are about drugs, the more informed your decisions and opinions about them will be. Accordingly, this Application is intended to provide you with nonjudgmental, realistic coverage of issues related to recreational drug use. We begin by reviewing key drug-related concepts and then examine the effects and risks of six types of widely abused drugs: narcotics, sedatives, stimulants, hallucinogens, marijuana, and ecstasy (MDMA).

Learn More Online

National Institute on Drug Abuse (NIDA)

This government-sponsored site houses a great deal of information on the medical consequences of abusing various drugs. It is also a resource for statistics on trends in drug abuse.

Drug-Related Concepts

The principal types of recreational drugs are described in **Figure 5.22**. This table lists representative drugs in each of the five categories and indicates how the drugs are taken, their principal medical uses, their desired effects, and their common side effects.

Most drugs produce tolerance effects. **Tolerance is a progressive decrease in a person's responsiveness to a drug with continued use.** Tolerance effects usually lead people to consume larger and larger doses of a drug to attain the effects they desire. Tolerance builds more rapidly to some drugs than to others. The first column in **Figure 5.23** (which lists the risks associated with drug abuse) indicates whether various categories of drugs tend to produce rapid or gradual tolerance.

When evaluating potential problems associated with using specific drugs, a key consideration is the likelihood of either physical or psychological dependence. Although both forms of drug dependence have a physiological basis (Di Chiara, 1999), important differences exist between the two syndromes. **Physical dependence exists when a person must continue to take a drug to avoid withdrawal illness (which occurs when drug use is terminated).** The symptoms of *withdrawal illness* (also called *abstinence syndrome*) vary depending on the drug. Withdrawal from heroin and barbiturates can produce fever, chills, tremors, convulsions, seizures, vomiting, cramps, diarrhea, and severe aches and pains. The agony of withdrawal from these drugs virtually compels addicts to continue using them. Withdrawal from stimulants leads to a different and somewhat milder syndrome dominated by fatigue, apathy, irritability, depression, and disorientation.

Psychological dependence exists when a person must continue to take a drug to satisfy intense mental and emotional craving for it. Psychological dependence is more subtle than physical dependence, as it is not marked by a clear withdrawal reaction. However, psychological dependence can create a powerful, overwhelming need for a drug. The two types of dependence often coexist—that is, many people manifest both psychological and physical dependence on a specific drug. Both types of dependence are established gradually with repeated use of a drug. However, specific drugs vary greatly in their potential for creating dependence. The second and third columns in **Figure 5.23** provide estimates of the risk of each kind of dependence for the drugs covered in our discussion.

	COMPARISON OF MAJOR CATEGORIES OF ABUSED DRUGS			
Drugs	**Methods of administration**	**Principal medical uses**	**Desired effects**	**Short-term side effects**
Narcotics (opiates) Morphine Heroin	Injected, smoked, oral	Pain relief	Euphoria, relaxation, anxiety reduction, pain relief	Lethargy, drowsiness, nausea, impaired coordination, impaired mental functioning, constipation
Sedatives Barbiturates (e.g., Seconal) Nonbarbiturates (e.g., Quaalude)	Oral, injected	Sleeping pill, anticonvulsant	Euphoria, relaxation, anxiety reduction, reduced inhibitions	Lethargy, drowsiness, severely impaired coordination, impaired mental functioning, emotional swings, dejection
Stimulants Amphetamines Cocaine	Oral, sniffed, injected, freebased, smoked	Treatment of hyperactivity and narcolepsy; local anesthetic (cocaine only)	Elation, excitement, increased alertness, increased energy, reduced fatigue	Increased blood pressure and heart rate, increased talkativeness, restlessness, irritability, insomnia, reduced appetite, increased sweating and urination, anxiety, paranoia, increased aggressiveness, panic
Hallucinogens LSD Mescaline Psilocybin	Oral		Increased sensory awareness, euphoria, altered perceptions, hallucinations, insightful experiences	Dilated pupils, nausea, emotional swings, paranoia, jumbled thought processes, impaired judgment, anxiety, panic reaction
Cannabis Marijuana Hashish THC	Smoked, oral	Treatment of glaucoma; other uses under study	Mild euphoria, relaxation, altered perceptions, enhanced awareness	Bloodshot eyes, dry mouth, reduced memory, sluggish motor coordination, sluggish mental functioning, anxiety

Figure 5.22

Major categories of abused drugs. This chart summarizes the methods of ingestion, chief medical uses, and principal effects of five major types of recreational drugs. Alcohol is covered in the main body of the chapter. (Based on Julien, 2008; Levinthal, 2008; Lowinson et al., 2005)

RISKS ASSOCIATED WITH MAJOR CATEGORIES OF ABUSED DRUGS				
Drugs	Tolerance	Risk of physical dependence	Risk of psychological dependence	Fatal overdose potential
Narcotics (opiates)	Rapid	High	High	High
Sedatives	Rapid	High	High	High
Stimulants	Rapid	Moderate	High	Moderate to high
Hallucinogens	Gradual	None	Very low	Very low
Cannabis	Gradual	None	Low to moderate	Very low

© Cengage Learning

Figure 5.23

Specific risks for various categories of drugs. This chart shows the estimated risk potential for tolerance, dependence, and overdose for the five major categories of drugs discussed in this Application.

An *overdose* is an excessive dose of a drug that can seriously threaten one's life. Any drug can be fatal if a person takes enough of it, but some drugs carry more risk of overdose than others. In **Figure 5.23**, column 4 estimates the risk of accidentally consuming a lethal overdose of various drugs. Drugs that are central nervous system (CNS) depressants—narcotics and sedatives—carry the greatest risk of overdose. It's important to understand that the effects of these drugs are additive. Many overdoses involve lethal *combinations* of CNS depressants. What happens when people overdose on these drugs? Their respiratory system usually grinds to a halt, producing coma, brain damage, and death within a brief period. In contrast, fatal overdoses with CNS stimulants (cocaine and amphetamines) usually involve a heart attack, stroke, or cortical seizure.

Now that our basic vocabulary is spelled out, we can begin to examine the effects and risks of major recreational drugs. Of course, we'll be describing the *typical* effects of each drug. Please bear in mind that the effects of any drug depend on the user's age, body weight, physiology, personality, mood, expectations, and previous experience with the drug. The dose and potency of the drug, the method of administration, and the setting in which the drug is taken also influence its effects (Leavitt, 1995).

Narcotics

Narcotics (or opiates) are drugs derived from opium that are capable of relieving pain. In government regulations, the term *narcotic* is used in a haphazard way to refer to a variety of drugs besides opiates. The most widely abused opiates are heroin, morphine, and a relatively new painkiller called Oxycontin (oxycodone). However, less potent opiates, such as codeine, Demerol, and Vicodin, are also subject to misuse.

Effects

The most significant narcotics problem in modern, Western society is the use of heroin. Most users inject this drug intravenously with a hypodermic needle. The main effect is an overwhelming sense of euphoria. This "Who cares?" feeling makes the heroin high an attractive escape from reality. Common side effects include nausea, lethargy, drowsiness, constipation, and slowed respiration.

Risks

Narcotics carry a high risk for both *psychological and physical dependence* (Knapp, Ciraulo, & Jaffe, 2005). It is estimated that there are about 600,000 heroin addicts in the United States (Winick & Norman, 2005). Although heroin withdrawal usually isn't life threatening, it can be terribly unpleasant, so that "junkies" have a desperate need to continue their drug use. Once dependence is entrenched, users tend to develop a *drug-centered lifestyle* that revolves around the need to procure more heroin. This lifestyle occurs because the drug is expensive and available only through highly undependable black market channels. Obviously, it is difficult to lead a productive life if one's existence is dominated by a desperate need to "score" heroin. The inordinate cost of the drug forces many junkies to resort to criminal activities to support their habit. Heroin use in the United States has leveled off since the 1990s (Johnston et al., 2008). Still, heroin is blamed for over 4,000 deaths annually, so *overdose* is a very real danger. The effects of opiates are additive with those of other CNS depressants, and most narcotic overdoses occur in combination with the use of sedatives or alcohol. Junkies also risk *contracting infectious disease* because they often share hypodermic needles and tend to be sloppy about sterilizing them. The most common of these diseases used to be hepatitis, but in recent years

AIDS has been transmitted at an alarming rate through the population of intravenous drug users (Des Jarlais, Hagan, & Friedman, 2005).

Sedatives

Sedatives **are sleep-inducing drugs that tend to decrease central nervous system and behavioral activity.** In street jargon, they are often called "downers," as they induce a sense of relaxation accompanied by lowered metabolic function (Julien, 2008). Over the years, the most widely abused sedatives have been the barbiturates, which are compounds derived from barbituric acid. However, barbiturates have gradually become medically obsolete and diminished in availability, so sedative abusers have had to turn to drugs in the benzodiazepine family, such as Valium (Wesson et al., 2005).

Effects

People abusing sedatives generally consume larger doses than are prescribed for medical purposes. These overly large doses have a euphoric effect similar to that produced by drinking large amounts of alcohol (Wesson et al., 2005). Feelings of tension, anxiety, and depression are temporarily replaced by a relaxed, pleasant state of intoxication, in which inhibitions may be loosened. Sedatives carry a truckload of dangerous side effects. Motor coordination suffers badly, producing slurred speech and a staggering walk, among other things. Intellectual functioning also becomes sluggish, and judgment is impaired. The user's emotional tone may become unstable, with feelings of dejection often intruding on the intended euphoric mood.

Risks

Sedatives have the potential to produce *both psychological and physical dependence.* They are also among the leading causes of *overdoses* in the United States because of their additive interactions with other CNS depressants (especially alcohol) and because of the degree to which they impair judgment. In their drug-induced haze, sedative abusers are likely to take doses they would ordinarily recognize as dangerous. Sedative users also elevate their risk for *accidental injuries* because these drugs can have significant effects on motor coordination.

Stimulants

Whereas sedatives slow people's metabolic rate (Julien, 2008), stimulants create a feeling of alertness and energetic awareness. *Stimulants* **are drugs that tend to increase central nervous system and behavioral activity.** They range from mild, widely available forms, such as caffeine and nicotine, to stronger, carefully regulated stimulants, such as cocaine and amphetamines ("speed"). All stimulants have some mood-altering effect. Here we focus on the latter two drugs.

Cocaine, an organic substance extracted from the coca shrub, is usually consumed as a crystalline powder that is snorted through the nasal cavities, although it can be consumed orally or intravenously. "Crack" is a processed variant of cocaine, consisting of little chips of cocaine that are usually smoked. Smoking crack tends to be more dangerous than snorting cocaine powder because smoking leads to a more rapid absorption of the drug into the bloodstream and more concentrated delivery of the drug to the brain. That said, all the forms of cocaine and all the routes of administration can deliver highly toxic amounts of the drug to the brain (Repetto & Gold, 2005).

Synthesized in a pharmaceutical laboratory, amphetamines are usually consumed orally. However, speed is also sold as a crystalline powder (called "crank" or "crystal meth") that may be snorted or injected intravenously. A smokable form of methamphetamine, called "ice," is seen in some regions.

Effects

Amphetamines and cocaine have almost indistinguishable effects, except that cocaine produces a very brief high (20–30 minutes unless more is taken), while a speed high can last many hours (Gold, Miller, & Jonas, 1992). Stimulants create a euphoria very different from that created by narcotics or sedatives. They produce a buoyant, elated, enthusiastic, energetic, "I can conquer the world!" feeling accompanied by increased alertness. Common side effects include increased blood pressure, muscle tension, sweating, and restlessness. Some users experience unpleasant feelings of irritability, anxiety, and paranoia.

Risks

Stimulants can cause physical dependence, but the physical distress caused by withdrawal is mild compared to that caused by narcotic or sedative withdrawal. Psychological dependence on stimulants is a more common problem. Cocaine can create an exceptionally *powerful psychological dependence* that compels the user to pursue the drug with a fervor normally seen only when physical dependence exists (Gold & Jacobs, 2005).

Both cocaine and amphetamines can suppress appetite and disrupt sleep. Thus, heavy use of stimulants may lead to poor eating, poor sleeping, and ultimately, a *deterioration in physical health.* Furthermore, stimulant use increases one's risk for stroke, heart attack, and other forms of cardiovascular disease, and crack smoking is associated with a host of respiratory problems (Gourevitch & Arnsten, 2005). Regular cocaine users show greater incidence of cardiovascular disease than nonusers, but even novice users place themselves at risk for cardiac symptoms (Darke, Kaye, & Duflou,

2006). Heavy stimulant use occasionally leads to the onset of a severe psychological disorder called *amphetamine* or *cocaine psychosis* (depending on the drug involved), which is dominated by intense paranoia (King & Ellinwood, 2005). All of the risks associated with stimulant use increase when more potent forms of the drugs (crack and ice) are used. Overdoses on stimulants used to be relatively infrequent (Kalant & Kalant, 1979). However, in recent years, *cocaine overdoses have increased sharply* as more people experiment with more dangerous modes of ingestion.

Hallucinogens

Hallucinogens **are a diverse group of drugs that have powerful effects on mental and emotional functioning, marked most prominently by distortions in sensory and perceptual experience.** The principal hallucinogens are LSD, mescaline, and psilocybin, which have similar effects, although they vary in potency. Mescaline comes from the peyote plant, psilocybin comes from a particular type of mushroom, and LSD is a synthetic drug. Common street names for hallucinogens include "acid," "mushrooms," "fry," and "blotter."

Effects

Hallucinogens intensify and distort perception in ways that are difficult to describe, and they temporarily impair intellectual functioning as thought processes become meteoric and jumbled. These drugs can produce awesome feelings of euphoria that sometimes include an almost mystical sense of "oneness" with the human race. This is why they have been used in religious ceremonies in various cultures. Unfortunately, at the other end of the emotional spectrum, they can also produce nightmarish feelings of anxiety, fear, and paranoia, commonly called a "bad trip."

Risks

There is no potential for physical dependence on hallucinogens, and no deaths attributable to overdose are known to have occurred. Psychological dependence has been reported but appears to be rare. Reports that LSD increases chromosome breakage were based on poor methodology (Dishotsky et al., 1971). However, like most drugs, hallucinogens may be harmful to a fetus if taken by a pregnant woman.

Although the dangers of hallucinogens have probably been exaggerated in the popular press, there are some significant risks (Pechnick & Ungerleider, 2005). Emotion is highly volatile with these drugs, so users can never be sure they won't experience *acute panic* from a terrifying bad trip. Generally, this disorientation subsides within a few hours, leaving no permanent emotional scars. However, in such a severe state of disorientation, *accidents and suicide* are possible. *Flashbacks* are vivid hallucinogenic experiences occurring long after the original drug ingestion. They do not appear to be a common problem, but repetitious flashbacks have proved troublesome for some individuals. In a small minority of users, hallucinogens may contribute to the emergence of a *variety of psychological disorders* (psychoses, depressive reactions, paranoid states) that may be partially attributable to the drug (Pechnick & Ungerleider, 2005).

Marijuana

Cannabis **is the hemp plant from which marijuana, hashish, and THC are derived.** Marijuana (often called "pot," "weed," "reefer," or "grass"), the most commonly used and available illegal drug in the United States, is a mixture of dried leaves, flowers, stems, and seeds taken from the plant, while hashish comes from the plant's resin. THC, the active chemical ingredient in cannabis, can be synthesized for research purposes (for example, to give to lab animals).

Effects

When smoked, cannabis has an almost immediate impact that may last several hours. The effects of the drug vary greatly, depending on the user's expectations and experience with it, the drug's potency, and the amount smoked. The drug has subtle effects on emotion, perception, and cognition (Grinspoon, Bakalar, & Russo, 2005). Emotionally, the drug tends to create a mild, relaxed state of euphoria. Perceptually, it enhances the impact of incoming stimulation, thus making music sound better, food taste better, and so on. Cannabis tends to produce a slight impairment in cognitive functioning (especially short-term memory) and perceptual-motor coordination while the user is high. However, there are huge variations among users.

Risks

Overdose and physical dependence are not problems with marijuana, but as with any other drug that produces pleasant feelings, it has the potential to produce *psychological dependence* (Grinspoon, Bakalar, & Russo, 2005). Marijuana can also cause *transient problems with anxiety and depression* in some people. Of greater concern is recent research suggesting that marijuana use during adolescence *may help to precipitate schizophrenia* in young people who have a genetic vulnerability to the disorder (Compton, Goulding, & Walker, 2007; see Chapter 14). Studies also suggest that cannabis may have a more *negative effect on driving* than has been widely believed (Ramaekers, Robbe, & O'Hanlon, 2000). Indeed, people often make riskier decisions under the influence of marijuana (Lane et al., 2005), which may account for its link to increased risk for injuries (Kalant, 2004). Like tobacco smoke, marijuana smoke carries carcinogens and impurities into the lungs, thus increasing one's chances for *respiratory and pulmonary diseases, and probably lung cancer* (Kalant, 2004). However, the evidence on other widely publicized risks remains controversial. Here is a brief overview of the evidence on some of these controversies:

- *Does marijuana reduce one's immune response?* Research with animals clearly demonstrates that cannabis can suppress various aspects of immune system responding (Cabral & Pettit, 1998). However, infectious diseases do not *appear* to be more common among marijuana smokers than among nonsmokers. Thus, it is unclear whether marijuana increases susceptibility to infectious diseases in humans (Bredt et al., 2002).

- *Does marijuana lead to impotence and sterility in men?* Research with humans has yielded weak, inconsistent, and reversible effects on testosterone and sperm levels (Brown & Dobs, 2002). At present, the evidence suggests that marijuana has little lasting impact on male smokers' fertility or sexual functioning (Grinspoon, Bakalar, & Russo, 2005).

- *Does marijuana have long-term negative effects on cognitive functioning?* Some studies using elaborate and precise assessments of cognitive functioning *have* found an association between chronic, heavy marijuana use and measureable impairments in attention and memory (see **Figure 5.24**) that show up when users are not high (Ehrenreich et al., 1999; Solowij et al., 2002). However, the

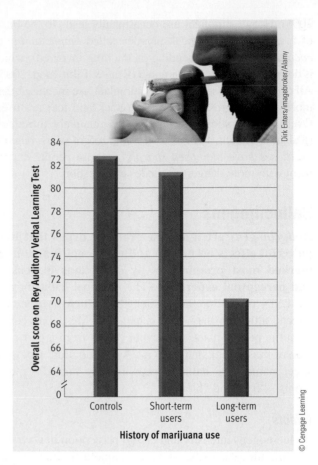

Figure 5.24

Chronic cannabis use and cognitive performance. Solowij and associates (2002) administered a battery of neuropsychological tests to fifty-one long-term cannabis users who had smoked marijuana regularly for an average of 24 years; fifty-one short-term cannabis users who had smoked marijuana regularly for an average of 10 years; and thirty-three control subjects who had little or no history of cannabis use. The cannabis users were required to abstain from smoking marijuana for a minimum of 12 hours prior to their testing. The study found evidence suggestive of subtle cognitive impairments among the long-term cannabis users on many of the tests. The graph shown here depicts the results observed for overall performance on the Rey Auditory Verbal Learning Test, which measures several aspects of memory functioning.

cognitive deficits that have been observed are modest and certainly not disabling, and one study found that the deficits vanished after a month of marijuana abstinence (Pope, Gruber, & Yurgelun-Todd, 2001).

Ecstasy (MDMA)

A relatively recent drug controversy in Western society centers on MDMA, better known as "ecstasy." Derived from methamphetamine, MDMA was originally formulated in 1912 but was not widely used in the United States until the 1990s, when it became popular in the context of "raves" and dance clubs (Millman & Beeder, 1994). Popu-

MDMA, better known as "ecstasy," surged in popularity in the 1990s in the context of "raves" and dance clubs. Although many people view MDMA as a relatively harmless drug, recent research suggests otherwise.

larity of the drug, which peaked around 2001 and then dropped (Johnston et al., 2008), is greater among high school students than young adults (Johnston et al., 2007). ***MDMA is a compound related to both amphetamines and hallucinogens, especially mescaline; it produces a high that typically lasts a few hours or more.*** Users report that they feel warm, friendly, euphoric, sensual, insightful, and empathetic, yet alert and energetic. Problematic side effects include increased blood pressure, muscle tension, sweating, blurred vision, insomnia, and transient anxiety.

Empirical research on ecstasy is still in its infancy, so assertions about its risks and dangers must be tentative and provisional. Data on adverse effects are also complicated by the fact that the vast majority of MDMA users ingest it in conjunction with many other drugs (Pedersen & Skrondal, 1999). There is some evidence that it creates problems regarding maintaining normal body temperature and the immune system (Connor, 2004). Yet another complicating factor is that MDMA often contains potentially harmful impurities, contaminants, and toxic by-products

introduced during its illicit manufacture (Grob & Poland, 2005).

MDMA does not appear to be especially addictive, but psychological dependence can clearly become a problem for some people. MDMA has been implicated in cases of stroke and heart attack, seizures, heat stroke, and liver damage, but its exact contribution is hard to gauge given all the other drugs that MDMA users typically consume (Burgess, O'Donohoe, & Gill, 2000; Grob & Poland, 2005). Chronic, heavy use of ecstasy appears to be associated with sleep disorders, depression, and elevated anxiety and hostility (Morgan, 2000). Moreover, studies of former MDMA users suggest that ecstasy may have subtle, long-term effects on cognitive functioning (Medina, Shear, & Corcoran, 2005; Parrott, 2000). Quite a few studies have found memory deficits in former users (Bhattachary & Powell, 2001; Zakzanis & Young, 2001). Other studies have found decreased performance on laboratory tasks requiring attention and learning (Gouzoulis-Mayfrank et al., 2000). Thus, although more research is needed, there are many reasons to be concerned about the possible effects of ecstasy.

CHAPTER 5 | Review

KEY IDEAS

STRESS, PERSONALITY, AND ILLNESS

● The biopsychosocial model holds that physical health is influenced by a complex network of biological, psychological, and sociocultural factors. Stress is one of the psychological factors that can affect physical health. In particular, cynical hostility has been implicated as a contributing cause of coronary heart disease. A number of mechanisms may contribute to this connection.

● Emotional reactions may also influence susceptibility to heart disease. Recent research has suggested that transient mental stress and the negative emotions that result may tax the heart. Yet another line of research has identified the emotional dysfunction of depression as a risk factor for heart disease.

● The connection between psychological factors and the onset of cancer is not well documented, but stress and personality do appear to influence the course of the disease. Researchers have found associations between stress and the onset of a variety of other diseases. Stress may play a role in a variety of diseases because it can temporarily suppress immune functioning. While there's little doubt that stress can contribute to the development of physical illness, the link between stress and illness is modest.

HABITS, LIFESTYLES, AND HEALTH

● People commonly engage in health-impairing habits and lifestyles. These habits creep up slowly, and their risks are easy to ignore because the dangers often lie in the distant future.

● Smokers have much higher mortality rates than nonsmokers because they are more vulnerable to a variety of diseases. Giving up smoking can reduce one's health risks, but doing so is difficult and relapse rates are high.

● Drinking rivals smoking as a source of health problems. In the short term, drinking can impair driving, cause various types of accidents, and increase the likelihood of aggressive interactions or reckless sexual behavior. In the long term, chronic, excessive alcohol consumption increases one's risk for numerous health problems, including cirrhosis of the liver, heart disease, hypertension, stroke, and cancer.

● Obesity elevates one's risk for many health problems. Body weight is influenced by genetic endowment, eating and exercise habits, and perhaps set point or settling point. Weight loss is best accomplished by decreasing caloric consumption while increasing exercise.

● Poor nutritional habits have been linked to many health problems, including cardiovascular diseases and some types of cancer, although some of the links are tentative. One's health can best be served by eating a balanced diet while limiting the intake of saturated fats, cholesterol, refined carbohydrates, sugar, and salt.

● Lack of exercise is associated with elevated mortality rates. Regular exercise can reduce one's risk for cardiovascular disease, cancer, and obesity-related diseases; buffer the effects of stress; and lead to desirable personality changes.

● Although misconceptions abound, HIV is transmitted almost exclusively by sexual contact and the sharing of needles by intravenous drug users. One's risk for HIV infection can be reduced by avoiding IV drug use, having fewer sexual partners, using condoms, and curtailing certain sexual practices.

REACTIONS TO ILLNESS

● Variations in seeking treatment are influenced by the severity, duration, and disruptiveness of one's symptoms and by the reactions of friends and family. The biggest problem is the tendency of many people to delay needed medical treatment. At the other extreme, a minority of people learn to like the sick role because it earns them attention and allows them to avoid stress.

● Good communication is crucial to effective health services, but many factors undermine communication between patients and health providers, such as short visits, overuse of medical jargon, and patients' reluctance to ask questions.

● Noncompliance with medical advice is a major problem, which appears to occur 30%–50% of the time. The likelihood of nonadherence is greater when instructions are difficult to understand, when recommendations are difficult to follow, and when patients are unhappy with their doctor.

APPLICATION: UNDERSTANDING THE EFFECTS OF DRUGS

● Recreational drugs vary in their potential for tolerance effects, psychological dependence, physical dependence, and overdose. The risks associated with narcotics use include both types of dependence, overdose, and the acquisition of infectious diseases.

● Sedatives can also produce both types of dependence, are subject to overdoses, and elevate the user's risk for accidental injuries. Stimulant use can lead to psychological dependence, overdose, psychosis, and a deterioration in physical health. Cocaine overdoses have increased greatly in recent years.

● Hallucinogens can in some cases contribute to accidents, suicides, and psychological disorders, and they can cause flashbacks. The risks of marijuana use include psychological dependence, impaired driving, transient problems with anxiety and depression, and respiratory and pulmonary diseases. Recent studies suggest that marijuana use may have some long-term negative effects on cognitive processes.

● More research is needed, but it appears that the use of ecstasy (MDMA) may contribute to a variety of acute and chronic physical maladies. MDMA may also have subtle, negative effects on cognitive functioning.

KEY TERMS

Acquired immune deficiency
  syndrome (AIDS)
  pp. 152–153
Alcohol dependence (alcohol-
  ism) p. 144
Atherosclerosis p. 131
Biopsychosocial model p. 129
Body mass index (BMI) p. 144
Cancer p. 134
Cannabis p. 161
Coronary heart disease p. 131
Hallucinogens p. 161
Health psychology p. 130
Hostility p. 132
Immune response pp. 136
MDMA p. 163

Narcotics p. 159
Nutrition p. 147
Overdose p. 159
Physical dependence p. 158
Psychological dependence
  p. 158
Sedatives p. 160
Set-point theory p. 146
Settling-point theory p. 146
Stimulants p. 160
Tolerance p. 158
Type A personality
  pp. 131–132
Type B personality p. 132
Unrealistic optimism p. 138

KEY PEOPLE

Robin DiMatteo p. 156
Meyer Friedman and Ray Rosenman p. 131
Janice Kiecolt-Glaser p. 136

CHAPTER 5 | Practice Test

1. The greatest threats to health in our society today are
   a. environmental toxins.
   b. accidents.
   c. chronic diseases.
   d. contagious diseases caused by specific infectious agents.

2. Which of the following is *not* associated with elevated coronary risk?
   a. Cynical hostility
   b. Strong emotional reactions to transient mental stress
   c. Obsessive-compulsive disorder
   d. Depression

3. Why do people tend to act in self-destructive ways?
   a. Because many health-impairing habits creep up on them
   b. Because many health-impairing habits involve activities that are quite pleasant at the time
   c. Because the risks tend to lie in the distant future
   d. All of the above

4. Some short-term risks of alcohol consumption include all but which of the following?
   a. Hangovers and life-threatening overdoses in combination with other drugs
   b. Poor perceptual coordination and driving drunk
   c. Increased aggressiveness and argumentativeness
   d. Transient anxiety from endorphin-induced flashbacks

5. Twin studies and other behavioral genetics research suggest that
   a. genetic factors have little impact on people's weight.
   b. heredity has scant influence on BMI but does influence weight.
   c. heredity accounts for 60% or more of the variation in weight.
   d. heredity is responsible for severe, morbid obesity but has little influence over the weight of normal people.

6. Which of the following has *not* been found to be a mode of transmission for AIDS?
   a. Sexual contact among homosexual men
   b. The sharing of needles by intravenous drug users
   c. Sexual contact among heterosexuals
   d. Sharing food

7. Regarding the seeking of medical treatment, the biggest problem is
   a. the tendency of many people to delay seeking treatment.
   b. the tendency of many people to rush too quickly for medical care for minor problems.
   c. not having enough doctors to cover peoples' needs.
   d. the tendency of people in higher socioeconomic categories to exaggerate their symptoms.

8. In which of the following cases are people most likely to follow the instructions they receive from health care professionals?
   a. When the instructions are complex and punctuated with impressive medical jargon
   b. When they do not fully understand the instructions but still feel the need to do something
   c. When they like and understand the health care professional
   d. All of the above

9. Which of the following risks is *not* typically associated with narcotics use?
   a. Overdose
   b. Infectious disease
   c. Physical dependence
   d. Flashbacks

10. The use of sedatives may result in personal injury because they
    a. cause motor coordination to deteriorate.
    b. enhance motor coordination too much, making people overconfident about their abilities.
    c. suppress pain warnings of physical harm.
    d. trigger hallucinations such as flying.

ANSWERS

1. c Page 129
2. c Pages 131–134
3. d Pages 137–138
4. d Page 143
5. c Page 146
6. d Pages 153–154
7. a Page 155
8. c Page 157
9. d Pages 159–160
10. a Page 160

COURSEMATE

Go to **CengageBrain.com** to access Psychology CourseMate, where you will find an interactive eBook, glossaries, flashcards, quizzes, videos, and more.

PERSONAL EXPLORATIONS WORKBOOK

Go to the *Personal Explorations Workbook* in the back of your textbook for exercises that can enhance your self-understanding in relation to issues raised in this chapter.

Exercise 5.1 *Self-Assessment:* Multidimensional Health Locus of Control Scales

Exercise 5.2 *Self-Reflection:* How Do Your Health Habits Rate?

CHAPTER 6

The Self

© iStockphoto.com/Klubovy

At last you are in college and on your own, away from home. You are a little nervous but excited about your new life and its challenges. Today is your first official day of college and psychology is your first class. You arrive early. You take a seat near the front of the lecture hall and immediately feel conspicuous. You don't know anyone in the class; in fact, you suddenly realize you don't know anyone at the university except your roommate, who is still a stranger. Many students seem to know one another. They are laughing, talking, and catching up while you just sit there, quiet and alone. They seem friendly, so why won't they talk to you? Should you speak to them first? Are you dressed okay—what about your hair? You begin to question yourself: Will you ever make any friends in this class or at the university? Oh, here comes the professor. She seems nice enough, but you wonder what she expects. Will this class be difficult? Well, you do plan to work hard and study a lot, but how will psychology help you in the future? Perhaps you should be taking a more practical class, maybe accounting, which will lead right to a career. Wait a minute: What if the professor calls on you in front of all these strangers who are already friends? Will you sound intelligent or look foolish? As the professor begins to take the class roll, your mind is racing. You feel tense and your stomach gets a little queasy as she gets closer in the alphabet to your name.

This scenario illustrates the process of self-perception and the effects it can have on emotion, motivation, and goal setting. People engage in this sort of self-reflection constantly, especially when they are trying to understand their own behavior or when they must decide how to act.

In this chapter, we highlight the self and its important role in adjustment. We begin by looking at two major components of the self: self-concept and self-esteem. Then we review some key principles of the self-perception process. Next, we turn to the important topic of self-regulation. Finally, we focus on how people present themselves to others. In this chapter's Application, we offer some suggestions for building self-esteem.

SELF-CONCEPT

LEARNING OBJECTIVES

- Identify some key aspects of the self-concept.
- Cite two types of self-discrepancies, and describe their effects and ways to cope with them.

- Discuss important factors that help form the self-concept.
- Explain how individualism and collectivism influence the self-concept.

If you were asked to describe yourself, what would you say? You'd probably start off with some physical attributes such as "I'm tall," "I'm of average weight," or "I'm blonde." Soon you'd move on to psychological characteristics: "I'm friendly," "I'm honest," "I'm reasonably intelligent," and so forth. People usually identify whatever makes them unique in a particular situation. These distinctive qualities fit into their self-definitions. As we will see, the self is both a cognitive and a social construct (Baumeister, 2012), one that emerges in early childhood and unfolds through adolescence (Harter, 2012). How did you develop beliefs about yourself? Have your self-views changed over time? Read on.

The Nature of the Self-Concept

Although the self-concept is usually talked about as a single entity, it is actually a multifaceted structure (Oyserman, Elmore, & Smith, 2012). That is, **the self-concept is an organized collection of beliefs about the self.** The self-concept entails your beliefs about your personality (Markus & Cross, 1990), those things than come to mind when you think about yourself (Stets & Burke, 2003), and what you believe to be true about yourself (Forgas & Williams, 2002). These beliefs, also called *self-schemas*, shape social perception (Showers & Zeigler-Hill, 2012), are developed from past experience, and are concerned with your personality traits, abilities, physical features, values, goals, and social roles (Campbell, Assanand, & DiPaula, 2000). People have self-schemas on dimensions that are important to them, including both strengths and weaknesses. **Figure 6.1** depicts the self-concepts of two hypothetical individuals.

Each self-schema is characterized by relatively distinct thoughts and feelings. For instance, you might have considerable information about your social skills and feel quite self-assured about them but have limited information and less confidence about your physical skills. Your self-concept is apt to be "relational"—that is, your sense of self is based on your current and past relationships with significant others in your life, such as friends, family, and romantic partners (Andersen & Chen, 2002).

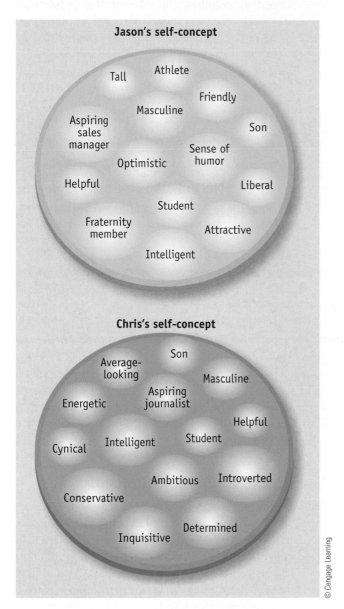

Figure 6.1

The self-concept and self-schemas. The self-concept is composed of various self-schemas, or beliefs about the self. Jason and Chris have different self-concepts in part because they have different self-schemas.

Hazel Markus

Beliefs about the self influence not only current behavior but also future behavior. According to social psychologist Hazel Markus, *possible selves* **are one's conceptions about the kind of person one might become in the future** (Erikson, 2007; Markus & Nurius, 1986). If you have narrowed your career choices to personnel manager and psychologist, they would represent two possible selves in the career realm. Possible selves are developed from past experiences, current behavior, and future expectations. They make people attentive to goal-related information and role models and mindful of the need to practice goal-related skills. As such, they help individuals not only to envision desired future goals but also to achieve them (Hock, Deshler, & Schumaker, 2006; McElwee & Haugh, 2010) while moderating reactions to both positive and negative feedback (Niedenthal, Setterlund, & Wherry, 1992). Interestingly, it has been found that, for individuals who have experienced traumatic events, psychological adjustment is best among those who are able to envision a variety of positive selves (Morgan & Janoff-Bulman, 1994). Sometimes, however, possible selves are negative and represent what you fear you might become—such as an alcoholic like Uncle George or a recluse lacking intimate relationships like your next-door neighbor. In these cases, possible selves function as images to be avoided (e.g., Lee & Oyserman, 2009).

What motivates people to approach or avoid particular possible selves? One answer appears to be motives that enhance one's identity. Vignoles and colleagues (2008) found that people desired possible selves that enhanced their self-esteem, self-perceived effectiveness, and sense of meaning or purpose, among other motives. At the same time, however, they feared developing identities in which such desired motives would be blocked.

Individuals' beliefs about themselves are not set in concrete—but neither are they easily changed. People are strongly motivated to maintain a consistent view of the self across time and situations. Thus, once the self-concept is established, the individual has a tendency to preserve and de-

Yuri Arcurs/Shutterstock.com

© Cengage Learning

fend it. In the context of this stability, however, self-beliefs do have a certain dynamic quality (Markus & Wurf, 1987). For example, when coupled with educational strategies, "academic possible selves" led to positive changes in planning, test scores, grades, and attendance in a sample of low-income minority youth (Oyserman, Bybee, & Terry, 2006). Individuals with academic or career-oriented possible selves are also more persistent when it comes to scholastic achievement than those with different self-goals (Leondari & Gonida, 2008). Self-concepts seem to be most susceptible to change when people shift from an important and familiar social setting to an unfamiliar one, such as when they go off to college or to a new city for their first "real" job.

Self-Discrepancies

Some people perceive themselves pretty much the way they'd like to see themselves. Others experience a gap between what they actually see and what they'd like to see. For example, Nathan describes his actual self as "shy" but his ideal self as "outgoing." According to E. Tory Higgins (1987), individuals have several organized self-perceptions: an *actual self* (qualities you believe you *actually* possess), an *ideal self* (characteristics you would *like* to have), and an *ought self* (traits you believe you *should* possess). The ideal and ought selves serve as personal standards or self-guides that direct behavior. **Self-discrepancy consists of a mismatch between the self-perceptions that make up the actual self, ideal self, and ought self.** These self-discrepancies are measureable and have consequences for how people think, feel, and act (Hardin & Lakin, 2009; Phillips & Silvia, 2010).

Self-Discrepancies and Their Effects

The differences among one's actual, ideal, and ought selves influence how one feels about oneself and can create some particular emotional vulnerabilities (Higgins, 1999). According to Higgins, when people live up to their personal standards (ideal or ought selves), they experience high self-esteem; when they don't meet their own expectations, their self-esteem suffers (Moretti & Higgins, 1990). In addition, he says, certain types of self-discrepancies are associated with specific emotions (see **Figure 6.2**). One type of self-discrepancy occurs when the *actual* self is at odds with the *ideal* self. Such instances trigger *dejection-related* emotions (sadness, disappointment). As actual/ideal discrepancies outnumber actual/ideal congruencies, sadness increases and cheerfulness decreases (Silvia & Eddington, 2012). Consider Tiffany's situation: She knows that she's attractive, but she is also overweight and would like to be thinner. Self-discrepancy theory predicts that she would feel dissatisfied and dejected. Interestingly, research has shown an association between discrepant actual/ideal views of body shape and eating disorders (Sawdon, Cooper, & Seabrook, 2007).

A second type of discrepancy involves a mismatch between *actual* and *ought* selves. Let's say you don't stay in touch with your grandparents as often as you feel you should. According to Higgins and others (Silvia & Eddington, 2012), actual/ought self-discrepancies produce *agitation-related* emotions (irritability, anxiety, and guilt). As actual/ought discrepancies outnumber actual/ought congruencies, anxiety increases and calm emotions decrease (Higgins, Shah, & Friedman, 1997). Extreme discrepancies of this type can result in anxiety-related psychological disorders.

Everyone experiences self-discrepancies, yet most people manage to feel reasonably good about themselves. How is this possible? Three factors seem to be important: the amount of discrepancy experienced, the person's awareness of the discrepancy, and whether the discrepancy is actually important to the person (Higgins, 1999). Thus, a pre-med major who gets a C in calculus will probably feel a lot worse than an English major who gets a C in the course.

Figure 6.2

Types of self-discrepancies, their effects on emotional states, and possible consequences. According to E. Tory Higgins (1989), discrepancies between actual and ideal selves produce disappointment and sadness, whereas discrepancies between actual and ought selves result in irritability and guilt. Such self-discrepancies can make individuals vulnerable to more serious psychological problems, such as depression and anxiety-related disorders.

© Cengage Learning

Coping with Self-Discrepancies

Can individuals do anything to blunt the negative emotions and blows to self-esteem associated with self-discrepancies? Yes! For one thing, people can *change their behavior* to bring it more in line with their ideal or ought selves. For instance, if your ideal self is a person who gets above-average grades and your actual self just got a D on a test, you can study more effectively for the next test to improve your grade. But what about the times you can't match your ideal standards? Perhaps you had your heart set on being on the varsity tennis team but didn't make the cut. One way to ease the discomfort associated with such discrepancies is to bring your ideal self a bit more in line with your actual abilities. You may not achieve your ideal self right away, if ever, but by behaving in ways that are consistent with that self, you will get closer to it and be more content (Haidt, 2006; T. D. Wilson, 2011). Alternatively, subtle encouragement to consider ways to approach an ideal self (perhaps a constructive, friendly suggestion from a friend or a teacher) is apt to raise your spirits in a positive way (Shah & Higgins, 2001).

Another, less positive, approach is to *blunt your self-awareness,* or how much you focus on what you like or dislike about yourself, your self-perceived strengths and shortcomings, and so on. You can do so by avoiding situations that increase your self-awareness—if you don't want to appear to be shy, don't attend a party where you expect to spend a miserable evening talking to yourself. If your weight is bothering you, you might stay off the scale or avoid shopping for new clothes (as well as gazing into full-length mirrors).

Some people use alcohol to blunt self-awareness. In one study, college students were put into either a high or a low self-awareness group based on test scores (Hull & Young, 1983). Then both groups were given a brief version of an intelligence test as well as false feedback on their test performance. Half of the high self-awareness group were told that they had done quite well on the test and the other half were told that they had done quite poorly. Next, supposedly as part of a separate study, these participants were asked to taste and evaluate various wines for 15 minutes. The experimenters predicted that the high self-awareness

When people don't live up to their personal standards, self-esteem suffers, and some turn to alcohol to blunt their awareness of the discrepancy.

participants who had been told that they had done poorly on the IQ test would drink more than the other groups, and this is precisely what the study found (see **Figure 6.3**). Those who couldn't escape negative information about themselves drank more alcohol to reduce their self-awareness. Similarly, in the real world it has been found that alcoholics who have high self-awareness and who experience negative or painful life events relapse more quickly and completely (Hull, Young, & Jouriles, 1986).

Heightened self-awareness intensifies people's internal sensations (Silvia & Duval, 2001; Silvia & Gendolla, 2001), but it doesn't always make people focus on self-discrepancies and negative aspects of the self. If that were true, most people would feel a lot worse about themselves than they actually do. As you recall, self-concepts are made up of numerous self-beliefs—many positive, some negative. Because individuals have a need to feel good about themselves, they tend to focus on their positive features rather than their "warts" (Tesser, Wood, & Stapel, 2005). In fact, when a person's self-concept is threatened (a job interview doesn't go well), the individual can recover by affirming competence in an unrelated domain

Figure 6.3

Self-awareness and alcohol consumption. Individuals who were high in self-awareness drank significantly more wine in a 15-minute period if they believed they had performed poorly on an IQ test than did any other group. This finding shows how people sometimes try to blunt self-awareness to cope with self-discrepancies.

Source: Adapted from Hull, J. G., & Young, R. D. (1983). Self-consciousness, self-esteem, and success—failure as determinants of alcohol consumption in male social drinkers. *Journal of Personality and Social Psychology, 44,* 1097–1109. Copyright © 1983 American Psychological Association. Reprinted by permission of the author.

(focusing on extraordinary talent as a salsa dancer) (Aronson, Cohen, & Nail, 1999; Steele, Spencer & Lynch, 1993). Alternatively, people can affirm their self-identities by focusing on the important values they believe in, which in turn can help them reflect on larger life issues that matter more than self-related setbacks (Wakslak & Trope, 2009).

Factors Shaping the Self-Concept

A variety of sources influence one's self-concept. Chief among them are one's own observations, feedback from others, and cultural values.

One's Own Observations

Individuals begin observing their own behavior and drawing conclusions about themselves early in life. Children will make statements about who is the tallest, who can run fastest, or who can swing the highest. Leon Festinger's (1954) *social comparison theory* **proposes that individuals compare themselves with others in order to assess their abilities and opinions.** People compare themselves to others to determine how attractive they are, how they did on the history exam, how their social skills stack up, and so forth (Alicke, 2007; Dijkstra, Gibbons, & Buunk, 2010). Individuals cannot help themselves: They compare their own behavior with that of their peers (Stapel & Suls, 2004). In fact, social comparisons can be ego enhancing (Helgeson & Mickelson, 1995), especially when comparing one's self to a close friend or peer. The direction of social comparison appears to matter, however, as less self-positivity is generated when one is asked to compare a friend or a peer with oneself (Pahl, Etser, & White, 2009).

Although Festinger's original theory claimed that people engage in social comparison for the purpose of accurately assessing their abilities, research suggests that they also engage in social comparison to improve their skills and to maintain their self-image (Wheeler & Suls, 2005). Sometimes social comparison is self-focused, such as when a successful professional woman compares her "current self" to the passive, withdrawn "past self" of high school (Ross & Wilson, 2002). Generally, however, people compare themselves against others with particular qualities. **A *reference group* is a set of people who are used as a gauge in making social comparisons.** People choose their reference groups strategically. For example, if you want to know how you did on your first test in social psychology (ability appraisal), your reference group would likely be the entire class. In terms of acquiring accurate self-knowledge about your performance, this sort of comparison is a good one if you are confident your classmates are similar to you (Wheeler, Koestner,

& Driver, 1982). Thus, people use others, even complete strangers (Mussweiler, Rütter, & Epstude, 2004), as social benchmarks for comparison (Mussweiler & Rütter, 2003).

What happens when people compare themselves to others who are better or worse off than themselves? For instance, if you want to improve your tennis game (skill development), your reference group should be limited to superior players, whose skills give you a goal to pursue. Such *upward social comparisons* can motivate you and direct your future efforts (Blanton et al., 1999). On the other hand, if your self-esteem needs bolstering, you will probably make a *downward social comparison,* looking to those you perceive to be worse off, thereby enabling you to feel better about yourself (Lockwood, 2002). We'll have more to say about downward social comparison a little later in the chapter.

People's observations of their own behavior are not entirely objective. The general tendency is to distort reality in a positive direction (see **Figure 6.4** on the next page). In other words, most people tend to evaluate themselves in a more positive light than they really merit (Taylor & Brown, 1988). The strength of this tendency was highlighted in a large survey of high school seniors conducted as part of the SAT (Myers, 1980). By definition, 50% of students must be "above average" and 50% "below average" on specific questions. However, 100% of the respondents saw themselves as above average in "ability to get along with others." And 25% of the respondents thought that they belonged in the top 1%! This better-than-average effect seems to be a common phenomenon (Kuyper & Dijkstra, 2009). One explanation for these sorts of inflated self-findings is that the respondents attended high school with mostly average peers (Marsh, Kong, & Hau, 2000), thus they perceived themselves as "big fish in a small pond," at least until they encounter more competitive peers (Shepperd & Taylor, 1999).

In some academic situations, however, social comparisons may be reduced by circumstantial information. Garcia and Tor (2009) introduced what they call the "N-effect," in which the number of recognized or known competitors (or N, which refers to their number) appears to reduce the motivation to compete, a result of making particular social comparisons. One study found that some individuals completing an easy quiz did so much faster if they believed they were competing against 10 rather than 100 other people. Another study revealed that social comparisons become less important to individuals as N rises. And what about SAT scores? Garcia and Tor also found evidence suggesting that SAT scores drop as the average number of test takers increases at the testing site. Think about the N-effect with respect to your own academic achievement behavior: Do smaller classes encourage you to be more competitive than larger ones?

Figure 6.4

Distortions in self-images. How people see themselves may be different from how others see them. These pictures and text illustrate the subjective quality of self-concept and people's perception of others. Generally, self-images tend to be distorted in a positive direction.

As she sees herself: Unchanged since age 22. Sociable, scintillating, sexy.

As the husband sees her: Older than her years. Someone more suited to suburban domesticity and the PTA.

As he sees himself: Stylish haircut, benevolent, generous, powerful. A smooth operator.

As the wife sees him: Somewhat of a slob, moody, not very decisive or strong.

Photos: Pat Bruno/Positive Images; Graphic: © Cengage Learning

Feedback from Others

Individuals' self-concept is shaped significantly by the feedback they get from important people in their lives. Early on, parents and other family members play a dominant role. Parents give their children a great deal of direct feedback, saying such things as "We're so proud of you" or "If you just tried harder, you could do a lot better in math." Most people, especially when young, take this sort of feedback to heart. Thus, it comes as no surprise that studies find a link between parents' views of a child and the child's self-concept (Burhans & Dweck, 1995). There is even stronger evidence for a relationship between children's *perceptions* of their parents' attitudes toward them and their own self-views (Felson, 1989, 1992).

Teachers, Little League coaches, Scout leaders, classmates, and friends also provide feedback during childhood. In later childhood and adolescence, parents and classmates are particularly important sources of feedback and support (Harter, 2003). Later in life, feedback from close friends and marriage partners assumes importance. In fact, there is evidence that a close partner's support and affirmation can bring the loved one's actual self-views and behavior more in line with his or her ideal self (Drigotas, 2002). For this situation to happen, the partner needs to hold views of the loved one that match the target person's ideal self and behave in ways to bring out the best in the person. If the target person's behavior can closely match the ideal self, then self-views can move nearer to the ideal self. Researchers have labeled this process the *Michelangelo phenomenon* to reflect the partner's role in "sculpting" into reality the ideal self of a loved one (Rusbult, Finkel, & Kumashiro, 2009).

Learn More Online

Research Sources: Concepts of Person and Self

Over the past century psychologists, philosophers, and many others have wondered what is meant by terms like *person* and *self*. Professor Shaun Gallagher of the Department of Philosophy at the University of Memphis provides visitors with a variety of resources to explore these concepts.

Whether positive or negative, feedback from others plays an important role in shaping a youngster's self-concept.

Keep in mind that people filter feedback from others through their existing self-perceptions. That is, individuals don't see themselves exactly as others see them but rather as they *believe* others see them (Baumeister & Twenge, 2003; Tice & Wallace, 2003). Thus, feedback from others usually reinforces people's self-views. When feedback about the self conflicts with a person's central self-conceptions, he or she is quite capable of selectively forgetting it; yet the person can recall the feedback when motivated toward self-improvement, including the way he or she regulates close relationships with others (Green et al., 2009).

Social Context

Receiving feedback from others reveals that the self-concept does not develop in isolation. Of course, it's not only people that matter; so do the social contexts where interactions occur. Think about it: You're much more boisterous (and less self-conscious) when you are out with friends at a dance or a diner than when you are sitting in class. Social context affects how people think and feel about others as well, including the impressions they may knowingly convey to others in different situations (Carlson & Furr, 2009). In office settings, for example, a superior will act and feel like a leader with subordinates but will quickly change demeanor and outlook in the presence of an equal (Moskowitz, 1994).

Cultural Values

Self-concept is also shaped by cultural values. Among other things, the society in which one is reared defines what is desirable and undesirable in personality and behavior. For example, American culture puts a high premium on individuality, competitive success, strength, and skill. When individuals meet cultural expectations, they feel good about themselves and experience increases in self-esteem (Cross & Gore, 2003). In the United States, for example, friends heap praise on one another with great

regularity. Such self-congratulatory behavior puzzles Japanese visitors, who are apt to be more restrained when doling out praise. Kitayama (1996) found that Americans report praising a peer every day. When asked the same question, Japanese citizens, who are socialized to feel less pride in personal achievement, reported praising a peer once every four days or so.

Cross-cultural studies suggest that different cultures shape different conceptions of the self (Adams, 2012; Cross & Gore, 2003). One important way cultures differ is on the dimension of individualism versus collectivism (Triandis, 2001). ***Individualism* involves putting personal goals ahead of group goals and defining one's identity in terms of personal attributes rather than group memberships.** In contrast, *collectivism* **involves putting group goals ahead of personal goals and defining one's identity in terms of the groups one belongs to** (such as one's family, tribe, work group, social class, caste, and so on). Although it's tempting to think of these perspectives in either/or terms, it is more appropriate to view them as qualities that vary in degree and that can be assessed (Fischer et al., 2009). Thus, it is more accurate to say that certain cultures are more or less individualistic (or collectivist) than others rather than see them as either one or the other.

Here is a clever but telling example illustrating the difference between individualistic and collectivist cultures when simple choice is concerned. American students and Indian students selected a pen from a group composed of one blue pen and four red ones. American students consistently picked the singular blue pen, while the Indian students always chose a red pen (Nicholson, 2006; see also Connor Snibe & Markus, 2005; Kim & Markus, 1999; Stephens, Markus, & Townsend, 2007). In Western culture, we need to remember that "agency," or how people express their sense of power or influence in the social world, is not always found in other cultures or cultural contexts (Markus & Kitayama, 2004). In a follow-up study, once the students made their choice, some were told "Actually, you can't have that pen. Here, take this one instead." All students were then told to try their new pen, either the one "chosen" for them or the one "given" to them, and to rate it. The Americans preferred the pens they originally chose, thus devaluing the pen they were "given." How did the Indian students react? They showed no preference for either the pen they freely chose or the one given to them. Individualistic cultures promote freedom and choice, and people who live in these cultures do not like to have either threatened.

A variety of factors influence societies' tendencies to cherish individualism or collectivism. Among other things, increases in a culture's affluence, education, urbanization, and social mobility tend to foster more individualism (Triandis, 1995). Many contemporary societies are in transition, but generally speaking North American and Western

European cultures tend to be individualistic, whereas Asian, African, and Latin American cultures tend to be collectivist (Hofstede, 1983).

Culture shapes thought (Nisbett, 2004; Nisbett et al., 2001). Individuals reared in individualistic cultures usually have an *independent view of the self,* perceiving themselves as unique, self-contained, and distinct from others. In contrast, individuals reared in collectivist cultures typically have an *interdependent view of the self.* They see themselves as inextricably connected to others and believe that harmonious relationships with others are of utmost importance. Thus, in describing herself, a person living in an individualistic culture might say, "I am kind," whereas someone in a collectivist culture might respond, "My family thinks I am kind" (Triandis, 2001). **Figure 6.5** depicts the self-conceptions of representatives of these contrasting worldviews.

Researchers have noted parallels between the self-views promoted by individualistic and collectivist cultures and the self-views of some groups. For example, women usually have more interdependent self-views than men (Cross & Madson, 1997). But don't take this finding to mean that men are less social than women; rather, it means that men and women get their social needs met in different ways (Baumeister & Sommer, 1997). Thus women are usually involved in close relationships involving intimate friends and family members (*relational* interdependence), while men tend to interact in social groups such as clubs and sports teams (*collective* interdependence) (Gabriel & Gardner, 1999). These gender differences in self-views may explain other observed gender differences, such as women being more likely than men to share their feelings and thoughts with others.

Figure 6.5

Independent and interdependent views of the self. (a) Individuals in cultures that support an independent view perceive the self as clearly separated from significant others. **(b)** Individuals in cultures that support an interdependent view perceive the self as inextricably connected to others.

Source: Adapted from Markus, H. R., & Kitayama, S. (1991). Culture and the self: Implications for cognition, emotion, and motivation. *Psychological Review, 98,* 224–253. Copyright 1991 American Psychological Association. Adapted by permission of the publisher and author. American Psychological Association. Reprinted by permission of the author.

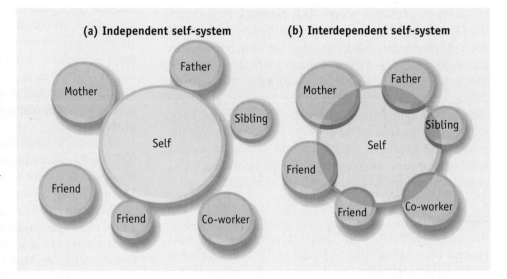

SELF-ESTEEM

LEARNING OBJECTIVES

- Clarify the implications of self-concept confusion and self-esteem instability.
- Explain how high and low self-esteem are related to adjustment.

- Distinguish between high self-esteem and narcissism, and discuss narcissism and aggression.
- Discuss some key influences in the development of self-esteem.

Do you think of yourself in primarily positive or negative terms? One of the functions of the self-concept is to evaluate the self; the result of this self-evaluation is termed *self-esteem.* **Self-esteem refers to one's overall assessment of one's worth as a person.** Self-esteem is a global self-evaluation that blends many specific evaluations about one's adequacy as a student, an athlete, a worker, a spouse, a parent, or whatever is personally relevant. **Figure 6.6** shows how specific elements of the self-concept may contribute to self-esteem. If you feel basically good about yourself, you probably have high self-esteem.

People with high self-esteem are confident, taking credit for their successes in various ways (Blaine & Crocker 1993) while seeking venues for demonstrating their skills (Baumeister, 1998). High-self-esteem folks are not unduly discouraged by failure, because they usually create personal strategies for downplaying or ignoring negative criticism (Heimpel et al., 2002). Compared to individuals with low self-esteem, they are also relatively sure of who they are (Campbell, 1990). In reality, the self-views of people with low self-esteem are not more negative; rather, they are more confused and tentative (Campbell &

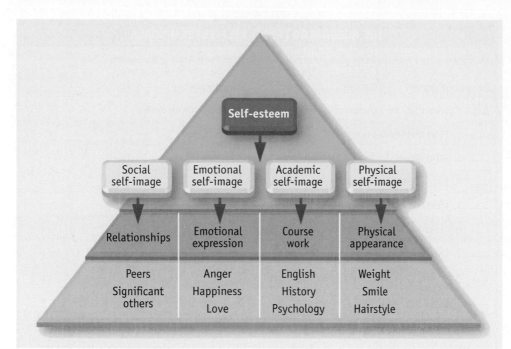

Figure 6.6
The structure of self-esteem. Self-esteem is a global evaluation that combines assessments of various aspects of one's self-concept, each of which is built up from many specific behaviors and experiences. (Adapted from Shavelson, Hubner, & Stanton, 1976)

Roy Baumeister

Lavallee, 1993), as such individuals often experience emotional highs and lows as well as mood swings (Campbell, Chew, & Scratchley, 1991). In other words, their self-concepts seem to be less clear, less complete, more self-contradictory, and more susceptible to short-term fluctuations than the self-views of high-self-esteem individuals. According to Roy Baumeister (1998), an eminent researcher on the self, this "self-concept confusion" means that individuals with low self-esteem simply don't know themselves well enough to strongly endorse many personal attributes on self-esteem tests, which results in lower self-esteem scores. People with low self-esteem are more focused on self-protection—maintaining and not losing whatever favorable sense of worth they possess—than on self-enhancement (Baumeister, Hutton, & Tice, 1989).

Although self-concept confusion may resolve itself over time if people learn who they truly are, there is compelling evidence that low self-esteem is a challenge at all phases of the adult life span. Recent longitudinal research reveals that self-esteem has a pronounced impact on real-life outcomes (Orth, Robins, & Widaman, 2012) and that low self-esteem is found to be a consistent risk factor for depressive symptoms among people ages 18 to 88 (Orth et al., 2009b). Further, low self-esteem's link to people's risk for depression is independent of other factors, such as stressful life events (Orth et al., 2009a).

Self-esteem can be construed in two primary ways: as a trait or as a state. *Trait self-esteem* refers to the ongoing sense of confidence people have regarding their abilities (athletic, assertive) and characteristics (friendliness, helpfulness). People's traits tend to stay with them and to remain constant; if one has high or low self-esteem in childhood, chances are one will have a similar level as an adult (Trzesniewski, Donnellan, & Robins, 2003). **Figure 6.7** on the next page presents a basic self-report measure often used in research when self-esteem is studied as a trait. In contrast, *state self-esteem* is dynamic and changeable, referring to how individuals feel about themselves in the moment (Heatherton & Polivy, 1991). Feedback from others, self-observation, one's point in the life span, moods, a temporary financial setback, even the loss of one's alma mater's team (Hirt et al., 1992)—all can lower one's current sense of self-worth. Those whose self-esteem fluctuates in response to daily experiences are highly sensitive to interactions and events that have potential relevance to their self-worth, and they may even mistakenly view irrelevant events as having significance (Kernis & Goldman, 2002). They always feel their self-worth is on the line.

There is a third way to construe self-esteem: as domain specific (Brown & Marshall, 2006). When self-esteem is linked to a particular area of one's life, it is best described as consisting of one's self-evaluations. Thus, people may think of themselves as athletic (i.e., trait self-esteem) and feel good after winning a round of golf (i.e., state self-esteem), but when asked, they may not feel very good about their running speed when playing tennis (i.e., self-evaluation within a domain). Domain-specific self-esteem predicts performance relatively well, much better than general self-esteem does. So, someone with high academic self-esteem (this individual feels good about her

Figure 6.7

A popular measure of self-esteem: The Rosenberg Self-Esteem Scale. The scale shown here is a widely used research instrument that taps respondents' feelings of general self-esteem.

Source: Adapted from Rosenberg, M. (1965). *Society and the adolescent self-image.* Princeton, NJ: Princeton University Press. Copyright © by Princeton University Press. http://www.bsos .umd.edu/socy/grad/socpsy_rosenberg.html

THE ROSENBERG (1965) SELF-ESTEEM SCALE

Using the scale below, indicate your agreement with each of the following statements.

1	2	3	4
Strongly disagree	Disagree	Agree	Strongly agree

_____ 1. I feel that I am a person of worth, at least on an equal basis with others.

_____ 2. I feel that I have a number of good qualities.

_____ 3. All in all, I am inclined to feel that I am a failure.

_____ 4. I am able to do things as well as most other people.

_____ 5. I feel I do not have much to be proud of.

_____ 6. I take a positive attitude toward myself.

_____ 7. On the whole, I am satisfied with myself.

_____ 8. I wish I could have more respect for myself.

_____ 9. I certainly feel useless at times.

_____ 10. At times I think I am no good at all.

To calculate your score, first reverse the scoring for the five negatively worded items (3, 5, 8, 9, and 10) as follows: 1 = 4, 2 = 3, 3 = 2, 4 = 1. Then, sum your scores across the 10 items. Your total score should fall between 10 and 40. A higher score indicates higher self-esteem.

academic prowess) is likely to earn good grades (Marsh & O'Mara, 2008).

Investigating self-esteem is challenging for several reasons. For one thing, obtaining accurate measures of self-esteem is difficult. The problem is that researchers tend to rely on self-reports from subjects, which obviously may be biased. As you've seen, most individuals typically hold unrealistically positive views about themselves (Buss, 2012); moreover, some people may choose not to disclose their actual self-esteem on a questionnaire. (What about you? Did you answer the questions in **Figure 6.7** truthfully and without any self-enhancing biases? How can you be sure?) Second, in probing self-esteem it is often quite difficult to separate cause from effect. Thousands of correlational studies report that high and low self-esteem are associated with various behavioral characteristics. For instance, self-esteem is a correlate of happiness, which was introduced in Chapter 1. However, it is hard to tell whether high self-esteem causes happiness or vice versa. You should keep this problem in pinpointing causation in mind as we learn more about this fascinating topic.

The Importance of Self-Esteem

Popular wisdom holds that self-esteem is the key to practically all positive outcomes in life. In fact, its actual benefits are much fewer—but, we hasten to add, not unimportant (Krueger, Vohs, & Baumeister, 2009; Swann, Chang-Schneider, & McClarty, 2007). A comprehensive review of research examined the purported and actual advantages of self-esteem (Baumeister et al., 2003). Let's look at the findings that relate to self-esteem and adjustment.

Self-Esteem and Adjustment

The clearest advantages of self-esteem are in the *emotional sphere.* Namely, self-esteem is strongly and consistently related to happiness. In fact, Baumeister and his colleagues are persuaded that high self-esteem actually leads to greater happiness, although they acknowledge that research has not clearly established the direction of causation. On the other side, low self-esteem is more likely than high self-esteem to lead to depression.

In the area of *achievement,* high self-esteem has not been shown to be a reliable cause of good academic performance (Forsyth et al., 2007). In fact, it may actually be the (weak) result of doing well in school. Baumeister and his colleagues speculate that other factors may underlie both self-esteem and academic performance. Regarding job performance, the results are mixed. Some studies find that high self-esteem is linked to better performance, but others find no difference. And it may be that occupational success leads to high self-esteem.

Stephen Coburn/Shutterstock.com

In the *interpersonal realm,* Baumeister and his colleagues report that people with high self-esteem claim to be more likable and attractive, to have better relationships, and to make better impressions on others than people with low self-esteem do. Interestingly, these advantages seem to exist mainly in the minds of the beholders, because objective data (ratings of peers) do not support these views. In fact, Mark Leary's *sociometer theory* suggests that self-esteem is actually a subjective measure of one's interpersonal popularity and success (Leary, 2004b; Leary & Baumeister, 2000). Regarding romantic relationships, for example, those with low self-esteem are more likely to distrust their partners' expressions of love and support and to worry about rejection when compared to high-self-esteem individuals. Still, there is no evidence that self-esteem (high or low) is related to how quickly relationships end.

What about self-esteem and *coping,* a key aspect of adjustment? Individuals with low self-esteem *and* a self-blaming attributional style are definitely at a disadvantage here. For one thing, they become more demoralized after a failure than those with high self-esteem do. For them, failure contributes to depression and undermines their motivation to do better the next time. By contrast, individuals with high self-esteem persist longer in the face of failure. Second, as can be seen in **Figure 6.8**, individuals with low self-esteem often have negative expectations about their performance (in a social situation, at a job interview, on a test). Because self-esteem affects expectations, it operates

in a self-perpetuating fashion. As a result, such people feel anxious and may not prepare for the challenge. Then, if they blame themselves when they do poorly, they feel depressed and deliver one more blow to their already battered self-esteem. Of course, this cycle also works (in the opposite way) for those with high self-esteem. In either case, the important point is that self-esteem can affect not only the present, but also the future.

High Self-Esteem Versus Narcissism

Although feeling good about oneself is desirable, problems arise when people's self-views are inflated and unrealistic. Indeed, high self-esteem may not be all it's cracked up to be (Crocker & Park, 2004). As we noted in Chapters 1 and 2, narcissism is the tendency to regard oneself as grandiosely self-important. Narcissistic individuals passionately want to think well of themselves and are highly sensitive to criticism (Twenge & Campbell, 2003). They are preoccupied with fantasies of success, believe that they deserve special treatment, and react aggressively when they experience threats to their self-views (ego threats). Those with fragile (unstable) self-esteem also respond in this manner (Kernis, 2003a, 2003b). Compared to narcissists, however, high-self-esteem individuals are able to moderate rather than exploit available self-enhancement opportunities (Horvath & Morf, 2010). Individuals whose positive self-appraisals are secure or realistic are not so susceptible to ego threats and are less likely to resort to hostility and aggression in the face of them. Note that narcissists' aggression must be provoked; without provocation, they are no more likely to aggress than non-narcissists (Twenge & Campbell, 2003).

Baumeister and his colleagues speculate that narcissists who experience ego threats have an elevated propensity to engage in aggressive acts such as partner abuse,

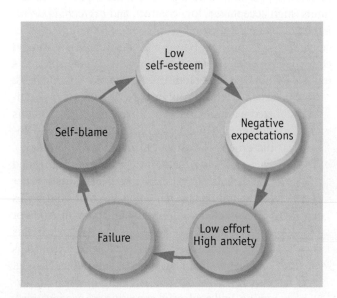

Figure 6.8

The vicious circle of low self-esteem and poor performance.
Low self-esteem is associated with low or negative expectations about performance. These low expectations often result in inadequate preparation and high anxiety, heightening the likelihood of poor performance. Unsuccessful performance triggers self-blame, which feeds back to lower self-esteem.

Source: Adapted from Brehm, S. S., Kassin, S. M., & Fein, S. (2002). *Social psychology* (5th ed.). Boston: Houghton Mifflin.

"Can you believe this is happening to me? Her scores are very low in self-esteem."

Nicholas Monu/Vetta/Getty Images

rape, gang violence, individual and group hate crimes, and political terrorism (Baumeister, 1999; Bushman et al., 2003). Is there any evidence to support this idea? In a series of studies, researchers gave participants the opportunity to aggress against someone who had either insulted or praised an essay they had written (Bushman & Baumeister, 1998). The narcissistic participants reacted to their "insultors" with exceptionally high levels of aggression (see **Figure 6.9**). Another study compared male prisoners and college men on narcissism and self-esteem. Violent offenders scored significantly higher in narcissism, but their self-esteem scores were similar to those of the college men (Bushman & Baumeister, 2002).

These findings have important practical implications (Thomaes & Bushman, 2011). Most rehabilitation programs for spousal abusers, delinquents, and criminals are based on the faulty belief that these individuals suffer from low self-esteem. So far, there is little empirical evidence that low self-esteem leads to either direct (e.g., hitting someone) or indirect (e.g., giving someone a negative evaluation) aggression (Bushman et al., 2009). Indeed, current research suggests that efforts to boost (already inflated) self-esteem are misguided; a better approach is to help such individuals develop more self-control and more realistic views of themselves.

The Development of Self-Esteem

Although people's sense of self-worth emerges in early childhood, individual differences in self-esteem begin to stand out in middle childhood and adolescence (Erol & Orth, 2011) and remain across the lifespan (Harter, 2006). The typical pattern found involves high self-esteem in childhood, an observed fall in adolescence (especially among girls), a gradual return and rise in adulthood, and a precipitous decline once more during old age (Robins & Trzesniewski, 2005). Because the foundations of self-esteem are laid early in life (Harter, 2003), psychologists have focused much of their attention on the role of parenting in self-esteem development. Indeed, there is ample evidence that parental involvement, acceptance, support, and exposure to clearly defined limits have marked influence on children's self-esteem (Harter, 1998).

Two major dimensions underlie parenting behavior: acceptance and control (Maccoby & Martin, 1983). Diana Baumrind (1971, 1978) identified four distinct parenting styles as interactions between these two dimensions (see **Figure 6.10**). *Authoritative parenting* uses high emotional support and firm, but reasonable limits (high acceptance, high control). *Authoritarian parenting* entails low emotional support with rigid limits (low acceptance, high control). *Permissive parenting* uses high emotional support with few limits (high acceptance, low control), and *neglectful parenting* involves low emotional support and few limits (low acceptance, low control). Baumrind and others have found correlations between these parenting styles and children's traits and behaviors, including self-esteem (Furnham & Cheng, 2000). Authoritative parenting is associated with the highest self-esteem scores, and this finding generally holds true across different ethnic groups (Wissink, Dekovic, & Meijer, 2006). One study conducted in Spain, however, found that permissive parenting was sometimes better than authoritative parenting but that both styles yielded better outcomes than the authoritarian or neglectful styles (García & Gracia, 2009). In this study, permissive parenting was characterized as indulgent—that is, as lenient and understanding. Usually, authoritarian parenting, permissive parenting, and neglectful parenting are second, third, and fourth in line. These results suggest that cultural differences and traditions may have some bearing on the benefits of one parenting style over another. In any case, all of these studies were correlational, so keep in mind they don't demonstrate that parenting style *causes* high or low self-esteem.

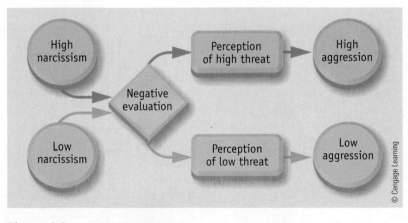

© Cengage Learning

Figure 6.9

The path from narcissism to aggression. Individuals who score high on narcissism perceive negative evaluations by others to be extremely threatening. This experience of ego threat triggers strong hostile feelings and aggressive behavior toward the evaluator in retaliation for the perceived criticism. Low scorers are less likely to perceive negative evaluations as threatening and, therefore, behave much less aggressively toward evaluators. (Adapted from Bushman & Baumeister, 1998).

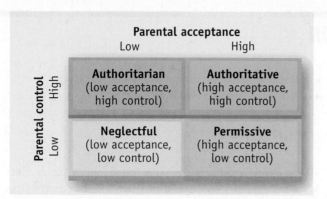

Figure 6.10

Baumrind's parenting styles. Four parenting styles result from the interactions of parental acceptance and parental control, as theorized by Diana Baumrind.

Source: Adapted from Baumrind, D. (1971). Current patterns of parental authority [Monograph]. *Developmental Psychology, 4*(1, Part 2), 1–103. Copyright 1971 American Psychological Association. Adapted by permission of the author.

Perhaps authoritative parenting leads to appropriate levels of self-esteem that have important consequences for children's later behavior. One study found that authoritative parenting served a protective function by decreasing adolescent smoking and drinking (Piko & Balázs, 2012).

Ethnicity, Gender, and Self-Esteem

Because prejudice and discrimination are still pervasive in the United States, people commonly assume that members of minority groups have lower self-esteem than members of the majority group. Research both supports and contradicts this assumption. On the one hand, the self-esteem of Asians, Hispanics, and Native Americans is lower than that of whites, although the differences are small (Twenge & Crocker, 2002). On the other hand, the self-esteem of blacks is higher than that of whites (Gray-Little & Hafdahl, 2000; Twenge & Crocker, 2002). Adding gender to the mix complicates the picture even more. White males have higher self-esteem than white females, but minority males have lower self-esteem than minority females (Twenge & Crocker, 2002).

Thus, ethnicity and gender interact in complex ways in self-esteem. The role of cultural differences in the self-concept may provide some insight here. Recall our earlier discussion of individualism and collectivism. Note that differences on this dimension are found not only between nations but also within a given country. And here's another fact: High individualism is associated with high self-esteem. What's interesting here is that the pattern of ethnic differences in individualism closely mirrors the pattern of ethnic differences in self-esteem (Twenge & Crocker, 2002). That is, blacks score higher than whites, whites do not differ significantly from Hispanics, and Hispanics score higher than Asian Americans. Thus, the ethnic differ-

Parents, teachers, coaches, and other adults play a key role in shaping self-esteem.

ences in self-esteem are likely rooted in how the different groups view themselves, based on cultural messages.

Although females are not a minority group, they resemble ethnic minorities in that they tend to have lower status and less power than males. The popular press abounds with reports of low self-esteem in adolescent girls and women (Pipher, 1994). Is there any empirical basis for this assertion? One meta-analysis of 115 studies found that men had higher domain-specific self-esteem for physical appearance, athleticism, personal self (self-evaluation of personality independent of body or relationships to others), and self-satisfaction (happiness with self), while women did so in the domains of behavioral conduct (socially acceptable actions) and moral-ethical self-esteem (Gentile et al., 2009). Interestingly, the difference in self-esteem for physical appearance only appeared after 1980 and was largest among adult participants. The reason, Gentile and colleagues speculate, is increased media focus on how people look. Interestingly, men and women did not differ in their self-esteem levels for academic ability, social acceptance, family, or affect (emotional well-being).

In an earlier and more extensive meta-analysis, researchers examined gender differences in self-esteem by statistically summarizing the results of several hundred studies (with respondents ranging from 7 to 60 years of age) as well as the data from three nationally representative surveys of adolescents and young adults (Kling et al., 1999). In both analyses, males scored higher on self-esteem than females, although the differences were small for the most part. The largest difference occurred in the 15- to 18-year-old age group. Consider an important qualification regarding these results: It's not the case that girls have particularly low self-esteem; rather, it is more likely that boys tend to be more egotistical during their teens. Also, white girls have lower self-esteem than minority girls do. The fact that white girls tend to have more negative body images than minority girls may be a factor in their lower self-esteem (Twenge & Crocker, 2002).

BASIC PRINCIPLES OF SELF-PERCEPTION

LEARNING OBJECTIVES

- Distinguish between automatic and controlled processing.
- Define self-attributions, and identify the key dimensions of attributions.
- Explain how optimistic and pessimistic explanatory styles are related to adjustment.

- Identify three motives that guide self-understanding.
- Discuss four methods of self-enhancement.

Now that you're familiar with some of the major aspects of the self, let's consider how people construct and maintain a coherent and positive view of the self. First we look at the basic cognitive processes involved and then at the fascinating area of self-attributions. Then we move on to discuss explanatory style and the key motives guiding self-understanding, with a special emphasis on self-enhancement techniques.

Cognitive Processes

People are faced with an inordinate number of decisions on a daily basis. How do they keep from being overwhelmed? The key lies in how people process information. According to Shelley Taylor (1981), people are "cognitive misers." Because cognitive resources (attention, memory, and so forth) are limited, the mind works to "hoard" them by taking cognitive shortcuts. For example, you probably have the same morning routine—shower, drink coffee, eat breakfast, check email, and so forth. Because you do these things without a lot of thought, you can conserve your attentional, decision-making, and memory capacities for important cognitive tasks. This example illustrates the default mode of handling information: *automatic processing.* On the other hand, when important decisions arise or when you're trying to understand why you didn't get that job you wanted, you spend those precious cognitive resources. This mode is termed *controlled processing.* Ellen Langer (1989) describes these two states as *mindlessness* and *mindfulness,* respectively. Mindfulness promotes cognitive flexibility, which in turn can lead to self-acceptance (Carson & Langer, 2006), stress reduction (Carmody & Baer, 2008), and well-being (Langer, 2009a, 2009b) In contrast, mindlessness leads to rigid thinking in which details and important distinctions are lost.

Another way that cognitive resources are protected is through *selective attention,* with high priority given to information pertaining to the self (Bargh, 1997). An example of this tendency is a phenomenon known as the "cocktail party effect"—the ability to pick out the mention of your name in a roomful of chattering people (Wood & Cowan, 1995). Sometimes our selective self-attention works against us, as when we vastly overestimate how conspicuous we are in the minds of other people, a phenomenon known as the *spotlight effect* (Gilovich, Medvec, & Savitsky, 2000). What would happen if you were to wear an embarrassing T-shirt—one emblazoned with none other than Barry Manilow on it—into a room of peers? Self-conscious participants guessed that half of the peers would notice their dorky fashion choice; in reality, less than 25% did.

Another principle of self-cognition is that people strive to understand themselves. One way they do so, as you saw in our discussion of social comparison theory, is to compare themselves with others (Wood & Wilson, 2003). Yet another is to engage in attributional thinking, our next topic.

Self-Attributions

Let's say that you win a critical match for your school's tennis team. To what do you attribute your success? Is your new practice schedule starting to pay off? Did you have the home court advantage? Was your opponent playing with a minor injury? This example from everyday life illustrates the nature of the self-attribution process. *Self-attributions are inferences that people draw about the causes of their own behavior.* People routinely make attributions to make sense out of their experiences (Malle, 2006, 2011). These attributions involve inferences that ultimately represent guesswork on each person's part.

Fritz Heider (1958) was the first to assert that people tend to locate the cause of a behavior either within a person, attributing it to personal factors, or outside a person, attributing it to environmental factors. He thus established one of the crucial dimensions along which attributions are made: internal versus external. The other two dimensions are stable-unstable and controllable-uncontrollable. Let's discuss these various types of attributions in greater detail.

Internal or external. Elaborating on Heider's insight, various theorists have agreed that explanations of behavior and events can be categorized as internal or external attributions (Bastian & Haslam, 2006; Kelley, 1967; Robins et al., 2004; Weiner, 2006). *Internal attributions ascribe the causes of behavior to personal dispositions, traits, abilities, and feelings. External attributions ascribe the causes of behavior to situational demands and environmental constraints.* For example, if you credit your poor statistics grade to your failure to prepare adequately for the test or to getting overly anxious during the test, you are making internal attributions. An external attribution could be that the course is simply too hard, that the teacher is

COMPARING INTERNAL VERSUS EXTERNAL ATTRIBUTIONS	
Internal attributes	**External attributes**
Personality factors or characteristics	Setting (e.g., classroom, clinic, park, concert hall)
Age	Other people
Gender	Rules guiding behavior
Skills	Weather
Ethnicity	Time of day
Education	Environment (e.g. quiet, crowded, hot)
Intelligence	

Figure 6.11

Comparing internal versus external attributions. Internal attributions are characteristics or qualities linked to a person and his or her actions. In contrast, external attributions are characteristics or qualities linked to the context or the environment where the individual's behavior occurs. Some sample sources for each type of attribution are included here.

© Cengage Learning 2015

unfair, or that the book is incomprehensible. **Figure 6.11** provides sample sources for both types of attributions.

Whether one's self-attributions are internal or external can have a tremendous impact on one's personal adjustment. Studies suggest that people who attribute their setbacks to internal, personal causes while discounting external, situational explanations may be more prone to depression than people who display the opposite tendencies (Riso et al., 2003).

Stable or unstable. A second dimension people use in making causal attributions is the stability of the causes underlying behavior (Weiner, 1994). A *stable* cause is one that is more or less permanent and unlikely to change over time. A sense of humor and intelligence are *stable internal* causes of behavior. *Stable external* causes of behavior include such things as laws and rules (speed limits, no-smoking areas). *Unstable* causes of behavior are variable or subject to change. *Unstable internal* causes of behavior include such things as mood (good or bad) and motivation (strong or weak). *Unstable external* causes could be the weather and the presence or absence of other people. According to Bernard Weiner (1994), the stable-unstable dimension in attribution cuts across the internal-external dimension, creating four types of attributions for success and failure, as shown in **Figure 6.12**.

Let's apply Weiner's model to a concrete event. Imagine that you are contemplating why you just landed the job you wanted. You might credit your situation to internal factors that are stable (excellent ability) or unstable (hard work on your attractive résumé). Or you might attribute the outcome to external factors that are stable (lack of top-flight competition) or unstable (luck). If you didn't get the job, your explanations would fall into the same four categories: internal-stable (lack of ability), internal-unstable (inadequate effort on your résumé), external-stable (too much competition in your field), and external-unstable (bad luck).

Controllable or uncontrollable. A third dimension in the attribution process acknowledges the fact that sometimes

events are under one's control and sometimes they are not (Weiner, 1994). For example, the amount of effort you expend on a task is typically perceived as something under your control, whereas an aptitude for music is viewed as something you are born with (beyond your control). Controllability can vary with each of the other two factors.

These three dimensions appear to be the central ones in the attribution process. Research has documented that self-attributions are motivational, guiding one toward or away from possible courses of action. Thus, one's self-beliefs can influence future expectations (success or failure) and emotions (pride, hopelessness, guilt), and these expectations and emotions can combine to influence subsequent performance (Weiner, 2006, 2012). Self-attributions, then, play a key role in one's feelings, motivational state, and behavior.

Figure 6.12

Key dimensions of attributional thinking. Weiner's model assumes that people's explanations for success and failure emphasize internal versus external causes and stable versus unstable causes. For example, if you attribute an outcome to great effort or to lack of effort, you are citing causes that lie within the person. Since effort can vary over time, the causal factors at work are unstable. Other examples of causal factors that fit into each of the four cells in Weiner's model are shown in the diagram.

Source: From Weiner, B., Frieze, I., Kukla, A., Reed, L.. & Rosenbaum, R. M. (1972). Perceiving the causes of success and failure. In E. E. Jones, D. E. Kanuouse, H. H. Kelly, R. E. Nisbett, S. Valins, & B. Weiner (Eds.), *Perceiving causes of behavior*. Morristown, NJ: General Learning Press. Reprinted by permission of the author.

Explanatory Style

Julio and Josh are freshmen who have just struck out trying to get their first college dates. After experiencing disappointment, they reflect on the possible reasons for it. Julio speculates that his approach was too subtle. Looking back, he realizes that he wasn't very direct because he was nervous about asking the woman out. When she didn't reply, he didn't follow up for fear that she didn't really want to go out with him. On further reflection, he reasons that she probably didn't respond because she wasn't sure of his intentions. He vows to be more direct the next time. Josh, on the other hand, responds to the situation by moping: "I'll never have a relationship. I'm a total loser." On the basis of these comments, who do you think is likely to get a date in the future? If you guessed Julio, you are probably correct. Let's see why.

According to Martin Seligman (1991), people tend to exhibit, to varying degrees, an *optimistic explanatory style* or a *pessimistic explanatory style* (see **Figure 6.13**). As we saw in Chapter 3, *explanatory style* **refers to the tendency to use similar causal attributions for a wide variety of events in one's life.** The person with an optimistic explanatory style usually attributes setbacks to external, unstable, and specific factors (Peterson & Steen, 2009). A person who failed to get a desired job, for example, might attribute this misfortune to factors in the interview situation ("The room was really hot," "The questions were slanted") rather than to personal shortcomings. This style can be psychologically protective (Wise & Rosqvist, 2006), helping people to discount their setbacks and thus maintain a favorable self-image (Gordon, 2008). It also helps people bounce back from failure.

In contrast, people with a pessimistic explanatory style tend to attribute their setbacks to internal, stable, and global (or pervasive) factors. These attributions make them feel bad about themselves and doubtful about their ability to handle challenges in the future. As noted in Chapter 4, such a style can foster passive behavior and make people more vulnerable to *learned helplessness* and depression (Peterson, Maier, & Seligman, 1993), especially when they expect that things won't work out in their favor (Peterson & Vaidya, 2001). Of more concern is some suggestive evidence from a longitudinal sample of people that "catastrophizing"—attributing negative events to global causes—predicted accidental and violent deaths (Peterson et al., 1998). Luckily, explanatory style can be measured (Haeffel et al., 2008), and cognitive-behavioral therapy appears to be effective at helping individuals at risk for depression (Seligman, Schulman, & Tryon, 2007) and at encouraging depressed individuals to change their pessimistic explanatory style (Seligman et al., 1999).

Motives Guiding Self-Understanding

Whether people evaluate themselves by social comparisons, attributional thinking, or other means, they are highly motivated to pursue self-understanding. In this pursuit, they are driven by three major motives: assessment, verification, and enhancement (Biernat & Billings, 2001).

Self-Assessment

The *self-assessment motive* is reflected in people's desire for truthful information about themselves (Trope, 1986).

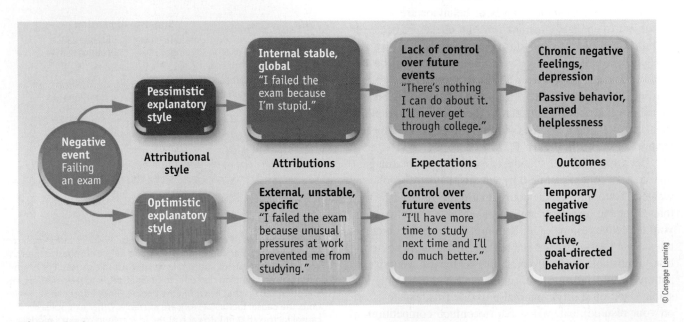

Figure 6.13

The effects of explanatory style on expectations, emotions, and behavior. The pessimistic explanatory style is seen in the top row of boxes. This attributional style, which attributes setbacks to internal, stable, and global causes, tends to result in an expectation of lack of control over future events, depressed feelings, and passive behavior. A more adaptive, optimistic attributional style is shown in the bottom row of boxes.

The problem is straightforward: Individuals don't know themselves all that well (Dunning, 2006). Unfortunately, many self-assessments are quite flawed; the only good news is that people are typically unaware of this fact (Dunning, Heath, & Suls, 2004), presumably because evaluating one's own abilities is a formidable challenge (Carter & Dunning, 2008).

Let's consider an example illustrating a limit to one's ability to engage in self-assessment. Recently, social psychologists have become interested in the issue of emotional accuracy: How well do people predict their future feelings in response to good and bad events? As noted in Chapter 1, this process is known as *affective forecasting* (Gilbert, Driver-Linn, & Wilson, 2002; Wilson & Gilbert, 2003). Wilson and Gilbert (2005) have demonstrated repeatedly that people mispredict how much pleasure or displeasure they will feel once future events come to pass. The challenge people face is not the valence—or direction—of their feelings; individuals are reasonably good at judging what makes them happy or unhappy. Instead, the problem is the *intensity* and the *duration* of positive or negative feelings.

One source of bias in affective forecasting is the *impact bias,* which occurs when people misjudge the eventual intensity and duration of their emotional response to some future event. In this case, they overestimate rather than underestimate their feelings. Here's an example many readers can relate to: where they live on campus. Dunn, Wilson, & Gilbert (2003) asked college students to estimate how happy or unhappy they would be a year after being assigned to a desirable or an undesirable dormitory. As shown in **Figure 6.14**, the students expected that where they ended up living would have a fairly substantial impact on their overall levels of happiness. As you can see, however, a year after moving into the desired or less desired housing, self-reported happiness was virtually identical for the two groups (see **Figure 6.14**). In other words, people often overestimate the emotional impact of a single event because of what researchers call *focalism*, the tendency to overemphasize how much one will think about an event in the future while also underestimating how other events will compete for one's thoughts and feelings (Schkade & Kahneman, 1998; Wilson et al., 2000).

Dorm life may not seem to be a very dramatic backdrop for adventures in affective forecasting, but other, more consequential life events have been studied. Research has found that people overestimate how unhappy they will be a couple months after a romance ends; women miscalculate their level of unhappiness on getting unwanted results from a pregnancy test; and untenured college faculty misjudge how unhappy they will be 5 years after being turned down for tenure (Loewenstein, O'Donoghue, & Rabin, 2003; Wilson & Gilbert, 2003). Thus, impact bias and focalism can distort expectations great and small, suggesting that the ability to accurately engage in self-assessment is limited.

Still, there is some hope. Individuals do seek accurate feedback about many types of information, including their personal qualities, abilities, physical features, and so forth. It's obvious why people look for accurate information. After all, it helps them set realistic goals and behave in appropriate ways (Oettingen & Gollwitzer, 2001).

Self-Verification

The *self-verification motive* drives people toward information that matches what they already believe about themselves, whether positive or negative (North & Swann, 2009a; Swann, 2012). This tendency to strive for a consistent self-image ensures that individuals' self-concepts are relatively stable. Individuals maintain consistent self-perceptions in a number of subtle ways and are often unaware of doing so (Schlenker & Pontari, 2000). For example, people maintain consistency between their past and present behavior by erasing past memories that conflict with present ones. To illustrate, people who were once shy and who later became outgoing have been shown to recall memories about themselves that indicate that they perceive themselves as always having been outgoing (Ross & Conway, 1986).

Another way people maintain self-consistency is by seeking out feedback and situations that will confirm their

Figure 6.14

Biased impact: Students' predicted versus actual levels of happiness a year after being assigned to a desirable or undesirable dormitory. Using a 7-point scale (where 1 = unhappy and 7 = happy), college students predicted how happy they would be a year later if they were randomly assigned to live in a desirable or an undesirable dormitory. Students anticipated that their dorm assignment would have a pronounced positive or negative impact on their overall happiness (yellow bars); however, a year later, those who ended up living in undesirable housing versus the desirable dorms showed nearly identical levels of happiness (green bars).

Source: Wilson, T. D., & Gilbert, D. T. (2005). Affective forecasting: Knowing what to want. *Current Directions in Psychological Science, 14,* 131–134, Fig. 1. Copyright © 2006 Blackwell Publishing. Reprinted by permission of Sage Publications.

existing self-perceptions and avoiding potentially discon-firming situations or feedback. Thus, self-verification processes are not only adaptive, they have other positive qualities as well (North & Swann, 2009b; Swann, 2012). According to William Swann's *self-verification theory,* **people prefer to receive feedback from others that is consistent with their own self-views.** Thus, people with positive self-concepts should prefer positive feedback from others and those with negative self-concepts should prefer negative feedback. Research usually finds this situation to be the case (Swann, Rentfrow, & Guinn, 2003). In one study, college men were divided into positive and negative self-concept groups based on test scores. They were then asked to choose a partner for a subsequent 2- to 3-hour interaction. Participants were led to believe that one of the prospective partners held views of him that were consistent with his self-view and that the other held views of him that were inconsistent with his self-view. As predicted, subjects with positive self-views preferred partners who viewed them positively, whereas those with negative self-views chose partners who viewed them negatively (Swann, Stein-Seroussi, & Geisler, 1992). Among depressed persons, the persistent self-views predicted by self-verification processes may account for treatment setbacks or an ongoing sense of unease or dissatisfction with life (Petit & Joiner, 2006).

Interestingly, when the opportunity to verify their self-views is blocked, people subsequently engage in the relevant behavior as a way to verify their identities. Brooks, Swann, and Mehta (2011), for example, found that when assertive people were deprived of the chance to express their assertive natures in one setting, they later did so in the context of a different social interaction.

Self-Enhancement

Finally, people are motivated by the *self-enhancement motive.* *Self-enhancement* **is the tendency to seek positive (and reject negative) information about oneself.** Psychologically, self-enhancement can appear in at least four ways: as an observed response or behavior, a process, a personality trait, or an underlying motive (Sedikides & Alicke, 2012). One example of self-enhancement is the tendency to hold flattering views of one's personal qualities, a tendency termed the *better-than-average effect* (Buckingham & Alicke, 2002). You've already seen an example of this effect in our earlier report that 100% of students who took the SAT rated themselves above average in the ability to get along with others—a mathematical impossibility. Students can take perverse pleasure in knowing that faculty also succumb to this bias: 94% of them regard their teaching as above average (Cross, 1977)!

A second example of self-enhancement concerns *illusions of control* (Langer, 1975), in which people overestimate their degree of control over outcomes. Thus, indi-viduals who pick their own "lucky" numbers on lottery tickets falsely believe that they can influence the outcome of such random events, an act and inference that makes them feel good (Dunn & Wilson, 1990; Wohl & Enzle, 2002).

Methods of Self-Enhancement

The powerful self-enhancement motive drives individuals to seek positive (and reject negative) information about themselves (Sanjuán, Magallares, & Gordillo, 2011). Let's examine four cognitive strategies people commonly use in this process.

Downward Comparisons

We've already mentioned that people routinely compare themselves to others as a means of learning more about themselves (social comparison). However, once a threat to self-esteem enters the picture, people often adjust their strategy and choose to compare themselves with those who are worse off than they are (Wood, 1989). *Downward social comparison* **is a defensive tendency to compare oneself with someone whose troubles are more serious than one's own.** Why do people change strategies under threat? Because they need to feel better, often doing so by connecting to the experience of others (Wayment & O'Mara, 2008). Research shows that downward social comparisons are associated with increases in both mood and self-esteem (Reis, Gerrard, & Gibbons, 1993).

If you have ever been in a serious traffic accident in which your car was "totaled," you probably reassured yourself by reflecting on the fact that at least no one was seriously injured. Similarly, people with chronic illnesses may compare themselves with those who have life-threatening diseases. The protective power of downward comparisons is apt to be quite robust. One recent study indicates that these strategic contrasts with the experience of others can save people from experiencing feelings of regret across their lives (Bauer & Wrosch, 2011).

Self-Serving Bias

Suppose that you and three other individuals apply for a part-time job in the parks and recreation department and you are selected for the position. How do you explain your success? Chances are, you tell yourself that you were hired because you were the most qualified for the job. But how do the other three people interpret their negative outcome? Do they tell themselves that you got the job because you were the most able? Unlikely! Instead, they probably attribute their loss to "bad luck" or to not having had time to prepare for the interview. These different explanations for success and failure reflect **the *self-serving bias,* or the tendency to attribute one's successes to personal factors and one's failures to situational factors** (Mezulis et al., 2004; Shepperd, Malone, & Sweeny, 2008). One explanation for the self-serving bias is that unbiased self-judgments require a high degree of self-control, which is usually overridden by one's automatic drive toward self-enhancement (Krusemark, Campbell, & Clementz, 2008).

For example, in one experiment, two strangers jointly took a test. They then received bogus success or failure feedback about their test performance and were asked to assign responsibility for the test results. Successful participants claimed credit, but those who failed blamed their partners (Campbell et al., 2000). Still, people don't always rush to take credit. In another experiment in the just-cited study, participants were actual friends. In this case, participants shared responsibility for both successful and unsuccessful outcomes. Thus, friendship places limits on the self-serving bias.

Although the self-serving bias has been documented in a variety of cultures (Fletcher & Ward 1988), it seems to be particularly prevalent in individualistic, Western societies, where the emphasis on competition and high self-esteem motivates people to try to impress others, as well as themselves. In contrast, Japanese subjects exhibit a *self-effacing bias* in explaining successes (Akimoto & Sanbonmatsu, 1999), as they tend to attribute their successes to the help they receive from others or to the ease of the task, while downplaying the importance of their ability. When they fail, Japanese subjects tend to be more self-critical than subjects from individualistic cultures (Heine & Renshaw, 2002).

Still, the self-serving bias is so strong that people are even biased against seeing it in themselves but are quite happy to claim that it is robust and recognizable in the actions and beliefs expressed by others (Pronin, Gilovich, & Ross, 2004; Pronin, Lin, & Ross, 2002). Perhaps this bias is one reason that people are often so convinced of their inherent correctness that they are willing to argue and even fight with others over matters great and small (Kennedy & Pronin, 2008; Pronin & Ross, 2006).

Basking in Reflected Glory

When your favorite sports team won the national championship last year, did you make a point of wearing the team cap? And when your best friend won that special award, do you remember how often you told others the good news about him? If you played a role in someone's success, it's understandable that you would want to share in the recognition; however, people often want to share recognition even when they are on the sidelines of an outstanding achievement. **Basking in reflected glory is the tendency to enhance one's image by publicly announcing one's association with those who are successful.**

Robert Cialdini and his colleagues (1976) studied this phenomenon at colleges with nationally ranked football teams. The researchers predicted that, when asked how their team had fared in a recent football game, students would be more likely to say, "We won" (in other words, to bask in reflected glory, or to "BIRG"—pronounced with a soft "g") when the home team had been successful than to respond "We lost" when it had been defeated. Indeed, the researchers found that students were more likely to BIRG when their team won than when it lost. Also, subjects who believed that they had just failed a bogus test were more likely to use the words "We won" than those who believed they had performed well on the test. Besides football fans (Spinda, 2011), BIRGing has also been found in the text of soccer fan magazines (Bernache-Assollant, Lacassagne, & Braddock, 2007).

BIRGing is not limited to team sports. Apparently it has a place in people's political beliefs, as well. A field study done following the 2008 presidential election found that people with window or yard signs endorsing Barack Obama kept their signs up longer than homeowners who had signs endorsing the other candidate, John McCain (Miller, 2009). Obama won a second term in November 2012: Do you think people with pro-Obama signs displayed them longer after the election than those who campaigned for Mitt Romney, the losing candidate?

A related self-enhancement strategy is "CORFing," or *cutting off reflected failure.* Because self-esteem is partly tied to an individual's associations with others, people often protect their self-esteem by distancing themselves from those who are unsuccessful (Boen, VanBeselaere, & Feys,

People frequently claim association with others who are successful (basking in the reflected glory) to maintain positive feelings about themselves.

2002; Miller, 2009). Thus, if your cousin is arrested for drunk driving, you may tell others that you don't really know him very well. Interestingly, BIRGing and CORFing are apparently not limited to the United States or to public settings. For example, websites of Belgian and Dutch soccer teams receive significantly more "surfers" after the teams win matches (BIRGing) than when they lose (CORFING) (Boen, VanBeselaere, & Feys, 2002).

Self-Handicapping

When people fail at an important task, they need to save face. In such instances, individuals can usually come up with a face-saving excuse ("I had a terrible stomachache"). Curiously, some people actually behave in a way that sets them up to fail so that they have a readymade excuse for failure, should it occur. ***Self-handicapping* is the tendency to sabotage one's performance to provide an excuse for possible failure.** For example, when a big test is looming, they put off studying until the last minute or go out drinking the night before the test. If, as is likely, they don't do well on the exam, they explain their poor performance by saying they hadn't prepared. (After all, wouldn't you rather have others believe that your poor performance is due to inadequate preparation rather than to lack of ability?) Lack of effort is often indicative of self-handicapping, as is a lack of self-control (Uysal & Knee, 2012); however, one recent study demonstrated that sometimes exerting too much effort—ironically, an active behavioral strategy—can reveal it, too. A group of men were led to believe that *too much* practice could hurt their future performance on a task. Within the group, those who scored high on a trait measure of self-handicapping were found to practice more compared to those low on this trait. Ironically, by over-preparing to ensure a poor performance, the high self-handicappers were able to save face—they could readily attribute their failure to their overpractice rather than a lack of skill, which is a more psychologically threatening explanation (Smith, Hardy, & Arkin, 2009). People use a variety of other tactics for handicapping their performance: alcohol, drugs, procrastination, a bad mood, a distracting stimulus, anxiety, depression, and being overcommitted (Baumeister, 1998).

Self-handicapping should not be confused with *defensive pessimism,* a trait causing some people to mentally identify the worst possible outcome and then to work hard to make sure it never occurs (Norem, 2008, 2009; Norem & Smith, 2006; Thomas, 2011). Although the two constructs appear similar, defensive pessimists are motivated to avoid bad outcomes, whereas self-handicappers undermine their own efforts (Elliot & Church, 2003; Martin et al., 2003). Imagine working on a huge end-of-term project for a class—one that will make or break your final course grade. Optimists cope with anxiety by anticipating they will do their best. Defensive pessimists will expect the worst and then get right to work, ending up pleasantly

surprised when they do well. People engaging in self-handicapping, however, might procrastinate or do any number of things that can undermine their successful completion of the project.

Self-handicapping seems like a "win-win" strategy: If you fail, you have a face-saving excuse ready, and if you happen to succeed, you can claim that you are unusually gifted! However, it probably has not escaped your attention that self-handicapping is highly risky. By giving yourself an attributional "out" in case of failure, your self-defeating behavior will likely result in poor performance (Zuckerman, Kieffer, & Knee, 1998). Moreover, while self-handicapping may save you from negative self-attributions about your ability, it does not prevent others from making different negative attributions about you. Others may perceive you as lazy, inclined to drink too much, or highly anxious, depending on the means you use to self-handicap—perceptions that are sometimes accurate (Zuckerman & Tsai, 2005). Consequently, this self-enhancement tactic has serious drawbacks.

Potentially, anyone can engage in self-handicapping behavior (surely, you have come up with an excuse or two when things did not go your way), but research suggests that men self-handicap more than women, possibly because women place more importance on displaying effort

RECOMMENDED reading

···

The Positive Power of Negative Thinking: Using Defensive Pessimism to Harness Anxiety and Perform at Your Peak

by Julie Norem (Basic Books, 2002)

Can negative thoughts, such as fear of failing or of performing poorly, ever be a good thing? Perhaps a little anxiety can help rather than harm. Surprisingly, social-personality psychologist Julie Norem of Wellesley College argues that some negative self-views can actually galvanize one's resolve and lead to success. How so? Imagine the benefits of "defensive pessimism" by envisioning worst case scenarios prior to undertaking a difficult or challenging task and then working hard to avoid them. Once you identify the demons and dangers blocking you from your goal, you can plan a strategy for moving forward. Setting expectations at low or even moderate levels can lead to large emotional dividends if you end up outperforming your beginning benchmarks. If nothing else, defensive pessimism is a compelling antidote to unrealistic optimism or maladaptive self-strategies, such as denial, procrastination, or self-handicapping.

Log on to CourseMate at www.cengagebrain.com *for descriptions of other recommended books.*

(McCrea et al., 2008). Individuals with low self-esteem tend to have low self-confidence, which encourages them to engage in self-handicapping behaviors (Coudevylle, Gernigon, & Martin Ginis, 2011). High-status individuals are also likely to use self-handicapping as a social strategy (Lucas & Lovaglia, 2005). Why? Self-handicapping commonly occurs when self-esteem is threatened. Thus, high-status individuals will be more motivated to preserve their level of self-worth than people of a lower status. Interestingly, when gender is controlled, race and ethnicity matter somewhat: European Americans self-handicap more than non-European Americans (Lucas & Lovaglia, 2005), as do narcissists, who tend to be arrogant or conceited (Rhodewalt, Tragakis, & Finnerty, 2006).

SELF-REGULATION

LEARNING OBJECTIVES

- Define self-regulation, and explain the ego-depletion model of self-regulation.
- Explain how self-efficacy develops and why it is important to psychological adjustment.
- Describe the three categories of self-defeating behavior.

"Should I have that hot fudge sundae or not?" "I guess I'd better get started on that English paper." "Would I be better off checking Facebook one more time or going to bed?" People are constantly trying to resist impulses and make themselves do things they don't really want to do. **Self-regulation is the process of directing and controlling one's behavior.** Clearly, the ability to manage and direct what you think, how you feel, and how you behave is tied to your success at work, your relationships, and your mental and physical health (Baumeister & Vohs, 2007; Vohs & Baumeister, 2011; Vohs, Baumeister, & Tice, 2008). Being able to forgo immediate gratification (studying instead of partying) and focus your behavior on important, longer-range goals (graduating and getting a good job) is of paramount importance for success in life (Doerr & Baumeister, 2010; Forgas, Baumeister, & Tice, 2009).

It's possible that people have a limited amount of self-control resources. If you tax these resources resisting temptation in a given situation, you may have a hard time resisting the next temptation or persisting at a new task. As a result, self-control can have a cost (Baumeister & Alquist, 2009). At least that's the idea behind the *ego depletion model of self-regulation* (Baumeister et al., 1998). To investigate this hypothesis, researchers asked college students to participate in a study of taste perception (the study was actually on self-control) (Baumeister et al., 1998). Some participants were asked to eat two or three radishes in 5 minutes but not to touch the chocolate candy and chocolate chip cookies that were nearby. Others were asked to eat some candy or some cookies but were told not to eat any of the nearby radishes. A control group didn't participate in this part of the study. Then all subjects were asked to solve what were, unbeknownst-to-them, unsolvable puzzles while they supposedly waited for another part of the study. Researchers measured the subjects' self-control by the amount of time they persisted at the puzzles and the number of attempts they made. According to the

ego depletion model, the radish eaters would use more self-control resources (resisting the chocolate) than the chocolate eaters (resisting the radishes) or the subjects in the no-food control group. Thus, this group should have the fewest self-control resources left to use for persisting at a difficult task. As you can see in **Figure 6.15**, the radish eaters gave up sooner and made fewer attempts on the puzzles than the chocolate eaters or the control group.

One of the reasons people rely so often on habit and automatic processing is to conserve these important self-control resources (Baumeister, Muraven, & Tice, 2000). By not doing so, people can inadvertently undermine their own positive qualities. For example, ego depletion has been found to make people less helpful to strangers but

Figure 6.15

Persistence on unsolvable puzzles. Participants who were instructed to eat radishes and not to eat chocolate treats used more self-control resources than participants who were instructed to eat the chocolate and not touch the radishes or participants in the no-food control group. Because the radish eaters had relatively few self-control resources remaining to help them persist at a difficult task (unsolvable puzzles), they persisted for the shortest time and made the fewest attempts to solve the puzzles when compared to the other two groups. (Adapted from Baumeister et al., 1998)

Log on to CourseMate at www.cengagebrain.com **to watch this video.**

People practice self-regulation, also referred to as self-control, in their everyday lives—whether to avoid eating too much or becoming overly upset. Roy Baumeister, social psychologist at Florida State University, demonstrates how self-regulation requires energy in this Reel Research video. According to Baumeister, most of the major social and emotional problems Americans face stem from a lack of self-control.

Two of Baumeister's studies are demonstrated in this video. The first study, involving radishes and cookies, is covered earlier in this chapter (see results in **Figure 6.15**). The video shows how the study was conducted and shows that self-control requires energy. In the second study, researchers tested participants' glucose levels before asking them to watch a video. On the left was a video of a woman speaking inaudibly; on the right was a series of words. Some participants (Group A) were asked to watch the video without further instruction. Other participants (Group B) were asked to watch the video but avoid looking at the words. After they completed this task, glucose levels were tested again. The participants in Group B were given lemonade; Jessica received lemonade sweetened with sugar while Hallie's lemonade had a sugar substitute. Participants from both groups were asked to submerge their arm in an ice bath. Hallie—who was asked to exhibit self-control and was given a sugar substitute—pulled her arm from the ice bath in less than 4 seconds, while the other participants tolerated it for over twice that time.

Watch the *Exerting Self Control* video to learn more about the relationship between visual cues and addiction. Delve even deeper by responding to the following discussion questions.

DISCUSSION QUESTIONS

1. Researchers told participants in the first study that the goal was to understand their reaction to food. What was the actual goal of the study, and what were its findings?
2. Good self-control and intelligence are predictive of life success, according to Baumeister. Name the benefits of good self-control described in the video. What is his advice about self-control as a muscle?
3. Create a study similar to the ones covered in the video. What task would you give your participants to exhibit self-control? How would you measure energy spent and its relationship with self-control?

not, fortunately, family members (DeWall et al., 2008). Being asked to make too many choices or decisions can also reduce people's self-control (Vohs et al., 2008).

Self-regulation seems to develop early and remain relatively stable. One study reported that 4-year-olds who were better at delaying gratification did better in terms of both academic performance and social competence some 10 years later (Mischel, Shoda, & Peake, 1988; Shoda, Mischel, & Peake, 1990). Recent evidence suggests that self-regulation is malleable and can be strengthened like a muscle, which means that with regular "exercise," people can become less vulnerable to ego depletion effects (Baumeister et al., 2006). Being in a good mood (Tice et al., 2007) and ingesting sugar, which fuels energy (Gailliot et al., 2009), can restore people's self-control. In the next section, we examine self-efficacy, a key aspect of self-regulation, and then discuss self-defeating behavior, a case of self-control failure.

Self-Efficacy

Albert Bandura

As explained in Chapter 2, *self-efficacy* refers to one's belief about one's ability to perform behaviors that should lead to expected outcomes. It represents people's conviction that they can achieve specific goals. According to Albert Bandura (2000, 2008a,b), efficacy beliefs vary according to the person's skills. You may have high self-efficacy when it comes to making friends but low self-efficacy when it comes to speaking in front of a group. However, simply having a skill doesn't guarantee that you will be able to put it into practice. Like the Little Engine That Could, you must also *believe* that you are capable of doing so ("I *think* I can, I *think* I can . . ."). In other words, self-efficacy is concerned not with the skills you have, but with your *beliefs about what you can do* with these skills.

Correlates of Self-Efficacy

A number of studies have shown that self-efficacy affects individuals' commitments to goals, their performance on tasks, and their persistence toward goals in the face of obstacles (Maddux & Gosselin, 2003). Self-efficacy is related to health promotion (Bandura, 2004), academic performance (Brady-Amoon & Fuertes, 2011; Prat-Sala & Redford, 2012), career choice (Betz & Klein, 1996), job performance and worker productivity (Stajkovic & Luthans, 1998), and coping with unemployment (Creed, Lehman, & Hood, 2009). Because of the importance of self-efficacy in psychological adjustment (Bandura, 2008a), it is worth keeping in mind that self-efficacy is learned and can be changed. Research shows that increasing self-efficacy is an effective way to improve health (losing weight, stopping smoking) (Maddux & Gosselin, 2003) and to treat a variety of psychological problems, including test anxiety (Smith, 1989), fear of computer use (Wilfong, 2006), phobias (Williams, 1995), fear of sexual assault (Ozer & Bandura, 1990), eating disorders (Goodrick et al., 1999), and substance abuse (DiClemente, Fairhurst, & Piotrowski, 1995), including marijuana dependence (Lozano, Stephens, & Roffman, 2006).

Developing Self-Efficacy

Self-efficacy is obviously a valuable quality. How does one acquire it? Bandura (1997, 2000) identifies four sources of self-efficacy: mastery experiences, vicarious experiences, persuasion/encouragement, and interpretation of emotional arousal.

1. *Mastery experiences.* The most effective path to self-efficacy is through mastering new skills. Sometimes new skills come easily—learning how to use the copy machine in the library, for instance. Some things are harder to master, such as learning how to drive a stick-shift in a standard transmission car or how to play the piano. In acquiring more difficult skills, people usually make mistakes. If they persist through failure experiences to eventual success, they learn the lesson of self-efficacy: I *can* do it!

2. *Vicarious experiences.* Another way to improve self-efficacy is by watching others perform a skill you want to learn. It's important that you choose a model who is competent at the task, and it helps if the model is similar to you (in age, gender, and ethnicity). For example, if you're shy about speaking up for yourself, observing someone who is good at doing so can help you develop the confidence to do it yourself.

3. *Persuasion and encouragement.* Although it is less effective than the first two approaches, a third way to develop self-efficacy is through the encouragement of others. For example, if you're having a hard time asking someone for a date, a friend's encouragement might give you just the push you need.

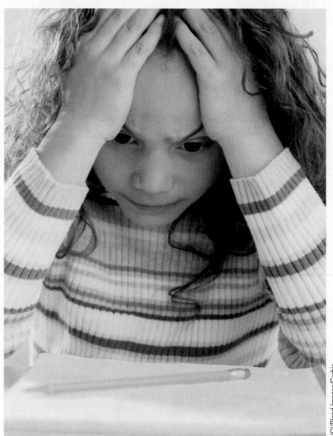

Ironically, difficulties and failures can ultimately contribute to the development of a strong sense of self-efficacy. Self-efficacy tends to improve when youngsters learn to persist through difficulties and overcome failures.

4. *Interpretation of emotional arousal.* The physiological responses that accompany feelings and interpretations of these responses are another source of self-efficacy. Let's say you're sitting in class waiting for your professor to distribute an exam. You notice that your palms are moist, your stomach feels a little queasy, and your heart is pounding. If you attribute these behaviors to fear, you can temporarily dampen your self-efficacy, thus decreasing your chances of doing well. Alternatively, if you attribute your sweaty palms and racing heart to the arousal everyone needs in order to perform well, you may be able to boost your self-efficacy and increase your chances of doing well. Of course, self-regulation doesn't always succeed. That's the case in self-defeating behavior, our next topic.

Self-Defeating Behavior

People typically act in their own self-interest. But sometimes they knowingly do things that are bad for them—such as smoking, having unprotected sex, and completing important assignments at the last minute. *Self-defeating behaviors* **are seemingly intentional actions that thwart a person's self-interest.** Self-defeating behaviors generally provide short-term or immediate pleasures but lay the ground work for long-term problems rather than gains (Baumeister & Bushman, 2011; Twenge, 2008). According to Roy Baumeister (1997; Baumeister & Scher, 1988), there are three categories of intentional self-defeating behaviors: deliberate self-destruction, tradeoffs, and counterproductive strategies. The key difference among these three behaviors lies in how intentional they are. As **Figure 6.16** shows, attempts at deliberate self-destruction involve the most intent; counterproductive strategies are the least intentional, and tradeoffs fall in between.

In *deliberate self-destruction,* people want to harm themselves and choose courses of action that will forseeably lead to that result. This type of behavior typically occurs in individuals with psychological disorders; deliberate self-destruction appears to be infrequent in normal populations.

Marc Vaughn/Masterfile

Self-defeating behaviors come in many forms with many underlying motivations. Overeating is a matter of *tradeoffs*. People realize that excessive eating may be harmful in the long run, but it is enjoyable at the time.

THREE CATEGORIES OF SELF-DEFEATING BEHAVIOR		
Type of self-defeating behavior	Harm foreseen?	Harm desired?
Deliberate self-destruction	Yes	Yes
Tradeoffs	Yes	No
Counterproductive strategies	No	No

© Cengage Learning

Figure 6.16

Three categories of self-defeating behavior. Roy Baumeister and Steven Scher (1988) distinguished three categories of self-defeating behaviors, based on how intentional the behaviors are. Intentionality is determined by two factors: an individual's awareness that a behavior could bring possible harm and an individual's desire to harm himself or herself. Deliberate self-destruction is the most intentional, followed by tradeoffs, then counterproductive strategies.

In *tradeoffs,* people foresee the possibility of harming themselves but accept it as a necessary accompaniment to achieving a desirable goal. Overeating, smoking, and drinking to excess are examples that come readily to mind. Other examples include procrastinating (putting off tasks feels good in the short run, but the struggle to meet looming deadlines results in poor performance and increased stress and illness), failing to follow prescribed health care advice (it's easier to slack off now, but doing so leads to future problems), shyness (avoiding social situations protects against anxiety but makes loneliness more likely), and self-handicapping (getting drunk before an exam explains poor performance but increases the chances of failure). People engage in tradeoffs because they bring immediate, positive, and reliable outcomes, not because they want to hurt themselves in the short or the long run.

In *counterproductive strategies,* a person pursues a desirable outcome but misguidedly uses an approach that is bound to fail. Of course, you can't always know in advance if a strategy will pay off. Thus, people must *habitually* use this strategy for it to qualify as self-defeating. For example, some people tend to persist in unproductive endeavors, such as pursuing an unreachable career goal or an unrequited love. People persist in these behaviors because they erroneously believe they'll be successful, not because they are intent on self-defeat.

To conclude, although most people engage in self-defeating behavior at some time, there is little evidence that they deliberately try to harm themselves or to fail at a task. Instead, self-defeating behavior appears to be the result of people's distorted judgments or strong desires to escape from immediate, painful feelings (Twenge, Catanese, & Baumeister,, 2002). Such feelings can occur as a result of social exclusion (Twenge et al., 2002) or impulsivity linked to people's narcissism (Vazire & Funder, 2006).

SELF-PRESENTATION

LEARNING OBJECTIVES

- Define impression management, and cite some strategies people use to make positive impressions.
- Understand how high self-monitors are different from low self-monitors.

Whereas your self-concept involves how you see yourself, your public self involves how you want others to see you. **A public self is an image presented to others in social interactions.** This presentation of a public self may sound deceitful, but it is perfectly normal, and everyone does it (Schlenker, 2003). Many self-presentations (ritual greetings, for example) take place automatically and without awareness. But when it really counts (job interviews, for example), people consciously strive to make the best possible impression so they are perceived favorably. In fact, when people exert effort by putting their "best face forward" they are likely to convey their true selves to others (Human et al., 2012). Long-term couples who plan "date nights" do the same thing by actively presenting themselves and create a positive mood in the process (Dunn, Akin, & Norton, 2008).

Typically, individuals have a number of public selves that are tied to certain situations and certain people. For instance, you may have one public self for your parents and another for your peers. You may have still others for your teachers, your boss, your co-workers, and so forth. Also, people differ in the degree of overlap or congruence among their various public selves (see **Figure 6.17**). Does it matter whether you perceive yourself to be essentially the same person in different situations? It seems so. People who see themselves as being similar across different social roles (with friends, at work, at school, with parents, with romantic partners) are better adjusted than those who perceive less integration in their self-views across these roles (Lutz & Ross, 2003; but see Baird, Le, & Lucas, 2006).

Impression Management

As noted earlier, the *spotlight effect* leads people to think others notice and evaluate them more than is the actual case (Gilovich, Kruger, & Medvec, 2002). In a related phenomenon, the *guilty by association effect,* people erroneously assume their social standing suffers as a result of embarrassing actions or blunders perpetrated by those they associate with ("My friend is making me look bad!")

(Fortune & Newby-Clark, 2008). These two self-focused responses remind us that people normally strive to make a positive impression on others in order to be liked, respected, hired, and so forth (Baumeister & Twenge, 2003), just as they must be careful not to alienate others by bragging or drawing too much attention to themselves (Anderson et al., 2006). The sociologist Erving Goffman (1959) used the term *face* to describe the idealized image people try to create in the minds of others. *Impression management* **refers to usually conscious efforts by people to influence how others think of them.** As a skill, impression management is vital to social life (Koslowsky & Pindek, 2011). Consider how what you post on Facebook, for example, is a way for you to share your doings while still controlling what others know about you.

To see impression management in operation, let's look at a study of behavior in simulated job interviews (von Baeyer, Sherk, & Zanna, 1981). In this study, female job applicants were led to believe that the man who would

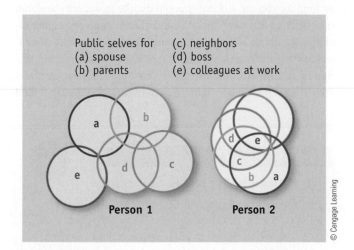

Figure 6.17

Public selves and adjustment. Person 1 has divergent public selves with relatively little overlap among them. Person 2, whose public selves are more congruent with each other, is likely to be better adjusted than Person 1.

interview them held either traditional, chauvinistic views of women or just the opposite. The researchers found that applicants who expected a chauvinist presented themselves in a more traditionally feminine manner than subjects in the other condition. Their self-presentation efforts extended to both their appearance (they wore more makeup) and their communication style (they talked less and gave more traditional answers to a question about marriage and children). In a job interview, people are particularly attentive to making a good impression, but impression management also operates in everyday interactions, although individuals may be less aware of it (Schlenker, 2003). Let's look at some common impression management strategies.

Impression Management Strategies

One reason people engage in impression management is to claim a particular identity (Baumeister, 1998). Thus, you select a type of dress, hairstyle, and manner of speech to present a certain image of yourself. Tattoos and body piercings also create a specific image. A second motive for impression management is to gain liking and approval from others—by editing what you say about yourself and by using various nonverbal cues such as smiles, gestures, and eye contact. Because self-presentation is practiced so often, people usually do it automatically. At other times, however, impression management may be used intentionally—to get a job, a date, a promotion, and so forth. Some common self-presentation strategies include ingratiation, self-promotion, exemplification, intimidation, and supplication (Jones, 1990). To this list, we add a rarely recognized strategy, negative acknowledgment:

1. *Ingratiation.* Of all the self-presentation strategies, ingratiation is the most fundamental and most frequently used. **Ingratiation is behaving in ways to make oneself likable to others.** For example, *giving compliments* is effective, as long as you are sincere (people dislike insincerity and can often detect it). One study found that waitresses could increase their tips simply by praising the food choices of customers as they ordered (Seiter, 2007). *Doing favors for others* is also a common tactic, as long as your gestures aren't so spectacular they leave others feeling indebted

(Gordon, 1996). At the same time they are being "helpful," however, ingratiators run the risk of raising suspicion about their motives for doing so (Ham & Vonk, 2011).

2. *Self-promotion.* The motive behind self-promotion is earning respect. You do so by playing up your strong points so you will be perceived as competent. For instance, in a job interview, you might find ways to mention that you earned high honors at school and that you were president of the student body and a member of the soccer team. To keep from coming across as a braggart, you shouldn't go overboard with self-promotion. For this reason, false modesty ("Oh, thanks, but it was nothing special") often works well. Still, being somewhat direct is better than being indirect, which can be perceived to be manipulative (Tal-Or, 2010).

3. *Exemplification.* Setting an example is not always easy. Because most people try to project an honest image, you have to demonstrate exemplary behavior to claim special credit for integrity or character. Occupations fraught with danger, such as those in the military or law enforcement, provide obvious opportunities to exemplify moral virtue or to demonstrate courage. A less dramatic, but still effective, strategy is to behave consistently according to high ethical standards—as long as you don't come across as self-righteous. Also, your words and deeds need to match unless you want to be labeled a hypocrite.

4. *Intimidation.* This strategy sends the message, "Don't mess with me" or "Do as I say." Intimidation usually works only in nonvoluntary relationships—for instance, when it's hard for workers to find another employer or for an economically dependent spouse to leave a relationship. Obvious intimidation tactics include threats and the withholding of valuable resources (salary increases, promotions, sex). A more subtle tactic is emotional intimidation—holding over a person's head the threat of an aggressive outburst if you don't get your way. The other self-presentation strategies work by creating a favorable impression; intimidation usually generates dislike and resentment. Nonetheless, it can work.

5. *Supplication.* This is usually the tactic of last resort. To get favors from others, individuals try to present themselves as weak and dependent—as in the song, "Ain't Too Proud to Beg" (Van Kleef, De Dreu, & Manstead, 2006). Students may plead or break into tears in an instructor's office in an attempt to get a grade changed. Because of the social norm to help those in need, supplication may work; however, unless the supplicator has something to offer the potential benefactor, it's not an effective strategy.

6. *Negative acknowledgment.* Can confessing you've made a relatively minor error motivate people to like you a bit more? Ward and Brenner (2006) found that making negative acknowledgments—candidly admitting to possessing some negative quality—triggered positive responses. In one study, when a hypothetical college student

Learn More Online

International Society for Self and Identity

The International Society for Self and Identity (ISSI) is an interdisciplinary association of social and behavioral scientists who are interested in studying the human self. This site provides membership information, announcements, information about conferences, and links to related sites concerning self and identity.

"I'm told that you respond very well to intimidation."

Learn More Online

Impression Management

This short article at TheFreeDictionary.com explains impression management and provides a number of links to other articles on related issues.

divulged that his high school record was by no means an outstanding one, his grades were judged more favorably than when he did not comment on his academic history. Perhaps negative acknowledgment leads people to see one as honest. As long as the quality does not define the person, admitting that one is not perfect and that everyone makes small mistakes may sometimes be an advantage.

Individuals tailor their use of self-presentation strategies to match the situation. For instance, it's unlikely that you'd try intimidating your boss; you'd be more likely to ingratiate or promote yourself with him or her. All of these strategies carry risks. Thus, to make a good impression, you must use these strategies skillfully.

Perspectives on Impression Management

Curiously, almost all research on self-presentation has been conducted on first meetings between strangers, yet the vast majority of actual social interactions take place between people who already know each other. Noting the gap between reality and research, Dianne Tice and her colleagues (1995) investigated whether self-presentation varied in these two situations. They found that people strive to make positive impressions when they interact with strangers but shift toward modesty and neutral self-presentations when they are with friends. Why the difference? Because strangers don't know you, you want to give them positive information so they'll form a good impression of you. Besides, strangers have no way of knowing whether you are bending the truth. On the other hand, your friends already know your positive qualities. Thus, belaboring them is unnecessary and may make you seem boastful. Likewise, your friends know you well enough to know whether you are grandstanding, so you don't bother. The best approach to managing impressions may be a balanced one. Robinson, Johnson, and Shields (1995) found that people who presented themselves using a mix of self-promoting and self-deprecating comments were viewed as more genuine and likeable than those who relied exclusively on either type of descriptions.

Self-Monitoring

According to Mark Snyder (1986; Fuglestad & Snyder, 2009; Gangestad & Snyder, 2000), people vary in their awareness of how they are perceived by others. ***Self-monitoring* refers to the degree to which people attend to and control the impressions they make on others.** People who are high self-monitors seem to be very sensitive to their impact on others. Low self-monitors, on the other hand, are less concerned about impression management and behave more spontaneously.

Mark Snyder

Compared to low self-monitors, high self-monitors want to make a favorable impression and try to tailor their actions accordingly; they are skilled at deciphering what others want to see. In fact, high self-monitors manage their social relations well, earning status from others by offering them aid while avoiding asking for assistance themselves (Flynn et al., 2006; Fuglestad & Snyder, 2010). Because they are able to control their emotions and deliberately regulate nonverbal signals, they are talented at self-presentation (Gangestad & Snyder, 2000). In contrast, low self-monitors are more likely to express their true beliefs or, possibly, to try to convey the impression that they are sincere and genuine individuals.

As you might infer, these two personality types view themselves differently (Gangestad & Snyder, 2000). Low self-monitors see themselves as having strong principles and behaving in line with them, whereas high self-monitors perceive themselves as flexible and pragmatic. Because high self-monitors don't perceive a necessary connection between their private beliefs and their public actions, they aren't troubled by discrepancies between beliefs and behavior, even when it involves mimicking group-based prejudice (Klein, Snyder, & Livingston, 2004).

In the upcoming Application, we redirect our attention to the critical issue of self-esteem and outline seven steps for boosting it.

BUILDING SELF-ESTEEM

LEARNING OBJECTIVES

- List seven ways to build self-esteem.

Answer the following "yes" or "no."

____ **1.** I worry that others don't like me.

____ **2.** I have very little confidence in my abilities.

____ **3.** I often feel awkward in social situations and just don't know how to take charge.

____ **4.** I have difficulty accepting praise or flattery.

____ **5.** I have a hard time bouncing back from failure experiences.

If you answered "yes" to most of these questions, you may suffer from low self-esteem. As we noted earlier, people with low self-esteem are less happy and more prone to depression, become demoralized after failures, and are anxious in relationships. Moreover, even people with high global self-esteem may have pockets of low self-esteem. For example, you may feel great about your "social self" but not so good about your "academic self." Thus, this Application can be useful to many people, as research demonstrates clearly that people are willing to forgo other pleasures in order to boost their self-esteem (Bushman, Moeller, & Crocker, 2011).

We have one caveat, however: It is possible for self-esteem to be too high—recall our earlier discussion about narcissism, ego threats, and violence. Better adjustment is associated with realistically high (and stable) self-esteem. Thus, our suggestions are directed to those whose self-esteem could use a legitimate boost, not to those whose self-esteem is already inflated. The latter group can benefit from developing more realistic self-views.

As you saw in our discussion of self-efficacy, there is ample evidence that efforts at self-improvement can pay off by boosting self-esteem. Following are seven guidelines for building self-esteem. These suggestions are distilled from the advice of many experts, including Baumeister et al. (2003), Ellis (1989), McKay and Fanning (2000), and Zimbardo (1990).

Learn More Online

National Association for Self-Esteem (NASE)

This site is dedicated to fostering self-esteem. It explains the nature of self-esteem, permits visitors to estimate their self-esteem, discusses parenting and self-esteem, and provides links to other relevant websites.

1. Recognize That You Control Your Self-Image

Recognize that *you* ultimately control how you see yourself. You *do* have the power to change your self-image. True, we have discussed at length how feedback from others influences your self-concept. Yes, social comparison theory suggests that people need such feedback and that it would be unwise to ignore it completely. However, the final choice about whether to accept or reject such feedback rests with you. Your self-image resides in your mind and is a product of your thinking. Although others may influence your self-concept, you are the final authority.

2. Learn More About Yourself

People with low self-esteem don't seem to know themselves in as much detail as those with high self-esteem. Accordingly, to boost your self-esteem, you need to take stock of yourself. To do so, review what you know about your physical appearance, personality characteristics, relations with others, school and job performance, intellectual functioning, and sexuality. By thinking through each area, you may discover that you're fuzzy about certain aspects of yourself. To get a clearer picture, pay careful attention to your thoughts, feelings, and behavior and utilize feedback from others.

3. Don't Let Others Set Your Goals

A common trap that many people fall into is letting others set the standards by which they evaluate themselves. Oth-

LOW SELF-ESTEEM

Mike Twohy/The New Yorker Collection/www.cartoonbank.com

If you like singing star Taylor Swift, that's fine, but she is not a sensible benchmark for evaluating your attractiveness or success. Some people distort the social comparison process.

ers are constantly telling you that you should do this or ought to do that. You may hear that you "should study accounting" or "ought to lose weight." Most of this advice is well intentioned and may contain good suggestions. Still, it is important that you make your *own* decisions about what you will do and what you will believe in. Think about the source of and basis for your personal goals and standards. Do they really represent ideals that *you* value? Or are they beliefs that you have passively accepted from others without thinking?

4. Recognize Unrealistic Goals

Are your goals realistic? Many people demand too much of themselves. They want to always perform at their best, which is obviously impossible. For instance, you may have a burning desire to achieve national acclaim as an actress. However, the odds against such an achievement are enormous. It is important to recognize this reality so that you do not condemn yourself to failure. Some overly demanding people pervert the social comparison process by always comparing themselves to the *best* rather than to similar others. They assess their looks by comparing themselves with famous models, and they judge their finances by comparing themselves with the wealthiest people they know or hear about in the media. Such comparisons are unrealistic and almost inevitably undermine self-esteem. Set reasonable, realistic goals for yourself.

5. Modify Negative Self-Talk

How you think about your life influences how you see yourself (and vice versa). People who are low in self-esteem tend to engage in counterproductive modes of thinking. For example, when they succeed, they may attribute their success to good luck, and when they fail, they may blame themselves. Quite to the contrary, you should take credit for your successes and consider the possibility that your failures may not be your fault. As discussed in Chapter 4, Albert Ellis has pointed out that people often think irrationally and draw unwarranted negative conclusions about themselves. If someone breaks off a romantic relationship with you, do you think, "He doesn't love me. I

must be a worthless, unlovable person?" The conclusion that you are a "worthless person" does *not* follow logically from the fact of the breakup. Such irrational thinking and negative self-talk breed poor self-esteem. Recognize the destructive potential of negative self-talk and bring it to a halt.

6. Emphasize Your Strengths

This advice may seem trite, but it has some merit. People with low self-esteem often derive little satisfaction from their accomplishments and virtues. They pay little heed to their good qualities while talking constantly about their defeats and frailties. The fact is that everyone has strengths and weaknesses. You should accept those personal shortcomings that you are powerless to change and work on those that are changeable, without becoming obsessed about it. At the same time, you should embrace your strengths and learn to appreciate them.

7. Approach Others with a Positive Outlook

Some people with low self-esteem try to cut others down to their (subjective) size through constant criticism. This fault finding and negative approach does not go over well. Instead, it leads to tension, antagonism, and rejection. This rejection lowers self-esteem still further (see **Figure 6.18**). You can boost your esteem-building efforts by recognizing and reversing this self-defeating tendency. Cultivate the habit of maintaining a positive, supportive outlook when you approach people. Doing so will promote rewarding interactions and help you earn others' acceptance. There is probably nothing that enhances self-esteem more than acceptance and genuine affection from others.

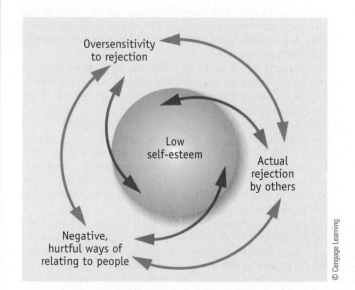

Figure 6.18

The vicious circle of low self-esteem and rejection. A negative self-image can make expectations of rejection a self-fulfilling prophecy, because people with low self-esteem tend to approach others in negative, hurtful ways. Real or imagined rejections lower self-esteem still further, creating a vicious circle.

CHAPTER 6 | Review

KEY IDEAS

SELF-CONCEPT

- The self-concept is composed of a number of beliefs about what one is like, and it is not easily changed. It governs both present and future behavior. Discrepancies between one's ideal self and one's actual or ought self can produce negative emotions and lowered self-esteem. To cope with these negative states, individuals may bring their behavior in line with their ideal selves or blunt their awareness of self-discrepancies.
- The self-concept is shaped by several factors, including individuals' observations of their own behavior, which often involve social comparisons with others. Self-observations tend to be biased in a positive direction. In addition, feedback from others shapes the self-concept; this information is also filtered to some extent. Cultural guidelines also affect the way people see themselves. Members of individualistic cultures usually have an independent view of the self, whereas those in collectivist cultures often have an interdependent view of the self.

SELF-ESTEEM

- Self-esteem is a person's global evaluation of his or her worth. Like the self-concept, it tends to be stable, but it can fluctuate in response to daily ups and downs.
- Compared to those with high self-esteem, individuals with low self-esteem are less happy, more likely to be depressed, more likely to give up after failure, and less trusting of others.
- Narcissistic individuals are prone to aggression when their self-esteem is threatened. Self-esteem develops through interactions with significant others. Self-esteem, ethnicity, and gender interact in complex ways.

BASIC PRINCIPLES OF SELF-PERCEPTION

- To avoid being overwhelmed with information, people tend to use automatic processing, but for important decisions, they shift to controlled processing. To explain the causes of their behavior, individuals make self-attributions. Generally, people attribute their behavior to internal or external factors and to stable or unstable factors. Controllability-uncontrollability is another key dimension of self-attributions.
- People tend to use either an optimistic explanatory style or a pessimistic explanatory style to understand various events that occur in their lives, and these attributional styles are related to psychological adjustment.
- People are guided by three distinct motives in seeking to understand themselves. The self-assessment motive directs people toward accurate feedback about the self. The self-verification motive drives people toward information that matches their current self-views, even though doing so may involve some distortion of reality. The self-enhancement motive enables people to maintain positive views of themselves.
- Common self-enhancement strategies include making downward comparisons to others whose problems are more serious than one's own, attributing successes to personal factors and failures to external factors (the self-serving bias), basking in the reflected glory of others who are successful, and sabotaging one's performance to provide an excuse for possible failure (self-handicapping).

SELF-REGULATION

- Self-regulation involves setting goals and directing behavior to meet those goals. Engaging in self-control can temporarily deplete what appears to be a limited underlying resource. A key aspect of self-regulation is self-efficacy—an individual's belief that he or she can achieve specific goals. Self-efficacy plays a key role in adjustment and can be learned through mastery experiences, vicarious experiences, persuasion, and positive interpretations of emotional arousal.
- Sometimes normal people knowingly do things that are bad for them. These self-defeating actions fall into three categories: deliberate self-destruction, tradeoffs, and counterproductive strategies.

SELF-PRESENTATION

- Public selves are the various images that individuals project to others. Generally, people try to manage the impressions they make by using a variety of strategies, including ingratiation, self-promotion, exemplification, intimidation, supplication, and negative acknowledgment. High self-monitors pay more attention to the impressions they make on others and tend to be more concerned about making favorable impressions than low self-monitors do.

APPLICATION: BUILDING SELF-ESTEEM

- The seven building blocks to higher self-esteem are (1) recognize that you control your self-image, (2) learn more about yourself, (3) don't let others set your goals, (4) recognize unrealistic goals, (5) modify negative self-talk, (6) emphasize your strengths, and (7) approach others with a positive outlook.

KEY TERMS

Basking in reflected glory p. 186
Collectivism p. 173
Downward social comparison p. 184
Explanatory style p. 182
External attributions p. 180
Impression management p. 191
Individualism p. 173
Ingratiation p. 192
Internal attributions p. 180
Possible selves p. 168
Public self p. 191
Reference group p. 171

Self-attributions p. 180
Self-concept p. 167
Self-defeating behaviors p. 190
Self-discrepancy p. 169
Self-efficacy p. 189
Self-enhancement p. 184
Self-esteem p. 174
Self-handicapping p. 186
Self-monitoring p. 193
Self-regulation p. 187
Self-serving bias p. 184
Self-verification theory p. 184
Social comparison theory p. 171

KEY PEOPLE

Albert Bandura p. 189
Roy Baumeister pp. 175–178

Hazel Markus pp. 167–169
Mark Snyder p. 193

CHAPTER 6 | Practice Test

1. Which of the following statements is *not true* about the self-concept?
   a. It is composed of one dominant belief about the self.
   b. It is composed of many self-beliefs.
   c. It is relatively stable over time.
   d. It influences present as well as future behavior.

2. Mismatches between one's actual and ought selves result in lower self-esteem and
   a. dejection-related feelings.
   b. agitation-related feelings.
   c. feelings of self-enhancement.
   d. no particular feelings.

3. A person reared in a collectivist culture is likely to have a(n) _____ self-view, whereas a person reared in an individualistic culture is likely to have a(n) _____ self-view.
   a. self-discrepant; self-consistent
   b. self-consistent; self-discrepant
   c. independent; interdependent
   d. interdependent; independent

4. Low self-esteem is associated with
   a. happiness.
   b. high trust of others.
   c. self-concept confusion.
   d. recovering after failure experiences.

5. Aggression in response to self-esteem threats is more likely to occur in people who are
   a. high in self-esteem.
   b. low in self-esteem.
   c. narcissistic.
   d. self-defeating.

6. Which of the following is *not* a basic principle of self-perception?
   a. People are "cognitive spenders."
   b. People's explanatory style is related to adjustment.
   c. People want to receive information that is consistent with their self-views.
   d. People want to maintain positive feelings about the self.

7. Keisha is upset when a textbook is stolen, but she feels better after she hears that a classmate's book bag, including her cell phone and wallet, was stolen. This is an example of
   a. the self-serving bias.
   b. basking in reflected glory.
   c. downward comparison.
   d. self-handicapping.

8. Which of the following statements about self-efficacy is true?
   a. It can be developed by persevering through failure until one achieves success.
   b. It is something that one is born with.
   c. It is essentially the same as self-esteem.
   d. It refers to conscious efforts to make a certain impression on others.

9. The self-presentation strategy of ingratiation involves trying to make others
   a. respect you.
   b. fear you.
   c. feel sorry for you.
   d. like you.

10. Which of the following will *not* help you build higher self-esteem?
    a. Minimizing negative self-talk
    b. Comparing yourself with those who are the best in a given area
    c. Working to improve yourself
    d. Approaching others with positive expectations

ANSWERS

1. a Pages 167–168
2. b Page 169
3. d Pages 173–174
4. c Page 175
5. c Pages 177–178
6. a Pages 180–184
7. c Page 184
8. a Pages 189–190
9. d Page 192
10. b Pages 194–195

COURSEMATE

Go to **CengageBrain.com** to access Psychology CourseMate, where you will find an interactive eBook, glossaries, flashcards, quizzes, videos, and more.

PERSONAL EXPLORATIONS WORKBOOK

Go to the *Personal Explorations Workbook* in the back of your textbook for exercises that can enhance your self-understanding in relation to issues raised in this chapter.

Exercise 6.1 *Self-Assessment:* Self-Monitoring Scale

Exercise 6.2 *Self-Reflection:* How Does Your Self-Concept Compare to Your Self-Ideal?

Social Thinking and Social Influence

Jim West/Alamy

You have a new boss at work. Your old boss was let go because of poor performance. The new boss looks very serious. He always wears a white shirt and a conservative tie, and he rarely smiles. Unlike your old boss, who was friendly and joked around a lot, this fellow is very reserved. He rarely even says hello to you when your paths cross in the halls or out in the parking lot. You wonder whether he doesn't like you or happens to treat everyone that way. Maybe he's just driven by his work. You resolve to ask around the office to see how he acts with your co-workers. You do know that he fired a woman who worked a few doors down the hall. You're not sure why; she seemed nice, always smiling and saying hello. She sure looked like a hard worker. Maybe he thought she was too friendly? The new boss is also not much older than you—in fact, he might be your age. What if he thinks you are not working hard enough? Maybe he feels you should have advanced farther in the company, or that you are too nice? Could he be thinking about firing you?

This situation illustrates the process of person perception in everyday life. Everyone asks and answers "why" questions about the people around them. Individuals constantly form impressions to try to make sense of the people they encounter, not only to understand them but also to predict how they will behave. This chapter explores how people form impressions of others, as well as how and why such judgments can be incorrect. Our consideration of *social cognition* (how people think about others, as well as themselves) then broadens to examine the problems posed by prejudice. We then look at how others try to influence one's beliefs and behavior. To do so, we explore the power of persuasive messages and the social pressures to conform and obey. As you will learn, social thinking and social influence play important roles in personal adjustment.

FORMING IMPRESSIONS OF OTHERS

LEARNING OBJECTIVES

- Cite the five sources of information people use to form impressions of others.
- Explain the key differences between snap judgments and systematic judgments.
- Define attributions and describe two attribution-based expectations that can distort an observer's perceptions.

- Recognize four important cognitive distortions and how they operate.
- Identify some ways in which perceptions of others are efficient, selective, and consistent.

Do you recall the first time you met your roommate? She seemed friendly but a little shy, and perhaps a bit on the neat side—so much so that you wondered whether you would get along. You like things less structured; not messy, but decidedly lived-in or comfortable. You were worried that you'd have to change your ways, straightening up your space all the time. Happily, once you got to know her better, she warmed up to you and your clutter, and now you are close friends. As people interact with others, they constantly engage in **person perception, the process of forming impressions of others.** Because impression formation is usually such an automatic process, people are unaware that it is taking place. Nonetheless, the process is a complex one, involving perceivers, their social networks, and those who are perceived (Baumeister,

2010b; Leising & Borkenau, 2011; Waggoner, Smith, & Collins, 2009). Let's review some of its essential aspects.

Key Sources of Information

Because you can't read other people's minds, you are dependent on *observations* of others to determine what they are like (Uleman & Saribay, 2012). In forming impressions of others, people rely on five key sources of observational information: appearance, verbal behavior, actions, nonverbal messages, and situational cues.

1. *Appearance.* Despite the admonition "You can't judge a book by its cover," people frequently do exactly that. Physical features such as height, weight, skin color, and hair color are some of the cues used to "read" other

people. Regardless of their accuracy, beliefs about physical features are used to form impressions of others (Olivola & Todorov, 2010), including people's personalities (Naumann et al., 2009). Styles of dress, clothing or jewelry that designate religious beliefs, body piercings, and tattoos also provide clues about others. Failing to dress appropriately for a job interview, for example, can reduce the chances of being hired (Turner-Bowker, 2001).

2. *Verbal behavior.* Another obvious source of information about others is what they say. People form impressions based on what and how much others self-disclose, how often they give advice and ask questions, and how judgmental they are (Tardy & Dindia, 2006). If Tanisha speaks negatively about most of the people she knows, you will probably conclude that she is a critical person.

3. *Actions.* Because people don't always tell the truth, you have to rely on their behavior to provide insights about them. For instance, when you learn that Wade volunteers 5 hours a week at the local homeless shelter, you are likely to infer that he is a caring person. In impression formation, actions speak louder than words.

4. *Nonverbal messages.* As discussed in Chapter 8, a key source of information about others is nonverbal communication: facial expressions, eye contact, body language, and gestures (Ekman, 2007; Knapp & Hall, 2006). These nonverbal cues provide information about people's emotional states and dispositions. For example, in our culture, we make judgments about others based on their faces (Ito, 2011; Montpare, 2010; Zebrowitz & Montepare, 2008); thus, a bright smile and steady eye contact signal friendliness and openness, just as a handshake can indicate extraversion (Bernieri & Petty, 2011). Also, because people know that verbal behavior is easily manipulated, they often rely on nonverbal cues to determine the truth of what others say (Frank & Ekman, 1997). And we should not forget about nonverbal cues that appear in written form (*how* we say what we say), as the content of email messages can suggest personality traits or emotional states of the sender (McAndrew & De Jonge, 2011).

5. *Situations.* The setting in which behavior occurs provides crucial information about how to interpret a person's behavior (Cooper & Withey, 2009; Reis & Holmes, 2012; Trope & Gaunt, 2003). For instance, without situational cues (such as being at a wedding versus a funeral), it would be hard to know whether a person crying is happy or sad.

When it comes to drawing inferences about people, one bad piece of information can outweigh or undo a collection of positive characteristics. Social psychological research repeatedly demonstrates that the presence of a trait perceived to be negative ("untrustworthy") can have more influence on forming impressions than several positive qualities ("warm," "open," "friendly," "clever") (Vonk, 1993). When an immoral act is performed, other good or virtuous

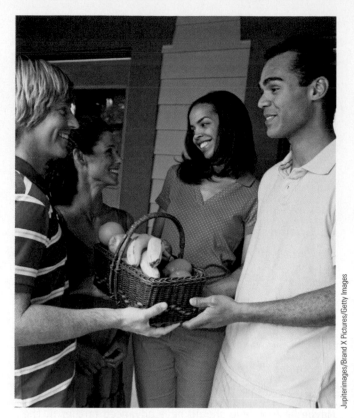

In forming impressions of others, people rely on cues such as appearance, actions, and verbal and nonverbal messages, as well as the nature of the situation.

behaviors cannot undo the damage to people's perceptions of the offender's character (Riskey & Birnbaum, 1974). In fact, a single bad deed can eliminate a good reputation, but one good deed cannot redeem an otherwise bad standing in the eyes of others (Skowronski & Carlston, 1992). Thus, in the realm of perception *bad impressions tend to be stronger than good ones* (Baumeister et al., 2001).

Snap Judgments Versus Systematic Judgments

In their interactions with others, people are bombarded with more information than they can possibly handle. To avoid being overwhelmed, they rely on alternative ways to process information (Kahneman, 2011). *Snap judgments* about others are those made quickly and based on only a few bits of information and preconceived notions. Thus, they may not be particularly accurate. Indeed, there is evidence that when a stranger looks very similar to someone we know well, such as a romantic partner, we automatically, effortlessly, and more or less nonconsciously like the person (Günaydin et al., 2012). Nevertheless, people can get by with superficial assessments of others quite often. As Susan Fiske (2004) puts it, "Good-enough accuracy in forming impressions allows us to navigate our so-

Susan Fiske

cial seas and not collide or run aground too often" (p. 132). Often, interactions with others are so fleeting or inconsequential that it makes little difference that such judgments are imprecise.

On the other hand, when it comes to selecting a friend, a mate, or an employee, it's essential that impressions be as accurate as possible. Thus, it's not surprising that people are motivated to take more care in such assessments. In forming impressions of those who can affect their welfare and happiness, people make *systematic judgments* rather than snap decisions (see **Figure 7.1**). That is, they take the time to observe the person in a variety of situations and to compare that person's behavior with that of others in similar situations. To determine the cause of others' behavior, people engage in the process of causal attribution.

Attributions

As we have noted in earlier chapters, *attributions* **are inferences that people draw about the causes of their own behavior, others' behavior, and events.** In Chapter 6, we focused on self-attributions. Here, we'll apply attribution theory to the behavior of *other people* (Jones et al., 1972). For example, suppose that your boss bawls you out for doing a sloppy job on an insignificant project. To what do you attribute this tongue lashing? Was your work really that bad? Is your boss just in a grouchy mood? Is your boss under too much pressure?

In Chapter 6, we noted that attributions have three key dimensions: internal versus external, stable versus unstable, and controllable versus uncontrollable (Jones & Davis, 1965; Weiner, 1974). For this discussion, we focus only on the internal/external dimension (Heider, 1958). When people ascribe the causes of someone's behavior to personal dispositions, traits, abilities, or feelings, they are

making *internal* attributions. When they impute the causes of a person's behavior to situational demands and environmental constraints, they are making *external* attributions. For example, if a friend's business fails, you might attribute the failure to your friend's lack of business skills (an internal factor) or to negative trends in the economy (an external factor).

The types of attributions people make about others can have a tremendous impact on everyday social interactions. Consider the judgments people make about the nature of others' emotional experiences or reactions, for example. People often assume that women are the more emotional gender when, in fact, they are no more emotional than men except where outward displays of emotion are concerned (DeAngelis, 2001; see Chapter 11). This bias can color the conclusions observers make about the emotional experiences of men and women in similar circumstances. In two experiments, participants were given either situational ("was having a rough day") or dispositional ("so emotional") information as the cause of expressions in a series of photographs of male and female faces (Barrett & Bliss-Moreau, 2009). Even when the information was attributed to situational sources, the women's expressions were more likely to be characterized as being due to their personalities. These findings may explain why men, but not women, are often give an attributional "pass" when they show too much feeling in front of others (Mendoza-Denton, Park, & O'Connor, 2008).

Obviously, people don't make attributions about every person they meet. Research suggests that people are relatively selective in this process (Malle, 2004; Malle & Knobe, 1997). It seems they are most likely to make attributions (1) when others behave in unexpected or negative ways, (2) when events are personally relevant, and (3) when they are suspicious about another person's motives. For example, if Serena laughs loudly at the local student hangout, no one bats an eye. But if she does so in the middle of a serious lecture, it raises eyebrows and generates speculation about why she behaved this way.

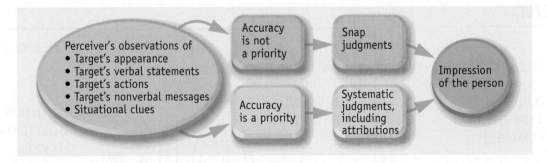

Figure 7.1

The process of person perception. In forming impressions of others, perceivers rely on various sources of observational information. When it's important to form accurate impressions of others, people are motivated to make systematic judgments, including attributions. When accuracy isn't a priority, people make snap judgments about others. (Adapted from Kassin, Fein, & Markus, 2011)

Some aspects of the attribution process are logical (Trope & Gaunt, 2003). Nonetheless, research also shows that the process of person perception is sometimes illogical and unsystematic, as in the case of snap judgments. Perceivers may agree on the nature of people's behavior but because of their own implicit biases get the cause of the behavior wrong (Robins et al., 2004). Other sources of error also creep into the process, a topic we take up next.

Perceiver Expectations

Remember Evan, that bully from the fourth grade? He made your life miserable—constantly looking for opportunities to poke fun at you and beat you up. Now when you meet someone named Evan, your initial reaction is negative, and it takes a while to warm up to him (Andersen & Chen, 2002). Why? Your negative past experiences with an Evan have led you to expect the worst, whether or not it's warranted (Andersen, Reznik, & Manzella, 1996). This is just one example of how *perceiver expectations* can influence the perception of others (de Calvo & Reich, 2009). Let's look at two of the principles governing perceiver expectations: confirmation bias and self-fulfilling prophecy.

Confirmation Bias

Shortly after you begin interacting with someone, you start forming hypotheses about what the person is like. In turn, these hypotheses can influence your behavior toward that person in such a way as to confirm your expectations. Thus, if on your first encounter with Xavier he has a camera around his neck, you will probably hypothesize that he has an interest in photography and question him selectively about his shutterbug activities. You might also neglect to ask more wide-ranging questions that would give you a more accurate picture of him. **Confirmation bias is the tendency to seek information that supports one's beliefs while not pursuing disconfirming information.**

Confirmation bias is a well-documented phenomenon (Dougherty, Turban, & Callander, 1994; Nickerson, 1998). It occurs in casual social interactions and in gender relations (Traut-Mattausch et al., 2011), as well as in job interviews and in courtrooms, where the interviewer or attorney may ask leading questions (Fiske & Taylor, 1991). Law enforcement officers, for example, should be careful to evaluate evidence without any preconceived notion of a suspect's guilt or innocence (Lilienfeld & Landfield, 2008b). When it comes to forming first impressions of others, the principle is not so much "seeing is believing" as "believing is seeing" (see **Figure 7.2**), and some people may be more susceptible to displaying confirmation biases than others (Rassin, 2008). In other words, some people's personalities may predispose them to focus on facts that fit their theories instead of weighing all of the available information more critically.

Confirmation bias also occurs because individuals selectively recall facts to fit their views of others. In one experiment, participants watched a videotape of a woman engaging in a variety of activities, including listening to classical music, drinking beer, and watching TV (Cohen, 1981). Half of them were told that the woman was a waitress and the other half were told that she was a librarian. When asked to recall the woman's actions on the videotape, participants tended to remember activities consistent with their stereotypes of waitresses and librarians. Thus, those who thought that the woman was a waitress recalled her drinking beer; those who thought she was a librarian recalled her listening to classical music.

DILBERT

DILBERT Scott Adams/Dist. by United Feature Syndicate, Inc.

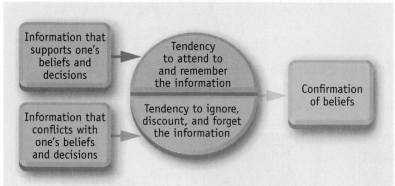

© Cengage Learning

Figure 7.2

Confirmation bias. Confirmation bias is a two-pronged process in which people seek and remember information that supports their beliefs while discounting and forgetting information that is inconsistent with their beliefs. This common cognitive slant often distorts the process of person perception, leading to inaccurate impressions of people.

Can a confirmation bias be used to characterize perceptions of group behaviors as well as individual actions? Apparently so. A recent study considered whether confirmation bias is linked to the pervasive belief in a sexual double standard, namely that men are rewarded for sexual activity while women are derogated for it (Marks & Fraley, 2006). Think about it: In our culture, isn't promiscuity sometimes praised (or at least ignored) when men engage in it? However, women run the risk of losing their reputations if they become known to have a variety of sexual partners. Participants in the study by Marks and Fraley (2006) read brief accounts about either a male or a female that contained an equal number of positive and negative observations about the individual's sexual behavior. Despite perceived advances in sexual equality and living in a society that is increasingly open minded about sexual behavior, people were more likely to recall information that "confirmed" the double standard (pro-male, anti-female) than contradicted it. In other words, "boys will be boys" and they can get away with promiscuity, but women cannot without sullying their reputations.

Can anything be done to reduce conformation bias? There is some evidence that intentionally presenting people with information that is inconsistent with their perceptions and preferences can encourage them to engage in more divergent thinking (Schwind et al., 2012), but this is unlikely to happen very often in daily life.

Self-Fulfilling Prophecies

Sometimes a perceiver's expectations can actually change another person's behavior (Madon et al., 2011). **A *self-fulfilling prophecy* occurs when expectations about a person cause him or her to behave in ways that confirm the expectations.** This term was originally coined by sociologist Robert Merton (1948) to explain phenomena such as "runs" on banks that occurred during the Depression. That is, when unfounded rumors would circulate that a bank couldn't cover its deposits, people would rush to the bank and withdraw their funds, thereby draining the deposits from the bank and making real what was initially untrue.

Figure 7.3 depicts the three steps in a self-fulfilling prophecy. First, the perceiver has an initial impression of someone. (A teacher believes that Jennifer is highly intelligent.) Then the perceiver behaves toward the target person according to his or her expectations. (He asks her interesting questions and praises her answers.) The third step occurs when the target person adjusts his or her behavior to the perceiver's actions, confirming the perceiver's hypothesis about the target person. (Jennifer performs well in class.) Note that both individuals are unaware that this process is operating. Also note that because perceivers are unaware of their expectations and of the effect they can have on others, they mistakenly attribute the target per-

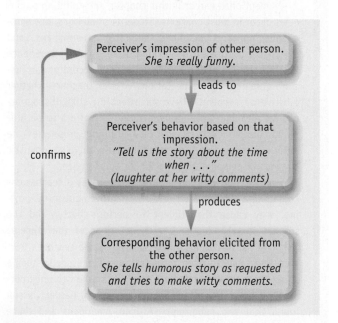

Figure 7.3

The three steps of the self-fulfilling prophecy. Through a three-step process, your expectations about a person can cause that person to behave in ways that confirm those expectations. First, you form an impression of someone. Second, you behave toward that person in a way that is consistent with your impression. Third, the person exhibits the behavior that you encourage, which confirms your initial impression.

Source: Adapted from Smith, E. R., & Mackie, D. M. (1995). *Social psychology*. New York: Worth, p. 103. Copyright © 1995 Worth Publishing. Reprinted with permission.

Log on to CourseMate at www.cengagebrain.com to watch this video.

Researchers often study how self-fulfilling prophecies operate in the classroom, between instructor and student. In this video, Lee Jussim, social psychologist at Rutgers University, discusses the power of self-fulfilling prophecies, as well as the most affected groups and environments.

As mentioned earlier in this chapter, self-fulfilling prophecies occur in most contexts. Students of all ages, businesspeople, military personnel, laboratory technicians, and psychiatric professionals—among other groups—experience the effects of self-fulfilling prophecies. According to Jussim's research, the expectations of the teacher—whether positive or negative—have an effect on student's performance. Although past research found the effect to be profound, Jussim explains that self-fulfilling prophecies are fairly widespread but do not ordinarily involve dramatic changes in personality, behavior, or competence.

Positive self-fulfilling prophecies, such as a teacher encouraging a student after noticing improvement in her writing, may cause the student to perform better and the teacher to raise his or her expectations of the student. Negative self-fulfilling prophecies, such as a teacher's lowered and falsely biased expectations of a student from a stigmatized background, may cause the student to underperform, as he or she is not encouraged to try harder. Jussim found that two subgroups—African Americans and those with lower social class backgrounds—in the elementary and junior high school groups showed large self-fulfilling prophecy effects. Members of these subgroups are more vulnerable because they come from stigmatized backgrounds, and the effects of the self-fulfilling prophecies were positive. Students in the two subgroups experienced an increase in competence comparable to a 100-point increase on the SATs.

Watch the *Self-Fulfilling Prophecies and School Performance* video to learn more about self-fulfilling prophecies and how to make their effects positive. Delve even deeper by responding to the following discussion questions.

DISCUSSION QUESTIONS

1. Why do researchers want to understand self-fulfilling prophecy? How might it influence human performance, whether positively or negatively?

2. Jussim explains that school systems need to design a different learning context. Why is a new learning context needed to foster positive self-fulfilling prophecies? What might a new learning environment include? Explain your answers.

3. Create a scenario in which a self-fulfilling prophecy occurs. What is the context? Who is the perceiver, and do his or her expectations have positive or negative effect?

son's behavior to an internal cause (Jennifer is smart), rather than an external one (their own expectations).

How does self-fulfilling prophecy play out in daily life? Stinson and colleagues (2009) suggest that we often treat others the way we hope to be treated by them—that is, by displaying interpersonal warmth (smiling; saying "hello," "please," and "thank you"; being sincere). When we anticipate acceptance, we behave warmly toward others ("Thanks for your help!") and usually receive the same treatment back ("You're very welcome! I was glad to help!"). However, when we expect rejection, we act coldly toward others ("Your airline made me miss my flight! You need to get me on the very next plane!") and then they repay us in kind ("I'm on my break; I can't help you").

The best-known experiments on self-fulfilling prophecy have been conducted in classroom settings, looking at the effect of teachers' expectations on students' academic performance (Rosenthal, 1985; see also Rosenthal, 2002). A review of 400 studies of this phenomenon over a period of 30 years reported that teacher expectations significantly influenced student performance in 36% of the experiments. In a related vein, perhaps the "storm and stress" of early adolescence, particularly teen rebellion and risk taking and the predictable parental reactions, are sometimes expectation based (Buchanan & Hughes, 2009). When both teens and parents anticipate tension and alienation, for example, they may look for, instigate, or see other behaviors as fitting their respective perceptions. Other research suggests the belief in self-fulfilling prophecies among psychologists may itself be something of a self-fulfilling prophecy in that researchers overestimate both the presence and impact of the bias (Jussim, 2012).

Cognitive Distortions

Another source of error in person perception comes from distortions in the minds of perceivers. These errors in judgment are most likely to occur when a perceiver is in a hurry, is distracted, or is not motivated to pay careful attention to another person.

Social Categorization

One of the ways people efficiently process information is to classify objects (and people) according to their distinctive features (Macrae & Bodenhausen, 2001). Thus, people quite often categorize others on the basis of nationality, race, ethnicity, gender, age, religion, sexual orientation, and so forth (Crisp & Hewstone, 2006). People frequently take the easy path of categorizing others to avoid expending the cognitive effort that would be necessary for a more accurate impression.

People classify those who are similar to them as members of their *ingroup* ("us") and those who are dissimilar to them as being in the *outgroup* ("them"). Such categorizing has three important results. First, people usually have less favorable attitudes toward outgroup members than ingroup members (Brewer & Brown, 1998), such that empathic reactions to those perceived to be in their ingroup are often exaggerated (Brewer, 2007). Second, individuals usually see outgroup members as being much more alike than they really are, whereas they see members of their ingroup as unique individuals (Oakes, 2001). In other words, people frequently explain the behavior of outgroup members on the basis of the characteristic that sets them apart ("Those *Nerdians* are *all* drunks") but attribute the same behavior by an ingroup member to individual personality traits ("*Brett* is a heavy drinker"). This phenomenon, in which

others are seen as "all alike" and one's own group is perceived to be "diverse," is termed the *outgroup homogeneity effect* (Ostrom & Sedikides, 1992).

The third result of categorizing is that it heightens the visibility of outgroup members when there are only a few of them within a larger group. In other words, minority group status in a group makes more salient the quality that distinguishes the person—ethnicity, gender, whatever. When people are perceived as being unique or distinctive, they are also seen as gaining more attention in a group, and their good and bad qualities are given extra weight (Crocker & McGraw, 1984). Significantly, distinctiveness—some quality that makes one person stand out from others—can also trigger stereotyping. Nelson and Miller (1995) found that when observers were told that an individual was both a tennis player and a skydiver, they thought of the person primarily as a skydiver. People tend to define others by those traits or actions that are rare, uncommon, or otherwise distinctive. When later asked to select a gift book for the same individual, observers were apt to choose a skydiving book over one about tennis.

Finally, based on their proclivity to categorize, people are even likely to see outgroup members as looking more like each other than they actually do. Various studies clearly show that eyewitnesses are better at identifying people of their own race than those who belong to a different racial group (Meissner & Brigham, 2001). The exception to this rule occurs when outgroup members are angry (Ackerman, Zuroff, & Moskowitz, 2000). That is, angry outgroup members are much easier to identify than angry ingroup members, suggesting that the human mind carefully tracks strangers who may pose a threat.

Stereotypes

Stereotypes **are widely held beliefs that people have certain characteristics because of their membership in a particular group.** For example, many people assume that Jews are shrewd and ambitious, that African Americans have special athletic and musical abilities, and that Muslims are religious fanatics. Although a kernel of truth may underlie some stereotypes, it should be readily apparent that not all Jews, African Americans, Muslims, and so forth behave alike. If you take the time to think about it, you will recognize that there is enormous diversity in behavior within any group. The problem, of course, is that stereotypes are linked with prejudice and discrimination (Bodenhausen & Richeson, 2010).

What happens when we meet someone who is an exception to our stereotype—say, an accountant who is not quiet and reserved, but rather boisterous and outgoing? Instead of adjusting or broadening our stereotype, we are likely to categorize such an exception as a misfit or a *subtype* (Altermatt & DeWall, 2003; Richards & Hewstone, 2001). Subtypes are categories people rely on for understanding those who do not fit their general stereotypes.

Earlier in this chapter we noted that women are erroneously thought of as being much more emotional than men. Imagine that you endorse this stereotypic view but have a good female friend who rarely displays any emotions, whether positive or negative. As her behavior neither conforms to nor confirms your prevailing stereotype, you store information and thoughts about her in a subtype reserved for "unemotional women."

Stereotypes may also be based on physical appearance. In particular, there is plenty of evidence that physically attractive people are believed to have desirable personality traits. This widespread perception is termed the *"what-is-beautiful-is-good" stereotype* (Dion, Berscheid, & Walster, 1972). Specifically, beautiful people are usually viewed as happier, more socially competent, more assertive, better adjusted, and more intellectually competent than those who are less attractive (Eagly et al., 1991; Jackson, Hunter, & Hodge, 1995). In fact, people believe they remember more positive qualities associated with attractive people and more negative characteristics with unattractive individuals (Rohner & Rasmussen, 2012). This attractiveness stereotype is not exclusively Western, but it can vary somewhat in other cultures. Koreans, for example, consider honesty and concern for others to be extremely important, and they tend to believe that attractive others will score above average on these traits (Wheeler & Kim, 1997). Yet most such perceptions have little basis in fact.

Attractive people *do* have an advantage in the social arena. Attractive children, for example, tend to be perceived as more popular than less attractive ones; sad to say, their teachers like them better, too (Dion, 1973; Dion, Berscheid, & Walster, 1972). Is there a long-term consequence? Well, good-looking adults have better social skills, are more popular, are less socially anxious (especially about interactions with the other gender), are less lonely, and are more sexually experienced (Feingold, 1992b). However, they are not any different from others in intelligence, happiness, mental health, or self-esteem (Feingold, 1992b; Langlois et al., 2000). Thus, attractive people are perceived in a more favorable light than is actually justified. Unfortunately, the positive biases toward attractive people also operate in reverse. Hence, unattract-

ive people are unjustifiably seen as less well adjusted and less intellectually competent than others.

How does the attractiveness stereotype affect most people? First, the bad news: Highly attractive people end up with one another (all else being equal, a perfect "10" might marry a "9," for example, but is unlikely to pair off with a "4" or a "5"). If there is any solace in this news, it's this: Most of people pair up with others who match their own level of attractiveness. Thus, individuals are likely to date those who match their own level of attractiveness (Berscheid et al., 1971). In fact, the correlation between lovers' respective levels of attractiveness is fairly robust (Feingold, 1988). Interestingly, close to the same level of association in rated appearance is found between male friends. Thus, the attractiveness stereotype can have profound effects in people's lives.

Stereotypes can be spontaneously triggered when people—even in those who are not prejudiced—encounter members of commonly stereotyped groups, (Devine, 1989; Dunning & Sherman, 1997). Worse still, racially based stereotypes can cause regrettable—and potentially dangerous—split-second decisions in which people see a weapon that isn't actually there (Payne, 2006). Stereotypes can exist outside a person's awareness (Bodenhausen, Macrae, & Hugenberg, 2003; Dasgupta, 2009). Because stereotyping is automatic, some psychologists are pessimistic about being able to control it (Bargh, 1999); others take a more optimistic view (Uleman et al., 1996). For example, a recent study found less automatic race bias when men and women of different races (except blacks) were surreptitiously induced to smile while looking at photographs of blacks (Ito et al., 2006). If people put forth effort to respond in a friendly and open manner to individuals who are different from them on some important dimension (race, sexual orientation), perhaps the positive behaviors will lead to a reduction in automatic biases when reacting to others.

One conclusion from such studies is that exerting some degree of self-control is a way to reduce prejudice. Maintaining such self-control can be a challenge, however, as research suggests that exerting self-control depletes available energy, which means a drop in blood sugar or glucose (Gailliot, 2008). Could the tendency to stereotype be reduced if perceivers ingested sugar, which would replenish energy and promote more self-control? In a study by Gailliot and colleagues (2009), participants drank lemonade that contained either sugar or Splenda (a no-calorie sugar substitute) and then engaged in an impression formation task. Those who consumed sugar used fewer stereotypes when writing an essay about a gay man than did those in the control (no-sugar) condition. Further, persons high in prejudice in the glucose group offered fewer derogatory statements in their essays than did the high-prejudice individuals in the control group. Thus, under some circumstances, people may be able to override the predilection to stereotype.

There is also some intriguing new evidence that imagining an encounter between oneself and an outgroup member can reduce hostile feelings linked to stereotyping. Brambilla, Ravenna, and Hewstone (2012) had participants imagine interacting with someone from an outgroup usually rated as either high or low on warmth and competence. The imagined encounters promoted feelings of warmth and competence toward the members of groups usually dehumanized (e.g., poor people), envied (e.g., wealthy people), or otherwise targeted for condescending behavior (e.g., elderly people).

Why do stereotypes persist? For one thing, they are functional (Quinn, Macrae, & Bodenhausen, 2003) and require little or no effort (Allport, 1954). Recall from Chapter 6 that people are "cognitive misers." Because they are deluged with much more information than they can process, the tendency is to reduce complexity to simplicity (Bodenhausen & Macrae, 1994) and to save energy (Macrae, Milne, & Bodenhausen, 1994). But, as we noted earlier, the tradeoff for simplification is inaccuracy. Stereotypes also endure because of confirmation bias. Thus, when individuals encounter members of groups that they view with prejudice, they are likely to see what they expect to see. Self-fulfilling prophecy is a third reason stereotypes persist: Beliefs about another person may actually elicit the anticipated behavior and thus confirm biased expectations.

The Fundamental Attribution Error

When explaining the causes of others' behavior, people invoke personal attributions and discount the importance of situational factors. Although this tendency is not universal (Choi, Nisbett, & Norenzayan, 1999; Miyamoto & Kitayama, 2002), it is strong enough that Lee Ross (1977) called it the "*fundamental* attribution error." **The *fundamental attribution error* refers to the tendency to explain other people's behavior as the result of personal, rather than situational, factors.**

This tendency (sometimes termed *correspondence bias;* Jones, 1990) differs from stereotyping in that inferences are based on actual behavior. Nonetheless, those inferences may still be inaccurate. If Jeremy leaves class early, you may be correct in inferring that he is inconsiderate, but he might also have had a previously scheduled job interview. Thus, a person's behavior at a given time may or may not reflect his or her personality or character—but observers tend to assume that it does. The situations people encounter can have profound effects on their behavior, often overpowering the influence of their dispositions—they just don't realize it (Ross & Ward, 1996).

What's behind this tendency to discount situational influences on people's behavior? Once again, the culprit is people's tendency to be cognitive misers. It seems that making attributions is a two-step process (Gilbert & Malone, 1995). As you can see in **Figure 7.4**, in the first step, which occurs automatically, observers make an internal attribution because they are focusing on the person rather than the situation. (At your bank, if you observe the man ahead of you yell at the teller, you might infer that he is a hostile person.) In the second step, observers weigh the impact of the situation on the target person's behavior and adjust their inference. (If you overhear the customer claim this is the third time in three weeks that the bank has made the same error in his account, you're likely to temper your initial judgment about his hostile tendencies.)

The first step in the attribution process occurs spontaneously, but the second step requires cognitive effort and attention. Thus, it is easy to stop after step one—especially if one is in a hurry or distracted. Failure to take the effortful second step can result in the fundamental attribution error. However, when people are motivated to form accurate impressions of others (Webster, 1993) or when they are suspicious about another's motives (Fein, 1996), they do expend the effort to complete the second step. In these cases, they are more likely to make accurate attributions. Some evidence suggests that these two steps may be re-

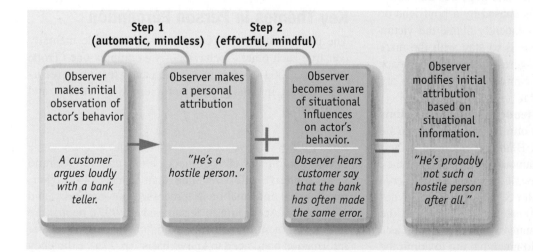

Step 1
(automatic, mindless)

Step 2
(effortful, mindful)

Observer makes initial observation of actor's behavior	Observer makes a personal attribution	Observer becomes aware of situational influences on actor's behavior.	Observer modifies initial attribution based on situational information.
A customer argues loudly with a bank teller.	*"He's a hostile person."*	*Observer hears customer say that the bank has often made the same error.*	*"He's probably not such a hostile person after all."*

Figure 7.4

Explaining the fundamental attribution error. People automatically take the first step in the attribution process (making a personal attribution). However, they often fail to take the second step (considering the possible influence of situational factors on a person's behavior), because that requires extra effort. The failure to consider situational factors causes observers to exaggerate the role of personal factors in behavior—that is, they make the fundamental attribution error. (Adapted from Kassin, Fein, & Markus, 2011) lated to different types of brain activity (Lieberman et al., 2004). Unfortunately, much of the time people are busy with their work and social lives, which severely limits opportunities for attributional corrections while interpreting the intentions and behavior of others (Geeraert et al., 2004). Only when people are forced or seriously motivated to do a thorough analysis of possible causes for the behavior of another or others can they reduce the impact of the fundamental attribution error (e.g., Stalder, 2009).

Cultural values seem to promote different attributional errors. In *individualistic* cultures, where independence is valued, it is assumed that individuals are responsible for their actions. In *collectivist* societies, conformity and obedience to group norms are valued, so it is assumed that an individual's behavior reflects adherence to group expectations (see Chapter 6). Some experts speculate that different styles of thinking underlie cultural differences in attributional styles (Nisbett & Miyamoto, 2005; Nisbett et al., 2001). They suggest that the Western mentality is *analytical* (attention is focused on an object, and causality is ascribed to it), whereas the East Asian mentality is *holistic* (attention is focused on the field surrounding an object, and causality is understood to reside in the relationship between the object and its field) (Masuda & Nisbett, 2006; Miyamoto, Nisbett, & Masuda, 2006). Consistent with both of these views, researchers have found that Americans explain others' behavior in terms of internal attributions more often than Hindus (Miller, 1984), Chinese (Chua, Leu, & Nisbett, 2005; Morris & Peng, 1994), Japanese (Weisz, Rothbaum, & Blackburn, 1984), or Koreans (Choi et al., 2003; Norenzayan, Choi, & Nisbett, 2002). Religion, too, may matter where the fundamental attribution error is concerned. Li and colleagues (2012) found that Protestants are more likely to make internal attributions than Roman Catholics, presumably because Protestantism focuses more on the inward condition of the soul.

Defensive Attribution

Observers are especially likely to make internal attributions in trying to explain the calamities and tragedies that befall other people. When a woman is abused by a boyfriend or husband, for example, people frequently blame the victim by remarking on how stupid she is to stay with the man, rather than condemning the aggressor for his behavior (Summers & Feldman, 1984). Similarly, rape victims are often judged to have "asked for it" (Abrams et al., 2003).

Defensive attribution is a tendency to blame victims for their misfortune, so that one feels less likely to be victimized in a similar way. Blaming victims for their calamities also helps people maintain their belief that they live in a "just world" where people get what they deserve and deserve what they get (Hafer & Bègue, 2005; Haynes & Olson, 2006; Lerner, 1998). Acknowledging that the world is not just—that unfortunate events can happen as a result of chance factors—would mean having to admit the

A common example of defensive attribution is the tendency to blame the homeless for their plight.

frightening possibility that the catastrophes that happen to others could also happen to oneself (Lambert, Burroughs, & Nguyen, 1999), especially when the victim is perceived to be like oneself (Correia, Vala, & Aguiar, 2007). Defensive attributions are a self-protective, but irrational, strategy that allows people to avoid such unnerving thoughts and helps them feel in control of their lives (Hafer, 2000; Lipkus, Dalbert, & Siegler, 1996). Unfortunately, when victims are blamed for their setbacks, people unfairly attribute undesirable traits to them, such as incompetence, foolishness, and laziness. Thus, people do not like "losers," even when the decision that brought about the failure was a reasonable one (Baron & Hershey, 1988).

What about random good events? Can defensive attributions be harnessed to explain luck while still providing a sense of control? Apparently they can. One study found that children see lucky peers, such as someone who just found some money laying on the street, as more likely to perform positive acts and to be nice to others than unlucky children (Olson et al., 2008).

Key Themes in Person Perception

The process of person perception—how people mentally construe each others' behavior—is a complex one (Trope & Gaunt, 2003). Nonetheless, we can detect three recurrent themes in this process: efficiency, selectivity, and consistency.

Efficiency

In forming impressions of others, people prefer to exert no more cognitive effort or time than is necessary. Thus, much social information is processed automatically and effortlessly. According to Susan Fiske (1993), people are like government bureaucrats, who "only bother to gather information on a 'need to know' basis" (p. 175). Efficiency has two important advantages: People can make judgments quickly, and it keeps things simple. The big disadvantage is that snap judgments are error-prone. Still, on balance, efficiency works pretty well as an operating principle.

Selectivity

The old saying that "people see what they expect to see" has been confirmed repeatedly by social scientists. In a classic study, Harold Kelley (1950) showed how a person is preceded by his or her reputation. Students in a class at the Massachusetts Institute of Technology were told that a new lecturer would be speaking to them that day. Before the instructor arrived, the students were given a short description of him, with one important variation. Half the students were led to expect a "warm" person, while the other half were led to expect a "cold" one (see **Figure 7.5**). All the participants were exposed to exactly the same 20 minutes of lecture and interaction with the new instructor. However, those who were led to expect a warm person rated the instructor as significantly more considerate, sociable, humorous, good-natured, informal, and humane than those who expected a cold person.

Consistency

How many times did your parents remind you to be on your best behavior when you were meeting someone for the first time? As it turns out, they were onto something! Considerable research supports the idea that first impressions are powerful (Asch, 1956; Belmore, 1987). **A *primacy effect* occurs when initial information carries more weight than subsequent information.** Primacy effects are likely to occur when perceivers—the people who meet us for the first time—are in good rather than bad moods (Forgas, 2011). We risk being labeled a hypocrite, for example, if we say one thing and then do another (such as claiming to have an open mind and then make a cutting, judgmental remark about someone) rather than the reverse (Barden, Rucker, & Petty, 2005). Initial negative impressions may be especially hard to change (Mellers, Richards, & Birnbaum, 1992). Thus, getting off on the wrong foot may be particularly damaging. As noted earlier in this

Mr. Blank is a graduate student in the Department of Economics and Social Science here at M.I.T. He has had three semesters of teaching experience in psychology at another college. This is his first semester teaching Ec. 70. He is 26 years old, a veteran, and married. People who know him consider him to be a rather cold person, industrious, critical, practical, and determined.	Mr. Blank is a graduate student in the Department of Economics and Social Science here at M.I.T. He has had three semesters of teaching experience in psychology at another college. This is his first semester teaching Ec. 70. He is 26 years old, a veteran, and married. People who know him consider him to be a very warm person, industrious, critical, practical, and determined.

© Cengage Learning

Figure 7.5

Descriptions of the guest lecturer in Kelley's (1950) study. These two descriptions, provided to two groups of students before the lecturer spoke, differ by only an adjective. But this seemingly small difference caused the two groups to form different perceptions of the lecturer.

chapter, negative information can outweigh positive factors; bad can indeed be stronger than good. Only if people are motivated to form an accurate impression and are not tired will they be less likely to lock in their initial impressions (Webster, Richter, & Kruglanski, 1996).

Why are primacy effects so potent? Because people find comfort in cognitive *consistency;* cognitions that contradict each other tend to create tension and discomfort. Hence, once people believe that they have formed an accurate picture of someone, they tend to tune out or discount subsequent information that seems to contradict that picture (Belmore, 1987). It is not impossible to override an initial impression, but the built-in preference for consistency makes doing so more difficult than most people realize.

To conclude, although the process of person perception is highly subjective, people are relatively accurate perceivers of others (Fiske, 1998). Even when misperceptions occur, they are often harmless. However, there clearly are occasions when such inaccuracies are problematic. This is certainly true in the case of prejudice, which we consider next.

THE PROBLEM OF PREJUDICE

LEARNING OBJECTIVES

- Explain how "old-fashioned" and modern discrimination differ.
- Understand how authoritarianism and cognitive distortions can contribute to prejudice.

- Clarify how intergroup competition and threats to social identity can foster prejudice.
- Describe the operation of several strategies for reducing prejudice.

Let's begin our discussion by clarifying a couple of terms that are often confused. ***Prejudice* is a negative attitude toward members of a group;** *discrimination* **involves** **behaving differently, usually unfairly, toward the members of a group.** Prejudice and discrimination do tend to go together, but that is not always the case (see

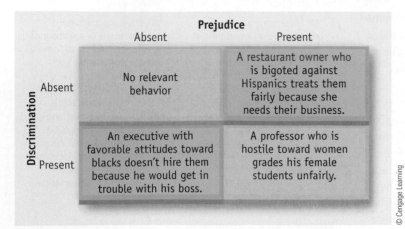

Figure 7.6
Prejudice and discrimination. Prejudice and discrimination are highly correlated, but they don't necessarily go hand in hand. As the examples in the blue cells show, prejudice can exist without discrimination and discrimination without prejudice.

Figure 7.6). One classic social psychology study found almost no discriminatory behavior aimed at a Chinese couple traveling around the country with a white professor in the 1930s. Before making the trips, the professor anticipated that they would encounter some prejudice about where they could stay or dine, but the three were declined service only a few times. Months later, when the professor wrote to all the establishments they had visited to ask whether Chinese guests were welcome, however, the majority of the responses were, in fact, prejudiced and rather uninviting, showing that attitudes don't always predict behavior (LaPiere, 1934). Why can people respond in discriminatory ways sometimes but not always? It is possible that a restaurant owner would be prejudiced against Chinese individuals and yet treat them like anyone else because he needed their business. This is an example of prejudice without discrimination. Although it is probably less common, discrimination without prejudice may also occur. For example, an executive who has favorable attitudes toward blacks may not hire them because he thinks his boss would be upset.

Sometimes, too, prejudices and stereotypes can be triggered without conscious awareness (Wittenbrink & Schwartz, 2007) and can have consequences for behavior. For example, in one study, college students were given a sentence completion task in which half of them received a

Learn More Online

Implicit Association Test

Visit this website sponsored by psychologists at Harvard University who study people's nonconscious prejudices by using what are called implicit measures of social cognition. You can learn about the Implicit Association Test (IAT) here as well as participate in some online research.

word list containing words stereotypically associated with elderly people (wrinkle, gray, Florida). Once the idea of old age was surreptitiously "primed" in their thoughts, these same college students were later found to take 13% longer to walk to an elevator than a control group that received a neutral word list (Bargh, Chen, & Burrows, 1996).

"Old-Fashioned" Versus Modern Discrimination

Over the past 40 years, prejudice and discrimination against minority groups have diminished in the United States. Racial segregation is no longer legal, and discrimination based on race, ethnicity, gender, and religion is much less common than it was in the 1950s and 1960s. Thus, the good news is that overt, or *"old-fashioned," discrimination* against minority groups has declined. The bad news is that a more subtle form of prejudice and discrimination has emerged (Dovidio & Gaertner, 1996; Gawronski et al., 2012). That is, people may privately harbor racist or sexist attitudes but express them only when they feel such views are justified or when it's safe to do so. This new phenomenon has been termed *modern discrimination* (also called *modern racism*). Modern discrimination is also operating when people endorse equality as an abstract principle but oppose programs intended to promote equality on the grounds that discrimination against minority groups no longer exists (Wright & Taylor, 2003). In **Figure 7.7**, you can see the kinds of items used to measure old-fashioned and modern sexism, for example.

While modern racists do not wish to return to the days of segregation, they also feel that minority groups should not push too fast for advancement or receive special treatment by the government. Individuals who endorse statements that favor "modern" discrimination are much more likely to vote against a black political candidate, to oppose affirmative action, and to favor tax laws that benefit whites at the expense of blacks, compared to those who do not endorse such views (Murrell et al., 1994).

One important trend in the study of prejudice is the recognition that most white people consider the possibility that they might hold racist views to be very upsetting; indeed, they are conflicted about it. As a result, they avoid acting in any way that might be construed as racist by others or even by themselves. The upshot is that well-intentioned whites can engage in *aversive racism,* an indirect, subtle, ambiguous form of racism that occurs when their conscious endorsement of egalitarian ideals is in conflict with unconscious, negative reactions to minority group members (Dovidio, Gaertner, & Pearson, 2005; Dovidio et al., 2009; Hodson, Dovidio, & Gaertner, 2010). One study found that black patients had less positive interactions with white physicians who harbored feelings consistent with aversive rac-

ITEMS RELATED TO OLD-FASHIONED SEXISM

1. Women are generally not as smart as men.

2. It is more important to encourage boys than to encourage girls to participate in athletics.

ITEMS RELATED TO MODERN SEXISM

1. Discrimination against women is no longer a problem in the United States.

2. Over the past few years, the government and news media have been showing more concern about the treatment of women than is warranted by women's actual experiences.

Scoring: Possible responses to the statements range from "strongly agree" to "strongly disagree." Individuals who moderately or strongly agree with the above items reflect old-fashioned or modern sexism, respectively.

Figure 7.7

Measuring old-fashioned and modern sexism. Research shows similarities between old-fashioned and modern beliefs about both racism and sexism. Janet Swim and colleagues (1995) have developed a scale to measure the presence of both old-fashioned and modern sexism. Four items from the 13-item scale are shown here. Old-fashioned sexism is characterized by endorsement of traditional gender roles and acceptance of stereotypes that portray females as less competent than males. In contrast, subtle, modern sexism is characterized by denial of continued discrimination and rejection of policies intended to help women.

Source: From Swim, J. K., Aikin, K. J., Hall, W. S., & Hunter, B. A. (1995). Sexism and racism: Old-fashioned and modern prejudices. *Journal of Personality and Social Psychology, 68,*199–214. Copyright © 1995 American Psychological Association. Adapted by permission of the publisher and the author.

ism (Penner et al., 2010). An aversive racist might act in a racist manner when a nonracist excuse is available ("I interviewed several qualified blacks for the job but I had to hire the best candidate, who happened to be white"). Fortunately, researchers are seeking ways to combat such unintended but real bias toward others (Gaertner & Dovidio, 2005). When people cannot reconcile the conflict between their expressed attitudes and how they act, for example, their prejudice decreases (Son Hing, Li, & Zanna, 2002).

Causes of Prejudice

Prejudice is obviously a complex issue and has multiple causes. Although we can't thoroughly examine all of the causes of prejudice, we'll examine some of the major psychological and social factors that contribute to this vexing problem.

Authoritarianism

In some of the earliest research on prejudice, Theodor Adorno and his colleagues (1950) identified the *authoritarian personality,* a personality type characterized by prejudice toward *any* group perceived to be different from oneself. Subsequent research found serious methodologi-

cal weaknesses in the study, calling into question the validity of the personality type.

Over the past 50 years, both the definition and measurement of authoritarianism have evolved (Dion, 2003). The construct is now termed *right-wing authoritarianism* (RWA) (Altemeyer, 1988a), and it is characterized by authoritarian submission (exaggerated deference to those in power), authoritarian aggression (hostility toward targets sanctioned by authorities), and conventionalism (strong adherence to values endorsed by authorities). Because authoritarians tend to support established authority, RWA is more commonly found among political conservatives than among political liberals (who are more likely to challenge the status quo). RWA has even been linked to the Big Five personality traits (recall Chapter 2) in that authoritarian individuals tend to score low on openness to experience and conscientiousness (Sibley & Duckitt, 2008).

What causes RWAs to be prejudiced? According to Robert Altemeyer (1998), there are two key factors. First, they organize their social world into ingroups and outgroups, and they view outgroups as threatening their cherished traditional values. Second, they tend to be self-righteous: They believe that they are more moral than others, and they feel justified in derogating groups that authority figures define as immoral. RWAs have typically been reared in highly religious and socially homogeneous groups, with little exposure to minority groups and unconventional behavior. They feel unduly threatened by social change—a fear picked up from their parents who believe that "the world is a dangerous and hostile place" (Altemeyer, 1988b, p. 38). Altemeyer also notes that fearful attitudes are reinforced by the mass media's emphasis on crime and violence. Exposure to cultural empathy and open-mindedness (Nesdale, De Vries Robbé, & Van Oudenhoven, 2012) and to diverse kinds of people and perspectives can reduce RWA (Dhont & Van Hiel, 2012).

Authoritarian behavior has been linked with other types of personalities. Recently, a related personality type, *social dominance orientation* (SDO), has received much research attention (Ho et al., 2012; Kahn et al., 2009; Sidanius & Pratto, 1999; Son Hing, Bobocel, & Zanna, 2007). People high in SDO prefer inequality among social groups, believing in a hierarchy where some are destined to dominate others, such as men over women, majorities over minorities, or heterosexuals over homosexuals (Kteily, Ho, & Sidanius, 2012). Those low in SDO are less likely to think in terms of a social pecking order where society's "haves" should control over what happens to the "have nots." **Figure 7.8** on the next page illustrates some sample items from a scale designed to assess SDO.

Can socially dominant feelings like those held by members of a majority race toward minority-group members be reduced? Although changing someone's personality is quite a challenge, there is some evidence that exposing those who believe in inequality between groups to morally worthy

Figure 7.8

A preference for social hierarchies. Social dominance orientation (SDO) refers to a person's preference for maintaining inequality among groups (based on race, gender, religion, or social class) in society, so that some groups dominate the others. These five sample items are from the longer 16-item SDO questionnaire. Responses are scored on a 9-point scale ranging from "very negative" to "very positive."

Source: From Pratto, F., Sidanius, J., Stallworth, L. M., & Malle, B. F. (1994). Social dominance orientation: A personality variable predicting social and political attitudes. *Journal of Personality and Social Psychology, 67,* 741–763.

behavior can make them more open minded, if only for a short time. Freeman and colleagues (2009) elicited feelings of warmth and admiration in participants by having them watch a film clip of actors committing morally good deeds. Later, even individuals high in group-based dominance, a component of SDO, were more likely to donate money to a black-oriented charity compared to those in a control group.

Cognitive Distortions and Expectations

Much of prejudice is rooted in automatic cognitive processes that operate without conscious intent (Wright & Taylor, 2003). As you recall, *social categorization* predisposes people to divide the social world into ingroups and outgroups. This distinction can trigger negativity toward outgroup members.

Perhaps no factor plays a larger role in prejudice than *stereotyping* (D. J. Schneider, 2004). Many people subscribe to derogatory stereotypes of various ethnic groups. Although racial stereotypes have declined over the last 50 years, they're not entirely a thing of the past (Dovidio et al., 2003). Racial profiling, in which law enforcement officers stop motorists, pedestrians, or airline passengers solely on the basis of skin color, is a case in point. Similarly, the events of September 11, 2001 caused some Americans to view all Muslims and Arabs as potential terrorists (Hendricks et al., 2007).

People are more likely to make the *fundamental attribution error* when evaluating targets of prejudice (Levy, Stroessner, & Dweck, 1998). Thomas Pettigrew (2001) suggests that perceiving negative characteristics as being dispositional (personality based) and due to group membership is the *ultimate attribution error*. Thus, when people take note of ethnic neighborhoods dominated by crime

and poverty, they blame these problems on the residents (they're lazy and ignorant) and downplay or ignore situationally based explanations (job discrimination, poor police service, and so on). The old saying, "They should pull themselves up by their own bootstraps" is a blanket dismissal of how situational factors may make it especially difficult for minorities to achieve upward mobility.

Defensive attributions, in which people unfairly blame victims of adversity to reassure themselves that the same thing won't happen to them, can also contribute to prejudice. For example, individuals who claim that people who contract AIDS deserve it may be trying to reassure themselves that they won't suffer a similar fate (Buunk & Dijkstra, 2001).

Expectations can also foster and maintain prejudice. You already know that once people have formed impressions, they are invested in maintaining them. For instance, people note and recall behavior that confirms their stereotypes better than information that is inconsistent with their beliefs (Bodenhausen, 1988). Also, when an outgroup member's behavior contradicts a stereotype, people often "ex-

Which man looks guilty? If you picked the man on the right, you're wrong. Wrong for judging people based on the color of their skin. Because if you look closely, you'll see they're the same man. Unfortunately, racial stereotyping like this happens every day. On America's highways, police stop drivers based on their skin color rather than for the way they are driving. For example, in Florida 80% of those stopped and searched were black and Hispanic, while they constituted only 5% of all drivers. These humiliating and illegal searches are violations of the Constitution and must be fought. Help us defend your rights. Support the ACLU. www.aclu.org **american civil liberties union**

Bill Aron/PhotoEdit

This clever poster, sponsored by the American Civil Liberties Union, focuses a spotlight on the sensitive issue of racial profiling. Racial profiling, which is a manifestation of modern racism, reflects the influence of stereotyping. The phenomenon of racial profiling shows how simple, often automatic, cognitive distortions can have unfortunate consequences in everyday life.

plain away" such behavior to leave their stereotype intact (Ickes et al., 1982). Unfortunately, the fact that social thinking is automatic, selective, and consistent means that people usually see what they expect to see when they look through prejudiced eyes, even when viewing objective presentations from media sources (Vallone, Ross, & Lepper, 1985).

Competition Between Groups

Back in 1954, Muzafer Sherif and his colleagues conducted a now-classic study at Robbers' Cave State Park in Oklahoma to look at competition and prejudice (Sherif et al., 1961). In this study, 11-year-old boys were invited, with parental permission, to attend a three-week summer camp. What the boys didn't know was that they were participants in an experiment. The boys were randomly assigned to one of two groups; at camp, they went directly to their assigned campsites and had no knowledge of the other group's presence. During the first week, the boys got to know members of their own group through typical camp activities (hiking, swimming, and camping out); each group also chose a name (the Rattlers and the Eagles).

In the second week, the Rattlers and Eagles were introduced to each other through intergroup competitions. Events included a football game, a treasure hunt, and a tug of war, with medals, trophies, and other desirable prizes for the winning team. Almost immediately after competitive games were introduced, hostile feelings erupted between the two groups and quickly escalated to highly aggressive behavior: Food fights broke out in the mess hall, cabins were ransacked, and group flags were burned. This classic study and more recent research (Schopler & Insko, 1992) suggest that groups often respond more negatively to competition than individuals do.

This experimental demonstration of the effects of competition on prejudice is often mirrored in the real world. For example, disputes over territory often provoke antagonism, as is the case in the Israeli-Palestinian conflict. A lack of empathy for members of another group is a powerful force (Castano, 2012), but a scarcity of jobs or other important resources can also create competition between social groups. Still, competition does not always breed prejudice. In fact, the *perception* of threats to one's ingroup (loss of status, for example) is much more likely to cause hostility between groups than actual threats to the ingroup are (Dovidio et al., 2003). Unfortunately, such perceptions are quite common, because ingroup members usually assume that outgroup members are competitive and will try to thwart the ingroup's success (Fiske & Ruscher, 1993). To conclude, there is ample evidence that conflict over actual and perceived scarcity of resources can prejudice individuals toward outgroup members.

Threats to Social Identity

Although group membership provides individuals with a sense of identity and pride, it can also foster prejudice and discrimination, as we just noted. Members' individual psychologies become merged with group and even societal processes (Turner & Reynolds, 2004). To explore a different facet of this idea, we turn to *social identity theory,* developed by Henri Tajfel (1982) and John Turner (1987). According to this theory, self-esteem is partly determined by one's *social identity,* or collective self, which is tied to one's group memberships (nationality, religion, gender, major, occupation, political party affiliation, and so forth) (Ellemers & Haslam, 2012; Sidanius et al., 2004). Whereas your personal self-esteem is elevated by individual accomplishments (you got an A on a history exam), your collective self-esteem is boosted when an ingroup is successful (your team wins the football game). Likewise, your self-esteem can be threatened on both the personal level (you didn't get called for that job interview) and the collective level (your football team loses the championship game).

Threats to both personal and social identity motivate individuals to restore self-esteem, but threats to social identity are more likely to provoke responses that foster prejudice and discrimination (Crocker & Luhtanen, 1990). When collective self-esteem is threatened, individuals react in two key ways to bolster it. The most common response is to show *ingroup favoritism*—for example, tapping an ingroup member for a job opening or rating the performance of an ingroup member higher than that of an outgroup member (Stroebe, Lodewijkx, & Spears, 2005). In fact, when individuals become wrapped up in identifying with a group, they respond to group criticism as if it were a critique of the self (McCoy & Major, 2003). The second way to deal with threats to social identity is to engage in *outgroup derogation*—in other words, to "trash" outgroups perceived to be threatening. This latter tactic is especially likely to be used by individuals who identify strongly with an ingroup (Perreault & Bourhis, 1999). **Figure 7.9** depicts the various elements of social identity theory.

Significantly, it is "ingroup love," not "outgroup hate" that underlies most discrimination (Brewer, 1999). In other

Figure 7.9

Social identity theory. According to Tajfel (1982) and Turner (1987), individuals have both a personal identity (based on a unique sense of self) and a social identity (based on group memberships). When social identity is threatened, people are motivated to restore self-esteem by either showing favoritism to ingroup members or derogating outgroup members. These tactics contribute to prejudice and discrimination. (Adapted from Kassin, Fein, & Markus, 2011) words, ingroups reward their own members and withhold rewards from outgroups, rather than deliberately blocking outgroups from desired resources (Fiske, 2002). And here's the final rub: Ingroup favoritism is often subtle and can be triggered by arbitrary and inconsequential factors, such as shared musical tastes (Lonsdale & North, 2009).

Stereotype Threat

Our discussion in this chapter has focused on stereotypes that are directed at others—that is, how each person relies on simplified beliefs associating groups of people with particular traits. What happens when individuals are the targets of a stereotype used by others to characterize the group they belong to? Is the stereotype ignored, or does the person internalize its impact?

Consider African Americans, for example. One pernicious stereotype is that African American students perform poorly on standardized tests compared to, say, white students. Claude Steele (1992, 1997) of Stanford University suggests that while socioeconomic disadvantages can serve as an explanatory factor for the underperformance of blacks relative to whites on such tests, there may be other legitimate reasons. How so? Steele suggests that the availability and awareness of derogatory stereotypes connected to various stigmatized groups, including blacks, leads to *stereotype vulnerability*, otherwise known as *stereotype threat*. Feelings of stereotype vulnerability can undermine group members' performance on standardized tests, as well as other measures of academic achievement.

In a study by Steele and Aronson (1995), for example, black and white college students who scored well above average in academic ability were recruited (their comparable academic backgrounds ruled out cultural disadvantage as a factor in the research). All participants were asked to take a challenging 30-minute test of verbal ability composed of items drawn from the Graduate Record Exam (GRE). In one condition, stereotype vulnerability was made salient: The test was described as being an excellent index of a person's general verbal ability. In the other condition, the test was described as a means for researchers to analyze people's problem-solving strategies (thus, not as a measure of intellectual ability). What did Steele and Aronson find? When the African American students' stereotype vulnerability was not emphasized, the performances of black and white students did not differ (see the bars on the left side of **Figure 7.10**). Yet when the same test was presented in a way that increased stereotype threat, the black students scored significantly lower than the white test takers (see the two bars on the right side of **Figure 7.10**).

The impact of stereotype threat has been replicated numerous times (Cadinu et al., 2005; Croizet et al., 2004; Shapiro & Neuberg, 2007). Steele and his colleagues have demonstrated the stereotype threat can influence the performance of a variety of groups, not just minorities, suggesting its applicability to a variety of behavioral phenom-

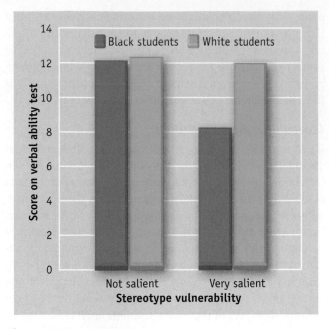

Figure 7.10

Stereotype vulnerability and test performance. Steele and Aronson (1995) compared the performances of African American and white students of equal ability on a 30-item verbal ability test constructed from difficult GRE questions. When the black students' stereotype vulnerability was not obvious, their performance did not differ from that of the white students; but when the threat of stereotype vulnerability was raised, the black students performed significantly worse than the white students.

Source: Adapted from Steele, C. M., & Aronson, J. (1995). Stereotype threat and the intellectual test performance of African Americans. *Journal of Personality and Social Psychology, 69,* 797–811. Copyright © 1995 by the American Psychological Association. Reprinted by permission of the author.

ena (Steele, 2011). Thus, for example, women have been shown to be vulnerable to stereotype threat concerning the belief that men perform better on math-related tasks (Spencer, Steele, & Quinn, 1999; Stone & McWhinnie, 2008). In turn, white men have been found to be "threatened" by the stereotype that men of Asian descent are superior when it comes to doing well at mathematics (Aronson et al., 1999).

Reducing Prejudice

For decades, psychologists have searched for ways to reduce prejudice. Such a complicated problem requires solutions on a number of levels. Let's look at a few interventions that have been shown to help.

Cognitive Strategies

Because stereotypes are part of the social air that people breathe, practically everyone learns stereotypes about various groups. This means that stereotyped thinking about others becomes a mindless habit—even for individuals who have been taught to be tolerant of those who are different from themselves (Fiske, 2002).

Although it's true that stereotypes kick in automatically, unintentionally, and unconsciously, individuals *can* override them—with some cognitive effort (Fiske, 2002). Thus, if you meet someone who speaks with an accent, your initial, automatic reaction might be negative. However, if you believe that prejudice is wrong and if you are aware that you are stereotyping, you can intentionally inhibit such thoughts and work to avoid speaking or behaving in a biased manner. One problem is that such self-regulation is demanding, like a muscle that becomes tired with use (Richeson & Shelton, 2003; Richeson, Trawalter, & Shelton, 2005). According to Patricia Devine's (1989) model of prejudice reduction, this process requires an intentional shift from *automatic processing* to *controlled processing*—or from *mindlessness* to *mindfulness,* in Ellen Langer's terms (see Chapters 6 and 16). Thus, you can reduce prejudice if you are motivated to pay careful attention to what and how you think.

Intergroup Contact

Let's return to the Robbers' Cave study. When we left them, the Rattlers and Eagles were engaged in food fights and flag burning. Understandably, the experimenters were eager to restore peace. First, they tried speaking with each group, talking up the other group's good points and minimizing their differences. They also made the Eagles and the Rattlers sit together at meals and "fun" events like movies. Unfortunately, these tactics fell flat.

Next, the experimenters designed intergroup activities based on the principle of *superordinate goals*—goals that require two or more groups to work together to achieve mutual ends. For example, each boy had to contribute in some way (building a fire, preparing the food) on a cookout so that all could eat. After the boys had participated in a variety of such activities, the hostility between the two groups was much reduced. In fact, at the end of the three-week camping period, the Eagles and the Rattlers voted to ride the same bus back home. Cooperating to reach common goals, then, can reduce conflict (Bay-Hinitz, Peterson, & Quilitch, 1994).

Researchers have identified four necessary ingredients in the recipe for reducing intergroup hostility (Brewer & Brown, 1998). First, groups must *work together for a common goal*—merely bringing hostile groups into contact is not effective in reducing intergroup antagonism and may in fact worsen it. Second, cooperative efforts must have *successful outcomes*—if groups fail at a cooperative task, they are likely to blame each other for the failure. Third, group members must have the opportunity to establish *meaningful connections* with one another and not merely go through the motions of interacting. The fourth factor of *equal status contact* requires bringing together members of different groups in ways that ensure that everyone has equal status. A large meta-analysis demonstrated clear support for intergroup contact that meets these conditions as a means of reducing prejudice (Pettigrew & Tropp, 2006).

What about the contact hypothesis in college life? Shook and Fazio (2008) conducted a field experiment in which white college students were randomly assigned to share a dorm room with a white or a black roommate. Although students in the interracial situation did report less satisfaction with their roommates than those with same-race assignments, there was an important positive outcome of contact in this housing experiment: Those students living in the interracial rooms were found to be less prejudiced across time compared to those with same-race living arrangements. Other research supports the argument that contact can reduce prejudiced feelings between members of different groups (Binder et al., 2009; Tropp & Molina, 2012).

THE POWER OF PERSUASION

LEARNING OBJECTIVES

- Cite the key elements in the persuasion process, and describe how each one operates.
- Discuss the evidence on one-sided versus two-sided messages and the value of arousing fear or positive feelings in persuasion.
- Explain how the two cognitive routes to persuasion operate.

Every day you are bombarded by attempts to alter your attitudes through persuasion. You may not even be out of bed before you start hearing radio advertisements meant to persuade you to buy specific toothpastes, cell phones, and athletic shoes. When you watch the morning news, you hear statements from numerous government officials, all of which have been carefully crafted to shape your opinions. On your way to school, you see billboards showing attractive models draped over cars in the hopes that they can induce positive feelings that will transfer to the vehicles. Walking to class, a friend tries to get you to vote for his candidate for student body president. "Does it ever let up?" you wonder.

When it comes to persuasion, the answer is "no." As Anthony Pratkanis and Elliot Aronson (2000) note, Americans live in the "age of propaganda." In light of this situation, let's examine some of the factors that determine whether persuasion works.

Persuasion **involves the communication of arguments and information intended to change another person's attitudes.** What are attitudes? For the purposes of our discussion, we'll define *attitudes* **as beliefs and feelings about people, objects, and ideas.** Let's look more closely at two of the terms in this definition. We use the term *beliefs* to mean thoughts and judgments about people, objects, and ideas. For example, you may *believe* that equal pay for equal work is a fair policy or that capital punishment is not an effective deterrent to crime. The "feeling" component of

attitudes refers to the positivity and negativity of one's feelings about an issue as well as how strongly one feels about it. For example, you may *strongly favor* equal pay for equal work but only *mildly disagree* with the idea that capital punishment reduces the crime rate. Psychologists assume that attitudes predict behavior (Briñol & Petty, 2012; Petty & Fazio, 2008)—if you are favorably disposed toward some new product, you are likely to buy it; if not, you won't (Eagly & Chaiken, 1998). Of course, there is more to the persuasion side of the attitude-behavior relation: Read on.

Elements of the Persuasion Process

The process of persuasion or attitude change (Crano & Prislin, 2008) includes four basic elements (see **Figure 7.11**). The *source* **is the person who sends a communication, and the** *receiver* **is the person to whom the message is sent.** Thus, if you watched a presidential address on TV, the president would be the source, and you and millions of other viewers would be the receivers in this persuasive effort. **The** *message* **is the information transmitted by the source; the** *channel* **is the medium through which the message is sent.** In examining communication channels, investigators have often compared face-to-face interaction with appeals sent via mass media (such as television and radio). Although the research on communication channels is interesting, we'll confine our discussion to source, message, and receiver variables.

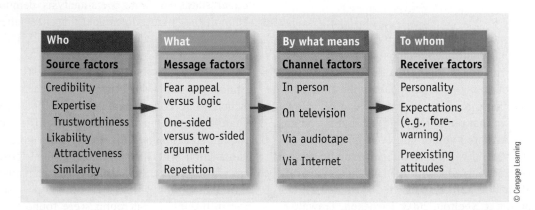

Figure 7.11

Overview of the persuasion process. The process of persuasion essentially boils down to *who* (the source) communicates *what* (the message) *by what means* (the channel) *to whom* (the receiver). Thus, four sets of variables influence the process of persuasion: source, message, channel, and receiver factors. The diagram lists some of the more important factors in each category (including some that are not discussed in the text because of space limitations).

Source Factors

Persuasion tends to be more successful when the source has high *credibility* (Petty, Wegener, & Fabrigar, 1997) or when perceivers believe the communicator will actually deliver on a promise (Clark, Evans, & Wegener, 2011). Two subfactors make a communicator credible: expertise and trustworthiness (Hovland & Weiss, 1951). People try to convey their *expertise* by mentioning their degrees, their training, and their experience or by showing an impressive grasp of the issue at hand (Clark et al., 2012). As to *trustworthiness,* whom would you believe if you were told that your state needs to reduce corporate taxes to stimulate its economy—the president of a huge corporation in your state or an economics professor from out of state? Probably the latter. Trustworthiness is undermined when a source, such as the corporation president, appears to have something to gain. In contrast, trustworthiness is enhanced when people appear to argue against their own interests (Petty et al., 2001). This effect explains why salespeople often make remarks like "Frankly, my snowblower isn't the best and they have a better brand down the street if you're willing to spend a bit more . . ."

Likability is a second major source factor and includes a number of subfactors (Petty et al., 1997). A key consideration is a person's *physical attractiveness* (Petty et al., 1997). For example, one researcher found that attractive students were more successful than less attractive ones in obtaining signatures for a petition (Chaiken, 1979). People also respond better to sources who are *similar* to them in ways that are relevant to the issue at hand (Mackie, Worth, & Asuncion, 1990). Thus, politicians stress the values they and their constituents hold in common.

Source variables are used to great effect in advertising. Many companies spend a fortune to obtain a spokesperson such as Ellen DeGeneres or Rachel Ray who combines trustworthiness, likability, and a knack for connecting with the average person. Companies quickly abandon spokespersons whose likability declines. For example, many companies canceled endorsement contracts with basketball star Kobe Bryant and golf legend Tiger Woods after they were implicated in tawdry sexual affairs. Lance Armstrong's fall from grace following accusations of performance-enhancing drug use has no doubt affected his standing with the public as well as with corporate sponsors. Thus, source variables are extremely important factors in persuasion.

Message Factors

Imagine that you are going to advocate the selection of a high-profile entertainer as the speaker at your commencement ceremony. In preparing your argument, you ponder the most effective way to structure your message. On the one hand, you're convinced that having a well-known entertainer on campus would be popular with students and would boost the image of your university in the commu-

Advertisers frequently employ well-liked celebrities such as Pink to pitch their products, hoping that the positive feelings of the audience toward the source will transfer to the product.

nity and among alumni. Still, you realize that this performer would cost a lot and that some people believe that an entertainer is not an appropriate commencement speaker. Should you present a *one-sided argument* that ignores the possible problems? Or should you present a *two-sided argument* that acknowledges concern about the problems and then downplays them?

In general, two-sided arguments seem to be more effective (Crowley & Hoyer, 1994). In fact, just mentioning that there are two sides to an issue can increase your credibility with an audience (Jones & Brehm, 1970). One-sided messages work only when your audience is uneducated about the issue or when they already favor your point of view.

Persuaders also use emotional appeals to shift attitudes, as message factors are more likely to be attended to as a problem's seriousness increases (Feng, & MacGeorge, 2010). Insurance companies show scenes of homes on fire to arouse fear. Antismoking campaigns emphasize the threat of cancer. Deodorant ads prey on the fear of embarrassment. Does *fear arousal* work? Yes. Studies involving a wide range of issues (nuclear policy, auto safety, and dental hygiene among others) have shown that the arousal of fear often increases persuasion (Perloff, 1993). And fear appeals are influential if people feel susceptible to the

Angela Weiss/Stringer/Getty Images

threat (De Hoog, Stroebe, & De Wit, 2007). If you induce strong fear in your audience without providing a workable solution to the problem (such as a surefire stop-smoking or weight-loss program), however, you may make your audience defensive, causing them to tune you out (Petty & Wegener, 1998).

Generating *positive feelings*, too, can sometimes be an effective way to persuade people. Familiar examples of such tactics include the use of music and physically attractive actors in TV commercials, the use of laugh tracks in TV programs, and the practice of wining and dining prospective customers. People attend better to humorous messages than to sober ones (Duncan & Nelson, 1985); later, they may recall that something was funny but forget what it was about (Cantor & Venus, 1980). Producing positive feelings to win people over *can* be effective—provided they don't care too much about the issue. If people do care about the topic, it takes more than good feelings to move them. For example, one study showed that the use of music in TV commercials was effective in persuading viewers, but only when the message concerned a trivial topic (Park & Young, 1986).

Receiver Factors

What about the receiver of the persuasive message? Are some people easier to persuade than others? Yes, but the answer is complicated. For instance, receptivity to a message can sometimes depend on people's *moods:* Optimistic people process uplifting messages better than pessimists, who are drawn to counterattitudinal communications, or those opposing their current views (Wegener & Petty, 1994). Other people want to think deeply about issues, having a so-called **need for cognition, the tendency to seek out and enjoy effortful thought, problem-solving activities, and in-depth analysis.** Such people, who truly relish intellectual give-and-take as well as debate, are more

likely to be convinced by high-quality arguments than those who prefer more superficial analyses (Nettelhorst & Brannon, 2012). Moreover, they are more likely to be motivated to process complex messages more carefully (See et al., 2009).

Transient factors also matter in receptivity to persuasive messages. *Forewarning* the receiver about a persuasive effort and a receiver's initial position on an issue, for instance, seem to be more influential than a receiver's personality. When you shop for a new TV or a car, you expect salespeople to work at persuading you. To some extent, this forewarning reduces the impact of their arguments (Petty & Wegener, 1998). When receivers are forewarned about a persuasion attempt on a personally important topic, it is harder to persuade them than when they are not forewarned (Wood & Quinn, 2003). But when they are told to expect a persuasive message on an unimportant topic, their attitudes shift in the direction of the persuasive appeal even before it occurs—to avoid appearing gullible! Thus, the old saying, "To be forewarned is to be forearmed" is often true.

Understandably, receivers are harder to persuade when they encounter a position that is incompatible with their existing beliefs. In general, people display a *disconfirmation bias* in evaluating such arguments (Edwards & Smith, 1996). Also, people from different cultures respond to different themes in persuasive messages. In one study, participants from an individualistic culture (the United States) preferred magazine ads that stressed the theme of uniqueness, while those from a collectivist culture (Korea) preferred ads that stressed conformity (Kim & Markus, 1999).

The Whys of Persuasion

Why do people change their attitudes in response to persuasive messages? Thanks to the work of Richard Petty and John Cacioppo (1986), psychologists have a good understanding of the cognitive processes that underlie attitude change.

Richard Petty

According to the *elaboration likelihood model,* **an individual's thoughts about a persuasive message (rather than the actual message itself) determine whether attitude change will occur** (Benoit & Benoit, 2008; Petty & Briñol, 2012; Petty et al., 2005; Wagner & Petty, 2011). As we have noted, sometimes people make quick, sloppy decisions (automatic processing, mindlessness, snap judgments), whereas at other times they process information carefully (controlled processing, mindfulness, systematic judgments). Some-

John Cacioppo

"You're right. It does send a powerful message."

times people choose to think; others times they choose not to. These processes also operate in persuasion, with messages sometimes persuading receivers through a *peripheral* route and sometimes through a *central* route.

When people are distracted, tired, or uninterested in a persuasive message, they fail to key in on the true merits of the product or issue. They do process information, but not mindfully. Being in a happy mood can produce the same effect (Sinclair, Mark, & Clore, 1994). Surprisingly, even when people do not carefully evaluate a message, attitude change can occur (Petty & Cacioppo, 1990). What happens is that the receiver is persuaded by cues that are peripheral to the message—thus the term *peripheral route* (see **Figure 7.12**). Just because you're not mindfully analyzing a TV commercial for a new fruit drink doesn't mean that you're totally tuned out. You may not be paying attention to the substance of the commercial, but you are aware of superficial aspects of the ad—you like the music, your favorite basketball player is pitching the product, and boy, that beach scene sure looks nice.

Although persuasion usually occurs via the peripheral route, senders can also use another route to attitude change— the *central route* (see **Figure 7.12**). In this case, receivers process persuasive messages mindfully, by thinking about the logic and merits of the pertinent (or central) arguments. In other words, the receiver cognitively *elaborates* on the persuasive message—hence, the name of the model—and messages that receive greater and deeper processing are more resistant to persuasion (Blankenship & Wegener, 2008). If people have a favorable reaction to their thoughtful evaluation of a message, positive attitude change occurs; an unfavorable reaction results in negative attitude change.

For the central route to override the peripheral route, two requirements must be met. First, receivers must be *motivated* to process the persuasive message carefully. Motivation is triggered when people are interested in the issue, find it personally relevant, have a high need for cognition, and have time and energy to think about it carefully. For example, if your university is considering changing its grading system, you will probably make a point of thinking carefully about the various options and their implications. Second, receivers must have the *ability* to grasp the

Political candidates use music, flags, and slogans to persuade via the peripheral route; when they present their views on an issue, they are going for the central route.

message—that is, the message must be comprehensible, and individuals must be capable of understanding it. If people are distracted, tired, or find the message uninteresting or irrelevant, they will not pay careful attention, and superficial cues will become salient.

Ultimately, the two routes to persuasion are not equally effective. Attitudes formed via the central route are longer lasting and more resistant to challenge than those formed via the peripheral route (Petty & Wegener, 1998). They are also better predictors of a person's behavior (Petty, Priester, & Wegener, 1994). In any case, the elaboration likelihood model can predict when persuasion is apt to be effective and it holds particular promise for applications regarding health-related behavior (Petty, Barden, & Wheeler, 2009), including preventing smoking (Flynn et al., 2011).

To conclude, although we can't stem the tide of persuasive messages bombarding you every day, we hope we've alerted you to the need to be a vigilant recipient of persuasion attempts. Of course, persuasion is not the *only* method through which people try to influence you, as you'll see in the next section.

Figure 7.12

The peripheral and central routes to persuasion. Persuasion can occur via two different routes. The central route, which results in high elaboration, tends to produce longer-lasting attitude change and stronger attitudes than the peripheral route.

THE POWER OF SOCIAL PRESSURE

LEARNING OBJECTIVES

- Summarize what Asch discovered about conformity.
- Distinguish between normative and informational influences on conformity.
- Describe Milgram's research on obedience, and explain how to resist demands from an authority.

In the previous section, we showed you how others attempt to change your *attitudes*. Now you'll see how others attempt to change your *behavior*—by trying to get you to agree to their requests and demands. **Figure 7.13** shows that social influence occurs on a continuum. On one end of the continuum, behavior change—yielding to social pressure—can lead to conformity, compliance, and even obedience. At the other end, resisting social pressure allows people to remain independent, be assertive, or even act defiant.

Conformity and Compliance Pressures

If you extol the talent of popular group Maroon 5 or keep a well-manicured lawn, are you exhibiting conformity? According to social psychologists, it depends on whether your behavior is freely chosen or the result of group pressure. *Conformity* **occurs when people yield to real or imagined social pressure.** For example, if you like Maroon 5 because you truly enjoy their music, that's not conformity. However, if you like them because it's "cool" and your friends would question your taste if you didn't, then you're conforming. Similarly, if you maintain a well-groomed lawn just to avoid complaints from your neighbors, you're yielding to social pressure. In short, people are apt to explain the behavior of others as conforming but not think of their own actions this way (Pronin, Berger, & Moluki, 2007). Your friends may buy iPods because they are conformists; you buy one for what seem to be justifiable personal reasons (failing to realize that all those "conformists" believe this to be their motivation, too). As you read this section, remember that individuals often believe they are "alone in a crowd of sheep" because everyone else is conforming (Pronin et al., 2007). And use of the animal metaphor is apt, as conformity is now being studied by comparative biologists as an important form of social influence among animals (Claidière & Whiten, 2012).

Conformity is far more common than most people appreciate. We all conform to social expectations in an endless variety of ways. There is nothing inherently good or bad about conforming to social pressures; it all depends on the situation. However, it is prudent to be aware of how social expectations can sometimes have a profound influence on our behavior.

The Dynamics of Conformity

To introduce this topic, we'll re-create a classic experiment devised by Solomon Asch (1955). The participants are male undergraduates recruited for a study of visual perception. A group of seven participants are shown a large card with a vertical line on it and asked to indicate which of three lines on a second card matches the original "standard line" in length (see **Figure 7.14**). All seven participants are given a turn at the task, and each announces his choice to the group. The subject in the sixth chair doesn't know it, but everyone else in the group is an accomplice of the experimenter.

Yielding to Influence   **Resisting Influence**

Obedience   Compliance   Conformity   Independence   Assertiveness   Defiance

Figure 7.13

Continuum of social influence. Social influences vary in the degree of pressure they bring to bear on the individual. People may conform to group norms or maintain their independence, comply with requests or be assertive; and obey or defy the demands of authority.

Source: Adapted from Kassin, S. M., Fein, S., & Markus, H. (2011). *Social psychology* (8th ed.), Figure 7.1 on page 252. Belmont, CA: Wadsworth/Cengage. Adapted with permission.

Figure 7.14

Stimuli used in Asch's conformity studies. Subjects were asked to match a standard line (top) with one of three other lines displayed on another card (bottom). The task was easy—until experimental accomplices started responding with obviously incorrect answers, creating a situation in which Asch evaluated subjects' conformity.

Source: Adapted from illustration on p. 35 by Sarah Love in Asch, S. (1955, November). Opinions and social pressure. *Scientific American, 193*(5), 31–35. Copyright © 1955 by Scientific American, Inc.

The accomplices give accurate responses on the first two trials. On the third trial, line 2 is clearly the correct response, but the first five participants all say that line 3 matches the standard line. The genuine subject can't believe his ears. Over the course of the experiment, the accomplices all give the same incorrect response on 12 out of 18 trials. Asch wanted to see how the subject would respond in these situations. The line judgments are easy and unambiguous. Without group pressure, people make matching errors less than 1% of the time. So, if the subject consistently agrees with the accomplices, he isn't making honest mistakes—he is conforming. Will the subject stick to his guns, or will he go along with the group? Asch found that the men conformed (made mistakes) on 37% of the 12 trials. The subjects varied considerably in their tendency to conform, however. Of the 50 participants, 13 never caved in to the group, while 14 conformed on more than half the trials. One could argue that the results show that people confronting a unanimous majority generally tend to *resist* the pressure to conform. But given how clear and easy the line judgments were, most social scientists viewed the findings as a dramatic demonstration of humans' propensity to conform.

In subsequent studies, Asch (1956) determined that group size and group unanimity are key determinants of conformity. To examine group size, Asch repeated his procedure with groups that included one to fifteen accomplices. Little conformity was seen when a subject was pitted against just one accomplice. Conformity increased rapidly as group size went from two to four, peaked at a group size of seven, and then leveled off (see **Figure 7.15**). Thus, Asch concluded that as group size increases, conformity increases—up to a point. Significantly, Asch found that group size made little difference if just one accomplice "broke" with the others, wrecking their unanimous agreement. The presence of another dissenter lowered conformity to about one-quarter of its peak, even when the dissenter made inaccurate judgments that happened to conflict with the majority view. Apparently, the participants just needed to hear a second person question the accuracy of the group's perplexing responses. Asch's classic study has been replicated without the use of confederates and similar results were observed (Mori & Arai, 2010). Recent research suggests that when individuals have a high need for uniqueness—that is, when they feel indistinguishable from others and are motivated to reestablish a sense of individuality—they can resist majority pressures to conform (Imhoff & Erb, 2009).

Conformity Versus Compliance

Did the conforming participants in Asch's study really change their beliefs in response to social pressure, or did they just pretend to change them? Subsequent studies asked participants to make their responses privately, instead of publicly (Deutsch & Gerard, 1955; Insko et al., 1985). Conformity declined dramatically when participants wrote down their responses. Thus, it is likely that Asch's participants did not really change their beliefs. Based on this evidence, theorists concluded that Asch's experiments evoked a particular type of conformity, called

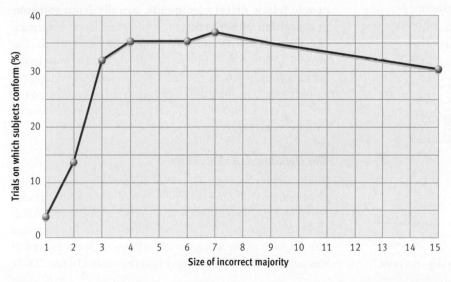

Figure 7.15

Conformity and group size. This graph shows the percentage of trials on which participants conformed as a function of the number of individuals with an opposing view. Asch found that conformity became more frequent as group size increased, up to about seven persons, and then leveled off.

Source: Adapted from illustration on p. 32 by Sarah Love in Asch, S. (1955, November). Opinions and social pressure. *Scientific American, 193*(5), 31–35. Copyright © 1955 by Scientific American, Inc.

compliance. *Compliance* **occurs when people yield to social pressure in their public behavior, even though their private beliefs have not changed.** For example, many people comply with modest group pressure daily—they "dress up" for work by wearing suits, ties, dresses, and so on—when they would prefer to wear more casual clothing.

The Whys of Conformity

People often conform or comply because they are afraid of being criticized or rejected. *Normative influence* **operates when people conform to social norms for fear of negative social consequences.** Compliance often results from subtle, implied pressure. For example, for fear of making a negative impression, you may remove your eyebrow ring for a job interview. However, compliance also occurs in response to explicit rules, requests, and commands. Thus, you'll probably follow your boss's instructions even when you think they're lousy ideas.

People are also likely to conform when they are uncertain how to behave (Cialdini, 2001). Thus, if you're at a nice restaurant and don't know which fork to use, you may watch others to see what they're doing. *Informational influence* **operates when people look to others for how to behave in ambiguous situations.** In such cases, using others as a source of information about appropriate behavior is a good thing. But relying on others to know how to behave in unfamiliar situations can sometimes be problematic, as you'll see shortly.

Resisting Conformity Pressures

Sometimes conforming is just harmless fun—such as participating in Internet-generated "flash mobs." At other times, people conform on relatively trivial matters—such as dressing up for dinner at a nice restaurant. In this case, conformity and compliance minimize the confusion and anxiety people experience in unfamiliar situations. However, when individuals feel pressured to conform to antisocial norms, tragic consequences may result. Negative examples of "going along with the crowd" include drinking more than one knows one should because others say, "C'mon, have just

"*He's one of our own, so let's give him a big welcome.*"

Charles Barsotti/The New Yorker Collection/
www.cartoonbank.com

one more" and driving at someone's urging when under the influence of alcohol or drugs. Other instances include refusing to socialize with someone simply because the person isn't liked by one's social group and failing to come to another's defense when it might make one unpopular.

The above examples all concern normative influence, but pressure can come from informational influence as well. A useful example concerns a paradox called **the bystander effect—the tendency for individuals to be less likely to provide help when others are present than when they are alone.** Numerous studies have confirmed that people are less helpful in emergency situations when others are around (Fischer et al., 2011; Levine et al., 1994). Thankfully, the bystander effect is less likely to occur when the need for help is very clear (Fischer, Greitemeyer, & Pollozek, 2006) or when people experience heightened self-awareness (van Bommel et al., 2012).

What accounts for the bystander effect? A number of factors are at work, and conformity is one of them. The bystander effect is most likely to occur in *ambiguous situations,* because people look around to see whether others are acting as if there's an emergency (Harrison & Wells, 1991). If everyone hesitates, this inaction (informational influence) suggests that help isn't needed. So the next time you witness what you think might be an emergency, don't automatically give in to the informational influence of inaction.

To resist conformity pressures, we offer these suggestions: First, make an effort to pay more attention to the social forces operating on you. Second, if you find yourself in a situation where others are pressuring you, try to identify someone in the group whose views match yours. Recall that just one dissenter in Asch's groups significantly reduced conformity pressures. And, if you know in advance that you're heading into this kind of situation, consider inviting a friend with similar views to go along.

Pressure from Authority Figures

Obedience **is a form of compliance that occurs when people follow direct commands, usually from someone in a position of authority.** In itself, obedience isn't good or bad; it depends on what one is being told to do. For example, if the fire alarm goes off in your classroom building and your instructor "orders" you to leave, obedience is a good idea. On the other hand, if your boss asks you to engage in an unethical or illegal act, *disobedience* is probably in order.

The Dynamics of Obedience

Like many other people after World War II, social psychologist Stanley Milgram was troubled by how readily the citizens of Germany had followed the orders of dictator Adolf Hitler, even when the orders required morally repugnant actions, such as the slaughter of millions of Jews, as well as Russians, Poles, Gypsies, and homosexuals (Blass, 2004).

Hugo Jaeger/Timepix/Time Life Pictures/Getty Images

Learn More Online

Stanley Milgram

This site provides a wealth of accurate information about the work of Stanley Milgram, arguably one of the most controversial and creative social psychologists in the field's history. The site is maintained by Thomas Blass, a psychology professor at the University of Maryland (Baltimore County), who has published many articles and books on the life and work of Milgram.

© 1981 Eric Kroll, courtesy of Alexandra Milgram

Stanley Milgram

This observation was Milgram's motivation to study the dynamics of obedience. Milgram's (1963) participants were a diverse collection of forty men from the local community who volunteered for a study on the effects of punishment on learning. When they arrived at the lab, they drew slips of paper from a hat to get their assignments. The drawing was rigged so that the subject always became the "teacher" and an experimental accomplice (a likable 47-year-old accountant) became the "learner."

The teacher watched while the learner was strapped into a chair and electrodes were attached to his arms (to be used to deliver shocks whenever he made a mistake on the task). The subject was then taken to an adjoining room that housed the shock generator that he would control in his role as the teacher. Although the apparatus looked and sounded realistic, it was a fake, and the learner was never shocked. The experimenter played the role of the authority figure who told the teacher what to do and who answered any questions that arose.

The experiment was designed such that the learner would make many mistakes, and the teacher was instructed to increase the shock level after each wrong answer. At 300 volts, the learner began to pound on the wall between the two rooms in protest and soon stopped responding to the teacher's questions. From this point forward, participants frequently turned to the experimenter for guidance. Whenever they did so, the experimenter (authority figure) firmly stated that the teacher should continue to give stronger and stronger shocks to the now-silent learner. Milgram wanted to know the maximum shock the teacher was willing to administer before refusing to cooperate.

As **Figure 7.16** shows, 65% of the subjects administered all 30 levels of shock. Although they tended to obey

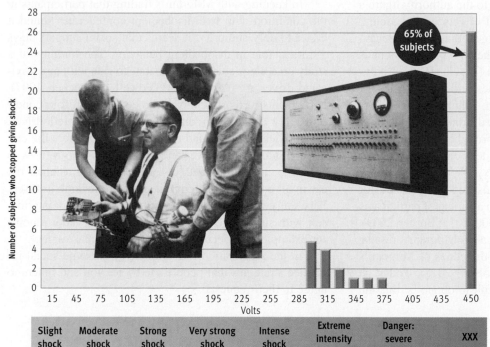

Figure 7.16

Milgram's (1963) experiment on obedience. The photos show the fake shock generator and the "learner" being connected to the shock generator during an experimental session. The results of the study are summarized in the bar graph. The vast majority of subjects (65%) delivered the entire series of shocks to the learner.

From the film *Obedience*, copyright © 1968 by Stanley Milgram; copyright renewed 1993 by Alexandra Milgram and distributed by Alexander Street Press. Reprinted by permission of Alexandra Milgram.

the experimenter, many participants voiced and displayed considerable distress about harming the learner. They protested, groaned, bit their lips, trembled, and broke into a sweat—but they continued administering the shocks. Based on these findings, Milgram concluded that obedience to authority was even more common than he or others had anticipated. A recent replication by Burger (2009) suggests Milgram's conclusion still stands: Although participants were stopped at the 150-volt level for ethical reasons, 70% continued to shock the learner despite hearing cries of anguish (Milgram found that 80% of his participants continued to shock after 150 volts).

The Causes of Obedience

After his initial demonstration, Milgram (1974) tried about twenty variations on his experimental procedure, looking for factors that influenced participants' obedience. For instance, he studied female participants to look at gender differences in obedience (he found no evidence of such differences). In another condition, two confederates played the role of teachers who defied the experimenter's demands to continue, one at 150 volts and one at 210 volts. In this condition, only 10% of the subjects shocked at the maximum level.

What caused the obedient behavior observed by Milgram? First, the demands on the participants (to shock the learner) escalated gradually, so that very strong shocks were demanded only after the participant was well into the experiment. Second, participants were told that the authority figure, not the teacher, was responsible if anything happened to the learner. Third, subjects evaluated their actions in terms of how well they lived up to the authority figure's expectations, not by their harmful effects on the victim. Taken together, these findings suggest that human behavior is determined not so much by the *kind of person* one is as by the *kind of situation* one is in (Lewin, 1935). Applying this insight to Nazi war crimes and other atrocities, Milgram made a chilling assertion: Inhuman and evil visions may originate in the disturbed mind of an authority figure like Hitler, but it is only through the obedient actions of normal people that such ideas can be turned into frightening reality.

Milgram's study has been consistently replicated for many years, in diverse settings, with a variety of participants and procedural variations (Blass, 2000, 2012; Burger, 2009). Overall, the weight of evidence supports Milgram's results. Of course, critics have questioned the ethics of Milgram's procedure (Baumrind, 1964; Nicholson, 2011). Today, at most universities it would be difficult to obtain permission

to replicate Milgram's study—an ironic epitaph for what may be psychology's best-known experiment.

To Obey or Not to Obey?

The findings of obedience research confront us with the chilling fact that most people can be coerced into engaging in actions that violate their morals and values. Perhaps you've heard of the 1968 My Lai incident, an American "crime of obedience," in which U.S. military forces killed 400–500 Vietnamese women, children, and elderly men (Kelman & Hamilton, 1989). The Abu Ghraib prisoner abuse scandal in Iraq in 2004 is a more recent reminder that strong social pressures can produce morally repugnant behavior (Fiske, Harris, & Cuddy, 2004; Post, 2011). One recent study suggests that engaging in synchrony—following a leader literally in a step-by-step manner—can lead to destructive obedience (Wiltermuth, 2012).

In keeping with Milgram's finding that participants in the condition with two disobedient confederates found it easier to defy authority, it seems that social support plays a critical role in disobedient behavior. The findings of a study on college students' decisions to ride with an intoxicated driver are relevant here (Powell & Drucker, 1997). Participants were randomly assigned to one of four conditions: (1) driver with one beer, (2) intoxicated driver, (3) intoxicated driver and confederate who enters the car, and (4) intoxicated driver and confederate who refuses to enter the car. Participants consistently chose to enter the car in all conditions except when the confederate refused. Especially when disobedience involves risk, aligning oneself with supportive others (family, friends, labor unions, for example) can decrease anxiety and increase safety.

In the Application, we'll alert you to some social influence strategies that people use to get you and others to agree to their requests.

SEEING THROUGH COMPLIANCE TACTICS

LEARNING OBJECTIVES

- Describe compliance strategies based on the principles of consistency and reciprocity.
- Discuss how the principle of scarcity can increase a person's desire for something.

Which of the following statements is true?
____ **1.** It's a good idea to ask for a small favor before soliciting the larger favor that you really want.
____ **2.** It's a good idea to ask for a large favor before soliciting the smaller favor that you really want.

Would you believe that *both* of these conflicting statements are true? Although the two approaches work for different reasons, both can be effective ways to get people to do what you want. It pays to understand these and other social influence strategies because advertisers, salespeople, and fundraisers (not to mention friends and neighbors) use them frequently to influence people's behavior. So you can see the relevance of these strategies to your own life, we've grouped them by the principles that make them work. Much of our discussion is based on the work of Robert Cialdini (2007), a social psychologist who spent years observing social influence tactics used by compliance professionals.

Courtesy Robert Cialdini

Robert Cialdini

The Consistency Principle

Once people agree to something, they tend to stick with their initial commitment (Cialdini, 2007). This tendency to prefer consistency in one's behavior is used to gain compliance in two ways. Both involve a person getting another individual to commit to an initial request and then changing the terms of the agreement to the requestor's advantage. Because people often stay with their initial commitments, the target will likely agree to the revised proposal, even though it may not be to his or her benefit.

The Foot-in-the-Door Technique

Door-to-door salespeople have long recognized the importance of gaining a *little* cooperation from sales targets (getting a "foot in the door") before hitting them with the real sales pitch. **The *foot-in-the-door* (FITD) *technique* involves getting people to agree to a small request to increase the chances that they will agree to a larger request later** (see **Figure 7.17a** on the next page). This technique is widely used. For example, groups seeking donations often ask people to simply sign a petition first.

Salespeople routinely ask individuals to try a product with "no obligations" before they launch their hard sell. In a similar vein, a wife might ask her husband to get her a cup of coffee, and when he gets up to fetch it say, "While you're up, would you fix me a peanut butter sandwich?"

The FITD technique was first investigated by Jonathon Freedman and his colleagues. In one study (Freedman & Fraser, 1966), the large request involved telephoning homemakers to ask whether a team of six men doing consumer research could come into their home to classify all their household products. Imagine six strangers trampling through your home, pulling everything out of your closets and cupboards, and you can understand why only 22% of the subjects in the control group agreed to this outlandish request. Subjects in the experimental group were contacted three days before the unreasonable request was made and asked to answer a few questions about the soaps used in their home. When the large request was made three days later, 53% of the experimental group complied with that request. Other studies find that odd or unusual initial requests can enhance compliance (Dolinski, 2012), as can a pleasant smell emanating from the person making the request (Saint-Bauzel & Fointiat, 2012). Even requests made over the Internet instead of in person can elicit compliance (Guéguen & Jacob, 2001; Markey, Wells, & Markey, 2002).

Why does this strategy work? The best explanation is rooted in Daryl Bem's *self-perception theory* or the idea that people sometimes infer their attitudes by observing their own behavior (Burger & Guadagno, 2003). When Joe agrees to sign a petition, he infers that he is a helpful person. So when he is confronted with a second, larger request to collect petition signatures, "helpful person" comes to mind, and Joe complies with the request.

The Lowball Technique

A second commitment-based strategy is **the *lowball technique,* which involves getting someone to commit to an attractive proposition before its hidden costs are revealed.** The name for this technique derives from a common practice in automobile sales, in which a customer is offered a terrific bargain on a car. The bargain price gets the customer to commit to buying, but soon after, the dealer starts revealing some hidden costs. Typically, the customer discovers that options expected to be included in the original price are actually going to cost extra. Once they have committed to buying a car, most customers are unlikely to cancel the deal. Car dealers aren't the only ones who use this technique. For instance, a friend might ask if you want to spend a week with him at his charming lakeside cabin. After you accept this seemingly generous offer, he may add, "Of course, there's a little work to do. We need to paint the doors, repair the pier, and . . ." You might think that people would become angry and back out of a deal once its hidden costs are revealed. Sometimes this does happen, but lowballing is a surprisingly effective strategy (Burger & Cornelius, 2003).

The Reciprocity Principle

Most people have been socialized to believe in the *reciprocity principle*—the rule that one should pay back in kind what one receives from others. Charities frequently make use of this principle. Groups seeking donations for the disabled, the homeless, and so forth routinely send "free" address labels, key rings, and other small gifts with their pleas for donations. The belief that people should reciprocate others' kindness is a powerful norm; thus, people often feel obliged to reciprocate by making a donation in return for the gift. According to Cialdini (2007), the reciprocity norm is so powerful that it often works even when (1) the gift is uninvited, (2) the gift comes from someone you dislike, or (3) the gift results in an uneven exchange. Let's review some basic influence tactics that take advantage of our belief in reciprocity.

The Door-in-the-Face Technique

The door-in-the-face technique reverses the sequence of requests used with the foot-in-the-door technique. **The door-in-the-face (DITF) technique involves making a large request that is likely to be turned down in order to increase the chances that people will agree to a smaller request later** (see **Figure 7.17b**). The name for this strategy is derived from the expectation that the initial

(a) Foot-in-the-door technique

Small request first → "Would you donate some old clothes for one of our charity programs?" → If yes, then . . . → Larger request (the one desired in the first place) → "Would you donate $50 to our organization?"

(b) Door-in-the-face technique

Large request first → "Would you volunteer to run a weekly program for our youth group?" → If no, then . . . → Smaller request (the one desired in the first place) → "Would you donate $50 to our organization?"

Figure 7.17

The foot-in-the-door and door-in-the-face techniques. These two influence techniques are essentially the reverse of each other, but both can work. **(a)** In the foot-in-the-door technique, you begin with a small request and work up to a larger one. **(b)** In the door-in-the-face technique, you begin with a large request and work down to a smaller one.

request will be quickly rejected. For example, a wife who wants to coax her frugal husband into buying a $30,000 sports car might begin by proposing that they purchase a $40,000 sports car. By the time he has talked his wife out of the more expensive car, the $30,000 price tag may look quite reasonable to him. For the DITF technique to work, there must be no delay between the two requests (O'Keefe & Hale, 2001). Guéguen, Jacob, and Meineri (2011) found that restaurant customers who declined to order dessert were more likely to order coffee or tea when the waitress proposed a beverage immediately rather than a few minutes later. Another study found that the door-in-the-face technique encouraged students to do academic work, such as completing a 20-item math worksheet (Chan & Au, 2011). Interestingly, the effect has been shown to increase solicited donations online and in the absence of face-to-face interaction (Guéguen, 2003).

Other Reciprocity-Based Techniques

Salespeople who distribute free samples to prospective customers are also using the reciprocity principle. Cialdini (2007) describes the procedures used by the Amway Corporation, which sells such household products as detergent, floor wax, and insect spray. Amway's door-to-door salespeople give homemakers many bottles of their products for a "free trial." When they return a few days later, most of the homemakers feel obligated to buy some of the products.

The reciprocity norm is meant to promote fair exchanges in social interactions. However, when people manipulate the reciprocity rule, they usually give something of minimal value in the hopes of getting far more in return. College students were found to be more likely to make a pledge to a charity when it happened to be the charity of a confederate who previously purchased some candy for them (Whatley et al., 1999). In a business exchange, for example, a person selling large computer systems may treat a potential customer at an exclusive restaurant in an effort to close a deal worth hundreds of thousands of dollars.

The Scarcity Principle

It's no secret that telling people they can't have something only makes them want it more. According to Cialdini (2007), this principle derives from two sources. First, people have learned that items that are hard to get are of

Advertisers often try to artificially create scarcity to make their products seem more desirable.

better quality than items that are easy to get. From there, they often assume, erroneously, that anything that is scarce must be good. Second, when people's choices (of products, services, romantic partners, job candidates) are constrained in some way, they often want what they can't have even more (Williams et al., 1993). The psychological term for this is *reactance* (Brehm, 1966; Chadee, 2011; Shen & Dillard, 2007).

Companies and advertisers frequently use the scarcity principle to drive up the demand for their products. Thus, you constantly see ads that scream "limited supply available," "for a limited time only," "while they last," and "time is running out." Although both messages work, research suggests that limited-quantity messages are more effective (Aggarwal, Jun, & Huh, 2011). Perhaps the scarcity principle accounts for the reason so many antique and "vintage" items on eBay generate so much interest and auction dollars.

In summary, people use a variety of methods to coax compliance from one another. Despite the fact that many of these influence techniques are more or less dishonest, they're still widely used. There is no way to completely avoid being hoodwinked by influence strategies, and sometimes individuals may be more susceptible to such influence, as appears to be the case when someone feels ostracized and wants to get back into the good graces of a group (Carter-Sowell, Chen, & Williams, 2008). However, being alert to these techniques can reduce the likelihood that you'll be a victim of influence artists. As we noted in our discussion of persuasion, "to be forewarned is to be forearmed."

Learn More Online

Influence at Work

This website, by researchers Robert Cialdini and Kelton Rhodes, offers an intriguing set of pages that explore a wide variety of social influence phenomena: persuasion, propaganda, brainwashing, and the tactics of various types of cults.

CHAPTER 7 | Review

KEY IDEAS

FORMING IMPRESSIONS OF OTHERS

- In forming impressions of other people, individuals rely on appearance, verbal behavior, actions, nonverbal messages, and situational cues. Individuals usually make snap judgments about others unless accurate impressions are important. To explain the causes of other people's behavior, individuals make attributions (either internal or external).
- People often try to confirm their expectations about what others are like, which can result in biased impressions. Self-fulfilling prophecies can actually change a target person's behavior in the direction of a perceiver's expectations.
- Categorization of people into ingroups and outgroups can slant social perceptions. Stereotypes, which are widely held beliefs about the typical characteristics of various groups, can distort one's perceptions of others. When people make the fundamental attribution error, they discount situational factors and explain others' behavior in terms of internal attributions. Defensive attribution often leads people to blame victims for their misfortunes. The process of person perception is characterized by the themes of efficiency, selectivity, and consistency.

THE PROBLEM OF PREJUDICE

- Prejudice is a particularly unfortunate outcome of the tendency to view others inaccurately. Blatant ("old-fashioned") discrimination occurs relatively infrequently today, but subtle expressions of prejudice and discrimination ("modern discrimination," aversive racism) have become more common.
- Common causes of prejudice include right-wing authoritarianism, a strong social dominance orientation, cognitive distortions due to stereotyping and attributional errors, actual competition between groups, and threats to one's social identity. Stereotype threat represents a case of internalized prejudice that can be countered. Strategies for reducing prejudice are rooted in social thinking and collaborative intergroup contact.

THE POWER OF PERSUASION

- The success of persuasive efforts depends on several factors. A source of persuasion who is expert, trustworthy, likable, physically attractive, and similar to the receiver tends to be relatively effective. Although there are some limitations, two-sided arguments, arousal of fear, and generation of positive feelings are effective elements in persuasive messages. Persuasion is undermined when receivers are forewarned or have beliefs that are incompatible with the position being advocated.
- Persuasion takes place via two processes. The central route to persuasion requires a receiver to be motivated to process persuasive messages carefully (elaboration). A favorable reaction to such an evaluation will result in positive attitude change. When a receiver is unmotivated or unable to process persuasive messages carefully, persuasion may take place via the peripheral route (on the basis of simple cues such as a catchy tune). Persuasion undertaken via the central route tends to have more enduring effects on attitudes.

THE POWER OF SOCIAL PRESSURE

- Asch found that subjects often conform to the group, even when the group reports inaccurate judgments. Asch's experiments may have produced public compliance while subjects' private beliefs remained unchanged. Both normative and informational influence can produce conformity. Being mindful of social pressures and getting support from others with similar views are ways to resist conformity pressures.

- In Milgram's landmark study of obedience to authority, subjects showed a remarkable tendency to follow orders to shock an innocent stranger. Milgram's findings highlight the influence of situational pressures on behavior. Although people often obey authority figures, sometimes they are disobedient, usually because they have social support.

APPLICATION: SEEING THROUGH COMPLIANCE TACTICS

- Although they work for different reasons, all compliance tactics have the same goal: getting people to agree to requests. The foot-in-the-door and the lowball technique are based on the fact that people prefer consistency in their behavior.
- The door-in-the-face technique and the tactic of offering "giveaway" items are manipulations of the principle of reciprocity, the rule that one should pay back in kind what one receives from others. When advertisers suggest that products are in short supply, they are taking advantage of the scarcity principle. Understanding these strategies can make you less vulnerable to manipulation.

KEY TERMS

Attitudes p. 216
Attributions p. 201
Bystander effect p. 222
Channel p. 216
Compliance p. 222
Confirmation bias p. 202
Conformity p. 220
Defensive attribution p. 208
Discrimination p. 209
Door-in-the-face technique p. 226
Elaboration likelihood model p. 218
Foot-in-the-door technique p. 225
Fundamental attribution error p. 207
Informational influence p. 222
Lowball technique p. 225
Message p. 216
Need for cognition p. 218
Normative influence p. 222
Obedience p. 222
Person perception p. 199
Persuasion p. 216
Prejudice p. 209
Primacy effect p. 209
Receiver p. 216
Reciprocity principle p. 226
Self-fulfilling prophecy p. 203
Source p. 216
Stereotypes p. 205

KEY PEOPLE

Solomon Asch pp. 220–222
Robert Cialdini pp. 225–227
Susan Fiske pp. 200–201, 208
Stanley Milgram pp. 222–224
Richard Petty and John Cacioppo pp. 218–219
Muzafer Sherif p. 213
Claude Steele p. 214

CHAPTER 7 | Practice Test

1. Inferences that people draw about the causes of events, their own behavior, and others' behavior are called
   a. snap judgments.
   b. self-fulfilling prophecies.
   c. attributions.
   d. attitudes.

2. Which of the following is *not* a potential source of cognitive distortion in perception?
   a. Categorizing
   b. The bystander effect
   c. Stereotypes
   d. Defensive attribution

3. Which of the following is *not* a theme in person perception?
   a. Efficiency
   b. Selectivity
   c. Consistency
   d. Mindfulness

4. "Old-fashioned" discrimination is _____; "modern" discrimination is _____.
   a. blatant; subtle
   b. legal; illegal
   c. common; rare
   d. race-based; gender-based

5. Which of the following is a cause of prejudice?
   a. Mindfulness
   b. Right-wing authoritarianism
   c. The fundamental attribution error
   d. Activities based on superordinate goals

6. Receivers who are forewarned that someone will try to persuade them will most likely
   a. be very open to persuasion.
   b. listen intently but openly argue with the speaker.
   c. be more resistant to persuasion.
   d. heckle the persuader.

7. Compared to attitudes formed via the peripheral route, those formed via the central route
   a. operate subliminally.
   b. are more enduring and harder to change.
   c. last only a short time.
   d. are poor predictors of behavior.

8. When people change their outward behavior but not their private beliefs, _____ is operating.
   a. conformity
   b. persuasion
   c. obedience
   d. compliance

9. The results of Milgram's (1963) study imply that
   a. situational factors can exert tremendous influence over behavior.
   b. in the real world, most people resist pressures to act in harmful ways.
   c. most people are willing to give obviously wrong answers on rigged perceptual tasks.
   d. disobedience is far more common than obedience.

10. When charities send prospective donors free address labels and the like, which of the following social influence principles are they manipulating?
    a. The consistency principle
    b. The scarcity principle
    c. The reciprocity principle
    d. The foot-in-the-door principle

ANSWERS

1. c Page 201
2. b Pages 205–208
3. d Pages 208–209
4. a Pages 210–211
5. b Pages 211–214
6. c Page 218
7. b Pages 218–219
8. d Page 222
9. a Page 224
10. c Pages 226–227

COURSEMATE

Go to **CengageBrain.com** to access Psychology CourseMate, where you will find an interactive eBook, glossaries, flashcards, quizzes, videos, and more.

PERSONAL EXPLORATIONS WORKBOOK

Go to the *Personal Explorations Workbook* in the back of your textbook for exercises that can enhance your self-understanding in relation to issues raised in this chapter.

Exercise 7.1 *Self-Assessment:* Argumentativeness Scale

Exercise 7.2 *Self-Reflection:* Can You Identify Your Prejudicial Stereotypes?

Interpersonal Communication

© Yuri Arcurs/Alamy

Veronica, a high school senior, is getting ready for the prom. Her date, Javier, is waiting downstairs. As she fixes her hair, checks her makeup for what is probably the tenth time in the last hour, and smoothes the front of her new and costly dress, her 13-year-old sister, Amy, wanders into the room. As Veronica looks at her own reflection in a full-length mirror, she hears Amy snort, *"Nice* dress. Really *nice."* Amy's voice brims with the sort of sarcasm that is refined in middle-school hallways, but it is enough to shake Veronica's confidence. "What do you mean? What's wrong with this dress? It's beautiful—isn't it?" she says quickly, worry creeping into her voice. *"Oh, that* dress," grins Amy. "Why there's *not* a thing wrong with it, I am *so* sure Javier will just *love* it." While making that last statement Amy rolls her eyes. A shouting match ensues. Veronica's mother intervenes, telling Veronica she "must have misunderstood—Amy would never make fun of such a nice dress."

Minutes later, her confidence still a bit rattled, Veronica descends the stairs, wondering if it is too late to put on something else—maybe the dress she wore to the junior-senior dance last year? Would anyone remember she wore it before? Would Javier? A moment later, she hears Javier say, "Wow—that is a *really* nice dress. You look terrific, even amazing." Thoughts of changing dresses flee her mind as quickly as they arrived. She smiles at Javier and says, "Thanks, Javier, I think it's a nice dress, too." A memorable night begins.

Sometimes it's not so much what people say that matters but how they say it. The same word—like the word *nice*—can drip with sarcasm (as Amy demonstrated) or sincerity (as Javier showed us). Learning to manage the interpersonal communication in daily life is an important way to deal with people and to interpret their intentions accurately.

Communication skills are highly relevant to adjustment because they can be critical to happiness and success in life. In this chapter, we begin with an overview of the communication process and then turn to the important topic of nonverbal communication. Next, we discuss ways to communicate more effectively and examine common communication problems. Finally, we look at interpersonal conflict, including constructive ways to deal with it. In the Application, we consider ways to develop an assertive communication style.

THE PROCESS OF INTERPERSONAL COMMUNICATION

LEARNING OBJECTIVES

- Outline various aspects of the communication process.
- Discuss important differences between face-to-face and computer-mediated communication.

Communication can be defined as the process of sending and receiving messages that have meaning (Williams et al., 2012). Your personal thoughts have meaning, of course, but when you "talk to yourself," you are engaging in *intra*personal communication. In this chapter, we will focus on *inter*personal communication—the transmission of meaning between two or more people (Smith & Wilson, 2010). For the most part, we'll concentrate on two-person interactions.

We define ***interpersonal communication*** **as an interactional process in which one person sends a message to another.** Note several points about this definition. First, for communication to qualify as *interpersonal,* at least two people must be involved. Second, interpersonal communication is a *process* (Hargie, 2011). By this, we simply mean that it usually involves a series of actions: Kelli talks/Jason listens, Jason responds/Kelli listens, and so on. Third, this process is *interactional.* Effective communication is not a one-way street: Both participants send as well as receive information when they're interacting. Communicators also interpret and create messages by reflecting on their own experiences. People with similar backgrounds are apt to understand each other better (at least initially) than individuals with different frames of reference (Schramm, 1955). A key implication of these facts is that you need to pay attention to both *speaking* and *listening* if you want to be an effective communicator, just as you should learn to ask focused questions to clarify the meaning or intent of the communications you receive.

Components and Features of the Communication Process

Let's take a look at the essential components of the interpersonal communication process. The key elements (most of which were introduced in Chapter 7) are (1) the sender, (2) the receiver, (3) the message, (4) the channel through which the message is sent, (5) noise or interference, and (6) the context in which the message is communicated. As we describe these components, refer to **Figure 8.1** to see how they work together.

The *sender* **is the person who initiates the message.** In a typical two-way conversation, both people serve as senders (as well as receivers). Keep in mind that each person brings a unique set of expectations and understandings to each communication situation. **The *receiver* is the person to whom the message is targeted.**

The *message* **refers to the information or meaning that is transmitted from the sender to the receiver.** The message is the *content* of the communication—that is, the ideas and feelings conveyed. Two important cognitive processes underlie the transmission of messages: Speakers *encode* or transform their ideas and feelings into symbols and organize them into a message; receivers *decode* or translate a speaker's message into their own ideas and feelings (see **Figure 8.1**). Generally, fluent speakers of a language are unaware of these processes. If you've ever learned a new language, however, you have consciously experienced encoding (groping for the right word to express an idea) and decoding (trying to discover a word's meaning by how it is used).

The *channel* **refers to the sensory means through which the message reaches the receiver.** Typically, people receive information from multiple channels simultaneously. They not only hear what the other person says, they also see the person's facial expressions, observe his or her gestures, experience eye contact, and sometimes feel the person's touch. Note that the messages in the various channels may be consistent or inconsistent with each other, making their interpretation more or less difficult. Sometimes sound is the only channel available for receiving information—when you talk on the telephone, for instance. Through sound, people hear both the literal content of messages and vocal inflections. In computer-mediated communication (email, chat rooms, and so on), only the visual channel is called into play, as individuals communicate in writing.

Whenever two people interact, miscommunication can occur. *Noise* **refers to any stimulus that interferes with accurately expressing or understanding a message.** Sources of noise include environmental factors (street traffic, loud music, computer spam or pop-ups, crowded rooms), physical factors (poor hearing, poor vision), and physiological factors (hunger, headaches, medications). Noise can also have semantic origins (Verderber, Verderber, & Berryman-Fink, 2008). For instance, profanity, ethnic slurs, or sexist language can cause a listener to disregard the larger message. In addition, psychological factors such as defensiveness and anxiety can contribute to noise, as we'll see later in the chapter.

All social communication occurs in and is influenced by a *context,* **the environment in which communication takes place.** Context includes the *physical environment*—such as location, time of day, and noise level—and how a conversation takes place: face to face, in a telephone call, or via the Internet. Other important aspects of context include the nature of the participants' *relationship* (work associates, friends, family), their *history* (previous interactions), their current *mood* (happy, stressed), and their *cultural backgrounds* (Verderber et al., 2008). In other words, context refers to how people are influenced by their situations (Reis & Holmes, 2012). Culture is especially important in the United States because of the varieties of subcultures, many with different rules of communication. The Recommended Reading *Multicultural Manners* is an excellent guide to the cultural variety in communication practices in our diverse nation.

Most person-to-person communications are characterized by common features. For example, you are probably

Figure 8.1

A model of interpersonal communication. Interpersonal communication involves six elements: the sender, the receiver, the message, the channel through which the message is transmitted, distorting noise, and the context in which the message is sent. In conversations, both participants function as sender and receiver.

people's past communications affect their present and future communications (Wood, 2006) because they cannot edit or "unsay" sent messages.

Technology and Interpersonal Communication

The recent explosion in electronic and wireless communication technology has revolutionized our notions of interpersonal communication (Kock, 2012). Today, communication via email, Skype, mailing lists, text or instant messaging, "tweets," Facebook, blogs and vlogs, chat rooms, and videoconferencing must be considered along with face-to-face interactions. ***Electronically mediated communication* is interpersonal communication that takes place via technology** (cell or smart phones, computers, and tablet or other hand-held devices). Even a new type of slang ("netlingo") has developed to facilitate quick and easy communication for use in text messaging, email messages, and chat rooms (Ellis, 2006). **Figure 8.2** provides some examples of this slang.

EXAMPLES OF NETLINGO	
Acronymn	**Meaning**
B4N or BFN	Bye For Now
CYM	Check Your Mail
GTG	Got To Go
IDK	I Don't Know
LOL	Laughing Out Loud
NBD	No Big Deal
PAL	Parents Are Listening
RUOK	Are You OK?
TY	Thank You
WKEWL	Way Cool
DGT	Don't Go There
F2F	Face to Face
LDR	Long Distance Relationship
SAPFU	Surpassing All Previous Foul Ups
ZZZ	Sleeping, Bored, Tired

Figure 8.2

Cyberspace slang. A new type of slang has developed that allows quick and easy communication in email messages, text messages, and chat rooms. Here you can see some frequently used text messaging acronyms and their meanings. These acronyms are variously termed netlingo, techspeak, or e-talk. Although netlingo is obviously useful for cybercommunication, its use in more formal settings (school, work) is problematic. (Information from NetLingo.com)

not interested in engaging in intimate or private exchanges with everyone you meet. Instead, you are *selective* in initiating or responding to communications. Communications between people are not isolated events; rather, they have a *systemic* quality because of time, situation, social class, education, culture, personal histories, and other influences that are beyond individuals' control but that nonetheless affect how they interact with each other. Communications within a given relationship (such as those between you and a close friend) are also *unique*, possessing special patterns, vocabulary, even rhythms (Nicholson, 2006). When you become close to a given person, you may establish particular roles and rules for how you interact with each other that are distinct from the roles or rules used in your other relationships (Duck, 2006). For example, close friends often share private or "inside" jokes with one another that a bystander simply would not understand. Finally, communications are said to be *processual*—that is, part of a continuous and evolving process that becomes more personal as people interact with greater frequency. More to the point,

Cell phones have both advantages and disadvantages. On the positive side, they are a convenient way to keep in touch with others, provide a sense of security, and can summon aid in an emergency. Camera and video features on smart phones allow your friends and family to share your experiences even when they are hundreds or thousands of miles away. On the down side, however, they erode the barrier between private and pubic life. Some phone features automatically update your friends about your current location ("Sally Dean is at Taco Junction") as you go about your daily life. Cell phones also tie people to their jobs, can disrupt classrooms and public events, and bring private conversations into public places. Who hasn't been forced to listen to someone yelling his or her personal business into a cell phone in a public place? By now, most people are familiar with the basic rules of etiquette for cell phone use in public: (1) turn off your phone (or put it on "vibrate" mode) when the ringing will disturb others,

(2) keep your calls short, and (3) make and receive calls unobtrusively or out of earshot from others.

In the area of computer-mediated communication, email is by far the most widely used application, but chat rooms are also popular, especially among teens and those in their early and middle 20s (Nie & Erbring, 2002). Shy, less sociable students, for example, have been found to rely on email and social networking sites (Facebook) more often than on instant messaging or chat rooms (Chan, 2011). One explanation is that introverted individuals are less anxious when they communicate to others in an asynchronous or intermittent manner rather than a synchronous or simultaneous back and forth.

As we have noted, face-to-face communication relies on the spoken word, while Internet communication depends on the written word. You can see other important differences in **Figure 8.3**. The absence of nonverbal cues in computer-mediated communication also means that you

FACE-TO-FACE VERSUS ELECTRONIC COMMUNICATION		
Dimension	**Face-to-Face**	**Internet**
Physical distance	People need to be in the same place at the same time to meet.	People can meet and develop a relationship with someone thousands of miles away.
Anonymity	One can't be anonymous in real-life interactions.	People take greater risks in disclosing personal information than they otherwise do. Thus, feelings of intimacy can develop more quickly.
Richness of communication	People have access to nonverbal cues such as facial expressions and tone of voice to detect nuances in meaning or deception.	In cyberspace, these cues are absent, making social and status cues, such as gender, age, social class, race, and ethnicity less discernible.
Visual cues	Physical appearance and visual cues play a big role in attraction in face-to-face relationships.	These cues are generally absent on the Internet (although people can exchange photographs online).
Time	Two people have to connect at the same time.	Although instant messaging and chat room conversations take place in real time, there is no need for an immediate response, so time becomes relatively unimportant. On the Internet, you can take as long as you like to craft a response so you can more completely explain yourself.

Figure 8.3

Differences between face-to-face and electronically mediated communication. Electronically mediated communication applications (cell phone text messaging, email, chat rooms, news groups, and so forth) have dramatically changed the ways people interact and develop relationships. Face-to-face and electronic communication differ from each other in five important ways. (Adapted from Bargh & McKenna, 2004; Boase & Wellman, 2006; Verderber & Verderber, 2004)

Cell phone etiquette in public places calls for turning off your phone or putting it on vibrate mode, keeping your voice low, and making your calls short.

need to take special care that the other person understands your intended meaning. Thus, you should choose your words carefully, provide clarifying details, and describe your feelings, if necessary. It's also a good idea to review what you have written before you send it!

Social Networking Sites: Privacy and Security Issues

Do you take part in any social networking site (SNS), such as Facebook or Twitter? If you are a typical college student or a young adult, there is a good chance you have posted a profile of yourself on one of these popular Internet destinations. The primary benefit of any SNS is being able to present yourself virtually to other people who may already know you, remember you from a shared past (high school, for example), or want to connect with you ("friend you," in Internet parlance) because of some common interest. Most online profiles contain all kinds of personal or private information, everything from your favorite books, movies, or food to your political, social, and even religious beliefs. In effect, an SNS allows you to express yourself and your personality (Carpenter, Green, & LaFlam, 2011).

Is there any drawback or down side to taking part in an SNS? There can be if you do not take appropriate steps to maintain your online privacy. Why should privacy be a concern? Simply put, you never know who is reading your profile or what they are doing with the information you have shared (Lewis, Kaufman, & Christakis, 2008). Surely, you are already aware that you should be careful what financial information (such as PIN numbers) you share online and that interfacing with a website is never a good idea unless you know it is a secure one (LaRose &

Rifon, 2007). But what about the information you post on your SNS? Should you worry about that?

Possibly yes. Consider the fact that Facebook has over 800 million active users (Facebook, 2011), yet users assume others, not they themselves, are at risk when it comes to posting private information (Debatin et al., 2009). To presume that all of those users are well intentioned seems somewhat foolhardy. There is also ample evidence that the content of student postings has been used to raid student parties (Hass, 2006) and to keep individuals from getting jobs (Finder, 2006). In short, private information is not always so private. Think for a moment: Is your SNS profile set so that it cannot be read, accessed, or searched by nonfriends (strangers)? Or can anyone see your personal pages?

Based on their analyses of an SNS dataset composed of user profiles, Lewis et al. (2008) claim that students are likely to act to maintain their online privacy based on two factors: social influence and personal incentives. Where social influence is concerned, students follow the lead of those close to them; thus, they are likely to keep their profiles private if their roomates and friends do so. Perhaps not surprisingly, women are more likely to maintain private profiles than men are.

What about those "personal incentives"? Interestingly, people with private profiles are online with greater regularity than those with public profiles. Within their dataset, Lewis et al. (2008) found that people who maintained their privacy were also likely to have more esoteric tastes in music, books, and movies compared to those whose pages are public. So, maintaining privacy is not only wise from a security perspective, it may also represent a way to demonstrate one's sociocultural tastes (albeit to friends rather than strangers).

Communication and Adjustment

Before we plunge further into the topic of interpersonal communication, let's take a moment to emphasize its significance. Communication with others—friends, lovers, parents, spouses, children, employers, workers—is such an essential and commonplace aspect of everyday life that it's hard to overstate its role in adjustment. Many of life's gratifications (and frustrations and heartaches, as well) hinge on one's ability to communicate effectively with others. Numerous studies have shown that good communication can enhance satisfaction in relationships (Egeci & Gençöz, 2006; Estrada, 2012) and that poor communication ranks high as a cause of breakups among both straight and gay couples (Angulo, Brooks, & Swann, 2011; Kurdek, 1998).

NONVERBAL COMMUNICATION

LEARNING OBJECTIVES

- List five general principles of nonverbal communication.
- Discuss the dynamics of personal space and what can be discerned from facial cues and eye contact.
- Summarize the research findings on body movement, posture, gestures, touch, and paralanguage in communication.

- Recognize the difficulty in detecting deception, and clarify the nonverbal cues linked to deception.
- Assess the significance of nonverbal sensitivity in interpersonal interactions.

You're standing at the bar in your favorite hangout, gazing across a dimly lit room filled with people drinking, dancing, and talking. You signal to the bartender that you'd like another drink. Your companion comments on the loudness of the music, and you nod your head in agreement. You spot an attractive stranger across the bar; your eyes meet for a moment and you smile. In a matter of seconds, you have sent three messages without uttering a syllable. To put it another way, you have just sent three *nonverbal* messages. **Nonverbal communication is the transmission of meaning from one person to another through means or symbols other than words.** Communication at the nonverbal level takes place through a variety of behaviors: interpersonal distance, facial expression, eye contact, body posture and movement, gestures, physical touch, and tone of voice (e.g., Gifford, 2011; Murphy, 2012).

Clearly, a great deal of information is exchanged through nonverbal channels—more than most people realize. You can significantly enhance your communication skills by learning more about this important aspect of communication.

General Principles

Let's begin by examining some general principles of nonverbal communication.

1. *Nonverbal communication conveys emotions.* People can communicate their feelings without saying a word—for example, "a look that kills." Nonverbal demonstrations of positive feelings include sitting or standing close to those you care for, touching them often, and looking at them frequently. Still, nonverbal signals on their own are not the precise indicators of emotional states that they were once believed to be (App et al., 2011), so you should be cautious in making inferences.

2. *Nonverbal communication is multichanneled.* Nonverbal communication typically involves simultaneous messages sent through a number of channels. For instance, information may be transmitted through gestures, facial expressions, eye contact, and vocal tone at the same time. In contrast, verbal communication is limited to a single channel: speech. If you have ever tried to follow two people speaking at once, you understand how difficult it is to process multiple inputs of information. This means that many nonverbal transmissions can sail by the receiver unnoticed.

3. *Nonverbal communication is ambiguous.* A shrug or a raised eyebrow can mean different things to different people. Moreover, receivers may have difficulty determining whether nonverbal messages are being sent intentionally. Although some popular books on body language imply otherwise, few nonverbal signals carry universally accepted meanings, even within the same culture. Thus, nonverbal cues are informative, but they are most reliable when accompanied by verbal messages and embedded in a familiar cultural and social context (Samovar, Porter, & McDaniel, 2007).

4. *Nonverbal communication may contradict verbal messages.* How often have you seen people proclaim "I'm not angry" even though their bodies shout that they are positively furious? When confronted with such an inconsistency, which message should you believe? Because of their greater spontaneity, you're probably better off heeding the nonverbal signs. Research shows that when someone is instructed to tell a lie, deception is most readily detected through nonverbal signals (Sporer & Schwandt, 2007).

5. *Nonverbal communication is culture-bound.* Like language, nonverbal signals are different in different cultures (Samovar et al., 2007; Weisbuch & Ambady, 2008). Culture influences how people notice, retain, and decode nonverbal behaviors they witness (Matsumoto & Yoo, 2005). Sometimes cultural differences can be quite dramatic. For example, in Tibet people greet their friends by sticking out their tongues (Ekman, 1975).

Elements of Nonverbal Communication

Nonverbal signals can provide a great deal of information in interpersonal interactions. As we discuss specific nonverbal behaviors, we will focus on what they communicate about interpersonal attraction and social status.

Personal Space

Proxemics is the study of people's use of interpersonal space. *Personal space* is a zone of space surrounding a person that is felt to "belong" to that person. Personal space is like an invisible bubble you carry around with you in your social interactions. The size of this mobile zone is related to your cultural background, social status, personality, age, and gender.

Distance in relationships is psychological (Hess, 2002, 2003) as well as physical. The amount of interpersonal dis-

In Tibet, friends greet their friends by sticking out their tongue.

tance people prefer depends on the nature of the relationship and the situation (E. T. Hall, 2008; J. A. Hall, 1990). The appropriate distance between people is also regulated by social norms and varies by culture (Hall & Whyte, 2008; Samovar et al., 2007). For instance, people of Northern European heritage tend to engage in less physical contact and keep a greater distance between themselves than people of Latin or Middle Eastern heritage. The United States is usually characterized as a medium-contact culture, but there is a lot of variability among ethnic groups. The situation matters, too: Consider how much distance from others people desire when they are using an ATM. Those waiting behind you in line know that you want your privacy in order to preserve the personal information you enter into the machine during a transaction (Li & Li, 2007). They, in turn, expect the same courtesy. Similarly, when strangers expect to interact with one another directly in a group setting, they are likely to move their seats closer to one another (Novelli, Drury, & Reicher, 2010). When no expectation of direct interaction exists, people automatically retain greater personal space between one another.

Anthropologist Edward T. Hall (1966) has described four interpersonal distance zones that are appropriate for middle-class encounters in American culture, as shown in **Figure 8.4**. The general rule is that the more you like someone, the more comfortable you feel being physically close to that person. Women seem to have smaller personal-space zones than men do (Holland et al., 2004). When talking, women sit or stand closer together than men do. Of course, there are obvious exceptions, such as in crowded subways and elevators, but these situations are often

Figure 8.4

Interpersonal distance zones. According to Edward Hall (1966), people like to keep a certain amount of distance between themselves and others. The distance that makes one feel comfortable depends on whom one is interacting with and the nature of the situation.

Zone and distance

Zone 1: Intimate distance zone	Zone 2: Personal distance zone	Zone 3: Social distance zone	Zone 4: Public distance zone
(0–18")	(18"–4')	(4'–12')	(12'+)

Appropriate people and situations

| Parents and children, lovers, spouses/partners | Close friends | Co-workers, social gatherings, friends, work situations | Actors, total strangers, important officials |

experienced as stressful. For example, one study examined train commuters' experiences during rush hour (Evans & Wener, 2007). Interestingly, density (crowding) within the train car had little impact on commuters' stress, but stress associated with seating density (the proximity of other passengers) was quite high, as indicated by self-reports, physiological measures, and behavioral measures of feeling "closed in." Imagine the long-term impact of such personal space distress on people who commute twice a day for five or more days per week.

Personal distance can also convey information about status. People generally stand farther away from high-status communication partners versus partners of lower power (Holland et al., 2004). Moreover, it is the prerogative of the more powerful person in an interaction to set the "proper" distance (Henley, 1986). One study in Japan found that female subordinates kept male superiors at the greatest distance as compared to male or female peers (Aono, 2003).

Facial Expression

More than anything else, *facial expressions* convey emotions (Hess & Thibault, 2009). Paul Ekman and Wallace Friesen have identified six distinctive facial expressions that correspond with six basic emotions: anger, disgust, fear, happiness, sadness, and surprise (Ekman, 1994; Ekman & Friesen, 1984). Early research involving participants from many countries supported the idea that these six emotions are universally recognized (Ekman, 1972). In such studies, researchers showed photographs depicting different emotions to subjects from a variety of Western and non-Western cultures and asked them to match the photographs with an emotion. Some representative results from this research are depicted in **Figure 8.5**.

A more recent meta-analysis of 97 studies (based on studies in over 40 countries) looked at whether these six emotions are universally recognized or are culturally spe-

Display rules require unsuccessful contestants in beauty pageants to suppress the display of resentful, envious, or angry feelings.

cific (Elfenbein & Ambady, 2002). Interestingly, there was evidence for both perspectives. In support of the universal view, individuals do accurately recognize emotions in photographs of people from other cultures. Favoring cultural specificity, there was evidence of an "ingroup advantage." Thus, observers are better at recognizing the emotions in photographs from their own cultural groups than those from other cultural groups. A few basic facial expressions are universally recognizable, but other emotional expressions vary from culture to culture—as we noted in the earlier example of Tibetans sticking out their tongues to greet their friends.

Interestingly, recent research suggests that there may also be a seventh distinct facial expression for anxiety that occurs in ambiguous situations where perceived threats (e.g., feelings of being watched or followed) are unclear.

Figure 8.5

Facial expressions and emotions.
Ekman and Friesen (1984) found that people in highly disparate cultures showed fair agreement on the emotions portrayed in these photos. This consensus across cultures suggests that the facial expressions associated with certain emotions may have a biological basis.

Source: Photos courtesy of Paul Ekman, Ph.D./ Paul Ekman Group, LLC.

	Emotion displayed			
	Fear	Disgust	Happiness	Anger
Country	Agreement in judging photos (%)			
United States	85	92	97	67
Brazil	67	97	95	90
Chile	68	92	95	94
Argentina	54	92	98	90
Japan	66	90	100	90
New Guinea	54	44	82	50

Anxiety is marked by darting of the eyes and head swivels (see **Figure 8.6**). As an emotion, anxiety is often confused with fear, a reaction that occurs when perceived threats are more apparent (e.g., confronting a snarling dog) (Perkins et al., 2012).

Each society has rules that govern whether and when it is appropriate to express one's feelings (Koopmann-Holm & Matsumoto, 2011; Matsumoto, 2006). *Display rules* **are norms that govern the appropriate display of emotions in a culture.** In the United States, for instance, it is considered bad form to gloat over one's victories or to show envy or anger in defeat.

Besides cultural differences, there are gender differences in facial expression (LaFrance, Hecht, & Paluck, 2003). For example, men typically show less facial expression than women do, a finding linked to social pressures for males to inhibit such displays (Kilmartin, 2007). Also, as you might expect, people high in self-monitoring (see Chapter 6) are better than low self-monitors at managing their facial expressions (Gangestad & Snyder, 2000).

What about decoding the emotion displayed on faces? There is some evidence that age matters. In one study on facial identification and memory, it was found that when compared to younger people, older individuals were less able to identify angry expressions on either young or older faces. Moreover, once the older participants categorized the faces they viewed, they remembered angry faces less well than happy ones (Ebner & Johnson, 2009). Although people's abilities to decode facial expressions of emotion do decrease with age, such changes are not entirely explained by other age-related declines such as in vision and memory (Lambrecht, Kreifelts, & Wildgruber, 2012).

Figure 8.6
Anxiety: A new universal facial expression? Perkins and colleagues (2012) argue that anxiety may represent a seventh universal facial expression. As shown here, humans recognize anxiety when they see darting eyes accompanied by swiveling of the head.

Is it possible to deliberately deceive others through facial expression? Absolutely. In fact, people are better at sending deceptive messages with their faces than with other areas of their bodies (Porter, ten Brinke, & Wallace, 2012). As an example, you are no doubt familiar with the term "poker face," an allusion to poker players who are experts at controlling their excitement about a good hand of cards (or their dismay about a bad one).

Eye Contact

Eye contact (also called mutual gaze) is another major channel of nonverbal communication. The duration of eye contact is its most meaningful aspect. The ability to use eye contact as a means to gauge the mental and emotional states of others appears in humans over 6 years of age (Vida & Maurer, 2012). Among European Americans, people who engage in high levels of eye contact are usually judged to have effective social skills and credibility. Similarly, speakers, interviewers, and experimenters receive higher ratings of competence when they maintain high rather than low eye contact with their audience. As a rule, people engage in more eye contact when they're listening than when they're talking (Bavelas, Coates, & Johnson, 2002). People display an interesting self-serving bias with respect to eye contact: They assume attractive people are more likely to make eye contact with them than persons deemed less attractive (Kloth, Altmann, & Schweinberger, 2011). Where listening is concerned, mutual gaze can even promote music appreciation: More eye contact between a musician and audience actually leads to greater levels of enjoyment of the musical performance (Antonietti, Cocomazzi, & Iannello, 2009).

There may be times when some types of communication either enhance or reduce eye contact. For example, researchers have long speculated that people are more likely to make eye contact with others when making sincere statements. Conversely, psychologists assumed that speakers making sarcastic or derisive comments become gaze averse—that is, they are more likely to break eye contact with listeners. A controlled study using speaker-listener pairs confirmed these expectations (Williams, Burns, & Harmon, 2009).

Gaze also communicates the *intensity* (but not the positivity or negativity) of feelings. For example, couples who say they are in love spend more time gazing at each other than other couples do (Patterson, 1988). Also, maintaining moderate (versus constant or no) eye contact with others typically generates positive feelings in them. When women make eye contact with men, a longer gaze can generate the latter's interest, sustaining it when smiling is part of the interaction (Guéguen et al., 2008).

In a negative interpersonal context, a steady gaze becomes a stare that causes most people to feel uncomfortable (Kleinke, 1986). Moreover, like threat displays among nonhuman primates such as baboons and rhesus monkeys,

© iStockphoto.com/drbimages

a stare can convey aggressive intent (Henley, 1986). Thus, if you want to avoid road rage incidents, avoid making eye contact with hostile motorists. People also communicate by *reducing* eye contact with others. Unpleasant interactions, embarrassing situations, or invasions of personal space usually trigger this behavior (Kleinke, 1986). Indeed, in the absence of verbal or contextual information, such looking away can communicate fear; in effect, people sometimes "point" to danger with their eyes (Hadjikhani et al., 2008).

Culture strongly affects patterns of eye contact (Samovar et al., 2007). For example, Americans should be sensitive to the fact that direct eye contact is perceived as an insult in Mexico, Latin America, Japan, and Africa, and in some Native American tribes. By contrast, people from Arab countries look directly into the eyes of their conversational partners for longer periods than Americans are used to.

In the United States, gender and racial differences have been found in eye contact. For instance, women tend to gaze at others more than men do (Briton & Hall, 1995). However, the patterning of eye contact also reflects status, and gender and status are often confounded. Higher-status individuals look at the other person more when speaking than when listening, while lower-status people behave just the opposite. Women usually show the lower-status visual pattern because they are typically accorded lower status than men. As you can see in **Figure 8.7**, when women are in high-power positions, they show the high-status visual pattern to the same extent that men do (Dovidio et al., 1988). African Americans use more continuous eye contact than European Americans when speaking, but less when listening (Samovar & Porter, 2004). Misunderstandings can arise if gaze behaviors that are intended to convey interest and respect are interpreted as being disrespectful or dishonest.

Body Language

Body movements—those of the head, trunk, hands, legs, and feet—also provide nonverbal avenues of communication (Sinke, Kret, & de Gelder, 2012; Streeck, Goodwin, & LeBaron, 2011). **Kinesics is the study of communication through body movements.** By noting a person's body movements, observers may be able to tell an individual's level of tension or relaxation, or whether a person's expressed remorse is sincere and genuine or merely fabricated "crocodile tears" (ten Brinke et al., 2012). For instance,

© Cengage Learning

Figure 8.7

Visual dominance, status, and gender. Women typically show low visual dominance (see control condition) because they are usually accorded lower status than men (Dovidio et al. 1988). However, when researchers placed women in a high power position and measured their visual behavior, women showed the high visual dominance pattern and men showed the low visual dominance pattern. When men were placed in the high power position, the visual dominance patterns reversed. Thus, visual dominance seems to be more a function of status than of gender.

frequent touching or scratching suggests nervousness (Harrigan et al., 1991).

Posture also conveys information. Leaning back with arms or legs arranged in an asymmetrical or "open" position conveys a feeling of relaxation. Posture can also indicate someone's attitude toward you (McKay, Davis, & Fanning, 1995). A body leaning toward you typically indicates interest and a positive attitude. Conversely, a body angled away from you or a position with crossed arms may indicate a negative attitude or defensiveness.

Posture can also convey status differences. Generally, a higher-status person will look more relaxed. By contrast, a lower-status person will tend to exhibit a more rigid body posture, often sitting up straight with feet together, flat on the floor, and arms close to the body (a "closed" position) (Vrugt & Luyerink, 2000). Again, status and gender differences are frequently parallel. That is, men are more likely to exhibit the high-status "open" posture and women the lower-status "closed" posture (Cashdan, 1998).

People use *hand gestures* to describe and emphasize the words they speak, as well as to persuade (Maricchiolo et al., 2009). You might point to give directions or slam your fist on a desk to emphasize an assertion. To convey "no," you can extend the index finger of your dominant hand and wave it back and forth from left to right. Children know that when adults slide their right index finger up and down their left index finger, it means "shame on you." As travelers frequently discover, the meaning of gestures is not universal

Both hand photos: Irena Misevic/Shutterstock.com

The potential force of body language can be seen in these photos showing Lyndon Baines Johnson, who was the U. S. Senate majority leader at the time (1957), working over a fellow senator (Theodore Green). The status difference between Johnson and his colleague is obvious and the way Johnson leans into Green is a clear attempt at intimidation.

(Samovar et al., 2007). For instance, a circle made with the thumb and forefinger means that everything is "OK" to an American, but it is considered an obscene gesture in some countries.

Touch

Touch takes many forms and can express a variety of meanings, including support, consolation, and sexual intimacy. Touch can also convey messages of status and power (Hall, 2006a). In the United States, people typically "touch downward"—i.e., higher-status individuals are freer to touch subordinates than vice versa (Henley & Freeman, 1995). Higher-status people who touch others while making requests ("I'm conducting a survey—will you answer some questions for me?") actually increase compliance rates (Guéguen, 2002). How people interpret the possible messages communicated by touch depends on the age and gender of the individuals involved, the setting in which the touching takes place, and the relationship between the toucher and recipient, among other things (Major, Schmidlin, & Williams, 1990). For example, consider the impact of being touched while you are out shopping. Consumers who are accidentally touched by a stranger (a confederate of the researcher) while shopping end up rating products more negatively and then spend less time in stores compared to their untouched counterparts (Martin, 2012). There are also gender differences related to status and touch: Adult women use touch to convey closeness or intimacy, whereas men use touch as a means to control or indicate their power in social situations (DiBaise & Gunnoe, 2004; Hall, 2006a). Finally, there are strong norms about *where* on the body people are allowed to touch their friends. These norms are quite different for

"O.K., big cheer here, but nothing that might be construed as pressure. Quiet now, but a supportive quiet. Watch your body language."

same-gender as opposed to cross-gender interactions, as can be seen in **Figure 8.8**.

Other findings about touching behavior have come from an observational study of 4,500 pairs of Bostonians interacting in a variety of public places, such as shopping malls, hotel lobbies, and subway stations (Hall & Veccia, 1990, 1991). For one thing, female-female pairs touched

Figure 8.8

Where friends touch each other. Social norms govern where friends tend to touch each other. As these figures show, the patterns of touching are different in same-gender as opposed to cross-gender interactions.

Source: Based on Marsh, P. (Ed.). (1988). *Eye to eye: How people interact.* Topsfield, MA: Salem House. Copyright © 1988 by Andromeda Oxford Ltd and HarperCollins, Publishers.

each other significantly more than male-male pairs. Second, in younger pairs men touched women more, but in older pairs the pattern was reversed. Comparable age changes were not found for same-gender pairs.

More recently, a simple but provocative study found that a 5-second touch from one person to another can often convey a specific emotion (Hertenstein, Holmes et al., 2009). Undergraduate research recruits were to touch or be touched by a stranger. Touchers were instructed to convey one of eight specific emotions via their fingers: sympathy, love, gratitude, anger, disgust, sadness, fear, or happiness. Touchers made contact by selecting the face, head, arms, hands, shoulders, trunk, or back. Those receiving were blindfolded so as not to know the sex of the touchers. Afterward, recipients reviewed a list of the eight emotions and were told to choose the one they believed was conveyed by the touch. Strikingly, judgments of emotional accuracy ranged between 50% and 78% (if they had simply guessed about the emotion linked to each touch, average precision would have been around 12.5%). One tentative conclusion is that intimate interactions—those in which people touch others they know very well—can convey as much emotion as facial expressions.

Paralanguage

The term *paralanguage* refers to *how* something is said rather than to *what* is said. Thus, **paralanguage includes all vocal cues other than the content of the verbal message itself.** Cues to paralanguage include grunts, sighs, murmurs, gasps, and other vocal sounds. It can also entail how loudly or softly people speak, how fast they talk, and the pitch, rhythm, and quality (such as accent, pronunciation, sentence complexity) of their speech. Each of these vocal characteristics can affect the message being transmitted.

Variations in vocal emphasis can give the same set of words very different meanings. Consider the sentence "I really enjoyed myself." By varying the word that is accented, you can speak this sentence in three ways, each suggesting a different meaning:

- *I* really enjoyed myself! (Even though others may not have had a good time, I did.)
- I *really* enjoyed myself! (My enjoyment was exceptional.)
- I really *enjoyed* myself! (Much to my surprise, I had a great time.)

As you can see from these examples, you can actually reverse the meaning of a verbal message by how you say it (such as with sarcasm). The vignette that opens this chapter also illustrates how paralanguage can change the meaning of words.

Aspects of vocalization can also communicate emotions (Banse & Scherer, 1996). For example, rapid speech may mean that a person is happy, frightened, or nervous. Slower speech might be used when people are uncertain or

when they want to emphasize a point. Loud vocalization often signals anger. A relatively high pitch may indicate anxiety. Slow speech, low volume, and low pitch are often associated with sadness. Thus, vocal quality provides another window on someone's true feelings.

In cyberspace communication, emailers use various substitutes for the paralanguage cues found in spoken communication. For instance, capital letters are used for emphasis ("I had a GREAT vacation"); however, using capital letters throughout a message is viewed as shouting and considered rude behavior. Using *emoticons* (punctuation marks arranged to indicate the writer's emotions) has also become a common practice; thus, :-) indicates a smile and :-(indicates a frown. Other common emoticons are shown in **Figure 8.9**.

Detecting Deception

Like it or not, lying is a part of everyday life (DePaulo, 2004). People typically tell one to two lies a day (DePaulo et al., 1997). Most of these everyday lies are inconsequen-

Figure 8.9

Conveying emotion in cyberspace by using emoticons. People sometimes complain that online communication, chiefly email or text messaging, does not allow recipients to read senders' emotional states. Emoticons, or punctuation marks and some letters joined to convey emotion visually, can fill in this digital age gap in interpersonal communication.

Source: "List of Emoticons" Wikipedia entry, accessed on June 24, 2009.

Bella DePaulo

tial "white lies," such as claiming to be better than one actually is or lying to avoid hurting someone's feelings ("Say, I like your new haircut—really, I do"). Of course, people tell more serious lies, too. When they do, such lies are used to gain some advantage—that is, to get what they want or to obtain something they feel entitled to, such as gaining credit for an idea (DePaulo et al., 2004). People tell serious lies, too, when they want to avoid conflict or to protect or even harm other people.

Is it possible to catch people in a lie? Yes, but it's difficult—even for experts (Bond & DePaulo, 2006, 2008). As shown in **Figure 8.10**, some studies have found that professionals whose work involves detecting lies (police officers, FBI agents, and psychiatrists, for example) are slightly more accurate judges of liars than nonexperts are (Ekman, O'Sullivan, & Frank, 1999). Still, even these individuals have accuracy rates around 57%—not much better than chance (50%), which means their "edge" is slight. Even married people cannot necessarily tell when their spouse is lying unless the marital bond has been disrupted for whatever reason and suspicion is running high (McCormack & Levine, 1990). Moreover, recent meta-analyses found no significant differences in the accuracy rates of experts and nonexperts (Bond & DePaulo, 2008; Ekman, 2009), yet people routinely overestimate their ability to detect liars (DePaulo et al., 1997).

The popular stereotypes about how liars give themselves away don't necessarily correspond to the actual clues related to dishonesty. For example, observers tend to focus on the face (the least-revealing channel) and to ignore more useful information (Burgoon, 1994). In **Figure 8.11** on the next page, you can review the research findings on the nonverbal behaviors actually associated with deception (based on DePaulo, Stone, & Lassiter, 1985). By comparing the second and third columns in the figure, you can see which cues are actually associated with deception and which are erroneously linked with it. Contrary to popular belief, lying is *not* associated with slow talking, long pauses before speaking, excessive shifting of posture, reduced smiling, or lack of eye contact. A meta-analysis of over 300 studies generally supported these findings, concluding that liars say less, tell less-compelling stories, make a more negative impression, are more tense, and include less unusual content in their stories than truth tellers do (DePaulo et al., 2003).

So, how *do* liars give themselves away? As you will note in **Figure 8.11** on the next page, many of the clues "leak" from nonverbal channels, because speakers have a harder time controlling these channels (DePaulo & Friedman, 1998). For example, liars may blink less than usual while telling a lie because of cognitive demand (Leal & Vrij, 2008). Eye blinks then accelerate once the lie has been told. Vocal cues include speaking with a higher pitch, giving relatively short answers, and excessive hesitations. Visual cues include dilation of the pupils. It's also helpful to look for inconsistencies between facial expressions and lower body movements. For example, a friendly smile accompanied by a nervous shuffling of feet could signal deception.

People can also deplete their self-presentational resources over time—they tire of creating and conveying the same impression over and over—thereby rousing observers' suspicions that they are being deceptive (Vohs, Baumeister, & Ciarocco, 2005). For example, during a campaign, a politician might continually renounce belief in a previously held policy (raising taxes is necessary for public safety) to different audiences (e.g., business leaders, retirees) made up of skeptical voters. Problems might arise when poor management of the candidate's self-presentation occurs during the routine stump speech.

Bella DePaulo (1994), a noted researcher in this area, isn't too optimistic about the prospects of teaching people to spot lies, because the cues are usually subtle. If she's correct, perhaps *machines* can do better. **The polygraph is a device that records fluctuations in physiological arousal as a person answers questions.** Although called a "lie detector," it's really an emotion detector. The polygraph monitors key indicators of autonomic arousal such as heart rate, blood pressure, respiration rate, and perspiration, or galvanic skin response (GSR). The assumption is that when people lie, they experience

Figure 8.10

How well do experts distinguish truth and deception? Lie-detection experts with experience making judgments of truth and deception were shown brief videotapes of ten women telling the truth or lying about their feelings (Ekman & O'Sullivan, 1991). Considering that there was a 50–50 chance of guessing correctly, the accuracy rates were remarkably low. Only a sample of U.S. Secret Service agents posted a better-than-chance performance. (Adapted from Kassin, Fein, & Markus, 2011) emotion that produces noticeable changes in these physiological indicators (see **Figure 8.12**).

Polygraph experts claim that lie detector tests are 85%–90% accurate and that there is research support for the validity of polygraph testing (Honts, Raskin, & Kircher, 2002). These claims are clearly not supported by the evidence. Methodologically sound research on this question is surprisingly sparse (largely because the research is difficult to do), and the limited evidence available is not very impressive (Branaman & Gallagher, 2005; Iacono, 2009). One problem is that when people respond to incriminating questions, they may experience emotional arousal even when they are telling the truth. Thus, polygraph tests often lead to accusations against the innocent. Another problem is that some people can lie without experiencing physiological arousal. Thus, because of high error rates, polygraph results are not admitted as evidence in most types of courtrooms (Iacono, 2008).

NONVERBAL CUES AND DECEPTIONS		
Kind of cue	**Are cues associated with actual deception?**	**Are cues believed to be a sign of deception?**
Vocal cues		
Speech hesitations	YES: Liars hesitate more	YES
Voice pitch	YES: Liars speak with higher pitch	YES
Speech errors (stutters, stammers)	YES: Liars make more errors	YES
Speech latency (pause before starting to speak or answer)	NO	YES: People think liars pause more
Speech rate	NO	YES: People think liars talk slower
Response length	YES: Liars give shorter answers	NO
Visual cues		
Pupil dilation	YES: Liars show more dilation	(No research data)
Adapters (self-directed gestures)	YES: Liars touch themselves more	NO
Blinking	YES: Liars blink less	(No research data)
Postural shifts	NO	YES: People think liars shift more
Smile	NO	YES: People think liars smile less
Gaze (eye contact)	NO	YES: People think liars engage in less eye contact

Figure 8.11

Detecting deception from nonverbal behaviors. This chart summarizes evidence on which nonverbal cues are *actually* associated with deception and which are *believed* to be a sign of deception, based on a research review by DePaulo, Stone, and Lassiter (1985).

One promising method is the use of brain-imaging procedures for detecting lies. Such tools enable researchers to create computer images of brain structures and to assess changes, such as blood flow, during thought tasks. Some preliminary evidence is that, under highly controlled conditions, brain-imaging technology can separate liars from those who are telling the truth with a higher degree of success than the conventional polygraph (Simpson, 2008).

Figure 8.12

The polygraph measures emotional reactions. A lie detector measures the physiological arousal that most people experience when they tell a lie. After using nonthreatening questions to establish a baseline, a polygraph examiner looks for signs of arousal (such as the sharp change in GSR shown here) on incriminating questions.

Suspicion and the Minnesota Trust Game

Log on to CourseMate at www.cengagebrain.com to watch this video.

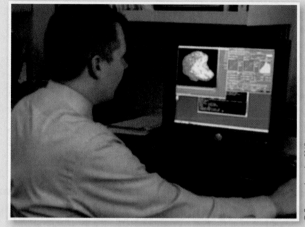

Considering that people lie every day, suspicion has its advantages and disadvantages. Although it can guard us from harm, suspicion can also cause unnecessary distress. Angus MacDonald III, psychologist at University of Minnesota, discusses suspicion in this Reel Research video.

Using a functional MRI (fMRI) scanner to examine a participant's brain activity while playing a game, researchers identify specific areas associated with suspicion. Through such studies, MacDonald hopes to determine more effective psychological and pharmacological solutions for patients suffering from mental health disorders in which suspicion is a symptom. People suffering from schizophrenia, neurological disorders associated with aging, and overuse of methamphetamines often have suspicion as a symptom—which can complicate treatment and endanger the safety of the person and others.

MacDonald demonstrates how suspicion influences social interactions in a study involving graduate students Jim and Melissa enaging in the Minnesota Trust Game. In this game, players have the choice to select $10 for both players, represented in the left column, or give their partner the choice to choose from either the center or right columns. The right column, like the left, is always valued at the same amount for both players ($20) while the center column offers values that could be beneficial or detrimental to one or both of the players. Although the players do not know what their partner chooses, Jim shows higher levels of suspicion while Melissa is more trusting. When Jim does not trust Melissa to choose to his benefit, he becomes threatened and suspicious. What MacDonald found is that certain areas in the brain become more active when suspicion rises, and these same areas may be overactive in people suffering from mental disorders.

Watch the *Suspicion and Minnesota Trust Game* video to learn more about the study. Delve even deeper by responding to the following discussion questions.

DISCUSSION QUESTIONS

1. "I think most people would lie to get ahead." Do you agree or disagree? What does this say about your level of trust in others? How do you think Jim and Melissa responded to this statement during the study, based on the video?
2. Why didn't researchers give Jim and Melissa feedback about their partner's selections? How does this affect the outcome of the study and their behavior?
3. Why does suspicion complicate treatment for those suffering from illnesses like schizophrenia or Alzheimer's disease? How might studying the brain lead to more specialized treatments?

Drawbacks include the practicality of implementing such technology, the costs involved, and ethical issues surrounding the ability to peer inside people's heads. A less-expensive and more practical method may involve the use of a reaction time (RT) paradigm for detecting concealed information in non-criminal contexts (Verschuere et al., 2010). Slower response times to controlled questions, for example, might point to deception, and preliminary evidence indicates the approach is as valid as the polygraph.

To summarize, deception is potentially detectable, but the nonverbal behaviors that accompany lying are subtle and difficult to spot.

The Significance of Nonverbal Communication

Good nonverbal communication skills are associated with good social adjustment and with relationship satisfaction (Schachner, Shaver, & Mikulincer, 2005). Experts give particular attention to *nonverbal sensitivity—the ability to accurately encode (express) and decode (understand) nonverbal cues.* Nonverbal sensitivity is related to social, emotional, and academic competence (Bänziger et al., 2011), even in children (Izard et al., 2001).

In a study of college students' romantic relationships, nonverbal sensitivity was correlated with relationship well-being (Carton, Kessler, & Pape, 1999). And it's been found that spouses with poor nonverbal communication skills are more dissatisfied with their marriages (Noller, 1987). Since these are correlational studies, we can't tell whether nonverbal insensitivity leads to marital dissatisfaction or whether unhappy relationships cause couples to make less effort at communicating. Both possibilities probably play a role. And nonverbal insensitivity and dissatifaction can set up a vicious cycle that spirals downward (Miller, Perlman, & Brehm, 2007).

What about sensitivity for decoding and responding to facial expressions of emotion? Generally, women are better encoders and decoders of nondeceptive messages than men (Hall, 1998, 2006b). It is not that women are innately better at these skills or that they have lower status than men, but rather that women are more motivated than men to exert effort at these skills (Hall, Coats, & Smith-LeBeau, 2005). The good news is that men (and women) who are willing to use some effort can improve their nonverbal communication skills—and enjoy happier and more satisfying relationships.

TOWARD MORE EFFECTIVE COMMUNICATION

LEARNING OBJECTIVES

- Identify five steps involved in making small talk.
- Explain why self-disclosure is important to adjustment, citing ways to reduce risks associated with it.
- Discuss the role of self-disclosure in relationship development.
- Analyze cultural and gender differences in self-disclosure, and discuss how disclosure varies due to cultural and gender differences.
- Cite four points good listeners need to keep in mind.

If you are like most people, you probably overestimate how effectively you communicate with others (Keysar & Henly, 2002). In this section, we turn to some practical issues that will help you become a more effective communicator with your family, friends, romantic partner, and co-workers. We'll review conversational skills, self-disclosure, and effective listening.

Conversational Skills

When it comes to meeting strangers, some people launch right into a conversation, while others break into a cold sweat as their minds go completely blank. If you fall into the second category, don't despair! The art of conversation is actually based on conversational *skills.* And these skills can be learned. To get you started, we'll offer a few general principles, gleaned primarily from *Messages: The Communication Skills Book* by McKay and associates (1995). If you want to explore this topic in greater depth, their book is an excellent source of practical advice.

First, follow the Golden Rule: Give to others what you would like to receive from them. In other words, give others your attention and respect and let them know that you like them. Second, focus on the other person instead of yourself. Concentrate on what the person is saying, rather than on how you look, what you're going to say next, or how you are going to win the argument. Third, as we have noted, use nonverbal cues to communicate your interest in the other person. Like you, others also find it easier to interact with a person who signals friendliness. A welcoming smile can make a big difference in initial contacts.

Now, how do you actually get the conversational ball rolling? Psychologist Bernardo Carducci (1999) suggests five steps for making successful small talk. We'll use his template and fill in with additional suggestions:

1. *Indicate that you are open to conversation by commenting on your surroundings.* ("This line sure is slow.") Of course, you can begin with other topics, too, but you should be careful about your opening line. Because cute lines often backfire ("Hi, I'm easy—are you?"), your best bet is probably the conventional approach.

Learn More Online

Tools for Communication: A Model of Effective Communication

Communicating effectively is essential to success in most aspects of life, including relationships and work. This online manual provides helpful advice on key issues related to effective communication. It is one of many online manuals on coping with various life stresses at JamesJMessina.org, a site maintained by James J. Messina and Constance M. Messina.

2. *Introduce yourself.* You don't have to be an extravert to behave like one in an unfamiliar situation. If no one is saying anything, why not make the first move by extending your hand, looking the person in the eye, and introducing yourself? Do this early in the conversation and use specifics to give the other person information to help find common ground ("I'm Adam Weaver. I'm a psychology major at the university").

3. *Select a topic others can relate to.* Keep an eye out for similarities and differences between you and your conversational partner. Look for things you have in common—a tattoo, a class, a hometown—and build a conversation around that ("I heard a great band last night"). Alternatively, work off your differences ("How did you get interested in science fiction? I'm a mystery fan myself").

4. *Keep the conversational ball rolling.* You can keep things going by elaborating on your initial topic ("After the band finished, a bunch of us walked to the new coffeehouse and tried their death-by-chocolate dessert special"). Alternatively, you can introduce a related topic or start a new one.

5. *Make a smooth exit.* Politely end the conversation ("Well, I've got to run. I enjoyed talking with you"). When you see the person again, be sure to give a friendly smile and a wave. You need not become friends in order to be friendly.

After you've learned a little about another person, you may want to move the relationship to a deeper level. This is where self-disclosure comes into play, the topic we address next.

Self-Disclosure

Self-disclosure **is the act of sharing information about yourself with another person.** In other words, self-disclosure involves opening up about yourself to others. The information you share doesn't have to be a deep, dark secret, but it may be. Conversations with strangers and acquaintances typically start with superficial self-disclosure—your opinion of the TV show you saw last night or your views on who will win the World Series. Typically, only when people have come to like and trust each other do they begin to share private information—such as self-consciousness about one's weight, worries about one's health (Park, Bharadwaj, & Blank, 2011), or jealousy of one's brother (Greene, Derlega, & Mathews, 2006). **Figure 8.13** illustrates how self-disclosure varies according to type of relationship.

In discussing self-disclosure, we focus on verbal communication—how disclosers and recipients decide to share information with each other (Ignatius & Kokkonen, 2007). But keep in mind that *non*verbal communication plays an equally important role in self-disclosure (Laurenceau & Kleinman, 2006). For example, you have already seen how nonverbal cues can support or completely change the

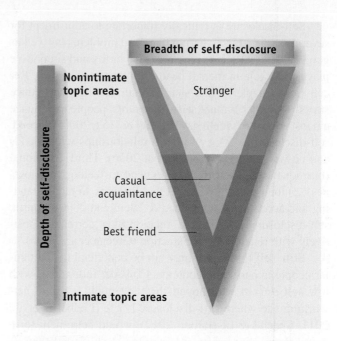

Figure 8.13

Breadth and depth of self-disclosure. Breadth of self-disclosure refers to how many topics one opens up about; depth refers to how far one goes in revealing private information. Both the breadth and depth of one's disclosures are greater with best friends as opposed to casual acquaintances or strangers. (Adapted from Altman & Taylor, 1973)

meaning of the words they accompany. Also, nonverbal behaviors can determine whether interactions have positive, neutral, or negative outcomes. Thus, if you tell a friend about a distressing experience and she signals her concern via sympathtic nonverbal cues (eye contact, leaning forward, intent facial expression), your feelings about the interaction will be positive. But if she conveys a lack of interest (looks around the room, has bored facial expression), you will walk away with negative feelings.

"I'm sorry. I was so busy listening to myself talk that I forgot what I was saying."

Self-disclosure is critically important to adjustment for several reasons. First, sharing fears and problems (as well as good news) with others who are trustworthy and supportive plays a key role in mental health (Greene et al., 2006). Recall from Chapter 4 that sharing your feelings can reduce stress. And after mutual self-disclosures, people experience a boost in positive feelings (Vittengl & Holt, 2000). Second, self-disclosure is a way to build relationships with friends and co-workers (Tardy & Dindia, 2006). Third, emotional (but not factual) self-disclosures lead to feelings of closeness, as long as disclosers feel that listeners are understanding and accepting (Laurenceau & Kleinman 2006). Fourth, self-disclosure in romantic relationships correlates positively with relationship satisfaction (Greene et al., 2006).

Still, self-disclosure may not be beneficial for particular people in particular contexts. Consider individuals with low self-esteem who hoped that Facebook, a social networking site where self-disclosure is rife (Ledbetter et al., 2011; Special & Li-Barber, 2012), would help them form social connections with others. One study found that although these people found Facebook to be a low-threat way to engage in self-disclosure, the content of their online disclosures, which were either too low in positivity or too high in negativity, led to undesired reactions from their online "friends" (Forest & Wood, 2012). Other research confirms that recognition of others' low self-esteem hinders positive self-disclosure because the respondent fears the exchange will go poorly, but not because they are worried about hurting others' feelings (MacGregor & Holmes, 2011). Interestingly, too, people don't actually disclose more online as compared to face-to-face meetings (Nguyen, Bin, & Campbell, 2012).

Self-Disclosure: What People Tell and Don't Tell Others About Themselves

What sorts of information do people share about themselves with others? What do they hold back? One common thing all people do is recount stories about themselves. The emotional content of these narrative experiences may determine what they share and what they keep to themselves. Three studies on self-disclosure and narrative identity found some intriguing results (Pasupathi, McLean, & Weeks, 2009). While individuals may disclose some emotional events, they are less likely to do so if the events are social transgressions. For example, consider a common indiscretion such as shoplifting. A first-year college student who once acted on a youthful dare may be ashamed to tell her new roommate and potential friend about the experience. In addition, when an event is memorable (such as the death of a beloved grandparent in a hospice), even if the emotion surrounding the event is negative, disclosure is likely to occur. But when an event is important but distant in time (such as a parental divorce during one's childhood), more negative feelings and less positive emotions regarding it predict a decreased likelihood of disclosure.

Self-Disclosure and Relationship Development

Earlier, we noted that self-disclosure leads to feelings of intimacy. Actually, the process is a little more complicated than that. Research suggests that only certain types of disclosures lead to feelings of closeness (Laurenceau, Barrett, & Rovine, 2005). For instance, emotional-evaluative self-disclosures (how you feel about your sister, for instance) do, but factual-descriptive self-disclosures (that you have three siblings, for example) do not. Moreover, for intimacy to develop in a relationship, a discloser must feel understood and cared for (Lin & Huang, 2006; Reis & Patrick, 1996). In other words, self-disclosure alone doesn't lead to intimacy—how listeners respond matters, too (Maisel, Gable, & Strachman, 2008). Interestingly, people seem to feel strongly that their expressions of values and what they care about reveal a great deal about themselves. However, such self-disclosure is not necessarily viewed as revealing by observers (Pronin, Fleming, & Steffel, 2008).

Self-disclosure varies over the course of relationships. At the beginning of a relationship, high levels of mutual disclosure prevail (Taylor & Altman, 1987). Once a relationship is well established, the level of disclosure tapers off, although responsiveness remains high (Reis & Patrick, 1996). Also, in established relationships people are less likely to reciprocate disclosures in the same conversation. Thus, when a lover or a good friend reveals private information, you frequently respond with words of sympathy and understanding rather than a similar disclosure. This movement away from equal exchanges of self-disclosure appears to be based on twin needs that emerge as intimate relationships develop: (1) the need for connection (via openness) and (2) the need for autonomy (via privacy) (Planalp, Fitness, & Fehr, 2006). By reciprocating support (versus information), individuals can strengthen relationships while maintaining a sense of privacy. In fact, successfully balancing these contradictory needs seems to be an important factor in relationship satisfaction (Finkenauer & Hazam, 2000).

When relationships are in distress, self-disclosure patterns change. For example, one or both individuals may decrease the breadth and depth of their self-disclosures, indicating that they are emotionally withdrawing (Baxter, 1988). Sometimes people's personalities influence the quality and consequences of self-disclosure in their intimate relationships. Besides engaging in less self-disclosure, for example, people who suffer from social phobia—anxiety when interacting with others—often report less intimacy, emotional expression, and satisfaction in their romantic relationships (Sparrevohn & Rapee, 2009).

Culture, Gender, and Self-Disclosure

Americans generally assume that personal sharing is essential to close friendships and happy romantic partnerships. This view is consistent with an individualistic culture that emphasizes the expression of each person's unique feelings and experiences. In collectivist cultures such as China and Japan, people are open about their group memberships and status because these factors guide social interactions; however, sharing personal information is reserved for established relationships (Samovar et al., 2007). One explanation for higher levels of self-disclosure in individualistic cultures is relational mobility—the idea that individuals have opportunities to create and terminate social relationships with regularity or when necessary (Schug, Yuki, & Maddux, 2010). Cultures that are high in relational mobility, like the United States, produce strong incentives for self-disclosure as a way to demonstrate social commitment. Someone forming a business relationship with another person may engage in a high-level self-disclosure in order to "seal the deal," only to later dissolve the relationship when another client with bigger sales potential appears.

What about gender? In the United States, it has been found that females tend to be more openly self-disclosing than males, although the disparity seems smaller than once believed (Fehr, 2004). This gender difference is strongest in *same-gender* friendships, with female friends sharing more personal information than male friends (Wright, 2006). In *other-gender* relationships, self-disclosure is more equal, although men with traditional gender-role attitudes are less likely to self-disclose, because they view sharing personal information as a sign of weakness. Also, women share more personal information and feelings, whereas men share more nonpersonal information, both in conversations and in email messages (Kilmartin, 2007).

What about the disclosure styles of men and women in more intimate relationships? One theory argues that such intimate interactions are best fostered by a combination of self-disclosure and empathic responding—that is, being a compassionate listener and supportive partner (Reis & Shaver, 1988). Men and women appear to differ in the emphasis placed on these two behaviors. A recent study found that men's degree of disclosure and empathic responding predicted their own feelings of closeness and confidence in the relationship. Women's feelings of intimacy, however, were more likely to be based on their male partner's degree of disclosure and empathic responding (Mitchell et al., 2008).

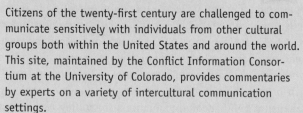

Gender disparities in self-disclosure are attributed to socialization. In American culture, most men are taught to conceal tender emotions and feelings of vulnerability, especially from other men (Kilmartin, 2007). But different gender patterns are found in other countries (Reis & Wheeler, 1991). For example, in Jordan and Japan, where early intimacy between male and female friends is discouraged, close contact between same-gender friends is encouraged. Japanese college students have also been found to score lower on self-disclosure measures that their American counterparts (Kito, 2005).

And, in the early stages of other-gender relationships, American men often disclose more than women (Derlega et al., 1985). This finding is consistent with the traditional expectations that males should initiate relationships and females should encourage males to talk. Thus, it is an oversimplification to say that American women are always more open than men.

Effective Listening

Listening and hearing are two distinct processes that are often confused. *Hearing* is a physiological process that occurs when sound waves come into contact with our eardrums. In contrast, **listening is a mindful activity and complex process that requires one to select and organize information, interpret and respond to communications, and recall what one has heard.** Listening well is an active skill, one that even has devoted following (visit the website of the International Listening Association).

Effective listening is a vastly underappreciated skill. There's a lot of truth in the old saying, "We have two ears and only one mouth, so we should listen more than we speak." Because listeners process speech much more rapidly than people speak (between 500 and 1000 words per minute versus 125–175 words per minute), it's easy for them to become bored, distracted, and inattentive (Hanna, Suggett, & Radtke, 2008). Fatigue and preoccupation with one's own thoughts are other factors that interfere with effective listening.

Ting Hoo/Riser/Getty Images

To be a good listener, you need to keep four points in mind. First, *signal your interest in the speaker by using nonverbal cues.* Face the speaker squarely and lean toward him or her (rather than slouching or leaning back in a chair). This posture shows that you are interested in what the other person has to say. Communicate your feelings about what the speaker is saying by nodding your head or raising your eyebrows.

Second, *hear the other person out before responding.* Listeners often tune out or interrupt a conversational partner when (1) they know someone well (because they believe that they already know what the speaker will say), (2) a speaker has mannerisms listeners find frustrating (stuttering, mumbling, speaking in a monotone), and (3) a speaker discusses ideas (abortion, politics) that generate strong feelings or uses terms (*welfare cheat, redneck*) that push "hot buttons." Although it is challenging not to tune out a speaker or lob an insult in these situations, you'll be better able to formulate an appropriate response if you allow the speaker to complete his or her thought.

Third, *engage in active listening* (Verderber et al., 2008). Pay attention to what the speaker is saying and mindfully process the information. Active listening also involves the skills of clarifying and paraphrasing. Inevitably, a speaker will skip over an essential point or say something that is confusing. When this happens, you need to ask for clarification. "Was Bill her boyfriend or her brother?" Clarifying ensures that you have an accurate picture of the message and also tells the speaker that you are interested. Paraphrasing takes clarifying another step. To paraphrase means to state concisely what you believe the speaker said. You might say, "Let me see if I've got this right . . ." or "Do you mean . . . ?" It's obviously silly to paraphrase every single thing the speaker says; you need to paraphrase only when the speaker says something important. Paraphrasing has a number of benefits: It reassures the speaker that you are "with" him or her, it derails misinterpretations, and it keeps you focused on the conversation.

"Of course I'm listening. I'm in a heightened state of alert."

Paraphrasing can take several forms (Verderber et al., 2008). In *content paraphrasing,* you focus on the literal meaning of the message. In *feelings paraphrasing,* you focus on the emotions connected to the content of the message. If your friend declares, "I just can't believe he showed up at the party with his old girlfriend!" a feelings paraphrase is obviously in order ("You were really hurt by that").

Finally, *pay attention to the other person's nonverbal signals.* Listeners use a speaker's words to get the "objective" meaning of a message, but they rely on nonverbal cues for the emotional and interpersonal meanings of a message. Your knowledge of body language, tone of voice, and other nonverbal cues can give you deeper understanding of what others are communicating (Akhtar, 2007). Remember that these cues are available not only when the other person is speaking but also when you are talking. If you often get signals that your listener is drifting away, you might be going overboard on irrelevant details or, perhaps, hogging the conversation. The antidote is active listening.

COMMUNICATION PROBLEMS

LEARNING OBJECTIVES

- Discuss some common responses to communication apprehension.
- Identify four barriers to effective communication.

In this section, we focus on two problems that can interfere with effective communication: anxiety and communication barriers.

Communication Apprehension

It's the first day of your child psychology class and you have just learned that 30-minute oral presentations are a course requirement. Do you welcome this requirement as an opportunity to polish your public speaking skills or, panic-stricken, do you race to the nearest computer station to drop the class? If you opted for the latter, you may suffer from *communication apprehension,* **or anxiety caused by having to talk with others.** Some people experience communication apprehension in all speaking situations (including one-on-one encounters), but most people who have the problem notice it only when they have to speak before groups.

Communication apprehension is a concern for students as well as teachers because it can adversely affect general academic success as well as performance related to public speaking requirements in the classroom (Bourhis, Allen, & Bauman, 2006). One study found that when it is treated as a personality variable, individuals with higher levels of communication apprehension were found to have lower critical thinking skills as well as less-developed oral communication skills (Blume, Dreher, & Baldwin, 2010). Other research suggests that communication apprehension can disrupt skills needed for effective career planning (Meyer-Griffith, Reardon, & Hartley, 2009). Interestingly, greater confidence in one's communication skills is positively associated with better listening skills. However, more-confident people apparently have a more difficult time extracting emotional content from communications than those who are less certain of themselves (Clark, 1989). The explanation may be that less-certain individuals review emotional communications with greater care.

Culture, too, can influence whether one is anxious when communicating with others. Students from universities in Japan and American universities completed McCroskey's (1982) self-report measure of communication apprehension. Japanese students were found to have significantly higher levels of communication apprehension compared to their American counterparts (Pryor, Butler, & Boehringer, 2005).

Bodily experiences associated with communication apprehension can range from "butterflies" in the stomach to cold hands, dry mouth, and a racing heart rate. There is some evidence linking communication apprehension with irrtable bowel syndrome, as well (Bevan, 2009). These

physiological effects are stress-induced "fight or flight" responses of the autonomic nervous system (see Chapter 3). The physiological responses themselves aren't the root of communication apprehension; rather, the problem lies in the speaker's *interpretation* of these bodily responses. That is, high scorers on measures of communication apprehension frequently interpret these bodily changes as indications of fear. In contrast, low scorers often chalk up these reactions to the normal excitement in such a situation (Richmond & McCroskey, 1995).

Researchers have identified four responses to communication apprehension (Richmond & McCroskey, 1995). The most common is *avoidance,* or choosing not to participate when confronted with a voluntary communication opportunity. If people believe that speaking will make them uncomfortable, they will typically avoid the experience. *Withdrawal* occurs when people unexpectedly find themselves trapped in a communication situation they can't escape. Here they may clam up entirely or say as little as possible. *Disruption* refers to the inability to make fluent oral presentations or to engage in appropriate verbal or nonverbal behavior. Of course, inadequate communication skills can produce this same behavioral effect, and it isn't always possible for the average person to identify the actual cause of the problem. *Overcommunication* is a relatively unusual response to high communication apprehension, but it does occur. An example would be someone who attempts to dominate social situations by talking nonstop. Although such individuals are seen as poor communicators, they are not usually perceived as having communication apprehension. That's because we expect to see this problem only in those who talk very little. Of course, overcommunication may be caused by other factors as well.

Obviously, avoidance and withdrawal tactics are merely short-term strategies for coping with communication apprehension (Richmond & McCroskey, 1995). Because it is unlikely that you can go through life without having to speak in front of a group, it is important to learn to cope with this stressful event rather than avoid it time and again. Allowing the problem to get out of hand can result in self-limiting behavior, such as refusing a job promotion that entails public speaking. People with high communication

Jupiterimages/Comstock Images/Getty Images

apprehension are likely to have difficulties in relationships, at work, and at school (Richmond & McCroskey, 1995).

Happily, there are effective ways to reduce speech anxiety. With the technique of visualization, for example, you picture yourself successfully going through all of the steps involved in preparing for and making a presentation. Research shows that people who practice visualization have less anxiety and fewer negative thoughts when they actually speak compared to previsualization levels (Ayres, Hopf, & Ayres, 1994). Other research demonstrates that repeatedly practicing a presentation while being digitally videoed can help some people with communication apprehension (Leeds & Maurer, 2009). In particularly acute cases of communication apprehension, substituting a recorded talk may be preferable to a live presentation (Leeds & Maurer, 2009). Both *positive reinterpretation* (see Chapter 4) and *systematic desensitization* (Chapter 15) are highly effective methods for dealing with this problem as well.

Barriers to Effective Communication

Earlier in the chapter, we discussed noise and its disruptive effects on interpersonal communication. Now we want to check out some psychological factors that contribute to noise. These barriers to effective communication can reside in the sender, in the receiver, or sometimes in both. Common obstacles include defensiveness, ambushing, motivational distortion, and self-preoccupation.

Defensiveness

Perhaps the most basic barrier to effective communication is *defensiveness*—**an excessive concern with protecting oneself from being hurt.** People usually react defensively when they feel threatened, such as when they believe that others are evaluating them or trying to control or manipulate them (Trevithick & Wengraf, 2011). Defensiveness is also triggered when others act in a superior manner. Thus, those who flaunt their status, wealth, brilliance, or power often put receivers on the defensive. Dogmatic people who project "I'm always right" also breed defensiveness.

A threat need not be real to elicit defensive behavior. If you persuade yourself that Brandon won't like you, your interactions with him will probably not be very positive. And, if a self-fulfilling prophecy kicks in, you may produce the negative reaction you fear. Strive to cultivate a communication style that minimizes defensiveness in others. On the other hand, if you think about the importance of maintaining your own integrity when feeling threatened, you may be able to reduce or eliminate your own defensiveness (Critcher, Dunning, & Armor, 2010). At the same time, keep in mind that you don't have complete control over others' perceptions and reactions.

Ambushing

Some listeners are really just looking for the opportunity to attack a presenter. Although the person who is about to attack—we might label such people verbal "bushwhackers"—is really listening carefully and intently to what is being said, his or her purpose in doing so is simply to assail or harass the speaker (Wood, 2010). Understanding, discussing, or having an otherwise thoughtful exchange of ideas and opinions is not the point. People who engage in ambushing almost always arouse defensiveness from others, especially those whom they attack. Sadly, ambushing can be an effective barrier to communication because few people relish being hassled or bullied in front of others.

Motivational Distortion

In Chapter 7, we discussed distortions and expectancies in person perception. These same processes operate in communication. That is, motivational distortion occurs when people hear what they want to hear instead of what is actually being said. Each person has a unique frame of reference—certain attitudes, values, and expectations—that can influence what he or she hears. Information that contradicts an individual's own views often produces emotional distress. One way people avoid such unpleasant feelings is to engage in *selective attention,* or actively choosing to attend to information that supports their beliefs and ignoring information that contradicts them (Stevens & Bavelier, 2012). Similarly, an individual may read unintended meanings into statements or jump to erroneous conclusions. This tendency to distort information occurs most often when people are discussing issues they feel strongly about, such as politics, racism, sexism, homosexuality, or abortion.

Self-Preoccupation

Who hasn't experienced the frustration of trying to communicate with someone who is so self-focused that two-way conversation is impossible? Self-preoccupied people are engaging in what is called *pseudolistening,* or pretending to listen while their minds are occupied with other topics that have captured their attention (O'Keefe, 2002). These annoying, self-centered individuals seem to talk to hear themselves speak. If you try to slip in a word about *your* problems, they cut you off by proclaiming, "That's nothing. Listen to what happened to me!" Further, self-preoccupied people are poor listeners. When someone else is talking, they're mentally rehearsing their next comments. Because they are self-focused, these individuals are usually oblivious to their negative impact on others.

INTERPERSONAL CONFLICT

LEARNING OBJECTIVES

- Assess the pros and cons of avoiding versus facing conflict.
- Describe five types of conflict and five personal styles for dealing with them.
- Articulate six tips for coping effectively with interpersonal conflict.

People do not have to be enemies to be in conflict, and being in conflict does not make people enemies. *Interpersonal conflict exists whenever two or more people disagree.* By this definition, conflict occurs between friends and lovers as well as between competitors and enemies. Interpersonal conflict is present anytime people have disparate views, opposing perspectives, incompatible goals, emotional reactions, and a desire to try to address and resolve their differences (Ruz & Tudela, 2011; Wilmot & Hocker, 2006). The discord may be caused by a simple misunderstanding, or it may be a product of incompatible goals, values, attitudes, or beliefs. Because conflict is an unavoidable aspect of interactions, knowing how to deal constructively with it is essential. Many studies report associations between effective conflict management and relationship satisfaction (Kline et al., 2006).

Beliefs About Conflict

How do you respond when a conflict arises between yourself and another person? Why do you react that way? Your approach to or avoidance of conflict may be rooted in how conflict was dealt with in your family (Ben-Ari & Hirshberg, 2009; Larkin, Frazer, & Wheat, 2011; Mikulincer & Shaver, 2011).

Many people assume that any kind of conflict is bad and that it should be suppressed if at all possible. In reality, conflict is neither inherently bad nor inherently good. It is a natural phenomenon that may lead to either good or bad outcomes, depending on how people deal with it. When people see conflict as negative, they tend to avoid dealing with it. Of course, sometimes avoiding conflict can be good. If a relationship or an issue is of little importance to you, or if you believe that the costs of confrontation are too high (your boss might fire you), avoidance might be the best way to handle a conflict. Also, cultures differ in how conflict should be handled. Collectivist cultures (such as China and Japan) often avoid conflict, whereas individualistic cultures tend to encourage direct confrontations (Samovar et al., 2007; Zhang, Harwood, & Hummert, 2005). In individualistic cultures, the consequences of avoiding conflict depend on the nature of the relationship. When relationships and issues are important, avoiding conflict is generally counterproductive. For one thing, it can lead to a self-perpetuating cycle (see **Figure 8.14**). Of course, individuals who are exposed to both types of cultures (Korean Americans, for example) are apt to display a combination of approaches to resolving conflicts (Kim-Jo, Benet-Martínez, & Ozer, 2010).

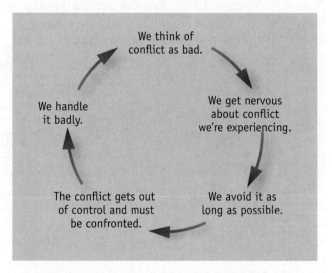

Figure 8.14

The conflict avoidance cycle. Avoiding conflict can lead to a self-perpetuating cycle: (1) People think of conflict as bad, (2) they get nervous about a conflict they are experiencing, (3) they avoid the conflict as long as possible, (4) the conflict gets out of control and must be confronted, and (5) they handle the confrontation badly. In turn, this negative experience sets the stage for avoiding conflict the next time—usually with the same negative outcome. (Adapted from Lulofs, 1994)

Radius Images/Alamy

Disagreements are a fact of everyday life, so effective communicators need to learn how to deal with them constructively.

Let's consider an example of a cultural difference: a comparison of Japanese and American styles of negotiation, a situation where conflict may arise (McDaniel & Quasha, 2000). Japanese values urge those involved in negotiations to seek ways to avoid conflict. In contrast, American values encourage a bit of competition as well as assertiveness (see **Figure 8.15**). As you review the figure's content, imagine you were involved in delicate negotiations regarding some business transaction: Which cultural style for dealing with conflict would you prefer?

When dealt with openly and constructively, interpersonal conflict can lead to a variety of valuable outcomes (Clark & Grote, 2003). Among other things, constructive confrontation may (1) bring problems out into the open where they can be solved, (2) put an end to chronic sources of discontent in a relationship, and (3) lead to new insights through the airing of divergent views.

Styles of Managing Conflict

How do you react to conflict? Some approaches are more constructive than others (Deutsch, 2011). Most people have a habitual way or personal style of dealing with dissension. Studies have consistently revealed five distinct patterns of dealing with conflict: avoiding/withdrawing, accommodating, competing/forcing, compromising, and collaborating (Lulofs & Cahn, 2000). Two dimensions underlie these different styles: interest in satisfying one's own concerns and interest in satisfying others' concerns (Rahim & Magner, 1995). You can see the location of these five styles on the two dimensions in **Figure 8.16**. As you read about these styles, try to determine where you fit.

● *Avoiding/withdrawing* (low concern for self and others). Some people simply find conflict extremely distasteful. When a conflict emerges, the avoider will change the subject, deflect discussion with humor, make a hasty exit, or pretend to be preoccupied with something else. Usually, people who prefer this style hope that ignoring a problem will make it go away. Yet some researchers argue this style is actually very goal directed and not at all a passive response to conflict (Wang, Fink, & Cai, 2012). For minor problems, this tactic is often a good one—there's no need to react to every little annoyance.

For bigger conflicts, avoiding/withdrawing is not a good strategy; it usually just delays the inevitable clash.

● *Accommodating* (low concern for self, high concern for others). Like the avoider, the accommodator feels uncomfortable with conflict. However, instead of ignoring the disagreement, this person brings the conflict to a quick end by giving in easily. People who are overly concerned about acceptance and approval from others commonly use this strategy of surrender. Habitual accommodating is a poor way of dealing with conflict because it does not generate creative thinking and effective solutions. Moreover, feelings of resentment (on both sides) may develop because the accommodator often likes to play the role of a martyr. Of course, when you don't have strong preferences (for instance, where to eat out), occasional accommodating is perfectly appropriate.

● *Competing/forcing* (high concern for self, low concern for others). The competitor turns every conflict into a black-and-white, win-or-lose situation. Competitors will do virtually anything to emerge victorious from confrontations; thus, they can be deceitful and aggressive—including using verbal attacks and physical threats. They rigidly adhere to one position and will use threats and coercion to force the other party to submit. This style is undesirable because, like accommodation, it fails to generate creative solutions to problems. Moreover, this approach is especially likely to lead to postconflict tension, resentment, and hostility.

● *Compromising* (moderate concern for self and others). Compromising is a pragmatic approach to conflict that acknowledges the divergent needs of both parties.

| JAPANESE AND AMERICAN STYLES OF NEGOTIATION ||
American style	**Japanese style**
Overstate your initial position to establish a strong image.	Understate your initial position or state it vaguely to allow the other side to state their position.
Keep your bottom line secret from the other person to preserve your power and gain the most.	Find informal ways to let the other person know your bottom line to move agreement forward without directly confronting the other with your bottom line.
Where there are differences, assert your position and attempt to win the other's assent.	Look for areas of agreement and focus talk on them.
Be adversarial.	Avoid confrontation or explicit disagreement.
Work to win all you can.	Work to make sure that neither you nor the other person fails.
Push to reach decisions as rapidly as possible.	Plan to spend a long time discussing issues before even moving toward a decision.

Figure 8.15

Navigating conflict by negotiation through cultural values. Different cultures have different ways of navigating conflicts and reaching agreements. Visitors to other cultures, particularly those from the business world, risk ruining deals or possible partnerships if they fail to interpret their colleagues correctly. Here are some examples of how Japanese and Americans differ in their typical style of negotiation.

Source: Adapted from Wood, J. T. (2010). *Interpersonal communication: Everyday encounters* (6th ed.). Boston, MA: Wadsworth (p. 232), based on McDaniel & Quasha (2000) and Weiss (1987).

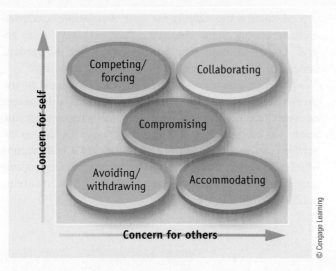

Figure 8.16
Five styles of handling interpersonal conflict. In dealing with discord, individuals typically prefer one of five styles. The two dimensions of *concern for self* and *concern for others* underlie each of the five styles.

Compromisers are willing to negotiate and to meet the other person halfway. With this approach, each person gives up something so both can have partial satisfaction. Because both parties gain some satisfaction, compromising is a fairly constructive approach to conflict, especially when the issue is moderately important.

- *Collaborating* (high concern for self and others). Whereas compromising simply entails "splitting the difference" between positions, collaborating involves a sincere effort to find a solution that will optimally satisfy both parties. In this approach, conflict is viewed as a mutual problem to be solved as effectively as possible. Collaborating thus encourages openness and honesty. It also stresses the importance of criticizing the other person's *ideas* in a disagreement rather than the other *person*. To collaborate, you have to work on clarifying differences and similarities in positions so that you can build on the similarities. Generally, this is the most productive approach for dealing with conflict. Instead of resulting in a postconflict residue of tension and resentment, collaborating tends to produce a climate of trust.

Dealing Constructively with Conflict

As you have seen, the most effective approach to conflict management is collaborating. To help you implement such an approach, we will offer some specific suggestions. But, before we get down to specifics, there are a few principles to keep in mind (Alberti & Emmons, 2001; Verderber et al., 2007). First, in a conflict situation, try to give the other person the benefit of the doubt; don't automatically assume that those who disagree with you are ignorant or mean-spirited. Show respect for their position, and do your best to empathize with, and fully understand, their frame of reference. Second, approach the other person as an

equal. If you have a higher status or more power (parent, supervisor), try to set this difference aside. Third, define the conflict as a mutual problem to be solved cooperatively, rather than as a win-lose proposition. Fourth, choose a mutually acceptable time to sit down and work on resolving the conflict. It is not always best to tackle the conflict when and where it first arises. Finally, communicate your flexibility and willingness to modify your position.

Here are some explicit guidelines for dealing effectively with interpersonal conflict (Alberti & Emmons, 2001; De Dreu et al., 2006; Verderber et al., 2007):

- *Make communication honest and open.* Don't withhold information or misrepresent your position. Avoid deceit and manipulation. Try being agreeable (Barry & Friedman, 1998).
- *Exhibit trust.* Being trustworthy and dependable can lead to smooth and successful negotiations (De Dreu et al., 2006).
- *Use specific behaviors to describe another person's annoying habits rather than general statements about their personality.* You'll probably get further with your roommate if you say something like, "Please throw your clothes in the hamper" rather than "You're such an inconsiderate slob." Remarks about specific actions are less threatening and are less likely to be taken personally. They also clarify what you hope will change.
- *Avoid "loaded" words.* Certain words are "loaded" in the sense that they tend to trigger negative emotional reactions in listeners. For example, you can discuss politics without using terms such as "right-winger" and "knee-jerk liberal."
- *Try using grace.* The word "grace" refers to honoring the needs of others by putting aside one's own desires (Wood, 2010). Graceful acts occur when one person shows kindness that is likely never to be repaid; indeed, the person doesn't expect to receive any compensation in return. Perhaps you and your roommate agreed to split chores. She fails to live up to her part of the agreement one week, presumably because she has an inordinate amount of schoolwork to do. Instead of instigating a conflict, you do her chores and say nothing about it. Your gracious act helps her and at the same time avoids creating a conflict; in a sense, you are helping yourself as well.
- *Use a positive approach and help the other person save face.* Saying "I love it when we cook dinner together" will go

Learn More Online

The Conflict Resolution Information Source

This excellent resource on conflict management is provided by the University of Colorado's Conflict Information Consortium. The site is actually a gateway to a huge variety of resources on conflict management and is easy to navigate.

over better than "You never help with dinner, and I resent it." Similarly, you can increase your chances of having a request accepted if you say, "I realize that you are very busy, but I'd really appreciate it if you would look at my paper again. I've marked the places I'd like you to reconsider."

• *Limit complaints to recent behavior and to the current situation.* Dredging up past grievances only rekindles old resentments and distracts you from the current problem. And avoid saying things like "You *always* say you're too busy" or "You *never* do your fair share of the housework." Such categorical statements are bound to put the other person on the defensive.

• *Assume responsibility for your own feelings and preferences.* Rather than "*You* make me mad," say "*I* am angry." Or, try "I'd appreciate it if you'd water the garden" instead of "Do you think the garden needs watering?"

• *Use an assertive (as opposed to submissive or aggressive) communication style.* This approach will make it easier to head off and deal constructively with conflict situations. In the upcoming Application, we elaborate on *assertive communication* and its usefulness in a wide variety of interpersonal communication situations, such as making acquaintances, developing relationships, and resolving conflicts.

Application

DEVELOPING AN ASSERTIVE COMMUNICATION STYLE

LEARNING OBJECTIVES

• Distinguish among assertive, submissive, and aggressive communications.
• List five steps that lead to more assertive communication.

Answer the following questions "yes" or "no."

___ **1.** When someone asks you for an unreasonable favor, is it difficult to say no?

___ **2.** Do you feel timid about returning flawed merchandise?

___ **3.** Do you have a hard time requesting even small favors from others?

___ **4.** When a group is hotly debating an issue, are you shy about speaking up?

___ **5.** When a salesperson pressures you to buy something you don't want, is it hard for you to resist?

If you answered "yes" to several of these questions, you may need to increase your assertiveness. Many people have a hard time being assertive; however, this problem is more common among females because they are socialized to be more submissive than males—to "be nice." Consequently, assertiveness training is especially popular among women. Men, too, find assertiveness training helpful, both because some have been socialized to be passive and because others want to learn to be less aggressive and more assertive. In this Application we elaborate on the differences among assertive, submissive, and aggressive behavior and discuss some procedures for increasing assertiveness, which can build self-esteem (Sazant, 2010).

One last point: Generally, people tend to associate assertiveness with direct person-to-person social interactions. Don't forget, however, that assertiveness is also important in indirect exchanges as well. Learning to be assertive in email or text messages or on social networking sites is also important (Alberti & Emmons, 2008).

The Nature of Assertiveness

Assertiveness **involves acting in one's own best interests by expressing one's thoughts and feelings directly and honestly.** Essentially, assertiveness involves standing up for your rights when someone else is about to infringe on them. To be assertive is to speak out rather than pull your punches.

The nature of assertive communication can best be clarified by contrasting it with other types of communication. *Submissive communication* is deferential, as it involves giving in to others on points of possible contention. Submissive people often let others take advantage of them. Typically, their biggest problem is that they cannot say no to unreasonable requests. A common example is the college student who can't tell her roommate not to borrow her clothes. Submissive people also have difficulty voicing disagreement with others and making requests themselves. In traditional trait terminology, they are timid.

Although the roots of submissiveness have not been investigated fully, they appear to lie in excessive concern about gaining the social approval of others. However, the strategy of "not making waves" is more likely to garner others' contempt than their approval. Moreover, individuals who use this style often feel bad about themselves (for being "pushovers") and resentful of those they allow to take advantage of them. These feelings often lead the submissive individual to try to punish the other person by withdrawing, sulking, or crying (Bower & Bower, 1991, 2004). These manipulative attempts to get one's own way are sometimes referred to as "passive aggression" or "indirect aggression" (Hopwood & Wright, 2012).

At the other end of the spectrum, *aggressive communication* focuses on saying and getting what one wants at the expense of others' feelings and rights. With assertive behavior, however, one strives to respect others' rights and defend one's own. The problem in real life is that assertive and aggressive behaviors *may* overlap. When someone is about to infringe on their rights, people often lash out at the other party (aggression) while defending their rights (assertion). The challenge, then, is to be firm and assertive without becoming aggressive. Advocates of assertive communication argue that it is much more adaptive than either submission or aggression (Alberti & Emmons, 2001; Bower & Bower, 1991, 2004). They maintain that submissive behavior leads to poor self-esteem, self-denial, emotional suppression, and strained interpersonal relationships. Conversely, aggressive communication tends to promote guilt, alienation, and disharmony. In contrast, assertive behavior is said to foster high self-esteem, satisfactory interpersonal relationships, and effective conflict management. Here are three different ways to express the same desire:

Aggressive: I want Chinese food tonight, so that is what we are going to eat. End of story.

Assertive: I feel like having Chinese food tonight—do you?

Submissive: It's okay with me if we don't have Chinese food tonight; whatever you feel like having is fine with me.

The essential point with assertiveness is that you are able to state what you want clearly and directly. Being able to do so makes you feel good about yourself and will usually make others feel good about you, too. And, although being assertive doesn't guarantee you will get what you want, it certainly enhances your chances.

Steps in Assertiveness Training

Numerous assertiveness training programs are available in book form, on CDs or DVDs, or through seminars. Most of the programs are behavioral and emphasize gradual improvement and reinforcement of appropriate behavior. Here we summarize the key steps in assertiveness training.

1. Understand What Assertive Communication Is

To produce assertive behavior, you need to understand what it looks and sounds like. Thus, most programs begin by clarifying the nature of assertive communication. Assertiveness trainers often ask clients to imagine situations calling for assertiveness and compare hypothetical submissive (or passive), assertive, and aggressive responses. Let's consider one such comparison. In this example, a woman in assertiveness training is asking her roommate to cooperate in cleaning their apartment once a week. The roommate, who is uninterested in the problem, is listening to music when the conversation begins. In this example, the roommate is playing the role of the antagonist—called a "downer" in the following scripts (excerpted from Bower & Bower, 2004, pp. 8, 9, 11).

The Passive Scene

she: Uh, I was wondering if you would be willing to take time to decide about the housecleaning.

downer: (listening to music) Not now, I'm busy.

she: Oh, okay.

The Aggressive Scene

she: Listen, I've had it with you not even talking about cleaning this damn apartment. Are you going to help me?

downer: (listening to the music) Not now, I'm busy.

she: Why can't you look at me when you turn me down? You don't give a damn about the housework or me! You only care about yourself!

downer: That's not true.

she: You never pay any attention to the apartment or to me. I have to do everything around here!

downer: Oh, shut up! You're just neurotic about cleaning all the time. Who are you, my mother? Can't I relax with my stereo for a few minutes without you pestering me? This was my apartment first, you know!

The Assertive Scene

she: I know housework isn't the most fascinating subject, but it needs to be done. Let's plan when we'll do it.

downer: (listening to music) Oh, c'mon—not now! I'm busy.

she: This won't take long. I feel that if we have a schedule, it will be easier to keep up with the chores.

downer: I'm not sure I'll have time for all of them.

she: I've already drawn up a couple of rotating schedules for housework, so that each week we have an equal division of tasks. Will you look at them? I'd like to hear your decisions about them, say, tonight after supper?

downer: (indignantly) I have to look at these now?

she: Is there some other time that's better for you?

downer: Oh, I don't know.

she: Well, then let's discuss plans after supper for 15 minutes. Is that agreed?

downer: I guess so.

she: Good! It won't take long, and I'll feel relieved when we have a schedule in place.

A helpful way to distinguish among the three types of communication is in terms of how people deal with their own rights and the rights of others. Submissive people sacrifice their own rights. Aggressive people tend to ignore the rights of others. Assertive people consider both their own rights *and* the rights of others. You'll find some additional guidelines for behaving assertively in **Figure 8.17**.

RULES FOR ASSERTIVE SCRIPTS	
Do	**Don't**
Describe	
Describe the other person's behavior objectively.	Describe your emotional reaction to it.
Use concrete terms.	Use abstract, vague terms.
Describe a specified time, place, and frequency of the action.	Generalize for "all time."
Describe the action, not the "motive."	Guess at your Downer's motives or goals.
Express	
Express your feelings.	Deny your feelings.
Express them calmly.	Unleash emotional outbursts.
State feelings in a positive manner, as relating to a goal to be achieved.	State feelings negatively, making Downer attack.
Direct yourself to the specific offending behavior, not to the whole person.	Attack the entire character of the person.
Specify	
Ask explicitly for change in your Downer's behavior.	Merely imply that you'd like a change.
Request a small change.	Ask for too large a change.
Request only one or two changes at one time.	Ask for too many changes.
Specify the concrete actions you want stopped and those you want performed.	Ask for changes in nebulous traits or qualities.
Take account of whether your Downer can meet your request without suffering large losses.	Ignore your Downer's needs or ask only for your satisfaction.
Specify (if appropriate) what behavior you are willing to change to make the agreement.	Consider that only your Downer has to change.
Consequences	
Make the consequences explicit.	Be ashamed to talk about rewards and penalties.
Give a positive reward for change in the desired direction.	Give only punishments for lack of change.
Select something that is desirable and reinforcing to your Downer.	Select something that only you might find rewarding.
Select a reward that is big enough to maintain the behavior change.	Offer a reward you can't or won't deliver.
Select a punishment of a magnitude that "fits the crime" of refusing to change behavior.	Make exaggerated threats.
Select a punishment that you are actually willing to carry out.	Use unrealistic threats or self-defeating punishment.

Figure 8.17

Guidelines for assertive behavior. Gordon and Sharon Bower (1991, 2004) outline a four-step program intended to help readers create successful assertive scripts for themselves. The four steps are (1) *describe* the unwanted behavior from another person (called your "Downer") that is troubling you, (2) *express* your feelings about the behavior to the other person, (3) *specify* the changes needed, and (4) try to provide rewarding *consequences* for the change. Using this framework, the table shown here provides some useful dos and don'ts for achieving effective assertive behavior.

Source: Adapted from Bower, S. A., & Bower, G. H. (1991). *Asserting yourself: A practical guide for positive change* (2nd ed.). Reading, MA: Addison-Wesley. Copyright © 1991 by Sharon Anthony Bower and Gordon H. Bower. Reprinted by permission of Perseus Books Publishers, a member of Perseus Books, L.L.C.

2. Monitor Your Assertive Communication

Most people's assertiveness varies from one situation to another. In other words, they may be assertive in some social contexts and timid in others. Consequently, once you understand the nature of assertive communication, you should monitor yourself and identify when you are nonassertive. In particular, you should figure out *who* intimidates you, on *what topics,* and in *which situations.*

3. Observe a Model's Assertive Communication

Once you have identified the situations in which you are nonassertive, think of someone who communicates assertively in those situations and observe that person's behavior closely. In other words, find someone to model yourself after. This is an easy way to learn how to behave assertively in situations crucial to you. Your observations should also allow you to see how rewarding assertive communication can be, which should strengthen your assertive tendencies.

4. Practice Assertive Communication

The key to achieving assertive communication is to practice it and work toward gradual improvement. Practice can take several forms. In *covert rehearsal,* you imagine a situation requiring assertion and the dialogue you would engage in. In *role playing,* you ask a friend or therapist to play the role of an antagonist, then practice communicating assertively in this artificial situation. Eventually, of course, you want to transfer your assertiveness skills to real-life situations.

5. Adopt an Assertive Attitude

Most assertiveness training programs have a behavioral orientation and focus on specific responses for specific situations (see **Figure 8.18**). However, it's obvious that real-life situations rarely match those portrayed in books. Thus, some experts maintain that acquiring a repertoire of verbal responses for certain situations is not as important as developing a new attitude that you're not going to let people push you around (or let yourself push others around, if you're the aggressive type) (Alberti & Emmons, 2001). Although most programs don't talk explicitly about attitudes, they do appear to instill a new attitude indirectly. A change in attitude is probably crucial to achieving flexible, assertive behavior.

ASSERTIVE RESPONSES TO SOME COMMON PUTDOWNS		
Nature of remark	**Put-down sentence**	**Suggested assertive reply**
Nagging about details	"Haven't you done this yet?"	"No, when did you want it done?" (Answer without hedging, and follow up with a question.)
Prying	"I know I maybe shouldn't ask, but ..."	"If I don't want to answer, I'll let you know." (Indicate that you won't make yourself uncomfortable just to please this person.)
Putting you on the spot socially	"Are you busy Tuesday?"	"What do you have in mind?" (Answer the question with a question.)
Pigeonholing you	"That's a woman for you!"	"That's one woman, not *all* women." (Disagree—assert your individuality.)
Using insulting labels for your behavior	"That's a dumb way to ..."	"I'll decide what to call my behavior." (Refuse to accept the label.)
Basing predictions on an amateur personality analysis	"You'll have a hard time. You're too shy."	"In what ways do you think I'm too shy?" (Ask for clarification of the analysis.)

Figure 8.18

Assertive responses to common put-downs. Having some assertive replies at the ready can increase your confidence in difficult social interactions.

Source: Adapted from Bower, S. A., & Bower, G. H. (1991). *Asserting yourself: A practical guide for positive change* (2nd ed.). Reading, MA: Addison-Wesley. Copyright © 1991 by Sharon Anthony Bower and Gordon H. Bower. Reprinted by permission of Perseus Books Publishers, a member of Perseus Books, L.L.C.

CHAPTER 8 | Review

KEY IDEAS

THE PROCESS OF INTERPERSONAL COMMUNICATION

- Interpersonal communication is the interactional process that occurs when one person sends a message to another. Communication takes place when a sender transmits a message to a receiver either verbally or nonverbally. The widespread use of electronic communication devices has raised new issues in interpersonal communication. Although people often take it for granted, effective communication contributes to their adjustment in school, in relationships, and at work.

NONVERBAL COMMUNICATION

- Nonverbal communication conveys emotions, above all. It tends to be more spontaneous than verbal communication, and it is more ambiguous. Sometimes it contradicts what is communicated verbally. It is often multichanneled and, like language, is culturally bound.
- The amount of personal space that people prefer depends on culture, gender, social status, and situational factors. Facial expressions can convey a great deal of information about people's emotions. Variations in eye contact can influence nonverbal communication in a host of ways.
- Body postures can hint at interest in communication, and they often reflect status differences. Touch can communicate support, consolation, intimacy, status, and power. Paralanguage refers to *how* something is said rather than *what* is said.
- Certain nonverbal cues are associated with deception, but many of these cues do not correspond to popular beliefs about how liars give themselves away. Discrepancies between facial expressions and other nonverbal signals may suggest dishonesty. The vocal and visual cues associated with lying are so subtle, however, that the detection of deception is difficult. Machines used to detect deception (polygraphs) are not particularly accurate.
- Nonverbal communication, particularly nonverbal sensitivity, plays an important role in adjustment, especially in the quality of interpersonal relationships. Women are typically more nonverbally sensitive than men because they exert more effort at it.

TOWARD MORE EFFECTIVE COMMUNICATION

- To be an effective communicator, it's important to develop good conversational skills, including knowing how to make small talk with strangers.
- Self-disclosure—opening up to others—is associated with good mental health, happiness, and satisfying relationships. The emotional content of an experience may determine whether individuals will share it with others or keep it to themselves.
- Self-disclosure can foster emotional intimacy in relationships. Emotional-evaluative self-disclosures lead to feelings of closeness, but factual-descriptive disclosures do not. The level of self-disclosure varies over the course of relationships. Cultures vary in their preferred level of self-disclosure. American women tend to disclose more than men, but this disparity is not as large as it once was. Effective listening is an essential aspect of interpersonal communication.

COMMUNICATION PROBLEMS

- A number of problems can arise that interfere with effective communication. Individuals who become overly anxious when they talk with others suffer from communication apprehension. This difficulty can cause problems in relationships and in work and educational settings. Sometimes communication can produce negative interpersonal outcomes. Barriers to effective communication include defensiveness, ambushing, motivational distortion, and self-preoccupation.

INTERPERSONAL CONFLICT

- Dealing constructively with interpersonal conflict is an important aspect of effective communication. Individualistic cultures tend to encourage direct confrontations, whereas collectivist cultures often avoid them. Nonetheless, many Americans have negative attitudes about conflict.
- In dealing with conflict, most people have a preferred style: avoiding/withdrawing, accommodating, competing, compromising, or collaborating. This last style is the most effective in managing conflict.

APPLICATION: DEVELOPING AN ASSERTIVE COMMUNICATION STYLE

- Assertiveness enables individuals to stand up for themselves while respecting the rights of others. To become more assertive, individuals need to understand what assertive communication is, monitor their assertive communication, observe a model's assertive communication, practice being assertive, and adopt an assertive attitude.

KEY TERMS

Assertiveness p. 256
Channel p. 232
Communication apprehension p. 250
Context p. 232
Defensiveness p. 252
Display rules p. 239
Electronically mediated communication p. 233
Interpersonal communication p. 231
Interpersonal conflict p. 253
Kinesics p. 240
Listening p. 249
Message p. 232
Noise p. 232
Nonverbal communication p. 236
Nonverbal sensitivity p. 246
Paralanguage p. 242
Personal space p. 236
Polygraph p. 243
Proxemics p. 236
Receiver p. 232
Self-disclosure p. 247
Sender p. 232

KEY PEOPLE

Bella DePaulo pp. 241–244
Paul Ekman and Wallace Friesen p. 238
Edward T. Hall pp. 237–238

CHAPTER 8 | Practice Test

1. Which of the following is *not* a component of the interpersonal communication process?
   a. The sender
   b. The receiver
   c. The channel
   d. The monitor

2. Research shows that individuals from a variety of cultures
   a. agree on the facial expressions that correspond with all emotions.
   b. agree on the facial expressions that correspond with fifteen basic emotions.
   c. agree on the facial expressions that correspond with six basic emotions.
   d. do not agree on the facial expressions that correspond with any emotions.

3. Which of the following is *not* an aspect of nonverbal communication?
   a. Facial expressions
   b. Homogamy
   c. Posture
   d. Gestures

4. According to research, which of the following cues is associated with dishonesty?
   a. Speaking with a higher-than-normal pitch
   b. Speaking slowly
   c. Giving relatively long answers to questions
   d. Lack of eye contact

5. With regard to self-disclosure, it is best to
   a. share a lot about yourself when you first meet someone.
   b. share very little about yourself for a long time.
   c. gradually share information about yourself.
   d. give no personal information on a first encounter, but share a lot the next time.

6. Paraphrasing is an important aspect of
   a. nonverbal communication.
   b. active listening.
   c. communication apprehension.
   d. assertiveness.

7. When people hear what they want to hear instead of what is actually said, _____ is operating.
   a. assertiveness
   b. self-preoccupation
   c. motivational distortion
   d. active listening

8. The conflict style that reflects low concern for self and low concern for others is:
   a. competing/forcing.
   b. compromising.
   c. accomodating.
   d. avoiding/withdrawing.

9. Generally, the most productive style for managing conflict is
   a. collaboration.
   b. compromise.
   c. accommodation.
   d. avoidance.

10. Expressing your thoughts directly and honestly without trampling on other people is a description of which communication style?
   a. Aggressive
   b. Empathic
   c. Submissive
   d. Assertive

ANSWERS

1. d Page 232
2. c Pages 238–239
3. b Pages 236–242
4. a Page 243
5. c Page 247
6. b Page 250
7. c Page 252
8. d Page 254
9. a Page 255
10. d Pages 256–259

COURSEMATE

Go to **CengageBrain.com** to access Psychology CourseMate, where you will find an interactive eBook, glossaries, flashcards, quizzes, videos, and more.

PERSONAL EXPLORATIONS WORKBOOK

Go to the *Personal Explorations Workbook* in the back of your textbook for exercises that can enhance your self-understanding in relation to issues raised in this chapter.

Exercise 8.1 *Self-Assessment:* Opener Scale

Exercise 8.2 *Self-Reflection:* How Do You Feel About Self-Disclosure?

Friendship and Love

© Picture Press/Alamy

ntonio was so keyed up, he tossed and turned all night. When morning finally arrived, he was elated. In less than two hours, he would be meeting Sonia for coffee! In his first class that morning, thoughts and images of Sonia constantly distracted him from the lecture. When class was finally over, he had to force himself not to walk too fast to the Student Union, where they had agreed to meet. Sound familiar? Chances are that you recognize Antonio's behavior as that of someone falling in love.

Friendship and love play a major role in psychological adjustment. Social connectedness is a strong pre-dictor of happiness. Conversely, social isolation is associated with poor physical and mental health and antisocial behavior (Smith, McPherson, & Smith-Lovin, 2009). We begin this chapter by defining close relationships. Next, we consider why people are attracted to each other, how relationships develop, and why they stay in or leave relationships. Then we probe more deeply into friendship and romantic love and discuss how the Internet influences relationships. Finally, in the Application section, we focus on the painful problem of loneliness and how to overcome it.

THE INGREDIENTS OF CLOSE RELATIONSHIPS

LEARNING OBJECTIVES

- Describe typical characteristics of close relationships.
- Explain the paradox of close relationships.

Typically, *close relationships* **are those that are important, interdependent, and long lasting.** In other words, people in close relationships spend a lot of time and energy maintaining the relationship, and what one person says and does affects the other. Close relationships are characterized by partners who are irreplaceable, whereas in casual social relationships (such as between store clerk and customer), partners can be interchangeable (Livesay & Duck, 2009).

Close relationships come in many forms, from family relationships, friendships, and work relationships to romantic relationships and marriage. When college students were asked to identify the person to whom they felt closest, 47% named a romantic partner, 36% listed a friend, 14% mentioned a family member, and 3% named another indi-vidual such as a co-worker (Berscheid, Snyder, & Omoto, 1989). Regardless of the type of relationship, humans are social animals, and social acceptance is central to our lives (DeWall & Bushman, 2011).

As you are aware, close relationships can arouse intense feelings—both positive (passion, concern, caring) and negative (rage, jealousy, despair). This phenomenon is termed the *paradox of close relationships* (Perlman, 2007). Close relationships are related to some of the best aspects of life (well-being, happiness, health), but they do have a dark side (abuse, deception, rejection) (Perlman & Carcedo, 2011). This paradox makes friendship and love perennial interests for poets, philosophers, and psychologists alike. Let's examine how relationships develop.

mangostock/Shutterstock.com

Learn More Online

The Unabridged Student Counseling Virtual Pamphlet Collection

This site includes links to online information for the problems and issues faced by students. The section on relationships provides advice on a diverse array of topics, including getting along with a roommate, dating online, fighting fair, preventing violence, and dealing with loneliness.

RELATIONSHIP DEVELOPMENT

LEARNING OBJECTIVES

- Discuss the roles of proximity, familiarity, and physical attractiveness in initial attraction.
- Understand the roles of reciprocal liking and similarity in getting acquainted.
- Outline some commonly used relationship maintenance strategies, and explain what is meant by "minding" relationships.
- Summarize interdependence theory, and explain how rewards, costs, and investments influence relationship satisfaction and commitment.

Attraction is the initial desire to form a relationship. Individuals use a multitude of factors to assess another person's appeal as a mate or a friend. Furthermore, because attraction is a two-way street, intricate interactions occur among variables. To simplify this complex issue, we divide our coverage into four segments. First, we review the factors that operate in initial encounters. Then we consider elements that come into play as people become acquainted and relationships deepen. Finally, we review what's involved in maintaining relationships.

Our review of research in this section pertains to both friendships and romantic relationships. In some cases, a particular factor (such as physical attractiveness) may play a more influential role in love than in friendship, or vice versa. However, all the factors discussed in this section enter into both types of relationships. These factors also operate in the same way in both straight and gay friendships and romantic relationships (Peplau & Fingerhut, 2007). But we should note that homosexuals face three unique dating challenges (Peplau & Spalding, 2003): They have a smaller pool of potential partners; they are often under pressure to conceal their sexual orientation; and they have limited ways to meet prospective partners. Also, fears of hostility or rejection may cause them to guard their self-disclosures to acquaintances and friends.

Initial Encounters

Sometimes initial encounters begin dramatically with two strangers' eyes locking across a room. More often, two people become aware of their mutual attraction, usually triggered by each other's looks and early conversations. What draws two strangers together as either friends or lovers? Three factors stand out: proximity, familiarity, and physical attractiveness.

Proximity

Attraction usually depends on proximity: People have to be in the same place at the same time. *Proximity* **refers to geographic, residential, and other forms of spatial closeness.** Of course, proximity is not an issue in cyberspace interactions (Fehr, 2008). But in everyday life people become attracted to, and acquainted with, someone who lives, works, shops, or plays nearby. Proximity effects may

seem self-evident, but it is sobering to realize that your friendships and love interests are often shaped by seating charts, apartment availability, shift assignments, and office locations.

The importance of proximity was apparent in a study that examined friendship development in a real-life context (Back, Schmukle, & Egloff, 2008). College students in a psychology course were randomly assigned to sit in neighboring seats, in the same row but not in neighboring seats, or without any physical relation to one another (control). One year later, the researchers measured the friendship development among classmates. As proximity would suggest, those who sat in neighboring seats were more likely to be friends than those in the same row, while those in the same row were more likely to be friends than those in the control condition (see **Figure 9.1**).

■ High closeness ■ Medium closeness ■ Low closeness

© Cengage Learning

Figure 9.1

Friendship intensity as a function of initial seat assignment. To show that friendships are sometimes the result of mere chance, Back, Schmukle, and Egloff (2008) found that college students' initial seat assignments predicted how close the students would be a year later. Sitting in neighboring seats yielded the closest friendships, followed by sitting in the same row, and finally sitting in no obvious proximity.

Source: Adapted from Back, M. D., Schmukle, S. C., & Egloff, B. (2008). Becoming friends by chance. *Psychological Science, 19*(5), 439–440.

REEL RESEARCH

Emotional Reactions to Rejection

Log on to CourseMate at www.cengagebrain.com to watch this video.

As mentioned in the chapter, humans are social animals, and social acceptance is central to people's lives. As a result, fear of rejection can deter many from becoming more intimate with others. Although not the most favorable experience, rejection has a powerful effect on emotions. Roy Baumeister, social psychologist at Florida State University, conducts experiments involving college students, rejection, and emotional responses (pain tolerance and empathy to be specific) in this Reel Research video.

In Baumeister's study, a small group of students are placed in a room and asked to get to know one another. After a short time together, they are separated into individual rooms and experimenters randomly assign them to experience either "rejection" or "acceptance." After the students are given the rejection or acceptance information, the experimenter conducts a physical test of the participants' pain threshold and another test involving their emotional response to a story in which someone is rejected. The rejected students show a high tolerance for pain during the physical test and a lack of empathy toward the character in the rejection story, while accepted students show low tolerance for pain and high empathy for the character.

Not only does rejection cause people to become numb to physical and emotional pain, it can cause temporary but strong changes in behavior. According to Baumeister, people tend to become more aggressive, more short-sighted, less helpful, and less emotional when confronted with even small forms of rejection.

Watch the *Emotional Reactions to Rejection* video to learn more about Baumeister's research and the relationship between rejection and pain. Delve even deeper by responding to the following discussion questions.

DISCUSSION QUESTIONS

1. How did Brittany and Michael respond to the physical pain and rejection story? How did being accepted or rejected affect their behavior and reactions?
2. Discuss the demonstration in the video. How did Baumeister measure pain tolerance and empathy, and why are these elements related to the experience of rejection?
3. According to Baumeister, how do people react to emotional and physical pain after experiencing rejection? How do these reactions protect them from experiencing further pain?

How does proximity increase attraction? Goodfriend (2009) asserts that first, people who are near each other are more likely to get acquainted and find out their similarities. Second, individuals who live or work close by may be seen as more convenient and less costly (in terms of time and energy) than those further away. Finally, people might develop attraction just because someone in close proximity becomes familiar to them.

Familiarity

You probably walk the same route to your classes several times a week. As the term progresses, you begin to recognize some familiar faces along the way. Have you found yourself nodding or smiling at these people? If so, you've experienced **the *mere exposure effect*, or an increase in positive feelings toward a novel stimulus (person) based on frequent exposure to it** (Zajonc, 1968). Note that the positive feelings arise just on the basis of seeing someone frequently—not because of any interaction.

The implications of the mere exposure effect on initial attraction should be obvious. Generally, the more familiar someone is, the more you will like him or her (Le, 2009; Reis et al., 2011). And greater liking increases the probability that you will strike up a conversation and, possibly, develop a relationship with the person. Of course, people can be attracted to total strangers, so familiarity isn't the only factor involved in initial attraction (Fitness, Fletcher, & Overall, 2007).

Physical Attractiveness

Physical attractiveness plays a major role in initial face-to-face encounters. Among American college students, physical attractiveness in a dating partner has increased in importance over the past 50 years—for both sexes, but especially for men (Buss et al., 2001). As you might expect, the importance of physical appearance is different for a future spouse or life partner than it is for casual relationships. For a marriage partner, both male and female college students ranked the traits of honesty and trustworthiness most highly (Regan & Berscheid, 1997). For a sexual partner, both men and women ranked "attractive appearance" the highest. Good looks play a role in friendships as well. People, especially males, prefer attractiveness in their same- and other-gender friends (Fehr, 2000).

Do gays and straights differ in the importance they place on the physical attractiveness of prospective dating partners? It seems not (Peplau & Spalding, 2000). In fact, researchers often find gender rather than sexual orientation to be the more important factor in partner preferences. For example, in the wording of gay and straight personal advertisements in newspapers, both heterosexual and homosexual men are more likely than heterosexual or homosexual women to request physically attractive partners (Bailey et al., 1997; Deaux & Hanna, 1984). Similar findings emerge when gay and straight participants rate their desire to date hypothetical partners: men value attractiveness more than women do (Ha et al., 2012).

The emphasis on beauty may not be quite as great as the evidence reviewed thus far suggests. In a classic, cross-cultural study conducted in thirty-seven countries on the characteristics commonly sought in a mate, Buss (1989) found that personal qualities, such as kindness and intelligence, were ranked higher by both genders than physical attractiveness was. Similarly, in a 2005 Internet survey of over 200,000 participants, intelligence, humor, honesty, and kindness were ranked as the most important traits in a partner, with good looks coming in fifth. However, when results were separated by gender, attractiveness was still ranked higher by men than by women (Lippa, 2007). Keep in mind that verbal reports don't always predict people's actual priorities and behavior, and some people might not be aware of what actually attracts them (Sprecher & Felmlee, 2008). Finally, it should be noted that judgments about physical attractiveness can and do change as one learns about the personality of the individual in question (Lewandowski, Aron, & Gee, 2007).

What makes someone attractive? Although people can hold different views about what makes a person attractive, they tend to agree on the key elements of good looks. Researchers who study attractiveness focus almost exclusively on facial features and physique. Both aspects are important in perceived attractiveness, but an unattractive body is seen as a greater liability than an unattractive face (Alicke, Smith, & Klotz, 1986). Males, whether gay or straight, place more emphasis on body build and physical attractiveness than females do (Franzoi & Kern, 2009). In fact, when evaluating potential short-term partners, if they could only see a portion of the potential mate men were more likely to look at the body than the face (Confer, Perilloux, & Buss, 2010).

Michael Cunningham (2009a), a pioneer in this area of research, identified four categories of qualities that cause someone to be seen as more or less attractive: neonate (baby-face) qualities, mature features, expressiveness, and grooming. Even across different ethnic groups and countries, there seems to be strong agreement on attractive facial features (Cunningham et al., 1995; Langlois et al., 2000). Women who have *neonate qualities* such as large eyes, prominent cheekbones, a small nose, and full lips get high ratings (Jones, 1995). Although softer- and finer-featured male faces are also rated as attractive (Leonardo DiCaprio's, for example) (Perrett et al., 1998), neonate qualities contribute more to the attractiveness of females (Cunningham, 2009a).

In particular, the combination of these youthful features with *mature features* (prominent cheekbones, wide smile) seems to be the winning ticket—think of Angelina Jolie (Cunningham, Druen, & Barbee, 1997). Men who have mature features such as a strong jaw and a broad forehead get high ratings on attractiveness (George Clooney and Denzel Washington come to mind) (Cunningham, Barbee, & Pike, 1990). Mature features also play a role when it comes to physique. Males who have broad shoulders, slim waists and legs, and small buttocks receive high attractiveness ratings (Singh, 1995). In recent years, the ideal body shape for males has become more muscular (Martins, Tiggeman, & Kirkbride, 2007). Tall men are also considered attractive (Lynn & Shurgot, 1984). Women of average weight with an "hourglass" figure and medium-sized breasts are rated high in attractiveness (Singh, 1993). African American men and women prefer a larger body type than European American men and women do (Franko & Roehrig, 2011). Nonetheless, being considerably overweight is viewed very negatively in the United States, despite the increasing incidence of obesity (Hebl & Mannix, 2003).

Expressive traits, such as a large smile and high-set eyebrows, are also related to perceptions of attractiveness (Cunningham, 2009a). A broad smile is seen as more attractive, perhaps because it can indicate friendliness, and high-set eyebrows could be seen as a sign of interest and agreeableness. *Grooming qualities* are characteristics people use to enhance their other physical qualities, such as cosmetics, hairstyle, clothing, and accessories (Cunningham, 2009a). Individuals will go to great lengths to enhance their physical attractiveness, as demonstrated by the increased rate of cosmetic surgery. Between 1997 and 2011, the number of cosmetic surgeries performed on Americans increased by a whopping 73%. In 2011, over 9 million cosmetic procedures were performed (see **Figure 9.2**), with liposuction and breast augmentations being the top two (American Society for Aesthetic Plastic Surgery, 2011).

Currently in the United States, thinness receives heightened emphasis, especially for girls and women. Many studies show that repeated exposure to media portrayals of the thin ideal are associated with body dissatisfaction (Groesz, Levine, & Murnen, 2002; Nouri, Hill, & Orrell-Valente, 2011). Thus, it is not surprising that high school girls underestimate the body size that boys find attractive (Paxton et al., 2005). High school girls also believe that other girls have thinner bodies and that the ideal body shape is smaller than their own (Sanderson et al., 2008). Also, many college women perceive themselves to be heavier than they actually are and wish to be thinner (Vartanian, Giant, & Passino, 2001). Not surprisingly, women who associate positive attributes with being underweight have a higher incidence of eating disorders (Ahern, Bennett, & Hetherington, 2008). Further, eating disorders affect all ethnic groups (Levine & Smolak, 2010; Marques et al., 2011). We explore the important issue of eating disorders in the Chapter 14 Application.

Gay males also live in a subculture that emphasizes physical appearance. A study that experimentally induced self-objectification (by having participants wear a swimsuit versus a turtleneck sweater) showed that gay males felt more body shame, had more body dissatisfaction, and ate less when given the opportunity than straight males did (Martins et al., 2007). Interestingly, these findings match the results of a similar study where women wore a swimsuit (Fredrickson, et al., 1998). Although gay men show greater dissatisfaction with their overall body, studies indicate that they are most dissatisfied with their body hair and muscularity (Martins, Tiggemann, & Churchett, 2008).

On average, both gay and heterosexual men desire to be thinner and more muscular, and this dissatisfaction increases with age (Tiggemann, Martins, & Kirkbride, 2007). As American culture increasingly objectifies male bodies, and as men feel greater pressure to meet the ideals of the male body shape, appearance may become more central to men's self-concept, leading to greater body dissatisfaction and more eating disorders in this group (Martins et al., 2007), prompting experts to call for more research on these underdiagnosed and undertreated disorders in men (Strother et al., 2012).

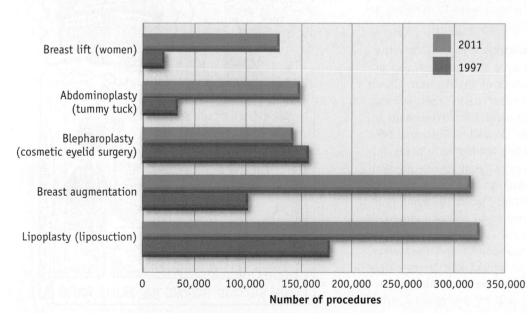

Figure 9.2

Top five surgical cosmetic procedures in 2011. The number of cosmetic surgeries annually is on the rise. In 2011, over 9 million cosmetic procedures were performed.

Source: Retrieved from the American Society for Aesthetic Plastic Surgery (2011), www.surgery.org/media/statistics

According to the matching hypothesis, people tend to wind up with someone similar to themselves in attractiveness. However, other factors, such as personality, intelligence, and social status, also influence attraction.

Matching up on looks. Thankfully, people can enjoy rewarding social lives without being spectacularly good-looking. In the process of dating and mating, people apparently take into consideration their own level of attractiveness. **The *matching hypothesis* proposes that people of similar levels of physical attractiveness gravitate toward each other.** This hypothesis is supported by findings that both dating and married heterosexual couples tend to be similar in physical attractiveness (Feingold, 1988; Hatfield & Sprecher, 2009). That is, individuals tend to partner with others who are "in their same league." There is some debate, however, about the relevance of this principle in partner selection (Taylor et al., 2011). Some theorists believe that individuals mostly pursue highly attractive partners and that their matching is the result of social forces beyond their control, such as rejection by more attractive others. Another theory maintains that physical attractiveness is a resource that partners bring to the relationship and, in general, partners want to maintain an equitable balance (Hatfield & Sprecher, 2009).

Attractiveness and resource exchange. Physical attractiveness can be viewed as a resource that partners can exchange in relationships. A number of studies have shown that, in heterosexual dating, males "trade" their occupational status for youth and physical attractiveness in females, and vice versa (Fletcher, Overall, & Friesen, 2006; Fletcher et al., 2004). This finding holds true in many cultures. As noted earlier, men in most countries rate physical attractiveness in a prospective mate as more important than women do, whereas women rate "good financial prospects" and "ambitious and industrious" as more important characteristics than men do (Buss, 1989). In reviewing the content of personal ads in newspapers and magazines, Wiederman (1993) reported that female advertisers sought financial resources in prospective partners eleven times more often than the men did.

David Buss

Evolutionary social psychologists such as David Buss (1988, 2009) believe that these findings on age, status, and physical attractiveness reflect gender differences in inherited reproductive strategies that have been sculpted over thousands of generations by natural selection. Their thinking has been guided by *parental investment theory,* **which maintains that a species' mating patterns depend on what each sex has to invest—in the way of time, energy, and survival risk—to produce and nurture offspring.** According to this model, members of the gender that makes the smaller investment will compete with each other for mating opportunities with the gender that makes the larger investment, and the gender with the larger investment will tend to be more discriminating in selecting its partners (Webster, 2009).

How does this analysis apply to humans? Like many mammalian species, human males are required to invest little in the production of offspring beyond the act of copulation, so their reproductive potential is maximized by mating with as many females as possible (Buss & Schmitt, 2011). Also, males should prefer young and attractive females because these qualities are assumed to signal fertility, which should increase the chances of conception and passing genes on to the next generation. The situation for females is quite different. Females have to invest nine months in pregnancy, and our female ancestors typically had to devote at least several additional years to nourishing offspring through breastfeeding. These realities limit the

BIZARRO

ONE SECOND BEFORE THE BLIND DATE

Evolutionary theory can explain why attractive women often become romantically involved with much older men who happen to be wealthy.

rial resources. These preferences should increase the likelihood that a male partner will be committed to a long-term relationship and will be able to support the woman and their children, thus ensuring that her genes will be passed on (see **Figure 9.3**).

Are there alternatives to the evolutionary explanation for patterns of mate selection and resource exchange in heterosexual relationships? Yes, sociocultural models can also provide plausible explanations that center on traditional gender-role socialization and men's greater economic power (Li & Tausczik, 2009; Sprecher, Sullivan, & Hatfield, 1994). Some theorists argue that women have learned to value men's economic clout because their own economic potential has been severely limited in virtually all cultures by a long history of discrimination. Consistent with this hypothesis, it is women in countries with limited educational and career opportunities for females who show the strongest preferences for men with high incomes (Eagly & Wood, 1999). Moreover, when women's economic power increases, so does their preference for a physically attractive mate (Gangestad, 1993).

Now that we have explored initial attraction, let's consider the factors that are important as individuals get to know one another.

Getting Acquainted

After several initial encounters, people typically begin the dance of getting to know each other. Is it possible to predict which budding relationships will flower and which will die on the vine? We'll examine two factors that can keep the ball rolling: reciprocal liking and perceived similarity.

Reciprocal Liking

An old adage advises, "If you want to *have* a friend, *be* a friend." This suggestion captures the idea of the reciprocity principle in relationships. **Reciprocal liking refers to liking those who show that they like you.** Many studies show that

number of offspring women can produce, regardless of how many males they mate with. Hence, females have little or no incentive for mating with many males. Instead, females can optimize their reproductive potential by selectively mating with reliable partners who have greater mate-

	Biological reality	**Evolutionary significance**	**Behavioral outcomes**
Males	Reproduction involves minimal investment of time, energy, and risk	Maximize reproductive success by seeking more sexual partners with high reproductive potential	More interest in uncommitted sex, greater number of sex partners over lifetime, look for youth and attractiveness in partners
Females	Reproduction involves substantial investment of time, energy, and risk	Maximize reproductive success by seeking partners willing to invest material resources in your offspring	Less interest in uncommitted sex, smaller number of sex partners over lifetime, look for income, status, and ambition in partners

Figure 9.3

Parental investment theory and mating preferences. Parental investment theory suggests that basic differences between males and females in parental investment have great adaptive significance and lead to gender differences in mating propensities and preferences, as outlined here.

if you believe another person likes you, you will like him or her (Montoya & Horton, 2012), especially if you find that other person attractive (Stambush & Mattingly, 2010). Think about it. You respond positively when others sincerely flatter you, do favors for you, and use nonverbal behavior to signal their interest in you (eye contact, leaning forward). These interactions are enjoyable, validating, and positively reinforcing (Smith & Caprariello, 2009). As such, you usually reciprocate such behavior.

You can see a self-fulfilling prophecy at work here. If you believe that someone likes you, you behave in a friendly manner toward that person. Your behavior encourages him or her to respond positively, which confirms your initial expectation. A study by Rebecca Curtis and Kim Miller (1986) showed self-fulfilling prophecy in action. College students who were strangers were divided into pairs for a 5-minute "get acquainted" conversation. Afterward, one member of each pair was led to believe that the other student either did or didn't like him or her. Then the pairs met again and talked about current events for 10 minutes. Raters, blind to the experimental condition of the participants, listened to tape recordings of the 10-minute interactions and rated the participants on a number of behaviors. As predicted, the participants who believed that they were liked were rated as disclosing more about themselves, behaving more warmly, disagreeing less, and having a more positive tone of voice and general attitude than those who believed that they were disliked.

The common strategy of "playing hard to get" (nonreciprocity) is at odds with the reciprocity principle. The thought behind this tactic is that people should not reciprocate prematurely lest they be seen as desperate or unselective (Cupach & Spitzberg, 2008). Eastwick and colleagues (2007) assert that "not all reciprocity is created equal"; it's best when it's exclusive. They found that romantic desires directed at one person are viewed positively, but not when they are directed toward many individuals. The conclusion? In general, you should probably avoid playing hard to get.

Similarity

Do "birds of a feather flock together," or do "opposites attract"? Research offers far more support for the first adage than the second (Montoya, Horton, & Kirchner, 2008; Surra et al., 2006). Despite the increasing diversity of the United States, similarity continues to play a key role in attraction, and the similarity principle operates in both friendships and romantic relationships regardless of sexual orientation (Morry, 2007, 2009). In a longitudinal study of best friends, researchers found that similarity among friends in 1983 actually predicted their closeness in 2002—19 years later (Ledbetter, Griffin, & Sparks, 2007). We've already explored similarity in physical attractiveness (the matching hypothesis). Now, let's consider other similarities that contribute to attraction.

Heterosexual married and dating couples tend to be similar in *demographic characteristics* (age, race, religion, socioeconomic status, and education), *physical attractiveness, intelligence,* and *attitudes* (Watson et al., 2004). According to Donn Byrne's two-stage model, people first "sort" for dissimilarity, avoiding those who appear to be different. Then, from among the remaining group, they gravitate toward those who are most similar (Byrne, Clore, & Smeaton, 1986).

Support for similarity in *personality* as a factor in attraction is weaker and mixed (Luo & Klohnen, 2005). Preliminary results indicate that perceived similarity in personality might be more important than actual similarity, at least in the early phases of getting acquainted (Selfhout et al., 2009). Once people are in committed relationships, however, similarity in personality is associated with relationship satisfaction (Gonzaga, Campos, & Bradbury, 2007).

What is the appeal of similarity? For one thing, you assume that a similar person will probably like you (Montoya & Horton, 2012). Second, when others share your beliefs, you feel validated (Byrne & Clore, 1970). Finally, people who are similar are more likely to react to situations in the same way, thus reducing the chances for conflicts and stress (Gonzaga, 2009).

Established Relationships

Over time, some acquaintanceships evolve into established relationships. Individuals mutually determine the desired level of intimacy they want in a relationship, whether friendship or romantic. Not all relationships need to be highly intimate to be satisfying. For others, intimacy is an essential ingredient of relationship satisfaction. In either case, if they are to continue, close relationships need to be maintained.

Maintenance of Ongoing Relationships
Relationship maintenance involves the actions and activities used to sustain the desired quality of a relationship. In Figure 9.4 on the next page, you can see a list of commonly used relationship maintenance behaviors. Often, these behaviors occur spontaneously (calling to check in, eating meals together); at other times, behaviors are more intentional and require more planning (traveling to visit family and friends) (Canary & Stafford, 2001). Obviously, strategies vary depending on the nature of a relationship (familial, friendship, romantic) and its stage of development (new, developing, mature). For example, married couples engage in more assurances and social networking than dating partners do (Stafford & Canary, 1991). Partners in long-distance relationships often rely on communication for effective relationship maintenance (Stafford, 2010). When coding the content of emails for long-distance romantic partners, Johnson and colleagues (2008) found that the most common categories used were assurances, openness, and positivity, in that order.

RELATIONSHIP MAINTENANCE STRATEGIES	
Strategy	**Behavioral example**
Positivity	Try to act nice and cheerful
Openness	Encourage him/her to disclose thoughts and feelings to me
Assurances	Stress my commitment to him/her
Social networking	Show that I am willing to do things with his/her friends and family
Task sharing	Help equally with tasks that need to be done
Joint activities	Spend time hanging out
Mediated communication	Use email to keep in touch
Avoidance	Respect each other's privacy and need to be alone
Antisocial behaviors	Act rude to him/her
Humor	Call him/her by a funny nickname
No flirting	Do not encourage overly familiar behavior (relevant in cross-gender friendships)

Figure 9.4

Relationship maintenance strategies. College students were asked to describe how they maintained three different personal relationships over a college term. Their responses were grouped into eleven categories. You can see that, ironically, some people behave negatively in an attempt to enhance relationships. Openness was the most commonly nominated strategy. (Adapted from Canary & Stafford, 1994)

Both spontaneous and intentional maintenance activities are correlated with relationship satisfaction and commitment (Canary & Dainton, 2006). Even in same-sex friendships, maintenance behaviors such as positivity, assurances, and sharing tasks are related to friendship closeness (Ledbetter, 2009). Also, relationship satisfaction is higher when the frequency of one partner's maintenance activities is in line with the other's expectations or when maintenance contributions are equitable (Stafford & Canary, 2006). Gay and lesbian couples generally use the same maintenance behaviors as heterosexual couples (Hass & Stafford, 1998).

Another approach to relationship maintenance is the use of "minding" (Harvey & Omarzu, 1997). *Minding* is an active and ongoing process of continuing mutual self-disclosure and maintaining relationship-enhancing beliefs and attributions about one's partner. This model asserts that a high level of minding is associated with satisfying and intimate long-term relationships, and vice versa. To elaborate, a high degree of minding involves using good listening skills, having detailed knowledge about your partner's opinions, making generally positive attributions

for your partner's behaviors, expressing feelings of trust and commitment, recognizing your partner's support and effort, and having an optimistic view of the future of the relationship. By contrast, a low degree of minding is characterized by a lack of interest in your partner's self-disclosures, generally negative attributions for your partner's behavior, dwelling on your partner's faults, and a pessimistic view of the future of the relationship. As you can see, this model has a strong cognitive flavor. Although Harvey and Omarzu focus on committed romantic relationships, they suggest that their model likely applies to family and friendship relationships as well (Omarzu, 2009).

Relationship Satisfaction and Commitment

How do you gauge your satisfaction in a relationship? What determines whether you will stay in or get out of a relationship? *Interdependence* or *social exchange theory* **postulates that interpersonal relationships are governed by perceptions of the rewards and costs exchanged in interactions.** Basically, this model predicts that interactions between acquaintances, friends, and lovers will continue as long as the participants feel that the benefits they derive from the relationship are reasonable in comparison to the costs of being in the relationship. Harold Kelley and John Thibaut's interdependence theory (Kelley & Thibaut, 1978; Thibaut & Kelley, 1959) is based on B. F. Skinner's principle of reinforcement, which assumes that people try to maximize their rewards in life and minimize their costs (see Chapter 2).

Rewards include such things as emotional support, status, and sexual gratification (in romantic relationships); costs are such things as the time and energy that a relationship requires, emotional conflicts, and the inability to engage in other rewarding activities because of relationship obligations. According to interdependence theory, people assess a relationship by its *outcome*—their subjective perception of the rewards of the relationship minus its costs (see **Figure 9.5** on the next page).

Individuals assess their *satisfaction* with a relationship by comparing the relationship outcomes (rewards minus costs) to their subjective expectations. **A *comparison level* is a personal standard of what constitutes an accept-**

Learn More Online

Psychology Today: Relationships

This site from *Psychology Today* includes current, cutting-edge research on all types of relationships. The editors do a good job of making scientific research accessible and practical.

Figure 9.5

The key elements of social exchange theory and their effects on a relationship. According to social exchange theory, relationship *outcome* is determined by the rewards minus the costs of a relationship. Relationship *satisfaction* is based on the outcome matched against comparison level (expectations). *Commitment* to a relationship is determined by one's satisfaction minus one's comparison level for alternatives plus one's investments in the relationship.

Source: Adapted from Brehm, S. S., & Kassin, S, M. (1993). *Social psychology*. Boston: Houghton Mifflin. Copyright © 1993 by Houghton Mifflin Company.

able balance of rewards and costs in a relationship. It is based on the outcomes you have experienced in previous relationships and the outcomes you have seen others experience in their relationships. Your comparison level may also be influenced by your exposure to fictional relationships, such as those you have read about or seen on television. Consistent with the predictions of exchange theory, research shows that relationship satisfaction is higher when rewards are perceived to be high and costs are viewed as relatively low.

To understand the role of *commitment* in relationships, we need to consider two additional factors. The first is **the comparison level for alternatives, or one's estimation of the available outcomes from alternative relationships.** In using this standard, individuals assess their current relationship outcomes in comparison to the potential outcomes of other, similar relationships that may be available to them. This principle helps explain why many unsatisfying relationships are not terminated until another love interest actually appears. It also explains why someone might leave a seemingly happy relationship, if that person's expectations and standards were not being met. The second factor that figures in relationship commitment is **investments, or things that people contribute to a relationship that they can't get back if the relationship ends.** Investments include past costs (time, money) that they can never recover if the relationship fails. Understandably, putting investments into a relationship strengthens one's commitment to it.

Figure 9.5 demonstrates how interdependence theory works. If both members of a couple feel that they are getting a lot out of the relationship (lots of strokes, high status) compared to its costs (a few arguments, occasionally giving up preferred activities), they will probably perceive the relationship as satisfactory and will keep it going. However, if either one begins to feel that the ratio of re-

wards to costs is falling below his or her comparison level, dissatisfaction is likely to occur. The dissatisfied person may attempt to alter the balance of costs and rewards or try to ease out of the relationship. The likelihood of ending the relationship depends on the number of important investments a person has in the relationship and whether the person believes that an alternative relationship is available that could yield greater satisfaction.

Research generally supports interdependence theory and its extensions (Rusbult, Agnew, & Arriaga, 2012). Social exchange principles seem to operate in a similar fashion regardless of a couple's sexual orientation (Peplau & Fingerhut, 2007). However, many people resist the idea that close relationships operate according to an economic model. Much of this resistance probably comes from discomfort with the idea that self-interest plays such an important role in the maintenance of relationships. Resistance may also stem from doubts about how well social exchange principles apply to close relationships. In fact, there is some empirical support for this position (Harvey & Wenzel, 2006). Margaret Clark and Judson Mills (1993) distinguish between *exchange relationships* (with strangers, acquaintances, co-workers) and *communal relationships* (with close friends, lovers, family members). Research suggests that in exchange relationships, the usual principles of social exchange dominate, but in communal relationships these principles seem to be applied differently (Morrow, 2009). For example, in communal relationships, rewards are usually given freely, without any expectation of prompt reciprocation. Also, individuals pay more attention to the needs of a partner in a communal relationship than in an exchange relationship. In other words, you use a need-based norm with people who are close to you and help them without calculating whether and when they will reward you in kind.

FRIENDSHIP

LEARNING OBJECTIVES

- Summarize the research on what makes a good friend.
- Describe some key gender and sexual orientation differences in friendships.
- Explain the friendship repair ritual as a way of dealing with conflict in friendships.

It's hard to overestimate the importance of friends. They give help in times of need, advice in times of confusion, consolation in times of failure, and praise in times of achievement. Friends clearly are important to individuals' adjustment. In fact, friendship quality is predictive of overall happiness, in part because friends satisfy basic psychological needs (Demir & Özdemir, 2010). College students with strong friendships are more optimistic and deal better with stressful life events (Brissette, Scheir, & Carver, 2002). Intimate and stable friendships are associated with less stress in adulthood and less troublesome behavior in adolescence (Hartup & Stevens, 1999).

bikeriderlondon/Shutterstock.com

What Makes a Good Friend?

Exactly what makes someone a good friend? One approach to this question comes from a cross-cultural study of students in England, Italy, Japan, and Hong Kong (Argyle & Henderson, 1984). Notably, in this diverse sample there was enough agreement on how friends should conduct themselves to identify six informal rules governing friendships, including sharing good news, providing emotional support, helping in times of need, making each other happy when together, trusting and confiding in each other, and standing up for each other. Notice that the common thread running through these rules seems to be providing emotional and social support.

We can also look at the common themes that underlie friendships of all ages in order to understand the nature of friendship. Researchers have identified three such themes (de Vries, 1996). The first involves the emotional dimension of friendship (self-disclosure, expressing affection and support, and so forth). A second theme concerns the communal nature of friendship (participating in or supporting each other in mutually shared activities). The third dimension entails sociability and compatibility (friends are sources of fun and recreation). These studies and others show that the most important element of friendship is emotional support (Collins & Madsen, 2006).

Gender and Sexual Orientation Issues

Men's and women's same-gender friendships have a lot in common (Wright, 2006); both sexes value intimacy, self-disclosure, and trust (Winstead, 2009). However, some interesting differences appear to be rooted in traditional gender roles and socialization. In the United States, women's friendships are more often emotionally based, whereas men's tend to be activity based. Although some researchers have challenged this characterization (Walker, 1994), the current belief is that men's friendships are typically based on shared interests and doing things together, whereas women's friendships more often focus on talking—usually about personal matters (Fehr, 1996, 2004).

We can also compare American men's and women's friendships on *preferred topics* of conversation. Women are far more likely than men to discuss personal problems, people, relationships, and feelings (Fehr, 2004). Men, on the other hand, are much more likely to talk about sports, work, vehicles, and computers than personal concerns. Email communications also reflect this gender difference (Colley & Todd, 2002). So whose friendships are more intimate, men's or women's? Currently, there is controversy over this question. The most widely accepted view is that women's friendships are closer and more satisfying because they involve more self-disclosure (Fehr, 2004).

What short-circuits intimate connections between men? Several factors stand out for American men (Way, 2011). First, men are socialized to be self-sufficient, which inhibits self-disclosure. Second, homophobia, which is stronger in males than females, is a barrier to intimacy among males and contributes to inconsistent and often ambiguous standards for emotional expression and intimacy between men (Nardi, 2007). Third, traditional gender-role expectations encourage men to see each other as competitors. Why reveal weaknesses to someone who might take advantage of you? Studies indicate that interpersonal competition is highest in male-male friendships (Singleton & Vacca, 2007).

The boundaries between the friendship and romantic or sexual relationships of gay men and lesbians appear to be more complex than those of heterosexuals. Many intimate relationships among lesbians begin as friendships and progress to romance and then to a sexual relationship (Diamond, 2007). Obviously, discerning and negotiating these shifts can be difficult. Also, both lesbians and gay men are much more likely than heterosexuals to maintain social contacts with former sexual partners (Solomon, Rothblum, & Balsam, 2004). One possible explanation for this phenomenon is the small size of some gay and lesbian social networks (Peplau & Fingerhut, 2007). Also, compared to heterosexual couples, gay and lesbian couples have less support from families and societal institutions (Kurdek, 2005). So, maintaining close connections with friends and creating "safe spaces" through these connections is especially important (Goode-Cross & Good, 2008).

Conflict in Friendships

Friends, especially long-term ones, are bound to experience conflicts. As with other types of relationships, conflicts can result from incompatible goals, mismatched expectations, or changes in individuals' interests over time. If the conflicts are great enough, they can result in the friendship ending. Alternatively, individuals can engage in behavior to preserve the relationship. Cahn (2009) describes three steps in friendship repair rituals. First, there is a *reproach,* in which the offended party acknowledges the problem and asks the offender for an explanation. Second, the offender offers a *remedy* by taking responsibility and offering a justification, a concession, an apology, or a combination of these three. Finally in the *acknowledgment* stage the offended party acknowledges the remedy and the friendship progresses. Of course at any point, either party can call off the ritual and dissolve the friendship. Ultimately, conflict is a reality in all relationships, whether platonic or romantic (Reis, Snyder, & Roberts, 2009).

ROMANTIC LOVE

LEARNING OBJECTIVES

- Clarify the research findings on the experience of love in gay and straight couples, and identify some gender differences regarding love.
- Compare Sternberg's triangular theory of love with the theory of adult attachment styles.

- Discuss the course of romantic love over time, including what couples go through as they dissolve a relationship.
- Explain why relationships fail and what couples can do to help relationships last.

Wander through a bookstore and you'll see an overwhelming array of titles such as *Men Who Can't Love, Women Who Love Too Much,* and *Getting the Love You Want.* Turn on your radio and you'll hear the refrains of "All You Need Is Love," "Crazy in Love," and "Love You Like a Love Song." Although there are other forms of love, such as parental love and platonic love, these books and songs are all about *romantic love,* a subject of consuming interest for almost everyone.

Although there are cultural differences in romantic attitudes and behaviors, romantic love is experienced in all cultures (Hatfield & Rapson, 2010). Love is difficult to define, difficult to measure, and frequently difficult to understand. Nonetheless, psychologists have conducted thousands of studies and developed a number of interesting theories on love and romantic relationships.

Sexual Orientation and Love

Sexual orientation refers to a person's preference for emotional and sexual relationships with individuals of the same gender, the other gender, or either gender. *Heterosexuals* seek emotional-sexual relationships with members of the other gender. *Homosexuals* seek emotional-sexual relationships with members of the same gender.

Bisexuals seek emotional-sexual relationships with members of both genders. In recent years, the terms *gay* and *straight* have become widely used to refer to homosexuals and heterosexuals, respectively. *Gay* can refer to homosexuals of either gender, but most homosexual women prefer to call themselves *lesbians.* Chapter 12 goes into more details regarding sexual orientation.

Many studies of romantic love and relationships suffer from **heterosexism, or the assumption that all individuals and relationships are heterosexual.** For instance, most questionnaires on romantic love and romantic relationships fail to ask participants about their sexual orientation. Thus, when data are analyzed, there is no way to know whether subjects are referring to same- or other-gender romantic partners. Assuming that their subjects are all heterosexuals, some researchers proceed to describe their

Dotshock/Shutterstock.com

findings without any mention of homosexuals. Because most people identify themselves as heterosexual, heterosexism in research isn't likely to distort conclusions about heterosexuals; however, it renders homosexual relationships invisible. Further, research on same-sex relationships tends to focus on white, middle class Americans (Peplau & Ghavami, 2009). Consequently, psychologists don't know as much about the range of homosexual relationships as they would like to. Researchers are now devoting much more attention to this issue.

We discuss gay and lesbian committed relationships more in Chapter 10, so we will just touch on the basics here. We *do* know that homosexual romances and relationships are essentially the same as those of heterosexuals. Both groups experience romantic and passionate love and make commitments to relationships (Kurdek, 1994, 1998; Peplau & Ghavami, 2009). Both heterosexual and homosexual couples hold similar values about relationships, report similar levels of relationship satisfaction, perceive their relationships to be loving and satisfying, and say they want their partners to have characteristics similar to theirs (Peplau & Fingerhut, 2007). Further, both groups desire positive qualities, such as caring and friendliness, in a partner (Felmlee, Hilton, & Orzechowicz, 2012). When relationship differences are found, they are much more likely to be rooted in gender than in sexual orientation, as we'll see next.

Gender Differences

Stereotypes hold that women are more romantic than men. Nonetheless, research suggests just the opposite—that men are the more romantic gender (Dion & Dion, 1988). For example, men hold more romantic beliefs ("Love lasts forever" or "There is one perfect love in the world for everyone") (Peplau, Hill, & Rubin, 1993). In addition, men fall in love more easily than women, whereas women fall out of love more easily than men (Hill, Rubin, & Peplau, 1976; Rubin, Peplau, & Hill, 1981). Research has found that although participants (both male and female) *believe* that women are more likely to confess love first, in *reality,* men are more likely to say "I love you" first, and they report more happiness when receiving confessions of love (Ackerman, Griskevicius, & Li, 2011) (see **Figure 9.6**).

In contrast, women are more likely to report physical symptoms associated with being in love—for instance, feeling as though they are "floating on a cloud" (Peplau & Gordon, 1985)—and they are somewhat more likely to verbalize and display tender emotions (Dindia & Allen, 1992). We should note, however, that men and women have more similarities than differences when it comes to relationships (Marshall, 2010). It appears that the notion that men and women are from different relational planets is somewhat of an exaggeration.

Figure 9.6

Who is the more romantic gender? Ackerman and colleagues (2011) found that although both males and females believe that women are more likely to confess love first, in reality men are more likely to say "I love you" first.

Source: Adapted from Ackerman, J. M., Griskevicius, V., & Li, N. P. (2011). Let's get serious: Communicating commitment in romantic relationships. *Journal of Personality and Social Psychology 100*(6), 1079–1094.

Theories of Love

Can the experience of love be broken down into certain key components? How are romantic love relationships similar to other types of close relationships? These are the kinds of questions that two current theories of love address.

Triangular Theory of Love

Robert Sternberg's (1986, 1988, 2006) *triangular theory of love* posits that all love experiences are made up of three components: intimacy, passion, and commitment. Each of the components is represented as a point of a triangle, from which the theory derives its name (see **Figure 9.7** on the next page).

Robert Sternberg

***Intimacy* refers to warmth, closeness, and sharing in a relationship.** Signs of intimacy include giving and receiving emotional support, valuing the loved one, wanting to promote the welfare of the loved one, and sharing one's self and one's possessions with another. Self-disclosure is necessary in order to achieve and maintain feelings of intimacy in a relationship, whether platonic or romantic.

***Passion* refers to the intense feelings (both positive and negative) experienced in love relationships, including sexual desire.** Passion is related to drives that lead to romance, physical attraction, and sexual consummation. Although sexual needs may be dominant in many close relationships, other needs also figure in the experience of passion, including the needs for nurturance, self-esteem, dominance, submission, and self-actualization. For example, self-esteem is threatened when someone experiences

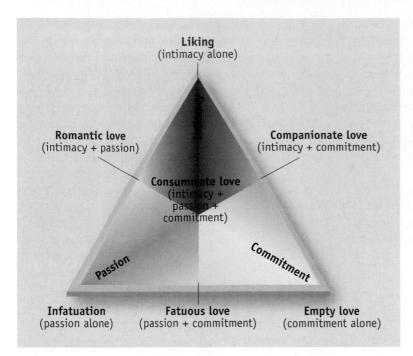

Figure 9.7

Sternberg's triangular theory of love. According to Robert Sternberg (1986), love includes three components: intimacy, passion, and commitment. These components are portrayed here as points on a triangle. The possible combinations of these three components yield the seven types of relationships mapped out here. The absence of all three components is called nonlove, which is not shown in the diagram.

Source: From Sternberg, R. J. (1986). A triangular theory of love. *Psychological Review, 93,* 119–135. Copyright © 1986 by the American Psychological Association. Reprinted by permission of the author.

jealousy. Passion obviously figures most prominently in romantic relationships.

Commitment involves the decision and intent to maintain a relationship in spite of the difficulties and costs that may arise. According to Sternberg, commitment has both short-term and long-term aspects. The short-term aspect concerns the conscious decision to love someone. The long-term aspect reflects the determination to make a relationship endure. Although the decision to love someone usually comes before commitment, that is not always the case (in arranged marriages, for instance).

Sternberg has described eight types of relationships that can result from the presence or absence of each of the three components of love, as depicted in **Figure 9.7**. One of these relationship types, nonlove, is not pictured in the diagram because it is defined as the absence of any of the three components. Most casual interactions are of this type. When all three components are present, *consummate love* is said to exist.

Sternberg's model has generated considerable interest and research. In support of his theory, researchers report that Sternberg's three components characterize not only how people think about love in general but also how they personally experience love (Aron & Westbay, 1996). All three components are positively related to satisfaction in

dating relationships (Madey & Rodgers, 2009). In an Internet survey of over 16,000 participants, all three components were related to the personality trait of agreeableness, perhaps because agreeable individuals perceive others more positively and find it easier to maintain relationships (Ahmeto-glu, Swami, & Chamorro-Premuzic, 2010). The researchers also looked at the changes in each component over time and found that commitment increased over the course of a relationship, whereas passion decreased. In a cross-cultural study of Chinese and American heterosexual couples in their 20s, questionnaires were used to measure intimacy, passion, and commitment (Gao, 2001). Scores on these three components of love increased as relationships became more serious. Although there were no significant differences between the two groups on intimacy and commitment scores, Americans scored significantly higher on the passion scale than the Chinese did. Finally, Sternberg's three components are applicable to same-sex romantic relationships as well (Bauermeister et al., 2011).

The triangular theory alone doesn't fully capture the complexity of love (Hsia & Schweinle, 2012). It seems that how people bond with others plays a role. Madey and Rodgers (2009) found that the way one bonds with others (or one's attachment style) predicts intimacy and commitment levels, which in turns predicts relationship satisfaction. To see why that might be the case, let's turn our attention to attachment theory.

Romantic Love as Attachment

In a groundbreaking theory of love, Cindy Hazan and Phillip Shaver (1987) asserted that romantic love can be conceptualized as an attachment process, with similarities to the bond between infants and their caregivers. According to these theorists, adult romantic love and infant attachment share a number of features: intense fascination with the other person, distress at separation, and efforts to stay close and spend time together. Of course, there are also differences: Infant-caregiver relationships are one-sided, whereas caregiving in romantic relationships works both ways. A second difference is that romantic relationships usually have a sexual component, whereas infant-caregiver relationships do not.

Cindy Hazan

Phillip Shaver

Today, adult attachment theory is one of the most influential approaches to the study of close relationships

(Shaver & Mikulincer, 2012). Researchers who study attachment are keenly interested in the nature and development of *attachment styles*, **or typical ways of interacting in close relationships.** Their interest is fueled by the belief that attachment styles develop during the first year of life and strongly influence individuals' interpersonal interactions from then on.

Infant attachment. Hazan and Shaver's ideas build on earlier work in attachment theory by John Bowlby (1980) and Mary Ainsworth (Ainsworth et al., 1978). Based on actual observations of infants and their primary caregivers, they identified three attachment styles. Over half of infants develop a *secure attachment style*. However, other infants develop insecure attachments. Some infants are very anxious when separated from their caretaker and show resistance at reunion, a response characterized as an *anxious-ambivalent attachment style*. A third group of infants never connect very well with their caretaker and are classified in the *avoidant attachment style*. How do attachments in infancy develop? As you can see in **Figure 9.8**, three parenting styles have been identified as likely determinants of attachment quality. A *warm/responsive* approach seems to promote secure attachments, whereas a *cold/rejecting* style is associated with avoidant attachments. An *ambivalent/inconsistent* style seems to result in anxious-ambivalent attachments.

OLJ Studio/Shutterstock.com

Parent's caregiving style	Infant attachment	Adult attachment style
Warm/responsive— She/he was generally warm and responsive; she/he was good at knowing when to be supportive and when to let me operate on my own; our relationship was always comfortable, and I have no major reservations or complaints about it.	**Secure attachment—** An infant-caregiver bond in which the child welcomes contact with a close companion and uses this person as a secure base from which to explore the environment.	**Secure—**I find it relatively easy to get close to others and am comfortable depending on them and having them depend on me. I don't often worry about being abandoned or about someone getting too close to me.
Cold/rejecting—She/he was fairly cold and distant, or rejecting, not very responsive; I wasn't her/his highest priority, her/his concerns were often elsewhere; it's possible that she/he would just as soon not have had me.	**Avoidant attachment—** An insecure infant-caregiver bond, characterized by little separation protest and a tendency for the child to avoid or ignore the caregiver.	**Avoidant—**I am somewhat uncomfortable being close to others; I find it difficult to trust them, difficult to allow myself to depend on them. I am nervous when anyone gets too close, and often love partners want me to be more intimate than I feel comfortable being.
Ambivalent/ inconsistent— She/he was noticeably inconsistent in her/his reactions to me, sometimes warm and sometimes not; she/he had her/his own agenda, which sometimes got in the way of her/his receptiveness and responsiveness to my needs; she/he definitely loved me but didn't always show it in the best way.	**Anxious/ambivalent attachment—**An insecure infant-caregiver bond, characterized by strong separation protest and a tendency of the child to resist contact initiated by the caregiver, particularly after a separation.	**Anxious/ambivalent—** I find that others are reluctant to get as close as I would like. I often worry that my partner doesn't really love me or won't want to stay with me. I want to merge completely with another person, and this desire sometimes scares people away.

Figure 9.8

Infant attachment and romantic relationships. According to Hazan and Shaver (1987), romantic relationships in adulthood are similar in form to attachment patterns in infancy, which are determined in part by parental caregiving styles. The theorized relations between parental styles, attachment patterns, and intimate relations are outlined here. Hazan and Shaver's (1987) study sparked a flurry of follow-up research, which has largely supported the basic premises of their groundbreaking theory, although the links between infant experiences and close relationships in adulthood appear to be somewhat more complex than those portrayed here. (Based on Hazan and Shaver, 1986, 1987; Shaffer, 1989)

Adult attachment. What do these attachment styles look like in adulthood? To answer this question, we'll summarize the findings of a number of studies (Mickelson, Kessler, & Shaver, 1997; Shaver & Hazan, 1993). You can also see capsule summaries of adult attachment styles in **Figure 9.8.**

• *Secure adults* (about 55% of participants). These people trust others, find it easy to get close to them, and are comfortable with mutual dependence. They rarely worry about being abandoned by their partner. Secure adults have the longest-lasting relationships and the fewest divorces. They describe their parents as behaving warmly toward them and toward each other.

• *Avoidant adults* (about 25% of participants). These individuals both fear and feel uncomfortable about getting close to others. They are reluctant to trust others and prefer to maintain emotional distance from others. They have the lowest incidence of positive relationship experiences of the three groups. Avoidant adults describe their parents as less warm than secure adults do and see their mothers as cold and rejecting.

• *Anxious-ambivalent adults* (about 20% of participants). These adults are obsessive and preoccupied with their relationships. They want more relationship closeness than their partners do and suffer extreme feelings of jealousy, based on fears of abandonment. Their relationships have the shortest duration of the three groups. Ambivalent adults describe their relationship with their parents as less warm than secure adults do and feel that their parents had unhappy marriages.

Although there are cultural variations, adult attachment theory appears to apply across cultures (Hatfield, & Rapson, 2010). Studies in Australia and Israel have confirmed that people are distributed across the three attachment styles with similar percentages in those countries (Feeney & Noller, 1990). Also, males and females are distributed similarly across the three styles, and the proportions of gay men and lesbians in the different attachment styles match those of straight men and women (Ridge & Feeney, 1998).

The current thinking assumes that attachment style is determined by where people fall on two continuous dimensions (Brennan, Clark, & Shaver, 1998). *Attachment anxiety* reflects how much a person worries that a partner will not be available when needed. This fear of abandonment stems, in part, from a person's doubts about his or her lovability. *Attachment avoidance* reflects the degree to which a person distrusts a partner's goodwill and has tendencies to maintain emotional and behavioral distance from a partner. People's scores on these two dimensions as measured by self-report data yield four attachment styles: secure, preoccupied (anxious-ambivalent), avoidant-dismissing, and avoidant-fearful. You are already familiar with the se-

cure style, and "preoccupied" is just a different label for the anxious-ambivalent style. The dismissing and fearful styles are two variations of the avoidant style.

As you can see in **Figure 9.9,** securely attached individuals (low on both anxiety and avoidance) enjoy close relationships and are not worried that others will leave them. Those in the *preoccupied* category (high on anxiety, low on avoidance) desire closeness with others but fear rejection. Those with an *avoidant-dismissing* style (high on avoidance, low on anxiety) prefer to maintain their distance from others and are not concerned about rejection, while those with an *avoidant-fearful* style (high on both avoidance and anxiety) are uncomfortable being close to others but still worry about rejection. There is evidence that this type of anxiety is at its highest in the early stages of a relationship, before it becomes established (Eastwick & Finkel, 2008).

Although it might appear from **Figure 9.9** that the four attachment styles are distinctly different categories or typologies, that is not the case (Shaver & Mikulincer, 2006). Recall that the two underlying dimensions of anxiety and avoidance are distributed along a continuum (as indicated by the arrows in the figure) from low to high. This means that people are *more or less* anxious (or avoidant) versus totally consumed by anxiety or totally without anxiety. So, as you read about the four attachment styles, keep in mind that they are "convenient labels for sets of anxiety and avoidance scores rather than distinctly different categories that have nothing in common" (Miller, Perlman, & Brehm, 2007).

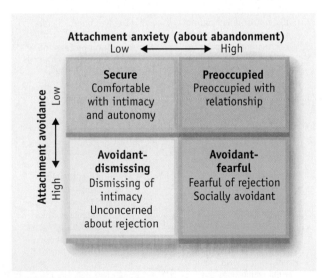

Figure 9.9

Attachment styles and their underlying dimensions. Attachment styles are determined by where people fall along two continuous dimensions that range from low to high: attachment avoidance and attachment anxiety (about abandonment). This system yields four attachment styles, which are described here. (Adapted from Brennan, Clark, & Shaver, 1998; Fraley & Shaver, 2000)

Correlates of attachment styles. The idea of adult attachment styles has stimulated a huge body of research. Among other findings, studies consistently show that securely attached individuals have more-committed, satisfying, interdependent, and well-adjusted relationships compared to those who are insecurely attached (Bartholomew, 2009). Also, high attachment anxiety is associated with lower dating relationship quality (Holland, Fraley, & Roisman, 2012). An avoidant style is associated with shorter relationships (Shaver & Brennan, 1992). Attachment styles have also been related to sexual satisfaction in heterosexual relationships: Anxious attachment in men is predictive of their female partners' sexual dissatisfaction, whereas avoidant attachment in women is related to male partners' sexual dissatisfaction (Brassard et al., 2012).

When researchers subject couples to stress in order to study the connection between attachment style and relationship health, the findings generally support attachment theory predictions (Feeney, 2004). That is, securely attached individuals both seek out and provide support under stress. By contrast, avoidant people withdraw from their partners and may become angry either when they are asked for support or when they don't receive the support they want. Anxious individuals become fearful and sometimes exhibit hostility. When discussing conflicts with their partners, anxiously attached individuals report more personal distress and escalate the severity of the conflict (Campbell et al., 2005).

In terms of psychological adjustment, securely attached people typically have better mental health than insecurely attached people (Haggerty, Hilsenroth, & Vala-Stewart, 2009). Individuals who are insecurely attached are more vulnerable to a number of problems, including low self-esteem, low self-confidence, self-consciousness, anger, resentment, anxiety, loneliness, and depression (Cooper et al., 2004; Mikulincer & Shaver, 2003).

Given these findings, you might ask yourself, how do insecure individuals find partners? To explore this question, Brumbaugh and Fraley (2010) observed participants interacting with people they thought to be potential dating partners. The researchers found that insecure people were especially good at reaching out to potential partners, presenting themselves as interesting, and conveying their positive qualities such as humor, warmth, and attentiveness. The authors speculate that "because insecure people have a great deal going against them in terms of their relative attractiveness, this may explain why they attempt to conceal or obscure their negative features through the use of positive ones that they do possess" (p. 609).

Stability of attachment styles. It appears that early bonding experiences do influence relationship styles later in life. A meta-analysis of longitudinal studies concluded that attachment styles are moderately stable over the first 19 years

of life (Fraley, 2002). However, despite the relative stability of attachment styles, they are not set in stone. In childhood, changes from secure to insecure attachment are typically related to negative life events (divorce or death of parents, parental substance abuse, maltreatment) (Waters et al., 2000). Experiences later in life, such as consistent support (or lack thereof) from one's partner, can either increase or decrease one's attachment anxiety (Shaver & Mikulincer, 2008). One study reported that a significant number of individuals (ages 26–64) in short-term psychotherapy shifted from an insecure to a secure attachment style (Travis et al., 2001). Thus, therapy may be a helpful option for those with attachment difficulties. Contemporary researchers argue that social scientists should continue to explore how social experiences "accumulate" over the course of growing up to influence adult romantic relationships (Simpson, Collins, & Salvatore, 2011).

The Course of Romantic Love

Most people find being in love exhilarating and wish the experience could last forever. Must passion fade? Regrettably, the answer to this question seems to be "yes." Consistent with this view, Sternberg's (1986) triangular theory holds that passion peaks early in a relationship and then declines in intensity. In contrast, both intimacy and commitment increase as time progresses, although they develop at different rates (see **Figure 9.10**). Research supports the idea that the intense attraction and arousal one feels for a lover does tend to subside over time—for both gays and straights (Aron, Fisher, & Strong, 2006; Kurdek, 2005).

Why does passion fade? It seems that three factors kick into high gear early, then begin to dissipate: fantasy,

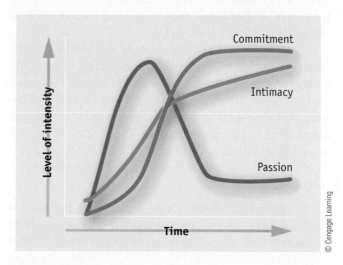

Figure 9.10

The course of love over time. According to Sternberg (1986), the three components of love typically progress differently over time. He theorizes that passion peaks early in a relationship and then declines. In contrast, intimacy and commitment are thought to build gradually.

novelty, and arousal (Miller et al., 2007). At first, love is "blind," so individuals usually develop a fantasy picture of their lover (often a projection of their own needs). However, as time passes, the intrusion of reality undermines this idealized view. Also, the novelty of a new partner fades with increased interactions and knowledge. Finally, people can't exist in a state of heightened physical arousal forever.

Does the decline of passion mean the demise of a relationship? Not necessarily. Some relationships do dissolve when early passion fades. However, many others evolve into different, but deeply satisfying, mixtures of passionate-companionate love. And while passion *does* fade over time, researchers note that passion is typically defined based on the type experienced in new relationships—the type that includes a high obsession component. Acevedo and Aron (2009) found that when you factor out obsession, romantic love (which is both engaging and sexual) does indeed exist in long-term marriages, and it is associated with relationship satisfaction. In fact, in a random sample of American adults married for more that 10 years, over 50% said they were intensely or very intensely in love with their spouse (O'Leary et al., 2012).

Why Relationships End

The question of why some relationships last while others end is a popular issue in relationship research. Nonetheless, the matter is complex, so easy answers have not been forthcoming. When it comes to break-ups, there are often differences in what people report publicly as the cause, what they actually think is the cause, and what the cause actually is (Powell & Fine, 2009). In a meta-analysis of 137 studies, Le and colleagues (2010) found that relationship factors such as commitment and love were better predictors of break-ups than individual factors such as personality or attachment style.

Let's take a look at a classic study, the Boston Couples Study (Hill et al., 1976). Here, 200 couples (predominantly college students in Boston) were followed over two years. To participate, couples had to be "going steady" and believe that they were in love. If couples split, researchers asked them to give their reasons. The results of this and other studies (Buss, 1989; Powell & Fine, 2009; Sprecher, 1994) suggest that five prominent factors contribute to romantic break-ups:

1. *Premature commitment.* Virtually all the reasons for break-ups involved things that could only be known by interacting over time. Hence, it seems that many couples make romantic commitments without taking the time to get to know each other. These individuals may find out later that they don't really like each other or that they have little in common. For these reasons, "whirlwind courtships" are risky. Intimacy needs to be combined with commitment if

relationships are to survive. Additionally, perceiving that a partner's commitment is wavering predicts the end of a relationship, regardless of one's own commitment and satisfaction level (X. Arriaga et al., 2006).

2. *Ineffective communication and conflict management skills.* All couples have disagreements. Not surprisingly, disagreements increase as couples learn more about each other and become more interdependent. Poor conflict management skills are a key factor in relationship distress and can lead to a break-up. Distressed couples tend to have more negativity in their communication, which can decrease problem solving and increase withdrawal (Cordova & Harp, 2009). As we saw in Chapter 8, the solution to this problem is not to stifle all disagreements, because conflict can be helpful to relationships. The key is to manage conflict constructively.

3. *Becoming bored with the relationship.* Couples who break up rank "boredom with the relationship" high on the list of reasons for splitting. As we have noted, novelty usually fades as people get to know each other, and boredom can set in. Individuals have needs for both novelty and predictability in close relationships (Sprecher, 1994). Balancing the two can be tricky for couples.

4. *Availability of a more attractive relationship.* Whether a deteriorating relationship actually ends depends, in great part, on the availability and awareness of a more attractive alternative (Miller, 2008). We all know of individuals who remained in unsatisfying relationships only until they met a more appealing prospect. Further, those without desirable alternatives experience more distress during break-ups than those who have desirable alternatives (Simpson, 1987).

5. *Low levels of satisfaction.* All of these factors can contribute to low levels of relationship satisfaction. Becoming dissatisfied in a relationship can erode one's commitment and increase the chances of relationship dissolution. Obviously, many other factors play a role in relationship satisfaction, including one's expectations of a partner, attachment style, and stress level (Powell & Fine, 2009).

How Relationships End

Sometimes relationships deteriorate to the point where one or both partners decide the relationship should end. Break-ups are not single events; they are instead a process (Sprecher, Zimmerman, & Abrahams, 2010). Steve Duck and colleagues proposed a model describing six processes that partners go through in relationship dissolution (Duck, 1982; Rollie & Duck, 2006). First, the relationship experiences *breakdown processes,* in which one or both partners become dissatisfied. If this breakdown becomes extreme, either partner might engage in *intrapsychic processes*— ruminating about his or her dissatisfaction, the cost of the relationship, and attractive alternatives. If commitment wavers, the couple will engage in *dyadic processes* by discussing and negotiating the conflict. At this point the relationship can be repaired. However, if partners reach the decision to end their relationship, *social processes* occur as friends and family are alerted to the problem. As the couple move toward breaking up, *grave-dressing processes* occur in which each partner develops a separate accounts of the break-up for his or her social network. Finally, each partner engages in *resurrection processes* to prepare for his or her new life. This model appears to apply to both romantic relationships and friendships (Norwood & Duck, 2009).

Helping Relationships Last

Close relationships are important to our health and happiness, so how can we increase the likelihood that they will last? Research supports the following suggestions:

1. *Take plenty of time to get to know the other person before you make a long-term commitment.* Research based on Sternberg's theory shows that intimacy built through meaningful self-disclosure is a good predictor of whether dating couples' relationships will continue (Madey & Rodgers, 2009). Other advice comes from long-married couples who were asked why they thought their relationship had lasted (Lauer & Lauer, 1985). The most frequently cited responses of 351 couples who had been married for 15 years or more were (1) friendship ("I like my spouse as a person"); (2) commitment to the relationship ("I want the relationship to succeed"); (3) similarity in values and relationship issues ("We agree on how and how often to show affection"); and (4) positive feelings about each other ("My spouse has grown more interesting"). Thus, early attention to the intimacy foundations of a relationship and ongoing, mutual efforts to build a commitment can foster more enduring love. **Figure 9.11** offers some key questions for couples to discuss before they decide to commit to their partner.

2. *Emphasize the positive qualities in your partner and relationship.* It is essential to communicate more positive than negative feelings to your partner. Early in a relationship, this is easy to do, but it gets harder as relationships continue. Recall that in well-minded relationships, people explain their partner's behaviors in ways that enhance the relationship (Harvey & Pauwels, 2009). Oddly, married couples generally make more negative and fewer positive statements to their spouse than to strangers, and we presume this situation holds for those in other types of committed relationships as well (Fincham, 2001; Fincham & Beach, 2006). Unfortunately, when one partner engages in this behavior, the other often responds in kind, which can set in motion a pattern of reciprocal negativity that makes things worse. Partners who see the best in each other, even in conflict, are more likely to stay together and experience greater

SHOULD WE MARRY?
1. What are our separate professional goals in terms of positions or jobs desired? One year from now? Five years? Fifteen years?
2. How do we decide to spend our money? Is there an amount ($50? $500? $5,000?) over which we need to discuss a purchase before committing to it?
3. Who is responsible for grocery shopping, cooking, and other tasks connected with meals? Do we eat out? A lot? A little?
4. Am I comfortable giving and receiving love, sexually? In sex, does my partner feel my love for him or her?
5. Who will take care of our child if we both work? How does each partner feel about day care?

© Cengage Learning

Figure 9.11

Key questions for dating couples to discuss before deciding to marry. To increase their chances for satisfying and long-lasting marriages and partnerships, experts advise dating couples to get to know each other well. Author Susan Piver (2000) has developed a list of 100 essential questions for couples to discuss before they make long-term commitments. The questions cover home, money, work, sex, health and food, family, children, community and friends, and spiritual life. Here is a sample of five questions to consider.

Source: From Piver, S. (2000). *The hard questions: 100 essential questions to ask before you say "I do."* New York: Jeremy P. Tarcher/Putnam.

satisfaction (Murray, Holmes, & Griffin, 1996). Hence, as the old song advises, it helps to "accentuate the positive."

3. *Develop effective conflict management skills.* Conflicts arise in all relationships, so it's essential to handle them well. For one thing, it's helpful to distinguish between minor annoyances and significant problems. You need to learn to see minor irritations in perspective and recognize how little they matter. With big problems, however, it's usually best to avoid the temptation to sweep them under the rug in the hope that they'll disappear. Important issues rarely vanish on their own, and if you postpone the inevitable discussion, the "sweepings" will have accumulated, making it harder to sort out the various issues. An interaction pattern common to dissatisfied couples is "demand-withdraw" (Eldridge, 2009). Typically, this pattern involves the woman pressing the man to discuss a relationship problem and the man avoiding or withdrawing from the interaction. This pattern is associated with the "closeness versus separateness dilemma," in which one partner wants more intimacy and closeness and the other wants more privacy and independence (Sagrestano, Heavey, & Christensen, 2006). For more specific suggestions on handling conflict, refer to our discussion in Chapter 8.

4. *Find ways to bring novelty to long-term relationships.* As romantic partners learn more about each other and develop feelings of intimacy, they also become more predictable to each other. But, too much predictability can translate into loss of interest and, possibly, boredom. As you can see in **Figure 9.12**, central to relationship boredom is the lack of novelty (Harasymchuk & Fehr, 2010). One way to keep things interesting is to engage in new activities together. In fact, one study reported that couples who participated in exciting activities together (versus just spending time together) showed increases in relationship satisfaction over a 10-week period (Reissman, Aron, & Bergen, 1993).

Rank	Dating	Married
1	Doing same things	Doing same things
2	Fighting/arguments	Not going out, staying in
3	Watching movies together all the time	Not seeing partner
4	Spend too much time together	No communication
5	Routine	Work spillover
6	Not going out, staying in	Partner does things without spouse
7	Talk about the same things	Routine
8	Doing something partner likes, but you do not	Not socializing with others
9	Nothing to talk about	Watching movies together all the time
10	No communication	Talk about the same things

© Cengage Learning

Figure 9.12

Most frequently cited causes of boredom in dating and married relationships. In a 2010 study of dating and married individuals, Harasymchuk and Fehr (2010) obtained participants' perceived causes of relational boredom. Many of these factors—including "doing the same things," which was the most frequently cited for both groups—overlap, but some are unique to one of the groups. As you can see, central to relational boredom is the lack of novelty.

Source: Adapted from Harasymchuk, C., & Fehr, B. (2010). A script analysis of relational boredom: Causes, feelings, and coping strategies. *Journal of Social and Clinical Psychology, 29*(9), 988–1019.

THE INTERNET AND RELATIONSHIPS

LEARNING OBJECTIVES

- Clarify how differences between Internet and face-to-face interactions affect relationship development.
- Describe the pros and cons of building intimacy online.
- Discuss the role of the Internet in face-to-face interactions.

To meet prospective friends and romantic partners, people used to be limited to school, work, and church settings. Then came the "bar scene," personal ads, and speed dating. Now, the Internet has dramatically expanded opportunities for people to meet and develop relationships through social networking services (Facebook, Twitter, Instagram), online dating services (eHarmony, Match.com), interactive virtual worlds, online multiple player games, chat rooms, and blogs. It is becoming increasingly common for the Internet to play a role in social interactions.

Critics of these social networking trends fear the demise of face-to-face interactions, widespread loneliness and alienation, and millions being lured into dangerous liaisons by unscrupulous people. But research to date generally paints a positive picture of the Internet's impact on people's connections with one another. For example, the web offers a wealth of interaction opportunities for those normally sepa-

rated because of geography or physical infirmity. Also, Internet groups provide a safer venue than "real life" for individuals with social anxiety or those with stigmatized identities (for example, transgendered people) to interact. Similarly, Internet groups for those with grave illnesses (cancer, multiple sclerosis, diabetes, AIDS) provide important support and information to their subscribers.

Developing Close Relationships Online

In a short period of time, the Internet has become an indispensable vehicle for making acquaintances and developing relationships. One survey based on a nationally representative sample of American adults reported that 31% (representing 63 million people) knew someone who had used a dating website, and 11% (representing 16 million adults) had visited such a site to meet people (Madden & Lenhart,

2006). Among those who used online dating sites, a majority (52%) reported "mostly positive" experiences, although a sizable number (29%) had "mostly negative" experiences. Further, McKenna, Green, and Gleason (2002) reported that 22% of their participants said that they were living with, had become engaged to, or were married to someone they had first met on the Internet. Madden and Lenhart (2006) asked the Internet users who said they were single and looking for a romantic partner to identify how they used the Internet for dating. You can see their responses in **Figure 9.13**.

The differences between Internet and face-to-face communication require psychologists to reexamine the established theories and principles of relationship development that we discuss in this chapter. For example, good looks and close physical proximity are powerful factors in initial attraction in the real world. On the Internet, where people often form relationships sight unseen, these factors are less relevant. In the absence of physical appearance, similarity of interests and values kicks in earlier and assumes more power than it does in face-to-face relationships (McKenna, 2009). Research indicates that the more similar an online friend, the stronger the

Justin Pumfrey/Taxi/Getty Images

bond (Mesch & Talmud, 2007). One study found that pairs of strangers who chatted on the Internet liked each other more than if they had talked face-to-face (McKenna et al., 2002). But in another study of pairs randomly assigned to either face-to-face or Internet chat conversations, the face-to-face group felt more satisfied with the experience and felt a higher degree of closeness and self-disclosure with their partners (Mallen, Day, & Green, 2003). Even in long-term friendships, enhanced self-disclosure through emails or instant messaging increases feelings of closeness (McKenna, 2009).

Building Online Intimacy

Although critics are concerned that Internet relationships are superficial, research suggests that virtual relationships can be just as intimate as face-to-face ones and are sometimes even closer (Bargh, McKenna, & Fitzsimons, 2002). Because the Internet is shrouded in the cloak of anonymity, people can take greater risks in online self-disclosure. Thus, feelings of intimacy can develop more quickly (McKenna & Bargh, 2000). Sometimes this experience can set up a false sense of intimacy, which can create uncomfortable feelings if a face-to-face meeting ensues—that is, meeting with a stranger who knows "too much" about you (Hamilton, 1999). Of course, such face-to-face meetings can also go smoothly. Experts caution that whenever you share private information online, you are sharing it in a public space (DeAndrea, Tong, & Walther, 2011).

In addition to facilitating self-disclosure, anonymity also allows people to construct a virtual identity. Obviously, this can be a problem if one person adopts a fictional persona and another assumes that it is authentic and begins to take the relationship seriously. A related concern is truthfulness. In one survey, only 25% of online daters admitted to using deception (Byrm & Lenton, 2001), yet a whopping 86% of participants in an online dating site felt that others misrepresented their physical appearance (Gibbs, Ellison, & Heino, 2006). The most common factors that online daters

DATING-RELATED ACTIVITIES ONLINE	
Online activities	Single and looking Internet users (%)
Flirt with someone	40
Go to an online dating website	37
Ask someone out on a date	28
Find a place offline, like a nightclub or singles event, where you might meet someone to date	27
Been introduced to a potential date by a third party using email or instant messaging	21
Participate in an online group where you hope to meet people to date	19
Search for information about someone you dated in the past	18
Maintain a long-distance relationship	18
Search for information about someone you are currently dating or are about to meet for a first date	17
Break up with someone you are dating	9

Figure 9.13

Dating-related activities online. Researchers asked Internet users who were single and looking for a romantic partner how they used the Internet (including email and instant messaging) for dating (Madden & Lenhart, 2006). Flirting and going to an online dating website were most frequently mentioned. Most respondents engaged in three or fewer of these activities.

Source: Adapted from Madden & Lenhart (2006). *Online dating.* Retrieved April 29, 2007 from http://www.pewinternet.org/pdfs/PIP_Online_Dating.pdf. (Dating-Related Activities Online table, p. 5) Reprinted by permission of PEW Internet & American Life Project. Washington, D.C.

misrepresent are age, appearance, and marital status (Byrm & Lenton, 2001). In fact, one study found that the lower the online daters' attractiveness, the more likely they were to lie about their physical descriptors such as height, weight, and age (Toma & Hancock, 2010).

Some people rationalize lying online because it has practical advantages: Men on dating sites who claim to earn high salaries receive more replies than those who say they earn less money (Epstein, 2007). In addition, there are semantic misunderstandings: One person's "average" may be another person's "plump." Another reason some people "stretch the truth" is to work around frustrating constraints imposed by the technological design of dating websites (such as age cutoffs). Finally, creating an accurate online representation of oneself is a complex process: Individuals need to put their best self forward to attract potential dates, but they also need to present themselves authentically—especially if they expect to meet a person face to face (Gibbs et al., 2006). One study found that online daters dealt with this tension by constructing profiles that reflected their "ideal self" rather than their "actual self" (Ellison, Heino, & Gibbs, 2006). Sprecher (2011) notes that such misrepresentations are typical in any early courtship; however, they are more common online because people are forced to provide comprehensive self-descriptions that ordinarily would come up gradually over time.

Moving Beyond Online Relationships

Many virtual relationships migrate to face-to-face interactions. When people do decide to move beyond an Internet-based relationship, actual meetings usually take place only after telephone contact. Researchers find that romantic

relationships that begin on the Internet seem to be just as stable over two years as traditional relationships (McKenna, Green, & Gleason, 2002).

The Internet has also assumed importance in maintaining established relationships. In a poll of 1,000 Internet users, 94% reported that the Internet made it easier for them to communicate with friends and family who live far away, and 87% said that they use it regularly for that purpose (D'Amico, 1998). **Figure 9.14** depicts the most commonly reported uses of social networking sites. Although some social critics predicted that online activity would reduce face-to-face interactions, Internet users typically maintain their social involvements while cutting back on TV time (Boase & Wellman, 2006). Additionally, online communication is linked to increased closeness in existing friendships for adolescents (Valkenburg & Peter, 2007). However, playing Internet games and visiting chat rooms are negatively related to the quality of best friendship and romantic relationships (Blais et al., 2008).

The Internet has definitely changed the relationship landscape, and not just in the initial stages of relationships (Finkel et al., 2012). Individuals can use the Internet to

"Your online profile stated that you were tall, dark and handsome. Have you ever considered a career in fiction writing?"

REPORTED USES OF SOCIAL NETWORK SITES BY MYSPACE AND FACEBOOK USERS	
Use	**Percent reporting**
To keep in touch with old friends	96
To keep in touch with current friends	91
To post/look at pictures	57
To make new friends	56
To locate old friends	55
For dating purposes	8

Figure 9.14

How social networking sites are used. With the help of social networking sites, the Internet has dramatically expanded opportunities for people to meet and develop relationships. When surveyed, the majority of MySpace and Facebook users used their accounts to locate and keep in touch with friends, both old and new. Only a small percentage reported using their accounts for dating purposes.

Source: Adapted from Raacke & Bonds-Raacke, (2008). MySpace and Facebook: Applying the uses and gratifications theory in exploring friend-networking sites. *CyberPsychology and Behavior,11*(2), 169–174.

sustain contacts, reconnect, and even break up with others. Additional research in this fascinating area will not only provide valuable information about virtual relationships but also reveal interesting new perspectives on face-to-face relationships. Experts caution that excessive reliance on the Internet for social relationships has drawbacks and can lead to the "illusion of companionship" (Turkle, 2011) while actually fostering loneliness.

OVERCOMING LONELINESS

LEARNING OBJECTIVES

- Describe loneliness, and discuss its prevalence.
- Explain how early experiences and current social trends contribute to loneliness.
- Understand how shyness, poor social skills, and self-defeating attributions contribute to loneliness.
- Summarize the suggestions for conquering loneliness.

Answer the following "true" or "false."

____ **1.** Adolescents and young adults are the loneliest age group.

____ **2.** Many people who are lonely are also shy.

____ **3.** The seeds of loneliness are often sown early in life.

____ **4.** Effective social skills can be learned relatively easily.

All of the above are true, as you'll learn shortly. But let's start with a couple of general points. First, being alone doesn't necessarily produce feelings of loneliness. In these fast-paced times, solitude can provide needed down time to recharge your batteries. Also, people need time alone to deepen self-understanding, wrestle with decisions, and contemplate important life issues. Second, people can feel lonely even when surrounded by others (at a party or concert, for instance). It's possible to have a large social network but not feel close to anyone in particular.

The Nature and Prevalence of Loneliness

Loneliness occurs when a person has fewer interpersonal relationships than desired or when these relationships are not as satisfying as desired. Of course, people vary in their needs for social connections. Thus, if you're not distressed by the quantity or quality of your social and emotional ties, you wouldn't be considered lonely.

We can think about loneliness in various ways. One approach is to look at the type of relationship deficit involved (Weiss, 1973). *Emotional loneliness* stems from the absence of an intimate attachment figure. For a child, this figure is typically a parent; for an adult, it is usually a spouse or partner or a best friend. *Social loneliness* results from the lack of a friendship network (typically provided in school, work, or church settings and in community groups). For example, a married couple who move to a new city will experience social loneliness until they make new social connections; however, because they have each other, they should not experience emotional loneliness. On the other hand, a recently divorced person will probably feel emotional loneliness but should not experience social loneliness if work and friendship networks remain intact (which is not always the case).

Emotional loneliness seems to be tied to the absence of a romantic partner in both college students and senior adults (Green et al., 2001). Social loneliness, however, seems to spring from different roots, depending on age. In college students, it's the *quantity* of friendship contacts that counts; among the older group, it's the *quality* of contacts. It's also worth noting that social support can't compensate for emotional loneliness—for example, the presence of friends and family cannot substitute for a loved one who has died. Of course, this is not to say that social support is unimportant. The point is that different types of loneliness require different responses; therefore, you need to pinpoint the exact nature of your social deficits to cope effectively with loneliness.

A second way to look at loneliness is in terms of its duration (Young, 1982). *Transient loneliness* involves brief and sporadic feelings of loneliness, which many people may experience even when their social lives are reasonably adequate. *Transitional loneliness* occurs when people who have had satisfying social relationships in the past become lonely after experiencing a disruption in their social network (the death of a loved one, say, or a divorce or a move). *Chronic loneliness*

Piotr Marcinski/Shutterstock.com

is a condition that affects people who have been unable to develop a satisfactory interpersonal network over a period of years. Here we focus on chronic loneliness.

How many people are plagued by loneliness? Although we don't have a precise answer to this question, anecdotal evidence suggests that the number is substantial. Telephone hotlines for troubled people report that complaints of loneliness dominate their calls. No doubt some of the popularity of social network sites, instant messaging, and chat rooms can be traced to loneliness.

The prevalence of loneliness in specific age groups actually contradicts stereotypes. For example, many assume that the loneliest age group is the elderly, but this "distinction" actually belongs to adolescents and young adults (Snell & March, 2008). Gay and lesbian adolescents are particularly likely to be lonely (Westefeld et al., 2001). Loneliness is also common among college students (Knox, Vail-Smith, & Zusman, 2007). A second surprising finding is that loneliness decreases with age, at least until the much later years of adulthood when one's friends begin to die or one becomes widowed (DePaulo, 2011; Schnittker, 2007).

In line with expectations, people who live alone are lonelier than those who live with a partner (Pinquart, 2003). In a national survey of individuals ages 57 to 85, researchers found that the number of friends and relatives, as well as the frequency of contact, was related to reduced loneliness (Shiovitz-Ezra & Leitsch, 2010). For participants who were not married, there was a negative relationship between the number of relatives and loneliness.

Women are found to be lonelier than men, but only on measures that use words such as "lonely" or "loneliness" (Borys & Perlman, 1985). Thus, it is likely that this apparent gender difference is really men's reluctance to admit to feeling lonely. In fact, when surveying men and women in the Netherlands, researchers found that divorced men are more likely to suffer from emotional loneliness than divorced women are (Dykstra & Fokkema, 2007).

The Roots of Loneliness

Any event that ruptures the social fabric of a person's life may lead to loneliness, so no one is immune. We'll consider the roles of early experience and social trends.

Early Experiences

A key problem in chronic loneliness seems to be early negative social behavior that leads to rejection by peers (Pedersen et al., 2007). Children who are aggressive or withdrawn are likely to suffer peer rejection even in preschool (Ray et al., 1997). What prompts inappropriate social behavior in young children? One factor is an insecure attachment style. Because of difficult early parent-infant interactions, children often develop social behaviors (aggression, aloofness, competitiveness, overdependence)

that "invite" rejection by adults and peers (Bartholomew, 1990). You can see how a vicious cycle gets set up. A child's inappropriate behavior prompts rejection, which in turn triggers negative expectations about social interactions in the child, which can lead to more negative behavior, and so on. To help break this self-defeating cycle (and head off the loneliness that can result), it is crucial to help children learn appropriate social skills early in life. Without intervention, this vicious cycle can continue and result in chronic loneliness. Indeed, one study found that attachment style at the age of only 24 months was predictive of later childhood loneliness (Raikes & Thompson, 2008).

Social Trends

Some social commentators and social scientists are concerned that recent trends are undermining social connections in our culture (McPherson, Smith-Lovin, & Brashears, 2006). Cacioppo and Patrick (2008) discuss "being lonely in a social world." A number of factors come into play. Parents (especially if they are single) may be so pressed for time that they have little time to cultivate adult relationships (Olds & Schwartz, 2009). Because of busy schedules, face-to-face interactions at home are reduced as family members eat on the run, on their own, or in front of the TV without meaningful family conversation. Further, superficial social interactions become prevalent as people order their meals and do their banking at drive-up windows, purchase their groceries via automated checkout stations, and so forth. While tech-

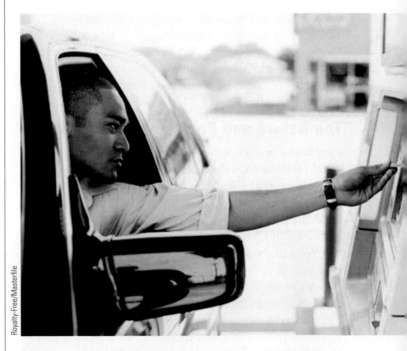

Royalty-Free/Masterfile

Thanks to automation and online technology, people today are able to take care of many of life's necessities without interacting with other human beings. These reduced opportunities for social interaction help fuel increased loneliness.

nology makes life easier in some respects and does provide opportunities for developing relationships, it has its downsides. As previously mentioned, online relationships that are void of true connection and intimacy can leave us feeling lonely (Turkle, 2011).

Correlates of Loneliness

For people who are chronically lonely, painful feelings are a fact of life. Three factors that figure prominently in chronic loneliness are shyness, poor social skills, and a self-defeating attributional style. Of course, the link between these factors and loneliness could go either way. Feeling lonely might cause a person to make negative attributions about others, but making negative attributions can also lead to loneliness.

Shyness

Shyness is positively related to loneliness (Woodhouse, Dykas, & Cassidy, 2012). *Shyness* **refers to discomfort, inhibition, and excessive caution in interpersonal relations.** Specifically, shy people tend to (1) be timid about expressing themselves, (2) be overly self-conscious about how others react to them, (3) embarrass easily, and (4) experience physiological symptoms of their anxiety, such as a racing pulse, blushing, or an upset stomach. In pioneering research on shyness, Philip Zimbardo (1977, 1990) and his associates report that 60% of shy people indicated that their shyness was *situationally specific*. That is, their shyness was triggered only in certain social contexts, such as asking someone for help or interacting with a large group of people. Supporting the importance of the situation, one study found that self-reported shyness was related to decreased self-disclosures in an online conversation, but only when a webcam was present. Shyness was not related to self-disclosure when there was no webcam (Brunet & Schmidt, 2007).

Poor Social Skills

A variety of problematic social skills are associated with loneliness (Gierveld, van Tilburg, & Dykstra, 2006). A common finding is that lonely people show lower responsiveness to their conversational partners and are more self-focused (Rook, 1998). Similarly, researchers report that lonely people are relatively inhibited and unassertive, speaking less than nonlonely people. They also seem to disclose less about themselves than those who are not lonely or who are less socially anxious (Cuming & Rapee, 2010). This (often unconscious) tendency has the effect of keeping people at an emotional distance and limits interactions to a relatively superficial level. These interactional problems are based, in part, on heightened fears of rejection (Jackson et al., 2002). It seems that people with "rejection anxiety" believe that their signaled interest is obvious to others when it is not (Vorauer et al., 2003). Thus, unaware that their signal was invisible, those with rejection anxiety may perceive rejection where none exists. The fact that social skills deficits and peer acceptance are predictive of loneliness isn't simply a Western phenomenon; it has been demonstrated among Japanese and Chinese students as well (Aikawa, Fujita, & Tanaka, 2007; Liu & Wang, 2009).

Self-Defeating Attributional Style

It's easy to see how repeated rejections can foster negative expectations about social interactions. Thus, lonely people are prone to irrational thinking about their social skills, the probability of their achieving intimacy, the likelihood of being rejected, and so forth. Unfortunately, once people develop these negative ideas, they often behave in ways that confirm their expectations, again setting up a vicious cycle of behavior.

Jeffrey Young (1982) points out that lonely people engage in *negative self-talk* that prevents them from pursuing intimacy in an active and positive manner. He has identified some clusters of ideas that foster loneliness. **Figure 9.15** on the next page gives examples of typical thoughts from six of these clusters of cognitions and the overt behaviors that result. As you can see, several of the cognitions in **Figure 9.15** are stable, internal self-attributions. This tendency to attribute loneliness to stable, internal causes constitutes a self-defeating attributional style (Anderson et al., 1994). That is, lonely people tell themselves that they're lonely because they're basically unlovable individuals. Not only is this a devastating belief, it is self-defeating because it offers no way to change the situation. Happily, it *is* possible to reduce loneliness, as you'll see.

Conquering Loneliness

The personal consequences associated with chronic loneliness can be painful and sometimes overwhelming: low self-esteem, hostility, depression, alcoholism, psychosomatic illness, and, possibly, suicide (McWhirter, 1990). Chronic loneliness is also associated with immune system deficits and is a predictor of a number of diseases, including cardiovascular disease and cancer (Hawkley & Cacioppo, 2009), and it has been linked to poor sleep quality

Learn More Online

The Shyness Homepage

The Shyness Institute (Portola Valley, CA) offers a "gathering of network resources for people seeking information and services for shyness." The Institute is co-directed by psychologists Lynne Henderson and Philip Zimbardo.

Clusters	Cognitions	Behaviors
A	1. I'm undesirable. 2. I'm dull and boring.	Avoidance of friendship
B	1. I can't communicate with other people. 2. My thoughts and feelings are bottled up inside.	Low self-disclosure
C	1. I'm not a good lover in bed. 2. I can't relax, be spontaneous, and enjoy sex.	Avoidance of sexual relationships
D	1. I can't seem to get what I want from this relationship. 2. I can't say how I feel, or he/she might leave me.	Lack of assertiveness in relationships
E	1. I won't risk being hurt again. 2. I'd screw up any relationship.	Avoidance of potentially intimate relationships
F	1. I don't know how to act in this situation. 2. I'll make a fool of myself.	Avoidance of other people

CLUSTERS OF COGNITIONS TYPICAL OF LONELY PEOPLE

Figure 9.15

Patterns of thinking underlying loneliness. According to Young (1982), negative self-talk contributes to loneliness. Six clusters of irrational thoughts are illustrated here. Each cluster of cognitions leads to certain patterns of behavior (right) that promote loneliness.

Source: From a paper presented at the annual convention of the American Psychological Association, 9/2/79. An expanded version of this paper appears in G. Emery, S. D. Hollan, & R. C. Bedrosian (Eds.) (1981). *New directions in cognitive therapy.* New York: Guilford Press and in L. A. Peplau & D. Perlman (Eds.) (1982). *Loneliness: A sourcebook of current theory, research and therapy.* New York: Wiley. Copyright © 1982 by John Wiley & Sons, Inc. and Jeffrey Young.

(Hawkley & Cacioppo, 2010). Although there are no simple solutions to loneliness, there are some effective ones. Let's look at four useful strategies.

One option is to use the Internet to overcome loneliness, although this approach can be a double-edged sword. On the plus side, the Internet is an obvious boon to busy people, those with stigmatized social identities, and those who find physical mobility difficult (the infirm and people with serious medical conditions). Among lonely persons, Internet use is associated with benefits such as reduced loneliness, improved social support, and formation of online friendships (Morahan-Martin & Schumacher, 2003; Shaw, & Gant, 2002). Moreover, socially anxious people can interact without the pressure involved in face-to-face communication (Bonetti, Campbell, & Gilmore, 2010). On the other hand, if lonely people spend a lot of time online, they might devote less time to face-to-face relationships and might not develop the self-confidence to pursue relationships offline. One study found that lonely individuals more often reported that Internet use caused disturbances in their daily functioning (Morahan-Martin & Schumacher, 2003), raising concerns about Internet addiction.

A second suggestion is to resist the temptation to withdraw from social situations. A study that asked people what they did when they felt lonely found the top responses to be "read" and "listen to music" (Rubenstein & Shaver, 1982). These days, playing computer games and

using the Internet are also options. If done occasionally, these activities can be constructive ways of dealing with loneliness. However, as long-term strategies, they do nothing to help a lonely person acquire new "real-world" friends. This situation is particularly relevant to those with an avoidant attachment style. Research indicates that, for first-year college students, involvement in extracurricular activities is related to a lower degree of loneliness (Bohnert, Aikins, & Edidin, 2007). The importance of staying active socially cannot be overemphasized. Recall that proximity is a powerful factor in the development of close relationships. To make friends, you have to be around people.

A third strategy is to break out of the habit of the self-defeating attributional style we just discussed ("I'm lonely because I'm unlovable"). There are other attributions a lonely person could make, and these alternative explanations point to solutions (see **Figure 9.16**). If someone says, "My conversational skills are weak" (unstable, internal cause), the solution would be: "I'll try to find out how to improve them." Or, if someone thinks, "It always takes time to meet people when you move to a new location" (unstable, external cause), this attribution suggests the solution of trying harder to establish new relationships and giving them time to develop. The attribution "I've really searched, but I just can't find enough compatible people at my workplace" (stable, external cause) may lead to the decision, "It's time to look for a new job." As you can see, the last three attribu-

Figure 9.16

Stability dimension

Internal-external dimension		Unstable cause (temporary)	Stable cause (permanent)
	Internal cause	I'm lonely now, but won't be for long. I need to get out and meet some new people.	I'm lonely because I'm unlovable. I'll never be worth loving.
	External cause	My lover and I just split up. I guess some relationships work and some don't. Maybe I'll be luckier next time.	The people here are cold and unfriendly. It's time to look for a new job.

Attributions and loneliness. Lonely people often have a self-defeating attributional style, in which they attribute their loneliness to stable, internal causes (see upper right quadrant). Learning to make alternative attributions (see other quadrants) can bring to light ways to deal with loneliness and facilitate active coping.

Source: Based on Shaver, P., & Rubenstein, C. (1980). Childhood attachment experience and adult loneliness. In L. Wheeler (Ed.), *Review of personality and social psychology* (Vol.1, pp. 42–73). Thousand Oaks, CA: Sage Publications.

tions lead to active modes of coping rather than the passivity fostered by a self-defeating attributional style.

Finally, to thwart loneliness, people need to cultivate their social skills. You'll find a wealth of information on this important topic in Chapter 8 (Interpersonal Communication). Lonely people, especially, should focus on attending to others' nonverbal signals, deepening the level of their self-disclosure, engaging in active listening, improving their conversational skills, and developing an assertive communication style.

Anyone who feels overwhelmed at the prospect of tackling loneliness on his or her own should consider seeing a counselor or therapist. Dealing with loneliness and shyness usually involves work on two fronts. First, counselors help people improve social skills through *social skills training*. In this program, individuals learn and practice the skills involved in initiating and maintaining relationships. Second, counselors use *cognitive therapy* (see Chapter 15) to help lonely and shy individuals break the habit of automatic negative thoughts and self-defeating attributions. Over a series of sessions, individuals learn to change their negative views of themselves ("I'm boring") and other people ("They're cold and unfriendly"). Both of these approaches have high success rates, and they can pave the way to more positive social interactions that are critical to adjustment.

RECOMMENDED reading

Loneliness: Human Nature and the Need for Social Connection

by John T. Cacioppo and William Patrick (W. W. Norton & Company, 2008)

John T. Cacioppo is an internationally recognized expert on social and emotional influences on human behavior. With William Patrick he has compiled a readable book summarizing decades of research on one of the most difficult interpersonal problems: loneliness. The first part, "The Lonely Heart," discusses the roots and implications of loneliness in the modern world. In the second part, "From Selfish Genes to Social Beings," the authors use an evolutionary perspective to explore people's need for connectedness. The last part, "Finding Meaning in Connection," offers suggestions for identifying and reducing one's own loneliness. Whether you are lonely or not, this book is an interesting and insightful read.

Log on to CourseMate at **www.cengagebrain.com** *for descriptions of other recommended books.*

CHAPTER 9 | Review

KEY IDEAS

THE INGREDIENTS OF CLOSE RELATIONSHIPS

- Close relationships are those that are important, interdependent, and long-lasting. They include friendships as well as work, family, and romantic relationships. They can elicit both positive and negative emotions.

RELATIONSHIP DEVELOPMENT

- People are initially drawn to others who are nearby, who are seen often, and who are physically attractive. Although physical attractiveness plays a key role in initial attraction, people also seek other desirable characteristics, such as kindness and intelligence. There is general agreement about what makes a person attractive. People often match up on looks, but sometimes men trade status for physical attractiveness in women, and vice versa.
- As people get acquainted, they prefer others who like them and who are similar to them in various ways. Couples tend to be similar in age, race, religion, education, and attitudes.
- Once relationships are established, people engage in various maintenance behaviors and actions to sustain them. Interdependence (social exchange) theory uses principles of reinforcement to predict relationship satisfaction and commitment. How individuals apply social exchange principles depends on whether they are in exchange or communal relationships.

FRIENDSHIP

- A key component of friendship is emotional support. Women's same-gender friendships are usually characterized by self-disclosure and intimacy, whereas men's same-gender friendships typically involve doing things together. Some friendship issues are more complex for homosexuals than heterosexuals. Friends must engage in friendship repair if they are dealing with conflict.

ROMANTIC LOVE

- Research indicates that the experience of romantic love is similar for heterosexual and homosexual individuals. Contrary to stereotypes, men may be more romantic in some ways than women. In choosing a partner, women are more selective than men.
- Sternberg's triangular theory of love proposes that passion, intimacy, and commitment combine into eight types of love. Hazan and Shaver theorize that love relationships follow the form of attachments developed in infancy.
- Researchers subsequently expanded the number of attachment styles from three to four: secure, preoccupied, avoidant-dismissing, and avoidant-fearful. Each style has a characteristic profile. Although attachment styles show stability over time, it is possible for them to change.
- Initially, romantic love is usually characterized by passion, but strong passion appears to fade over time for a number of reasons. In relationships that continue, passionate love evolves into a less intense, more mature form of love.
- The chief causes of relationship failure are the tendency to make premature commitments, ineffective conflict management

skills, boredom with the relationship, and the availability of a more attractive relationship. To help relationships last, couples should take the time to know each other very well, emphasize the positive qualities in their partner and relationship, develop effective conflict management skills, and engage in novel activities together.

THE INTERNET AND RELATIONSHIPS

- The Internet offers many new vehicles for meeting others and developing relationships. The differences between Internet and face-to-face communication have important implications for established psychological theories and principles of relationship development.
- Virtual relationships can be just as intimate as face-to-face ones. However, people often misrepresent themselves online. Many online relationships go on to become face-to-face ones.

APPLICATION: OVERCOMING LONELINESS

- Loneliness involves discontent with the extent and quality of one's interpersonal network. A surprisingly large number of people in our society are troubled by loneliness. The age groups most affected by loneliness contradict stereotypes.
- The origins of chronic loneliness can often be traced to early negative behavior that triggers rejection by peers and teachers. Social trends may also promote loneliness. Loneliness is associated with shyness, poor social skills, and self-defeating attributions.
- The keys to overcoming loneliness include resisting the temptation to withdraw from social situations, avoiding self-defeating attributions, and working on one's social skills.

KEY TERMS

Attachment styles p. 277
Close relationships p. 263
Commitment p. 276
Comparison level pp. 271–272
Comparison level for
  alternatives p. 272
Heterosexism p. 274
Interdependence theory p. 271
Intimacy p. 275
Investments p. 272
Loneliness p. 285
Matching hypothesis p. 268
Mere exposure effect p. 265
Parental investment theory
  p. 268
Passion p. 275
Proximity p. 264
Reciprocal liking p. 269
Relationship maintenance
  p. 270
Sexual orientation p. 274
Shyness p. 287
Social exchange theory p. 271

KEY PEOPLE

Michael Cunningham p. 266
David Buss p. 268
Cindy Hazan and Philip Shaver pp. 276–278
Harold Kelley and John Thibaut pp. 271–272
Robert Sternberg pp. 275–276
Philip Zimbardo p. 287

1. The *mere exposure effect* refers to an increase in positive feelings due to
   a. seeing someone often.
   b. interacting with someone.
   c. communicating via email often.
   d. seeing someone once.

2. Jack and Liz have been dating for two years. They are a good example of the matching hypothesis. This means that they are matched on the basis of
   a. religion.
   b. personality.
   c. socioeconomic status.
   d. looks.

3. A sociocultural explanation for the finding that women are more selective than men in choosing partners is that women
   a. have better vision than men.
   b. have less economic power than men.
   c. are less superficial than men.
   d. have to compensate for being more romantic than men.

4. Women's same-gender friendships are typically based on _____; men's are typically based on _____.
   a. shopping together; hunting together
   b. attending sports events; attending sports events
   c. shared activities; intimacy and self-disclosure
   d. intimacy and self-disclosure; shared activities

5. If a researcher fails to determine the sexual orientation of her research participants and reports her findings without any mention of homosexuals, her study suffers from
   a. homosexism.
   b. social exchange.
   c. heterosexism.
   d. homophobia.

6. Tracey's personal standard of what constitutes an acceptable balance of rewards and costs in a relationship is termed
   a. social exchange.
   b. comparison level.
   c. proximity level.
   d. relationship satisfaction.

7. Jenna tends to keep her distance from others and is unconcerned about social rejection. She would be classified in which of the following attachment styles?
   a. Secure
   b. Preoccupied
   c. Avoidant-dismissing
   d. Avoidant-fearful

8. Ross is going through a painful break-up. He is ruminating about his dissatisfaction, the costs of his relationship, and his alternatives. Steve Duck would say Ross going through which of the following processes?
   a. Breakdown
   b. Intrapsychic
   c. Dyadic
   d. Social

9. Which of the following statements regarding self-disclosure in online communication is accurate?
   a. Because online communication is anonymous, people take fewer risks in online self-disclosure.
   b. Because online communication is anonymous, people take greater risks in online self-disclosure.
   c. Because there is a potential record of one's online communication, people take fewer risks in online self-disclosure.
   d. There is no difference in self-disclosure in online versus face-to-face communication.

10. A self-defeating attributional style associated with loneliness involves attributing loneliness to
    a. internal, stable factors.
    b. internal, unstable factors.
    c. external, stable factors.
    d. external, unstable factors.

ANSWERS

1. a Pages 265–266
2. d Page 268
3. b Page 269
4. d Page 273
5. c Pages 274–275
6. b Pages 271–272
7. c Page 278
8. b Pages 280–281
9. b Page 283
10. a Page 287

COURSEMATE

Go to **CengageBrain.com** to access Psychology CourseMate, where you will find an interactive eBook, glossaries, flashcards, quizzes, videos, and more.

PERSONAL EXPLORATIONS WORKBOOK

Go to the *Personal Explorations Workbook* in the back of your textbook for exercises that can enhance your self-understanding in relation to issues raised in this chapter.

Exercise 9.1 *Self-Assessment:* Social Avoidance and Distress Scale

Exercise 9.2 *Self-Reflection:* How Do You Relate to Friends?

CHAPTER 10

Marriage and Intimate Relationships

Stockbyte/Getty Images

"My hands are shaky. I want to call her again but I know it is no good. She'll only yell and scream. It makes me feel lousy. I have work to do but I can't do it. I can't concentrate. I want to call people up, go see them, but I'm afraid they'll see that I'm shaky. I just want to talk. I can't think about anything besides this trouble with Nina. I think I want to cry."—A recently separated man quoted in Marital Separation *(Weiss, 1975, p. 48)*

This man is describing his feelings a few days after he and his wife broke up. He is still hoping for reconciliation. In the meantime, he feels overwhelmed by anxiety, remorse, and depression. He feels very alone and is scared at the prospect of remaining alone. His emotional distress is so great that he can't think straight or work effectively. His reaction to the loss of an intimate relationship is not all that unusual. Break-ups are devastating for most people—a reality that illustrates the enormous importance of intimate relationships in people's lives.

In the previous chapter, we explored the important role of close relationships in personal adjustment. In this chapter we focus on marriage and committed intimate relationships. We discuss why people marry and how they progress toward the selection of a mate. To shed light on marital adjustment, we describe the life cycle of the family, highlighting key vulnerable spots in marital relations and issues related to divorce. We also address alternative relationship lifestyles, including gay partnerships, cohabitation, and singlehood. Finally, in the Application we examine the tragic problem of violence in intimate relationships. Let's begin by discussing recent challenges to the traditional concept of marriage.

CHALLENGES TO THE TRADITIONAL MODEL OF MARRIAGE

LEARNING OBJECTIVE

- Discuss six social trends that are affecting the institution of marriage.

Marriage is the legally and socially sanctioned union of sexually intimate adults. Traditionally, the marital relationship has included economic interdependence, common residence, sexual fidelity, and shared responsibility for children. Although the institution of marriage remains popular, it sometimes seems to be under assault from shifting social trends. The percentage of married adults has been decreasing gradually since the 1960s. In 2011, a record low 51% of adults were married (Cohn et al., 2011), prompting many experts to ask whether marriage is in serious trouble. Although it appears that the institution of marriage will weather the storm, we should note some of the social trends that are shaking up the traditional model:

1. *Increased acceptance of singlehood.* Remaining single is a trend that has been on the rise for several decades (Morris & DePaulo, 2009). In part, this trend reflects longer postponement of marriage than before. **Figure 10.1** on the next page shows that the median age at which people marry has been increasing gradually since the mid-1960s. In 2011, the median age of first marriages was 26.5 years for women and 28.7 years for men (Cohn et al.,

2011). Thus, remaining single is becoming a more acceptable lifestyle. As a result, the negative stereotype of people who remain single—lonely, frustrated, and unchosen—is gradually evaporating.

2. *Increased acceptance of cohabitation.* **Cohabitation is living together in a sexually intimate relationship without the legal bonds of marriage.** Although many people continue to disapprove of the practice, negative attitudes toward couples living together have clearly declined (Cherlin, 2004). The prevalence of cohabitation has grown dramatically in recent decades. Moreover, cohabiting relationships increasingly include children (Stanley & Rhoades, 2009).

3. *Reduced premium on permanence.* Most people still view marriage as a permanent commitment, but an increasing number of people regard divorce as justifiable if their marriage fails to foster their interests. Accordingly, the social stigma associated with divorce has lessened, and divorce rates are about 45% (Whitehead & Popenoe, 2001).

4. *Transitions in gender roles.* Gender-role expectations are different for people entering marriage today than

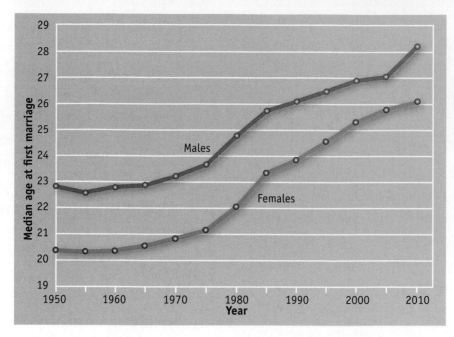

Figure 10.1

Median age at first marriage. The median age at which people in the United States marry for the first time has been creeping up for both males and females since the mid-1960s. This trend indicates that more people are postponing marriage. (Data from U.S. Bureau of the Census)

they were a generation or two ago. The traditional breadwinner and homemaker roles for the husband and wife are being discarded by many couples as more and more married women enter the workforce (Halpern, 2005; see **Figure 10.2**). Role expectations for husbands and wives are becoming more varied, more flexible, and more ambiguous. Many people regard this trend as a step in the right direction. However, changing gender roles create new potential for conflict between marital partners.

5. *Increased voluntary childlessness.* In the past two decades, the percentage of women without children has climbed in all age groups as an increasing number of married couples have chosen not to have children or to delay having children (Bulcroft & Teachman, 2004; Shaw, 2011). Researchers speculate that this trend is a result of new career opportunities for women, the tendency to marry at a later age, and changing attitudes (such as a desire for independence or concerns about overpopulation) (Hatch, 2009).

6. *Decline of the traditional nuclear family.* Thanks to endless reruns of television shows like *Happy Days, The Cosby Show,* and *Everybody Loves Raymond,* in the eyes of many American adults the ideal family should consist of a husband and wife married for the first time, rearing two or more children, with the man serving as the primary breadwinner. As McGraw and Walker (2004), put it, "Many people today, both in academic settings and popular culture, continue to idealize the image of the traditional

nuclear family—one consisting of a breadwinner father and a homemaker mother. . . . Because this ideology remains strong, a dearth of support exists for families that do not conform to the image" (p. 177). In reality, this image was never all that accurate, and in 2010 only 66% of

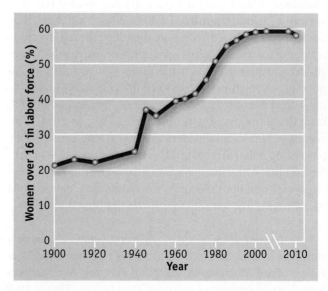

Figure 10.2

Women in the workforce. The percentage of women in the United States (over age 16) who work outside the home has been rising steadily, although it has leveled off in recent years. (Data from U.S. Bureau of Labor Statistics)

children under the age of 18 lived with two married parents (U.S. Census Bureau, 2010). The increasing prevalence of single-parent households, stepfamilies, childless marriages, and unwed parents make the traditional nuclear family a highly deceptive mirage that does not reflect the diversity of family structures in America. Interestingly, this change is reflected in the fact that many television shows today depict alternative family structures (for instance, *Two and a Half Men* and *Modern Family*).

In summary, traditional marriage is no longer the only acceptable lifestyle that defines a family (Laumann, Mahay, & Youm, 2007). The norms that mold marital and intimate relationships have been restructured in fundamental ways in recent decades. Thus, the institution of marriage is in a period of transition, creating new adjustment challenges for modern couples. Support for the concept of monogamy remains strong, but changes in society are altering the traditional model of marriage. The impact of these changes can be seen throughout this chapter as we discuss various facets of married life.

© Andrzej Tokarski/Shutterstock.com

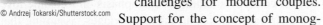

DECIDING TO MARRY

LEARNING OBJECTIVES

- Describe some cultural influences on marriage.
- Identify several factors influencing the selection of a mate.
- Summarize evidence on predictors of marital success.

"I am (sadly) not married to my long time boyfriend. . . . I would really like to have a ring on my finger not necessarily with a wedding to follow, but just as a sign of commitment. Whenever I talk to my boyfriend about planning our future life together his answer is always the same: 'You know that I love you and we already share money, an apartment, and (formerly) a car so what more do you need.' I am not sure if I absolutely want to be married, but I do know that I want our relationship to progress and move forward. After 12 years I am tired (and bored) of living the same life."—Kristina, a blogger, writing about whether she should give her boyfriend a marriage ultimatum (www.dinksfinance.com)

This woman is trying to decide if she wants to be married. Although alternatives to marriage are more viable than ever, experts project that over 90% of Americans will marry at least once (Cordova & Harp, 2009). Some will do it several times! Why? As shown in **Figure 10.3** on the next page, American women overwhelmingly cite *love* as the reason they decided to marry. But how does culture influence marriage? How do individuals choose their partners? And what are some predictors of successful marriages? We'll address these questions as we discuss the factors that influence the decision to marry.

Cultural Influences on Marriage

Although it appears that romantic love is experienced in all cultures, there are cultural differences in romantic attitudes and behaviors (Hatfield & Rapson, 2010). For instance, cultures vary in their emphasis on romantic love as a prerequisite for marriage. Modern Western cultures are somewhat unusual in permitting free choice of one's marital partner. According to Elaine Hatfield and Richard Rapson (1993), "Marriage-for-love represents an ultimate expression of individualism" (p. 2). By contrast, marriages arranged by families and other go-betweens remain common in cultures high in collectivism (Merali, 2012), such as those in India (Gupta, 1992), Japan (Iwao, 1993), China

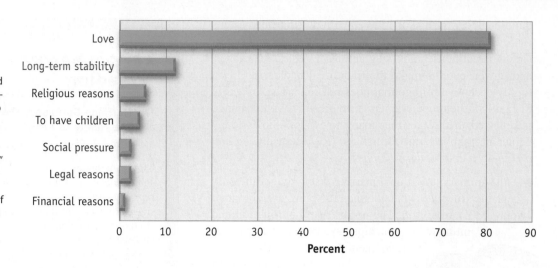

Figure 10.3

Why do women decide to marry? There are many reasons women choose to get married. Campbell, Wright, and Flores (2012) conducted an online survey of 197 women who had been married less than 2 years and asked them the primary reasons they got married. As the figure shows, "love" was by far the most common response, but "long-term stability" was a concern for 13% of the women, and other reasons received some responses as well. (Adapted from Campbell, Wright, & Flores, 2012).

(Xiaohe & Whyte, 1990), and West African countries (Adams, Anderson, & Adonu, 2004). In fact, experts estimate that up to 80% of world cultures have arranged marriage (Pasupathi, 2009). This practice is declining in some societies, especially in urban settings, as a result of Westernization (Moore & Wei, 2012). Still, when people in collectivist societies contemplate marriage, they strongly weigh the impact the relationship will have on their family, rather than relying solely on what their heart says (Triandis, 1994).

Cultural views of marriage are linked to both a country's values and its economic health. In one study, researchers asked college students in eleven countries the following question: "If a man (woman) had all the other qualities you desired, would you marry this person if you were not in love with him (her)?" (Levine et al., 1995). Students in countries with more individualistic values and higher standards of living were significantly more likely to answer "no" to the question than were those in countries with more collectivist values and lower standards of living.

People from Western societies often hold a simplistic view of collectivist cultures' deemphasis on romantic love and their penchant for arranged marriages, assuming that the modern conception of romantic love as the basis for marriage must result in better marital relationships than collectivist cultures' "antiquated" beliefs and practices (Grearson & Smith, 2009). However, there is little empirical support for this ethnocentric view. Take, for example, a study of couples in India, which found that love grew over the years in arranged marriages, whereas it declined among couples who married for romantic love (Gupta & Singh, 1982). Another study found that Indian couples in arranged marriages living in the United States reported higher marital satisfaction than U.S. couples who married by choice (Madathil & Benshoff, 2008). It appears that smug assumptions about the superiority of Western ways are misguided, given our extremely high divorce rates. Culture is but one influence on marital decisions; let's look at some specific factors that influence one's choice of a mate.

Marriages based on romantic love are the norm in Western cultures, whereas arranged marriages prevail in collectivist cultures.

Selecting a Mate

Mate selection in American culture is a gradual process that begins with dating and moves on to sometimes lengthy periods of courtship. Let's look at some of the factors that influence this important process.

Monogamy and Polygamy

Monogamy **is the practice of having only one spouse at a time.** In our society, monogamous marital relationships are the norm and the law. Many cultures, however, practice *polygamy,* **having more than one spouse at a time.** Westerners typically associate it with the Mormon religion, even though the Mormon Church officially denounced polygamy in the late 19th century (Hatch, 2009). However, polygamy is practiced worldwide in countries such as Algeria, Chad, Kuwait, and Saudi Arabia and in some Islamic groups. The practice of polygamy tends to be most common in societies where women have little to no independence, access to education, or political power (Cunningham, 2009b). Research found that Jordanian women in polygamous marriages (also called plural marriages) report more problems in family functioning and marital relations, lower self-esteem, less life satisfaction with life, and more depression, anxiety, and hostility than their monogamous counterparts (Al-Krenawi, Graham, & Al Gharaibeh, 2011). Women report that unhappiness, loneliness, sense of competition, and jealousy are disadvantages of polygamy. Commonly reported ways of dealing with these disadvantages include believing that this way of life is God's will, allocating household resources equally, and maintaining an attitude of respect for the other wives (Slonim-Nevo & Al-Krenawi, 2006).

Endogamy and Homogamy

As we saw in Chapter 9, birds of a feather do seem to flock together (Montoya, Horton, & Kirchner, 2008). *Endogamy* **is the tendency for people to marry within their own social group.** Research demonstrates that people tend to marry others of the same race, religion, ethnic background, and social class (McPherson, Smith-Lovin, & Cook, 2001). This behavior is promoted by cultural norms and by the way similarity fosters interpersonal attraction. Although endogamy appears to be declining, this decrease has been gradual. For example, in 2010, 10% of all households reported an interracial marriage, up from 7% in 2000 (U.S. Bureau of the Census, 2012). This is up from just 1% in 1970 (Gaines, 2009). Although some people speculate that interracial relationships carry an extra burden, recent research suggests that there are no differences between interracial couples and same-race couples in terms of relationship quality, conflict patterns, and attachment. In fact, interracial couples tend to report higher relationship satisfaction than others (Troy, Lewis-Smith, & Lauren-

People tend to marry others who are similar in race, religion, and social class—a phenomenon called endogamy.

ceau, 2006), especially partners who feel positive about their own race while being accepting of others (Leslie & Letiecq, 2004).

Homogamy **is the tendency for people to marry others who have similar personal characteristics.** Among other things, marital partners tend to be similar in age and education (Fu & Heaton, 2008), physical attractiveness (Hatfield & Sprecher, 2009), attitudes and values (Luo & Klohnen, 2005), marital history (Ono, 2006), and even vulnerability to psychological disorders (Mathews & Reus, 2001). Interestingly, homogamy is associated with longer-lasting and more satisfying marital relations (Gonzaga, 2009). Even in dating relationships, similarity on a variety of characteristics is related to stability and satisfaction (Peretti & Abplanalp, 2004).

Gender and Mate Selection Preferences

Research reveals that males and females exhibit both similarities and differences in what they look for in a marital partner. Many characteristics, such as physical attractiveness, intelligence, humor, honesty, and kindness, are rated highly by both sexes (Lippa, 2007). Both male and female college students gave high ratings to the traits of honesty and trustworthiness for marriage partners (Regan & Berscheid, 1997). However, a few reliable differences between men's and women's priorities have been found, and these differences appear to be nearly universal across cultures.

As we saw in Chapter 9, women tend to place a higher value than men on potential partners' socioeconomic status, intelligence, ambition, and financial prospects. In contrast, men consistently show more interest than women in potential partners' youthfulness and physical attractiveness (Buss & Kenrick, 1998). Fletcher (2002) asserts that mate selection criteria can be grouped in three major categories: warmth/loyalty, vitality/attractiveness, and status/resources. Compared to men, women tend to place a greater emphasis on warmth/loyalty and status/resources and less of an emphasis on vitality/attractiveness. This gender difference is greater for long-term as opposed to short-term mate selection (Fletcher et al., 2004). Most theorists explain these gender disparities in terms of evolutionary concepts (Buss, 2009).

Predictors of Marital Success

Are there any factors that reliably predict marital success? A great deal of research has been devoted to this question. This effort has been plagued by one obvious problem: How do you measure "marital success"? Some researchers have simply compared divorced and intact couples in regard to premarital characteristics. The problem with this strategy is that it only assesses commitment and not satisfaction. Many intact couples obviously do not have happy or successful marriages. Other researchers have used elaborate questionnaires to measure couples' marital satisfaction. Unfortunately, these scales appear to measure complacency and lack of conflict more than satisfaction (Fowers et al., 1994). Although research shows some thought-provoking correlations between couples' premarital characteristics and marital adjustment, most of the correlations are relatively small. Thus, there are no foolproof predictors of marital success. Nevertheless, here are some of the factors that researchers have looked at.

Family background. The marital adjustment of partners is correlated with the marital satisfaction of their parents. People whose parents were divorced are more likely than others to experience divorce themselves (Frame, Mattson, & Johnson, 2009). Researchers speculate that this intergenerational "divorce cycle" may be due in part to how individuals learn to resolve conflicts. For better or worse, they often learn this behavior from their parents. Rhoades (2012) found that spouses whose parents were divorced reported more negative communication than those with parents who were still married. Further, Whitton and colleagues (2008) found that hostility levels of parents in family interactions predicted the marital hostility levels of their offspring 17 years later. This, in turn, was predictive of marital adjustment, especially for men. The researchers note, however, that other factors, such as the development of insecure attachment styles, might be at play here.

Age. The age at which one marries is also related to the likelihood of marriage success. Couples who marry young have higher divorce rates (Bramlett & Mosher, 2002), as **Figure 10.4** shows. Perhaps people who marry later have more carefully selected their mate or are less likely to undergo dramatic personal change that would render them incompatible with their partners. Researchers speculate that as more individuals choose to marry later in life, divorce rates could actually decrease.

Length of courtship. Longer periods of courtship are associated with a greater probability of marital success (Cate & Lloyd, 1988). Longer courtships may allow couples to evaluate their compatibility more accurately. Alternatively, the correlation between courtship length and marital success may exist because people who are cautious about marriage have attitudes and values that promote marital stability.

Personality. Generally, studies have found that partners' specific personality traits are not strong predictors of marital success. That said, there are some traits that show modest correlations with marital adjustment. For example, two negative predictors of marital success are perfectionism (Haring, Hewitt, & Flett, 2003) and insecurity (Crowell, Treboux, & Waters, 2002).

Recently, researchers have had more success exploring the link between people's underlying emotional dispositions and marital adjustment. They found that intensity of smiling in college yearbooks (an indicator of positive emotional expression) was predictive of a lower likelihood of divorce in later life (Hertenstein et al., 2009). These researchers found similar results when they rated childhood photos of older adults; smiling in photos negatively predicted divorce later in life. While Hertenstein acknowledges that there are other explanations for the link (such as that smiling people might attract more friends and have more social support), he asserts that these results demonstrate the important role of positive emotional dispositions in life.

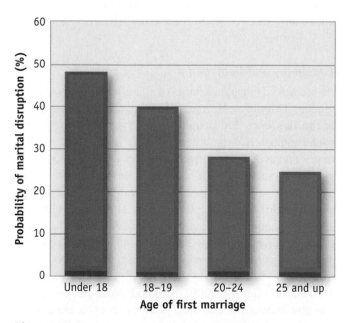

Figure 10.4

Age at marriage and probability of marital disruption after 10 years. Researchers have estimated the likelihood of marital disruption (either divorce or separation) after 10 years for various age groups. The data summarized here show that the probability of marital disruption is substantially higher among those who marry young. (Data from the Centers for Disease Control)

Premarital communication. As you might expect, the degree to which couples get along well during their courtship is predictive of their marital adjustment. The quality of premarital communication appears to be especially crucial (Markman et al., 2010). For example, the more that prospective mates are negative, sarcastic, insulting, and unsupportive during courtship, the greater the likelihood of marital distress and divorce (Clements, Stanley, & Markman, 2004). Close relationships that include self-disclosure and acceptance of what is learned through disclosure are likely to be the most satisfying over long periods of time (Harvey & Omarzu, 1999). Further, research shows that shared decision making is predictive of less marital conflict (Kamp Dush & Taylor, 2012).

Although most research in the area of communication has focused on discussions of conflict, one study found that being understood and validated in conversation is strongly related to satisfaction, even when the conversation is about a positive event (Gable, Gonzaga, & Strachman, 2006). While this research focused on dating couples, Gable and his colleagues speculate that "positive emotional exchanges may serve as a foundation on which stable and satisfying relationships rest" (p. 916). In fact, playfulness and positive emotion in mundane, everyday interactions in couples seem to be emerging as important components in marital adjustment (Driver & Gottman, 2004).

Stressful events. So far we have talked about issues that individual partners bring to a marriage, but these relation-

ships don't exist in a vacuum. Stressful situations surrounding a marriage (unemployment, chronic illness, caregiving for an aging parent) can cause conflict, increase distress, and harm marital stability (Frame et al., 2009). Partners who report higher levels of external stress also report more stress and tension in their close relationships (Bodenmann, Ledermann, & Bradbury, 2007; Ledermann et al., 2010). Research has also found that the stress from work can spill over to affect mood at home, which ultimately can erode a marriage (Lavee & Ben-Ari, 2007). Neff (2012) suggests that stress harms marriages over time by limiting one's ability to engage in relationship-promoting behaviors. One exception to the stress-distress link is the stress related to becoming new parents, a topic we will talk about in more detail shortly.

MARITAL ADJUSTMENT ACROSS THE FAMILY LIFE CYCLE

LEARNING OBJECTIVES

- Explain each stage of the family life cycle.
- Identify factors couples weigh in deciding whether to have children, and analyze the dynamics of the transition to parenthood.

- Identify common problems that surface as a family's children reach adolescence, and discuss the transitions that occur in the later stages of the family life cycle.

"Jennifer has taken a lot of time away from us, the time that we normally spend doing things together or talking. It seems like maybe on a weekend when we would normally like to sleep in, or just have lazy sex, Jennifer wakes up and needs to be fed. . . . But I'm sure that will pass as soon as Jennifer gets a little older. We're just going through a phase."—A new mother quoted in American Couples (Blumstein & Schwartz, 1983, p. 205)

"We're just going through a phase." That statement highlights an important point: There are predictable patterns of development for families, just as there are for individuals. These patterns make up **the** *family life cycle,* **an orderly sequence of developmental stages that families tend to progress through.** The institutions of marriage and family are inevitably intertwined. With the advent of marriage,

two persons create an entirely new family. Typically, this new family forms the core of one's life as an adult.

Sociologists have proposed a number of models to describe family development. Our discussion is organized around a six-stage model outlined by Carter and McGoldrick (1988, 1999). **Figure 10.5** on the next page provides an overview of their model. It spells out the developmental tasks during each stage of the life cycle for families that eventually have children and remain intact. Admittedly, not all families progress through the family life cycle in an orderly fashion, and some researchers find that marital problems are similar whether a couple are newly married, have young children, or have been married for many years. Nevertheless, the model does appear to be a useful predictive tool for the marriage experience (Kapinus & Johnson, 2003). Although Carter and McGoldrick have described

THE FAMILY LIFE CYCLE		
Family life cycle stage	**Key developmental task**	**Additional changes in family status required to proceed developmentally**
1. Between families: The unattached young adult	Accepting parent/offspring separation	a. Differentiation of self in relation to family of origin b. Development of intimate peer relationships c. Establishment of self in work
2. The joining of families through marriage: The newly married couple	Commitment to new system	a. Formation of marital system b. Realignment of relationships with extended families and friends to include spouse
3. The family with young children	Accepting new members into the system	a. Adjusting marital system to make space for child(ren) b. Taking on parenting roles c. Realignment of relationships with extended family to include parenting and grandparenting roles
4. The family with adolescents	Increasing flexibility of family boundaries to include children's independence	a. Shifting of parent-child relationships to permit adolescent to move in and out of system b. Refocus on midlife marital and career issues c. Beginning shift toward concerns for older generation
5. Launching children and moving on	Accepting a multitude of exits from and entries into the family system	a. Renegotiation of marital system as a dyad b. Development of adult-to-adult relationships between grown children and their parents c. Realignment of relationships to include in-laws and grandchildren d. Dealing with disabilities and death of parents (grandparents)
6. The family in later life	Accepting the shifting of generational roles	a. Maintaining own and/or couple functioning and interests in face of physiological decline; exploration of new familial and social role options b. Support for a more central role for middle generation c. Making room in the system for the wisdom and experience of the elderly; supporting the older generation without over-functioning for them d. Dealing with loss of spouse, siblings, and other peers and preparation for own death; life review and integrations

Figure 10.5

Stages of the family life cycle. The family life cycle can be divided into six stages, as shown here (based on Carter & McGoldrick, 1988). The family's key developmental task during each stage is identified in the second column. The third column lists additional developmental tasks at each stage.

variations on this basic pattern that are associated with remaining childless or going through a divorce (McGoldrick & Carter, 2003), we will focus primarily on the typical, basic pattern in this section. We will also focus on heterosexual couples in this section.

Between Families: The Unattached Young Adult

As young adults become independent of their parents, they go through a transitional period during which they are "between families" until they form a new family through marriage. What is interesting about this stage is that more and more people are prolonging it. As we saw in **Figure 10.1,** the median age for marriage has been gradually increasing for several decades. The extension of this stage is probably the result of a number of factors, including the availability of new career options for women, increased educational requirements in the world of work, an increased emphasis on personal autonomy, and more positive attitudes about remaining single.

Joining Together: The Newly Married Couple

The next phase begins when the unattached adult becomes attached. If marriage is chosen, the newly married, heterosexual couple gradually settle into their roles as husband and wife. For some couples, this phase can be quite troublesome, as the early years of marriage are often marred by numerous problems and disagreements. When reporting on marital satisfaction, 8%–14% of newlyweds score in the distressed range; the most commonly reported problems are balancing work and marriage and financial concerns (Schramm et al., 2005). In general, however, this stage tends to be characterized by great happiness—the proverbial "honeymoon stage" and "marital bliss." Spouses' satisfaction with their relationship tends to be relatively high early in marriage, before the arrival of the first child.

The prechildren phase used to be rather short for most newly married couples, as they quickly went about the business of starting a family. Traditionally, couples simply *assumed* that they would proceed to have children. In recent decades, however, ambivalence about having children has clearly increased, and the Pew Research Center (2010) reports that about 20% of women will not have children by age 44, up from 10% in the 1970s. Thus, more and more couples find themselves struggling to *decide* whether to have children. Often, the decision to remain childless occurs after numerous postponements, when the couple finally acknowledges that "the right time" is never going to arrive.

Couples who choose to remain childless cite the great costs incurred in raising children. In addition to the financial burdens, they mention such costs as giving up educational or career opportunities, loss of time for leisure activities and each other, loss of autonomy, worry about the responsibility associated with childrearing, and concerns about overpopulation (Hatch, 2009). Women especially cite career issues as playing a role in their decisions (Park, 2005), and voluntarily childless women tend to have higher incomes and more work experience than other women (Abma & Martinez, 2006).

Although voluntary childlessness is becoming more common, couples who make this choice are still in the minority. Most couples decide to have children, citing the responsibility to procreate, the joy of watching youngsters mature, the sense of purpose that children create, and the satisfaction associated with emotional nurturance and the challenges of childrearing (Cowan & Cowan, 2000). The vast majority of parents rate parenthood as a positive and satisfying experience and report no regret about their choice (Demo, 1992). Similarly, most voluntarily childless women do not regret their decision (DeLyser, 2012). Note that we have been discussing *voluntary* childlessness. Those who wish to have children but cannot (because of infertility for instance) express concerns over their childlessness (McQuillan et al., 2012).

Family with Young Children

Although most parents are happy with their decision to have children, the arrival of the first child represents a major transition, and the disruption of routines can be emotionally draining, negatively affecting parents' well-being (Umberson, Pudrovska, & Reczek, 2010). The transition to parenthood tends to have a greater impact on mothers than fathers (Nomaguchi & Milkie, 2003). The new mother, already physically exhausted by the birth process, is particularly prone to postpartum distress. According to the Centers for Disease Control (2012) approximately 11% to

18% of women report postpartum depressive symptoms. Risk factors for developing postpartum depression include past depression, high stress levels, and marital dissatisfaction (O'Hara, 2009). Issues such as infants' sleep patterns and crying are associated with mothers' depressive symptoms (Meijer & van den Wittenboer, 2007). Interestingly, the risk for depression is not just for those who give birth, but for adoptive mothers too. Mott and colleagues (2011) compared both groups and found no differences in levels of depressive symptoms. Further, the same stressors (for instance sleep deprivation and less marital satisfaction) were related to depression among adoptive mothers.

The transition to parenthood is more difficult when a mother's expectations regarding how much the father will be involved in child care are not met (Fox, Bruce, & Combs-Orme, 2000). A review of decades of research on parenthood and marital satisfaction found that (1) parents exhibit lower marital satisfaction than comparable nonparents, (2) mothers of infants report the steepest decline in marital satisfaction, and (3) the more children couples have, the lower their marital satisfaction tends to be (Twenge, Campbell, & Foster, 2003).

Crisis during the transition to first parenthood is not a forgone conclusion, however. The key to making this transition less stressful may be to have *realistic expectations* about parental responsibilities (Belsky, 2009). Studies find that stress tends to be greatest in new parents who have

Learn More Online

American Academy of Child and Adolescent Psychiatry (AACAP): Facts for Families

Many new parents may need help coping with emerging problems in their children. The brochures here (in a variety of languages, including English, Spanish, and Chinese) cover a wide range of psychological issues and psychiatric conditions.

overestimated the benefits and underestimated the costs of their new role. Reactions to parenthood may also depend on how well a couple's marriage is going (Lawrence et al., 2008). Couples with high levels of affection and commitment prior to the first child's birth are likely to maintain a stable level of satisfaction after the child's birth (Shapiro, Gottman, & Carrère, 2000). Although children bring their share of trials and tribulations to a marriage, divorce rates are clearly higher for those who remain childless (Shapiro et al., 2000).

Family with Adolescent Children

Parents overwhelmingly rate adolescence as the most difficult stage of parenting (Gecas & Seff, 1990). However, problematic parent-teen relationships appear to be the exception rather than the rule (Smetana, 2009). As adolescent children seek to establish their own identities, parental influence tends to decline while the influence of peer groups tends to increase. Parents tend to retain more influence than peers over important matters, such as educational goals and career plans, but peers gradually gain more influence over less critical matters, such as style of dress and recreational plans (Gecas & Seff, 1990). Thus, conflicts between adolescent children and their parents tend to involve everyday matters such as chores and dress more than substantive issues such as sex and drugs (Barber, 1994). Adolescents tend to exhibit better adjustment in families in which they are encouraged to participate in decision making but parents ultimately maintain control (Smetana, 2009). Parents seem to learn from their experience in dealing with an adolescent child, as they report less conflict with their second adolescent child than their first (Whiteman, McHale, & Crouter, 2003).

In addition to worrying about their adolescent children, middle-aged couples often worry about the care of their aging parents. Adults caught between these conflicting responsibilities have been called the *sandwich generation* (Riley & Bowen, 2005). Based on national survey data from Great Britain and the United States, one-third of women between the ages of 55 and 69 simultaneously provide help to both generations (Grundy & Henretta, 2006). Females tend to assume most of the responsibility for elderly relatives, and it is estimated that in the future women can expect to spend more years caring for their aging parents than for their dependent children (Bromley & Blieszner, 1997). Many theorists are concerned that these multigenerational caregiving responsibilities may prove burdensome and lead to burnout (Fruhauf, 2009). Supporting this concern, one study found that the number of hours spent caring for an aging parent was correlated with wives' psychological distress (Voydanoff & Donnelly, 1999). On the positive side, many caregivers describe the experience as gratifying in that it al-

lowed them to repair or enhance damaged relationships (Fruhauf, 2009). Additionally, these situations allow for increased interaction between children and grandparents (Silverstein & Ruiz, 2009).

Launching Children into the Adult World

When children begin to reach their twenties, the family has to adapt to a multitude of exits and entries, as children leave and return, sometimes with their own spouses. This period, during which children normally progress from dependence to independence, brings a variety of transitions. In many instances, conflict subsides and parent-child relations become closer and more supportive.

One might argue that launching children into the adult world tends to be a lengthier and more difficult process today than it once was (Furstenberg, 2001). As shown in **Figure 10.6**, the number of adults living with their parents is increasing (U.S. Bureau of the Census, 2011a). The rapidly rising cost of a college education and the shrinking job market have probably led many young adults to linger in their parents' homes. Moreover, crises such as separation, divorce, job loss, and single-parent pregnancy force many children who have ventured out on their own to return to their parents. Interestingly, young adults have more negative attitudes about returning home than their parents do (Veevers, Gee, & Wister, 1996).

When parents do manage to get all their children launched into the adult world, they find themselves faced with an "empty nest." This period was formerly thought to be a difficult transition for many parents, especially mothers who were familiar only with the maternal role. In recent decades, however, more women have experience with other roles outside the home and look forward to their "liberation" from childrearing responsibilities. Most parents adjust effectively to the empty nest situation, and this period is associated with increased marital satisfaction for mothers (Gorchoff, John, & Helson, 2008). In fact, parents are more likely to have problems if their children *return* to

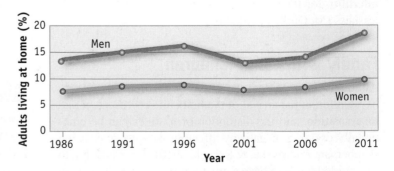

Figure 10.6

The percentage of adults living at home. According to 2011 U.S. Census data, the percentage of adults ages 25–34 living at home has increased over the past 25 years, especially for men. The recent upturn might be a result of the economic recession. (Data from U.S. Bureau of the Census)

the once-empty nest, especially if these returns are frequent (Bookwala, 2009).

The Family in Later Life

Marital satisfaction tends to climb in the postparental period as couples find they have more time to devote attention to each other. This trend appears to be the result of partners' time together being more relaxed and enjoyable (Gorchoff, John, & Helson, 2008). Older couples rate children or grandchildren, good memories, and traveling together as the top three sources of pleasure (Levenson, Carstersen, & Gottman, 1993). However, spouses do have to adapt to spending more time with each other and often need to renegotiate role expectations (Walsh, 1999). Of course, age-related considerations that are independent of the relationship, such as the increased likelihood of physical illness, can make the later years stressful. The three most commonly reported problems in late-life marriages

are disagreements or disappointments about leisure activities, intimacy, and finances (Henry, Miller, & Giarrusso, 2005). Some gender differences in disappointments are apparent in older couples: Men are more likely to be disappointed about financial matters, whereas women are more likely to be disappointed about personal habits and health matters.

VULNERABLE AREAS IN MARITAL ADJUSTMENT

LEARNING OBJECTIVES

- Discuss how role expectations, work, and financial issues may affect marital adjustment.

- Summarize evidence on the relationship between communication quality and marital adjustment.

"When we first got married, the first six months of conflicts were all about getting him to take account of what I had planned for him at home. . . . He would come waltzing in an hour and a half late for dinner, or cancel an evening with friends, because he had to close a deal. . . . We would argue and argue . . . not because I didn't want him to make a living . . . but because I thought he had to be more considerate."—A wife quoted in American Couples *(Blumstein & Schwartz, 1983, p. 174)*

During courtship, couples tend to focus on pleasurable activities. But once couples are married, they deal with a variety of problems, such as arriving at acceptable role compromises, paying bills, and raising a family. Marital conflict is associated with several negative outcomes for partners and their family members, including increased depression, alcoholism, physical health problems, domestic violence, and divorce (Fincham, 2009). All couples encounter problems, but successful marriages depend on couples' ability to handle their problems. In this section we analyze the major kinds of difficulties that are likely to emerge. Although there are no simple solutions for these problems, it helps to know where you're likely to encounter them.

Gaps in Role Expectations

When heterosexual individuals marry, they assume new roles—those of husband and wife. Each role comes with

certain expectations that the partners hold about how wives and husbands should behave. These expectations may vary greatly from one person to another. Gaps between partners in their role expectations can have a negative effect on couples' marital satisfaction. Unfortunately, substantial differences in role expectations seem particularly likely in this era of transition in gender roles, a topic we discuss in depth in Chapter 11.

The traditional role expectations for husbands and wives used to be fairly clear. A husband was supposed to act as the principal breadwinner, make the important decisions, and take care of certain household chores, such as car or yard maintenance. A wife was supposed to raise the children, cook, clean, and follow the leadership of her husband. Spouses had different spheres of influence (Coltrane & Shih, 2010). The working world was the domain of the

SALLY FORTH

husband, the home the domain of the wife. In recent decades, however, forces of social change have led to new expectations about marital roles. Thus, modern couples need to negotiate and renegotiate role responsibilities throughout the family life cycle.

Women may be especially vulnerable to ambivalence about shifting marital roles. More and more women are aspiring to demanding careers, yet husbands' careers continue to take priority over their wives' ambitions (Haas, 1999). Typically, it is wives who are expected to interrupt their career to raise young children, stay home when children are sick, and abandon their jobs when husbands' careers require relocation. Moreover, even when both spouses are employed, many husbands maintain traditional role expectations about housework, child care, and decision making.

Men's contribution to housework has increased noticeably since the 1960s (Calasanti & Harrison-Rexrode, 2009), but wives are still doing the bulk of the household chores in America, even when they work outside the home (Sayer, 2005). For example, research indicates that wives take responsibility for about 65% of total housework (not including child care), while husbands do the remaining 35%. Moreover, wives still account for 78% of the essential "core housework" such as cooking, cleaning, and laundry, while men continue to handle more discretionary, traditional "male chores," such as yard or auto maintenance (Bianchi et al., 2000).

Although married women perform the majority of all housework, only about one-third of wives characterize their di-

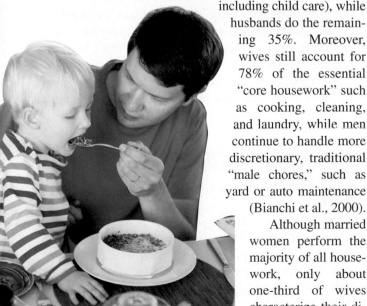

© Aleksei Potov/Shutterstock.com

vision of labor as unfair, because most women don't expect a 50–50 split (Coltrane, 2001). Nevertheless, these one-third of wives constitute a sizable population of women for whom housework is a source of discontent. Research shows that women are more likely to perceive their share of housework as unfair when they have nontraditional attitudes about gender roles and when they work outside the home (Coltrane, 2001). As you might expect, wives who perceive their housework burden to be unfair tend to report lower levels of marital satisfaction (Coltrane & Shih, 2010). Interestingly, men who have lived independently for a longer period of time (that is, not with their parents, partners, or in dorms) are more egalitarian in their views about housework than are those who have had less of an independent "bachelorhood" (Pitt & Borland, 2008).

Couples in which the husband holds egalitarian gender role attitudes have higher levels of marital happiness than those where the husband holds more traditional attitudes (Frieze & Ciccocioppo, 2009). Given this finding, it is imperative that couples discuss role expectations in depth before marriage. If they discover that their views are divergent, they need to take the potential for problems seriously. Many people casually dismiss gender role disagreements, thinking they can "straighten out" their partner later on. But assumptions about marital roles, whether traditional or not, may be deeply held and not easily changed.

Work and Career Issues

The possible interactions between one's occupation and one's marriage are numerous and complex. Although the data on the effect of income and employment on marital stability are inconsistent (Rodrigues, Hall, & Fincham, 2006), individuals' job satisfaction and involvement can affect their own marital satisfaction, their partner's marital satisfaction, and their children's development.

Work and Marital Adjustment

Many studies have compared the marital adjustment of male-breadwinner versus dual-career couples. The interest in this comparison arises from traditional views that regard men's *lack* of employment and women's *employment* as departures from the norm. Typically, these studies simply categorize women as working or nonworking and evaluate couples' marital satisfaction. Most of these studies find little in the way of consistent differences in the marital adjustment of male-breadwinner versus dual-career couples, and they often find some benefits for dual-career couples, such as increased social contacts, self-esteem, and egalitarian attitudes (Haas, 1999; Steil, 2009). Although dual-career couples do face special problems in negotiating career priorities, child-care arrangements, and other practical matters, their marriage need not be negatively affected.

However, the frustration and stress of an unsatisfying job might spill over to contaminate one's marriage. When pressures at work increase, husbands and wives report more role conflicts and often feel overwhelmed by their multiple commitments (Crouter et al., 1999). Furthermore, studies find that spouses' stress at work can have a substantial negative effect on their marital and family interactions (Perry-Jenkins, Repetti, & Crouter, 2001). For example, after highly stressful days at work, spouses tend to withdraw from family interactions (Repetti & Wang, 2009).

Negative work-to-family spillover seems to be more common for mothers than for fathers and is especially problematic when preschool children are involved (Dilworth, 2004; Stevens et al., 2007). Perhaps this difference is due to the fact that even when working, women continue to do more household labor than men (Sayer, 2005). Work-related demands that increase the likelihood of family conflict and stress include enduring long commutes, bringing work home, and receiving job contacts at home (Voydanoff, 2005). The stress associated with working night shifts appears to be especially tough on spouses and families (Presser, 2000), as is the experience of jobs that require travel (Zvonkovic et al., 2005).

Although the difficulties involved in juggling work and family roles can be challenging, some theorists have argued that in the long run multiple roles are beneficial to both men and women. Barnett and Hyde (2001) assert that negative effects of stress in one role can be buffered by success and satisfaction in another role. They also note that multiple roles can increase sources of social support and opportunities to experience success. Moreover, when both spouses work outside the home, income tends to be greater, and spouses often find they have more in common.

Parents' Work and Children's Development

Another issue of concern has been the potential impact of parents' employment on their children. Virtually all of the research in this area has focused on the effects of mothers' employment outside the home. In 2010, approximately 21 million mothers were employed (U.S. Bureau of the Census, 2011b). What does the research on maternal em-

ployment show? Although many Americans seem to believe that maternal employment is detrimental to children's development, the vast majority of empirical studies have found little evidence that a mother's working is harmful to her children (Gottfried & Gottfried, 2008). A meta-analysis of 69 studies found no link between maternal employment and children's achievement or behavioral problems (Lucas-Thompson, Goldberg, & Prause, 2010). Additionally, studies generally have not found a link between mothers' employment status and the quality of infant-mother emotional attachment (NICHD Early Child Care Research Network, 1997). In a longitudinal study spanning two decades, early maternal employment showed no "sleeper effects." That is, there were no negative outcomes that showed up later in life, leading researchers to conclude that the adverse outcomes of maternal employment are a "public myth" (Gottfried & Gottfried, 2008, p. 30).

In fact, maternal employment has been shown to have positive effects on children's development in some cases. Recent data from the Canadian National Longitudinal Survey of Children and Youth indicate that maternal employment is related to decreased hyperactivity, lower levels of anxiety, and increased prosocial behavior at age 4 (Nomaguchi, 2006). Further, while maternal employment doesn't

Ariel Skelley/Blend Images/Getty Images

Although many Americans seem to believe that maternal employment is detrimental to children's development, the vast majority of empirical studies have found little evidence that a mother's working is harmful to her children.

eliminate poverty, it does mean that fewer children are raised in poverty (Esping-Anderson, 2007; Lichter & Crowley, 2004). Children brought up in poverty exhibit poorer physical health, reduced mental health, lower academic performance, and increased delinquency in comparison to other children (Seccombe, 2001). However, experts are careful to note that any benefits of maternal employment might also come at the cost of fewer positive interactions between the mother and child (Nomaguchi, 2006).

Financial Difficulties

Neither financial stability nor wealth can ensure marital satisfaction. However, financial difficulties can cause stress in a marriage, and finances are one of the top concerns for newlyweds (Schramm et al., 2005). Without money, families live in constant dread of financial drains such as illness, layoffs, or broken appliances. Spontaneity in communication may be impaired by an understandable reluctance to talk about financial concerns. Indeed, money is a "taboo" topic for many couples (Atwood, 2012). Thus, it is not surprising that serious financial worries among couples are associated with increased hostility in husbands, increased depression in wives, and lower marital happiness in both husbands and wives (White & Rogers, 2001). Similarly, husbands' job insecurity is predictive of wives' reports of marital conflict and their thoughts of divorce (Fox & Chancey, 1998). Moreover, evidence consistently demonstrates that the risk of separation and divorce increases as husbands' income declines (Ono, 1998).

Even when financial resources are plentiful, money can be a source of marital strain. Quarrels about how to spend money are common and are potentially damaging at all income levels. For instance, studies have found that perceptions of financial problems (regardless of a family's actual income) are associated with decreased marital satisfaction (Dean, Carroll, & Yang, 2007). Differences in spending habits (tightwad, spendthrift) can also lead to marital conflict (Rick, Small, & Finkel, 2011). Further, newlywed couples who increase their consumer debt spend less time together and argue more about money than those who pay off their debt (Dew, 2008). In a study that examined how happily married couples handled their money in comparison to couples that eventually divorced, Schaninger and Buss (1986) found that the happy couples engaged in more joint decision making on finances. Thus, the best way to avoid troublesome battles over money is probably to engage in extensive planning of expenditures together—that is, to *communicate*.

Inadequate Communication

Effective communication is crucial to the success of a marriage and is consistently associated with greater marital satisfaction (Litzinger & Gordon, 2005). Further, the marital communication–satisfaction link seems to be robust across cultures (Rehman & Holtzworth-Munroe, 2007). In a study of couples in the process of divorce, researchers found that communication difficulties were the most frequently cited problem among both husbands and wives (Bodenmann et al., 2007; Cleek & Pearson, 1985). In addition, communication is a highly ranked source of conflict for long-term married couples (Levenson et al., 1993). Because the ability to communicate emotions is associated with better marital adjustment, couples need to feel safe discussing conflict (Cordova, Gee, & Warren, 2005). Research supports the notion that marital adjustment depends not on whether there is conflict (conflict is virtually inevitable) but rather on how conflict is handled when it occurs (Driver et al., 2003).

A number of studies have compared communication patterns in happy and unhappy marriages. This research indicates that unhappily married couples (1) find it difficult to convey positive messages, (2) misunderstand each other more often, (3) are less likely to recognize that they have been misunderstood, (4) use more frequent, and more intense, negative messages, and (5) often differ in the amount of self-disclosure they prefer in the relationship (Noller & Fitzpatrick, 1990; Noller & Gallois, 1988; Sher & Baucom, 1993). They often fall into a demand-withdraw pattern where one partner engages in a demand behavior (such as a complaint or criticism) and the other responds by withdrawing (ignoring or changing the topic, for instance) (Eldridge & Baucom, 2012). Above all else, unhappy couples tend to get caught up in escalating cycles of conflict from which they cannot escape, whereas happy couples find ways to exit the cycles (Fincham, 2003).

The importance of marital communication was underscored in a widely cited study by John Gottman and his colleagues that attempted to predict the likelihood of divorce in a sample of fifty-two married couples (Buehlman, Gottman, & Katz, 1992). Each couple provided an oral history of their relationship and a 15-minute sample of their interaction style, during which they discussed two problem areas in their marriage. The investigators rated the spouses on a variety of factors that mostly reflected the subjects' ways of communicating with each other. Based on these ratings, they were able to predict which couples would divorce within three years with 94% accuracy!

Gottman, who is probably the world's foremost authority on marital communication, asserts that conflict and anger are normal in marital interactions and are not, in and of themselves, predictive of marital dissolution. Instead, Gottman (1994, 2011) identifies four other communication patterns, which he

John Gottman

calls the "Four Horsemen of the Apocalypse," that are risk factors for divorce: contempt, criticism, defensiveness, and stonewalling. *Contempt* involves communicating insulting feelings that one's spouse is inferior. *Criticism* involves constantly expressing negative evaluations of one's partner. It typically begins with the word *you* and involves sweeping negative statements. *Defensiveness* refers to responding to contempt and criticism by invalidating, refuting, or denying the partner's statements. This obstructive communication escalates marital conflict. *Stonewalling* is refusing to listen to one's partner, especially to the partner's complaints. Gottman eventually added a fifth troublesome communication pattern, *belligerence,* which involves provocative, combative challenges to the partner's power and authority (Gottman, Gottman, & DeClaire, 2006). Given the importance of good communication, many approaches to marital therapy emphasize the development of better communication skills in partners (Gottman & Gottman, 2008).

DIVORCE AND ITS AFTERMATH

LEARNING OBJECTIVES

- Describe the evidence on changing divorce rates and the factors that go in to deciding to divorce.
- Analyze how spouses and children tend to adjust to divorce.

- Summarize data on remarriage and the impact of stepfamilies on children.

"In the 10 years that we were married I went from 24 to 34, and they were a very significant 10 years. I started a career, started to succeed, bought my first house, had a child, you know, very significant years. And then all of a sudden, every goddamn thing, I'm back to zero. I have no house. I don't have a child. I don't have a wife. I don't have the same family. My economic position has been shattered. And nothing recoverable. All these goals which I had struggled for, every goddamn one of them, is gone."
—*A recently divorced man quoted in* Marital Separation *(Weiss, 1975, p. 75)*

***Divorce* is the legal dissolution of a marriage.** It tends to be a painful and stressful event for most people, as this bitter quote illustrates. Any of the problems discussed in the previous section might lead a couple to consider divorce. However, people appear to vary in their threshold for divorce, just as they do in their threshold for marriage. Some couples will tolerate a great deal of disappointment and bickering without seriously considering divorce. Other couples are ready to call their attorney as soon as it becomes apparent that their expectations for marital bliss were somewhat unrealistic. Typically, however, divorce is the culmination of a gradual disintegration of the relationship brought about by an accumulation of interrelated problems, which often date back to the beginning of a couple's relationship (Huston, Niehuis, & Smith, 2001).

Divorce Rates

Although relatively accurate statistics are available on divorce rates, it is still difficult to estimate the percentage of marriages that end in divorce. It is clear that divorce rates in the United states increased dramatically between the 1950s and 1980s, but they appear to have stabilized and even declined slightly since then (Teachman, 2009). When divorce rates were at their peak, the most widely cited estimates of future divorce risk were around 50%. However, the modest reductions in divorce rates in recent years appear to have lowered the risk of divorce to 43%-46% for couples (Schoen & Canudas-Romo, 2006). Nevertheless, because some marriages end in permanent separation instead of legal divorce, Amato (2010) suggests that the common belief that about half of marriages end is reasonable. Although most people realize that divorce rates are high, they have a curious tendency to underestimate the likelihood that they will personally experience a divorce.

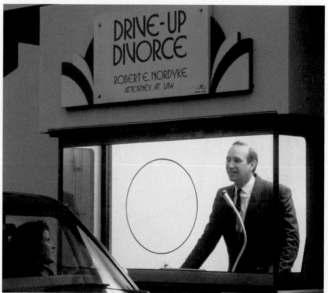

The high divorce rate has led to some novel ways of dealing with its worrisome legal aspects. Attorney Robert Nordyke discovered that the drive-up window at his new office—a former savings and loan branch in Salem, Oregon—was perfect for serving legal papers on his clients' spouses.

When asked directly, newlywed women pegged their probability of divorce at about 13%. Further, a full 97% of these women said they expected to remain married to their current spouse for life (Campbell, Wright, & Flores, 2012). Obviously these estimations are far beyond the actual probability for the population as a whole.

Divorce rates are higher among blacks than whites or Hispanics, among lower-income couples, among couples with less education, among couples who cohabitated, among people who marry at a relatively young age, and among those whose parents divorced (Amato, 2010). As **Figure 10.7** shows, the vast majority of divorces occur during the first decade of a marriage (Copen et al., 2012). What types of marital problems are predictive of divorce? Frequently cited problems include communication difficulties (not talking; being moody, critical, and easy to anger), infidelity, jealousy, growing apart, foolish spending behavior, and substance abuse problems (Amato & Previti, 2003).

A wide variety of social trends have probably contributed to increasing divorce rates. The stigma attached to divorce has gradually eroded. Many religious denominations are becoming more tolerant of divorce, and marriage has thus lost some of its sacred quality. The shrinking size of families probably makes divorce a more viable possibility. The entry of more women into the workforce has made many wives less financially dependent on the continuation of their marriage. New attitudes emphasizing individual fulfillment seem to have counterbalanced older attitudes that encouraged dissatisfied spouses to suffer in silence. Reflecting all these trends, the legal barriers to divorce have also diminished (de Vas, 2012; Teachmen, 2009).

To address these trends, pro-marriage advocates campaign for policies that would make divorces more difficult to obtain. For example, several states have enacted covenant marriage laws (Sanchez, 2009). Couples who choose to enter into a covenant marriage agree to complete premarital education programs and pledge to divorce only in response to severe problems (such as spouse abuse or a lengthy prison term), and only after seeking extensive marriage counseling (Adams & Coltrane, 2006). However, critics point out that making divorces harder to get may not be a realistic option in today's society. Although a majority of adults agree—in the abstract—that divorce laws should be tougher, they do not want their own personal freedom in this area to be impeded. For instance, only around 2% of couples have chosen covenant marriage in the state (Louisiana) that first offered this option, and overall divorce rates have not dropped there (Allman, 2009). Still, those who choose a covenant marriage do appear to have reduced divorce rates (Sanchez, 2009).

Deciding on a Divorce

Divorces are often postponed repeatedly, and they are rarely executed without a great deal of agonizing forethought. The decision to divorce is usually the outcome of a long series of smaller decisions or relationship stages that may take years to unfold, so divorce should be viewed as a process rather than as a discrete event (Demo & Fine, 2009). Wives' judgments about the likelihood of their marriages ending in divorce tend to be more accurate than husbands' judgments (South, Bose, & Trent, 2004). This finding may be related to the fact that wives initiate the majority of divorce actions (Hetherington, 2003).

It is difficult to generalize about the relative merits of divorce as opposed to remaining in an unsatisfactory marriage. Extensive research shows that people who are currently divorced suffer a higher incidence of both physical and psychological maladies and are less happy than those who are currently married (Amato, 2001; Trotter, 2009). In a meta-analysis involving thirty-two studies across eleven countries, Sbarra and colleagues (2011) found that divorce was associated with early death risk, especially for men. Nevertheless, as painful as marital dissolution may be, remaining in an unhappy marriage is also potentially detrimental. Research has shown that in comparison to divorced individuals, unhappily married people tend to show poorer physical health, lower levels of happiness, less life satisfaction, and lower self-esteem (Hawkins & Booth, 2005; Wickrama et al., 1997). In addition, divorce is often related to higher rates of autonomy, self-awareness, and job success, especially when individuals have a stable financial

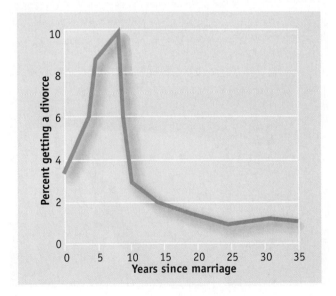

Figure 10.7

Divorce rate as a function of years married. This graph shows the distribution of divorces in relation to how long couples have been married. As you can see, the vast majority of divorces occur in the early years, with divorce rates peaking between the fifth and tenth years of marriage. (Data from National Center for Health Statistics)

"That's right, Phil. A separation will mean—among other things—watching your own cholesterol."

situation and a strong social support network (Trotter, 2009). Moreover, like other stressful life events, divorce can lead to personal growth and positive changes in the self (Tashiro, Frazier, & Berman, 2006), so the picture is not entirely negative.

Adjusting to Divorce

Although divorce seems to have a more negative impact on men's health and mortality (Amato, 2010), it appears to be more difficult and disruptive for women in terms of finances (Trotter, 2009). Women are more likely to assume the responsibility of raising the children, whereas men tend to reduce their contact with their children, some losing contact with their kids altogether. Another key consideration is that divorced women are less likely than their ex-husbands to have adequate income or a satisfying job (Smock, Manning, & Gupta, 1999). Although the economic consequences of divorce can be more severe for women than for men, in this era of two-income families, many men also experience a noticeable decline in their standard of living after going through a divorce (McManus & DiPrete, 2001).

The process of getting divorced is stressful for both spouses. Researchers do *not* find consistent gender differences in psychological adjustment to divorce (Amato, 2001). In the aggregate, the magnitude of the negative effects of divorce on individuals' psychological well-being seems to be pretty similar for husbands and wives. Factors associated with favorable postdivorce adjustment include

having higher income, getting remarried, having more positive attitudes about divorce, and being the partner who initiated the divorce (Wang & Amato, 2000). After a divorce, having social relationships, including both one-to-one friendships and a circle of friends, is important to adjustment (Krumrei et al., 2007). Forgiveness of the ex-spouse is also associated with increased well-being and lowered depression (Rye et al., 2004). Similarly, evidence suggests that self-compassion (showing kindness to and forgiving oneself about the divorce) is associated with less post-divorce distress (Sbarra, Smith, & Mehl, 2012).

Effects of Divorce on Children

As divorce rates increase, so do the number of children from divorced families. When couples have children, decisions about divorce must take into account the potential impact on their offspring. Widely publicized research by Judith Wallerstein and her colleagues has painted a rather bleak picture of how divorce affects youngsters (Wallerstein & Blakeslee, 1989; Wallerstein, Lewis, & Blakeslee, 2000). This research followed a sample of 60 divorced couples and their 131 children for 25 years, beginning in 1971. At the 10-year follow-up, almost half of the participants were characterized as "worried, underachieving, self-deprecating, and sometimes angry young men and women" (Wallerstein & Blakeslee, 1989, p. 299). Even *25 years* after their parents' divorce, a majority of subjects were viewed as troubled adults who found it difficult to maintain stable and satisfying intimate relationships (Wallerstein, 2005; Wallerstein & Lewis, 2004).

Wallerstein died in 2012 at the age of 90. In writing about her friend and long-time collaborator, Sandra Blakeslee (2012) summed up the heart of their findings as follows: (1) Divorce can have profound effects on children,

Learn More Online

Divorce Central

Divorce Central is one of a number of practical sites that provide information and advice on legal, emotional, and financial issues for individuals contemplating or going through a divorce. Annotated links to other divorce-related sites can also be found here.

effects that can last well into adulthood; (2) the supportive quality of the postdivorce family is critical; (3) the age of the children at the time of the divorce can predict the nature of the effects on those children; and (4) stepfamilies present a number of hazards that are difficult to anticipate.

The enduring, long-term effects of divorce reported by Wallerstein were particularly disturbing and generated great interest from the media, resulting in an abundance of TV interviews, magazine articles, and so forth. However, critics point out that her study suffered from a variety of flaws (Amato, 2003; Cherlin, 1999). It was based on a small sample of children from a wealthy area in California that clearly was not representative of the population at large. There was no comparison group, and conclusions were based on impressions from clinical interviews, in which it is easy for interviewers to see what they expect to see. Further, critics caution against drawing causal conclusions from correlational data (Gordon, 2005).

Another complicated issue in assessing the effects of divorce is the choice of who should serve as a baseline for comparison. One can argue that children of divorce should be compared to children from intact homes characterized by persistent marital discord, a group that also shows elevated rates of many types of adjustment problems (Papp, Cummings, & Schermerhorn, 2004).

E. Mavis Hetherington

Are Wallerstein's findings consistent with other research? Yes and no. The results of another long-running study by E. Mavis Hetherington (1993, 1999, 2003), which used a larger and more representative sample, a control group, and conventional statistical comparisons, suggest that Wallerstein's conclusions are unduly pessimistic. According to Hetherington, divorce can be traumatic for children, but a substantial majority adjust reasonably well after 2 to 3 years, and only about 25% show serious psychological or emotional problems in adulthood (versus 10% in the control group). That is, most children of divorce do not show long-term adjustment problems (Lansford, 2009). Other research has highlighted some positive outcomes of parental divorce for children: enhancing personal growth, teaching life management skills, encouraging realistic relationship expectations, and enhancing empathy (Demo & Fine, 2009). Research has found only limited support, however, for the notion of a "good divorce" (Amato, Kane, & James, 2011).

Although Wallerstein's conclusions appear overly negative, *they differ from the results of other research only in degree* (Amato, 2003). After a divorce, many children exhibit depression, anxiety, nightmares, dependency, aggression, withdrawal, distractibility, lowered academic performance, reduced physical health, precocious sexual

behavior, and substance abuse (Barber & Demo, 2006; Kelly & Emery, 2003; Knox, 2000). Experiencing divorce during childhood is a risk factor for many subsequent problems in one's adult years, including maladjustment, marital instability, and reduced occupational attainments (Amato, 1999). Children have more adjustment problems when their parents have a history of particularly bitter, acrimonious conflict (Amato, 2001). Other factors that influence the impact of divorce on children's adjustment include their age, coping resources, and adjustment prior to the divorce (Lansford, 2009; Shelton & Harold, 2007).

So what can we conclude about the effects of divorce on children? Ahrons (2007) cautions that that the extensive body of research on divorce suggests a "nuanced picture of divorce, one that defies sound-bite conclusions" (p. 4). It is reasonable to conclude that divorces have highly varied effects on children that depend on a complex constellation of interacting factors. As such, Amato (2010) suggests that the question for researchers is not whether divorce affects children but how it affects them and under what circumstances.

Remarriage and Stepfamilies

Evidence that adequate courtship opportunities exist for the divorced is provided by the statistics on remarriage: The majority of divorced people eventually remarry. The mean length of time between divorce and remarriage is 3 to 4 years (Kreider, 2005).

How successful are second marriages? The answer depends on your standard of comparison. Divorce rates *are* higher for second than for first marriages, though the average duration for second marriages is about the same as for first, about 8 to 9 years (Kreider, 2005). However, this statistic may simply indicate that this group of people see divorce as a reasonable alternative to an unsatisfactory marriage. Nonetheless, studies of marital adjustment suggest that second marriages are slightly less successful than first marriages, especially for women who bring children into the second marriage (Teachman, 2008). Of course, if you consider that in this pool of people *all* the first marriages ran into serious trouble, then the second marriages look rather good by comparison. As with first marriages, communication plays a major role in marital satisfaction for both spouses (Beaudry et al., 2004).

Another major issue related to remarriage is its effect on children. For example, as the traditional nuclear family declines, children's living arrangements are becoming increasingly unstable and diverse, which might contribute to decreased well-being (Brown, 2010). *Stepfamilies* or *blended families* (where both spouses bring in children from a previous relationship) are an established part of modern life, and adaptation to remarriage can be difficult for children (Bray, 2009). **Figure 10.8** summarizes the developmental stages through which most stepfamilies progress. Wallerstein and Lewis (2007) argue that there is an inherent instability in parenting, as parents are caught between their desires to create a new intimate relationship and to maintain their parenting role. This can be a negative experience for children who feel powerless or who undergo dramatic changes in living spaces, rules, and expectations (Stoll et al., 2005). Research indicates that on the average, interaction in stepfamilies appears to be somewhat less cohesive and warm than interaction in first-marriage families, and stepparent-stepchild relations tend to be more negative and distant than parent-child relations in first marriages (Pasley & Moorefield, 2004), though it is important to note that this doesn't mean that these relationships are necessarily problematic or dysfunctional.

The evidence suggests that children in stepfamilies are a little less well adjusted than children in first marriages and are roughly similar in adjustment to children in single-parent homes (Sweeney, Wang, & Videon, 2009). In an analysis of sixty-one studies, Jeynes (2006) found that children in stepfamilies tend to show lower academic achievement and psychological well-being than those from

PATTERNS OF DEVELOPMENT IN STEPFAMILIES		
Stage	**Description**	**Example**
Stage One: Fantasy	Family has unrealistic, ideal expectations.	I love my new wife, so I'll certainly love her children.
Stage Two: Immersion	Real life challenges expectations.	It seems like my husband is closer to his daughter than he is to me.
Stage Three: Awareness	Family members attempt to make sense out of the new arrangements.	I understand that my stepchildren are resistant to the new family structure, not because they are bad kids, but because it is hard for them.
Stage Four: Mobilization	Family members attempt to negotiate difficulties.	Eating together as a family is important enough to me that I am willing to speak with my husband about it.
Stage Five: Action	Family creates strategies to resolve differences.	We will have weekly family meetings to air frustrations.
Stage Six: Contact	Positive emotional bonds begin to form.	My stepson and I can resolve this issue by having a heart-to-heart.
Stage Seven: Resolution	Norms are established and new family rituals emerge.	My teenage stepdaughter appreciates my perspective on her new boyfriend.

Figure 10.8

Patterns of development in stepfamilies. Papernow (1993) developed a model of seven stages through which most stepfamilies pass as they move from fantasy toward resolution.

Source: Adapted from Papernow, P. L. (1993). *Becoming a stepfamily: Patterns of development in remarried families.* San Francisco: Jossey-Bass. Reprinted by permission of the author.

intact or single-parent families. However, the differences between stepfamilies and other types of families in the adjustment of their children tend to be modest.

In sum, much research remains to be conducted in the area of divorce and its impact on the family. For instance, there is very little research on the impact of separation on spouses and children. Further, with the legalization of same-sex marriages in several states, a topic we turn to next, researchers will no doubt began to examine the effects of marital dissolution on same-sex spouses and families (Amato, 2010).

ALTERNATIVE RELATIONSHIP LIFESTYLES

LEARNING OBJECTIVES

- Compare homosexual and heterosexual couples in regard to the dynamics of their intimate relationships and the adjustment of children.
- Discuss the prevalence of cohabitation and its relationship to marital success.

- Describe stereotypes of single life, and summarize evidence on the adjustment of single people.

So far we have been discussing the traditional model of marriage, which, as we noted at the beginning of the chapter, has been challenged by a variety of social trends. More and more people are experiencing alternative relationship lifestyles, including gay couples, singles, and partners choosing cohabitation.

Gay Relationships

Up until this point, we have, for purposes of simplicity, focused our attention on *heterosexuals,* those who seek emotional-sexual relationships with members of the other gender. However, we have been ignoring a significant minority group: *homosexual* men and women, who seek committed, emotional-sexual relationships with members of the same gender. (In everyday language, the term *gay* is used to refer to homosexuals of both genders, although many homosexual women prefer the term *lesbian* for themselves.)

Popular stereotypes suggest that gays rarely get involved in long-term intimate relationships. In reality, most homosexual men, and nearly all homosexual women, prefer stable, long-term relationships, and at any one time roughly 40%–60% of gay males and 45%–80% of lesbians are involved in committed relationships (Kurdek, 2004). Lesbian relationships are generally sexually exclusive (Goldberg, 2010a). It is more common for committed male couples to have "open" relationships, allowing for the possibility of sexual activity (but not affection) with outsiders.

Same-Sex Marriage

Americans continue to be divided over the morality of homosexual partnerships. In fact, as shown in **Figure 10.9**, a 2012 Gallup poll found that half of Americans think that same-sex marriages should be legally recognized, a percentage that has been increasing over time (Newport, 2012). Still, gay couples in most states cannot choose to legally formalize their unions by getting married. They are therefore denied many economic benefits available to married couples. For example, they can't file joint tax returns, and gay individuals often can't obtain employer-provided health insurance for their partner. Thus, gay and lesbian rights raise major political issues that affect gays and lesbians both socially and psychologically (Fingerhut, Riggle, & Rostosky, 2011).

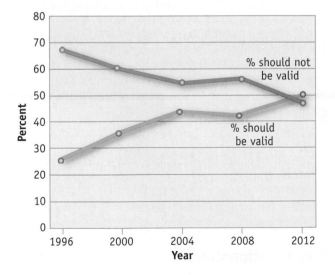

Figure 10.9

Attitudes toward legal same-sex marriage. Americans' attitudes toward same-sex marriage have grown increasingly positive over time and reached a record high in 2012. (Adapted from Newport, 2012

Same-sex marriage is now a legal right in states such as Massachusetts, Connecticut, and Vermont, and civil unions and domestic partnerships are legally recognized in other states, such as New Jersey and California. However, during the past decade many states (such as Alabama and Texas) have passed laws prohibiting same-sex marriages, and constitutional amendments banning gay marriage have been introduced in the U.S. Congress. Some argue that allowing gay marriages would erode traditional family values. A study using over a decade of data, however, does not bear this out. This research found no adverse effects on factors such as divorce, abortion rates, or single parenthood as a result of allowing (or banning) gay marriage (Langbein & Yost, 2009). The public discussion of gay marriage, as difficult as it is, has highlighted the realities of homosexual couples and their family relationships.

Comparisons to Heterosexual Couples

Devoting a separate section to gay couples may seem to imply that the dynamics of their close relationships are different from those seen in heterosexual couples. As Garnets and Kimmel (1991) point out, gay relationships "develop within a social context of societal disapproval with an absence of social legitimization and support; families and other social institutions often stigmatize such relationships and there are no prescribed roles and behaviors to structure such relationships" (p. 170). Although gay relationships evolve in a different social context, research has documented that close relationships, gay or heterosexual, function in similar ways (Herek, 2006). Both heterosexual and

REEL RESEARCH

Sexual Prejudice in America

Log on to CourseMate at www.cengagebrain.com **to watch this video.**

Personal values can influence one's attitudes toward other groups of people. One group often victimized by others is homosexuals, both male and female. In this Reel Research video, Gregory Herek, a psychologist at University of California, Davis, discusses the influences on sexual prejudice and investigates attitudes of heterosexual males and females across the nation. The purpose of Herek's research is to explore the psychological processes associated with sexual prejudice.

Herek explains that public opinion about the acceptability of homosexuality and gay marriage fluctuates and is often linked to discussions about moral values. Using a national sample population of heterosexual males and females from varying ages and socioeconomic and ethnic backgrounds, researchers asked participants how they would rate different groups of people. Some questions involved gay men and women and bisexual men and women as groups; other questions involved ethnic groups. On a scale of zero to 100, respondents rated homosexual and bisexual groups below the median, with ratings between 43 and 47. Conversely, white, black, Mexican American, and Puerto Rican groups were rated above the median, between 63 and 70. A large number of respondents gave gay and bisexual groups a

rating of zero, meaning they felt strong hostility toward these groups. Herek explains that negative attitudes, particularly expressed by heterosexual men toward homosexual men, may be the product of a number of factors, including devout religious background, internal psychological conflict about one's own masculinity, societal pressures to prove heterosexuality, and peer pressure to ostracize those from "appropriately unacceptable" groups.

Watch the *Sexual Prejudice in America* video to learn more about Herek's study. Delve even deeper by responding to the following discussion questions.

DISCUSSION QUESTIONS

1. Explain the study demonstrated in the video. How did researchers collect their data? What findings were highlighted, and what influence does society have over people's attitudes toward homosexual men and women?

2. How do current events affect public opinion about homosexuality?

3. According to Herek, how can a negative attitude toward homosexuality be improved or made positive? What activity might be necessary?

homosexual couples hold similar values about relationships, report similar levels of relationship satisfaction, perceive their relationships to be loving and satisfying, and say they want their partners to have characteristics similar to theirs (Peplau & Fingerhut, 2007). Furthermore, homosexual and heterosexual couples are similar in terms of the factors that predict relationship satisfaction, the sources of

conflict in their relationships, and their patterns of conflict resolution (Kurdek, 2004; Peplau & Ghavami, 2009).

Given the lack of moral, social, legal, and economic support for gay relationships, are gay unions less stable than heterosexual unions? Researchers have not yet been able to collect adequate data on this question, but the limited data available suggest that gay couples' relationships

MARRIAGE AND INTIMATE RELATIONSHIPS

are somewhat briefer and more prone to break-ups than heterosexual marriages (Peplau, 1991). If that's the case, it might be because gay relationships face fewer barriers to dissolution—that is, fewer practical problems that make break-ups difficult or costly (Kurdek, 1998).

Gay Parenting

Although research indicates striking similarities between homosexual and heterosexual relationships, basic misconceptions about the nature of gay relationships remain widespread. For example, lesbians and gay men tend to be thought of as individuals rather than as members of families. This thinking reflects a bias that homosexuality and family just don't mesh (Allen & Demo, 1995). In reality, gays are very much involved in families as sons and daughters, as parents and stepparents, and as aunts, uncles, and grandparents. According to the 2010 U.S. Census, out of the 594,000 same-sex households, 115,000 (19%) are rearing children, 84% of whom are their own biological children. Many of these parental responsibilities are left over from previous marriages, as about 20%–30% of gays have

Children reared by gay or lesbian parents do not seem more poorly adjusted than other children. Research indicates that the quality of child-parent interactions is much more important to a child's development than parental sexual orientation.

been heterosexually married (Kurdek, 2004). But an increasing number of homosexuals are opting to have children in the context of their gay relationships (Falk, 1994; Gartrell et al., 1999).

What do we know about gays and lesbians as parents? The evidence suggests that homosexuals are similar to their heterosexual counterparts in their approaches to parenting and that their children are similar to the children of heterosexual parents in terms of personal development and peer relations (C. J. Patterson, 2001, 2006, 2009). The overall adjustment of children with gay parents appears similar in quality to that of children of heterosexual parents (Goldberg, 2010b; Tasker, 2005). Moreover, the vast majority of children of gay parents grow up to identify themselves as heterosexual (Bailey & Dawood, 1998), and studies suggest that they are no more likely than others to become homosexual (Flaks et al., 1995). In sum, children reared by gay and lesbian parents do not appear to suffer any special ill effects and do not seem noticeably different from other children. Decades of research indicates that the quality of child-parent interactions is much more important to a child's development than parental sexual orientation (Crowl, Ahn, & Baker, 2008; Patterson, 2006, 2009).

Cohabitation

As we noted earlier in the chapter, *cohabitation* refers to living together in a sexually intimate relationship outside of marriage. Recent years have witnessed a tremendous increase in the number of cohabiting couples (see **Figure 10.10**). Although cohabitation is still illegal in four states (Florida, Michigan, Mississippi, and Virginia), there were about 7.6 million unmarried couples living together in 2011 (U.S. Bureau of the Census, 2011a). Increasing rates of cohabitation are not unique to the United States and are even higher in many European countries (Kiernan, 2004). However, the percentage of couples living together in the U.S. at any one time does not accurately convey how widespread this phenomenon has become, because cohabiting unions tend to be shorter than marriages (Seltzer, 2004).

Cohabitation tends to conjure up images of college students or other well-educated young couples without children, but these images are misleading. In reality, cohabitation rates have always been higher in the less-educated and lower-income segments of the population (Bumpass & Lu, 2000). Moreover, many cohabitating couples have children (Bianchi, Raley, & Casper, 2012).

Although many people see cohabitation as a threat to the institution of marriage, many theorists see it as a new stage in the courtship process—a sort of trial marriage. Consistent with this view, about 30% of teenagers indicated that they would probably or definitely cohabitate (Manning, Longmore, & Giordano, 2007). Further, three-quarters of female cohabitants expect to marry their cur-

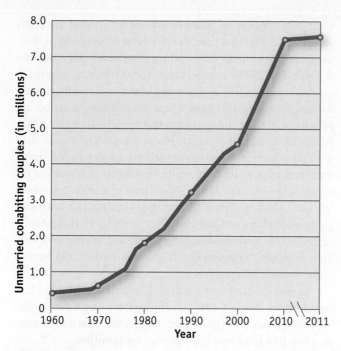

Figure 10.10

Cohabitation in the United States. The number of unmarried couples living together has been increasing rapidly since 1970 (based on U.S. Census data). This increase shows no signs of leveling off.

fact, studies have consistently found an association between premarital cohabitation and *increased* marital discord and divorce rates (Teachman, 2003). This association is referred to as the *cohabitation effect* (Jose, O'Leary, & Moyer, 2010), and it holds true even for second marriages (Stanley et al., 2010). However, preliminary research suggests that the cohabitation effect might be weakening for recent cohorts of married couples (Manning & Cohen, 2012).

What accounts for the cohabitation effect? Many theorists argue that this nontraditional lifestyle has historically attracted a more liberal and less conventional segment of the population with a weak commitment to the institution of marriage and relatively few qualms about getting divorced. This explanation has considerable empirical support (Stanley, Whitton, & Markman, 2004), but some support also exists for the alternative explanation—that the experience of cohabitation changes people's attitudes, values, or habits in ways that somehow increase their vulnerability to divorce (Kamp Dush, Cohan, & Amato, 2003; Seltzer, 2001).

Remaining Single

The pressure to marry is substantial in our society (Sharp & Ganong, 2011). People are socialized to believe that they are not complete until they have found their "other half" and have entered into a partnership for life. And reference is often made to people's "failure" to marry. In spite of this pressure, an increasing proportion of young adults are remaining single (Morris & DePaulo, 2009). In 2010, over a quarter of all households in the United States were one-person (Lofquist et al., 2012) (see **Figure 10.11**).

Does the greater number of single adults mean that people are turning away from the institution of marriage? Perhaps a little, but for the most part, no. A variety of factors have contributed to the growth of the single population. Much of this growth is a result of the higher median age at which people marry and the increased rate of divorce. The vast majority of single, never-married people *do* hope to marry eventually. In a national survey of never-

rent partner (Lichter, Batson, & Brown, 2004). In spite of these expectations, however, research shows that most individuals cohabitate for practical reasons (such as financial necessity, convenience, or to meet housing needs), rather than as a trial marriage (Sassler & Miller, 2011). Conceiving a child during cohabitation tends to increase couples' chances of staying together (Manning, 2004).

As a prelude to marriage, cohabitation should allow people to experiment with marital-like responsibilities and reduce the likelihood of entering marriage with unrealistic expectations, suggesting that couples who cohabit before they marry should go on to more successful marriages than those who do not. Although this analysis sounds plausible, researchers have *not* found that premarital cohabitation increases the likelihood of subsequent marital success. In

Figure 10.11

One-person households in the United States. This graph depicts the increase in the number of U.S. households with only one person living in them. It shows that the percentage has more than doubled in the last 50 years. (Data from U.S. Bureau of the Census)

married adults, only 12% reported that they did not want to eventually get married (Cohn et al., 2011).

Singles continue to be stigmatized and plagued by two disparate stereotypes. On the one hand, single people are sometimes portrayed as carefree swingers who are too busy enjoying the fruits of promiscuity to shoulder marital responsibilities. On the other hand, they are seen as losers who have not succeeded in snaring a mate and they may be portrayed as socially inept, maladjusted, frustrated, lonely, and bitter. These stereotypes do a great injustice to the diversity that exists among those who are single. In fact, the negative stereotypes of singles have led some researchers to coin the term *singlism* to capture how single people can be victims of prejudice and discrimination (DePaulo, 2011; DePaulo & Morris, 2005, 2006).

Moving beyond stereotypes, what do scientists know about singlehood? It is true that single people exhibit poorer mental and physical health than married people (Waite, 1995), and they rate themselves as less happy than their married counterparts (Waite, 2000). However, we must use caution in interpreting these results; in many studies, "singles" include those who are divorced or widowed, which inflates this finding (DePaulo, 2011; Morris & DePaulo, 2009). Furthermore, the differences are modest, and the happiness gap has shrunk, especially among women. The physical health benefits of being married appear to be greater for men than for women (Amato, 2010). But most studies find that single women are more satisfied with their lives and less distressed than comparable single men, and various lines of evidence suggest that women get along without men better than men get along without women (Marker, 1996). When interviewing life-long single women between the ages of 65 and 77, Baumbusch (2004) found that these women expressed satisfaction with their decision to remain single and emphasized the importance of their independence.

In sum, as traditional married households become less common in modern life, psychological researchers must answer the call to explore and understand alternative relationship lifestyles and their impact on families.

Application

UNDERSTANDING INTIMATE PARTNER VIOLENCE

LEARNING OBJECTIVES

- Discuss the incidence of partner abuse and the characteristics of batterers, and explain why some partners stay in abusive relationships.

- Discuss the incidence and consequences of date rape as well as the factors that contribute to it.
- Understand ways to reduce the likelihood of date rape.

Answer the following statements "true" or "false."

____ **1.** Most rapes are committed by strangers.

____ **2.** Women are almost never perpetrators of intimate violence.

____ **3.** Most women in abusive relationships are attracted to violent men.

____ **4.** Most men who have witnessed domestic violence as children will batter their intimate partners.

All of the above statements are false, as you will see in this Application, which examines the darker side of intimate relationships. Most people assume they will be safe with those they love and trust. Unfortunately, some people are betrayed by individuals to whom they feel closest. *Intimate partner violence* **is aggression toward those who are in close relationship to the aggressor.** Intimate partner violence takes many forms: psychological, physical, and sexual abuse. Tragically, this violence sometimes ends in homicide. In this Application, we'll focus on two serious social problems: partner abuse and date rape. Much of our discussion is based on the work of the Rape, Abuse, and Incest National Network (RAINN).

Partner Abuse

Celebrity cases such as those involving Chris Brown and Rihanna have dramatically heightened public awareness of partner violence, particularly wife battering. *Battering* **encompasses physical abuse, emotional abuse, and sexual abuse of an intimate partner.** *Physical abuse* can include kicking, biting, punching, choking, pushing, slapping, hitting with an object, and threatening with or using a weapon. Examples of *emotional abuse* include humiliation, name calling, controlling what the partner does and with whom the partner socializes, refusing to communicate, unreasonably withholding money, and questioning the partner's sanity. *Sexual abuse* is characterized as using sexual behavior to control, manipulate, or demean the other person. Let's explore the research on physical abuse of partners.

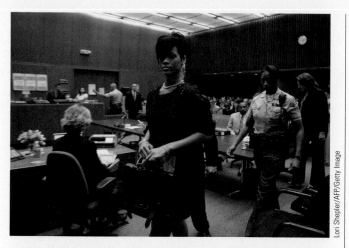

Celebrity cases such as Rihanna's abuse by Chris Brown have dramatically heightened public awareness of intimate partner violence. Sadly, in addition to sustaining physical injuries, victims of partner abuse often suffer from severe anxiety, depression, feelings of helplessness and humiliation, and symptoms of posttraumatic stress disorder.

Incidence and Consequences

As with other taboo topics, obtaining accurate estimates of physical abuse is difficult. According to the Centers for Disease Control (2011), twenty-four people per minute are victims of rape, physical violence, or stalking by an intimate partner in the United States. As shown in **Figure 10.12**, most first-time victims of intimate partner violence are young adults. Men, as well as women, are victims.

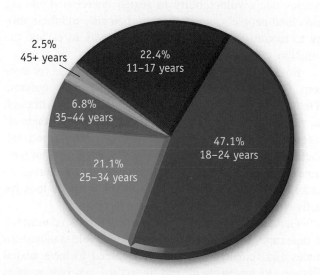

Figure 10.12

Age and intimate partner violence. This graph shows the ages of women when they first experienced intimate partner violence. As you can see, most were young adults. A similar pattern holds for men. (Data from the Centers for Disease Control)

About one man in seven has experienced physical violence by an intimate partner at some point in his lifetime. That said, women are more likely to be victims of abuse. In 2010, females accounted for 91.9% of reported rape and sexual assault incidents (Bureau of Justice Statistics, 2011). Further, a woman is the victim in 85% of nonfatal violent crimes committed by intimate partners and in 75% of murders by spouses (Rennison & Welchans, 2000). It is also inaccurate to assume that intimate violence is seen only in marital relationships—partner abuse is also a significant problem for cohabiting heterosexual couples and for gay couples.

The effects of battering reverberate beyond the obvious physical injuries. Victims of partner abuse tend to suffer from severe anxiety, depression, feelings of helplessness and humiliation, stress-induced physical illness, and symptoms of posttraumatic stress disorder (Lundberg-Love & Wilkerson, 2006). Children who witness marital violence also experience ill effects, such as anxiety, depression, reduced self-esteem, and increased delinquency (Johnson & Ferraro, 2001).

Characteristics of Batterers

Sexual assault perpetrators are a diverse group, so a single profile has not emerged. Some factors associated with an elevated risk for domestic violence include unemployment, drinking and drug problems, a tendency to anger easily, attitudes that condone aggression, and high stress (Stith et al., 2004). Studies indicate that men who were beaten as children or who witnessed their mothers being beaten are more likely to abuse their wives, although most men who grow up in these difficult circumstances do *not* become batterers themselves (Wareham, Boots, & Chavez, 2009). Batterers tend to be jealous in relationships, have unrealistic expectations of their partners, blame others for their own problems, and have their feelings hurt easily (Lundberg-Love & Wilkerson, 2006). Other relationship factors associated with domestic violence include having frequent disagreements, exhibiting a heated style of dealing with disagreements, and pairing a man holding traditional gender-role attitudes with a woman who has nontraditional views of gender roles (DeMaris et al., 2003).

Learn More Online

Office on Violence Against Women

This U.S. Department of Justice office was created in 1995 after federal legislation mandated national efforts to reduce domestic violence, sexual assault, and stalking. The site provides a wide variety of legal and social scientific resources in support of this mission.

Why Do People Stay in Abusive Relationships?

Individuals leave abusive partners more often than popular stereotypes suggest, but people are still perplexed by the fact that many partners remain in abusive relationships that seem horrible and degrading. However, research shows that this phenomenon is not really that perplexing. A number of seemingly compelling reasons explain why some individuals feel that leaving is not a realistic option, and many of the reasons revolve around fear. Some individuals lack financial independence and fear that they won't be able to survive financially without their partner (Kim & Gray, 2008). Others simply have no place to go and fear becoming homeless (Browne, 1993a). Still others feel guilty and ashamed about their failing relationship and don't want to face disapproval from family and friends, who are likely to fall into the trap of blaming the victim (Barnett & LaViolette, 1993). Above all else, many fear that if they try to leave, they may precipitate more brutal violence and even murder (Grothues & Marmion, 2006). Unfortunately, this fear is not altogether unrealistic, as many abusers have shown remarkable persistence in tracking down, stalking, threatening, beating, and killing their ex-partners. Although it is important to understand why people stay, it is also important to explore why individuals batter and what interventions can prevent partners from being brutalized or killed when they do leave.

Date Rape

Intimate violence is not limited to marital relations. **Date rape refers to forced and unwanted intercourse in the context of dating.** It can occur on a first date, with someone you've dated for a while, or with someone to whom you're engaged. The key factor in distinguishing this type of abuse is a partner's *consent*. There are two important considerations to keep in mind regarding consent. First, relationship status (either current or previous) and past acts of intimacy are *not* indicators of consent. Second, to ensure that activity is consensual, partners should seek consent with each sexual activity as the level of sexual intimacy increases (for instance when kissing, moving from kissing to petting, and from petting to oral sex).

Incidence and Consequences

It's difficult to estimate how often date rape occurs because the majority of instances go unreported (Frazier, 2009). Although the rate of intimate partner violence has declined since the 1990s (Catalano, 2012), it's much more common than widely realized. Most people naively assume that the vast majority of rapes are committed by strangers who leap from bushes or dark alleys to surprise their victims. In reality, research indicates that most victims are raped by someone they know (Frazier, 2009).

In the aftermath of date rape, victims typically experience a variety of emotional reactions, including fear, anger, anxiety, self-blame, and guilt (Kahn & Andreoli Mathie, 1999). Many rape victims suffer from depression, symptoms of posttraumatic stress disorder, and increased risk for suicide (Foa, 1998; Slashinski, Coker, & Davis, 2003; Ullman, 2004). Negative reactions can be exacerbated if the victim's family and friends are not supportive—particularly if family or friends blame the victim for the attack. In addition to the trauma of the rape, women also have to cope with the possibilities of pregnancy. Meanwhile, male victims (both gay and straight) have to deal with fears of social evaluation related to gender role stereotypes (for example, "I am less of a man for not being able to defend myself"). For either gender, the possibility of a sexually transmitted disease is a concern. Further, if the rape survivor presses charges against the attacker, he or she may have to deal with difficult legal proceedings, negative publicity, and social stigma.

Contributing Factors

To understand the phenomenon of date rape, it's essential to know something about the factors that contribute to this behavior. It probably comes as no surprise to learn that alcohol contributes to about half of sexually aggressive incidents (Abbey, 2009). Alcohol impairs judgment and reduces inhibitions, making people more willing to assert their power. Drinking also undermines one's ability to interpret ambiguous social cues, making one more likely to overestimate a date's interest in sex. The more intoxicated perpetrators are, the more aggressive they tend to be (Abbey, 2009; Abbey et al., 2003). Alcohol also increases one's vulnerability to sexual coercion. Drinking can cloud people's assessments of their risk and their ability to mount firm resistance or find a way to escape the situation.

So-called "date rape drugs" are also a cause for concern. Rohypnol ("roofies") and gamma hydroxybutyrate (GHB) are two drugs used to subdue individuals. Although these drugs are colorless, odorless, and tasteless, their effects are anything but benign, and they can even be fatal. Victims typically pass out and have no recall of what happened while they were under the influence of the drug. To make it easier to spike a drink, predators typically look for individuals who are already intoxicated.

Gender differences in sexual standards also contribute to date rape. Society still encourages a double standard for males and females. Men are encouraged to have sexual feelings, to act on them, and to "score," whereas women are socialized to be coy about their sexual desires. These social norms can encourage game playing, so dating partners may not always say what they mean or mean what they say. For instance, whereas the majority of women say

Alcohol contributes to about half of sexually aggressive incidents.

"no" and mean it, some women may say "no" to sexual activity when they actually mean "maybe" or "yes." This response, referred to as "token resistance," is less common than once thought (Muehlenhard, 2011). Unfortunately, token resistance clouds the issue of whether a woman has consented to sex.

Protecting Oneself from Date Rape

To protect oneself, the Rape, Abuse, and Incest National Network suggests that is useful to understand the three stages of date rape. First, *intrusion* is when an offender violates the victim's personal space or level of comfort with unwelcomed touches, stares, or sharing of information. *Desensitization*, the second stage, occurs when the victim gets used to the intrusive actions and sees them as less threatening. In this stage the victim might still feel uncomfortable but might convince herself that the feeling is un-

founded. Finally, *isolation* occurs when the offender isolates the victim from others. Understanding these three stages can help one identify warning signs of sexual aggression.

It is imperative to recognize date rape for what it is: an act of sexual aggression, and victims are never to blame for others' acts of aggression. There are steps one can take, however, to reduce one's likelihood of victimization: (1) Beware of excessive alcohol and drug use, which may undermine self-control and self-determination in sexual interactions. (2) Don't leave your drink unattended or accept drinks from people you don't know or trust. (3) When dating someone new, agree to go only to public places, and always carry enough money for transportation back home. (4) Watch out for your friends and have them watch out for you. (5) Finally, clearly and accurately communicate your feelings and expectations about sexual activity by engaging in appropriate self-disclosure.

KEY IDEAS

CHALLENGES TO THE TRADITIONAL MODEL OF MARRIAGE

● The traditional model of marriage is being challenged by the increasing acceptability of singlehood, the increasing popularity of cohabitation, the reduced premium on permanence, changes in gender roles, the increasing prevalence of voluntary childlessness, and the decline of the traditional nuclear family. Nonetheless, marriage remains quite popular.

DECIDING TO MARRY

● A multitude of factors influence an individual's decision to marry, including one's culture. The norm for our society is to select a mate and engage in a monogamous marriage. Mate selection is influenced by endogamy, homogamy, and gender. Women place more emphasis on potential partners' ambition and financial prospects, whereas men are more interested in a partner's youthfulness and physical attractiveness.

● There are some premarital predictors of marital success, such as family background, age, length of courtship, and personality, but the relations are weak. The nature of a couple's premarital communication is a better predictor of marital adjustment. Stressful events surrounding the marriage influence marital stability.

MARITAL ADJUSTMENT ACROSS THE FAMILY LIFE CYCLE

● The family life cycle is an orderly sequence of developmental stages through which families tend to progress. Newly married couples tend to be very happy before the arrival of children. Today more couples are struggling with the decision about whether to have children. The arrival of children is a major transition that is handled best by parents who have realistic expectations about the difficulties inherent in raising a family.

● As children reach adolescence, parents should expect more conflict as their influence declines. They must learn to relate to their children as adults and help launch them into the adult world. Most parents no longer struggle with the empty nest syndrome. Adult children returning home may be more of a problem.

VULNERABLE AREAS IN MARITAL ADJUSTMENT

● Gaps in expectations about marital roles may create marital stress. Disparities in expectations about gender roles and the distribution of housework may be especially common and problematic. Work concerns can clearly spill over to influence marital functioning, but the links between parents' employment and children's adjustment are complex.

● Wealth does not ensure marital happiness, but a lack of money can produce marital problems. Inadequate communication is a commonly reported marital problem, which is predictive of divorce.

DIVORCE AND ITS AFTERMATH

● Divorce rates have increased dramatically in recent decades, but they appear to be stabilizing. Most couples underestimate their likelihood of divorce. Deciding on a divorce tends to be a gradual process rather than a single event.

● Wallerstein's research suggests that divorce tends to have negative effects on children. Hetherington's research suggests that most children recover from divorce after a few years. The effects of divorce on children vary, but negative effects can be long-lasting.

● A substantial majority of divorced people remarry. These second marriages have a somewhat lower probability of success than first marriages. The adjustment of children in stepfamilies appears to be somewhat lower than for other families, but differences are modest.

ALTERNATIVE RELATIONSHIP LIFESTYLES

● Gay relationships develop in a starkly different social context than marital relationships, and acceptance of same-sex relationships have increased over time. Most homosexuals desire long-term intimate relationships, and studies have found that heterosexual and homosexual couples are similar in many ways. Children raised by gay parents do not show poorer adjustment than other children.

● The prevalence of cohabitation has increased dramatically. Logically, one might expect cohabitation to facilitate marital success, but research has consistently found an association between cohabitation and marital instability.

● An increasing proportion of the young population are remaining single, but this fact does not mean that people are turning away from marriage. Although singles generally have the same adjustment problems as married couples, evidence suggests that singles tend to be somewhat less happy and less healthy.

APPLICATION: UNDERSTANDING INTIMATE PARTNER VIOLENCE

● Intimate partner violence takes many forms including psychological, physical, and sexual abuse. Women are the principal victims of serious, dangerous abuse. Perpetrators of intimate partner violence are diverse, but they tend to anger easily, be jealous, and have unrealistic expectations of their partner. Partners stay in abusive relationships for a variety of compelling, practical reasons, including economic realities.

● The majority of rapes are committed by someone the victim knows. Rape is a traumatic experience that has many serious consequences. Alcohol abuse, drug use, and gender-based sexual standards all contribute to date rape. Miscommunication revolving around token resistance is particularly problematic. There are steps one can take to protect oneself from date rape.

KEY TERMS

Battering p. 316	Homogamy p. 297
Cohabitation p. 293	Intimate partner violence
Date rape p. 318	p. 316
Divorce p. 307	Marriage p. 293
Endogamy p. 297	Monogamy p. 297
Family life cycle p. 299	Polygamy p. 297

KEY PEOPLE

John Gottman pp. 306–307
E. Mavis Hetherington p. 310
Judith Wallerstein pp. 309–310

1. Which of the following is a recent social trend that is undermining the traditional model of marriage?
   a. Decreased acceptance of singlehood
   b. Less voluntary childlessness
   c. Reduced acceptance of cohabitation
   d. Reduced premium on permanence in marriage

2. Endogamy refers to
   a. the tendency to marry within one's social group.
   b. the tendency to marry someone with similar characteristics.
   c. the final marriage in serial monogamy.
   d. norms that promote marriage outside one's social unit.

3. Based on trends in the data, which of the following couples has the greatest likelihood of marital success?
   a. Stephanie and David, whose parents are divorced
   b. Jessica and Carlos, who are both perfectionists
   c. Ruth and Randy, who had a long courtship
   d. Carla and Turk, who married at a very young age

4. The transition to parenthood tends to be easier when
   a. the newborn child was planned for.
   b. the parents have realistic expectations.
   c. the new parents are relatively young.
   d. the father is not heavily involved in child care.

5. Which of the following characteristics in young children is related to maternal employment?
   a. Increased hyperactivity
   b. Higher anxiety
   c. Increased positive interactions with the mothers
   d. Increased prosocial behavior

6. Truc and Hiroshi have plenty of financial resources. In their marriage, arguments about money
   a. may be common.
   b. don't occur.
   c. are a big problem only if the wife earns more than her husband.
   d. are unrelated to marital satisfaction.

7. The evidence suggests that the negative effects of divorce on former spouses' *psychological* adjustment are
   a. exaggerated for both sexes.
   b. greater for men than women.
   c. greater for women than men.
   d. about the same for men and women.

8. Which of the following has been supported by research on intimate relationships among gay men and lesbians?
   a. The majority of gay couples have open relationships.
   b. Gay couples avoid becoming involved in long-term relationships.
   c. Gay couples have impoverished family relations.
   d. Gay couples want the same things out of intimate relationships that heterosexuals want.

9. Research on cohabitation indicates that
   a. most cohabitants are just not interested in marriage.
   b. most cohabitants would eventually like to marry.
   c. cohabitation is declining.
   d. cohabitation experience improves the chances that one's marriage will be successful.

10. Which of the following can an individual do to reduce the likelihood of being victimized by date rape?
    a. Be coy about sexual desires and offer token resistance to sexual advances
    b. Avoid communicating about sex altogether
    c. Beware of excessive alcohol and drug use
    d. View intrusive actions as nonthreatening

ANSWERS

1. d Pages 293–294
2. a Page 297
3. c Pages 298–299
4. b Page 301
5. d Page 305
6. a Page 306
7. d Page 309
8. d Page 312
9. b Pages 314–315
10. c Page 319

COURSEMATE

Go to **CengageBrain.com** to access Psychology CourseMate, where you will find an interactive eBook, glossaries, flashcards, quizzes, videos, and more.

PERSONAL EXPLORATIONS WORKBOOK

Go to the *Personal Explorations Workbook* in the back of your textbook for exercises that can enhance your self-understanding in relation to issues raised in this chapter.

Exercise 10.1 *Self-Assessment:* Passionate Love Scale

Exercise 10.2 *Self-Reflection:* Thinking Through Your Attitudes About Marriage and Cohabitation

Gender and Behavior

© Zhu difeng/Shutterstock.com

On January 14, 2005, the then-president of Harvard University Lawrence H. Summers spoke publicly about Harvard's policies regarding diversity. Dr. Summers focused his remarks on the issue of women's underrepresentation in tenured positions in science and engineering at top universities. He offered three broad hypotheses about this gender disparity. The one that attracted the most media attention was what he called a "different availability of aptitude at the high end." While he acknowledged that there are differences in socialization and patterns of discrimination between men and women, he cited innate gender differences in mathematical and scientific ability as having greater "importance" in explaining the gender disparity (*Harvard Crimson*, 2005).

Summers's remarks on this issue sparked a contentious debate among academics, scientists, and the public. The war of words lingered for months and eventually led to Summers' resignation as president of Harvard. This scenario demonstrates in a highly compelling way that gender research is relevant, important, and frequently controversial. Obviously, psychologists have a lot to offer in this area. In this chapter, we explore some intriguing and controversial questions: Are there genuine behavioral and cognitive differences between males and females? If so, what are their origins? Are traditional gender-role expectations healthy or unhealthy? Why are gender roles in our society changing, and what does the future hold? After addressing those questions, in the Application we explore gender and communication styles.

GENDER STEREOTYPES

LEARNING OBJECTIVES

- Explain the nature of gender stereotypes and their connection with instrumentality and expressiveness.
- Discuss four important points about gender stereotypes.

Let's begin by clarifying some terms. Surprisingly, there is little consensus about when to use the term *sex* and when to use the term *gender*. Some scholars prefer to use the term *gender* to refer to male-female differences that are learned and *sex* to designate biologically based differences between males and females. Others argue that making this sharp distinction fails to recognize that biology and culture interact (Hyde, 2004). Still others use the terms interchangeably (Vanwesenbeeck, 2009). This inconsistency has prompted some scholars to speculate that the distinction has become less meaningful over time (Muehlenhard & Peterson, 2011), while others argue that precision in language is important for scientific studies (Smith et al., 2010). For the sake of simplicity, we'll use **gender to mean the state of being male or female.** (When we use the term *sex,* we're referring to sexual behavior.) It's important to note that, as we use the term, gender says nothing about the *causes* of behavior. In other words, if we say that there are gender differences in aggressive behavior, we are simply stating that males and females differ in this area. This behavioral disparity might be caused by biological factors, by environmental factors, or

by both. **Figure 11.1** on the next page sorts out a number of gender-related terms that we will use in our discussions.

Obviously, males and females differ biologically—in their genitals and other aspects of anatomy, and in their physiological functioning. These readily apparent physical disparities between males and females lead people to expect other differences as well, especially with regard to social roles (McCreary & Chrisler, 2010). Recall from Chapter 7 that *stereotypes* are widely held beliefs that people possess certain characteristics simply because of their membership in a particular group. Thus, **gender stereotypes are widely shared beliefs about males' and females' abilities, personality traits, and social behavior.** Research indicates that beliefs about the typical attributes characteristic of men and women are widely shared (Desert & Leyens, 2006). For example, a survey of gender stereotypes in twenty-five countries revealed considerable similarity of views (Williams, Satterwhite, & Best, 1999). Because of the widespread gains in educational and occupational attainment by American women since the 1970s, you might expect to find changes in contemporary gender stereotypes for both genders. However, although gender stereotypes in this country have become more complex, they remain largely stable.

Gender stereotypes are too numerous to summarize here. Instead, you can examine **Figure 11.2**, which lists a number of characteristics people commonly link with femininity and masculinity. Note that the stereotyped attributes for males generally reflect the quality of *instrumentality,* **an orientation toward action and accomplishment,** whereas the stereotypes for females reflect the quality of *expressiveness,* **an orientation toward emotion and relationships**.

When it comes to stereotypes, there are some important points to keep in mind. First, despite the general agreement on a number of gender stereotypes, variability also occurs. The characteristics in **Figure 11.2** represent the prototypic American male or female: white, middle-class, heterosexual, and Christian. But it is obvious that not everyone fits this set of characteristics. For example, the stereotypes for African American males and females are more similar on the dimensions of competence and expressiveness than those for white American males and females (Kane, 2000).

A second point about gender stereotypes is that since the 1980s, the boundaries between male and female stereotypes have become less rigid. Earlier, male and female stereotypes were seen as separate and distinct categories (for example, men are strong and women are weak). Now it seems that people perceive gender as a continuum as opposed to a dichotomy (Beall, Eagly, & Sternberg, 2004).

A third consideration is that the traditional male stereotype is more complimentary than the conventional female stereotype. This fact is related to *androcentrism,* **or the belief that the male is the norm**. There is considerable evidence that, in the United States, masculinity is associated with higher overall status and competence (Ridgeway & Bourg, 2004). For instance, in the workplace a man might be described as "good at details," whereas a woman is viewed as "picky." Likewise, a man might be viewed as "exercising authority," whereas a woman would be described as "controlling" for the same behaviors. Ironically, this bias is evident even in psychological studies of gender. Hegarty and Buechel (2006) examined 388 articles on gender differences from journals published by the American Psychological Association and found evidence of androcentric reporting. Specifically, gender differences were reported in terms of *women* being different, as opposed to men. The implicit assumption, then, is that men are the

GENDER-RELATED CONCEPTS	
Term	**Definition**
Gender	The state of being male or female
Gender identity	An individual's perception of himself or herself as male or female
Gender stereotypes	Widely held and often inaccurate beliefs about males' and females' abilities, personality traits, and social behavior
Gender differences	Actual disparities in behavior between males and females, based on research observations
Gender roles	Culturally defined expectations about appropriate behavior for males and females
Gender-role identity	A person's identification with the traits regarded as masculine or feminine (one's sense of being masculine or feminine)
Sexual orientation	A person's preference for sexual partners of the other gender (heterosexual), the same gender (homosexual), or both genders (bisexual)

© Cengage Learning

Figure 11.1

Terminology related to gender. The topic of gender involves many closely related ideas that are easily confused. The gender-related concepts introduced in this chapter are summarized here for easy comparison.

GENDER STEREOTYPES	
Masculine	**Feminine**
Active	Artistic
Analytical	Aware of others' feelings
Athletic	Creative
Competitive	Devotes self to others
Financial provider	Emotional
Good at numbers	Gentle
Good at problem solving	Graceful
Independent	Kind
Physically strong	Soft voice
Self-confident	Takes care of children
Stands up to pressure	Tends the house
Takes a stand	Understanding

Figure 11.2

Traditional gender stereotypes. Gender stereotypes are widely known and relate to many diverse aspects of psychological functioning. This is a partial list of the characteristics that college students associate with a typical man and a typical woman. Gender stereotypes have remained remarkably stable in spite of all the recent changes relating to gender issues in modern societies.

Source: Adapted from Kite, M. E. (2001). Gender stereotypes in J. Worell (Ed.). *Encyclopedia of women and gender: Sex similarities and differences and the impact of society on gender* (Vol. 1). (pp. 561–570). San Diego, CA US: Academic Press.

Learn More Online

Resources for Women's Studies

This database at Vanderbilt University has a wealth of resources for issues related to women's and gender studies.

SIX CHIX

© Isabella Bannerman, Margaret Shulock, Rina Piccolo, Ann C. Telnaes, Kathryn LeMieux and Stephanie Piro. 2002 KING FEATURES SYNDICATE

norm from which women deviate. Look for evidence of this bias as you read about studies in this chapter.

Finally, keep in mind what you learned about stereotypes in Chapter 7: They can bias your perceptions and expectations of others as well as your interactions.

Let's shift from gender stereotypes to what males and females are actually like. Keep in mind that our discussion focuses on modern Western societies; the story may be different in other cultures.

GENDER SIMILARITIES AND DIFFERENCES

LEARNING OBJECTIVES

- Explain how meta-analyses have helped researchers who study gender.
- Articulate the gender similarities hypothesis.
- Summarize the research on gender similarities and differences in verbal, mathematical, and spatial abilities.

- Understand the research on gender similarities and differences in personality, social behavior, and psychological disorders.
- Give two explanations for why gender differences appear larger than they actually are.

Are men more aggressive than women? Do more women than men suffer from depression? Hundreds of studies have attempted to answer these and related questions about gender and behavior. Moreover, new evidence is pouring in constantly, and many researchers report conflicting findings. To add to the confusion, gender differences are not clear cut; they are complex and often subtle. It is an oversimplification, for instance, to say that women are verbal and men are spatial (Spelke, 2005).

It is an almost overwhelming task to keep up with the research in this area. Thankfully, a statistical technique called meta-analysis helps clarify this body of research (Murnen & Smolak, 2010). *Meta-analysis* **combines the statistical results of many studies of the same question, yielding an estimate of the size and consistency of a variable's effects**. This approach allows a researcher to assess the overall trends across all the previous studies of how gender is related to, say, math abilities or conformity. Meta-analysis has been a great boon to researchers, and quite a few meta-analyses on gender differences have now been conducted.

Based on the results of over forty-six meta-analyses, Janet Shibley Hyde, a noted authority in the field, proposed the *gender similarities hypothesis*. Hyde (2005, 2007a) notes that men and women are similar on most psychological variables and that most of the time when researchers report a difference, it is quite small. She further asserts that overinflated claims of gender differences have costs associated with

Janet Shibley Hyde

them for the workplace and relationships. Critics of this hypothesis argue that Hyde omitted several important variables from her review and that methodological limitations led her to underestimate true gender differences (Davies & Shackelford, 2006; Lippa, 2006). It will be interesting to see where this dispute leads in the future.

Researchers also debate as to whether gender differences are largely attributable to environmental factors as opposed to biological ones, and there is evidence on both sides (Halpern, 2000). Before we examine the possible causes of these differences, let's thread our way through the available research in three areas: cognitive abilities, personality traits and social behavior, and psychological disorders.

Cognitive Abilities

We should first point out that gender differences have *not* been found in *overall* intelligence (Priess & Hyde, 2010). Of course, this fact shouldn't be surprising, because intelligence tests are intentionally designed to minimize differences between the scores of males and females. But what about gender differences in *specific* cognitive skills? Let's start with verbal abilities.

© Rob Marmion/Shutterstock.com

Learn More Online

Women in Science, Technology, Engineering, and Mathematics ON THE AIR!

At this website, sponsored by the National Science Foundation, you can listen to stories about women working in science, technology, engineering, and mathematics (STEM) fields.

Verbal Abilities

Verbal abilities include a number of distinct skills, such as vocabulary, reading, writing, spelling, and grammar abilities. Girls and women generally have the edge in the verbal area, although the gender differences are small (Hyde, 2007b). Among the findings worth noting are that girls usually start speaking a little earlier, have larger vocabularies and better reading scores in grade school, and are more verbally fluent (on tests of writing, for instance). Boys seem to fare better on verbal analogies (Priess & Hyde, 2010). However, they are three to four times more likely to be stutterers (Skinner & Shelton, 1985) and five to ten times more likely than girls to be dyslexic (Vandenberg, 1987). It is important to remember that while gender differences in verbal abilities generally favor females, the overlap between males and females in verbal abilities is much greater than the gap between them.

Mathematical Abilities

Researchers have looked extensively at gender differences in *mathematical abilities,* including performing computations and solving word and story problems. Although it is conventional wisdom that males have greater mathematical abilities than females, a recent meta-analysis representing the data of over a million participants over the past 20 years indicates otherwise (Lindberg et al., 2010). This research led Lindberg and colleagues to

conclude that that there are no longer gender differences in general mathematical performance. Another meta-analysis including almost 500,000 students from over sixty-nine countries found that "on average, males and females differ very little in math achievement," even though males have a more positive attitude toward math (Else-Quest, Hyde, & Linn, 2010, p. 125).

Thus, the current view is that gender differences in mathematical abilities in the general population are essentially nil. However, this conclusion has a few exceptions. In mathematical *complex problem solving,* boys start to slightly outperform girls when they reach high school (Lindberg et al., 2010). Given that this pattern does not emerge until later in life, researchers do not see it as an innate cognitive difference, but as a difference in socialization. For instance, boys take more high school math and physics courses, where complex problem solving is taught. Still, because problem-solving ability is essential for success in scientific courses and careers (arenas currently underpopulated by women), this finding is a concern. Also, males outperform females at the high end of the mathematical ability distribution (Dweck, 2007). This gap, however, has been shrinking since the 1980s (Ceci, Williams, &

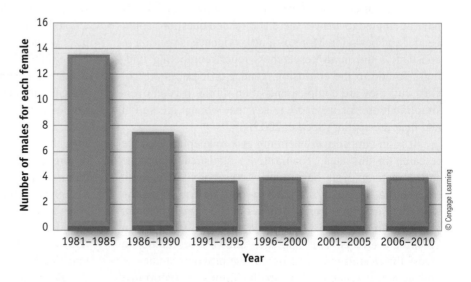

Figure 11.3

Male-to-female ratio for math SAT scores of 700 and above. Research shows that males outperform females at the high end of the mathematical ability distribution. As you can see in this graph, this gap has shrunk since the 1980s. Between 1981 and 1985 boys who scored a 700 and above outnumbered girls 13 to 1; by 2010 this ratio was only 4 to 1.

REEL RESEARCH

Stereotype Threat and Test Performance

Many college students experience stereotype threat, or feeling judged by others and reduced to stereotypes about their gender or race, and their performance can suffer because of it. For example, negative stereotypes about women's mathematical abilities could cause women in male-dominated fields to underperform, even though they are intellectually equivalent. Similarly, African American students have shown negative effects of stereotype threat in research studies like the demonstration in this Reel Research video.

Claude Steele, a psychologist at Stanford University, discusses how stereotype threat affects various groups of people—in this case, college students. Steele explains that some students underperform when preoccupied by thoughts and anxiety about stereotypes. Steele conducts a study involving two demonstrations. All the participants in each demonstration have similar skill levels. In the first demonstration, male and female students are asked to take a difficult standardized test and are told that the test showed gender differences. With another group of students, the same test is given but the researcher frames it differently, stating that some tests are biased against women but that this test is not. Male and female students then take the test separately. The results? Women dramatically underperformed when told there were gender differences and performed as well as men when told the test was not biased.

In the second demonstration, the performance of black and white students is examined. Researchers tell one group

that they are taking a standardized test, while they tell the other group that it is a problem-solving test, not a measure of ability—as with most standardized tests. Again, black students and white students take the test separately. Similar to the findings of the first demonstration, the black students performed as well as white students when told it was a test of their problem-solving skills, rather than ability. Steele demonstrates that introducing stereotype threat causes dramatic changes in the students' performance on standardized tests.

Watch the *Stereotype Threat and Test Performance* video to learn more about how stereotype threat affects performance. Delve even deeper by responding to the following discussion questions.

DISCUSSION QUESTIONS

1. In each demonstration, what factors changed the performance of all students in a positive way? What was eliminated?
2. Describe the groups researchers are studying to reduce the risk of stereotype threat, according to the video. Why are these groups important?
3. Framing allowed researchers to introduce stereotype threat during the test. How would you frame a verbal ability test to favor the abilities of women over men?

Barnett, 2009) (see **Figure 11.3**). As with verbal abilities, there is more support for gender similarities than differences in mathematics, but when small differences do emerge they appear to favor boys.

Spatial Abilities

In the cognitive area, the most compelling evidence for gender differences is in *spatial abilities,* which include perceiving and mentally manipulating shapes and figures

(Lawton, 2010). Males typically outperform females in most spatial abilities, and gender differences favoring males are consistently found in the ability to perform mental rotations of a figure in three dimensions—a skill important in occupations such as engineering, chemistry, and the building trades (see **Figure 11.4**). This gender gap in the ability to handle mental rotations is relatively large and has been found repeatedly (Halpern, 2000, 2004), and using creative methods, researchers have demonstrated this difference in infants as young as 5 months old (Moore & Johnson, 2008). However, experience and training can improve mental rotation in both girls and boys (Newcombe, 2007). In fact, playing action video games has been shown to improve mental rotation skills for both genders (Spence et al., 2009). Feng and colleagues (2007) found benefits, especially for women, in rotation skills after only 10 hours of training on an action video game.

Personality Traits and Social Behavior

Turning to personality and social behavior, let's examine those factors for which gender differences are reasonably well documented.

Self-Esteem

Females typically score lower than males on tests of global self-esteem, but the difference in scores is small (Stake & Eisele, 2010), and Hyde (2005) argues that this difference has been exaggerated in the popular press. For example, a meta-analysis of several hundred studies that included respondents from 7 to 60 years of age found only a small difference in self-esteem that favored males (Kling et al., 1999). The authors found no support for claims that girls' self-esteem drops dramatically during adolescence. A second meta-analysis also reported only a small overall gender difference favoring males (Major et al., 1999). Other research consistently reports self-esteem differences between white men and women, but findings are mixed for other ethnic groups (Twenge & Crocker, 2002).

Obviously, the findings on self-esteem are complex. To add to the complexity, a recent meta-analysis of 115 studies examined gender differences in specific self-esteem domains (Gentile et al., 2009). As noted in Chapter 6, the researchers found gender differences favoring males with regard to self-esteem domains of physical appearance, athleticism, and self-satisfaction, but they found differences in behavioral conduct and morality/ethics favoring females. No gender differences were found for domains such as academics and social acceptance. **Figure 11.5** summarizes these findings.

Aggression

Aggression **involves behavior that is intended to hurt someone, either physically or verbally** (see Chapter 4). Common stereotypes hold that males are more aggressive than females, but the picture is more complex (Frieze & Yu Li, 2010). Gender differences in aggression vary depending on the form aggression takes. Cross-cultural meta-analyses conclude that males consistently engage in more *physical aggression* than females (Archer, 2005). This difference is evident even in young children (Baillargeon et al., 2007). In the area of *verbal aggression* (insults, threats of harm), the findings are inconsistent (Geen, 1998). When it comes to *relational aggression,* such as giving someone the "silent treatment" to get one's way, talking behind another's back, or trying to get others to dislike someone, females are rated higher (Archer, 2005). *Indirect aggression* overlaps to some degree with relational aggression; it involves covert behaviors in which the target is not directly confronted—spreading rumors, for instance.

GENDER DIFFERENCES IN SPECIFIC SELF-ESTEEM DOMAINS	
Specific self-esteem domain	**Actual finding**
Physical appearance	Males higher
Athletic	Males higher
Academic	No difference
Social acceptance	No difference
Family	No difference
Behavioral conduct	Females higher
Self-satisfaction	Males higher
Moral-ethical	Females higher

Figure 11.5

Gender differences in specific self-esteem domains. Females typically score lower than males on tests of self-esteem. However, a recent meta-analysis examined gender differences in specific self-esteem domains. As you can see, gender differences in self-esteem are more complex than previously thought. (Adapted from Gentile et al. 2009)

Can the set of blocks on the left be rotated to match the set at the right?

Figure 11.4

Mental rotation test. Spatial reasoning tasks can be divided into a variety of subtypes. Studies indicate that males perform slightly better than females on most, but not all, spatial tasks. The tasks on which males are superior often involve mentally rotating objects, such as in the problem shown here, for which the answer is "no."

Source: From Kalat, J. W. (2013). *Biological psychology* (11th ed.). Belmont, CA: Wadsworth. Reproduced with permission. www.cengage.com/permissions

© iStockphoto.com/Christopher Futcher

and, based on self-reports of victims, women make up 14% of violent offenders (Carson & Sabol, 2012). Further, males are nine times more likely to commit murder than females (Cooper & Smith, 2011). **Figure 11.6** shows the stark gender differences in such crimes as assault, robbery, rape, and homicide.

Sexual Attitudes and Behavior

We cover the relation between gender and sexuality in more depth in Chapter 12, so we will address only the basics here. In the sexual domain, a meta-analysis by Petersen and Hyde (2010a, 2011) found that men are slightly more likely to engage in sexual activity and tend to have more sexual partners. Men are slightly more permissive in their attitudes toward sex in general, while women are more likely than men to feel negative emotions (such as shame or guilt) in response to sex. The researchers found larger differences for some aspects of sexuality. Specifically, males are more likely than females to engage in casual sex, use pornography, and masturbate (Peterson & Hyde, 2010b). Again, it's important to note that, in line with the gender similarities hypothesis, most gender differences regarding sexuality are relatively small.

Emotional Expression

Conventional wisdom holds that women are more "emotional" than men. Does research support this belief? If by being "emotional" we mean outwardly displaying one's emotions, the answer is yes. A number of studies have found that women express more emotion than men (Brody & Hall, 2010). Gender differences "favoring" women have been found on such emotions as sadness, disgust, fear, surprise, happiness, and anger. Similarly, women are better than men at recognizing emotions in others based on facial expressions or other nonverbal cues (Hampson, van Anders, & Mullin, 2006).

In a study of 8-, 11-, and 15-year-olds from Finland, Israel, Italy, and Poland, researchers looked at gender differences in three types of aggression: physical, verbal, and indirect (Oesterman et al., 1998). Across nations, boys were equally likely to use physical and verbal aggression and less likely to use indirect aggression. Girls most often used indirect aggression, followed by verbal aggression, then physical aggression. Even in controlled laboratory settings where male and female participants are exposed to the same aggression-evoking stimulus, women are more likely than men to aggress indirectly (Gianciola et al, 2009).

However, when you consider extreme forms of aggression, there is no getting around the fact that men commit a grossly disproportionate share of violent crimes. According to the U.S. Department of Justice, in 2011 only about 7% of all state and federal inmates were women,

Do women actually *experience* more emotion? To answer this question, Ann Kring and Albert Gordon (1998) had college students view films selected to evoke sadness, happiness, and fear. The researchers videotaped the participants' facial expressions and asked them to describe their emotional experiences. As expected, the researchers found gender differences in the facial expression of emotion. However, they failed to find any gender differences in *experienced* emotions. Thus, gender differences in emotional functioning may be limited to the outward expression of feelings and could stem from the different rules parents teach their sons and daughters about displaying emotions (DeAngelis, 2001).

Figure 11.6

Gender differences in violent crime convictions. Males are much more likely to be sentenced to prison for violent crimes than women are. These data support the findings of laboratory studies showing that males are more physically aggressive than females. (Data from Bureau of Justice Statistics, 2011)

Communication

Gender differences in communication are quite complex (McHugh & Hambaugh, 2010). Popular stereotypes suggest that females are much more talkative than males. In fact, the opposite seems to be true: Men talk more than women (Cameron, 2007). Men do tend to interrupt women more than women interrupt men, although this difference is small (Eckert & McConnell-Ginet, 2003). However, when women have more power in work or personal relationships, women interrupt more (Aries, 1998). Perhaps some gender differences in communication are better seen as a status difference. For more on gender and communication, see this chapter's Application.

Psychological Disorders

In terms of the *overall* incidence of mental disorders, only minimal gender differences have been found. When researchers assess the prevalence of *specific* disorders, however, they do find some rather consistent gender differences (Nolen-Hoeksema & Keita, 2003). Antisocial behavior, alcoholism, and other drug-related disorders are far more prevalent among men than among women. On the other hand, women are about twice as likely as men to suffer from depression and anxiety disorders (Hatzenbuehler et al., 2010; Nolen-Hoeksema, 2012). Even when comparing opposite-sex fraternal twins, females have a higher rate of mood disorders than males (Kendler, Myers, & Prescott, 2005).

In Chapter 3, we discussed posttraumatic stress disorder (PTSD). In a set of meta-analyses, Tolin and Foa (2006) found that females are more likely than males to develop PTSD, even when the traumatic events are the same. In addition, women *attempt* suicide more often than men, but men *complete* suicides (actually kill themselves) more frequently than women (Canetto, 2008; Schrijvers, Bollen, & Sabbe, 2012). Throughout the lifespan, females are more likely to engage in deliberate self-harm than males (Hawton & Harriss, 2008).

Females also show higher rates of eating disorders (see the Chapter 14 Application), which have been linked to distorted body images (Calogero & Thompson, 2010). *Body image* consists of one's attitudes, beliefs, and feelings about one's body. Weight is particularly important for women. Typically women have a greater drive for thinness and are more concerned with dieting than are men (Herman & Polivy, 2010). For many years, this concern with thinness has existed among white and Asian Americans, but has been a lesser concern among Hispanics and black Americans (Polivy & Herman, 2002). Unfortunately, some evidence suggests that the very-thin female ideal may be spreading to these two groups as well (Barnett, Keel, & Conoscenti, 2001). While ultra-thinness for women has been a longtime media message, muscular body types for men are becoming more heavily promoted

(Martins, Tiggeman, & Kirkbride, 2007). Studies show that males of all ages wish to be more muscular (Morrison, Morrison, & Hopkins, 2003; Olivardia, Pope, & Phillips, 2000). Thus, the pressure to live up to an ideal body shape is a significant adjustment challenge facing both males and females today. Failure to live up to these ideals can create body dissatisfaction and lead to eating disorders (Smolak, 2006).

Putting Gender Differences in Perspective

It pays to be cautious when interpreting gender differences. Although research has uncovered some genuine differences in behavior, remember that these are *group* differences. That is, they tell us nothing about individuals. Essentially, we are comparing the "average man" with the "average woman." **Figure 11.7** shows how scores on a trait might be distributed for men and women. Although the group averages are detectably different, you can see that there is great variability within each group (gender) and huge overlap between the two group distributions. Furthermore, as we have repeatedly noted, the differences between these groups are usually relatively small (Hyde, 2005, 2007b). *Ultimately, the similarities between women and men greatly outweigh the differences.*

A second essential point is that gender accounts for only a minute proportion of the differences between individuals. Using complicated statistical procedures, it is possible to gauge the influence of gender (or other factors) on behavior. These tests often show that factors other than gender (for example, the social context in which behavior occurs) are far more important determinants of differences between individuals (Yoder & Kahn, 2003).

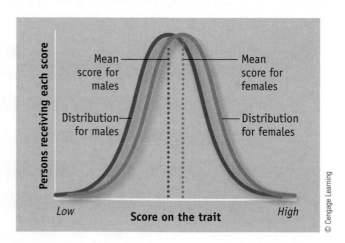

Figure 11.7
The nature of group differences. Gender differences are group differences that tell us little about individuals because of the great overlap between the groups. For a given trait, one gender may score higher on the average, but there is far more variation within each gender than between the genders.

Another point to keep in mind is that when gender differences are found, they do not mean that one gender is better than the other. As Diane Halpern (1997) humorously notes, "It is about as meaningful to ask 'Which is the smarter sex?' . . . as it is to ask 'Which has the better genitals?'" (p. 1092). The problem is not with gender differences, but with how these differences are evaluated by the larger society.

Although gender differences in abilities, personality and behavior are relatively few in number and small in size, sometimes it seems otherwise. How come? One explanation focuses on gender-based differences in social roles. Alice Eagly's (1987) *social role theory* **asserts that minor gender differences are exaggerated by the different social roles that males and females occupy**. For example, because women are assigned the role of care-giver, they learn to behave in nurturing ways. Over time, people come to associate such role-related behaviors with individuals of a given gender, not with the roles they play. In other words, people come to see nurturing as a female trait rather than as a characteristic that anyone in a nurturing role would demonstrate. This is one way that gender stereotypes develop and persist.

Courtesy of Alice Eagly

Alice Eagly

Another explanation for discrepancies between beliefs and reality is that the differences actually reside in the eye of the beholder, not the beholdee. *Social constructionism* **asserts that individuals construct their own reality based on societal expectations, conditioning, and self-socialization** (Hyde, 1996). According to social constructionists, people's specific beliefs about gender (as well as their tendency to look for gender differences) are rooted in the "gendered" messages and conditioning that permeate socialization experiences. To better understand these issues, we next explore the role of biological and environmental factors as likely sources of gender differences.

BIOLOGICAL ORIGINS OF GENDER DIFFERENCES

LEARNING OBJECTIVES

- Summarize evolutionary explanations for gender differences.
- Review the evidence linking gender differences in cognitive abilities to brain organization.
- Describe the evidence relating hormones to gender differences, both prenatally and after birth.

Are the gender differences that *do* exist biologically built in, or are they acquired through socialization? This is the age-old question of nature versus nurture. The "nature" theorists concentrate on how biological disparities between the genders contribute to differences in behavior. "Nurture" theorists, on the other hand, emphasize the role of learning and environmental influences. Although we will discuss biological and environmental influences separately, keep in mind that most contemporary researchers and theorists in this area recognize that biological and environmental factors interact. Further, biological factors can influence gender differences without specifically determining them (Berenbaum, Blakemore, & Beltz, 2011). Let's first look at three biologically based lines of inquiry on this topic: evolutionary explanations, brain organization, and hormonal influences.

Evolutionary Explanations

Evolutionary psychologists suggest that gender differences in behavior reflect different natural selection pressures operating on the genders over the course of human history (Geary, 2007). That is, natural selection favors behaviors that maximize the chances of passing on genes to the next generation (reproductive success).

To support their assertions, evolutionary psychologists look for gender differences that are consistent across cultures. Is there consistency across cultures for the better-documented gender differences? Despite some fascinating exceptions, gender differences in personality, cognitive abilities, aggression, and sexual behavior *are* found in many cultures (Buss & Schmitt, 2011; Halpern, 2000; Lippa, 2010). According to evolutionary psychologists, these consistent differences have emerged because males and females have been confronted with different adaptive demands. For example, males are thought to be more *sexually active and permissive* because they invest less than females in the process of procreation and can maximize their reproductive success by seeking many sexual partners (Webster, 2009). However, it is important to remember that even in cross-cultural work, there are more differences *within* each gender than *between* the genders, especially when it comes to cognitive abilities (Kenrick et al., 2004).

The gender gap in *aggression* is also explained in terms of reproductive fitness. Because females are more selective about mating than males are, males have to engage in more competition for sexual partners than females do. Greater aggressiveness is thought to be adaptive for males in this competition for sexual access because it should foster social dominance over other males (Kenrick & Trost, 1993). Evolutionary theorists assert that gender differences in *spatial abilities* reflect the division of labor in ancestral hunting-and-gathering societies in which males typically handled the hunting and females the gathering. Males' superiority on most spatial tasks has been attributed to the adaptive demands of hunting (Newcombe, 2010).

Evolutionary analyses of gender differences are interesting, but controversial. While it is eminently plausible that evolutionary forces could have led to some divergence between males and females in typical behavior, evolutionary hypotheses are highly speculative and difficult to test empirically. In addition, evolutionary theory can be used to claim that the status quo in society is the inevitable outcome of evolutionary forces. Thus, if males have dominant status over females, natural selection must have favored this arrangement. The crux of the problem is that evolutionary analyses can be used to explain almost anything. For instance, if the situation regarding mental rotation were reversed—if females scored higher than males—evolutionary theorists might attribute females' superiority to the adaptive demands of gathering food, weaving baskets, and making clothes—and it would be difficult to prove otherwise.

Brain Organization

Some theorists propose that male and female brains are organized differently, which might account for gender differences in some gender-specific abilities (Lippa, 2005). As you may know, the human brain is divided into two halves. **The *cerebral hemispheres* are the right and left halves of the cerebrum, which is the convoluted outer layer of the brain.** The cerebrum, the largest and most complicated part of the human brain, is responsible for most complex mental activities. Some evidence suggests that the right and left cerebral hemispheres are specialized to handle different cognitive tasks (Sperry, 1982; Springer & Deutsch, 1998). For example, it appears that the *left hemisphere* is more actively involved in *verbal and mathematical processing,* while the *right hemisphere* is specialized to handle *visual-spatial and other nonverbal processing.* Still, it is important to note that the brain functions as a unified structure, in that these two hemispheres do not act completely independently.

After these findings on hemispheric specialization surfaced, some researchers began looking for disparities between male and female brain organization as a way to explain the then-observed gender differences in verbal and spatial skills. Some thought-provoking findings have been reported. For instance, males exhibit more cerebral specialization than females (Hines, 1990). In other words, males tend to depend more heavily than females on the left hemisphere in verbal processing and on the right hemisphere in spatial processing. Gender differences have also been found in the size of the *corpus callosum,* **the band of fibers connecting the two hemispheres of the brain** (Gur & Gur, 2007). More specifically, some studies suggest that females tend to have a larger corpus callosum. This greater

size might allow for better interhemispheric transfer of information, which in turn might underlie the more bilateral organization of female brains (Lippa, 2005). Thus, some theorists have argued that these differences in brain organization are responsible for gender differences in verbal and spatial ability (Clements et al. 2006).

Although this idea is intriguing, there are some important limitations in this line of reasoning. First, studies have not consistently found that males have more specialized brain organization than females (Kaiser et al., 2007, 2009), and the finding of a larger corpus callosum in females does not always emerge (Fine, 2010). Second, because a significant amount of brain development occurs over the first 5 to 10 years after birth, during which time males and females are socialized differently, it is possible that different life experiences may accumulate to produce slight differences in brain organization (Hood et al., 1987). In other words, because the brain responds to the environment, the biological factors that supposedly cause gender differences in cognitive functioning may actually reflect the influence of environmental factors (Berenbaum et al., 2011). Third, gender accounts for only a small amount of the variance in lateralization; it's more dependent on the type of task

Studies have shown that the brain's cerebral hemispheres, shown here, are somewhat specialized in the kinds of cognitive tasks they handle and that such specialization is more pronounced in males than in females. Whether this difference bears any relation to gender differences in behavior is yet to be determined.

(Boles, 2005). Finally, it's important to remember that male and female brains are much more similar than they are different.

Consequently, even though the popular press has often touted the idea that there are "male brains" and "female brains" that are fundamentally different, the notion that cerebral specialization is linked to gender differences in mental abilities is still under debate. As brain-imaging techniques such as MRIs become more sophisticated, the research in this area will certainly advance.

Hormonal Influences

As we discussed in Chapter 3, *hormones* are chemical substances released into the bloodstream by the endocrine glands. Biological gender is determined by sex chromosomes: An XX pairing produces a female, and an XY pairing produces a male. However, both male and female embryos are essentially the same until about 8 to 12 weeks after conception. Around this time, male and female gonads (sex glands) begin to produce different hormonal secretions. The high level of *androgens* (male hormones such as testosterone) in males and the low level of androgens in females lead to the differentiation of male and female genital organs.

The influence of prenatal hormones on genitalia is clear, but their impact on behavior is harder to establish. However, researchers have found that hormones play an important role in the development of sex-typical childhood behavior, including toy preferences (Hines, 2010, 2011). Much of what researchers know about this topic comes from studying endocrine disorders—that is, those caused by interference with normal prenatal hormonal secretions (Saucier & Ehresman, 2010). Scientists have studied children born to mothers given an androgen-like drug to prevent miscarriage. Two trends have been noted in this research (Collaer & Hines, 1995). First, girls exposed prenatally to abnormally high levels of androgens exhibit more male-typical behavior than other girls do. Second, boys exposed prenatally to abnormally low levels of androgens exhibit more female-typical behavior than other boys.

These findings suggest that prenatal hormones shape gender differences in humans. But there are a number of problems with this evidence (Basow, 1992; Fausto-Sterling, 1992). First, there is much more and much stronger evidence for hormonal influence for females than for males. Second, behavior is always subject to social factors after birth. Third, it's always dangerous to draw conclusions about the general population based on small samples of people who have abnormal conditions, although recent research has replicated the link between prenatal hormones and sex-typical childhood behaviors in the general population (Auyeung et al., 2009). Fourth, most of the endocrine disorders studied have multiple effects (besides altering hormone level) that make it difficult to isolate actual causes. Finally, most of the research is necessarily correlational, and it is always risky to draw causal conclusions from correlational data.

Postnatally, the hormone testosterone plays an important role in *sexual desire* for both men and women (Petersen & Hyde, 2010a). That is, when testosterone is reduced or eliminated, both men and women show decreases in sexual drive. Additionally, high levels of testosterone in men and women correlate with higher rates of *sexual activity* (Petersen & Hyde, 2011). Testosterone has also been linked with higher levels of *aggression* (impulsive and antisocial behavior) in humans, but the picture is complicated because aggressive behavior can produce increases in testosterone (Dabbs, 2000). In fact, one study demonstrated that simply interacting with a gun increased testosterone levels in males (Klinesmith, Kasser, & McAndrew, 2006).

The overall evidence suggests that, aside from obvious physical differences, biological factors such as evolution, brain structure, and hormones play a relatively minor role in gender differences. In contrast, efforts to link gender differences to disparities in the way males and females are socialized have proved more fruitful. We consider this perspective next.

ENVIRONMENTAL ORIGINS OF GENDER DIFFERENCES

LEARNING OBJECTIVES

- Define socialization and gender roles, and describe Margaret Mead's findings on the variability of gender roles and their implications.
- Explain how reinforcement and punishment, observational learning, and self-socialization operate in gender-role socialization.
- Describe how parents, peers, schools, and the media serve as sources of gender-role socialization.

Socialization is the acquisition of the norms and roles expected of people in a particular society. This process includes all the efforts made by a society to ensure that its members learn to behave in a manner that's considered appropriate. Teaching children about gender roles is an important aspect of the socialization process. *Gender roles* are cultural expectations about what is appropriate behavior for each gender. For example, in our culture women have traditionally been expected to rear children, cook meals, clean house, and do laundry. On the other hand, men have been expected to be the family breadwinner, do yardwork, and tinker with cars.

Are gender roles in other cultures similar to those seen in our society? Generally, yes—but not necessarily. Despite a fair amount of cross-cultural consistency in gender roles, some dramatic variability occurs as well. For instance, anthropologist Margaret Mead (1950) conducted a now-classic study of three tribes in New Guinea. In one tribe, *both* genders followed our masculine role expectations (the Mundugumor); in another, *both* genders approximated our feminine role (the Arapesh). In a third tribe, the male and female roles were roughly the *reverse* of our own (the Tchambuli). Such remarkable discrepancies between cultures existing within 100 miles of one another demonstrate that gender roles are not a matter of biological destiny. Instead, like other roles, gender roles are acquired through socialization.

Keep in mind that gender roles and gender stereotypes are intertwined, each fueling the other. As we noted earlier, Eagly's social role theory suggests that gender differences often occur (and seem bigger than they actually are) because males and females are guided by different role expectations. In the next section, we'll discuss how society teaches individuals about gender roles.

Processes in Gender-Role Socialization

How do people acquire gender roles? Several key learning processes come into play, including reinforcement and punishment, observational learning, and self-socialization.

Reinforcement and Punishment

In part, gender roles are shaped by the power of rewards and punishment—the key processes in operant conditioning (see Chapter 2). Parents, teachers, peers, and others often reinforce (usually with tacit approval) "gender-appropriate" behavior. For example, a young boy who has hurt himself may be told that "big boys don't cry." If he succeeds in inhibiting his crying, he may get a pat on the back or a warm smile—both powerful reinforcers. Over time, a consistent pattern of such reinforcement will strengthen the boy's tendency to "act like a man" and suppress emotional displays.

Most parents (and peers) take gender-appropriate behavior for granted and don't go out of their way to reward it. However, others are much less tolerant of gender-inappropriate behavior, especially for males. For instance, a 10-year-old boy who enjoys playing with dollhouses will probably elicit strong disapproval. Reactions usually involve ridicule or verbal reprimands rather than physical punishment. We will learn more about parents as a source of gender socialization shortly.

Observational Learning

Younger children commonly imitate the behavior of a parent or an older sibling. This imitation, or *observational learning*, occurs when a child's behavior is influenced by observing others. These others are called *models*. Parents serve as models for children, as do siblings, teachers, relatives, and others who are important in children's lives. Models are not limited to real people; television, movie, and cartoon characters can also serve as models.

According to *social cognitive theory* (see Chapter 2), young children are more likely to imitate people who are nurturant, powerful, and similar to them (Bussey & Bandura, 1984, 1999, 2004). Children imitate both genders, but most children are prone to imitate same-gender models. Interestingly, same-gender peers may be even more influential models than parents are (Maccoby, 2002).

Self-Socialization

Children are not merely passive recipients of gender-role socialization. Rather, they play an active role in this process,

Children learn behaviors appropriate to their gender roles very early in life. According to social learning theory, girls tend to do the sorts of things their mothers do, while boys tend to follow in their fathers' footsteps.

beginning early in life (Halim & Ruble, 2010). Because society labels people, characteristics, behavior, and activities by gender, children learn that gender is an important social category. Around 2 to 3 years of age, children begin to identify themselves as male or female (Martin, Ruble, & Szkrybalo, 2002). Once children have these labels, they begin to organize the various pieces of gender-relevant information into gender schemas. *Gender schemas* **are cognitive structures that guide the processing of gender-relevant information**. Basically, gender schemas work like lenses that cause people to view and organize the world in terms of gender (Bem, 1993).

Self-socialization begins when children link the gender schema for their own gender to their self-concept. Once this connection is made, children are motivated to selectively attend to activities and information that are consistent with the schema for their own gender. For example, Terrance knows that he is a boy and also has a "boy" schema that he attaches to himself. Now his self-esteem is dependent on how well he lives up to his boy schema. In this way, children get involved in their own socialization. They are "gender detectives," working diligently to discover the rules that are supposed to govern their behavior (Halim & Ruble, 2010).

Sources of Gender-Role Socialization

Four major sources of gender-role messages are parents, peers, schools, and the media. Keep in mind that gender-role socialization varies depending on one's culture. For example, black families typically make fewer distinctions between girls and boys when compared to white families (Hill, 2002); as a result, gender roles are more flexible for black women (Littlefield, 2003). By contrast, gender roles are relatively rigidly defined in Asian and Hispanic families (Chia et al., 1994; Comas-Diaz, 1987). Also, gender roles are changing, so the generalizations that follow may say more about how *you* were socialized than about how your children will be.

Parents

Although a meta-analysis of 172 studies of parental socialization practices suggests that parents don't treat girls and boys as differently as one might expect (Lytton & Romney, 1991), there are some important disparities. For one thing, there is a strong tendency for both mothers and fathers to emphasize and encourage *play activities* that are "gender appropriate." For example, studies show that parents encourage boys and girls to play with different types of toys (Wood, Desmarais, & Gugula, 2002). Gender differences are found in toy preferences, and children as young as preschoolers have a clear definition of girl toys and boy toys (Freeman, 2007). Generally, boys have less leeway to play with "feminine" toys than girls do with "masculine" toys. Preliminary evidence suggests, however, that these

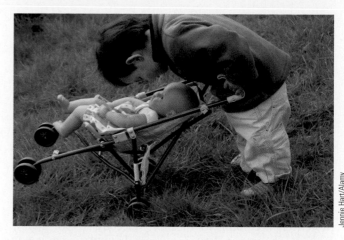

Jennie Hart/Alamy

Boys are under more pressure than girls to behave in gender-appropriate ways. Little boys who show an interest in dolls are likely to be chastised by both parents and peers.

differences in play activities are less pronounced among children of same-sex couples (Goldberg, Kashy, & Smith, 2012).

In addition to toys, the *picture books* parents buy for their children typically depict characters engaging in gender-stereotypic activities (Gooden & Gooden, 2001). An analysis of 200 bestselling and award-winning children's books found nearly twice as many male as female main characters; also, the male characters were more likely to be in the illustrations, and the female characters were more nurturing and less likely to have an occupation (Hamilton et al., 2006). Further, a content analysis of 20 years of award-winning children's books revealed that females were more often depicted using household items (spoons, sewing machines), whereas male characters were more often depicted using production items outside the home (like cars and tools), a pattern that has not changed over time (Crabb & Marciano, 2011). Even books that parents and teachers rate as "nonsexist" portray female characters with stereotypic personalities, chores, and leisure activities (Diekman & Murnen, 2004). Interestingly, this gender bias holds for representations of parents in these books as well. In a content analysis of 200 prominent children's picture books, Anderson and Hamilton (2005) found that fathers were underrepresented and, when they did appear, were often withdrawn and ineffectual.

Another way parents reinforce gender roles is through the way they communicate with their children. For instance, one study found that fathers were more attentive to their daughters' submissive emotions such as sadness, whereas they were more attentive to their sons' disharmonious emotions like anger (Chaplin, Cole, & Zahn-Waxler, 2005). Another study found that when talking to sons, parents tend to discuss more action-based activities, but they discuss physical appearance more in conversations with their daughters (Cristofaro & Tamis-LeMonda, 2008).

Through these conversational patterns, parents subtly (or not so subtly) reinforce what emotions and behaviors are appropriate for girls and boys to display.

Peers

Peers form an important network for learning about gender-appropriate and gender-inappropriate behavior (Clemans et al., 2010). Between the ages of 4 and 6, children tend to separate into same-gender groups, and these preferences appear to be child- rather than adult-driven (Fabes, Hanish, & Martin, 2003). From 6 to about age 12, boys and girls spend much more time with same-gender than other-gender peers. Moreover, according to Eleanor Maccoby (1998, 2002), over time boys' and girls' groups develop different "subcultures" (shared understandings and interests) that strongly shape youngsters' gender-role socialization.

Play among same-gender peers takes different forms for boys and girls as well (Maccoby, 1998, 2002). Boys play in larger groups and roam farther away from home, whereas girls prefer smaller groups and stay near the house. In addition, high status in boys' groups tends to be achieved by engaging in dominant behavior (telling others what to do and enforcing orders). In contrast, girls usually express their wishes as suggestions rather than demands. Also, boys engage in rough-and-tumble play much more frequently than girls do (Lippa, 2005).

Because both boys and girls are critical of peers who violate traditional gender norms, they perpetuate stereotypical behavior. Among children ages 3–11, boys are devalued more than girls for dressing like the other gender, whereas girls are evaluated more negatively than boys for playing like the other gender—for instance, loudly and roughly versus quietly and gently (Blakemore, 2003). Further, "gender atypical boys" report more often being victims of bullying, more loneliness, and greater distress than their "typical" peers (Young & Sweeting, 2004). Associations between negative adjustment and gender atypical behavior, however, appear to be reduced with positive parenting styles (Alanko et al., 2008).

Schools

The school environment figures importantly in socializing gender roles (Meece & Scantlebury, 2006). Children's grade-school *textbooks* have often ignored or stereotyped girls and women (AAUW Educational Foundation, 1992). Although the depiction of stereotypical gender roles has declined considerably since the 1970s, researchers still find significant differences in how males and females are portrayed, even in supposedly nonsexist books (Diekman & Murnen, 2004). Gender bias has even been reported in popular medical textbooks, where relevant gender-specific information is scarce (Dijkstra, Verdonk, & Largro-Janssen, 2008). These discrepancies can have subtle effects. For instance, one study found that female students had higher scores on a science test after viewing counter-stereotypic images (female scientists) than after viewing stereotypic images (male scientists) (Good, Woodzicka, & Wingfield, 2010). The reverse was true for male students.

Gender bias in schools also shows up in *teachers' treatment of boys and girls* (Basow, 2010). Preschool and grade-school teachers often reward gender-appropriate behavior in their pupils. Teachers also tend to pay greater attention to boys—helping them, praising them, and scolding them more than girls (Beaman, Wheldall, & Kemp, 2006). By contrast, girls tend to be less visible in the classroom and to receive less encouragement for academic achievement from teachers. Further, even teachers' own stereotypes about ability (boys' being good at math, for example) can bias their treatment of students (Riegle-Crumb & Humphries, 2012). Overall, these teacher-student interactions reinforce the gender stereotype of male competence and dominance (Meece & Scantlebury, 2006). It is important to consider that even with this bias, there is still concern in education today about the "underachieving male" (Beaman et al., 2006).

Gender bias also shows up in *academic and career counseling*. Despite the fact that females obtain higher grades than males (on the average) in all subjects from elementary school through college, many counselors continue to encourage male students to pursue high-status careers in medicine or engineering while guiding female students toward less-prestigious careers (Halpern, 2004, 2006). Stereotypic beliefs that lead to differential treatment by counselors and teachers can facilitate barriers to women's career choices, especially in the areas of science and math.

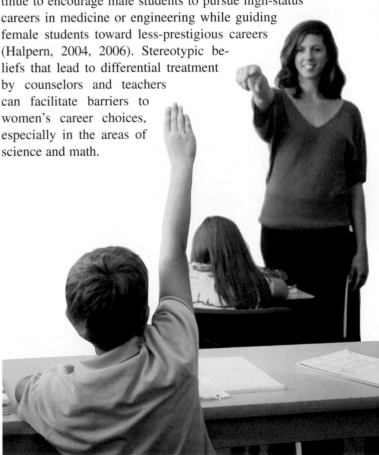

© Blend Images/Shutterstock.com

The Media

Television is yet another source of gender-role socialization. American youngsters spend a lot of time watching TV. According to a Nielsen Media Research (2012) report, the average American spends 4 hours, 38 minutes a day watching live TV (the time is even greater if you include recorded shows). A systematic review of the literature indicates that contemporary youth view an average of 1.8–2.8 hours of TV a day, with 28% watching more than 4 hours per day (Marshall, Gorely, & Biddle, 2006). Approximately 35% of children are raised in homes where the TV is on "always" or "most of the time" (Vandewater et al., 2005). In one study nearly two-thirds of adolescents had a television in their bedroom, and those who did were less likely to engage in healthy behaviors than those without (Barr-Anderson et al., 2008).

In traditional children's adventure *cartoons* (as opposed to educational cartoons), male characters appear more often and engage in more physical aggression, whereas female characters are much more likely to show fear, act romantic, be polite, and act supportive (Leaper et al., 2002). An analysis of male and female characters on *prime-time television programs* showed that the number and variety of roles of female TV characters have increased but that these shifts lag behind the actual changes in women's lives (Glascock, 2001). Women are still portrayed in stereotypic and often sexualized ways (Collins, 2011). Compared to males, females appear less often, are less likely to be employed in prestigious positions, are more likely to be younger, and are more likely to appear in secondary and comedy roles. As compared to female characters, males are still more likely to demonstrate competence-related behaviors such as reaching

a goal, showing ingenuity, and answering questions (Aubrey & Harrison, 2004).

Television commercials are even more gender-stereotyped than TV programs (Lippa, 2005). When analyzing over 450 after-school commercials from the popular children's network Nickelodeon, researchers found that gender-role stereotypes were pervasive (Kahlenberg & Hein, 2010). Commercials were gender oriented, and even gender-neutral toys were often marketed toward one gender (see **Figure 11.8**). Further, boys tended to be depicted outdoors more than girls, and they were shown engaged in a wider variety of activities. In another content analysis of 1,337 prime time commercials from the three major networks, Ganahl and colleagues (2003) found that women were underrepresented in commercials (except for beauty products) and that they often played support roles for men. In another content analysis comparing the major U.S. networks to an African American niche station (Black Entertainment Television—BET), researchers found that the majority of the characters in prime-time commercials are male and white, even on BET (Messineo, 2008).

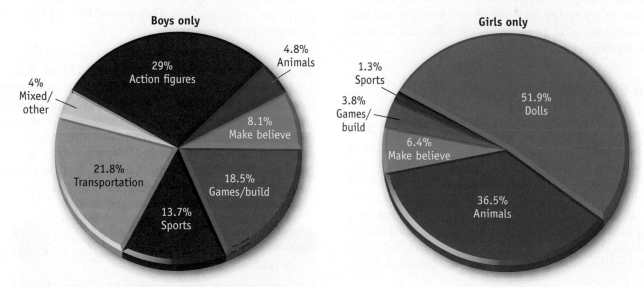

Figure 11.8

Toys presented in commercials with boys or girls in them. A content analysis of commercials airing on Nickelodeon demonstrated that commercials with only boys promoted very different toys than those with only girls. These differences highlight the role of gender-role stereotypes in the media. (Adapted from Kahlenberg & Hein, 2010)

TV is not the only medium that perpetuates gender stereotypes; gender-role socialization is a multimedia event. Most *video games* push a hypermasculine stereotype featuring search-and-destroy missions, fighter pilot battles, and male sports (Lippa, 2005). Of the few video games directed at girls, the great majority are highly stereotypic (shopping and Barbie games). Also, *music videos* frequently portray women as sex objects, a pattern that has increased over time (Hall, West, & Hill, 2012). As demonstrated in a content analysis of *educational software* for young children, most software programs had more male than female characters, portrayed males in more stereotypical ways, and focused more on gender-stereotypic appearance for females (Sheldon, 2004). Even daily newspaper *comics* follow these gender-stereotypic patterns (Glascock & Preston-Schreck, 2004).

Do the media actually influence children's views about gender? Evidence suggests that the answer is yes. A meta-analysis reported a link between children's exposure to gender stereotyping in the media and the acquisition of gender-stereotyped beliefs (Oppliger, 2007). Even among adults, viewing sexualized portrayals of women appears to influence viewers' gender-role and sexual attitudes (Kistler & Lee, 2010). Admittedly, gender-role socialization is complex, and other factors such as parental values come into play as well. Nonetheless, Greenwood and Lippman (2010) argue that our perceptions of gender differences might be an "artifact of the gender-stereotyped landscape of the mass media" (p. 662).

GENDER-ROLE EXPECTATIONS

LEARNING OBJECTIVES

- List the key elements of the traditional male role, and identify common problems associated with the traditional male role.
- List the major expectations of the female role, and identify common problems associated with the female role.
- Describe two ways in which women are victimized by sexism.

Traditional gender roles are based on several unspoken assumptions: that all members of the same gender have basically the same traits, that the traits of one gender are very different from the traits of the other gender, and that masculine traits are more highly valued. In recent decades, many social critics and theorists in psychology and other fields have scrutinized gender roles, identifying the essential features and the ramifications of traditional roles. In this section, we review the research and theory in this area and note changes in gender roles over the past 30 to 40 years. We begin with the male role.

Role Expectations for Males

A number of psychologists have sought to pinpoint the essence of the traditional male role (Levant, 1996, 2003, 2011; Pleck, 1995). Many consider *anti-femininity* to be the central theme that runs through the male gender role. That is, "real men" shouldn't act in any way that might be perceived as feminine. For example, men should not publicly display vulnerable emotions, should avoid feminine occupations, and should not show obvious interest in relationships—especially homosexual ones. Five key attributes constitute the traditional male role (Brannon, 1976; Jansz, 2000):

   1. *Achievement.* To prove their masculinity, men need to beat out other men at work and at sports. Having a high-status job, driving an expensive car, and making lots of money are aspects of this element.

   2. *Aggression.* Men should be tough and fight for what they believe is right. They should aggressively defend themselves and those they love against threats.

   3. *Autonomy.* Men should be self-reliant and not admit to being dependent on others.

   4. *Sexuality.* Real men are heterosexual and are highly motivated to pursue sexual activities and conquests.

   5. *Stoicism.* Men should not share their pain or express their "soft" feelings. They should be cool and calm under pressure.

There is evidence that manhood, as opposed to womanhood, is more precarious (Bosson et al., 2009). That is, it is more susceptible to threat and requires social proof and validation. Unfortunately, harmful demonstrations of masculinity such as displays of physical aggression are typical ways of defending one's manhood when this status is threatened (Bosson et al., 2009). This behavior is often at odds with modern gender-role expectations. According to Joseph Pleck (1995), who has written extensively on this

Learn More Online

American Men's Studies Association

This site collects academic resources to advance "the critical study of men and masculinities." It includes links to many other sites and organizations interested in the male experience.

issue, in the *traditional male role,* masculinity is validated by individual physical strength, aggressiveness, and emotional inexpressiveness. In the *modern male role,* however, masculinity is validated by economic achievement, organizational power, emotional control (even over anger), and emotional sensitivity and self-expression, but only with women.

Thus, in modern societies, the traditional male role coexists with some new expectations. Some theorists use the plural "masculinities" to describe these variations in the male gender role (Schrock & Schwalbe, 2009; Smiler, 2004). This flux in expectations means that males are experiencing role inconsistencies and pressures to behave in ways that conflict with traditional masculinity: to communicate personal feelings, to nurture children and share in housework, to integrate sexuality with love, and to curb aggression. Some psychologists believe that these pressures have shaken traditional masculine norms sufficiently that many men are experiencing a masculinity crisis and diminished pride in being a man (Levant, 1996, 2003). Brooks (2010) argues that distress over ever-changing gender roles fuels three major problems—violence, substance abuse, and sexual misconduct—as men channel their distress into these destructive behaviors. The good news is that boys and men are beginning to get more attention from psychological theorists, researchers, and clinicians.

Problems with the Male Role

It is often assumed that only females suffer from the constricting binds of traditional gender roles. Not so. As we just discussed, the costs of the male role are an increasing cause for concern. As we examine the relevant research, keep in mind that male gender roles "are not to be regarded as 'given,' neither psychological nor biologically, but rather as socially constructed" (Levant & Richmond, 2007, p. 141). Therefore, many researchers are calling for a closer examination of the influence of culture on gender-role stress.

Pressure to Succeed

Most men are socialized to be highly competitive and are taught that a man's masculinity is measured by the size of his paycheck and job status. The majority of men who have internalized the success ethic are unable to fully realize their dreams. This is a particular problem for African American and Hispanic men, who experience more barriers to financial success than European American men do. How does this "failure" affect men? Although many are able to adjust to it, many are not. The men in this latter group are likely to suffer from shame and low self-esteem (Kilmartin, 2000). Men's emphasis on success also makes it more likely that they will spend long hours on the job. This pattern in turn decreases the amount of time families can spend together and increases the amount of time partners spend on housework or child care.

© Prodakszyn/Shutterstock.com

Gender differences in pressure to succeed might be more perceived than real. When asked about *perceptions,* college students rated the typical man as worrying about achievement more that the typical woman. However, when asked about their *own* worry, females reported more worry about achievement that male students did (Wood et al., 2005). Perhaps this finding reflects men's not wanting to express that they are worrying about anything.

The Emotional Realm

Most young boys are trained to believe that men should be strong, tough, cool, and detached (Jansz, 2000). Thus, they learn early to hide vulnerable emotions such as love, joy, and sadness because they believe that such feelings are feminine and imply weakness. As a result, over time, some men lose touch with their own emotional lives. With the exception of anger, men with traditional views of masculinity are more likely to suppress outward emotion, supposedly because having feelings may lead to a loss of composure (Jakupcak et al., 2003). Keep in mind, however, that some researchers challenge this view. As with many gender gaps, differences in emotionality tend to be small, inconsistent, and dependent on the situation.

Males' difficulty with "tender" emotions has serious consequences. First, suppressed emotions can contribute to stress-related disorders. And worse, men are less likely than women to seek social support or help from health professionals (Lane & Addis, 2005). Second, men's emotional inexpressiveness can cause problems in their relationships with partners and children. For example, compared to husbands who endorse traditional masculine roles, those who endorse egalitarian gender roles report greater marital happiness, as do their wives (Frieze & Ciccocioppo, 2009). Further, children whose fathers are warm, loving, and accepting toward them have higher self-esteem and lower rates of aggression and behavior problems (Rohner & Veneziano, 2001).

Sexual Problems

Men often experience sexual problems that derive partly from their gender-role socialization, which gives them a "macho" sexual image to live up to. There are few things that men fear more than a sexual encounter in which they are unable to achieve an erection. Unfortunately, these very fears often *cause* the dysfunction that men dread (see Chapter 12). The upshot is that men's obsession with sexual performance can produce anxiety that may interfere with their sexual responsiveness.

Another problem is that many men learn to confuse feelings of intimacy and sex. In other words, if a man experiences strong feelings of connectedness, he is likely to interpret them as sexual feelings. This confusion has a number of consequences (Kilmartin, 2000). For one thing, sex may be the only way some men can allow themselves to feel intimately connected to another. Thus, men's keen interest in sex may be driven, in part, by strong needs for emotional intimacy that don't get satisfied in other ways. The confusion of intimacy and sex may underlie the tendency for men (compared to women) to perceive eye contact, a compliment, an innocent smile, a friendly remark, or a brush against the arm as a sexual invitation (Kowalski, 1993). Finally, the sexualization of intimate feelings causes inappropriate anxiety when men feel affection for another

man, thus promoting *homophobia* or sexual prejudice, *the intense intolerance of homosexuality*. Indeed, endorsement of traditional gender roles and hypermasculinity are related to negative attitudes toward homosexuality (Parrott et al., 2008).

Role Expectations for Females

The role expectations for American women have undergone dramatic changes, especially with regard to work. Prior to the 1970s, a woman was expected to be a housewife and a stay-at-home mother. Today, there are three major expectations for women:

1. *The marriage mandate.* Remaining single is a trend that has been on the increase for several decades (DePaulo, 2011); however, there is still a stigma attached to singlehood in a society where marriage is the norm (Sharp & Ganong, 2011). Most women are socialized to feel incomplete until they find a mate. Women attain adult status when they get married. In the context of marriage, women are expected to be responsible for cooking, cleaning, and other housework.

2. *The motherhood mandate.* A major imperative of the female role is to have children. This expectation has been termed the "motherhood mandate" (Rice & Else-Quest, 2006). The prevailing ideology of today's motherhood mandate is that women should desire to have children, mothering should be wholly child-centered, and mothers should be self-sacrificing rather than persons who have their own needs and interests (Arendell, 2000; Vandello et al., 2008).

3. *Work outside the home.* Most of today's young women, especially those who are college educated, expect to work outside the home, and they also want a satisfying family life. As you can see in **Figure 11.9**, the percentage of women in the labor force has been steadily rising over the last 30 years. Yet even when they work outside the

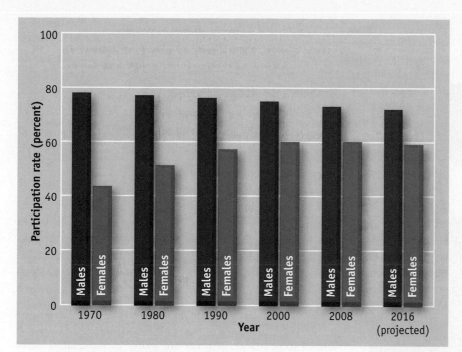

Figure 11.9

Increases in women's workforce participation. The percentage of women who work outside the home has increased steadily over the past century, especially since 1970, although it appears to be stabilizing at around 60%. (Data from the *Statistical Abstract of the United States*, 2010)

home, women still perform the bulk of the household chores (Sayer, 2005).

Problems with the Female Role

Writers in the feminist movement generated some compelling analyses of the problems associated with the pre-1970s traditional role of wife and mother (Friedan, 1964; Millett, 1970). Many criticized the assumption that women, unlike men, did not need an independent identity; it should be sufficient to be Jim Smith's wife and Jason and Robin's mother. Since that time, girls and women have increasingly been encouraged to develop and use their talents, and work opportunities for women have greatly expanded. Still, there are problems with the female role.

Diminished Career Aspirations

Despite recent efforts to increase women's opportunities for achievement, young women are more likely to underestimate their achievement than boys (who overestimate theirs), especially when estimating performance on "masculine" tasks such as science and math (Eccles, 2001, 2007; Watt et al., 2012). This is a problem because science

and math are the foundations for many high-paying, high-status careers, and the lack of a math background (as opposed to ability) often contributes to the inferior performance of some women (Dweck, 2007).

The discrepancy between women's abilities and their level of achievement has been termed the *ability-achievement gap* (Hyde, 1996). The roots of this gap seem to lie in the conflict between achievement and femininity that is built into the traditional female role. The marriage and motherhood mandates fuel women's focus on *heterosexual success*—learning how to attract and interest males as prospective mates. The resulting emphasis on dating and marriage can lead some women away from a challenging career—they worry that they will be seen as unfeminine if they boldly strive for success. Of course, this is not a concern for all women. And, because younger men are more supportive of their wives' working than older men are, this conflict should ease for younger women.

Juggling Multiple Roles

Another problem with the female role is that societal institutions have not kept pace with the reality of women's lives, especially if women choose motherhood. In 2010, approximately 21 million mothers were employed (U.S. Bureau of the Census, 2011b). Yet some workplaces (and many husbands and fathers) still operate as if all women were stay-at-home moms and as if there were no single-parent families. This gap between policies based on outdated assumptions and reality means that women who "want it all" experience burdens and conflicts that most men do not. That's because most men typically have *major*

Learn More Online

Feminist Majority Foundation

This site brings together a massive set of resources dealing with issues from a feminist perspective.

day-to-day responsibilities in only *one* role: worker. But most women have major day-to-day responsibilities in *three* roles: spouse, parent, and worker.

One way today's college-educated women deal with these conflicts is to postpone marriage and motherhood (and to have small families) in order to pursue more education or to launch their careers (Hoffnung, 2004). Additionally, they are more likely than men to expect childrearing to disrupt their careers (Singer, Cassin, & Dobson, 2005). Once women in high-powered careers are established, some are temporarily "stepping out" of the workforce to focus on childbearing and rearing their young children (Wallis, 2004). Given the three-role reality of their lives, they trade off the worker role and income for a slower pace and less stress to rear young children. Their strategy: "You can have it all, just not all at the same time" (Wallis, 2004, p. 53).

Of course multiple roles, in themselves, are not inherently problematic. In fact, there is some evidence that multiple roles can be beneficial for mental health, as you'll see in Chapter 13. Rather, the problem stems from the tensions among these roles and the unequal sharing of role responsibilities. Greater participation in household tasks and child care by husbands or others, as well as family-friendly workplaces and subsidized quality child-care programs, help alleviate women's stress in this area. However, this issue is not clear cut. Goldberg and Perry-Jenkins (2004) note that women with traditional gender roles and whose husbands did *more* child care after the birth of their first child experienced substantial distress. Of course, this might be due to the fact that these women performed *less*

child care than they expected and experienced distress because they were not living up to their own gender-role expectations.

Ambivalence About Sexuality

Like men, women may have sexual problems that stem, in part, from their gender-role socialization. For many women, the problem is difficulty in enjoying sex. Why? Research shows that adherence to traditional gender roles is associated with a decrease in women's sexual satisfaction (Sanchez, Fetterrolf, & Rudman, 2012). For instance, many girls are still taught to suppress or deny their sexual feelings (Petersen & Hyde, 2010). Further, they are told that a woman's role in sex is a passive one. In addition, girls are encouraged to focus on romance rather than on gaining sexual experience. As a result, many women feel uncomfortable (guilty, ashamed) with their sexual urges. Indeed, girls associate shame and guilt with sex more than boys do (Cuffee, Hallfors, & Waller, 2007). Thus, when it comes to sexuality, women are likely to have ambivalent feelings instead of the largely positive feelings that men have (Hyde, 2004). Unfortunately, this ambivalence is often viewed as sexual "dysfunction" for women, as opposed to an attitude resulting from narrow gender roles and beliefs (Drew, 2003).

Sexism: A Special Problem for Females

Intimately intertwined with the topic of gender roles is the issue of sexism. *Sexism* **is discrimination against people on the basis of their gender**. Sexism usually refers to discrimination by men against women. However, sometimes *women* discriminate against other women and sometimes *men* are the victims of gender-based discrimination. Sexism is not limited to American culture; it is a cross-cultural phenomenon (Brandt, 2011). In this section, we'll discuss two specific problems: economic discrimination and aggression toward women.

Economic Discrimination

Women are victimized by two forms of economic discrimination: differential access to jobs and differential treatment once on the job. Concerning *job access,* the problem is that women still lack the same employment opportunities as men. For example, in 2011 women were more than twice as likely as men to have occupations with wages below the poverty level (Institute for Women's Policy Research, 2012). Ethnic minority women are even less likely than white women to work in high-status, male-dominated occupations. Across all economic sectors, men are more likely than women to hold positions with decision-making authority (Eagly & Sczesny, 2009). In contrast, women are overrepresented in "pink-collar ghetto" occupations, such as secretary and preschool and kindergarten teacher. Additionally, motherhood can be a liability on the job market. One study found that, there is a bias against mothers (but not fathers) applying for a job, in terms of anticipated competence (Heilman & Okimoto, 2007).

The second aspect of economic discrimination is *differential treatment* on the job. For example, women typically earn lower salaries than men in the same jobs (see **Figure 11.10**). And occupations that are male dominated typically pay more than those that are female dominated (Pratto & Walker, 2004). Further, when women demonstrate leadership qualities such as confidence, ambitiousness, and assertiveness, they are evaluated less favorably than men, perhaps because this behavior contradicts the female gender stereotype (Lyness & Heilman, 2006). Thus, they are often penalized for their success. There appears to be a *glass ceiling* that prevents most women and ethnic minorities from being advanced to top-level professional positions (Reid, Miller, & Kerr, 2004). For example, in 2012 there were only eighteen female CEOs of Fortune 500 companies—still an all-time record high (Huffington Post, 2012). One of the reasons for the glass ceiling is the perception by bosses that female subordinates have greater family-work conflict than their male counterparts (Hoobler, Lenmon, & Wayne, 2011). Ironically, men employed in traditionally female fields are promoted more quickly than their female counterparts, a phenomenon dubbed the *glass escalator* (Hultin, 2003).

Aggression Toward Females

Forms of aggression toward girls and women include rape, intimate violence, sexual harassment, sexual abuse, incest, and violent pornography. We've discussed a number of these problems elsewhere (in particular, consult the Application for Chapter 10), so we'll focus here on sexual harassment. **Sexual harassment is unwelcome conduct on the basis of gender**. It can include sexual advances, requests for sexual favors, and other verbal or physical harassment of a sexual nature. Sexual harassment has become recognized as a widespread problem that occurs not only on the job but also at home (obscene telephone calls), while walking outside (catcalls and whistles), and in medical and psychotherapy settings. It also takes place in schools and colleges. Sexual harassment is more about dominance and power than desire. Women in male-dominated organizations are more likely to be harassed than those in female-dominated ones, and women who break traditional gender roles (such as being assertive and showing leadership abilities) in male-dominated organizations are the most likely to be targets (Berdahl, 2007).

Betz (2006) distinguishes between two categories of sexual harassment in the workplace. In *quid pro quo harassment* employees are expected to give in to sexual demands in exchange for employment, raises, promotions, and so forth. In *hostile environment harassment* employees are exposed to sexist or sexually oriented comments, cartoons, posters, and so forth. Research shows that minority women experience a form of "double jeopardy" when it comes to workplace harassment. When Berdahl and Moore (2006) surveyed employees from five ethnically diverse companies, they found that women experience more harassment than men, that minorities experience more harassment than whites, and that minority women experience more harassment than any other group. The experience of sexual harassment is related to poorer job outcomes (Settles et al., 2006), as well as increased psychological distress (Nielsen & Einarsen, 2012). Given that harassment continues to be a major problem in the workplace, future researchers will no doubt continue to explore this issue.

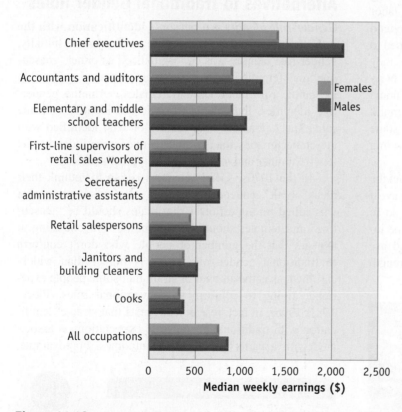

Figure 11.10

The gender gap in weekly wages. Women continue to earn less than men in almost all occupational categories, as these 2011 data for selected occupations make clear. Many factors can contribute to this gender gap in earned income, but economic discrimination is probably a major consideration. (Data from the Institute for Women's Policy Research, 2012)

GENDER IN THE PAST AND IN THE FUTURE

LEARNING OBJECTIVES

- Explain the basis for traditional gender roles and why they are changing.
- Define gender-role identity, and discuss two alternatives to traditional gender roles.

In Western society, gender roles are in a state of transition. As we have noted, sweeping changes have already occurred in the female role. It's hard to imagine today, but less than 100 years ago, women were not allowed to vote or to manage their own finances. It wasn't that long ago when it was virtually unheard of for a woman to initiate a date, manage a corporation, or run for public office. In this section, we discuss why gender roles are changing and what the future might bring.

Why Are Gender Roles Changing?

A number of theories attempt to explain why gender roles are in transition. Basically, these theories look at the past to explain the present and the future. A key consideration is that gender roles have always constituted a division of labor. In earlier societies, such as hunting-and-gathering and herding societies, the gender-based division of labor was a natural outgrowth of some simple realities. Men tend to be stronger than women, so they were better equipped to handle such jobs as hunting and farming; therefore, they got those assignments. Women were responsible for nursing young children and so were assigned gathering, home maintenance, and childrearing. Although people might have worked out other ways of doing things (and some cultures did), there were some basic reasons for dividing labor according to gender in premodern societies.

Thus, traditional gender roles are a carryover from the past. Once traditions are established, they have a way of perpetuating themselves. Over the last century or so in Western society, these divisions of labor have become increasingly antiquated. For example, the widespread use of machines to do work has rendered physical strength relatively unimportant. Therein lies the prime reason for changes in gender roles. *Traditional gender roles no longer make economic sense.*

The future is likely to bring even more dramatic shifts in gender roles. We can see the beginnings of these changes now. For example, although women still bear children, nursing responsibilities are now optional. Moreover, as women become more economically independent, they have less need to get married solely for economic reasons. The possibility of developing a fetus outside the uterus may seem farfetched now, but some experts predict that it is only a matter of time. If so, "motherhood" would not be the domain of women only. In light of these and other changes in modern society, it is safe to say that gender roles are likely to remain in flux for some time to come.

Alternatives to Traditional Gender Roles

Gender-role identity **is a person's identification with the qualities regarded as masculine or feminine.** Initially, gender-role identity was conceptualized as either "masculine" or "feminine." All males were expected to develop masculine role identities and females, feminine gender-role identities. Individuals who did not identify with the role expectations for their gender or who identified with the characteristics for the other gender were judged to be few in number and to have psychological problems.

In the 1970s, social scientists began to rethink their ideas about gender-role identity. One assumption that was called into question is that males should be "masculine" and females should be "feminine." For one thing, it appears that the number of people who don't conform to traditional gender-role norms is higher than widely assumed, as is the amount of strain that some people experience trying to conform to conventional roles (Pleck, 1981, 1995). In fact, research suggests that strong identification with traditional gender-role expectations is associated with a variety of negative outcomes. For example,

The Photo Works/Alamy

Learn More Online

Voice of the Shuttle: Gender Studies

The VOS maintains one of the broadest databases of web resources across many topics. The multiple links cited here cover the spectrum of gender-related issues from women's and men's studies to gay and lesbian identity resources.

high femininity in females is correlated with low self-esteem (Whitley, 1983) and increased psychological distress (Helgeson, 1994). High masculinity in males has been linked to increased Type A behavior (see Chapter 5), chronic self-destructiveness (Van Volkom, 2008), increased bullying in adolescence (Steinfeldt et al., 2012), and greater sexual prejudice and homophobia (Barron et al., 2008). Males high in masculinity have a greater likelihood of committing physical and sexual aggression in intimate relationships (Mosher, 1991), including same-sex relationships (Oringher & Samuelson, 2011). Furthermore, relationship satisfaction tends to be lower in heterosexual couples with traditional gender-role identities (Burn & Ward, 2005). Thus, contrary to earlier thinking, the evidence suggests that "masculine" males and "feminine" females may be less well adjusted, on the average, than those who are less traditional.

As people have become aware of the possible costs of conventional gender roles, there has been much debate about moving beyond them. A big question has been: What should we move toward? To date, two ideas have received the most attention: (1) androgyny and (2) gender-role transcendence. Let's examine these options.

Androgyny

Like masculinity and femininity, androgyny is a type of gender-role identity. *Androgyny* **refers to the coexistence of both masculine and feminine personality traits in a single person**. In other words, an androgynous person is one who scores above average on measures of *both* masculinity and femininity.

To help you fully appreciate the nature of androgyny, we need to briefly review other kinds of gender identity (see **Figure 11.11**). Males who score high on masculinity and low on femininity, and females who score high on femininity and low on masculinity, are said to be *gender-typed*. Males who score high on femininity but low on masculinity, and females who score high on masculinity but low on femininity, are said to be *cross-gender-typed*. Finally, males and females who score low on both masculinity and femininity are characterized as *gender-role undifferentiated*.

Keep in mind that we are referring to individuals' descriptions of themselves in terms of personality traits traditionally associated with each gender (dominance, nurturance, and so on). People sometimes confuse gender-role identity with sexual orientation, but they are not the same. A person can be homosexual, heterosexual, or bisexual (sexual orientation) and be androgynous, gender-typed, cross-gender-typed, or gender-role undifferentiated (gender-role identity).

In groundbreaking research four decades ago, Sandra Bem (1975) challenged the then-prevailing view that males who scored high in masculinity and females who scored

Sandra Bem

high in femininity are better adjusted than "masculine" women and "feminine" men. She argued that traditionally masculine men and feminine women feel compelled to adhere to rigid and narrow gender roles that unnecessarily restrict their behavior. In contrast, androgynous individuals ought to be able to function more flexibly. She also advanced the idea that androgynous people are psychologically healthier than those who are gender-typed.

How have Bem's ideas played out over time? First, androgynous people do seem more flexible than others. That is, they can be nurturing (feminine) or independent (masculine), depending on the situation (Bem, 1975). In contrast, gender-typed males tend to have difficulty behaving nurturantly, while gender-typed females often have trouble with independence. Also, individuals whose partners are either androgynous or feminine (but not masculine or undifferentiated) report higher relationship satisfaction and fewer depressive symptoms (Bradbury, Campbell, & Fincham, 1995). This finding holds for both cohabiting heterosexuals and lesbian and gay couples (Kurdek & Schmitt, 1986b). Thus, in these areas androgyny seems to be advantageous.

Bem's second assertion—that androgynous people are psychologically healthier than gender-typed individuals—requires a more complicated analysis. Decades of studies have been conducted to try to answer this question. Some early studies *did* find a positive correlation between androgyny and mental health. Ultimately, however, the weight of the evidence did not support Bem's hypothesis that androgyny is especially healthy.

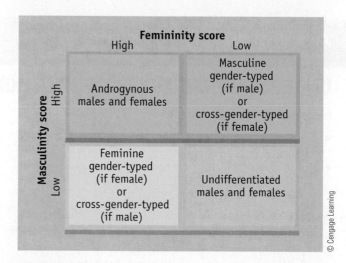

Figure 11.11

Possible gender-role identities. This diagram summarizes the relations between participants' scores on measures of masculinity and femininity and four possible gender identities.

One resolution to these contradictory findings might lie in the *type* of masculine and feminine traits an androgynous person adopts. Obviously, there are both positive and negative masculine and feminine traits. Therefore someone who adopts predominantly positive traits for both would be desirably androgynous, whereas someone who adopts predominantly negative traits for both would be undesirably androgynous. In support of differentiating androgyny into categories, Woodhill and Samuels (2003) found that positively androgynous individuals show higher levels of psychological health and well-being than those who were negatively androgynous. However, researchers speculate that, due to changing gender roles, the traits Bem used to categorize gender identities are now outdated. Case in point—in a sample of college students, Auster and Ohm (2000) found that although eighteen of the twenty feminine traits still qualified as feminine, only eight of the twenty masculine traits were still perceived as strictly masculine. These problems with the concept of androgyny and its measurement have led Bem and other psychologists to take a different view of gender roles, as you'll see next.

Gender-Role Transcendence

As psychologists thought more about androgyny, they realized that the concept had some additional problems. For one thing, the idea that people should have both masculine and feminine traits reinforces the assumption that gender is an integral part of human behavior (Bem, 1983). As such, the androgyny perspective sets up self-fulfilling prophecies. That is, if people use gender-based labels ("masculine" and "feminine") to describe certain human characteristics and behavior, they are likely to associate these traits with one gender or the other. Another criticism of androg-

yny is that it implies that the solution to gender bias is to change the individual rather than to address the gender inequities in society and its institutions (Matlin, 2004).

Many gender theorists maintain that masculinity and femininity are really only arbitrary labels that we have learned to impose on certain traits through societal conditioning. This assertion is the foundation for the *gender-role transcendence* perspective (Bem, 1983, 1993; Spence, 1983). **The *gender-role transcendence perspective* proposes that to be fully human, people need to move beyond gender roles as a way of organizing their perceptions of themselves and others**. This goal requires that instead of dividing human characteristics into masculine and feminine categories (and then combining them, as the androgyny perspective suggests), we should dispense with the artificially constructed gender categories and labels altogether. How would this work? Instead of the labels "masculine" and "feminine," we would use gender-neutral terms such as "instrumental" and "expressive," respectively, to describe personality traits and behaviors. This "decoupling" of traits and gender could reduce the self-fulfilling prophecy problem.

Given that individuals today have had years of exposure to gender messages, moving toward gender-role transcendence would likely be a gradual process. According to James O'Neil and Jean Egan (1992), such a gender-role journey moves from initial acceptance of traditional gender roles (Stage 1) to a growing ambivalence about gender roles (Stage 2). From there, it evolves to anger about sexism (Stage 3) and then to actions to reduce sexist restrictions (Stage 4). Finally, in Stage 5, people integrate their gender-role beliefs, which enables them to see themselves and the world in less gender-stereotypic ways.

Application

UNDERSTANDING MIXED-GENDER COMMUNICATION

LEARNING OBJECTIVES

- Distinguish between expressive and instrumental styles of communication.
- Describe gender differences in nonverbal communication and speaking styles.

- Explain how the different socialization experiences of males and females might contribute to communication differences.
- Discuss four reasons one should use caution in analyzing theories of mixed-gender communication.

Answer the following questions "true" or "false."

____ **1.** Men talk more than women in mixed-gender groups.

____ **2.** Women are more likely to ask for help than men.

____ **3.** Women are more willing to initiate confrontations in relationships than men.

____ **4.** Men talk more about nonpersonal issues with their friends more than women do.

If you answered true to all of these statements, you were correct. They are just some of the observed differences in communication styles between males and females. While not characteristic of all men and women, or of all mixed-gender conversations, these style differences appear to be the source of many misunderstandings between males and females.

When people experience frustrating communication situations in their personal or work relationships, they often attribute them to the other person's quirks or failings. Instead, it seems that some of these frustrating experiences may result from gender differences in communication style. Before we go any further, it is important to remember that scholars who advocate the gender similarities hypothesis argue that gender differences in many areas, including communication, are exaggerated and that males and females are similar on most psychological variables (see Hyde, 2005). As with many of the gender differences we have discussed in this chapter, differences in communication are often small and inconsistent (MacGeorge et al., 2004). In general, they are a matter of degree, not kind. In other words, it's not a matter of men being from Mars and women from Venus, but more like men are from North Dakota and women are from South Dakota (Dindia, 2006).

Tetra Images/Getty Images

Instrumental and Expressive Styles

Experts distinguish between instrumental and expressive (also called affective) communication. An *instrumental style* focuses on reaching practical goals and finding solutions to problems; an *expressive style* is characterized by being able to express tender emotions easily and being sensitive to the feelings of others. Because of the differences in their socialization experiences, men are more likely to value an "instrumental" style of communication and women, an "expressive" style, according to many researchers (Block, 1973; Tannen, 1990). Of course, many individuals use both styles, depending on the situation.

In conflict situations, men's instrumental style means that they are more likely to stay calm and problem oriented and to make more efforts to find compromise solutions to problems. However, an instrumental style can have a darker side. When the instrumental behavior of calmness changes to coldness and unresponsiveness, it becomes negative. Research has shown that this emotional unresponsiveness is characteristic of many men and that it seems to figure importantly in marital dissatisfaction (Larson & Pleck, 1998).

Nonverbal Communication

Many studies indicate that women are more skilled than men in nonverbal communication—a key component of the expressive style. For example, they are better at reading and sending nonverbal messages (Hall & Matsumoto, 2004) and are more facially expressive (Brody & Hall, 2010). **Figure 11.12** on the next page illustrates some of the gender differences in common nonverbal behaviors (Mast & Sczesny, 2010).

Women engage in some "negative" expressive behaviors as well. For example, during relationship conflicts, women are more likely to (1) display strong negative emotions (Noller, 1985, 1987); (2) use psychologically coercive tactics, such as guilt manipulations, verbal attacks, and power plays (Barnes & Buss, 1985); and (3) reject attempts at reconciliation (Barnes & Buss, 1985). Interestingly, women appear to value online expressive communication (often via social networking sites) more than men (Tufekci, 2008).

Speaking Styles

Most studies have found that women speak more tentatively ("I may be wrong, but . . .") than men, especially when discussing masculine topics in mixed-gender groups (McHugh & Hambaugh, 2010; Palomares, 2009). In a meta-analysis of over twenty-nine studies, Leaper and Robnett (2011) found support for this phenomenon, though the difference was small. In her classic model of gender differences in communication, Lakoff (1973) suggested that this discrepancy in speaking style is responsible in part

COMMON GENDER COMMUNICATION CHARACTERISTICS

Female	Male
Accurate emotion expression	Body movement (e.g., fidgeting)
Expressiveness (face)	Bodily expansiveness
Forward leaning	Filled pauses
Gazing	Interruptions
Gesturing	Loud voice
Nodding	Speaking longer
Self-touch	Speech errors
Smiling	Visual dominance

Figure 11.12

Communication characteristics more common to each gender. Research shows that women are more skilled than men in nonverbal communication—a key component of the expressive style. This figure illustrates some of the gender differences in common nonverbal bahaviors (based on Mast & Sczesny, 2010).

for gender inequalities. To "remediate" this difference, contemporary researchers suggest assertiveness training (see the Application in Chapter 8).

Why might this difference exist? One explanation is that women's tentative language can be used to expressive sensitivity in a conversation. Another explanation attributes women's greater use of tentative and polite language to their lower status and still another to gender-specific socialization (Athenstaedt, Haas, & Schwab, 2004). Let's explore some theories about gender socialization specific to language and communication.

The Clash of Two "Cultures"

According to sociolinguist Deborah Tannen (1990), males and females are typically socialized in different "cultures." That is, males are likely to learn a language of "status and independence," while females learn a language of "connection and intimacy" (p. 42). Tannen likens male-female communications to other "cross-cultural" communications—full of opportunities for misunderstandings to develop. For

Learn More Online

Deborah Tannen's Homepage

Georgetown University Professor Deborah Tannen has won considerable recognition for her work on communication differences between men and women in diverse settings such as the home and office. Visitors to her homepage will find a complete bibliography of professional and general interest publications.

some hints on how to improve gender-based communication, see **Figure 11.13**.

These differences in communication styles develop in childhood and are fostered by traditional gender stereotypes and the socializing influences of parents, teachers, media, and childhood social interactions—usually with same-gender peers. As we noted earlier, boys typically play in larger groups, usually outdoors, and farther away from home than girls. Thus, boys are less under the scrutiny of adults and are therefore more likely to engage in activities that encourage exploration and independence. Also, boys' groups are often structured in terms of high- and low-status roles. Boys achieve high status in their groups by engaging in dominant behavior (telling others what to do and enforcing compliance). The games that boys play often result in winners and losers, and boys frequently bid for dominance by interrupting each other, calling each other names, boasting to each other about their abilities, and refusing to cooperate with each other (Maccoby, 1998, 2002; Maltz & Borker, 1998).

In contrast, girls usually play in small groups or in pairs, often indoors, and gain high status through popularity—the key to which is intimacy with peers. Many of the games girls play do not have winners or losers. And, while it is true that girls vary in abilities and skills, to call attention to oneself as better than others is frowned upon. Girls are likely to express their wishes as suggestions rather than as demands or orders (Maccoby, 1998, 2002; Maltz & Borker, 1998). Dominance tends to be gained by verbal persuasion rather than by the direct bids for power characteristic of boys' social interactions (Charlesworth & Dzur, 1987). These two cultures shape the functions of speech in different ways. According to Eleanor Maccoby (1990), among boys, "speech serves largely egoistic functions and is used to establish and

"Norman won't collaborate."

HINTS TO IMPROVE COMMUNICATION

Hints for men	Hints for women
1. Notice whether or not you have a tendency to interrupt women. If you do, work on breaking this habit. When you catch yourself interrupting, say, "I'm sorry, I interrupted you. Go ahead with what you were saying."	1. When others interrupt you, politely but firmly redirect the conversation back to you. You can say, for example, "Excuse me. I haven't finished my point."
2. Avoid responding to a woman's questions in monosyllables ("Yep," "Nope," "Uh-huh"). Give her more details about what you did and explain why.	2. Look the person you're talking with directly in the eye.
3. Learn the art of conversational give and take. Ask women questions about themselves. And listen carefully when they respond.	3. A lower-pitched voice gets more attention and respect than a higher-pitched one, which is associated with little girls. Keeping your abdominal muscles firm as you speak will help keep your voice low.
4. Don't order women around. For example, don't say, "Get me the newspaper." First, notice whether it might be an inconvenience for her to do something for you. If it isn't, say, "Would you mind giving me the newspaper?" or "Would you please give me the newspaper?"	4. Learn to be comfortable claiming more space (without becoming a space hog). If you want your presence to be noted, don't fold yourself up into an unobtrusive object.
5. Don't be a space hog. Be more aware of the space you take up when you sit with others (especially women). Watch that you don't make women feel crowded out.	5. Talk more about yourself and your accomplishments. This isn't offensive as long as others are doing the same and the circumstances are appropriate. For example, if the conversation turns to photography and you know a lot about the topic, it's perfectly OK to share your expertise.
6. Learn to open up about personal issues. Talk about your feelings, interests, hopes, and relationships. Talking about personal things helps others know who you are (and probably helps you clarify your self-perceptions, too).	6. Make a point of being aware of current events so you'll be knowledgeable about what others are discussing and have an opinion to contribute.
7. Don't be afraid to ask for help if you need it.	7. Resist the impulse to be overly apologetic. Although many women say "I'm sorry" to convey sympathy or concern (not apology), these words are likely to be interpreted as an apology. Because apologizing puts one in a lower-power position, women who use apologetic words inappropriately put themselves at a disadvantage.

Figure 11.13

Hints to improve communication between women and men. To have productive personal and work relationships in today's world demands that people be knowledgeable about gender and communication styles. Both men and women may be able to benefit from the suggestions listed here. (Compiled by the authors based on insights from Tannen, 1990)

protect an individual's turf. Among girls, conversation is a more socially binding process" (p. 516).

Some Caveats

The idea that there are two cultures founded on gender-based communication styles has intuitive appeal because it confirms people's stereotypes and reduces complex issues to simple explanations. But there are some an important caveats here. First, as we have noted, status, power, and gender-role differences can lurk behind what seem to be gender differences. Second, many of the assertions of theorists such as Lakoff and Tannen are based on casual observation, and, when put to the empirical test, the findings are mixed (McHugh & Hambaugh, 2010). Third, there are individual differences in preferred styles: Some women use the "male style" and some men use the "female style." Finally, the social context is a much stronger influence on behavior than gender is, which means that many people use either style, depending on the situation. For example, one study found expected gender differences in willingness to initiate negotiations (women were less willing then men), but these differences disappeared when the negotiations were framed in terms of *asking* for something (as opposed to negotiating) (Small et al., 2007).

Therefore, we caution you to avoid reducing *all* communication problems between males and females to gender-based style differences. Many scholars argue that we need to look at gender communication in more complex, less stereotypic ways and that our current way of thinking has far-reaching implications for issues such as expectations for achievement, communication of sexual consent and date rape, and sexual harassment (Cameron, 2007). It is simply not true that men and women come from different planets. In fact, MacGeorge et al. (2004) suggests that the idea of "different cultures is a myth that should be discarded" altogether (p. 143).

CHAPTER *11* | Review

KEY IDEAS

GENDER STEREOTYPES

• Many stereotypes have developed around behavioral differences between the genders, although the distinctions between the male and female stereotypes are less rigid than they used to be. Gender stereotypes may vary depending on ethnicity, and they typically favor males.

GENDER SIMILARITIES AND DIFFERENCES

• Some contemporary researchers have adopted the gender similarity hypothesis, emphasizing the fact that males and females are more similar than different on most psychological variables.

• There are no gender differences in general intelligence. When it comes to verbal abilities, gender differences are small, and they generally favor females. Gender differences in mathematical abilities are typically small as well, and they favor males. Males perform much better than females on the spatial ability of mental rotation; however, this skill can be improved through practice.

• Research shows that males typically are somewhat higher in self-esteem, although the findings are complex. Males tend to be more physically aggressive than females, whereas females are higher in relational aggression. Males have more permissive attitudes about casual sex and are more sexually active than females. Males and females are similar in the experience of emotions, but females are more likely to outwardly display emotions. Gender differences in communication are complex. Males and females are similar in overall mental health, but they differ in prevalence rates for specific psychological disorders.

• Gender differences that do exist are quite small. Moreover, they are group differences that tell us little about individuals. Nonetheless, some people still adhere to the belief that psychological differences between the genders are substantial. Social role theory and social constructionism provide two explanations for this phenomenon.

BIOLOGICAL ORIGINS OF GENDER DIFFERENCES

• Biological explanations of gender differences include those based on evolution, brain organization, and hormones. Evolutionary psychologists explain gender differences on the basis of their purported adaptive value in ancestral environments. These analyses are speculative and difficult to test empirically.

• Regarding brain organization, some studies suggest that males exhibit more cerebral specialization than females. However, linking this finding to gender differences in cognitive abilities is questionable for a number of reasons.

• Efforts to tie hormone levels to gender differences have also been troubled by interpretive problems. Nonetheless, there probably is some hormonal basis for gender differences in aggression and in some aspects of sexual behavior.

ENVIRONMENTAL ORIGINS OF GENDER DIFFERENCES

• The socialization of gender roles appears to take place through the processes of reinforcement and punishment, observational learning, and self-socialization. These processes operate through many social institutions, but parents, peers, schools, and the media are the primary sources of gender-role socialization.

GENDER-ROLE EXPECTATIONS

• Five key attributes of the traditional male role include achievement, aggression, autonomy, sexuality, and stoicism. The theme of anti-femininity cuts across these dimensions. Problems associated with the traditional male role include excessive pressure to succeed, difficulty in dealing with emotions, and sexual problems. Homophobia is a particular problem for men.

• Role expectations for females include the marriage mandate, the motherhood mandate, and working outside the home. Among the principal costs of the female role are diminished career aspirations, juggling of multiple roles, and ambivalence about sexuality. In addition to these psychological problems, women also face sexist hurdles in the economic domain and may be victims of aggression.

GENDER IN THE PAST AND IN THE FUTURE

• Gender roles have always represented a division of labor. They are changing today, and they seem likely to continue changing because they no longer mesh with economic reality. Consequently, an important question is how to move beyond traditional gender roles. The perspectives of androgyny and gender-role transcendence provide two possible answers to this question.

APPLICATION: UNDERSTANDING MIXED-GENDER COMMUNICATION

• Because of different socialization experiences, many males and females learn different communication styles. These differences, however, appear to be a matter of degree, not type.

• Men are more likely to use an instrumental style of communication, whereas women favor an expressive style. Women appear to be more skilled at nonverbal communication and tend to use more tentative language. This could be related to gender socialization, including how children use language in play.

• Although the idea of gender-based communication styles has intuitive appeal, the research is mixed. Other factors besides gender play an important role in these differences. In addition, men and women can alter their communication styles to fit the situation. Scholars suggest we explore mixed-gender communication in less stereotypic ways.

KEY TERMS

Aggression p. 328
Androcentrism p. 324
Androgyny p. 345
Body image p. 330
Cerebral hemispheres p. 332
Corpus callosum p. 332
Expressiveness p. 324
Gender p. 323
Gender-role identity p. 344
Gender-role transcendence perspective p. 346
Gender roles p. 333
Gender schemas p. 335
Gender stereotypes p. 323
Hormones p. 333
Instrumentality p. 324
Meta-analysis p. 325
Sexism p. 342
Sexual harassment p. 343
Social constructionism p. 331
Social role theory p. 331
Socialization p. 333

KEY PEOPLE

Sandra Bem p. 345
Alice Eagly p. 331
Janet Shibley Hyde p. 325
Joseph Pleck pp. 338–339
Deborah Tannen p. 348

1. Taken as a whole, gender differences in verbal abilities are
   a. small and favor females.
   b. large and favor females.
   c. nonexistent.
   d. small and favor males.

2. Among the following traits, the largest gender differences are found in
   a. verbal abilities.
   b. mathematical abilities.
   c. physical aggression.
   d. conformity.

3. Which of the following statements about gender differences is true?
   a. Males have lower self-esteem than females.
   b. Males show more relational aggression than females.
   c. Males have less permissive attitudes about sex than females.
   d. Males express fewer emotions than females.

4. The finding that males exhibit more cerebral specialization than females supports which of the following biologically based explanations for gender differences?
   a. Evolutionary theory
   b. Brain organization
   c. Hormones
   d. Social constructionism

5. Four-year-old Rachel seems to pay particular attention to what her mother and her older sister do, and she often imitates them. What is taking place?
   a. Sexism
   b. Observational learning
   c. Operant conditioning
   d. Androcentric bias

6. Parents tend to respond negatively to _____ behavior, especially in _____ .
   a. gender appropriate; boys
   b. gender appropriate; girls
   c. gender inappropriate; boys
   d. gender inappropriate; girls

7. Which of the following statements about peer socialization is true?
   a. Peer groups appear to influence gender-role socialization more in boys than in girls.
   b. Girls play in smaller groups and boys in larger groups.
   c. High status in boys' groups is achieved by making suggestions to others.
   d. Peers have relatively little impact on gender-role socialization.

8. Which of the following is *not* a problem with the male role?
   a. Pressure to succeed
   b. Emotional inexpressiveness
   c. Sexual problems
   d. Androgyny

9. Which of the following is *not* a problem with the female role?
   a. Poor nonverbal communication skills
   b. Diminished career aspirations
   c. Juggling multiple roles
   d. Ambivalence about sexuality

10. Sara exhibits both masculine and feminine personality traits. According to gender identity theory, she would be classified as
    a. cross-gender-typed.
    b. undifferentiated.
    c. androcentric.
    d. androgynous.

ANSWERS

1. a Page 326
2. c Pages 328–329
3. d Page 329
4. b Page 332
5. b Page 334
6. c Page 335
7. b Page 336
8. d Pages 339–340
9. a Pages 341–342
10. d Page 345

COURSEMATE

Go to **CengageBrain.com** to access Psychology CourseMate, where you will find an interactive eBook, glossaries, flashcards, quizzes, videos, and more.

PERSONAL EXPLORATIONS WORKBOOK

Go to the *Personal Explorations Workbook* in the back of your textbook for exercises that can enhance your self-understanding in relation to issues raised in this chapter.

Exercise 11.1 *Self-Assessment*: Personal Attributes Questionnaire (PAQ)

Exercise 11.2 *Self-Reflection*: How Do You Feel About Gender Roles?

CHAPTER 12

Development and Expression of Sexuality

© michaeljung/Shutterstock.com

R achel and Marissa, both college students and new roommates, headed out to a local club on a Friday night. After a while, they were joined by Luis and Jim, whom they knew a little from one of their classes. As the evening progressed, they all got along well. After a couple of hours, Rachel took Marissa aside and asked if she would drive the car back to their apartment so Rachel could leave with Luis. Marissa agreed and went home. When she woke up the next morning, Marissa realized that Rachel hadn't come home yet. Questions raced through Marissa's mind. How could Rachel have spent the night with a guy she barely even knew? Was it being prudish to think that? Did Rachel or Luis have a con- dom? Marissa knew she would have been afraid of getting pregnant, or maybe getting a disease of some kind.

As this scenario illustrates, sexuality raises a lot of issues in people's lives. In this chapter we consider sexuality and adjustment. Specifically, we look at the development of sexuality and the interpersonal dynamics of sexual relationships. Then we discuss sexual arousal, varieties of sexual expression, and patterns of sexual behavior. We also address the important topics of contraception and sexually transmitted diseases. In the Application, we offer some suggestions for enhancing sexual relationships.

BECOMING A SEXUAL PERSON

LEARNING OBJECTIVES

- Identify the key aspects of sexual identity.
- Explain how both physiological and psychosocial factors influence aspects of sexuality such as sexual differentiation, attitudes, and behavior.
- Understand gender differences in sexual socialization and how they affect individuals.

- Summarize the current thinking on the origins of sexual orientation, attitudes toward homosexuality, the process of disclosing one's sexual orientation, and the adjustment of lesbians and gay males.

People vary greatly in how they express their sexuality. While some eagerly reveal the intimate details of their sex lives, others can't even utter sexual words without embarrassment. Some people need to turn out the lights before they can have sex; others would like to be on camera with spotlights shining. To understand this diversity, we need to examine developmental influences on human sexual behavior.

Before beginning, we should note that sex research has some unique problems. Given the difficulties in conducting direct observation, sex researchers depend mostly on interviews and questionnaires. As a result, sex studies are especially susceptible to participant bias (McCallum & Peterson, 2012). People who are willing to volunteer information tend to be more liberal and more sexually experienced than the general population (Wiederman, 2004). In addition, respondents may shade the truth about their sex lives because of shame, embarrassment, boasting, wishful thinking, or simply wanting to be viewed favorably. Thus, you need to evaluate the results of sex research with more than the usual caution.

Key Aspects of Sexual Identity

Identity refers to a clear and stable sense of who one is in the larger society. We'll use the term **sexual identity to refer to the complex set of personal qualities, self-perceptions, attitudes, values, and preferences that guide one's sexual behavior.** In other words, your sexual identity is your sense of yourself as a sexual person. It includes three key features: sexual orientation, sexual values and ethics, and erotic preferences.

1. *Sexual orientation.* Sexual orientation is an individual's preference for emotional and sexual relationships with individuals of one gender or the other. **Heterosexuals seek emotional-sexual relationships with members of the other gender. Homosexuals seek emotional-sexual relationships with members of the same gender. Bisexuals seek emotional-sexual relationships with members of both genders.** However, sexual orientation is more complicated than this categorization implies, and research supports the notion of unique subgroups within each category (Worthington & Reynolds, 2009).

The terms *gay* and *straight* are widely used to refer to homosexuals and heterosexuals, respectively. Male homosexuals are called *gay,* whereas female homosexuals prefer to be called *lesbians.* Frequently, the term *LGB* is used to refer, collectively, to lesbians, gay men, and bisexuals. *Transgendered* individuals are those whose sense of gender "does not line up with the sex they were labeled with at birth" (Teich, 2012, p. 135). As such, transgendered individuals typically don't adhere to traditional gender roles in terms of physical appearance or sexual behaviors. Although often used interchangeably, the terms *transgendered* and *transsexual* are different, in that transgender is an umbrella term for a number of sexual identities of which transsexual is just one (Jenness & Geis, 2011). Because the lesbian, gay male, bisexual, and transgendered communities often have intersecting interests, the term *LGBT* is used to refer to these groups, although the word *queer* is now replacing this designation in the academic literature (Newmahr, 2011).

Chaz Bono (born Chastity Bono) is a transgendered man who, growing up, felt like a male trapped in a female's body. After struggling with gender-identity issues, he underwent a female-to-male gender transition between 2008 and 2010. He is now an LBGT advocate.

2. *Sexual values and ethics.* Sexual values can take the form of absolutism (no sexual activity outside of marriage), relativism (the relationship determines whether sexual activity is appropriate), or hedonism (anything goes) (Richey, Knox, & Zusman, 2009). In forming their values, people are taught that certain expressions of sexuality are "right," while others are "wrong." The nature of these sexual messages is culture-specific and varies depending on gender, race, ethnicity, and socioeconomic status. For example, a sexual double standard encourages sexual experimentation in males, but not females. Individuals are faced with the daunting task of sorting through these often-conflicting messages to develop their own sexual values and ethics, and ultimately their values predict their sexual behavior (Balkin et al., 2009).

3. *Erotic preferences.* Within the limits imposed by sexual orientation and values, people still differ in what they find enjoyable. One's erotic preferences encompass one's attitudes about self-stimulation, oral sex, intercourse, and other sexual activities. For instance, researchers found that although men and women were equally interested in erotic photos, they differed in terms of their preferences for the sexual activities depicted (Rupp & Wallen, 2009). Such preferences develop through a complex interplay of physiological and psychosocial influences—issues we take up next.

Physiological Influences

Among the various physiological factors involved in sexual behavior, hormones have been of particular interest to researchers.

Hormones and Sexual Differentiation

During the prenatal period, a number of biological developments result in a fetus that is male or female. Hormones play an important role in this process, which is termed *sexual differentiation.* Around the third month of prenatal development, different hormonal secretions begin to be produced by male and female *gonads*—the sex glands. In males, the testes produce *androgens,* **the principal class of male sex hormones.** Testosterone is the most important of the androgens. In females, the ovaries produce *estrogens,* **the princi-**

Learn More Online

American Psychological Association: Psychology Topics

APA's website offers information and resources on many important contemporary psychological issues. Under the heading of Psychology Topics, the sexuality site provides answers to common questions as well as links to additional web resources.

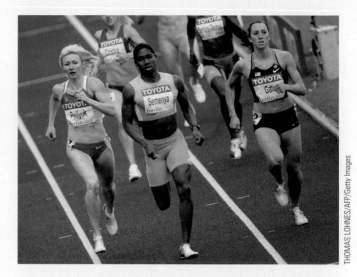

THOMAS LOHNES/AFP/Getty Images

After Caster Semenya, a South African athlete who is intersex, won the 800-meter world championship, questions were raised about her eligibility to compete as a woman. This controversy brought gender issues to the forefront of athletics.

pal class of female sex hormones. Actually, both classes of hormones are present in both genders, but in different proportions. During prenatal development, the differentiation of the genitals depends primarily on the level of testosterone produced—high in males, low in females.

There are instances, though rare, in which sexual differentiation is incomplete and individuals are born with ambiguous genitals, sex organs, or sex chromosomes. These persons, called *intersex individuals* (previously called *hermaphrodites*), typically have both testicular and ovarian tissue (Vilain, 2000). Though their gender is usually difficult to determine at birth, some intersex individuals might not be identified until puberty, and it is often difficult for them to determine their "true" sexual identity (Gough et al., 2008).

At puberty, hormones reassert their influence on sexual development. Adolescents attain reproductive capacity as hormonal changes trigger the maturation of the *primary sex characteristics,* the structures necessary for reproduction (sex organs). Hormonal shifts also regulate the development of *secondary sex characteristics* (physical features that distinguish the genders but are not directly involved in reproduction). In females, more estrogen leads to breast development, widened hips, and rounded body contours. In males, more androgen results in developing facial hair, a deeper voice, and angular body contours.

In females, the onset of puberty is typically signaled by *menarche*—**the first occurrence of menstruation.** American girls typically reach menarche between ages 12 and 13 (Chandra et al., 2005), with further sexual maturation continuing until approximately age 16 (Susman, Dorn, & Schiefelbein, 2003). Pregnancy is a possibility for girls at this age, so any girl who has begun to menstruate should assume that she could become pregnant.

In males, there is no clear-cut marker of the onset of sexual maturity, although the capacity to ejaculate is used as an index of puberty (the onset of sperm production not being a visible event). *Spermarche,* **or the first ejaculation,** usually occurs through masturbation (Hyde, 1994a). Experts note that ejaculation may not be a valid index of actual maturity, as early ejaculations may contain seminal fluid but not active sperm. The average age of spermarche in American boys is around 13 to 14 (Archibald, Graber, & Brooks-Gunn, 2003), with complete sexual maturation occurring at about 18 (Susman, Dorn, & Schiefelbein, 2003).

Hormones and Sexual Behavior

Hormonal fluctuations play a modest role in sex drive. *Androgen* levels appear to be related to sexual motivation in both men and women, although the effect is less strong in women (Apperloo et al., 2003). High levels of *testosterone* in men and women correlate with higher rates of sexual activity (Petersen & Hyde, 2011). Curiously, *estrogen* levels among women do not correlate well with sexual interest. In fact, researchers found no hormonal fluctuation differences between women diagnosed with hypoactive (low) sexual desire disorder and those without the diagnosis (Schreiner-Engel et al., 1989). In summary, physiological factors have important effects on sexual development. Their influence on sexual *anatomy,* however, is much greater than their influence on sexual *activity*.

Psychosocial Influences

The principal psychosocial influences on sexual identity are essentially the same as the main sources of gender-role socialization discussed in Chapter 11. Sexual identity is shaped by one's family, peers, schools, and religion, as well as the media.

Families

Parents and the home environment are significant influences on sexual identity in the early years. Before they reach school age, children usually engage in some sex play and exploration, such as "playing doctor." They also display curiosity about sexual matters, asking questions such as "Where do babies come from?" Parents who punish innocent, exploratory sex play and who stutter and squirm when kids ask sexual questions convey the idea that sex is "dirty." As a result, children may begin to feel guilty about their sexual urges and curiosity.

Some studies suggest that direct communication between parents and children about issues related to sex is declining (Robert & Sonenstein, 2010). As you can see in **Figure 12.1**, almost 50% of teens report getting information about birth control from someone other than their parents. When it comes to sex in general, 79% of girls report talking to their parents as opposed to 70% of boys (Martinez, Abma, & Casey, 2010). And even when communication does occur, many young people feel dissatisfied with the sexual information they receive from their parents, both in terms of quantity and quality. Although most parents recognize that it is important to communicate with their children about issues related to sexuality, many don't because they simply don't know how. Further, even when parents do provide information, it is not uncommon for their knowledge about sexually related topics to be incorrect, incomplete, or outdated, prompting experts to encourage sex education for the parents of teens (Brookes et al., 2010).

Parents who are able to talk honestly to their kids about sex tend to be those who have open family communi-

I don't know what you've been hearing at the playground, but there's no such thing as sex.

nication styles and whose own parents talked with them about sex (Fisher, 1990). Adolescents who feel close to their parents and who believe that their parents support them are likely to adopt sexual attitudes similar to their parents' and to limit or delay their sexual activities (Sprecher, Christopher, & Cate, 2006). The parents who do not discuss sex with their children are often the same ones who send restrictive sexual messages, especially to their daughters (Kim & Ward, 2007). Parents who make sex a taboo topic reduce their influence on their kids' evolving sexual identity, as the children turn elsewhere for information.

Peers

Friends provide a lot of information regarding sex, and positive peer influence is associated with less risky sexual behavior (Dunn, Gilbert, & Wilson, 2011). Indeed, the

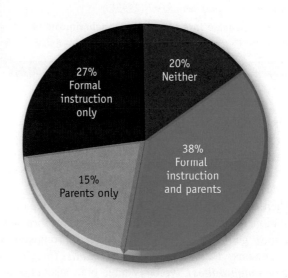

27% Formal instruction only

20% Neither

38% Formal instruction and parents

15% Parents only

Figure 12.1

Sources of information about birth control among teens. Many young people do not get their information about contraception from either their parents or their schools. (Adapted from Alan Guttmacher Institute, 2012b)

sexual behavior of one's friends is a strong predictor of one's own sexual behavior (Lyons et al., 2011). But it's not just actual *behaviors* that individuals use for information; adolescents' sexual attitudes and behavior are also positively associated with their *perceptions* of their friends' sexual attitudes and behavior (Sprecher et al., 2006). Unfortunately, peers can be a source of highly misleading information and often champion sexual behavior at odds with parents' views. While researchers acknowledge that the sexual socialization that comes from parents and peers is important for healthy sexual development, sexual education that comes from school-based programs is also significant.

Schools

Surveys show that the vast majority of parents and other adults support sex education programs in the schools, despite the media attention given to isolated, vocal protests (Tortolero et al., 2011). As of 2012, twenty-one states and the District of Columbia mandate sex education (Alan Guttmacher Institute, 2012b). When surveyed, the vast majority of teens reported receiving formal instruction about sexually transmitted diseases or infections (93%), HIV (89%), and abstinence (84%). However, only 62% of boys and 70% of girls received any formal instruction about contraception (Martinez et al., 2010).

The type of sexual education schools offer varies. "Abstinence only" programs offer no information about contraceptive methods, while "abstinence plus" programs include information about sexually transmitted diseases as well as contraception. "Comprehensive programs" offer information on a wide variety topics such as contraception, abortion, sexually transmitted diseases, relationships, sexual orientation, and responsible decision making.

What is the effectiveness of these various programs? *Abstinence only* programs do not deter adolescents from engaging in sex, nor do they delay first intercourse or reduce the number of sexual partners (U.S. Department of Health and Human Services, 2007). In fact, they have been associated with a decrease in reliable contraceptive use (Isley et al., 2010). In contrast, *comprehensive programs* result in a wide range of positive outcomes: increased use of contraception, reduced pregnancies, and reduced high-risk sexual behavior (Chin et al., 2012). In addition, these programs do not promote (and may even delay) having early sex and do not increase (and may decrease) the number of sexual partners.

Religion

One's religious background (or lack thereof) can play a major role in the development of sexual identity. There is evidence that teens and young adults who view religion as very important and who frequently attend church are less likely to have had sex and to have had fewer sex partners than their nonreligious peers (Haglund & Fehring, 2010). Religious teachings and traditions can dictate what is seen as sexually natural or unnatural. Historically, religious institutions have had a lot to say about issues such as guilt, monogamy, and homosexuality, for example (Francoeur, 2007). Using data from three national surveys, Regnerus (2007) found that the predominant message that teens receive about sex from their religious institutions is "Don't do it until you're married." This message is conveyed through church-based initiatives such as abstinence pledges, chastity vows, and purity rings. This message is largely ineffective, however. Teens who take these pledges tend to be just as sexually active (but less likely to use condoms or other forms of birth control) as their equally religious nonpledging peers. On the other hand, they do tend to feel more guilty about it (Rosenbaum, 2009). These findings suggest that although religious teachings might affect sexual attitudes, they do not always influence behavior.

Teens who take abstinence pledges or wear purity rings tend to be just as sexually active as their peers who don't.

Learn More Online

SIECUS (Sexuality Information and Educational Council of the United States)

This site is produced by one of the oldest organizations in the United States devoted to educating the public about matters of sexuality. It contains an annotated set of web-based links to a variety of topics related to sexuality.

The Media

Americans see thousands of sexual encounters a year on television, videos, DVDs, and computers. And the portrayal of sexual content, both in terms of sex talk and behavior, appears to be on the rise. In movies, sexual content has increased over the years, especially for female characters (Bleakley, Hennessy, & Fishbein, 2012). The percentage of television shows containing sexual content has been increasing as well. When analyzing over 2,000 television programs, Kunkel and his colleagues (2007) found that depictions of sexual intercourse doubled over a 5-year period. They also found that topics related to sexual risks and responsibilities, though increasing, were still incredibly rare, with such references appearing in only 6% of all sexual scenes. **Figure 12.2** shows how sexual content is distributed over common television genres.

As highlighted by the popularity of the *Twilight* series, movies and televisions shows aimed at young people also contain sexual content. One study found that 16% of characters involved in sexual intercourse on television are teenagers or young adults (Eyal & Finnerty, 2009). Television portrayals of sexual behavior can influence an individual's beliefs about typical sexual practices. For adolescents, viewing sexual content on television is linked to increased sexual activity as well as intentions to engage in sexual behavior in the future (Fisher at al., 2009).

Books and magazines are another source of information about sex. Some 20% of adolescents and young adults reported that they had learned "a lot" about relationships and sexual health from magazines (Kaiser Family Foundation, 2003). Regrettably, sexual content in magazines often reinforces gender stereotypes and sexual myths under the pretense of offering ideas for "improvement" (Johnson, 2007). Although some publications provide accurate and useful information, many perpetuate myths about sex and miseducate young (and older) readers. In addition to content, the *images* in magazines convey sexual messages. In a content analysis of over four decades of *Rolling Stone*

As highlighted by the popularity of series such as the *Twilight* trilogy, movies that are aimed at young people contain sexual content.

magazine covers, researchers found that women were more sexualized than men and that this trend has increased over time (Hatton & Trautner, 2011).

Music lyrics and music videos are additional vehicles of sexual socialization, and the sexualization of music has also increased over time (Hall, West, & Hill, 2012). Listening to music with sexually explicit and degrading lyrics is associated with higher levels of sexual behaviors in teenagers (Primack et al., 2009). In addition, male college students who viewed sexually explicit music videos were

Figure 12.2

Percent of programs in various genres that depict any sexual content. Kunkel and colleagues (2007) examined over 100 hours of television per week for the 2001–2002 television season. They measured both sexual talk (conversations about sex, comments about sexual actions) and sexual behavior (intimate touching, implied sexual intercourse). As you can see, sexual content is common in a variety of television genres.

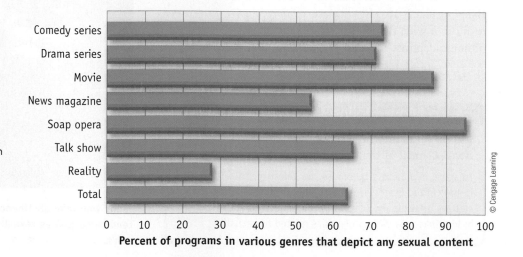

Percent of programs in various genres that depict any sexual content

more sexually permissive, were more likely to objectify women, expressed more stereotypic gender attitudes, and showed a greater acceptance of rape (Kistler & Lee, 2010). Even for middle-school males, exposure to music videos has been linked to greater rape acceptance (Kaestle, Halpern, & Brown, 2007).

Researchers find that the highest proportion of negative sexual messages occur in rap and rap-rock music (Martino et al., 2006). After analyzing 120 videos from the major music networks Turner (2011) reported that videos targeting African Americans (those shown on BET) were significantly more sexual in content than those on the other networks (MTV, VH1). Further, rap music videos tend to sexualize female characters more than male ones, and for African American adolescents, exposure to these stereotypes is associated with increases in sexual partners and negative body image (Conrad, Dixon, & Zhang, 2009; Peterson et al., 2007).

Turning to cyberspace, experts estimate that there were about 2.27 billion (32.7% of the total world population) Internet users worldwide in 2011 (Internet World Stats, 2011). Websites with sexually explicit images are extremely popular, especially among males. Parents are understandably alarmed about children having easy access to sexually explicit material online. On the up side, the Internet provides easy and private access to useful information on a variety of sexual topics, including contraceptive methods and resources for the LGBT communities.

Note that the causal link between sexual behavior and sexual media viewing can go both ways. While those exposed to sex in the media are more sexually active, those who are more sexually active tend to seek out more sexual content. In fact, 50% of adolescents (males more than females) report actively seeking out sexual content in the media (Bleakley, Hennessy, & Fishbein, 2011). Other experts argue that the link between media exposure and sexual behaviors may actually be due to outside factors, such as permissive parenting or having sexually active peers—factors that could influence both the viewing and the sexual behavior simultaneously (Steinberg & Monahan, 2010).

Admittedly, the media can promote responsible sexual behavior and an understanding of issues such as sexual orientation. However, whatever advantages there might be to sexual content in the media, experts agree that media depictions of sexuality would have to change dramatically for consumption of sexual media to be considered a healthy part of sexual development (Hust, Brown, & L'Engle, 2008).

Gender Differences in Sexual Socialization

Americans have many deeply held beliefs about how men and women express themselves sexually, and decades of research exist regarding gender differences in sexuality.

From an early age we are taught that men simply like sex more than women do—they are more interested in it, want more of it, and are more open in their attitudes than women are. As we saw in Chapter 11, such gender differences can become exaggerated, leading to harmful gender stereotypes, so how do these commonly held beliefs hold up under scientific scrutiny? To explore this question, Jennifer Petersen and Janet Shibley Hyde (recall that she is the proponent of the *gender similarity hypothesis*) conducted a large-scale meta-analysis that included over 800 published articles and 7 large national data sets. Petersen and Hyde (2010b, 2011) conclude that while gender differences exist both in sexual behaviors and attitudes, most of these differences are quite small—the sexes have a lot more in common than was previously thought. Here is a summary of some of smaller differences they uncovered:

- Men are slightly more likely to engage in sex (although this difference appears to be decreasing over time).
- Men have sex somewhat more frequently and have more sex partners.
- Men are more permissive in their attitudes toward sex in general (again, the magnitude of this difference has decreased over time).
- Women are more likely than men to feel negative emotions (e.g., shame, guilt, fear) in response to sex.

There were a few exceptions to the gender similarity hypothesis, areas in which larger differences emerged. For instance, men are more likely to engage in casual sex (sex with a stranger or acquaintance). Further, men are more likely to engage in masturbation and pornography use.

Although biological and evolutionary factors can explain some of these differences, societal values and gender roles obviously come into play here. American males are encouraged to experiment sexually, to initiate sexual activities, and to enjoy sex without emotional involvement. They also get the message to be conquest oriented and to desire multiple partners. Thus, men may emphasize "sex for fun" in casual relationships and reserve "sex with love" for committed relationships (Oliver & Hyde, 1993).

Females are typically taught to view sex in the context of a loving relationship with one partner. They learn about romance and the importance of physical attractiveness and catching a mate. Unlike males, they are not encouraged to experiment with sex or to have numerous sexual partners. Whereas social norms encourage males to be sexually active, these norms discourage such behavior in females—in fact, sexually active women may be chastised for their behavior.

In addition to this sexual double standard, other factors have the potential to influence sexual socialization for females (Petersen & Hyde, 2010a). One such factor is *concern about sexual performance*. Accepting the belief that women should not enjoy sex might increase a woman's sexual inhibitions. A second factor is *fear of preg-

nancy. The media reinforce the gender stereotype that females are the ones responsible for pregnancy (Hust, Brown, & L'Engle, 2008). As a result, concerns about becoming pregnant can inhibit a woman's enthusiasm for sex. A third factor is *sexual guilt*. A recent national survey supported the idea that girls associate more shame and guilt with sex than boys do (Cuffee, Hallfors, & Waller, 2007). When you combine these factors with the positive rewards of dating and emotional intimacy, it's no surprise that many women feel ambivalent about sex. These feelings can tilt in the negative direction if early sexual partners are impatient, selfish, or unskilled.

With differing views of sexuality and relationships, males and females can be out of sync with each other—particularly in adolescence and early adulthood. For instance, college men are more likely to believe that oral sex isn't sex, cybersex isn't cheating, and the frequency of intercourse decreases after marriage. College women, on the other hand, are likely to think exactly the opposite (Knox, Zusman, & McNeely, 2008). These gender differences can lead to confusion and mean that communication is essential for mutually satisfying sexual relationships.

Because both members of homosexual couples have been socialized similarly, they are less likely than straight couples to have problems with incompatible expectations. Let's consider sexual orientation next.

Sexual Orientation

Gay, straight, or in between? In this section, we'll explore the intriguing and controversial topic of sexual orientation.

Key Considerations

Most people view heterosexuality and homosexuality as two distinct categories: you're either one or the other. However, many individuals who define themselves as heterosexuals have had homosexual experiences, and vice versa. Thus, it is more accurate to view heterosexuality and homosexuality as end points on a continuum. Indeed,

Alfred Kinsey and colleagues (1948) devised a seven-point scale, shown in **Figure 12.3**, to characterize sexual orientation.

Alfred Kinsey

Some researchers argue that even Kinsey's model is too simplistic. For instance, how would you categorize a person who was married for 10 years, has children, is divorced, and is now involved in a committed homosexual relationship? What about a woman who only dates men but who has homosexual fantasies and engages in same-gender sex on the Internet? And what about someone who self-identifies as straight but has had homosexual encounters in the past? Research supports a complex and malleable view of sexual orientation (Diamond, 2003). Savin-Williams (2009) argues that sexual orientation has several components, including sexual attraction (which gender one desires as a sexual partner), romantic attraction (which gender one establishes warm, loving relationships with), sexual behavior (which gender one is sexually involved with), and sexual identity (self-reported orientation). To add to the complexity, these components aren't always consistent with each other and aren't always stable over time.

How many gays and lesbians are there? The answer is, it depends on what question you ask. In the 2010 census, more than 1.8 million Americans indicated they were living with a same-sex partner (O'Connell & Feliz, 2011). Experts at the Williams Institute estimate that there are 8 million adults (about 3.5% of the adult population) in the United States who identify as lesbian, gay, or bisexual, although 19 million (8.2%) report having engaged in sexual activity with a same-sex partner, and 25.6 million (11%) report having a degree of sexual attraction to a same-sex other (Gates, 2011). However, as we've seen, there are multiple components to sexual orientation, and estimates of prevalence depend greatly on which component one measures and when.

0	1	2	3	4	5	6
Exclusively heterosexual	Predominantly heterosexual only incidentally homosexual	Predominantly heterosexual more than incidentally homosexual	Equally heterosexual and homosexual	Predominantly homosexual more than incidentally heterosexual	Predominantly homosexual only incidentally heterosexual	Exclusively homosexual

Figure 12.3

Heterosexuality and homosexuality as end points on a continuum. Kinsey and other sex researchers view heterosexuality and homosexuality as ends of a continuum rather than as all-or-none distinctions. Kinsey created this seven-point scale (from 0 to 6) for describing sexual orientation.

REEL RESEARCH ▶

Sexual Assertiveness and Gender

Log on to CourseMate at www.cengagebrain.com to watch this video.

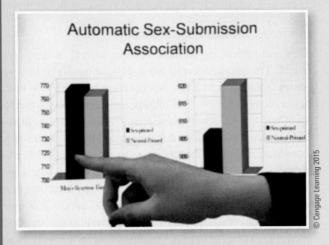

Automatic Sex-Submission Association

© Cengage Learning 2015

© Cengage Learning 2015

Gender norms are shaped by cultural and societal values and can cause men and women to behave differently in intimate relationships. Traditional gender norms place importance on masculine, dominant men and feminine, submissive women. Diana Sanchez, social psychologist at Rutgers University, studies women's unconscious association of sex with submissiveness in this Reel Research video.

Sanchez explains that women tend to behave passively in relationships, adopting a submissive attitude and treating their sexuality as if it is not their own. In the video, some female students are interviewed about their perspective on gender norms. They discuss how society and the media accept submissive women as "sexy," while men are expected to be dominant. To determine whether women's association between sex and submission is unconscious, Sanchez asks male and female participants to respond to words displayed on a screen, categorizing them as either real or nonsense words. Participants are told that the game measures their reaction time; however, sexually charged and neutral words flash across the screen during the game, priming their reaction. Sanchez believed that women participants who quickly associate sex with submission would also be quicker to respond to submissive words directly preceded by sex-primed words. Her prediction proved correct, as women responded faster to submissive terms when sex-primed than men. Also,

women who showed associations between submission and sex were more likely to self-report difficulty becoming sexually aroused, passive or submissive behavior with their partner, and lack of control in their relationships.

Researchers hope to make women feel sexually satisfied and content with their partners by changing gender norms. According to Sanchez, partners should encourage each other to take control and rewrite gender role scripts, empowering women to become more sexually assertive and share control over their relationship.

Watch the *Sexual Assertiveness and Gender* video to learn more about gender norms and sexual assertiveness. Delve even deeper by responding to the following discussion questions.

DISCUSSION QUESTIONS

1. How do gender norms reinforce dominance in men and submission in women?
2. Describe the demonstration conducted in the video. Why would the researcher mislead the participants to think the study is a measure of reaction time? What information did researchers collect? Explain your answers.
3. Find examples of submissive and assertive women in media. Explain why these women are exemplary of either submissive or assertive behavior.

Origins

There is no consensus among researchers as to *why* some people are straight and others gay, and people experience little or no sense of choice either way. A number of *environmental explanations* have been suggested as causes of sex-

ual orientation. Freud believed that homosexuality originates from an unresolved Oedipus complex (see Chapter 2). That is, instead of coming to identify with the parent of the same gender, the child continues to identify with the parent of the other gender. Learning theorists assert that homosexuality results from early negative heterosexual encounters or early positive homosexual experiences. Sociologists propose that homosexuality develops because of poor relationships with same-gender peers or because being labeled a homosexual sets up a self-fulfilling prophecy. Surprisingly, a comprehensive review of the causes of sexual orientation found no compelling support for *any* of these explanations (Bell, Weinberg, & Hammersmith, 1981).

Jason Merritt/Staff/Getty Images

Similarly, there is no evidence that parents' sexual orientation is linked to that of their children (Patterson, 2003). That is, heterosexual parents are as likely to produce homosexual (or heterosexual) offspring as homosexual parents are. Children who grow up in gay or lesbian families are predominantly heterosexual (Bailey & Dawood, 1998).

Some theorists speculate that *biological factors* are involved in the development of sexual orientation. Several lines of research suggest that hormonal secretions during prenatal development may shape sexual development, organize the brain in a lasting manner, and influence subsequent sexual orientation (Byne, 2007). Because of advances in technology that allow researchers to actually map the activity in the brain, we can begin to explore brain differences in sexual orientation. However, it is important to keep in mind that it is difficult to determine whether any brain differences are the cause or the consequence of sexual orientation (Safron et al., 2007).

Genetic factors are also of interest. In an important study, investigators identified gay and bisexual men who had a twin brother or an adopted brother (Bailey & Pillard, 1991). They found that 52% of the participants' identical twins were gay, 22% of their fraternal twins were gay, and only 11% of their adoptive brothers were gay. A companion study of lesbian women with twin or adopted sisters reported a similar pattern of results (Bailey et al., 1993; see **Figure 12.4**). Although separating genetic and environmental factors within families is difficult, there is evidence for the partial heritability of sexual orientation (Dawood, Bailey, & Martin, 2009). Nevertheless, contemporary researchers endorse a more interactive, biopsychosocial

model of sexual orientation to capture the influence of biological, psychological, and social factors.

The bottom line is that there probably isn't a single determining factor for an individual's sexual orientation. It is likely that there are a variety of types of homosexuality—and heterosexuality for that matter—that will require a variety of explanations rather than a single account. This issue is exceedingly complex and research is still needed.

Attitudes Toward Homosexuality

Gay and lesbian rights have become central in the political arena. The legalization of same-gender marriage in several states (such as New York, Massachusetts, and Iowa) and the legal recognition of civil unions and domestic partnerships in other states (such as New Jersey and California) have set off contentious public debates. Fueling the controversy, constitutional amendments banning gay marriage have been introduced in the U.S. Congress and in many state legislatures. Although the public discussion of gay marriage can be divisive, some believe that it has value (Garnets & Kimmel, 2003). First, it has allowed the gay community to educate straight citizens about the realities and diversity of same-gender couples and their family relationships. Second, it has helped raise the nation's awareness about the facets of discrimination against gays and lesbians.

Homophobia **is the intense fear and intolerance of homosexuals.** Because few people with negative attitudes toward homosexuals have the psychopathology that "phobia" implies, some psychologists believe that *sexual preju-*

Figure 12.4

Genetics and sexual orientation. A concordance rate indicates the percentage of twin pairs or other pairs of relatives that exhibit the same characteristic. If relatives who share more genetic relatedness show higher concordance rates than relatives who share less genetic overlap, this evidence suggests a genetic predisposition to the characteristic. Studies of both gay men and lesbian women have found higher concordance rates among identical twins than fraternal twins, who in turn exhibit more concordance than adoptive siblings. These findings are consistent with the hypothesis that genetic factors influence sexual orientation. If *only* genetic factors were responsible for sexual orientation, the identical twin concordance rates would push 100%; because they are much lower, environmental factors must also play a role. (Data from Bailey & Pillard, 1991; Bailey et. al., 1993) *dice* is a more appropriate term (Herek, 2009b). The lowest levels of sexual prejudice are associated with individuals who personally know someone who is gay (Fingerhut, 2011). Higher levels of sexual prejudice are associated with being older, male, less educated, and living in the South or Midwest and in rural areas (Herek & Capitanio, 1996). Sexual prejudice is also correlated with such psychological factors as authoritarianism (see Chapter 6), traditional gender-role attitudes (see Chapter 11), and conservative religious and political beliefs.

Unfortunately, negative attitudes sometimes translate into violence. In 2010, 18.6% of reported hate crimes were based on the offender's bias against the victim's sexual orientation (Federal Bureau of Investigation, 2011). In a national survey, 23% of the LGB participants had been threatened with violence, and 49% reported verbal harassment. These percentages were even higher when just considering gay males (35% for violence and 63% for harassment; Herek, 2009a). Clinicians note that most middle-aged LGBT individuals know someone who has been a victim of violence because of their sexual orientation (Scott & Levine, 2010).

Although many Americans still exhibit sexual prejudice, general attitudes appear to moving in a positive direction. A 2012 Gallup poll found that half of Americans think same-sex marriages should be legally recognized, a proportion that has been increasing over time (Newport, 2012). Greater acceptance is due, in part, to the increasing visibility of lesbians and gays in society. For instance, homosexual content on television has increased dramatically over the past two decades, including having more openly gay characters (*Glee, Modern Family*) and celebrities (Ellen).

Perhaps we shouldn't be surprised that people's explanations of sexual orientation play a role in their attitudes. Viewing homosexuality as biological or genetic in origin (that is, uncontrollable) is associated with more favorable attitudes than attributing it to choice (Savin-Williams et al., 2010). Black Americans are more likely than white Americans to endorse choice as an explanation for sexual orientation (Jayaratne et al., 2009), which may explain some of the cultural differences in acceptance of homosexuality. For instance, in a national survey, 72% of black respondents, compared to 52% of whites, indicated that homosexuality was "always wrong" (See **Figure 12.5**).

Disclosing One's Sexual Orientation

Coming to terms with one's sexual identity is complicated and difficult when it must take place in a climate of sexual prejudice. For gays, lesbians, and bisexuals, *coming out* involves recognizing and accepting one's sexual orientation, then disclosing it to others (Scott & Levine, 2010). Recent generations are becoming aware of and are disclosing gay, lesbian, or bisexual identities earlier in life (Floyd & Bakeman, 2006).

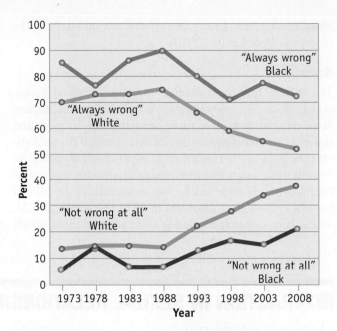

Figure 12.5
Racial differences in attitudes toward homosexuality. A national survey indicates that racial differences in acceptance of homosexuality still exist. Black respondents tend to be less accepting than whites. (Adapted from Glick & Golden, 2010).

Coming out can be a difficult process for many people. Gay and lesbian teenagers report losing more friends and worrying more about friendship loss than their heterosexual counterparts (Diamond & Lucas, 2004). With regard to families, the quality of a parent-child relationship prior to disclosure may be the best predictor of how parents will initially react and adjust to their child's coming out (Savin-Williams, 2001). Because of cultural differences in acceptance of homosexuality, LGBT people of color must contend with the additional stress of negative reactions in their families and communities (Iwasaki & Ristock, 2007).

In deciding to disclose one's sexual orientation to others, individuals must balance the psychological and social benefits (being honest, having social support) against the costs (losing friends, being fired, falling victim to hate crimes, losing custody of children). When the costs are too high or fear is too great, some individuals choose not to make known their sexual identity and are said to be *in the closet* (Scott & Levine, 2010).

Adjustment

The mental health community initially classified homosexuality as a psychological disorder. But researchers demonstrated that view to be a myth; that is, gays and straights are indistinguishable in their general psychological processes and on measures of psychological health. As a result of research, changes in public attitudes, and political lobbying, homosexuality was deleted from the official list of psychological disorders in 1973 (Newmahr, 2011). Since then, research continues to demonstrate that sexual orientation doesn't impair psychological adjustment in gay, straight, and bisexual individuals, couples, and parents (Hancock & Greenspan, 2010).

Although there is no reliable evidence that homosexual orientation per se impairs psychological functioning, exposure to sexual prejudice and discrimination can cause acute distress. Some studies suggest that gay males and lesbians are at greater risk than their straight peers for anxiety, depression, self-injurious behavior, substance dependence, suicidal ideation, and suicide attempts (Balsam et al., 2005; Cochran, 2001). Fortunately, like their heterosexual counterparts, most LGBT individuals are able to cope with this stress and thrive despite adversity.

INTERACTION IN SEXUAL RELATIONSHIPS

LEARNING OBJECTIVES

- Identify several approach and several avoidance sexual motives.
- Describe common barriers in communicating about sex.

People have many motives for engaging in sexual activity. In all cases, however, communication is critical for healthy sexual relationships. In this section, we'll briefly discuss the interpersonal dynamics of sexual relationships.

Motives for Engaging in Sex

Sexual motives are numerous and diverse, ranging from purely physical to deeply emotional. One conceptual framework for understanding sexual motives is to classify them as approach and avoidance motives (Impett, Peplau, & Gable, 2005). *Approach motives* focus on obtaining positive outcomes: (1) pursuing one's own sexual pleasure, (2) feeling good about oneself, (3) pleasing one's partner, (4) promoting intimacy in a relationship, and (5) expressing love for one's partner. *Avoidance motives* center on evading negative outcomes: (1) avoiding relationship conflict, (2) avoiding hurting a partner's feelings, (3) preventing a partner's anger, and (4) preventing a partner from losing interest. Researchers report that sexual encounters based on approach motives are positively associated with personal and relationship well-being. By contrast, sexual interactions based on avoidance motives are negatively associated with relationship satisfaction and are especially detrimental to the continuation of relationships (Katz & Tirone, 2009).

Communicating About Sex

Because individuals differ in sexual motives, attitudes, and appetites, disagreements about sex are to be expected. Couples have to negotiate whether, how often, and when they will have sex. They also have to decide what kinds of erotic activities will take place and what sexual behavior means to their relationship. This negotiation process may not be explicit, but it's there. Unresolved disparities can be an ongoing source of frustration in a relationship. Still, many people find it difficult to talk with their partner about sex. Couples can encounter four common barriers to sexual communication:

1. *Fear of appearing ignorant.* Many Americans are ignorant and misinformed about sex, often because media sources present incorrect information or perpetuate sexual myths. (You can test your own knowledge about some aspects of sex by responding to the questions in **Figure 12.6**). Because most people feel that they should be experts about sex and know that they are not, they feel ashamed. To hide their lack of knowledge, they avoid talking about sex.

2. *Concern about partner's response.* Both men and women say they want their partners to tell them what they want sexually. Ironically, neither feels comfortable doing so. People usually hold back because they're afraid of hurting the other's feelings. Or they fear that their partner won't respect and love them if they are truthful. Research shows that more extensive disclosure of sexual likes and dislikes positively predicts sexual and relationship satisfaction in committed relationships (Byers, 2011). Individuals who keep their preferences to themselves are likely to remain frustrated and unsatisfied.

3. *Conflicting attitudes about sex.* Many people, particularly women, are burdened with the negative sexual messages they learned as children. Also, most individuals have contradictory beliefs about sex ("Sex is 'beautiful'" and "Sex is 'dirty'"), and this dissonance produces psychological conflicts.

4. *Negative early sexual experiences.* Some people have had negative sexual experiences that inhibit their enjoyment of sex. If these experiences are due to ignorant or inconsiderate sexual partners, subsequent positive sexual interactions will usually resolve the problem over time. If earlier sexual experiences have been traumatic, as in the case of rape or incest, counseling may be required to help a person view sex positively and enjoy it.

A person's sexual self-esteem is a strong predictor of his or her ability to communicate about sex (Oattes & Offman, 2007). To communicate more easily and effectively about sex, you may want to review Chapter 8. Most of the advice on how to improve verbal and nonverbal communication can be applied to sexual relationships. Assertive communication and constructive conflict resolution strategies can keep sexual negotiations healthy. A basic rule is to accentuate the positive ("I like it when you . . .") rather than the negative ("I don't like it when you . . .").

Figure 12.6

How knowledgeable about sex are you? Check your basic sexual knowledge by answering these five questions. Information about each of the questions is discussed in this chapter.

THE HUMAN SEXUAL RESPONSE

LEARNING OBJECTIVES

- Describe the four phases of the human sexual response cycle.
- Discuss gender differences in patterns of orgasm, and give some reasons for them.

When people engage in sexual activity, exactly how does the body respond? Surprisingly, until William Masters and Virginia Johnson conducted their groundbreaking research in the 1960s, little was known about the physiology of the human sexual response. Masters and Johnson used physiological recording devices to monitor the bodily changes of volunteers engaging in sex. Their observations and interviews with these subjects yielded a detailed description of the human sexual response that won them widespread acclaim.

The Sexual Response Cycle

Masters and Johnson's (1966, 1970) description of the sexual response cycle is a general one, outlining typical rather than inevitable patterns—people vary considerably. **Figure 12.7** on the next page shows how the intensity of sexual arousal changes as women and men progress through the four phases of the sexual response cycle.

Excitement Phase

During the initial phase of excitement, the level of arousal usually escalates rapidly. In both sexes, muscle tension, respiration rate, heart rate, and blood pressure increase quickly. In males *vasocongestion—***engorgement of blood vessels**—produces penile erection, swollen testes, and the movement of the scrotum (the sac containing the testes) closer to the body. In females, vasocongestion leads to a swelling of the clitoris and vaginal lips, vaginal lubrication, and enlargement of the uterus. Most women also experience nipple erection and a swelling of the breasts.

Plateau Phase

The name given to the "plateau" stage is misleading because physiological arousal does not level off. Instead, it continues to build, but at a much slower pace. In women, further vasocongestion produces a tightening of the lower

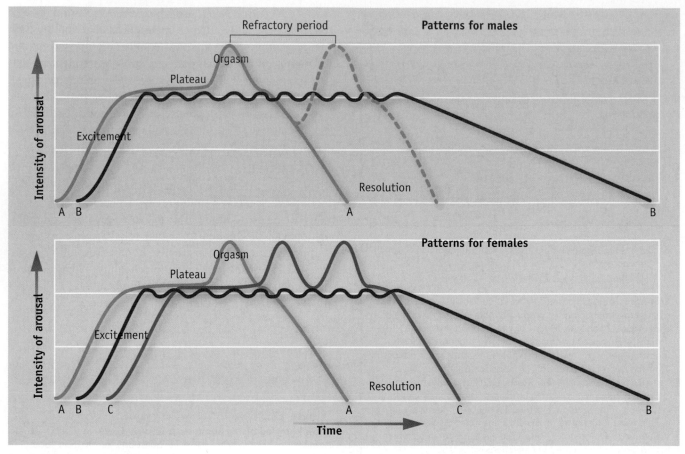

Figure 12.7

The human sexual response cycle. There are similarities and differences between men and women in patterns of sexual arousal. Pattern A, which culminates in orgasm and resolution, is the most typical sequence for both sexes. Pattern B, which involves sexual arousal without orgasm followed by a slow resolution, is also seen in both genders, but it is more common among women. Pattern C, which involves multiple orgasms, is seen almost exclusively in women, as men go through a refractory period before they are capable of another orgasm. (Based on Masters & Johnson, 1966)

third of the vagina and a "ballooning" of the upper two-thirds, which lifts the uterus and cervix away from the end of the vagina. In men, the head of the penis may swell, and the testicles typically enlarge and move closer to the body. Many men secrete a bit of pre-ejaculatory fluid from the tip of the penis that may contain sperm.

Distractions during the plateau phase can delay or stop movement to the next stage. These include ill-timed interruptions like a telephone ringing or a child's knocking—or not!—on the bedroom door. Equally distracting can be such things as physical discomfort, pain, guilt, frightening thoughts, feelings of insecurity or anger toward one's partner, and anxiety about not having an orgasm.

Orgasm Phase

Orgasm **occurs when sexual arousal reaches its peak intensity and is discharged in a series of muscular contractions that pulsate through the pelvic area.** Heart rate, respiration rate, and blood pressure increase sharply during this exceedingly pleasant spasmodic response. The male orgasm is usually accompanied by ejaculation of

seminal fluid. Some women report that they ejaculate some kind of fluid at orgasm, but the prevalence of female ejaculation and the source and nature of the fluid are matters still under debate. The subjective experience of orgasm appears to be essentially the same for men and women, although the relationship between subjective experience and physical response seems to be greater for men (Suschinsky, Lalumiere, & Chivers, 2009). That is, there is a higher degree of agreement between a man's physical response (erection) and his self-report of arousal than there is for a woman.

Resolution Phase

During the resolution phase, the physiological changes produced by sexual arousal subside. If one has not had an orgasm, the reduction in sexual tension may be relatively slow and sometimes unpleasant. After orgasm, men generally experience a *refractory period,* **a time following male orgasm during which males are largely unresponsive to further stimulation.** The refractory period varies from a few minutes to a few hours and increases with age.

Critics note that the Masters and Johnson model focuses entirely on genital changes during sex and ignores cognitive factors. An alternative is the three-stage model of noted sex therapist Helen Singer Kaplan (1979), which begins with desire, followed by excitement and then orgasm. Since people's thoughts and views about sex underlie many sexual problems, it is helpful to keep in mind that the sexual response involves more than just physical factors.

Gender Differences in Patterns of Orgasm

As a whole, the sexual responses of women and men parallel each other fairly closely. Nonetheless, there are some interesting differences between the genders in their patterns of experiencing orgasm. During *intercourse,* women are less likely than men to reach orgasm (that is, they are more likely to follow pattern B in **Figure 12.7**). Women are more likely to orgasm when they engage in a variety of sexual behaviors such as oral sex, whereas men are more likely to orgasm when sex includes intercourse. According to a national survey (Herbenick et al., 2010b), 91% of men report having had an orgasm during their sexual activities in the past year compared to 64% of women (see **Figure 12.8**).

How do we account for these disparities? First, although most women report that they enjoy intercourse, it is not the optimal mode of stimulation for them. This is because intercourse provides rather indirect stimulation to the clitoris, the most sexually sensitive genital area in most women. Thus, more lengthy *foreplay,* including manual or oral stimulation of the clitoris, is usually the key to enhancing women's sexual pleasure. Many men mistakenly assume that women experience the same degree of pleasurable sensations that they do during sexual intercourse. But this is not the case, as the upper two-thirds of the vagina has relatively few nerve endings—a good thing, since the vagina serves as the birth canal! Manual or oral stimulation of the clitoris is typically more effective in produc-

ing female orgasm than sexual intercourse alone. Unfortunately, many couples are locked into the idea that orgasms should be achieved only through intercourse (as often depicted in movies). Even the word *foreplay* suggests that any other form of sexual stimulation is merely preparation for the "main event."

Research suggests that lesbians have orgasms more often and more easily in sexual interactions than heterosexual women do (Diamond, 2006). Kinsey and colleagues (1953) attributed this difference to female partners' knowing more about women's sexuality and how to optimize women's sexual satisfaction than male partners do. Also, female partners are more likely to emphasize the emotional aspects of lovemaking than male partners (Peplau, Fingerhut, & Beals, 2004). Taken together, these facts support a socialization-based explanation of gender differences in orgasmic consistency.

Because women reach orgasm through intercourse less consistently than men, they are more likely than men to fake an orgasm. Some 67% of women and 28% of men report that they have faked an orgasm (Muehlenhard & Shippee, 2010). People typically do so to make their partner feel better or to bring sexual activity to an end when they're tired. Frequent faking is not a good idea, because it can become a vicious cycle and undermine communication about sex.

Figure 12.8

Gender differences in sexual experiences within the past year. A national survey regarding Americans' most recent sexual experiences revealed that men were more likely than women to report having experienced orgasm and to report experiencing high levels of pleasure during sex. (Adapted from Herbenick et al., 2010a)

SEXUAL EXPRESSION

LEARNING OBJECTIVES

- Describe six different forms of sexual expression.
- Discuss the preferred sexual activities of gay males and lesbians.

People experience and express sexuality in myriad ways. Most individuals engage in a variety of sexual practices (see **Figure 12.9** on the next page) and the menu of sexual activities is quite similar for heterosexual and same-sex

couples (Holmberg & Blair, 2009). **Erogenous zones are areas of the body that are sexually sensitive or responsive.** The genitals and breasts usually come to mind when people think of erogenous zones, as these areas are particu-

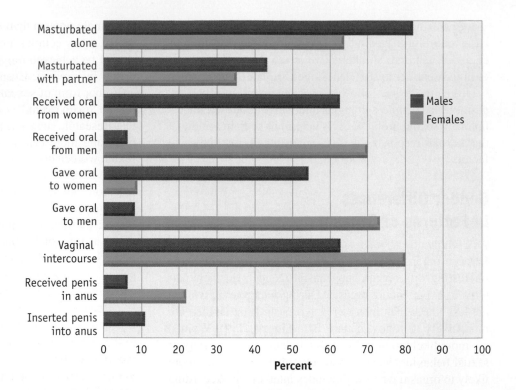

Figure 12.9

Percentages of sexual activities for American men and women, ages 20–24. Data from a national survey shows the distribution of reported sexual activities for men and women, ages 20–24, in the past year. It is clear that young adults engage in a variety of sexual activities. (Adapted from Herbenick et al., 2010b)

larly sensitive for most people. But it's worth noting that many individuals fail to appreciate the potential that lies in other areas of the body. Virtually any area of the body can function as an erogenous zone. Indeed, the ultimate erogenous zone may be the mind. That is, an individual's mental set is extremely important to sexual arousal. Skillful genital stimulation by a partner may have absolutely no impact if a person is not in the mood. Yet fantasy in the absence of any other stimulation can produce great arousal. In this section, we'll consider the most common forms of sexual expression.

Fantasy

Have you ever fantasized about having sex with someone other than your partner? If so, you've had one of the most commonly reported fantasies (Kahr, 2008). In fact, a study of university students and employees reported that 98% of men and 80% of women had sexual fantasies involving someone other than their current partner (Hicks & Leitenberg, 2001). As you might expect, women's fantasies tend to be more romantic, while men's tend to contain more explicit imagery (Impett & Peplau, 2006). Most sex therapists view sexual fantasies as a harmless, and even healthy, way to enhance sexual excitement and achieve orgasm either during masturbation or with a partner.

Dominance and submission fantasies are not uncommon. Research indicates that 31%–57% of women have submission fantasies in which they are forced into sex (Critelli & Bivona, 2008). Still, just because one fantasizes about a particular encounter, such as coercive sex, doesn't mean that one really wants to have such an experience.

Kissing and Touching

Most two-person sexual activities begin with kissing and mutual caressing. Kissing usually starts at the lips but may be extended to almost any area of the partner's body. In fact, there seems to be something special about kissing as a form of nonverbal communication. Floyd and colleagues (2009) randomly assigned heterosexual partners to either increase their romantic kissing frequency or not. After 6 weeks, they found that those who had increased kissing had less perceived stress levels and higher relationship satisfaction. These differences were still significant even after the researchers controlled for increased verbal affections and decreased conflict, two factors that might be expected with increased romantic kissing.

Men often underestimate the importance of kissing and touching (including clitoral stimulation). It is not surprising, therefore, that heterosexual women commonly complain that their partners are in too much of a hurry (King, 2005). Partners who seek to learn about each other's preferences and who try to accommodate each other are much more likely to have mutually satisfying sexual experiences than those who don't.

Self-Stimulation

Masturbation, **or the stimulation of one's own genitals,** has historically been condemned as immoral because it is nonreproductive. Disapproval and suppression of masturbation (often referred to as *self-abuse* at the time) were truly intense in the 19th and early 20th centuries, when people believed that the practice was harmful to physical and mental health. Masturbation is also referred to as *self-stimulation* or *autoeroticism.*

Kinsey discovered over six decades ago that most people masturbate with no ill effects. Sexologists now recognize that self-stimulation is normal and healthy. In fact, sex therapists often prescribe masturbation to treat both male and female sexual problems (see this Chapter's Application). Nonetheless, many of those who engage in the practice feel guilty about it.

Self-stimulation is common in our society. In a national survey, as many as 85% of women and 94% of men reported having engaged in self-stimulation at some point in their lives (Herbenick et al., 2010b). Among married couples, up to 71% of men and 51% of women report engaging in self-stimulation (Herbenick et al., 2010c; Reece et al., 2010). In fact, masturbation in marriage is often associated with a greater degree of marital and sexual satisfaction (Leitenberg, Detzer, & Srebnik, 1993). Perhaps self-stimulation leads to greater satisfaction, or perhaps those who are more satisfied are more likely to engage is self-stimulation. The direction of this relationship has yet to be determined.

Sometimes people, more often women, use vibrators or other "sex toys" for self-stimulation (as well as during sexual interactions). One study found that 46% of women reported having used a vibrator during masturbation (Herbenick et al., 2010d). Recent evidence suggests that vibrator use for women is associated with more positive sexual functioning and better sexual health practices (Herbenick et al., 2009). The findings are similar for men who incorporate vibrators into foreplay with their partners (Reece at al., 2009).

Oral Sex

Oral sex refers to oral stimulation of the genitals. ***Cunnilingus* is oral stimulation of the female genitals; *fellatio* is oral stimulation of the penis.** Oral sex is a common practice in adolescent sexual experiences and most couples' (both gay and straight) sexual relationships. According to the National Survey of Family Growth, about two-thirds of males and females ages 15–24 have had oral sex (Copen, Chandra, & Martinez, 2012).

When engaging in oral-genital contact, partners may stimulate each other simultaneously, or one partner may stimulate the other without immediate reciprocation. Oral sex may be one of several activities in a sexual encounter, or it may be the main event. It is a major source of orgasms for many heterosexual couples, and it plays a central role in homosexual relationships.

There is debate as to whether oral sex counts as "sex." One study found that only 20% of college students would say they "had sex" with someone with whom they only had oral-genital contact (Hans, Gillen, & Akande, 2010). Further, most individuals see engaging in oral sex as consistent with abstinence (Hans & Kimberly, 2011).

A positive aspect of oral sex for some people is that it does not result in pregnancy. This fact partly accounts for the finding that younger teens are more likely to engage in oral sex than in intercourse. However, some sexually transmitted diseases (HIV, for example) can be contracted through oral-genital stimulation, especially if there are small cracks in the mouth or if the mouth is exposed to semen. And a person with a cold sore can pass along the herpes virus during oral sex or kissing. Unfortunately, data suggest that up to 40% of sexually active teens either don't know that one can become infected with HIV through unprotected oral sex or are unsure about it (Centers for Disease Control, 2009c).

Anal Sex

***Anal intercourse* involves insertion of the penis into a partner's anus and rectum.** Legally, it is termed *sodomy* (and it is still illegal in some states). In a national survey, up to 27% of men and 22% women reported having practiced anal sex in the past year (Herbenick et al., 2010b). Anal intercourse is more popular among homosexual male couples than among heterosexual couples. However, even among gay men it ranks behind oral sex and mutual masturbation in prevalence.

Anal sex is risky. Gay men who engage in it without a condom (referred to as bareback sex) run a high risk for HIV infection in that rectal tissues are easily torn, facilitating HIV transmission (Bauermeister et al., 2009).

Intercourse

Vaginal intercourse, known more technically as ***coitus,* involves inserting the penis into the vagina and (typically) pelvic thrusting.** It is the most widely endorsed and widely practiced sexual act in our society. In a national survey, 80% of male and 86% of female respondents said that they had practiced penile-vaginal sex the last time they had sex (Herbernick et al., 2010a). Frequent intercourse is associated with greater sexual and relationship satisfaction, higher life satisfaction, and better mental health (Brody & Costa, 2009).

Inserting the penis generally requires adequate vaginal lubrication, or intercourse may be difficult and painful for

Learn More Online

Kaiser Family Foundation

This foundation sponsors multiple programs and educational efforts in the United States and South Africa to promote health generally, and its site provides a large set of resources regarding human sexuality.

the woman. This is another good reason for couples to spend plenty of time on mutual kissing and touching, since sexual excitement induces vaginal lubrication. In the absence of adequate lubrication, partners may choose to use artificial lubricants.

Couples use a variety of positions in intercourse and may use more than one position in a single encounter. The man-above, or "missionary," position is the most common, but the woman-above, side-by-side, and rear-entry positions are also popular. Each position has its advantages and disadvantages. Although people are fascinated by the relative merits of various positions, specific positions may not be as important as the tempo, depth, and angle of move-

ments in intercourse. As with other aspects of sexual relations, the crucial consideration is that partners talk to each other about their preferences.

What kinds of sexual activities do homosexuals prefer in the absence of coitus (which is, by definition, a heterosexual act)? As is true with heterosexual couples, the preliminary activities of gay and lesbian couples include kissing, hugging, and caressing. Gay men also engage in fellatio, mutual masturbation, and anal intercourse, in that order of prevalence (Lever, 1994). Lesbians engage in cunnilingus, mutual masturbation, and *tribadism* (also known as humping or scissoring), in which partners rub their genitals together so that both receive genital stimulation at the same time.

PATTERNS OF SEXUAL BEHAVIOR

LEARNING OBJECTIVES

- Outline the research on sex outside of as well as within committed relationships.
- Compare and contrast sexual behavior in married couples versus committed homosexual couples.
- Discuss the research on infidelity in committed relationships.

The context of a sexual interaction influences the interaction itself. In this section we examine how the type of relationship one is in relates to sexual behavior.

Sex Outside of Committed Relationships

"Hooking up," a phenomenon that arose in the late 1990s, involves two strangers or briefly acquainted people having a single sexual encounter. Hookups don't always involve intercourse (manual stimulation and oral sex are common). Owen and colleagues (2010) found that 50%–55% of college students report having had at least one hookup in the past year. When looking at hookups that did include sexual intercourse, Eshbaugh and Gute (2008) found that 36% of sexually active women reported having sex with someone

only once, and 29% reported having sex with someone they had known less than 24 hours. Further, hookups that included sex were linked to regret for women. Hookups typically result from flirting, drinking, and hanging out and typically end when one or both partners reach orgasm or one person leaves or passes out (Paul, Wenzel, & Harvey, 2008). **Figure 12.10** depicts men's and women's comfort levels with various hooking-up behaviors.

"Friends with benefits" (FWB) refers to friends who engage in sex but who don't label their relationship as romantic. This situation is different from hooking up because participants in a FWB relationship anticipate maintaining their friendship. In one study, 54% of young adult men and 43% of women reported maintaining this kind of relationship (Owen & Fincham, 2011). People who engage in a

Figure 12.10

Gender differences in comfort level with hooking-up behaviors. College men and women were asked to rate their comfort level with four hooking-up behaviors. The ratings were made on an 11-point scale (11 = *very comfortable*; 1 = *not at all comfortable*). As you can see from the mean ratings shown here, men's comfort levels significantly exceeded women's for all four behaviors

Source: From Lambert, T. A., Kahn, A. S., & Apple, K. J. (2003). Pluralistic ignorance and hooking up. *The Journal of Sex Research*, 40(2) 129–133. Copyright 1979 Society for the Scientific Study of Sexuality. Reprinted by permission.

© Monkey Business Image/Shutterstock.com

FWB arrangement are more likely to be casual daters, to be nonromantics, and to hold more hedonistic sexual values (Puentes, Knox, & Zusman, 2008). Obviously, negotiating such relationships can be tricky. Friendships are jeopardized if unreciprocated desires for romantic commitment develop or if one person wants to end the sexual relationship.

Sex in Committed Relationships

Sex is a key aspect of most committed, romantic relationships. In this section, we examine patterns of sexual activity in dating couples, married couples, and gay couples.

Sex Between Dating Partners

With the average age of first marriage rising, most couples confront the issue of premarital sex (Bogle, 2011). Some

worry that sex might adversely affect the relationship; others fear that not having sex will cause trouble. Is there evidence to support either view? As it turns out, sexual intimacy is a positive predictor of relationship stability (Sprecher & Cate, 2004). However, gender and sexual and relationship satisfaction are also part of this equation. For men, sexual (but not relationship) satisfaction is significantly correlated with relationship stability; for women, relationship (but not sexual) satisfaction is significantly associated with relationship stability (Sprecher, 2002).

Marital Sex

Couples' overall marital satisfaction is strongly related to their satisfaction with their sexual relationship (Sprecher et al., 2006). Of course, it is difficult to know whether good sex promotes good marriages or good marriages promote good sex. In all probability, it's a two-way street. Relationship satisfaction is also correlated with satisfaction in other areas of a relationship (fairness in distribution of household labor, for example) (Impett & Peplau, 2006).

Married couples vary greatly in how often they have sex (see **Figure 12.11**). The majority of couples report engaging in sex in a range of two to three times per week to a few times per month, with the frequency of sex decreasing as the years pass (Herbenick et al., 2010c; Reece et al., 2010). Biological changes play some role in this trend, but social factors are also compelling. Many couples attribute this decline to increasing fatigue from work and childrearing and to growing familiarity with their sexual routine.

As men and women age, sexual arousal tends to build more slowly and orgasms tend to diminish in frequency and intensity. Males' refractory periods lengthen, and females' vaginal lubrication and elasticity decrease. Nevertheless, older people, especially those in good health, remain capable of and interested in rewarding sexual

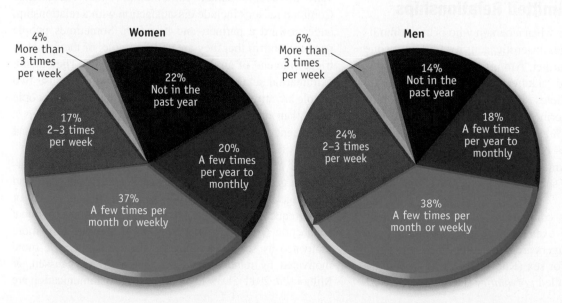

Figure 12.11

Frequency of sex among married men and women. In a large-scale national survey, married individuals were asked how often they had vaginal intercourse. Their responses were wide ranging. The majority of couples report engaging in sex between two to three times per week and a few times per month. (Adapted from Herbenick et al., 2010c, and Reece et al., 2010) encounters (Zahn, 2012). In a national survey, 43% of men and 22% of women over the age of 70 reported having had sex in the previous year (Herbenick, 2010b). Marrying for love, still being in love, and being financially stable are associated with sexual activity in later adulthood (Papaharitou et al., 2008). Unfortunately, restrictive health-care institutions and professionals often present barriers to sexuality by either explicitly or implicitly discouraging sexual expression among those in late adulthood.

Sex in Homosexual Relationships

What about the frequency of sex among lesbian, gay, and heterosexual couples? Peplau and her colleagues (2004) report three patterns. First, there is a general decline in the frequency of sexual behavior over time. Second, in the early stages of a relationship, gay males engage in sex more frequently than the other types of couples. Third, lesbian couples have sex less often than other couples.

© mangostock/Shutterstock.com

Like heterosexual women, most lesbians believe that sex and love are intertwined. In contrast (and like straight males), gay men find casual sex more acceptable (Sanders, 2000). Comparative studies find comparable levels of sexual satisfaction in gay, lesbian, and heterosexual couples (Kurdek, 2005). And for both lesbians and gay men, sexual satisfaction is correlated with overall relationship satisfaction.

Infidelity in Committed Relationships

Sexual infidelity occurs when a person who is in a committed relationship engages in erotic activity with someone other than his or her partner. Among married couples, this behavior is also called "adultery" or "extramarital sex." Infidelity among couples in committed relationships (straight and gay) is termed "extradyadic sex." The vast majority of people (91%) in our society believe that extramarital sex is "always" or "almost always wrong" (Saad, 2007). Nonetheless, Americans are fascinated by infidelity, if the popularity of such TV series as *The Good Wife* is any gauge.

Although it's not common, some couples condone extramarital sex. Two examples include "swinging" and "open marriage." Swingers are married couples who agree to exchange partners for sex (Rubin, 2001). In open marriage, now typically called *polyamory* (Hatch, 2009), both partners agree that it is okay for each to have sex with others (O'Neill & O'Neill, 1972). As we noted, gay male couples are more likely to have open relationships than are lesbian or heterosexual couples.

Precisely what kind of erotic activity qualifies as "cheating" is debatable, especially between men and women. Are you unfaithful if you develop a deep emotional involvement without sex? No doubt many people would say "yes," and research supports the notion that both sexual and emotional infidelity are upsetting (Lishner et al., 2008). Is it "cheating" if a person in a committed relationship uses the Internet for sexual arousal or masturbation? What about exchanging sexually explicit email messages with someone you've never met face to face? Those are definite issues, and therapists are seeing more couples for problems related to cyber affairs.

Prevalence

Because of the associated stigma and secrecy, accurate estimates of infidelity are difficult to come by. A national Internet survey found that about 28% of married men and about 18% of married women admitted having had a sexual affair at least once (Weaver, 2007). In one study of over 1300 undergraduates, approximately 20% had engaged in extradyadic oral sex or intercourse without telling their partner (Knox, Vail-Smith, & Zusman, 2008).

As we noted, sexual openness is more common in committed gay male relationships, and the rates of extradyadic sex for this group are higher than for all other groups (Peplau & Fingerhut, 2007). Committed lesbian relationships are much more exclusive, in principle and in practice, than gay male relationships (Peplau & Fingerhut, 2007). Rates of lesbian extradyadic sex are also lower than those for married women.

Motivations

Why do people pursue extramarital sexual encounters? Common reasons include dissatisfaction with a relationship, anger toward a partner, and boredom. Sometimes people need to confirm that they are still desirable, or they want to trigger the end of an unsatisfying relationship. Then again, extramarital sexual activity can occur simply because two people are attracted to each other. Erotic reactions to people other than one's partner do not cease when one makes a permanent commitment. Most people suppress these sexual desires because they disapprove of adultery.

The gender differences in motivations for infidelity parallel the gender differences in sexual socialization. Men tend to engage in extradyadic affairs to obtain sexual variety or more frequent sex, whereas women usually seek an emotional connection (Buunk & Dijkstra, 2006). Men are also more motivated by sexual excitement, whereas women are more motivated by relationship unhappiness (Mark, Janssen, & Milhousen, 2011). Low levels of positive communication are associated with infidelity for both genders (Allen at al., 2008). Age is also a factor. People between the ages of 18 and 30 are twice as likely to engage in sex outside a committed relationship than people over 50 (Treas & Giesen, 2000).

Impact

Infidelity can lead to breaking up or divorce. Still, it's hard to know in these cases whether extradyadic sex is a symptom of a disintegrating relationship or its cause. When a partner cheats, men tend to react with anger and violence, whereas women tend to show sadness and seek out support from friends (Miller & Maner, 2008). The type of cheating matters as well. Women are more distressed by emotional infidelity, while men are more distressed by sexual infidelity (Cramer et al., 2008). Participants in extramarital affairs, whether or not they are discovered, may experience loss of self-respect, guilt, stress, and complications of sexually transmitted diseases. Occasionally, extramarital affairs can have a positive effect on a marriage if they motivate a couple to resolve relationship problems through marital counseling.

PRACTICAL ISSUES IN SEXUAL ACTIVITY

LEARNING OBJECTIVES

- Identify constraints on effective contraception, and discuss the merits of hormone-based contraceptives and male condoms.
- Describe the various types of STDs, and discuss their prevalence and means of transmission.
- List some suggestions for safer sexual practices.

Regardless of the context of sexual activity, two practical issues are often matters of concern: contraception and sexually transmitted diseases. These topics are more properly in the domain of medicine than of psychology, but birth control and sex-related infections certainly do have their behavioral aspects.

Contraception

Most people want to control whether and when they will conceive a child, so they need reliable contraception and need to know how to use it effectively. Despite the availability of effective contraceptive methods, however, many people fail to exercise much control. Between 2006 and 2010, 14% of births were not only unplanned but were unwanted by the mother (Mosher, Jones, & Abma, 2012). Teenage birth rates are also a concern. According to the Centers for Disease Control, teen birth rates showed a decline in 2007 through 2009; however, they still account for almost 38 out of 1000 (3.79%) births (Ventura & Hamilton, 2011).

Constraints on Effective Contraception

Effective contraception requires that intimate couples negotiate their way through a complex sequence of steps. First, both people must define themselves as sexually active. Second, both must have accurate knowledge about fertility and conception. Third, their chosen method of contraception must be readily accessible. Finally, both must have the motivation and skill to use the method correctly and consistently. Failure to meet even one of these conditions can result in an unintended pregnancy.

Many high school students use either withdrawal or no contraception at all. In fact, withdrawal (or pulling out) is the second most common method of contraception for teenagers, after the condom (Martinez, Copen, & Abma, 2011). These who engage in this practice are at high risk for pregnancy and sexually transmitted diseases. In addition, any couples who do not use condoms (even if they use another contraceptive method) can contract sexually transmitted diseases unless both partners have tested negatively for such infections.

Why do some individuals and couples engage in risky sexual behavior? When asking women, researchers have identified various individual, interpersonal, and societal factors that come into play. Individual reasons include technical problems using the method, forgetting to use it, or having unexpected sex. Examples of interpersonal reasons include discomfort discussing contraception with a partner or having friends that don't support contraception use. Limited access to contraception, high cost, or incorrect information are commonly reported societal reasons for not using contraception.

Once again, conflicting norms about gender and sexual behavior play a role. Men are socialized to be the initiators of sexual activity, but when it comes to birth control, they often rely on women to take charge. It is hard for a woman to maintain an image of sexual naïveté and also

Learn More Online

Sexual Health Network

The health professionals who staff this Connecticut-based site have assembled a comprehensive set of resources related to all aspects of human sexual health, including sexual functioning for persons with physical injuries or disabilities.

Most excuses provided by women for having unprotected sex fall into three categories: individual (such as forgetting or having unexpected sex), interpersonal (for example, fear of partner's reaction), or societal (for instance, limited access or incorrect information).

be responsible for contraception. Insisting on condom use might be too "risky" to her feminine identity (Cook, 2012). The mixed messages sent by some sexual education programs or parents ("Use a condom but we can't supply you with one") add to the confusion. Finally, alcohol can undermine condom use, although this is not always the case. Some individuals drink as a socially acceptable way to avoid potentially embarrassing discussions about sex.

Selecting a Contraceptive Method

If a couple are motivated to control their fertility, how should they go about selecting a technique? A rational choice requires accurate knowledge of the effectiveness, benefits, costs, and risks of the various methods. **Figure 12.12** summarizes information on most of the methods currently available. The *ideal failure rate* estimates the probability of conception when the technique is used correctly and consistently. The *typical failure rate* is what occurs in the real world, when users' negligence is factored in.

The greater one's knowledge about birth control, the more likely one is to communicate with one's partner before sex. Although male contraception is currently limited to withdrawal,

condoms, and vasectomy, contraception is a joint responsibility. Hence, it's essential for partners to discuss their preferences, to decide what method(s) they are going to use, and to *act* on their decision. Let's look in more detail at two of the most widely used birth control methods in the Western world: hormone-based contraceptives and condoms.

Hormone-based contraceptives contain synthetic forms of estrogen and progesterone (or progesterone only, in the minipill), which inhibit ovulation in women. Types of hormone-based contraceptives include "the pill," hormonal injectables (Depo-Provera), the transdermal patch (worn on the skin), the vaginal ring (inserted once a month), and contraceptive implants. Many couples prefer these birth control options because contraceptive use is not tied to the sex act. But these contraceptives do not protect against sexually transmitted diseases.

Except for Depo-Provera, which has been linked to a slightly increased risk of breast cancer, use of hormone-based contraceptives does not appear to increase a woman's overall risk for cancer (Trussell, 2004). In fact, the likelihood of certain forms of cancer (such as uterine and ovarian cancer) is reduced in women who use low-dosage *oral* contraceptives. These methods do slightly increase the risk of certain cardiovascular disorders, such as heart disease and stroke. Thus, women who smoke, are over age 35, have any suspicion of cardiovascular disease, have liver disease, or have breast or uterine cancer should consider alternative methods of contraception.

The male *condom*, a barrier method of contraception, is a sheath worn over the penis during intercourse to collect ejaculated semen. The condom is the only widely available contraceptive device for use by males. In fact, 80% of adolescent males (and 69% of females) reported

CONTRACEPTIVE METHODS

Hormonal Methods	Ideal failure rate (%)	Typical failure rate (%)	Advantages	Disadvantages
Birth control pills combination	0.3	9	Highly reliable; coitus-independent; has some health benefits	Side effects; daily use; continual cost; health risks for some women; no protection against STDs
Minipill (progestin only)	0.5	3	Thought to have low risk of side effects; coitus-independent; has some health benefits	Breakthrough bleeding; daily use; continual cost; health risks for some women; no protection against STDs
Hormonal injectables (Depo-Provera)	0.2	6	Highly reliable; coitus-independent; no memory or motivation required for use; reduces risk of endometrial and ovarian cancer	Side effects; use may increase risk of certain cancers; continual cost; injection every 3 months; no protection against STDs
Hormonal ring (NuvaRing)	0.3	9	Highly reliable; coitus-independent; no memory or motivation required for use; may offer protection against endometrial and ovarian cancer	Side effects; no data on extended use; no protection against STDs
Subdermal implants (Implanon)	0.05	0.05	Highly reliable; coitus-independent; no memory or motivation required for use	Side effects; painful removal; possible scarring at site; no protection from STDs
Transdermal patch	.03	9	No memory or motivation required to use; coitus-independent; very reliable; has some health benefits	Continual cost; skin irritation for some women; no protection against STDs
Barrier methods				
IUD	0.2–0.6	0.2–0.8	No memory or motivation required for use; very reliable; some health benefits	Cramping, bleeding, expulsion; risk of pelvic inflammatory disease; no protection against STDs
Diaphragm with spermicidal cream or jelly	6	12	No major health risks; inexpensive	Aesthetic objections; initial cost
Condom (male)	2	18	Protects against STDs; simple to use; male responsibility; no health risks; no prescriptions required	Unaesthetic to some; requires interruption of sexual activity; continual cost
Condom (female)	5	21	Protects against STDs; reduces post-coital drip; can be used without partner knowledge	Difficult to insert; uncomfortable; can be noisy during intercourse
Sponge	9–20	12–24	24-hour protection; simple to use; no taste or odor; inexpensive; effective with several acts of intercourse	Aesthetic objections; continual cost; no protection against STDs
Cervical cap with spermicidal cream or jelly	9–20	20–40	48-hour protection; no major health risks	May be difficult to insert; may irritate cervix; initial cost
Spermicides	18	28	No major health risks; no prescription required	Unaesthetic to some; must be properly inserted; continual cost; no protection against STDs
Fertility awareness (rhythm)	1–9	24	No cost; acceptable to Catholic church	Requires high motivation and periods of abstinence; unreliable; no protection against STDs

Note: STDs = Sexually transmitted diseases

(continued on next page)

Figure 12.12

A comparison of widely used contraceptive techniques. Couples can choose from a variety of contraceptive methods. This chart summarizes the advantages and disadvantages of each method. Note that the typical failure rate is much higher than the ideal failure rate for all methods, because couples sometimes do not use contraceptive techniques consistently and correctly. (Based on Alan Guttmacher Institute, 2012a)

Surgical Methods	Ideal failure rate (%)	Typical failure rate (%)	Advantages	Disadvantages
Female sterilization (tubal ligation)	0.5	0.5	Effective; permanent; doesn't interfere with sexual activity; reduces risk of ovarian cancer	Side effects associated with surgery; doesn't protect against STDs; expensive; irreversible
Male sterilization (vasectomy)	0.1	0.15	Effective; permanent; doesn't interfere with sexual activity	Side effects associated with surgery; doesn't protect against STDs; expensive; irreversible
Other methods				
Withdrawal	4	22	No cost or health risks	Reduces sexual pleasure; unreliable; requires high motivation; no protection against STDs
No contraception	85	85	No immediate monetary cost	High risk of pregnancy and STDs

Note: STDs = Sexually transmitted diseases

Figure 12.12 (*continued*)
A comparison of widely used contraceptive techniques.

using a condom the most recent time they had intercourse (Fortenberry et al., 2010). Other barrier methods include female condoms (which are inserted into the vagina), diaphragms, and spermicides.

Condoms can be purchased in any drugstore without a prescription. If used correctly, the condom is highly effective in preventing pregnancy (see **Figure 12.12**). It must be placed over the penis after erection but before any contact with the vagina, and space must be left at the tip to collect the ejaculate. The man should withdraw before completely losing his erection and firmly hold the rim of the condom during withdrawal to prevent any semen from spilling into the vagina.

Condoms are made of polyurethane, latex rubber, or animal membranes ("skin"). Polyurethane condoms are thinner than latex condoms; however, they are more likely to break and to slip off than latex condoms. Using latex condoms definitely reduces the chances of contracting or passing on various sexually transmitted diseases. However, oil-based creams and lotions (petroleum jelly, massage oil, baby oil, and hand and body lotions, for example) should never be used with latex condoms (or diaphragms). Within 60 seconds, these products can make microscopic holes in the rubber membrane that are large enough to allow passage of HIV and organisms produced by other sexually transmitted diseases. Water-based lubricants such as Astroglide or K-Y Warming Liquid do not cause this problem. Polyurethane condoms are impervious to oils. Skin condoms do *not* offer protection against sexually transmitted diseases.

Emergency Contraception

There are a variety of reasons that individuals have unprotected sex, and in some cases they might turn to emergency contraception after the fact. Women may seek emergency contraception in cases of sexual assault, contraceptive fail-

ure, or unplanned sex. Progestin pills (also called Plan B or "morning after" pills) are available from pharmacies without a prescription for women ages 18 and older (girls under 18 must have a prescription) (Alan Guttmacher Institute, 2012b). Plan B pills are 89% effective when started within 72 hours after unprotected sex. The drug works like birth control pills, by preventing ovulation or fertilization and implantation of the fertilized egg into the uterine wall (Planned Parenthood Federation of America, 2012b). If the fertilized egg is already implanted into the wall of the uterus, progestin will not harm it. By contrast, mifepristone (also called the "abortion pill" and formerly RU 486) is a drug that can induce a miscarriage in pregnancies in pregnancies of less than 9 weeks. Prescribed by a physician, mifepristone is typically administered in the form of two pills taken several days apart (Planned Parenthood Federation of America, 2012a). Although no substitute for regular birth control, these drugs can be used after unprotected sex and are particularly helpful in cases of rape. They do not, however, provide any protection against sexually transmitted diseases.

Sexually Transmitted Diseases

A *sexually transmitted disease* (STD) is a disease or infection transmitted primarily through sexual contact. The principal types of sexually transmitted diseases are listed in **Figure 12.13**, along with their symptoms and modes of transmission. When people think of STDs (also referred to as sexually transmitted infections or STIs), they typically think of chlamydia and gonorrhea, but these diseases are only the tip of the iceberg. There are actually around twenty-five sexually transmitted diseases. Some of them—for instance, pubic lice—are minor nuisances that can readily be treated. Others, however, are severe afflic-

STD	Transmission	Symptoms
Acquired immune deficiency syndrome (AIDS)	The AIDS virus is spread by coitus or anal intercourse. There is a chance the virus may also be spread by oral-genital sex, particularly if semen is swallowed. (AIDS can also be spread by nonsexual means: contaminated blood, contaminated hypodermic needles, and transmission from an infected woman to her baby during pregnancy or childbirth.)	Most people infected with the virus show no immediate symptoms; antibodies usually develop in the blood 2–8 weeks after infection. People with the virus may remain symptom-free for 5 years or more. No cure for the disease has yet been found. Common symptoms include fevers, night sweats, weight loss, chronic fatigue, swollen lymph nodes, diarrhea and/or bloody stools, atypical bruising or bleeding, skin rashes, headache, chronic cough, and a whitish coating on the tongue or throat.
Chlamydia infection	The *Chlamydia trichomatis* bacterium is transmitted primarily through sexual contact. It may also be spread by fingers from one body site to another.	In men, chlamydial infection of the urethra may cause a discharge and burning during urination. Chlamydia-caused epidydimitis may produce a sense of heaviness in the affected testicle(s), inflammation of the scrotal skin, and painful swelling at the bottom of the testicle. In women, pelvic inflammatory disease caused by chlamydia may disrupt menstrual periods, temperature, and cause abdominal pain, nausea, vomiting, headache, infertility, and ectopic pregnancy.
Human papillomavirus (HPV)	Virus is often on genital skin areas not covered by a condom (vulva, scrotum, etc.); virus is spread primarily through penile-vaginal, oral-genital, oral-anal, or genital-anal contact; transmission most often occurs by asymptomatic individuals.	Often asymptomatic; 10% of infections lead to contagious genital warts, which may appear 3 to 8 months after contact with infected person; HPV is associated with various cancers.
Gonorrhea ("clap")	The *Neisseria gonorrhoeae* bacterium (gonococcus) is spread through penile-vaginal, oral-genital, or genital-anal contact.	Most common symptoms in men are a cloudy discharge from the penis and burning sensations during urination. If the disease is untreated, complications may include inflammation of the scrotal skin and swelling at the base of the testicle. In women, some green or yellowish discharge is produced, but the disease commonly remains undetected. At a later stage, pelvic inflammatory disease may develop.
Herpes	The genital herpes virus (HSV-2) appears to be transmitted primarily by penile-vaginal, oral-genital, or genital-anal contact. The oral herpes virus (HSV-1) is transmitted primarily by kissing, or oral-genital contact.	Small red, painful bumps (papules) appear in the region of the genitals (genital herpes) or mouth (oral herpes). The papules become painful blisters that eventually rupture to form wet, open sores.
Pubic lice ("crabs")	*Phthirus pubis*, the pubic louse, is spread easily through body contact or through shared clothing or bedding.	Persistent itching. Lice are visible and may often be located in pubic hair or other body hair.
Syphilis	The *Treponema pallidum* bacterium (spirochete) is transmitted from open lesions during penile-vaginal, oral-genital, oral-anal, or genital-anal contact.	*Primary stage:* A painless chancre (sore) appears at the site where the spirochetes entered the body. *Secondary stage:* The chancre disappears and a generalized skin rash develops. *Latent stage:* There may be no observable symptoms. *Tertiary stage:* Heart failure, blindness, mental disturbance, and many other symptoms may occur. Death may result.
Trichomoniasis	The protozoan parasite *Trichomonas vaginalis* is passed through genital sexual contact or less frequently by towels, toilet seats, or bathtubs used by an infected person.	In women, white or yellow vaginal discharge with an unpleasant odor; vulva is sore and irritated. Men are usually asymptomatic.
Viral hepatitis	The hepatitis B virus may be transmitted by blood, semen, vaginal secretions, and saliva. Manual, oral, or penile stimulation of the anus is strongly associated with the spread of this virus. Hepatitis A seems to be spread primarily via the fecal-oral route. Oral-anal sexual contact is a common mode of sexual transmission for hepatitis A.	Vary from nonexistent to mild, flulike symptoms to an incapacitating illness characterized by high fever, vomiting, and severe abdominal pain.

Figure 12.13

Overview of common sexually transmitted diseases (STDs). This chart summarizes the symptoms and modes of transmission of nine STDs. Note that intercourse is not required to transmit all STDs—many can be contracted through oral-genital contact or other forms of physical intimacy. (Adapted from Carroll, 2007; Crooks & Baur, 2008; Hatcher et al., 2004) tions that are difficult to treat. For instance, if it isn't detected early, syphilis can cause heart failure, blindness, and brain damage, and AIDS is eventually fatal. Most of these infections are spread from one person to another through intercourse, oral-genital contact, or anal-genital contact.

Prevalence and Transmission

No one is immune to sexually transmitted diseases. Even monogamous partners can develop some STDs (yeast infections, for instance). Health authorities estimate that about 19 million new cases occur in the United States each year, with nearly half occurring in the under-25 age group (Centers for Disease Control, 2012c).

The Centers for Disease Control (2012b) estimate that 1.2 million people are living with HIV/AIDS (see Chapter 5 for more information on HIV). The United States has seen a surge of HIV infections stemming from heterosexual transmission. Although most young people are knowledgeable about HIV and AIDS, the Centers for Disease Control estimates that 8300 young people ages 13–24 had HIV infection in 2009. Further, the rate of HIV infections is up among young gay and bisexual men, especially those of color (Centers for Disease Control, 2012b). Unfortunately, the availability of new drug treatments for HIV—obviously welcome news for the most part—seems to have increased risk taking among gay and bisexual men (Peterson & Bakeman, 2006). Additionally, these new drugs are quite costly, well out of the reach of those without health insurance (Freedberg et al., 2001).

HIV is increasing more rapidly among blacks and Latinos than whites (Kaiser Family Foundation, 2012a, 2012b). **Figure 12.14** shows the racial breakdown of new HIV infections. Women whose sexual partners have had multiple sex partners or inject drugs are especially at risk. An increasing concern is that a woman's partner may be secretly having sex with other men and may deny that he is gay or bisexual. This phenomenon, known as being on the "down low," is more common among black and Latinos than white men, presumably because of cultural differences in attitudes toward homosexuality and bisexuality (Barnshaw & Letukas, 2010). In one study, 22% of men on the down low had

recently had both unprotected anal and vaginal sex (Siegel et al., 2008). These men report that they didn't use protection because the didn't always have condoms available, they enjoyed sex more without a condom, and they perceived their females partners as "safe" (Dodge, Jeffries, & Sandfort, 2008). Obviously, this lifestyle has serious implications for unknowing female partners in terms of increasing their risk for HIV infection or any STD.

Human papillomavirus (HPV) infections cause about half of STDs diagnosed among 15- to 24-year-olds (Alan Guttmacher Institute, 2006). HPV is increasingly common; it's estimated that 50% of sexually active men and women acquire genital HPV infection (Centers for Disease Control, 2012a). HPV tends to be more serious for women than men because certain types of HPV can lead to cervical cancer. In 2006, the U.S. Food and Drug Administration approved a vaccine (Gardisil) that prevents infection with the types of HPV that lead to cervical cancer. The vaccination is recommended for both girls and boys, starting at age 11 (Alan Guttmacher Institute, 2012b).

© Elena Elisseeva/
Shutterstock.com

Prevention

Abstinence is obviously the best way to avoid acquiring STDs. Of course, for many people this is not an appealing or realistic option. Short of abstinence, the best strategy is to engage in sexual activity only in the context of a long-

Figure 12.14

A racial breakdown of new HIV infections. This graph illustrates the estimated rate of new HIV infections by gender and race. As you can see, HIV is increasing more rapidly among blacks and Latinos than whites (Adapted from Centers for Disease Control, 2012b).

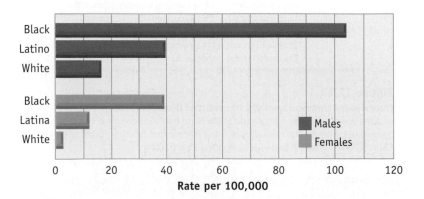

term relationship, where partners have an opportunity to know each other reasonably well. Casual sex greatly increases the risk for STDs, including HIV.

Along with being judicious about sexual relations, you need to talk openly about safer sexual practices with your partner. But if you don't carry the process one step further and practice what you preach, you remain at risk.

We offer the following suggestions for safer sex:

- If you are not involved in a sexually exclusive relationship with someone free of disease, always use latex condoms with spermicides. They have a good track record of preventing STDs and offer effective protection against the AIDS virus. (And never use oil-based lubricants with latex condoms; use water-based lubricants instead.)
- If there is any possibility that you or your partner has an STD, abstain from sex, always use condoms, or use other types of sexual expression such as hand-genital stimulation. People can be carriers of sexually transmitted diseases without knowing it. For instance, in its early stages gonorrhea may cause no readily apparent symptoms in women, who may unknowingly transmit the infection to their partners.
- Don't have sex with lots of people. You increase your risk of contracting STDs.
- Don't have sex with someone who has had lots of previous partners. People won't always be honest about their sexual history, so it's important to know whether you can trust a prospective partner's word.
- Don't assume that the labels people attach to themselves (heterosexual or homosexual) accurately describe their actual sexual behavior. According to a study based on a nationally representative sample of individuals ages 15–44, 6% of males and 11% of females reported that they had had at least one same-gender sexual experience in their lives (Mosher, Chandra, & Jones, 2005). As we discussed previously, many people keep these encounters secret from their partners.

- You should consider *any* activity that exposes you to blood (including menstrual blood), semen, vaginal secretions, urine, feces, or saliva as high-risk behavior *unless* you and your partner are in a mutual, sexually exclusive relationship and neither of you is infected.
- Because HIV is easily transmitted through anal intercourse, it's a good idea to avoid this type of sex. Rectal tissues are delicate and easily torn, thus letting the virus pass through the membrane. Always use a condom during anal sex.
- Oral-genital sex may also transmit HIV, particularly if semen is swallowed.
- Wash your genitals with mild soap and warm water before and after sexual contact.
- Urinate shortly after intercourse.
- Watch for sores, rashes, or discharge around the vulva or penis, or elsewhere on your body, especially the mouth. If you have cold sores, avoid kissing or oral sex.

If you have any reason to suspect that you have an STD, find a health clinic and get tested *as soon as possible*. It's normal to be embarrassed or afraid of getting bad news, but don't delay. Health professionals are in the business of helping people, not judging them. To be sure, get tested twice. If you have several sexual partners in a year, you should have regular STD checkups. You will have to ask for them, as most doctors and health clinics won't perform them otherwise.

Remember that the symptoms of some STDs disappear as the infection progresses. If your test results are positive, it's essential to get the proper treatment *right away*. Notify your sexual partners so they can be tested immediately, too. And avoid sexual intercourse and oral sex until you and your partner are fully treated and a physician or clinic says you are no longer infectious.

Even with these risks, sexual activity is a normal part of intimate relationships. In the Application, we focus on enhancing sexual satisfaction and treating common sexual problems.

Application

ENHANCING SEXUAL RELATIONSHIPS

LEARNING OBJECTIVES

- List five general suggestions for enhancing sexual relationships.
- Discuss the nature, prevalence, and causes of common sexual dysfunctions, as well as some strategies to cope with them.

Answer the following statements "true" or "false."

_____ 1. Sexual problems are unusual.

_____ 2. Sexual problems belong to couples rather than individuals.

_____ 3. Sexual problems are highly resistant to treatment.

_____ 4. Sex therapists sometimes recommend masturbation as a treatment for certain types of problems.

The answers are (1) false, (2) true, (3) false, and (4) true. If you missed several of these questions, you are by no means unusual. Misconceptions about sexuality are the norm rather than the exception. Fortunately, there is plenty of useful information on how to improve sexual relationships.

For the sake of simplicity, our advice is directed to heterosexual couples, but much of what we have to say is also relevant to same-gender couples. For advice aimed specifically at same-gender couples, we recommend *Permanent Partners: Building Gay and Lesbian Relationships That Last* by Betty Berzon (2004).

General Suggestions

Let's begin with some general ideas about how to enhance sexual relationships. Even if you are satisfied with your sex life, these suggestions may be useful as "preventive medicine."

1. *Become knowledgeable about sex.* A surprising number of people are ignorant about the realities of sexual functioning. So the first step in promoting sexual satisfaction is to acquire accurate information about sex. The shelves of most bookstores are bulging with popular books on sex, but many of them are loaded with inaccuracies. A good bet is to pick up a college textbook on human sexuality. Enrolling in a course on human sexuality is also a good idea. Most colleges offer such courses today.

2. *Review your sexual values system.* Many sexual problems stem from a negative sexual values system that associates sex with immorality. The guilt feelings caused by such an orientation can interfere with sexual functioning. Thus, sex therapists often encourage adults to examine the sources and implications of their sexual values.

3. *Learn to communicate about sex.* Sexual communication is linked to both sexual and relationship satisfaction (Montesi et al., 2011). It is essential in a sexual relationship. Many common problems—such as choosing an inconvenient time, too little erotic activity before intercourse, and too little tenderness afterward—are traceable largely to poor communication. Your partner is not a mind reader! You have to share your thoughts and feelings. Remember that both men and women say they want more instructions from their partner. If you are unsure about your partner's preferences, ask. And provide candid (but diplomatic) feedback when your partner asks for your reactions.

4. *Avoid focusing on sexual performance.* Sexual encounters are not tests or races. People can get overly concerned with issues like both partners reaching orgasm simultaneously. A grim determination to climax typically makes it harder to do so. This mental set can lead to disruptive habits like judging one's performance. Sexual experiences are usually best when people relax and enjoy themselves. It's better to adopt the philosophy that getting there is at least half the fun.

5. *Enjoy your sexual fantasies.* As we noted earlier, the mind is the ultimate erogenous zone. Although Freudian theory originally saw sexual fantasy as an unhealthy by-product of sexual frustration and immaturity, research shows that sexual fantasies are quite common and not indicative of sexual dysfunction (Kahr, 2008). Men and women both report that their sexual fantasies increase their excitement. So don't be afraid to use fantasy to enhance your sexual arousal.

Understanding Sexual Dysfunction

Many people struggle with *sexual dysfunctions—impairments in sexual functioning that cause subjective distress.* Figure 12.15 shows the prevalence of some of the most common sexual problems. Physical, psychological, and interpersonal factors can contribute to sexual problems. *Physical factors* include chronic illness, disabilities, some medications, alcohol, and drugs. *Individual psychological factors* include performance anxiety, negative attitudes about sexuality learned during childhood, fears of pregnancy and STDs, life stresses such as unemployment, and prior sexual abuse. *Interpersonal factors* include ineffective communication about sexual matters and unresolved relationship issues that fuel anger and resentment.

People commonly assume that a sexual problem resides in just one partner (physical or individual psychological factors). While this is sometimes the case, most sexual problems emerge out of partners' unique ways of relating to each other (interpersonal factors). Moreover, even in those cases where a problem may lie more with

Figure 12.15

Gender differences in reported sexual difficulties within the past year. This graph shows the results of a national survey of sexual behavior in Americans ages 18–59. The most commonly reported problem among men is erectile difficulties; in women common problems include orgasmic and lubrication difficulties. (Adapted from Herbenick et al., 2010a)

Unresolved sexual problems can be a source of tension and frustration in relationships. Physical, psychological, and interpersonal factors can contribute to sexual difficulties.

© Lucky Business/Shutterstock.com

one partner than another, the couple needs to work together for an acceptable solution. In other words, sexual problems belong to couples rather than to individuals.

Now let's examine the symptoms and causes of four common sexual dysfunctions: erectile difficulties, premature ejaculation, orgasmic difficulties, and low sexual desire.

Erectile difficulties occur when a man is persistently unable to achieve or maintain an erection adequate for intercourse. The traditional name for this problem is *impotence,* but sex therapists have discarded the term because of its demeaning connotation. A man who has never had an erection sufficient for intercourse is said to have *lifelong erectile difficulties.* A man who has had intercourse in the past but who is currently having problems achieving erections is said to have *acquired erectile difficulties.* The latter problem is more common and easier to overcome.

In a study of twenty-seven countries, nearly half the men surveyed reported having erectile difficulties if a broad criterion (the inability to get an erection adequate for satisfactory sexual performance) is used (Mulhall et al., 2008). In a national survey of American adults over the age of 50, 44% of men reported some erectile difficulty (Schick et al., 2010).

Physical factors besides aging can play a role in erectile dysfunction. For example, many cases may be the result of side effects from medication. A host of common diseases (such as obesity, diabetes, heart disease, and high blood pressure) can produce erectile problems as a symptom. Many temporary conditions, such as fatigue, worry

about work, an argument with one's partner, a depressed mood, or too much alcohol can cause such incidents. The most common psychological cause of erectile difficulties is anxiety about sexual performance. Anxiety may stem from doubts about virility or conflict about the morality of sexual desires. Interpersonal factors can have an effect if one's partner turns an incident into a major catastrophe. If the man allows himself to get unduly concerned about his sexual response, the seeds of anxiety may be sown.

Premature ejaculation occurs when sexual relations are impaired because a man consistently reaches orgasm too quickly. What is "too quickly"? To address this question, researchers asked a random sample of sex therapists from the United States and Canada for their expert opinions (Corty & Guardiani, 2008). They found that sustaining intercourse for 3 to 13 minutes is not worthy of concern. Obviously, time estimates, even from "experts," are arbitrary. The critical consideration is the subjective feelings of the partners. If either partner feels that the ejaculation is persistently too fast for sexual gratification, the couple have a problem. Although estimates of the pervasiveness of premature ejaculation vary, as many as one in three men might deal with this issue at some point in their lives (Mayo Clinic, 2011).

What causes this dysfunction? Some men who have a lifelong history of quick ejaculation may have a neurophysiological predisposition to the condition. Biological causes include hormones, thyroid problems, or inflammation of the prostate. Psychological causes can include stress, depression, or anger at one's partner. Some therapists believe that early sexual experiences in which a rapid climax was advantageous (or necessary to avoid being discovered) can establish a habit of rapid ejaculation (Mayo Clinic, 2009).

***Orgasmic difficulties* occur when people experience sexual arousal but have persistent problems in achieving orgasm.** When this problem occurs in men, it is often called *male orgasmic disorder*. The traditional name for this problem in women, *frigidity,* is no longer used because of its derogatory implications. Since this problem is much more common among women, we'll limit our discussion to them. A woman who has never experienced an orgasm through any kind of stimulation is said to have *generalized lifelong orgasmic difficulties*. Women who experience orgasms in some situations or only rarely are said to have *situational orgasmic difficulties*. Although lifelong orgasmic difficulties would seem to be the more severe problem, they are actually more responsive to treatment than situational orgasmic difficulties.

Physical causes of orgasmic difficulties are rare (medications can be a problem). One of the leading psychological causes is a negative attitude toward sex. Women who have been taught that sex is dirty or sinful are likely to approach it with shame and guilt. These feelings can undermine arousal, inhibit sexual expression, and impair orgasmic responsiveness. Arousal may also be inhibited by fear of pregnancy or excessive concern about achieving orgasm.

Some women have orgasmic difficulties because intercourse is too brief. Others fail to experience orgasms because their partners are unconcerned about their needs and preferences. But many couples simply need to explore sexual activities such as manual or oral stimulation of the clitoris that are more effective in producing female orgasm than sexual intercourse alone.

***Hypoactive sexual desire* is the lack of interest in sexual activity.** Individuals with this problem rarely initiate sex or tend to avoid sexual activities with their partner. It occurs in both men and women, but it is more common among women and tends to increase with age (Davison & Davis, 2011). In fact, low desire was the most commonly reported sexual problem for women in a national sample of adults age 57 to 85 (Lindau et al., 2007). In women, low sexual desire is most often associated with relationship difficulties. Other factors related to hypoactive desire include sexual abuse in childhood, stress, distraction, anxiety, depression, and body image dissatisfaction (Brotto et al., 2010). In men, low sexual desire is often related to embarrassment about erectile dysfunction (Carvalho & Nobre, 2011).

Coping with Specific Problems

With the advent of modern sex therapy, sexual problems no longer have to be chronic sources of frustration and shame. *Sex therapy* **involves the professional treatment of sexual dysfunctions.** Masters and Johnson reported high success rates for their treatments of specific problems, and there is a consensus that sexual dysfunctions can be overcome with regularity. The advent of medications (such as Viagra) to treat sexual problems has resulted in an increased emphasis on medical and individual treatments over relationship interventions. Nonetheless, couple-based treatment approaches definitely have their place and are often recommended (Goldhammer & McCabe, 2012). If you're looking for a sex therapist, be sure to find someone who is qualified to work in this specialized field. One professional credential to look for is that provided by the American Association of Sex Educators, Counselors, and Therapists (AASECT).

William Masters and Virginia Johnson

Bettmann/Corbis

Erectile Difficulties

According to Pfizer, the company that makes Viagra, the much-touted pill for treating erectile disorders is effective for up to four out of five men. Still, it is not without its drawbacks— some of them life threatening. Cialis and Levitra are two similar pills that enhance erec-

Jack Sullivan/Alamy

tions over a longer period (24 to 36 hours) than Viagra. These drugs affect the muscles in the penis, allowing them to relax, which in turn increases the blood flow and results in an erection. To work effectively, these pills must be incorporated into the couple's lovemaking style. The expectation that a pill alone will solve sexual problems that stem from relationship or psychological issues can set men up for additional sexual dysfunction (McCarthy, Bodnar, & Handal, 2004). There is evidence that exercising and staying physically active help maintain healthy erectile functioning (Janiszewski, Janssen, & Ross, 2009).

To overcome psychologically based erectile difficulties, the key is to decrease the man's performance anxiety. It is a good idea for a couple to discuss the problem openly. The woman (or other man, in a gay couple) should be reassured that the difficulty does not reflect lack of affection by her partner. Obviously, it is crucial for her to be emotionally supportive rather than hostile and demanding.

Masters and Johnson introduced an effective procedure for the treatment of erectile difficulties and other dysfunctions. *Sensate focus* **is an exercise in which part-**

ners take turns pleasuring each other while giving guided verbal feedback and in which certain kinds of stimulation are temporarily forbidden. One partner stimulates the other, who simply lies back and enjoys it while giving instructions and feedback about what feels good. Initially, the partners are not allowed to touch each other's genitals or to attempt intercourse. This prohibition should free the man from feelings of pressure to perform. Over a number of sessions, the couple gradually include genital stimulation in their sensate focus, but intercourse is still banned. With the pressure to perform removed, many men spontaneously get erections. Repeated arousals should begin to restore the man's confidence in his sexual response. As his confidence returns, the couple can move on gradually to attempts at intercourse.

Premature Ejaculation

Men troubled by premature ejaculation range from those who climax almost instantly to those who cannot last the time that their partner requires. In the latter case, simply slowing down the tempo of intercourse may help. Sometimes the problem can be solved indirectly by discarding the traditional assumption that orgasms should come through intercourse. If the female partner enjoys oral or manual stimulation, these techniques can be used to provide her with an orgasm either before or after intercourse. This strategy can reduce the performance pressure for the male partner, and couples may find that intercourse starts to last longer.

For the problem of instant ejaculation, two treatments are very effective: the *stop-start method* (Semans, 1956) and the *squeeze technique* (Masters & Johnson, 1970). With both, the woman brings the man to the verge of orgasm through manual stimulation. Then, she either stops stimulating him (stop-start technique) or squeezes the base or the end of his penis firmly for 3–5 seconds (squeeze technique) until he calms down. She repeats this procedure three or four times before bringing him to orgasm. These exercises can help a man recognize preorgasmic sensations and teach him that he can delay ejaculation. Medications such as certain antidepressants and topical anesthetic creams may also help (Mayo Clinic, 2009).

Orgasmic Difficulties

Negative attitudes and embarrassment about sex are often at the root of women's orgasmic difficulties. Thus, therapeutic discussions are usually geared toward helping nonorgasmic women reduce their ambivalence about sexual expression, become more clear about their sexual needs, and become more assertive about them. Sex therapists often suggest that women who have never had an orgasm try to have one by first using a vibrator and then shifting to masturbation, as the latter more closely approximates stimulation by a partner. Sensate focus is also an effective technique for treating orgasmic difficulties (Donahey, 2010).

When a woman's orgasmic difficulties stem from not feeling close to her partner, treatment usually focuses on couples' relationship problems more than on sexual functioning per se. Therapists also focus on helping couples improve their communication skills.

Hypoactive Sexual Desire

Therapists consider reduced sexual desire the most challenging sexual problem to treat (Aubin & Heiman, 2004). This is because the problem usually has multiple causes, which can also be difficult to identify. If the problem is a result of fatigue from overwork, couples may be encouraged to allot more time to personal and relationship needs. Sometimes hypoactive sexual desire reflects relationship problems. Treatment for reduced sexual desire is usually more intensive than that for more specific sexual disorders, and it is usually multifaceted to deal with the multiple aspects of the problem.

Medications can be used for low sexual desire. Hormonal therapies are used for both men and women. The medical and financial success of Viagra has encouraged pharmaceutical companies to develop drugs that will boost women's sexual desire (Marshall, 2005). Still, drugs will not solve relationship problems. For these, couples therapy is needed. And as we have seen for most problematic issues in this chapter, communication between partners is crucial.

CHAPTER 12 | Review

KEY IDEAS

BECOMING A SEXUAL PERSON

- One's sexual identity is made up of sexual orientation, sexual values and ethics, and erotic preferences. Physiological factors such as hormones influence sexual differentiation and anatomy more than they do sexual activity. Psychosocial factors appear to have more impact on sexual behavior. Sexual identity is shaped by families, peers, schools, religion, and the media. Because of differences in sexual socialization, sexuality usually has different meanings for males and females.
- Experts believe that sexual orientation is complex, with multiple components. The determinants of sexual orientation are not yet known but appear to be a complex interaction of biological and environmental factors.
- General attitudes toward homosexuals are negative but appear to be moving in a positive direction. Coming to terms with and disclosing sexual orientation is a complicated process. Recent evidence suggests that homosexuals are at greater risk for depression and suicide attempts than are heterosexuals, a phenomenon that might be linked to their membership in a stigmatized group.

INTERACTION IN SEXUAL RELATIONSHIPS

- Sexual motives can be grouped into approach and avoidance motives. One's motives for sex are linked to personal and relationship well-being. Men tend to be motivated more by physical gratification, whereas women are more likely to have emotional motives.
- Disparities between partners in sexual interest and erotic preferences lead to disagreements that require negotiation. Effective communication plays an important role in sexual and relationship satisfaction.

THE HUMAN SEXUAL RESPONSE

- The physiology of the human sexual response was described by Masters and Johnson. They identified four phases in the sexual response cycle: excitement, plateau, orgasm, and resolution. For a more complete view of this process, individuals' cognitive experiences during sexual encounters also need to be factored in.
- Women reach orgasm in intercourse less consistently than men, usually because foreplay and intercourse are too brief and because of gender differences in sexual socialization.

SEXUAL EXPRESSION

- Sexual fantasies are normal and are an important aspect of sexual expression. Kissing and touching are important erotic activities, but their importance is often underestimated by heterosexual males. Despite historically negative attitudes about masturbation, this practice is quite common, even among married people. Oral-genital sex has become a common element in most couples' sexual repertoires. Anal sex is less common.
- Coitus is the most widely practiced sexual act in our society. Sexual activities between gay males include mutual masturbation, fellatio, and, less often, anal intercourse. Lesbians engage in mutual masturbation, cunnilingus, and tribadism.

PATTERNS OF SEXUAL BEHAVIOR

- Hooking up, a phenomenon that has been on the rise since the 1990s, is a common practice for young adults. The casual sex associated with hookups is risky. Many young adults also engage in friends-with-benefits arrangements. These relationships can be tricky to negotiate.

- Sexual intimacy is a predictor of relationship stability. Younger married couples tend to have sex about two or three times a week. This frequency declines with age in both heterosexual and same-sex couples, though sexual activity in late adulthood is common.
- Most Americans strongly disapprove of extramarital sex. Infidelity is less common among married couples and lesbians and more common among gay male couples. People become involved in extradyadic relationships for a variety of reasons.

PRACTICAL ISSUES IN SEXUAL ACTIVITY

- Contraception and sexually transmitted diseases are two practical issues that concern many sexually active individuals. Many people who do not want to conceive a child fail to use contraceptive procedures effectively, if at all. Contraceptive methods differ in effectiveness and have various advantages and disadvantages.
- STDs are increasing in prevalence, especially among those under 25. The danger of contracting STDs is higher among those who have had more sexual partners. In the United States, the rates of HIV infections stemming from heterosexual sex are on the rise, particularly among black and Latino individuals. Using condoms decreases the risk of contracting STDs. Early treatment of STDs is important.

APPLICATION: ENHANCING SEXUAL RELATIONSHIPS

- To enhance their sexual relationships, individuals need to have adequate sex education and positive values about sex. They also need to be able to communicate with their partners about sex and avoid focusing on sexual performance. Enjoying sexual fantasies is also important.
- Common sexual dysfunctions include erectile difficulties, premature ejaculation, orgasmic difficulties, and hypoactive sexual desire. Treatments for low sexual desire are less effective than those for more specific sexual problems. Sex therapy can be useful.

KEY TERMS

Anal intercourse p. 369
Androgens p. 354
Bisexuals p. 353
Coitus p. 369
Cunnilingus p. 369
Erectile difficulties p. 381
Erogenous zones p. 367
Estrogens pp. 354–355
Fellatio p. 369
Gonads p. 354
Heterosexuals p. 353
Homophobia p. 362
Homosexuals p. 353
Hypoactive sexual desire p. 382
Masturbation pp. 368–369
Menarche p.355
Orgasm p. 366
Orgasmic difficulties p. 382
Premature ejaculation p. 381
Refractory period p. 366
Sensate focus pp. 382–383
Sex therapy p. 382
Sexual dysfunctions p. 380
Sexual identity p. 353
Sexually transmitted disease (STD) p. 376
Spermarche p. 355
Vasocongestion p. 365

KEY PEOPLE

Alfred Kinsey p. 360
William Masters and Virginia Johnson pp. 365–367, 382

CHAPTER 12 | Practice Test

1. Anthony has an "anything goes" attitude about sex. His partner thinks the type of relationship should determine what sexual activities are appropriate. Anthony has _____ sexual values whereas his partner has _____ sexual values.
   a. absolute; relativistic
   b. hedonistic; absolute
   c. relativistic; hedonistic
   d. hedonistic; relativistic

2. Which of the following statements about sexual orientation is true?
   a. Heterosexuality and homosexuality are best viewed as two distinct categories.
   b. Sexual orientation is complex and malleable.
   c. Biological factors alone probably determine sexual orientation.
   d. Environmental factors alone probably determine sexual orientation.

3. Stacy is in the initial phase of sexual arousal. Her muscles are tense and her heart rate and blood pressure are elevated. She is in which phase of Masters and Johnson's sexual response cycle?
   a. Foreplay
   b. Orgasm
   c. Excitement
   d. Resolution

4. Sexual fantasies
   a. are signs of abnormality.
   b. are quite normal.
   c. rarely include having sex with someone other than one's partner.
   d. are an excellent indication of what people want to experience in reality.

5. Regarding overall marital satisfaction and sexual satisfaction, research indicates there is
   a. a strong relationship.
   b. a weak relationship.
   c. no relationship.
   d. a strong relationship, but only in the first year of marriage.

6. Who of the following are most likely to have an "open" relationship?
   a. A heterosexual married couple
   b. A gay male couple
   c. A lesbian couple
   d. All are equally likely

7. Which of the following statements is true regarding infidelity?
   a. Women are more distressed by emotional infidelity, while men are more distressed by sexual infidelity.

   b. Women are more motivated by sexual excitement, whereas men are more motivated by relationship unhappiness.
   c. People between the ages of 18 and 30 are less likely to engage in sex outside a committed relationship than people over 50.
   d. The majority of people in American society today approve of extramarital sex.

8. Which of the following statements about condoms is true?
   a. It's okay to use oil-based lubricants with latex condoms.
   b. Polyurethane condoms are thicker than latex condoms.
   c. Skin condoms provide protection against STDs.
   d. It's okay to use water-based lubricants with latex condoms.

9. Sexually transmitted diseases
   a. are all very serious.
   b. have immediate symptoms.
   c. are most common among people under age 25.
   d. are most common among people between 26 and 40.

10. Which of the following is one of the text's suggestions for enhancing your sexual relationships?
    a. Set clear goals for each sexual encounter.
    b. Adhere to negative sexual values.
    c. Avoid giving your partner feedback.
    d. Pursue adequate sex education.

ANSWERS

1. d Page 354   6. b Page 372
2. b Page 360   7. a Page 373
3. c Page 365   8. d Page 376
4. b Page 368   9. c Page 378
5. a Page 371   10. d Page 380

COURSEMATE

Go to **CengageBrain.com** to access Psychology CourseMate, where you will find an interactive eBook, glossaries, flashcards, quizzes, videos, and more.

PERSONAL EXPLORATIONS WORKBOOK

Go to the *Personal Explorations Workbook* in the back of your textbook for exercises that can enhance your self-understanding in relation to issues raised in this chapter.

Exercise 12.1 *Self-Assessment:* Sexuality Scale

Exercise 12.2 *Self-Reflection:* How Did You Acquire Your Attitudes About Sex?

Careers and Work

© Stephen Coburn/Shutterstock.com

"Love and work . . . work and love, that's all there is." This quote is attributed to Sigmund Freud, whose opinions on love and sex are well known, if sometimes misunderstood. Less well known, however, is the fact that Freud viewed work as an important element in understanding the human condition. Working is a defining characteristic in the lives of many people; it may be *the* defining characteristic for Americans. Consider this: Do most of the people you know identify themselves by what they do in their careers? When you meet someone new, isn't one of the first things you ask something like, "So, what do you do for a living?" How people reply to this question reveals information not only about their occupation but also about their social status, educational background, lifestyle, personality, interests, aspirations, and aptitudes. In other words, work plays a pivotal role in adult life, particularly in the United States. According to a Gallup poll, 73% of Americans rate work as either "extremely" or "very important" in their life (Moore, 2003). In **Figure 13.1**, you can see that how people view their jobs is strongly correlated with their income. In a very real sense, people *are* what they do at work. If that observation makes sense to you, it should come as no surprise that being unemployed can have devastating consequences for people's sense of self and well-being.

Because work is such a significant aspect of life, psychologists take a great interest in it. ***Industrial/ organizational (I/O) psychology* is the study of human behavior in the workplace.** Industrial/ organizational psychologists strive to increase the dignity and performance of workers and the organizations for which they labor (Islam & Zyphur, 2009; Zedek, 2011). Among other issues, I/O psychologists study worker motivation and satisfaction, job performance, ethics in the workplace, leadership, occupational hazards, personnel selection, and diversity in organizations. A recent concern is how individuals balance work and

family life (Greenhaus & Powell, 2006; Major & Morganson, 2011). An imbalance between these two spheres can lead to what I/O psychologists call work-family conflict (e.g., Glavin & Schieman, 2012; Odle-Dusseau, Britt, & Greene-Shortridge, 2012).

We begin this chapter by reviewing some important considerations in choosing a career. Then we explore two models of career development and discuss women's career issues. Next, we examine how the workplace and workforce are changing and look at some occupational hazards such as job stress, sexual harassment, and unemployment. Finally, we address the important issues involved in balancing work, relationships, and leisure. In the Application, we offer some concrete suggestions for enhancing your chances of landing a desirable job.

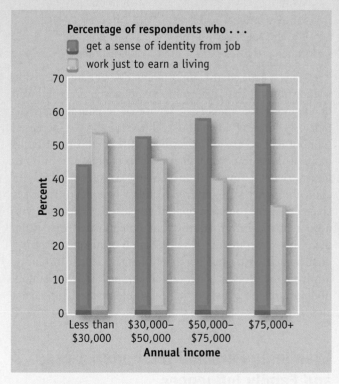

Figure 13.1

How workers view their jobs. The way workers view their jobs is strongly related to their income. Those who earn higher salaries are more likely to obtain a sense of identity from their work, whereas those who earn lower salaries typically see their jobs merely as a way to make a living. (Data from Moore, 2001)

CHOOSING A CAREER

LEARNING OBJECTIVES

- Describe personal and family influences on job choice.
- List helpful sources of career information and important aspects of potential occupations.
- Clarify the role of occupational interest inventories in career decisions.
- Outline six important considerations in choosing an occupation.

One of your biggest decisions in life is choosing a career. Think about it: The average person works at least 8 hours a day, 5 days a week, 50 weeks a year, for 40 to 45 years. Some people work much more and, admittedly, some work considerably less. Still, such a time commitment—really, a lifetime commitment—implies that you should both enjoy and be proficient at what you do for a living. Imagine the dissatisfaction, if not drudgery, that people who neither like their careers nor are adept at them feel all the time. Aside from sleeping, most people spend more time working than any other activity. Just consider a typical weekday:

Sleep	6–8 hours
Commute to and from work	1–2 hours
Work	8 hours
Prepare and eat meals	2 hours
TV and Internet time	1–3 hours
Other activities	1–2 hours

As you can see, the importance of your career decision is enormous. It may determine whether you are employed or unemployed, financially secure or insecure, happy or unhappy. Rapidly advancing technology and the increased training and education required to break into most fields make it more important than ever to choose carefully. In theory, what's involved in making a successful career choice is pretty straightforward. First, you need to have a clear grasp of your personal characteristics. Second, you need realistic information about potential careers. From there, it's just a matter of selecting an occupation that is a good match with your personal characteristics. In reality, however, the process is a lot more complicated than simply finding a match between these two elements. Let's take a closer look.

Examining Personal Characteristics and Family Influences

People with limited job skills and qualifications (education, training, experience) have limited job options. As a result, they often have to take whatever job is available rather than a job that is well suited for them. In a real sense, these individuals do not choose their jobs—the jobs choose them. In fact, *choosing* a career is a luxury usually afforded to the middle and upper classes. For those who *are* able to select a career, personal qualities and family influences come into play.

Personal Characteristics

Making career decisions can be scary. Individuals who exhibit *secure attachment* (see Chapter 9) and who have a sense of *self-efficacy* about career-relevant abilities (see Chapter 6) find it easier to make career choices (Fouad, 2007; Meredith, Merson, & Strong, 2007; Song & Chon, 2012). What other personal characteristics affect career choice? Although *intelligence* does not necessarily predict occupational success (Griffeth, Hom, & Gaertner, 2000), it does predict the likelihood of entering particular occupations. That's because intelligence is related to academic success—the ticket required to enter certain fields. Professions such as law, medicine, and engineering are open only to those who can meet increasingly selective criteria as they advance from high school to college to graduate education and professional training. The relationship between intelligence and occupational level generally holds well for men, but an ability-achievement gap exists for women, as we noted in Chapter 11.

Some psychologists have also wondered about the link between intelligence and job satisfaction. Although the topic has not received much attention, one study indicates that smart people tend to have lower job satisfaction than less-intelligent workers when the work in question is less complex or challenging (Ganzach, 1998). Thus, pursuing a career that matches one's intellectual abilities may be a wise decision.

Still, in many occupations, special talents are more important than general intelligence. *Specific aptitudes* that might make a person well suited for certain occupations include creativity, artistic or musical talent, mechanical ability, clerical skill, mathematical ability, and persuasive talents. A particularly crucial characteristic is *social skills,* since the teams and networking are increasingly important in a wide variety of organizations (de Janasz & Forret, 2008; Kozlowski & Bell, 2003). A worker must be able not only to get along well with peers but also to counsel or supervise them. Certainly, social-emotional or interpersonal intelligence—the ability to behave wisely in human relations and to accurately interpret emotions and intentions—is an important part of such social skills (Albrecht, 2009; Kafetsios et al., 2009; Lievens & Chan, 2010; Mayer, Salovey, & Caruso, 2008).

As people travel through life, they acquire a variety of *interests.* Are you intrigued by the business world? the academic world? international affairs? the outdoors? physical sciences? music? athletics? art and culture? human services? hospitality and recreation? The list of potential interests is virtually infinite. Because interests underlie your motivation for work and your job satisfaction, they should definitely be considered in your career planning.

Finally, it is important to choose an occupation that is compatible with your *personality* (Swanson & D'Achiardi, 2005). We'll examine the relationship between personality types and career choice in a later section.

Family Influences

Individuals' career choices are strongly influenced by their family background (Whiston & Keller, 2004). That is, the jobs that appeal to people tend to be like those of their parents. For instance, people who grow up in middle-class homes are likely to aspire to high-paying professions in law, medicine, or engineering. On the other hand, individuals from low-income families often lean toward blue-collar jobs in construction work, office work, and food services.

Family background influences career choice for several reasons. For one thing, a key predictor of occupational status is the number of years of education an individual has completed (Arbona, 2005). And because parents and children often attain similar levels of education, they are likely to have similar jobs. Second, career attainment is related to socioeconomic status. The factors that mediate this relationship are educational aspirations and attainment during the school years (Schoon & Parsons, 2002). This means that parents and teachers can help boost children's career aspirations and opportunities by encouraging them to do well in school. Although socioeconomic status seems to have more influence on career aspirations than ethnicity does (Rojewski, 2005), ethnic differences in aspirations are still found. For example, a cross-cultural and multiethnic study reported that Chinese and Asian American college students more often choose investigative (analytical, intellectual, mathematical) occupations, and their career decisions are more influenced by parents than European American college students' decisions are (Tang, 2002).

Finally, parenting practices come into play. Most children from middle-class homes are encouraged to be curious and independent, qualities that are essential to success in many high-status occupations. By contrast, children from lower-status families are often taught to conform and obey (Hochschild, 2003). As a result, they may have less opportunity to develop the qualities demanded in high-status jobs. As we noted in Chapter 11, parents' gender-role expectations also influence their children's aspirations and sometimes interact with socioeconomic status and ethnicity.

Researching Job Characteristics

The second step in selecting an occupation is seeking out information about jobs. Because the sheer number of jobs is overwhelming, you have to narrow the scope of your search before you can start gathering information.

Sources of Career Information

Once you have selected some jobs that might interest you, the next question is: Where do you get information about them? A helpful place to start is the *Occupational Outlook Handbook,* available in most libraries and on the Internet. This government document, published every two years by the U.S. Bureau of Labor Statistics, is a comprehensive guide to occupations. It includes job descriptions, education and training requirements, salaries, and employment outlooks for over 800 occupations.

If you want more detailed information on particular occupations, you can usually get it by doing some online

Kevin Winter/Staff/Getty Images

Ben Stiller decided to emulate his father, Jerry Stiller, by pursuing an acting career.

Learn More Online

Occupational Outlook Handbook (OOH) Online

Every two years the Bureau of Labor Statistics publishes the OOH, now available via the Internet. This guide to every occupation in the United States includes descriptions of the nature of each job and its working conditions, educational requirements, future employment, and earnings prospects. You can also find information about job and workforce trends here.

searching. If you're interested in a career in psychology, you can obtain a number of pamphlets or books from the American Psychological Association (APA) or consult a book dedicated to careers in psychology (Helms & Rogers, 2010; Kuther & Morgan, 2012; Landrum, 2009). Also, the APA website provides links to other sites describing more than 50 subfields in psychology, many of which provide useful career information. Related professions (social work, school psychology, and so on) also have webpages. You will find the addresses of these pages on Marky Lloyd's Careers in Psychology website.

Essential Information About Occupations

When you examine occupational literature and interview people, what kinds of information should you seek? To some extent, the answer depends on your unique interests, values, and needs. However, some things are of concern to virtually anyone. Workers typically give high ratings to good health insurance, retirement plans, limited job stress, and recognition for performing well (Saad, 1999). Some key issues you need to know about include:

- *The nature of the work.* What would your duties and responsibilities be on a day-to-day basis?
- *Working conditions.* Is the work environment pleasant or unpleasant, low key or high pressure?
- *Job entry requirements.* What education and training are required to break into this occupational area?
- *Ongoing training or education.* Will you need to continue learning within or outside the workplace in order to remain proficient at your occupation?
- *Potential earnings.* What are entry-level salaries, and how much can you hope to earn if you're exceptionally successful? What does the average person earn? What are the fringe benefits?
- *Potential status.* What is the social status associated with this occupation?
- *Opportunities for advancement.* How do you move up in this field? Are there adequate opportunities for promotion and advancement?
- *Intrinsic job satisfaction.* Apart from money and formal fringe benefits, what can you derive in the way of personal satisfaction from this job? Will it allow you to help people, have fun, be creative, or shoulder responsibility?

Learn More Online

Marky Lloyd's Careers in Psychology Page

For those who think they might want a job or career in psychology or allied fields, Professor Marky Lloyd has put together a fine set of resources to help in both planning and making the choice. Many of the resources are helpful to any student seeking career guidance and employment tips.

- *Future outlook.* What is the projected supply and demand for this occupational area?
- *Security.* Is the work apt to be stable, or can the job disappear if there is an economic downturn?

By the way, if you're wondering whether your college education will be worth the effort in terms of dollars and cents, the answer is yes. As we'll discuss shortly, the jobs that you can obtain with a college degree typically yield higher pay than those that require less education (Crosby & Moncarz, 2006). Indeed, by current estimates, across a lifetime a typical bachelor's degree leads to over $1 million of earnings more than a high school diploma (Reuters, 2012). But educational attainment alone does not predict who performs well in a given job setting (Hunter & Hunter, 1984). In other words, having a college degree is not as important as the grades you earn during college. Why? Higher grade point averages (GPAs) point to the ability to be trained (Dye & Reck, 1989), which in turn influences subsequent job performance (Roth et al., 1996), salary level (Roth & Clarke, 1998), and frequency of promotions (Cohen, 1984). Still, experts agree that the future belongs to those who are better educated (Gordon, 2006), and a main reason is the appeal education has for employers. Ng and Feldman (2009) found that employees with more education performed better at work, were good citizens of their organizations, were absent less frequently, and were much less likely to engage in on-the-job substance abuse than workers with less education.

Using Psychological Tests for Career Decisions

If you are undecided about an occupation, you might consider taking some tests at your campus counseling center. *Occupational interest inventories* **measure your interests as they relate to various jobs or careers.** These inventories help users identify vocational areas for choosing potential careers. Two widely used tests of this type are the Strong Interest Inventory (SII) (Kantamneni & Fouad, 2011) and the Self-Directed Search (SDS) (Brown, 2007). Another popular interest inventory is the Kuder Career Search with Placement Match (Zytowski & Kuder, 1999).

Occupational interest inventories do not attempt to predict whether you would be successful in various occupations (Aamodt, 2004). Rather, they focus more on the likelihood of job *satisfaction* than job *success* (Nye et al., 2011). When you take an occupational interest inventory, you receive many scores indicating how similar your interests are to the typical interests of people in various occupations. For example, a high score on the accountant scale of a test means that your interests are similar to those of the average accountant. This correspondence in interests does not guarantee that you would enjoy a career in accounting,

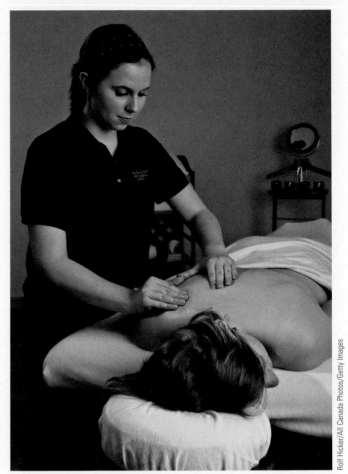

Randy Duchaine/Alamy

Rolf Hicker/All Canada Photos/Getty Images

People vary in their preferences for work environments. Some like high-pressure work; others prefer more low-key jobs.

but it is a moderately good predictor of job satisfaction (Hansen, 2005).

Although interest inventories can be helpful in working through career decisions, several cautions are worth noting. First, you may score high on some occupations that you're sure you would hate. Given the sheer number of occupational scales on the tests, this can easily happen by chance. However, you shouldn't dismiss the remainder of the test results just because you're sure that a few specific scores are "wrong." Second, don't let the test make career decisions for you. Some students naively believe that they should pursue whatever occupation yields their highest score. That is not how the tests are meant to be used. They merely provide information for you to consider. Ultimately, you have to think things out for yourself.

Third, you should be aware that most occupational interest inventories have a lingering gender bias (Einarsdóttir & Rounds, 2009). Many of these scales were originally developed 30 to 40 years ago when outright discrimination or more subtle discouragement prevented women from entering many traditionally "male" occupations. Critics assert that interest inventories have helped channel women into gender-typed careers, such as nursing and teaching, while guiding them away from more prestigious "male" occupations, such as medicine and engineering. Undoubtedly, this was true in the past. Recently, progress has been made toward reducing gender bias in occupational tests, although it has not been eliminated (Hansen, 2005). Research suggests that ethnic bias on interest tests is less of a concern than gender bias (Hansen, 2005), although some concerns remain (Fouad & Walker, 2005).

Taking Important Considerations into Account

As you contemplate your career options, here are some important points to keep in mind.

1. *You have the potential for success in a variety of occupations.* Career counselors stress that people have multiple potentials (Spokane & Cruza-Guet, 2005). Considering the huge variety of job opportunities, it's foolish to believe that only one career would be right for you. If you expect to find one job that fits you perfectly, you may spend your entire lifetime searching for it.

2. *Career success is apt to be linked to mobility.* Career paths are now more turbulent and subject to sudden, unexpected changes than in the past. Career success can hinge on your willingness to embrace moving from one job to another as expected and as a positive rather than negative quality associated with career evolution (Chudzikowski, 2011).

3. *Be cautious about choosing a career solely on the basis of salary.* Because of the tremendous emphasis on material success in America, people are often tempted to choose a career solely on the basis of income or status. However, research suggests that meaning and purpose, rather than money, lead to happiness and well-being (e.g., Diener & Biswas-Diener, 2008). Experts advise against following a strategy aimed at choosing a career based solely on projected earnings (Pollack, 2007). When people ignore personal characteristics in choosing a career, they risk being mismatched. Such job mismatching can result in boredom, frustration, and unhappiness with one's work, and these negative feelings can spill over into other spheres of life.

4. *There are limits on your career options.* Entry into a particular occupation is not simply a matter of choosing what you want to do. It's a two-way street. You get to make choices, but you also have to persuade schools and employers to choose you. Your career options will be limited to some extent by factors beyond your control, including fluctuations in the economy and the job market.

5. *Career choice is a developmental process that extends throughout life.* Occupational choice involves not a single decision but a series of decisions. Although this process was once believed to extend only from prepuberty to the early 20s, authorities now recognize that the process continues throughout life. Some experts predict that the average person will have ten jobs over the course of his or her working life (Levitt, 2006). Nonetheless, middle-aged people may underestimate the options available to them and therefore miss opportunities to make constructive changes. We want to emphasize that making occupational choices is not limited to youth.

6. *Some career decisions are not easily undone.* Although it's never too late to strike out in new career directions, it is important to recognize that many decisions are not readily reversed. Learning to exercise control over your career and the environment where you work is important (Converse et al., 2012). Few middle-aged lawyers suddenly decide to attend medical school or become elementary school teachers, for example, but it does happen. Once you invest time, money, and effort in moving along a particular career path, it may not be easy to change paths. And family responsibilities, especially child care and elder care, can make major career changes difficult. This potential problem highlights why it is important to devote careful thought to your occupational choice as soon as you can.

In the next section, we explore in greater detail how personal characteristics are related to career choice and career development.

MODELS OF CAREER CHOICE AND DEVELOPMENT

LEARNING OBJECTIVES

- Summarize Holland's model of career choice and Super's stage model of career development.
- Identify some differences between women's and men's career development.

How do people choose a career? Before interest inventories came along, career counselors routinely asked people to share their likes and dislikes, to identify individuals they admired, and to catalog their hobbies (Reardon et al., 2009). Self-reports and interest tests have their place, but psychologists are interested in more theoretically based approaches aimed at understanding how individuals make career choices and how their careers evolve over time. Theorists have developed several approaches to these issues. Here we examine two influential models.

Holland's Person-Environment Fit Model

The most influential trait model of career choice is that developed by John Holland (1996, 1997). According to Holland, career choice is related to an individual's personality characteristics (e.g., values, interests, needs, skills, learning styles, attitudes), which are assumed to be relatively stable over time. In Holland's system, people can be classified into one of six personality types, called *personal orientations.* Similarly, occupations can be classified into six ideal *work environments.*

According to Holland, people search for environments that allow them to exercise their abilities and skills, share their attitudes or values with others, and adopt agreeable problems and roles. They flourish when their personality type is matched with a work environment that is congruent with their abilities, interests, and self-beliefs. The term "work environment" should be viewed broadly, not narrowly, as it can be a job or an occupation, a field of study, an educational program, a college or a university, a leisure time activity, or the particular culture found within an organization. In fact, in Holland's view, a work environment can even be construed as a social relationship with another person or persons (Reardon et al.,

2009). A good match between one's personality and a work environment typically results in career satisfaction, achievement, and stability. Workers who fit well in their professional environments, for example, are less likely to report conflicts on the job or to display aggression in the workplace (Pseekos, Bullock-Yowell, & Dahlen, 2011). Holland's six personal orientations and their optimal work environments are shown in **Figure 13.2**.

Obviously, the six personal orientations are ideal types, and no one person will fit perfectly into any one type. In fact, most people are a combination of two or three types (Holland, 1996). You can take a rough stab at categorizing your own personal orientation by studying **Figure 13.2**. Look at the matching work environments to get some ideas for possible career options.

More research has been conducted on Holland's model than any other theory in vocational psychology—to date, around 1600 publications have examined it (Ruff, Reardon, & Bertoch, 2008)—and much of this research is supportive (Spokane & Cruza-Guet, 2005). For instance, researchers report that Holland's model describes the career preferences of ethnically diverse male and female college students relatively accurately (Fouad & Mohler, 2004). On

Bob Daemmrich/The Image Works

Those with a social personal orientation in Holland's theory are understanding and want to help others. Teachers typically score high on social orientation.

the other hand, people with good job-personality matches should be more satisfied with their jobs and likely to remain in these jobs longer than those who are less well matched, but research shows that job-personality fit contributes very little (5%) to job satisfaction (Fouad, 2007).

HOLLAND'S PERSONAL ORIENTATIONS AND RELATED WORK ENVIRONMENTS		
Themes	**Personal orientations**	**Work environments**
Realistic	Values concrete and physical tasks. Perceives self as having mechanical skills and lacking social skills.	*Settings:* concrete, physical tasks requiring mechanical skills, persistence, and physical movement *Careers:* machine operator, pilot, draftsperson, engineer
Investigative	Wants to solve intellectual, scientific, and mathematical problems. Sees self as analytical, critical, curious, introspective, and methodical.	*Settings:* research laboratory, diagnostic medical case conference, work group of scientists *Careers:* marine biologist, computer programmer, clinical psychologist, architect, dentist
Artistic	Prefers unsystematic tasks or artistic projects: painting, writing, or drama. Perceives self as imaginative, expressive, and independent.	*Settings:* theater, concert hall, library, radio or TV studio *Careers:* sculptor, actor, designer, musician, author, editor
Social	Prefers educational, helping, and religious careers. Enjoys social involvement, church, music, reading, and dramatics. Is cooperative, friendly, helpful, insightful, persuasive, and responsible.	*Settings:* school and college classrooms, psychiatrist's office, religious meetings, mental institutions, recreational centers *Careers:* counselor, nurse, teacher, social worker, judge, minister, sociologist
Enterprising	Values political and economic achievements, supervision, and leadership. Enjoys leadership control, verbal expression, recognition, and power. Perceives self as extraverted, sociable, happy, assertive, popular, and self-confident.	*Settings:* courtroom, political rally, car sales room, real estate firm, advertising company *Careers:* realtor, politician, attorney, salesperson, manager
Conventional	Prefers orderly, systematic, concrete tasks with verbal and mathematical data. Sees self as conformist and having clerical and numerical skills.	*Settings:* bank, post office, file room, business office, Internal Revenue office *Careers:* banker, accountant, timekeeper, financial counselor, typist, receptionist

Figure 13.2

Overview of Holland's theory of occupational choice. According to John Holland (1985), people can be divided into six personality types (personal orientations) that prefer different work environments, as outlined here.

Source: Adapted from Holland, J. L. (1985). *Making occupational choices: A theory of occupational personalities and work environments* (2nd ed.). Englewood Cliffs, NJ: Prentice-Hall.

In contrast to trait models such as Holland's that view occupational choice as a specific event, stage theories view occupational choice as a developmental process. We look at that approach next.

Super's Developmental Model

Columbia University Archives-Columbiana Library

Donald Super

A highly influential developmental model of career choice is that outlined by Donald Super (1988, 1990). He views occupational development as a process that begins in childhood, unfolds and matures gradually across most of the lifespan (Patton & Lokan, 2001), and ends with retirement (Giannantonio & Hurley-Hanson, 2006). Super asserts that the person's *self-concept* is the critical factor in this process. In other words, decisions about work and career commitments reflect people's attempts to express their changing views of themselves. To map these changes, Super breaks the occupational life cycle into five major stages and a variety of substages (see **Figure 13.3**).

Growth Stage

The growth stage occurs during childhood, when youngsters fantasize about exotic jobs they would enjoy. Generally, they imagine themselves as detectives, airplane pilots, and brain surgeons rather than plumbers, salespersons, and bookkeepers. Until near the end of this period, children are largely oblivious to realistic considerations such as the abilities or education required for specific jobs. Naturally, children's aspirations and expectations may vary widely because of their home and educational environments (Cook et al., 1996).

Exploration Stage

Pressures from parents, teachers, and peers to develop a general career direction begin to intensify during high school. By the end of high school, individuals are expected to have narrowed a general career direction into a specific one. Young people try to get a real taste of their intended occupation through reading about it or taking on part-time work. During the later part of this stage, youths typically seek full-time work. If their initial work experiences are gratifying, their tentative commitment will be strengthened. However, unrewarding early experiences may motivate individuals to shift to another occupation, where they will continue the exploration process. In effect, it's better to explore a particular career and discover it does not meet one's expectations sooner rather than later. Helwig (2008) found that while parent and teacher support is important, not enough career preparation occurs during the high school years, which means that the subsequent stage in Super's model becomes a very important one.

Establishment Stage

Vacillation in career commitment continues to be common during the first part of the establishment stage. Once people make gratifying occupational choices, their career commitment is strengthened. With few exceptions, future job moves will take place *within* the preferred occupational area. Having made a commitment, the person now needs to demonstrate the ability to function effectively in the area. To succeed, individuals must use previously acquired skills, learn new skills, and display flexibility in adapting to organizational changes.

Maintenance Stage

As the years go by, opportunities for further career advancement and occupational mobility decline. However, both formal and informal forms of lifelong learning are often necessary so that workers can keep pace with the ever-changing aspects of their current and future jobs (Pang, Chua, & Chu, 2008). Around their mid-40s, many people cross into the maintenance stage, during which they worry more about *retaining* their achieved status than *improving* it. Although middle-aged employees may need to update their skills to compete with younger workers, their primary goal is to protect the security, power, advantages, and perks that they have attained. With decreased emphasis on career advancement, many people shift energy and attention away from work in favor of family or leisure activities.

Decline Stage

Deceleration involves a decline in work activity in the years prior to retirement. People redirect their energy and attention toward planning for this major transition. Super's original formulation, which was based on research in the 1950s, projected that deceleration ought to begin at around age 65. Since the 1970s, however, the large Baby Boom cohort has created an oversupply of skilled labor and professional talent. This social change has created pressures that promote early retirement. Because of these conditions, deceleration often begins earlier than Super initially indicated. On the other hand, the recent economic recession and accompanying financial worries experienced by people in the United States and around the world may change things yet again. People who have lost their job or retirement savings may be planning a longer time horizon, so that their career deceleration may not begin until closer to age 70. A recent Gallup poll (2001), for example, revealed that 8 out of every 10 American workers believe they will continue working full- or part-time after they reach retirement age. A greater proportion of these workers, 44% to 36%, claim they will do so because they "want to" rather than because they "will have to."

Retirement brings work activity to a halt. People approach this transition with highly varied attitudes. Many

STAGES OF OCCUPATIONAL DEVELOPMENT		
Stage	Approximate ages	Key events and transitions
Growth stage	**0–14**	**A period of general physical and mental growth**
Prevocational substage	0–3	No interest or concern with vocations
Fantasy substage	4–10	Fantasy is basis for vocational thinking
Interest substage	11–12	Vocational thought is based on individual's likes and dislikes
Capacity substage	13–14	Ability becomes the basis for vocational thought
Exploration stage	**15–24**	**General exploration of work**
Tentative substage	15–17	Needs, interests, capacities, values, and opportunities become bases for tentative occupational decisions
Transition substage	18–21	Reality increasingly becomes basis for vocational thought and action
Trial substage	22–24	First trial job is entered after the individual has made an initial vocational commitment
Establishment stage	**25–44**	**Individual seeks to enter a permanent occupation**
Trial substage	25–30	Period of some occupational change due to unsatisfactory choices
Stabilization substage	31–44	Period of stable work in a given occupational field
Maintenance stage	**45–65**	**Continuation in one's chosen occupation**
Decline stage	**65+**	**Adaptation to leaving workforce**
Deceleration substage	65–70	Period of declining vocational activity
Retirement substage	71+	A cessation of vocational activity

Figure 13.3

Overview of Super's theory of occupational development. According to Donald Super, people go through five major stages (and a variety of substages) of occupational development over the life span.

Source: Adapted from Zaccaria, J. (1970). *Theories of occupational choice and vocational development.* Boston: Houghton Mifflin. Copyright © 1970 by Time Share Corporation, New Hampshire.

individuals look forward to it eagerly. Others approach it with apprehension, unsure about how they will occupy themselves and worried about their financial viability. Still others approach retirement with a combination of hopeful enthusiasm and anxious concern. Although retirement may mean less income, it can also mean more time to spend with friends and on hobbies, travel, and meaningful volunteer or charity work. For some, retirement from a primary career may prompt the launching of a new career.

As a stage theorist, Super deserves credit for recognizing that people follow different patterns in their career development. For example, he identified several patterns for both men and women that do not coincide with the conventional pattern we have described. In support of Super's model, it has been found that career maturity is correlated with self-esteem and self-efficacy (Creed, Prideaux, & Patton, 2005; Kornspan & Etzel, 2001). A more serious prob-

lem with Super's theory is that it assumes that people will remain in the same careers all of their working lives. But today's American workers will have many career changes, a reality that is incompatible with the assumptions of long-term models like Super's. The current thinking about career stages or cycles is that they are shorter and recur periodically over the course of a person's career (Greenhaus, 2003). To be useful, stage models must reflect today's workplace realities (Patton & Lokan, 2001).

Women's Career Development

It is currently estimated that 58.6% of adult women (versus 71.2% of men) are in the labor force (Hall & Solis, 2011; U.S. Bureau of the Census, 2006b; see also Toossi, 2007). Moreover, the odds that a woman will work outside the home during her adult life are greater than 90% (U.S. Department of Labor, 2003). In the last 50 years, women's employment has positively affected the U.S. economy, as well as the social and economic lives of families and the women themselves (Sloan Work and Family Research Network, 2009). Although women's labor force participation is approaching that of men's, important gender differences remain when it comes to career choice and development. For one thing, most women still subordinate their career goals to their husband's (Betz, 2005). This is even the case with academically gifted women (Arnold, 1995). If a married man wants or needs to move to another job, his wife typically follows him and takes the best job she can find in the new location. Hence, married women usually have less control over their careers than married men do. Also, the high divorce rate (around 45%) means that many women will have to provide for themselves and their children (Betz, 2006). One study reported that after a divorce, the woman's standard of living drops 27% (Weitzman, 1996). Today's women need to take these factors into account as they consider their career options.

Another gender difference concerns career paths. Men's career paths are usually *continuous,* whereas women's tend to be *discontinuous* (Betz, 1993). In other words, once men start working full-time, they usually continue to work. Women are more likely to interrupt their careers to concentrate on child-drearing or family crises (Hynes & Clarkberg, 2005). Because women are having fewer children and are returning to work sooner, the amount of time they are out of the labor force is decreasing. Although labor force discontinuity is a factor in women's lower salaries and status, there is also evidence that women are simply paid less than men (Dey & Hill,

2007). Women who do not have children usually remain in the labor force and tend to have a pattern of career advancement similar to men's (Blair-Loy & DeHart, 2003).

What about women whose husbands fit the traditional breadwinner model (i.e., he works, she cares for the home and children)? Interestingly, women whose spouses earned incomes in the top and bottom 20% of income levels had the lowest workforce participation rates (Cohany & Sok, 2007). Presumably, women who reside in households where the breadwinner model is still practiced have elected not to work outside the home.

THE CHANGING WORLD OF WORK

LEARNING OBJECTIVES

- Identify seven work-related trends.
- Describe the relationship between education and salary.
- Summarize demographic changes transforming the workforce, highlighting challenges posed by diversity.

Before you enter the working world, it's important to get your bearings. In this section we look at several important background issues: contemporary trends in the workplace, the relationship between education and earnings, and diversity in the workforce.

Workplace Trends

Work **is an activity that produces something of value for others.** For some people, work is just a way to earn a living; for others, work is a way of life. For both types of workers, the nature of work is undergoing dramatic changes, affecting people's identities (Reissner, 2010). Because such changes can affect your future job prospects, you need to be aware of seven important trends:

1. *Technology is changing the nature of work.* Computers and electronic equipment have dramatically transformed the workplace. From the worker's point of view, these changes have both down sides and up sides. On the negative side, computers automate many tasks that people perform, eliminating jobs. The digital workplace also demands that employees have more education and skills than were previously required (Cetron & Davies, 2003). And workers have to keep upgrading their technology skills, which can be stressful. On the positive side, technological advances allow employees to work at home and to communicate with others in distant offices and while traveling. Working at home while being electronically connected to the office is called *telecommuting* (Lautsch, Kossek, & Ernst, 2011), and approximately 45% of organizations use some form of it (SHRM, 2011). Telecommuting provides psychological as well as obvious practical benefits for workers, including lower levels of work-family life conflict, lower employee turnover, and higher job satisfaction (Gajendran & Harrison, 2007).

2. *New work attitudes are required.* Yesterday's workers could usually count on job security. Thus, many could afford a somewhat passive attitude in shaping their careers. But today's workers have job security only as long as they can add value to a company; organizational change is a frequent event (Burke, 2011). This situation means that workers must take a more active role in shaping their careers (Smith, 2000). In addition, they must develop a variety of valuable skills, be productive workers, and skillfully market themselves to prospective employers. In the new work environment, the keys to job success are self-direction, self-management, up-to-date knowledge and skills, flexibility, and mobility (Smith, 2000). Conscientious workers, then, would be wise to engage in ongoing self-assessment aimed at improving and expanding their skills.

The growth of technology is significantly changing the nature of work, with both positive and negative effects.

3. *Lifelong learning is a necessity.* Experts predict that today's jobs are changing so rapidly that in many cases, work skills will become obsolete over a 10- to 15-year period (Lock, 2005a). Thus, lifelong learning and training will become essential for employees. Every year, nearly one-third of American workers take courses to improve their job skills (American Council on Education, 1997). In some cases, retraining occurs on the job; in others, community colleges and technical institutes provide continuing education. Distance learning courses and programs are also available, although you have to watch out for bogus programs (Mariani, 2001). For suggestions on how to evaluate the quality and accreditation claims of distance education programs. Workers who know "how to learn" will be able to keep pace with the rapidly changing workplace and will be highly valued. Those who cannot, may be left behind.

4. *Independent workers are increasing.* Corporations are downsizing and restructuring to cope with the changing economy and to be competitive globally. In doing so, they are slashing thousands of permanent jobs and doling out the work to temporary employees or to workers in other countries, a practice termed *outsourcing.* By reducing the number of regular workers, companies can chop their expenditures on payroll, health insurance, and pension plans, as temporary employees don't typically receive such benefits. A leaner workforce also enables organizations to respond quickly to fast-changing markets. According to Daniel Pink (2001), one way to survive in this new environment is to become a "free agent" and hire out your skills to one or more organizations on a contract basis. Many professionals thrive on contract work; they have freedom, flexibility, and high incomes. But for those who are short on skills and entrepreneurial spirit, this work can be stressful and risky. About a third of independent employees would prefer to work for someone else than to work for themselves (Bond et al., 2003).

5. *The boundaries between work and home are breaking down.* As already noted, today's technological advances allow people to work at home and stay in touch with the office via the Internet, telephones, and fax machines. Working at home is convenient—workers save time (no commuting) and money (on gas, parking, clothes).

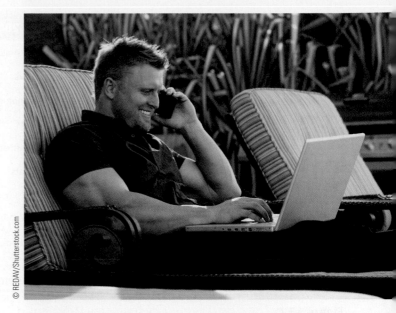

People who telecommute have the flexibility to work at home.

Still, family members and friends may interrupt home-workers, necessitating setting rules to protect work time. With the advent of smart phones, expanding wireless networks, and handheld computers, employees can be contacted any time and any place, making some workers feel as though they are on an "electronic leash." Looking at the flip side, the availability of onsite day care in some large companies means that a traditional home function has moved to the office (Drago, 2007). This development is largely a response to increases in the number of single-parent families and ***dual-earner households,* in which both partners are employed.** Consider this fact: Over 70% of today's workers have children under the age of 18 (U.S. Bureau of the Census, 2012b). Thus, quality onsite day care is a big draw to workers because it allows parents to interact with their children during the day.

6. *The highest job growth will occur in the professional and service occupations.* The United States, like many other industrialized nations, continues to shift from a manufacturing, or "goods-producing," economy to a service-producing one (U.S. Bureau of Labor Statistics, 2006). Whereas the bulk of yesterday's jobs were in manufacturing, construction, agriculture, and mining, the jobs of the next decade will be in the professional (and related technical) occupations and service occupations. Among the professional occupations, jobs in the computer and health-care industries are expected to expand dramatically. In psychology, jobs in health, clinical, counseling, and school psychology are expected to show strong growth. In the service occupations, strong job growth should occur in education, health services, social services, professional services, and business services. **Figure 13.4** on the next page depicts twenty occupations expected to grow the most and pay the most between now and 2018.

Learn More Online

DegreeInfo.com

If you need assistance evaluating distance learning programs, this site can help you. Its purpose is to disseminate accurate information about quality distance-based higher education programs. None of the writers for this site are currently affiliated with any school, although some of them are alumni of regionally accredited distance learning programs.

"BEST BET" OCCUPATIONS, 2008–2018	
Biomedical engineers	Physical therapist aides
Network systems and data communications analysts	Dental hygienists
	Veterinary technologists and technicians
Home health aides	Dental assistants
Personal and home care aides	Computer software engineers, applications
Financial examiners	Medical assistants
Medical scientists, except epidemiologists	Physical therapist assistants
Physician assistants	Veterinarians
Skin care specialists	Self-enrichment education teachers
Biochemists and biophysicists	Compliance officers, except agriculture, construction, health and safety, and transportation
Athletic trainers	

Figure 13.4

Fastest growth high-salary occupations. According to the U.S. Bureau of Labor Statistics, between 2008 and 2018 these 20 occupations will have the largest number of job openings and will provide the highest pay. Median annual salaries range from $85,430 (computer software engineers, applications) to $20,460 (home health aides). (Adapted from *Occupational Outlook Handbook*, 2010–2011)

7. *Job sharing is becoming more common.* Not everyone wants to work a 40-hour week or is able to do so. Having the opportunity to job share—that is, to share one job between two people—may be beneficial. Approximately 13% of organizations currently provide this option (Burke, 2005; Society for Human Resource Management, 2011). Job sharing often occurs when both spouses work in similar professions. For example, high school teaching is a good fit; the husband, a history instructor, can teach his classes in the morning, while his wife, a math teacher, can schedule her courses in the afternoons. When sharing a job, each person usually works 20 hours per week at separate times. A few hours per week may be conjoined so that each partner can update the other, as well as meet with their supervisor and other workforce members. As you can imagine, job sharing is ideal for couples who have small children or other family obligations (caring for elderly parents), are enrolled in degree programs, want to work part-time, or are considering gradually winding down their careers. Employers like job sharing because it promotes commitment to the organization while also attracting well-qualified individuals who could not otherwise accept a full-time position.

Education and Earnings

Although many jobs exist for individuals without a college degree, these jobs usually offer the lowest pay and benefits. In fact, all but 1 of the 50 highest-paying occupations require a college degree or higher (U.S. Bureau of Labor Statistics, 2004). (The high-paying job that doesn't require a college degree is air traffic controller.) Many construc-

tion management jobs, too, do not require a bachelor's degree (U.S. Bureau of Labor Statistics, 2012a). In **Figure 13.5**, you can see that the more you learn, the more you earn. Having a college degree is also associated with more career options, greater opportunities for professional advancement, and lower unemployment (Dohm & Wyatt, 2002). The link between learning and earning holds for both males and females, although, as you can see, men are paid approximately $7000 to $30,000 more than women with the same educational credentials. Despite legislation aimed at reducing discrepancies related to gender, research indicates that women continue to receive lower wages than men for holding the same or similar jobs (Blau & Khan, 2007). One estimate indicates women are now earning about 81% of what men earn (Kelleher, 2007). Pay parity has increased somewhat; in 1979, for example, women made only 63% of what their male counterparts earned (Kelleher, 2007).

On the other hand, a college diploma is no guarantee of a great job. In fact, many college graduates are underemployed. **Underemployment is settling for a job that does not fully utilize one's skills, abilities, and training.** Besides having implications for worker satisfaction, underemployment poses social and psychological challenges (Maynard & Feldman, 2011; McKee-Ryan & Harvey, 2011). About 18% of college graduates take jobs that don't usually require a college degree, and experts predict that this situation is unlikely to change in the near future (Lock, 2005a). And while it's true that the jobs one can obtain with a college degree pay more than those requiring less education, the higher-paying jobs go to college graduates with *college-level* reading, writing, and quantitative skills. College graduates without these skills more often end up in high-school-level jobs (Pryor & Schaffer, 1997).

Current employers are not very happy with the academic skills of many of their employees. According to a survey by the College Board's National Commission on Writing, a majority of U.S. employers say that about a third of their workers do not meet the writing requirements for their positions (College Entrance Examination Board, 2004). The ability to write clearly, concisely, and well is a skill that any savvy college graduate should tout to potential employers. As new jobs develop, they will require more education and higher skill levels. International com-

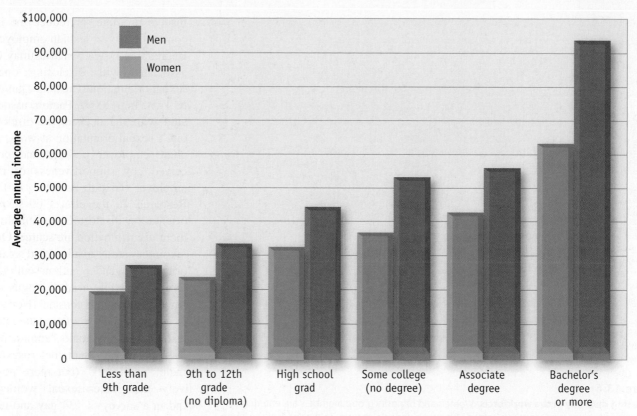

Figure 13.5

Education and income. This graph shows the average incomes of year-round, full-time workers age 18 and over, by gender and educational attainment. As you can see, the more education people have, the higher their income tends to be. However, at all levels women earn less than men with comparable education. (Data from U.S. Bureau of the Census, 2012a)

petition and technology are the two driving forces here (Toossi, 2009). Thus, computer literacy is also an essential complement to a good basic education.

The Changing Workforce

The *labor force* consists of all those who are employed as well as those who are currently unemployed but are looking for work. In this section, we look at some of the changes affecting the labor force and consider how women and other minorities fare in the workplace.

Demographic Changes

The workforce is becoming increasingly diverse with regard to both gender and ethnicity (Howard, 1995). In 2005, 61% of married women worked, compared to 41% in 1970 (U.S. Bureau of the Census, 2012a). This percentage increase holds even for women with very young children. For instance, in 1975 only 33% of women with children under the age of 3 worked outside the home; by 2005, this number had grown to 57% (U.S. Bureau of the Census, 2012b). These changes have implications not only for work and family life but also for men's and women's roles.

The workforce is also becoming more ethnically diversified (see **Figure 13.6** on the next page) (U.S. Bureau of

Labor Statistics, 2006). High school graduation rates for Asian Americans match those for European Americans, but college graduation rates for Asian Americans exceed those of European Americans. Both high school and college graduation rates of Hispanics and African Americans lag behind those of European Americans, although they have been improving in recent decades (Worthington, Flores, & Navarro, 2005). Consequently, both groups are at a disadvantage when it comes to competing for the better jobs.

Although gay, lesbian, and bisexual workers have been longstanding participants in the workplace, they are often "closeted" for fear of discrimination. Most of these workers do not have the same legal protections against employment discrimination as their heterosexual counterparts (Badgett,

Learn More Online

U.S. Department of Labor

With primary responsibility for many job- and work-related matters in the U.S. government, the Labor Department offers a site that can serve as a base to explore a variety of topics, including wages and compensation, worker productivity, and the legal rights of workers (such as protection from sexual harassment).

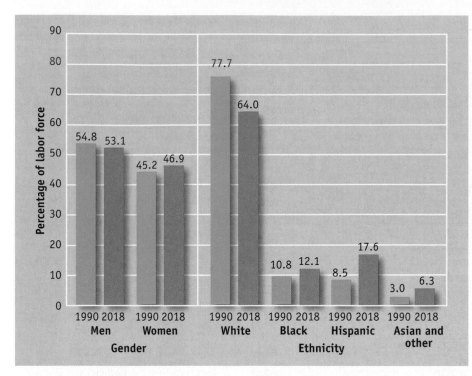

Figure 13.6

Increasing diversity in the workforce. Women and minority group members are entering the workforce in greater numbers than before. This graph projects changes in the share of the labor force by gender and by ethnicity between 1990 and 2018. (Data from Toossi, 2009)

2003); thus, wage gaps can exist because of sexual orientation. One recent study suggests that gay men tend to earn somewhat less than heterosexual men, while lesbians may earn somewhat *more* than heterosexual women (Antecol, Jong, & Steinberger, 2008). Further, disclosing one's sexual orientation may cause a homophobic supervisor to fire, re-

John Browne, the long-time chief executive of British Petroleum and close associate of former British Prime Minister Tony Blair, had little choice but to resign after a judge cleared the way for a newspaper to publish allegations made by a former boyfriend. The exposé of Browne's private life ended his 41-year career at British Petroleum. The stunning demise of Browne's career demonstrates why many gay individuals choose to remain "closeted" in the workplace out of concern about recriminations.

fuse to promote, or reduce the income of a gay or lesbian employee. Regrettably, wage penalties may be associated with disclosing one's sexual orientation (Cushing-Daniels & Tsz-Ying, 2009). Factors associated with the decision to disclose one's sexual orientation at work include employer policies and perceived gay supportiveness of the employer (Griffith & Hebl, 2002). Research on the effects of sexual orientation disclosure and employment discrimination are scarce. One laboratory study manipulated sexual orientation, gender, and masculinity/ femininity while holding bogus résumé qualifications constant (Horvath & Ryan, 2003). Participants rated lesbian and gay male "applicants" less positively than heterosexual male "applicants" (but more positively than heterosexual women). And in a survey of 534 gay and lesbian employees, more heterosexism— showing discriminatory favoritism for heterosexuals over homosexuals—was reported with male supervisors or male work teams, and these effects were stronger for lesbians than for gay men (Ragins, Cornwell, & Miller, 2003).

Today's Workplace for Women and Minorities

Recent years have seen a dramatic upsurge in the number of females and ethnic minorities in the workplace. Is today's workplace essentially the same for these groups as it is for white males? In many respects, the answer appears to be no (Denmark, German, & Brodsky, 2011). Although job discrimination on the basis of race and gender has been illegal for more than 40 years, women and minority group members continue to face obstacles to occupational success. Foremost among these obstacles is *job segregation.* Jobs are simultaneously typed by gender and by race. For example, skycaps are typically African American males, and most hotel maids are minority females. Most white women and minority workers tend to be concentrated in jobs where there is little opportunity for advancement or increase in salary (Equal Employment Opportunity Commission, 2007). Also, as we discussed in Chapter 11, workers in female-dominated fields typically earn less than those in male-dominated fields, even when the jobs require similar levels of training, skill, and responsibility.

More women and ethnic minorities are entering higher-status occupations, but they still face discrimination because they are frequently *passed over for promotion* in

REEL RESEARCH

Using Groups to Change Prejudice

Log on to CourseMate at www.cengagebrain.com to watch this video.

By encouraging co-workers to collaborate with people from different racial backgrounds, managers can help promote positive attitudes among members of a group. Although being part of a team can reduce negative feelings, unconscious or implicit associations can influence people's reactions, as demonstrated in this Reel Research video.

Mahzarin Banaji, a social psychologist at Harvard University, helped develop the Implicit Associations Test (IAT), which demonstrated that white participants made more negative associations when presented with black faces than with white faces. In a related study, researchers scanned subjects' brains while images of black and white faces were displayed subliminally on a screen. Results from this study corroborated Banaji's findings by demonstrating a stronger reaction in the amygdala—the fear center of the brain—when white participants viewed black faces than when they saw white faces.

Jay Van Bavel and Wil Cunningham, social cognitive neuroscientists at Ohio State University, study how implicit associations affect behavior. They have determined that the amygdala responds to both negative and positive stimuli—but most importantly that it detects what is relevant. By making race less relevant, the researchers believe they can reduce unconscious racial prejudice.

In another demonstration, white participants are assigned to a team (Tigers or Lions) and told to become familiar with all of the faces on both teams. Each team includes

four white males and four black males. Participants play a game in which they view words, half positive and half negative, along with the faces of team members from both the Tigers and Lions. They are asked to categorize the words as either good or bad and are given very little time to make a choice. As Van Bavel and Cunningham had hoped, belonging to the same group improved the likelihood that a participant would associate white and black faces from their own team with positive words. Interestingly, white members of the outgroup, or other team, also received positive associations, while black members of the outgroup received negative associations.

Watch the *Reducing Racial Prejudice* video to learn more about implicit associations. Delve even deeper by responding to the following discussion questions.

DISCUSSION QUESTIONS

1. Describe the first demonstration discussed in the video. How is the Implicit Associations Test conducted? Why are the participants' reactions considered unconscious responses?

2. How does Van Bavel and Cunningham's study place less relevance on race? What important factors are necessary to make race less relevant?

3. How can people shape their emotional responses to members of outgroups? How can outgroup members be made a part of the ingroup?

favor of white men (Whitley & Kite, 2006). This seems to be a problem especially at higher levels of management (Cotter et al., 2001). For example, in 2010, about 14.4% of corporate officer positions in Fortune 500 companies were

held by women (Catalyst, 2011), while an earlier estimate found that only about 1.5% were held by women of color (Catalyst, 2007). Furthermore, discrimination toward women and ethnic and other minorities (gays, lesbians) is now more covert, subtle, and indirect (Nadal, 2011; Nadal & Haynes, 2012). Employers and fellow employees are less likely to display overt discriminatory behaviors. Instead, however, they may hold onto prejudices that leak out unconsciously in their exchanges with members of diverse groups (Nadal, 2008; Sue et al., 2008).

There appears to be a *glass ceiling*, **or invisible barrier that prevents most women and ethnic minorities from advancing to the highest levels of occupations** (see **Figure 13.7**). The fact that very few black women are in managerial positions has caused some to term the glass ceiling a "concrete wall" for women of color. Women continue to be underrepresented at the upper levels of corporate life (Barreto, Ryan, & Schmitt, 2009). Largely because of these reduced opportunities for career advancement, some female corporate managers are quitting their jobs and starting their own firms. In 2007 women owned 28.7% of nonfarm U.S. businesses (National Association of Women Business Owners, 2010). At the other end of the job spectrum, there seems to be a "sticky floor" that causes women and minorities to get stuck in low-paying occupations (Brannon, 2005).

When only one woman or minority person is employed in an office, that person becomes a *token*—**or a symbol of all the members of that group.** Tokens are more distinctive or visible than members of the dominant majority (Richard & Wright, 2010). And, as we discussed in Chapter 7, distinctiveness makes a person's actions subject to intense scrutiny, stereotyping, and judgments. Thus, if a white male makes a mistake, it is explained as an *individual* problem. When a token woman or minority person makes a mistake, it is seen as evidence that *all* members of that group are incompetent. Hence, tokens experience a

great deal of *performance pressure,* an added source of job stress (King et al., 2010). Interestingly, if tokens are perceived as being "too successful," they may be labeled "workaholics" or may be accused of trying to "show up" members of the dominant majority. These unfavorable perceptions may be reflected in performance appraisals. The performance of successful white men is less likely to be interpreted in these negative ways.

Another way the world of work is different for women, ethnic, and gay and lesbian minorities is that they have *less access to same-gender or same-group role models and mentors* (Murrell & James, 2001). Finally, *sexual harassment,* a topic we'll take up later, is much more likely to be a problem for working women than for working men. In sum, women and minority individuals must contend with discrimination on the job in a number of forms.

The Challenges of Change

The increasingly diverse workforce presents challenges to both organizations and workers. These challenges can occur within the workplace as well as within the community where the workplace and workers reside (Pugh et al., 2008). Important cultural differences exist in managing time and people, in identifying with work, and in making decisions (Thomas, 2005). These differences can contribute to conflict. Not surprisingly, perhaps, members of majority groups (generally white males) do not perceive discrimination as often as the members of minority groups do (Danaher & Branscombe, 2010). Another challenge is that some individuals feel that they are personally paying the price of prejudice in the workplace, and this perception causes resentment. Recognizing the problem, some corporations offer diversity training programs for their employees.

Figure 13.7

The glass ceiling for women and minorities. A longitudinal study looked at the chances of promotion to a managerial position in a sample of more than 26,000 adults over 30 years of career experience. This graph shows that promotion chances increased along with career experience for white men. By contrast, the promotion chances of white women and black men were much lower. As you can see, black women lagged far behind all groups. These trends are consistent with the existence of a glass ceiling for women and minorities.

Source: From Maume, D. J. (2004). Is the glass ceiling a unique form of inequality? *Work and Occupations, 31*(2), 250–274. Copyright © 2004 by Sage Publications. Reprinted by permission of Sage Publications.

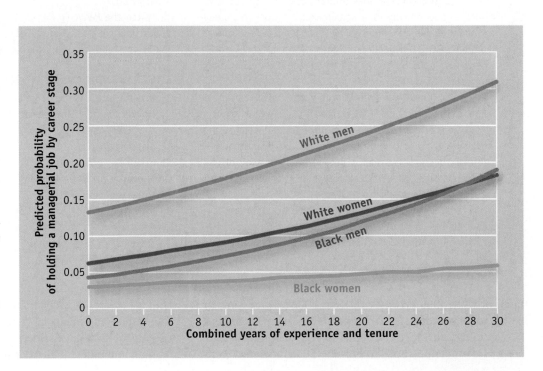

Many who advocate abandoning affirmative action programs that are intended to promote access to jobs for women and minorities argue that these programs promote "reverse discrimination" through the use of unfair hiring and promotion practices. For some, this perception may reflect a sense of *privilege,* an unquestioned assumption that white males should be guaranteed a place in society and that others should compete for the remaining jobs (Jacques, 1997). Not surprisingly, women and ethnic minority group members hold more positive views of affirmative action than do males and people who are not minority group members (Harrison et al., 2006). Some also argue that affirmative action undercuts the role of merit in employment decisions and sets up (supposedly) underprepared workers for failure. Many laboratory studies show that individuals have negative feelings about employees who may have been hired under affirmative action (Crosby et al., 2003; Evans, 2003). However, studies conducted with actual workers have not found this situation (Taylor, 1995). Regardless, this potential negative effect can be counteracted when workers know that decisions are based on merit as well as on group membership.

To minimize conflict and to maintain worker productivity and satisfaction, companies can provide well-designed diversity programs, and managers can educate themselves about the varied values and needs of their workers (Ocon, 2006). Similarly, both majority and minority employees must be willing to learn to work comfortably with those who come from other backgrounds.

Let's close this section with some good news regarding diversity. According to one survey, 92% of human resources directors connect recruiting diverse employees to their organizations' strategic hiring plans (Koc, 2007). Within the contemporary world of work, diversity is here to stay.

COPING WITH OCCUPATIONAL HAZARDS

LEARNING OBJECTIVES

- Recognize some important sources of job stress.
- Summarize the effects of job stress on physical and mental health.

- Describe the prevalence and consequences of sexual harassment.
- Identify some causes and effects of unemployment.

Work can bring people deep satisfaction; indeed, it can promote psychological health and well-being (Blustein, 2008). Yet work can also be a source of frustration and conflict. In this section, we explore three challenges to today's workers: job stress, sexual harassment, and unemployment.

Job Stress

You saw in Chapter 3 that stress can emerge from any corner of your life. However, many theorists suspect that the workplace is the primary source of stress in modern society. To begin, let's consider this sobering statistic: Over 75% of the workers in the United States claim that their jobs are stressful (Smith, 2003). To put this statistic into context, let's compare the typical stressors experienced by younger adults (ages 17–21) and those of older (25+), working adults. As you can see in the left column of **Figure 13.8** on the next page, younger people are troubled more by personal stressors, whereas older adults are troubled primarily by work-related stressors (right column). Let's examine the pervasive problem of job stress and see what employers and workers can do about it.

Sources of Stress on the Job

Between 2001 and 2004, the number of Americans claiming to feel overworked rose from 28% to 44% (Galinsky et al., 2005). Current estimates clock the average full-time

CATHY

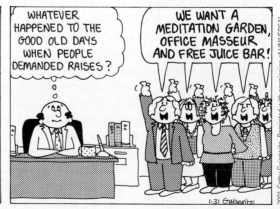

COMMON STRESSORS FOUND IN YOUNGER AND OLDER ADULTS	
Young adults (age 17–21)	**Older adults (age 25 and beyond)**
Graduating from high school	Organizational change
Beginning college	Job insecurity (downsizing)
Leaving home	Balancing work and family demands
Nagging parents	Paying bills
Peer pressure	Increasing job demands
Taking exams	Dull or unchallenging work
Fear of the future	Work overload (time pressure)
Graduating from college	Lack of supervisor or co-worker support
Job search	Unpleasant or dangerous work settings
Starting a new job	Pay inequity
Interviewing for jobs	Attending school while working full time
Financial concerns (school loans)	Job relocation
	Planning for retirement

Figure 13.8

Common stressors found in younger and older adults. Compare and contrast the typical sources of stress reported by younger and older adults. Do any of these stressors reflect your own experiences? As you can see, as people get older, their stress increasingly comes from work-related issues.

Source: Adapted from Aamodt, M. (2010). *Industrial/organizational psychology: An applied approach.* Belmont, CA: Wadsworth/Cengage. © 2010 Wadsworth, a part of Cengage Learning, Inc. Reproduced by permission.www.cengage.com/permissions.

workweek at 48 hours; in law and finance, 60-hour weeks are common (Hodge, 2002). According to a United Nations report, the average American worked 1,978 hours in 2000, up from 1,942 hours in 1990 (International Labour Office, 2002). That's an increase of nearly a full week over the previous decade. Compare this situation to that in Canada, Japan, and Mexico, where the average worker put in about 100 hours, or 2.5 weeks, less than American workers in 2000. Germans worked nearly 12.5 weeks less than Americans in 2000. Also, among affluent nations, only the United States does not require a minimum number of sick days for workers (Heymann et al., 2004).

In addition to long hours, common job stressors include lack of privacy, high noise levels, unusual hours (such as rotating shifts), the pressure of deadlines, lack of control over one's work, inadequate resources to do a job, and perceived inequities at work (Fairbrother & Warn, 2003). Environmental conditions, such as workplace temperature (e.g., extreme heat in a steel mill, excessive cold in a meat-packing plant), can affect physical, cognitive, and perceptual tasks (Evans et al., 2012). Fears of being downsized, concerns about health-care benefits (losing them or paying increasingly higher premiums), and worries about losing pension plans also dog workers in today's

economy. Office politics and conflict with supervisors, subordinates, and co-workers also make the list of job stressors (Chang, Rosen, & Levy, 2009; Miller, Rutherford, & Kolodinsky, 2008). People are also stressed when their personal philosophies are at odds with their company's views (Kristof-Brown, Zimmerman, & Johnson, 2005). For example, imagine the psychological challenges of being an environmentalist while working for an oil company advocating drilling in the Arctic reserve.

Having to adapt to changing technology and automated offices is another source of work stress. Firefighters, law enforcement officers, and coal miners face frequent threats to their physical safety. High-pressure jobs such as air traffic controller and surgeon demand virtually perfect performance, as errors can have disastrous consequences. Ironically, "underwork" (boring, repetitive tasks) can also be stressful.

Women may experience certain workplace stressors, such as sex discrimination and sexual harassment, at higher rates than men (Betz, 2006). African Americans and ethnic minorities must cope with racism and other types of discrimination on the job (Betz, 2006), which means members of minority groups may experience higher levels of stress than nonminorities do (Sulsky & Smith, 2005). Discrimination is also a problem for gay and lesbian employees (Badgett, 2003). Workers from lower socioeconomic groups typically work in more dangerous jobs than workers from higher socioeconomic status do.

Why are American workers so stressed out? According to Gwendolyn Keita and Joseph Hurrell (1994), four factors are the culprits:

1. *More workers are employed in service industries.* Workers in these jobs must interact with a variety of individuals on a daily basis. While most customers are civil and easy to deal with, some are decidedly difficult. Nonetheless, even obnoxious and troublesome customers are "always right," so workers have to swallow their frustration and anger, and doing so is stressful. Such situations may contribute to residual stress, where strain and tension from work are carried over because workers have a hard time "letting go." Imagine the frustration some workers must feel if their jobs do not allow them to be "right" or to speak candidly to customers.

David Young-Wolff/Photographer's Choice/Getty Images

2. *The economy is unpredictable.* In the age of takeovers and bankruptcies, even excellent workers aren't assured of keeping their jobs like workers in the past. Change in response to economic pressures often comes in the form of downsizing or restructuring (Robinson & Griffiths, 2005). Thus, the fear of job loss may lurk in the back of workers' minds. People may expend considerable time and emotional energy worrying about various "what if?" scenarios about their future, a future they cannot directly control. Sometimes, even those who get to keep their jobs following corporate upheavals are not spared psychological challenges, as they may develop a "survivor syndrome" (Marks & De Meuse, 2005).

3. *Rapid changes in computer technology tax workers' abilities to keep up.* Computers have taken over some jobs, forcing workers to develop new skills and to do so quickly. In other jobs, the stress comes from rapid and ongoing advances in technology (software as well as hardware) that force workers to keep pace with the changes. Workers may feel that they do not have the appropriate skills or the needed resources to complete tasks in allotted timeframes (Bolino & Turnley, 2005).

4. *The workplace is becoming more diverse.* As more women and minority group members enter the workplace, individuals from all groups must learn to interact more with people who are unfamiliar to them. Developing these skills takes time and may be stressful.

Taking a broader view, Robert Karasek contends that the two key factors in occupational stress are the *psychological demands* made on a worker and a worker's amount of *decision control* (Karasek & Theorell, 1990). Psychological demands are measured by asking employees questions such as "Is there excessive work?" and "Must you work fast (or hard)?" To measure decision control, employees are asked such questions as "Do you have a lot of say in your job?" and "Do you have freedom to make decisions?" In Karasek's demand-control model, *stress is greatest in jobs characterized by high psychological demands and low decision control.* Based on survey data obtained from workers, he has tentatively mapped out where various jobs fall on these two key dimensions of job stress, as shown in **Figure 13.9**. The jobs thought to be most stressful are those with heavy psychological demands and little control over decisions (see the lower right area of the figure). Considerable research has been conducted on the demand-control model, most of which has been supportive (Sonnentag & Frese, 2003).

Still, some criticize the model as being too simplistic (Ippolito et al., 2005).

Effects of Job Stress

As with other forms of stress, occupational stress is associated with numerous negative effects. In the work arena itself, job stress has been linked to an increased number of industrial accidents, increased absenteeism, poor job performance, and higher turnover rates (Colligan & Higgins, 2005). Experts estimate that stress-related reductions in workers' productivity may cost American industry hundreds of billions per year. Just under 3% of the workforce is absent on any given workday in the United States, and 13% of all employee absences can be chalked up to the impact of stress (Commerce Clearing House, 2007).

When job stress is temporary, as when important deadlines loom, workers usually suffer only minor and brief effects of stress, such as sleeplessness or anxiety. Prolonged high levels of stress are more problematic, as those who work in people-oriented jobs such as human services, education, and health care can attest (Maslach, 2005). A chief reason for the prevalence of burnout in these professions is ongoing amount of "people work," that

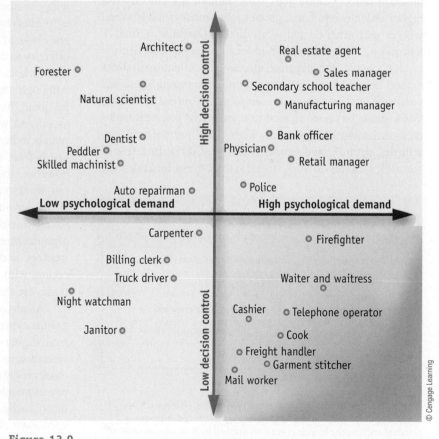

Figure 13.9

Karasek's model of occupational stress as related to specific jobs. Robert Karasek (1979) theorizes that occupational stress is greatest in jobs characterized by high psychological demands and low decision control. Based on survey data, this chart shows where various familiar jobs fall on these two dimensions. According to Karasek's model, the most stressful jobs are those shown in the shaded area on the lower right.

Sally Forth

is, performing the emotional labor required by clients, customers, students, and patients (Brotherridge & Grandey, 2002). As we noted in Chapter 3, prolonged stress can lead to *burnout,* characterized by exhaustion, cynicism, and poor job performance (Maslach, 2005). People's personalities and the nature of the work and careers they choose, too, can influence burnout (Lohmer, 2012). **Figure 13.10** lists some of the most common signs of burnout among workers. The feelings of listlessness, detachment, and potential for depression among employees with burnout are linked with higher absenteeism rates, greater job turnover, and lowered worker performance and work quality (Jawahar, Stone, & Kisamore, 2007; Ybema, Smulders, & Bongers, 2010).

Of course, the negative effects of occupational stress extend beyond the workplace. Foremost among these adverse effects are those on employees' *physical health.* Work stress has been related to a variety of physical maladies, including heart disease, high blood pressure, ulcers, arthritis, asthma, and cancer (Thomas, 2005). In a test of Karasek's model of work stress, symptoms of heart disease

were more prevalent among Swedish men whose jobs were high in psychological demands and low in decision control (Karasek et al., 1981). Job stress can also have a negative impact on workers' *psychological health.* Occupational stress has been related to distress, anxiety, and depression (Blackmore et al., 2007; Melchior et al., 2007).

Dealing with Job Stress

There are essentially three avenues of attack for dealing with occupational stress (Ivancevich et al., 1990). The first is to intervene at the *individual* level by modifying workers' ways of coping with job stress. For example, workers often try to deal with job stress by taking themselves out of the workplace for a short time, such as taking a vacation. Although vacations can help people recharge their professional batteries by reducing stress and the feelings associated with burnout, the benefits are temporary. Research indicates symptoms of stress and burnout do drop just before, during, and immediately following vacations; however, they tend to return to their original levels a few weeks later (Etzion, 2003). The second is to intervene at the *organizational* level by redesigning the work environment itself. The third is to intervene at the *individual-organizational interface* by improving the fit between workers and their companies. Concrete suggestions for coping with stressors, including those found in the workplace, are discussed in Chapter 4.

As already noted, workers from lower socioeconomic groups typically experience more work stress than those from higher-status groups. Ironically, these are the workers who receive less attention through stress management and other programs (Ilgen, 1990). Researchers are beginning to pay more attention to working-class and low-income families (Crosby & Sabattini, 2006). Perhaps their findings will encourage changes in the workplace.

COMMON SIGNS OF BURNOUT AMONG WORKERS	
Low energy	Negativity and complaining attitude
Lessened productivity	Increased forgetfulness
Apathy	Dread of going to work
Routinely late for work	Sense of being overwhelmed
Limited concentration	Frustration and tension
Feelings of low impact on organization or peers	

Figure 13.10

Common signs of job burnout among workers. Here are some of the commonly observed symptoms of stress-induced burnout, a physical and psychological condition marked by fatigue, pessimism, and a lowered quality of work or job performance. Burnout is most likely to occur when the stress and strain of work is continuous rather than occasional or sporadic. (Adapted from Aamodt, 2010)

Source: Adapted from Aamodt, M. (2010). *Industrial/organizational psychology: An applied approach.* Belmont, CA: Wadsworth/Cengage. © 2010 Wadsworth, a part of Cengage Learning, Inc. Reproduced with permission. www.cengage.com/permissions

Sexual Harassment

Sexual harassment burst into the American consciousness in 1991 during the televised confirmation hearings for the nomination of Clarence Thomas as a Justice of the U.S. Supreme Court. Although Justice Thomas survived the confirmation process, many would argue that his reputation was damaged by Anita Hill's public allegations of sexual harassment (while she had been his assistant in the U.S. Department of Education a decade earlier), and so was Hill's. Allegations of sexual harassment also caused serious problems for President Bill Clinton. These highly publicized examples of sexual harassment charges have served as a wake-up call to individuals and companies, as both can be sued for harassment (regulations were instituted in 1980). Sexual harassment is an ongoing problem around the globe (McDonald, 2012). Although most workers recognize that they need to take the problem of sexual harassment seriously, many people remain relatively naive about what constitutes sexual harassment.

Sexual harassment occurs when employees are subjected to unwelcome sexually oriented behavior. According to law, there are two types of sexual harassment. The first is *quid pro quo* (from the Latin expression that translates as "something given or received in exchange for something else"). In the context of sexual harassment, quid pro quo involves making submission to unwanted sexual advances a condition of hiring, advancement (raise, promotion), or not being fired. In other words, the worker's survival on the job depends on agreeing to engage in unwanted sex. The second type of harassment is *hostile environment,* or any type of unwelcome sexual behavior that creates hostile work situations that can inflict psychological harm and interfere with job performance.

Sexual harassment can take a variety of forms: unsolicited and unwelcome flirting, sexual advances, or propositions; insulting comments about an employee's appearance, dress, or anatomy; unappreciated dirty jokes and sexual gestures; intrusive or sexual questions about an employee's personal life; explicit descriptions of the harasser's own sexual experiences; abuse of familiarities such as "honey" and "dear"; unnecessary and unwanted physical contact such as touching, hugging, pinching, or kissing; catcalls; exposure of genitals; physical or sexual assault; and rape. As experts have pointed out, sexual harassment is an abuse of power by a person in authority. To determine what legally constitutes sexual harassment, the courts take into account "whether the behavior is motivated by the gender of the victim, whether it is unwelcome, whether it is repetitive, and whether it could lead to negative psychological or organizational outcomes" (Goldberg & Zhang, 2004, p. 823). Same-sex sexual harassment also occurs and is prosecuted according to the same standards applied in cross-sex sexual harassment, although little research has been done on the topic (but see Ryan & Wessel, 2012).

Prevalence and Consequences

Sexual harassment in the workplace is more widespread than most people realize, but the topic is now better understood because of increased research (O'Leary-Kelly et al., 2009). By one estimate, nearly a quarter of all women in the United States have experienced some form of sexual harassment in the workplace (Ilies et al., 2003). A reasonable estimate for male workers is 16.3% (Catalyst, 2012). The typical female victim is young, divorced or separated, in a nonsenior position, and in a masculine-stereotyped field (Davidson & Fielden, 1999). A review of studies on women in the military reported rates of sexual harassment ranging from 55% to 79% (Goldzweig et al., 2006). Women in blue-collar jobs are also at high risk, but sexual harassment also occurs in the professions. Sadly, sexual harassment is often associated with other forms of workplace discrimination for blacks and members of other ethnic or minority groups (Rospenda, Richman, & Shannon, 2009).

Experiencing sexual harassment can have negative effects on psychological and physical health (Norton, 2002). Problematic reactions include anger, reduced self-esteem, depression, and anxiety. Victims may also have difficulties in their personal relationships and in sexual adjustment (loss of desire, for example). Increased alcohol consumption, smoking, and dependence on drugs are also reported (Rospenda et al., 2008). In addition, sexual harassment can produce fallout on the job: Women who are harassed may be less productive, less satisfied with their jobs, and less committed to their work and employer (Woodzicka & LaFrance, 2005). Women who are sexually harassed also report lower job satisfaction and may withdraw from work as the result of physical and mental health problems. Some of these women are even found to display symptoms of posttraumatic stress disorder (Willness, Steel, & Lee, 2007). Finally, sexual harassment can heighten the incidence of job withdrawal while decreasing job satisfaction and undermining an individual's organizational commitment (Kath et al., 2009).

Stopping Sexual Harassment

To predict the occurrence of sexual harassment, researchers have developed a two-factor model based on the person (prospective harasser) and the social situation (Pryor, Giedd, & Williams, 1995). According to this model, individuals vary in their proclivity for sexual harassment, and organizational norms regarding the acceptability of sexual harassment also vary. Sexual harassment is most likely to occur when individual proclivity is high and organizational norms are accepting. Thus, it follows that organizations can reduce the incidence of sexual harassment by promoting norms that are intolerant of it.

Responses to sexual harassment may be personal as well as organizational. Researchers have developed a typology of possible responses to this problem (see **Figure 13.11**) and have studied their relative effectiveness (Bowes-Sperry & Tata, 1999; Knapp et al., 1997). Unfortunately, the most frequently used strategy—avoidance/denial—is also the least effective one. Confrontation/negotiation and advocacy seeking are two effective strategies but are infrequently used.

Unemployment

A major consequence of recent economic upheavals is *displaced workers*—**individuals who are unemployed because their jobs have disappeared.** Between 1999 and 2001, roughly 5 million workers with three or more years of experience were displaced as a result of plant closings, slack or insufficient work, or positions being eliminated (U.S. Bureau of the Census, 2006b). Losing one's job is difficult at best and devastating at worst; research suggest that job loss is in the top ten most stressful events a person can experience (Maysent & Spera, 1995). Given the high U.S. unemployment rate in late 2012 (around 8.1%) (U.S. Bureau of Labor Statistics, 2012b), many Americans have found themselves out of work and worried about their futures. Not only can unemployment cause economic distress, it can cause health problems and such psychological difficulties as loss of self-esteem, depression, and anxiety

(Bobek & Robbins, 2005; Wanberg, 2012). A recent meta-analysis found that the rate of psychological problems was more than doubled among unemployed persons compared to those who were working (Paul & Moser, 2009). Also, the rate of attempted and completed suicides is higher among those who are unemployed (Yang, Tsai, &Huang, 2011). Longer unemployment is also a risk factor linked with higher rates of suicide (Classen & Dunn, 2012). Gender does not affect the amount of distress experienced as the result of job loss (Kulik, 2000). Even "survivors," those who retain their jobs following a round of layoffs during downsizing, are not immune from psychological distress (Paulsen et al., 2005).

While losing a job at any age is highly stressful, those who are laid off in middle age seem to find the experience most difficult (Breslin & Mustard, 2003). For one thing, they typically have more financial responsibilities than

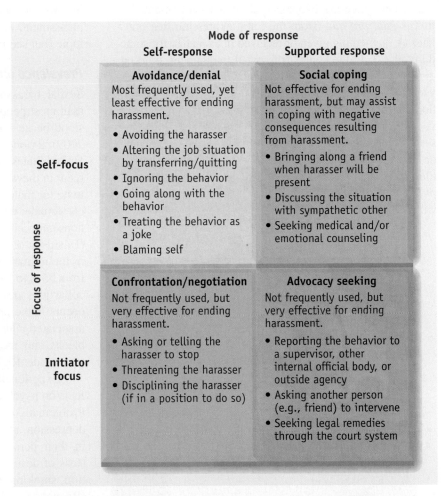

Figure 13.11

Effectiveness of responses to sexual harassment. Responses to sexual harassment can be classified into four categories based on the focus of the response (directed toward self or toward the harasser) and the mode of the response (involving the self or others). Unfortunately, the most frequent reactions turn out to be the least helpful. Effective strategies are available, but they are infrequently used.

Source: From Bowes-Sperry, L., & Tata, J. (1999). A multiperspective framework of sexual harassment. In G. N. Powell (Ed.), *Handbook of gender and work* (pp. 263–280). Thousand Oaks, CA: Sage Publications. Copyright © 1999 by Sage Publications. Reprinted with permission of Sage Publications, Inc.

"The dip in sales seems to coincide with the decision to eliminate the sales staff."

those in other age groups. Second, if other family members aren't able to provide health insurance, the entire family's health and welfare is jeopardized. Third, older workers typically remain out of work longer than younger workers. Thus, economic hardship can be a real possibility and can threaten quality of life for the worker's family. Finally, middle-aged workers have been on the job for a number of years. Because they typically feel highly involved in their work, being cut off from this important source of life satisfaction is painful (Broomhall & Winefield, 1990). Of course, not all middle-aged workers are affected negatively by loss of work (Leana & Feldman, 1991). Individuals who are in their 50s and close to retirement and those who are motivated to try their hand at something new seem the least affected. In fact, having goals to pursue while searching for work is associated with mental health among older individuals (Niessen, Heinrichs, & Dorr, 2009).

Coping with Unemployment

Following the recent recession in the United States, the unemployment rate crept up to 10% of the workforce before it began to recede, with even higher rates seen in many states. Many people lost their jobs through layoffs, downsizing, or the closing of various businesses. Mental health experts view job loss as a devastating life experience—similar to death, divorce, and serious illness or disability. Foremost, people are hit with the frightening prospect of loss of income and must deal with the stressful practicalities of how to live on less. Job loss also deals a psychological blow because it strikes at a key component of adult identity—having a job. And victims of downsizing must deal with the anger and resentment that stem from the unfairness of the situation.

Understandably, job loss negatively affects mental health (Paul & Moser, 2009) and is associated with de-creases in self-confidence, feelings of failure and rejection, and increases in anxiety and depression (Bobek & Robbins, 2005). Unfortunately, job loss also increases the likelihood of marital problems. Being aware of the psychological aspects can help one cope with the experience. Some experts suggest that individuals' reactions to job loss are similar to what they experience when they confront their own death (Bobek & Robbins, 2005).

For some practical suggestions for coping with job loss, we draw on the advice of career experts Michael Laskoff (2004) and Robert Lock (2005b):

1. *Apply for unemployment benefits as soon as possible.* The average length of unemployment in 2012 was 38 weeks (U.S. Bureau of Labor Statistics, 2012b). Thus, you need to look into unemployment benefits, which you may be able to collect for 26 weeks (or longer in some cases). Contact the nearest office of your state's Employment Security Commission or Department of Labor.

2. *Determine your income and expenses.* Determine precisely your sources of income (unemployment benefits, spouse or partner's income, savings) and how much you can count on per month. Itemize your monthly expenses. Set up a realistic budget and stick to it. Talk with your creditors if you need to.

3. *Lower your expenses and think of ways to bring in extra income.* Cut out unnecessary expenses for now. Minimize your credit card purchases and pay off the credit card bills every month to avoid building up huge debt. For extra income, consider selling a car, having a garage sale, or putting items up for auction on eBay. Use your skills as a temporary or seasonal worker.

4. *Stay healthy.* To save money on medical expenses, eat well-balanced meals, maintain an exercise regimen, and get adequate sleep. Use relaxation techniques to manage your stress (see Chapter 4). Keep yourself in a positive frame of mind by recalling past successes and imagining future ones.

5. *Reach out for support.* Although it is difficult to do, explain your job situation to your family and friends. You need their support, and they need to know how your unemployment will affect them. If you are having relationship problems, consult a counselor. Let your friends know that you are looking for work; they may have job leads.

6. *Get organized and get going.* Start by setting aside time and space to work on your job search. Then consider your situation. Is your résumé up to date? Can you find the same type of job, or do you need to think about other options? Do you need to relocate? Do you need more education or retraining? Some people decide to go into business for themselves, so don't overlook this option. Check out some of the excellent career planning books (for example, see this chapter's recommended reading, *What Color Is Your Parachute?*) and visit relevant websites. Expect to spend 15–25 hours a week on job-searching activities.

LEARNING OBJECTIVES

- Articulate current perspectives on workaholism.
- Explain work-family conflict, and discuss the benefits of multiple roles.
- Define leisure and list several leisure activities.

A major challenge for individuals today is balancing work, family, and leisure activities in ways that are personally satisfying (Cleveland, 2008; Major & Morganson, 2011; Warr, 2007). We noted earlier that dual-earner families are becoming increasingly common and that the traditional boundaries between family and paid work life are breaking down (Voydanoff, 2005). These two developments are related. Historically, traditional gender roles assigned women's work to the home and men's work outside the home. This division of labor created boundaries between family and work life. With more women entering the workforce, these boundaries have become blurred. The technology-based changes in the workplace are also eroding these distinctions between family and work life (Jackson, 2005). Here we examine three issues related to balancing various life roles.

Workaholism

Most people cherish their leisure activities and relationships with their families and friends. However, *workaholics* devote nearly all their time and energy to their jobs; for them, work is addictive (Griffiths, 2011). They put in lots of overtime, take few vacations, regularly bring work home from the office, sacrifice other roles in their lives, and think about work most of the time, yet they may not necessarily enjoy the job they hold (Ng, Sorenson, & Feldman, 2007). They are energetic, intense, and ambitious, which are generally positive traits; however, two unfavorable traits, perfectionism and negative emotionality, also predict workaholism (Bovornusvakool et al., 2012; Clark, Lelchook, & Taylor, 2010). In addition to personal factors, situational forces can also promote workaholism (Murphy & Zagorski, 2005). Thus, it is more common where the organizational climate supports imbalances between work and personal life (Burke, 2001). Recent evidence suggests a link exists between workaholism and the incidence of aggression (interpersonal conflict) in the workplace (Balducci et al., 2012). Workaholism has even been labeled a twenty-first-century addiction (Griffths, 2011; Shifron & Reysen, 2011).

Although workaholism has received considerable attention in the popular press, empirical research on the topic is relatively limited (Harpaz & Snir, 2003). A survey of 800 senior-level managers reported that nearly one in four considered themselves to be workaholics (Joyner, 1999). Psychologists are divided on the issue of whether workaholism is problematic. Should workaholics be praised for their dedication and encouraged in their single-minded pursuit of fulfillment through work (Baruch, 2011; Burke, 2009), or what is sometimes termed *work centrality* (Paullay, Alliger, & Stone-Romero, 1994)? Or is workaholism a form of addiction (Shifron & Reysen, 2011), a sign that an individual is driven by compulsions he or she cannot control? In support of the former view is evidence that some workaholics tend to be highly satisfied with their jobs and with their lives (Bonebright, Clay, & Ankenmann, 2000). They work hard simply because work is the most meaningful activity they know. Yet other evidence suggests that workaholics may have poorer emotional and physical well-being than nonworkaholics (Bonebright et al., 2000). How can these conflicting findings be reconciled?

It seems that there are two types of workaholics (Aziz & Zickar, 2006). One type, the *enthusiastic workaholic*, works for the pure joy of it. Such people derive immense satisfaction from work and generally perform well in highly demanding jobs. These individuals may also qualify as being high in *work engagement*, an emerging positive and fulfilling construct linked to absorption in work (Bakker et al., 2008). The other type, the *nonenthusiastic workaholic*, feels driven to work but reports low job enjoyment.

"If only I'd thought to take my damn phone with me, I could be getting some work done."

Moreover, these people tend to report lower life satisfaction and less purpose in life than enthusiastic workaholics. Thus, it is not surprising that the nonenthusiastic group are more likely to develop *burnout* (Maslach, 2005).

Both types of workaholics experience an imbalance between work and personal time. Not surprisingly, this situation translates into a high degree of work-family conflict for both groups (Bakker, Demerouti, & Burke, 2009). Moreover, the families of both groups suffer (Robinson, Flowers, & Ng, 2006). A recent study found that students whose parents were workaholics tended to report lower levels of psychological well-being and self-acceptance and high numbers of physical health complaints (Chamberlin & Zhang, 2009). So, although enthusiastic workaholics really love their work, their devotion to their jobs has a price, one often paid by their families.

Work and Family Roles

One of the biggest recent changes in the labor force has been the emergence of dual-earner households, now the dominant family form in the United States (U.S. Bureau of the Census, 2006b). Dual-earner couples are struggling to discover better ways of balancing family life and the demands of work. These changes in work and family life have sparked the interest of researchers in many disciplines, including psychology.

An important fact of life for dual-earner couples is that they juggle *multiple roles:* spouse or partner and employee. TICKS (two-income couples with kids) add a third role: parent. Thus, today's working parents experience **work-family conflict, or the feeling of being pulled in multiple directions by competing demands from the job and the family.** In heterosexual dual-earner families, men are taking on more household chores and child care, but most wives still have greater responsibilities in these areas (Drago, 2007). In gay and lesbian dual-earner house-

© Dirk Ercken/Shutterstock.com

holds, responsibilities are more evenly divided (Kurdek, 2005; Patterson, 2003). Single parents are especially likely to have work-family conflicts.

Although employers are reducing their contributions to employee benefits such as pension and retirement plans, health-care benefits, and the like, they do not seem to be cutting back on flexible work schedules, family leave, and child and elder care support (SHRM, 2011). A key reason employers are retaining these programs is that they help recruit and retain employees. Still, the fact is that most employees do not have access to such programs. Some believe that this situation is partly to blame for the downward drift in the percentage of mothers with infant children who are in the labor force (Stone & Lovejoy, 2004). In 1998, the participation rate for this group had reached a high of 59%; by 2005, it had fallen to 56%. According to Ellen Galinsky, president of the Families and Work Institute, "They're not fleeing work—they're fleeing the demanding way of work" (Armour, 2004). Indeed, the more hours women work, the more their marital satisfaction tends to suffer (but keep in mind that this is a correlational relationship and not a causal one). However, it makes sense that longer work hours can spill over into time once reserved for family commitments, thereby introducing strain in family life (Hughes & Parkes, 2007). To gain more control over their lives, some women are temporarily opting out of the workforce; others are going into business for themselves.

To be fair, some of the decline in women's labor force participation rates can probably be attributed to generational shifts in the views of the optimal balance of work and family roles. As you can see in **Figure 13.12** on the next page, more Gen-X employees with children endorse a family-centric view over a work-centric view compared to a comparable group of Boomers. Some suggest that these generational differences are due, in part, to many Gen-Xers seeing their hardworking parents lose their jobs because of downsizing (Families and Work Institute, 2004).

Although today's working parents may feel stressed, researchers find that multiple roles are beneficial for both men's and women's mental, physical, and relationship health, at least in middle-class couples (Barnett, 2005). For women, the benefits of multiple roles are attributed primarily to the effects of the employee role. For men, family involvement is important, especially in the area of relationship health. According to Rosalind Barnett and Janet Hyde (2001), a number of factors contribute to the positive outcomes associated with multiple roles, including added income, social support, opportunities to experience success, and buffering. The latter refers to the idea that successes and satisfactions in one role provide a buffer against the negative effects of stress or failure in another role. Of course, there are outside limits to the number of roles and the amount of work that people can take on before they sacrifice the benefits of multiple roles (Barnett & Hyde, 2001). Role overload likely causes psychological distress.

Figure 13.12

Generational differences in work and family priorities.

Gen-X parents are significantly more likely than Boomer parents to be family-centric (place more emphasis on family than work), whereas Boomer parents are significantly more likely than Gen-Xers to be work-centric (place greater emphasis on work than family). The fact that both groups have children under 18 living at home suggests that this is a generational, rather than a life cycle, difference.

Source: From Families and Work Institute (2004, October). *Generation and gender in the workplace.* New York: Families and Work Institute.

Gen-X
Age 23–37

13% Work-centric

55% Family-centric

33% Dual-centric

Boomers
Age 38–57

20% Work-centric

46% Family-centric

35% Dual-centric

Leisure and Recreation

As noted earlier, most Americans are putting in 48-hour workweeks, and many work more hours than that. Some workers put in extra hours because their employers mandate it. Others choose to work more hours to maintain their standard of living, because real earning power, especially for low-wage workers, has fallen behind what it was 25 years ago (Joyner, 2001). And when workers arrive home, unpaid family work awaits them. Given the pace of contemporary American life, it's no surprise that almost 60% of Americans say that having leisure time is either "extremely important" or "very important" in their lives, according to a Gallup poll (Moore, 2003).

American workers take an average of 14 days of paid annual vacation after 5 years of service (U.S. Bureau of Labor Statistics, 2009). The paid vacation time of American workers lags far behind that of many European workers (see **Figure 13.13**). Moreover, workers in most European Union countries get 4 weeks of vacation time by law (Roughton, 2001). A generous number of public holidays pushes the average vacation time in the E.U. to about 7 weeks!

We define *leisure* **as unpaid activities people choose to engage in because the activities are personally meaningful.** How might we distinguish activities that are meaningful from those that aren't? Although people may lounge in front of the TV set for hours at a time, most would also acknowledge that an important difference exists between this use of time and, say, hiking around a beautiful lake. While one activity merely provides respite from a boring or exhausting day (which you sometimes need), the other can be genuinely revitalizing. Being a couch potato will probably contribute nothing to your state of mind and may even contribute to feelings of apathy and depression. On the other hand, participating in activities that are meaningful and fulfilling can contribute to one's well-being and quality of life (Brajša-Žganec, Merkaš, & Šverko, 2011; Iwasaki et al., 2006).

Types of Leisure Activities

The types of leisure activities that people prefer are quite diverse. Popular leisure pursuits include:

- *Hobbies.* Among the most popular hobbies are photography; acting; music (playing and listening); dancing; gardening; knitting; drawing; collecting stamps, autographs, and so forth; hiking; camping; fishing; and birdwatching.

- *Reading.* Although fewer individuals read now than in the past, plenty of people still love to curl up with a good book. Books allow readers to escape from daily cares, solve mysteries, travel to real or imaginary places, learn useful information, and find inspiration.

- *Surfing the Internet.* A relatively new entry into the world of leisure, the Internet offers an amazing array of activities: emailing friends and relatives, social networking on Facebook, posting on message boards or Twitter, playing multiuser games, and listening to music are just a few options.

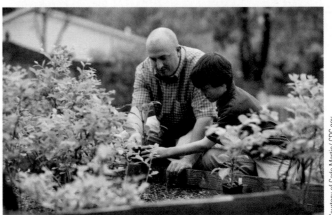

Leisure time should be relaxing and personally meaningful; cultivating a garden can be both of those things. Some research suggests that being satisfied with one's job and one's leisure activities is predictive of psychological health.

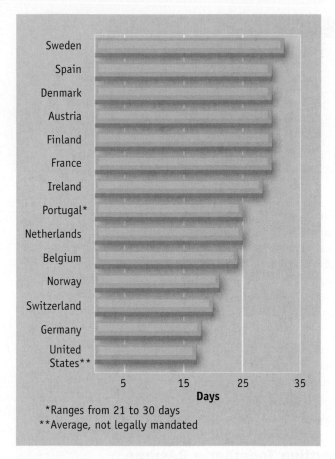

Figure 13.13

American and European vacation days. American workers average 16 paid vacation days a year. Most European workers get considerably longer vacations. Moreover, these are benefits mandated by law.

Source: Adapted from Mischel, L., Bernstein, J., & Schmitt, J. (2001). *The state of working America 2000–2001.* Ithaca, NY: Cornell University Press. Copyright © 2001 by Cornell University Press. Adapted by permission of the publisher, Cornell University Press.

● *Travel.* Many choose their destinations spontaneously, but others are more systematic in their travel plans. For example, some individuals want to travel to all the U.S. national parks or to every state in the Union. Those who can afford it may travel to other countries—to get a taste of real French cooking or a firsthand look at what remains of ancient Egyptian civilization.

● *Games and puzzles.* Some individuals enjoy playing bridge for relaxation; others like to play board games such as Scrabble or chess. Computerized and video games are highly popular, especially with children and adolescents. For some, the day isn't complete without the daily crossword or Sudoku puzzle.

● *Sports.* Many people like to play team sports such as bowling or softball, enjoying the benefits of both physical exercise and social interaction. Others enjoy individual sports such as jogging, swimming, surfing, ice skating, or skiing.

● *Volunteer activities.* Helping others appeals to individuals in almost all age groups. Moreover, individuals can use their skills to help others in an incredibly diverse array of settings: homeless shelters, hospitals, schools, battered women's shelters, boys' and girls' clubs, and sports teams, for example.

Being aware of the broad range of leisure activities heightens your chances of selecting those that are most meaningful to you.

In the upcoming Application, we describe how to conduct a productive job search and offer a few tips for more effective job interviews.

Application

GETTING AHEAD IN THE JOB GAME

LEARNING OBJECTIVES

● Summarize some guidelines for putting together an effective résumé.

● Discuss strategies for targeting companies where you would like to work.

● Outline several strategies for landing an interview, and discuss how to behave when interviewing for a job.

● Identify some factors that can influence an interviewer's rating of a job candidate.

● List the dos and don'ts of interviewing for jobs.

Answer the following statements "true" or "false."

____ **1.** The most common and effective job-search method is answering classified ads.

____ **2.** Your technical qualifications are the main factor in determining the success of your job search.

____ **3.** Employment agencies are a good source of leads to high-level professional jobs.

____ **4.** Your résumé should be very thorough and include everything you have ever done.

____ **5.** It's a good idea to inject some humor into your job interviews to help you and your interviewer relax.

Most career counselors would agree that all these statements are generally false. Although there is no one "tried and true" method for obtaining desirable jobs, experts do have guidelines that can increase your chances of success. Their insights are summarized in this Application. To ensure that you get the best job you can, you'll need to know more details than we can provide here. A good place to start is to read *What Color Is Your Parachute?*, one of the best job search manuals available (see the Recommended Reading box).

Above all else, it is important to conduct a job search that is well organized, thorough, and systematic. Sending out a hastily written résumé to a few randomly selected companies is a waste of effort. An effective job search requires lots of time and careful planning. Thus, it is crucial that you begin your search well in advance of the time when you will need a job.

Of course, no amount of planning and effort can guarantee favorable results in a job search. Luck is definitely a part of the picture. Success may hinge on being in the right place or on meeting the right person at the right time. Also keep in mind that employers are often inundated with applicants who have all of the required training and experience. In fact, the candidate who is ultimately selected may not be the one with the best technical qualifications.

RECOMMENDED reading

What Color Is Your Parachute? 2013: A Practical Manual for Job-Hunters and Career-Changers

by Richard Nelson Bolles (Ten Speed Press, 2013)

Richard Bolles is a clever, creative writer who has put together a landmark book on the process of hunting for a job. *Parachute* was first published in 1970 and has become so successful that it's updated yearly. If you have time to read only one book about getting a job or changing careers, this is the one to choose. Bolles's writing is humorous and opinionated. However, his opinions have merit because he has done his homework. The book is thoroughly researched and documented. The author destroys many of the myths about what does and does not work in seeking jobs. He discusses a variety of practical topics, including where the jobs are, what will get you hired, how to get in to see the boss, whom to see, whom to avoid, and how to start your own business. His discussion of transferable skills is must-reading. Readers will also appreciate helpful hints on using the Internet for career information and job searching. Bolles also has an interesting chapter on integrating work and faith. The book contains a number of useful appendixes, including exercises to help people determine their ideal job and locate a career counselor or coach.

Log on to CourseMate at www.cengagebrain.com for descriptions of other recommended books.

Rather, most hiring decisions are made on the basis of subjective impressions gleaned from résumés, telephone conversations, and face-to-face interviews. These impressions are based on perceptions of personality, appearance, social skills, and body language. Knowing this, you can practice certain strategies that may increase the odds in your favor.

No matter what type of job you're looking for, successful searches have certain elements in common. First, you must prepare a résumé. Next, you need to target specific companies or organizations you would like to work for. Then, you must inform these companies of your interest in such a way as to get them interested in you.

Putting Together a Résumé

No matter what your job search strategy, an excellent résumé is a critical ingredient. The purpose of a résumé is not to get you a job, but to get you an interview. To be effective, your résumé must show that you have at least the minimum technical qualifications for the position, know the standard conventions of the work world, and are a person who is on the fast track to success. Furthermore, it must achieve these goals without being flashy or gimmicky. Especially, it must contain no spelling or grammatical mistakes.

Here are a few basic guidelines for a résumé that projects a positive, yet conservative image (Lock, 2005a). For more tips on constructing a résumé, type "how to write a résumé" or "examples of résumés" into your favorite search engine.

1. Use high-quality white, ivory, or beige paper for hard copies.

2. Make sure the résumé contains not a single typographical error.

3. Keep it short. One side of an 8.5" × 11" sheet of paper will suffice for most college students; do not go over two pages.

4. Don't write in full sentences, and avoid using the word *I*. Instead, begin each statement with an "action" word that describes a specific achievement, such as "Supervised a staff of fifteen" or "Handled all customer complaints."

5. Avoid giving any personal information that is unrelated to the job. Such information is an unnecessary distraction and may give the reader cause to dislike you and therefore reject your application.

An effective résumé will generally contain the following elements, laid out in an easy-to-read format (**Figure 13.14** shows an attractively prepared résumé):

Heading. At the top of the page, give your name, address, phone number, and email address. (By the way, be sure your voice-mail greeting and your email address reflect a "professional" impression.) This is the only section of the résumé that is not given a label. (You do not need to label the document "Résumé.")

Objective. State precisely and concisely the kind of position you are seeking, remembering to use action words and to avoid the use of *I.* An example might be "Challenging, creative position in the communication field requiring extensive background in newspaper, radio, and television."

Education. List any degrees you've earned, giving major field of study, date, and granting institution for each. You should list the highest degree you received first. If you have a college degree, you don't need to mention your high school diploma. If you have received any *academic* honors or awards, mention them in this section.

Experience. This section should be organized chronologically, beginning with your most recent job and working backward. For each position, give the dates of employment and describe your responsibilities and accomplishments. Be specific, and make sure your most recent position is the one with the greatest achievements. Don't bother listing trivial attainments. Readers find such material annoying, and it just calls attention to the fact that you don't have more important items to list.

Also, beware of padding your résumé with misrepresentations or outright untruths. One résumé-writing business reported that 43% of 1,000 résumés they received over a 6-month period contained one or more "significant inaccuracies" (Cullen, 2007). If you are wondering whether to include a questionable entry on your résumé, use the "sniff test" (Theisen, 2002). Could you talk easily with an interviewer about what you claim on your résumé without feeling nervous? If not, delete the information. Remember, too, that information and photographs you post to your blog or personal website or to sites like Facebook or LinkedIn are available for anyone to see unless you use privacy protections (Chamberlin, 2007).

If you are currently a student or are a recent graduate, your schooling will provide the basis for both your experience and your qualifications. You can get a jump on the competition by gaining experience in the field in which you want to work—through internships or part-time or summer jobs. If this option isn't feasible, do some volunteer work in this area and list it under an "Honors and Activities" section on your résumé.

TERESA M. MORGAN

Campus Address	**Permanent Address**
1252 River St., Apt. 808	1111 W. Franklin
East Lansing, MI 48823	Jackson, MI 49203
(517)332-6086	(517)782-0819
tmorgan@michstate.edu	tmmor@gmail.com

OBJECTIVE
To pursue a career in interior design, or a related field, in which I can utilize my design training. Willing to relocate after June 2013.

EDUCATION

Sept. 2011– June 2013
Michigan State University, East Lansing, MI 48825. Bachelor of Arts–Interior Design, with emphasis in Design Communication and Human Shelter. Courses include Lighting, Computers, Public Relations and History of Art. (F.I.D.E.R. accredited) 3.0 GPA (4.0 = A).

July 2012– Aug. 2012
Michigan State University overseas study, England and France, Decorative Arts and Architecture. 4.0 GPA (4.0 = A).

Sept. 2009– June 2011
Jackson Community College, Jackson, MI 49201. Associate's Degree. 3.5 GPA (4.0 = A).

EMPLOYMENT

Dec. 2012– June 2013
Food Service and Maintenance, Owen Graduate Center, Michigan State University.
• Prepared and served food.
• Managed upkeep of adjacent Van Hoosen Residence Hall.

Sept. 2011– June 2012
Food Service and Maintenance, McDonel Residence Hall, Michigan State University.
• Served food and cleaned facility.
• Handled general building maintenance.

June 2008– Dec. 2008
Waitress, Charlie Wong's Restaurant, Jackson, MI.
• Served food, dealt with a variety of people on a personal level.
• Additional responsibilities: cashier, hostess, bartender, and employee trainer.

HONORS AND ACTIVITIES
• Community College Transfer scholarship from MSU.
• American Society of Interior Design Publicity Chairman; Executive Board, MSU Chapter.
• Sigma Chi Little Sisters.
• Independent European travel, summer 2008.
• Stage manager and performer in plays and musicals.

REFERENCES and PORTFOLIO available upon request.

Figure 13.14

Example of an attractively formatted résumé. The physical appearance of a résumé is very important. This example shows what a well-prepared résumé should look like. (Adapted from Lock, 2005b)

"Oops! The padding just fell out of your résumé."

Leo Cullum/The New Yorker Collection/www.cartoonbank.com

Ariel Skelley/Blend Images/Getty Images

To be successful on a job interview, candidates need to dress appropriately and convey confidence, enthusiasm, and interest in the job.

Technology is changing a number of aspects of the job-search process, including the preparation and screening of résumés. Increasingly, companies are likely to electronically scan résumés for key words that match job specifications (Lock, 2005a). Thus, it's helpful to know how to create an electronic résumé in addition to the traditional paper version. You can get this information at your campus Career Services office or at Learn More Online. Also, many organizations post formatting instructions on their websites for people who want to submit electronic résumés. The "next big thing" in résumés may be 2- to 3-minute video résumés. Because they're new, they're risky. And employers worry that they will provoke lawsuits based on claims of bias because race, gender, and age cues are visible (Cullen, 2007). An alternative is to list links to your website or blog on your résumé—if it is relevant and conveys a "professional" impression (Richter, 2007).

Finding Companies You Want to Work For

Initially, you need to determine what general type of organization will best suit your needs. Do you want to work in a school? a hospital? a small business? a large corporation? a government agency? a human services agency? To select an appropriate work environment, you need an accurate picture of your personal qualities and knowledge of various occupations and their characteristics. Job search manu-

als like *Parachute* can provide you with helpful exercises in self-exploration. To learn about the characteristics of various occupations, check out relevant websites such as the Occupational Outlook Handbook or visit your Career Services office.

Landing an Interview

No one is going to hire you without first "checking out the goods." This inspection process typically involves one or more formal interviews. So, how do you get invited for an interview? If you are applying for an advertised vacancy, the traditional approach is to send a résumé with a cover letter to the hiring organization. If your letter and résumé stand out from the crowd, you may be invited for an interview. A good way to increase your chances is to persuade the prospective employer that you are interested enough in the company to have done some research on the organization (Pollak, 2007). By taking the time to learn something about a company, you should be able to make a convincing case about the ways in which your expertise will be particularly useful to the organization.

If you are approaching an organization in the absence of a known opening, your strategy may be somewhat different. You may still opt to send a résumé, along with a more detailed cover letter explaining why you have selected this particular company. Another option, suggested

Learn More Online

CollegeGrad.com

This site bills itself as "The #1 entry-level job site." Key sections include "Job Preparation" (explore careers, résumés, and cover letters), "Job Searching" (advice and posting résumés), and "Offers" (salary, negotiating, and new job advice). You can also search for internships here.

Learn More Online

CareerRookie.com

This site is geared to college students seeking internships, part-time jobs, and entry-level careers. Check out the section on internships, where you can search by city, state, or category.

by Bolles (2007), is to introduce yourself (by phone or in person) directly to the person in charge of hiring and request an interview. You can increase your chances of success by using your network of personal contacts to identify some acquaintance that you and the person in charge have in common. Then you can use this person's name to facilitate your approach.

Polishing Your Interview Technique

The final, and most crucial, step in the process of securing a job is the face-to-face interview. If you've gotten this far, the employer already knows that you have the necessary training and experience to do the job. Your challenge is to convince the employer that you're the kind of person who would fit well in the organization. Your interviewer will attempt to verify that you have the intangible qualities that will make you a good team player. Even more important, he or she will try to identify any "red flag" behaviors, attitudes, or traits that mark you as an unacceptable risk.

To create the right impression, you must come across as confident, enthusiastic, and ambitious. By the way, a firm (not wishy-washy or bone-crushing) handshake helps create a positive first impression, especially for women (Chaplin et al., 2000). Your demeanor should be somewhat formal and reserved, and you should avoid any attempts at humor—you never know what might offend your interviewer. Above all, never give more information than the interviewer requests, especially negative information. If asked directly what your weaknesses are—a common ploy—respond with a "flaw" that is really a positive, as in "I tend to work too hard at times." Finally, don't ever blame or criticize anyone, especially previous employers, even if you feel that the criticism is justified (Lock, 2005b).

Developing an effective interview technique requires practice. Many experts suggest that you never turn down an interview, because you can always benefit from the practice even if you don't want the job. Preparation is crucial: Never go into an interview cold. Find out all you can about the company before you go. Try to anticipate the questions that will be asked and have some answers ready. You can review commonly asked interview questions on websites and in career books (Yate, 2006). Know, however, that many untrained interviewers treat interviews as informal and unplanned, which means they rely on unstructured questions. In contrast, trained interviewers usually rely on a set of standardized questions for prospective employees. Sample questions associated with both interviewer styles are shown in **Figure 13.15**. In general, you will not be asked simply to reiterate information from your résumé. Remember, it is your personal qualities that are being assessed at this point.

A final word of advice: If possible, avoid any discussion of salary in an initial interview. The appropriate time for salary negotiation is *after* a firm offer of employment

Unstructured interview questions

1. What are your weaknesses?
2. Why should we hire you?
3. What are your goals?
4. Why do you want to work here?
5. What are three positive things a former boss would say about you?
6. What salary are you seeking?
7. If you were an animal, what animal would you want to be? Why?

Structured interview questions

1. Tell me in specific detail about a time when you had to deal with a difficult person.
2. Give me an example of a time when you had to make a decision without having a supervisor present to help you.
3. Give me a specific example of when you demonstrated initiative in your last job.
4. Tell me about a time when you had to work with a team of other people.
5. Describe a situation where you had to be creative when it came to solving some problem.

Figure 13.15

Some typical unstructured and structured interview questions. Untrained interviewers treat interviews as informal and unplanned; they tend to ask unstructured questions. In contrast, trained interviewers usually rely on a set of standardized questions for prospective employees. Sample questions associated with unstructured or structured interviews, respectively, are shown here. (Adapted from Baumeister & Bushman, 2011)

has been extended. You can scope out salary information for many jobs by visiting Learn More Online. And you can find additional tips on interviewing at some of the other Learn More Online boxes in this chapter.

After you have an interview, you should follow up with a thank-you note and a résumé that will jog the prospective employer's memory about your training and talents.

Learn More Online

Salary.com

This useful site allows you to determine median salaries for numerous occupations at different experience levels and in different geographical areas and compare them to national averages. You can probably get all the information you need for free, but you can also pay (a lot) for a customized salary report.

CHAPTER 13 | Review

KEY IDEAS

CHOOSING A CAREER

- Ideally, people look for jobs that are compatible with their personal characteristics. Thus, individuals need to have a sense of their own abilities, interests, and personality. Family background also influences career choices.
- There are abundant resources for those who want to learn about possible career options. In researching prospective careers, it is important to find out about the nature of the work, working conditions, entry requirements, potential earnings, potential status, opportunities for advancement, intrinsic satisfactions, and the future outlook for jobs.
- Individuals who have trouble making career decisions may find it helpful to take an occupational interest inventory. People have the potential for success in a variety of occupations, and they need to keep this and other considerations in mind as they make career decisions.

MODELS OF CAREER CHOICE AND DEVELOPMENT

- John Holland's person-environment fit model of career development asserts that people select careers based on their own personality characteristics. Holland's well-supported theory includes six personal orientations and matching work environments.
- Super's stage theory holds that self-concept development is the basis for career choice. According to this model, there are five stages in the occupational life cycle: growth, exploration, establishment, maintenance, and decline. However, the assumption that people will remain in the same career all of their working lives is out of sync with current workplace realities.
- Models of career development in women are still being developed. Women's career paths are often less orderly and predictable than men's because of the need to juggle multiple roles and because many women interrupt their careers to devote time to childrearing.

THE CHANGING WORLD OF WORK

- Work is an activity that produces something of value for others. A number of contemporary trends are changing the world of work. Generally, the more education individuals obtain, the higher their salaries will be.
- In the future, more women and minorities will join the labor force. Although women and minorities participate in the workforce at all occupational levels, they tend to be concentrated in lower-paying and lower-status positions. Furthermore, women and minorities face discrimination in a number of areas. Increasing diversity in the workforce presents challenges to both organizations and workers.

COPING WITH OCCUPATIONAL HAZARDS

- Major hazards related to work include job stress, sexual harassment, and unemployment. Stress affects both employers and employees. Interventions to manage stress in the workplace can be made at the individual level, the organizational level, and the individual-organizational interface.
- Victims of sexual harassment often develop physical and psychological symptoms of stress that can lead to decreased work motivation and productivity. Many organizations are educating their workers about this problem. Individuals can also take steps to reduce sexual harassment, although the most popular strategies tend to be the least effective.

- Because of dramatic changes in the economy, unemployment is a problem for both skilled and unskilled workers. Job loss is highly stressful. Middle-aged workers are most distressed by the experience. Unemployed workers who believe that they have been treated unfairly and arbitrarily often feel angry. In coping with unemployment, social support is critical.

BALANCING WORK AND OTHER SPHERES OF LIFE

- A major challenge for workers today is balancing work, family, and leisure activities in ways that are personally satisfying. Workaholism may be based on positive or negative motives, but it still creates work-family conflict for workaholics and their families.
- As dual-earner families have become the norm, juggling multiple roles has emerged as a challenge, especially for women. Nonetheless, multiple roles are generally beneficial to mental, physical, and relationship health. Leisure plays an important role in promoting well-being and quality of life.

APPLICATION: GETTING AHEAD IN THE JOB GAME

- The essential elements of a successful job search include (1) determining the type of organization that will best suit one's needs, (2) constructing an effective résumé, (3) obtaining a job interview, and (4) developing an effective interview technique.
- Résumés should be brief and project a positive, yet conservative image. To locate prospective employers, it is good to use a variety of strategies.
- Nonverbal communication skills can be crucial in job interviews. You should try to appear confident and enthusiastic. Try to avoid salary discussions in your initial interview.

KEY TERMS

Displaced workers p. 408	Occupational interest inventories p. 390
Dual-earner households p. 397	
Glass ceiling p. 402	Sexual harassment p. 407
Industrial/organizational (I/O) psychology p. 387	Token p. 402
	Underemployment p. 398
Labor force p. 399	Work p. 396
Leisure p. 412	Work-family conflict p. 411

KEY PEOPLE

Richard Nelson Bolles p. 414
John Holland pp. 392–394
Robert Karasek pp. 405–406
Donald Super pp. 394–395

CHAPTER *13* | Practice Test

1. Individuals' career choices are often
   a. much higher in status than those of their parents.
   b. similar to those of their parents.
   c. much lower in status than those of their parents.
   d. unrelated to their family background.

2. Findings on education and earnings show that
   a. at all levels of education, men earn more than women.
   b. at all levels of education, women earn more than men.
   c. there are no gender differences in education and earnings.
   d. there is no relationship between education and earnings.

3. Occupational interest inventories are designed to predict
   a. how successful an individual is likely to be in a job.
   b. how long a person will stay in a career.
   c. how satisfied a person is likely to be in a job.
   d. all of the above.

4. Holland's theory of occupational choice emphasizes
   a. the role of self-esteem in job choice.
   b. the unfolding of career interests over time.
   c. parental influences and job choice.
   d. matching personality traits and job environments.

5. Which of the following is *not* a work-related trend?
   a. Technology is changing the nature of work.
   b. New work attitudes are required.
   c. Most new jobs will be in the manufacturing sector.
   d. Lifelong learning is a necessity.

6. When there is only one woman or minority person in a workplace setting, that person becomes a symbol of his or her group and is referred to as a
   a. token.
   b. scapegoat.
   c. sex object.
   d. protected species.

7. Job stress has been found to lead to all but one of the following negative effects. Which one?
   a. Burnout
   b. Bipolar disorder
   c. High blood pressure
   d. Anxiety

8. According to law, the two types of sexual harassment are
   a. quid pro quo and environmental.
   b. legal and illegal.
   c. caveat emptor and confrontational.
   d. industrial and organizational.

9. Compared to European workers, American workers receive
   a. much less paid vacation time.
   b. about the same amount of paid vacation time.
   c. much more paid vacation time, but less sick leave.
   d. much more paid vacation and more sick leave.

10. Which of the following is a good tip for preparing an effective résumé?
    a. Make your résumé as long as possible.
    b. Use complete sentences.
    c. Keep it short.
    d. Provide a lot of personal information.

ANSWERS

1. b Page 389
2. a Pages 398–399
3. c Page 390
4. d Pages 392–394
5. c Pages 396–398
6. a Page 402
7. b Pages 403–406
8. a Page 407
9. a Pages 412–413
10. c Pages 414–416

COURSEMATE

Go to **CengageBrain.com** to access Psychology CourseMate, where you will find an interactive eBook, glossaries, flashcards, quizzes, videos, and more.

PERSONAL EXPLORATIONS WORKBOOK

Go to the *Personal Explorations Workbook* in the back of your textbook for exercises that can enhance your self-understanding in relation to issues raised in this chapter.

Exercise 13.1 *Self-Assessment:* Assertive Job Hunting Survey

Exercise 13.2 *Self-Reflection:* What Do You Know About the Career That Interests You?

Psychological Disorders

© Image Source/Alamy

Actress Jessica Alba used to unplug every single appliance in her house because she worried it would catch fire. She would also check and recheck her doors to ensure that they were locked. Soccer star David Beckham acknowledges more elaborate concerns that involve symmetry and matching. He is not comfortable unless everything is arranged in straight lines or in pairs. For instance, if he has five cans of Pepsi in a refrigerator, he has to get rid of one to restore even pairs. When he enters a hotel room he immediately has to put away all the leaflets and books to restore order to the room.

For Alba and Beckham, these aren't just little eccentricities of being a celebrity. They're manifestations of obsessive-compulsive disorder (OCD). Comedian and talk show host Howie Mandel explains it in his 2009 autobiography, *Here's the Deal: Don't Touch Me*. Mandel doesn't shake hands, due to his fear of germs, but "it's not just that I'm scared of germs," he says. There's nothing wrong with shaking hands with someone and then washing your hands. But "there *is* something wrong with being totally consumed that you didn't get everything off your hand, that there's things crawling, so you wash it again, and you're so consumed that you wash it again, and you wash it again and you wash it again and you wash it again," Mandel says. "When you can't get past that, that's obsessive-compulsive disorder. It's not that you're afraid of germs, it's that you obsess about that thought and have to do things like hand-washing to relieve the worry. I always have intrusive thoughts and rituals."

What causes such abnormal behavior? Does Mandel have a mental illness, or does he just behave strangely? What is the basis for judging behavior as normal versus abnormal? How common are such disorders? Can they be cured? These are just a few of the questions that we address in this chapter as we discuss psychological disorders and their complex causes.

ABNORMAL BEHAVIOR: GENERAL CONCEPTS

LEARNING OBJECTIVES

- Describe and evaluate the medical model of abnormal behavior, and identify the key criteria of abnormality.
- Discuss the development of DSM-5.
- Summarize data on the prevalence of various psychological disorders.

Misconceptions about abnormal behavior are common. We therefore need to clear up some preliminary issues before we describe the various types of psychological disorders. In this section, we discuss (1) the medical model of abnormal behavior, (2) the criteria of abnormal behavior, (3) the classification of psychological disorders, and (4) the prevalence of such disorders.

The Medical Model Applied to Abnormal Behavior

There's no question that Howie Mandel's extreme fear of germs is abnormal. But does it make sense to view his unusual and irrational behavior as an *illness*? This is a controversial question. **The *medical model* proposes that it is useful to think of abnormal behavior as a disease.** This point of view is the basis for many of the terms used to refer to abnormal behavior, including mental *illness*, psychological *disorder*, and psycho*pathology* (*pathology* refers to manifestations of disease). The medical model gradually became the conventional way of thinking about abnormal behavior during the 19th and 20th centuries, and its influence remains dominant today.

The medical model clearly represented progress over earlier models of abnormal behavior. Prior to the eighteenth century, most conceptions of abnormal behavior were based on superstition. People who behaved strangely were thought to be possessed by demons, to be witches in league with the devil, or to be victims of God's punishment. Their disorders were "treated" with chants, rituals, exorcisms, and such. If the people's behavior was seen as threatening, they were candidates for chains, dungeons, torture, and death (see Figure 14.1).

The rise of the medical model brought improvements in the treatment of those who exhibited abnormal behavior. As victims of an illness, they were viewed with more sympathy and less hatred and fear. Although living conditions in early asylums were often deplorable, gradual progress was made toward more humane care of the mentally ill. It took time, but ineffectual approaches to treatment eventually gave way to scientific investigation of the causes and cures of psychological disorders.

However, in recent decades, some critics have suggested that the medical model may have outlived its usefulness (Boyle, 2007; Kiesler, 1999). A particularly vocal critic has been the late Thomas Szasz (1974, 1993). He asserted that "strictly speaking, disease or illness can affect only the body; hence there can be no mental illness. . . . Minds can be 'sick' only in the sense that jokes are 'sick' or economies are 'sick'" (1974, p. 267). He further argued that abnormal behavior usually involves a deviation from social norms rather than an illness. He contended that such deviations are "problems in living" rather than medical problems. According to Szasz, the medical model's disease analogy converts moral and social questions about what is acceptable behavior into medical questions.

Some critics are also concerned because medical diagnoses of abnormal behavior pin potentially derogatory labels on people (Overton & Medina, 2008). Being labeled

as psychotic, schizophrenic, or mentally ill carries a social stigma that can be difficult to shake. Those characterized as mentally ill are viewed as erratic, dangerous, incompetent, and inferior (Corrigan & Larson, 2008). These stereotypes promote distancing, disdain, prejudice, and rejection. Even after a full recovery, someone who has been labeled mentally ill may have difficulty finding a place to live or getting a job. The stigma of mental illness creates additional difficulties for people who already have more than their share of problems (Hinshaw, 2007). Unfortunately, this stigma appears to be deep-rooted and not easily reduced. In recent decades research has increasingly demonstrated that many psychological disorders are at least partly attributable to genetic and biological factors, making them appear more similar to physical illnesses (Pescosolido et al., 2010). You would think that these trends would lead to a reduction in the stigma associated with mental illness, but research suggests that the stigmatization of mental disorders has increased rather than decreased (Hinshaw & Stier, 2008; Schnittker, 2008).

Although critics' analyses of the medical model have some merit, we'll take the position that the disease analogy continues to be useful, although you should keep in mind that it is *only* an analogy. Medical concepts such as *diagnosis, etiology,* and *prognosis* have proven valuable in the treatment and study of abnormality. **Diagnosis involves distinguishing one illness from another. Etiology refers to the apparent causation and developmental history of an illness. A prognosis is a forecast about the probable course of an illness.** These medically based concepts have widely shared meanings that permit clinicians, researchers, and the public to communicate more effectively in their discussions of abnormal behavior.

Criteria of Abnormal Behavior

If your next-door neighbor scrubs his front porch twice every day and spends virtually all his time cleaning and recleaning his house, is he normal? If your sister-in-law goes to one physician after another seeking treatment for ailments that appear imaginary, is she psychologically healthy? How are we to judge what's normal and what's abnormal? More important, who's to do the judging?

These are complex questions. In a sense, *all* people make judgments about normality in that they all express opinions about others' (and perhaps their own) mental health. Of course, formal diagnoses of psychological disorders are made by mental health professionals. In making these diagnoses, clinicians rely on a variety of criteria, the foremost of which are the following:

Figure 14.1

Historical conceptions of mental illness. Throughout most of history, psychological disorders were thought to be caused by demonic possession, and the mentally ill were candidates for chains, torture, or as depicted here, exorcism.

Mary Evans Picture Library/The Image Works

1. *Deviance.* As Szasz pointed out, people are often said to have a disorder because their behavior deviates from what their society considers acceptable. What constitutes normality varies somewhat from one culture to another, but all cultures have such norms. When people ignore these standards and expectations, they may be labeled mentally ill. For example, *transvestic fetishism* is a sexual disorder in which a man achieves sexual arousal by dressing in women's clothing. This behavior is regarded as disordered because a man who wears a dress, brassiere, and nylons is deviating from our culture's norms. This example illustrates the arbitrary nature of cultural standards regarding normality, as the same overt behavior (cross-gender dressing) is acceptable for women yet deviant for men.

2. *Maladaptive behavior.* In many cases, people are judged to have a psychological disorder because their everyday adaptive behavior is impaired. This is the key criterion in the diagnosis of substance use (drug) disorders. In and of itself, alcohol and drug use is not terribly unusual or deviant. However, when the use of cocaine, for instance, begins to interfere with a person's social or occupational functioning, a substance use disorder exists. In such cases, it is the maladaptive quality of the behavior that makes it disordered.

3. *Personal distress.* Frequently, the diagnosis of a psychological disorder is based on an individual's report of great personal distress. This is usually the criterion met by people who are troubled by depression or anxiety disorders. Depressed people, for instance, may or may not exhibit deviant or maladaptive behavior. Such people are usually labeled as having a disorder when they describe their subjective pain and suffering to friends, relatives, and mental health professionals.

Although two or three criteria may apply in a particular case, people are often viewed as disordered when only one criterion is met. As you may have already noticed, diagnoses of psychological disorders involve *value judgments* about what represents normal or abnormal behavior (Sadler, 2005). The criteria of mental illness are not nearly as value-free as the criteria of physical illness. In evaluating physical diseases, people can usually agree that a weak heart or a malfunctioning kidney is pathological, regardless of their personal values. However, judgments about mental illness reflect prevailing cultural values, social trends, and political forces, as well as scientific knowledge (Kutchins & Kirk, 1997; Mechanic, 1999).

Antonyms such as *normal* versus *abnormal* and *mental health* versus *mental illness* imply that people can be divided neatly into two distinct groups: those who are normal and those who are not. In reality, it is often difficult to draw a line that clearly separates normality from abnormality. Everyone occasionally experiences personal distress. Everybody acts in deviant ways once in a while. And everyone displays some maladaptive behavior. People are judged to have psychological disorders only when their behavior becomes *extremely* deviant, maladaptive, or distressing. Thus, normality and abnormality exist on a continuum. It's a matter of degree, not an either-or proposition (see **Figure 14.2** on the next page).

Psychodiagnosis: The Classification of Disorders

Lumping all psychological disorders together would make it extremely difficult to understand them better. A sound taxonomy of mental disorders can facilitate empirical research and enhance communication among scientists and clinicians (First, 2008; Zimmerman & Spitzer, 2009). Thus, a great deal of effort has been invested in devising an elaborate system for classifying psychological disorders. This classification system, published by the American Psychiatric Association, is outlined in a book titled the *Diagnostic and Statistical Manual of Mental Disorders*. The fourth edition, referred to as DSM-IV, was released in 1994, and revised slightly in 2000. DSM-IV used a *multiaxial* system of classification. That is, it asked for judgments about individuals on five separate "axes." The diagnoses of disorders were made on Axes I and II, while the other axes involved assessments of patients' physical

John Henshall/Alamy

This man's hoarding behavior clearly represents a certain type of deviance, but does that mean he has a psychological disorder? The criteria of mental illness are more subjective and complicated than most people realize. To some extent, judgments of mental health represent value judgments.

Learn More Online

Psych Central

Psych Central is arguably the premier site for all aspects of mental health, including psychological disorders and treatment, professional issues, and information for mental health care consumers. This site offers nearly 2,000 annotated listings to information sources.

Figure 14.2

Normality and abnormality as a continuum.
No sharp boundary divides normal and abnormal
behavior. Behavior is normal or abnormal in degree,
depending on the extent to which it is deviant, personally distressing, or maladaptive.

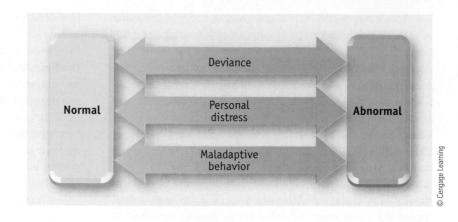

disorders, their level of stress, and their current level of
adaptive functioning.

Experts on psychodiagnosis worked for over a decade
to formulate a new edition of the diagnostic system (e.g.,
Andrews et al., 2009; Helzer et al., 2008b; Regier et al.,
2009), which is identified as DSM-5 (instead of DSM-V),
to facilitate incremental updates (such as DSM-5.1). Clinical researchers collected extensive data, held conferences,
and engaged in heated debate about whether various syndromes should be added, eliminated, or renamed. After all
this work, DSM-5 was published in May of 2013. One
major change was that the multiaxial system was retired.
The distinction between Axis I and Axis II disorders was
discarded. Clinicians are still encouraged to make nota-
tions about patients' physical illnesses, stressors, and
global functioning, but there are no formal axes for this
additional information.

One major issue in the development of DSM-5 was
whether to reduce the system's commitment to a categorical approach. In recent years many critics of the DSM
system have questioned the fundamental axiom that the
diagnostic system is built on: the assumption that people
can reliably be placed in discontinuous (nonoverlapping)
diagnostic categories (Helzer et al., 2008a; Widiger &
Trull, 2007). These critics note that there is enormous
overlap among various disorders in symptoms, making the
boundaries between diagnoses much fuzzier than would be
ideal. Critics have also pointed out that people often qualify for more than one diagnosis, a condition called **comorbidity—the coexistence of two or more disorders.** Widespread comorbidity raises the possibility that specific
diagnoses may not reflect distinct disorders, but merely
variations on the same underlying disorder (Lilienfeld &
Landfield, 2008a). Because of problems such as these,
some theorists have argued that the current *categorical approach* to diagnosis should be replaced by a *dimensional
approach,* which would describe disorders in terms of how
people score on a limited number of continuous dimensions, such as the degree to which they exhibit anxiety,
depression, agitation, hypochondria, paranoia, and so forth

(Kraemer, 2008). The practical logistics of shifting to a
dimensional approach are formidable. Agreement would
have to be reached about what dimensions to assess and
how to measure them. Because of such difficulties, the ar-
chitects of DSM-5 chose to retain a categorical approach,
although they supplemented the traditional system with a
dimensional approach to one major category of disorders
(personality disorders).

The Prevalence of Psychological Disorders

What percentage of the population is afflicted with mental
illness? Is it 10%? Perhaps 25%? Could the figure range as
high as 40% or 50%? Such estimates fall in the domain of
epidemiology—**the study of the distribution of mental
or physical disorders in a population.** The 1980s and
1990s brought major advances in psychiatric epidemiology. A number of large-scale investigations at the time
provided a huge, new database on the distribution of mental disorders (Wang et al., 2008). In epidemiology, *prevalence* **refers to the percentage of a population that exhibits a disorder during a specified time period.** In the
case of mental disorders, the most interesting data are the
estimates of *lifetime prevalence,* the percentage of people
having a specific disorder at any time in their lives.

Learn More Online

**NAMI: The National Alliance
for the Mentally Ill**

Professional and lay evaluators have consistently found
NAMI among the most helpful and informative organizations
dealing with the entire spectrum of mental disorders, including schizophrenia and depression. The NAMI site offers
a rich array of information on specific mental disorders and
on how patients and their families can find support.

Studies published in the 1980s and early 1990s found psychological disorders in roughly *one-third* of the population (Regier & Kaelber, 1995). Subsequent research, which focused on a somewhat younger sample (ages 18–54 instead of over age 18), suggested that about 44% of the adult population will struggle with some sort of psychological disorder at some point in their lives (Kessler & Zhao, 1999; Regier & Burke, 2000). The most recent large-scale epidemiological study estimated the lifetime risk of a psychiatric disorder to be 51% (Kessler et al., 2005a). Obviously, all these figures are *estimates* that depend to some extent on the sampling methods and assessment techniques used (Wakefield, 1999). Some experts believe that recent estimates are implausibly high and that they may trivialize psychiatric diagnoses (Wakefield & Spitzer, 2002).

In any event, the prevalence of psychological disorders is quite a bit higher than most people assume. The data that yielded the 44% estimate of total lifetime prevalence are summarized in **Figure 14.3**, which shows prevalence estimates for the most common classes of disorders. As you can see, the most common types of psychological disorders are (1) substance (alcohol and drugs) use disorders, (2) anxiety disorders (including obsessive-compulsive disorder), and (3) depressive and bipolar disorders, which until recently were lumped together as mood disorders.

The high prevalence of psychological disorders means that the economic costs of mental illness in modern societies are enormous. The annual cost of treating psychiatric illness in the United States was estimated to be about $150

billion in a 2003 report (New Freedom Commission on Mental Health, 2003). Another study estimated that more than 1.3 billion days of role performance (being able to go to work, function as a homemaker, and so forth) are lost each year in the United States to mental disorders (Merikangas et al., 2007). To put this exorbitant number in perspective, psychological disorders cause about three times as many disability days as cardiovascular diseases and vastly more than cancer. And there is no way to put a price on the extraordinary anguish suffered by the families of the mentally ill. Thus, the socioeconomic costs of psychological disorders are staggering.

We are now ready to start examining the specific types of psychological disorders. Obviously, we cannot cover all of the diverse disorders listed in the DSM system.

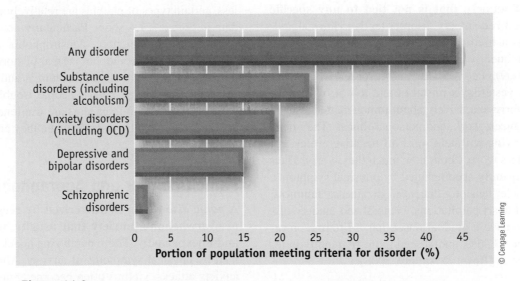

Figure 14.3

Lifetime prevalence of psychological disorders. The estimated percentage of people who have, at any time in their life, suffered from one of four types of psychological disorders or from a disorder of any kind (top bar) is shown here. Prevalence estimates vary somewhat from one study to the next, depending on the exact methods used in sampling and assessment. The estimates shown here are based on pooling data from Waves 1 and 2 of the Epidemiological Catchment Area studies and the National Comorbidity Study, as summarized by Regier and Burke (2000) and Dew, Bromet, and Switzer (2000). These studies, which collectively evaluated over 28,000 subjects, provide the best data to date on the prevalence of mental illness in the United States.

However, we will introduce most of the major categories of disorders to give you an overview of the many forms abnormal behavior takes. In discussing each set of disorders, we begin with brief descriptions of the specific syndromes or subtypes that fall in the category. Then we focus on the *etiology* of the disorders in that category. Although many paths can lead to specific disorders, some are more common than others. We highlight some of the common paths in order to enhance your understanding of the roots of abnormal behavior.

ANXIETY DISORDERS AND OBSESSIVE-COMPULSIVE DISORDER

LEARNING OBJECTIVES

- Describe three types of anxiety disorders, and discuss obsessive-compulsive disorder.
- Discuss how biology, conditioning, cognition, and stress contribute to the etiology of these disorders.

Everyone experiences anxiety from time to time. It is a natural and common reaction to many of life's difficulties. For some people, however, anxiety becomes a chronic problem. They experience high levels of anxiety with disturbing regularity. **Anxiety disorders are a class of disorders marked by feelings of excessive apprehension and anxiety.** In DSM-IV the principal types of anxiety disorders were generalized anxiety disorder, phobic disorder, obsessive-compulsive disorder, and panic disorder. DSM-5 removed obsessive-compulsive disorder from the anxiety disorders category and put it in its own special category, but for the sake of simplicity we will cover it here.

Generalized Anxiety Disorder

Generalized anxiety disorder is marked by a chronic high level of anxiety that is not tied to any specific threat. Generalized anxiety disorder tends to have a gradual onset, has a lifetime prevalence of about 5%, and is seen more frequently in females than males (Brown & Lawrence, 2009). People with this disorder worry constantly about yesterday's mistakes and tomorrow's problems. They worry excessively about minor matters related to family, finances, work, and personal illness. They hope that their worrying will help ward off negative events, but they nonetheless worry about how much they worry. Their anxiety is frequently accompanied by physical symptoms, such as muscle tension, diarrhea, dizziness, faintness, sweating, and heart palpitations. Generalized anxiety disorder tends to have a gradual onset, has a lifetime prevalence of about 5%–6%, and is seen more frequently in females than males (Rowa & Antony, 2008).

Phobic Disorder

In a phobic disorder, an individual's troublesome anxiety has a specific focus. **A phobic disorder is marked by a persistent and irrational fear of an object or situation that presents no realistic danger.** Although mild phobias are extremely common, people are said to have a phobic disorder only when their fears seriously interfere with their everyday behavior. Phobic reactions tend to be accompanied by physical symptoms of anxiety, such as trembling and palpitations (Rapee & Barlow, 2001). The following case provides an example of a phobic disorder:

Hilda is 32 years of age and has a rather unusual fear. She is terrified of snow. She cannot go outside in the snow. She cannot even stand to see snow or hear about it on the weather report. Her phobia severely constricts her day-to-day behavior. Probing in therapy revealed that her phobia was caused by a traumatic experience at age 11. Playing at a ski lodge, she was buried briefly by a small avalanche of snow. She had no recollection of this experience until it was recovered in therapy. (Adapted from Laughlin, 1967, p. 227)

As Hilda's unusual snow phobia illustrates, people can develop phobic responses to virtually anything. Nonetheless, certain types of phobias are relatively common, as the data in **Figure 14.4** show. Particularly common are acrophobia (fear of heights), claustrophobia (fear of small, enclosed places), brontophobia (fear of storms), hydrophobia (fear of water), and various animal and insect phobias (McCabe & Antony, 2008). People troubled by phobias typically realize that their fears are irrational, but they still are unable to calm themselves when they encounter a phobic object.

Panic Disorder and Agoraphobia

A *panic disorder* is characterized by recurrent attacks of overwhelming anxiety that usually occur suddenly and unexpectedly. These paralyzing attacks are accompanied by physical symptoms of anxiety. After a number of anxiety attacks, victims often become apprehensive, wondering when their next attack will occur. Their concern about exhibiting panic in public sometimes escalates to the point where they are afraid to leave home. This creates a condition called *agoraphobia.*

Agoraphobia is a fear of going out to public places. (its literal meaning is "fear of the marketplace or open places"). Because of this fear, some people become prisoners confined to their homes, although many can venture out if

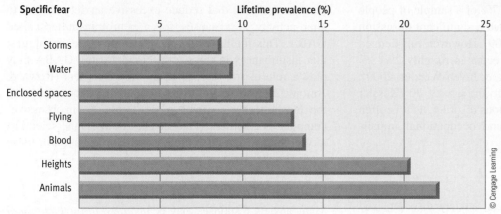

Figure 14.4

Common phobic fears. This graph shows the lifetime prevalence of the most common types of phobic fears reported by participants in a study by Curtis et al. (1998). As you can see, a substantial number of people struggle with a variety of specific phobias. Bear in mind that only a portion of these people qualify for a diagnosis of phobic disorder, which is merited only if individuals' phobias seriously impair their everyday functioning.

© Cengage Learning

accompanied by a trusted companion (Hollander & Simeon, 2008). As its name suggests, agoraphobia was once viewed as a phobic disorder. However, in DSM-III and DSM-IV it was characterized as a common complication of panic disorder. In DSM-5 it is listed as a separate anxiety disorder that may or may not coexist with panic disorder.

About two-thirds of people who are diagnosed with panic disorder are female (Taylor, Cox, & Asmundson, 2009). The onset of panic disorder typically occurs during late adolescence or early adulthood (McClure-Tone & Pine, 2009).

Obsessive-Compulsive Disorder

Obsessions are *thoughts* that repeatedly intrude on one's consciousness in a distressing way. Compulsions are *actions* that one feels forced to carry out. Thus, **an *obsessive-compulsive disorder (OCD)* is marked by persistent, uncontrollable intrusions of unwanted thoughts (obsessions) and urges to engage in senseless rituals (compul-**

Sciencecartoonsplus.com 1990 by Sidney Harris

sions). To illustrate, let's examine the bizarre behavior of a man once reputed to be the wealthiest person in the world:

The famous industrialist Howard Hughes was obsessed with the possibility of being contaminated by germs. This led him to devise extraordinary rituals to minimize the possibility of such contamination. He would spend hours methodically cleaning a single telephone. He once wrote a three-page memo instructing assistants on exactly how to open cans of fruit for him. The following is just a small portion of the instructions that Hughes provided for a driver who delivered films to his bungalow. "Get out of the car on the traffic side. Do not at any time be on the side of the car between the car and the curb. . . . Carry only one can of film at a time. Step over the gutter opposite the place where the sidewalk dead-ends into the curb from a point as far out into the center of the road as possible. Do not ever walk on the grass at all, also do not step into the gutter at all. Walk to the bungalow keeping as near to the center of the sidewalk as possible." (Adapted from Barlett & Steele, 1979, pp. 227–237)

Obsessions often center on fear of contamination, inflicting harm on others, suicide, or sexual acts. Compulsions usually involve rituals that temporarily relieve anxiety. Common examples include constant handwashing; repetitive cleaning of things that are already clean; endless rechecking of locks, faucets, and such; and excessive arranging, counting, and hoarding of things (Pato et al., 2008). Specific types of obsessions tend to be associated with specific types of compulsions. For example, obsessions about contamination tend to be paired with cleaning compulsions, and obsessions about symmetry tend to be paired with ordering and arranging compulsions.

Many of us can be compulsive at times. In-

g215/Shutterstock.com

deed, a recent study found that 17% of a sample of people without a mental disorder reported a significant obsession or compulsion (Fullana et al., 2009). However, full-fledged obsessive-compulsive disorders occur in roughly 2%–3% of the population (Zohar, Fostick, & Juven-Wetzler, 2009). Most cases (75%) emerge before the age of 30 (Kessler et al., 2005a). OCD can be a serious disorder, as it is often associated with severe social and occupational impairments (Torres et al., 2006).

Etiology

Like most psychological disorders, anxiety disorders and OCD develop out of complicated interactions among a variety of factors. Conditioning and learning appear especially important, but biological factors may also contribute.

Biological Factors

Recent studies suggest that there may be a weak to moderate genetic predisposition to anxiety disorders, depending on the specific type of disorder (Fyer, 2009). These findings are consistent with the idea that inherited differences in temperament might make some people more vulnerable than others to anxiety disorders. Kagan and his colleagues (1992) found that about 15%–20% of infants display an *inhibited temperament,* characterized by shyness, timidity, and wariness, which appears to have a strong genetic basis. Research suggests that this temperament is a risk factor for the development of anxiety disorders (Coles, Schofield, & Pietrefesa, 2006).

One influential theory holds that *anxiety sensitivity* may make people vulnerable to anxiety disorders (McWilliams et al., 2007). According to this notion, some people are very sensitive to internal physiological symptoms of anxiety and are prone to overreact with fear when they experience these symptoms. Anxiety sensitivity may fuel an inflationary spiral in which anxiety breeds more anxiety, which eventually spins out of control in the form of an anxiety disorder.

Recent evidence suggests that a link may exist between anxiety disorders and neurochemical activity in the brain. *Neurotransmitters* **are chemicals that carry signals from one neuron to another.** Therapeutic drugs (such as Valium) that reduce excessive anxiety appear to alter activity at synapses for a neurotransmitter called GABA. This finding and other lines of evidence suggest that disturbances in the neural circuits using GABA may play a role in some types of anxiety disorders (Rowa & Antony, 2008). Abnormalities in other neural circuits using the transmitter serotonin have been implicated in obsessive-compulsive disorders (Pato et al., 2008). Thus, scientists are beginning to unravel the neurochemical bases for these kinds of disorders.

Conditioning and Learning

Many anxiety responses may be *acquired through classical conditioning* and *maintained through operant conditioning* (see Chapter 2). According to Mowrer (1947), an originally neutral stimulus (the snow in Hilda's case, for instance) may be paired with a frightening event (the avalanche) so that it becomes a conditioned stimulus eliciting anxiety (see **Figure 14.5**). Once a fear is acquired through classical conditioning, the person may start avoiding the anxiety-producing stimulus. The avoidance response is *negatively reinforced* because it is followed by a reduction in anxiety. This process involves operant conditioning (also shown in **Figure 14.5**). Thus, separate conditioning processes may create and then sustain specific anxiety responses (Levis, 1989). Consistent with this view, studies find that a substantial portion of people suffering from phobias can identify a traumatic conditioning experience that probably contributed to their anxiety disorder (McCabe & Antony, 2008).

People tend to develop phobias to snakes very easily but to hot stoves rarely, even though the latter can be just as painful. Preparedness theory can explain this paradox.

snake: © paytai/Shutterstock.com; fry pan: © Kzenon/Shutterstock.com

Figure 14.5

Conditioning as an explanation for phobias. (1) Many phobias appear to be acquired through classical conditioning when a neutral stimulus is paired with an anxiety-arousing stimulus. (2) Once acquired, a phobia may be maintained through operant conditioning, because avoidance of the phobic stimulus leads to a reduction in anxiety, resulting in negative reinforcement.

The tendency to develop phobias of certain types of objects and situations may be explained by Martin Seligman's (1971) concept of *preparedness*. Like many theorists, Seligman believes that classical conditioning creates most phobic responses. *However, he suggests that people are biologically prepared by their evolutionary history to acquire some fears much more easily than others.* His theory would explain why people develop phobias of ancient sources of threat (such as snakes, spiders, and heights) much more readily than modern sources of threat (such as electrical outlets, hammers, or hot irons). Arne Öhman and Susan Mineka (2001) have updated the notion of preparedness, which they call an *evolved module for fear learning*. They maintain that this evolved module is automatically activated by stimuli related to survival threats in evolutionary history and is relatively resistant to intentional efforts to suppress the resulting fears. Consistent with this view, they have found that phobic stimuli associated with evolutionary threats (snakes, spiders) tend to produce more rapid conditioning of fears and stronger fear responses than modern fear-relevant stimuli, such as guns and knives (Mineka & Öhman, 2002).

Critics note a number of problems with conditioning models of phobias. For instance, many people with phobias cannot recall or identify a traumatic conditioning experience that led to their phobia. Conversely, many people endure extremely traumatic experiences that should, according to this rationale, create a phobia but do not (Coelho & Purkis, 2009). Moreover, phobic fears can be acquired indirectly, by observing another's fear response to a specific stimulus or by absorbing fear-inducing information (imagine a parent harping on how dangerous lightning is) (Coelho & Purkis, 2009). Thus, the development of phobias may depend on synergistic interactions among a variety of learning processes.

Cognitive Factors

Cognitive theorists maintain that certain styles of thinking make some people particularly vulnerable to anxiety disorders (Craske & Waters, 2005). According to these theorists, some people are prone to suffer from problems with anxiety because they tend to (a) misinterpret harmless situations as threatening, (b) focus excessive attention on perceived threats, and (c) selectively recall information that seems threatening (Beck, 1997; McNally, 1996). In one intriguing test of the cognitive view, anxious and nonanxious subjects were asked to read thirty-two sentences that could be interpreted in either a threatening or a nonthreatening manner (Eysenck et al., 1991). For instance, one such sentence was "The doctor examined little Emma's growth," which could mean that the doctor checked her height or the growth of a tumor. As **Figure 14.6** shows, the anxious subjects interpreted the sentences in a threatening way more often than the nonanxious subjects did. Thus, the cognitive view holds that some people are prone to anxiety disorders because they see threat in every corner of their lives (Riskind, 2005).

Figure 14.6

Cognitive factors in anxiety disorders. Eysenck and his colleagues (1991) compared how subjects with anxiety disorders and nonanxious subjects tended to interpret sentences that could be viewed as threatening or nonthreatening. Consistent with cognitive models of anxiety disorders, anxious subjects were more likely to interpret the sentences in a threatening light.

Stress

Finally, studies have supported the long-held suspicion that anxiety disorders are stress related (Beidel & Stipelman, 2007). For instance, Faravelli and Pallanti (1989) found that patients with panic disorder had experienced a dramatic increase in stress in the month prior to the onset of their disorder. In another study, Brown et al. (1998) found an association between stress and the development of social phobia. Thus, there is reason to believe that high stress often helps precipitate the onset of anxiety disorders.

DISSOCIATIVE DISORDERS

LEARNING OBJECTIVES

- Distinguish between two types of dissociative disorders.
- Summarize what is known about the causes of dissociative disorders.

Dissociative disorders are probably the most controversial set of disorders in the diagnostic system, sparking heated debate among normally subdued researchers and clinicians (Simeon & Loewenstein, 2009). *Dissociative disorders are a class of disorders in which people lose contact with portions of their consciousness or memory, resulting in disruptions in their sense of identity.* Here we describe two dissociative syndromes—dissociative amnesia and dissociative identity disorder—both of which are relatively uncommon.

Dissociative Amnesia

Dissociative amnesia is a sudden loss of memory for important personal information that is too extensive to be due to normal forgetting. Memory losses may occur for a single traumatic event (such as an automobile accident or home fire) or for an extended period of time surrounding the event. Cases of amnesia have been observed after people have experienced disasters, accidents, combat stress, physical abuse, and rape, or after they have witnessed the violent death of a parent, among other things (Cardeña & Gleaves, 2007). In some cases, having forgotten their name, their family, where they live, and where they work, these people wander away from their home area. In spite of this wholesale forgetting, they remember matters unrelated to their identity, such as how to drive a car and how to do math.

Dissociative Identity Disorder

Dissociative identity disorder (DID) involves the coexistence in one person of two or more largely complete, and usually very different, personalities. The name for this disorder used to be *multiple personality disorder,* which still enjoys informal usage. In dissociative identity disorder, the divergences in behavior go far beyond those that people normally display in adapting to different roles in life. People with "multiple personalities" feel that they have more than one identity. Each personality has his or her own name, memories, traits, and physical mannerisms. Although rare, this "Dr. Jekyll and Mr. Hyde" syndrome is frequently portrayed in novels, movies, and television shows. In popular media portrayals, the syndrome is often mistakenly called *schizophrenia.* As you will see later, schizophrenic disorders are entirely different and do not involve "split personality."

In dissociative identity disorder, the various personalities generally report that they are unaware of each other (Eich et al., 1997), although doubts have been raised about the accuracy of this assertion (Allen & Iacono, 2001). The alternate personalities commonly display traits that are quite foreign to the original personality. For instance, a shy, inhibited person might develop a flamboyant, extraverted alternate personality. Transitions between identities often occur suddenly. The disparities between identities can be bizarre, as personalities may assert that they are different in age, race, gender, or sexual orientation (Kluft, 1996). Dissociative identity disorder is seen more in women than men (Simeon & Loewenstein, 2009).

Starting in the 1970s, a dramatic increase occurred in the diagnosis of multiple personality disorder (Kihlstrom, 2001, 2005). Only seventy-nine well-documented cases had accumulated up through 1970, but by the late 1990s about 40,000 cases were estimated to have been reported (Lilienfeld & Lynn, 2003). Some theorists believe that these disorders used to be underdiagnosed—that is, they

Learn More Online

International Society for the Study of Dissociation

Dissociative disorders, including dissociative identity disorder, are the focus of this organization of research and clinical professionals. In addition to a selective bibliography and a set of treatment guidelines, the site provides links to other professional groups involved in studying and treating dissociation.

often went undetected (Maldonado & Spiegel, 2008). However, other theorists argue that a handful of clinicians had begun overdiagnosing the condition and that some clinicians even *encouraged and contributed* to the emergence of DID (McHugh, 1995; Powell & Gee, 1999). Consistent with this view, a survey of all the psychiatrists in Switzerland found that 90% of them had never seen a case of dissociative identity disorder, whereas 3 of the psychiatrists had each seen more than 20 DID patients (Modestin, 1992). The data from this study suggest that 6 psychiatrists (out of 655 surveyed) accounted for two-thirds of the dissociative identity disorder diagnoses in Switzerland.

Etiology

Dissociative amnesia is usually attributed to excessive stress. However, relatively little is known about why this extreme reaction occurs in a tiny minority of people but not in the vast majority who are subjected to similar stress. Some theorists speculate that certain personality traits—fantasy proneness and a tendency to become intensely absorbed in personal experiences—may make some people more susceptible to dissociative disorders, but adequate evidence is lacking on this line of thought (Kihlstrom, Glisky, & Angiulo, 1994).

The causes of dissociative identity disorder are particularly obscure. Some skeptical theorists (Gee, Allen, & Powell, 2003; Lilienfeld et al., 1999; Spanos, 1996), believe that people with multiple personalities are engaging in intentional role playing to use mental illness as a face-saving excuse for their personal failings. Nicholas Spanos (1996) also argues that a small minority of therapists help create multiple personalities in their patients by subtly encouraging the emergence of alternate personalities. According to Spanos, dissociative identity disorder is a creation of modern Western culture, much as demonic possession was a creation of early Christianity.

To bolster his argument, Spanos discusses how DID patients' symptom presentations seem to have been influenced by popular media. For example, the typical patient with dissociative identity disorder used to report having two or three personalities, but since the publication of *Sybil* (Schreiber, 1973) and other books describing patients with many personalities, the average number of alternate personalities has climbed to about fifteen. In a similar vein, a dramatic upsurge occurred in the number of dissociative patients reporting that they were victims of ritual satanic abuse during childhood after the publication of *Michelle Remembers* (Smith & Pazder, 1980), a book about a DID patient who purportedly was tortured by a satanic cult.

In spite of these concerns, many clinicians are convinced that DID is an authentic disorder (van der Hart & Nijenhuis, 2009). They argue that there is no incentive for either patients or therapists to manufacture cases of multiple personalities, which are often greeted with skepticism and outright hostility. They maintain that most cases of DID are rooted in severe emotional trauma that occurred during childhood (Maldonado & Spiegel, 2008). A substantial majority of people with DID report a history of disturbed home life, beatings and rejection from parents, and sexual abuse (Van der Hart & Nijenhuis, 2009). However, this abuse typically has not been independently verified (Lilienfeld & Lynn, 2003). Moreover, this link would not be unique to DID, as a history of child abuse elevates the likelihood of *many* disorders, especially among females (MacMillan et al., 2001).

In the final analysis, little is known about the causes of dissociative identity disorder, which remains a controversial diagnosis (Lilienfeld & Arkowitz, 2011). In one survey of American psychiatrists, only one-quarter of the respondents indicated that they felt there was solid evidence for the scientific validity of the DID diagnosis (Pope et al., 1999). Consistent with this finding, a more recent study found that scientific interest in DID has dwindled since the mid-1990s (Pope et al., 2006).

DEPRESSION AND BIPOLAR DISORDER

LEARNING OBJECTIVES

- Describe depressive and bipolar disorders, discuss their prevalence, and explain their relation to suicide risk.
- Explain how genetic, neurochemical, neuroanatomical, and hormonal factors contribute to the development of depressive and bipolar disorders.

- Discuss how cognitive processes, interpersonal factors, and stress contribute to the development of depressive and bipolar disorders.

What might Abraham Lincoln, Leo Tolstoy, Marilyn Monroe, Vincent Van Gogh, Ernest Hemingway, Winston Churchill, Virginia Woolf, Sheryl Crow, Owen Wilson, Irving Berlin, Kurt Cobain, Francis Ford Coppola, Carrie Fisher, Ted Turner, Sting, Mike Wallace, Larry Flynt, and Ben Stiller have in common? Yes, they all achieved great

prominence, albeit in different ways at different times. But, more pertinent to our interest, they all suffered from depression or bipolar disorder. Although these disorders can be terribly debilitating, people afflicted with them may still achieve greatness, because such disorders tend to be *episodic*. In other words, the disorders often come and go.

Mood disorders are common and have afflicted many successful, well-known people, such as Jon Hamm and Anne Hathaway.

Thus, episodes of disturbance are interspersed among periods of normality. These episodes of disturbance can vary greatly in length, but they typically last 3 to 12 months (Akiskal, 2005).

In DSM-III and DSM-IV, *major depressive disorder* and *bipolar disorder* were lumped together in a category called mood disorders. In DSM-5 they each get their own chapter or category, but we will discuss them together here. **Figure 14.7** depicts the main ways in which these disorders differ. People with major depressive disorder experience emotional extremes at just one end of the mood continuum as they experience periodic bouts of depression. People with bipolar disorders experience emotional extremes at both ends of the mood continuum, going through periods of both *depression* and *mania* (excitement and elation).

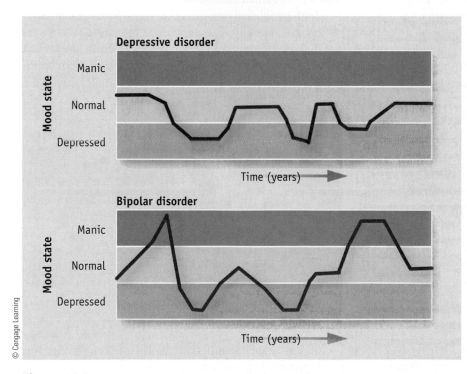

Figure 14.7

Episodic patterns in depressive and bipolar disorders. Episodes of emotional disturbance come and go unpredictably in depressive and bipolar disorders. People with major depressive disorders suffer from bouts of depression only, while people with bipolar disorders experience both manic and depressive episodes. The time between episodes of disturbance varies greatly.

Major Depressive Disorder

The line between normal and abnormal depression can be difficult to draw (Akiskal, 2009). Ultimately, a subjective judgment is required. Crucial considerations in this judgment include the duration of the depression and its disruptive effects. When depression significantly impairs everyday adaptive behavior for more than a few weeks, there is reason for concern.

In *major depressive disorder* people show persistent feelings of sadness and despair and a loss of interest in previous sources of pleasure. **Figure 14.8** summarizes the most common symptoms of depressive episodes and compares them to the symptoms of manic episodes. A central feature of depression is *anhedonia*—a diminished ability to experience pleasure. Depressed people lack the energy or motivation to tackle the tasks of living, to the point where they often have trouble getting out of bed (Craighead et al., 2008). Hence, depressed people

COMPARISON OF DEPRESSIVE AND MANIC SYMPTOMS		
Symptoms	Depressive episode	Manic episode
Emotional symptoms	Dysphoric, gloomy mood Diminished ability to experience pleasure Sense of hopelessness	Euphoric, enthusiastic mood Excessive pursuit of pleasurable activities Unwarranted optimism
Behavioral symptoms	Fatigue, loss of energy Insomnia Slowed speech and movement Social withdrawal	Energetic, tireless, hyperactive Decreased need for sleep Rapid speech and agitation Increased sociability
Cognitive symptoms	Impaired ability to think and make decisions Slowed thought processes Excessive worry, rumination Guilt, self-blame, unrealistic negative evaluations of one's worth	Grandiose planning, indiscriminate decision making Racing thoughts, easily distracted Impulsive behavior Inflated self-esteem and self-confidence

© Cengage Learning

Figure 14.8

Common symptoms in manic and depressive episodes. The emotional, cognitive, and motor symptoms exhibited in manic and depressive episodes are largely the opposite of each other.

often give up activities they used to find enjoyable. For example, a depressed person might quit going bowling or give up a favorite hobby like photography. Reduced appetite and insomnia are common. People with depression often lack energy. They tend to move sluggishly and talk slowly. Anxiety, irritability, and brooding are frequently observed. Self-esteem tends to sink as the depressed person begins to feel worthless. Depression plunges people into feelings of hopelessness, dejection, and boundless guilt. To make matters worse, people who suffer from depression often exhibit other disorders as well. Coexisting anxiety disorders and substance use disorders are particularly frequent (Boland & Keller, 2009).

The first onset of a depressive disorder can occur at any point in the life span, but a substantial majority of cases emerge before age 40 (Hammen, 2003). Depression occurs in children and adolescents, as well as adults (Wijlaars, Nazareth, & Petersen, 2012). The vast majority of people who suffer from depression experience more than one episode over the course of their lifetime. The average number of depressive episodes is five to six, and the average length of these episodes is about 6 months (Akiskal, 2009). Evidence suggests that an earlier age of onset is associated with more episodes of depression, more severe symptoms, and greater impairment of social and occupational functioning (Zisook et al., 2007). Although depression tends to be episodic, some people suffer from chronic major depression that may persist for years (Klein, 2010). Chronic major depression is associated with a particularly severe impairment of functioning. People with chronic depression tend to have a relatively early onset and high rates of comorbidity (additional disorders).

How common are depressive disorders? Well, estimates of the prevalence of depression vary quite a bit from one study to another because of the previously mentioned difficulty in drawing a line between normal dejection and abnormal depression. That said, depression is clearly a common disorder. The pooled data from the large-scale studies cited in **Figure 14.3** yielded a lifetime prevalence estimate of 13%–14%.

Research indicates that the prevalence of depression is about twice as high in women as it is in men (Nolen-Hoeksema & Hilt, 2009). The many possible explanations for this gender gap are the subject of considerable debate. The gap does *not* appear to be attributable to differences in genetic makeup (Kessler et al., 2003). A small portion of the disparity may be the result of women's elevated vulnerability to depression at certain points in their reproductive life cycle (Nolen-Hoeksema & Hilt, 2009). Obviously, only women have to worry abut the phenomena of postpartum and postmenopausal depression. Susan Nolen-Hoeksema (2001) argues that women experience more depression than men because they are far more likely to be victims of sexual abuse and somewhat more likely to endure poverty, harassment, and role constraints. In other words, she attributes the higher prevalence of depression among women to their experience of greater stress and adversity. Nolen-Hoeksema also believes that women have a greater tendency than men to *ruminate* about setbacks

Courtesy of Susan Nolen-Hoeksema

Susan Nolen-Hoeksema

Learn More Online

Dr. Ivan's Depression Central

Some might suggest that psychiatrist Ivan Goldberg's site would be better titled "Everything You Ever Wanted to Know About Depression . . ." He offers visitors a great depth of resources regarding depression and mood disorders.

and problems. Evidence suggests that this tendency to dwell on one's difficulties elevates vulnerability to depression, as we will discuss momentarily.

Bipolar Disorder

Bipolar disorder (**formerly known as** *manic-depressive disorder*) **is marked by the experience of both depressed and manic periods.** The symptoms seen in manic periods are generally the opposite of those seen in depression (see **Figure 14.8** for a comparison). In a manic episode, a person's mood becomes elevated to the point of euphoria. Self-esteem skyrockets as the person bubbles over with optimism, energy, and extravagant plans. Individuals become hyperactive and may go for days without sleep. They talk rapidly and shift topics wildly as their minds race at breakneck speed. Judgment is often impaired. Some people in manic periods gamble impulsively, spend money frantically, or become sexually reckless. Like depressive disorders, bipolar disorders vary considerably in severity.

You may be thinking that the euphoria in manic episodes sounds appealing. If so, you are not entirely wrong. In their milder forms, manic states can seem attractive. The increases in energy, self-esteem, and optimism can be deceptively seductive. Because of their increased energy, many bipolar patients report temporary surges of productivity and creativity (Goodwin & Jamison, 2007).

Although manic episodes may have some positive aspects, bipolar disorder ultimately proves to be troublesome for most victims. Manic periods often have a paradoxical negative undertow of uneasiness and irritability. Moreover, mild manic episodes usually escalate to higher levels that become scary and disturbing. Impaired judgment leads many victims to do things that they greatly regret later, as illustrated in the following case:

Robert, a dentist, awoke one morning with the idea that he was the most gifted dental surgeon in his tri-state area. He decided that he should try to provide services to as many people as possible, so that more people could benefit from his talents. Thus, he decided to remodel his two-chair dental office, installing 20 booths so that he could simultaneously attend to 20 patients. That same day he drew up plans for this arrangement, telephoned a number of remodelers, and invited bids for the work. Later that day, impatient to get going on his remodeling, he rolled up his sleeves, got himself a sledgehammer, and began to knock down the walls in his office. Annoyed when that didn't go so well, he smashed his dental tools, washbasins, and X-ray equipment. Later, Robert's wife became concerned about his behavior and summoned two of her adult daughters for assistance.

"Those? Oh, just a few souvenirs from my bipolar-disorder days."

The daughters responded quickly, arriving at the family home with their husbands. In the ensuing discussion, Robert—after bragging about his sexual prowess—made advances toward his daughters. He had to be subdued by their husbands. (Adapted from Kleinmuntz, 1980, p. 309)

Although not rare, bipolar disorder is much less common than depression. Bipolar disorder affects roughly about 1% of the population (Merikangas & Pato, 2009). Unlike depressive disorder, bipolar disorder is seen equally in men and women (Rihmer & Angst, 2009). As **Figure 14.9** shows, the onset of bipolar disorder is age related, with 25 being the

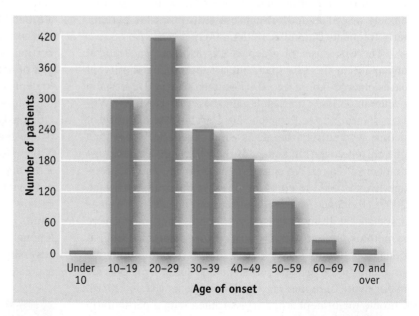

Figure 14.9

Age of onset for bipolar disorder. The onset of bipolar disorder typically occurs in adolescence or early adulthood. The data graphed here, which were combined from ten studies, show the distribution of age of onset for 1304 bipolar patients. As you can see, bipolar disorder emerges most frequently during the 20s decade.

Source: From Goodwin, F. K., & Jamison, K. R. (1990). *Manic-depressive illness.* New York: Oxford University Press. Copyright © 1990 Oxford University Press, Inc. Used by permission of Oxford University Press, Inc.

median age of onset (Miklowitz & Johnson, 2007). The mood swings in bipolar disorder can be patterned in many ways. Manic episodes typically last about 4 months. Episodes of depression tend to run somewhat longer, and most bipolar patients end up spending more time in depressed states than manic states (Bauer, 2008).

Mood Dysfunction and Suicide

A tragic, heartbreaking problem associated with depressive and bipolar disorders is suicide, which is the eleventh leading cause of death in the United States, accounting for about 30,000 deaths annually. Official statistics may underestimate the scope of the problem, as many suicides are disguised as accidents, either by the suicidal person or by the survivors who try to cover up afterward. Moreover, experts estimate that suicide attempts may outnumber completed suicides by a ratio of as much as ten to one (Sudak, 2009). Anyone can commit suicide, but some groups are at higher risk than others (Carroll-Ghosh, Victor, & Bourgeois, 2003). Evidence suggests that women *attempt* suicide three times more often than men. But men are more likely to actually kill themselves in an attempt, so they *complete* four times as many suicides as women. In regard to age, completed suicides peak in the over-75 age bracket.

With the luxury of hindsight, it is recognized that about 90% of the people who complete suicide suffer from some type of psychological disorder, although in some cases this disorder may not be readily apparent beforehand (Melvin et al., 2008). As you might expect, both bipolar disorder and depression are associated with dramatic elevations in suicide rates. Studies suggest that the lifetime risk of completed suicide is about 15%–20% in people with bipolar disorder and about 10%–15% in those who have grappled with depression (Sudak, 2009), but some experts believe that these estimates are overly high (Joiner et al., 2009). Smaller elevations in suicide rates are seen among people who suffer from schizophrenia, alcoholism, and substance abuse (Mann & Currier, 2006). Unfortunately, there is no foolproof way to prevent suicidal persons from taking their own life, but some useful tips are discussed in **Figure 14.10**.

© erics/Shutterstock.com

Etiology

We know quite a bit about the etiology of depressive and bipolar disorders, although the puzzle hasn't been assembled completely. There appear to be a number of routes into these disorders, involving in-

---

Figure 14.10
Preventing suicide. As Sudak (2005) notes, "it is not possible to prevent all suicides or to totally and absolutely protect a given patient from suicide. What is possible is to reduce the likelihood of suicide" (p. 2449). Hence, the advice summarized here may prove useful if you ever have to help someone through a suicidal crisis. (Based on American Association of Suicidology, 2007; American Foundation for Suicide Prevention, 2007; Fremouw, de Perczel, & Ellis, 1990; Rosenthal, 1988; Shneidman, Farberow, & Litman, 1994)

tricate interactions between psychological and biological factors.

Genetic Vulnerability

The evidence strongly suggests that genetic factors influence the likelihood of developing major depression or bipolar disorder (Lohoff & Berrettini, 2009). In studies that assess the impact of heredity on psychological disorders, investigators look at *concordance rates*. **A concordance rate indicates the percentage of twin pairs or other pairs of relatives who exhibit the same disorder.** If relatives who share more genetic similarity show higher concordance rates than relatives who share less genetic overlap, this finding supports the genetic hypothesis. Twin studies, which compare identical and fraternal twins (see Chapter 2), suggest that genetic factors *are* involved in depressive and bipolar disorders (Kelsoe, 2009). Concordance rates average around 65%–72% for identical twins but only 14%–19% for fraternal twins, who share less genetic similarity.

Thus, evidence suggests that heredity can create a *predisposition* to these disorders. Environmental factors probably determine whether this predisposition is converted into an actual disorder. Some promising results have been reported in *genetic mapping* studies that have attempted to pinpoint the specific genes that shape vulnerability to depressive and bipolar disorders (Levinson, 2009). However, results have been disturbingly inconsistent, and scientists do *not* appear to be on the verge of unraveling the genetic code for these disorders, which probably depend on subtle variations in constellations of many genes (Bearden, Jasinka, & Freimer, 2009).

Neurochemical and Neuroanatomical Factors

Heredity may influence susceptibility to depressive and bipolar disorders by creating a predisposition toward certain types of neurochemical abnormalities in the brain. Correlations have been found between these disorders and abnormal levels of two neurotransmitters in the brain: norepinephrine and serotonin (Duman, Polan, & Schatzberg, 2008), although other neurotransmitter disturbances may also contribute (Dunlop, Garlow, & Nemeroff, 2009). The details remain elusive, but low levels of serotonin appear to be a crucial factor underlying most forms of depression (Johnson et al., 2009). A variety of drug therapies are fairly effective in the treatment of depressive disorders. Most of these drugs are known to affect the availability (in the brain) of the neurotransmitters that have been related to depressive disorders (Bhagwagar & Heninger, 2009). Since this effect is unlikely to be a coincidence, it bolsters the plausibility of the idea that neurochemical changes contribute to depressive and bipolar disturbances.

Studies have also found some interesting correlations between

depressive disorders and a variety of structural abnormalities in the brain (Kempton et al., 2011). Perhaps the best-documented correlation is the association between depression and *reduced hippocampal volume* (Davidson, Pizzagalli, & Nitschke, 2009). The *hippocampus,* which is known to play a major role in memory (see **Figure 14.11**), tends to be about 8%–10% smaller in depressed subjects than in normal subjects (Videbech & Ravnkilde, 2004).

A fascinating theory of the biological bases of depression may be able to account for this finding. The springboard for this theory is the discovery that the human brain continues to generate new neurons in adulthood, especially in the hippocampal formation (Gage, 2002). This process is called *neurogenesis.* Evidence suggests that depression occurs when major life stress causes neurochemical reactions that suppress neurogenesis, resulting in reduced hippocampal volume (Duman et al., 2008; Jacobs, 2004). According to this view, the suppression of neurogenesis is the central cause of depression, and antidepressant drugs

Cerebral cortex

Hippocampus

© Jenn Huls/Shutterstock.com

Wadsworth Collection

© Cengage Learning

Figure 14.11

The hippocampus and depression. This graphic shows the hippocampus in blue. The photo inset shows a brain dissected to reveal the hippocampus in both the right and left hemispheres. It has long been known that the hippocampus plays a key role in memory, but its possible role in depression has only come to light in recent years. Research suggests that shrinkage of the hippocampal formation due to suppressed neurogenesis may be a key causal factor underlying depressive disorders.

that relieve depression do so because they promote neurogenesis (Duman & Monteggia, 2006). A great deal of additional research will be required to fully test this innovative model of the biological bases of depressive disorders.

Hormonal Factors

In recent years researchers have begun to focus on how hormonal changes may contribute to the emergence of depression. As we discussed in Chapter 3, in times of stress the brain sends signals along two pathways. One of them runs from the hypothalamus to the pituitary gland to the adrenal cortex, which releases corticosteroid hormones. This pathway is often referred to as the hypothalamic-pituitary-adrenocortical (HPA) axis. Evidence suggests that overactivity along the HPA axis in response to stress may often play a role in the development of depression (Goodwin, 2009). Consistent with this hypothesis, depressed patients tend to show elevated levels of cortisol, a key stress hormone produced by HPA activity (Thase, 2009). Some theorists believe that these hormonal changes eventually have an impact in the brain, where they may be the trigger for the suppression of neurogenesis just discussed (Duman et al., 2008).

Cognitive Factors

A variety of theories emphasize how cognitive factors contribute to depressive disorders. We will discuss Aaron Beck's (1987, 2008) influential cognitive theory of depression in Chapter 15, where his approach to therapy is described. In this section, we examine Martin Seligman's *learned helplessness model* of depression. Based largely on animal research, Seligman (1974) proposed that depression is caused by *learned helplessness*—passive "giving up" behavior produced by exposure to unavoidable aversive events (such as uncontrollable shock in the laboratory). He originally considered learned helplessness to be a product of conditioning but eventually revised his theory, giving it a cognitive slant. The reformulated theory of learned helplessness postulates that the roots of depression lie in how people explain the setbacks and other negative events that they experience (Abramson, Seligman, & Teasdale, 1978). According to Seligman (1990), people who exhibit a *pessimistic explanatory style* are especially vulnerable to depression. These people tend to attribute their setbacks to their personal flaws instead of to situational factors, and they tend to draw global, far-reaching conclusions about their personal inadequacies based on these setbacks.

In accord with cognitive models of depression, Susan Nolen-Hoeksema (1991, 2000) has found that people who *ruminate* about their problems and setbacks have elevated rates of depression and tend to remain depressed longer than those who do not ruminate. People who tend to ruminate repetitively focus their attention on their depressing feelings, thinking constantly about how sad, lethargic, and unmotivated they are. Excessive rumination tends to foster and amplify episodes of depression by increasing negative thinking, impairing problem solving, and undermining social support (Nolen-Hoeksema, Wisco, & Lyubomirsky, 2008). Nolen-Hoeksema believes that women have a greater tendency to ruminate than men and that this disparity may be a major reason that depression is more prevalent in women. Moreover, the effects of rumination are not limited to aggravating depressive disorders. Rumination is also associated with increased anxiety, binge eating, and binge drinking (Nolen-Hoeksema et al., 2008).

In sum, cognitive models of depression maintain that negative thinking is what leads to depression in many people. The principal problem with cognitive theories is their difficulty in separating cause from effect (Feliciano & Areán, 2007). Does negative thinking cause depression? Or does depression cause negative thinking (see **Figure 14.12**)? A *clear* demonstration of a causal link between negative thinking and depression is not possible because it would require manipulating people's explanatory style (which is not easy to change) in sufficient degree to produce full-fledged depressive disorders (which would not be ethical). However, a study by Lauren Alloy and her colleagues (1999) provided impressive evidence consistent with a causal link between negative thinking and vulnerability to depression. They assessed the explanatory style of a sample of first-year college students who were not depressed at the outset of the study. The students were characterized as being at high risk or low risk for depression based on whether they exhibited a negative cognitive style.

Figure 14.12

Interpreting the correlation between negative thinking and depression. Cognitive theories of depression assert that consistent patterns of negative thinking cause depression. Although these theories are highly plausible, depression could cause negative thoughts, or both could be caused by a third factor, such as neurochemical changes in the brain.

Figure 14.13

Negative thinking and prediction of depression. Alloy and colleagues (1999) measured the explanatory styles of first-year college students and characterized them as being high risk or low risk for depression. This graph shows the percentage of students who experienced major or minor episodes of depression over the next 2.5 years. As you can see, the high-risk students, who exhibited a negative thinking style, proved to be much more vulnerable to depression.

The follow-up data over the ensuing two and a half years on students who had no prior history of depression showed dramatic differences between the two groups in vulnerability to depression. During this relatively brief period, a major depressive disorder emerged in 17% of the high-risk students in comparison to only 1% of the low-risk students (see **Figure 14.13**). These findings and other data from the study suggest that negative thinking makes people more vulnerable to depression.

Interpersonal Roots

Some theorists suggest that inadequate social skills put people on the road to depressive disorders (Ingram, Scott, & Hamill, 2009). According to this notion, depression-prone people lack the social finesse needed to acquire many important kinds of reinforcers, such as good friends, top jobs, and desirable spouses. This paucity of reinforcers could understandably lead to negative emotions and depression (see **Figure 14.14**). Consistent with this theory, researchers have indeed found correlations between poor social skills and depression (Petty, Sachs-Ericsson, & Joiner, 2004).

Another interpersonal factor is that depressed people tend to be depressing (Joiner & Timmons, 2009). Individuals suffering from depression are often irritable and pessimistic. They complain a lot and aren't particularly enjoyable companions. They also alienate people by constantly asking for reassurances about their relationships and their

worth (Burns et al., 2006). As a consequence, depressed people tend to court rejection from those around them (Joiner & Timmons, 2009). Another problem is that depressed people tend to have fewer sources of social support than nondepressed people. This is unfortunate in that low social support can increase vulnerability to depression (Lakey & Cronin, 2008).

Precipitating Stress

Depressive and bipolar disorders sometimes appear mysteriously "out of the blue" in people who seem to be leading benign, nonstressful lives. For this reason, experts used to believe that these disorders were relatively uninfluenced by stress. However, recent advances in the measurement of personal stress have altered this picture. The evidence available today suggests a moderately strong link between stress and the onset of depressive and bipolar disorders (Monroe, Slavich, & Georgiades, 2009). Stress also appears to affect how people with these disorders respond to treatment and whether they experience a relapse of their disorder (Monroe & Hadjiyannakis, 2002).

Of course, the majority of people who experience severe stress endure it without getting depressed (Monroe & Reid, 2009). The impact of stress varies in part because different people have different degrees of *vulnerability* to depression or bipolar disorder. Variations in vulnerability appear to depend primarily on biological makeup. Similar interactions between stress and vulnerability probably influence the development of many kinds of disorders, including those that are next on our agenda: the schizophrenic disorders.

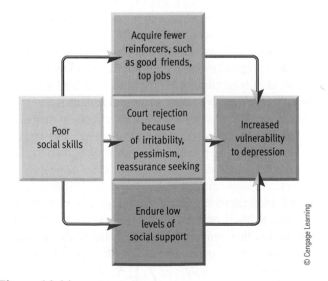

Figure 14.14

Interpersonal factors in depression. Interpersonal theories about the etiology of depression emphasize how inadequate social skills may contribute to the development of the disorder. Recent studies suggest that excessive reassurance seeking may play a particularly critical role in the social dynamics promoting depression.

SCHIZOPHRENIC DISORDERS

LEARNING OBJECTIVES

- Describe the prevalence and symptoms of schizophrenia.
- Outline the course and outcome of schizophrenia.
- Explain how genetic vulnerability, neurochemical factors, and structural abnormalities in the brain contribute to the development of schizophrenia.

- Summarize how neurodevelopmental insults to the brain, expressed emotion, and stress contribute to the development of schizophrenia.

Literally, *schizophrenia* means "split mind." However, when Eugen Bleuler coined the term in 1911, he was referring to the fragmenting of thought processes seen in the disorder—not to a "split personality." Unfortunately, writers in the popular media often assume that the split-mind notion refers to the syndrome in which a person manifests two or more personalities. As you have already learned, this syndrome is actually called *dissociative identity disorder.* Schizophrenia is a much more common, and altogether different, type of disorder.

Schizophrenic disorders are a class of disorders marked by disturbances in thought that spill over to affect perceptual, social, and emotional processes. How common is schizophrenia? Prevalence estimates suggest that about 1% of the population may suffer from schizophrenic disorders (Lauriello, Bustillo, & Keith, 2005). That may not sound like much, but it means that in North American alone there may be several million people troubled by schizophrenic disturbances. Moreover, schizophrenia is an extremely costly disorder for society, because it is a severe, debilitating illness that tends to have an early onset and often requires lengthy hospital care (Samnaliev & Clark, 2008). Because of these considerations, the financial impact of schizophrenia is estimated to exceed the costs of all types of cancers combined (Buchanan & Carpenter, 2005).

Symptoms

Schizophrenia is a severe disorder that wreaks havoc in victims' lives. Many of the key symptoms of schizophrenia are apparent in the following case history (adapted from Sheehan, 1982). Sylvia was first diagnosed as schizophrenic at age 15. She has been in and out of many types of psychiatric facilities since then. She has never been able to hold a job for any length of time. During severe flare-ups of her disorder, her personal hygiene deteriorates. She rarely washes, wears clothes that neither fit nor match, smears makeup on heavily but randomly, and slops food all over herself. Sylvia occasionally hears voices talking to her. Sylvia tends to be argumentative, aggressive, and emotionally volatile. Over the years, she has been involved in innumerable fights with fellow patients, psychiatric staff members, and strangers. Her thoughts can be highly irrational, as is apparent from the following quotation:

"Mick Jagger wants to marry me. If I have Mick Jagger, I don't have to covet Geraldo Rivera. Mick Jagger is St. Nicholas and the Maharishi is Santa Claus. I want to form a gospel rock group called the Thorn Oil, but Geraldo wants me to be the music critic on Eyewitness News, so what can I do? Got to listen to my boyfriend. Teddy Kennedy cured me of my ugliness. I'm pregnant with the son of God. I'm going to marry David Berkowitz and get it over with. Creedmoor is the headquarters of the American Nazi Party. They're eating the patients here. Archie Bunker wants me to play his niece on his TV show. I work for Epic Records. I'm Joan of Arc. I'm Florence Nightingale. The door between the ward and the porch is the dividing line between New York and California. Divorce isn't a piece of paper, it's a feeling. Forget about Zip Codes. I need shock treatment." (Sheehan, 1982, pp. 104–105)

Sylvia's case clearly shows that schizophrenic thinking can be bizarre and that schizophrenia is a brutally serious, psychologically disfiguring disorder. No single symptom is inevitably present, but the following symptoms are commonly seen in schizophrenia (Lewis, Escalona, & Keith, 2009; Liddle, 2009):

1. *Irrational thought.* Cognitive deficits and disturbed thought processes are the central, defining feature of schizophrenic disorders (Heinrichs, 2005). Various kinds of delusions are common. **Delusions are false beliefs that are maintained even though they clearly are out of touch with reality.** For example, one patient's delusion that he was a tiger (with a deformed body) persisted for 15 years (Kulick, Pope, & Keck, 1990). More typically, affected persons believe that their private thoughts are being broadcast to other people, that thoughts are being injected into their mind against their will, or that their thoughts are being controlled by some external force (Maher, 2001). In *delusions of grandeur,* people maintain that they are extremely famous or important. Sylvia expressed an endless array of grandiose delusions, such as thinking that Mick Jagger wanted to marry her, that she dictated the hobbit stories to Tolkien, and that she was going to win the Nobel Prize for medicine. In addition to delusions, the schizophrenic person's train of thought deteriorates. Thinking becomes chaotic rather than logical and linear. There is a "loosening of associations" as the schizophrenic shifts topics in disjointed ways. The quotation from Sylvia illustrates this symptom dramatically. The entire passage involves a wild "flight of ideas," but at one point (beginning with the sentence "Creedmoor is the headquarters . . .") she rattles off ten consecutive sentences that have no apparent connection to each other.

2. *Deterioration of adaptive behavior.* Schizophrenia involves a noticeable deterioration in the quality of the person's routine functioning in work, social relations, and personal care. Friends will often make remarks such as "Hal just isn't himself anymore." This deterioration is readily apparent in Sylvia's inability to get along with others or function in the work world. It's also apparent in her neglect of personal hygiene.

3. *Distorted perception.* A variety of perceptual distortions may occur in schizophrenia, with the most common being auditory hallucinations, which are reported by about 75% of patients (Combs & Mueser, 2007). ***Hallucinations* are sensory perceptions that occur in the absence of a real external stimulus or that represent gross distortions of perceptual input.** Schizophrenics frequently report that they hear voices of nonexistent or absent people talking to them. Sylvia, for instance, heard messages from Paul McCartney. These voices often provide an insulting running commentary on the person's behavior ("You're an idiot for shaking his hand"). The voices may be argumentative ("You don't need a bath"), and they may issue commands ("Prepare your home for visitors from outer space").

4. *Disturbed emotion.* Normal emotional tone can be disrupted in schizophrenia in a variety of ways. Although it may not be an accurate indicator of their underlying emotional experience, some victims show little emotional responsiveness, a symptom referred to as "blunted or flat affect." Others show inappropriate emotional responses that don't jell with the situation or with what they are saying. People with schizophrenia may also become emotionally volatile. This pattern was displayed by Sylvia, who often overreacted emotionally in erratic, unpredictable ways.

Traditionally, four subtypes of schizophrenic disorders were recognized: paranoid, catatonic, disorganized, and undifferentiated schizophrenia (Minzenberg, Yoon, & Carter, 2008). As its name implies, *paranoid schizophrenia* was thought to be dominated by delusions of persecution, along with delusions of grandeur. *Catatonic schizophrenia* was marked by striking motor disturbances, ranging from the muscular rigidity seen in a withdrawn state called a catatonic stupor to random motor activity seen in a state of catatonic excitement. *Disorganized schizophrenia* was viewed as a particularly severe syndrome marked by frequent incoherence, obvious deterioration in adaptive behavior, and virtually complete social withdrawal. People who were clearly schizophrenic but who could not be placed into any of the three previous categories were said

RECOMMENDED reading

What Is Mental Illness?
by Richard J. McNally (Harvard University Press, 2011)

In *What Is Mental Illness?* Richard McNally thoughtfully sifts through some of the most contentious and complicated issues confronting scholars in the field of mental health. A prominent clinical psychologist at Harvard University, McNally has published influential research on trauma, panic disorder, posttraumatic stress disorder, and recovered memories of child abuse (see Chapter 15), while contributing to the revision of both DSM-IV and DSM-5.

McNally begins by outlining the current controversy about whether there has been an "epidemic" of mental illness in recent decades. He explains why some critics have argued that prevalence rates for mental illness have become implausibly high. With this vexing issue as a backdrop, he moves on to examine the argument that the DSM system has pathologized and medicalized everyday adjustment problems.

His review of the history and politics underlying the DSM is very informative. After showing why it is so difficult to precisely define the boundary conditions of mental disorders, he examines recent proposed solutions developed by evolutionary psychologists. He then tackles the issue of whether society creates some mental disorders. Among other things, he analyzes how cultural contexts have shaped the presentation of certain disorders, such as bulimia nervosa, dissociative amnesia, dissociative identity disorder, and PTSD. In subsequent chapters he discusses the degree to which psychological disorders are genetic in origin and the debate about categorical versus dimensional approaches to diagnosis.

McNally does an admirable job of analyzing all these controversial issues in an even-handed, objective, and sophisticated manner. As its title suggests, this is not a book about how to deal with mental illness. Rather it is about whether all those syndromes that we view as mental illness ought to be conceptualized as mental disorders. McNally does not offer simple answers, but readers will come away with a whole new appreciation for the complexity and subjectivity of modern diagnostic systems.

Log on to CourseMate at* www.cengagebrain.com *for descriptions of other recommended books.

to have *undifferentiated schizophrenia*, which involved idiosyncratic mixtures of schizophrenic symptoms.

However, in a radical departure from tradition, DSM-5 discarded the four subtypes of schizophrenia. Why? For many years researchers pointed out that there were not meaningful differences between the classic subtypes in etiology, prognosis, or response to treatment. The absence of such differences cast doubt on the value of distinguishing among the subtypes. Critics also noted that the catatonic and disorganized subtypes were rarely seen in contemporary clinical practice and that undifferentiated cases did not represent a subtype as much as a hodgepodge of "leftovers."

Nancy Andreasen

Another approach to understanding and describing schizophrenia, advocated by Nancy Andreasen (1990), and others is to distinguish between the *positive symptoms* and *negative symptoms* of the disorder (Carpenter, 1992). *Negative symptoms* involve behavioral deficits, such as flattened emotions, social withdrawal, apathy, impaired attention, poor grooming, lack of persistence at work or school, and poverty of speech. *Positive symptoms* involve behavioral excesses or peculiarities, such as hallucinations, delusions, incoherent thought, agitation, bizarre behavior, and wild flights of ideas. Most patients exhibit both types of symptoms but vary in the *degree* to which positive or negative symptoms dominate (Andreasen, 2009). A relative predominance of positive symptoms is associated with better adjustment prior to the onset of schizophrenia and greater responsiveness to treatment (Combs & Mueser, 2007).

Course and Outcome

Schizophrenic disorders usually emerge during adolescence or early adulthood, with 75% of cases manifesting by the age of 30 (Perkins, Miller-Anderson, & Lieberman, 2006). Those who develop schizophrenia usually have a long history of peculiar behavior and cognitive and social deficits, although most do not manifest a full-fledged psychological disorder during childhood (Walker et al., 2004). The emergence of schizophrenia may be sudden, but it usually is insidious and gradual. Once it clearly emerges, the course of schizophrenia is variable, but patients tend to fall into three broad groups. Some patients, presumably those with milder disorders, are treated successfully and enjoy a full recovery. Other patients experience a partial recovery so that they can return to independent living for a time. However, they experience regular relapses and are in and out of treatment facilities for much of the remainder of their lives. Finally, a third group of patients endure chronic illness that sometimes results in permanent hospitalization. Estimates of the percentage of patients falling in each category vary.

Overall, the preponderance of studies have suggested that only about 20% of schizophrenic patients enjoy a full recovery (Perkins et al., 2006). However, to some extent, this low recovery rate may reflect the poor to mediocre quality of mental health care available for severe disorders in the vast majority of countries, including wealthy ones. When comprehensive, well-coordinated, quality care is initiated promptly, higher recovery rates in the vicinity of 50% have been found (Hopper et al., 2007; Liberman & Kopelowicz, 2005). Although schizophrenia is often viewed as a disorder marked by relentless deterioration, it is clear that a decent portion of patients experience a reasonable degree of recovery (Jablensky, 2009). Thus, the outlook for schizophrenia may not need to be as pervasively negative as it has been.

A number of factors are related to the likelihood of recovery from schizophrenic disorders (Cancro & Lehmann, 2000; Liberman et al., 2002). A patient has a relatively *favorable prognosis* when (1) the onset of the disorder has been sudden rather than gradual, (2) the onset has occurred at a later age, (3) the patient's social and work adjustment were relatively good prior to the onset of the disorder, (4) the proportion of negative symptoms is relatively low, (5) the patient's cognitive functioning is relatively preserved, (6) the patient shows good adherence to treatment interventions, and (7) the patient has a relatively

John Nash, the Nobel Prize–winning mathematician whose story was told in the film *A Beautiful Mind,* has struggled with paranoid schizophrenia since 1959.

healthy, supportive family situation to return to. Many of these predictors are concerned with the etiology of schizophrenic illness, which is the matter we turn to next.

Etiology

Most of us can identify, at least to some extent, with people who suffer from depression, obsessive-compulsive disorders, and phobic disorders. You can probably imagine events that might leave you struggling with depression or grappling with anxiety. But what could account for Sylvia thinking that she was Joan of Arc, or that she had dictated the hobbit novels to Tolkien? As mystifying as these delusions may seem, you'll see that the etiology of schizophrenic disorders is not all that different from the etiology of other disorders.

Genetic Vulnerability

Evidence is plentiful that hereditary factors play a role in the development of schizophrenic disorders (Kirov & Owen, 2009). For instance, in twin studies, concordance rates for schizophrenia average around 48% for identical twins, in comparison to about 17% for fraternal twins (Gottesman, 2001). Studies also indicate that a child born to two schizophrenic parents has about a 46% probability of developing a schizophrenic disorder (as compared to the probability of about 1% for the population as a whole). These and other findings that demonstrate the genetic roots of schizophrenia are summarized in **Figure 14.15**. Overall, the picture is similar to that seen for depressive and bipolar disorders. Several converging lines of evidence indicate

that people inherit a genetically transmitted *vulnerability* to schizophrenia (Cornblatt et al., 2009). Some theorists suspect that genetic factors may account for as much as 80% of the variability in susceptibility to schizophrenia (Pogue-Geile & Yokley, 2010). However, genetic mapping studies have made only modest progress in identifying the specific genes at work (Gunter, 2009).

Neurochemical Factors

Like depressive and bipolar disorders, schizophrenic disorders appear to be accompanied by changes in the activity of one or more neurotransmitters in the brain. Excess *dopamine* activity has been implicated as a likely cause of schizophrenia (Patel, Pinals, & Breier, 2008). This hypothesis makes sense because most of the drugs that are useful in the treatment of schizophrenia are known to dampen dopamine activity in the brain. However, the evidence linking schizophrenia to high dopamine levels is riddled with inconsistencies, complexities, and interpretive problems (Bobo et al., 2008), and in recent years, the dopamine hypothesis has become more nuanced and complex. Researchers believe that dysregulation occurs in dopamine circuits and that the nature of this dysregulation may vary in different regions of the brain (Howes & Kapur, 2009). Scientists are also investigating whether dysfunctions in neural circuits using glutamate play a role in schizophrenia (Downar & Kapur, 2008).

Recent research has suggested that marijuana use during adolescence may help precipitate schizophrenia in young people who have a genetic vulnerability to the disorder (McGrath et al., 2010). For example, a recent meta-analysis of 83 studies found that the onset of psychotic disorder tended to occur 2.7 years earlier in cannabis users as compared to nonusers (Large et al., 2011). This finding has generated considerable debate about whether and how cannabis might contribute to the emergence of schizophrenia (Castle, 2008). Some critics have suggested that schizophrenia might lead to cannabis use rather than vice versa. In other words, emerging psychotic symptoms may prompt young people to turn to marijuana to self-medicate. However, a carefully controlled long-term study in Germany found no evidence to support the self-medication explanation (Kuepper et al., 2011). After controlling for age, sex, social class, use of other drugs, occurrence of childhood trauma, and the presence of other disorders, the study found that marijuana use roughly doubled the risk of psychotic disturbance. The current thinking is that the key chemical ingredient in marijuana (THC) may amplify neurotransmitter activity in dopamine circuits (Kuepper et al., 2010).

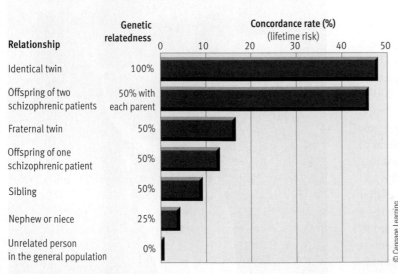

Figure 14.15

Genetic vulnerability to schizophrenic disorders. Relatives of schizophrenic patients have an elevated risk for schizophrenia. This risk is greater among closer relatives. Although environment also plays a role in the etiology of schizophrenia, the concordance rates shown here suggest that there must be a genetic vulnerability to the disorder. These concordance estimates are based on pooled data from 40 studies.

Structural Abnormalities in the Brain

For decades, studies have suggested that individuals with schizophrenia exhibit a variety of deficits in attention, perception, and information processing (Belger & Barch, 2009; Harvey, 2010). Impairments in working (short-term) memory are especially prominent. These cognitive deficits suggest that schizophrenic disorders may be caused by neurological defects. Until recent decades, however, this theory was based more on speculation than on actual research. However, advances in brain-imaging technology have yielded mountains of intriguing data since the mid-1980s. Research with various types of brain scans suggests an association between enlarged brain ventricles (the hollow, fluid-filled cavities in the brain depicted in **Figure 14.16**) and schizophrenic disturbance (Shenton & Kubicki, 2009). Enlarged ventricles are assumed to reflect either the degeneration or failure to develop of nearby brain tissue. The significance of enlarged ventricles is hotly debated, however. Structural deterioration in the brain could be a contributing *cause* or a *consequence* of schizophrenia.

The Neurodevelopmental Hypothesis

Several new lines of evidence have led to the emergence of the *neurodevelopmental hypothesis* of schizophrenia, which posits that schizophrenia is caused in part by various disruptions in the normal maturational processes of the brain before or at birth (Fatemi & Folsom, 2009). According to this hypothesis, insults to the brain during sensitive phases of prenatal development or during birth can cause subtle neuorological damage that elevates individuals' vulnerability to schizophrenia years later in adolescence and early adulthood (see **Figure 14.17**). What are the sources of these early insults? Thus far, research has focused mainly on viral infections or malnutrition during prenatal development and obstetrical complications during the birth process.

The evidence on viral infections has been building since Sarnoff Mednick and his colleagues (1988) discovered an

Figure 14.16

Schizophrenia and the ventricles of the brain. Cerebrospinal fluid (CSF) circulates around the brain and spinal cord. The hollow cavities in the brain filled with CSF are called *ventricles*. The four ventricles in the human brain are depicted here. Studies with modern brain-imaging techniques suggest that an association exists between enlarged ventricles in the brain and the occurrence of schizophrenic disturbance.

elevated incidence of schizophrenia among the children of women who were in their second trimester of prenatal development during a 1957 influenza epidemic in Finland. Quite a number of subsequent studies have found a link between exposure to influenza and other infections during prenatal development and increased prevalence of schizophrenia (Brown & Derkits, 2010). Another study, which investigated the possible impact of prenatal malnutrition, found an elevated incidence of schizophrenia in a cohort of people who were prenatally exposed to a severe famine in 1944–1945

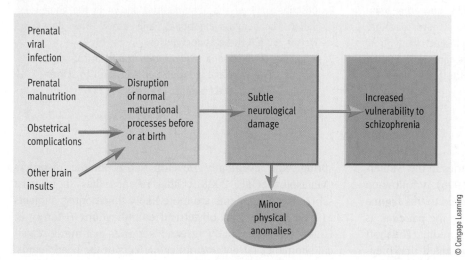

Figure 14.17

The neurodevelopmental hypothesis of schizophrenia. Research suggests that insults to the brain sustained during prenatal development or at birth may disrupt crucial maturational processes in the brain, resulting in subtle neurological damage that gradually becomes apparent as youngsters develop. This neurological damage is believed to increase both vulnerability to schizophrenia and the incidence of minor physical anomalies.

REEL RESEARCH

Identifying Early Signs of Schizophrenia

Log on to CourseMate at www.cengagebrain.com to watch this video.

Although the symptoms of schizophrenia generally emerge in late adolescence and early adulthood, some researchers have turned to home movies to learn more about how the condition can be diagnosed earlier in life. By analyzing home movies of children later diagnosed with schizophrenia, Elaine Walker, clinical psychologist at Emory University, discovers important predictors of the condition in this Reel Research video.

Walker hopes to answer the question: Why is schizophrenia dormant until late adolescence, and what triggers its onset then? By watching home movies collected from adult patients with schizophrenia, Walker identified abnormal motor development and emotional behavior in infants and children that can predict the emergence of schizophrenia. Walker noticed consistent abnormalities in their posture and movement as well as a display of general distress and negative emotions during infancy and childhood. These findings suggest that abnormalities in how the brain works—particularly the parts that control motor development and emotional response—were present, likely from birth. Prenatal insults and complications can also influence the brain development of infants, making them more vulnerable to schizophrenia.

Because puberty brings increases in hormonal fluctuations throughout the body, Walker believes schizophrenia is awakened by certain hormones. Cortisol, a stress hormone, can be detected in saliva samples. Walker studies the cortisol levels of participants who are vulnerable to schizophrenia. Participants who showed the most pronounced rise in cortisol levels during adolescent development were the most likely to show a progression of symptoms and to be diagnosed with schizophrenia.

Watch the *Identifying Early Signs of Schizophrenia* video to learn more about Walker's research. Delve even deeper by responding to the following discussion questions.

DISCUSSION QUESTIONS

1. What is required of the sample of patients Walker used in her home video study? Why is their age and mental health important?

2. Describe some of the abnormalities shown in the home videos—behavioral, emotional, and other. How does Walker explain these abnormalities?

3. Why does the hormone study demonstrated in the video include those with and without predisposition to schizophrenia? What is their age group?

---

because of a Nazi blockade of food deliveries in the Netherlands during World War II (Susser et al., 1996). A follow-up study of some schizophrenic patients exposed to this famine found increased brain abnormalities among the patients, as the neurodevelopmental hypothesis would predict (Hulshoff et al., 2000). Recent research has demonstrated that pregnant women exposed to extreme stress also have more off-spring who eventually develop schizophrenic disorders (Malaspina et al., 2008). Other research has shown that schizophrenic patients are more likely than control subjects to have a history of obstetrical complications (Murray & Bramon, 2005). Finally, research suggests that minor physical anomalies (slight anatomical defects of the head, hands, feet, and face) that would be consistent with prenatal neurological damage are more common in people with schizophrenia than in other people (Schiffman et al., 2002). Collectively, these diverse studies argue for a relationship between early neurological trauma and a predisposition to schizophrenia (King, St-Hilaire, & Heidkamp, 2010).

Expressed Emotion

Studies of expressed emotion have primarily focused on how this element of family dynamics influences the *course* of schizophrenic illness after the onset of the disorder (Leff & Vaughn, 1985). *Expressed emotion (EE)* reflects the degree to which a relative of a schizophrenic patient displays highly critical or emotionally overinvolved attitudes toward the patient. Audiotaped interviews of relatives' communication are carefully evaluated for critical comments, hostility toward the patient, and excessive emotional involvement (overprotective, overconcerned attitudes) (Hooley, 2004).

Studies show that a family's expressed emotion is a good predictor of the course of a schizophrenic patient's illness. After release from a hospital, patients who return to a family high in expressed emotion show relapse rates two to three times those of patients who return to a family low in expressed emotion (Hooley, 2009). Part of the problem for patients returning to homes high in expressed emotion is that their families are probably sources of stress rather than of social support. However, Rosenfarb et al. (1995) caution against placing all the blame on the families high in expressed emotion. They found that patients returning to high-EE homes exhibited more odd and disruptive behavior than patients returning to low-EE homes. Thus, the more critical, negative attitudes experienced by patients in high-EE homes may be caused in part by their own behavior.

Stress

Many theories of schizophrenia assume that stress plays a role in triggering schizophrenic disorders (Walker & Tessner, 2008). According to this notion, various biological and psychological factors influence individuals' *vulnerability* to schizophrenia. High stress may then serve to precipitate a schizophrenic disorder in someone who is vulnerable. Research indicates that high stress can also trigger relapses in patients who have made progress toward recovery (Walker, Mittal, & Tessner, 2008).

Until relatively recently, interest in the connection between stress and schizophrenia was limited to how adverse events in adolescence or early adulthood may contribute to provoking the onset of the disorder. However, in recent years there has been a surge of research on how severe stress in early childhood may increase individuals' vulnerability to schizophrenia 10–20 years later (Larkin & Read, 2008). In particular, quite a number of studies have reported a link between early childhood trauma and later psychotic disorders and symptoms (Bendall, Jackson, & Hulbert, 2010). For example, one recent study found an association between psychotic symptoms and exposure to sexual abuse, physical abuse, bullying, and institutional care during childhood (Bentall et al., 2012). In a similar vein, another study found a correlation between schizophrenic illness and the experience of abuse or neglect during childhood (Heins et al., 2011). It is not clear, however, whether the long-term negative effects of childhood trauma are specific to schizophrenia. For example, one recent study found that childhood sexual abuse elevates vulnerability to a wide range of disorders, including depression, anxiety disorders, eating disorders, and alcohol and drug dependence (Jonas et al., 2011).

AUTISM SPECTRUM DISORDER

LEARNING OBJECTIVES

● Describe the symptoms, prevalence, and etiology of autistic disorder.

Unlike the other disorders we have discussed, autism, by definition, manifests itself very early in life. This diagnosis has garnered increased attention in recent years. **Autism, or autism spectrum disorder, is characterized by profound impairment of social interaction and communication and by severely restricted interests and activities, apparent by the age of 3.** Originally called *infantile autism,* this disorder was first described by child psychiatrist Leo Kanner in the 1940s.

Symptoms and Prevalence

The central feature of autistic disorder is the child's lack of interest in other people. Children with autism act as though people in their environment are no different than nearby

Catchlight Visual Services/Alamy

Children with autism often fail to make eye contact with others and tend to find social attention unpleasant.

inanimate objects, such as toys, pillows, or chairs. They tend not to make eye contact with others or to need physical contact with their caretakers. They make no effort to connect with people and fail to bond with their parents or to develop normal peer relationships. Verbal communication can be very impaired, as about one-third of autistic children fail to develop speech (Wetherby & Prizant, 2005). Among those who do develop speech, their ability to initiate and sustain a conversation is very limited. And their use of language tends to be marked by peculiarities, such as *echolalia,* which involves rote repetition of others' words. Autistic children's interests are restricted in that they tend to become preoccupied with objects or repetitive body movements (spinning, body rocking, playing with their hands, and so forth). They can also be extremely inflexible, in that minor changes in their environment can trigger rages and tantrums. Some autistic children exhibit self-injurious behavior, such as banging their heads, pulling their hair, or hitting themselves. About half of autistic children exhibit subnormal IQ scores (Volkmar et al., 2009).

Parents of autistic children typically become concerned about their child's development by about 15–18 months of age and usually seek professional consultation by about 24 months. The diagnosis of autism is almost always made before affected children reach 3 years of age. More often than not, autism turns out to be a lifelong affliction requiring extensive family and institutional support throughout adulthood. However, with early and effective intervention, around 15%–20% of autistic individuals are able to live independently in adulthood and another 20%–30% approach this level of functioning (Volkmar et al., 2009).

Until relatively recently, the prevalence of autism was thought to be well under 1% (Newschaffer, 2007). Since the mid-1990s, however, a dramatic (roughly fourfold) increase has occurred in the diagnosis of autism, with prevalence estimates approaching 1% (Brugha et al., 2011). Most experts believe that this surge in autism is largely due to the result of greater awareness of the syndrome and the use of broader diagnostic criteria (Wing & Potter, 2009). Contemporary prevalence estimates usually include related syndromes, such as *Asperger's disorder,* that are milder forms of the disorder that used to go uncounted. Although these explanations make sense, scientists have not ruled out the possibility that a genuine increase has occurred in the prevalence of autism (Weintraub, 2011). Males account for about 80% of autism diagnoses, although curiously females tend to exhibit more severe impairments (Ursano, Kartheiser, & Barnhill, 2008). DSM-5 recognizes that autism involves several related disorders of varied severity—hence the renaming as *autism spectrum disorder.*

Etiology

Autism was originally blamed on cold, aloof parenting (Bettelheim, 1967), but that view was eventually discredited by research (Bhasin & Schendel, 2007). Given its appearance so early in life, most theorists today view autism as a disorder that originates in biological dysfunctions. Consistent with that viewpoint, twin studies and family studies have demonstrated that genetic factors make a major contribution to autistic disorders (Robinson et al., 2011). Many theorists believe that autism must be due to some sort of brain abnormality, but only modest progress has been made in pinpointing the nature of this abnormality. The most reliable finding has been that autism is associated with generalized brain enlargement that is apparent by age 2 (Hazlett et al., 2011; Schumann et al., 2010). MRI studies suggest that this brain overgrowth begins some time around the end of the first year, which, with the luxury of hindsight, is right around the same time that autistic symptoms usually start to surface. It is not clear yet whether this brain overgrowth plays a causal role in the emergence of autism, but theorists speculate that the overgrowth might produce disruptions in neural circuits.

One hypothesis that has garnered a great deal of publicity is the idea that autism may be caused by the mercury used as a preservative in some childhood vaccines (Kirby, 2005). However, the 1998 study that first reported a link between vaccinations and autism has been discredited as fraudulent (Deer, 2011; Godlee, Smith, & Marcovitch, 2011). Moreover, independent efforts to replicate the purported association between vaccinations and autism have consistently failed (Paul, 2009; Wing & Potter, 2009). Widespread belief in the apparently spurious relationship between autism and vaccinations may simply be due to the fact that children get scheduled vaccinations around the same age (12–15 months) that parents first start to realize that their children are not developing normally (Doja & Roberts, 2006). The popularity of the vaccination hypothesis may also be due to the explanatory void that it fills, as science has yet to achieve a sound understanding of the causes of autism.

UNDERSTANDING EATING DISORDERS

LEARNING OBJECTIVES

- Describe the subtypes, history, prevalence, and gender distribution of eating disorders.
- Explain how genetic factors, personality, culture, family dynamics, and disturbed thinking contribute to the development of eating disorders.

Answer the following "true" or "false."

____ **1.** Although they have attracted attention only in recent years, eating disorders have a long history and have always been fairly common.

____ **2.** Eating disorders are universal problems found in virtually all cultures.

____ **3.** People with anorexia nervosa are much more likely to recognize their eating behavior as pathological than are people suffering from bulimia nervosa.

____ **4.** The prevalence of eating disorders is twice as high in women as it is in men.

____ **5.** The binge-and-purge syndrome seen in bulimia nervosa is not common in anorexia nervosa.

All five of these statements are false, as you will see in this Application. The psychological disorders discussed in the main body of the chapter have largely been recognized for centuries and generally are found in one form or another in all cultures and societies. Eating disorders, however, present a sharp contrast to this picture: They have only been recognized in recent decades, and initially they were largely confined to affluent, Westernized cultures. In spite of these fascinating differences, eating disorders have much in common with traditional forms of pathology.

Types of Eating Disorders

Although most people don't seem to take eating disorders as seriously as other types of psychological disorders, you will see that they are dangerous and debilitating (Thompson, Roehrig, & Kinder, 2007). No psychological disorder is associated with a greater elevation in mortality (Striegel-Moore & Bulik, 2007). **Eating disorders** *are severe disturbances in eating behavior characterized by preoccupation with weight and unhealthy efforts to control weight.* Three syndromes are described in DSM-5: *anorexia nervosa, bulimia nervosa,* and a new syndrome called *binge-eating disorder.* We will devote most of our attention in this Application to anorexia and bulimia, but we will briefly outline the symptoms of binge-eating disorder as well.

Anorexia Nervosa

Anorexia nervosa *is characterized by intense fear of gaining weight, disturbed body image, refusal to maintain normal weight, and dangerous measures to lose weight.* Two subtypes have been distinguished. In *restricting type anorexia nervosa,* people drastically reduce their intake of food, sometimes literally starving themselves. In *binge-eating/purging type anorexia nervosa,* victims attempt to lose weight by forcing themselves to vomit after meals, by misusing laxatives and diuretics, and by engaging in excessive exercise.

Both types entail a disturbed body image. No matter how frail and emaciated the victims become, they insist that they are too fat. Their morbid fear of obesity means that they are never satisfied with their weight. If they gain a pound or two, they panic. The only thing that makes them happy is to lose more weight. The common result is a relentless decline in body weight—in fact, patients entering treatment for anorexia nervosa are typically 25%–30% below their normal weight (Hsu, 1990). Because of their disturbed body image, people suffering from anorexia generally do *not* appreciate the maladaptive quality of their behavior and rarely seek treatment on their own. They are typically coaxed or coerced into treatment by friends or family members who are alarmed by their appearance.

Anorexia nervosa eventually leads to a cascade of medical problems, including *amenorrhea* (a loss of menstrual cycles in women), gastrointestinal problems, low blood pressure, *osteoporosis* (a loss of bone density), and metabolic disturbances that can lead to cardiac arrest or circulatory collapse (Halmi, 2008; Russell, 2009). Anorexia is a debilitating illness that is associated with greatly elevated mortality rates (Arcelus et al., 2011). Steinhausen (2002) estimated that anorexia leads to death in 5%–10% of patients.

Bulimia Nervosa

Bulimia nervosa *involves habitually engaging in out-of-control overeating followed by unhealthy compensatory efforts, such as self-induced vomiting, fasting, abuse of laxatives and diuretics, and excessive exercise.* The eating binges are usually carried out in secret and are followed by intense guilt and concern about gaining weight. These feelings motivate ill-advised strategies to undo the effects of the overeating. However, vomiting prevents the absorption of only about half of recently consumed food, and laxatives and diuretics have negligible impact on caloric intake, so people suffering from bulimia

Eating disorders have become distressingly common among young women in Western cultures. No matter how frail they become, people suffering from anorexia insist that they are too fat.

Motte Jules/Abaca/Newscom

nervosa typically maintain a reasonably normal weight (Fairburn, Cooper, & Murphy, 2009).

Medical problems associated with bulimia nervosa include cardiac arrythmias, dental problems, metabolic deficiencies, and gastrointestinal problems (Halmi, 2008). Bulimia often coexists with other psychological disturbances, including depression, anxiety disorders, and substance abuse (Hudson et al., 2007).

Obviously, bulimia nervosa shares many features with anorexia nervosa, such as a morbid fear of becoming obese, preoccupation with food, and rigid, maladaptive approaches to controlling weight that are grounded in naive all-or-none thinking. The close relationship between the disorders is demonstrated by the fact that many patients who initially develop one syndrome cross over to display the other syndrome. However, the syndromes also differ in crucial ways. First and foremost, bulimia is a less life-threatening condition. Second, although their weight and appearance usually is more "normal" than that seen in anorexia, people with bulimia are much more likely to recognize that their eating behavior as pathological and are more prone to recognize their need for treatment (Guarda et al., 2007). Like anorexia, bulimia is associated with elevated mortality rates (Crow et al., 2009), although this elevation is only about one-third as great as that seen for anorexia (Arcelus et al., 2011).

Binge-Eating Disorder

Binge-eating disorder **involves distress-inducing eating binges that are not accompanied by the purging, fasting, and excessive exercise seen in bulimia.** Obviously, this syndrome resembles bulimia, but it is less severe. Still, this disorder creates great distress, as binge eaters tend to be disgusted by their bodies and distraught about their overeating. People with binge-eating disorder are frequently overweight. Their excessive eating is often triggered by stress (Gluck, 2006). Research suggests that this comparatively mild syndrome may be more common than anorexia or bulimia (Hudson et al., 2007).

History and Prevalence

Historians have been able to track down descriptions of anorexia nervosa that date back centuries, so the disorder is not entirely new, but anorexia nervosa did not become a *common* affliction until the middle of the 20th century (Vandereycken, 2002). Although binging and purging have a long history in some cultures, they were not part of a pathological effort to control weight, and bulimia nervosa appears to be a new syndrome that emerged gradually in the middle of the 20th century and was first recognized in the 1970s (Steiger & Bruce, 2009).

Both disorders are products of modern, affluent Western culture, where food is generally plentiful and the desirability of being thin is widely endorsed. Until relatively recently, these problems were not seen outside of Western cultures (Hoek, 2002). However, advances in communication have exported Western culture to farflung corners of the globe, and eating disorders have started showing up in many non-Western societies, especially affluent Asian countries (Becker & Fay, 2006).

A huge gender gap exists in the likelihood of developing eating disorders. About 90%–95% of individuals who are treated for anorexia nervosa and bulimia nervosa are female (Thompson & Kinder, 2003). This staggering discrepancy appears to be a result of cultural pressures rather than biological factors. Western standards of attractiveness emphasize being slender more for females than for males, and women generally experience heavier pressure to be physically attractive than men do (Strahan et al., 2008). The prevalence of eating disorders is also elevated in certain groups that place

Learn More Online

The Alliance for Eating Disorders Awareness

This site offers a great deal of information on eating disorders. Visitors can find statistics, suggested readings, information on symptoms and treatments, self-tests, success stories from people who have overcome their eating disorders, and links to other worthwhile websites.

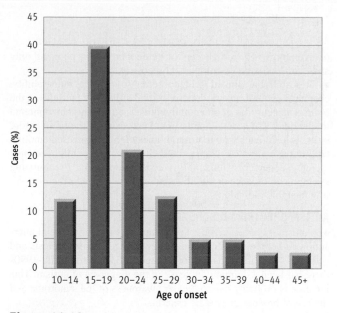

Figure 14.18

Age of onset for anorexia nervosa. Eating disorders emerge primarily during adolescence, as these data for anorexia nervosa show. This graph depicts how age of onset was distributed in a sample of 166 female patients from Minnesota. As you can see, over half experienced the onset of their illness before the age of 20, with vulnerability clearly peaking between the ages of 15 and 19. (Data from Lucas, et al., 1991)

an undue emphasis on thinness, such as fashion models, dancers, actresses, and athletes. Eating disorders mostly afflict *young* women. The typical age of onset for anorexia is 14–18, and for bulimia it is 15–21 (see **Figure 14.18**).

How common are eating disorders in Western societies? Research suggests that among females about 1% develop anorexia nervosa, roughly 1.5% develop bulimia nervosa, and about 3.5% exhibit binge-eating disorder (Hudson et al., 2007). Recent data also suggest that there may be more eating disorders among men than generally appreciated. In some respects, these figures may only scratch the surface of the problem. Evidence suggests that another 2%–4% of people may struggle with serious eating problems that do not quite qualify for a formal diagnosis (Swanson et al., 2011).

Etiology

Like other types of psychological disorders, eating disorders are caused by multiple determinants that work interactively.

Genetic Vulnerability

The scientific evidence is not nearly as strong or complete for eating disorders as it is for many other types of psychopathology, but some people may inherit a genetic vulnerability to these problems (Thornton, Mazzeo, & Bulik, 2011). Studies show that relatives of patients with eating disorders have elevated rates of anorexia nervosa and bulimia nervosa (Bulik, 2004). And studies of female twins

report higher concordance rates for identical twins than fraternal twins, suggesting that a genetic predisposition may be at work (Steiger, Bruce, & Israël, 2003).

Personality Factors

Genetic factors may exert their influence indirectly by fostering certain personality traits that make people more vulnerable to eating disorders. Although there are innumerable exceptions, victims of anorexia nervosa tend to be obsessive, rigid, neurotic, and emotionally restrained, whereas victims of bulimia nervosa tend to be impulsive, overly sensitive, and low in self-esteem (Wonderlich, 2002). Research also suggests that perfectionism is a risk factor for anorexia (Steiger & Bruce, 2009).

Cultural Values

The contribution of cultural values to the increased prevalence of eating disorders can hardly be overestimated (Striegel-Moore & Bulik, 2007). In Western society, young women are socialized to believe that they must be attractive and that to be attractive they must be as thin as the actresses and fashion models that dominate the media (Levine & Harrison, 2004). Thanks to this cultural milieu, many young women are dissatisfied with their weight because the societal ideals promoted by the media are unattainable for most of them (Thompson & Stice, 2001). Unfortunately, in a small portion of these women, the pressure to be thin, in combination with genetic vulnerability, family pathology, and other factors, leads to unhealthy efforts to control weight.

The Role of the Family

Many theorists emphasize how family dynamics can contribute to the development of anorexia nervosa and bulimia nervosa in young women (Haworth-Hoeppner, 2000). The principal issue appears to be that some mothers contribute to eating disorders simply by endorsing society's message that "you can never be too thin" and by modeling unhealthy dieting behaviors of their own (Francis & Birch, 2005). In conjunction with media pressures, this role modeling leads many daughters to internalize the idea that the thinner you are, the more attractive you are.

Cognitive Factors

Many theorists emphasize the role of disturbed thinking in the etiology of eating disorders (Williamson et al., 2001). For example, anorexic patients' typical belief that they are fat when they are really wasting away is a dramatic illustration of how thinking goes awry. Patients with eating disorders display rigid, all-or-none thinking and many maladaptive beliefs, such as "I must be thin to be accepted," "If I am not in complete control, I will lose all control," and "If I gain one pound, I'll go on to gain enormous weight." Additional research is needed to determine whether distorted thinking is a *cause* or merely a *symptom* of eating disorders.

CHAPTER 14 | Review

KEY IDEAS

ABNORMAL BEHAVIOR: GENERAL CONCEPTS

● The medical model views abnormal behavior as a disease. There are some problems with the medical model, but the disease analogy is useful. Three criteria are used in deciding whether people suffer from psychological disorders: deviance, personal distress, and maladaptive behavior. Often, it is difficult to draw a clear line between normality and abnormality.

● Some critics are concerned that medical diagnoses of abnormal behavior pin stigmatizing labels on people, but with or without labels, the stigma associated with mental illness appears difficult to reduce. DSM-5 is the official psychodiagnostic classification system in the United States. Some critics have questioned the categorical approach used by the DSM system, but DSM-5 mostly retains the categorical approach. Psychological disorders are more common than widely believed, with a lifetime prevalence of roughly 44%. The economic costs of mental illness are enormous.

ANXIETY DISORDERS AND OBSESSIVE-COMPULSIVE DISORDER

● The anxiety disorders include generalized anxiety disorder, phobic disorder, and panic disorder. After decades of being lumped with the anxiety disorders, obsessive-compulsive disorder (OCD) was given its own category in DSM-5. These disorders have been linked to a genetic predisposition, an inhibited temperament, anxiety sensitivity, and neurochemical abnormalities in the brain.

● Many anxiety responses, especially phobias, may be caused by classical conditioning and maintained by operant conditioning. Cognitive theorists maintain that some people are vulnerable to anxiety disorders because they see threats everywhere. Stress may also contribute to the onset of these disorders.

DISSOCIATIVE DISORDERS

● Dissociative disorders include dissociative amnesia and dissociative identity disorder (DID). These disorders appear to be uncommon, although there is some controversy about the prevalence of DID. Stress and childhood trauma may contribute to DID, but overall, the causes of dissociative disorders are not well understood. Some theorists believe that people with DID are engaging in intentional role playing to use mental illness as a face-saving excuse for their failings.

DEPRESSION AND BIPOLAR DISORDER

● Major depressive disorder and bipolar disorder used to be lumped together as mood disorders, but in DSM-5 they each get their own chapter. Both of these disorders are associated with an elevated risk for suicide. People vary in their genetic vulnerability to depressive and bipolar disorders, which are accompanied by changes in neurochemical activity in the brain. Reduced hippocampal volume and suppressed neurogenesis may be factors in depression.

● Hormonal changes along the HPA axis in response to stress may often play a role in the development of depression. Cognitive models posit that a pessimistic explanatory style, rumination, and other types of negative thinking contribute to depression. Depression is often rooted in interpersonal inadequacies, as people who lack social finesse often have difficulty acquiring life's reinforcers. Depressive and bipolar disorders are sometimes stress related.

SCHIZOPHRENIC DISORDERS

● Schizophrenic disorders are characterized by deterioration of adaptive behavior, irrational thought, distorted perception, and disturbed mood. The distinction between positive and negative symptoms has proven useful, but most patients exhibit both types of symptoms. The prognosis for schizophrenia is poor, as only about 20% of patients enjoy a full recovery.

● Research has linked schizophrenia to genetic vulnerability, changes in neurotransmitter activity, and enlarged ventricles in the brain. The neurodevelopmental hypothesis attributes schizophrenia to disruptions of normal maturational processes in the brain before or at birth. Patients who return to homes high in expressed emotion tend to have elevated relapse rates. Stress in early childhood may increase a person's vulnerability to schizophrenia. Precipitating stress in adolescence or adulthood may help to trigger the disorder in vulnerable individuals.

AUTISM SPECTRUM DISORDER

● Autism is characterized by profound impairment of social interaction and communication and by severely restricted interests and activities, which is apparent by the age of 3. Since the mid-1990s there has been a dramatic increase in the diagnosis of autism. This increase is probably due to greater awareness of the syndrome and the use of broader diagnostic criteria.

● Genetic factors contribute to autistic disorders, but little else is known about the etiology of autism. Research has failed to find an association between vaccinations and the development of autism.

APPLICATION: UNDERSTANDING EATING DISORDERS

● The principal eating disorders are anorexia nervosa, bulimia nervosa, and binge-eating disorder. Anorexia and bulimia are both associated with other psychopathology, and both lead to a cascade of medical problems. Eating disorders appear to be a product of modern, affluent, Westernized culture.

● Females account for 90%–95% of eating disorders. The typical age of onset is roughly 15 to 20. There appears to be a genetic vulnerability to eating disorders, which may be mediated by heritable personality traits. Cultural pressures on young women to be thin clearly help foster eating disorders. Some theorists emphasize how family dynamics and disturbed thinking can contribute to the development of eating disorders.

KEY TERMS

Agoraphobia p. 426
Anhedonia p. 432
Anorexia nervosa p. 447
Anxiety disorders p. 426
Autism p. 445
Autism spectrum disorder p. 445
Binge-eating disorder p. 448
Bipolar disorder p. 434
Bulimia nervosa p. 447
Comorbidity p. 424
Concordance rate p. 435
Delusions p. 439
Diagnosis p. 422
Dissociative amnesia p. 430
Dissociative disorders p. 430
Dissociative identity disorder (DID) p. 430
Eating disorders p. 447
Epidemiology p. 424
Etiology p. 422
Generalized anxiety disorder p. 426
Hallucinations p. 440
Major depressive disorder p. 432
Manic-depressive disorder p. 434
Medical model p. 421
Multiple-personality disorder p. 430
Neurotransmitters p. 428
Obsessive-compulsive disorder (OCD) p. 427
Panic disorder p. 426
Phobic disorder p. 426
Prevalence p. 424
Prognosis p. 422
Schizophrenic disorders p. 439

KEY PEOPLE

Nancy Andreasen p. 441
Susan Nolen-Hoeksema pp. 433, 437
Martin Seligman pp. 429, 437
Thomas Szasz p. 422

1. Sergio has just entered treatment for bipolar disorder, and he is informed that most patients respond to drug treatment within a month. This information represents
   a. a prognosis.
   b. an etiology.
   c. a histology.
   d. a concordance.

2. Although Sue always feels high levels of dread, worry, and anxiety, she still meets her daily responsibilities. Sue's behavior
   a. should not be considered abnormal, since her adaptive functioning is not impaired.
   b. should not be considered abnormal, since everyone sometimes experiences worry and anxiety.
   c. can still be considered abnormal, since she feels great personal distress.
   d. both a and b.

3. Recent epidemiological studies have found that the most common types of psychological disorders are
   a. dissociative disorders and anxiety disorders.
   b. anxiety disorders and schizophrenic disorders.
   c. substance use disorders and anxiety disorders.
   d. substance use disorders and autistic disorders.

4. People who repeatedly perform senseless rituals to overcome their anxiety are said to have a(n)
   a. generalized anxiety disorder.
   b. manic disorder.
   c. obsessive-compulsive disorder.
   d. phobic disorder.

5. Which of the following statements about dissociative identity disorder is true?
   a. The original personality is always aware of the alternate personalities.
   b. Dissociative identity disorder is an alternate name for schizophrenia.
   c. The multiple personalities are typically all quite similar to one another.
   d. Starting in the 1970s, there was a dramatic increase in the diagnosis of dissociative identity disorder.

6. After several months during which he was always gloomy and dejected, Mario has suddenly perked up. He feels elated and energetic and works around the clock on a writing project. He has also started to bet heavily on sporting events over the Internet, which he never did previously. Mario's behavior is consistent with
   a. schizophrenia.
   b. obsessive-compulsive disorder.
   c. bipolar disorder.
   d. dissociative identity disorder.

7. A concordance rate indicates
   a. the percentage of twin pairs or other relatives who exhibit the same disorder.
   b. the percentage of people with a given disorder who are currently receiving treatment.
   c. the prevalence of a given disorder in the general population.
   d. the rate of cure for a given disorder.

8. Which of the following would be a negative symptom of schizophrenia?
   a. Auditory hallucinations
   b. Delusions of persecution
   c. Having virtually no friendships
   d. Delusions of grandeur

9. Research suggests that there is an association between schizophrenia and
   a. serotonin depletion.
   b. enlarged brain ventricles.
   c. hippocampal degeneration.
   d. abnormalities in the cerebellum.

10. About _____ % of patients with eating disorders are female.
   a. 40
   b. 50–60
   c. 75
   d. 90–95

ANSWERS

1. a Page 422
2. c Page 423
3. c Page 425
4. c Page 427
5. d Pages 430–431
6. c Pages 433–434
7. a Page 435
8. c Page 441
9. b Page 443
10. d Page 448

COURSEMATE

Go to **CengageBrain.com** to access Psychology CourseMate, where you will find an interactive eBook, glossaries, flashcards, quizzes, videos, and more.

PERSONAL EXPLORATIONS WORKBOOK

Go to the *Personal Explorations Workbook* in the back of your textbook for exercises that can enhance your self-understanding in relation to issues raised in this chapter.

Exercise 14.1 *Self-Assessment:* Manifest Anxiety Scale

Exercise 14.2 *Self-Reflection:* What Are Your Attitudes on Mental Illness?

CHAPTER *15*

Psychotherapy

© BSIP SA/Alamy

What do you picture when you hear the term *psychotherapy*? If you're like most people, you probably envision a troubled patient lying on a couch in a therapist's office, with the therapist asking penetrating questions and providing sage advice. Typically, people believe that psychotherapy is only for those who are "sick" and that therapists have special powers that allow them to "see through" their clients. It is also widely believed that therapy requires years of deep probing into a client's innermost secrets. Many people further assume that therapists routinely tell their patients how to lead their lives. Like most stereotypes, this picture of psychotherapy is a mixture of fact and fiction, as you'll see in the upcoming pages.

In this chapter, we take a down-to-earth look at the process of *psychotherapy*, using the term in its broadest sense to refer to all the diverse approaches to the treatment of psychological problems. We start by discussing some general questions about the provision of treatment. Who seeks therapy? What kinds of professionals provide treatment? How many types of therapy are there? After considering these general issues, we examine some of the more widely used approaches to treating psychological maladies, analyzing their goals, techniques, and effectiveness. The Application at the end of the chapter focuses on practical issues involved in finding a therapist, in case you ever have to advise someone about seeking help.

ELEMENTS OF THE TREATMENT PROCESS

LEARNING OBJECTIVES

- Identify the three major categories of therapy, and discuss patterns of treatment seeking.
- Distinguish among the various types of mental health professionals involved in the provision of therapy.

Today people have a bewildering array of psychotherapy approaches to choose from. In fact, the immense diversity of therapeutic treatments makes defining the concept of *psychotherapy* difficult. After organizing a landmark conference that brought together many of the world's leading authorities on psychotherapy, Jeffrey Zeig (1987) commented, "I do not believe there is any capsule definition of psychotherapy on which the twenty-six presenters could agree" (p. xix). In lieu of a definition, we can identify a few basic elements that the various approaches to treatment have in common. All psychotherapies involve a helping relationship (the treatment) between a professional with special training (the therapist) and another person in need of help (the client). As we look at each of these three elements, you'll see the diverse nature of modern psychotherapy.

Treatments: How Many Types Are There?

In their efforts to help people, mental health professionals use many methods of treatment, including discussion, emotional support, persuasion, conditioning procedures, relaxation training, role playing, drug therapy, biofeedback, and group therapy. Some therapists also use a variety of less-conventional procedures, such as rebirthing, poetry therapy, and primal therapy. No one knows exactly how many ap-

proaches to treatment there are. One expert (Kazdin, 1994) estimates that there may be over 400 distinct types of psychotherapy! Fortunately, we can impose some order on this chaos. As varied as therapists' procedures are, approaches to treatment can be classified into three major categories:

1. *Insight therapies.* Insight therapy is "talk therapy" in the tradition of Freud's psychoanalysis. This is probably the approach to treatment that comes to mind when you think of psychotherapy. In insight therapies, clients engage in complex verbal interactions with their therapist. The goal in these discussions is to pursue increased insight regarding the nature of the client's difficulties and to sort through possible solutions. Insight therapy can be conducted with an individual or with a group.

2. *Behavior therapies.* Behavior therapies are based on the principles of learning and conditioning, which were introduced in Chapter 2. Instead of emphasizing personal insights, behavior therapists make direct efforts to alter problematic responses (phobic behaviors, for instance) and maladaptive habits (drug use, for instance). Behavior therapists work on changing clients' overt behaviors. They use different procedures for different kinds of problems.

3. *Biomedical therapies.* Biomedical approaches to therapy involve interventions into a person's physiological

functioning. The most widely used procedures are drug therapy and electroconvulsive therapy. In recent decades, drug therapy has become the dominant mode of treatment for psychological disorders. As **Figure 15.1** shows, one large-scale study found that 57% of mental health patients were treated with medication only, up from 44% just 9 years earlier (Olfson & Marcus, 2010). As the name bio-*medical* therapies suggests, these treatments have traditionally been provided only by physicians with a medical degree (usually psychiatrists). This situation is changing, however, as psychologists have been campaigning for prescription privileges (Price, 2008a). The chief rationale for this campaign is that many rural areas and underserved populations have inadequate access to psychiatrists (Ax et al., 2008). To date, psychologists have obtained prescription authority in two states (New Mexico and Louisiana), and they have made legislative progress toward this goal in many other states (Munsey, 2008b).

In this chapter we examine approaches to therapy that fall into each of these three categories. Although different methods are used in each, the three major classes of treatment are not entirely incompatible. For example, a client being seen in insight therapy may also be given medication.

Clients: Who Seeks Therapy?

People seeking mental health treatment show up with the full range of human problems: anxiety, depression, unsatisfactory interpersonal relations, troublesome habits, poor self-control, low self-esteem, marital conflicts, self-doubt, a sense of emptiness, and feelings of personal stagnation. Among adults, the

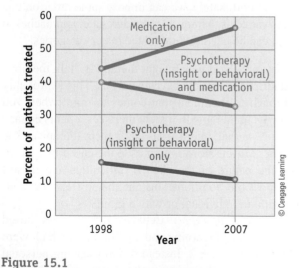

Figure 15.1
Escalating reliance on drug therapy. Using data from an ongoing national survey focusing on patterns of health care, Olfson and Marcus (2010) found some interesting trends in outpatient treatment for psychological disorders. Comparing treatment procedures in 1998 and 2007, they found that the percentage of patients treated with medication exclusively increased from 44% to 57%. During the same time period, the percentage of patients treated with insight or behavioral therapy alone, or in combination with drug therapy, declined.

two most common presenting problems are depression and anxiety (Olfson & Marcus, 2010).

A client in treatment does *not* necessarily have an identifiable psychological disorder. Some people seek professional help for everyday problems (career decisions, for instance) or vague feelings of discontent. One surprising finding in recent research has been that only about half of the people who use mental health services in a given year meet the criteria for a full-fledged mental disorder (Kessler et al., 2005b).

People vary considerably in their willingness to seek psychotherapy. Some people delay for many years before finally seeking treatment for their psychological problems (Wang et al., 2005a). As you can see in **Figure 15.2**, women are more likely than men to receive treatment, and whites are more likely than blacks or Hispanics to obtain therapy. Treatment is also more likely when people have medical insurance and when they have more education (Olfson & Marcus, 2010). *Unfortunately, it appears that many people who need therapy don't receive it.* Research suggests that only about one-third of the people who need treatment get it (Kessler et al., 2005b). People who could benefit from therapy do not seek it for a variety of reasons. Lack of health insurance and cost concerns appear to be major barriers to obtaining needed care for many people. Perhaps the biggest roadblock is the stigma surrounding the receipt of mental health treatment. Unfortunately, many people equate seeking therapy with admitting personal weakness.

Therapists: Who Provides Professional Treatment?

Friends and relatives may provide excellent advice about personal problems, but their assistance does not qualify as therapy. Psychotherapy refers to *professional* treatment by someone with special training. However, a common source of confusion about psychotherapy is the variety of "helping professions" available to offer assistance. Psychology and psychiatry are the principal professions involved in psychotherapy, providing the lion's share of mental health care. However, therapy is also provided by social workers, psychiatric nurses, counselors, and marriage and family therapists, as outlined in **Figure 15.3**.

Psychologists

Two types of psychologists may provide therapy, although the distinction between them is more theoretical than real. *Clinical psychologists* and *counseling psychologists* **specialize in the diagnosis and treatment of psychological disorders and everyday behavioral problems.** In theory, the training of clinical psychologists emphasizes treatment of full-fledged disorders, whereas the training of counseling psychologists is slanted toward treatment of everyday adjustment problems in normal people. In practice, how-

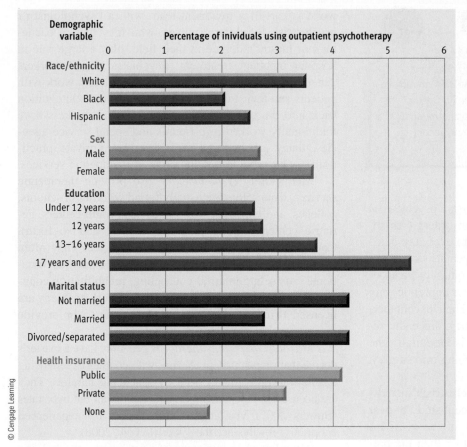

Figure 15.2

Therapy utilization rates. Olfson and Marcus (2010) analyzed data on the use of outpatient mental health services in the United States in relation to various demographic variables. In regard to marital status, utilization rates are particularly high among those who are divorced or not married. The use of therapy is also greater among those who have more education. Females are more likely to pursue therapy than males are, but utilization rates are relatively low among ethnic minorities and those who lack health insurance.

ever, there is great overlap between clinical and counseling psychologists in training, in skills, and in the clientele they serve (Morgan & Cohen, 2008).

Both types of psychologists must earn a doctoral degree (Ph.D., Psy.D., or Ed.D.). A doctorate in psychology requires 5 to 7 years of training beyond a bachelor's degree. The process of gaining admission to a Ph.D. program in clinical psychology is highly competitive (about as competitive as for medical school). Psychologists receive most of their training on university campuses, although they also serve a 1- to 2-year internship in a clinical setting, such as a hospital.

In providing therapy, psychologists use either insight or behavioral approaches. In comparison to psychiatrists, they are more likely to use behavioral techniques and less likely to use psychoanalytic methods. Clinical and counseling psychologists do psychological testing as well as psychotherapy, and many also conduct research.

Psychiatrists

Psychiatrists **are physicians who specialize in the treatment of psychological disorders.** Many psychiatrists also treat everyday behavioral problems.

TYPES OF THERAPISTS			
Profession	**Degree**	**Education beyond Bachelor's degree**	**Typical roles and activities**
Clinical psychologist	PhD or PsyD	5–7 years	Psychological testing, diagnosis, treatment with insight or behavior therapy
Counseling psychologist	PhD, PsyD or EdD	5–7 years	Similar to clinical psychologist, but more focus on work, career, and adjustment problems
Psychiatrist	MD	8 years	Diagnosis and treatment, primarily with biomedical therapies, but also insight therapies
Clinical social worker	MSW, DSW	2–5 years	Insight and behavior therapy, often help inpatients with their return to the community
Psychiatric nurse	RN, MA, or PhD	0–5 years	Inpatient care, insight and behavior therapy
Counselor	BA or MA	0–2 years	Vocational counseling, drug counseling, rehabilitation counseling
Marriage and family therapist	MA or PhD	2–5 years	Marital/couples therapy, family therapy

Figure 15.3

The principal mental health professions. Psychotherapists come from a variety of professional backgrounds. This chart provides an overview of various types of therapists' education and typical professional activities.

However, in comparison to psychologists, psychiatrists devote more time to relatively severe disorders (schizophrenia, mood disorders) and less time to everyday marital, family, job, and school problems. Psychiatrists have an M.D. degree. Their graduate training requires 4 years of course work in medical school and a 4-year apprenticeship in a residency at an approved hospital. Their psychotherapy training occurs during their residency, since the required course work in medical school is essentially the same for all students, whether they are going into surgery, pediatrics, or psychiatry.

In their provision of treatment, psychiatrists increasingly emphasize drugs. Indeed, in one recent study of over 14,000 visits to psychiatrists, only 29% of the visits involved the provision of some therapy other than the prescription and management of medications (Mojtabai & Olfson, 2008). Less than a decade earlier, that figure was 44% of visits, so psychiatrists are clearly abandoning talk therapies and behavioral interventions in favor of drug treatments.

Other Mental Health Professionals

Several other mental health professions also provide psychotherapy services. In hospitals and other institutions, *psychiatric social workers* and *psychiatric nurses* often work as part of a treatment team with a psychologist or psychiatrist. Psychiatric nurses, who may have a bachelor's or master's degree in their field, play a large role in hospital inpatient treatment. Psychiatric social workers generally have a master's degree and typically work with patients and their families to ease the patient's integration back into the community. Although social workers have traditionally worked in hospitals and social service agencies, many are licensed as independent, private practitioners who provide a wide range of therapeutic services.

Many kinds of *counselors* also provide therapeutic services. Counselors are usually found working in schools, colleges, and human services agencies (youth centers, geriatric centers, family planning centers, and so forth). Counselors typically have a master's degree. They often specialize in particular types of problems, such as vocational counseling, marital counseling, rehabilitation counseling, and drug counseling. Like social workers, many are licensed as independent, private practitioners who provide diverse services for a diverse clientele.

Marriage and family therapists generally have a master's degree that prepares them to work with couples experiencing relationship problems or with dysfunctional families. They are licensed as independent practitioners in all but two states (Bowers, 2007). Marital and family therapy has experienced enormous growth since the 1980s (Lebow, 2008).

Although clear differences exist among the helping professions in education and training, their roles in the treatment process overlap considerably. In this chapter, we refer to psychologists or psychiatrists as needed, but otherwise we use the terms *clinician, therapist,* and *mental health professional* to refer to psychotherapists of all kinds, regardless of their professional degree.

Now that we have discussed the basic elements in psychotherapy, we can examine specific approaches to treatment in terms of their goals, procedures, and effectiveness. We begin with a few representative insight therapies.

INSIGHT THERAPIES

LEARNING OBJECTIVES

- Understand the logic of psychoanalysis, and describe the techniques used to probe the unconscious.
- Describe client-centered therapy and new approaches to insight therapy inspired by positive psychology.
- Describe how group therapy, couples therapy, and family therapy are generally conducted.
- Assess the efficacy of insight therapies.
- Review both sides of the recovered memories controversy.

Many schools of thought exist as to how to conduct insight therapy. Therapists with different theoretical orientations use different methods to pursue different kinds of insights. What these varied approaches have in common is that *insight therapies* **involve verbal interactions intended to enhance clients' self-knowledge and thus promote healthful changes in personality and behavior.** Although there may be hundreds of insight therapies, the leading eight or ten approaches appear to account for the lion's share of treatment. In this section, we delve into psychoanalysis, client-centered therapy, treatments growing out of positive psychology, and group therapy.

Psychoanalysis

Sigmund Freud worked as a psychotherapist for almost 50 years in Vienna. Through a painstaking process of trial and error, he developed innovative techniques for the treatment of psychological disorders and distress. His system of *psychoanalysis* dominated psychiatry for more than half a century. Although this dominance has eroded in recent decades, a diverse array of psychoanalytic approaches to therapy continue to evolve and remain influential today (Luborsky, O'Reilly-Landry, & Arlow, 2011; Ursano, Sonnenberg, & Lazar, 2008).

Sigmund Freud

Psychoanalysis **is an insight therapy that emphasizes the recovery of unconscious conflicts, motives, and defenses through techniques such as free association, dream analysis, and transference.** To appreciate the logic of psychoanalysis, we have to look at Freud's thinking about the roots of mental disorders. Freud treated mostly anxiety-dominated disturbances, such as phobic, panic, obsessive-compulsive, and conversion disorders, which were then called *neuroses.* He believed that neurotic problems are caused by unconscious conflicts left over from early childhood. As explained in Chapter 2, he thought that these inner conflicts involve battles among the id, ego, and superego, usually over sexual and aggressive impulses. Freud theorized that people depend on defense mechanisms to avoid confronting these conflicts, which remain hidden in the depths of the unconscious. However, he noted that defensive maneuvers often lead to self-defeating behavior. Furthermore, he asserted that defenses tend to be only partially successful in alleviating anxiety, guilt, and other distressing emotions. With this model in mind, let's take a look at the therapeutic procedures used in psychoanalysis.

Probing the Unconscious

Given Freud's assumptions, we can see that the logic of psychoanalysis is very simple. The analyst attempts to probe the murky depths of the unconscious to discover the unresolved conflicts causing the client's neurotic behavior. In a sense, the analyst functions as a psychological detective. In this effort to explore the unconscious, he or she relies on two techniques: free association and dream analysis.

In *free association,* **clients spontaneously express their thoughts and feelings exactly as they occur, with as little censorship as possible.** Clients lie on a couch so they will be better able to let their minds drift freely. In free associating, clients expound on anything that comes to mind, regardless of how trivial, silly, or embarrassing it might be. Gradually, most clients begin to let everything pour out without conscious censorship. The analyst studies these free associations for clues about what is going on in the unconscious.

In *dream analysis,* **the therapist interprets the symbolic meaning of the client's dreams.** For Freud, dreams were the "royal road to the unconscious," the most direct means of access to patients' innermost conflicts, wishes, and impulses. Clients are encouraged and trained to remember their dreams, which they describe in therapy. The therapist then analyzes the symbolism in these dreams to interpret their meaning.

To better illustrate these matters, let's look at an actual case treated through psychoanalysis (adapted from Greenson, 1967, pp. 40–41). Mr. N was troubled by an unsatisfactory marriage. He claimed to love his wife, but he preferred sexual relations with prostitutes. Mr. N reported that his parents also endured lifelong marital difficulties. His childhood conflicts about their relationship appeared to be related to his problems. Both dream analysis and free association can be seen in the following description of a session in Mr. N's treatment:

Mr. N reports a fragment of a dream. All that he can remember is that he is waiting for a red traffic light to change when he feels that someone has bumped into him from behind. . . . The associations led to Mr. N's love of cars, especially sports cars. He loved the sensation, in particular, of whizzing by those fat, old, expensive cars. . . . His father always hinted that he had been a great athlete, but he never substantiated it. . . . Mr. N doubted whether his father could really perform. His father would flirt with a waitress in a cafe or make sexual remarks about women passing by, but he seemed to be showing off. If he were really sexual, he wouldn't resort to that.

As is characteristic of free association, Mr. N's train of thought meanders about with little direction. Nonetheless, clues about his unconscious conflicts are apparent. What did Mr. N's therapist extract from this session? The therapist saw sexual overtones in the dream fragment, where Mr. N was bumped from behind. The therapist also inferred that Mr. N had a competitive orientation toward his father, based on the free association about whizzing by fat, old, expensive cars. As you can see, analysts must *interpret* their clients' dreams and free associations. This is a critical process throughout psychoanalysis.

Interpretation

Interpretation **involves the therapist's attempts to explain the inner significance of the client's thoughts, feelings, memories, and behaviors.** Contrary to popular belief, analysts do not interpret everything, and they generally don't try to dazzle clients with startling revelations. Instead, analysts move forward inch by inch, offering interpretations that should be just out of the client's own

In psychoanalysis, the therapist encourages the client to reveal thoughts, feelings, dreams, and memories that can then be interpreted in relation to the client's current problems.

Rolf Bruderer/Flirt/Corbis

reach (Samberg & Marcus, 2005). Mr. N's therapist eventually offered the following interpretations to his client:

I said to Mr. N near the end of the hour that I felt he was struggling with his feelings about his father's sexual life. He seemed to be saying that his father was sexually not a very potent man. . . . He also recalls that he once found a packet of condoms under his father's pillow when he was an adolescent and he thought "My father must be going to prostitutes." I then intervened and pointed out that the condoms under his father's pillow seemed to indicate more obviously that his father used the condoms with his mother, who slept in the same bed. However, Mr. N wanted to believe his wish-fulfilling fantasy: mother doesn't want sex with father and father is not very potent. The patient was silent and the hour ended.

As you may already have guessed, the therapist had concluded that Mr. N's difficulties were rooted in an Oedipal complex (see Chapter 2). Mr. N had unresolved sexual feelings toward his mother and hostile feelings about his father. These unconscious conflicts, rooted in his childhood, were distorting his intimate relations as an adult.

Resistance

How would you expect Mr. N to respond to his therapist's suggestion that he was in competition with his father for the sexual attention of his mother? Obviously, most clients would have great difficulty accepting such an interpretation. Freud fully expected clients to display some resistance to therapeutic efforts. **Resistance involves largely unconscious defensive maneuvers intended to hinder the progress of therapy.** Resistance is assumed to be an inevitable part of the psychoanalytic process (Samberg & Marcus, 2005). Why do clients try to resist the helping process? Because they don't want to face up to the painful, disturbing conflicts they have buried in their unconscious. Although they have sought help, they are reluctant to confront their real problems.

Resistance may take many forms. Patients may show up late for their sessions, merely pretend to engage in free association, or express hostility toward the therapist. For instance, Mr. N's therapist noted that after the session just described, "The next day he began by telling me that he was furious with me." Analysts use a variety of strategies to deal with their clients' resistance. Often, a key consideration is the handling of *transference,* which we consider next.

Transference

Transference occurs when clients start relating to their therapist in ways that mimic critical relationships in their lives. Thus, a client might start relating to a therapist as if the therapist were an overprotective mother, rejecting brother, or passive spouse. In a sense, the client *transfers* conflicting feelings about important people onto the therapist (Høglend et al., 2011). For instance, in his treatment, Mr. N transferred some of the competitive hostility he felt toward his father onto his analyst.

Psychoanalysts often encourage transference so that clients begin to reenact relations with crucial people in the context of therapy. These reenactments can help bring repressed feelings and conflicts to the surface, allowing the client to work through them. The therapist's handling of transference is complicated and difficult because transference may arouse confusing, highly charged emotions in the client.

Undergoing psychoanalysis is not easy. It can be a slow, painful process of self-examination that routinely requires 3 to 5 years of hard work. It tends to be a lengthy process because patients need time to gradually work through their problems and genuinely accept unnerving revelations (Williams, 2005). Ultimately, if resistance and transference can be handled effectively, the therapist's interpretations should lead the client to profound insights. For instance, Mr. N eventually admitted, "The old boy is probably right, it does tickle me to imagine that my mother preferred me and I could beat out my father. Later, I wondered whether this had something to do with my own screwed-up sex life with my wife." According to Freud, once clients recognize the unconscious sources of their conflicts, they can resolve these conflicts and discard their neurotic defenses.

Learn More Online

The American Psychoanalytic Association

The site for this professional organization provides a great deal of useful information about psychoanalytic approaches to treatment. The resources include news releases, background information on psychoanalysis, an engine for literature searches, and a bookstore.

Modern Psychodynamic Therapies

Although still available, classical psychoanalysis as done by Freud is not widely practiced anymore (Kay & Kay, 2008). Freud's psychoanalytic method was geared to a particular kind of clientele that he was seeing in Vienna a century ago. As his followers fanned out across Europe and America, many found that it was necessary to adapt psychoanalysis to different cultures, changing times, and new kinds of patients. Thus, many variations on Freud's original approach to psychoanalysis have developed over the years. These descendants of psychoanalysis are collectively known as *psychodynamic approaches* to therapy.

Today we have a rich variety of psychodynamic approaches to therapy (Magnavita, 2008). Recent reviews of these treatments suggest that interpretation, resistance, and transference continue to play key roles in therapeutic efforts (Høglend et al., 2008). Other central features of modern psychodynamic therapies include (1) a focus on emotional experience, (2) exploration of efforts to avoid distressing thoughts and feelings, (3) identification of recurring patterns in patients' life experiences, (4) discussion of past experience, especially events in early childhood, (5) analysis of interpersonal relationships, (6) a focus on the therapeutic relationship itself, and (7) exploration of

dreams and other aspects of fantasy life (Shedler, 2010; see **Figure 15.4**). Recent research suggests that psychodynamic approaches can be helpful in the treatment of a diverse array of disorders, including depression, anxiety disorders, personality disorders, and substance abuse (Gibbons, Crits-Christoph, & Hearon, 2008; Shedler, 2010).

Client-Centered Therapy

You may have heard of people going into therapy to "find themselves" or to "get in touch with their real feelings." These now-popular phrases emerged out of the human potential movement, which was stimulated in part by the work of Carl Rogers (1951, 1986). Taking a humanistic perspective, Rogers devised *client-centered therapy* (also known as *person-centered therapy*) in the 1940s and 1950s.

Courtesy of Carl Rogers Memorial Library

Carl Rogers

Client-centered therapy is an insight therapy that emphasizes providing a supportive emotional climate for clients, who play a major role in determining the pace and direction of their therapy. You may wonder why the troubled, untrained client is put in charge of the pace and direction of the therapy. Rogers (1961) provides a compelling justification:

It is the client who knows what hurts, what directions to go, what problems are crucial, what experiences have been deeply buried. It began to occur to me that unless I had a need to demonstrate my own cleverness and learning, I would do better to rely upon the client for the direction of movement in the process. (pp. 11–12)

Rogers's theory about the principal causes of neurotic anxieties is quite different from the Freudian explanation. As discussed in Chapter 2, Rogers maintained that most personal distress is due to inconsistency, or "incongruence," between a person's self-concept and reality (see **Figure 15.5** on the next page). According to his theory, incongruence makes people prone to feel threatened by realistic feedback about themselves from others. For example, if you inaccurately viewed yourself as a hardworking, dependable person, you would feel threatened by contradictory feedback from friends or co-workers. According to Rogers, anxiety about such feedback often leads to reliance on defense mecha-

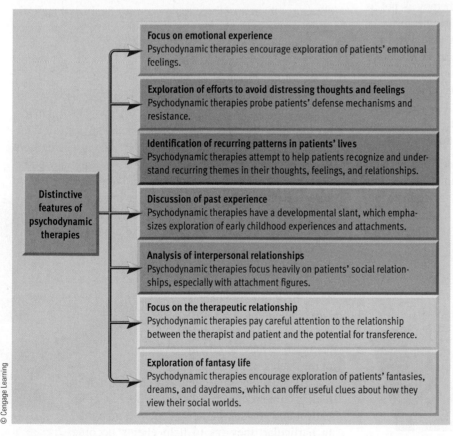

© Cengage Learning

Distinctive features of psychodynamic therapies

Focus on emotional experience
Psychodynamic therapies encourage exploration of patients' emotional feelings.

Exploration of efforts to avoid distressing thoughts and feelings
Psychodynamic therapies probe patients' defense mechanisms and resistance.

Identification of recurring patterns in patients' lives
Psychodynamic therapies attempt to help patients recognize and understand recurring themes in their thoughts, feelings, and relationships.

Discussion of past experience
Psychodynamic therapies have a developmental slant, which emphasizes exploration of early childhood experiences and attachments.

Analysis of interpersonal relationships
Psychodynamic therapies focus heavily on patients' social relationships, especially with attachment figures.

Focus on the therapeutic relationship
Psychodynamic therapies pay careful attention to the relationship between the therapist and patient and the potential for transference.

Exploration of fantasy life
Psychodynamic therapies encourage exploration of patients' fantasies, dreams, and daydreams, which can offer useful clues about how they view their social worlds.

Figure 15.4
Core features of psychodynamic therapies. In an article on the efficacy of psychodynamic therapies, Jonathan Shedler (2010) outlined the distinctive aspects of modern psychodynamic techniques and processes. The seven features described here represent the core of contemporary psychodynamic treatment.

Figure 15.5

Rogers's view of the roots of disorders. Carl Rogers's theory posits that anxiety and self-defeating behavior are rooted in an incongruent self-concept that makes one prone to recurrent anxiety, which triggers defensive behavior, which fuels more incongruence.

nisms, distortions of reality, and stifled personal growth. Excessive incongruence is thought to be rooted in clients' overdependence on others for approval and acceptance.

Given Rogers's theory, client-centered therapists seek insights that are quite different from the repressed conflicts that psychoanalysts try to track down. Client-centered therapists help clients realize that they do not have to worry constantly about pleasing others and winning acceptance. They encourage clients to respect their own feelings and values. They help people restructure their self-concept to correspond better to reality. Ultimately, these therapists try to foster self-acceptance and personal growth.

Therapeutic Climate

In client-centered therapy, the *process* of therapy is not as important as the emotional *climate* in which the therapy takes place. According to Rogers, it is critical for the therapist to provide a warm, supportive, accepting climate in which clients can confront their shortcomings without feeling threatened. The lack of threat should reduce clients' defensive tendencies and thus help them to open up. To create this atmosphere of emotional support, Rogers believed that client-centered therapists must provide three conditions:

1. *Genuineness.* The therapist must be genuine with the client, communicating in an honest and spontaneous manner. The therapist should not be phony or defensive.

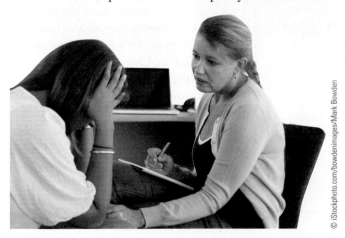

Client-centered therapists emphasize the importance of a supportive emotional climate in therapy. They also work to clarify, rather than interpret, the feelings expressed by their patients.

2. *Unconditional positive regard.* The therapist must also show complete, nonjudgmental acceptance of the client as a person. The therapist should provide warmth and caring for the client with no strings attached. This mandate does not mean that the therapist has to approve of everything that the client says or does. A therapist can disapprove of a particular behavior while continuing to value the client as a human being.

3. *Empathy.* Finally, the therapist must provide accurate empathy for the client. This means that the therapist must understand the client's world from the client's point of view. Furthermore, the therapist must be articulate enough to communicate this understanding to the client.

Rogers firmly believed that a supportive emotional climate is the major force that promotes healthy changes in therapy. However, some client-centered therapists place more emphasis on the therapeutic process.

Therapeutic Process

In client-centered therapy, the client and therapist work together almost as equals. The therapist provides relatively little guidance and keeps interpretation and advice to a minimum (Raskin, Rogers, & Witty, 2011). So, just what does the client-centered therapist do, besides creating a supportive climate? Primarily, the therapist provides feedback to help clients sort out their feelings. The therapist's key task is *clarification.* Client-centered therapists try to function like a human mirror, reflecting statements back to their clients, but with enhanced clarity. They help clients become more aware of their true feelings by highlighting themes that may be obscure in the clients' rambling discourse.

By working with clients to clarify their feelings, client-centered therapists hope to gradually build toward more far-reaching insights. In particular, they try to help clients become more aware of and comfortable with their genuine selves. Obviously, these are ambitious goals. Client-centered therapy resembles psychoanalysis in that both seek to achieve a major reconstruction of a client's personality.

Therapies Inspired by Positive Psychology

The growth of the positive psychology movement has begun to inspire new approaches to insight therapy (Peterson & Park, 2009). As noted in Chapter 3, *positive psychology* uses theory and research to better understand the positive, adaptive, creative, and fulfilling aspects of human existence. The advocates of *positive psychology* maintain that therapy has historically focused far too heavily on pathology, weakness, and suffering (and how to heal these conditions) rather than on health and resilience (Seligman, 2003a). They argue for increased research on contentment, well-being, human strengths, and positive emotions (see Chapter 16 for an in-depth discussion of positive psychology).

This philosophical approach has led to new therapeutic interventions. For example, *well-being therapy,* developed by Giovanni Fava and colleagues (Ruini & Fava, 2004), seeks to enhance clients' self-acceptance, purpose in life, autonomy, and personal growth. It has been used successfully in the treatment of mood disorders and anxiety disorders (Fava & Tomba, 2009).

Another new approach is *positive psychotherapy,* developed by Martin Seligman and colleagues (Rashid & Anjum, 2008; Seligman, Rashid, & Parks, 2006). Thus far, positive psychotherapy has been used mainly in the treatment of depression, although it was recently adapted for the treatment of schizophrenia (Meyer et al., 2012). *Positive psychotherapy* **attempts to get clients to recognize their strengths, appreciate their blessings, savor positive experiences, forgive those who have wronged them, and find meaning in their lives.** Preliminary research suggests that positive psychotherapy can be an effective treatment for depression. For example, in one study positive psychotherapy was compared to treatment as usual (whatever the therapist would normally do) and treatment as usual with medication. The data shown in **Figure 15.6** compare mean depression scores at the end of the study for participants in these three conditions (Seligman et al., 2006). As you can see, the lowest depression scores were observed in the group that received positive psychotherapy. These innovative interventions spurred by the positive psychology movement are in their infancy, but the early findings seem promising, and it will be interesting to see what the future holds.

Group Therapy

Although it dates back to the early part of the twentieth century, group therapy came of age during World War II and its aftermath in the 1950s. During this period, the expanding demand for therapeutic services forced clinicians to use group techniques (Burlingame & Baldwin, 2011). *Group therapy* **is the simultaneous treatment of several or more clients in a group.** Most major insight therapies

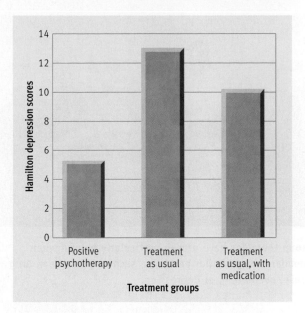

Figure 15.6

Positive psychotherapy for depression. In a study of the efficacy of positive psychotherapy, it was compared to treatment as usual (clinicians delivered whatever treatment they deemed appropriate) and to treatment as usual combined with antidepressant medication. At the end of 12 weeks of treatment, symptoms of depression were measured with the widely used Hamilton Rating Scale for Depression. The mean depression scores for each group are graphed here. As you can see, the positive psychotherapy group showed less depression than the other two treatment groups, suggesting that positive psychotherapy can be an effective intervention for depression. (Adapted from Seligman, Rashid, & Parks, 2006)

have been adapted for use with groups. Because of economic pressures in mental health care, the use of group therapy appears likely to grow in future years. Although group therapy can be conducted in a variety of ways, we can provide a general overview of the process as it usually unfolds (see Cox, Vinogradov, & Yalom, 2008; Spitz, 2009; Stone, 2008).

Participants' Roles

A therapy group typically consists of four to twelve people, with six to eight participants regarded as an ideal number (Cox et al., 2008). The therapist usually screens the participants, excluding anyone who seems likely to be disruptive. Some theorists maintain that judicious selection of participants is crucial to effective group treatment (Schlapobersky & Pines, 2009). There is some debate about whether it is better to have a homogeneous group (people who are similar in age, gender, and presenting problem) than a heterogeneous one. Practical necessities usually dictate that groups be at least somewhat diversified.

In group treatment the therapist's responsibilities include selecting participants, setting goals for the group, initiating and maintaining the therapeutic process, and protecting clients from harm (Cox et al., 2008). The therapist often plays a relatively subtle role, staying in the back-

Group therapies have proven particularly helpful when members share similar problems, such as alcoholism, drug abuse, overeating, or depression.

ground and focusing mainly on promoting group cohesiveness. The therapist always retains a special status, but the therapist and clients are on much more equal footing in group therapy than in individual therapy. The leader in group therapy expresses emotions, shares feelings, and copes with challenges from group members. In other words, group therapists participate in the group's exchanges and "bare their own souls" to some extent.

In group therapy, participants essentially function as therapists for one another (Schachter, 2011). Group members describe their problems, trade viewpoints, share experiences, and discuss coping strategies. Most important, they provide acceptance and emotional support for each other. In this supportive atmosphere, group members work at peeling away the social masks that cover their insecurities. Once their problems are exposed, members work at correcting them. As members come to value one another's opinions, they work hard to display healthy changes to win the group's approval.

Advantages of the Group Experience

Group therapies obviously save time and money, which can be critical in understaffed mental hospitals and other institutional settings (Cox et al., 2008). Therapists in private practice usually charge less for group than individual therapy. Obviously, this makes group therapy affordable for more people. However, group therapy is *not* just a less costly substitute for individual therapy. For many types of patients and problems, group therapy can be just as effective as individual treatment (Knauss, 2005; Stone, 2008). Moreover, group therapy has unique strengths of its own. For example, in group therapy participants often come to realize that their misery is not unique. They are reassured to learn that many other people have similar or even worse problems. Another advantage is that group therapy pro-

vides an opportunity for participants to work on their social skills in a safe environment. Yet another plus is that certain types of problems and clients respond especially well to the social support that group therapy can provide.

Couples and Family Therapy

Like group therapy, marital and family therapy rose to prominence after World War II. As their names suggest, these interventions are defined in terms of who is being treated. *Couples* or *marital therapy* **involves the treatment of both partners in a committed, intimate relationship, in which the main focus is on relationship issues.** Couples therapy is not limited to married couples. It is frequently provided to cohabiting couples, including gay couples. *Family therapy* **involves the treatment of a family unit as a whole, in which the main focus is on family dynamics and communication.** Family therapy often emerges out of efforts to treat children or adolescents with individual therapy. A child's therapist, for instance, might come to the realization that treatment is likely to fail because the child returns to a home environment that contributes to the child's problems and thus proposes a broader family intervention.

As with other forms of insight therapy, there are different schools of thought about how to conduct couples and family therapy (Goldenberg, Goldenberg, & Pelavin, 2011). Some of these diverse systems are extensions of influential approaches to individual therapy, including psychodynamic, humanistic, and behavioral treatments. Other approaches are based on innovative models of families as complex systems and explicit rejection of individual models of treatment. Although the various approaches to couples and family therapy differ in terminology and their theoretical models of relationship and family dysfunction, they tend to share common goals. First, they seek to understand the entrenched patterns of interaction that produce distress. In this endeavor they view individuals as parts of a family ecosystem, and they assume that people behave as they do because of their role in the system (Lebow, 2008). Second, they seek to help couples

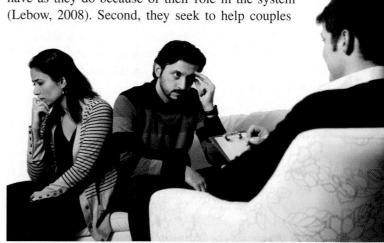

© iStockphoto.com/101dalmatians

and families improve their communication and move toward healthier patterns of interaction.

What kinds of problems bring partners in for couples therapy? The full range of relationship problems, such as constant arguments without resolution, resentment about power imbalances, perceptions of emotional withdrawal, the discovery or disclosure of affairs, sexual difficulties, the threat of relationship dissolution, and concern about how relationship issues are affecting the couple's children (Spitz & Spitz, 2009). Marital therapists attempt to help partners clarify their needs and desires in the relationship, appreciate their mutual contribution to problems, enhance their communication patterns, increase role flexibility and tolerance of differences, work out their balance of power, and learn to deal with conflict more constructively (Glick, Ritvo, & Melnick, 2008).

What are some of the indications for family therapy? It is likely to be helpful when a youngster's psychological difficulties appear to be rooted in family pathology, when families are buffeted by severe stress such as a serious illness or a major transition, when blended families experience adjustment problems, when sibling conflicts spin out of control, or when someone tries to sabotage another family member's individual therapy (Bloch & Harari, 2009; Spitz & Spitz, 2009). Family therapists attempt to help family members recognize how their patterns of interaction contribute to family distress, to achieve more effective communication, to help them rethink inflexible roles and coalitions, to wrestle with power issues in the family system, and, when relevant, to help them better understand children's psychiatric problems (Ritvo, Glick, & Berman, 2008).

Evaluating Insight Therapies

Evaluating the effectiveness of any approach to treatment is a complex challenge (Crits-Christoph & Gibbons, 2009; Staines & Cleland, 2007). Evaluating treatment results is especially complicated for insight therapies. If you were to undergo insight therapy, how would you judge its effectiveness? By how you felt? By looking at your behavior? By asking your therapist? By consulting your friends and family? What would you be looking for? Various schools of therapy pursue entirely different goals. And clients' ratings of their progress are likely to be slanted toward a favorable evaluation because they want to justify their effort, their heartache, their expense, and their time. Even evaluations by professional thera-

pists can be highly subjective (Luborsky et al., 1999). Moreover, people enter therapy with diverse problems of varied severity, creating huge confounds in efforts to assess the effectiveness of therapeutic interventions.

Despite these difficulties, thousands of outcome studies have been conducted to evaluate the effectiveness of insight therapy. These studies have examined a broad range of clinical problems and used diverse methods to assess therapeutic outcomes, including scores on psychological tests and ratings by family members, as well as therapists' and clients' ratings. These studies consistently indicate that insight therapy *is* superior to no treatment or to placebo treatment and that the effects of therapy are reasonably durable (Lambert, 2011; Torres & Saunders, 2009). And when insight therapies are compared head to head against drug therapies, they usually show roughly equal efficacy (Arkowitz & Lilienfeld, 2007). Studies generally find the greatest improvement early in treatment (the first 13–18 weekly sessions), with further gains gradually diminishing over time (Lambert, Bergin, & Garfield, 2004). Overall, about 50% of patients show a clinically meaningful recovery within about twenty sessions, and another 25% of patients achieve this goal after about forty-five sessions (Lambert & Ogles, 2004) (see **Figure 15.7**). Of course, these broad generalizations mask considerable variability in outcome, but the general trends are encouraging.

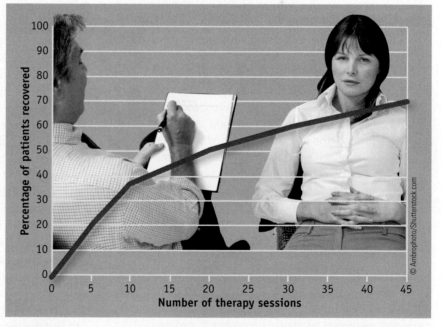

Figure 15.7

Recovery as a function of number of therapy sessions. Based on a national sample of over 6,000 patients, Lambert, Hansen, and Finch (2001) mapped out the relationship between recovery and the duration of treatment. These data show that about half of the patients had experienced a clinically significant recovery after twenty weekly sessions of therapy. After forty-five sessions of therapy, about 70% had recovered.

Source: Adapted from Lambert, M. J., Hansen, N. B., & Finch, A. E. (2001). Patient-focused research: Using patient outcome data to enhance treatment effects. *Journal of Consulting and Clinical Psychology, 69,* 159–172. Copyright © 2001 by the American Psychological Association. Used by permission of the authors.

Therapy and the Recovered Memories Controversy

While debate about the efficacy of insight therapy has simmered for many decades, the 1990s brought an entirely new controversy to rock the psychotherapy profession like never before. This emotionally charged debate was sparked by a spate of reports of people recovering repressed memories of sexual abuse and other childhood trauma through therapy. You've no doubt read or seen media stories about people—including some celebrities—who dredged up long-lost recollections of sexual abuse, typically with the help of their therapist. Such recovered memories have led to a rash of lawsuits in which adult plaintiffs have sued their parents, teachers, neighbors, pastors, and so forth for alleged child abuse 20 or 30 years earlier. For the most part, those who are accused have denied the allegations. Many of them have seemed genuinely baffled by the charges, which have torn apart some previously happy families (McHugh et al., 2004). In an effort to make sense of the charges, many accused parents have argued that their children's recollections are false memories created inadvertently by well-intentioned therapists through the power of suggestion.

The crux of the debate is that child abuse usually takes place behind closed doors, and in the absence of corroborative evidence, no way exists to reliably distinguish genuine recovered memories from those that are false. A handful of recovered memory cases have been substantiated by independent witnesses or belated admissions of guilt from the accused (Brewin, 2007; Shobe & Schooler, 2001). But in the vast majority of situations, the allegations of abuse have been vehemently denied, and independent corroboration has not been available. Recovered recollections of sexual abuse have become so common, a support group has been formed for accused people who feel that they have been victimized by "false memory syndrome."

Psychologists are sharply divided on the issue of recovered memories, leaving the public understandably confused. Many psychologists, especially therapists in clinical practice, accept most recovered memories at face value (Banyard & Williams, 1999; Gleaves & Smith, 2004; Legault & Laurence, 2007). They assert that it is common for patients to bury traumatic incidents in their unconscious. Citing evidence that sexual abuse in childhood is far more widespread than most people realize, they argue that most repressed memories of abuse are probably genuine.

In contrast, many other psychologists, especially memory researchers, have expressed skepticism about the recovered memories phenomenon (Kihlstrom, 2004; Loftus, 2003; McNally, 2007; Takarangi et al., 2008). They maintain that some suggestible, confused people struggling to understand profound personal problems have been convinced by persuasive therapists that their emotional problems must be the result of abuse that occurred years

before. Critics blame a small minority of therapists who presumably have good intentions but operate under the dubious assumption that virtually all psychological problems are attributable to childhood sexual abuse (Lindsay & Read, 1994; Loftus & Davis, 2006). Using hypnosis, dream interpretation, and leading questions, they supposedly prod and probe patients until they inadvertently create the memories of abuse they are searching for (Thayer & Lynn, 2006).

Psychologists who doubt the authenticity of repressed memories support their analysis by pointing to discredited cases of recovered memories (Brown, Goldstein, & Bjorklund, 2000). For example, with the help of a church counselor, one woman recovered memories of how her minister father repeatedly raped her, got her pregnant, and then aborted the pregnancy with a coat hanger. However, subsequent evidence revealed that the woman was still a virgin and that her father had had a vasectomy years before (Brainerd & Reyna, 2005). The skeptics also point to published case histories that clearly involved suggestive questioning and to cases in which patients have recanted recovered memories of sexual abuse after realizing that these memories were implanted by their therapists (Loftus, 1994; Shobe & Schooler, 2001). Indeed, quite a number of malpractice lawsuits have been filed against therapists for allegedly implanting false memories in patients (Brainerd & Reyna, 2005; Ost, 2006). Those who question recovered memories also point to several lines of carefully controlled laboratory research demonstrating that creating "memories" of events that never happened is not all that difficult (Lindsay et al., 2004; Loftus & Cahill, 2007). Skeptics also note that many repressed memories of abuse have been recovered under the influence of hypnosis, but research indicates that hypnosis tends to increase memory distortions while paradoxically making people feel more confident about their recollections (Mazzoni, Heap, & Scoboria, 2010).

So, what can we conclude about the recovered memories controversy? It seems pretty clear that therapists can unknowingly create false memories in their patients and that a significant portion of recovered memories of abuse are the product of suggestion (Follette & Davis, 2009; Ost, 2009). But it also seems likely that some cases of recovered memories are authentic (Brewin, 2007; Smith & Gleaves, 2007). It is difficult to estimate what proportion of recovered memories of abuse fall in each category. That said, recent evidence suggests that memories of abuse recovered through therapy are more likely to be false memories than those that are recovered spontaneously (McNally & Geraerts, 2009). People who report recovered memories of abuse seem to fall into two very different groups (Geraerts, Raymaekers, & Merckelbach, 2008). Some gradually recover memories of abuse with the assistance of suggestive therapeutic techniques, whereas others suddenly and unexpectedly recover such memories when they encounter a relevant retrieval cue (such as returning to the scene of the abuse). A study that sought to corroborate reports of abuse from both groups found a much higher corroboration rate among those who recovered their memories spontaneously (37%) as opposed to those who recovered their memories in therapy (0%) (Geraerts et al., 2007).

Thus, the matter needs to be addressed with great caution. On the one hand, people should be extremely careful about accepting recovered memories of abuse in the absence of convincing corroboration. On the other hand, such recovered memories cannot be summarily dismissed, and it would be tragic if the repressed memories controversy made people overly skeptical about the all-too-real problem of childhood sexual abuse.

BEHAVIOR THERAPIES

LEARNING OBJECTIVES

- Describe the goals and procedures of systematic desensitization and exposure therapies.
- Describe the use of aversion therapy and social skills training.
- Understand the logic, goals, and techniques of cognitive therapy.
- Assess the evidence on the efficacy of behavior therapies.

Behavior therapy is different from insight therapy in that behavior therapists make no attempt to help clients achieve grand insights about themselves. Why not? Because behavior therapists believe that such insights aren't necessary in order to produce constructive change. Consider a client troubled by compulsive gambling. The behavior therapist doesn't care whether this behavior is rooted in unconscious conflicts or parental rejection. What the client needs is to get rid of the maladaptive behavior. Consequently, the therapist simply designs a program to eliminate the compulsive gambling. The crux of the difference between insight therapy and behavior therapy lies in how each views symptoms. Insight therapists treat pathological symptoms as signs of an underlying problem. In contrast, behavior therapists think that the symptoms *are* the problem. Thus, **behavior therapies involve the application of the principles of learning to direct efforts to change clients' maladaptive behaviors.**

Behaviorism has been an influential school of thought in psychology since the 1920s. But behaviorists devoted little attention to clinical issues until the 1950s, when behavior therapy emerged out of three independent lines of research fostered by B. F. Skinner (1953) and his colleagues in the United States, Hans Eysenck (1959) and his colleagues in Britain, and Joseph Wolpe (1958) and his colleagues in South Africa (Wilson, 2011). Since then, there has been an explosion of interest in behavioral approaches to psychotherapy.

Behavior therapies are based on two main assumptions (Stanley & Beidel, 2009). *First, it is assumed that behavior is a product of learning.* No matter how self-defeating or pathological a client's behavior might be, the behaviorist believes that it is the result of past conditioning. *Second, it is assumed that what has been learned can be unlearned.* The same learning principles that explain how the maladaptive behavior was acquired can be used to get rid of it. Thus, behavior therapists attempt to change clients' behavior by applying the principles of classical conditioning, operant conditioning, and observational learning.

Systematic Desensitization

Devised by Joseph Wolpe (1958, 1987), systematic desensitization revolutionized psychotherapy by giving therapists their first useful alternative to traditional "talk therapy" (Fishman, Rego, & Muller, 2011). **Systematic desensitization is a behavior therapy used to reduce clients' anxiety responses through counterconditioning.** The treatment assumes that most anxiety responses are acquired through classical conditioning (as we discussed in Chapter 14). According to this model, a harmless stimulus (for instance, a bridge) may be paired with a frightening event (lightning striking it), so that it becomes a conditioned stimulus eliciting anxiety. The goal of systematic desensitization is to weaken the association between the conditioned stimulus (the bridge) and the conditioned response of anxiety (see **Figure 15.8** on the next page).

Systematic desensitization involves three steps. *In the first step, the therapist helps the client build an anxiety hierarchy.* This is a list of anxiety-arousing stimuli related to the

What's the nature of the trouble, and when did it begin?

Let's drive it around and see what happens.

FREUDIAN

BEHAVIOR THERAPIST

Sciencecartoonsplus.com by Sidney Harris

Figure 15.8

The logic underlying systematic desensitization. Behaviorists argue that many phobic responses are acquired through classical conditioning, as in the example diagrammed here. Systematic desensitization targets the conditioned associations between phobic stimuli and fear responses.

specific source of anxiety, such as flying, academic tests, or snakes. The client ranks the stimuli from the least anxiety arousing to the most anxiety arousing. *The second step involves training the client in deep muscle relaxation.* This second phase may begin during early sessions while the therapist and client are still constructing the anxiety hierarchy. *In the third step, the client tries to work through the hierarchy, learning to remain relaxed while imagining each stimulus.* Starting with the least anxiety-arousing stimulus, the client imagines the situation as vividly as possible while relaxing. If the client experiences strong anxiety, he or she drops the imaginary scene and concentrates on relaxation. The client keeps repeating this process until he or she can imagine a scene with little or no anxiety. Once a particular scene is conquered, the client moves on to the next stimulus situation in the anxiety hierarchy. Gradually, over a number of therapy sessions, the client progresses through the hierarchy, unlearning troublesome anxiety responses.

The effectiveness of systematic desensitization in reducing phobic responses is well documented (Spiegler & Guevremont, 2010). That said, interventions emphasizing direct exposures to anxiety-arousing situations have become behavior therapists' treatment of choice for phobic and other anxiety disorders (Rachman, 2009). **In** *exposure therapies* **clients are confronted with situations that they fear so that they learn that these situations are really harmless.** The exposures take place in a controlled setting and often involve a gradual progression from less-feared to more-feared stimuli. These real-life exposures to anxiety-arousing situations usually prove harmless, and individuals' anxiety responses decline. In recent decades, some therapists have resorted to highly realistic virtual-reality presentations of feared situations via computer-generated imagery (Meyerbröker & Emmelkamp, 2010; Reger et al., 2011). Exposure therapies are versatile in that they can be used with the full range of anxiety disorders, including obsessive compulsive disorder, posttraumatic stress disorder, and panic disorder.

Effective exposure treatments for phobias can even be completed in a single session! Onc-session treatment (OST) of phobias, pioneered by Lars-Göran Öst (1997), involves an intensive 3-hour intervention that depends primarily on gradually increased exposures to specific phobic objects and situations. A person with a spider phobia, for instance, would be asked to approach a small spider in a series of steps. Once anxiety subsides at a particular distance, the person comes closer and waits again until anxiety diminishes. When the person manages to endure a close encounter with the small spider, the therapist may move on to a larger, or more intimidating spider. OST has proven effective with a variety of specific phobias, including snakes, spiders, cats, dogs, darkness, thunderstorms, heights, and elevators (Ollendick et al., 2009; Öst, 1997; Öst et al., 2001).

Aversion Therapy

Aversion therapy is far and away the most controversial of the behavior therapies. It's not something that you would sign up for unless you were pretty desperate. Psychologists usually suggest it only as a treatment of last resort, after other interventions have failed. What's so terrible about aversion therapy? The client has to endure decidedly unpleasant stimuli, such as shocks or drug-induced nausea.

Aversion therapy **is a behavior therapy in which an aversive stimulus is paired with a stimulus that elicits an undesirable response.** For example, alcoholics have had drug-induced nausea paired with their favorite drinks during therapy sessions (Landabaso et al., 1999). By pairing an *emetic drug* (one that causes vomiting) with alcohol, the therapist hopes to create a conditioned aversion to alcohol (see **Figure 15.9**).

Figure 15.9

Aversion therapy. Aversion therapy uses classical conditioning to create an aversion to a stimulus that has elicited problematic behavior. For example, in the treatment of drinking problems, alcohol may be paired with a nausea-inducing drug to create a conditioned aversion to alcohol.

Log on to CourseMate at www.cengagebrain.com to watch this video.

Although phobias may seem difficult to overcome, effective treatment can be quite brief. As discussed in the text, Lars-Göran Öst developed a *one-session treatment* (*OST*) for phobias (also referred to as *brief exposure therapy*) that reduces or eliminates fear of an object or situation. In this Reel Research video, Öst demonstrates the effectiveness of OST with Mariam Dum, a research technician who has a fear of snakes.

David Barlow, director of the Center for Anxiety and Related Disorders at Boston University, is a pioneer in exposure therapy. Barlow invited Öst to demonstrate how OST works with Mariam, who has always had an unexplained fear of snakes. Although she has had little contact with them throughout her life, Mariam fears and tries to limit exposure to snakes. In the 3-hour session, Öst interviews her, explains how the treatment will go, and then gives Mariam control over how she is exposed to the snake. Öst starts out holding the snake with his back to Mariam. After 3 minutes, she allows Öst to face her with the snake. Gradually, when she feels more comfortable, she allows him to approach her with the snake. He asks Mariam about her level of anxiety at various stages throughout the session. After a while, Mariam touches and carries the snake, whom she has named Alf, and allows Öst to place it on the floor and slither across the room.

Gaining experience with a feared object or situation is essential to overcoming a phobia, because it is important for the patient to realize that feeling anxious or overwhelmed is natural and that there is no real danger. When Alf did not behave as Mariam predicted, her anxiety about the snake diminished. Öst demonstrates that a patient's motivation to succeed is far more predictive of success than his or her level of anxiety. Even though Mariam could barely look at the snake at the beginning of the session, being motivated to change gave her the self-confidence to help unhook Alf from Öst's belt loops without feeling scared at the end of the session.

Watch the *Phobias and One-Session Treatments* video to learn more about OST and how to overcome phobias. Delve even deeper by responding to the following discussion questions.

DISCUSSION QUESTIONS

1. What psychological explanations can be made about Mariam, according to Öst? How are habituation, self-efficacy, and modeling displayed in this demonstration?
2. Describe other treatment methods for phobias discussed in the video. Why are they effective or ineffective in eliminating phobias of the feared object or situation?
3. How is Mariam's anxiety level throughout the 3-hour treatment: stable, increasing, fluctuating, or declining? How does Öst practice OST with Mariam? When, if ever, does Mariam say her anxiety level is at zero? Describe the step-by-step process in detail.

Aversion therapy takes advantage of the automatic nature of responses produced through classical conditioning. Admittedly, alcoholics treated with aversion therapy know that they won't be given an emetic outside of their therapy sessions. However, their reflex response to the stimulus of alcohol may be changed so that they respond to it with nausea and distaste. Obviously, this response should make it much easier to resist the urge to drink.

Aversion therapy is not a widely practiced technique, and when it is used it is usually only one element in a larger treatment program. Troublesome behaviors treated successfully with aversion therapy have included drug and alcohol abuse, sexual deviance, gambling, shoplifting, stuttering, cigarette smoking, and overeating (Bordnick et al., 2004; Grossman & Ruiz, 2004; Maletzky, 2002).

Social Skills Training

Many psychological problems grow out of interpersonal difficulties. Behavior therapists point out that humans are not born with social finesse. They acquire their social skills through learning. Unfortunately, some people have not learned how to be friendly, how to make conversation, how to express anger appropriately, and so forth. Social ineptitude can contribute to anxiety, feelings of inferiority, and various kinds of disorders. In light of these findings, therapists are increasingly using social skills training in efforts to improve clients' social abilities. This approach to therapy has yielded promising results in the treatment of social anxiety (Bögels & Voncken, 2008), autism (Cappadocia & Weiss, 2011), attention deficit disorder (Monastra, 2008), and schizophrenia (Kurtz & Mueser, 2008).

Social skills training **is a behavior therapy designed to improve interpersonal skills that emphasizes modeling, behavioral rehearsal, and shaping.** This type of behavior therapy can be conducted with individual clients or in groups. Social skills training depends on the principles of operant conditioning and observational learning. The therapist makes use of *modeling* by encouraging clients to watch socially skilled friends and colleagues, so that the clients can acquire responses (eye contact, active listening, and so on) through observation.

In *behavioral rehearsal*, the client tries to practice social techniques in structured role-playing exercises. The therapist provides corrective feedback and uses approval to reinforce progress. Eventually, clients try their newly acquired skills in real-world interactions. Usually, they are given specific homework assignments. *Shaping* is used in that clients are gradually asked to handle more complicated and delicate social situations. For example, a nonassertive client may begin by working on making requests of friends. Only much later will the client be asked to tackle standing up to his or her boss.

Cognitive-Behavioral Treatments

In Chapter 3 we saw that people's cognitive interpretations of events make all the difference in the world in how well they handle stress. In Chapter 14 we learned that cognitive factors play a key role in the development of depression and other disorders. Citing the importance of findings such as these, behavior therapists started to focus more attention on

their clients' cognitions in the 1970s (Hollon & Digiuseppe, 2011). *Cognitive-behavioral treatments* **use varied combinations of verbal interventions and behavior modification techniques to help clients change maladaptive patterns of thinking.** Some of these treatments, such as Albert Ellis's (1973) *rational-emotive behavior therapy* and Aaron Beck's (1976) *cognitive therapy* emerged out of an insight therapy tradition, whereas other treatments, such as the systems developed by Donald Meichenbaum (1977) and Michael Mahoney (1974), emerged from the behavioral tradition. Since we covered the main ideas underlying Ellis's approach in our discussion of coping strategies in Chapter 4, we focus here on Beck's system of cognitive therapy (Beck, 1987; Newman & Beck, 2009).

Cognitive therapy **uses specific strategies to correct habitual thinking errors that underlie various types of disorders.** Cognitive therapy was originally devised as a treatment for depression, but in recent years it has been applied fruitfully to a wide range of disorders (Beck & Weishaar, 2011), and it has proven particularly valuable as a therapy for anxiety disorders (Rachman, 2009). According to cognitive therapists,

Aaron Beck

depression is caused by "errors" in thinking (see **Figure 15.10**). They assert that depression-prone people tend to (1) blame their setbacks on personal inadequacies without considering circumstantial explanations, (2) focus selectively on negative events while ignoring positive ones, (3) make unduly pessimistic projections about the future, and (4) draw negative conclusions about their worth as a person based on insignificant events. For instance, imagine that you got a low grade on a minor quiz in a class. If you made the kinds of errors in thinking just described, you might blame the grade on your woeful stupidity, dismiss comments from a classmate that it was an unfair test, gloomily predict that you will surely flunk the course, and conclude that you are not genuine college material.

COGNITIVE ERRORS THAT PROMOTE DEPRESSION	
Cognitive error	**Description**
Overgeneralizing	If it is true in one case, it applies to any case that is even slightly similar.
Selective abstraction	The only events that matter are failures, deprivation, and so on. I should measure myself by errors, weaknesses, etc.
Excessive responsibility (assuming personal causality)	I am responsible for all bad things, failures, and so on.
Assuming temporal causality (predicting without sufficient evidence)	If it has been true in the past, then it is always going to be true.
Self-references	I am the center of everyone's attention, especially when it comes to bad performances or personal attributes.
"Catastrophizing"	Always think of the worst. It is most likely to happen to you.
Dichotomous thinking	Everything is either one extreme or another (black or white; good or bad).

Figure 15.10

Beck's cognitive theory of depression. Beck's theory initially focused on the causes of depression, although it was gradually broadened to explain other disorders. According to Beck, depression is caused by the types of negative thinking shown here.

Source: Adapted from Beck, A. T. (1976). *Cognitive therapy and the emotional disorders.* New York: International Universities Press. Copyright © 1976 by International Universities Press, Inc. Adapted by permission of the publisher.

The goal of cognitive therapy is to change clients' negative thoughts and maladaptive beliefs (Kellogg & Young, 2008). To begin, clients are taught to detect their automatic negative thoughts, the sorts of self-defeating statements that people are prone to make when analyzing problems. Examples might include "I'm just not smart enough," "No one really likes me," or "It's all my fault." Clients are then trained to subject these automatic thoughts to reality testing. The therapist helps them to see how unrealistically negative the thoughts are.

Cognitive therapy uses a variety of behavioral techniques, including modeling, systematic monitoring of one's behavior, and behavioral rehearsal (Beck & Weishaar, 2011). Clients are given "homework assignments" that focus on changing their overt behaviors. They may be instructed to engage in responses on their own, outside of the clinician's office. For example, one shy, insecure young man in cognitive therapy was told to go to a singles bar and engage three different women in conversations for up to 5 minutes each (Rush, 1984). He was instructed to record his thoughts before and after each of the conversations. This assignment revealed various maladaptive patterns of thought that gave the young man and his therapist plenty to work on in subsequent sessions.

Evaluating Behavior Therapies

Behavior therapists have historically placed more emphasis than insight therapists on the importance of measuring therapeutic outcomes. As a result, there is ample research on the effectiveness of behavior therapy (Stanley & Beidel, 2009). Of course, behavior therapies are not well suited to the treatment of some types of problems (vague feelings of discontent, for instance). Furthermore, it's misleading to make global statements about the effectiveness of behavior therapies, because they include a variety of procedures designed for different purposes. For example, the value of systematic desensitization for phobias has no bearing on the value of aversion therapy for sexual deviance. For our purposes, it is sufficient to note that there is favorable evidence on the efficacy of most of the widely used behavioral interventions (Zinbarg & Griffith, 2008). Behavior therapies can make significant contributions to the treatment of depression, anxiety problems, phobias, obsessive-compulsive disorders, sexual dysfunction, schizophrenia, drug-related problems, eating disorders, hyperactivity, autism, and mental retardation (Emmelkamp, 2004; Hollon & Dimidjian, 2009; Wilson, 2011).

Learn More Online

The Beck Institute of Cognitive Therapy and Research

This site offers a diverse array of materials relating to Aaron Beck's cognitive therapy. Resources found here include newsletters, a referral system, a bookstore, recommended readings for clients, and questions and answers about cognitive therapy.

BIOMEDICAL THERAPIES

LEARNING OBJECTIVES

● Describe the principal drug therapies used in the treatment of psychological disorders, and summarize evidence regarding their efficacy.

● Identify some of the problems associated with drug therapies and drug research.

● Describe ECT, and discuss its efficacy and risks.

In the 1950s, a French surgeon was looking for a drug that would reduce patients' autonomic response to surgical stress. The surgeon noticed that chlorpromazine produced a mild sedation. Based on this observation, Delay and Deniker (1952) decided to give chlorpromazine to hospitalized schizophrenic patients to see whether it would have a calming effect on them. Their experiment was a dramatic success. Chlorpromazine became the first effective antipsychotic drug—and a revolution in psychiatry had begun. Hundreds of thousands of severely disturbed patients—patients who had appeared doomed to lead the remainder of their lives in mental hospitals—were gradually sent home thanks to the therapeutic effects of antipsychotic drugs (see **Figure 15.11**). Today, biomedical therapies, such as drug treatment, lie at the core of psychiatric practice.

Biomedical therapies **are physiological interventions intended to reduce symptoms associated with psychological disorders.** These therapies assume that psychological disorders are caused, at least in part, by biological malfunctions. As we discussed in the previous chapter, this assumption clearly has merit for many disorders, especially the more severe ones. We will discuss two biomedical approaches to psychotherapy: drug therapy and electroconvulsive therapy.

Treatment with Drugs

Psychopharmacotherapy **is the treatment of mental disorders with medication.** We will refer to this kind of treatment more simply as *drug therapy*. Therapeutic drugs for psychological problems fall into four major groups: antianxiety drugs, antipsychotic drugs, antidepressant drugs, and mood stabilizers.

Antianxiety Drugs

Most of us know someone who pops pills to relieve anxiety. The drugs involved in this common coping strategy are *antianxiety drugs,* **which relieve tension, apprehension, and nervousness.** The most popular of these drugs are Valium and Xanax, which are the trade names (the proprietary names that pharmaceutical companies use in marketing drugs) for diazepam and alprazolam, respectively.

Valium, Xanax, and other drugs in the benzodiazepine family are often called *tranquilizers.* These drugs are routinely prescribed for people diagnosed with anxiety disorders. They are also given to millions of people who simply suffer from chronic nervous tension. In the mid-1970s, pharmacists in the United States were filling nearly *100 million* prescriptions each year for Valium and similar antianxiety drugs. Many critics characterized this level of use as excessive. However, since the 1990s, benzodiazepine prescriptions have declined noticeably (Raj & Sheehan, 2004).

Antianxiety drugs exert their effects almost immediately. They can be fairly effective in alleviating feelings of anxiety (Dubovsky, 2009). However, their effects are measured in hours, so their impact is relatively short-lived. Common side effects of antianxiety drugs include drowsiness, depression, nausea, and confusion. These drugs also have some potential for abuse, dependency, and overdose, although the prevalence of these problems has been exaggerated (Martinez, Marangell, & Martinez, 2008). Another drawback is that patients who have been on antianxi-

Figure 15.11

The declining inpatient population in mental hospitals. The number of inpatients in public mental hospitals has declined dramatically since the late 1950s. In part, this drop has been due to "deinstitutionalization"—a philosophy that emphasizes outpatient care whenever possible. However, above all else, this decline was made possible by the development of effective antipsychotic medications.

© Cengage Learning 2015

ety drugs for a while often experience withdrawal symptoms when their drug treatment is stopped (Edwards et al., 2008).

Antipsychotic Drugs

Antipsychotic drugs are used primarily in the treatment of schizophrenia. They are also given to people with severe mood disorders who become delusional. The trade names (and generic names) of some prominent drugs in this category are Thorazine (chlorpromazine), Mellaril (thioridazine), and Haldol (haloperidol). **Antipsychotic drugs are used to gradually reduce psychotic symptoms, including hyperactivity, mental confusion, hallucinations, and delusions.**

Studies suggest that antipsychotics reduce symptoms in about 70% of patients, albeit in varied degrees (Kane, Stroup, & Marder, 2009). When antipsychotic drugs are effective, they work their magic gradually, as shown in **Figure 15.12**. Patients usually begin to respond within one

to three weeks, but considerable variability in responsiveness is seen. Further improvement may occur for several months. Many schizophrenic patients are placed on antipsychotics indefinitely because these drugs can reduce the likelihood of a relapse into an active schizophrenic episode (van Kammen, Hurford, & Marder, 2009).

Antipsychotic drugs undeniably make a major contribution to the treatment of severe mental disorders, but they are not without problems. They have many unpleasant side effects (Dolder, 2008; Muench & Hamer, 2010). Drowsiness, constipation, and cotton mouth are common. Patients may also experience tremors, muscular rigidity, and impaired coordination. After being released from a hospital, many schizophrenic patients, supposedly placed on antipsychotics indefinitely, discontinue their drug regimen because of the disagreeable side effects. Unfortunately, after patients stop taking their medication, about 70% relapse within a year (van Kammen et al., 2009). One recent study found that even brief periods of partial noncompliance with a drug regimen increased the risk of relapse (Subotnik et al., 2011). In addition to minor side effects, antipsychotics may cause a severe and lasting problem called *tardive dyskinesia,* which is seen in about 20%–30% of patients who receive long-term treatment with traditional antipsychotics (Kane et al., 2009). **Tardive dyskinesia is a neurological disorder marked by chronic tremors and involuntary spastic movements.** Once this debilitating syndrome emerges, there is no cure, although spontaneous remission sometimes occurs after the discontinuation of antipsychotic medication.

Psychiatrists currently rely primarily on a newer class of antipsychotic agents called *atypical* or *second-generation antipsychotic drugs,* such as clozapine, olanzapine, and quetiapine (Marder, Hurford, & van Kammen, 2009). These drugs appear to be roughly similar to the first-generation antipsychotics in therapeutic effectiveness, but they offer some advantages over the older drugs (Meltzer & Bobo, 2009). For instance, they can help some treatment-resistant patients who do not respond to traditional antipsychotics. And the second-generation antipsychotics produce fewer unpleasant side effects and carry less risk for tardive dyskinesia. Of course, like all powerful drugs, they carry some risks. This drug class appears to increase patients' vulnerability to diabetes and cardiovascular problems. Although they are much more expensive than traditional, first-generation antipsychotics, the second-generation antipsychotics have become the first line of defense in the treatment of schizophrenia.

Figure 15.12

The time course of antipsychotic drug effects. Antipsychotic drugs reduce psychotic symptoms gradually, over a span of weeks, as graphed here. In contrast, patients given placebo pills show little improvement.

Source: From Cole, J. O., Goldberg, S. C., & Davis, J. M. (1966). Drugs in the treatment of psychosis. In P. Solomon (Ed.), *Psychiatric drugs.* New York: Grune & Stratton. From data in the NIMH-PSC Collaborative Study I. Reprinted by permission of J. M. Davis.

Antidepressant Drugs

As their name suggests, *antidepressant drugs* **gradually elevate mood and help bring people out of a depression.** Reliance on antidepressants has increased dramatically in the last 10 to 15 years, as they have become the most frequently prescribed class of medication in the United States (Olfson & Marcus, 2009). Prior to 1987, there were two principal types of antidepressants: *tricyclics* (such as Elavil) and *MAO inhibitors* (such as Nardil). These two sets of drugs affect neurochemical activity in different ways and tend to work with different patients. Overall, they are beneficial for about two-thirds of depressed patients (Gitlin, 2009). The tricyclics have notably fewer problems with side effects and complications than the MAO inhibitors.

Today, psychiatrists are more likely to prescribe a newer class of antidepressants called *selective serotonin reuptake inhibitors (SSRIs),* which slow the reuptake process at serotonin synapses. The drugs in this class, which include Prozac (fluoxetine), Paxil (paroxetine), and Zoloft (sertraline), yield therapeutic gains similar to the tricyclics in the treatment of depression (Boland & Keller, 2008) while producing fewer unpleasant or dangerous side effects (Sussman, 2009). SSRIs have also proven valuable in the treatment of obsessive-compulsive disorders, panic disorders, and other anxiety disorders (Mathew, Hoffman, & Charney, 2009; Ravindran & Stein, 2009). However, there is some doubt about how effective the SSRIs (and other antidepressants) are in relieving episodes of depression among patients suffering from bipolar disorder (Berman, Jonides, & Kaplan, 2009).

Kumikomura/Dreamstime.com

Like antipsychotic drugs, the various types of antidepressants exert their effects gradually over a period of weeks, but about 60% of patients' improvement tends to occur in the first two weeks (Gitlin, 2009). A recent analysis that looked carefully at the severity of patients' depression when medication was initiated found that people with serious depression benefit the most from antidepressants (Fournier et al, 2010). This analysis focused on six studies that precisely measured patients' initial level of depression and included patients with the full range of symptom severity (many drug trials exclude patients with mild illness). The most provocative aspect of the findings was that antidepressants provided a relatively modest benefit for patients with mild to moderate depression.

A major concern in recent years has been evidence from a number of studies that SSRIs may increase the risk for suicide, primarily among adolescents and young adults (Healy & Whitaker, 2003; Holden, 2004). The challenge of collecting definitive data on this issue is much more daunting than one might guess, in part because suicide rates are already elevated among people who exhibit the disorders for which SSRIs are prescribed (Berman, 2009). Some researchers have collected data suggesting that suicide rates have *declined* slightly because of widespread prescription of SSRIs (Isacsson et al., 2009), while others have found no association between SSRIs and suicide (Simon et al., 2006).

Overall, when antidepressants are compared to placebo treatment, the data suggest that antidepressants lead to a slight elevation in the risk of suicidal behavior (Bridge et al., 2007; Hammad, Laughren, & Racoosin, 2006), although a recent analysis of forty-one antidepressant drug trials failed to find an increase in suicidal risk (Gibbons et al., 2012). When studies find an elevation in suicide risk, it appears to be a problem mainly among a small minority of children and adolescents. Regulatory warnings from the U.S. Food and Drug Administration (FDA) have led to a decline in the prescription of SSRIs for adolescents. This trend has prompted concern that increases in suicide may occur among untreated individuals (Dudley et al., 2008). This concern seems legitimate in that suicide risk clearly peaks in the month prior to people beginning treatment for depression, whether that treatment involves SSRIs or psychotherapy (Simon & Savarino, 2007). This pattern presumably occurs because the escalating agony of depression finally prompts people to seek treatment, but it also suggests that getting treatment with drugs or therapy reduces suicidal risk. In the final analysis, this is a complex issue, but the one thing experts seem to agree on is that adolescents starting on SSRIs should be monitored closely.

Mood Stabilizers

Mood stabilizers **are drugs used to control mood swings in patients with bipolar disorders.** For many years, lithium was the only effective drug in this category. Lithium has proven valuable in preventing *future* episodes of both mania and depression in patients with bipolar illness (Post & Altshuler, 2009). Lithium can also be used in efforts to bring patients with bipolar illness out of *current* manic or depressive episodes, although antipsychotics and antidepressants are also used for these purposes. On the negative side of the ledger, lithium does have some dangerous side effects if its use isn't managed skillfully (Jefferson & Greist, 2009). Lithium levels in the patient's blood must be monitored carefully, because high concentrations can be toxic and even fatal. Kidney and thyroid gland complications are the other major problems associated with lithium therapy.

In recent years a number of alternatives to lithium have been developed. The most popular of these newer mood stabilizers is an anticonvulsant agent called *valproate,* which has become more widely used than lithium in the treatment of bipolar disorders (Thase & Denko, 2008). Valproate appears to be roughly as effective as lithium in efforts to treat current manic episodes and to prevent future affective disturbances with fewer side effects (Muzina, Kemp, Calabrese, 2008).

Evaluating Drug Therapies

Drug therapies can produce clear therapeutic gains for many kinds of patients. What's especially impressive is that they can be effective in severe disorders that otherwise defy therapeutic endeavors. Nonetheless, drug therapies are controversial. Critics of drug therapy have raised a number of issues (Andrews et al., 2012; Bentall, 2009; Breggin, 2008; Healy, 2004; Kirsch, 2010). First, some critics argue that drug therapies often produce superficial curative effects. For example, Valium does not really solve problems with anxiety—it merely provides temporary relief from an unpleasant symptom. Moreover, this temporary relief may lull patients into complacency about their problem and prevent them from working toward a more lasting solution.

Second, critics charge that many drugs are overprescribed and many patients overmedicated. According to these critics, many physicians habitually hand out prescriptions without giving adequate consideration to more complicated and difficult interventions. Consistent with this line of criticism, a recent study of office visits to psychiatrists found that they increasingly prescribe two and even three medications to patients, even though relatively little is known about the interactive effects of psychiatric drugs (Mojtabai & Olfson, 2010). Third, some critics charge that the side effects of therapeutic drugs are worse than the illnesses the drugs are supposed to cure. Citing problems such as tardive dyskinesia, lithium toxicity, and addiction to antianxiety agents, these critics argue that the risks of therapeutic drugs aren't worth the benefits. Some critics have also

© Lisa S/Shutterstock.com

argued that psychiatric drugs may be helpful in the short term but that they disrupt neurotransmitter systems in ways that actually *increase* patients' vulnerability to psychological disorders in the long term (Andrews et al., 2011).

Critics maintain that the negative effects of psychiatric drugs are not fully appreciated because the pharmaceutical industry has managed to gain undue influence over the research enterprise as it relates to drug testing (Angell, 2004; Insel, 2010; L. J. Weber, 2006). Today, most researchers who investigate the benefits and risks of medications and craft diagnostic criteria and treatment guidelines have lucrative financial arrangements with the pharmaceutical industry, which they often fail to disclose (Bentall, 2009; Cosgrove & Krimsky, 2012). Their studies are funded by drug companies and they often receive substantial consulting fees. Unfortunately, these financial ties appear to undermine the objectivity required in scientific research, as studies funded by pharmaceutical and other biomedical companies are far more likely to report favorable results than nonprofit-funded studies (Bekelman, Li, & Gross, 2003; Perlis et al., 2005).

Consistent with this finding, when specific antipsychotic drugs are pitted against each other in clinical trials, the sponsoring company's drug is reported to be superior to the other drugs in 90% of studies (Heres et al., 2006). Industry-financed drug trials also tend to be too brief to detect the long-term risks associated with new drugs (Vandenbroucke & Psaty, 2008), and when unfavorable results emerge, the data are often withheld from publication (Rising, Bacchetti, & Bero, 2008; Turner et al., 2008). Also, research designs are often slanted in a multitude of ways so as to exaggerate the positive effects and minimize the negative effects of the drugs under scrutiny (Carpenter, 2002; Chopra, 2003). The conflicts of interest that appear to be pervasive in contemporary drug research raise grave concerns that require attention from researchers, universities, and federal agencies.

Obviously, drug therapies have stirred up some debate. However, this controversy pales in comparison to the furi-

DILBERT

ous debates inspired by electroconvulsive (shock) therapy (ECT). ECT is so controversial that the residents of Berkeley, California, voted to outlaw ECT in their city. However, in subsequent lawsuits the courts ruled that scientific questions cannot be settled through a vote, and they overturned the law. What makes ECT so controversial? You'll see in the next section.

Electroconvulsive Therapy (ECT)

In the 1930s, a Hungarian psychiatrist named Ladislas Meduna speculated that epilepsy and schizophrenia could not coexist in the same body. On the basis of this observation, which turned out to be inaccurate, Meduna theorized that it might be useful to induce epileptic-like seizures in schizophrenic patients. Initially, a drug was used to trigger these seizures. However, by 1938, a pair of Italian psychiatrists (Cerletti & Bini, 1938) demonstrated that it was safer to elicit the seizures with electric shock. Thus, modern electroconvulsive therapy was born.

***Electroconvulsive therapy (ECT)* is a biomedical treatment in which electric shock is used to produce a cortical seizure accompanied by convulsions.** In ECT, electrodes are attached to the skull over one or both temporal lobes of the brain (see the photo above). A light anesthesia is induced, and the patient is given a variety of drugs to minimize the likelihood of complications, such as spinal fractures. An electric current is then applied either to the right side or to both sides of the brain for about a second. Unilateral shock delivered to the right hemisphere is the preferred method of treatment today (Sackeim et al.,

2009). The current triggers a brief (about 30-second) convulsive seizure, during which the patient usually loses consciousness. Patients normally awaken in an hour or two. People typically receive three treatments a week over a period of two to seven weeks (Fink, 2009).

The clinical use of ECT peaked in the 1940s and 1950s, before effective drug therapies were widely available. ECT is not a rare treatment today, but its use has been declining. A recent study reported that the portion of hospitals with psychiatric units that offered ECT declined from 55% in 1993 to 35% in 2009 (Case et al., 2013). During the same period the number of patients treated with ECT decreased 43%. ECT advocates argue that ECT is underutilized because the public harbors many misconceptions about its risks and side effects (Kellner et al., 2012). Conversely, some critics of ECT have argued that it is overused because it is a lucrative procedure that boosts psychiatrists' income while consuming relatively little of their time in comparison to insight therapy (Frank, 1990).

Effectiveness of ECT

The evidence on the therapeutic efficacy of ECT is open to varied interpretations. Proponents of ECT maintain that it is a remarkably effective treatment for major depression (Fink, 2009; Prudic, 2009). Moreover, they note that many patients who do not benefit from antidepressant medication improve in response to ECT. However, opponents of ECT argue that the available studies are flawed and inconclusive and that ECT is probably no more effective than a placebo (Rose et al., 2003). Overall, enough favorable evidence seems to exist to justify *conservative* use of ECT in treating severe mood disorders in patients who have not responded to medication (Carney & Geddes, 2003). Unfortunately, relapse rates after ECT are distressingly high. For example in one well-controlled study, 64% of patients relapsed within 6 months, and the median time to relapse was only 8.6 weeks (Prudic et al., 2004). These relapse rates, however, can be reduced by giving ECT patients antidepressant drugs (Sackeim et al., 2009).

This patient is being prepared for electroconvulsive therapy. The mouthpiece keeps the patient from biting her tongue during the electrically induced seizures.

The debate about whether ECT works does *not* make ECT unique among approaches to the treatment of psychological disorders. Controversies exist regarding the effectiveness of most therapies. However, this controversy is especially problematic because ECT carries some risks.

Risks Associated with ECT

Even ECT proponents acknowledge that memory loss, impaired attention, and other cognitive deficits are common short-term side effects of electroconvulsive therapy (Nobler & Sackeim, 2006; Rowny & Lisanby, 2008). However, ECT proponents assert that these deficits are mild and usually disappear within a month or two (Glass, 2001). An American Psychiatric Association task force (2001) concluded that there is no objective evidence that ECT causes structural damage in the brain or that it has any lasting negative effects on the ability to learn and remember information. In contrast, ECT critics maintain that ECT-induced cognitive deficits are often significant and sometimes permanent (Breggin, 1991; Rose et al., 2003), although their evidence seems to be largely anecdotal. Given the concerns about the risks of ECT and the doubts about its efficacy, it appears that the use of ECT will remain controversial for some time to come.

CURRENT TRENDS IN TREATMENT

LEARNING OBJECTIVES

- Describe the merits of blending approaches to therapy, and discuss why therapy is underutilized by ethnic minorities.
- Explain how technology is being used to increase access to clinical services.

The controversy about ECT is only one of many contentious issues and shifting trends in the world of mental health care. In this section, we discuss the continuing trend toward blending various approaches to therapy, efforts to respond more effectively to increasing cultural diversity in Western societies, and innovations in how treatment is delivered.

Blending Approaches to Treatment

In this chapter we have reviewed many approaches to treatment. However, there is no rule that a client must be treated with just one approach. Often, a clinician will use several techniques in working with a client. For example, a depressed person might receive group therapy (an insight therapy), social skills training (a behavior therapy), and antidepressant medication (a biomedical therapy). Multiple approaches are particularly likely when a treatment *team* provides therapy. Studies suggest that combining approaches to treatment has merit (Glass, 2004; Szigethy & Friedman, 2009).

The value of multiple approaches may explain why a significant trend seems to have crept into the field of psychotherapy: a movement away from strong loyalty to individual schools of thought and a corresponding move toward integrating various approaches to therapy (Castonguay et al., 2003). Most clinicians used to depend exclusively on one system of therapy while rejecting the utility of all others. This era of fragmentation may be drawing to a close. One survey of psychologists' theoretical orientations, summarized in **Figure 15.13**, found that 36% of the respondents described themselves as *eclectic* in approach (Norcross, Hedges, & Castle, 2002). *Eclecticism* involves drawing ideas from two or more systems of therapy, instead of committing to just one system. Eclectic therapists borrow ideas, insights, and techniques from a variety of sources while tailoring their intervention strategy to the unique needs of each client. Advocates of eclecticism, such as Arnold Lazarus (1995, 2008), maintain that therapists should ask themselves, "What is the best approach for this specific client, problem, and situation?" and then adjust their strategy accordingly.

Increasing Multicultural Sensitivity in Treatment

Research on how cultural factors influence the process and outcome of psychotherapy has burgeoned in recent years, motivated in part by the need to improve mental health services for ethnic minority groups in American society

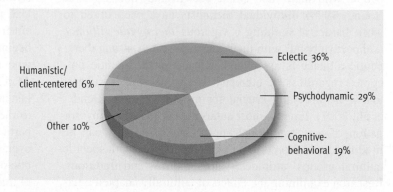

Figure 15.13

The leading approaches to therapy among psychologists. These data, from a survey of 531 psychologists who belong to the American Psychological Association's Division of Psychotherapy, provide some indication of how common an eclectic approach to therapy has become. The findings suggest that the most widely used approaches to therapy are eclectic, psychodynamic, and cognitive-behavioral treatments. (Based on data from Norcross, Hedges, & Castle, 2002)

(Worthington et al., 2007). Studies suggest that American minority groups generally underutilize therapeutic services (Bender et al., 2007; Sue et al., 2009). Why? A variety of barriers appear to contribute to this problem (Snowden & Yamada, 2005; Zane et al., 2004). One major consideration is that many members of minority groups have a history of frustrating interactions with American bureaucracies. Therefore, they are distrustful of large, intimidating institutions, such as hospitals and community mental health centers. Another issue is that most hospitals and mental health agencies are not adequately staffed with therapists who speak the languages used by minority groups in their service areas.

Yet another problem is that the vast majority of therapists have been trained almost exclusively in the treatment of white middle-class Americans. As a result, they are not familiar with the cultural backgrounds and unique characteristics of various ethnic groups. This culture gap often leads to misunderstandings, ill-advised treatment strategies, and reduced rapport. Consistent with this assertion, one study found that psychiatrists spent less time with African American patients than white patients (Olfson, Cherry, & Lewis-Fernández, 2009). Another study of over 3500 African American participants found that only 27% of their mental health visits resulted in "minimally adequate care" (Neighbors et al., 2007). And a recent study of over 15,000 people suffering from depression found that Mexican Americans and African Americans were notably less likely to receive treatment than whites, as can be seen in **Figure 15.14** (González et al., 2010).

What can be done to improve mental health services for American minority groups? Researchers in this area have offered a variety of suggestions (Hong, Garcia, & Soriano, 2000; Miranda et al., 2005; Pedersen, 1994). Discussions of possible solutions usually begin with the need to recruit and train more ethnic minority therapists. Studies show that ethnic minorities are more likely to go to mental health facilities that are staffed by a higher proportion of people who share their ethnic background (Sue, Zane, & Young, 1994). Individual therapists have been urged to work harder at building a vigorous *therapeutic alliance* (supportive bond) with their ethnic clients. A strong therapeutic alliance is associated with better therapeutic outcomes regardless of ethnicity, but some studies suggest that it is especially crucial for minority clients (Bender et al., 2007). Finally, most authorities urge further investigation of how traditional approaches to therapy can be modified and tailored to be more compatible with specific cultural groups' attitudes, values, norms, and traditions. Research examining the effects of culturally adapted interventions has found evidence that this tailoring process tends to yield positive effects (Griner & Smith, 2006; Sue et al., 2009). The benefits are particularly prominent when a treatment is tailored to a single, specific cultural group rather than a mixture of several cultural groups.

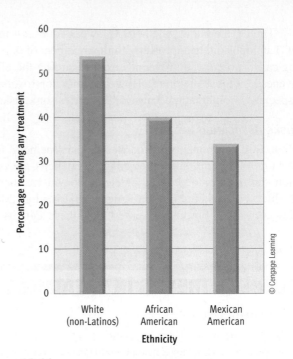

Figure 15.14

Ethnicity and treatment for depression. In a nationally representative sample of almost 16,000 subjects, Gonzáles and colleagues (2010), identified participants suffering from depression and ascertained what types of treatment they had received. When they analyzed these data in relation to ethnicity, they found that members of minority groups were less likely than whites to get treatment. The data graphed here show the percentage of patients receiving treatment of any kind.

Using Technology to Expand the Delivery of Clinical Services

Although the problem is especially acute among ethnic minorities, inadequate availability of mental health care is a broad problem that reaches into every corner of our society. As discussed in Chapter 14, psychological disorders are far more common than most people realize. Prevalence estimates suggest that in any given year about 25% of the U.S. population—roughly 75 million people—might benefit from therapeutic interventions. But as we noted at the beginning of this chapter, only about one-third of those who need treatment receive it. In an influential article, Alan Kazdin and Stacey Blase (2011) argue that there are just not enough clinicians and treatment facilities available to meet America's mental health needs. This shortage is particularly serious in small towns and rural areas. Moreover, Kazdin and Blase note that the traditional model of one-on-one therapy imposes constraints on the availability of treatment. The substantial costs of traditional treatments also contribute to the underutilization of psychotherapy services and the growing burden of mental illness. To address these problems, clinicians are increasingly attempting to harness technology to expand the delivery of mental health services and to reduce the costs of therapy.

Crazy: A Father's Search Through America's Mental Health Madness
by Pete Earley (Putnam, 2006)

This book will make you feel outraged. This book will make you cry. Above all else, this book will educate you about how incredibly difficult it can be to get effective mental health care for people troubled by severe disturbances such as schizophrenia and bipolar disorder. You will learn that the American mental health system sometimes seems insane.

The author is a former *Washington Post* investigative reporter who was suddenly drawn into the quagmire of America's mental health system when his son, Mike, developed bipolar disorder at the age of 23. Mike became seriously psychotic—at one point he wrapped aluminum foil around his head so people wouldn't be able to read his thoughts. His behavior became erratic. He crashed his car while trying to drive with his eyes closed, informed strangers at a coffeeshop that he had supernatural powers, and broke into a residence where he ignored a wailing burglar alarm and proceeded to pee on the carpet, turn on all the water faucets thereby flooding the home, and give himself a bubble bath—until the police arrived to detain him. In his disoriented state, Earley's son was not willing to voluntarily cooperate with treatment. So the family repeatedly found themselves in hospital emergency rooms where they were told that their son could not be admitted because—as an adult—he had the right to refuse treatment, even though his judgment was obviously severely impaired.

This frustrating experience motivated Earley to conduct a wide-ranging investigation of mental health care in the United States today. His journey took him to mental hospitals, prisons, courts, alternative facilities for the mentally ill, meetings of mental health advocacy groups, and street corners where the homeless mentally ill congregated. He learned that "What was happening to Mike was not an oddity. It was a tiny piece in a bigger story. A major shift had occurred in our country. The mentally ill, who used to be treated in state mental hospitals, were now being arrested. Our nation's jails and prisons were our new asylums" (p. 2).

This book tells two intertwined stories—Earley's personal battle to obtain meaningful treatment for his son and his investigative analysis of modern mental health care. Both stories are compelling, heart-wrenching, and enlightening. And both stories demonstrate that American society is not providing adequate care for a sizable segment of the mentally ill population.

Log on to CourseMate at **www.cengagebrain.com** *for descriptions of other recommended books.*

Efforts to use technology to create new platforms for the delivery of therapeutic services have taken many forms. One of the simpler approaches is to deliver both individual and group therapy over the phone. This method has been used in the treatment of elderly clients with anxiety problems (Brenes, Ingram, & Danhauer, 2012) and veterans suffering from loneliness and depression (Davis, Guyker, & Persky, 2012). A meta-analysis of studies examining phone-administered therapies found that they appear to be effective in reducing depressive symptoms and that they have lower dropout rates than traditional individual treatments (Mohr et al., 2008). Another relatively simple innovation has been to use videoconferencing technology to provide both individual and group therapy. For example, Tuerk et al. (2010) used this method in the treatment of posttraumatic stress disorder. Videoconferencing therapy has been used in the treatment of a variety of disorders, including mood disorders, anxiety disorders, and eating disorders. A recent review of research on this approach to treatment concluded that clinical outcomes are about the same as for face-to-face therapy and that clients tend to report high satisfaction (Backhaus et al., 2012).

Interventions delivered via the Internet hold even more promise for reaching large swaths of people who might otherwise go untreated. For example, software programs have been created for the treatment of depression (Thompson et al., 2010), generalized anxiety disorder (Amir & Taylor, 2012), obsessive-compulsive disorder (Andersson et al., 2011), and phobic disorders (Opris et al., 2012). Most of these treatments involve online, interactive, multimedia adaptations of cognitive-behavioral therapies. The computerized treatments typically consist of a series of modules that educate individuals about the nature and causes of their disorder and offer cognitive strategies for ameliorating their problems, along with practice exercises and homework assignments. In most cases the interventions include limited access to an actual therapist through the Internet, but some programs are fully automated with no therapist contact. Studies of computerized therapies suggest that they can be effective for many types of disorders, but more research and higher-quality research are needed before solid conclusions can be drawn on their value (Kiluk et al., 2011). Still, the early results look promising. Obviously, automated Internet interventions could greatly reduce treatment costs and increase access to therapy. That said, evidence suggests that dropout rates tend to be high, and little attention has been paid to the potential for adverse effects, so some clinicians are skeptical about the value of Internet therapy (Waller & Gilbody, 2009). Nonetheless, it appears likely that the future will see increased efforts to improve access to treatment through innovations in technology.

LOOKING FOR A THERAPIST

LEARNING OBJECTIVES

● Discuss where to seek therapy and the importance of a therapist's gender and professional background.

● Evaluate the importance of a therapist's theoretical approach and understand what one should expect from therapy.

Answer the following "true" or "false."

_____ **1.** Psychotherapy is an art as well as a science.

_____ **2.** The type of professional degree that a therapist holds is relatively unimportant.

_____ **3.** Psychotherapy can be harmful or damaging to a client.

_____ **4.** Psychotherapy does not have to be expensive.

_____ **5.** It is a good idea to shop around when choosing a therapist.

All of these statements are true. Do any of them surprise you? If so, you're in good company. Many people know relatively little about the practicalities of selecting a therapist. The task of finding an appropriate therapist is no less complex than shopping for any other major service. Should you see a psychologist or a psychiatrist? Should you opt for individual or group therapy? Should you see a client-centered therapist or a behavior therapist? The unfortunate part of this decision process is that people seeking psychotherapy often feel overwhelmed by personal problems. The last thing they need is to be confronted by yet another complex problem.

Nonetheless, the importance of finding a good therapist cannot be overestimated. Therapy can sometimes have harmful rather than helpful effects. We have already discussed how drug therapies and ECT can sometimes be damaging, but problems are not limited to these interventions. Talking about your problems with a therapist may sound pretty harmless, but studies indicate that insight therapies can also backfire (Lilienfeld, 2007). Although a great many talented therapists are available, psychotherapy, like any other profession, has incompetent practitio-

Learn More Online

Psych Central

The work of John Grohol, Psych Central is a source for learning about all aspects of mental health, including psychological disorders and treatment, professional issues, and information for mental health care consumers. Almost 2000 annotated listings to information sources are offered here.

ners as well. Therefore, you should shop for a skilled therapist, just as you would for a good attorney or a good mechanic.

In this Application, we present some information that should be helpful if you ever have to look for a therapist for yourself or for a friend or family member (based on Beutler, Bongar, & Shurkin, 2001; Ehrenberg & Ehrenberg, 1994; Pittman, 1994).

Where Do You Find Therapeutic Services?

Psychotherapy can be found in a variety of settings. Contrary to general belief, most therapists are not in private practice. Many work in institutional settings such as community mental health centers, hospitals, and human service agencies. The principal sources of therapeutic services are described in **Figure 15.15**. The exact configuration of therapeutic services available will vary from one community to another. To find out what your community has to offer, it is a good idea to consult your friends, your local phone book, or your local community mental health center.

Is the Therapist's Profession or Sex Important?

Psychotherapists may be trained in psychology, psychiatry, social work, counseling, psychiatric nursing, or marriage and family therapy. Researchers have *not* found any reliable associations between therapists' professional background and therapeutic efficacy (Beutler et al., 2004), probably because many talented therapists can be found in all of these professions. Thus, the kind of degree that a therapist holds doesn't need to be a crucial consideration in your selection process.

Whether a therapist's sex is important depends on your attitude (Nadelson, Notman, & McCarthy, 2005). If *you* feel that the therapist's sex is important, then for you it is. The therapeutic relationship must be characterized by trust and rapport. Feeling uncomfortable with a therapist of one sex or the other could inhibit the therapeutic process. Hence, you should feel free to look for a male or female therapist if you prefer to do so.

PRINCIPAL SOURCES OF THERAPEUTIC SERVICES	
Source	**Comments**
Private practitioners	Self-employed therapists are listed in the Yellow Pages under their professional category, such as psychologists or psychiatrists. Private practitioners tend to be relatively expensive, but they also tend to be highly experienced therapists.
Community mental health centers	Community mental health centers have salaried psychologists, psychiatrists, and social workers on staff. The centers provide a variety of services and often have staff available on weekends and at night to deal with emergencies.
Hospitals	Several kinds of hospitals provide therapeutic services. There are both public and private mental hospitals that specialize in the care of people with psychological disorders. Many general hospitals have a psychiatric ward, and those that do not will usually have psychiatrists and psychologists on staff and on call. Although hospitals tend to concentrate on inpatient treatment, many provide outpatient therapy as well.
Human services agencies	Various social service agencies employ therapists to provide short-term counseling. Depending on your community, you may find agencies that deal with family problems, juvenile problems, drug problems, and so forth.
Schools and workplaces	Most high schools and colleges have counseling centers where students can get help with personal problems. Similarly, some large businesses offer in-house counseling to their employees.

© Cengage Learning

Figure 15.15

Sources of therapeutic services. Therapists work in a variety of organizational settings. Foremost among them are the five described here.

Speaking of sex, you should be aware that sexual exploitation is an occasional problem in the context of therapy. Studies indicate that a small minority of therapists take advantage of their clients sexually (Pope, Keith-Spiegel, & Tabachnick, 1986). These incidents almost always involve a male therapist making advances to a female client. The available evidence indicates that these sexual liaisons are usually harmful to clients (Gabbard, 1994). There are absolutely no situations in which therapist-client sexual relations are an ethical therapeutic practice. If a therapist makes sexual advances, a client should terminate treatment.

Is Therapy Always Expensive?

Psychotherapy does not have to be prohibitively expensive. Private practitioners tend to be the most expensive, charging between $25 and $140 per (50-minute) hour. These fees may seem high, but they are in line with those of similar professionals, such as dentists and attorneys. Community mental health centers and social service agencies are usually supported by tax dollars. Hence, they can charge lower fees than most therapists in private practice. Many of these organizations use a sliding scale, so that clients are charged according to how much they can afford. Thus, most communities have inexpensive opportunities for psychotherapy. Moreover, many health insurance plans provide at least partial reimbursement for the cost of treatment.

Is the Therapist's Theoretical Approach Important?

Logically, you might expect that the diverse approaches to therapy vary in effectiveness. For the most part, that is *not* what researchers find, however. After reviewing the evidence, Jerome Frank (1961) and Lester Luborsky and his colleagues (1975) both quote the dodo bird who has just judged a race in *Alice in Wonderland:* "Everybody has won, and *all* must have prizes." Improvement rates for various theoretical orientations usually come out pretty close in most studies (Lambert & Ogles, 2004; Luborsky et al., 2002). In their landmark review of outcome studies, Smith and Glass (1977) estimated the effectiveness of many major approaches to therapy. As **Figure 15.16** on the next page shows, the estimates cluster together closely.

However, these findings are a little misleading, as they have been averaged across many types of patients and many types of problems. Most experts seem to think that *for certain types of problems, some approaches to therapy are more effective than others* (Beutler, 2002; Crits-Christoph, 1997). For example, Martin Seligman (1995) asserts that panic disorders respond best to cognitive therapy, that specific phobias are most amenable to treatment with systematic desensitization, and that obsessive-compulsive disorders are best treated with behavior ther-

Figure 15.16

Efficacy of various approaches to therapy. Smith and Glass (1977) reviewed nearly 400 studies in which clients who were treated with a specific type of therapy were compared with a control group made up of people with similar problems who went untreated. The bars indicate the percentile rank (on outcome measures) attained by the average client treated with each type of therapy when compared to control subjects. The higher the percentile, the more effective the therapy was. As you can see, the different approaches were fairly close in their apparent effectiveness.

Source: Adapted from Smith, M. L., & Glass, G. V. (1977). Meta-analysis of psychotherapy outcome series. *American Psychologist, 32,* 752–760. Copyright © 1977 by the American Psychological Association. Adapted by permission of the authors.

apy or medication. Thus, for a specific type of problem, a therapist's theoretical approach *may* make a difference.

It is also important to point out that the finding that various approaches to therapy are roughly equal in overall efficacy does not mean that all *therapists* are created equal. Some therapists unquestionably are more effective than others. However, these variations in effectiveness appear to depend on individual therapists' personal skills rather than on their theoretical orientation (Beutler et al., 2004). Good, bad, and mediocre therapists are found within each school

of thought. Indeed, the tremendous variation among individual therapists in skills may be one of the main reasons that it is hard to find efficacy differences between theoretical approaches to therapy (Staines, 2008).

The key point is that effective therapy requires skill and creativity. Arnold Lazarus (1989), who devised an approach to treatment called multimodal therapy, emphasizes that therapists "straddle the fence between science and art." Therapy is scientific in that interventions are based on extensive theory and empirical research (Forsyth & Strong,

INSIDE WOODY ALLEN

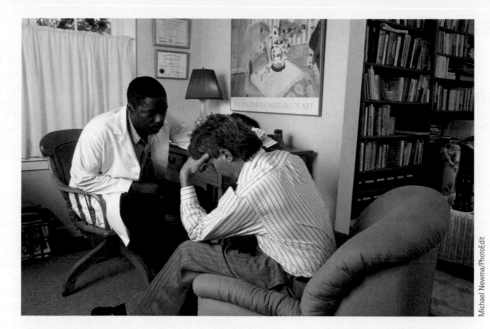

Therapy is both a science and an art. It is scientific in that practitioners are guided in their work by a huge body of empirical research. It is an art in that therapists often have to be creative in adapting their treatment procedures to individual patients and their idiosyncrasies.

1986). Ultimately, though, each client is a unique human being. The therapist has to creatively fashion a treatment program that will help that individual (Goodheart, 2006).

What Is Therapy Like?

It is important to have realistic expectations about therapy, or you may be unnecessarily disappointed. Some people expect miracles. They think they will turn their life around quickly with little effort. Others expect their therapist to run their lives for them. These are unrealistic expectations.

Therapy is usually a slow process. Your problems are not likely to melt away quickly. Moreover, therapy is hard work, and your therapist is only a facilitator. Ultimately, *you* have to confront the challenge of changing your behavior, your feelings, or your personality. You have to work out the problems that are undermining your sense of well-being. This process may not be pleasant. You may have to face up to some painful truths about yourself. As Ehrenberg and Ehrenberg (1994) point out, psychotherapy takes time, effort, and courage.

CHAPTER *15* | Review

KEY IDEAS

ELEMENTS OF THE TREATMENT PROCESS
- Psychotherapy involves three elements: treatments, clients, and therapists. Approaches to treatment are diverse, but they can be grouped into three categories: insight, behavior, and biomedical therapies. People vary considerably in their willingness to seek psychotherapy, and many people who need therapy do not receive it.
- Therapists come from a variety of professional backgrounds. Clinical and counseling psychologists, psychiatrists, social workers, psychiatric nurses, counselors, and marriage and family therapists are the principal providers of therapeutic services.

INSIGHT THERAPIES
- Insight therapies involve verbal interactions intended to enhance self-knowledge. In psychoanalysis, free association and dream analysis are used to explore the unconscious. When an analyst's probing hits sensitive areas, resistance can be expected. The transference relationship may be used to overcome this resistance. Classical psychoanalysis is not widely practiced anymore, but Freud's legacy lives on in modern psychodynamic therapies.
- Rogers pioneered client-centered therapy, which is intended to provide a supportive climate in which clients can restructure their self-concepts. This therapy emphasizes clarification of the client's feelings and self-acceptance. Positive psychotherapy attempts to get clients to recognize their strengths, appreciate their blessings, savor positive experiences, and find meaning in their lives.
- Most theoretical approaches to insight therapy have been adapted for use with groups. Group therapy has its own unique strengths and is not merely a cheap substitute for individual therapy. Marital and family therapists seek to understand the entrenched patterns of interaction that produce distress for their clients, view individuals as parts of a family ecosystem, and attempt to help couples and families improve their communication.
- The weight of the evidence suggests that insight therapies can be effective. Studies generally find the greatest improvement early in treatment. Repressed memories of childhood sexual abuse recovered through therapy are a source of controversy in the mental health field. Although many recovered memories of abuse may be the product of suggestion, some probably are authentic.

BEHAVIOR THERAPIES
- Behavior therapies use the principles of learning in direct efforts to change specific aspects of behavior. Wolpe's systematic desensitization is a treatment for phobias. It involves the construction of an anxiety hierarchy, relaxation training, and step-by-step movement through the hierarchy. In exposure therapies clients are confronted with situations that they fear so they learn that these situations are really harmless.
- In aversion therapy, a stimulus associated with an unwanted response is paired with an unpleasant stimulus in an effort to eliminate the maladaptive response. Social skills training can improve clients' interpersonal skills through modeling, behavioral rehearsal, and shaping. Beck's cognitive therapy concentrates on changing the way clients think about events in their lives. Ample evidence shows that behavior therapies are effective.

BIOMEDICAL THERAPIES
- Two examples of biomedical treatments are drug therapy and electroconvulsive therapy. A great variety of disorders are treated with drugs. The principal types of therapeutic drugs are antianxiety drugs, antipsychotic drugs, antidepressant drugs, and mood stabilizers.
- Drug therapies can be effective, but they have their pitfalls. Many drugs produce problematic side effects, and some are overprescribed. Critics are also concerned that the pharmaceutical industry has gained too much influence over drug testing research.
- Electroconvulsive therapy (ECT) is used to trigger a cortical seizure that is believed to have therapeutic value for depression. There is contradictory evidence and heated debate about the effectiveness of ECT and about possible risks associated with its use.

CURRENT TRENDS IN TREATMENT
- Combinations of insight, behavioral, and biomedical therapies are often used fruitfully in the treatment of psychological disorders. Many modern therapists are eclectic, using ideas and techniques gleaned from a number of theoretical approaches.
- Because of cultural, language, and access barriers, therapeutic services are underutilized by ethnic minorities in America. The crux of the problem is the failure of institutions to provide culturally sensitive forms of treatment for ethnic minorities.
- Clinicians are increasingly attempting to harness technology to expand the delivery and reduce the costs of therapy. These efforts to employ technology have included interventions via videoconferencing, telephone, and the Internet. The preliminary evidence on these innovative approaches to treatment looks promising.

APPLICATION: LOOKING FOR A THERAPIST
- Therapeutic services are available in many settings, and such services do not have to be expensive. Excellent and mediocre therapists can be found in all of the mental health professions. Thus, therapists' personal skills are more important than their professional degree. In selecting a therapist, it is reasonable to insist on a therapist of one gender or the other.
- The various theoretical approaches to treatment appear to be fairly similar in overall effectiveness. However, for certain types of problems, some approaches to therapy may be more effective than others. Therapy requires time, hard work, and the courage to confront your problems.

KEY TERMS

Antianxiety drugs p. 470
Antidepressant drugs p. 472
Antipsychotic drugs p. 471
Aversion therapy p. 466
Behavior therapies p. 465
Biomedical therapies p. 470
Client-centered therapy p. 459
Clinical psychologists p. 454
Cognitive-behavioral treatments p. 468
Cognitive therapy p. 468
Counseling psychologists p. 454
Couples therapy p. 462
Dream analysis p. 457
Electroconvulsive therapy (ECT) p. 474
Exposure therapies p. 466
Family therapy p. 462
Free association p. 457
Group therapy p. 461
Insight therapies p. 456
Interpretation p. 457
Marital therapy p. 462
Mood stabilizers p. 472
Positive psychotherapy p. 461
Psychiatrists p. 455
Psychoanalysis p. 457
Psychopharmacotherapy p. 470
Resistance p. 458
Social skills training p. 468
Systematic desensitization p. 465
Tardive dyskinesia p. 471
Transference p. 458

KEY PEOPLE

Aaron Beck pp. 468–469
Sigmund Freud pp. 457–459
Carl Rogers pp. 459–460
Joseph Wolpe pp. 465–466

CHAPTER *15* | Practice Test

1. Which of the following approaches to psychotherapy is based on the theories of Sigmund Freud and his followers?
   a. Behavior therapies
   b. Client-centered therapy
   c. Biomedical therapies
   d. Psychoanalytic therapy

2. Miriam is seeing a therapist who encourages her to let her mind ramble and say whatever comes up, regardless of how trivial or irrelevant it may seem. The therapist explains that she is interested in probing the depths of Miriam's unconscious mind. This therapist appears to practice _____ and the technique in use is _____.
   a. psychoanalysis; transference
   b. psychoanalysis; free association
   c. cognitive therapy; free association
   d. client-centered therapy; clarification

3. Because Suzanne has an unconscious sexual attraction to her father, she behaves seductively toward her therapist. Suzanne's behavior is most likely a form of
   a. resistance.
   b. transference.
   c. misinterpretation.
   d. spontaneous remission.

4. Client-centered therapy emphasizes
   a. interpretation.
   b. probing the unconscious.
   c. clarification.
   d. all of the above.

5. With regard to studies of the efficacy of various treatments, research suggests that
   a. insight therapy is superior to no treatment or placebo treatment.
   b. individual insight therapy is effective, but group therapy is not.
   c. group therapy is effective, but individual insight therapy rarely works.
   d. insight therapy is effective, but only if patients remain in therapy for at least 3 years.

6. According to behavior therapists, pathological behaviors
   a. are signs of an underlying emotional or cognitive problem.
   b. should be viewed as the expression of an unconscious sexual or aggressive conflict.
   c. can be modified directly through the application of established principles of conditioning.
   d. both a and b.

7. A stimulus that elicits an undesirable response is paired with a noxious stimulus in
   a. systematic desensitization.
   b. cognitive therapy.
   c. aversion therapy.
   d. psychoanalysis.

8. Bryce's psychiatrist has prescribed both an antidepressant and lithium for him. Bryce's diagnosis is probably
   a. schizophrenia.
   b. obsessive-compulsive disorder.
   c. bipolar disorder.
   d. dissociative disorder.

9. Drug therapies have been criticized on the grounds that
   a. they are ineffective in most patients.
   b. they temporarily relieve symptoms without addressing the real problem.
   c. many drugs are overprescribed and many patients are overmedicated.
   d. both b and c.

10. A therapist's theoretical approach is not nearly as important as his or her
    a. age.
    b. appearance.
    c. personal characteristics and skills.
    d. type of professional training.

ANSWERS

1. d Page 457
2. b Page 457
3. b Page 458
4. c Page 460
5. a Page 463
6. c Page 465
7. c Page 466
8. c Page 472
9. d Page 473
10. c Pages 478–480

COURSEMATE

Go to **CengageBrain.com** to access Psychology CourseMate, where you will find an interactive eBook, glossaries, flashcards, quizzes, videos, and more.

PERSONAL EXPLORATIONS WORKBOOK

Go to the *Personal Explorations Workbook* in the back of your textbook for exercises that can enhance your self-understanding in relation to issues raised in this chapter.

Exercise 15.1 *Self-Assessment:* Attitudes Toward Seeking Professional Psychological Help

Exercise 15.2 *Self-Reflection:* Thinking About Therapy

Positive Psychology

Kali9/E+/Getty Images

On January 15, 2009, a striking event galvanized the American public's attention and imbued people with feelings of joy. It was unprecedented: A passenger plane made a miraculous landing on the Hudson River in New York City. After the plane had taken off from LaGuardia Airport, the pilot, Chesley "Sully" Sullenberger, reported that a flock of birds had flown into the plane's engines, causing it to quickly lose power and altitude. Such bird strikes are perilous because they usually shut down one of the engines on an aircraft. This incident was much worse because the pilot believed that both engines were affected. Disaster was imminent, but moments later the pilot executed a near-perfect water landing, and all 155 on board were rescued from the icy waters. Images of the plane and the rescue of its passengers and crew by air and by boat flashed throughout the news media.

In addition to relief, elation was a common reaction to the plane's miraculous maneuver, which was quickly dubbed the "miracle on the Hudson." The event elevated the spirits of those who witnessed it, heard about it, or watched it on television or via the Internet. The pilot, a modest man who claimed that his training served him well, became an instant hero, one whose actions generated a sense of appreciative wonder in observers. What people shared in the aftermath of this event might be called a sense of *awe,* a state some psychologists refer to as a moral, spiritual, or even an aesthetic emotion (Haidt & Keltner, 2004; Keltner & Haidt, 2003; Schurtz et al., 2012). People who feel elation or a sense of awe report experiencing a warm feeling in their chests, an

The miraculous safe landing by US Air 1549 evoked feelings of awe that elevated the spirits of observers around the world.

expansion of their hearts, and a strong and sure sense of connection to other people.

Have you ever witnessed an event that touched you deeply and brought you a feeling of transcendence—that is, of goodness far beyond normal? Your experience need not have been a public "miracle" such as a disaster avoided. It might have been something as simple as observing a kind deed done selflessly or watching a glorious sunset. The point is that you felt changed for the better by what you witnessed.

This chapter is devoted to exploring the impact of such upbeat phenomena by presenting one of psychology's newest areas of inquiry: positive psychology. To do so, we define this new field and the three areas of research that compose it. We then discuss representative topics within each area in some detail. Our study of positive psychology concludes by considering the prospects and problems of studying how and why people thrive. This chapter's Application offers a variety of simple exercises you can use to boost your own level of happiness.

THE SCOPE OF POSITIVE PSYCHOLOGY

LEARNING OBJECTIVES

- Define positive psychology, and explain why it is a counterweight to the historic and dominant negative focus in the discipline.
- Explain why positive psychology provides a framework for new as well as older research on well-being.
- Identify positive psychology's three lines of inquiry.

You may have seen the popular bumpersticker suggesting that people "Commit Random Acts of Kindness and Senseless Acts of Beauty." If you have seen a car sporting this sentiment, you may well have concluded that the driver or owner is some sort of idealist or wide-eyed optimist. Perhaps the individual is someone who sees the proverbial glass as half-full rather than half-empty. But what if some serious psychological substance underlies the bumpersticker's message? Let's explore how a focus on what's good in life can be good for people.

Defining Positive Psychology and Its Brief History

Positive psychology **is a social and intellectual movement within the discipline of psychology that focuses on human strengths and how people can flourish and be successful** (Csikszentmihalyi & Nakamura, 2011; Lopez & Snyder, 2009; Peterson, 2006; Snyder & Lopez, 2007). In part, the emergence of positive psychology was a reaction to the predominantly negative focus found in most other areas of the discipline. Stop for a moment and think about your own perceptions of psychology. If you are like most students, you are likely to view psychology as a helping profession more than anything else. Fair enough. But consider how much of that "help" is based primarily on the study of weaknesses and problems—social, emotional, cognitive, and behavioral—that people exhibit (Seligman, 2002). Psychology's language is rooted in the negative, with words like "depression," "anxiety," and "disorder" (Bowers, 2008).

Until recently, the study of positive qualities and their impact on people's health and well-being occurred entirely outside of the discipline's mainstream. The advocates of positive psychology argue that it provides a needed balance in the discipline of psychology. Note that research in positive psychology does not deny the importance of negative states, experiences, feelings, and emotions. Failing to recognize the complete and complex range of human experience would make the approach incomplete (Brown & Holt, 2011). Though not always pleasant, for example, experiencing negative emotions can promote self-understanding and direct personal growth (Algoe, Fredrickson, & Chow, 2011; Lambert & Erekson, 2008). We learn to appreciate life's richness by recognizing its tragic elements (Woolfolk, 2002). So, let's be very clear: Positive psychology is not "happiology" (Seligman, 2011); rather, it represents a new direction of inquiry for the field.

Thus, this shift in perspective requires more than just donning the equivalent of rose-colored glasses or acting like a "Pollyanna," someone who is encumbered by foolish or even blind optimism. Advocates of positive psychology (including some who actually call themselves "positive psychologists") want to discover how to harness people's strengths, virtues, and other good qualities to help them enhance their lives. One of positive psychology's primary aims is to create tools and techniques for promoting well-being and psychological health, which have an impact on individuals, their connections with others, and physical health. A good way to think of positive psychology is as an

arm of psychology with potentially beneficial side effects, including the opportunity to prevent mental illness and reduce discontent by cultivating human strengths, such as courage, hope, and resilience, and helping people flourish in their lives (Seligman, 1998, 2011).

What led psychologists to consider developing a new subfield, especially one named positive psychology? As a researchable and teachable topic, positive psychology was not identified and named until 1998. During his year as president of the American Psychological Association (APA), psychologist Martin Seligman developed positive psychology as a counterweight to the discipline's negatively oriented history (Seligman, 1999). He was well

Martin E. P. Seligman

known for his research on learned helplessness, depression, and the acquisition of phobias—downbeat topics that fit comfortably within psychology's traditional emphasis on the negative. So what prompted his sudden interest in the potential power of people's positive natures? Seligman (2002) reported that an exchange with his 5-year-old daughter Nikki piqued his interest and triggered the chain of events that led to the founding of positive psychology. Quite simply, Nikki told her father that he was (as apparently was often the case) being a grump while the two of them were gardening. Seligman recalled that

Nikki . . . was throwing weeds into the air and dancing around. I yelled at her. She walked away, came back, and said . . . "Daddy, do you remember before my fifth birthday? From the time I was three to the time I was five, I was a whiner. I whined every day. When I turned five, I decided not to whine anymore. That was the hardest thing I've ever done. And if I can stop whining, you can stop being such a grouch." (2002, pp. 3–4)

By speaking some "truth to power," Nikki led her dad to experience something of an epiphany, a sudden flash of insight into an event. Raising children, for example, is not about telling them what to do (let alone yelling at them); rather, it is really about identifying and nurturing their good qualities and strengths (Carr, 2011). By extension, Seligman began to think about how the psychology of the past generations could have—*should* have—been about much more than negative, pathological states and human suffering (Seligman, 2003a).

But this is recent history—what about other events in psychology's past that led to present-day positive psychology? Since World War II, for example, psychology has focused on treating an increasing variety of psychological disorders (see Chapter 15). Indeed, clinical psychology was born out of the need to deal with the rise of pathology and psychological maladies linked to life in the modern world. Progress creates all kinds of stress, strains, and conflict. Consider the stressors found in daily life—work, money, love (or the lack thereof), family, purpose, and the need to find some meaning in all of them. Since the mid-twentieth century, the psychological community has responded to these changes and pressures by adhering to a disease model, in which the emphasis is on repairing damage rather than preventing it or, better still, inoculating people in advance against psychological distress (Maddux, 2009).

Seligman and like-minded researchers felt that the time was right to mount a campaign for change so that psychologists and the people they study, treat, and teach would learn to see their lives as fulfilling and flourishing rather than as stress-ridden and dysfunctional (Aspinwall & Staudinger, 2002; Keyes & Haidt, 2003; Seligman & Csikszentmihalyi, 2000). Informal gatherings were held, plans were laid, and then more formal efforts, such as conferences and workshops, were conducted where junior and senior psychologists met to develop a philosophy and identify goals for what became known as positive psychology. Soon after, scholarly articles, books, and even a journal dealing with positive psychology appeared (Linley, 2009). As Seligman and Mihaly Csikszentmihalyi (2000), another founder of the movement, claimed, "The aim of positive psychology is to begin to catalyze a change in the focus of psychology from preoccupation with only repairing the worst things in life to also building positive qualities" (p. 5).

If nothing else, positive psychology wants to change the traditional conception of mental health by helping people *flourish*—that is, to have high levels of well-being and low levels of mental illness (Keyes, 2009; Keyes & Lopez, 2002). Individuals who are *struggling* have high levels of both well-being and mental illness. Those who are *floundering* tend to have low levels of well-being but high levels of mental illness. Finally, a person who has low well-being and low mental illness is said to be *languishing*. **Figure 16.1** presents this combination in an alternative model of complete mental health. Note that when individuals truly flourish (possess high well-being and low mental illness), they also display a combination of high emotional well-being, high psychological well-being, and high social well-being (Keyes & Lopez, 2002).

Learn More Online

The World Database of Happiness

Are people living in one country happier than those in another? How do we know? To explore these and other questions, delve into the World Database of Happiness, which is maintained at Erasmus University Rotterdam, The Netherlands.

Reconsidering Older Research in Light of the New Positive Psychology

Positive psychology represents a turning point, even a change in the zeitgeist, for the discipline of psychology. The term *zeitgeist* refers to a timely intellectual state of mind that many people contribute to and share. The emergence of positive psychology seems to fit this description, but can we really conclude that this subdiscipline just "appeared" once Seligman and other like-minded psychologists began to communicate, organize, and then conceive and publish relevant research?

The answer is probably not, and here's why: Good ideas are often "in the air" before someone begins to study them or before a topical area is formally named. Thus, as an organized effort, the positive psychology movement *is* new, but many of the questions being studied are not; in fact, quite a few have been examined by psychologists for decades outside of the discipline's mainstream. A variety of theories, hypotheses, and research results pertaining to beneficial qualities and psychological themes in human experience, for example, have been around since the 1950s and 1960s (e.g., Allport, 1961; Maslow, 1973; Rogers, 1961). Indeed, the subdiscipline of humanistic psychology has long pursued questions that seem similar to those now asked by positive psychologists (Linley, 2009; Linley & Joseph, 2004a; Robbins, 2008). In fact, some humanistic psychologists have identified a tension between the two fields (Medlock, 2012), while others argue that positive psychology is overlooking,

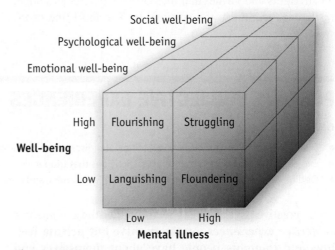

Figure 16.1

A proposed model of complete mental health based on positive psychological concepts. Keyes and Lopez (2002) proposed a model of complete mental health in which psychological assessments of flourishing, struggling, languishing, and floundering are considered across each of three levels of well-being (emotional, psychological, social), which leads to twelve classifications of mental health. The ideal state of complete mental health, flourishing, is marked by a low level of mental illness and high levels of emotional, psychological, and social well-being.

Source: Adapted from Figure 1.1 on page 6 in Compton, W. C., & Hoffman, E. (2013). *Positive psychology: The science of happiness and flourishing.* Belmont, CA: Wadsworth/Cengage.

even neglecting, established scholarly work in humanistic psychology (Friedman & Robbins, 2012; Rennie, 2012). And as many advocates of positive psychology are quick to acknowledge, questions about what constitutes a good life for an individual have been pursued by philosophers since Plato and Aristotle (Deci & Ryan, 2008; Schimmel, 2000).

As you read the remainder of this chapter, then, you will notice that older research studies and references are routinely mixed in with newer ones (those appearing after positive psychology's "birth" in 1998). Juxtaposing old with new research should not seem odd, as the questions asked and answers obtained earlier can now be examined fruitfully in light of new data linked to positive psychology's three areas of inquiry.

Introducing Positive Psychology's Three Lines of Inquiry

As originally conceived, positive psychology pursues three lines of inquiry, which, as shown in **Figure 16.2**, make up the "three legs" on which positive psychology stands (Gillham & Seligman, 1999; Seligman & Csikszentmihalyi, 2000). First, positive psychology is interested in people's *positive subjective experiences*. Such experiences include good moods, positive emotions, happiness, love, and other psychological processes that promote or maintain feelings of well-being in individuals. The second area of concern is *positive individual traits* that enable people to thrive. The traits falling under this heading are often said to be character strengths and virtues and include such qualities as hope, resilience, gratitude, and spirituality. The third line of in-

quiry focuses on *positive institutions,* or the settings and organizations that gather people together to promote civil discourse and enhance their positive subjective experiences and positive personal traits in a collective way. Positive institutions include close-knit families, quality schools, good work environments, and safe and supportive neighborhoods and communities.

Each of the three areas of inquiry seeks to understand the ways people can flourish in daily life. The next three sections in the chapter review concepts and illustrative research representing these areas. We begin with people's private feelings of well-being: positive subjective experiences.

Figure 16.2

The three legs of positive psychology. Research in positive psychology stands on "three legs," or lines of empirical, scientific inquiry: positive subjective experiences, positive individual traits, and positive institutions.

POSITIVE SUBJECTIVE EXPERIENCES

LEARNING OBJECTIVES

- Distinguish between moods and emotions, and discuss how thought speed and the broaden-and-build model are linked to positive states.
- Explain the flow experience and typical activities that trigger it.
- Outline the advantages of mindfulness over mindlessness, and define savoring.

Some positive psychologists focus on the study of *positive subjective experiences,* **or the positive but private feelings and thoughts people have about themselves and the events in their lives.** The frequency of positive subjective experiences has been linked to people's success in marriage, friendship, income, and health, among other areas of daily life; such personal accomplishments not only lead to good feelings, they also makes people more successful (Lyubomirsky, King, & Diener, 2005).

Subjective experiences tend to be present focused. In fact, a considerable amount of research has examined the most common positive subjective state, happiness, as discussed in detail in Chapter 1 (see also Diener & Biswas-

Diener, 2008; Gilbert, 2006b; Haidt, 2006). Sensual pleasures—pleasant tastes (chocolate) and smells (fresh-baked bread), for example, as well as touch (a friendly pat, a caress)—can trigger positive subjective states in people.

But subjective states are not just in the present. People can reflect on past experiences that conjure up feelings of contentment or satisfaction. Reviewing memories from childhood, such as holidays, birthdays, or family vacations, can be especially gratifying. Events need not be based in the distant past either. An office worker can call up feelings of satisfaction by recalling a successful performance review she received from her boss a month before or by remembering the goal her soccer-playing daughter made the previous week. Whether you reflect on a distant, recent, or current moment that was pleasant or even happy, you can experience a change in mood from a neutral state to a more positive one.

Positive Moods

When psychologists talk about moods, such as when someone reports being in a "good mood," they are not usually referring to emotion per se. Emotions are stronger subjective experiences, much more distinct than moods. Moods are more global responses to experience and tend to be more diffuse and pervasive, lasting much longer than emotions (Morris, 1999). Think about someone you know who is always cheerful and upbeat—that is, she is usually in a good mood. Imagine this friend returning to her parked car only to discover a parking ticket on her windshield. How does she react? She may become angry at herself for forgetting to put change in the meter, but a half-hour later, she has forgotten the costly ticket and returned to her usual smiling and placid self. In other words, she is once again experiencing a relatively good mood.

When people are in a good mood, they anticipate that good things will happen to them; as a consequence, they often make good things happen. In fact, being in a positive mood has several beneficial effects, including making people more agreeable, more helpful, less aggressive, and even better at decision making (Isen, 2002; Morris, 1999).

Positive Moods Can Promote Creative Solutions

We also know that being in a positive mood can enhance people's creativity. Isen and her colleagues, for example, hypothesized that positive mood would promote creative problem solving (Isen, Daubman, & Nowicki, 1987). For 5 minutes, groups of men and women watched either a funny "blooper" reel or an emotionally neutral film. Afterward, each participant was introduced to the "candle task," a standard measure of creative problem solving (Duncker, 1945). An experimenter read the following instructions aloud:

On the table [in front of you] are a book of matches, a box of tacks, and a candle. Above the table on the wall is a corkboard. Your task is to affix the candle to the corkboard in such a way that it will burn without dripping wax on the table or the floor beneath. You will be given 10 minutes to work on the problem.

Do you see how to solve the problem quickly and correctly? If you pour out the contents of the box and then tack the box to the corkboard, it becomes a candle holder (see **Figure 16.3**). The lit candle can then be placed upright in the box while being connected to the

"I don't sing because I am happy. I am happy because I sing."

corkboard. The solution prevents wax from dripping onto the floor. Once you recognize the solution, it seems obvious, yet many participants fail to identify the correct solution before the 10 minutes is up.

What was the impact of the mood manipulation (viewing one of the two films) on creativity and solving the candle task? As Isen and colleagues (1987) anticipated, the participants who saw the funny film were more likely to solve the problem correctly in the allotted time than those who watched the neutral film. Related studies support the

Figure 16.3

The Duncker candle task for demonstrating creativity: problem and solution.
Problem solvers are given a candle, a book of matches, and a box of tacks (left). They are then told to attach the candle to the wall in such a way that wax will not drip onto the table top. The correct solution—tacking the box to the wall so it can serve as a base to hold the lit candle (with no dripping onto the table) is shown on the right.

finding that good moods as well as positive emotions help people to be more creative in their thinking (Forgeard, 2011; Isen, 2004; Isen, Daubman, & Nowicki, 1987; To et al., 2012). One way to think about the impact of positive affect (feelings)—whether in the guise of milder moods or stronger emotions—is that it helps people see things in new, unconventional ways.

We have considered how positive mood can lead to particular outcomes, such as creative thinking. What if we reverse the process: Are there qualities associated with thinking that can lead to particular moods, especially positive ones? To answer that, let's take a look at some fascinating new research.

Positive Moods Are Linked with Quick Thoughts

When was the last time you felt your thoughts racing—that is, moving at a faster-than-usual rate? Chances are that if your thoughts were racing along at a brisk pace, you were probably in a good mood.

Pronin and Jacobs (2008) argue that faster thinking generally leads to a more positive mood (see also Pronin, Jacobs, & Wegner, 2008; Pronin & Wegner, 2006). However, when thoughts are too fast, they can be associated with feelings of *mania,* an abnormally elevated mood. What about slower thoughts? As you may have already surmised, they are often linked with negative moods. And very slow or sluggish thoughts can lead to depressive feelings. Thought speed is one property of a more general concept that Pronin and Jacobs call *mental motion.*

Besides speed of thought, mental motion also involves thought variability (Pronin & Jacobs, 2008). When one's thought is varied—thinking about many different things, not just one or two—one's mood is usually positive. Repetitive thoughts on the same topic, or what is sometimes referred to as *rumination,* are associated with negative affect. At the positive extreme of thought variation, people can experience mania or even a reverie or dreamlike state. Approaching the negative extreme, however, thoughts can become depressive or anxiety ridden. When quick thoughts and varied thinking meet, people feel elated; when thoughts are plodding and repetitive, however, people experience dejection. Naturally, thought speed and variability can oppose each other—when one is fast (or slow), the other can be varied (or repetitive). The consequences for various possible combinations of mental motion's properties for mood are shown in **Figure 16.4** (note where normal mood lies compared to the predictable deviations surrounding it as thought speed and variability change).

Finally, Pronin and Jacobs (2008) argue that thought speed and variability operate independently of the *content* of thought. In other words, you might assume that slow thoughts are necessary negative thoughts, but that is not always so. Although emotional problems such as depression and anxiety have been linked to nonrational or dysfunctional thinking (Beck, 2008), the arguments for mental motion's impact on mood do not require that thoughts have any particular content.

Let's review a simple experiment that illustrates the relationship between basic speed of thought and mood, as well as some of its psychological consequences. Pronin, Jacobs, and Wegner (2008) had a group of college students spend 10 minutes writing down solutions to a hypothetical problem (how to earn one year's private college tuition in a summer). Participants in the *fast-thought* group were told to produce "every idea you possibly can," whereas those in the *slow-thought* condition were asked to develop "as many good ideas as you can." The findings are summarized in **Figure 16.5**. People in the fast-thought group generated more ideas and felt themselves to be thinking at a faster rate compared to those in the other group (see the left side of **Figure 16.5**). Further, the fast-thought group experienced more positive mood levels and reported higher levels of energy than the slow-thought group (see the right side of **Figure 16.5**). Though preliminary, these findings may well have beneficial implications for developing thought-speed-based interventions for treating mood disorders (Pronin & Wegner, 2006).

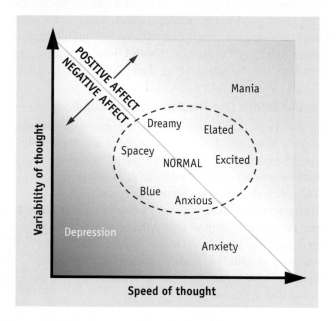

Figure 16.4

Mental motion and mood: The consequences of thought speed and variability for how people may feel. This diagram illustrates the theorized relationships between the speed and variability of thought and moods. Varied but fast thinking leads to feelings of elation, while slow, repetitive thinking causes feelings of dejection. When thought variability and speed oppose each other (one is low while the other is high), people's moods may depend on which of the two factors is more extreme. The mood states created by these combinations vary apart from their positive or negative valence. For example, repetitive thinking can create feelings of anxiety rather than depression if the thinking is rapid; indeed, anxious states of being are generally linked with more rapid thought than depressive states.

Source: Adapted from Pronin, E., & Jacobs, E. (2008). Thought speed, mood, and the experience of mental motion. *Perspectives on Psychological Science, 3,* 461–485. Copyright 2009 Sage Publications, Inc. Journals. Reproduced with permission of Sage Publications, Inc.

Figure 16.5

Results of the self-generated ideas, speed of thought, and mood experiment. Participants in the fast-thinking condition of the experiment generated more ideas in the allotted time than did their peers (see the graph on the far left). The crucial results are shown in the two graphs on the right. As you can see, those in the fast-thinking group reported having a more positive mood and higher levels of energy than those in the slow-thinking group.

Source: Adapted from Pronin, E., & Jacobs, E. (2008). Thought speed, mood, and the experience of mental motion. *Perspectives on Psychological Science, 3,* 461–485.

Are there any potential drawbacks to the link between speed of thought and positive mood? In some recent research, Chandler and Pronin (2012) identified one cause for concern: Besides good feelings, faster thoughts are also linked with greater risk taking. When participants were induced to think more quickly in experimental contexts, they were apt to take considerable chances with real money and to express greater intent to take part in risky acts, such as engaging in unprotected sex or using illegal drugs. Although the study of mental motion introduces a new dimension of study for positive psychology, as well as a new perspective on the power of positive thinking, it may have some limits worth noting. Let's now turn to the positive subjective states that represent feelings as specific responses—positive emotions.

Positive Emotions

Whereas moods are low-level feelings that can last for lengthy periods of time ("I was in a grumpy mood all last week"), emotions are stronger but shorter-lived feelings,

acute responses to some particular event ("I was overjoyed when I won the dance contest"). As noted in Chapter 3, *emotions* **are powerful, largely uncontrollable feelings, accompanied by physiological changes.** When psychologists speak of emotions, they usually divide them into two categories: positive and negative. *Positive emotions* **consist of pleasant responses to events that promote connections with others, including subjective states such as happiness, joy, euphoria, gratitude, and contentment.** When individuals experience positive emotions, they feel good about themselves, about other people, and often about whatever they are doing or thinking. Interestingly, some people are more prone to experiencing positive emotions than others are (Watson & Naragon, 2009). In contrast, *negative emotions* **consist of unpleasant responses to potential threats or dangers, including subjective states like sadness, disgust, anger, guilt, and fear.** Negative emotions are unpleasant disruptions that, while increasing vigilance, often cause people to turn inward or lead them to be snippy or disagreeable with others. And, as is true for positive emotions, some individuals experience negative emotions more routinely than others (Watson & Clark, 1984). In general, negative emotions draw more attention than positive ones, and this predisposition is likely an evolved process (Froh, 2009). The division of positive and negative emotions is basic, a structural fact of people's normal emotional lives (Watson, 2002).

Historically, negative emotions have been studied far more extensively than positive ones. One reason is that negative emotions have evolutionary significance. For example, experiencing negative emotions often alerts people

Learn More Online

Positive Psychology News Daily

Want a daily dose of positive psychology? Visit the Positive Psychology News Daily website, which contains up-to-date information on trends in parenting, education, health, exercise, and relationships. New books examining positive psychology are also reviewed here.

to possible threats. These emotions make people wary, narrowing the focus of attention (Derryberry & Tucker, 1994; Easterbrook, 1959). Second, negative emotions are implicated in the "flight or fight response," which occurs when an organism feels threatened. Negative emotions compel people to act through emotionally linked *specific action tendencies,* or behavioral reactions with survival value. The automatic response—tendency to act—is often to flee from a perceived threat (a mugger, a bully) or to fight off an attacker. Another reason that negative emotions receive so much attention is their sheer quantity; it is estimated that they outnumber positive emotions by about three to one (Ellsworth & Smith, 1988; Fredrickson, 1998), which may have contributed to the bias among psychologists to study them.

Barbara Fredrickson

But what about positive emotions—what value do they have? Some of the most intriguing answers to this question have come from Barbara Fredrickson, a social and positive psychologist who asserts that positive emotions play particular roles in people's mental and physical lives (Sekerka, Vacharkulksemsuk, & Fredrickson, 2012). Fredrickson (1998, 2007; Fredrickson & Branigan, 2005) developed the *broaden-and-build model* of positive emotions to explain how they benefit human beings. In contrast to negative emotions, positive ones spawn *nonspecific action tendencies* that nonetheless lead to adaptive responses. For example, when adults are experiencing positive emotions, they are much more likely to offer aid to people in need, engage others in social interaction, perform some creative activity, or try out some new experience (e.g., Fredrickson, 1998, 2002; see also, for example, Isen, 1987; 2004). Positive emotions can also serve as beneficial counterweights to the dysphoric or fearful feelings associated with emotional dysfunction and psychopathology (Garland et al., 2010). Put simply, positive emotions open people up to a variety of new behavioral options that promote and maintain psychosocial well-being.

At the same time, positive emotions broaden people's cognitive responses by promoting new and beneficial *thought-action tendencies,* in which established ways of positive thinking are associated with particular acts or behaviors. For example, when children are feeling joy, they become more playful and imaginative, often investigating their environments (Fredrickson, 1998; Frijda, 1986). This joyful exploration allows them to learn new things about the world and about themselves.

In one study, Fredrickson and Branigan (2005) demonstrated that the experience of joy did indeed broaden people's thought-action tendencies. After watching one of five emotion-eliciting film clips (joy, contentment, anger, fear, or a neutral condition), a group of research participants wrote down lists of everything they would like to have done at that moment. As shown in **Figure 16.6**, the participants who felt the emotion of either joy or contentment listed significantly more desired possible actions than the individuals in the negative or neutral emotion groups. Being joyful or contented apparently leads people to think of future possible activities they might engage in, whereas being in a negative or even neutral emotional state narrows people's thoughts and reduces the range of possible subsequent actions.

Thus, the broaden-and-build model proposes that positive emotions *broaden* people's outlooks and then they *build on* subsequent learning to develop future emotional and intellectual resources. Positive emotions create "bankable" social, cognitive, and affective resources that can be drawn on with emotional interest in the future. **Figure 16.7** illustrates the broaden-and-build model. Note that Fredrickson postulates that broader thought-action repertoires lead to increased well-being, which in turn triggers more positive emotions leading to happiness and what Fredrickson (2002) refers to as upward spirals of health.

What else do positive emotions accomplish besides broadening thought-action repertoires? Fredrickson also advanced what is known as **the *undoing hypothesis*, which posits that positive emotions aid the mind and the body by recovering a sense of balance and flexibility following an episode experiencing negative emotion** (Fredrickson & Joiner, 2002; Fredrickson & Levenson, 1998). When people are stressed, such as when a group of students take an unexpectedly difficult exam, the presence of positive emotions triggered by the shared experience

Figure 16.6

The broadening effects of positive emotions compared to neutral or negative emotions.
Experiencing an emotional state of joy or contentment led research participants to list a greater number of activities they might like to engage in at that moment than did individuals experiencing a neutral or negative emotional state.

Source: Adapted from Fredrickson, B. L. (2002). Positive emotions. In C. R. Snyder & S. J. Lopez (Eds.), *Handbook of positive psychology* (pp. 120–134). New York: Oxford University Press.

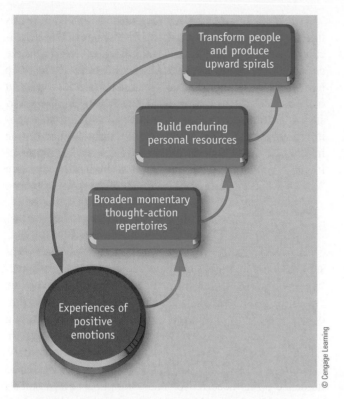

Figure 16.7

The broaden-and-build theory of positive emotions. According to Fredrickson (2002), the personal resources people gain during positive emotional states last for some time. This figure illustrates the three hypothesized sequential effects of positive emotions. First, positive emotions broaden people's range of thought-action sequences, which in turn builds personal resources, culminating in upward spirals of positive emotions. The cycle then repeats itself.

(e.g., the students meet after the test, discuss it, and share their anxiety about it) undo the aftereffects of the stressor more quickly. The students are likely to feel better once they realize they all felt the same way about the exam. They will smile at one another, roll their eyes, possibly even laugh at how absurdly difficult the questions were, leading to positive emotions that effectively wipe out the physiological and biochemical effects caused by the stressful test-taking experience. In addition, the resulting positive emotions reestablish flexible and open thinking after the narrowed perspective caused by the negative (stressful) emotions felt during the tough test.

Many times positive emotions are responses to events—that is, they are caused by good things that happen. We also need to consider the consequences of positive emotions that people intentionally create by pursuing particular activities.

Flow

Do you ever find yourself so happily or joyfully engaged in a challenging or interesting activity that you "lose yourself" in it? If you are an athlete, for example, you may describe the experience as "being in the zone" when you are playing basketball or tennis (Cooper, 1998; Kimiecik & Stein, 1992). Of course, the activity does not have to be particularly physical, as individuals who play video games routinely report losing all sense of time while engaged in a game. Likewise, surgeons report that the physical and intellectual challenges of doing an operation can place them into a zone for optimal performance. Musicians say the same thing about playing an instrument and performing for others. Psychologist Mihaly Csikszentmihalyi named this psychological phenomenon "flow." ***Flow* is the state of being in which a person becomes fully involved and engaged in the present time by some interesting, challenging, and intrinsically rewarding activity.**

Mihaly Csikszentmihalyi

Csikszentmihalyi recognized the pull of flow experiences in his own life when he played chess or went rock or mountain climbing (Diener & Biswas-Diener, 2008). He refers to flow as an optimal state, one he has studied for over three decades. To Csikszentmihalyi (1975):

Flow denotes the holistic sensation present when we act with total involvement . . . It is the state in which action follows upon action according to an internal logic which seems to need no conscious intervention on our part. We experience it as a unified flowing from one moment to the next, in which we feel in control of our actions, and in which there is little distinction between self and environment; between stimulus and response; or between past, present, and future. (p. 43)

When they enter this "optimal experience," people become less self-aware, lose all track of time, and focus their energies and attention on doing some engaging activity where skill and challenge are in balance. The flow experience is multifaceted (Ceja & Navarro, 2009; Delle Fave, 2009). Individuals who experience flow rarely worry about losing control over what they are doing, which, paradoxically, provides them with a sense of control. They often concentrate so deeply on what they are doing that they become oblivious to their surroundings and the people in them (Nakamura & Csikszentmihalyi, 2009). In Csikszentmihalyi's (1990) view, people's quality of life is at least partially determined by how well they are able to control their consciousness; more control promotes order and well-being, while less leads to psychological disorder and dissatisfaction.

Finding Flow

The good news is that everyone is familiar with the flow experience. Virtually anyone can find flow. According to Csikszentmihalyi, flow was originally conceived as a phenomenon falling between the opposite experiences of boredom and anxiety, and he believes that people experience flow when they find a balanced, meaningful place between these poles of experience. He also suggested that flow can be characterized as a balance between a person's current skill level and the challenges of the situation. Indeed, the flow experience is often found at the point where challenges are just manageable. This argument makes sense if you think about it: When the level of challenge in a task is right, people rise to the occasion to meet it. But if the challenge level is too high, people often begin to feel anxious about what they are doing—worrying about their performance, questioning their own competence—and, consequently, do not experience flow because they are distracted.

Similarly, if the task in question is monotonous or repetitive, people quickly become bored; it is not possible to achieve the flow state if one is not engaged by what one is doing. Think about a mundane task, such as stuffing envelopes. If you had to do it all day, every day, you would become fidgety, annoyed, and frustrated, as well as undeniably bored, because the task would be too easy (not to mention tiresome) for you. Once mastered, there would be no change in it and nothing new to learn in order to perform it.

Thus, to find flow and develop your creative potential, you must find a challenging activity that matches your skill level. Once an activity is chosen and the requisite challenge and skill levels are met, you can have a flow experience virtually whenever you wish.

A key element of a flow experience is that even if it is initially undertaken for other reasons, it becomes intrinsically rewarding. Thus, a child may be enrolled in a dance class by her parents, who tell her that the exercise will keep her weight down, give her poise, and keep her healthy. But once she begins to enjoy the challenge of learning new steps and routines, dancing becomes an activity worth doing for its own sake—her parents' reasons, though still true in one sense, have nothing to do with her reason for dancing. As William Butler Yeats put it in his 1928 poem "Among School Children":

> *O body swayed to music, O brightening glance,*
> *How can we know the dancer from the dance?*

When individuals experience flow, they have the pleasure of stretching themselves and their talents in new directions. For this reason, flow often occurs when people pursue creative or stimulating work, including aesthetic efforts (art, dance, music, drama, writing), hobbies, or sports, among other possibilities (Nakamura & Csikszentmihalyi, 2009). Further, anyone in almost any situation can experience flow. Factors such as social class, gender, culture, and age have no influence on its occurrence. Thus, the good news is that a person need only identify a domain and a skill-related activity within it that triggers flow.

Aside from the obvious fact that people find it to be a reinforcing state, why seek flow? For one thing, flow feels good and becomes a source of motivation. Aside from enhancing certain skills, flow provides positive emotions, staves off negative affect, and promotes goal commitment and achievement (Nakamura & Csikszentmihalyi, 2009).

If flow feels good and is reinforcing, shouldn't it be most likely to occur when people are having fun? Perhaps, but that all depends on how one defines "fun." For many people, their work is their play. Thus, there may be a some-

Jeff Greenberg/The Image Works

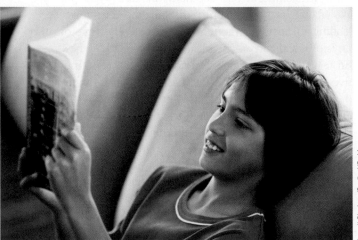

Russell Glenister/Cardinal/Corbis

Flow occurs when people are engaged in challenging activities that match their skill levels, such as creating a work of art or reading an exciting novel.

what paradoxical side to flow—namely, that people are most likely to experience this absorbing state when they are at work rather than play. Individuals who enjoy their work report being in flow quite often, and, not surprisingly, flow may be linked to job satisfaction (Csikszentmihalyi & LeFevre, 1989). Why does this happen? Presumably because the work often presents a good balance between challenge and skill. Of course, we need to acknowledge that work is something nearly everyone does and does quite often when compared to hobbies or recreational sports, for example.

Csikszentmihalyi originally began to recognize the force of flow when he was studying the creative processes of artists (Getzels & Csikszentmihalyi, 1976). He noticed that when artists were truly involved in what they were doing, the activity became highly focused and single-minded. The artists ignored their hunger or thirst, any tiredness, and virtually all other concerns for creature comforts in order to do their creative work. Once a piece of art was complete, however, the artists quickly lost interest in it. The joy was in the doing—the process of creating—and not really in the outcome or product of that process. Most people may not think of the work they do as being creative in an artistic or aesthetic sense, but becoming wrapped up in the moment-to-moment acts of work is similar. And self-imposed time pressures often lead workers to ignore a growling stomach or a dry throat in order to complete what they are doing. The point is that challenges and skill levels may allow people to enjoy what they do in a job, work, or career calling.

Of course, flow is found in all sorts of situations besides work and the workplace. We already mentioned sports (Cosma, 1999). Participating in a psychotherapy session (Grafanaki et al., 2007) or a religious ritual can lead to flow (Han, 1998), as can teaching (Beard, Stansbury, & Wayne, 2010; Coleman, 1994), taking part in online learning (Shin, 2006), driving a car (Csikszentmihalyi, 1997), reading for pleasure (McQuillan & Conde, 1996), engaging with one's family (Rathunde, 1988), and—surprisingly—cramming for a test (Brinthaupt & Shin, 2001). Even using a computer can lead to a flow state (Ghani & Deshpande, 1994). Oddly, perhaps, military combat can lead to flow as well (Harari, 2008). Boring tasks, such as housework, appear to prevent flow (Csikszentmihalyi, 1997) unless the situation is changed (listening to music while waxing the floor or scrubbing the tub can often do the trick).

Does Everyone Find Flow?

Csikszentmihalyi found that about 20% of respondents in American and European samples said they experienced flow quite frequently, usually several times a day. Very intense flow experiences were felt by a smaller percentage of respondents, however. Around 15% of a given sample will report that they have never had such an experience.

Are there any personality characteristics linked with the likelihood to experience flow? Teng (2011) examined how temperament and character can influence whether a given individual experiences flow. People who are persistent, seek novelty, and can rise above their own selves (self-transcendent) are apt to experience flow, while individuals who are highly self-directed are less likely to do so. Perhaps these results suggest that being overly focused can be counterproductive where optimal experience is concerned.

Mindfulness

Active engagement with a challenging and interesting activity—the flow experience—is one way to promote well-being. Surprisingly, there is another, simpler way to do so: by actively and mindfully noticing new things and drawing distinctions among them. Social psychologist Ellen Langer created the term *mindfulness* **to refer to a cultivated perspective in which people are sensitive to context and focused on the present.** People in a state of mindfulness notice novel features and readily attend to them, just as they draw novel distinctions in what they see. According to Langer (2002), to become more mindful people need to (1) resist the impulse to reduce or control the uncertainty found in daily living; (2) become less prone to evaluate themselves, others, and the situations they encounter; and (3) try to override their propensity to perform automatic (sometimes referred to as "stereotyped" or "scripted") behavior. To Langer, mindfulness "is a flexible state of mind—an openness to novelty, a process of actively drawing novel distinctions" (p. 214).

Mindfulness has been found to promote or enhance well-being in a variety of situations. In classroom settings, for example, mindfulness can improve student learning (Ritchart & Perkins, 2002), including helping young girls overcome gender differences when learning math (Anglin, Pirson, & Langer, 2008). Mindful practices have enabled musicians to play pieces that are more pleasurable for their audiences (Langer, Russell, & Eisenkraft, 2009) and allowed individuals to learn to regulate their heartbeats (Delizonna, Williams, & Langer, 2009). People in mindfully-based marriages are more satisfied (Burpee & Langer, 2005), and a mindful perspective can even reduce the tendency to use aging stereotypes (Djikie, Langer, & Stapleton, 2008).

Ellen J. Langer

One way to understand these benefits associated with mindfulness is to compare and contrast it with its problematic counterpart, mindlessness. Langer (1998) argues that people slip into a state of *mindlessness* **by engaging in rote behavior—performing familiar, scripted actions without much cognition, as if on autopilot** (e.g., Langer, 1990). In essence, when individuals are mindless, they are not doing much active thinking. Sometimes, of course, mindlessness can be adaptive; it frees up conscious attention and awareness when a task is familiar. Think back to when you learned to drive a car and how you had to pay rapt attention to what you were doing; by comparison, driving is likely to be a veritable breeze now. There is a down side to such mindless adaptation, however; you miss a great deal of information when you behave mindlessly. Sudden changes and novelties that appear in the environment are overlooked, for example, as are fine details. When driving mindlessly, you might miss a stop sign and drive right through it (or you might hit the car that stopped suddenly in front of you because you never saw it slow down). So, there are potential costs when attention and awareness are too free or loose. It's almost as if one is not really "there" to mentally follow what's happening. People are much better off when they take note of new information whatever the context happens to be.

Practically speaking, how can you become more mindful? You can do so by treating the facts you learn as conditional—that is, as linked to one and not necessarily other situations (cultivating a fresh perspective on experiences). Researchers who study mindfulness suggest there is another way: becoming aware of novelty and creating new distinctions by using *meditation*, or the disciplined, continuous, and focused contemplation of some subject or object (see Chapter 4). With regular meditation, people learn to train and direct their attention in nonanalytical and unemotional ways, subsequently becoming more mindful as a result (Marchand, 2012; Shapiro & Carlson, 2009; Shapiro, Schwartz, & Santerre, 2002). For example, Kabat-Zinn (1982) used Eastern meditative practices coupled with knowledge of mindfulness research to create a 10-week *mindfulness meditation* program that successfully reduced chronic pain and mood disturbances in a group of fifty-one patients (see also Kabat-Zinn, 1990, 1993; Shapiro, Schwartz, & Bonner, 1998). There is even some intriguing evidence that people who engage in mindfulness meditation are perceived to be happier by observers (Choi, Karremans, & Barendregt, 2012).

Shapiro, Schwartz, and Santerre (2002) suggest that when people experience moments of mindfulness,

some related qualities of this psychological state enter their consciousness. Some of these mindfulness qualities are shown in **Figure 16.8**. Note how well many of these qualities match up with the overall focus and goals of positive psychology. If you were to take up mindfulness meditation, which qualities would you hope to achieve or experience as a result?

If mindfulness meditation does not seem to be a likely course of action for you anytime soon, there is a simpler way for you to increase your attention, reduce your stress, and improve your subjective well-being: Go outside and experience nature. Recent research suggests that spending even a modest amount of time in natural surroundings—the forest or woods, a park, perhaps a garden—has restorative effects that make people more cognitively attentive and function better emotionally (Berman et al., 2012;

SOME QUALITIES ASSOCIATED WITH MINDFULNESS MEDITATION	
Quality	**Description**
Nonjudging	Impartial witnessing, observing the present moment by moment without explanation and categorization
Acceptance	Open to seeing things as they really are in the present moment with a clear understanding
Loving kindness	Being benevolent, compassionate, and forgiving, and demonstrating unconditional love
Patience	Allowing things to unfold in their time, bringing patience to oneself, to others, and to the present moment
Openness	Seeing things as if for the first time, creating possibility by paying attention to all feedback in the present moment
Nonstriving	Non-goal oriented, remaining unattached to outcome or achievement, not forcing things
Trust	Trusting the self, as well as one's body, intuitions, and emotions, and that life is unfolding as it is supposed to
Gentleness	Having a soft, tender, and considerate quality, but neither passive nor undisciplined
Gratitude	The quality of reverence, appreciating and being thankful for the present moment
Empathy	The quality of both feeling and understanding the situation of another person in the present time; communicating knowledge of the person's state to the person
Generosity	Giving in the present moment within a context of love and compassion, without attachment to gain or thought of return
Letting go	Demonstrating nonattachment or holding on to feelings, thoughts, or experiences; letting go does not refer to suppressing these states

Figure 16.8

Some qualities associated with mindfulness meditation. People who learn mindfulness meditation can expect to derive some benefits from the activity. As you can see, the qualities listed here fit well with established themes in positive psychology.

Source: Adapted from Shapiro, S. J., Schwartz, G. E. R., & Santerre, C. (2002). Meditation and positive psychology. In C. R. Snyder & S. J. Lopez (Eds.), *The handbook of positive psychology* (pp. 63–645). New York: Oxford University Press.

Encountering nature provides restorative benefits, including enhanced attention, lowered stress, and improved emotional function.

Berto, 2005; Hartig et al., 2003; Kaplan, 2001; Price, 2008b). In one study, for example, nineteen undergraduates spent half an hour walking around an arboretum near the University of Michigan's campus, while an equal number of students ambled around downtown Ann Arbor (Berman, Jonides, & Kaplan, 2008). When everyone returned to the lab to complete a battery of stress and short-term memory measures, the researchers found that the individuals who strolled in the arboretum had lower stress levels and heightened attention compared to the control group who ventured downtown. The explanation is that natural environments are much less mentally taxing than urban settings. Intuitively, individuals know that green and leafy settings are peaceful places that encourage them to relax and renew themselves. In contrast, even medium-sized cities are full of noise and busy distractions made by cars, buses, people, sirens, and the like. A second study found similar (though somewhat weaker) results by having participants look at slides of either nature scenes or cityscapes (Berman, Jonides, & Kaplan, 2008). One implication of

this second study is that hanging pictures of nature scenes indoors is a way to promote restorative effects on a modest but still helpful scale when going to a park or other green space is not always possible.

So, when the transcendentalist and author of *Walden* Henry David Thoreau (1817–1862) observed that "in wildness is the preservation of the world," he may well have been speaking of people's mental and emotional worlds. The implications of Berman and colleagues' (2008) results are clear: When you can, you should try to revitalize your heart and mind by enjoying nature and the great outdoors. Taking what we might call a "pastoral break" by going outside or even just looking at images of nature in picture hanging on the wall or in books or magazines will restore you intellectually, physically, and emotionally. These findings also have important implications for the design of cities, towns, or any urban public space: It should be done mindfully. Adding natural elements—trees, water, rocks, plants—provides benefits besides just beauty (Kaplan & Kaplan, 1989; Tennessen & Cimprich, 1995). Not only is the eye entertained; apparently so are the mind and the spirit.

Savoring: Deliberately Making Pleasures Last

How often do people slow down enough to really reflect on what they are doing and experiencing at that moment in time? Why don't people savor more of their daily experiences?

Savoring is a new concept in positive psychology but, as you will see, it has an excellent conceptual fit with the field and its goals. Psychologically, the term *savoring* **refers the power to focus on, value, and even boost the enjoyment of almost any experience, whether great or small** (Bryant & Veroff, 2007). To savor is to enjoy subjective states related to some current experience, one rooted in process and not outcome; the journey, if you will, is more important than arriving at the destination. You can savor a good, strong cup of coffee, a well-performed piece of music, or even the red, orange, and yellow foliage of autumn in New England. Researchers who study when and how people go about savoring their experiences claim it is an active process. Savoring is more than mere pleasure or the enjoyment of something or some activity. When you savor reading a book or watching a play or film, for example, a reflective quality is involved: Whether reader or viewer, you must attend to and consciously appreciate what is engaging your attention.

What factors affect the intensity of savoring? Bryant and Veroff (2007) suggest several, including:

1. *Duration.* The more time available for the experience, the greater the chance to savor it. Dedicated time like that reserved for exercise or socializing should be set aside for enjoying particular pleasures.

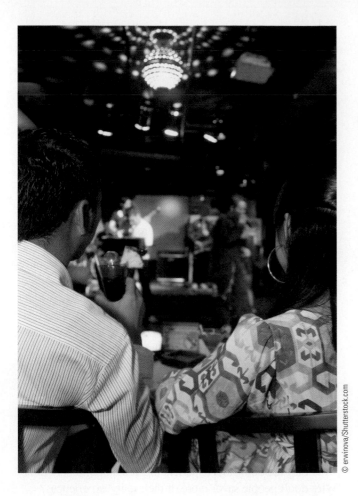
© erwinova/Shutterstock.com

in a subject—can experience more complex savoring when encountering a stimulus than can neophytes. Expert coffee, wine, or tea tasters, for instance, are likely to savor particular examples of these beverages more than the rest of us.

4. *Balanced self-monitoring.* If you think too much about what you are doing or if you become too self-focused, you can distort your ability to savor an experience.

5. *Social connection.* You might believe that savoring is a solitary pursuit. However, research reveals that savoring is that much more pleasurable if you have other people with whom to share the experience. Concerts, for example, are more enjoyable if you attend with a friend. But what about strangers—can you savor an experience with them? Bryant and Veroff (2007) give an example reported by the writer Frances Mayes, author of *Under the Tuscan Sun* (1996), who has long reflected on the special pleasures of her part-time life in Tuscany, Italy. In the following excerpt, she describes happening on several rainbows surrounding a local church:

Fog completely surrounds the church, and the dome floats above the clouds. Five intersecting rainbows dive and arch around the dome. I almost run off the road. At a curve I stop and get out, wishing everyone were with me. This is staggering. If it were the Middle Ages, I'd claim a miracle. Another car stops and a man dressed in fancy hunting clothes jumps out . . . he, too, looks stunned. We both just stare. As the clouds shift, the rainbows disappear one by one, but the dome still drifts, ready for any sign that might be about to happen. I wave to the hunter. "Auguri" [an Italian expression of good will, best wishes, and good luck] he calls. (pp. 218–219)

So, make time to savor the pleasures you encounter in your life. Research suggests that you may reduce depressive symptoms and negative emotions (Hurley & Kwon, 2012) and that you will be a happier, more relaxed person if you do (Jose, Lim, & Bryant, 2012).

2. *Stress reduction.* When distracting stress departs (you stop dwelling on all the homework you have to do over the weekend), savoring becomes possible (you can enjoy spending Friday evening with friends).

3. *Complexity.* More complex experiences produce greater quality and intensity of savoring. Examining a detailed work of art, such as an intricate painting, can lead to more sustained delight than perusing a simple drawing. It follows that experts—individuals with deep knowledge

POSITIVE INDIVIDUAL TRAITS

LEARNING OBJECTIVES

- Explain the concept of positive individual traits.
- Define hope, resilience, posttraumatic growth, and grit as beneficial qualities.
- Clarify why gratitude is a character strength and spirituality is a positive trait related to religious behavior.

Whereas subjective states account for people's positive feelings, *positive individual traits* **are dispositional qualities that account for why some people are happier and psychologically healthier than others.** Traits sway the interpretations people use to find meaning in events, influence their choices, help them select goals, and ultimately

drive what they do behaviorally. Think about someone you know who gets along well with other people. The fact that you see this person as being highly agreeable or cooperative represents what psychologists call a *trait*, an individual difference that makes your friend stand out from your other acquaintances (see Chapter 2). Another friend of yours might come across as reliable—that is, very organized and high in self-control, someone who takes few risks and works rather deliberately to achieve particular ends. An important quality of positive traits like these two is the assumption that they can be taught (Peterson & Seligman, 2004). Positive traits can also emerge as a response or reaction to life situations people experience. Here we discuss five examples of positive individual traits: hope, resilience, grit, gratitude, and spirituality.

Hope: Achieving Future Goals

Just as traits can explain much of what people do in the present, they can also predict how people will act in the future. Positive psychology is keenly interested in positive individual traits that encourage people to anticipate good rather than bad outcomes. Consider *hope,* **which refers to people's expectations that their goals can be achieved in the future** (Snyder, 1994). People become more excited by goals they can actually achieve than those that seem to be out of reach or too much of a challenge. Given its future directedness, hope is related to optimism, which is discussed in Chapters 3 and 5.

Doug Koch/KU University Relations

C. R. ("Rick") Snyder

The late C. R. Snyder (1994, 2002), a social and clinical psychologist, argued that these goal-directed expectations have two components: agency and pathways. *Agency* involves a person's judgment that his or her goals can be achieved. For example, a college student might determine whether obtaining a high grade in a required course in her major is possible. In other words, does Sarah expect that she can obtain the desired grade because she possesses the necessary drive or organizational skills? Agency, then, represents one's motivation to seek desired goals, and it appears to be linked with life satisfaction (Bailey et al., 2007). The second component in Snyder's theory, *pathways,* refers to Sarah's beliefs that successful plans can be crafted to reach the goal of a high grade. Pathways represent the realistic roadmap to achieving the goal. Note that a hopeful view would identify several paths to the goal (more hours of study, completing assigned readings in advance, faithfully attending class, doing homework, and so on), not merely one (Rand & Cheavens, 2009). A person's pathways complement his or her agency by serving as what Snyder (1994) called "waypower."

Snyder and colleagues (1991) developed the Trait Hope Scale to assess both agency and pathways (see **Figure 16.9**). Respondents rate how true each statement on the scale appears to be for them. A summary score of the agency and pathway items indicates a person's degree of hope (scores can range between 8 and 64; see **Figure 16.9**).

Separate scales also measure state hope (how a person feels at a single moment in time) (Snyder et al., 1996) and children's hope (Snyder et al.,1997), as well.

Why should anyone try to be a hopeful person? For several reasons, actually (Snyder, Rand, & Sigmon, 2002). Not surprisingly, hopeful people experience more positive emotions than those who have a more despairing outlook, and, as we have discussed, such emotions can be beneficial for a variety of reasons. Individuals who have hope expect to be better off in the future, just as they believe they will be better prepared than others to deal with any stressful circumstances that arise. Why might this be the case? Hopeful people are likely to be flexible thinkers, always on

A MEASURE OF HOPE AS A TRAIT

Read each item carefully. Using the scale shown below, please select the number that best describes YOU and put that number in the blank provided.

1 = Definitely false	5 = Slightly true
2 = Mostly false	6 = Somewhat true
3 = Somewhat false	7 = Mostly true
4 = Slightly false	8 = Definitely true

_____ **1.** I can think of many ways to get out of a jam.

_____ **2.** I energetically pursue my goals.

_____ **3.** I feel tired most of the time.

_____ **4.** There are lots of ways around any problem.

_____ **5.** I am easily downed in an argument.

_____ **6.** I can think of many ways to get the things in life that are important to me.

_____ **7.** I worry about my health.

_____ **8.** Even when others get discouraged, I know I can find a way to solve the problem.

_____ **9.** My past experiences have prepared me well for my future.

_____ **10.** I've been pretty successful in life.

_____ **11.** I usually find myself worrying about something.

_____ **12.** I meet the goals I set for myself.

Figure 16.9

Snyder's Trait Hope Scale. According to C. R. Snyder, as a trait, hope has two characteristics: agency and pathways. To determine your Agency subscale score, add items 2, 9, 10, and 12; your Pathways subscale score is derived by adding items 1, 4, 6, and 8. The total Hope Scale Score is the total of the four Agency and the four Pathway items. A higher total score reflects a greater degree of hope for the future. Scores can range from 8 to 64. In six samples of college students studied by Snyder et al. (1991), the average score was 25.

Source: From Snyder, C. R., Harris, C., Anderson, J. R., Holeran, S. A., Irving, L. M., Sigmon, S. T., Yoshinobu, L., Gibb, J., Langelle, C., & Harney, P. (1991). The will and the ways: Development and validation of an individual-differences measure of hope. *Journal of Personality and Social Psychology, 60,* 570–585.

the lookout for alternative pathways to attain their goals or to get around obstacles. They are also likely to be buoyed up by the positive social support they receive from those who are drawn to their encouraging, upbeat natures (Snyder, Rand & Sigmon, 2002).

Resilience: Reacting Well to Life's Challenges

Another important positive trait is *resilience,* **a person's ability to recover and often prosper following some consequential life event.** Such events are often traumatic—an accident, loss, or catastrophe causes an individual to confront and cope with a situation that can leave psychological scars. Resilient people cope with threats, maintaining, recovering, or even improving mental and physical health in the process of doing so (Masten, 2001; Ryff & Singer, 2003).

Resilience research examines a variety of tumultuous events, including how people deal with threats such as natural disasters, war, divorce, alcoholism and mental illness in parents, family violence, the demands of single parenting, and, of course, the loss of a loved one (Bonanno, 2009; Masten & Reed, 2002; Ryff & Singer, 2003). These threats range from extreme but rare events (war) to those that are tragically commonplace (family problems). Whatever its qualities, the threat is usually so severe and potentially damaging, if not life threatening, that most observers would expect negative rather than positive outcomes. Yet in spite of these traumatic "perfect storms," some people persevere and emerge psychologically resilient.

For example, imagine the future lives of children who are raised in abusive or neglectful households or in communities wracked by poverty, illness, and disease. Individuals born into such environments are said to be at higher risk than others for various mental, physical, social, and economic problems (Masten & Reed, 2002). Would anyone predict that children reared in such settings would eventually thrive and lead productive and happy lives? The surprising reality is that the resilient ones do (e.g., Garmezy, 1991; Masten & Coatsworth, 1998). Interestingly, resilience is not usually recognized by those who have it until they are called on to display it once a trauma occurs. Fortunately, resilience appears to be a relatively common trait among humans, including young children, and it may well emerge in reaction to everyday situations of stress and coping (DiCorcia & Tronick, 2011).

The good news is that a resilient outlook can be cultivated by anyone, as it is not a trait but a way of coping with adverse situations. Indeed, each person can be resilient in a different way. **Figure 16.10** lists ten factors that are believed to be important when cultivating resilience. How many of them do you already incorporate into your life? Which of the others can you learn?

In addition to resilience, some people display growth following a trauma such as an accident, a serious illness, or the onset of a disability. *Posttraumatic growth* **refers to enhanced personal strength, realization of what is truly important in life, and increased appreciation for life, friends, and family following trauma.** Posttraumatic growth provides empirical evidence that sometimes personal suffering can pave the way to positive insights (Davis & Nolen-Hoeksema, 2009; Groleau et al., 2012; Lechner, Tennen, & Affleck, 2009). Whereas resilience can help people rebound to their pretrauma levels, posttraumatic growth implies that people can also psychologically exceed those original levels by displaying enhanced functioning and positive changes. In fact, a surprising number of people actually claim that trauma "was the best thing that ever happened" to them (Park, 1998).

Figure 16.11 lists a variety of positive changes that are attributed to posttraumatic growth as grounded in the available research (Ryff & Singer, 2003; Tedeschi, Park, & Calhoun, 1998). As you can see, these changes can be categorized as being perceptual, relationship based, or a life priority. Advocates of positive psychology have helped reduce the skepticism associated with claims of posttraumatic growth and related coping strategies. Although verifying documented positive growth can be difficult, psychologists are now less likely to simply assume such change is due to

TEN WAYS TO CULTIVATE RESILIENCE
1. Foster connections with family members, friends, and people in the community.
2. Try not to catastrophize when a crisis happens; don't see an event as insurmountable.
3. Realize and accept that change is a part of life.
4. Move forward towards your goals.
5. Whenever possible be decisive but rely on problem-and-task-focused coping strategies.
6. Keep on the lookout for opportunities for self-discovery.
7. Develop and maintain a positive view of yourself.
8. Keep events, especially troubling ones, in perspective.
9. Maintain a hopeful outlook.
10. Take good care of yourself, paying special attention to your needs and feelings.

Figure 16.10

Ten ways to cultivate resilience. There are concrete things you can do in your life to develop resilience. The key is to select those that are likely to work well for you.

Source: http://www.apa.org/helpcenter/road-resilience.aspx

ASPECTS OF POSTTRAUMATIC GROWTH
Perceptual changes
Self is perceived as a survivor and not a victim
Increased feelings of personal strength, self-reliance, and self-confidence
Enhanced appreciation for life's fragile nature, including one's own
Relationship changes
Increases compassion for and willingness to give to others
Closer bonds with family
Feelings of closeness with others and greater willingness to disclose emotions
Life priority changes
Reduced concern with possessions, money, and social status
Greater willingness to take life easier
Enhanced clarity regarding what really matters in life
A deeper and more spiritual sense of the meaning of life

Figure 16.11

Positive changes attributed to posttraumatic growth. After experiencing a trauma, some people respond by exhibiting positive changes that generally fall into three areas: perceptual changes, relationship changes, and life priority changes. This figure illustrates examples of growth within each area.

Source: Adapted from Baumgardner, S. R., & Crothers, M. K. (2009). *Positive psychology.* Upper Saddle River, NJ: Prentice-Hall. Reproduced by permission of Pearson Education, Inc.

convenient rationalization, factual distortion, or unfounded self-report (Lechner, Tennen, & Affleck, 2009).

Grit: Harnessing Effort over the Long Term

What makes some people try harder to succeed at challenges than others? Casual observation reveals that some people are apt to accomplish more than others, even when both have equal levels of intelligence. Positive psychologist Angela Duckworth and her colleagues (2007) propose

"He appears to have lost all of his resilience."

Arnie Levin/The New Yorker Collection/www.cartoonbank.com

that some people have higher levels of a noncognitive trait they refer to as grit. **Grit is defined as possessing perseverance and passion for achieving long-term goals.** People who have higher levels of grit are apt to demonstrate serious effort and attention to accomplishing a goal despite setbacks, adversity, and slow-downs that impede their progress. According to Duckworth and colleagues, "The gritty individual approaches achievement as a marathon; his or her advantage is stamina" (p. 1088).

Duckworth and colleagues developed the Grit Scale to measure individual differences in grit (see **Figure 16.12** on the next page). How gritty are you? Why not complete the scale to find out? Note that a briefer version of the scale, the Short Grit Scale (GRIT-S), was developed by Duckworth and Quinn (2009) and yields the same results.

How does grit affect people's behavioral success? In one study, Duckworth and colleagues (2007) examined whether grit predicted the grade point averages (GPAs) of students attending an elite university. A group of 139 men and women completed the Grit Scale and reported their GPAs. As expected, gritty students had significantly higher GPAs than their less gritty counterparts. Another study explored grit's impact on the performance of child finalists in the 2005 Scripps National Spelling Bee. Duckworth and colleagues had the finalists complete the Grit Scale and other measures before the spelling competition began. They found that grittiness predicted who advanced to higher rounds in the competition. Why did those high on grit do so well in concrete terms? Gritty contestants were apt to stay in the competition longer because they studied longer, a factor attesting to their drive and stamina. The grittiest spellers were not necessarily the smartest or best spellers—they just stuck with and worked harder at preparing for the spelling bee.

Other researchers have explored how having grit propels people forward to achieve their goals (MacCann & Roberts, 2010; Maddi et al., 2012; Tough, 2012). Can grit be learned? That is, can individuals who have displayed less drive toward achieving long-term goals develop the grit to see them

THE GRIT SCALE

Please respond to the following 12 items using the below scale. Be honest—there are no right or wrong answers!

5 = Very much like me

4 = Mostly like me

3 = Somewhat like me

2 = Not much like me

1 = Not like me at all

_____ 1. I have overcome setbacks to conquer an important challenge.

_____ 2. New ideas and projects sometimes distract me from previous ones.*

_____ 3. My interests change from year to year.*

_____ 4. Setbacks don't discourage me.

_____ 5. I have been obsessed with a certain idea or project for a short time but later lost interest.*

_____ 6. I am a hard worker.

_____ 7. I often set a goal but later choose to pursue a different one.*

_____ 8. I have difficulty maintaining my focus on projects that take more than a few months to complete.*

_____ 9. I finish whatever I begin.

_____ 10. I have achieved a goal that took years of work.

_____ 11. I have become interested in new pursuits every few months.*

_____ 12. I am diligent.

Figure 16.12

Predicting who stays with a challenging course: The Grit Scale. According to Duckworth and colleagues (2007), higher levels of grit—the desire to persevere and have a passion for achieving long-term goals—enable some people to work harder and possess more stamina than others. To determine how gritty you are, score questions 1, 4, 6, 9, 10, and 12 using the scale values provided. Use reverse scoring for questions 2, 3, 5, 7, 8, and 11, as indicated by the *. If you assigned the item a score of 5, change it to 1; if you said 4, change it to 2; 3 remains 3; 2 becomes 4; and 1 becomes 5. After the conversion, add up all the points and divide by 12. The maximum score on this scale is 5 (extremely gritty), and the lowest score is 1 (not at all gritty).

Source: Page 1090 in Duckworth, A. L., Peterson, C., Matthews, M. D., & Kelly, D. R. (2007). Grit: Perseverance and passion for long-term goals. *Journal of Personality and Social Psychology, 92*(6), 1087–1101. doi:10.1037/0022-3514.92.6.1087

through? Duckworth believes the answer is yes, that grit may be a trait that can be changed, because its elements, such as self-discipline, can be developed (Hanford, 2012).

Gratitude: The Power of Being Thankful

One of the most promising positive individual traits that is receiving considerable research attention is gratitude, or

being grateful for what you have or others have done for you. As a human strength, *gratitude* **entails recognizing and concentrating on the good things in one's life and being thankful for them.** Gratitude is often considered within a moral context. In fact, being ungrateful—that is, expressing *in*gratitude—is considered to be a vice (Bono, Emmons, & McCullough, 2004). Yet experiencing gratitude (being thankful) and expressing it (thanking someone for being gracious to you) are among the most common ways to experience this beneficial, positive emotion (Emmons, 2005; Emmons & McCullough, 2004).

What are the psychosocial consequences of expressing gratitude? As might be expected, doing so enhances social connections with others: When people do nice things, they appreciate being thanked. More than that, however, expressing gratitude appears to extend the time people feel positive emotions linked to being thankful. Where negative affect tends to linger, positive moods tend to be shorter (Larsen & Prizmic, 2008). Besides benefiting others, conveying gratitude benefits the self, too. Feelings of gratitude make one feel happy, at times joyful, and can be a source of contentment (Emmons & McCullough, 2004; Watkins, Van Gelder, & Frias, 2009; Wood, Froh, & Geraghty, 2010). Experimental research also indicates that focusing on things to be thankful for improves people's moods, triggers coping behaviors, and motivates people to report experiencing health benefits (Emmons & McCullough, 2003; Sheldon & Lyubomirsky, 2006). Finally, when gratitude is treated as a personality trait, people who report being more thankful also tend to report higher levels of psychological well-being than less-appreciative others (Watkins et al., 2003).

Perhaps the best part of gratitude is that it is so easy to express, and, as a virtue, it can be performed almost anytime or anywhere. So, the next time someone does something nice for you, whether great or small, be sure to acknowledge the help or kindness by saying "Thank you" and expressing your appreciation in greater detail. Both you and your recipient will benefit psychologically from your simple act (see the Application section of this chapter for a gratitude-related exercise).

Spirituality: Seeking a Deeper Meaning

Some people are moved to question whether life has a deeper meaning than is apparent in daily experience. People who have the positive individual trait of spirituality possess a belief that life has transcendent or nonphysical qualities that are worth seeking and exploring (Pargament & Mahoney, 2002; Peterson & Seligman, 2004). Thus, spiritual individuals have a strong desire to search for the sacred (Pargament & Mahoney, 2009) and usually think of themselves as religious (Zinnebauer & Pargament, 2005; Zinnebauer et al., 1997). Although the terms are often used

People engage in religious activities to promote spirituality, which can lead to deeper meaning in daily life.

interchangeably, religion (or religiosity) and spirituality are distinct, albeit overlapping concepts. *Religion* refers primarily to what people do in a religious community (church, synagogue, temple, mosque), whereas *spirituality* refers to the human need for a deeper meaning that often motivates and guides religious behaviors. Religious behaviors are normally bound to the beliefs and rituals of some specific, formal religious institution (Zinnebauer, Pargament, & Scott, 1999).

Positive psychologists are interested in religion because participating in a religious community appears to enhance well-being (Myers, 2000a, 2008; Peterson & Seligman, 2004) and coping (Pargament, 2011). For example, people who engage in more religiously based activities (attending worship services, doing charity work) are generally mentally and physically healthier than others (Koenig, McCullough, & Larson, 2001). The more religious practice they engage in, the higher the rate of well-being and the lower the rates of alcohol and drug problems, criminal behavior, and other societal ills (Donahue & Benson, 1995; Myers, 1992, 2000b). Religious individuals also report fewer health problems, had lower rates of heart attacks and cancer, recover more quickly from surgery, and display higher levels of pain tolerance (George et al., 2000). They have even been found to live an average of 7 years longer than those who are less religious (Oman & Thoresen, 2005).

Does religion per se provide these psychological and physical benefits? Not all forms of religious behavior are apt to be helpful; indeed, some actually prove to be detrimental (Raiya, Pargament, & Magyar-Russell, 2010). Aside from faith alone, however, the social connections religious individuals form with others may discourage problematic or risky behaviors (George et al., 2000). Religion probably affects mental and physical health and well-being for a variety of reasons, including the social support

from like-minded others (Hill & Pargament, 2003) and the promotion of a healthier lifestyle (Emmons, 1999; Myers, 2000a). Religious individuals also tend to have higher levels of optimism, a trait that affects behaviors linked to well-being (Koenig & Cohen, 2002).

In contrast to organized religious practice, spirituality encompasses the human need for finding meaning in life and the assumption that such meaning involves something larger than the self or one's own existence (Zinnebauer, Pargament, & Scott, 1999). When psychologists talk about *meaning* in this context, they are referring to the ways in which people experience "perceptions of significance" (Park & Folkman, 1997, p. 116). From this perspective, when people search for or find meaning, they do so in ways that indicate that life is both significant and contains significance for them. Finding such meaning and significance can provide coherence and order to people's experiences (Park & Folkman, 1997; Yalom, 1980). According to Pargament and Mahoney (2009), "to envision, seek, connect, and hold onto, and transform the sacred may be what makes us uniquely human" (p. 616).

Let's consider a particular example of spirituality, one rooted in Eastern religion and philosophy: Buddhism. Buddhism is of interest to some positive psychologists because it offers some intriguing insights concerning the human pursuit of happiness and pleasure (Compton, 2005; Haidt, 2006; Keltner, 2009). To begin, Buddhists emphasize one truth: Life is ever changing. No matter what you do, you and the world around you will change. You, as well as your friends and family, were born; you will all grow old and, in time, die. These sobering changes represent a pure form of truth. Your response to this state of affairs is to attempt to control change by seeking security, finding things that are permanent, and trying to manage your worry (if not despair) by keeping things as stable and predictable as possible.

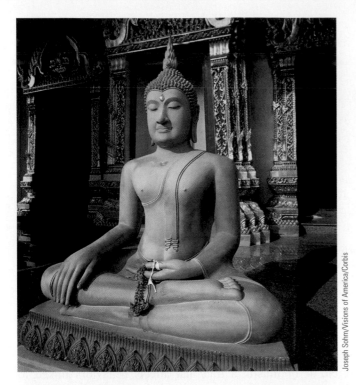

Positive psychologists are interested in Buddhism because it promotes awareness of life's challenges and encourages detachment from them.

The desire for a safe, permanent state of affairs is ill-founded; according to Buddhist doctrine, the belief that all will be well if only this state is reached is foolish. Change is inevitable, and still more change will follow. To Buddhists, this truth makes humans "suffer," as does the never-ending search for comfort and security. And one will suffer as changes come to pass. In actuality, life is really about seeking illusory security while experiencing inevitable suffering.

The way out of this suffering is to stop trying to control what cannot be controlled by accepting life's changes as routine and absolute. But how can this way of viewing life be achieved? Buddhism advocates embracing and developing two skills: awareness and detachment. Becoming more aware means increasing one's focus on everyday experiences in order to look for and find the sacred in the mundane. At the same time, by becoming "detached" from these experiences, people can release or "let go" of their desire to control what cannot be controlled so that change is allowed to occur in an unhindered fashion. By being both aware and detached, one can become more relaxed and accepting of one's life as it unfolds. Perhaps contentment is possible if people cease their struggles to make things as they wish and instead become conscious of the happiness present in every changing moment.

POSITIVE INSTITUTIONS

LEARNING OBJECTIVES

- Characterize the nature of positive institutions.
- Describe the characteristics of positive workplaces and positive schools, and identify some virtues associated with positive institutions.

Positive subjective experiences and positive individual traits both focus on and benefit the individual. What does positive psychology have to offer the community? Broader than the other two areas of inquiry, the third defining area of positive psychology encompasses the group level of analysis by examining positive institutions. *Positive institutions* **are those organizations that cultivate civic virtues, encouraging people to behave like good citizens while promoting the collective good.** Positive institutions, which include workplaces, schools, families, and organizations help build and maintain a beneficial society in which to live (Huang & Blumenthal, 2009). What qualities are fostered by positive institutions? When positive psychological socialization occurs, people who pass through and learn from positive institutions are focused on being nurturing, altruistic, tolerant, and responsible. Individuals who "graduate" from positive institutions tend to have a good work ethic.

Positive Workplaces

Some positive psychologists are interested in developing and maintaining organizations that provide a pleasant workplace and allow workers to thrive (Cameron, Dutton, & Quinn, 2003; Luthans & Youssef, 2009; Wright, 2003). In fact, a new movement known as *positive organizational behavior (POB)* is dedicated to studying beneficial human strengths and competencies and how they can be advanced, evaluated, and managed as a means to improve worker performance in businesses and organizations (Nelson & Cooper, 2007).

REEL RESEARCH

Positive Institutions and Volunteering

Log on to CourseMate at www.cengagebrain.com to watch this video.

© Cengage Learning 2015

© Cengage Learning 2015

One way to experience the benefits of working for a positive institution is to participate in a volunteer program. Mark Snyder, social psychologist at the University of Minnesota, studies the motivations behind volunteerism and describes it as an intriguing form of helping. Snyder and long-term volunteers discuss the reasons behind and benefits of volunteerism in this Reel Research video.

Volunteerism can be short or long term. Claudia and other bankers from Wells Fargo spent a day building houses with Habitat for Humanity, but this isn't Claudia's first time volunteering. She has already spent 30 years of her life volunteering for various organizations and often serves food at a homeless shelter with her family. Toni and Helen spend their time with Meals on Wheels, bringing food to those who cannot provide for themselves. Helen has been with the program for a year and a half, while Toni has been volunteering for 30 years. All of these people have volunteered 3 to 5 hours per week for most of the year, often for the majority of their lives.

Snyder explains the various motivations behind volunteerism, including familial or social influence, wanting to give back to the community, and—most important—benefiting oneself in some way. Among those who volunteer over a sustained period of time, Snyder found that volunteers benefited from their service in a number of ways, from furthering their career to learning new skills, making new friends, and improving self-esteem. Many volunteers share their experiences with others in their social network and promote a positive view of volunteerism, motivating their friends and family to participate. Also, participants build relationships with fellow volunteers and the people they serve. However, becoming a volunteer that services stigmatized groups, like those suffering from AIDS, can be challenging for others to accept. Snyder urges that future research determine how volunteerism affects the mental and physical health and well-being of the volunteer.

Watch the *Positive Institutions and Volunteering* video to learn more about why people volunteer. Delve even deeper by responding to the following discussion questions.

DISCUSSION QUESTIONS

1. Snyder explains the relationship between motivation behind volunteerism and actual volunteer experience. How do the relationships discussed predict whether a participant will be satisfied about his or her volunteer work? What do the relationships say about long- or short-term involvement?

2. Snyder describes individuals who volunteer long term. What relationships do they foster? Who benefits from performance of the service? Explain your answers.

3. Have you volunteered? If so, how did you become involved (chose to volunteer, volunteered with work group)? How long were you involved? If not, explain the reasons you have not volunteered and whether or not you would.

Within POB, there is a related emphasis on supporting organizational accomplishments and development of individuals by improving the quality of the relationships between co-workers (Harter, 2008; Luthans, Youssef, & Avolio, 2007).

A good way to think about the sorts of careers that positive organizations or workplaces spawn is by thinking about the distinction between a job and a calling. While studying people who worked in jobs ranging from clerical to professional, Wrzesniewski et al. (1997) found that workers viewed their chosen occupations in one of three ways.

- *Just a "job."* Money is necessary for survival, so work is done for pay. Individuals with this view often think of themselves as primary providers for their families.
- *A career.* Work satisfies this second group's desire and need to achieve, compete, and acquire status or prestige. Personal pride is clearly at stake here as well.
- *A "calling."* The third group view their work as a means for personal fulfillment and social purpose. They see their work as service to themselves as well as to other people. Thus, work becomes a form of community service while providing a sense of personal fulfillment.

Try putting these distinctions in more personal terms for yourself: Will you seek work that simply satisfies financial necessity (paying bills, providing security), or do you aspire to work that is personally fulfilling or even that "gives back" to your community?

Positive Schools

Most research on schools and the students' experiences within them has focused on the negative, emphasizing what is wrong with educational efforts (Snyder & Lopez, 2007). Recently, however, some psychologists have begun to focus on what they call school satisfaction, or students' judgments about their holistic school experiences (Huebner et al., 2009). As a psychological construct representing individual differences, *school satisfaction* is composed of both cognition (what students believe regarding educational experiences) and affect (students' reported frequency of positive and negative emotions in educational settings).

Thus far, a few findings regarding school satisfaction have emerged. First, school satisfaction is a good predictor of student engagement and academic progress as early as kindergarten (Ladd, Buhs, & Seid, 2000). Students who are high in school satisfaction tend to have higher GPAs than other students, as well as fewer reported psychological symptoms and a heightened sense of agency (Huebner & Gilman, 2006). It may come as no surprise that students

who are more engaged and performing well academically are also less likely to display adolescent problem behaviors (DeSantis et al., 2006). Thus, school satisfaction appears to be a promising and positive variable for the study of positive academic achievement in schools.

Virtuous Institutions?

Can positive institutions be like people? That is, can institutions both possess and promote positive virtues? Peterson (2006) notes that qualities that are intrinsically good can be found in everyday institutions like those we discussed in this section, as well as clubs, sports teams, government agencies, and organizations found throughout society. **Figure 16.13** lists the virtues that Peterson suggests

Positive schools promote student satisfaction, which is linked with student engagement and academic progress.

THE VIRTUES OF POSITIVE INSTITUTIONS	
Virtue	Description
Purpose	The institution provides a shared vision of the moral goals promoted by the institution; these goals are routinely remembered and celebrated.
Fairness	Rules exist and are known; rewards and punishments are administered consistently.
Humanity	The institution cares for its members, and vice versa.
Safety	The institution protects its members from threats, dangers, and exploitation.
Dignity	No matter what their status, all members of the institution are treated with respect.

Figure 16.13

Virtues found in positive institutions. Positive institutions are thought to offer a variety of benefits to the individuals who work within them, as well as to the communities in which they reside. This figure lists some of the basic virtues of such institutions. Can you think of any others?

Source: Adapted from Peterson, C. (2006). *A primer in positive psychology.* New York: Oxford University Press.

make institutions positive contributors to people's lives. As you examine the figure, think about the institutions you come into contact with regularly: How many of them display or enact these virtues?

POSITIVE PSYCHOLOGY: PROBLEMS AND PROSPECTS

LEARNING OBJECTIVES

- Identify some criticisms concerning positive psychology.
- Outline some opportunities for positive psychology's future.

Positive psychology has come a relatively long way in a fairly short time. Still, even positive psychology's creators and staunchest allies have wondered whether it is really here for the long run. Will this new subfield continue to attract interested students and researchers? Is it more of a fad or psychological fashion than a genuinely new area of empirical inquiry? To paraphrase two of its midwives, Christopher Peterson and Martin Seligman (2003), will it have the evergreen popularity of the Beatles—or suffer the "has-been" fate of Duran Duran?

Problems

More to the point, positive psychology has not been without critics and skeptics (Lazarus, 2003b; Richardson & Guignon, 2008). For example, the late Richard Lazarus (2003a), a renowned psychologist and stress researcher, wondered whether its message is not only *not* very new but destined to be a fad that will pass, later return, and pass again. Why? Because many important conceptual and empirical issues will likely be left unresolved while new disciplinary fads will appear. Lazarus also questioned whether parsing the discipline of psychology into positive and

negative spheres is not only an oversimplification but a way to introduce theoretical as well as practical problems into psychological research. As Lazarus (2003a) humorously but effectively posed it:

God needs Satan, and vice versa. One would not exist without the other. We need the bad which is part of life, to fully appreciate the good. (p. 94)

Similarly, as you read this chapter, you might have wondered whether this new area is really all that new. For example, perhaps positive psychology is little more than the repackaging of "old wine in new bottles." Or, more charitably, perhaps the framework of positive psychology

Learn More Online

Positive Psychology Center

This site, maintained at the University of Pennsylvania, includes a variety of links pertaining to positive psychology. It provides a great deal of information on conferences and educational programs.

is useful for reorganizing how we think about positive events, thoughts, feelings, and even behaviors, but it might not be the paradigm shift its creators hoped it would be. As partisans on either side of the positive psychology debate will agree, only time will tell whether it has both staying power and ongoing influence in the wider discipline. That being the case, what should we look for, and forward to, if positive psychology is to flourish?

Prospects

Perhaps the success of positive psychology will be best judged by the research findings and successful applications emerge in the future. The late Christopher Peterson (2006) offers what may be the most telling indicator of success:

Will there be needed balance between the positive and negative aspects of psychology? Perhaps survival of the label "positive psychology" will matter less if this desired and needed balance is achieved. A close second criterion is whether research can address why people don't seek out those qualities of life that make them truly happy. In other words, if research identifies which activities enable people to lead a good life (Dunn & Brody, 2008; Park & Peterson, 2009), will they apply these findings to their own lives? As research evidence and intervention studies appear, it will be exciting to see whether people do indeed change the ways they live (the exercises in this next section of the chapter may provide you with an opportunity to see how easy it is to introduce new, positive routines into you own life).

Application

BOOSTING YOUR OWN HAPPINESS

LEARNING OBJECTIVES

- Explain how counting one's blessings and expressions of gratitude can promote happiness.
- Recognize the psychological benefits of sharing a positive story about oneself, sharing good news, and engaging in prosocial spending.

Answer the following "true" or "false."

___ **1.** Counting your blessings is a simple way to increase your own happiness.

___ **2.** Writing a sincere thank you note can enhance well-being in you as well as the recipient.

___ **3.** Sharing good things that happen to you with an interested other person (and vice versa) can generate beneficial positive emotions.

___ **4.** Sometimes spending money can make you happy.

If you answered "false" to any or all of these questions because you concluded that the described activities were too simple, there is still more you can learn about the nature of happiness. Enhancing your own well-being and happiness may be easier than you believe. You have spent this chapter reading and thinking about how positive psychological insights affect and benefit the lives of others. Now it's your turn: How can positive psychology be used to improve your own life? This Application contains five simple exercises, each of which can pay some serious psychosocial dividends (Mongrain & Anselmo-Matthews, 2012). All you have to do is give them a try. Good luck.

Counting Your Blessings for a Week

Some days life seems annoying, if not overwhelming. Often it is not life's big problems that lay one low, but the little ones—the hassles, upsets, and minor disruptions—that get one down. For some people, it's getting stuck in traffic; for others, it's forgetting to charge their cellphones. Sometimes a person is late to class, forgets a promise, or misses a deadline. A button pops off his shirt or coat. His room is a mess and there's still laundry to be done. The minor is perceived to be major, and suddenly the person feels diminished.

What to do? Several researchers (Emmons & McCullough, 2003; Lyubomirsky, Sheldon, & Schkade, 2005; Seligman et al., 2005) suggest looking on the bright side of your life by counting your blessings—literally. By "blessings," these positive psychologists are referring to the good things that happen to you each day—a warm smile from a stranger, a pleasant lunch with a co-worker, an unexpected contact (perhaps on Facebook) from a long-lost old friend. Your list of good things can also contain grand events like falling in love, starting an exciting new job, or learning that a loved one's health has dramatically improved.

Peterson (2006) offers a few guidelines for keeping a list of good things. First, don't try to list too many things. Three a day is fine—more than that decreases any benefits associated with the exercise. Second, for one week, try to write the list of good things toward the end of the day. Peterson reports that this recording keeping is less effective when done too early in the day. Finally, after making your end-of-day list, take a few minutes to jot down reasons that your choices constitute good things for you and your life. By doing so, you will become more mindful about the nature of these good things.

What are the apparent benefits of keeping track of the good things in your life? People who did so for a week were found to have higher levels of happiness and fewer depressive symptoms up to six months after they quit keeping the list (Peterson, 2006). Better still, close to 60% of the original participants maintained their daily lists on their own and without prompting from the investigators. Follow-up surveys found that the now daily habit encouraged an ongoing sense of well-being and led to enhanced relationships with important others.

Writing and Delivering a Gratitude Letter

No one writes real letters any more—they text, Tweet, or send email messages. Writing a real letter is a dying art. So, this exercise will not only allow you to revive a dying art, it will afford you a chance to make the recipient of your letter feel good.

Most of us are good at saying thank you to folks who have done something nice for us, but expressing gratitude is tougher. Take a few minutes and think of all the people who have gone out of their way to help you so far in your life. Your parents, siblings, and grandparents are likely candidates, as are some of your teachers or coaches, roommates, close friends, perhaps some neighbors, and select others. Pick one of these people, the one you believe did you the greatest kindness to date. If you have never properly expressed gratitude to that individual, here's your chance.

Write a personal letter to your chosen individual—an email won't do because such messages are usually brief and can seem impersonal—and explain in clear terms how he or she helped you and why you are so very grateful. Better yet, make your letter more spontaneous by writing it by hand instead of typing it. Make the letter as rich and detailed as possible. In the ideal case, visit the person, hand-deliver your letter, and have the individual read it while you are there (Peterson, 2006). If this face-to-face encounter is not possible, you can mail the letter (or email if you absolutely must—but no texting, please!), then later speak to the person by phone.

What will happen once your letter is read? You will move the recipient (possibly to tears), but your expression of gratitude will also gratify him or her. And both of you are likely to feel happy (Seligman et al., 2005). Such letters are more life affirming in the moment than they are life changing in the long run (that is, unless you decide to write a gratitude letter every so often for the foreseeable future!). Still, being grateful is a good thing, as those who feel gratitude turn out to be much happier than those who don't (Park, Peterson, & Seligman, 2004).

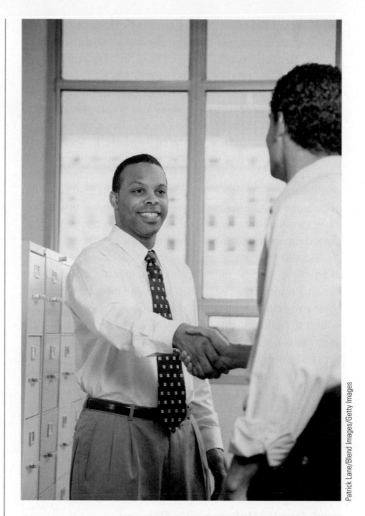

Patrick Lane/Blend Images/Getty Images

The expression of sincere gratitude benefits the person being thanked as well as the person doing the thanking.

What about people who are no longer with us, such as loved ones who have died? Is it possible to express gratitude for the kindness they gave when they were alive? Yes. If you wish, you can use the above directions as a model for writing a gratitude letter to a departed friend or loved one. You may not be able to directly share the letter with the person, but you are apt to bring up pleasant memories to reflect on as you express your gratitude in words on paper. These memories may allow you to once again have a "conversation" with a person to whom you owe a great deal.

Sharing a Story Illustrating the Best in You

Most people avoid blowing their own horns, but they can all remember times when they did things that brought out the best in them. Because people really don't like to brag, they often keep these stories to themselves. Although such modesty is admirable, there may be times when telling others about one's exemplary acts can serve as an example or even a source of inspiration. As you consider this activity, let this be one of these rare times when you disclose an act of private goodness to others.

What are the ground rules? Well, you should be honest and err on the side of modesty (again, no bragging) unless what you did was truly selfless and self-defining. Once you recall your example, be prepared to share it with others, probably members of the class in which you are using this book. You might ask the course instructor whether a class could be devoted to having people share their stories with one another. Alternatively, you could write a brief, one-page essay telling your tale. Your essay could then be posted on an online site where only other members of your class could access and read it. Or, copies could be made of everyone's stories and assigned as reading for a future class meeting. This last option lacks the passion and punch of hearing people tell their "personal best" stories, but this is one assignment that is likely to be read by all. If this exercise is not done in the context of your class, you could agree to swap stories with a classmate or two, which is a great way to make new friends as you explore the course material.

One last thing: Remember the golden rule of doing unto others what you'd have them do unto you. When people listen politely and with interest to your story, be sure to do the same for them (see the next exercise).

Sharing Good News and Capitalizing with Others

The humorist Fran Lebowitz (1982) once wrote that "the opposite of talking isn't listening. The opposite of talking is waiting" (p. 17). Is that how you often treat those who are close to you when they vie for your attention? Do you really listen closely to what they say and respond accordingly, especially when the news they are imparting is good? Do you focus more on wanting to tell the other person what good thing happened to you rather than celebrating his or her achievement? You of course want friends and loved ones to revel in your good fortune, but unless you do the same for them, you may not get the response you seek—or as we will see—any positive psychosocial benefits.

Positive psychologist Shelly Gable and her colleagues discovered that how people give and respond to good news from others has profound consequences for both the self and others (Gable et al., 2004). Specifically, sharing good news with those close to us can lead to "capitalization" when they respond with sincere interest and enthusiasm to what we say. *Capitalization* **refers to telling other people about whatever good things are happening in our own lives.** The term is admittedly unusual in this context, but one of the word's meanings is to "turn something into an advantage,"

which is what people do when they share good things with others. How so? Well, others' positive response to sharing creates positive emotions in the sharer, which capitalizes or builds on his or her already good feelings. These feelings of mutual respect, delight, and acknowledgment appear to enhance the qualities of the shared relationship. In short, both parties benefit socially and emotionally when good news is received and responded to in favorable ways.

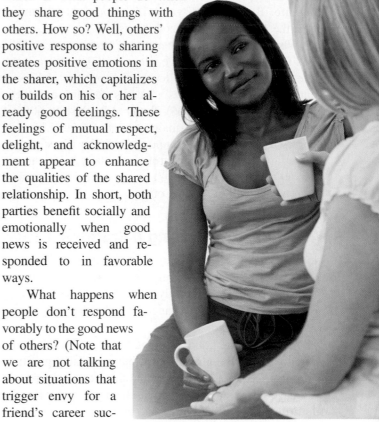

Darren Baker/Shutterstock.com

What happens when people don't respond favorably to the good news of others? (Note that we are not talking about situations that trigger envy for a friend's career success, say, or jealousy at her new romance—we are considering those times when people ignore sharing in some modest, if still happy, event.) Nothing happens: No positive emotions result, so neither self-reported well-being or relationship quality improves. Keep this in mind the next time you are tired at the end of the day and a friend or significant other wants to share some modest successes since you last talked. Rustling up some smiles and congratulations really won't take much effort on your part, and you are more likely to have the attention repaid to you sometime soon. Better still, you will focus less on your fatigue (always a good thing) and potentially improve your bonds with your pal or partner. Isn't that worth celebrating? This simple form of "paying it forward" can benefit everyone.

Prosocial Spending to Make You Happy

Let's close this Application with an interesting, if somewhat ironic, activity. Based on the research cited in Chapter 1, we know that money and material goods don't buy happiness, right (Diener & Biswas-Diener, 2008; Kasser, 2002)? Although many people believe that spending money on themselves will lead to happiness, there is ample evidence that such self-indulgence rarely leads to positive feelings. Can spending money ever make us happy? Well, it appears that under certain circumstances it can make us happier people.

"Who says you can't buy happiness!"

According to Dunn, Gilbert, and Wilson (2011), there are ways consumers can actually get more happiness when they choose to spend money. These include:

- Buying more experiences (plays, movies, concerts) rather than material goods (clothes, gadgets)
- Buying more small pleasures (a chocolate sundae) and fewer large ones (a new car)
- Using money to benefit others rather than oneself

This last possibility is intriguing: Can we spend money on behalf of others and make ourselves happy in the process?

Dunn, Aknin, and Norton (2008) gave research participants either $5 or $20 to spend on themselves or on another person. Those who spent the money on others were happier than those who spent it on themselves. Dunn and colleagues also found that people who spend a greater portion of their incomes on others or on charitable donations are much happier than those who simply spend their earnings on themselves. A related study by Aknin et al. (2010) found that when Ugandan and Canadian students reflected back on times they had been generous to others, they reported higher levels of happiness than students who thought back to times they had spent money on themselves (see also, Aknin et al., 2011a).

Why does spending on others—what researchers refer to as *prosocial spending*—heighten happiness? Giving to others makes us feel we are responsible, giving, and caring individuals. The act of giving makes us feel good about ourselves. When we spend our funds on others, we are also strengthening our social ties with them, and people with stronger social relationships are generally happier. Engaging in prosocial spending on others allows us to feel good about ourselves (Anik et al., 2011).

So, the next time you and a friend meet for coffee, go to a movie, or grab a quick bite, why not offer to pay? Or, if you see some small gift that you know will brighten a friend or loved one's day—a book, some chocolate, a flower, a charitable contribution, whatever—consider making the modest purchase in the interest of prosocial relations. You and your pal will be both very happy that you did (Aknin, Dunn, & Norton, 2012).

KEY IDEAS

THE SCOPE OF POSITIVE PSYCHOLOGY

- Positive psychology is a new area of psychology dedicated to the study of human strengths and how people can flourish in daily life. This subfield emerged as a reaction to the larger discipline's predominant focus on psychological problems. By providing needed balance, positive psychology can encourage people to focus on the positive aspects of daily living.
- Although it is a new area, many of the issues positive psychology explores have been studied outside the mainstream areas of the discipline for some time. Positive psychology provides an organizing framework for older and newer concepts related to well-being and the good life.
- Positive psychology explores three related lines of behavioral research: positive subjective experiences (such as good mood and positive emotions), positive individual traits (including hope, resilience, and gratitude), and positive institutions (such as beneficial work environments, good schools, and solid families).

POSITIVE SUBJECTIVE EXPERIENCES

- Positive subjective experiences entail the positive but usually private thoughts and feelings people have about their lives. Positive moods are global, longlasting reactions to events, whereas positive emotions are accute, distinct responses that last for shorter periods of time. Positive moods and emotions promote particular thoughts, feelings, and behaviors.
- Fredrickson's broaden-and-build model explains why positive emotions lead to new and beneficial ways of thinking and acting. Whereas negative emotions narrow people's thoughts, positive ones widen people's perspectives, creating future emotional and intellectual resources in the process.
- Flow is a psychological state marked by complete involvement and engagement with interesting, challenging, and intrinsically rewarding activities. Flow occurs when a person's skills are balanced by challenges that are just manageable.
- Mindful behavior is marked by attention and response to novel features of daily experience, whereas mindlessness occurs when individuals engage in familiar or rote actions that require little active thought.

POSITIVE INDIVIDUAL TRAITS

- Positive individual traits are qualities of character, some of which are learned while others are inherited. These positive dispositions explain why some people are happier and psychologically healthier than others.
- People who display hope anticipate that their desired goals can be met in the future. According to Snyder, hope consists of agency and pathways. The trait of hope is associated with the experience of positive emotions.
- Resilient people recover their psychological well-being following traumatic experiences better and faster than less-resilient people do. As evidence for such resilience, posttraumatic growth is marked by people's recogntion of what things truly matters, including enhanced appreciation for friends, loved ones, and life in general.
- Grit is a trait linked to perseverance and passion for successfully completing a long-term goal. People who have high levels of grit display stamina and a drive to achieve in spite of impediments.

- Gratitude occurs when people are thankful for the good things in their lives, particularly expressing appreciation for what others have done for them.
- As a trait, spirituality refers to people's belief that life has affirming transcendent or nonphysical qualities that warrant their attention.

POSITIVE INSTITUTIONS

- Positive institutions are organizations promoting civic virtues that help people act like good citizens who care about the general welfare. Schools can fall under this heading, as well. Positive institutions promote purpose, fairness, humility, safety, and dignity.

POSITIVE PSYCHOLOGY: PROBLEMS AND PROSPECTS

- Some critics argue that positive psychology is nothing more than old or exisiting ideas repackaged in a new, if positive, framework. Positive psychology's defenders counter that this subfield will achieve its goals if the larger discipline becomes more balanced where positive and negative psychological processes are concerned.

APPLICATION: BOOSTING YOUR OWN HAPPINESS

- Feelings of happiness can be achieved if people count the good things in their lives, express sincere gratitude to someone who helped them in the past, and share stories illustrating their own good actions that benefitted other people.
- There are psychologically beneficial qualities to sharing one's good news with others, enthusiastically listening to positive information other people share, and spending money on others rather than oneself.

KEY TERMS

Capitalization p. 510
Emotions p. 491
Flow p. 493
Gratitude p. 502
Grit p. 501
Hope p. 499
Mindlessness p. 495
Mindfulness p. 495
Negative emotions p. 491
Positive emotions p. 491

Positive individual traits p. 498
Positive institutions p. 504
Positive psychology p. 486
Positive subjective experiences p. 488
Posttraumatic growth p. 500
Resilience p. 500
Savoring, p. 497
Undoing hypothesis p. 492

KEY PEOPLE

Mihaly Csikszentmihalyi pp. 493–495
Barbara Fredrickson pp. 492–493
Ellen J. Langer p. 495
Martin Seligman pp. 486–487
C. R. Snyder pp. 499–500

1. As a social and intellectual movement within the larger discipline of psychology, positive psychology is concerned with
   a. human strengths.
   b. how people can flourish.
   c. creating a balance between the challenges and pleasures of daily life.
   d. all of the above.

2. Of positive psychology's three lines of inquiry, which one deals with psychological processes that promote favorable moods and emotions?
   a. Positive subjective experiences
   b. Positive individual traits
   c. Positive resilience
   d. Positive institutions

3. Being placed in a positive mood has been shown to make people
   a. less alert.
   b. more creative.
   c. more wary.
   d. think slowly.

4. Flow is a state of being in which a person
   a. perceives a sense of balance and well-being following a negative emotion.
   b. has positive thoughts linked with a broad range of subsequent actions.
   c. is fully engaged in an interesting, challenging, and rewarding activity.
   d. behaves in ways that have survival value.

5. A beneficial change in personal relations following some stressful event, such as developing closer bonds with one's family, is an example of
   a. postraumatic growth.
   b. capitalization.
   c. hope.
   d. mindfulness.

6. The human need for meaning in daily life is primarily associated with
   a. hope.
   b. meditation.
   c. postraumatic growth.
   d. spirituality.

7. Which of the following is *not* a virtue found within positive institutions?
   a. Dignity   c. Fairness
   b. Thrift   d. Humanity

8. Critics and skeptics of positive psychology sometimes argue that
   a. positive psychological research is unscientific.
   b. positive psychological processes are difficulty to demonstrate empirically.
   c. positive psychology's message is not new and may be nothing but a fad.
   d. positive psychology is misguided and that mainstream psychology should focus exclusively on the negative aspects of daily life.

9. Sharing good news about our lives with those we are close to is known as
   a. capitalization.   c. resilience.
   b. savoring.   d. mindfulness.

10. People can obtain happiness by spending money to
    a. benefit others.
    b. obtain small, not large, pleasures.
    c. buy experiences, not material goods.
    d. all of the above.

ANSWERS

1. d Page 486
2. a Page 488
3. b Pages 489–490
4. c Page 493
5. a Page 500
6. d Pages 502–503
7. b Page 507
8. c Pages 507–508
9. a Page 510
10. d Page 511

COURSEMATE

Go to **CengageBrain.com** to access Psychology CourseMate, where you will find an interactive eBook, glossaries, flashcards, quizzes, videos, and more.

PERSONAL EXPLORATIONS WORKBOOK

Go to the *Personal Explorations Workbook* in the back of your textbook for exercises that can enhance your self-understanding in relation to issues raised in this chapter.

Exercise 16.1 *Self-Assessment:* What Is Your Happiness Profile?

Exercise 16.2 *Self-Reflection:* Thinking About How You Construe Happiness

Psychology and Environmental Sustainability: What's Good for the Earth Is Good for Us

by Susan M. Koger (Willamette University) and Britain A. Scott (University of St. Thomas)

What do pollution, deforestation, the extinction of species, and climate change have in common? You might instantly respond, "They're all environmental problems." But is it really the *environment* that has the problems? What ties all these issues together is their cause: *maladaptive human behavior.* Particularly during the last 150 years, we humans have been behaving in ways that are *unsustainable.* We burn fossil fuels that pollute the air and change the climate, dump wastes into water and soil, overconsume resources, and invade the habitats of other species. Because the real problem is destructive human behaviors— and underlying thoughts, attitudes, feelings, values, and decisions—psychologists are increasingly applying their expertise to these issues (e.g., Clayton & Myers, 2009; Koger & Winter, 2010). As you will see, psychological insights are critical to the achievement of a *sustainable world*—one in which human activities and needs are balanced with those of other species and future generations, taking into account ecological as well as social and economic factors (Schmuck & Schultz, 2002).

Inspired by growing concern about environmental issues among the general public in the 1970s, some psychologists have been conducting research related to environmental issues for several decades. However, because their work does not fit neatly into a particular subdiscipline of the field, it generally receives little attention in psychology courses. You may have heard of *environmental psychologists,* who study how individuals are affected by, and interact with, their physical environments. However, the term *environment* in this label does not refer specifically to the natural environment. Only a minority of environmental psychologists study nature-related topics, such as people's cognitive responses to natural settings (e.g., Berman, Jonides, & Kaplan, 2008; Kaplan & Kaplan, 1989). Environmental psychologists are more likely to study the effects of noise, crowding, pollution, and urban living on aspects of human behavior. Numerous other researchers grounded in traditional branches of psychology (primarily social, behavioral, and cognitive psychology)

have investigated environmentally relevant behaviors such as energy conservation and material consumption. Over the past several years, a new label has emerged that promises to help tie together the work of nature-oriented environmental psychologists and other psychologists who study environmental behaviors. *Conservation psychology* **is the study of the interactive relationships between humans and the rest of nature, with a particular focus on how to enhance conservation of natural resources.** Conservation psychology is viewed as an applied field "that uses psychological principles, theories, or methods to understand and solve issues related to human aspects of conservation" (Saunders, 2003, p. 138).

So, "environmental problems" are really psychological problems; moreover, many of the disorders of adjustment highlighted in this text—anxiety, stress, depression, interpersonal difficulties—may be exacerbated, if not caused, by the same maladative behavior patterns that degrade the natural environment. That is, many psychological problems may result from humans' unhealthy relationship with nonhuman nature. In the 1990s, holistic thinkers known as *ecopsychologists* began promoting the idea that modern industrialized urban living erodes people's feeling of connectedness to nature, leaving them developmentally deprived and psychologically distressed. As Roszak (1992) put it, "When the Earth hurts, we hurt with it" (p. 308). Thus, some clinicians are incorporating ecopsychological therapies into their practices to foster mindfulness and a sense of place that may guide people to behave in more environmentally friendly ways (e.g., Buzzell & Chalquist, 2009; Clinebell, 1996; Conn, 1995; White & Heerwagen, 1998). Others promote wilderness experiences as a means of healing and self-expansion (Greenway, 1995; Harper, 1995) and as a catalyst toward more ecologically sustainable lifestyles (Kals & Ittner, 2003). Further, the expanding interdisciplinary field of *environmental health* is highlighting the interconnections among various consumer and industrial practices and adverse human impacts ranging from the neurological (developmental disabilities, Parkinson's disease) to various forms of cancer and reproductive and immune system dysfunction. Some *health psychologists* are thus turning their attention to "environmental" (i.e., toxic chemical) effects on cognitive and emotional development and various aspects of behavior.

In the following sections, we briefly review the current state of understanding about how we humans are negatively affecting the larger systems upon which our lives depend. We illustrate how many of the subdisciplines of psychology can aid in understanding—and hopefully solving—the foundational problems in people's thinking and behavior. We conclude that the health and well-being of humans is inextricably connected with the health of other species and the planet itself. (Note: A more thorough discussion of these issues is available in Koger & Winter, 2010.)

The Escalating Environmental Crisis

Unless you've been living in a cave without media access, you are at least somewhat familiar with the environmental issues currently confronting humanity. In fact, you may even feel tired of hearing the "gloom and doom" reports concerning melting ice caps and rising sea levels, toxic chemicals in the air and water, overpopulation, dwindling forests, and species losses. It may all seem too depressing, overwhelming, and perhaps even terrifying. Or maybe it doesn't seem to have much to do with you personally, and you feel powerless to make any difference.

Such responses are understandable and consistent with an evolutionary perspective. Human cognitive and perceptual systems evolved in an environment where the primary threats to safety were sudden and dramatic. As a result, people have difficulty responding to slowly developing but potentially calamitous conditions, especially when the consequences seem far away in terms of time or place. People discount distant dangers and take them less seriously than "risks with negative outcomes that occur for sure, now, here, and to us" (Gattig & Hendricks, 2007, p. 22). The tendency is to delay action until problems are large scale and readily apparent rather than work to prevent the problems. Unfortunately, by then it may be too late.

Let's take, for example, the problem of *global warming*. Gases such as carbon dioxide, methane, and nitrous oxide trap heat in the atmosphere. The naturally resulting *greenhouse effect* is necessary to maintain a climate suitable for life on this planet. Gas levels vary naturally to some extent, but as you have probably heard, modern living has created an unprecedented increase in greenhouse gas concentrations (see **Figure A.1**). Simultaneously, our forests, which act as the lungs of the earth by converting

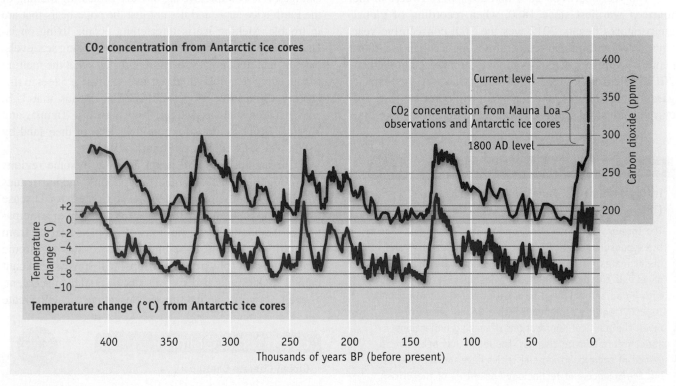

Figure A.1
Long-term trends in atmospheric carbon dioxide concentration and temperature. Scientists have sampled ice cores in Antarctica to study fluctuations in atmospheric concentrations of carbon dioxide (CO_2), the dominant greenhouse gas. Over the past 400,000 years, there has been a strong correlation between temperature variations and CO_2 levels. With the beginning of the Industrial Revolution in the 1800s, CO_2 concentrations began a dramatic and unprecedented increase, rising rapidly from 280 ppmv (parts per million by volume) to current levels of 376 ppmv. Note that this represents an increase of 77 ppmv relative to the highest concentrations reached during the course of the preceding 400,000 years (Woods Hole Research Center, 2009). Thus, it is highly unlikely that these recent trends reflect "natural" variability.

Figure A.2

Trends in global average temperature and carbon dioxide concentration since 1880. Evidence for a changing climate is also seen in average increases of global temperatures, which are correlated with escalating atmospheric CO_2 levels since the beginning of the Industrial Revolution in 1880. CO_2 measurements since 1958 are from the Mauna Loa Observatory in Hawaii; earlier data are from ice cores in Antarctica.

carbon dioxide to oxygen, have been rapidly shrinking because of logging and the clearing of forest land for other uses. As a result, carbon dioxide in the atmosphere is at the "highest level in 650,000 years" (Gardner & Prugh, 2008, p. 3) and is clearly correlated with planetary warming (see **Figure A.2**). Although it is not possible to establish causation from these correlational analyses, there is an "overwhelming consensus among scientists" that global warming is happening and that it is induced by human activity (Institute of Physics, 2013).

The years between 2001 and 2012 were twelve of the fourteen warmest since 1880, when recording of global temperatures began. 2012 was the 36th consecutive year since 1976 with global temperatures higher than the 20th-century average (NOAA National Climatic Data Center, 2012). The trends suggest that many warming greenhouse gases, including CO_2 and methane, will continue to rise if current industrial and social practices do not change dra-

matically and quickly. In its last report, the Intergovernmental Panel on Climate Change (2007) predicted that the planet could warm as much as 11 degrees Fahrenheit by 2100. That may not sound like much, but let's put that number in perspective: During the last Ice Age, the world was only 9 degrees cooler than it is today. Thus, we are facing the real possibility of planetary temperature changes of Ice Age magnitudes within this century.

You may be wondering why the warming of the planet matters. It matters because of the associated global *climatic changes*. For example, we are already witnessing melting of the Earth's ice caps, and it's not just the polar bears that are in trouble. Melting ice is threatening people living on islands and near the ocean because it leads to rising sea levels, erosion, and flooding. A recent report states that the melting is happening so quickly that sea levels may rise 5 feet in this century (Strauss & Kopp, 2012). This means that U.S. coastal cities such as Miami, New Orleans, Tampa, and Virginia Beach could lose more than 10% of their land by 2100 (Weiss, Overpeck, & Strauss, 2011).

Climate changes will mean flooding in some regions and drought in others. Tornados, typhoons, and hurricanes will likely become more intense. The Centers for Disease Control and Prevention (2009a) are gearing up in anticipation of the possibility of millions of people suffering from malnutrition, disease, and injury as a result of extreme weather. These physical hardships will have significant mental health impacts. Loss, disruption, and displacement, as well as worry about future consequences, will create

Learn More Online

Intergovernmental Panel on Climate Change (IPCC)

The Intergovernmental Panel on Climate Change (IPCC) is a U.N.-sponsored scientific organization that assesses and disseminates research related to world climate change. The panel was created in 1989 to provide member governments with broad and balanced information about climate change. Its 2007 report was honored with a Nobel Peace Prize. Given the political ramifications of making projections about future climate changes, the report has been controversial in some quarters, and critics have found some flaws, but the Science and Technology Committee of the British House of Commons recently determined that there was no basis for allegations of data misrepresentation. You can draw your own conclusions by visiting the IPCC website, where you will find a wealth of information on their procedures, data, and reports.

Learn More Online

Global Climate Change

NASA's Eyes on the Earth offers a quick look at the Planet's "vital signs," including decreases in Arctic sea ice and increases in carbon dioxide, sea level, and global temperatures since 1880. The site also describes the science behind climate change, including causes and anticipated effects.

profound stress. There will likely be an increase in acute and posttraumatic stress disorders and related problems such as anxiety, substance abuse, grief, depression, and suicide (Fritze et al., 2008). And, of course climate change will affect everyone, not just people in flooded or drought-ridden areas. As many as 20%–30% of known plant and animal species are at an increased risk for extinction because of climate change. Species extinction means a decrease in the *biodiversity* that is necessary to maintain healthy *ecosystems* (Lovejoy & Hannah, 2005)—ecosystems on which we all rely for basic life support.

Given the dire nature of these predicted outcomes, why aren't people responding collectively and as individuals to reduce use of fossil fuels and associated emissions? As Harvard Psychologist Daniel Gilbert (2006a) put it, "Environmentalists despair that global warming is happening so fast. In fact, it isn't happening fast enough." Humans respond best to threats that are "PAINful: i.e., Personal, Abrupt, Immoral, and happening Now" (Gilbert, 2008). But, despite the "hard-wiring" of the human brain that makes it difficult for people to anticipate and plan for long-term problems on the scale of global climate change, our species is capable of dramatic and rapid behavioral change. Consider, for example, the pace of the technological revolution. As undergraduates, the two of us relied on typewriters for writing papers after engaging in library research with massive printed publication indexes and bound volumes of journals. (Can you imagine?) Now, the idea of using anything other than high-speed computers and the Internet to conduct research and write papers seems horribly inefficient and cumbersome. In theory, the human capacity for behavioral adaptation could help reverse current ecological trends.

However, before someone changes his or her behaviors, that person must recognize which behaviors need changing, know how to change them, and feel that changing them is worthwhile. In fact, the majority of people will not even initiate change until they experience a personal crisis (Beddoe et al., 2009), commonly known as "hitting bottom," or until risks become salient and personally relevant. Breaking any *addiction*—whether to substances like alcohol or to unsustainable behaviors like compulsive shopping—requires patience and perseverance because most people relapse—that is, they fall back on old habits. This perspective from the psychology of addiction helps explain why many people don't feel galvanized to respond to issues like climate change: Such environmental risks don't seem personally relevant to most people. What does environmental destruction have to do with you as an individual? Although you yourself do not produce industrial wastes or log forests, like most people you probably engage in extravagant use and misuse of the world's natural resources.

Human impacts on the planet can be estimated by using the *ecological footprint*—a measure of how fast a person (or population) consumes resources and generates waste in comparison to how rapidly nature can absorb the waste and replenish the resources (see **Figure A.3**). People who live in the United States have the largest footprints in the world, consuming considerably more resources and generating more waste than any other people on the planet. Unfortunately, the gap between this ecological footprint and the planet's *carrying ca-*

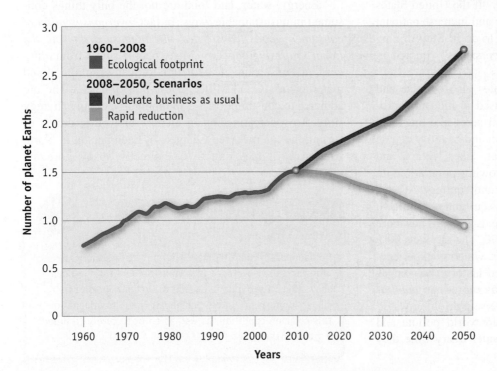

Figure A.3

World footprint: Do we fit on the planet? Humans use the equivalent of 1.5 planets to provide resources and absorb wastes. If current population and consumption trends continue, we will need the equivalent of two Earths to support us by 2030. And of course, we have only one.

Source: Global Footprint Network, www .footprintnetwork.org <http://www.footprintnetwork .org>, National Footprint Accounts 2011. Reprinted by permission.

pacity is growing at an alarming pace. "If everyone in the world had an ecological footprint equivalent to that of the typical North American or Western European, global society would overshoot the planet's biocapacity three to five fold" (Kitzes et al., 2008, p. 468). In other words, if everyone lived like those in the United States do, more than three additional planets would be needed to support this lifestyle!

People living in the U.S. are by far the biggest users of the world's energy. Less than 5% of the global population lives in the United States and the country holds only about 3% of the planet's oil (Kunstler, 2005), yet U.S. residents use a staggering 25% of the total commercial supply: 18,949,000 barrels of oil *per day*—the large majority of which is used for transportation (U.S. Energy Information Administration, 2013). The next largest consumer is China, but consider this: China has *four times* the population of the United States and uses less than half the amount of oil. Each person in the U.S. uses, on average, more than thirty times the amount of gasoline as the average person in a developing country (World Resources Institute, 2001). This "addiction to oil" is fostering a dangerously unstable international political situation. Middle Eastern countries rest on more than 60% of the planet's oil reserves, inspiring military-based foreign policies that emphasize control and access (e.g., Winter & Cava, 2006). Wars over access to resources including oil will likely become more common.

Amazingly, much of this huge expenditure of energy is wasted (G. T. Miller, 2007). People in North America waste more than 43% of their energy by selecting energy-inefficient automobiles, appliances, and home heating systems when more efficient choices are available. Energy expert Amory Lovins puts it plainly, "If the United States wants to save a lot of oil and money and increase national security, there are two simple ways to do it: Stop driving Petropigs and stop living in energy sieves" (quoted in G. T. Miller, 2007, p. 385).

Those living in the United States also overuse and abuse water. The toxic chemicals used in industrial production, as well as those used to kill pests like bugs and weeds, clean houses, and even groom and beautify people and pets, are polluting groundwater, lakes, rivers, and oceans. Demand for water from growing populations in arid locations is lowering reservoirs and aquifers. At least one quarter of the groundwater that is currently withdrawn is not being replenished. For example, Las Vegas has more than doubled in population since 1990. The city gets 90% of its water from the Colorado River, which is experiencing the worst drought in its recorded history (Las Vegas Valley Water District, 2013). Already more than *one billion* people on the planet do not have safe drinking water. In contrast, people in the developed world pollute and waste gallons of drinking-quality water every time they flush the toilet.

The wasteful use of energy and water are two of the primary contributors to the enormous ecological footprint of the U.S. population. Another major factor is diet. Livestock farming produces more greenhouse gases than transportation (Food and Agriculture Organization of the United Nations, 2006), and it was estimated that it takes 600 gallons of water to produce just one hamburger (Kreith, 1991). Japanese researchers calculated that the CO_2 emissions associated with the production of just 2.2 pounds of beef are equivalent to the amount emitted by an average European car every 155 miles (Bittman, 2008). Thus, if U.S. citizens merely decreased meat consumption by 20%, the energy savings and reduction in greenhouse gases would be equivalent to all of us trading in our gas-powered sedans for a Prius (Walsh, 2008). Yet, as a result of increasing affluence in other parts of the world and a rapidly expanding global population, worldwide meat consumption is projected to rise 53% by 2030 (World Resources Institute, 2001).

Most people in the U.S. regularly eat food that is out of season or does not grow in their region. This means that their food must travel long distances to get to them. It is typical in the United States for food to travel more than 1500 miles from its source to the dinner table (Pirog & Benjamin, 2003). Popular convenience foods are subject to energy-intensive processing and are packaged in containers and wrappers that cannot be reused or recycled. Further, 36 million tons of food is *wasted* every year in the United States (U.S. Environmental Protection Agency, 2013), more than a third of the edible food supply (Stokstad, 2009). Most of that food ends up in landfills, and as it rots it releases methane, a greenhouse gas that is twenty times more powerful than carbon dioxide at trapping heat in the atmosphere (U.S. EPA, 2013).

Energy, water, and food are not the only things consumed in unsustainable ways. In fact, *overconsumption of consumer goods constitutes the biggest drain on the Earth's carrying capacity*. Many people suffer from *affluenza,* an "unsustainable addiction to overconsumption and materialism" (G. T. Miller, 2007, p. 19). Those who are addicted to consumption use shopping as a coping strategy similar to overeating, using alcohol and other drugs, or surfing the Internet (see Chapter 4). Each person in North America consumes, directly or indirectly, vastly more raw

Learn More Online

Affluenza

Do you suffer from affluenza? Find out at this thought-provoking site developed in conjunction with a one-hour show filmed for public television in Oregon. The site includes information on the "diagnosis" and "treatment" of this common condition, as well as an opportunity to order a video of the show.

Learn More Online

The Story of Stuff

This site provides a charming, but disturbing, review of how material goods are produced, distributed, and disposed of in ways that are antagonistic to the goal of sustainability.

Learn More Online

Running the Numbers

Visit this site developed by Chris Jordan to see brilliant visual illustrations of the astonishing quantities of consumer goods used in the United States. For example, you can see 15 million sheets of office paper representing 5 minutes of paper use, or 106,000 aluminum cans for 30 seconds of can consumption. The artwork is clever, creative, and depressing.

materials than those in developing countries and even more than people in other developed nations. And the things people buy—clothes, electronics, cars, furnishings—are produced from materials that leave a long trail of pollution elsewhere that is invisible to the U.S. consumer. A pair of pants made of polyester and sold in an American department store may be sewn in a sweatshop in Indonesia, from synthetic material manufactured in Singapore, which comes from oil refined in Mexico. U.S. consumer culture is spreading quickly, so that people in developing countries are aiming for "the good life," hurrying to develop the same extravagant lifestyles modeled in movies, television, advertising, and tourism.

Conspicuous consumption of convenience foods and consumer goods yields astonishing amounts of solid waste. Each person in North America generates more than 4.5 pounds of garbage per day (G. T. Miller, 2007). People throw away approximately 2.5 million nonreturnable plastic bottles *every hour* and toss about 25 billion Styrofoam coffee cups in the garbage each year. Electronic "e-waste" is growing exponentially. Every year, people living in the United States discard an estimated 130 million cell phones and 100 million computers, monitors, and television sets, only recycling about 10% (G. T. Miller, 2007). But even careful household recycling will not change the biggest solid waste problem. Commercial and industrial activities generate 98.5% of the waste. Average citizens sponsor this enormous waste production every time they buy a product that was inefficiently manufactured, is overpackaged, is not recyclable or biodegradable, or has traveled a long distance to get to them (which describes the vast majority

of consumer products, including some that are misleadingly labeled "eco-friendly").

Ironically, there is evidence that overconsumption is not "delivering the goods." Rather, as you learned in Chapter 1, happiness is predicted by quality relationships, fulfilling work, and a positive outlook—not how much stuff one owns. In fact, the race to pay for material possessions is likely to detract from these primary ingredients of happiness. Thus, attempting to meet psychological needs through overconsumption jeopardizes not only one's physical habitat but also one's psychological well-being (Kasser & Kanner, 2004). You may have heard of the 3 R's: Reduce, Reuse, Recycle. But effective solutions to environmental problems must start with *Refusing* to buy things that aren't really necessary and choosing sustainably produced options for the things that are (G. T. Miller, 2007) (see **Figure A.4**).

As you were reading this section, did you feel despair? Anxiety? Irritation? Hopelessness? Did you scan the material, thinking to yourself that you already knew it? Did you find yourself growing overwhelmed, angry, or afraid? Did you feel guilty, defensive, or skeptical? Did you feel a sense of apathy? These *psychological* reactions are important because they determine how such problems are under-

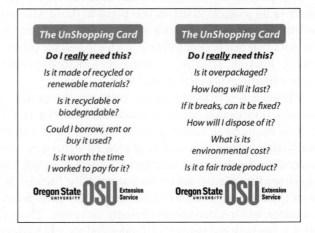

Figure A.4

An innovative effort to discourage overconsumption. This "UnShopping Card," developed by the Oregon State University Extension Service, was created to help people think more deliberately about their consumption decisions.

stood and what people are willing and able to do about them. In fact, the environmental crisis we face may well be the "pivotal psychological reality of our time" (Macy, 1995, p. 241). Although it would be naive to suggest that any one academic discipline will provide all the solutions to the environmental crisis, psychology has a lot to offer for understanding the roots of environmental destruction, the psychological forces maintaining it, and what it will take for people to change.

Insights from Social Psychology

As you may know, social psychology is primarily about the power of situational influence to shape behavior. Many environmentally damaging behaviors arise from *social norms*—informal, unwritten "rules" about what is appropriate or typical. Some researchers distinguish between *injunctive norms* (what is expected or approved of) and *descriptive norms* (what most people actually do) (Cialdini, Reno, & Kallgren, 1990). In the case of environmentally responsible behaviors, injunctive and descriptive norms often clash; that is, most people approve of environmentally responsible behaviors but don't actually engage in them. Cialdini (2003) argued that environmental campaigns that highlight people's environmentally irresponsible behavior may backfire, because they inadvertently focus attention on descriptive norms for *anti*-environmental behavior.

To test the importance of these two types of norms, researchers conducted a series of field experiments on littering. Thanks in large part to an aggressive nationwide anti-littering campaign in the 1970s, U.S. residents generally hold an injunctive norm against littering. Still, in some places the descriptive norm is to litter. Researchers tested how these norms interact to influence behavior. They found that in a littered setting, seeing a confederate litter made participants more likely to litter; however, in a *clean* setting, participants who saw a confederate litter were *less* likely to do so themselves, as compared to those who saw no littering behavior. Can you figure out why? It's because the stark contrast between the clean setting and the confederate's littering brought to mind the injunctive norm against littering (Cialdini et al., 1990).

Though social psychologists focus on the power of situational influence, they recognize that behavior is also shaped by internal factors such as attitudes and values. Individuals whose behavior is guided by *egocentric* and *materialistic* values that emphasize personal wealth and status tend to exhibit fewer environmentally friendly actions (Schultz et al., 2005). Still, *biocentric* values are no guarantee of environmentally friendly behavior. There is often a gap between people's attitudes and their behaviors. Even individuals with pro-environmental attitudes often find that situational constraints can make it difficult (or costly, inconvenient, or awkward) to act in an attitude-consistent manner (Kollmus & Agyeman, 2002).

Sometimes when individuals behave in an attitude-discrepant way, they experience *cognitive dissonance*, an uncomfortable state of arousal that motivates them to change their behaviors or attitudes to bring them in sync with each other (Festinger, 1954). In a few studies, researchers have successfully induced a state of cognitive dissonance that led to increased environmentally friendly behavior. For example, students on their way to the gym were intercepted and asked whether they ever waste water (all did) and whether they would sign their name to a public message about the importance of water conservation (all did); researchers lurking in the locker room found that these students took shorter showers after their workouts than did students who hadn't been reminded of their own hypocritical behavior (Dickerson et al., 1992). However, as long as individuals can justify their attitude-discrepant behavior to themselves, dissonance will not be aroused and their behavior is unlikely to change.

Many environmental problems result from people acting out of self-interest in the moment, ultimately harming the greater whole. Such *social dilemmas* contribute to environmental degradation in several ways (e.g., Gardner & Stern, 2002; Osbaldiston & Sheldon, 2002; Vlek & Steg, 2007):

- First, in *commons dilemmas,* individuals take more than their fair share of a communal resource (such as oil or water).
- Second, in *public goods dilemmas,* individuals contribute less than their fair share to a communal resource (i.e., not wanting to pay higher taxes for bus services).
- Third, in *risk dilemmas,* an individual's behavior exposes the greater whole to hazards (e.g., a homeowner uses toxic herbicides because she wants a green lawn).
- Fourth, *ecological dilemmas* occur when acting from self-interest upsets larger systems (e.g., a landowner fills in a wetland on his property, thereby interfering with waterfowl migration).

In these examples, rewards to the individual are more immediate and compelling than the delayed costs to the population. People don't always act in self-interest, however. Individuals will sometimes forgo personal benefits in favor of a common goal (such as driving less to reduce global emissions) if they identify with the group and feel responsible toward it (Dawes, 1980; Van Vugt, 2002) and if they perceive the long-term benefits as personally relevant (Milinski et al., 2008).

The founder of experimental social psychology, Kurt Lewin, emphasized that behavior is a function of both the situation and *the person*. How people define their *self-concepts* and their *social identities* certainly has implications for environmentally relevant behaviors. For example, negative stereotypes about environmentalists discourage some individuals from behaving in overtly sustainable ways. (Do you know anyone who is afraid of being perceived as a "tree-hugger"?) Recently, some social psychologists have turned their attention to the notion of the *ecologically connected self.* Theoretically, the more one defines oneself as *part of nature,* the more empathy one should have for other living things (Bragg, 1996). Several studies support the idea that an ecologically connected self is positively correlated with environmentally friendly attitudes and behaviors (e.g., Clayton, 2003; Mayer & Frantz, 2004; Schultz, 2001). Yet, it is probably safe to say that the self-concepts of most people living in industrialized countries today lack a sense of ecological connection.

Insights from Theories of Personality

As you learned in Chapter 2, one of the earliest personality theorists was Sigmund Freud, who believed that personality is shaped by how one resolves unconscious conflicts in early childhood. Because most of Freud's ideas cannot be empirically tested, they have inspired vigorous criticism. Still, his suggestion that people use unconscious defenses to ward off emotional discomfort seems relevant for understanding environmental issues. Awareness of the probable collapse of the planet's ecosystems *should* trigger powerful and uncomfortable feelings, but people often fail to act on those feelings. If people do use ego-protective *defense mechanisms* as proposed by Freud and his daughter Anna (A. Freud, 1936), this may explain how people can "know" about environmental problems and yet not change their behaviors.

Four defense mechanisms seem particularly applicable to people's ecologically unfriendly behaviors. *Rationalization* is one of the most common. For instance, though people may feel guilty about driving alone, they convince themselves, "I have to drive because carpooling is too inconvenient. *Identification* leads people to purchase nonessential status symbols so they can feel good about themselves. *Denial* about environmental problems includes minimizing their severity, seeing them as irrelevant,

and seeing oneself as not responsible (Opotow & Weiss, 2000). Finally, *projection* occurs when people perceive in others what they fail to perceive in themselves. One of us recalls vehemently grumbling about all the cars on the road during rush hour, only to be reminded by her 3-year-old in the backseat, "But Mommy, you're traffic, too!"

Contemporary personality theorists focus on individuals' traits, rather than unconscious motivations. Some personality traits are associated with caring for nonhuman nature. For example, Broida and colleagues (1993) found that college students classed as Intuitive and Feeling on the Myers-Briggs Type Inventory tended to be more ecologically concerned and more opposed to animal experimentation than other personality types. Mathews and Herzog (1997) administered the Sixteen Personality Factor Inventory to college students and found that two personality factors—sensitivity and imaginativeness—were positively correlated with attitudes toward animals. Furnham, McManus, and Scott (2004) measured the Big Five personality traits and found that openness to experience was positively related to liking of animals and believing that animals have feelings. More recently, researchers have found a positive relationship across cultures between the Big Five traits of openness, agreeableness, and conscientiousness and general pro-environmental attitudes and behaviors (Hirsh, 2010; Markowitz et al., 2012; Milfont & Sibley, 2012).

Insights from Behavioral Psychology

As you read in Chapter 2, one of the best-known behavioral psychologists, B. F. Skinner, argued that what people do depends on the consequences of their behavior: reinforcement encourages behavior, while punishment discourages it. Toward the end of his career, Skinner took a particular interest in environmental issues. In an address to the American Psychological Association, he criticized the efforts of environmental activists as inconsistent with operant learning principles. He said they should stop inspiring guilt, fear, and shame to motivate greener behaviors. Instead, they should help individuals see the potentially reinforcing consequences of sustainable lifestyles (Skinner, 1991). Yet, the benefits associated with environmentally *damaging* behaviors are often more obvious than the rewards of environmentally *sustainable* behaviors. For instance, can you think of any environmentally unfriendly behaviors that are rewarded by convenience or social status? Is it harder to think of environmentally friendly behaviors that are similarly reinforced?

One of the most common ways governments and companies can reinforce pro-environmental behavior is through financial rewards. Although temporary incentives, such as tax rebates, can help motivate greener choices, their effectiveness may be limited. Often, when the incentive goes away, so does the behavior (Abrahamse et al., 2005; Lehman & Geller, 1994). More powerful and enduring than financial rewards may be *social* reinforcers. For example, imagine being rewarded for energy-efficient driving by earning points that would show all of your Facebook friends how green you are—and how much greener you are than they (Pritchard, 2010). By creating social status competition, researchers have been able to motivate people to choose less desirable but greener products over more luxurious nongreen products, especially when the greener product was the more expensive option and their choices were made public (Griskevicius, Tybur, & Van den Bergh, 2010).

Besides the use of reinforcement, another behavior modification strategy involves altering *discriminative (antecedent stimuli)*. Prominent bins placed in areas where drinks are consumed serve as *prompts* to recycle cans and bottles (Lehman & Geller, 2004). Another example is placing signs over light switches reminding people to turn off the lights when they leave a room. Research suggests that the more specific the prompt, the greater its effectiveness. A sign saying "Faculty and students: Please turn off lights after 5 pm" is more effective than one reading "Conserve Electricity." Polite prompts are more effective than demanding ones (the word "please" can make a difference), and the closer the prompt is to the point of behavior, the better (a sign over a light switch is more effective than a sign across the room). Thus, polite, salient, and specific reminders can change behavior (Geller, Winett, & Everett, 1982; Lehman & Geller, 2004).

Although providing information is a technique widely used by environmental groups, there is little evidence that education alone changes what people actually do (see reviews by Abrahamse et al., 2005; Gardner & Stern, 2002; Lehman & Geller, 2004). *Modeling* environmentally friendly behavior can be more effective than simply describing it (see Bandura, 1977, and also Chapter 2). For instance, in one classic study, participants were exposed to a video showing a person turning down a thermostat, wearing warmer clothes, and using heavy blankets. With this treatment, viewers reduced their energy use by 28% (Winett et al., 1982). A more recent study involved users of a Facebook application who had been posting and commenting on climate change news stories. These participants reported increases in both their knowledge about climate change science and their pro-environmental behavior. Importantly, they claimed that it wasn't the information that motivated their behavior change; it was the peer modeling they witnessed in the online community (Robelia, Greenhow, & Burton, 2011).

Insights from Cognitive Psychology

From the perspective of cognitive psychology, much environmentally destructive behavior is maintained by cognitive biases. The tendency to depend on mental shortcuts called *heuristics* can lead to underestimation of the risks of environmental hazards. For example, the *availability heuristic* may explain why people downplay the significance of global warming. Most of us can't easily visualize melting icecaps and rising sea levels, so the perils of climate change don't easily come to mind. On the other hand, environmental hazards that have received dramatic media coverage, such as oil spills, feature prominently in our memories. Therefore, we may devote a lot of attention and resources to the vivid events, while neglecting the less vivid, but more insidious, hazards (Gardner & Stern, 2002).

Although the use of mental shortcuts is automatic, it is possible to temporarily override this tendency. When people are sufficiently motivated and not mentally overloaded, they are capable of careful, logical, effortful reasoning. The key may be for each person to increase his or her awareness of the potential for errors in thinking. In this way, individuals might become better environmental decision makers. Yet "coldly rational" judgments may not be superior to emotionally driven ones when it comes to environmental issues (Slovic et al., 2004). For example, after reading a description of nuclear energy that emphasized the negatives ("Waste is highly radioactive and contaminated with plutonium, a deadly element"), participants not only raised their estimates of the risks of nuclear power (as would be logically expected) but also *lowered* their estimates of the benefits of nuclear power—even though the description had not said anything about benefits. The researchers explained this change in participants' benefit estimates as being due to an overall increase in negative feelings about nuclear power (Finucane et al., 2000). Participants had used the *affect* (emotion-based) *heuristic* in making their judgments. Clearly, heuristics may sometimes bias people in an anti-environmental direction and sometimes in a pro-environmental direction.

Many cognitive biases protect individuals from threats to their self-esteem and feelings of security. They help people feel good about themselves in spite of their behavior or circumstances. *Comparative optimism* leads individuals to believe they are less vulnerable than others to all types of risks, including environmental threats, even though objectively there is no reason to think the risks are any different for one individual versus another (Pahl et al., 2005). *False consensus* helps people maintain positive self-esteem by convincing themselves that many others engage in the same undesirable behaviors as they do. For example, when a water shortage prompted a temporary shower ban at Princeton University in 1999, researchers conducted a 5-day field study during and after the ban (Benoît & Norton, 2003). They found that students who ignored the ban and showered as usual overestimated how many other people were similarly irresponsible. Finally, *false polarization* is the tendency to perceive the views of those on the opposing side of a debate as more extreme than they really are. In the shower ban study, participants believed that people who showered cared much less about the greater good than those who did not shower. However, self-report data suggested that the actual attitudinal positions of these two groups were quite close. Can you see how this cognitive bias might contribute to the political divide between Democrats and Republicans in the United States when it comes to environmental issues?

Insights from Developmental Psychology

The discipline of psychology emerged in an urban-industrialized context during the last century. This probably explains why developmental psychologists have largely overlooked the vital role that nature plays in humans' cognitive, emotional, and social development. Only since the 1990s have some developmentalists turned their attention toward topics such as children's relationship with animals, their understanding of life and ecological systems, their moral reasoning about environmental issues, and the implications of their experiences (or lack thereof) in natural settings.

Developmental psychologists have almost completely neglected the study of children's relationship with animals. This is surprising given that animals are a primary focus in children's lives: as companions (live, stuffed, or imaginary), as captive or wild specimens, as characters in books and film, and as creatures the children themselves pretend to be. Recently, however, a few developmental psychologists have proposed that in order to fully understand development, researchers must extend the list of important childhood influences to include animals—perhaps even putting them at the top of the list (Melson, 2001, 2003; Myers, 2007).

As you may know from personal experience, children often learn about death through having pets. But even without firsthand experience, young children intuitively perceive, categorize, and think about living things differently than nonliving things, and they see connections between plants, animals, and humans. This naïve understanding of nature is called *folkbiology* (Inagaki & Hatano, 2002). Seeing the similarities between themselves and other species inspires children to see nature as "something worthy of moral consideration" (Gebhard, Nevers, & Billmann-Mahecha, 2003, p. 92). Indeed, research on children's moral reasoning suggests that children sometimes adopt a *biocentric* perspective, where they view plants and animals as having rights and as deserving respect, just as people do. In several cross-cultural studies, children showed strong moral prohibitions against pollution, damage to natural systems, and other species (reviewed in Kahn, 2003). Research on children's folkbiology and environmentally related moral reasoning will not only broaden our understanding of cognitive development in general but may also help psychologists better understand why and how adults' unsustainable behaviors may be influenced by *anthropocentric* (human-centered) thinking and ignorance about ecology.

Increasingly, child development experts are becoming convinced that children need outdoor experiences to fully develop their emotional, physical, mental, and social capabilities (e.g., Kahn & Kellert, 2002), a theory that captured the attention of the general public with the publication of *Last Child in the Woods: Saving Our Children from Nature Deficit Disorder* (Louv, 2005). Children may need opportunities for spontaneous and independent play in natural areas to optimize their perceptual systems, their love relationships and empathy, and their sense of self (e.g., Kellert, 2002). Experiences in nature may also be vital for children's mental health. Children living in rural communities with more "nearby nature" have less psychological distress, including anxiety and depression, and fewer conduct disorders, such as bullying, than those living in urban areas (Wells & Evans, 2003). Recent studies suggest that even symptoms of *atten-*

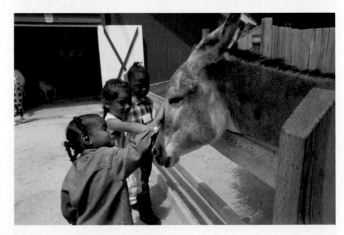

Experience with animals during childhood can have an impact on people's attitudes about nature in general, not to mention their feelings about the importance of preserving endangered species.

tion deficit hyperactivity disorders can be ameliorated by time spent in natural settings (Faber Taylor & Kuo, 2009; van den Berg & van den Berg, 2011).

Unfortunately, many children today spend very little time outside, and when they do go out they typically experience only degraded and polluted conditions, making identification with nature more difficult (Kahn, 2007). More time inside generally means more screen time—as much as 6 to 9 hours per day engaged with electronic media (Roberts, Foehr, & Rideout, 2005). Technology bombards children with images and advertisements that promote an environmentally destructive consumer culture (Kasser, 2002; Linn, 2008). Further, time spent inside stunts children's understanding of, and appreciation for, the natural world. Research on adults suggests that experiences in nature during childhood—and family members who modeled appreciation for nature—are significant predictors of a pro-environmental orientation (e.g., Guiney & Oberhauser, 2009; Horwitz, 1996). In fact, some investigators have argued that love of nature and concern about its protection are developed *only* with consistent outdoor experiences (Chawla, 1988). This means that children who spend most of their time indoors may ultimately be less likely to engage in pro-environmental actions.

Insights from Health and Clinical Psychology

You read in Chapter 3 about the physiology of stress and its associated behavioral and health consequences. It turns out that many aspects of contemporary environments that are ecologically unsound are also significant human stressors. Urban noise, traffic, crowding, pollution, and living near toxic industries or waste sites are all associated with increased stress and related symptoms such as anxiety, depression, anger, and aggression (Kuo & Sullivan, 2001; Lundberg, 1998). The effects of catastrophic environmental events can cause *posttraumatic stress disorder*. For example, mental health services were needed to treat depression, anxiety, and PTSD in approximately 250,000 survivors of Hurricane Katrina in 2005 (Siegel, 2007).

The manufacture, use, and disposal of tens of thousands of industrial and household chemicals are causing or contributing to increased rates of various forms of cancer, birth defects, reproductive abnormalities, immune system dysfunction, neurological impairments, and developmental disabilities, all significant stressors in their own right (e.g., Koger, Schettler, & Weiss, 2005; U.S. EPA, 2012). More than 85,000 chemicals are currently registered with the Environmental Protection Agency, including commonly used pesticides (such as flea or ant controls) and household chemicals (e.g., paint thinners, cleaning agents, bleach). In addition, certain ingredients in plastics, electronics, and cosmetics are known to be toxic to humans and other animals. The net result is deteriorating health of human beings on physical, mental, emotional, and social levels, as well as degradation of the planet.

The good news is that if individuals perceive a situation or product to be harmful to personal well-being and health, they will be more motivated toward problem solving and engaging in specific behaviors that act to reduce the risks (Homburg & Stolberg, 2006). One innovation in such *problem-focused coping* is reflected in a unique program developed at the Environmental Health Clinic at New York University. Analogous to other university health clinics, "impatients" (people who are tired of waiting for legislative action) make appointments to discuss environmental health concerns, including toxic chemicals and pollution, and receive "prescriptions" for actions: opportunities to engage in local data collection and projects aimed to improve environmental health. The goal is to convert people's anxiety and concern about environmental issues into specific, measurable, and significant actions (Schaffer, 2008).

Perhaps not surprisingly, people strongly prefer healthy, natural settings that include bodies of water, plants, trees, and sunlight over urban environments filled with buildings and cars (Kaplan & Kaplan, 1989; van den Berg, Hartig, & Staats, 2007). Walking in natural settings, or simply having views of plants, can alleviate symptoms of stress (e.g., Kaplan & Kaplan, 1989) by activating the *parasympathetic nervous system* (see Chapter 3), providing recovery by re-

Learn More Online

The Collaborative on Health and the Environment

The organization that maintains this site works to "advance knowledge and effective action to address growing concerns about the links between human health and environmental factors." The rich resources include access to a searchable database that summarizes research on the links between chemical contaminants and approximately 180 human diseases or conditions.

Learn More Online

Environmental Working Group

This nonprofit watchdog organization provides many useful resources (such as "Skin Deep" and "Pots, Pans, And Plastics: A Shopper's Guide to Food Safety") to consumers while simultaneously pushing for national policy change. The website offers recent research-based information on toxic chemicals and ways to avoid them.

In recent years, psychologists have conducted some interesting research on the effects of exposure to natural settings (like the top two photos) versus human-created urban environments (like the bottom two photos). This research indicates that natural environments can decrease individuals' response to stress.

ducing blood pressure and heart rate. Activities such as gardening, caring for indoor plants, and interacting with nonhuman animals such as pet dogs can all reduce stress (Frumkin, 2001). Spending time in nature can also provide recovery from prolonged work and concentration. You can probably relate to the worn out feeling that accompanies intense studying during midterm and final exams. As little as 20 minutes spent in a natural setting has been shown to relieve this attentional fatigue (Berman, et al., 2008).

Given their restorative benefits, natural environments have long been used in outpatient and nature-immersion therapies (Chalquist, 2009). For instance, Jordan and Marshall (2010) point out that Freud took his clients outside for analytic walks during the therapy hour. *Wilderness therapy* programs take advantage of nature as a backdrop for traditional therapeutic techniques or integrate wilderness skills and interaction as a part of therapy itself. Most wilderness therapy programs are designed for adolescents struggling with behavioral and emotional problems, but other client populations have included attachment-challenged adults (Bettmann & Jasperson, 2008), families

(Swank & Daire, 2010), and women who have suffered abuse (Cole, Erdman, & Rothblum, 1994; McBride & Korell, 2005). Because wilderness therapy programs have historically suffered from a lack of consistency in methods, quality, and practitioner credentials, as well as a lack of ethical oversight, some providers banded together in 1997 to form the Outdoor Behavioral Health Industry Council. Outcome research conducted by members of this organization and others is beginning to generate evidence for the effectiveness of nature-based therapy for improving self-perceptions, emotional well-being, resiliency, and social functioning (e.g., Chalquist, 2009; Russell, 2005).

Intact and healthy ecosystems are vital for human well-being, but valuing natural resources only for the ways in which they can benefit humankind is a limited and anthropocentric view. As Greenway (1995) put it, "Perhaps the clearest evidence of our recovery will be that we do not demand that wilderness heal us. We will have learned to let it be. For a wilderness that must heal us is surely a commodity, just as when we can only look at wilderness as a source of endless wealth" (pp. 134–135).

What You Can Personally Do

I am only one. But still I am one.
I cannot do everything, but still I can do something;
And because I cannot do everything,
I will not refuse to do the something that I can do.
—Quote from Edward Everett Hale (1822–1909),
original source unknown

Many excellent guides are available (both online and in print) on how to become more environmentally responsible. You can start by taking the online quiz at http://www.myfootprint.org/ to determine your own ecological footprint and consider ways to alter your daily life based on your quiz results. You might also consider developing a *behavior modification* project (see the Application section in Chapter 3) addressing some of your environmentally relevant behaviors.

Six aspects of human lifestyles most significantly and adversely affect the environment (Gardner & Stern, 2008; G. T. Miller, 2007): agriculture, transportation, home energy use, water use, overall resource consumption and waste, and toxic chemical production, use, and disposal. We recommend that you think about these issues and take the following steps toward walking more lightly on the Earth. If you don't feel you can do all of them, select at least a few to get you started on a more sustainable lifestyle, and then add a new one each month.

Agriculture

- Reduce your meat consumption by eating *no meat* one day per week, then increase to two days, and so forth.
- Buy locally grown food for at least one month a year, and then try to increase this.
- Buy organically produced food or grow some of your own.

Transportation

- Walk, bike, carpool, or take mass transit as much as you can.
- If possible, work at home or live near your work or school.
- When you have to drive, note that fuel efficiency can be dramatically increased by
  - reducing your speed;
  - avoiding rapid acceleration and sudden stops;
  - shutting off the engine rather than idling;
  - keeping tires inflated;
  - getting regular tune-ups; and
  - turning off your air conditioner.
- Record the distance you drive for one week, and then try to reduce the amount by 10%. Once you accomplish that, try reducing by 15% or more.
- When you purchase a new car, buy a small, fuel-efficient (greater than 35 mpg) model.

Home Energy Use

- Turn down the heat by at least a few degrees in winter, and avoid using air conditioning (or turn the thermostat up a few degrees in the summer).
- Turn off computers, printers, and other appliances when not in use.
- Replace your light bulbs with compact fluorescent bulbs.

Water Use

- Always turn off the water while brushing your teeth and shaving.
- Take showers instead of baths, and limit them to 5–10 minutes.
- Turn off the water while soaping up and shampooing.
- Reuse cups and plates when possible, rather than washing after each use.
- Only run dishwashers and clothes-washers with full loads.
- Use the flushing rule: "If it's yellow, let it mellow, if it's brown, flush it down" (urine is sterile).

Resource Consumption

- The two most important ways to reduce consumption and waste are:
  - *Refusing to buy things you don't really need, or that you could borrow or rent,* and
  - *Reusing* as many items as possible (coffee cups, canvas or other bags for groceries, and your own *to-go* container for leftovers when you eat out.

Refusing and reusing will save you money, and reduce your environmental impact. Recycling is important, but it still requires energy and encourages the production and use of more stuff. Keep a list of things you refused to buy or reused, and try to expand the list each month. (Refer to the "Unshopping Card" in **Figure A.4** on page A-7.)

- Beware of "green-washing"—many products are misleadingly labeled "eco-friendly" or "all natural."
- Buy secondhand items of all kinds whenever possible
- Give away, donate to charity, or sell items you no longer need or use, rather than throwing them away—especially during move out time at the end of the school year!
- Junk mail generates an astonishing amount of waste, utilizes an incredible amount of natural resources, and contributes to climate change. Let organizations know that you don't want to receive their newsletters, catalogs, and solicitations, and be sure to recycle mailings you can't refuse.

Toxic Chemicals

- Pesticides are designed to kill bugs (insecticides), weeds (herbicides), rodents, and so forth. They are directly toxic to humans as well, producing cancers and learning disabilities, among other health risks. Don't use any pesticides in your home, lawn, or garden, and educate others about their impacts on human health and neurological function, as well as detrimental effects on biodiversity.

• Avoid chemical cleansers. Baking soda and vinegar are excellent alternatives to many cleaning products; vinegar is also an effective weed killer.

• Many plastics, cosmetics, and personal care products contain chemicals that disrupt normal hormone functions (e.g., phthalates and bisphenol A or BPA). Don't buy bottled water, don't reheat or microwave foods in plastic containers, use fewer products with fewer ingredients, and don't trust claims like "dermatologist-tested," "natural," or "organic." Read the ingredient labels and avoid fragrances, dyes, parabens or -paraben, and things you can't pronounce.

• Reduce use of plastics by bringing your own refillable containers, buying in bulk, buying things with minimal packaging, and purchasing products in recyclable and recycled packaging.

• Dispose of household toxic products properly. Many items—paints, pesticides, batteries, and even energy-efficient compact fluorescent light bulbs—contain toxic ingredients. Drop these items off at a local household hazardous waste site.

GLOSSARY

acculturation Changing to adapt to a new culture.

acquired immune deficiency syndrome (AIDS) A disorder in which the immune system is gradually weakened and eventually disabled by the human immunodeficiency virus (HIV).

acute stressors Threatening events that have a relatively short duration and a clear end point.

adjustment The psychological processes through which people manage or cope with the demands and challenges of everyday life.

affective forecasting Efforts to predict one's emotional reactions to future events.

aggression Any behavior intended to hurt someone, either physically or verbally.

agoraphobia A fear of going out to public places.

alcohol dependence A chronic, progressive disorder marked by a growing compulsion to drink and impaired control over drinking that eventually interferes with health and social behavior.

alcoholism *See* alcohol dependence

ambient stress Chronic environmental conditions that, although not urgent, are negatively valued and place adaptive demands on people.

anal intercourse The insertion of the penis into a partner's anus and rectum.

androcentrism The belief that the male is the norm.

androgens The principal class of male sex hormones.

androgyny The coexistence of both masculine and feminine personality traits in an individual.

anhedonia A diminished ability to experience pleasure.

anorexia nervosa An eating disorder characterized by intense fear of gaining weight, disturbed body image, refusal to maintain normal weight, and use of dangerous methods to lose weight.

antecedents In behavior modification, events that typically precede a target response.

antianxiety drugs Drugs that relieve tension, apprehension, and nervousness.

anticipatory stressors Upcoming or future events that are perceived to be threatening.

antidepressant drugs Drugs that gradually elevate mood and help to bring people out of a depression.

antipsychotic drugs Drugs used to gradually reduce psychotic symptoms, including hyperactivity, mental confusion, hallucinations, and delusions.

anxiety disorders A class of psychological disorders marked by feelings of excessive apprehension and anxiety.

approach-approach conflict A conflict in which a choice must be made between two attractive goals.

approach-avoidance conflict A conflict in which a choice must be made about whether to pursue a single goal that has both attractive and unattractive aspects.

archetypes Emotionally charged images and thought forms that have universal meaning.

assertiveness Acting in one's own best interest by expressing one's feelings and thoughts honestly and directly.

atherosclerosis A disease characterized by gradual narrowing of the coronary arteries.

attachment styles Typical ways of interacting in close relationships.

attitudes Beliefs and feelings about people, objects, and ideas.

attributions Inferences that people draw about the causes of events, others' behavior, and their own behavior.

autism/autism spectrum disorder A psychological disorder characterized by profound impairment of social interaction and communication and by severely restricted interests and activities, apparent by the age of 3.

autonomic nervous system (ANS) That portion of the peripheral nervous system made up of the nerves that connect to the heart, blood vessels, smooth muscles, and glands.

aversion therapy A behavior therapy in which an aversive stimulus is paired with a stimulus that elicits an undesirable response.

avoidance-avoidance conflict A conflict in which a choice must be made between two unattractive goals.

basking in reflected glory The tendency to enhance one's image by publicly announcing one's association with those who are successful.

battering Physical abuse, emotional abuse, and sexual abuse, especially in marriage or relationships.

behavior Any overt (observable) response or activity by an organism.

behavior modification A systematic approach to changing behavior through the application of the principles of conditioning.

behavior therapies The application of the principles of learning to direct efforts to change clients' maladaptive behaviors.

behavioral contract A written agreement outlining a promise to adhere to the contingencies of a behavior modification program.

behaviorism A theoretical orientation based on the premise that scientific psychology should study observable behavior.

binge-eating disorder An eating disorder that involves distress-inducing eating binges

that are not accompanied by the purging, fasting, and excessive exercise seen in bulimia.

biomedical therapies Physiological interventions intended to reduce symptoms associated with psychological disorders.

biopsychosocial model The idea that physical illness is caused by a complex interaction of biological, psychological, and sociocultural factors.

bipolar disorder Psychological disorder marked by the experience of both depressed and manic periods.

bisexuals People who seek emotional-sexual relationships with members of both genders.

body image One's attitudes, beliefs, and feelings about one's body.

body mass index (BMI) Weight (in kilograms) divided by height (in meters) squared (kg/m^2).

brainstorming Generating as many ideas as possible while withholding criticism and evaluation.

bulimia nervosa An eating disorder characterized by habitual out-of-control overeating followed by unhealthy compensatory efforts, such as self-induced vomiting, fasting, abuse of laxatives and diuretics, and excessive exercise.

burnout Physical, mental, and emotional exhaustion that is attributable to work-related stress.

bystander effect The social phenomenon in which individuals are less likely to provide needed help when others are present than when they are alone.

cancer Malignant cell growth, which may occur in many organ systems in the body.

cannabis The hemp plant from which marijuana, hashish, and THC are derived.

capitalization Telling other people about whatever good things are happening in our own lives.

case study An in-depth investigation of an individual subject.

catastrophic thinking Unrealistic appraisals of stress that exaggerate the magnitude of one's problems.

catharsis The release of emotional tension.

cerebral hemispheres The right and left halves of the cerebrum, which is the convoluted outer layer of the brain.

channel The medium through which a message reaches the receiver.

chronic stressors Threatening events that have a relatively long duration and no readily apparent time limit.

classical conditioning A type of learning in which a neutral stimulus acquires the capacity to evoke a response that was originally evoked by another stimulus.

client-centered therapy An insight therapy that emphasizes providing a supportive emotional climate for clients, who play a major role in determining the pace and direction of their therapy.

clinical psychologists Psychologists who specialize in the diagnosis and treatment of psychological disorders and everyday behavioral problems.

clinical psychology The branch of psychology concerned with the diagnosis and treatment of psychological problems and disorders.

close relationships Relatively long-lasting relationships in which frequent interactions occur in a variety of settings and in which the impact of the interactions is strong.

cognitive-behavioral treatments Therapy approach that uses varied combinations of verbal interventions and behavior modification techniques to help clients change maladaptive patterns of thinking.

cognitive therapy An insight therapy that emphasizes recognizing and changing negative thoughts and maladaptive beliefs.

cohabitation Living together in a sexually intimate relationship without the legal bonds of marriage.

coitus The insertion of the penis into the vagina and (typically) pelvic thrusting.

collective unconscious According to Jung, a storehouse of latent memory traces inherited from people's ancestral past that is shared with the entire human race.

collectivism Putting group goals ahead of personal goals and defining one's identity in terms of the groups to which one belongs.

commitment The decision and intent to maintain a relationship in spite of the difficulties and costs that may arise.

communication apprehension The anxiety caused by having to talk with others.

comorbidity The coexistence of two or more disorders.

comparison level One's standard of what constitutes an acceptable balance of rewards and costs in a relationship.

comparison level for alternatives One's estimation of the available outcomes from alternative relationships.

compensation A defense mechanism characterized by efforts to overcome imagined or real inferiorities by developing one's abilities.

compliance Yielding to social pressure in one's public behavior, even though one's private beliefs have not changed.

concordance rate A statistic indicating the percentage of twin pairs or other pairs of relatives who exhibit the same disorder.

conditioned response (CR) A learned reaction to a conditioned stimulus that occurs because of previous conditioning.

conditioned stimulus (CS) A previously neutral stimulus that has, through conditioning, acquired the capacity to evoke a conditioned response.

confirmation bias The tendency to behave toward others in ways that confirm your expectations about them.

conformity Yielding to real or imagined social pressure.

conscious According to Freud, whatever one is aware of at a particular point in time.

conservation psychology The study of the interactive relationships between humans and the rest of nature, with a particular focus on how to enhance conservation of natural resources.

constructive coping Efforts to deal with stressful events that are judged to be relatively healthful.

context The environment in which communication takes place.

control group Subjects in an experiment who do not receive the special treatment given to the experimental group.

coping Active efforts to master, reduce, or tolerate the demands created by stress.

coronary heart disease A chronic disease characterized by a reduction in blood flow from the coronary arteries, which supply the heart with blood.

corpus callosum The band of fibers connecting the two hemispheres of the brain.

correlation The extent to which two variables are related to each other.

correlation coefficient A numerical index of the degree of relationship that exists between two variables.

counseling psychologists Psychologists who specialize in the treatment of everyday behavioral problems.

couples therapy The treatment of both partners in a committed, intimate relationship, in which the main focus is on relationship issues.

cunnilingus The oral stimulation of the female genitals.

date rape Forced and unwanted intercourse with someone in the context of dating.

defense mechanisms Largely unconscious reactions that protect a person from unpleasant emotions such as anxiety and guilt.

defensive attribution The tendency to blame victims for their misfortune, so that one feels less likely to be victimized in a similar way.

defensiveness An excessive concern wth protecting oneself from being hurt.

delusions False beliefs that are maintained even though they clearly are out of touch with reality.

dependent variable In an experiment, the variable that is thought to be affected by manipulations of the independent variable.

diagnosis Distinguishing one illness from another.

discrimination Behaving differently, usually unfairly, toward members of a group.

displaced workers Individuals who are unemployed because their jobs have disappeared.

displacement Diverting emotional feelings (usually anger) from their original source to a substitute target.

display rules Norms that govern the appropriate display of emotions.

dissociative amnesia A sudden loss of memory for important personal information that is too extensive to be due to normal forgetting.

dissociative disorders A class of psychological disorders characterized by loss of contact with portions of one's consciousness or memory, resulting in disruptions in one's sense of identity.

dissociative identity disorder (DID) Dissociative disorder involving the coexistence in one person of two or more largely complete, and usually very different, personalities. Also called multiple-personality disorder.

divorce The legal dissolution of a marriage.

door-in-the-face technique Making a very large request that is likely to be turned down to increase the chance that people will agree to a smaller request later.

downward social comparison The defensive tendency to compare oneself with someone whose troubles are more serious than one's own.

dream analysis A psychotherapeutic technique in which the therapist interprets the symbolic meaning of the client's dreams.

dual-earner households Households in which both partners are employed.

eating disorders Severe disturbances in eating behavior characterized by preoccupation with weight and unhealthy efforts to control weight.

ecstasy *See* MDMA.

ego According to Freud, the decision-making component of personality that operates according to the reality principle.

elaboration likelihood model The idea that an individual's thoughts about a persuasive message (rather than the message itself) determine whether attitude change will occur.

electroconvulsive therapy (ECT) A biomedical treatment in which electric shock is used to produce a cortical seizure accompanied by convulsions.

electronically mediated communication Interpersonal communication that takes place via technology.

emotional intelligence The ability to monitor, assess, express, or regulate one's emotions; the capacity to identify, interpret, and understand others' emotions; and the ability to use this information to guide one's thinking and actions.

emotions Powerful, largely uncontrollable feelings, accompanied by physiological changes.

empiricism The premise that knowledge should be acquired through observation.

endocrine system Glands that secrete chemicals called hormones into the bloodstream.

endogamy The tendency of people to marry within their own social group.

environmental psychologists Psychologists who study how individuals are affected by, and interact with, their physical environments.

epidemiology The study of the distribution of mental or physical disorders in a population.

erectile difficulties The male sexual dysfunction characterized by the persistent inability to achieve or maintain an erection adequate for intercourse.

erogenous zones Areas of the body that are sexually sensitive or responsive.

estrogens The principal class of female sex hormones.

etiology The apparent causation and developmental history of an illness.

evolutionary psychology A field of psychology that examines behavioral processes in terms of their adaptive value for members of a species over the course of many generations.

experiment A research method in which the investigator manipulates an (independent) variable under carefully controlled conditions and observes whether there are changes in a second (dependent) variable as a result.

experimental group The subjects in an experiment who receive some special treatment in regard to the independent variable.

explanatory style The tendency to use similar causal attributions for a wide variety of events in one's life.

exposure therapies An approach to behavior therapy in which clients are confronted with situations they fear so they learn these situations are really harmless.

expressiveness A style of communication characterized by the ability to express tender emotions easily and to be sensitive to the feelings of others.

external attributions Ascribing the causes of behavior to situational demands and environmental constraints.

extinction The gradual weakening and disappearance of a conditioned response tendency.

factor analysis Technique of analyzing correlations among many variables to identify closely related clusters of variables.

family life cycle An orderly sequence of developmental stages that families tend to progress through.

family therapy The treatment of a family unit as a whole, in which the main focus is on family dynamics and communication.

fellatio The oral stimulation of the penis.

fight-or-flight response A physiological reaction to threat that mobilizes an organism for attacking (fight) or fleeing (flight) an enemy.

fixation In Freud's theory, a failure to move forward from one stage to another as expected.

flow The state of being in which a person becomes fully involved and engaged in the present time by some interesting, challenging, and intrinsically rewarding activity.

foot-in-the-door technique Getting people to agree to a small request to increase the chances that they will agree to a larger request later.

forgiveness Counteracting the natural tendencies to seek vengeance or avoid an offender, thereby releasing this person from further liability for his or her transgression.

free association A psychotherapeutic technique in which clients spontaneously express their thoughts and feelings exactly as they occur, with as little censorship as possible.

frustration The feelings that occur in any situation in which the pursuit of some goal is thwarted.

fundamental attribution error The tendency to explain others' behavior as a result of personal rather than situational factors.

gender The state of being male or female.

gender identity The ability to correctly classify oneself as male or female.

gender-role identity A person's identification with the traits regarded as masculine or feminine.

gender-role transcendence perspective The idea that to be fully human, people need to move beyond gender roles as a way of organizing the world and of perceiving themselves and others.

gender roles Cultural expectations about what is appropriate behavior for each gender.

gender schemas Cognitive structures that guide the processing of gender-relevant information.

gender stereotypes Widely shared beliefs about males' and females' abilities, personality traits, and social behavior.

general adaptation syndrome A model of the body's stress response, consisting of three stages: alarm, resistance, and exhaustion.

generalized anxiety disorder A psychological disorder marked by a chronic high level of anxiety that is not tied to any specific threat.

glass ceiling An invisible barrier that prevents most women and ethnic minorities from advancing to the highest levels of an occupation.

gonads The sex glands.

gratitude Recognizing and concentrating on the good things in one's life and being thankful for them.

grit Possessing perseverance and passion for achieving long-term goals.

group therapy The simultaneous treatment of several or more clients in a group.

hallucinations Sensory perceptions that occur in the absence of a real external stimulus or that represent gross distortions of perceptual input.

hallucinogens A diverse group of drugs that have powerful effects on mental and emotional functioning, marked most prominently by distortions in sensory and perceptual experience.

hardiness A personality syndrome marked by commitment, challenge, and control that is purportedly associated with strong stress resistance.

health psychology The subfield of psychology concerned with the relation of psychosocial factors to the promotion and maintenance of health, and with the causation, prevention, and treatment of illness.

hedonic adaptation The phenomenon that occurs when the mental scale that people use to judge the pleasantness and unpleasantness of their experiences shifts so that their neutral point, or baseline for comparison, is changed.

heritability ratio An estimate of the proportion of trait variability in a population that is determined by variations in genetic inheritance.

heterosexism The assumption that all individuals and relationships are heterosexual.

heterosexuals People whose sexual desires and erotic behaviors are directed toward the other gender.

hierarchy of needs A systematic arrangement of needs, according to priority, in which basic needs must be met before less basic needs are aroused.

hindsight bias The common tendency to mold one's interpretation of the past to fit how events actually turned out.

homogamy The tendency of people to marry others who have similar personal characteristics.

homophobia The intense fear and intolerance of homosexuality.

homosexuals People who seek emotional/sexual relationships with members of the same gender.

hope People's expectations that their goals can be achieved in the future.

hormones Chemical substances released into the bloodstream by the endocrine glands.

hostility A persistent negative attitude marked by cynical, mistrusting thoughts, feelings of anger, and overtly aggressive actions.

humanism A theoretical orientation that emphasizes the unique qualities of humans, especially their free will and their potential for personal growth.

hypoactive sexual desire Lack of interest in sexual activity.

id In Freud's theory, the primitive, instinctive component of personality that operates according to the pleasure principle.

identification Bolstering self-esteem by forming an imaginary or real alliance with some person or group.

identity A relatively clear and stable sense of who one is and what one stands for.

immune response The body's defensive reaction to invasion by bacteria, viral agents, or other foreign substances.

impression management Usually conscious efforts to influence the way others think of one.

incongruence The disparity between one's self-concept and one's actual experience.

independent variable In an experiment, a condition or event that an experimenter varies in order to see its impact on another variable.

individualism Putting personal goals ahead of group goals and defining one's identity in terms of personal attributes rather than group memberships.

industrial/organizational (I/O) psychology The study of human behavior in the workplace.

informational influence Pressure to conform that operates when people look to others for how to behave in ambiguous situations.

ingratiation Efforts to make oneself likable to others.

insight therapies A group of psychotherapies in which verbal interactions are intended to enhance clients' self-knowledge and thus promote healthful changes in personality and behavior.

instrumentality A style of communication that focuses on reaching practical goals and finding solutions to problems.

interdependence theory *See* social exchange theory

internal attributions Ascribing the causes of behavior to personal dispositions, traits, abilities, and feelings rather than to external events.

internal conflict The struggle that occurs when two or more incompatible motivations or behavioral impulses compete for expression.

Internet addiction Spending an inordinate amount of time on the Internet and inability to control online use.

interpersonal communication An interactional process whereby one person sends a message to another.

interpersonal conflict Disagreement among two or more people.

interpretation A therapist's attempts to explain the inner significance of the client's thoughts, feelings, memories, and behaviors.

intimacy Warmth, closeness, and sharing in a relationship.

intimate partner violence Aggression toward those who are in close relationships to the aggressor.

investments Things that people contribute to a relationship that they can't get back if the relationship ends.

kinesics The study of communication through body movements.

labor force All people who are employed as well as those who are currently unemployed but are looking for work.

learned helplessness Passive behavior produced by exposure to unavoidable aversive events.

leisure Unpaid activities one chooses to engage in because they are personally meaningful.

life changes Any noticeable alterations in one's living circumstances that require readjustment.

listening A mindful activity and complex process that requires one to select and to organize information, interpret and respond to communications, and recall what one has heard.

loneliness The emotional state that occurs when a person has fewer interpersonal relationships than desired or when these relationships are not as satisfying as desired.

lowball technique Getting people to commit themselves to an attractive proposition before its hidden costs are revealed.

major depressive disorder Psychological disorder characterized by persistent feelings of sadness and despair and a loss of interest in previous sources of pleasure.

manic-depressive disorder *See* bipolar disorder.

marital therapy The treatment of both partners in a committed, intimate relationship, in which the main focus is on relationship issues.

marriage The legally and socially sanctioned union of sexually intimate adults.

masturbation The stimulation of one's own genitals.

matching hypothesis The idea that people of similar levels of physical attractiveness gravitate toward each other.

MDMA A compound related to both amphetamines and hallucinogens, especially mescaline; it produces a high that typically lasts a few hours or more. Also known as *ecstasy*.

medical model The idea that it is useful to think of abnormal behavior as a disease.

meditation A family of mental exercises in which a conscious attempt is made to focus attention in a nonanalytical way.

menarche The first occurrence of menstruation.

mere exposure effect An increase in positive feelings toward a novel stimulus (such as a person) based on frequent exposure to it.

message The information or meaning that is transmitted from one person to another.

meta-analysis A statistical technique that evaluates the results of many studies on the same question.

mindfulness A cultivated perspective in which people are sensitive to context and focused on the present.

mindlessness Engaging in rote behavior, performing familiar, scripted actions without much cognition, as if on autopilot.

mnemonic devices Strategies for enhancing memory.

monogamy The practice of having only one spouse at a time.

mood stabilizers Drugs used to control mood swings in patients with bipolar mood disorders.

multiple-personality disorder *See* dissociative identity disorder

narcissism The tendency to regard oneself as grandiosely self-important.

narcotics (opiates) Drugs derived from opium that are capable of relieving pain.

naturalistic observation An approach to research in which the researcher engages in careful observation of behavior without intervening directly with the subjects.

need for cognition The tendency to seek out and enjoy effortful thought, problem-solving activities, and in-depth analysis.

need for self-actualization The need to fulfill one's potential; the highest need in Maslow's motivational hierarchy.

negative emotions Unpleasant responses to potential threats or dangers, including subjective states like sadness, disgust, anger, guilt, and fear.

negative reinforcement The strengthening of a response because it is followed by the removal of a (presumably) unpleasant stimulus.

neuroticism A broad personality trait associated with chronic anxiety, insecurity, and self-consciousness.

neurotransmitters Chemicals that carry signals from one neuron to another.

noise Any stimulus that interferes with accurately expressing or understanding a message.

nonverbal communication The transmission of meaning from one person to another through means or symbols other than words.

nonverbal sensitivity The ability to accurately encode (express) and decode (understand) nonverbal cues.

normative influence Pressure to conform that operates when people conform to social norms for fear of negative social consequences.

nutrition A collection of processes (mainly food consumption) through which an organism uses the materials (nutrients) required for survival and growth.

obedience A form of compliance that occurs when people follow direct commands, usually from someone in a position of authority.

observational learning Learning that occurs when an organism's responding is influenced by observing others, who are called models.

obsessive-compulsive disorder (OCD) A psychological disorder marked by persistent uncontrollable intrusions of unwanted thoughts (obsessions) and by urges to engage in senseless rituals (compulsions).

occupational interest inventories Tests that measure one's interests as they relate to various jobs or careers.

Oedipal complex According to Freud, a child's erotically tinged desires for the other-sex parent, accompanied by feelings of hostility toward the same-sex parent.

operant conditioning A form of learning in which voluntary responses come to be controlled by their consequences.

optimism A general tendency to expect good outcomes.

orgasm The release that occurs when sexual arousal reaches its peak intensity and is discharged in a series of muscular contractions that pulsate through the pelvic area.

orgasmic difficulties Sexual disorders characterized by an ability to experience sexual arousal but persistent problems in achieving orgasm.

overcompensation Making up for frustration in one area by seeking overgratification in another area.

overlearning Continued rehearsal of material after one has first appeared to have mastered it.

overdose An excessive dose of a drug that can seriously threaten one's life.

panic disorder Recurrent attacks of overwhelming anxiety that usually occur suddenly and unexpectedly.

paralanguage All vocal cues other than the content of the verbal message itself.

parental investment theory The idea that a species' mating patterns depend on what each sex has to invest—in the way of time, energy, and survival risk—to produce and nurture offspring.

passion The intense feelings (both positive and negative) experienced in love relationships, including sexual desire.

person perception The process of forming impressions of others.

personal space A zone of space surrounding a person that is felt to "belong" to that person.

personality An individual's unique constellation of consistent behavioral traits.

personality trait A durable disposition to behave in a particular way in a variety of situations.

persuasion The communication of arguments and information intended to change another person's attitudes.

phobic disorder Anxiety disorder marked by a persistent and irrational fear of an object or situation that presents no realistic danger.

physical dependence The need to continue to take a drug to avoid withdrawal illness.

polygamy Having more than one spouse at one time.

polygraph A device that records fluctuations in physiological arousal as a person answers questions.

positive emotions Pleasant responses to events that promote connections with others, including subjective states such as happiness, joy, euphoria, gratitude, and contentment.

positive individual traits Dispositional qualities that account for why some people are happier and psychologically healthier than other people.

positive institutions Those organizations that cultivate civic virtues, encouraging people to behave like good citizens while promoting the collective good.

positive reinforcement The strengthening of a response because it is followed by the arrival of a (presumably) pleasant stimulus.

positive psychology A social and intellectual movement within the discipline of psychology that focuses on human strengths and how people can flourish and be successful.

positive psychotherapy Approach to therapy that attempts to get clients to recognize their strengths, appreciate their blessings, savor positive experiences, forgive those who have wronged them, and find meaning in their lives.

positive subjective experiences The positive but private feelings and thoughts people have about themselves and the events in their lives.

possible selves One's conceptions about the kind of person one might become in the future.

posttraumatic growth Enhanced personal strength, realization of what is truly important in life, and increased appreciation for life, friends, and family following trauma.

posttraumatic stress disorder (PTSD) Disturbed behavior that emerges sometime after a major stressful event is over.

preconscious According to Freud, material just beneath the surface of awareness that can be easily retrieved.

prejudice A negative attitude toward members of a group.

premature ejaculation Impaired sexual relations because a man consistently reaches orgasm too quickly.

pressure Expectations or demands that one behave in a certain way.

prevalence The percentage of a population that exhibits a disorder during a specified time period.

primacy effect The fact that initial information tends to carry more weight than subsequent information.

primary appraisal An initial evaluation of whether an event is (1) irrelevant to one, (2) relevant, but not threatening, or (3) stressful.

procrastination The tendency to delay tackling tasks until the last minute.

prognosis A forecast about the probable course of an illness.

projection Attributing one's own thoughts, feelings, or motives to another person.

projective tests Personality tests that ask subjects to respond to vague, ambiguous stimuli in ways that may reveal the subjects' needs, feelings, and personality traits.

proxemics The study of people's use of interpersonal space.

proximity Geographic, residential, and other forms of spatial closeness.

psychiatrists Physicians who specialize in the treatment of psychological disorders.

psychoanalysis An insight therapy that emphasizes the recovery of unconscious conflicts, motives, and defenses through techniques such as free association, dream analysis, and transference.

psychodynamic theories All the diverse theories descended from the work of Sigmund Freud that focus on unconscious mental forces.

psychological dependence The need to continue to take a drug to satisfy intense mental and emotional craving for it.

psychological test A standardized measure of a sample of a person's behavior.

psychology The science that studies behavior and the physiological and mental processes that underlie it and the profession that applies the accumulated knowledge of this science to practical problems.

psychopharmacotherapy The treatment of mental disorders with medication.

psychosexual stages In Freud's theory, developmental periods with a characteristic sexual focus that leave their mark on adult personality.

psychosomatic diseases Genuine physical ailments caused in part by psychological factors, especially emotional distress.

public self An image presented to others in social interactions.

punishment The weakening (decrease in frequency) of a response because it is followed by the arrival of a (presumably) unpleasant stimulus.

rational-emotive therapy An approach to therapy that focuses on altering clients' patterns of irrational thinking to reduce maladaptive emotions and behavior.

rationalization Creating false but plausible excuses to justify unacceptable behavior.

reaction formation Behaving in a way that is exactly the opposite of one's true feelings.

receiver The person to whom a message is targeted.

reciprocal liking Liking those who show they like you.

reciprocity principle The rule that one should pay back in kind what one receives from others.

reference group A set of people who are used as a guage in making social comparisons.

refractory period A time after orgasm during which males are unable to experience another orgasm.

regression A reversion to immature patterns of behavior.

relationship maintenance The actions and activities used to sustain the desired quality of a relationship.

reliability The measurement consistency of a test.

repression Keeping distressing thoughts and feelings buried in the unconscious.

resilience A person's ability to recover and often prosper following some consequential life event.

resistance Largely unconscious defensive maneuvers intended to hinder the progress of therapy.

savoring The power to focus on, value, and even boost the enjoyment of almost any experience, whether great or small.

schizophrenic disorders A class of disorders marked by disturbances in thought that spill over to affect perceptual, social, and emotional processes.

secondary appraisal An evaluation of one's coping resources and options for dealing with stress.

sedatives Sleep-inducing drugs that tend to decrease central nervous system and behavioral activity.

self-actualization *See* need for self-actualization.

self-attributions Inferences that people draw about the causes of their own behavior.

self-concept A collection of beliefs about one's basic nature, unique qualities, and typical behavior.

self-defeating behaviors Seemingly intentional acts that thwart a person's self-interest.

self-disclosure The voluntary act of verbally communicating private information about oneself to another person.

self-discrepancy The mismatching of self-perceptions.

self-efficacy One's belief about one's ability to perform behaviors that should lead to expected outcomes.

self-enhancement The tendency to seek positive (and reject negative) information about oneself.

self-esteem One's overall assessment of one's worth as a person; the evaluative component of the self-concept.

self-fulfilling prophecy The process whereby expectations about a person cause the person to behave in ways that confirm the expectations.

self-handicapping The tendency to sabotage one's performance to provide an excuse for possible failure.

self-monitoring The degree to which people attend to and control the impressions they make on others.

self-regulation Directing and controlling one's behavior.

self-report inventories Personality scales that ask individuals to answer a series of questions about their characteristic behavior.

self-serving bias The tendency to attribute one's successes to personal factors and one's failures to situational factors.

self-verification theory The idea that people prefer to receive feedback from others that is consistent with their own self-views.

sender The person who initiates a message.

sensate focus A sex-therapy exercise in which partners take turns pleasuring each other with guided verbal feedback while certain kinds of stimulation are temporarily forbidden.

sensation seeking A generalized preference for high or low levels of sensory stimulation.

set-point theory The idea that there is a natural point of stability in body weight, thought to involve the monitoring of fat cell levels.

settling-point theory The idea that weight tends to drift around the level at which the constellation of factors that determine food consumption and energy expenditure achieve an equilibrium.

sex therapy The professional treatment of sexual dysfunctions.

sexism Discrimination against people on the basis of their sex.

sexual dysfunction An impairments in sexual functioning that causes subjective distress.

sexual harassment The subjection of individuals to unwelcome sexually oriented behavior.

sexual identity The complex of personal qualities, self-perceptions, attitudes, values, and preferences that guide one's sexual behavior.

sexual orientation A person's preference for emotional and sexual relationships with individuals of the same gender, the other gender, or either gender.

sexually transmitted disease (STD) An illness that is transmitted primarily through sexual contact.

shaping Modifying behavior by reinforcing closer and closer approximations of a desired response.

shyness Discomfort, inhibition, and excessive caution in interpersonal relations.

social comparison theory The idea that people need to compare themselves with others in order to gain insight into their own behavior.

social constructionism The assertion that individuals construct their own reality based on societal expectations, conditioning, and self-socialization.

social exchange theory The idea that interpersonal relationships are governed by perceptions of the rewards and costs exchanged in interactions.

social role theory The assertion that minor gender differences are exaggerated by the different social roles that males and females occupy.

social skills training A behavior therapy designed to improve interpersonal skills that emphasizes shaping, modeling, and behavioral rehearsal.

social support Aid and succor provided by members of one's social networks.

socialization The process by which individuals acquire the norms and roles expected of people in a particular society.

source The person who initiates, or sends, a message.

spermarche An adolescent male's first ejaculation.

standardization The uniform procedures used to administer and score a test.

stereotypes Widely held beliefs that people have certain characteristics simply because of their membership in a particular group.

stimulants Drugs that tend to increase central nervous system and behavioral activity.

stress Any circumstances that threaten or are perceived to threaten one's well-being and thereby tax one's coping abilities.

subjective well-being Individuals' personal assessments of their overall happiness or life satisfaction.

sublimation Defense mechanism that occurs when unconscious, unacceptable impulses are channeled into socially acceptable, perhaps even admirable, behaviors.

superego According to Freud, the moral component of personality that incorporates social standards about what represents right and wrong.

surveys Structured questionnaires designed to solicit information about specific aspects of participants' behavior.

sustainable world A world in which human activities and needs are balanced with those of other species and future generations, taking into account ecological as well as social and economic factors.

systematic desensitization A behavior therapy used to reduce clients' anxiety responses through counterconditioning.

tardive dyskinesia A neurological disorder marked by chronic tremors and involuntary spastic movements.

test norms Statistics that provide information about where a score on a psychological test ranks in relation to other scores on that test.

token A symbol of all the members of a group.

token economy A system for doling out symbolic reinforcers that are exchanged later for a variety of genuine reinforcers.

tolerance A progressive decrease in responsiveness to a drug with continued use.

transference A phenomenon that occurs when clients start relating to their therapist in ways that mimic critical relationships in their lives.

twin studies A research method in which researchers assess hereditary influence by comparing the resemblance of identical twins and fraternal twins on a trait.

Type A personality A personality style marked by a competitive orientation, impatience and urgency, and anger and hostility.

Type B personality A personality style marked by relatively relaxed, patient, easygoing, amicable behavior.

unconditioned response (UCR) An unlearned reaction to an unconditioned stimulus that occurs without previous conditioning.

unconditioned stimulus (UCS) A stimulus that evokes an unconditioned response without previous conditioning.

unconscious According to Freud, thoughts, memories, and desires that are well below the surface of conscious awareness but that nonetheless exert great influence on our behavior.

underemployment Settling for a job that does not fully utilize one's skills, abilities, and training.

undoing hypothesis The idea that positive emotions aid the mind and the body by recovering a sense of balance and flexibility following an episode experiencing negative emotion.

unrealistic optimism Awareness that certain health-related behaviors are dangerous but erroneously viewing those dangers as risks for others rather than oneself.

validity The ability of a test to measure what it was designed to measure.

variables *See* dependent variable; independent variable.

vasocongestion Engorgement of blood vessels.

work An activity that produces something of value for others.

work-family conflict The feeling of being pulled in multiple directions by competing demands from job and family.

workforce *See* labor force.

REFERENCES

Aamodt, M. G. (2004). *Research in law enforcement selection.* Boca Raton, FL: BrownWalker.

Abbey, A. (2009). Alcohol and sexual assault. In H. T. Reis & S. Sprecher (Eds.), *Encyclopedia of human relationships* (Vol. 1). Los Angeles: Sage Reference Publication.

Abbey, A., Clinton-Sherrod, A. M., McAuslan, P., Zawacki, T., & Buck, P. O. (2003). The relationship between the quantity of alcohol consumed and the severity of sexual assaults committed by college men. *Journal of Interpersonal Violence, 18*(7), 813–833.

Abel, E. L., & Kruger, M. L. (2010). Smile intensity in photographs predicts longevity. *Psychological Science, 21*(4), 542–544. doi:10.1177/0956797610363775

Abi-Saleh, B., Iskanadar, S. B., Elgharib, N., & Cohen, M. V. (2008). C-reactive protein: The harbinger of cardiovascular diseases. *Southern Medical Journal, 101*, 525–533.

Abma, J. C., & Martinez, G. M. (2006). Childlessness among older women in the United States: Trends and profiles. *Journal of Marriage and Family, 68*, 1045–1056.

Abrahamse, W., Steg, L., Vlek, C., & Rothengatter, T. (2005). A review of intervention studies aimed at household energy conservation. *Journal of Environmental Psychology, 25*, 273–291.

Abrams, D., Viki, G. T., Masser, B., & Bohner, G. (2003). Perceptions of stranger acquaintance rape: The role of benevolent and hostile sexism in victim blame and rape proclivity. *Journal of Personality and Social Psychology, 84*, 111–125.

Abramson, L. Y., Seligman, M. E. P., & Teasdale, J. D. (1978). Learned helplessness in humans: Critique and reformulation. *Journal of Abnormal Psychology, 87*, 49–74.

Acevedo, B. P., & Aron, A. (2009). Does a long-term relationship kill romantic love? *Review of General Psychology 13*, 59–65.

Ackerman, J. M., Griskevicius, V., & Li, N. P. (2011). Let's get serious: Communicating commitment in romantic relationships. *Journal of Personality and Social Psychology, 100*(6), 1079–1094. doi:10.1037/a0022412

Ackerman, J. M., Shapiro, J. R., Neuberg, S. L., Kenrick, D. T., Schaller, M., Becker, D. V., et al. (2006). They all look the same to me (unless they're angry): From out-group homogeneity to out-group heterogeneity. *Psychological Science, 17*, 836–840.

Ackerman, S., Zuroff, D. C., & Moskowitz, D. S. (2000). Generativity in midlife and young adults: Links to agency, communion, and subjective well-being. *International Journal of Aging and Human Development, 50*(1), 17–41.

Adams, G. (2012). Context in person, person in context: A cultural psychology approach to social-personality psychology. In K. Deaux & M. Snyder (Eds.), *The Oxford handbook of personality and social psychology* (pp. 182–208). New York, NY: Oxford University Press.

Adams, G., Anderson, S. L., & Adonu, J. K. (2004). The cultural grounding of closeness and intimacy. In D. J. Mashek & A. Aron (Eds.), *Handbook of closeness and intimacy.* Mahwah, NJ: Erlbaum.

Adams, M., & Coltrane, S. (2006). Framing divorce reform: Media, morality, and the politics of family. *Family Process, 46*, 17–34.

Adler, A. (1917). *Study of organ inferiority and its psychical compensation.* New York, NY: Nervous and Mental Diseases Publishing.

Adler, A. (1927). *Practice and theory of individual psychology.* New York, NY: Harcourt, Brace & World.

Adorno, T. W., Frenkel-Brunswik, E., Levinson, D. J., & Sanford, B. W. (1950). *The authoritarian personality.* New York, NY: Harper & Row.

Aggarwal, P., Jun, S., & Huh, J. (2011). Scarcity messages: A consumer competition perspective. *Journal of Advertising, 40*(3), 19–30. doi:10.2753/JOA0091-3367400302

Ahern, A. L., Bennett, K. M., & Hetherington, M. M. (2008). Internalization of the ultra-thin ideal: Positive implicit associations with underweight fashion models are associated with drive for thinness in young women. *Eating Disorders, 16*, 294–307.

Ahmetoglu, G., Swami, V., & Chamorro-Premuzic, T. (2010). The relationship between dimensions of love, personality, and relationship length. *Archives of Sexual Behavior, 39*(5), 1181–1190. doi:10.1007/s10508-009-9515-5

Ahrons, C. R. (2007). Introduction to the special issue on divorce and its aftermath. *Family Process, 46*(1), 3–6.

Aikawa, A., Fujita, M., & Tanaka, K. (2007). The relationship between social skills deficits and depression, loneliness, and social anxiety: Rethinking a vulnerability model of social skills deficits. *The Japanese Journal of Social Psychology, 23*, 95–103.

Ainsworth, M. D. S., Blehar, M. C., Waters, E., & Wall, S. (1978). *Patterns of attachment: A psychological study of the strange situation.* Hillsdale, NJ: Erlbaum.

Akerstedt, T., Kecklund, G., & Axelsson, J. (2007). Impaired sleep after bedtime stress and worries. *Biological Psychology, 76*(3), 170–173.

Akgun, S., & Ciarrochi, J. (2003). Learned resourcefulness moderates the relationship between academic stress and academic performance. *Educational Psychology, 23*(3), 287-294.

Akhtar, S. (2007). *Listening to others: Developmental and clinical aspects of empathy and attunement.* Lanham, MD: Jason Aronson.

Akimoto, S. A., & Sanbonmatsu, D. M. (1999). Differences in self-effacing behavior between European and Japanese Americans: Effect on competence evaluations. *Journal of Cross-Cultural Psychology, 30*, 159–177.

Akiskal, H. S. (2005). Mood disorders: Clinical features. In B. J. Sadock & V. A. Sadock (Eds.), *Kaplan & Sadock's comprehensive textbook of psychiatry.* Philadelphia: Lippincott Williams & Wilkins.

Akiskal, H. S. (2009). Mood disorders: Clinical features. In B. J. Sadock, V. A. Sadock, & P. Ruiz (Eds.), *Kaplan & Sadock's comprehensive textbook of psychiatry* (pp. 1693–1733). Philadelphia: Lippincott Williams & Wilkins.

Aknin, L. B., Barrington-Leigh, C. P., Dunn, E. W., Helliwell, J. F., Biswas-Diener, R., Kemeza, I., Nyende, P., Ashton-James, C. E., & Norton, M. I. (2010). *Prosocial spending and well-being: Cross-cultural evidence for a psychological universal*, No 16415, NBER Working Papers, National Bureau of Economic Research, Inc.

Aknin, L. B., Dunn, E. W., & Norton, M. I. (2012). Happiness runs in a circular motion: Evidence for a positive feedback loop between prosocial spending and happiness. *Journal of Happiness Studies, 13*(2), 347–355. doi:10.1007/s10902-011-9267-5

Aknin, L. B., Sandstrom, G. M., Dunn, E. W., & Norton, M. I. (2011a). It's the recipient that counts: Spending money on strong social ties leads to greater happiness than spending on weak social ties. *Plos ONE, 6*(2). doi:10.1371/journal.pone.0017018

Aknin, L. B., Sandstrom, G. M., Dunn, E. W., & Norton, M. I. (2011b). Investing in others: Prosocial spending for (pro)social change. In R. Biswas-Diener (Ed.), *Positive psychology as social change* (pp. 219–234). New York, NY: Springer Science + Business Media. doi:10.1007/978-90-481-9938-9_13

Alan Guttmacher Institute. (2006). *Facts on sexually transmitted infections in the United States.* Retrieved from http://www.guttmacher.org/pubs/FIB_STI_US.html#11.

Alan Guttmacher Institute (2012a). Contraception use in the United States. *Fact Sheet.* Retrieved from http://www.guttmacher.org/pubs/fb_contr_use.html

Alan Guttmacher Institute (2012b). *Facts on American teens' sexual and reproductive health.* Retrieved from http://www.guttmacher.org/pubs/FB-Teen-SexEd.html

Alan Guttmacher Institute (2012c). Sex and HIV education. *State Policies in Brief.* Retrieved from http://www.guttmacher.org/statecenter/spibs/spib_SE.pdf

Alanko, K., Santtila, P., Harlaar, N., Witting, K., Varjonen, M., Jern, P., Johansson, A., von der Pahlen, B., & Sandnabba, N. K. (2008). The association between childhood gender atypical behavior and adult psychiatric symptoms is moderated by parenting style. *Sex Roles, 58*, 837–847.

Alberti, R. E., & Emmons, M. L. (2001). *Your perfect right.* San Luis Obispo, CA: Impact Publishers.

Alberti, R. E., & Emmons, M. L. (2008). *Your perfect right: Assertiveness and equality in your life and relationships* (9th ed.). Atascadero, CA: Impact Publishers.

Albrecht, K. (2009). *Social intelligence: The new science of success.* New York, NY: Pfeiffer.

Aldo, A., Nolen-Hoeksema, S., & Schweizer, S. (2010). Emotion-regulation strategies across psychopathology: A meta-analytic review. *Clinical Psychology Review, 30*(2), 217–237. doi:10.1016/j.cpr.2009.11.004

Aldwin, C. M. (2007). *Stress, coping, and development: An integrative perspective.* New York, NY: Guilford.

Algoe, S. B., Fredrickson, B. L., & Chow, S. (2011). The future of emotions research within positive psychology. In K. M. Sheldon, T. B. Kashdan, M. F. Steger (Eds.), *Designing positive psychology: Taking stock and moving forward* (pp. 115-132). New York, NY: Oxford University Press. doi:10.1093/acprof:oso/9780195373585.003.0008

Alicke, M. D. (2007). In defense of social comparison [Special issue]. *International Review of Social Psychology, 20*, 11-29.

Alicke, M. D., Smith, R. H., & Klotz, J. L. (1986). Judgments of personal attractiveness: The role of faces and bodies. *Personality and Social Psychology Bulletin, 12*, 381–389.

Al-Krenawi, A., Graham, J., & Al Gharaibeh, F. (2011). A comparison study of psychological, family function marital and life satisfactions of polygamous and monogamous women in Jordan. *Community Mental Health Journal, 47*(5), 594–602. doi:10.1007/s10597-011-9405-x

Allan, R. (2011). Type A behavior pattern. In R. Allen & J. Fisher (Eds.), *Heart and mind: The practice of cardiac psychology* (2nd ed., pp. 287–290). Washington, DC: American Psychological Association.

Allen, E. S., Rhoades, G. K., Stanley, S. M., Markman, H. J., Williams, T., Melton, J., & Clements, M. L. (2008). Premarital precursors of marital infidelity. *Family Process, 47*, 243–259.

Allen, J. J. B., & Iacono, W. G. (2001). Assessing the validity of amnesia in dissociative identity disorder: A dilemma for the DSM and the courts. *Psychology, Public Policy, and Law, 7*, 311–344.

Allen, K. R., & Demo, D. H. (1995). The families of lesbians and gay men: A new frontier in family research. *Journal of Marriage and the Family, 57*, 111–127.

Allgood, W. P., Risko, V. J., Alvarez, M. C., & Fairbanks, M. M. (2000). Factors that influence study. In R. F. Flippo & D. C. Caverly (Eds.), *Handbook of college reading and study strategy research.* Mahwah, NJ: Erlbaum.

Allison, D. B., Fontaine, K. R., Manson, J. E., Stevens, J., & VanItallie, T. B. (1999). Annual deaths attributable to obesity in the United States. *Journal of the American Medical Association, 282*(16), 1530–1538.

Allison, D. B., Heshka, S., Neale, M. C., Lykken, D. T., & Heymsfield, S. B. (1994). A genetic analysis of relative weight among 4,020 twin pairs, with an emphasis on sex effects. *Health Psychology, 13*, 362–365.

Allman, K. (2009). Covenant marriage laws in Louisiana. Retrieved from http://www.bestofneworleans.com/gambit/covenant-marriage-laws-in-louisiana/Content?oid=1252802

Almeida, D. M. (2005). Resilience and vulnerability to daily stressors assessed via diary methods. *Current Directions in Psychological Science, 14*(2), 64–68. doi:10.1111/j.0963-7214.2005.00336.x

Alloy, L. B., Abramson, L. Y., Whitehouse, W. G., Hogan, M. E., Tashman, N. A., Steinberg, D. L., Rose, D. T., & Donovan, P. (1999). Depressogenic cognitive styles: Predictive validity, information processing and personality characteristics, and developmental origins. *Behavioral Research and Therapy, 37*, 503–531.

Allport, G. W. (1937). *Personality: A psychological interpretation.* New York, NY: Holt.

Allport, G. W. (1954). *The nature of prejudice.* Reading, MA: Addison-Wesley.

Allport, G. W. (1961). *Pattern and growth in personality.* New York, NY: Holt, Rinehart, & Winston.

Altemeyer, B. (1988a). *Enemies of freedom: Understanding right-wing authoritarianism.* San Francisco: Jossey-Bass.

Altemeyer, B. (1988b). The good soldier, marching in step: A psychological explanation of state terror. *Sciences, March/April,* 30–38.

Altemeyer, B. (1998). The other "authoritarian personality." *Advances in Experimental Social Psychology, 30,* 47–92.

Altermatt, T. W., & DeWall, C. N. (2003). Agency and virtue: Dimensions underlying subgroups of women. *Sex Roles, 49,* 631–641.

Altman, I., & Taylor, D. A. (1973). *Social penetration: The development of interpersonal relationships.* New York, NY: Irvington.

Amato, P. R. (1999). Children of divorced parents as young adults. In E. M. Hetheringon (Ed.), *Coping with divorce, single parenting, and remarriage: A risk and resiliency perspective.* Mahwah, NJ: Erlbaum.

Amato, P. R. (2001). The consequences of divorce for adults and children. In R. M. Milardo (Ed.), *Understanding families into the new millennium: A decade in review.* Minneapolis, MN: National Council on Family Relations.

Amato, P. R. (2003). Reconciling divergent perspectives: Judith Wallerstein, quantitative family research, and children of divorce. *Family Relations: Interdisciplinary Journal of Applied Family Studies, 52*(4), 332–339.

Amato, P. R. (2010). Research on divorce: Continuing trends and new developments. *Journal of Marriage and Family, 72*(3), 650–666. doi:10.1111/j.1741-3737.2010.00723.x

Amato, P. R., Kane, J. B., & James, S. (2011). Reconsidering the "good divorce." *Family Relations: An Interdisciplinary Journal of Applied Family Studies, 60*(5), 511–524. doi:10.1111/j.1741-3729.2011.00666.x

Amato, P. R., & Previti, D. (2003). People's reasons for divorcing: Gender, social class, the life course, and adjustment. *Journal of Family Issues, 24*(5), 602–626.

American Association of Suicidology. (2007). *Understanding and helping the suicidal individual.* Retrieved from http://www.suicidology.org/associations/1045/files/Understanding.pdf.

American Association of University Women Educational Foundation. (1992). *How schools shortchange girls.* Washington, DC: AAUW.

American Cancer Society. (2008). *Cancer facts and figures 2008.* Atlanta, GA: American Cancer Society.

American Council on Education. (1997). Many college graduates participate in training courses to improve their job skills. *Higher Education and National Affairs, 46*(19), 3.

American Foundation for Suicide Prevention. (2007). *When you fear someone may take their own life.* Retrieved April 12, 2007 from http://www.afsp.org/index.cfm?page_id=F2F25092-7E90-9BD4-C4658F1D2B5D19A0.

American Psychiatric Association Task Force on Electroconvulsive Therapy. (2001). *The practice of electroconvulsive therapy: Recommendations for treatment* (2nd ed.). Washington, DC: American Psychiatric Association.

American Psychological Association. (2007, October 24). *Stress a major health problem in the U.S., Warns APA.* Retrieved from http://www.apa.org/news/press/releases/2007/10/stress.aspx

American Psychological Association. (2010). *Stress In America Findings.* Washington, DC: APA.

American Society for Aesthetic Plastic Surgery. (2008). Surgical and nonsurgical procedures: 12-year Comparison, 1997–2008. Retrieved from http://www.surgery.org.media/statistics

American Society for Aesthetic Plastic Surgery. (2011). Statistics 2011. Retrieved from http://www.surgery.org/media/statistics

Amir, N., & Taylor, C. T. (2012). Combining computerized home-based treatments for generalized anxiety disorder: An attention modification program and cognitive behavioral therapy. *Behavior Therapy, 43,* 546-559. doi:10.1016/j.beth.2010.12.008

Andersen, B. L., Golden-Kreutz, D. M., & DiLillo, V. (2001). Cancer. In A. Baum, T. A. Revenson, & J. E. Singer (Eds.), *Handbook of health psychology.* Mahwah, NJ: Erlbaum.

Andersen, B. L., Kiecolt-Glaser, J. K., & Glaser, R. (1994). A biobehavioral model of cancer stress and disease course. *American Psychologist, 49,* 389–404.

Andersen, S. M., & Chen, S. (2002). The relational self: An interpersonal social-cognitive theory. *Psychological Review, 109,* 619–645.

Andersen, S. M., Reznik, I., & Manzella, L. M. (1996). Eliciting facial affect, motivation, and expectancies in transference: Significant-other representations in social relations. *Journal of Personality and Social Psychology, 71,* 1108–1129.

Anderson, B., Wethington, E., & Kamarck, T. W. (2011). Interview assessment of stressor exposure. In R. J. Contrada & A. Baum (Eds.), *The handbook of stress science: Biology, psychology, and health* (pp. 1–9). New York, NY: Springer.

Anderson, C., Srivastava, S., Beer, J. S., Spataro, S. E., & Chapman, J. A. (2006). Knowing your place: Self-perceptions of status in face-to-face groups. *Journal of Personality and Social Psychology, 91,* 1094–1110.

Anderson, C. A. (2004). An update on the effects of playing violent video games. *Journal of Adolescence, 27*(1), 113–122.

Anderson, C. A., & Bushman, B. J. (2001). Effects of violent video games on aggressive behavior, aggressive cognition, aggressive affect, physiological arousal, and prosocial behavior: A meta-analytic review of the scientific literature. *Psychological Science, 12,* 353–359.

Anderson, C. A., Miller, R. S., Riger, A. L., Dill, J. C., & Sedikides, C. (1994). Behavioral and characterological attributional styles as predictors of depression and loneliness: Review, refinement, and test. *Journal of Personality and Social Psychology, 66,* 549–558.

Anderson, C. A., Shibuya, A., Ihori, N., Swing, E. L., Bushman, B. J., Sakamoto, A., & . . . Saleem, M. (2010). Violent video game effects on aggression, empathy, and prosocial behavior in Eastern and Western countries: A meta-analytic review. *Psychological Bulletin, 136*(2), 151–173. doi:10.1037/a0018251

Anderson, D. A., & Hamilton, M. (2005). Gender role stereotyping of parents in children's picture books: The invisible father. *Sex Roles, 52*(3–4), 145–151.

Andersson, E., Ljótsson, B., Hedman, E., Kaldo, V., Paxling, B., Andersson, G., . . . Rück, C. (2011). Internet-based cognitive behavior therapy for obsessive compulsive disorder: A pilot study. *BMC Psychiatry, 11*(125), 1–10. doi:10.1186/1471-244X-11-125

Andreasen, N. C. (1990). Positive and negative symptoms: Historical and conceptual aspects. In N. C. Andreasen (Ed.), *Modern problems of pharmacopsychiatry: Positive and negative symptoms and syndromes.* Basel: Karger.

Andreasen, N. C. (2009). Schizophrenia: A conceptual history. In M. C. Gelder, N. C. Andreasen, J. J. López-Ibor, Jr., & J. R. Geddes (Eds.), *New Oxford textbook of psychiatry* (2nd ed., Vol. 1). New York, NY: Oxford University Press.

Andrews, B., & Hejdenberg, J. (2007). Stress in university students. In G. Fink (Ed.), *Encyclopedia of stress: Vols. 1–4* (2nd ed., pp. 612–614). San Diego, CA: Elsevier Academic Press.

Andrews, G., Charney, D., Sirovatka, P., & Regier, D. (Eds.). (2009). *Stress-induced and fear circuitry disorders: Advancing the research agenda for DSM-V.* Arlington, VA: American Psychiatric Publishing.

Andrews, P. W., Kornstein, S. G., Halberstadt, L. J., Gardner, C. O., & Neale, M. C. (2011). Blue again: Perturbational effects of antidepressants suggest monoaminergic homeostasis in major depression. *Frontiers in Psychology, 2*(159), 1–24. doi:10.3389/fpsyg.2011.00159

Andrews, P. W., Thomson, J. A., Jr., Amstadter, A., & Neale, M. C. (2012). *Primum non nocere:* An evolutionary analysis of whether antidepressants do more harm than good. *Frontiers in Psychology, 3*(117), 1–19. doi:10.3389/fpsyg.2012.00117

Angell, M. (2004). *The truth about the drug companies: How they deceive us and what to do about it.* New York, NY: Random House.

Anglin, L. P., Pirson, M., & Langer, E. (2008). Mindful learning: A moderator of gender differences in mathematics performance. *Journal of Adult Development, 15*(3–4), 132–139.

Angrosino, M. V. (2007). *Naturalistic observation: Qualitative essentials.* Walnut Creek, CA: Left Coast Press.

Angst, J. (2009). Course and prognosis of mood disorders. In M. C. Gelder, N. C. Andreasen, J. J. López-Ibor, Jr., & J. R. Geddes (Eds.), *New Oxford textbook of psychiatry* (2nd ed., Vol. 1). New York, NY: Oxford University Press.

Angulo, S., Brooks, M. L., & Swann, W., Jr. (2011). Swimming serenely in a sea of words: Sexism, communication, and precarious couples. *Personal Relationships, 18*(4), 604–616. doi:10.1111/j.1475-6811.2010.01322.x

Anik, L., Aknin, L. B., Norton, M. I., & Dunn, E. W. (2011). Feeling good about giving: The benefits (and costs) of self-interested charitable behavior. In D. M. Oppenheimer & C. Y. Olivola (Eds.), *The science of giving: Experimental approaches to the study of charity* (pp. 3–13). New York, NY: Psychology Press.

Ansbacher, H. (1970, February). Alfred Adler, individual psychology. *Psychology Today,* pp. 42–44, 66.

Antecol, H., Jong, A., & Steinberger, M. (2008). The sexual orientation wage gap: The role of occupational sorting and human capital. *Industrial & Labor Relations Review, 61,* 518–543.

Anthony, I. C., & Bell, J. E. (2008). The neuropathology of HIV/AIDS. *International Review of Psychiatry, 20*(1), 15–24.

Antonietti, A., Cocomazzi, D., & Iannello, P. (2009). Looking at the audience improves music appreciation. *Journal of Nonverbal Behavior, 33,* 89–106.

Antoniou, A. G., & Cooper, C. L. (2005). *Research companion to organizational health psychology.* Northampton, MA: Edward Elgar.

Antony, M. M., & McCabe, R. E. (2003). Anxiety disorders: Social and specific phobias. In A. Tasman, J. Kay, & J. A. Lieberman (Eds.), *Psychiatry.* New York, NY: Wiley.

Aono, A. (2003). The effects of gender and status on interpersonal distance: From the viewpoint of the oppression hypothesis. *The Japanese Journal of Social Psychology, 19,* 51–58.

App, B., McIntosh, D. N., Reed, C. L., & Hertenstein, M. J. (2011). Nonverbal channel use in communication of emotion: How may depend on why. *Emotion, 11*(3), 603–617. doi:10.1037/a0023164

Apperloo, M. J. A., Van Der Stege, J. G., Hoek, A., & Weijmar Schultz, W. C. M. (2003). In the mood for sex: The value of androgens. *Journal of Sex and Marital Therapy, 29*(2), 87–102.

Arbona, C. (2005). Promoting the career development and academic achievement of at-risk youth: College access programs. In S. D. Brown & R. W. Lent (Eds.), *Career development and counseling: Putting theory and research to work.* New York, NY: Wiley.

Arcelus, J., Mitchell, A. J., Wales, J., & Nielsen, S. (2011). Mortality rates in patients with anorexia nervosa and other eating disorders: A meta-analysis of 36 studies. *Archives of General Psychiatry, 68*, 724–731. doi:10.1001/archgenpsychiatry.2011.74

Arcelus, J., Whight, D., Langham, C., Baggott, J., McGrain, L., Meadows, L., & Meyer, C. (2009). A case series evaluation of the modified version of interpersonal psychotherapy (IPT) for the treatment of bulimic eating disorders: A pilot study. *European Eating Disorders Review, 17*(4), 260–268. doi:10.1002/(ISSN)1099-096810.1002/erv.v17:410.1002/erv.932.

Archer, J. (2005). Are women or men the more aggressive sex? In S. Fein, G. R. Goethals, & M. J. Sandstrom (Eds.), *Gender and aggression: Interdisciplinary perspectives.* Mahwah, NJ: Erlbaum.

Archibald, A., Graber, J. A., & Brooks-Gunn, J. (2003). Pubertal processes and physiological growth in adolescence. In G. R. Adams & M. D. Berzonsky (Eds.), *Blackwell handbook of adolescence* (pp. 24–47). Malden, MA: Blackwell.

Arendell, T. (2000). Conceiving and investigating motherhood: The decade's scholarship. *Journal of Marriage and the Family, 62*(4), 1192–1207.

Argyle, M. (1999). Causes and correlates of happiness. In D. Kahneman, E. Diener, & N. Schwarz (Eds.), *Well-being: The foundations of hedonic psychology.* New York, NY: Sage.

Argyle, M. (2001). *The psychology of happiness* (2nd ed.). New York, NY: Routledge.

Argyle, M., & Henderson, M. (1984). The rules of friendship. *Journal of Social and Personal Relationships, 1*, 211–237.

Aries, E. (1998). Gender differences in interaction: A reexamination. In D. J. Canary & K. Dindia (Eds.), *Sex differences and similarities in communication: Critical essays and empirical investigations of sex and gender in interaction.* Mahwah, NJ: Erlbaum.

Arkowitz, H., & Lilienfeld, S. O. (2006). Do self-help books help? *Scientific American Mind, 17*(5), 78–79.

Arkowitz, H., & Lilienfeld, S. O. (2007). The best medicine? How drugs stack up against talk therapy for the treatment of depression. *Scientific American Mind, 18*(5), 80–83.

Arkowitz, H., & Lilienfeld, S. O. (2010, September/October). The "Just do it!" trap: Why Dr. Phil and Dr. Laura won't solve your problems. *Scientific American Mind,* 64–65.

Armbruster, B. B. (2000). Taking notes from lectures. In R. F. Flippo & D. C. Caverly (Eds.), *Handbook of college reading and study strategy research.* Mahwah, NJ: Erlbaum.

Armour, S. (2004, May 4). Some moms quit as offices scrap family-friendliness. *USA Today,* pp. 1A–2A.

Arnaut, G. L. Y. (2006). Sensation seeking, risk taking, and fearlessness. In J. C. Thomas & D. L. Segal (Eds.), *Comprehensive handbook of personality and psychopathology* (Vol 1, pp. 322–344). New York, NY: Wiley.

Arndt, J., & Vess, M. (2008). Tales from existential oceans: Terror management theory and how the awareness of our mortality affects us all. *Social and Personality Psychology Compass, 2*(2), 909–928. doi:10.1111/j.1751-9004.2008.00079.x

Arnold, K. D. (1995). *Lives of promise: What becomes of high school valedictorians.* San Francisco: Jossey-Bass.

Aron, A., Fisher, H., & Strong, G. (2006). Romantic love. In A. L. Vangelisti & D. Perlman (Eds.), *The Cambridge handbook of personal relationships.* New York, NY: Cambridge University Press.

Aron, A., & Westbay, N. (1996). Dimensions of the prototype of love. *Journal of Personality and Social Psychology, 70*, 535–551.

Aronson, J., Jannone, S., McGlone, M., & Johnson-Campbell, T. (2009). The Obama effect: An experimental test. *Journal of Experimental Social Psychology, 45*, 957–960.

Aronson, J., Lustina, M. J., Good, C., Keough, K., Steele, C. M., & Brown, J. (1999). White men can't do math: Necessary and sufficient factors in stereotype threat. *Journal of Experimental Social Psychology, 35*(1), 29–46.

Aronson, J. M., Cohen, G., & Nail, P. R. (1999). *Cooperation in the classroom: The jigsaw method.* New York, NY: Longman.

Arriaga, P., Esteves, F., Carneiro, P., & Monteiro, M. B. (2006a). Violent computer games and their effects on state hostility and physiological arousal. *Aggressive Behavior, 32*, 358–371.

Arriaga, X. B., Reed, J. T., Goodfriend, W., & Agnew, C. R. (2006b). Relationship perceptions and persistence: Do fluctuations in perceived commitment undermine dating relationships? *Journal of Personality and Social Psychology, 91*, 1045–1065.

Artham, S. M., Lavie, C. J., & Milani, R. V. (2008). Cardiac rehabilitation programs markedly improve high-risk profiles in coronary patients with high psychological distress. *Southern Medical Journal, 101*, 262–267.

Asch, S. E. (1955). Opinions and social pressures. *Scientific American, 193*(5), 31–35.

Asch, S. E. (1956). Studies of independence and conformity: A minority of one against a unanimous majority. *Psychological Monographs, 70* (9, Whole No. 416).

Ashcraft, K. A., & Bonneau, R. H. (2008). Psychological stress exacerbates primary vaginal herpes simplex virus type 1 (HSV-1) infection by impairing both innate and adaptive immune responses. *Brain, Behavior, & Immunity,* 1231–1240.

Aspinwall, L. G., & Staudinger, U. M. (2002). *A psychology of human strengths: Fundamental questions and future directions for a positive psychology.* Washington, DC: American Psychological Association.

Associated Press. (2005, October 22). How many survivors does it take to tell a joke? Retrieved from http://www.msnbc.msn.com/id/9783819/ns/us/us_news-katrina_the_long_road_back/

Athenstaedt, U., Haas, E., & Schwab, S. (2004). Gender role self-concept and gender-typed communication behavior in mixed-sex and same-sex dyads. *Sex Roles, 50*(1/2), 37–52.

Atwood, J. D. (2012). Couples and money: The last taboo. *American Journal of Family Therapy, 40*(1), 1–19. doi:10.1080/01926187.2011.600674

Aubin, S., & Heiman, J. R. (2004). Sexual dysfunction from a relationship perspective. In J. H. Harvey, A. Wenzel, & S. Sprecher (Eds.), *The handbook of sexuality in close relationships.* Mahwah, NJ: Lawrence Erlbaum.

Aubrey, J. S., & Harrison, K. (2004). The gender-role content of children's favorite television programs and its links to their gender-related perceptions. *Media Psychology, 6*, 11–146.

Auster, C. J., & Ohm, S. C. (2000). Masculinity and femininity in contemporary American society: A reevaluation using the Bem Sex-Role Inventory. *Sex Roles, 43*, 499–528.

Auyeung, B., Baron-Cohen, S., Ashwin, E., Knickmeyer, R., Taylor, K., Hackett, G., & Hines, M. (2009). Fetal testosterone predicts sexually differentiated childhood behavior in girls and in boys. *Psychological Science, 20*(2), 144–148. doi:10.1111/j.1467-9280.2009.02279.x

Ax, R. K., Bigelow, B. J., Harowski, K., Meredith, J. M., Nussbaum, D. & Taylor, R. R. (2008). Prescriptive authority for psychologists and the public sector: Serving underserved health care consumers. *Psychological Services, 5*(2), 184–197.

Ayanian, J. Z., & Cleary, P. D. (1999). Perceived risks of heart disease and cancer among cigarette smokers. *Journal of the American Medical Association, 281*(11), 1019–1021.

Ayar, A. A. (2006). Road Rage: Recognizing a psychological disorder. *Journal of Psychiatry & Law, 34*, 123–143.

Ayoola, A. B., Nettleman, M., & Brewer, J. (2007). Reasons for unprotected intercourse in adult women. *Journal of Women's Health, 16*, 302–310.

Ayotte, B. J., Margrett, J. A., & Hicks-Patrick, J. (2010). Physical activity in middle-aged and young-old adults: The roles of self-efficacy, barriers, outcome expectancies, self-regulatory behaviors and social support. *Journal of Health Psychology, 15*(2), 173–185. doi:10.1177/1359105309342283

Ayres, J., Hopf, T., & Ayres, D. M. (1994). An examination of whether imaging ability enhances the effectiveness of an intervention designed to reduce speech anxiety. *Communication Education, 43*(3), 252–258.

Aziz, S., & Zickar, M. J. (2006). A cluster analysis investigation of workaholism as a syndrome. *Journal of Occupational Health Psychology, 11*(1), 52–62.

Back, M. D., Schmukle, S. C., & Egloff, B. (2008). Becoming friends by chance. *Psychological Science, 19*(5), 439–440. doi:10.1111/j.1467-9280.2008.02106.x

Back, M. D., Schmukle, S. C., & Egloff, B. (2010). Why are narcissists so charming at first sight? Decoding the narcissism-popularity link at zero acquaintance. *Journal of Personality and Social Psychology, 98*(1), 132–145. doi:10.1037/a0016338

Backhaus, A., Agha, Z., Maglione, M. L., Repp, A., Ross, B., Zuest, D., . . . Thorp, S. R. (2012). Videoconferencing psychotherapy: A systematic review. *Psychological Services, 9*, 111–131. doi:10.1037/a0027924

Baddeley, J. L., & Pennebaker, J. W. (2011). The expressive writing method. In L. L'Abate & L. G. Sweeney (Eds.), *Research on writing approaches in mental health* (pp. 85–92). Bingley, United Kingdom: Emerald Group Publishing.

Badgett, M. V. L. (2003). Employment and sexual orientation: Disclosure and discrimination in the workplace. In L. D. Garnets & D. C. Kimmel (Eds.), *Psychological perspectives on lesbian, gay, and bisexual experiences* (2nd ed,). New York, NY: Columbia University Press.

Bailey, J. M., & Dawood, K. (1998). Behavior genetics, sexual orientation, and the family. In C. J. Patterson & A. R. D'Augelli (Eds.), *Lesbian, gay and bisexual identities in families: Psychological perspectives.* New York, NY: Oxford University Press.

Bailey, J. M., Kim, P. Y., Hills, A., & Linsenmeier, J. A. W. (1997). Butch, femme, or straight acting? Partner preferences of gay men and lesbians. *Journal of Personality and Social Psychology, 73*(5), 960–973.

Bailey, J. M., & Pillard, R. C. (1991). A genetic study of male sexual orientation. *Archives of General Psychiatry, 48*, 1089–1096.

Bailey, J. M., Pillard, R. C., Neale, M. C., & Agyei, Y. (1993). Heritable factors influence sexual orientation in women. *Archives of General Psychiatry, 50*, 217–223.

Bailey, T. C., Eng, W., Frisch, M. B., & Snyder, C. R. (2007). Hope and optimism as related to life satisfaction. *The Journal of Positive Psychology, 2*(3), 168–175. doi:10.1080/17439760701409546

Baillargeon, R. H., Zoccolillo, M., Keenan, K., Cote, S., Persusse, D., Wu, H., Boivin, M., & Tremblay, R. E. (2007). Gender differences in physical aggression: A prospective population-based survey of children before and after 2 years of age. *Developmental Psychology, 43*, 13–26.

Baird, B. M., Le, K., & Lucas, R. E. (2006). On the nature of intraindividual personality variability: Reliability, validity, and associations with well-being. *Journal of Personality and Social Psychology, 90*, 521–527.

Baker, F., Ainsworth, S. R., Dye, J. T., Crammer, C., Thun, M. J., Hoffmann, D., Repace, J. L., Henningfield, J. E., Slade, J., Pinney, J., Shanks, T., Burns, D. M., Connolly, G. N., & Shopland, D. R. (2000). Health risks associated with cigar smoking. *Journal of the American Medical Association, 284*, 735–740.

Bakker, A. B., Demerouti, E., & Burke, R. (2009). Workaholism and relationship quality: A spillover-crossover perspective. *Journal of Occupational Health Psychology, 14*(1), 23–33.

Bakker, A. B., Schaufeli, W. B., Leiter, M. P., & Taris, T. W. (2008). Work engagement: An emerging concept in occupational health psychology. *Work & Stress, 22*(3), 187–200.

Balducci, C., Cecchin, M., Fraccaroli, F., & Schaufeli, W. B. (2012). Exploring the relationship between workaholism and workplace aggressive behaviour: The role of job-related emotion. *Personality and Individual Differences.* doi:10.1016/j.paid.2012.05.004

Balkin, R. S., Perepiczka, M., Whitely, R., & Kimbrough, S. (2009). The relationship of sexual values and emotional awareness to sexual activity in young adulthood. *Adultspan Journal, 8,* 17–28.

Balsam, K. F., Beauchaine, T. P., Mickey, R. M., & Rothblum, E. D. (2005). Mental health of lesbian, gay, bisexual, and heterosexual siblings: Effects of gender, sexual orientation, and family. *Journal of Abnormal Psychology, 114,* 471–476.

Bandura, A. (1977). *Social learning theory.* Englewood Cliffs, NJ: Prentice-Hall.

Bandura, A. (1986). *Social foundations of thought and action: A social-cognitive theory.* Englewood Cliffs, NJ: Prentice-Hall.

Bandura, A. (1993). Perceived self-efficacy in cognitive development and functioning. *Educational Psychologist, 28,* 117–148.

Bandura, A. (1997). *Self-efficacy: The exercise of control.* New York, NY: W. H. Freeman.

Bandura, A. (1999a). A sociocognitive analysis of substance abuse: An agentic perspective. *Psychological Science, 10*(3), 214–217.

Bandura, A. (1999b). Social cognitive theory of personality. In L. A. Pervin & O. P. John (Eds.), *Handbook of personality: Theory and research* (2nd ed.). New York, NY: Guilford Press.

Bandura, A. (2000). Social cognitive theory: An agentic perspective. *Annual Review of Psychology, 52,* 1–26.

Bandura, A. (2004). Health promotion by social cognitive means. *Health Education & Behavior, 31*(2), 143–164.

Bandura, A. (2008a). An agentic perspective on positive psychology. In S. J. Lopez (Ed.), *Positive psychology: Exploring the best in people* (pp. 167–196). Westport, CT: Praeger.

Bandura, A. (2008b). Reconstrual of "free will" from the agentic perspective of social cognitive theory. In J. Baer, J. C. Kaufman, & R. F. Baumeister (Eds.), *Are we free? Psychology and free will* (pp. 86–127). New York, NY: Oxford University Press.

Banks, S., & Dinges, D. F. (2011). Chronic sleep deprivation. In M. H. Kryger, T. Roth, & W. C. Dement (Eds.), *Principles and practice of sleep medicine.* Philadelphia, PA: Elsevier Saunders.

Banse, R., & Scherer, K. R. (1996). Acoustic profiles in vocal emotion expression. *Journal of Personality and Social Psychology, 70*(3), 614636.

Banyard, V. L., & Williams, L. M. (1999). Memories for child sexual abuse and mental health functioning: Findings on a sample of women and implications for future research. In L. M. Williams & V. L. Banyard (Eds.), *Trauma & memory.* Thousand Oaks, CA: Sage.

Bänziger, T., Scherer, K. R., Hall, J. A., & Rosenthal, R. (2011). Introducing the MiniPONS: A short multichannel version of the Profile of Nonverbal Sensitivity (PONS). *Journal of Nonverbal Behavior, 35*(3), 189–204. doi:10.1007/s10919-011-0108-3

Barber, B. K. (1994). Cultural, family, and personal contexts of parent-adolescent conflict. *Journal of Marriage and the Family, 56,* 375–386.

Barber, B. L., & Demo, D. H. (2006). The kids are alright (at least, most of them): Links between divorce and dissolution and child well-being. In M. A. Fine & J. H. Harvey (Eds.), *Handbook of divorce and relationship resolution.* Mahwah, NJ: Erlbaum.

Barden, J., Rucker, D., & Petty, R. E. (2005). "Saying one thing and doing another": Examining the impact of event order on hypocrisy judgments of others. *Personality and Social Psychology Bulletin, 31,* 1463–1474.

Bargh, J. A. (1997). The automaticity of everyday life. In R. S. Wyer Jr.(Ed.), *Advances in social cognition* (Vol. 10). Mahwah, NJ: Erlbaum.

Bargh, J. A. (1999). The cognitive monster: The case against the controllability of automatic stereotype effects. In S. Chaiken & Y. Trope (Eds.), *Dual process theories in social psychology.* New York, NY: Guilford.

Bargh, J. A., Chen, M., & Burrows, L. (1996). Automaticity of social behavior: Direct effects of trait construct and stereotype activation on action. *Journal of Personality and Social Psychology, 71,* 230–244.

Bargh, J. A., & McKenna, K. Y. A. (2004). The Internet and social life. *Annual Review of Psychology, 55,* 573–590.

Bargh, J. A., McKenna, K. Y. A., & Fitzsimons, G. M. (2002). Can you see the real me? Activation and expression of the "true self" on the Internet. *Journal of Social Issues, 58*(1), 33–48.

Barlett, D. L., & Steele, J. B. (1979). *Empire: The life, legend and madness of Howard Hughes.* New York, NY: Norton.

Barnes, M. L., & Buss, D. M. (1985). Sex differences in the interpersonal behavior of married couples. *Journal of Personality and Social Psychology, 48,* 654–661.

Barnes, V. A., Treiber, F., & Davis, H. (2001). The impact of Transcendental Meditation on cardiovascular function at rest and during acute stress in adolescents with high norspeed in old age. *Current Directions in Psychological Science, 6,* 163–169.

Barnett, H. L., Keel, P. K., & Conoscenti, L. M. (2001). Body type preferences in Asian and Caucasian college students. *Sex Roles, 45* (11–12), 867–878.

Barnett, O. W., & LaViolette, A. D. (1993). *It could happen to anyone: Why battered women stay.* Thousand Oaks, CA: Sage.

Barnett, R. C. (2005). Dual-earner couples: Good/bad for her and/or him? In D. F. Halpern & S. E. Murphy (Eds.), *From work-family balance to work-family interaction: Changing the metaphor.* Mahwah, NJ: Erlbaum.

Barnett, R. C., & Hyde, J. S. (2001). Women, men, work, and family: An expansionist theory. *American Psychologist, 56*(10), 781–796.

Barnshaw, J., & Letukas, L. (2010). The low down on the down low: Origins, risk identification and intervention. *Health Sociology Review, 19*(4), 478–490. doi:10.5172/hesr.2010.19.4.478

Baron, J., & Hershey, J. C. (1988). Outcome bias in decision evaluation. *Journal of Personality and Social Psychology, 54,* 569–579.

Barr-Anderson, D., van den Berg, P., Neumark-Sztainer, D., & Story, M. (2008). Characteristics associated with older adolescents who have a television in their bedrooms. *Pediatrics, 121,* 718–724.

Barreto, M., Ryan, M. K., & Schmitt, M. T. (2009). *The glass ceiling in the 21st century: Understanding barriers to gender equality.* Washington, DC: American Psychological Association. doi:10.1037/11863-000

Barrett, L. F., & Bliss-Moreau, E. (2009). She's emotional, he's having a bad day: Attributional explanations for emotion stereotypes. *Emotion, 9*(5), 649–658.

Barron, J. M., Struckman-Johnson, C., Quevillon, R., & Banka, S. R. (2008). Heterosexual men's attitudes toward gay men: A hierarchical model including masculinity, openness, and theoretical explanations. *Psychology of Men & Masculinity, 9,* 154–166.

Barry, B., & Friedman, R. A. (1998). Bargainer characteristics in distributive and integrative negotiation. *Journal of Personality and Social Psychology, 74,* 345–359.

Barsky, A. J. (1988). The paradox of health. *New England Journal of Medicine, 318,* 414–418.

Bartholomew, K. (1990). Avoidance of intimacy: An attachment perspective. *Journal of Social and Personal Relationships, 7,* 47–178.

Bartholomew, K. (2009). Adult attachment, individual differences. In H. T. Reis & S. Sprecher (Eds.), *Encyclopedia of human relationships: Vol. 1* (pp. 34–39). Los Angeles: Sage Reference Publication.

Bartholow, B. D., Bushman, B. J., & Sestir, M. A. (2006). Chronic violent video game exposure and desensitization to violence: Behavioral and event-related brain potential data. *Journal of Experimental Social Psychology, 42,* 532–539.

Bartone, P., Roland, R., Picano, J., & Williams, T. (2008). Psychological hardiness predicts success in U.S. Army Special Forces candidates. *International Journal of Selections and Assessment, 16*(1), 78–81.

Baruch, Y. (2011). The positive well-being aspects of workaholism in cross cultural perspective: The chocoholism metaphor. *The Career Development International, 16*(6), 572–591. doi:10.1108/13620431111178335

Basow, S. A. (1992). *Gender stereotypes and roles* (3rd ed.). Pacific Grove, CA: Brooks/Cole.

Basow, S. A. (2010). Gender in the classroom. In J. C. Chrisler & D. R. McCreary (Eds.), *Handbook of gender research in psychology* (Vol. 1, pp. 277-295). New York, NY: Springer.

Bastian, B., & Haslam, N. (2006). Psychological essentialism and stereotype endorsement. *Journal of Personality and Social Psychology, 42,* 228–235.

Bauer, I., & Wrosch, C. (2011). Making up for lost opportunities: The protective role of downward social comparisons for coping with regrets across adulthood. *Personality and Social Psychology Bulletin, 37*(2), 215–228. doi:10.1177/0146167210393256

Bauer, M. S. (2008). Mood disorders: Bipolar (manicdepressive) disorders. In A. J. Kay, J. A. Lieberman, M. B. First, & M. Maj (Eds.), *Psychiatry* (3rd ed.). New York, NY: Wiley-Blackwell.

Bauermeister, J. A., Carballo-Dieguez, A., Ventuneac, A., & Bolezal, C. (2009). Assessing motivations to engage in intentional condomless anal intercourse in HIV risk contexts ("bareback sex") among men who have sex with men. *AIDS Education and Prevention, 21,* 156–168.

Bauermeister, J. A., Johns, M. M., Pingel, E., Eisenberg, A., Santana, M., & Zimmerman, M. (2011). Measuring love: Sexual minority male youths' ideal romantic characteristics. *Journal of LGBT Issues in Counseling, 5*(2), 102–121. doi:10.1080/15538605.2011.574573

Baum, A., Perry, N. W., Jr., & Tarbell, S. (2004). The development of psychology as a health science. In R. G. Frank, A. Baum, & J. L. Wallender (Eds.), *Handbook of clinical health psychology* (Vol. 3, pp. 9–28). Washington, DC: American Psychological Association.

Baum, A., Trevino, L. A., & Dougall, A. L. (2011). Stress and the cancers. In R. J. Contrada & A. Baum (Eds.), *The handbook of stress: Biology, psychology, and health* (pp. 411-423). New York, NY: Springer.

Baumbusch, J. L. (2004). Unclaimed treasures: Older women's reflections on lifelong singlehood. *Journal of Women & Aging, 16,* 105–121.

Baumeister, R. F. (1984). Choking under pressure: Self-consciousness and paradoxical effects of incentives on skillful performance. *Journal of Personality and Social Psychology, 46,* 610–620.

Baumeister, R. F. (1989). The optimal margin of illusion. *Journal of Social and Clinical Psychology, 8,* 176–189.

Baumeister, R. F. (1995). Disputing the effects of championship pressures and home audiences. *Journal of Personality and Social Psychology, 68,* 644–648.

Baumeister, R. F. (1997). Esteem threat, self-regulatory breakdown, and emotional distress as factors in self-defeating behavior. *Review of General Psychology, 1,* 145–174.

Baumeister, R. F. (1998). The self. In D. T. Gilbert, S. T. Fiske, & G. Lindzey (Eds.), *The handbook of social psychology.* Boston, MA: Mcgraw-Hill.

Baumeister, R. F. (1999). The nature and structure of the self: An overview. In R. F. Baumeister (Ed.), *The self in social psychology.* Ann Arbor, MI: Edwards Bros.

Baumeister, R. F. (2010a). The self. In R. F. Baumeister & E. J. Finkel (Eds.), *Advanced social psychology: The state of the science* (pp. 139–175). New York, NY: Oxford University Press.

Baumeister, R. F. (2010b). Social psychologists and thinking about people. In R. F. Baumeister & E. J. Finkel (Eds.), *Advanced social psychology: The state of the science* (pp. 5–25). New York, NY: Oxford University Press.

Baumeister, R. F. (2012). Self-control—The moral muscle. *The Psychologist, 25*(2), 112–115.

Baumeister, R. F., Bratslavsky, E., Finkenauer, C., & Vohs, K. D. (2001). Bad is stronger than good. *Review of General Psychology, 5*(4), 323–370.

Baumeister, R. F., Bratslavsky, E., Muraven, M., & Tice, D. M. (1998). Ego depletion: Is the active self a limited resource? *Journal of Personality and Social Psychology, 74*(5), 1252–1265.

Baumeister, R. F., & Bushman, B. C. (2011). *Social psychology and human nature* (2nd ed.). Belmont, CA: Wadsworth/Cengage.

Baumeister, R. F., Campbell, J. D., Krueger, J. I., & Vohs, K. D. (2003). Does high self-esteem cause better performance, interpersonal success, happiness, or healthier lifestyles? *Psychological Science in the Public Interest, 4*(1), 1–44.

Baumeister, R. F., Gailliot, M., DeWall, M., & Oaten, M. (2006). Self-regulation and personality: How interventions increase regulatory success, and how depletion moderates the effects of traits on behavior. *Journal of Personality, 74*, 1773–1801.

Baumeister, R. F., Hutton, D. G., & Tice, D. M. (1989). Cognitive processes during deliberate self-presentation: How self-presenters alter and misinterpret the behavior of their interaction partners. *Journal of Experimental Social Psychology, 25*, 59–78.

Baumeister, R. F., Muraven, M., & Tice, D. M. (2000). Ego depletion: A resource model of volition, self regulation, and controlled processing. *Social Cognition, 18*(2), 130–150.

Baumeister, R. F., & Scher, S. J. (1988). Self-defeating behavior patterns among normal individuals: Review and analysis of common self-destructive tendencies. *Psychological Bulletin, 104*(1), 3–22.

Baumeister, R. F., & Sommer, K. L. (1997). What do men want? Gender differences and two spheres of belongingness: Comment on Cross and Madson (1997). *Psychological Bulletin, 122*(1), 38–44.

Baumeister, R. F., & Steinhilber, A. (1984). Paradoxical effects of supportive audiences on performance under pressure: The home field disadvantage in sports championships. *Journal of Personality and Social Psychology, 47*, 85–93.

Baumeister, R. F., & Twenge, J. M. (2003). The social self. In T. Millon & M. J. Lerner (Eds.) *Handbook of psychology: Vol. 5. Personality and social psychology.* New York, NY: Wiley.

Baumeister, R. F., & Vohs, K. D. (2007). Self-regulation, ego depletion, and motivation. *Social and Personality Psychology Compass, 1*(1), 115–128.

Baumrind, D. (1964). Some thoughts on the ethics of reading Milgram's "Behavioral study of obedience." *American Psychologist, 19*, 421–423.

Baumrind, D. (1967). Child care practices anteceding three patterns of preschool behavior. *Genetic Psychology Monographs, 75*, 43–88.

Baumrind, D. (1971). Current patterns of parental authority. *Developmental Psychology Monographs, 4* (1, Part 2).

Baumrind, D. (1978). Parental disciplinary patterns and social competence in children. *Youth and Society, 9*, 239–276.

Bavelas, J. B., Coates, L., & Johnson, T. (2002). Listener responses as a collaborative process: The role of gaze. *Journal of Communication, 52*(3), 566–580.

Baxter, L. A. (1988). A dialectical perspective on communication strategies in relationship development. In S. Duck (Ed.), *Handbook of personal relationships.* New York, NY: Wiley.

Bay-Hinitz, A. K., Peterson, R. F., & Quilitch, H. R. (1994). Cooperative games: A way to modify aggressive and cooperative behaviors in young children. *Journal of Applied Behavior Analysis, 27*, 435–446.

Beall, A. E., Eagly, A. H., & Sternberg, R. J. (2004). Introduction. In A. H. Eagly, A. E. Beall, & R. J. Sternberg (Eds.), *The psychology of gender.* New York, NY: Guilford Press.

Beaman, R., Wheldall, K., & Kemp, C. (2006). Differential teacher attention to boys and girls in the classroom. *Educational Review, 58*, 339–366.

Beard, K., Stansberry, H., & Wayne, K. (2010). The nature, meaning and measure of teacher flow in elementary schools: A test of rival hypotheses. *Educational Administration Quarterly, 46*(3), 426–458.

Bearden, C. E., Jasinska, A. J., & Freimer, N. B. (2009). Methodological issues in molecular genetic studies of mental disorders. *Annual Review of Clinical Psychology, 5*, 549–569. doi:10.1146/annurev.clinpsy.032408.153545

Beaudry, M., Bousvert, J., Simard, M., Parent, C., & Blais, M. (2004). Communication: A key component to meeting the challenges of stepfamilies. *Journal of Divorce & Remarriage, 42*, 85–104.

Beck, A. T. (1976). *Cognitive therapy and the emotional disorders.* New York, NY: International Universities Press.

Beck, A. T. (1987). Cognitive therapy. In J. K. Zeig (Ed.), *The evolution of psychotherapy.* New York, NY: Brunner/Mazel.

Beck, A. T. (1997). Cognitive therapy: Reflections. In J. K. Zeig (Ed.), *The evolution of psychotherapy: The third conference.* New York, NY: Brunner/Mazel.

Beck, A. T. (2008). The evolution of the cognitive model of depression and its neurobiological correlates. *American Journal of Psychiatry, 165*, 969–977.

Beck, A. T., & Weishaar, M. E. (2011). Cognitive therapy. In R. J. Corsini & D. Wedding (Eds.), *Current psychotherapies* (9th ed.). Belmont, CA: Brooks/Cole.

Becker, A., & Fay, K. (2006). Sociocultural issues and eating disorders. In S. Wonderlich, J. Mitchell, M. de Zwaan, & H. Steiger (Eds.), *Annual review of eating disorders.* Oxon, England: Radcliffe.

Beckman, H., Regier, N., & Young, J. (2007). Effect of workplace laughter groups on personal efficacy beliefs. *The Journal of Primary Prevention, 28*(2), 167–182.

Beddoe, R., Costanza, R., Farley, J. U., Garza, E., Kent, J., Kubiszewski, I., Martinez, L., et al. (2009). Overcoming systematic roadblocks to sustainability: The evolutionary redesign of worldviews, institutions, and technologies. *Proceedings from the National Academy of Science (PNAS), 106*, 2483–2489.

Behar, R. (1991, May 6). The thriving cult of greed and power. *Time*, pp. 50–77.

Beidel, D. C., & Stipelman, B. (2007). Anxiety disorders. In M. Hersen, S. M. Turner, & D. C. Beidel (Eds.), *Adult psychopathology and diagnosis.* New York, NY: Wiley.

Beilock, S. (2010). *Choke: What the secrets of the brain reveal about getting it right when you have to.* New York, NY: Free Press.

Beisecker, A. E. (1990). Patient power in doctor-patient communication: What do we know? *Health Communication, 2*, 105–122.

Bekelman, J. E., Li, Y., & Gross, C. P. (2003). Scope and impact of financial conflicts of interests in biomedical research. *Journal of the American Medical Association, 289*, 454–465.

Bekkouche, N. S., Holmes, S., Whittaker, K. S., & Krantz, D. S. (2011). Stress and the heart: Psychosocial stress and coronary heart disease. In R.J. Contrada & A. Baum (Eds.), *The handbook of stress science: Biology, psychology, and health* (pp. 385–398). New York, NY: Springer.

Belar, C. D. (2008). Clinical health psychology: A health care specialty in professional psychology. *Professional Psychology: Research and Practice, 39*, 229–233.

Belger, A., & Barch, D. M. (2009). Cognitive neuroscience and neuroimaging in schizophrenia. In D. S. Charney & E. J. Nestler (Eds.), *Neurobiology of mental illness* (pp. 303–320). New York, NY: Oxford University Press.

Bell, A. P., & Weinberg, M. S. (1978). *Homosexualities: A study of diversity among men and women.* New York, NY: Simon & Schuster.

Bell, A. P., Weinberg, M. S., & Hammersmith, K. S. (1981). *Sexual preference—Its development in men and women.* Bloomington: Indiana University Press.

Belmore, S. M. (1987). Determinants of attention during impression formation. *Journal of Experimental Psychology: Learning, Memory, and Cognition, 13*, 480–489.

Belsky, J. (2009). Parenthood, transition to. In H. T. Reis & S. Sprecher (Eds.), *Encyclopedia of human relationships: Vol. 3* (pp. 1204–1207). Los Angeles: Sage Reference Publication.

Bem, S. L. (1975, September). Androgyny vs. the tight little lives of fluffy women and chesty men. *Psychology Today*, pp. 58–62.

Bem, S. L. (1983). Gender schema theory and its implications for child development: Raising gender-aschematic children in a gender-schematic society. *Signs, 8*, 598–616.

Bem, S. L. (1993). The lenses of gender: *Transforming the debate on sexual inequality.* New Haven, CT: Yale University Press.

Ben-Ari, R., & Hirshberg, I. (2009). Attachment styles, conflict perception, and adolescents' strategies of coping with interpersonal conflict. *Negotiation Journal, 25*(1), 59–82. doi:10.1111/j.1571-9979.2008.00208.x

Bendall, S., Jackson, H. J., & Hulbert, C. A. (2010). Childhood trauma and psychosis: Review of the evidence and directions for psychological interventions. *Australian Psychologist, 45*, 299–306. doi:10.1080/00050060903443219

Bender, D. S., Skodol, A. E., Dyck, I. R., Markowitz, J. C., Shea, M. T., Yen, S., et al. (2007). Ethnicity and mental health treatment utilization by patients with personality disorders. *Journal of Consulting and Clinical Psychology, 75*, 992–999.

Ben-Ezra, M. (2004). Trauma in antiquity: 4000 year old post-traumatic reactions? *Stress and Health, 20*, 121–125.

Benoît, M., & Norton, M. I. (2003). Perceptions of a fluid consensus: Uniqueness bias, false consensus, false polarization, and pluralistic ignorance in a water conservation crisis. *Personality and Social Psychology Bulletin, 29*, 559–567.

Benoit, W. L., & Benoit, P. J. (2008). *Persuasive messages: The process of influence.* Malden, MA: Blackwell Publishing.

Ben-Porath, Y. S. (2003). Assessing personality and psychopathology with self-report inventories. In J. R. Graham & J. A. Naglieri (Eds.), *Handbook of psychology: Vol. 10. Assessment psychology.* New York: Wiley.

Benson, H. (1975). *The relaxation response* (1st ed.). New York, NY: Morrow.

Bentall, R. P. (2009). *Doctoring the mind: Is our current treatment of mental illness really any good?* New York, NY: New York University Press.

Bentall, R. P., Wickham, S., Shevlin, M., & Varese, F. (2012). Do specific early-life adversities lead to specific symptoms of psychosis? A study from the 2007 Adult Psychiatric Morbidity Survey. *Schizophrenia Bulletin, 38*, 734–740. doi:10.1093/schbul/sbs049

Berdahl, J. L. (2007). The sexual harassment of uppity women. *Journal of Applied Psychology, 92*, 425–437.

Berdahl, J. L., & Moore, C. (2006). Workplace harassment: Double jeopardy for minority women. *Journal of Applied Psychology, 91*, 426–436.

Berenbaum, S. A., Blakemore, J., & Beltz, A. M. (2011). A role for biology in gender-related behavior. *Sex Roles, 64*(11–12), 804–825. doi:10.1007/s11199-011-9990-8

Berkowitz, L. (1989). Frustration-aggression hypothesis: Examination and reformulation. *Psychological Bulletin, 106*, 59–73.

Berman, A. L. (2009). Depression and suicide. In I. H. Gotlib & C. L. Hammen (Eds.), *Handbook of depression* (2nd ed.). New York, NY: Guilford Press.

Berman, M. G., Jonides, J., & Kaplan, S. (2008). The cognitive benefits of interacting with nature. *Psychological Science, 19*, 1207–1212.

Berman, M. G., Kross, E., Krpan, K. M., Askren, M. K., Burson, A., Deldin, P. J., & . . . Jonides, J. (2012). Interacting with nature improves cognition and affect for individuals with depression. *Journal of Affective Disorders.* doi:10.1016/j.jad.2012.03.012

Bernache-Assollant, I., Lacassagne, M.-F., & Braddock, J. H., II (2007). Basking in reflected glory and blasting: Differences in identity-management strategies between two groups of highly identified soccer fans. *Journal of Language and Social Psychology, 26*(4), 381–388.

Bernieri, F. J., & Petty, K. N. (2011). The influence of handshakes on first impression accuracy. *Social Influence, 6*(2), 78–87. doi:10.1080/15534510.2011.566706

Berry, C. M., & Sackett, P. R. (2009). Individual differences in course choice result in underestimation of the validity of college admissions systems. *Psychological Science, 20*(7), 822–830. doi:10.1111/j.1467-9280.2009.02368.x.

Berry, D., Sheehan, R., Heschel, R., Knafl, K., Melkus, G., & Grey, M. (2004). Family-based interventions for childhood obesity: A review. *Journal of Family Nursing, 10*, 429–449.

Berscheid, E., Dion, K., Walster, E., & Walster, G. (1971). Physical attractiveness and dating choice: A test of the matching hypothesis. *Journal of Personality and Social Psychology, 7*, 173–189.

Berscheid, E., Snyder, M., & Omoto, A. M. (1989). The relationship closeness inventory: Assessing the closeness of interpersonal relationships. *Journal of Personality and Social Psychology, 57*, 792–807.

Berthoud, H., & Morrison, C. (2008). The brain, appetite, and obesity. *Annual Review of Psychology, 59*, 55–92.

Berto, R. (2005). Exposure to restorative environments helps restore attentional capacity. *Journal of Environmental Psychology, 25*, 249–259.

Berzon, B. (2004). *Permanent partners: Building gay and lesbian relationships that last.* New York, NY: The Penguin Group.

Bettelheim, B. (1967). *The empty fortress.* New York, NY: Free Press.

Bettmann, J. E., & Jasperson, R. A. (2008). Adults in wilderness treatment: A unique application of attachment theory and research. *Clinical Social Work Journal, 36*, 51–61.

Betz, N. E. (1993). Women's career development. In F. L. Denmark & M. A. Paludi (Eds.), *Psychology of women: A handbook of issues and theories.* Westport, CT: Greenwood Press.

Betz, N. E. (2005). Women's career development. In S. D. Brown & R. W. Lent (Eds.), *Career development and counseling: Putting theory and research to work.* New York, NY: Wiley.

Betz, N. E. (2006). Women's career development. In J. Worell & C. D. Goodheart (Eds.), *Handbook of girls' and women's psychological health.* New York, NY: Oxford University Press.

Betz, N. E., & Klein, K. L. (1996). Relationships among measures of career self-efficacy, generalized self-efficacy, and global self-esteem. *Journal of Career Assessment, 4*(3), 285–298.

Beusterien, K. M., Davis, E. A., Flood, R., Howard, K., & Jordan, J. (2008). HIV patient insight on adhering to medication: A qualitative analysis. *AIDS Care, 20*, 251–259.

Beutler, L. E. (2002). The dodo bird is extinct. *Clinical Psychology: Science & Practice, 9*(1), 30–34.

Beutler, L. E., Bongar, B., & Shurkin, J. N. (2001). *A consumers guide to psychotherapy.* New York, NY: Oxford University Press.

Beutler, L. E., Malik, M., Alimohamed, S., Harwood, T. M., Talebi, H., Noble, S., & Wong, E. (2004). Therapist variables. In M. J. Lambert (Ed.), *Bergin and Garfield's handbook of psychotherapy and behavior change.* New York, NY: Wiley.

Bevan, J. L. (2009). Interpersonal communication apprehension, topic avoidance, and the experience of irritable bowel syndrome. *Personal Relationships, 16*(2), 147–165. doi:10.1111/j.1475-6811.2009.01216.x

Bevans, K., Cerbone, A., & Overstreet, S. (2008). Relations between recurrent trauma exposure and recent life stress and salivary cortisol among children. *Development and Psychopathology, 20*, 257–272.

Bhagwagar, Z., & Heninger, (2009). Antidepressants. In M. C. Gelder, N. C. Andreasen, J. J. López-Ibor, Jr., & J. R. Geddes (Eds.), *New Oxford textbook of psychiatry* (2nd ed., Vol. 1). New York, NY: Oxford University Press.

Bhasin, T., & Schendel, D. (2007). Sociodemographic risk factors for autism in a U.S. metropolitan area. *Journal of Autism and Developmental Disorders, 37*, 667–677.

Bhattachary, S., & Powell, J. H. (2001). Recreational use of 3,4-methylenedioxymethamphetamine (MDMA) or "ecstasy": Evidence for cognitive impairment. *Psychological Medicine, 31*(4), 647–658.

Bianchi, S., Milkie, M. A., Sayer, L. C., & Robinson, J. P. (2000). Is anyone doing the housework? Trends in the gender division of household labor. *Social Forces, 79*(1), 191–228.

Bianchi, S. M., Raley, S. B., Casper. L. M. (2012). Changing American families. In P. Noller & G. C. Karantzas (Eds.), *The Wiley-Blackwell handbook of couples and family relationships* (pp. 36–47). Malden, MA: Wiley-Blackwell.

Biernat, M., & Billings, L. S. (2001). Standards, expectancies and social comparison. In A. Tesser & N. Schwarz (Eds.), *Blackwell handbook of social psychology: Intraindividual processes.* Malden, MA: Blackwell.

Bin Kassim, M. A., Hanafi, S. R., & Hancock, D. R. (2008). Test anxiety and its consequences on academic performance among university students. *Advances in Psychology Research, 53*, 75–95.

Binder, J., Zagefka, H., Brown, R., Funke, F., Kessler, T., Mummendey, A., Maquil, A., Demoulin, S., & Leyens, J. P. (2009). Does contact reduce prejudice or does prejudice reduce contact? A longitudinal test of the contact hypothesis among majority and minority groups in three European countries. *Journal of Personality and Social Psychology, 96*, 843–856.

Biron, C., Brun, J., Ivers, H., & Cooper, C. L. (2006). At work but ill: Psychosocial work environment and well-being determinants of presenteeism propensity. *Journal of Public Mental Health, 5*, 26–37.

Bittman, M. (2008, January 27). Rethinking the meat guzzler. *The New York Times.* Retrieved from http://www.nytimes.com/2008/01/27/weekinreview/27bittman.html

Björntorp, P. (2002). Definition and classification of obesity. In C. G. Fairburn & K. D. Brownell (Eds.), *Eating disorders and obesity: A comprehensive handbook.* New York, NY: Guilford.

Blackmore, E. R., Stansfield, S. A., Weller, L., Munce, S., Zagorski, B. M., & Stewart, D. E. (2007). Major depressive episodes and work stress: Results from a national population survey. *American Journal of Public Health, 97*, 2088–2093.

Blaine, B., & Crocker, J. (1993). Self-esteem and self-serving biases in reaction to positive and negative events: An integrative review. In R. F. Baumeister (Ed.), *Self-esteem: The puzzle of low self-regard.* New York : Plenum.

Blair, C., Granger, D. A., Willoughby, M., Mills, Koonce, R., Cox, M., Greenberg, M. T., & . . . Fortunato, C. K. (2011). Salivary cortisol mediates effects of poverty and parenting on executive functions in early childhood. *Child Development, 82*(6), 1970–1984. doi:10.1111/j.1467-8624.2011.01643.x

Blair, S. N., Cheng, Y., & Holder, J. S. (2001). Is physical activity or physical fitness more important in defining health benefits? *Medicine and Science in Sports and Exercise, 33*, S379–S399.

Blair, S. N., Kohl, H. W., Paffenbarger, R. S., Clark, D. G., Cooper, K. H., & Gibbons, L. W. (1989). Physical fitness and all-cause mortality: A prospective study of healthy men and women. *Journal of the American Medical Association, 262*, 2395–2401.

Blair-Loy, M., & DeHart, G. (2003). Family and careeer trajectories among African American female attorneys. *Journal of Family Issues, 24*, 908–933.

Blais, J. J., Craig, W. M., Pepler, D., & Connolly, J. (2008). Adolescents online: The importance of Internet activity choices to salient relationships. *Journal of Youth and Adolescence, 37*, 522–536.

Blakemore, J. E. O. (2003). Children's beliefs about violating gender norms: Boys shouldn't look like girls, and girls shouldn't act like boys. *Sex Roles, 48*(9/10), 411–419.

Blakeslee, S. (2012). Divorce has consequences: But most people didn't think about them before Judith Wallerstein. Retrieved from http://www.slate.com/articles/double_x/doublex/2012/07/judith_wallerstein_and_divorce_how_one_woman_changed_the_way_we_think_about_breakups_.html

Blankenship, K. L., & Wegener, D. T. (2008). Opening the mind to close it: Considering a message in light of important values increases message processing and later resistance to change. *Journal of Personality and Social Psychology, 94*(2), 196–213.

Blanton, H., Buunk, B. P., Gibbons, F. X., & Kuyper, H. (1999). When better-than-others compare upward: Choice of comparison and comparative evaluation as independent predictors of academic performance. *Journal of Personality and Social Psychology, 76*, 420–430.

Blass, T. (Ed.). (2000). *Obedience to authority: Current perspectives on the Milgram paradigm.* Mahwah, NJ: Erlbaum.

Blass, T. (2004). *The man who shocked the world: The life and legacy of Stanley Milgram.* New York, NY: Basic Books.

Blass, T. (2012). A cross-cultural comparison of studies of obedience using the Milgram paradigm: A review. *Social and Personality Psychology Compass, 6*(2), 196–205. doi:10.1111/j.1751-9004.2011.00417.x

Blau, F. D., & Khan, L. M. (2007). The gender pay gap: Have women gone as far as they can? *Academy of Management Perspective, 21*, 7–23.

Bleakley, A., Hennessy, M., & Fishbein, M. (2011). A model of adolescents' seeking of sexual content in their media choices. *Journal of Sex Research, 48*(4), 309-315. doi:10.1080/00224499.2010.497985

Bleakley, A., Jamieson, P. E., & Romer, D. (2012). Trends of sexual and violent content by gender in top-grossing U.S. films, 1950–2006. *Journal of Adolescent Health.* doi:10.1016/j.jadohealth.2012.02.006

Bloch, S., & Harari, E. (2009). Family therapy in the adult psychiatric setting. In M. C. Gelder, N. C. Andreasen, J. J. López-Ibor, Jr., & J. R. Geddes (Eds.), *New Oxford textbook of psychiatry* (2nd ed., Vol. 1). New York, NY: Oxford University Press.

Block, J. H. (1973). Conceptions of sex role: Some cross-cultural and longitudinal perspectives. *American Psychologist, 28*, 512–526.

Bloor, M. (2005). Observations of shipboard illness behavior: Work discipline and the sick role in a residential work setting. *Qualitative Health Research, 15*(6), 766–777.

Blume, B. D., Dreher, G. F., & Baldwin, T. T. (2010). Examining the effects of communication apprehension within assessment centres. *Journal of Occupational and Organizational Psychology, 83*(3), 663–671. doi:10.1348/096317909X463652

Blumenthal, J. (2008). Depression and coronary heart disease: Association and implications for treatment. *Cleveland Clinic Journal of Medicine, 75*, S48–53.

Blumstein, P., & Schwartz, P. (1983). *American couples: Money, work, sex.* New York, NY: Morrow.

Blustein, D. L. (2008). The role of work in psychological health and well-being: A conceptual, historical, and public policy perspective. *American Psychologist, 63*(4), 228–240.

Boase, J., & Wellman, B. (2006). Personal relationships: On and off the internet. In A. L. Vangelisti & D. Perlman (Eds.), *The Cambridge handbook of personal relationships.* New York, NY: Cambridge University Press.

Bobek, B. L., & Robbins, S. B. (2005). Counseling for career transition: Career pathing, job loss, and reentry. In S. D. Brown & R. W. Lent (Eds.), *Career development and counseling: Putting theory and research to work.* New York, NY: Wiley.

Bobo, W. V., Rapoport, J. L., Abi-Dargham, A., Fatemi, H., & Meltzer, H. Y. (2008). The neurobiology of schizophrenia. In A. Tasman, J. Kay, J. A. Lieberman, M. B. First, & M. Maj (Eds.), *Psychiatry* (3rd ed.). New York, NY: Wiley-Blackwell.

Bodenhausen, G. V. (1988). Stereotypic biases in social decision making and memory: Testing process models of stereotype use. *Journal of Personality and Social Psychology, 55*, 726–737.

Bodenhausen, G. V., & Macrae, C. N. (1994). Coherence versus ambivalence in cognitive representations of persons. In R. S. Wyer (Ed.), *Advances in social cognition: Associated systems theory: A systematic approach to cognitive representations of persons* (Vol. 7, pp. 149–156). Hillsdale, NJ: Erlbaum.

Bodenhausen. G. V., Macrae, C. N., & Hugenberg, K. (2003). Social cognition. In T. Millon & M. J. Lerner (Eds.), *Handbook of psychology, Vol. 5: Personality and social psychology.* New York, NY: Wiley.

Bodenhausen, G. V., & Richeson, J. A. (2010). Prejudice, stereotyping, and discrimination. In R. F. Baumeister & E. J. Finkel (Eds.), *Advanced social psychology: The state of the science* (pp. 341–383). New York, NY: Oxford University Press.

Bodenmann, G, Ledermann, T., & Bradbury, T. N. (2007). Stress, sex, and satisfaction in marriage. *Personal Relationships, 14,* 551–569.

Bodenmann, G., Charvoz, L., Bradbury, T. N., Bertoni, A., Iafrate, R., Giuliani, C., & . . . Behling, J. (2007). The role of stress in divorce: A three-nation retrospective study. *Journal of Social and Personal Relationships, 24*(5), 707–728. doi:10.1177/0265407507081456

Boen, F., Van Beselaere, N., & Feys, J. (2002). Behavioral consequences of fluctuating group success; An Internet study of soccer-team fans. *Journal of Social Psychology, 142,* 769–781.

Bögels, S. M., & Voncken, M. (2008). Social skills training versus cognitive therapy for social anxiety disorder characterized by fear of blushing, trembling, or sweating. *International Journal of Cognitive Therapy, 1*(2), 138–150. doi:10.1521/ijct.2008.1.2.138

Bogle, K. (2011). Premarital adolescent sexual activity. In C. D. Bryant (Ed.), *The Routledge handbook of deviant behavior* (pp. 260–265). New York, NY: Routledge/Taylor & Francis Group.

Bohnert, A. M., Aikins, J. W., & Edidin, J. (2007). The role of organized activities in facilitating social adaption across the transition to college. *Journal of Adolescent Research, 22,* 189–208.

Boland, R. J., & Keller, M. B. (2008). Antidepressants. In A. Tasman, J. Kay, J. A. Lieberman, M. B. First, & M. Maj (Eds.), *Psychiatry* (3rd ed.). New York, NY: Wiley-Blackwell.

Boland, R. J., & Keller, M. B. (2009). Course and outcome of depression. In I. H. Gotlib & C. L. Hammen (Eds.), *Handbook of depression* (2nd ed., pp. 23–43). New York, NY: Guilford Press.

Boles, D. B. (2005). A large-sample study of sex differences in functional cerebral lateralization. *Journal of Clinical and Experimental Neuropsychology, 27,* 759–768.

Bolger, N. (1990). Coping as a personality process: A prospective study. *Journal of Personality and Social Psychology, 59,* 525–537.

Bolino, M. C., & Turnley, W. H. (2005). The personal costs of citizenship behavior: The relationship between individual initiative and role overload, job stress, and work-family conflict. *Journal of Applied Psychology, 90*(4), 740–748.

Bolles, R. N. (2007). *The 2007 what color is your parachute? A practical manual for job-hunters and career-changers.* Berkeley, CA: Ten Speed Press.

Bolles, R. N. (2013). *What color is your parachute? 2013: A practical manual for job-hunters and career-changers.* New York, NY: Ten Speed Press.

Bonanno, G. A. (2009). *The other side of sadness: What the new science of bereavement tells us about life after loss.* New York, NY: Basic Books.

Bond, C. F., Jr., & DePaulo, B. M. (2006). Accuracy of deception judgments. *Personality and Social Psychology Review, 10*(3), 214–234.

Bond, C. F., Jr., & DePaulo, B. M. (2008). Individual differences in judging deception: Accuracy and bias. *Psychological Bulletin, 134,* 477–492.

Bond, J. T., Thompson, C., Galinsky, E., & Prottas, D. (2003). *The 2002 national study of the changing workforce.* New York, NY: Families and Work Institute.

Bonebright, C. A., Clay, D. L., & Ankenmann, R. D. (2000). The relationship of workaholism with work-life conflict, life satisfaction, and purpose in life. *Journal of Counseling Psychology, 47,* 469–477.

Bonetti, L., Campbell, M., & Gilmore, L. (2010). The relationship of loneliness and social anxiety with children's and adolescents' online communication. *Cyberpsychology, Behavior, and Social Networking, 13*(3), 279–285. doi:10.1089/cyber.2009.0215

Bono, G., Emmons, R. A., & McCullough, M. E. (2004). Gratitude in practice and the practice of gratitude. In P. A. Linley & S. Joseph (Eds.), *Positive psychology in practice* (pp. 464–484). Hoboken, NJ: Wiley.

Bookwala, J. (2009). Couples in middle age. In H. T. Reis & S. Sprecher (Eds.), *Encyclopedia of human relationships: Vol. 2* (pp. 340–343). Los Angeles: Sage Reference Publication.

Bordnick, P. S., Elkins, R. L., Orr, T. E., Walters, P., & Thyer, B. A. (2004). Evaluating the relative effectiveness of three aversion therapies designed to reduce craving among cocaine abusers. *Behavioral Interventions, 19*(1), 1–24.

Bornstein, R. F. (2003). Psychodynamic models of personality. In T. Millon & M. J. Lerner (Eds.), *Handbook of psychology, Vol. 5: Personality and social psychology.* New York, NY: Wiley.

Borys, S., & Perlman, D. (1985). Gender differences in loneliness. *Personality and Social Psychology Bulletin, 11,* 63–74.

Bosson, J. K., Vandello, J. A., Burnaford, R. M., Weaver, J. R., & Wasti, S. A. (2009). Precarious manhood and displays of physical aggression. *Personality and Social Psychology Bulletin, 35,* 623–634.

Bouchard, C. (2002). Genetic influences on body weight. In C. G. Fairburn & K. D. Brownell (Eds.), *Eating disorders and obesity: A comprehensive handbook* (2nd ed., pp. 16–21). New York, NY: Guilford.

Bourhis, J., Allen, M., & Bauman, I. (2006). Communication apprehension: Issues to consider in the classroom. In B. M. Gayle, R. W. Preiss, N. Burrell, & M. Allen (Eds.), *Classroom communication and instructional processes: Advances through meta-analysis* (pp. 211–227). Mahwah, NJ: Erlbaum.

Bovornusvakool, W., Vodanovich, S. J., Ariyabuddhiphongs, K., & Ngamake, S. T. (2012). Examining the antecedents and consequences of workaholism. *The Psychologist-Manager Journal, 15*(1), 56–70. doi:10.1080/10887156.2012.649994

Bower, S. A., & Bower, G. H. (1991). *Asserting yourself: A practical guide for positive change* (2nd ed.). Reading, MA: Addison-Wesley.

Bower, S. A., & Bower, G. H. (2004). *Asserting yourself: A practical guide for positive change* (updated ed.). Cambridge, MA: Da Capo Press/Perseus.

Bowers, K. (2008). Making the most of human strengths. In S. J. Lopez (Ed.), *Positive psychology: Exploring the best in people* (Vol. 1, pp. 23–36). Westport, CT: Praeger.

Bowers, M. (2007, July/August). The making of the MFT profession: Standards, regulation. *Family Therapy Magazine,* pp. 12–18.

Bowes-Sperry, L., & Tata, J. (1999). A multiperspective framework of sexual harassment. In G. N. Powell (Ed.), *Handbook of gender and work.* Thousand Oaks, CA: Sage.

Bowins, B. (2004). Psychological defense mechanisms: A new perspective. *American Journal of Psychoanalysis, 64*(1), 1–26.

Bowlby, J. (1980). *Attachment and loss: Vol. 3. Loss: Sadness and depression.* New York, NY: Basic Books.

Boyce, C. J., Brown, G. A., & Moore, S. C. (2010). Money and happiness: Rank of income, not income, affects life satisfaction. *Psychological Science, 21*(4), 471–475.

Boyle, G. J. (2008). Critique of the five-factor model of personality. In G. J. Boyle, G. Matthews, & D. H. Saklofske (Eds.), *The Sage handbook of personality theory and assessment* (pp. 295–312). Los Angeles: Sage.

Boyle, M. (2007). The problem with diagnosis. *The Psychologist, 20,* 290–292.

Bradbury, T. N., Campbell, S. M., & Fincham, F. D. (1995). Longitudinal and behavioral analysis of masculinity and femininity in marriage. *Journal of Personality and Social Psychology, 68*(2), 328–341.

Brady, G. (2012, June 13). The sniff test. *Ever forward.* Retrieved from http://genebrady.me/2012/06/13/the-sniff-test/

Brady-Amoon, P., & Fuertes, J. N. (2011). Self-efficacy, self-rated abilities, adjustment, and academic performance. *Journal of Counseling & Development, 89* (4), 431-438.

Bragg, E. A. (1996). Towards ecological self: Deep ecology meets constructionist self-theory. *Journal of Environmental Psychology, 16,* 93–108.

Brainerd, C. J., & Reyna, V. F. (2005). *The science of false memory.* New York, NY: Oxford University Press.

Brajša-Žganec, A., Merkaš, M., & Šverko, I. (2011). Quality of life and leisure activities: How do leisure activities contribute to subjective well-being? *Social Indicators Research, 102*(1), 81–91. doi:10.1007/s11205-010-9724-2

Brambilla, M., Ravenna, M., & Hewstone, M. (2012). Changing stereotype content through mental imagery: Imagining intergroup contact promotes stereotype change. *Group Processes & Intergroup Relations, 15*(3), 305–315. doi:10.1177/1368430211427574

Bramlett, M. D., & Mosher, W. D. (2002). Cohabitation, marriage, divorce, and remarriage in the United States. *Vital Health Statistics, 23*(22).

Branaman, T. F., & Gallagher, S. N. (2005). Polygraph testing in sex offender treatment: A review of limitations. *American Journal of Forensic Psychology, 23*(1), 45–64.

Brandes, D., Ben-Schachar, G., Gilboa, A., Bonne, O., Freedman, & S., Shalev, A. Y. (2002). PTSD symptoms and cognitive performance in recent trauma survivors. *Psychiatry Research, 110,* 231–238.

Brandt, M. J. (2011). Sexism and gender inequality across 57 societies. *Psychological Science, 22*(11), 14131418. doi:10.1177/0956797611420445

Brannon, L. (2005). *Gender: Psychological perspectives.* Boston, MA: Allyn & Bacon.

Brannon, R. (1976). The male sex role: Our culture's blueprint of manhood, and what it's done for us lately. In D. David & R. Brannon (Eds.), *The forty-nine percent majority.* Reading, MA: Addison-Wesley.

Brassard, A., Péloquin, K., Dupuy, E., Wright, J., & Shaver, P. R. (2012). Romantic attachment insecurity predicts sexual dissatisfaction in couples seeking marital therapy. *Journal of Sex and Marital Therapy, 38*(3), 245-262. doi:10.1080/0092623X.2011.606881

Bratko, D., & Butkovic, A. (2003). Family study of sensation seeking. *Personality and Individual Differences, 35,* 1559–1570.

Bray, J. H. (2009). Remarriage. In H. T. Reis & S. Sprecher (Eds.), *Encyclopedia of human relationships: Vol. 3* (pp. 1359–1363). Los Angeles: Sage Reference Publication.

Bredt, B. M., Higuera-Alhino, D., Hebert, S. J., McCune, J. M., & Abrams, D. I. (2002). Short-term effects of cannabinoids on immune phenotype and function in HIV-1-infected patients. *Journal of Clinical Pharmacology, 42,* 90S–96S.

Breggin, P. R. (1991). *Toxic psychiatry.* New York, NY: St. Martin's Press.

Breggin, P. R. (2008). *Medication madness: A psychiatrist exposes the dangers of mood-altering medications.* New York, NY: St. Martin's Press.

Breggin, P. R., & Cohen, D. (2007). *Your drug may be your problem: How and why to stop taking psychiatric medications.* New York, NY: Da Capo Lifelong Books.

Brehm, J. W. (1956). Postdecision changes in the desirability of alternatives. *Journal of Abnormal and Social Psychology, 52,* 384–389.

Brehm, J. W. (1966). *A theory of psychological reactance.* New York, NY: Academic Press.

Brehm, S. S., Kassin, S. M., & Fein, S. (2002). *Social psychology.* Boston, MA: Houghton Mifflin.

Brenes, G. A., Ingram, C. W., Danhauer, S. C. (2012). Telephone-delivered psychotherapy for late-life anxiety. *Psychological Services, 9,* 219–220. doi:10.1037/a0025950

Brennan, K. A., Clark, C. L., & Shaver, P. R. (1998). Self-report measurement of adult attachment: An integrative overview. In J. A. Simpson & W. S. Rholes (Eds.), *Attachment theory and close relationships.* New York, NY: Guilford Press.

Breslin, F. C., & Mustard, C. (2003). Factors influencing the impact of unemployment on mental health among young and older adults in a longitudinal, population-based survey. *Scandinavian Journal of Work, Environment & Health, 29*(1), 5–14.

Brewer, M. B. (1999). The psychology of prejudice: Ingroup love or outgroup hate? *Journal of Social Issues, 55,* 429–444.

Brewer, M. B. (2007). The importance of being *we*: Human nature and intergroup relations. *American Psychologist, 62,* 726–738.

Brewer, M. B., & Brown, R. J. (1998). Inter-group relations. In D. T. Gilbert, S. T. Fiske, & G. Lindzey (Eds.), *The handbook of social psychology* (4th ed., Vol. 2). New York, NY: McGraw-Hill.

Brewin, C. R. (2007). Autobiographical memory for trauma: Update on four controversies. *Memory, 15,* 227–248.

Brickman, P., Coates, D., & Janoff-Bulman, R. (1978). Lottery winners and accident victims: Is happiness relative? *Journal of Personality and Social Psychology, 36,* 917–927.

Bridge, J. A., Iyengar, S., Salary, C. B., Barbe, R. P., Birmaher, B., Pincus, H. A., et al. (2007). Clinical response and risk for reported suicidal ideation and suicide attempts in pediatric antidepressant treatment: A meta-analysis of randomized controlled trials. *Journal of the American Medical Association, 297,* 1683–1969.

Bridges, K. R., & Roig, M. (1997). Academic procrastination and irrational thinking: A re-examination with context controlled. *Personality & Individual Differences, 22,* 941–944.

Brink, E., Alsén, P., Herlitz, J., Kjellgren, K., & Cliffordson, C. (2012). General self-efficacy and health-related quality of life after myocardial infarction. *Psychology, Health & Medicine, 17,* 346–355. doi:10 .1080/13548506.2011.608807

Briñol, P., & Petty, R. E. (2012). A history of attitudes and persuasion research. In A. W. Kruglanski & W. Stroebe (Eds.), *Handbook of the history of social psychology* (pp. 283–320). New York, NY: Psychology Press.

Brinthaupt, T. M., & Shin, C. M. (2001). The relationship of academic cramming to the flow experience. *College Student Journal, 35,* 457–471.

Brissette, I., Scheier, M. F., & Carver, C. S. (2002). The role of optimism in social network development, coping, and psychological adjustment during a life transition. *Journal of Personality and Social Psychology, 82*(1), 102–111.

Briton, N. J., & Hall, J. A. (1995). Beliefs about female and male nonverbal communication. *Sex Roles, 32*(1-2), 79–90.

Britton, B. K., & Tesser, A. (1991). Effects of time-management practices on college grades. *Journal of Educational Psychology, 83,* 405–410.

Brody, L. R., & Hall, J. A. (2010). Gender, emotion, and socialization. In J. C. Chrisler & D. R. McCreary (Eds.), *Handbook of gender research in psychology* (Vol. 1, pp. 429–454). New York, NY: Springer.

Brody, S., & Costa, R. M. (2009). Satisfaction (sexual, life, relationship, and mental health) is associated directly with penile and vaginal intercourse, but inversely with other sexual behavior frequencies. *Journal of Sexual Medicine, 6,* 1947–1954.

Broida, J., Tingley, L., Kimball, R., & Miele, J. (1993). Personality differences between pro- and anti-vivisectionists. *Society and Animals, 1,* 129–144.

Bromley, M., & Blieszner, R. (1997). Planning for long-term care: Filial behavior and relationship quality of adult children with independent parents. *Family Relations,* 155–162.

Brondolo, E., ver Halen, N. B., Libby, D., & Pencille, M. (2011). Racism as a psychosocial stressor. In R. J. Contrada & A. Baum (Eds.), *The handbook of stress science: Biology, psychology, and health* (pp. 167–184). New York, NY: Springer.

Brookes, R., Lehman, T. C., Maguire, S., Mitchell, P., Mejia, V. A., Johnson Aramaki, T., & Raboni, E. M. (2010). Real life. Real talk. Creating engagement in sexual and reproductive health among parents, teens, families, and communities. *Social Marketing Quarterly, 16*(1), 52–69. doi:10.1080/15245000903551839

Brooks, G. (2010). The crisis of masculinity. In *Beyond the crisis of masculinity: A transtheoretical model for male-friendly therapy* (pp. 13–22). Washington, DC: American Psychological Association. doi:10.1037/12073-001

Brooks, M. L., Swann, W. r., & Mehta, P. H. (2011). Reasserting the self: Blocking self-verifying behavior triggers compensatory self-verification. *Self and Identity, 10*(1), 77–84. doi:10.1080/15298861003593575

Broomhall, H. S., & Winefield, A. H. (1990). A comparison of the affective well-being of young and middle-aged unemployed men matched for length of employment. *British Journal of Medical Psychology, 63,* 43–52.

Brotherridge, C. M., & Grandey, A. A. (2002). Emotional labor and burnout: Comparing two perspectives of "people work." *Journal of Vocational Behavior, 60,* 17-39.

Brotto, L. A., Bitzer, J., Laan, E., Leiblum, S., & Luria, M. (2010). Women's sexual desire and arousal disorders. *Journal of Sexual Medicine, 7,* 586-614. doi:10.1111.j.17436109.2009.01630.x

Brown, A. S., & Derkits, E. J. (2010). Prenatal infection and schizophrenia: A review of epidemiologic and translational studies. *American Journal of Psychiatry, 167*(3), 261–280. doi:10.1176/appi.ajp.2009.09030361

Brown, D. (2007). *Career information, career counseling, and career development.* Boston, MA: Allyn & Bacon.

Brown, E. J., Juster, H. R., Heimberg, R. G., & Winning, C. D. (1998). Stressful life events and personality styles: Relation to impairment and treatment outcome in patients with social phobia. *Journal of Anxiety Disorders, 12*(3), 233–251.

Brown, J. D., & Marshall, M. A. (2006). The three faces of self-esteem. In M. H. Kernis (Ed.), *Self-esteem issues and answers: A sourcebook of current perspectives* (pp. 4–9). New York, NY: Psychology Press.

Brown, J. M., Stewart, J. C., Stump, T. E., & Callahan, C. M. (2011). Risk of coronary heart disease events over 15 years among older adults with depressive symptoms. *The American Journal of Geriatric Psychiatry, 19*(8), 721–729.

Brown, K., & Holt, M. (2011). Experiential processing and the integration of bright and dark sides of the human psyche. In K. M. Sheldon, T. B. Kashdan, & M. F. Steger (Eds.), *Designing positive psychology: Taking stock and moving forward* (pp. 147-159). New York, NY: Oxford University Press. doi:10.1093/acprof:oso/9780195373585.003.0010

Brown, R. D., Goldstein, E., & Bjorklund, D. F. (2000). The history and zeitgeist of the repressed–false memory debate: Scientific and sociological perspectives on suggestibility and childhood memory. In D. F. Bjorklund (Ed.), *False-memory creation in children and adults.* Mahwah, NJ: Erlbaum.

Brown, S. L. (2010). Marriage and child well-being: Research and policy perspectives. *Journal of Marriage and Family, 72*(5), 1059–1077. doi:10.1111/j.1741-3737.2010.00750.x

Brown, S. L., Nesse, R. M., Vinokur, A. D., & Smith, D. M. (2003). Providing social support may be more beneficial than receiving it: Results from a prospective study of mortality. *Psychological Science, 14*(4), 320–327.

Brown, S. L., Sanchez, L. A., Nock, S. L., & Wright, J. D. (2006). Links between premarital cohabitation and subsequent marital quality, stability, and divorce: A comparison of covenant versus standard marriages. *Social Science Research, 35,* 454–470.

Brown, T. A., & Lawrence, A. E. (2009). Generalized anxiety disorders and obsessive-compulsive disorder. In P. H. Blaney & T. Millon (Eds.), *Oxford textbook of psychopathology* (pp.146–175). New York, NY: Oxford University Press.

Brown, T. T., & Dobs, A. S. (2002). Endocrine effects of marijuana. *Journal of Clinical Pharmacology, 42,* 97S–102S.

Browne, A. (1993a). Family violence and homelessness: The relevance of trauma histories in the lives of homeless women. *American Journal of Orthopsychiatry, 63,* 370–384.

Browne, A. (1993b). Violence against women by male partners: Prevalence, outcomes, and policy implications. *American Psychologist, 48,* 1077–1087.

Brownell, K. D., & Wadden, T. A. (2000). Obesity. In B. J. Sadock, & V. A. Sadock (Eds.), *Kaplan and Sadock's comprehensive textbook of psychiatry* (7th ed.). Philadelphia: Lippincott/Williams & Wilkins.

Brugha, T. S., McManus, S., Bankart, J., Scott, F., Purdon, S., Smith, J., . . . & Meltzer, H. (2011). Epidemiology of autism spectrum disorders in adults in the community in England. *Archives of General Psychiatry, 68*(5), 459–466. doi:10.1001/archgenpsychiatry .2011.38

Brumbaugh, C., & Fraley, R. (2010). Adult attachment and dating strategies: How do insecure people attract mates? *Personal Relationships, 17*(4), 599–614. doi:10.1111/j.1475-6811.2010.01304.x

Brunell, A. B., Staats, S., Barden, J., & Hupp, J. M. (2011). Narcissism and academic dishonesty: The exhibitionism dimension and the lack of guilt. *Personality and Individual Differences, 50,* 323–328. doi:10.1016/j.paid.2010.10.006

Brunet, P. M., & Schmidt, L. A. (2007). Is shyness context specific? Relation between shyness and online disclosure. *Journal of Research in Personality, 41,* 938–945.

Bryant, F. B., & Veroff, J. (2007). *Savoring: A new model of positive experience.* Mahwah, NJ: Erlbaum.

Bryant, R. A., & Guthrie, R. M. (2005). Maladaptive appraisals as a risk factor for posttraumatic stress: A study of trainee firefighters. *Psychological Science, 16,* 749–752.

Buchanan, C. M., & Hughes, J. L. (2009). Construction of social reality during early adolescence: Can expecting storm and stress increase real or perceived storm and stress? *Journal of Research on Adolescence, 19*(2), 261–285.

Buchanan, R. W., & Carpenter, W. T. (2005). Concept of schizophrenia. In B. J. Sadock & V. A. Sadock (Eds.), *Kaplan & Sadock's comprehensive textbook of psychiatry.* Philadelphia: Lippincott Williams & Wilkins.

Buchwald, H., Avidor, Y., Braunwald, E., Jensen, M. D., Pories, W., Fahrbach, K., et al. (2004). Bariatric surgery: A systematic review and meta-analysis. *Journal of the American Medical Association, 292,* 1724–1737.

Buckingham, J. T., & Alicke, M. D. (2002). The influence of individual versus aggregate social comparison and the presence of others on self–evaluations. *Journal of Personality and Social Psychology, 83*(5), 1117–1130.

Buckman, R. (2002). Communications and emotions: Skills and effort are key. *British Medical Journal, 325,* 672.

Buehlman, K. T., Gottman, J. M., & Katz, L. F. (1992). How a couple views their past predicts their future: Predicting divorce from an oral history interview. *Journal of Family Psychology, 5,* 295–318.

Buffardi, L. E. (2011). Narcissism and the World Wide Web. In W. K. Campbell & J. D. Miller (Eds.), *The handbook of narcissism and narcissistic personality disorder: Theoretical approaches, empirical findings, and treatments* (pp. 371–381). New York, NY: Wiley.

Bulcroft, R., & Teachman, J. (2004). Ambiguous constructions: Development of a childless or child-free life course. In M. Coleman, & L. H. Ganong (Eds.), *Handbook of contemporary families: Considering the past, contemplating the future.* Thousand Oaks, CA: Sage.

Bulik, C. M. (2004). Genetic and biological risk factors. In J. K. Thompson (Ed.), *Handbook of eating disorders and obesity.* New York: Wiley.

Bumpass, L. L., & Lu, H. H. (2000). Trends in cohabitation and implications for children's family contexts in the United States. *Population Studies, 54,* 29–41.

Bureau of Justice Statistics. (2011). *Criminal Victimization, 2010,* (Washington, DC: U.S. Department of Justice, 2011), Table 1, http://bjs.ojp.usdoj.gov/content/pub/pdf/cv10.pdf (accessed September 28, 2011).

Burger, J. M. (2008). *Personality* (7th ed.). Belmont, CA: Wadsworth.

Burger, J. M. (2009). Replicating Milgram: Would people still obey today? *American Psychologist, 64*(1), 1–11.

Burger, J. M., & Cornelius, T. (2003). Raising the price of agreement: Public commitment and the lowball compliance procedure. *Journal of Applied Social Psychology, 33*(5), 923–934.

Burger, J. M., & Guadagno, R. E. (2003). Self-concept clarity and the foot-in-the-door procedure. *Basic and Applied Social Psychology, 25*(1), 79–86.

Burgess, C., O'Donohoe, A., & Gill, M. (2000). Agony and ecstasy: A review of MDMA effects and toxicity. *European Psychiatry, 15*(5), 287–294.

Burgoon, J. K. (1994). Nonverbal signals. In M. L. Knapp & G. R. Miller (Eds.), *Handbook of interpersonal communication* (2nd ed.). Thousand Oaks, CA: Sage.

Burhans, K. K., & Dweck, C. S. (1995). Helplessness in early childhood: The role of contingent worth. *Child Development, 66*, 1719–1738.

Burke, B. L., Martens, A., & Faucher, E. H. (2010). Two decades of terror management theory: A meta-analysis of mortality salience research. *Personality and Social Psychology Review, 14*(2), 155–195. doi:10.1177/1088868309352321

Burke, M. E. (2005). *2004 reference and background checking survey report.* Alexandria, VA: Society for Human Resource Management.

Burke, R. J. (2001). Workaholism in organizations: The role of organizational values. *Personnel Review, 30*, 637–645.

Burke, R. J. (2009). Working to live or living to work: Should individuals and organizations care? *Journal of Business Ethics, 84*(Suppl2), 167–172.

Burke, W. W. (2011). *Organizational change: Theory and practice* (3rd ed.). Thousand Oaks, CA: Sage.

Burlingame, G. M., & Baldwin, S. (2011). Group therapy. In J. C. Norcross, G. R. Vandenbos, & D. K. Freedheim (Eds.), *History of psychotherapy: Continuity and change* (2nd ed.). Washington, DC: American Psychological Association.

Burn, S. M., & Ward, A. Z. (2005). Men's conformity to traditional masculinity and relationship satisfaction. *Psychology of Men and Masculinity, 6*, 254–263.

Burns, A. B., Brown, J. S., Plant, E. A., Sachs-Ericsson, N., & Joiner, T. E. Jr. (2006). On the specific depressotypic nature of excessive reassurance-seeking. *Personality and Individual Differences, 40*(1), 135–145.

Burpee, L., & Langer, E. (2005). Mindfulness and marital satisfaction. *Journal of Adult Development, 12*(1), 43–51.

Bushman, B. J., & Anderson, C. A. (2001). Media violence and the American public. *American Psychologist, 56*, 477–489.

Bushman, B. J., & Baumeister, R. F. (1998). Threatened egotism, narcissism, self-esteem, and direct and displaced aggression: Does self-love or self-hate lead to violence? *Journal of Personality and Social Psychology, 75*(1), 219–229.

Bushman, B. J., & Baumeister, R. F. (2002). Does self-love or self-hate lead to violence? *Journal of Research in Personality, 36*(6), 543–545.

Bushman, B. J., Baumeister, R. F., Thomaes, S., Ryu, E., Begeer, S., & West, S. G. (2009). Looking again, and harder, for a link between self-esteem and aggression. *Journal of Personality, 77*(2), 427–446.

Bushman, B. J., Bonacci, A. M., van Dijk, M., & Baumeister, R. F. (2003). Narcissism, sexual refusal, and aggression: Testing a narcissistic reactance model of sexual coercion. *Journal of Personality and Social Psychology, 84*, 1027–1040.

Bushman, B. J., & Huesmann, L. (2012). Effects of violent media on aggression. In D. G. Singer & J. L. Singer (Eds.), *Handbook of children and the media* (2nd ed., pp. 231–248). Thousand Oaks, CA: Sage Publications, Inc.

Bushman, B. J., Moeller, S. J., & Crocker, J. (2011). Sweets, sex, or self-esteem? Comparing the value of self-esteem boosts with other pleasant rewards. *Journal of Personality, 79*(5), 993–1012. doi:10.1111/j.1467-6494.2011.00712.x

Buss, A. H. (2012). Self II: Self-esteem and identity. In *Pathways to individuality: Evolution and development of personality traits* (pp. 141–168). Washington, DC: American Psychological Association. doi:10.1037/13087-007

Buss, D. M. (1988). The evolution of human intrasexual competition: Tactics of mate attraction. *Journal of Personality and Social Psychology, 54*, 616–628.

Buss, D. M. (1989). Sex differences in human mate preferences: Evolutionary hypotheses tested in 37 cultures. *Behavioral and Brain Sciences, 12*, 1–14.

Buss, D. M. (1991). Evolutionary personality psychology. *Annual Review of Psychology, 42*, 459–491.

Buss, D. M. (1995). Evolutionary psychology: A new paradigm for psychological science. *Psychological Inquiry, 6*, 1–30.

Buss, D. M. (2009). The great struggles of life: Darwin and the emergence of evolutionary psychology. *American Psychologist, 64*(2), 140–148. doi:10.1037/a0013207

Buss, D. M., & Kenrick, D. T. (1998). Evolutionary social psychology. In D. T. Gilbert, S. T. Fiske, & G. Lindzey (Eds.), *The handbook of social psychology.* New York, NY: McGraw-Hill.

Buss, D. M., & Schmitt, D. P. (1993). Sexual strategies theory: A contextual evolutionary analysis of human mating. *Psychological Review, 100*, 204–232.

Buss, D. M., & Schmitt, D. P. (2011). Evolutionary psychology and feminism. *Sex Roles, 64*(9-10), 768–787. doi:10.1007/s11199-011-9987-3

Buss, D. M., Shackelford, T. K., Kirkpatrick, L. A., & Larsen, R. J. (2001). A half century of mate preferences: The cultural evolution of values. *Journal of Marriage and Family, 63*, 491–503.

Bussey, K., & Bandura, A. (1984). Influence of gender constancy and social power on sex-linked modeling. *Journal of Personality and Social Psychology, 47*, 1292–1302.

Bussey, K., & Bandura, A. (1999). Social cognitive theory of gender development and differentiation. *Psychological Review, 106*(4), 676–713.

Bussey, K., & Bandura, A. (2004). Social cognitive theory of gender development and functioning. In A. H. Eagly, A. E. Beall, & R. J. Sternberg (Eds.), *The psychology of gender.* New York, NY: Guilford Press.

Butler, A. C., Roediger, H. L., III. (2008). Feedback enhances the positive effects and reduces the negative effects of multiple-choice testing. *Memory & Cognition, 36*(3).

Butler, E. A., Egloff, B., Wlhelm, F. H., Smith, N. C., Erickson, E. A., & Gross, J. J. (2003). The social consequences of expressive suppression. *Emotion, 3*(1), 48–67.

Butler, J. L., & Baumeister, R. F. (1998). The trouble with friendly faces: Skilled performance with a supportive audience. *Journal of Personality and Social Psychology, 75*(5), 1213–1230.

Buunk, A. P., & Dijkstra, P. (2001). Rationalizations and defensive attributions for high-risk sex among heterosexuals. *Patient Education and Counseling, 45*(2), 127–132. doi:10.1016/S0738-3991(01)00114-8

Buunk, A. P., & Dijkstra, P. (2006). Temptation and threat: Extradyadic relations and jealousy. In A. L. Vangelisti & D. Perlman (Eds.), *The Cambridge handbook of personal relationships.* New York, NY: Cambridge University Press.

Buxton, M. N., Arkel, Y., Lagos, J., Deposito, F., Lowenthal, H., & Simring, S. (1981). Stress and platelet aggregation in hemophiliac children and their family members. *Research Communications in Psychology, Psychiatry and Behavior, 6*, 21–48.

Buzzell, L. & Chalquist, C. (2009). Ecotherapy: Healing with nature in mind. San Francisco: Sierra Club Books

Byers, E. (2011). Beyond the birds and the bees and was it good for you? Thirty years of research on sexual communication. *Canadian Psychology/Psychologie Canadienne, 52*(1), 20–28. doi:10.1037/a0022048

Byne, W. (2007). Biology and sexual minority status. In I. L. Meyer & M. E. Northridge (Eds.), *The health of sexual minorities: Public health perspectives on lesbian, gay, bisexual, and transgender populations* (pp. 65–90). New York, NY: Springer Science and Business Media.

Byrm, R. J., & Lenton, R. L. (2001). *Love online: A report on digital dating in Canada.* Retrieved April 30, 2007 from http://www.nelson.com/nelson/harcourt/sociology/newsociety3e/loveonline.pdf.

Byrne, D., & Clore, G. L. (1970). A reinforcement model of evaluative responses. *Personality: An International Journal, 1*(2), 103–128.

Byrne, D., Clore, G. L., & Smeaton, G. (1986). The attraction hypothesis: Do similar attitudes affect anything? *Journal of Personality and Social Psychology, 51*, 1167–1170.

Byrne, R. (2006). *The secret.* New York, NY: Atria Books.

Cabral, G. A., & Petit, D. A. D. (1998). Drugs and immunity: Cannabinoids and their role in decreased resistance to infectious disease. *Journal of Neuroimmunology, 83*, 116–123.

Cacioppo, J. T., & Patrick, W. (2008). *Loneliness.* New York, NY: Norton.

Cadinu, M., Maass, A., Rosablanca, A., & Kiesner, J. (2005). Why do women underperform under stereotype threat? Evidence for the role of negative thinking. *Psychological Science, 16*, 572–578.

Cahn, D. D. (2009). Friendship, conflict and dissolution. In H. T. Reis & S. Sprecher (Eds.), *Encyclopedia of human relationships: Vol. 1* (pp. 703–706). Los Angeles: Sage Reference Publication.

Calasanti, T., & Harrison-Rexrode, J. (2009). Gender roles in relationships. In H. T. Reis & S. Sprecher (Eds.), *Encyclopedia of human relationships: Vol. 1* (pp. 754–757). Los Angeles: Sage Reference Publication.

Calogero, R. M., & Thompson, J. K. (2010.) Gender and body image. In J. C. Chrisler & D. R. McCreary (Eds.), *Handbook of gender research in psychology* (Vol. 2, pp. 153-184). New York, NY: Springer.

Cameron, D. (2007). *The myth of Mars and Venus: Do men and women really speak different languages?* Oxford, UK: Oxford University Press.

Cameron, K. S., Dutton, J. E., & Quinn, R. E. (Eds.). (2003). *Positive organizational scholarship: Foundations of a new discipline.* San Francisco: Berrett-Koehler.

Cameron, L., Leventhal, E. A., & Leventhal, H. (1993). Symptom representations and affect as determinants of care seeking in a community-dwelling, adult sample population. *Health Psychology, 12*, 171–179.

Campbell, J. D. (1990). Self-esteem and clarity of the self-concept. *Journal of Personality and Social Psychology, 59*, 538–549.

Campbell, J. D., Assanand, S., & DiPaula, A. (2000). Structural features of the self-concept and adjustment. In A. Tesser, R. B. Felson, & J. M. Suls (Eds.), *Psychological perspectives on self and identity.* Washington, DC: American Psychological Association.

Campbell, J. D., Chew, B., & Scratchley, L. S. (1991). Cognitive and emotional reactions to daily events: The effects of self-esteem and self-complexity. *Journal of Personality, 59*, 473–505.

Campbell, J. D., & Lavallee, L. F. (1993). Who am I? The role of self-concept confusion in understanding the behavior of people with low self-esteem. In R. Baumeister (Ed.), *Self-esteem: The puzzle of low self-regard.* New York, NY: Plenum.

Campbell, K., Wright, D. W., & Flores, C. G. (2012). Newlywed women's marital expectations: Lifelong monogamy? *Journal of Divorce and Remarriage, 53*(2), 108–125. doi:10.1080/10502556.2012.651966

Campbell, L., Simpson, J. A., Boldry, J., & Kashy, D. A. (2005). Perceptions of conflict and support in romantic relationships: The role of attachment anxiety. *Journal of Personality and Social Psychology, 88*, 510–531.

Campbell, L. F., & Smith, T. P. (2003). Integrating self-help books into psychotherapy. *Journal of Clinical Psychology, 59*(2), 177–186.

Campbell, W. K., & Foster, J. D. (2007). The narcissistic self: Background, an extended-agency model, and ongoing controversies. In C. Sedikides & S. J. Spencer (Eds.), *The self* (pp. 115–138). New York, NY: Psychology Press.

Campbell, W. K., Sedikides, C., Reeder, G. D., & Elliot A. J. (2000). Among friends? An examination of friendship and the self-serving bias. *British Journal of Social Psychology, 39*(2), 229–239.

Canary, D. J., & Stafford, L. (1994). *Maintaining relationships through strategic and routine interaction.* In D. J. Canary & L. Stafford (Eds.), Communication and relationship maintenance (pp. 3–22). San Diego: Academic Press.

Canary, D. J., & Dainton, M. (2006). Maintaining relationships. In A. L. Vangelisti & D. Perlman (Eds.), *The Cambridge handbook of personal relationships.* New York, NY: Cambridge University Press.

Canary, D. J., & Stafford, L. (2001). Equity in the preservation of personal relationships. In J. H. Harvey & A. E. Wenzel (Eds.), *Close romantic relationships: Maintenance and enhancement.* Mahwah, NJ: Erlbaum.

Cancro, R., & Lehmann, H. E. (2000). Schizophrenia: Clinical features. In B. J. Sadock & V. A. Sadock (Eds.), *Kaplan and Sadock's comprehensive textbook of psychiatry* (7th ed., Vol. 1, pp. 1169–1198). Philadelphia: Lippincott/Williams & Wilkins.

Canetto, S. S. (2008). Women and suicidal behavior: A cultural analysis. *American Journal of Orthopsychiatry, 78,* 259–266.

Canli, T. (2008). Toward a "molecular psychology" of personality. In O. P. John, R. W. Robbins & L. A. Pervin (Eds.), *Handbook of personality: Theory and research* (Vol. 3, pp. 311–327). New York, NY: Guilford Press.

Cannon, W. B. (1929). *Bodily changes in pain, hunger, fear, and rage.* Oxford, England: Appleton.

Cannon, W. B. (1932). *The wisdom of the body.* New York, NY: Norton.

Cantor, J. R., & Venus, P. (1980). The effects of humor on recall of a radio advertisement. *Journal of Broadcasting, 24,* 13–22.

Canu, W., & Gordon, M. (2005). Mother nature as treatment for ADHD: Overstating the benefits of green. *American Journal of Public Health, 95,* 371.

Cappadocia, M., & Weiss, J. A. (2011). Review of social skills training groups for youth with Asperger syndrome and high functioning autism. *Research in Autism Spectrum Disorders, 5*(1), 70–78. doi:10.1016/j.rasd.2010.04.001

Carbonell, D. M., Reinherz, H. Z., & Beardslee, W. R. (2005). Adaptation and coping in childhood and adolescence for those at risk for depression in emerging adulthood. *Child and Adolescent Social Work Journal, 22,*, 395–416.

Cardeña, E., & Gleaves, D. H. (2007). Dissociative disorders. In M. Hersen, S. M. Turner, & D. C. Beidel (Eds.), *Adult psychopathology and diagnosis.* New York, NY: Wiley.

Carducci, B. J. (1999). *The pocket guide to making successful small talk.* New Albany, IN: Pocket Guide Publications.

Carey, M. P., & Vanable, P. A. (2003). AIDS/HIV. In A. M. Nezu, C. M. Nezu, & P. A. Geller (Eds.), *Handbook of psychology: Vol. 9. Health psychology.* New York, NY: Wiley.

Carlson, E. N., & Furr, R. M. (2009). Evidence of differential meta-accuracy: People understand the different impressions they make. *Psychological Science, 20*(8), 1033–1039.

Carlson, E. N., Vazire, S., & Oltmanns, T. F. (2011). You probably think this paper is about you: Narcissists' perceptions of their personality and reputation. *Journal of Personality and Social Psychology, 101,* 185–201. doi:10.1037/a0023781

Carlson, L., Specca, M., Faris, P., & Patel, K. (2007). One year pre-post intervention follow-up of psychological, immune, endocrine, and blood pressure outcomes of mindfulness-based stress reduction (MBSR) in breast cancer and prostate cancer outpatients. *Brain, Behavior, and Immunity, 21*(8), 1038–1049.

Carlson, R. (1997). *Don't sweat the small stuff . . . and it's all small stuff: Simple ways to keep the little things from taking over your life.* New York, NY: Hyperion.

Carmody, J., & Baer, R. A. (2008). Relationships between mindfulness practice and levels of mindfulness, medical and psychological symptoms and well-being in a mindfulness-based stress reduction program. *Journal of Behavioral Medicine, 31*(1), 23–33. doi:10.1007/s10865-007-9130-7

Carnagey, N. L., Anderson, C. A., & Bartholow, B. D. (2007). Media violence and social neuroscience: New questions and new opportunities. *Current Directions in Psychological Science, 16,* 178–182.

Carney, S., & Geddes, J. (2003). Electroconvulsive therapy. *British Medical Journal, 326,* 1343–1344.

Carpenter, C. J. (2012). Narcissism on Facebook: Self-promotional and anti-social behavior. *Personality and Individual Differences, 52,* 482–486. doi:10.1016/j.paid.2011.11.011

Carpenter, J. M., Green, M. C., & LaFlam, J. (2011). People or profiles: Individual differences in online social networking use. *Personality and Individual Differences, 50*(5), 538–541. doi:10.1016/j.paid.2010.11.006

Carpenter, W. T. (1992). The negative symptom challenge. *Archives of General Psychiatry, 49,* 236–237.

Carpenter, W. T. (2002). From clinical trial to prescription. *Archives of General Psychology, 59,* 282–285.

Carr, A. (2011). *Positive psychology: The science of happiness and human strengths* (2nd ed.). New York, NY: Routledge/Taylor & Francis Group.

Carroll, J. L. (2007). *Sexuality now: Embracing diversity.* Belmont, CA: Wadsworth.

Carroll-Ghosh, T., Victor, B. S., & Bourgeois, J. A. (2003). Suicide. In R. E. Hales & S. C. Yudofsky (Eds.), *Textbook of clinical psychiatry.* Washington, DC: American Psychiatric Publishing.

Carson, E. A., & Sabol, W. J. (2012). Prisoners in 2011. U.S. Department of Justice, Bureau of Justice Statistics. Retrieved from http://bjs.ojp.usdoj.gov/content/pub/pdf/p11.pdf

Carson, S. H., & Langer, E. J. (2006). Mindfulness and self-acceptance. *Journal of Rational-Emotive & Cognitive Behavior Therapy, 24,* 29–43.

Carter, B., & McGoldrick, M. (1988). Overview: The changing family life cycle—A framework for family therapy. In E. A. Carter & M. McGoldrick (Eds.), *The changing family life cycle: A framework for family therapy* (2nd ed.). New York, NY: Gardner Press.

Carter, B., & McGoldrick, M. (1999). Overview: The expanded family life cycle: Individual, family, and social perspectives. In B. Carter & M. McGoldrick (Eds.), *The expanded family life cycle: Individual, family, and social perspectives* (3rd ed.). Boston, MA: Allyn & Bacon.

Carter, T. J., & Dunning, D. (2008). Faulty self-assessment: Why evaluating one's own competence is an intrinsically difficult task. *Social and Personality Psychology Compass, 2*(1), 346–360.

Carter-Sowell, A. R., Chen, Z., & Williams, K. D. (2008). Ostracism increases social susceptibility. *Social Influence, 3*(3),143–153.

Carton, J. S., Kessler, E. A., & Pape, C. L. (1999). Nonverbal decoding skills and relationship well-being in adults. *Journal of Nonverbal Behavior, 23*(1), 91–100.

Carvalho, J., & Nobre, P. (2011). Biopsychosocial determinants of men's sexual desire: Testing an integrative model. *Journal of Sexual Medicine, 8*(3), 754–763. doi:10.1111/j.1743-6109.2010.02156.x

Carver, C. S. (2011). Coping. In R. J. Contrada & A. Baum (Eds.), *The handbook of stress science: Biology, psychology, and health* (pp. 221–229). New York, NY: Springer.

Carver, C. S., & Connor-Smith, J. (2010). Personality and coping. *Annual Review of Psychology, 61,* 679–704. doi:10.1146/annurev.psych.093008.100352

Carver, C. S., Pozo, C., Harris, S. D., Noriega, V., Scheier, M. F., Robinson, D. S., Ketcham, A. S., Moffat, F. L., Jr., & Clark, K. C. (1993). How coping mediates the effect of optimism on distress: A study of women with early-stage breast cancer. *Journal of Personality and Social Psychology, 65,* 375–390.

Carver, C. S., Scheier, M. F., & Segerstrom, S. C. (2010). Optimism. *Clinical Psychology Review, 30,* 879–889.

Carver, C. S., Scheier, M. F., & Weintraub, J. K. (1989). Assessing coping strategies: A theoretically based approach. *Journal of Personality and Social Psychology, 56,* 267–283.

Case, B. G., Bertollo, D. N., Laska, E. M., Price, L. H., Siegel, C. E., Olfson, M., & Marcus, S. C. (2013). Declining use of electroconvulsive therapy in United States general hospitals. *Biological Psychiatry, 73,* 119–126.

Cashdan, E. (1998). Smiles, speech, and body posture: How women and men display sociometric status and power. *Journal of Nonverbal Behavior, 22,* 209–228.

Cassel, R. N. (2000). Third force psychology and person-centered theory: From ego-status to ego-ideal. *Psychology: A Journal of Human Behavior, 37*(3), 44–48.

Castano, E. (2012). Antisocial behavior in individuals and groups: An empathy-based approach. In K. Deaux & M. Snyder (Eds.), *The Oxford handbook of personality and social psychology* (pp. 419–445). New York, NY: Oxford University Press.

Castle, D. (2008). Drawing conclusions about cannabis and psychosis. *Psychological Medicine, 38*(3), 459–460.

Castonguay, L. G., Reid Jr., J. J., Halperin, G. S., & Goldfried, M. R. (2003). Psychotherapy integration. In G. Stricker, & T. A. Widiger (Eds.), *Handbook of psychology: Vol. 8. Clinical psychology.* New York, NY: Wiley.

Catalano, S. (2012). Intimate partner violence, 1993–2010. U.S. Department of Justice. Retrieved from http://www.bjs.gov/content/pub/pdf/ipv9310.pdf

Catalyst. (2007). Catalyst releases 2006 census of women in Fortune 500 corporate officer and board positions. Retrieved on June 5, 2007 from http://www.catalyst.org/pressroom/press_releases/2006_Census_Release.pdf.

Catalyst. (2011). 2011 Catalyst census: Fortune 500 women executive offices and top earners. Retrieved from www.catalyst.org/file/534/2011_Fortune_500_census_weote.pdf

Catalyst. (2012). Sex discrimination and sexual harassment. Retrieved from www.catalyst.org/publication/213/sex-discrimination-and-sexual-harrassment

Cate, R. M., & Lloyd, S. A. (1988). Courtship. In S. Duck (Ed.), *Handbook of personal relationships.* New York, NY: Wiley.

Cattell, H. E. P. & Mead, A. D. (2008). The sixteen personality factor questionnaire (16 PF). In G. J. Boyle, G. Matthews, & D. H. Saklofske (Eds.), *The Sage handbook of personality theory and assessment* (Vol. 2, pp. 135–159). Los Angeles: Sage.

Cattell, R. B. (1950). *Personality: A systematic, theoretical and factual study.* New York, NY: McGraw-Hill.

Cattell, R. B. (1966). *The scientific analysis of personality.* Chicago: Aldine.

Cattell, R. B. (1990). Advances in Cattellian personality theory. In L. A. Pervin (Ed.), *Handbook of personality: Theory and research.* New York, NY: Guilford.

Cattell, R. B., Eber, H. W., & Tatsuoka, M. M. (1970). *Handbook of the Sixteen Personality Factor Questionnaire* (16PF). Champaign, IL: Institute for Personality and Ability Testing.

Caverly, D. C., Orlando, V. P., & Mullen, J. L. (2000). Textbook study reading. In R. F. Flippo & D. C. Caverly (Eds.), *Handbook of college reading and study strategy research.* Mahwah, NJ: Erlbaum.

Ceci, S. J., Williams, W. M., & Barnett, S. M. (2009). Women's underrepresentation in science: Sociocultural and biological considerations. *Psychological Bulletin, 135*(2), 218–261. doi:10.1037/a0014412

Ceja, L., & Navarro, J. (2009). Dynamics of flow: A nonlinear perspective. *Journal of Happiness Studies, 10*(6), 665–684.

Centers for Disease Control. (2006). Update: Trends in AIDS incidence-United States. *MMWR, 46*(37), 861–867.

Centers for Disease Control. (2009a). Climate change and public health. Retrieved from http://www.cdc.gov/ClimateChange/policy.htm

Centers for Disease Control. (2009b). *Oral sex and HIV risk.* Retrieved from http:www.cdc.gov/hiv

Centers for Disease Control. (2009c). *Sexual and reproductive health of persons aged 10–24 years—United States, 2002–2007.* Retrieved from http:www.cdc.gov/mmwr/preview/mmwrhtml/ss5806al.htm?s

Centers for Disease Control. (2011). *Sexual violence, stalking, and intimate partner violence widespread in the U.S.* Retrieved from http://www.cdc.gov/media/releases/2011/p1214_sexual_violence.html

Centers for Disease Control. (2012a). *Genital HPV infection—fact sheet.* Retrieved from http://www.cdc.gov/std/HPV/STDFact-HPV.htm

Centers for Disease Control. (2012b). *HIV in the United States*. Retrieved from http://www.cdc.gov/hiv/resources/factsheets/us.htm.

Centers for Disease Control. (2012c). *Sexual risk behavior: HIV, STD, & teen pregnancy prevention*. Retrieved from http://www.cdc.gov/healthyyouth/sexualbehaviors/index.htm

Centers for Disease Control. (2012d). *Depression among women of reproductive age and postpartum depression*. Retrieved from http://www.cdc.gov/reproductivehealth/Depression/

Cepeda, N. J., Pashler, H., Vul, E., Wixted, J. T., & Rohrer, D. (2006). Distributed practice in verbal recall tasks: A review and quantitative synthesis. *Psychological Bulletin, 132*, 354–380.

Cerletti, U., & Bini, L. (1938). Un nuovo metodo di shockterapie "L'elettro-shock." Boll. Acad. Med. *Roma, 64*, 136–138.

Cetron, M. J., & Davies, O. (2003, March–April). Trends shaping the future: Technological, workplace, management, and institutional trends. *The Futurist*, pp. 30–43.

Chadee, D. (2011). Toward freedom: Reactance theory revisited. In D. Chadee (Ed.), *Theories in social psychology* (pp. 13–43). New York, NY: Wiley-Blackwell.

Chaiken, S. (1979). Communicator's physical attractiveness and persuasion. *Journal of Personality and Social Psychology, 37*, 1387–1397.

Chalquist, C. (2009). Ecotherapy research and a psychology of homecoming. In L. Buzzell & C. Chalquist (2009), *Ecotherapy: Healing with nature in mind* (pp. 69-82). San Francisco, CA: Sierra Club Books.

Chamberlin, C. M., & Zhang, N. (2009). Workaholism, health, and self-acceptance. *Journal of Counseling & Development, 87*(2), 159–169.

Chamberlin, J. (2007, March). Too much information. *GradPSYCH*, pp. 14–16.

Chan, A., & Au, T. (2011). Getting children to do more academic work: Foot-in-the-Door versus Door-in-the-Face. *Teaching and Teacher Education, 27*(6), 982-985. doi:10.1016/j.tate.2011.04.007

Chan, M. (2011). Shyness, sociability, and the role of media synchronicity in the use of computer-mediated communication for interpersonal communication. *Asian Journal of Social Psychology, 14*(1), 84-90.

Chandler, J. J., & Pronin, E. (2012). Fast thought speed induces risk taking. *Psychological Science, 23*(4), 370–374. doi:10.1177/0956797611431464

Chandola, T. & Marmot, M. G. (2011). Socioeconomic status and stress. In R. J. Contrada & A. Baum (Eds.), *The handbook of stress science: biology psychology and health* (pp. 185–193). New York, NY: Springer.

Chandra, A., Martinez, G. M., Mosher, W. D., Abma, J. C., & Jones, J. (2005). Fertility, family planning, and reproductive health of U.S. women: Data from the 2002 National Survey of Family Growth. *Vital Health Stat 23*(25).

Chang, C. H., Rosen, C. C., & Levy, P. E. (2009). The relationship between perceptions of organizational politics and employee attitudes, strain, and behavior: A meta-analysis. *Academy of Management Journal, 52*, 779-801.

Chang, R. Y., & Kelly, P. K. (1993). *Step-by-step problem solving: A practical guide to ensure problems get (and stay) solved*. Irvine, CA: Richard Chang Associates.

Chaplin, T. M., Cole, P. M., & Zahn-Waxler, C. (2005). Parental socialization of emotion expression: Gender differences and relations to child adjustment. *Emotion, 5*(1), 80–88. doi:10.1037/1528-3542.5.1.80

Chaplin, W. F., Phillips, J. B., Brown, J. D., Clanton, N. R., & Stein, J. L. (2000). Handshaking, gender, personality, and first impressions. *Journal of Personality and Social Psychology, 79*(1), 110–117.

Chapman, B., Fiscella, K., Kawachi, I., & Duberstein, P. (2010). Personality, socioeconomic status, and all-cause mortality in the United States. *American Journal of Epidemiology, 171*(1), 83–92. doi:10.1093/aje/kwp323

Charlesworth, W. R., & Dzur, C. (1987). Gender comparisons of preschoolers' behavior and resource utilization in group problem-solving. *Child Development, 58*, 191–200.

Chawla, L. (1988). Children's concern for the natural environment. *Children's Environments Quarterly, 5*(3), 13–20.

Chen E., & Miller, G. E. (2007). Stress and inflammation in exacerbation of asthma. *Brain, Behavior, and Immunity, 21*, 993–999.

Chen, G., & Martin, R. A. (2007). A comparison of humor styles, coping humor, and mental health between Chinese and Canadian university students. *Humor, 20*, 215–234.

Chen, Y. Y., Gilligan, S., & Coups, E. J. (2005). Hostility and perceived social support: Interactive effects on cardiovascular reactivity to laboratory stressors. *Annals of Behavioral Medicine, 29*, 37–43.

Cheng, C. (2001). Assessing coping flexibility in real-life and laboratory settings: A multimethod approach. *Journal of Personality and Social Psychology, 80*(5), 814–833.

Cheng, C. (2003). Cognitive and motivational processes underlying coping flexibility: A dual-process model. *Journal of Personality and Social Psychology, 84*, 425–438.

Cheng, C., & Cheung, M. W. L. (2005). Cognitive processes underlying coping flexibility: Differentiation and integration. *Journal of Personality, 73*, 859–886.

Cherlin, A. J. (1999). Going to extremes: Family structure, children's well-being, and social science. *Demography, 36*, 421–428.

Cherlin, A. J. (2004). The deinstitutionalization of American marriage. *Journal of Marriage and Family, 66*, 848–861.

Cherlin, A. J. (2009). *The marriage-go-round: The state of marriage and the family in America today*. New York, NY: Knopf.

Chia, R. C., Moore, J. L., Lam, K. N., Chuang, C. J., & Cheng, B. S. (1994). Cultural differences in gender role attitudes between Chinese and American students. *Sex Roles, 31*, 23–29.

Chiappelli, F., & Hodgson, D. (2000). Immune suppression. In G. Fink (Ed.), *Encyclopedia of stress* (Vol. 2). San Diego: Academic Press.

Chida, Y., Hamer, M., Wardle, J., & Steptoe, A. (2008). Do stress-related psychosocial factors contribute to cancer incidence and survival? *Nature Clinical Practice Oncology, 5*(8), 466–475.

Chin, H. B., Sipe, T., Elder, R., Mercer, S. L., Chattopadhyay, S. K., Jacob, V., . . . & Santelli, J. (2012). The effectiveness of group-based comprehensive risk-reduction and abstinence education interventions to prevent or reduce the risk of adolescent pregnancy, human immunodeficiency virus, and sexually transmitted infections: Two systematic reviews for the Guide to Community Preventive Services. *American Journal of Preventive Medicine, 42*(3), 272–294. doi:10.1016/j.amepre.2011.11.006

Chiu, C.-Y., Kim, Y.-H., & Wan, W. W. N. (2008). Personality: Cross-cultural perspectives. In G. J. Boyle, G. Matthews, D. H. Saklofske (Eds.), *The Sage handbook of personality theory and assessment* (pp. 124–144). Los Angeles: Sage.

Choi, I., Dalal, R., Kim-Prieto, C., & Park, H. (2003). Culture and judgment of causal relevance. *Journal of Personality and Social Psychology, 84*(1), 46-59.

Choi, I., Nisbett, R. E., & Norenzayan, A. (1999). Causal attribution across cultures: Variation and universality. *Psychological Bulletin, 125*(1), 47–63.

Choi, Y., Karremans, J. C., & Barendregt, H. (2012). The happy face of mindfulness: Mindfulness meditation is associated with perceptions of happiness as rated by outside observers. *The Journal of Positive Psychology, 7*(1), 30–35. doi:10.1080/17439760.2011.626788

Chopra, D. (1993). *Ageless body, timeless mind*. New York, NY: Crown.

Chopra, S. S. (2003). Industry funding of clinical trials: Benefit or bias? *JAMA, 290*, 113–114.

Chou, C., Condron, L., & Belland, J. C. (2005). A review of the research on Internet addiction. *Educational Psychology Review, 17*, 363–388.

Chou, F., Holzemer, W. L., Portillo, C. J., & Slaughter, R. (2004). Self-care strategies and sources of information for HIV/AIDS symptom management. *Nursing Research, 53*, 332–339.

Chow, H. H. (2011). Procrastination among undergraduate students: Effects of emotional intelligence, school life, self-evaluation, and self-efficacy. *Alberta Journal of Educational Research, 57*(2), 234–240.

Christensen, A. J., & Johnson, J. A. (2002). Patient adherence with medical treatment regimens: An interactive approach. *Current Directions in Psychological Science, 11*(3), 94–97.

Chua, H. F., Leu, J., & Nisbett, R. E. (2005). Culture and diverging views of social events. *Personality and Social Psychology Bulletin, 31*, 925–934.

Chudzikowski, K. (2011). Career transitions and career success in the "new" career era. *Journal of Vocational Behavior*. doi:10.1016/j.jvb.2011.10.005

Church, A. T. (2010). Current perspectives in the study of personality across cultures. *Perspectives on Psychological Science, 5*, 441–449. doi:10.1177/1745691610375559

Church, A. T., Alvarez, J. M., Mai, N. T. Q., French, B. F., Katigbak, M. S., & Ortiz, F. A. (2011). Are cross-cultural comparisons of personality profiles meaningful? Differential item and facet functioning in the Revised NEO Personality Inventory. *Journal of Personality and Social Psychology, 101*, 1068–1089. doi:10.1037/a0025290

Cialdini, R. B. (2001). *Influence: Science and practice* (4th ed.). Boston, MA: Allyn & Bacon.

Cialdini, R. B. (2003). Crafting normative messages to protect the environment. *Current Directions in Psychological Science, 12*, 105–109.

Cialdini, R. B. (2007). *Influence: Science and practice*. New York, NY: HarperCollins.

Cialdini, R. B., Borden, R. J., Thorne, A., Walker, M. R., Freeman, S., & Sloan, L. R. (1976). Basking in reflected glory: Three (football) field studies. *Journal of Personality and Social Psychology, 34*, 366–375.

Cialdini, R. B., Reno, R. R., & Kallgren, C. A. (1990). A focus theory of normative conduct: Recycling the concept of norms to reduce littering in public places. *Journal of Personality and Social Psychology, 58*, 1015–1026.

Claidière, N., & Whiten, A. (2012). Integrating the study of conformity and culture in humans and nonhuman animals. *Psychological Bulletin, 138*(1), 126–145. doi:10.1037/a0025868

Clark, A. J. (1989). Communication confidence and listening competence: An investigation of the relationships of willingness to communicate, communication apprehension, and receiver apprehension to comprehension of content and emotional meaning in spoken messages. *Communication Education, 38*(3), 237–248.

Clark, J. K., Evans, A. T., & Wegener, D. T. (2011). Perceptions of source efficacy and persuasion: Multiple mechanisms for source effects on attitudes. *European Journal of Social Psychology, 41*(5), 596–607. doi:10.1002/ejsp.787

Clark, J. K., Wegener, D. T., Habashi, M. M., & Evans, A. T. (2012). Source expertise and persuasion: The effects of perceived opposition or support on message scrutiny. *Personality and Social Psychology Bulletin, 38*(1), 90–100. doi:10.1177/0146167211420733

Clark, M. A., Lelchook, A. M., & Taylor, M. L. (2010). Beyond the Big Five: How narcissism, perfectionism, and dispositional affect relate to workaholism. *Personality and Individual Differences, 48*(7), 786–791. doi:10.1016/j.paid.2010.01.013

Clark, M. S., & Grote, N. K. (2003). Close relationships. In T. Millon & M. J. Lerner (Eds.) *Handbook of psychology: Vol. 5. Personality and social psychology*. New York, NY: Wiley.

Clark, M. S., & Mills, J. (1993). The difference between communal and exchange relationships: What it is and is not. *Journal of Personality and Social Psychology Bulletin, 19*, 684–691.

Clark, R. (2003). Self-reported racism and social support predict blood pressure reactivity in Blacks. *Annals of Behavioral Medicine, 25*, 127–136.

Clarke, V. A., Lovegrove, H., Williams, A., & Machperson, M. (2000). Unrealistic optimism and the health belief model. *Journal of Behavioral Medicine, 23*, 367–376.

Classen, T. J., & Dunn, R. A. (2012). The effect of job loss and unemployment duration on suicide risk in the United States: A new look using mass layoffs and unemployment duration. *Health Economics, 21,* 338–350. doi:10.1002/hec.1719

Clayton, S. (2003). Environmental identity: A conceptual and an operational definition. In S. Clayton & S. Opotow (Eds.), *Identity and the natural environment* (pp. 4565). Cambridge, MA: MIT Press.

Clayton, S., & Myers, G. (2009). *Conservation psychology: Understanding and promoting human care for nature.* Chichester, West Sussex, UK: Wiley-Blackwell.

Cleek, M. G., & Pearson, T. A. (1985). Perceived causes of divorce: An analysis of interrelationships. *Journal of Marriage and the Family, 47,* 179–183.

Clemans, K. H., DeRose, L. M., Graber, J. A., & Brooks-Gunn, J. (2010). Gender on adolescence: Applying a person-in-context approach to gender identity and roles. In J. C. Chrisler & D. R. McCreary (Eds.), *Handbook of Gender Research in Psychology* (Vol. 1, pp. 527-557). New York, NY: Springer y.

Clements, A. M., Rimrodt, S. L., Abel, J. R., Blankner, J. G., Mostofsky, S. H., Pekar, J. J., et al. (2006). Sex differences in cerebral laterality of language and visuospatial processing. *Brain and Language, 98*(2), 150–158.

Clements, M. L., Stanley, S. M., & Markman, H. J. (2004). Before they said "I do": Discriminating among marital outcomes over 13 years. *Journal of Marriage and Family, 66,* 613–626.

Cleveland, J. N. (2008). Age, work, and family: Balancing unique challenges for the twenty-first century. In A. Marcus-Newhall, D. F. Halpern, & S. J. Tan (Eds.), *The changing realities of work and family: A multidisciplinary approach* (pp. 108–139). New York, NY: Wiley-Blackwell. doi:10.1002/9781444305272.ch6

Clifford, S., Barber, N., & Horne, R. (2008). Understanding different beliefs held by adherers, unintentional nonadherers, and intentional nonadherers: Application of the Necessity-Concerns Framework. *Journal of Psychosomatic Research, 64,* 41–46.

Clinebell, H. (1996). *Ecotherapy: Healing ourselves, healing the earth.* Minneapolis, MN: Augsburg Fortress.

Coates, D. D. (2011). Counseling former members of charismatic groups: Considering pre-involvement variables, reasons for joining the group and corresponding values. *Mental Health, Religion & Culture, 14,* 191–207. doi:10.1080/13674670903443404

Coates, T. J., & Collins, C. (1998). Preventing HIV infection. *Scientific American, 279*(1), 96–97.

Cochran, S. D. (2001). Emerging issues in research on lesbians' and gay men's mental health: Does sexual orientation really matter? *American Psychologist, 56,* 931–947.

Coelho, C., & Purkis, H. (2009). The origins of specific phobias: Influential theories and current perspectives. *Review of General Psychology, 13*(4), 335–348. doi:10.1037/a0017759

Cohany, S. R., & Sok, E. (2007, February). Trends in labor force participation of married mothers of infants. *Monthly Labor Review,* 9–16.

Cohen, C. E. (1981). Person categories and social perception: Testing some boundaries of the processing effects of prior knowledge. *Journal of Personality and Social Psychology, 40,* 441–452.

Cohen, F., & Solomon, S. (2011). The politics of mortal terror. *Current Directions in Psychological Science, 20,* 316–320. doi:10.1177/0963721411416570

Cohen, M. J. M., Kunkel, E. S., & Levenson, J. L. (1998). Associations between psychosocial stress and malignancy. In J. R. Hubbard & E. A. Workman (Eds.), *Handbook of stress medicine: An organ system approach.* Boca Raton: CRC Press.

Cohen, P. (1984). College grades and adult achievement. *Research in Higher Education, 20,* 281–293.

Cohen, S. (2005). Keynote presentation at the eighth International Congress of Behavioral Medicine. *International Journal of Behavioral Medicine, 12*(3), 123–131.

Cohen, S., Doyle, W. J., Turner, R., Alper, C. M., & Skoner, D. P. (2003). Sociability and susceptibility to the common cold. *Psychological Science, 14*(5), 389–395.

Cohen, S., Evans, G. W., Krantz, D. S., & Stokols, D. (1980). Physiological, motivational, and cognitive effects of aircraft noise on children: Moving from the laboratory to the field. *American Psychologist, 35,* 231–243.

Cohen, S., Frank, E., Doyle, W. J., Skoner, D. P., Rabin, B. S., & Gwaltney, J. M., Jr. (1998). Types of stressors that increase susceptibility to the common cold in healthy adults. *Health Psychology, 17,* 214–223.

Cohen, S., Kessler, R. C., & Gordon, L. U. (1995). Strategies for measuring stress in studies of psychiatric and physical disorders. In S. Cohen, R. C. Kessler, & L. U. Gordon (Eds.), *Measuring stress: A guide for health and social scientists.* New York, NY: Oxford University Press.

Cohen, S., Lichtenstein, E., Prochaska, J. O., Rossi, J. S., Gritz, E. R., Carr, C. R., . . . & Ossip-Klein, D. (1989). Debunking myths about self-quitting: Evidence from 10 prospective studies of persons who attempt to quit smoking by themselves. *American Psychologist, 44,* 1355–1365.

Cohen, S., & Pressman, S. D. (2006). Positive affect and health. *Current Directions in Psychological Science, 15*(3), 122–125. doi:10.1111/j.0963-7214.2006.00420.x

Cohn, V., Passel, J., Wang, W., & Livingston, G. (2011). Barely half of U.S. adults are married—a record low. Pew Research Center. Retrieved from http://www .pewsocialtrends.org/2011/12/14/barely-half-of-u-s-adults-are-married-a-record-low/?src=sdt-carousel

Cole, E., Erdman, E., & Rothblum, E. (Eds.) (1994). *Wilderness therapy for women: The power of adventure.* New York, NY: Haworth Press.

Coleman, L. J. (1994). "Being a teacher": Emotions and optimal experience while teaching gifted children. *Gifted Child Quarterly, 38,* 146–152.

Coles, M. E., Schofield, C. A., & Pietrefesa, A. S. (2006). Behavioral inhibition and obsessive-compulsive disorder. *Journal of Anxiety Disorders, 20,* 1118–1132.

Collaer, M. L., & Hines, M. (1995). Human behavioral sex differences: A role for gonadal hormones during early development? *Psychological Bulletin, 118,* 55–107.

College Entrance Examination Board. (2004). Writing a ticket to work . . . or a ticket out: a survey of business leaders. Retrieved from www.writingcommission.org/prod_downloads/writingcom/writing-ticket-to-work.pdf

Colley, A., & Todd, Z. (2002). Gender-linked differences in the style and content of e-mails to friends. *Journal of Language and Social Psychology, 21*(4), 380–392.

Colligan, T. W., & Higgins, E. M. (2005). Workplace stress: Etiology and consequences. *Journal of Workplace Behavioral Health, 21*(2), 89–97.

Collins, R. L. (2011). Content analysis of gender roles in media: Where are we now and where should we go? *Sex Roles, 64*(3–4), 290–298. doi:10.1007/s11199-010-9929-5

Collins, W. A., & Madsen, S. D. (2006). Personal relationships in adolescence and early adulthood. In A. L. Vangelisti & D. Perlman (Eds.), *The Cambridge handbook of personal relationships.* New York, NY: Cambridge University Press.

Coltrane, S. (2001). Marketing the marriage "solution": Misplaced simplicity in the politics of fatherhood. *Sociological Perspectives, 44*(4), 387–418.

Coltrane, S., & Shih, K. Y. (2010). Gender and the division of labor. In J. C. Chrisler & D. R. McCreary (Eds.), *Handbook of gender research in psychology, Vol 2. Gender research in social and applied psychology* (pp. 401–422). New York, NY: Springer Science + Business Media. doi:10.1007/978-1-4419-1467-5_17

Colvin, C. R., & Block, J. (1994). Do positive illusions foster mental health? An examination of the Taylor and Brown formulation. *Psychological Bulletin, 116,* 3–20.

Colvin, C. R., Block, J., & Funder, D. C. (1995). Overly positive self-evaluations and personality: Negative implications for mental health. *Journal of Personality and Social Psychology, 68,* 1152–1162.

Comas-Diaz, L. (1987). Feminist therapy with mainland Puerto Rican women. *Psychology of Women Quarterly, 11,* 461–474.

Comas-Diaz, L. (2006). Cultural variation in the therapeutic relationship. In C. D. Goodheart, A. E. Kazdin, &

R. J. Sternberg (Eds.), *Evidence-based psychotherapy: Where practice and research meet.* Washington, DC: American Psychological Association.

Combs, D. R., & Mueser, K. T. (2007). Schizophrenia. In M. Hersen, S. M. Turner, & D. C. Beidel (Eds.), *Adult psychopathology and diagnosis.* New York, NY: Wiley.

Commerce Clearing House. (2007). *2007 CCH unscheduled absenteeism survey.* Riverwoods, IL: Commerce Clearning House.

Compton, M. T., Goulding, S. M., & Walker, E. F. (2007). Cannabis use, first-episode psychosis, and schizotypy: A summary and synthesis of recent literature. *Current Psychiatry Reviews, 3,* 161–171.

Compton, W. C. (2005). *An introduction to positive psychology.* Belmont, CA: Thompson-Wadsworth.

Confer, J. C., Perilloux, C., & Buss, D. M. (2010). More than just a pretty face: Men's priority shifts toward bodily attractiveness in short-term versus long-term mating contexts. *Evolution and Human Behavior, 31*(5), 348–353. doi:10.1016/j.evolhumbehav.2010.04.002

Conkle, A., & West, C. (2008). Psychology on the road. *The Observer, 21,* 19–23.

Conley, K. M., & Lehman, B. J. (2012). Test anxiety and cardiovascular responses to daily academic stressors. *Stress and Health: Journal of the International Society for the Investigation of Stress, 28*(1), 41-50. doi:10.1002/smi.1399

Conn, S. (1995). When the earth hurts, who responds? In T. Roszak, M. E. Gomes, & A. D. Kanner (Eds.), *Eco-psychology: Restoring the earth, healing the mind* (pp. 156–171). San Francisco: Sierra Club.

Connor, T. (2004). Methylenedioxymethamphetamine (MDMA, "Ecstasy"): A stressor on the immune system. *Journal of Immunology, 111,* 357–367.

Connor Snibe, A., & Markus, H. R. (2005). You can't always get what you want: Educational attainment, agency, and choice. *Journal of Personality and Social Psychology, 88,* 703–720.

Conrad, K., Dixon, T., & Zhang, Y. (2009). Controversial rap themes, gender portrayals and skin tone distortion: A content analysis of rap music videos. *Journal of Broadcasting & Electronic Media, 53,* 134–156.

Consedine, N. S., Magai, C., & Chin, S. (2004). Hostility and anxiety differentially predict cardiovascular disease in men and women. *Sex Roles, 50,* 63–77.

Contrada, R. J. (2011). Stress, adaptation, and health. In R. J. Contrada & A. Baum (Eds.), *The handbook of stress science: Biology, psychology, and health* (pp. 1–9). New York, NY: Springer.

Converse, P. D., Pathak, J., DePaul-Haddock, A., Gotlib, T., & Merbedone, M. (2012). Controlling your environment and yourself: Implications for career success. *Journal of Vocational Behavior, 80*(1), 148–159. doi:10.1016/j.jvb.2011.07.003

Cook, C. (2012). "Nice girls don't": Women and the condom conundrum. *Journal of Clinical Nursing, 21*(3–4), 535–543. doi:10.1111/j.1365-2702.2011.03879.x

Cook, T., Church, M., Ajanaku, S., & Shadish, W. (1996). The development of occupational aspirations and expectations among inner-city boys. *Child Development, 67*(6), 3368–3385.

Cooper, A. (1998). *Playing in the zone: Exploring the spiritual dimensions of sports.* Boston, MA: Shambala.

Cooper, A., & Smith, E. (2011). *Homicide trends in the United States, 1980–2008.* Retrieved from http://bjs.ojp.usdoj.gov/index.cfm?ty=pbdetail&iid52221

Cooper, C., Bebbington, P., King, M., Jenkins, R., Farrell, M., Brugha, T., . . . Livingston, G. (2011). Happiness across age groups: Results from the 2007 National Psychiatric Morbidity Survey. *International Journal of Geriatric Psychiatry, 26,* 608–614. doi:10.1002/gps.2570

Cooper, C. L., & Dewe, P. (2004). *Stress: A brief history.* Malden, MA: Blackwell Publishing.

Cooper, D. C., & Waldstein, S. R. (2004). Hostility differentially predicts risk factors in African American and White young adults. *Journal of Psychosomatic Research, 57,* 491–497.

Cooper, M. L., Albino, A. W., Orcutt, H. K., & Williams, N. (2004). Attachment styles and intrapersonal adjustment: A longitudinal study from adolescence into young adulthood. In W. S. Rholes & J. A. Simpson (Eds.), *Adult attachment: Theory, research, and clinical implications.* New York, NY: Guilford.

Cooper, W. H., & Withey, M. J. (2009). The strong situation hypothesis. *Personality and Social Psychology Review, 13*(1), 62–72.

Cope, M. B., Fernández, J. R., & Allison, D. B. (2004). Genetic and biological risk factors. In J. K. Thompson (Ed.), *Handbook of eating disorders and obesity.* New York, NY: Wiley.

Copen, C. E., Chandra, A., & Martinez, G. (2012). Prevalence and timing of oral sex with opposite-sex partners among females and males aged 15–24 years: United States, 2007–2010. *National health statistics reports; no. 56.* Hyattsville, MD: National Center for Health Statistics.

Copen, C. E., Daniels, K., Vespa, J., & Mosher, W. D. (2012). First marriages in the United States: Data from the 2006–2010 National Survey of Family Growth. *National Health Statistics Reports; no. 49.* Hyattsville, MD: National Center for Health Statistics.

Cordova, J. V., & Harp, A. G. (2009). Deteriorating relationships. In H. T. Reis & S. Sprecher (Eds.), *Encyclopedia of human relationships: Vol. 2* (pp. 402–407). Los Angeles: Sage Reference Publication.

Cordova, J. V., Gee, C. B., & Warren, L. Z. (2005). Emotional skillfulness in marriage: Intimacy as a mediator of the relationship between emotional skillfulness and marital satisfaction. *Journal of Social and Clinical Psychology, 24,* 218–235.

Cornblatt, B. A., Green, M. F., Walker, E. F., & Mittal, V. A. (2009). Schizophrenia: Etiology and neurocognition. In P. H. Blaney & T. Millon (Eds.), *Oxford textbook of psychopathology* (pp. 298–332). New York, NY: Oxford University Press.

Cornell, D. G. (1997). Post hoc explanation is not prediction. *American Psychologist, 52,* 1380.

Correia, I., Vala, J., & Aguiar, P. (2007). Victim's innocence, social categorization, and the threat to the belief in a just world. *Journal of Experimental Social Psychology, 43,* 31–38.

Corrigan, P. W. & Larson, J. E. (2008). Stigma. In K. T. Mueser & D. V. Jeste (Eds.), *Clinical handbook of schizophrenia* (pp. 533–540). New York, NY: Guilford.

Corsica, J. A., & Perri, M. G. (2003). Obesity. In A. M. Nezu, C. M. Nezu, & P. A. Geller (Eds.), *Handbook of psychology: Vol. 9. Health psychology.* New York, NY: Wiley.

Corty, E. W., & Guardiani, J. M. (2008). Canadian and American sex therapists' perceptions of normal and abnormal ejaculatory latencies: How long should intercourse last? *Journal of Sexual Medicine, 5,* 1251–1256.

Cosgrove, L., & Krimsky, S. (2012). A comparison of DSM-IV and DSM-5 panel members' financial associations with industry: A pernicious problem persists. *PLoS Medicine, 9,* e1001190. doi:10.1371/journal.pmed .1001190

Cosma, J. B. (1999). Flow in teams. *Dissertation Abstracts International. 60*(6-A), 1901.

Costa, P. T., Jr., & McCrae, R. R. (1992). *Revised NEO Personality Inventory: NEO PI and NEO Five-Factor Inventory (Professional Manual).* Odessa, FL: Psychological Assessment Resources.

Costa, P. T., Jr., & McCrae, R. R. (2008). The revised NEO Personality Inventory (NEO-PI-R). In G. J. Boyle, G. Matthews, & D. H. Saklofske (Eds.), *The Sage handbook of personality theory and assessment* (Vol. 2, pp.179–198). Los Angeles: Sage.

Cotter, D. A., Hermsen, J. M., Ovadia, S., & Vanneman, R. (2001). The glass ceiling effect. *Social Forces, 80,* 655–682.

Coudevylle, G. R., Gernigon, C., & Martin Ginis, K. A. (2011). Self-esteem, self-confidence, anxiety and claimed self-handicapping: A mediational analysis. *Psychology of Sport and Exercise, 12*(6), 670–675. doi:10.1016/j.psychsport.2011.05.008

Covey, S. R. (1989). *The seven habits of highly effective people.* New York, NY: Simon & Schuster.

Cowan, C. P., & Cowan, P. A. (2000). *When partners become parents.* Mahwah, NJ: Erlbaum.

Cox, P. D., Vinogradov, S., & Yalom, I. D. (2008). Group therapy. In R. E. Hales, S. C. Yudofsky, & G. O. Gabbard (Eds.), *The American psychiatric publishing textbook of psychiatry* (pp. 1329–1376). Washington, DC: American Psychiatric Publishing, Inc.

Crabb, P. B., & Marciano, D. L. (2011). Representations of material culture and gender in award-winning children's books: A 20-year follow-up. *Journal of Research in Childhood Education, 25*(4), 390–398. doi:10 .1080/02568543.2011.605209

Craighead, W. E., Ritschel, L. A., Arnarson, E. O., & Gillespie, C. F. (2008). Major depressive disorder. In W. E. Craighead, D. J. Miklowitz, & L. W. Craighead (Eds.), *Psychopathology: History, diagnosis, and empirical foundations.* New York, NY: Wiley.

Craik, F. I. M., & Tulving, E. (1975). Depth of processing and the retention of words in episodic memory. *Journal of Experimental Psychology. General, 104,* 268–294.

Cramer, R., Lipinski, R. E., Meteer, J. D., & Houska, J. (2008). Sex differences in subjective distress to unfaithfulness: Testing competing evolutionary and violation of infidelity expectations hypotheses. *The Journal of Social Psychology, 148*(4), 389–405. doi:10.3200/SOCP.148.4.389-406

Cramp, F., & Daniel, J. (2008). Exercise for the management of cancer-related fatigue in adults. *Cochrane Database of Systematic Reviews,* Cochrane AN: CD006145.

Crano, W. D., & Prislin, R. (Eds.). (2008). *Attitudes and attitude change.* New York, NY: Psychology Press.

Craske, M. G., & Waters, A. M. (2005). Panic disorders, phobias, and generalized anxiety disorder. *Annual Review of Clinical Psychology, 1,* 197–225.

Crawford, S. A., & Caltabiano, N. J. (2011). Promoting emotional well-being through the use of humour. *The Journal of Positive Psychology, 6*(3), 237–252. doi:10.1080/17439760.2011.577087

Crede, M., & Kuncel, N. R. (2008). Study habits, skills, and attitudes: The third pillar supporting collegiate academic performance. *Perspectives on Psychological Science, 3*(6), 425–453. doi:10.1111/j.1745-6924.2008.00089.x

Creed, P., Lehmann, K., & Hood, M. (2009). The relationship between core self-evaluations, employment commitment, and well-being in the unemployed. *Personality and Individual Differences, 47*(4), 310–315.

Creed, P., Prideaux, L., & Patton, W. (2005). Antecedents and consequences of career decisional states in adolescence. *Journal of Vocational Behavior, 67,* 397–412.

Crews, F. (2006). *Follies of the wise: Dissenting essays.* Emeryville, CA: Shoemaker Hoard.

Crisp, R. J., & Hewstone, M. E. (2006). *Multiple social categorization: Processes, models, and applications.* New York, NY: Psychology Press.

Cristofaro, T. N., & Tamis-LeMonda, C. S. (2008). Lessons in mother-child and father-child personal narratives in Latino families. In A. McCabe, A. L. Bailey, & G. Melzi (Eds.), *Spanish-language narration and literacy: Culture, cognition, and emotion* (pp. 54–91). New York, NY: Cambridge University Press.

Critcher, C. R., Dunning, D., & Armor, D. A. (2010). When self-affirmations reduce defensiveness: Timing is key. *Personality and Social Psychology Bulletin, 36*(7), 947–959. doi:10.1177/0146167210369557

Critelli, J. W., & Bivona, J. M. (2008). Women's erotic rape fantasies: An evaluation of theory and research. *Journal of Sex Research, 45,* 57–70.

Crits-Christoph, P. (1997). Limitations of the dodo bird verdict and the role of clinical trials in psychotherapy research: Comment on Wampold, et al. (1997). *Psychological Bulletin, 122,* 216–220.

Crits-Christoph, P., & Gibbons, M. B. C. (2009). The evaluation of psychological treatment. In M. C. Gelder, N. C. Andreasen, J. J. López-Ibor, & J. R. Geddes (Eds.), *New Oxford textbook of psychiatry* (2nd ed., Vol. 1). New York, NY: Oxford University Press.

Crocker, J., & Luhtanen, R. (1990). Collective self-esteem and ingroup bias. *Journal of Personality and Social Psychology, 58,* 60–67.

Crocker, J., & McGraw, K. M. (1984). What's good for the goose is not good for the gander: Solo status as an obstacle to occupational achievement for males and females. *American Behavioral Scientist, 27,* 357–370.

Crocker, J., & Park, L. E. (2004). The costly pursuit of self-esteem. *Psychological Bulletin, 130,* 392–414.

Croizet, J., Despres, G., Gauzins, M. E., Huguet, P., Leyens, J., & Meot, A. (2004). Stereotype threat undermines intellectual performance by triggering a disruptive mental load. *Personality and Social Psychology Bulletin, 30,* 721–731.

Crooks, R., & Baur, K. (2008). *Our sexuality.* Belmont, CA: Wadsworth.

Crosby, F. J., & Sabattini, L. (2006). Family and work balance. In J. Worrell & C. D. Goodheart (Eds.), *Handbook of girls' and women's psychological health.* New York, NY: Oxford University Press.

Crosby, O., Iyer, A., Clayton, S., & Downing, R. A. (2003). Affirmative action: Psychological data and the policy debates. *American Psychologist, 58*(1), 93–115.

Crosby, O., & Moncarz, R. (2006, Fall). The 2004–14 job outlook for college graduates. *Occupational Outlook Quarterly,* pp. 42–57.

Cross, P. (1977). Not can but will college teaching be improved? *New Directions for Higher Education, 17,* 1–15.

Cross, S. E., & Gore, J. S. (2003). Cultural models of the self. In M.R. Leary & J. P. Tangney (Eds.), *Handbook of self and identity.* New York, NY: Guilford.

Cross, S. E., & Madson, L. (1997). Models of the self: Self-construal and gender. *Psychological Bulletin, 122*(1), 5–37.

Crouter, A. C., Bumpus, M. F., Maguire, M. C., & McHale, S. M. (1999). Linking parents' work pressure and adolescents' well-being: Insights into dynamics in dual-earner families. *Developmental Psychology, 35,* 1453–1461.

Crow, S. J., Peterson, C. B., Swanson, S. A., Raymond, N. C., Specker, S., Eckert, E. D., & Mitchell, J. E. (2009). Increased mortality in bulimia nervosa and other eating disorders. *American Journal of Psychiatry, 166*(12), 1342–1346. doi:10.1176/appi.ajp.2009.09020247

Crowell, J. A., Treboux, D., & Waters, E. (2002). Stability of attachment representations: The transition to marriage. *Developmental Psychology, 38,* 467–479.

Crowl, A., Ahn, S., & Baker, J. (2008). A meta-analysis of developmental outcomes for children of same-sex and heterosexual parents. *Journal of GLBT Family Studies, 4,* 385–407.

Crowley, A. E., & Hoyer, W. D. (1994). An integrative framework for understanding two-sided persuasion. *Journal of Consumer Research, 20,* 561–574.

Csikszentmihalyi, M. (1975). Play and intrinsic rewards. *Journal of Humanistic Psychology, 15,* 41–63.

Csikszentmihalyi, M. (1990). *Flow: The psychology of optimal experience.* New York, NY: Harper & Row.

Csikszentmihalyi, M. (1997). *Finding flow.* New York, NY: Basic Books.

Csikszentmihalyi, M., & LeFevre, J. (1989). Optimal experience in work and leisure. *Journal of Personality and Social Psychology, 56,* 815–822.

Csikszentmihalyi, M., & Nakamura, J. (2011). Positive psychology: Where did it come from, where is it going? In K. M. Sheldon, T. B. Kashdan, & M. F. Steger (Eds.), *Designing positive psychology: Taking stock and moving forward* (pp. 3–8). New York, NY: Oxford University Press.

Cuffee, J. J., Hallfors, D. D., & Waller, M. W. (2007). Racial and gender differences in adolescent sexual attitudes and longitudinal associations with coital debut. *Journal of Adolescent Health Care, 41,* 19–26.

Cullen, L. T. (2007, February 22). It's a wrap. You're hired! *Time,* p. 57.

Cuming, S., & Rapee, R. M. (2010). Social anxiety and self-protective communication style in close relationships. *Behaviour Research and Therapy, 48*(2), 87–96. doi:10.1016/j.brat.2009.09.010

Cunningham, C. O., & Selwyn, P. A. (2005). HIV-related medical complications and treatment. In J. H. Lowinson, P. Ruiz, R. B. Millman, & J. G. Langrod (Eds.), *Substance abuse: A comprehensive textbook.* Philadelphia: Lippincott/Williams & Wilkins.

Cunningham, M. R. (2009a). Physical attractiveness, defining characteristics. In H. T. Reis & S. Sprecher (Eds.), *Encyclopedia of human relationships: Vol. 3* (pp. 1237–1242). Los Angeles: Sage Reference Publication.

Cunningham, M. R. (2009b). Polygamy. In H. T. Reis & S. Sprecher (Eds.), *Encyclopedia of human relationships: Vol. 3* (pp. 1256–1259). Los Angeles: Sage Reference Publication.

Cunningham, M. R., Barbee, A. P., & Pike, C. L. (1990). What do women want? Facialmetric assessment of multiple motives in the perception of male facial physical attractiveness. *Journal of Personality and Social Psychology, 59*, 61–72.

Cunningham, M. R., Druen, P. B., & Barbee, A. P. (1997). Angels, mentors, and friends: Trade-offs among evolutionary, social, and individual variables in physical appearance. In J. A. Simpson & D. T. Kenrick (Eds.), *Evolutionary Social Psychology*. Mahwah, NJ: Erlbaum.

Cunningham, M. R., Roberts, A. R., Barbee, A. P., Druen, P. B., & Wu, C. (1995). "Their ideas of beauty are, on the whole, the same as ours": Consistency and variability in the cross-cultural perception of female physical attractiveness. *Journal of Personality and Social Psychology, 68*, 261–279.

Cupach, W. R., & Spitzberg, B. H. (2008). "Thanks, but no thanks. . ." The occurrence and management of unwanted relationship pursuit. In S. Sprecher, A. Wenzel, & J. Harvey (Eds.), *Handbook of relationship initiation* (pp. 409–424). New York, NY: Psychology Press.

Curioni, C. C., & Lourenco, P. M. (2005). Long-term weight loss after diet and exercise: A systematic review. *International Journal of Obesity, 29*, 1168–1174.

Curtis, G. C., Magee, W. J., Eaton, W. W., Wittchen, H., & Kessler, R. C. (1998). Specific fears and phobias: Epidemiology and classification. *British Journal of Psychiatry, 173*, 212–217. doi:10.1192/bjp.173.3.212

Curtis, R. C., & Miller, K. (1986). Believing another likes or dislikes you: Behaviors making the beliefs come true. *Journal of Personality and Social Psychology, 51*, 284–290.

Cushing-Daniels, B., & Tsz-Ying, Y. (2009). Wage penalties and sexual orientation: An update using the general social survey. *Contemporary Economic Policy, 27*(2), 164–175.

Czincz, J., & Hechanova, R. (2009). Internet addiction: Debating the diagnosis. *Journal of Technology in Human Services, 27*(4), 257–272. doi:10.1080/15228830903329815

Dabbs, J. M., with Dabbs, M. G. (2000). *Heroes, rogues, and lovers: Testosterone and behavior.* New York, NY: McGraw-Hill.

D'Amico, M. L. (1998). Internet has become a necessity, U.S. poll shows. *CNNinteractive* [Internet magazine], 1.

Danaher, K., & Branscombe, N. R. (2010). Maintaining the system with tokenism: Bolstering individual mobility beliefs and identification with a discriminatory organization. *British Journal of Social Psychology, 49*(2), 343–362. doi:10.1348/014466609X457530

Dantzer, R., & Mormede, P. (1995). Psychoneuroimmunology of stress. In B. E. Leonard & K. Miller (Eds.), *Stress, the immune system and psychiatry.* New York, NY: Wiley.

Darke, S., Kaye, S., & Duflou, J. (2006). Comparative cardiac pathology among deaths due to cocaine toxicity, opioid toxicity and non-drug related causes. *Addiction, 101*, 1771–1777.

Dasgupta, N. (2009). Mechanisms underlying the malleability of implicit prejudices and stereotypes: The role of automaticity and cognitive control. In T. D. Nelson (Ed.), *Handbook of prejudice, stereotyping, and discrimination* (pp. 267–284). New York, NY: Psychology Press.

David, D. H., & Lyons-Ruth, K. (2005). Differential attachment responses of male and female infants to frightening maternal behavior: Tend or befriend versus fight of flight? *Infant Mental Health Journal, 26*(1), 1–18.

Davidson, K. W., Mostofsky, E., & Whang, W. (2010). Don't worry, be happy: Positive affect and reduced 10-year incident coronary heart disease: The Canadian Nova Scotia Health Survey. *European Heart Journal, 31*, 1065–1070.

Davidson, M. J., & Fielden, S. (1999). Stress and the working woman. In G. N. Powell (Ed.), *Handbook of gender and work.* Thousand Oaks, CA: Sage.

Davidson, R. J., Pizzagalli, D. A., & Nitschke, J. B. (2009). Representation and regulation of emotion in depression: Perspectives from affective neuroscience. In I. H. Gotlib & C. L. Hammen (Eds.), *Handbook of Depression* (pp. 218–248). New York, NY: The Guilford Press.

Davies, A. P. C., & Shackelford, T. K. (2006). An evolutionary psychological perspective on gender similarities and differences. *American Psychologist, 32*, 640–641.

Davis, C. G., & Nolen-Hoeksema, S. (2009). Making sense of loss, perceiving benefits, and posttraumatic growth. In S. J. Lopez & C. R. Snyder (Eds.), *Oxford handbook of positive psychology* (2nd ed., pp. 641–649). New York, NY: Oxford.

Davis, M., Guyker, W., & Persky, I. (2012). Uniting veterans across distance through telephone-based reminiscence group therapy intervention. *Psychological Services, 9*, 206–208. doi:.10.1037/a0026117

Davis, R. A. (2001). A cognitive-behavioral model of pathological Internet use. *Computers in Human Behavior, 17*(2), 187–195.

Davison, S. L., & Davis, S. R. (2011). Androgenic hormones and aging—the link with female sexual function. *Hormones and Behavior, 59*, 745–753. doi:10.1016/j.yhbeh.2010.12.013

Dawes, R. M. (1980). Social dilemmas. *Annual Review of Psychology, 31*, 169–193.

Dawood, K., Bailey, J., & Martin, N. G. (2009). Genetic and environmental influences on sexual orientation. In Y. Kim (Ed.), *Handbook of behavior genetics* (pp. 269–279). New York, NY: Springer Science + Business Media.

Dean, L. R., Carroll, J. S., & Yang, C. (2007). Materialism, perceived financial problems, and marital satisfaction. *Family and Consumer Sciences Research Journal, 35*, 260–281.

DeAndrea, D. C., Tong, S., & Walther, J. B. (2011). Dark sides of computer-mediated communication. In W. R. Cupach & B. H. Spitzberg (Eds.), *The dark side of close relationships II* (pp. 95–118). New York, N: Routledge/Taylor & Francis Group.

DeAngelis, T. (2001, December). Are men emotional mummies? *Monitor on Psychology,* pp. 40–41.

DeAngelis, T. (2004). What's to blame for the surge in super-size Americans? *Monitor on Psychology, 35*(1), 46, 62.

Deaux, K., & Hanna, R. (1984). Courtship in the personals column: The influence of gender and sexual orientation. *Sex Roles, 11*, 363–375.

Debatin, B., Lovejoy, J. P., Horn, A., & Hughes, B. N. (2009). Facebook and online privacy: Attitudes, behaviors, and unintended consequences. *Journal of Computer-Mediated Communication, 15*(1), 83–108. doi:10.1111/j.1083-6101.2009.01494.x

de Calvo, M. P. C., & Reich, D. A. (2009). Detecting perceiver expectancies: The role of perceiver distraction in spontaneously triggering identity negotiation. *Basic and Applied Social Psychology, 31*(2), 174–187.

DeCarvalho, R. J. (1991). *The founders of humanistic psychology.* New York, NY: Praeger.

Deci, E. L., & Ryan, R. M. (2008). Hedonia, eudaimonia, and well-being: An introduction. *Journal of Happiness Studies, 9*, 1–11.

De Dreu, C. K., W., Beersma, B. Stroebe, K., & Euwema, M. C. (2006). Motivated information processing, strategic choice, and the quality of negotiated agreement. *Journal of Personality and Social Psychology, 90*, 927–943.

Deer, B. (2011). How the case against MMR vacine was fixed. *BMJ, 342*, 77–82.

de Geus, E., & Neumann, D. L. (2008). Psychophysiological measurement of personality. In G. J. Boyle, G. Matthews, & D. H. Saklofske (Eds.), *The Sage handbook of personality theory and assessment* (Vol. 2, pp. 313–333). Los Angeles: Sage.

de Geus, E., & Stubbe, J. H. (2007). Aerobic exercise and stress reduction. In G. Fink (Ed.), *Encyclopedia of stress: Vols. 1–4* (2nd ed., pp. 73–77). San Diego, CA: Elsevier Academic Press.

De Hoog, N., Stroebe, W., & De Wit, J. B. F. (2007). The impact of vulnerability to and severity of a health risk on processing and acceptance of fear-arousing communications: A meta-analysis. *Review of General Psychology, 11*(3), 258–285.

de Janasz, S. C., & Forret, M. L. (2008). Learning the art of networking: A critical skill for enhancing social capital and career success. *Journal of Management Education, 32*(5), 629–650. doi:10.1177/1052562907307637

Delay, J., & Deniker, P. (1952). *Trente-huit cas de psychoses traitees par la cure prolongee et continue de 4560 RP.* Paris: Masson et Cie.

Delizonna, L. L., Williams, R. P., & Langer, E. J. (2009). The effect of mindfulness on heart rate control. *Journal of Adult Development, 16*(2), 61–65.

Delle Fave, A. (2009). Optimal experience and meaning: Which relationship? *Psychological Topics, 18*(20), 284–302.

DeLyser, G. (2012). At midlife, intentionally child-free women and their experiences of regret. *Clinical Social Work Journal, 40*(1), 66–74. doi:10.1007/s10615-011-0337-2

DeMaris, A., Benson, M. L., Fox, G. L., Hill, T., & Van Wyk, J. (2003). Distal and proximal factors in domestic violence: A test of an integrated model. *Journal of Marriage and Family, 65*, 652–667.

Demir, M., & Özdemir, M. (2010). Friendship, need satisfaction and happiness. *Journal of Happiness Studies, 11*(2), 243–259. doi:10.1007/s10902-009-9138-5

Demo, D. H. (1992). Parent-child relations: Assessing recent changes. *Journal of Marriage and the Family, 54*, 104–117.

Demo, D. H., & Fine, M. A. (2009). Children and divorce. In H. T. Reis & S. Sprecher (Eds.), *Encyclopedia of human relationships: Vol. 2* (pp. 453–458). Los Angeles: Sage Reference Publication.

Deniz, O., Aygül, R., Koçak, N., Orhan, A., & Kaya, M. D. (2004). Precipitating factors of migraine attacks in patients with migraine with and without aura. *Pain Clinic, 16*, 451–456.

Denmark, F. L., German, S. T., & Brodsky, J. B. (2011). Sex discrimination. In M. A. Paludi, C. R. Paludi, & E. R. DeSouza (Eds.), *Praeger handbook on understanding and preventing workplace discrimination* (pp. 195–226). Santa Barbara, CA: Praeger/ABC-CLIO.

Denollet, J., Martens, E. J., Nyklicek, I., Conraads, V., & de Gelder, B. (2008). Clinical events in coronary patients who report low distress: Adverse effect of repressive coping. *Health Psychology, 27*, 302–308. doi:10.1037/0278-6133.27.3.302

Denson, T. F., Aviles, F. E., Pollock, V. E., Earleywine, M., Vasquez, E. A., & Miller, N. (2008). The effects of alcohol and the salience of aggressive cues on triggered displaced aggression. *Aggressive Behavior, 34*, 25–33.

Denson, T. F., DeWall, C., & Finkel, E. J. (2012). Self-control and aggression. *Current Directions in Psychological Science, 21*(1), 20–25. doi:10.1177/0963721411429451

DePaulo, B. M. (1994). Spotting lies: Can humans learn to do better? *Current Directions in Psychological Science, 3*(3), 83–86.

DePaulo, B. M. (2004). The many faces of lies. In A. G. Miller (Ed.), *The social psychology of good and evil* (pp. 303–326). New York, NY: Guilford.

DePaulo, B. M. (2011). Living single: Lightening up those dark, dopey myths. In W. R. Cupach & B. H. Spitzberg (Eds.), *The dark side of close relationships II* (pp. 409–439). New York, NY: Routledge/Taylor & Francis Group.

DePaulo, B. M., Ansfield, M. E., Kirkendol, S. E., & Boden, J. M. (2004). Serious lies. *Basic and Applied Social Psychology, 6*, 147–167.

DePaulo, B. M., Charlton, K., Cooper, H., Lindsay, J. J., & Muhlenbruck, L. (1997). The accuracy-confidence correlation in the detection of deception. *Personality and Social Psychology Review, 1*(4), 346–357.

DePaulo, B. M., & Friedman, H. (1998). Nonverbal communication. In D. T. Gilbert, S. T. Fiske, & G. Lindzey (Eds.), *The handbook of social psychology* (Vol. 2). Boston, MA: McGraw-Hill.

DePaulo, B. M., Lindsay, J. J., Malone, B. E., Muhlenbruck, L., Charlton, K., & Cooper, H. (2003). Cues to deception. *Psychological Bulletin, 129*(1), 74–118.

DePaulo, B. M., & Morris, W. L. (2005). Singles in society and in science. *Psychological Inquiry, 16,* 57–83.

DePaulo, B. M., & Morris, W. L. (2006). The unrecognized stereotyping and discrimination against singles. *Current Directions in Psychological Science, 15,* 251–254.

DePaulo, B. M., Stone, J., & Lassiter, G. D. (1985). Deceiving and detecting deceit. In B. R. Schlenker (Ed.), *The self and social life.* New York, NY: McGraw-Hill.

DePrince, A. P., Chu, A. T., & Pineda, A. S. (2011). Links between specific posttrauma appraisals and three forms of trauma-related distress. *Psychological Trauma: Theory, Research, Practice, and Policy, 3*(4), 430-441. doi:10.1037/a0021576

De Raad, B., Barelds, D. H., Levert, E., Ostendorf, F., Mlačić, B., Blas, L., et al. (2010). Only three factors of personality description are fully replicable across languages: A comparison of 14 trait taxonomies. *Journal of Personality and Social Psychology, 98*(1), 160–173. doi:10.1037/a0017184

Derlega, V. J., Winstead, B. A., Wong, P. T. P., & Hunter, S. (1985). Gender effects in an initial encounter: A case where men exceed women in disclosure. *Journal of Social and Personal Relationships, 2,* 25–44.

Derryberry, D., & Tucker, D. M. (1994). Motivating the focus of attention. In P. M. Neidenthal & S. Kitayama (Eds.), *The heart's eye: Emotional influences in perception and attention* (pp. 167–196). San Diego, CA: Academic Press.

DeSantis King, A., Huebner, E. S., Suldo, S. M., & Valois, R. F. (2006). An ecological view of school satisfaction in adolescence: Linkages between social support and behavior problems. *Applied Research in Quality of Life, 1,* 279–295.

Desert, M., & Leyens, J. (2006). Social comparisons across cultures I: Gender stereotypes in high and low power distance cultures. In S. Guimond (Ed.), *Social Comparison and Social Psychology: Understanding cognition, intergroup relations, and culture.* New York, NY: Cambridge University Press.

Des Jarlais, D. C., Hagan, H., & Friedman, S. R. (2005). Epidemiology and emerging public heath perspectives. In J. H. Lowinson, P. Ruiz, R. B. Millman, & J. G. Langrod (Eds.), *Substance abuse: A comprehensive textbook.* Philadelphia: Lippincott/Williams & Wilkins.

Deutsch, M. (2011). Constructive conflict management for the world today. In P. T. Coleman (Ed.), *Conflict, interdependence, and justice: The intellectual legacy of Morton Deutsch* (pp. 289–307). New York, NY: Springer Science + Business Media.

Deutsch, M., & Gerard, H. B. (1955). A study of normative and informational social influences upon individual judgment. *Journal of Abnormal and Social Psychology, 51,* 629–636.

De Vas, D. (2012). Social trends and relationships. In P. Noller & G. C. Karantzas (Eds.), *The Wiley-Blackwell handbook of couples and family relationships* (pp. 25–35). Malden, MA: Wiley-Blackwell.

Devine, P. G. (1989). Stereotypes and prejudice: Their automatic and controlled components. *Journal of Personality and Social Psychology, 56,* 5–18.

de Vries, B. (1996). The understanding of friendship: An adult life course perspective. In C. Magai & S. H. McFadden (Eds), *Handbook of emotion, adult development, and aging.* San Diego, CA: Academic Press.

Dew, J. (2008). Debt change and marital satisfaction change in recently married couples. *Family Relations, 57,* 60–71.

Dew, M. A., Bromet, E. J., & Switzer, G. E. (2000). Epidemiology. In M. Hersen & A. S. Bellack (Eds.), *Psychopathology in adulthood.* Boston, MA: Allyn & Bacon.

DeWall, C. N., Baumeister, R. F., Gailliot, M. T., & Maner, J. K. (2008). Depletion makes the heart grow less helpful: Helping as a function of self-regulatory energy and genetic relatedness. *Personality and Social Psychology Bulletin, 34,* 1653–1662.

DeWall, C., & Bushman, B. J. (2011). Social acceptance and rejection: The sweet and the bitter. *Current Directions in Psychological Science, 20*(4), 256–260. doi:10.1177/0963721411417545

Dey, J. G., & Hill, C. (2007). *Behind the pay gap.* Washington, DC: American Association of University Women Educational Foundation.

DeYoung, C. G., & Gray, J. R. (2009). Personality neuroscience: Explaining individual differences in affect, behaviour and cognition. In P. J. Corr & G. Matthews (Eds.), *The Cambridge handbook of personality psychology* (pp. 323–346). New York, NY: Cambridge University Press.

DeYoung, C. G., Hirsh, J. B., Shane, M. S., Papademetris, X., Rajeevan, N., & Gray, J. R. (2010). Testing predictions from personality neuroscience: Brain structure and the Big Five. *Psychological Science, 21*(6), 820–828.

Dhabhar, F. S. (2011). Effects of stress on immune function: Implications for immunoprotection and immunopathology. In R. J. Contrada & A. Baum (Eds.), *The handbook of stress science: Biology, psychology, and health* (pp. 47-64). New York, NY: Springer.

Dhont, K., & Van Hiel, A. (2012). Intergroup contact buffers against the intergenerational transmission of authoritarianism and racial prejudice. *Journal of Research in Personality, 46*(2), 231–234. doi:10.1016/j.jrp.2011.12.008

Diamond, L. E. (2003). Was it a phase? Young women's relinquishment of lesbian/bisexual identities over a 5-year period. *Journal of Personality and Social Psychology, 84,* 352–364.

Diamond, L. M. (2006). The intimate same-sex relationships of sexual minorities. In A. L. Vangelisti & D. Perlman (Eds.), *The Cambridge handbook of personal relationships.* New York, NY: Cambridge University Press.

Diamond, L. M. (2007). "Having a girlfriend without knowing it": Intimate friendships among adolescent sexual-minority women. In K. E. Lovaas & M. M. Jenkins (Eds.), *Sexualities & communication in everyday life* (pp. 107–115). Thousand Oaks, CA: Sage.

Diamond, L. M., & Lucas, S. (2004). Sexual-minority and heterosexual youths' peer relationships: Experiences, expectations, and implications for well-being. *Journal of Research on Adolescence, 14*(3), 313–340. doi:10.1111/j.1532-7795.2004.00077.x

DiBaise, R., & Gunnoe, J. (2004). Gender and culture differences in touching behavior. *Journal of Social Psychology, 144,* 49–62.

Di Chiara, G. (1999). Drug addiction as dopamine-dependent associative learning disorder. *European Journal of Pharmacology, 375,* 13–30.

Dickerson, C. A., Thibodeau, R., Aronson, E., & Miller, D. (1992). Using cognitive dissonance to encourage water conservation. *Journal of Applied Social Psychology, 22*(11), 841–854. doi:10.1111/j.1559-1816.1992.tb00928.x

DiClemente, C. C., Fairhurst, S. K., & Piotrowski, N. A. (1995). Self-efficacy and addictive behaviors. In J. E. Maddux (Ed.), *Self-efficacy, adaptation, and adjustment: Theory, research and application.* New York, NY: Plenum Press.

DiCorcia, J. A., & Tronick, E. (2011). Quotidian resilience: Exploring mechanisms that drive resilience from a perspective of everyday stress and coping. *Neuroscience and Biobehavioral Reviews, 35*(7), 1593–1602. doi:10.1016/j.neubiorev.2011.04.008

Diekman, A. B., & Murnen, S. K. (2004). Learning to be little women and little men: The inequitable gender equality of nonsexist children's literature. *Sex Roles, 50*(5/6), 373–385.

Diener, E., & Biswas-Diener, R. (2002). Will money increase subjective well-being? *Social Indicators Research, 57*(2), 119–169. doi:10.1023/A:1014411319119

Diener, E., & Biswas-Diener, R. (2008). *Happiness: Unlocking the mysteries of psychological wealth* London: Wiley-Blackwell.

Diener, E., & Diener, C. (1996). Most people are happy. *Psychological Science, 7,* 181–185.

Diener, E., Gohm, C. L., Suh, E., & Oishi, S. (2000). Similarity of the relations between marital status and subjective well-being across cultures. *Journal of Cross-Cultural Psychology, 31,* 419–436.

Diener, E., Kesebir, P., & Tov, W. (2009). Happiness. In M. R. Leary & R. H. Hoyle (Eds.), Handbook of individual differences in social behavior (pp. 147–160). New York, NY: Guilford.

Diener, E., & Seligman, M. E. P. (2002). Very happy people. *Psychological Science, 13,* 80–83.

Diener, E., & Seligman, M. E. P. (2004). Beyond money: Toward an economy of well-being. *Psychological Science in the Public Interest, 5*(1), 1–31.

Diener, E., Tay, L., & Myers, D. G. (2011). The religion paradox: If religion makes people happy, why are so many dropping out? *Journal of Personality and Social Psychology, 101,* 1278–1290. doi:10.1037/a00224402

Diener, E., Wolsic, B., & Fujita, F. (1995). Physical attractiveness and subjective well-being. *Journal of Personality and Social Psychology, 69,* 120–129.

Dijkstra, A. F., Verdonk, P., & Lagro-Janssen, A. L. M. (2008). Gender bias in medical textbooks: Examples from coronary heart disease, depression, alcohol abuse and pharmacology. *Medical Education, 42,* 1021–1028.

Dijkstra, P., Gibbons, F. X., & Buunk, A. P. (2010). Social comparison theory. In J. E. Maddux & J. P. Tangney (Eds.), *Social psychological foundations of clinical psychology* (pp. 195–211). New York, NY: Guilford.

Dillard, A. J., McCaul, K. D., & Klein, W, M. P. (2006). Unrealistic optimism in smokers: Implications for smoking myth endorsement and self-protective motivation. *Journal of Health Communication, 11,* 93–102.

Dilworth, J. E. L. (2004). Predictors of negative spillover from family to work. *Journal of Family Issues, 25,* 241–261.

DiMatteo, M. R. (1997). Health behaviors and care decisions: An overview of professional-patient communication. In D. S. Gochman (Ed.), *Handbook of health behavior research II: Provider determinants.* New York, NY: Plenum Press.

DiMatteo, M. R. (2004). Variations in patients' adherence to medical recommendations: A quantitative review of 50 years of research. *Medical Care, 42*(3), 200–209.

DiMatteo, M. R., Giordani, P. J., Lepper, H. S., & Croghan, T. W. (2002). Patient adherence and medical treatment outcomes: A meta-analysis. *Medical Care. 40,* 794–811.

Din, J. N., Newby, D. E., & Flapan, A. D. (2004). Omega 3 fatty acids and cardiovascular disease—fishing for a natural treatment. *British Medical Journal, 328,* 30–35.

Dindia, K. (2006). Men are from North Dakota, women are from South Dakota. In K. Dindia (Ed.), *Sex Differences and similarities in communication* (2nd ed., pp. 3–20). Mahwah, NJ: Lawrence Erlbaum Associates Publishers.

Dindia, K., & Allen, M. (1992). Sex differences in self-disclosure: A meta-analysis. *Psychological Bulletin, 112,* 106–124.

Dion, K. (1973). Young children's stereotyping of facial attractiveness. *Developmental Psychology, 9,* 183–188.

Dion, K. K., Berscheid, E., & Walster, E. (1972). What is beautiful is good. *Journal of Personality and Social Psychology, 24,* 285–290.

Dion, K. L. (2003). Prejudice, racism and discrimination. In T. Millon & M. J. Lerner (Eds.), *Handbook of psychology: Vol 5. Personality and social psychology.* New York, NY: Wiley.

Dion, K. L., & Dion, K. K. (1988). Romantic love: Individual and cultural perspectives. In R. J. Sternberg & M. L. Barnes (Eds.), *The psychology of love* (pp. 264–289). New Haven, CT: Yale University Press.

Dishotsky, N. I., Loughman, W. D., Mogar, R. E., & Lipscomb, W. R. (1971). LSD and genetic damage: Is LSD chromosome damaging, carcinogenic, mutagenic, or teratogenic? *Science, 172,* 431–440.

Dittner, A. J., Rimes, K., & Thorpe, S. (2011). Negative perfectionism increases the risk of fatigue following a period of stress. *Psychology and Health, 26*(3), 253–268. doi:10.1080/08870440903225892

Djikic, M., Langer, E. J., & Stapleton, S. F. (2008). Reducing stereotyping through mindfulness: Effects on automatic stereotype-activated behaviors. *Journal of Adult Development, 15*(2), 106–111.

Dodge, B., Jeffries, W. L., & Sandfort, T. G. M. (2008). Beyond the down low: Sexual risk, protection, and disclosure among at risk Black men who have sex with both men and women (MSMW). *Archive of Sexual Behavior, 37,* 683–696.

Doerr, C. E., & Baumeister, R. F. (2010). Self-regulatory strength and psychological adjustment: Implications of the limited resource model of self-regulation. In J. E. Maddux & J. Tangney (Eds.), *Social psychological foundations of clinical psychology* (pp. 71-83). New York, NY: Guilford Press.

Dohm, A., & Wyatt, I. (2002). College at work: Outlook and earnings for college graduates, 2000-10. *Occupational Outlook Quarterly, 46*(3), 3–15.

Doja, A., & Roberts, W. (2006). Immunizations and autism: A review of the literature. *Canadian Journal of Neurological Sciences, 33*(4), 341–346.

Dolby, S. K. (2005). *Self-help books: Why Americans keep reading them.* Urbana: University of Illinois Press.

Dolder, C. R. (2008). Side effects of antipsychotics. In K. T. Mueser & D. V. Jeste (Eds.), *Clinical handbook of schizophrenia* (pp. 168–177). New York, NY: Guilford.

Dolinski, D. (2012). The nature of the first small request as a decisive factor in the effectiveness of the foot-in-the-door technique. *Applied Psychology: An International Review, 61*(3), 437–453. doi:10.1111/j.1464-0597.2011.00477.x

Dollard, J., Doob, L. W., Miller, N. E., Mowrer, O. H., & Sears, R. R. (1939). *Frustration and aggression.* New Haven, CT: Yale University Press.

Donahey, K. M. (2010). Female orgasmic disorder. In S. B. Levine (Ed.), *Handbook of clinical sexuality for mental health professionals* (2nd ed., pp. 351–368). New York, NY: Routledge/Taylor & Francis Group.

Donahue, M. J., & Benson, P. L. (1995). Religion and the well-being of adolescents. *Journal of Social Issues, 51,* 145–160.

Dornelas, E. A. (2008). Depression. In *Psychotherapy with cardiac patients: Behavioral cardiology in practice* (pp. 51–65). Washington, DC: American Psychological Association. doi:10.1037/11809-004

Dougall, A. L., & Baum, A. (2000). Three Mile Island, stress effects of. In G. Fink (Ed.), *Encyclopedia of stress* (Vol. 3). San Diego: Academic Press.

Dougall, A. L., & Swanson, J. N. (2011). Physical health outcomes of trauma. In R. J. Contrada & A. Baum (Eds.), *The handbook of stress science: Biology, psychology, and health* (pp. 373–384). New York, NY: Springer.

Dougherty, J. (2009, October 22). For some seeking rebirth, Sweat Lodge was end. *The New York Times.* Retrieved from http://www.nytimes.com/2009/10/22/us/22sewat.html

Dougherty, T. W., Turban, D. B., & Callender, J. C. (1994). Confirming first impressions in the employment interview: A field study of interview behavior. *Journal of Applied Psychology, 79*(5), 659–665.

Dovidio, J. F., & Gaertner, S. L. (1996). Affirmative action, unintentional racial biases, and intergroup relations. *Journal of Social Issues, 52,* 51–75.

Dovidio, J. F., & Gaertner, S. L. (1999). Reducing prejudice: Combating intergroup biases. *Current Directions in Psychological Science, 8,* 101–105.

Dovidio, J. F., Ellyson, S. L., Keating, C. F., Heltman, K., & Brown, C. E. (1988). The relationship of social power to visual display of dominance between men and women. *Journal of Personality and Social Psychology, 54,* 233–242.

Dovidio, J. F., Gaertner, S. L., Esses, V. M., & Brewer, M. B. (2003). Social conflict, harmony, and integration. In T. Millon & M. J. Lerner (Eds.) *Handbook of psychology: Vol. 5. Personality and social psychology.* New York, NY: Wiley.

Dovidio, J. F., Gaertner, S. L., & Pearson, A. R. (2005). On the nature of prejudice: The psychological foundations of hate. In R. J. Sternberg (Ed.), *The psychology of hate.* Washington, DC: American Psychological Association.

Dovidio, J. F., Gaertner, S. L., Penner, L. A., Pearson, A. R., Norton, W. E. (2009). Aversive racism—how unconscious bias influences behavior: Implications for legal, employment, and health care contexts. In J. L. Chin (Ed.), *Diversity in mind and in action, Vol. 3: Social justice matters* (pp. 21–35). Santa Barbara, CA: Praeger/ABC-CLIO.

Downar, J., & Kapur, S. (2008). Biological theories. In K. T. Mueser & D. V. Jeste (Eds.), *Clinical handbook of schizophrenia* (pp. 25–34). New York, NY: The Guilford Press.

Downing, S. (2011). *On course: Strategies for creating success in college and life.* Belmont, CA: Wadsworth.

Drago, R. W. (2007). *Striking a balance: Work, family, life.* Boston, MA: Dollars & Sense.

Drew, J. (2003). The myth of female sexual dysfunction and its medicalization. *Sexualities, Evolution and Gender, 5*(2), 89–96.

Drigotas, S. M. (2002). The Michelangelo phenomenon and personal well-being. *Journal of Personality, 70,* 59–77.

Driver, J., Tabares, A., Shapiro, A., Nahm, E. Y., & Gottman, J. M. (2003). Interactional patterns in marital success and failure: Gottman laboratory studies. In F. Walsh (Ed.), *Normal family processes: Growing diversity and complexity.* New York, NY: Guilford.

Driver, J. L., & Gottman, J. M. (2004). Daily marital interactions and positive affect during marital conflict among newlywed couples. *Family Processes, 43,* 301–314.

Dubbert, P. M., King, A. C., Marcus, B. H., & Sallis, J. F. (2004). Promotion of physical activity through the life span. In J. M. Raczynski & L. C. Leviton (Eds.), *Handbook of clinical health psychology: Vol. 2. Disorders of behavior and health.* Washington, DC: American Psychological Association.

Dube, M. F., & Green, C. R. (1982). Methods of collection of smoke for analytical purposes. *Recent Advances in Tobacco Science, 8,* 42–102.

Dubovsky, S. L. (2009). Benzodiazepine receptor agonists and antagonists. In B. J. Sadock, V. A. Sadock, & P. Ruiz (Eds.), *Kaplan & Sadock's comprehensive textbook of psychiatry* (pp. 3044–3055). Philadelphia: Lippincott Williams & Wilkins.

Duck, S. W. (1982). A topography of relationship disengagement and dissolution. In S. W. Duck (Ed.), *Personal relationship 4: Dissolving personal relationships* (pp. 1–30). London: Academic Press.

Duck, S. W. (2006). *Human relationships* (4th ed.). London: Sage.

Duckworth, A. L., Peterson, C., Matthews, M. D., & Kelly, D. R. (2007). Grit: Perseverance and passion for long-term goals. *Journal of Personality and Social Psychology, 92*(6), 1087–1101. doi:10.1037/0022-3514.92.6.1087

Duckworth, A., & Quinn, P. D. (2009). Development and validation of the Short Grit Scale (GRIT–S). *Journal of Personality Assessment, 91*(2), 166–174. doi:10.1080/00223890802634290

Dudley, M., Hadzi-Pavlovic, D., Andrews, D., & Perich, T. (2008). New-generation antidepressants, suicide and depressed adolescents: How should clinicians respond to changing evidence? *Australian and New Zealand Journal of Psychiatry, 42*(6), 456–466. doi:10.1080/00048670802050538

Duhigg, C. (2012). *The power of habit: Why we do what we do in life and business.* New York, NY: Random House.

Duman, R. S., & Monteggia, L. M. (2006). A neurotrophic model for stress–related mood disorders. *Biological Psychiatry, 59,* 1116–1127.

Duman, R. S., Polan, H. J., & Schatzberg, A. (2008). Neurobiologic foundations of mood disorders. In A. Tasman, J. Kay, J. A. Lieberman, M. B. First, & M. Maj (Eds.), *Psychiatry* (3rd ed.). New York, NY: Wiley-Blackwell.

Dunbar-Jacob, J., & Schlenk, E. (2001). Patient adherence to treatment regimen. In A. Baum, T. A. Revenson, & J. E. Singer (Eds.), *Handbook of health psychology.* Mahwah, NJ: Erlbaum.

Duncan, C. P., & Nelson, J. E. (1985). Effects of humor in a radio advertising experiment. *Journal of Advertising, 14,* 33–40, 64.

Duncker, K. (1945). On problem solving. *Psychological Monographs, 58*(5, Whole No. 270).

Dunkel-Schetter, C., Gurung, R. A. R., Lobel, M., & Wadhwa, P. D. (2001). Stress processes in pregnancy and birth: Psychological, biological, and sociocultural influences. In A. Baum, T. A. Revenson, & J. E. Singer (Eds.), *Handbook of health psychology.* Mahwah, NJ: Erlbaum.

Dunlop, B. W., Garlow, S. J., & Nemeroff, C. B. (2009). The neurochemistry of depressive disorders: Clinical studies. In D. S. Charney & E. J. Nestler (Eds.), *Neurobiology of mental illness* (pp. 435–460). New York, NY: Oxford University Press.

Dunn, A. L., Trivedi, M. H., & O'Neal, H. A. (2001). Physical activity dose-response effects on outomes of depression and anxiety. *Medicine and Science in Sports and Exercise, 33,* S587–S597.

Dunn, D. S., & Brody, C. (2008). Defining the good life following acquired physical disability. *Rehabilitation Psychology, 53,* 413–425.

Dunn, D. S., & Wilson, T. D. (1990). When the stakes are high: A limit to the illusion-of-control effect. *Social Cognition, 8,* 305–323.

Dunn, E. W., Aknin, L. B., & Norton, M. I. (2008). Spending money on others promotes happiness. *Science, 319*(5870), 1687–1688. doi:10.1126/science.1150952

Dunn, E. W., Gilbert, D. T., & Wilson, T. D. (2011). If money doesn't make you happy, then you probably aren't spending it right. *Journal of Consumer Psychology, 21*(2), 115– 125. doi:10.1016/j.jcps.2011.02.002

Dunn, E. W., Wilson, T. D., & Gilbert, D. T. (2003). Location, location, location: The misprediction of satisfaction in housing lotteries. *Personality and Social Psychology Bulletin, 29,* 1421–1432.

Dunn, M. S., Kitts, C., Lewis, S., Goodrow, B., & Scherzer, G. D. (2011). Effects of youth assets on adolescent alcohol, tobacco, marijuana use, and sexual behavior. *Journal of Alcohol and Drug Education, 55*(3), 23–40.

Dunning, D. (2006). Strangers to ourselves? *The Psychologist, 19*(10), 600–603.

Dunning, D., & Sherman, D. A. (1997). Stereotypes and tacit inference. *Journal of Personality and Social Psychology, 73*(3), 459–471.

Dunning, D., Heath, C., & Suls, J. M. (2004). Flawed self-assessment: Implications for health, education, and the workplace. *Psychological Science in the Public Interest, 5*(3), 69–106.

Dutton, J. E., & Ragins, B. R. (Eds.). (2007). *Exploring positive relationships at work: Building a theoretical and research foundation.* Mahwah, NJ: Erlbaum.

Dweck, C. S. (2007). Is math a gift? Beliefs that put females at risk. In S. J. Ceci & W. M. Williams (Eds.), *Why aren't more women in science?* (pp. 47–56). Washington, DC: American Psychological Association.

Dye, D. A., & Reck, M. (1989). College grade point average as a predictor of adult success: A reply. *Public Personnel Management, 18*(2), 239–240.

Dykstra, P. A., & Fokkema, T. (2007). Social and emotional loneliness among divorced and married men and women: Comparing the deficit and cognitive perspectives. *Basic and Applied Social Psychology, 29,* 1–12.

Eagly, A. H. (1987). *Sex differences in social behavior: A social-role interpretation*. Hillsdale, NJ: Erlbaum.

Eagly, A. H., Ashmore, R. D., Makhijani, M. G., & Longo, L. C. (1991). What is beautiful is good, but . . . : A meta-analytic review of research on the physical attractiveness stereotype. *Psychology Bulletin, 110,* 107–128.

Eagly, A. H., & Chaiken, S. (1998). Attitude structure and function. In D. T. Gilbert, S. T. Fiske, & G. Lindzey (Eds.), *Handbook of social psychology.* New York, NY: McGraw-Hill.

Eagly, A. H., & Sczesny, S. (2009). Stereotypes about women, men, and leaders: Have times changed? In M. Barreto, M. K. Ryan, & M. T. Schmitt (Eds.), *The glass ceiling in the 21st century: Understanding barriers to gender equality* (pp. 21–47). Washington, DC: American Psychological Association.

Eagly, A. H., & Wood, W. (1999). The origins of sex differences in human behavior: Evolved dispositions versus social roles. *American Psychologist, 54*(6), 408–423.

Eaker, E. D., Sullivan, L. M., Kelly-Hayes, M., D'Agostino, R. B., & Benjamin, E. J. (2004). Anger and hostility predict the development of atrial fibrillation in men in the Framingham Offspring Study. *Circulation, 109*(10), 1267–1271.

Easterbrook, J. A. (1959). The effect of emotion on cue utilization and the organization of behavior. *Psychological Review, 66,* 183–201.

Easterlin, B. L., & Cardena, E. (1999). Cognitive and emotional differences between short- and long-term Vipassana meditators. *Imagination, Cognition and Personality, 18*(1), 68–81.

Eastwick, P. W., & Finkel, E. J. (2008). The attachment system in fledgling relationships: An activating role for attachment anxiety. *Journal of Personality and Social Psychology, 95,* 628–647.

Eastwick, P. W., Finkel, E. J., Mochon, D., & Ariely, D. (2007). Selective versus unselective romantic desire: Not all reciprocity is created equal. *Psychological Science, 18,* 317–319.

Ebner, N. C., & Johnson, M. K. (2009). Young and older emotional faces: Are there age group differences in expression identification and memory? *Emotion, 9,* 329–339.

Ebstein, R. P. (2006). The molecular genetic architecture of human personality: Beyond self-report questionnaires. *Molecular Psychiatry, 11*(5), 427–445. doi:10.1038/sj.mp.400181

Eccles, J. S. (2001). Achievement. In J. Worrell (Ed.), *Encyclopedia of women and gender.* San Diego: Academic Press.

Eccles, J. S. (2007). Where are all the women? Gender differences in participation in physical science and engineering. In S. J. Ceci & W. M. Williams (Eds.), *Why aren't more women in science?* (pp. 199–210). Washington, DC: American Psychological Association.

Eckert, P., & McConnell-Ginet, S. (2003). *Language and gender.* Cambridge, UK: Cambridge University Press.

Edenfield, T. M., & Blumenthal, J. A. (2011). Exercise and stress reduction. In R. J. Contrada & A. Baum (Eds.), *The handbook of stress science: Biology, psychology, and health* (pp. 301–319). New York, NY: Springer.

Edwards, D. M., Hale, K. L., Maddux, R. E., & Rapaport, M. H. (2008). Anxiolytic drugs. In A. Tasman, J. Kay, J. A. Lieberman, M. B. First, & M. Maj (Eds.), *Psychiatry* (3rd ed.). New York, NY: Wiley-Blackwell.

Edwards, K., & Smith, E. E. (1996). A disconfirmation bias in the evaluation of arguments. *Journal of Personality and Social Psychology, 71,* 5–24.

Egeci, I. S., & Gençöz, T. (2006). Factors associated with relationship satisfaction: Importance of communication skills. *Contemporary Family Therapy: An International Journal, 28,* 383–391.

Ehrenberg, O., & Ehrenberg, M. (1994). *The psychotherapy maze: A consumer's guide to getting in and out of therapy.* Northvale, NJ: Jason Aronson.

Ehrenreich, H., Rinn, T., Kunert, H. J., Moeller, M. R., Poser, W., Schilling, L., Gigerenzer, G., &

Hoehe, M. R. (1999). Specific attentional dysfunction in adults following early start of cannabis use. *Psychopharmacology, 142,* 295–301.

Eich, E., Macaulay, D., Loewenstein, R. J., & Dihle, P. H. (1997). Memory, amnesia, and dissociative identity disorder. *Psychological Science, 8,* 417–422.

Einarsdóttir, S., & Rounds, J. (2009). Gender bias and construct validity in vocational interest measurement: Differential item functioning in the Strong Interest Inventory. *Journal of Vocational Behavior, 74*(3), 295–307. doi:10.1016/j.jvb.2009.01.003

Einstein, G. O., & McDaniel, M. A. (2004). *Memory fitness: A guide for successful aging.* New Haven, CT: Yale University Press.

Ekman, P. (1972). Universals and cultural differences in facial expressions of emotion. In J. Cole (Ed.), *Nebraska symposium on motivation, 1971.* Lincoln, NE: University of Nebraska Press.

Ekman, P. (1975, September). The universal smile: Face muscles talk every language. *Psychology Today,* pp. 35–39.

Ekman, P. (1994). Strong evidence for universals in facial expressions: A reply to Russell's mistaken critique. *Psychological Bulletin, 115,* 268–287.

Ekman, P. (2007). *Emotions revealed: Recognizing faces and feelings to improve communication and emotional life* (2nd ed.). New York, NY: Holt.

Ekman, P. (2009). *Telling lies: Clues to deceit in the marketplace, politics, and marriage* (Rev. ed.). New York, NY: Norton.

Ekman, P., & Friesen, W. V. (1984). *Unmasking the face.* Palo Alto, CA: Consulting Psychologists Press.

Ekman, P., & O'Sullivan, M. (1991). Who can catch a liar? *American Psychologist, 44*(9), 913–920.

Ekman, P., O'Sullivan, M., & Frank, M. G. (1999). A few can catch a liar. *Psychological Science, 10*(3), 263–266.

Eldridge, K. A. (2009). Conflict patterns. In H. T. Reis & S. Sprecher (Eds.), *Encyclopedia of human relationships: Vol. 1* (pp. 307–310). Los Angeles: Sage Reference Publication.

Eldridge, K. A., & Baucom, B. (2012). Demand-withdraw communication in couples. In P. Noller & G. C. Karantzas (Eds.), *The Wiley-Blackwell handbook of couples and family relationships* (pp. 144–158). Malden, MA: Wiley-Blackwell.

Elfenbein, H. A., & Ambady, N. (2002). Universals and cultural differences in recognizing emotions of a different cultural group. *Current Directions in Psychological Science, 12*(5), 159–164.

Ellemers, N., & Haslam, S. (2012). Social identity theory. In P. M. Van Lange, A. W. Kruglanski, & E. Higgins (Eds.), *Handbook of theories of social psychology* (Vol. 2, pp. 379–398). Thousand Oaks, CA: Sage Publications Ltd.

Ellington, L., & Wiebe, D. J. (1999). Neuroticism, symptom presentation, and medical decision making. *Health Psychology, 18*(6), 634–643.

Elliot, A. J., & Church, M. A. (2003). A motivational analysis of defensive pessimism and self-handicapping. *Journal of Personality, 71,* 369–393.

Ellis, A. (1973). *Humanistic psychotherapy: The rational-emotive approach.* New York, NY: Julian Press.

Ellis, A. (1977). *Reason and emotion in psychotherapy.* Seacaucus, NJ: Lyle Stuart.

Ellis, A. (1985). *How to live with and without anger.* New York, NY: Citadel Press.

Ellis, A. (1987). The evolution of rational-emotive therapy (RET) and cognitive behavior therapy (CBT). In J. K. Zeig (Ed.), *The evolution of psychotherapy.* New York, NY: Brunner/Mazel.

Ellis, A. (1989). Rational-emotive therapy. In R. J. Corsini & D. Wedding (Eds.), *Current Psychotherapies.* Itasca, IL: Peacock.

Ellis, A. (1993). The advantages and disadvantages of self-help therapy materials. *Professional Psychology: Research and Practice, 24,* 335–339.

Ellis, A. (1996). How I learned to help clients feel better and get better. *Psychotherapy, 33,* 149–151.

Ellis, A. (2001a). *Feeling better, getting better, staying better: Profound self-help therapy for your emotions.* Atascadero, CA: Impact Publishers.

Ellis, A. (2001b). *Overcoming destructive beliefs, feelings, and behaviors: New directions for Rational Emotive Behavior Therapy.* Amherst, NY: Prometheus Books.

Ellis, A., & Ellis, D. (2011). Rational emotive behavior therapy. Washington, DC: American Psychological Association.

Ellis, J. (2006, January 28). "IM-speak" struggle for teachers. *Statesboro Herald,* pp. 1A, 14A.

Ellison, N., Heino, R., & Gibbs, J. (2006). Managing impressions online: Self-presentation processes in the online dating environment. *Journal of Computer-Mediated Communication, 11,* 415–441.

Ellsworth, P. C., & Smith, C. A. (1988). Shades of joy: Patterns of appraisal differentiating pleasant emotions. *Cognition and Emotion, 2,* 301–331.

Else-Quest, N. M., Hyde, J. S., & Linn, M. C. (2010). Cross-national patterns of gender differences in mathematics: A meta-analysis. *Psychological Bulletin, 136,* 103–127.

Emanuel, H. M. (1987). Put time on your side. In A. D. Timpe (Ed.), *The management of time.* New York, NY: Facts On File.

Emavardhana, T., & Tori, C. D. (1997). Changes in self-concept, ego defense mechanisms, and religiosity following seven-day Vipassana meditation retreats. *Journal for the Scientific Study of Religion, 36,* 194–206.

Emmelkamp, P. M. G. (2004). In M. J. Lambert (Ed.), *Bergin and Garfield's handbook of psychotherapy and behavior change.* New York, NY: Wiley.

Emmons, R. A. (1999). *The psychology of ultimate concerns: Motivation and spirituality in personality.* New York, NY: Guilford.

Emmons, R. A. (2003). Personal goals, life meaning, and virtue: Wellsprings of a positive life. In C. L. M. Keyes & J. Haidt (Eds.), *Flourishing: Positive psychology and the life well-lived.* Washington, DC: American Psychological Association.

Emmons, R.A. (2005). Giving thanks: Psychological research on gratitude and praise. In C. L. Harper, Jr. (Ed.), *Spiritual information: 100 perspectives* (pp. 451–456). Philadelphia, PA: Templeton Foundation Press.

Emmons, R. A., & McCullough, M. E. (2003). Counting blessings versus burdens: Experimental studies of gratitude and subjective well-being in daily life. *Journal of Personality and Social Psychology, 84,* 377–389.

Emmons, R. A., & McCullough, M. E. (2004). *The psychology of gratitude.* New York, NY: Oxford.

Epel, E. S., Blackburn, E. H., Lin, J., Dhabhar, F. S., Adler, N. E., Morrow, J. D., & Cawthon, R. M. (2004). Accelerated telomere shortening in response to life stress. *Proceedings of the National Academy of Sciences, 101,* 17312–17315.

Epstein, R. (2001). Physiologist Laura. *Psychology Today, 34* (4), 5.

Epstein, R. (2007, February–March). The truth about online dating. *Scientific American Mind, 18,* pp. 28–35.

Equal Employment Opportunity Commission. (2007). *Occupational employment in private industry by race/ethnic group/sex, and by industry, United States, 2005.* Retrieved from http://www.eeoc.gov/stats/jobpat/2005/national.html.

Erikson, M. G. (2007). The meaning of the future: Toward a more specific definition of possible selves. *Review of General Psychology, 11*(4), 348–358.

Erol, R. Y., & Orth, U. (2011). Self-esteem development from age 14 to 30 years: A longitudinal study. *Journal of Personality and Social Psychology, 101* (3), 607–619. doi:10.1037/a0024299

Eschleman, K. J., Bowling, N. A., & Alarcon, G. M. (2010). A meta-analytic examination of hardiness. *International Journal of Stress Management, 17*(4), 277–307. doi:10.1037/a0020476

Eshbaugh, E. M., & Gute, G. (2008). Hookups and sexual regret among college women. *Journal of Social Psychology, 148,* 77–89.

Esping-Andersen, G. (2007). Sociological explanations of changing income distributions. *American Behavioral Scientist, 50,* 639–658.

Esterson, A. (2001). The mythologizing of psychoanalytic history: Deception and self-deception in Freud's accounts of the seduction theory episode. *History of Psychiatry, 7,* 329–352.

Estrada, M. (2012). Romantic communication in intimate relationships: The romantic construal model. In M. A. Paludi (Ed.), *The psychology of love* (pp. 125-139). Santa Barbara, CA: Praeger/ABC-CLIO.

Etzion, D. (2003). Annual vacation: Duration of relief from job stressors and burnout. *Anxiety, Stress, and Coping, 16,* 213-226.

Evans, D. C. (2003). A comparison of the other-directed stigmatization produced by legal and illegal forms of affirmative action. *Journal of Applied Psychology, 88,* 121-130.

Evans, G. W., Becker, F. D., Zahn, A., Bilotta, E., & Keesee, A. M. (2012). Capturing the ecology of workplace stress with cumulative risk assessment. *Environment and Behavior, 44*(1), 136-154. doi:10.1177/0013916510389981

Evans, G. W., Hygge, S., & Bullinger, M. (1995). Chronic noise and psychological stress. *Psychological Science, 6,* 333–338.

Evans, G. W., & Stecker, R. (2004). Motivational consequences of environmental stress. *Journal of Environmental Psychology, 24*(2), 143–165.

Evans, G. W., & Wener, R. E. (2007). Crowding and personal space invasion on the train: Please don't make me sit in the middle. *Journal of Environmental Psychology, 27,* 90–94. doi:10.1016/j.jenvp.2006.10.002

Everett, M. D., Kinser, A. M., & Ramsey, M. W. (2007). Training for old age: Production functions for the aerobic exercise inputs. *Medicine and Science in Sports and Exercise, 39,* 2226–2233.

Everson, S. A., Kauhanen, J., Kaplan, G. A., Goldberg, D. E., Julkunen, J., Tuomilehto, J., & Salonen, J. T. (1997). Hostility and increased risk of mortality and acute myocardial infarction: The mediating role of behavioral risk factors. *American Journal of Epidemiology, 146*(2), 142–152.

Exline, J. J., Baumeister, R. F., Bushman, B. J., Campbell, W. K., & Finkel, E. J. (2004). Too proud to let go: Narcissistic entitlement as a barrier to forgiveness. *Journal of Personality and Social Psychology, 87,* 894–912.

Eyal, K, & Finnerty, K. (2009). The portrayal of sexual intercourse on television: How, who, and with what consequence? *Mass Communication & Society, 12,* 143–169.

Eysenck, H. J. (1959). Learning theory and behaviour therapy. *Journal of Mental Science, 195,* 61–75.

Eysenck, H. J. (1967). *The biological basis of personality.* Springfield, IL: Charles C Thomas.

Eysenck, H. J. (1982). *Personality, genetics and behavior: Selected papers.* New York, NY: Praeger.

Eysenck, H. J. (1991). Dimensions of personality: 16, 5, or 3?—Criteria for a taxonomic paradigm. *Personality and Individual Differences, 12,* 773–790.

Eysenck, M. W., Mogg, K., May, J., Richards, A., & Mathews, A. (1991). Bias in interpretation of ambiguous sentences related to threat in anxiety. *Journal of Abnormal Psychology, 100,* 144–150.

Faber Taylor, A., & Kuo, F. E. (2009). Children with attention deficits concentrate better after walk in the park. *Journal of Attention Disorders, 12,* 402–409.

Fabes, R. A., Hanish, L. D., & Martin, C.L. (2003). Children at play: The role of peers in understanding the effects of child care. *Child Development, 74,* 1039–1043.

Facebook. (2011). Statistics. Retrieved from http://www.facebook.com/press/info.php?statistics

Fairbrother, K., & Warn, J. (2003). Workplace dimensions, stress, and job satisfaction. *Journal of Managerial Psychology, 18*(1), 8–21.

Fairburn, C. G., Cooper, Z., & Murphy, R. (2009). Bulimia nervosa. In M. C. Gelder, N. C. Andreasen, J. J. López-Ibor, Jr., & J. R. Geddes (Eds.), *New Oxford textbook of psychiatry* (2nd ed., Vol. 1). New York, NY: Oxford University Press.

Falk, P. (1994). The gap between psychological assumptions and empirical research in lesbian-mother child custody cases. In A. E. Gottfried & A. W. Gottfried (Eds.), *Redefining families: Implications for children's development.* New York, NY: Plenum.

Falsetti, S. A., & Ballenger, J. C. (1998). Stress and anxiety disorders. In J. R. Hubbard & E. A. Workman (Eds.), *Handbook of stress medicine: An organ system approach.* New York, NY: CRC Press.

Families and Work Institute. (2004). *Generation and gender in the workplace.* New York, NY: Families and Work Institute.

Fang, C., Miller, S., Bovbjerg, D., Bergman, C., Edelson, M., Rosenblum, N., et al. (2008). Perceived stress is associated with impaired T-cell response to HPV 16 in women with cervical dysplasia. *Annals of Behavioral Medicine, 35*(1), 87–96.

Faravelli, C., & Pallanti, S. (1989). Recent life events and panic disorders. *American Journal of Psychiatry, 146,* 622–626.

Fassler, D. (2001). *Talking to children about war and terrorism: 20 tips for parents.* Retrieved November 20, 2001 from American Psychiatric Association Web site: http://www.psych.org/disaster/20tipsparents11801.cfm.

Fatemi, S., & Folsom, T. D. (2009). The neurodevelopmental hypothesis of schizophrenia, revisited. *Schizophrenia Bulletin, 35*(3), 528–548. doi:10.1093/schbul/sbn187

Faulenbach, M., Uthoff, H., Schwegler, K., Spinas, G. A., Schmid, C., & Wiesli, P. (2011). Effect of psychological stress on glucose control in patients with Type 2 diabetes [Short report: Care delivery]. *Diabetic Medicine, 29,* 128–131.

Fausto-Sterling, A. (1992). *Myths of gender: Biological theories about women and men* (2nd ed.). New York, NY: Basic Books.

Fava, G. A., & Sonino, N. (2008). The biopsychosocial model thirty years later. *Journal of Psychotherapy and Psychosomatics, 77,* 1–2.

Fava, G. A., & Tomba, E. (2009). Increasing psychological well-being and resilience by psychotherapeutic methods. *Journal of Personality, 77*(6), 1903–1934. doi:10.1111/j.1467-6494.2009.00604.x

Federal Bureau of Investigation. (2011). Hate Crime Statistics, 2010. http://www.fbi.gov/about-us/cjis/ucr/hate-crime/2010/narratives/hate-crime-2010-victims

Feeney, J. A. (2004). Adult attachment and relationship functioning under stressful conditions: Understanding partners' responses to conflict and challenge. In W. S. Rholes & J. A. Simpson (Eds.), *Adult attachment: Theory, research, and clinical implications.* New York, NY: Guilford.

Feeney, J. A., & Noller, P. (1990). Attachment style as a predictor of adult romantic relationships. *Journal of Personality and Social Psychology, 58,* 281–291.

Feeny, N. C., Stines, L. R., & Foa, E. B. (2007). Post-traumatic stress disorder-clinical. In G. Fink (Ed.), *Encyclopedia of stress: Vols. 1–4* (2nd ed., pp. 135–139). San Diego, CA: Elsevier Academic Press.

Fehr, B. (1996). *Friendship processes.* Thousand Oaks, CA: Sage.

Fehr, B. (2000). The life cycle of friendship. In C. Hendrick & S. S. Hendrick (Eds.), *Close relationships: A sourcebook.* Thousand Oaks, CA: Sage.

Fehr, B. (2004). Intimacy expectations in same-sex friendships: A prototype interaction-pattern model. *Journal of Personality and Social Psychology, 86*(2), 265–284.

Fehr, B. (2008). Friendship formation. In S. Sprecher, A. Wenzel & J. Harvey (Eds.), *Handbook of relationship initiation* (pp. 29–54). New York, NY: Psychology Press.

Fehr, B. (2009). Friendship formation and development. In H. T. Reis & S. Sprecher (Eds.), *Encyclopedia of human relationships: Vol. 1* (pp. 706–710). Los Angeles: Sage Reference Publication.

Fein, S. (1996). Effects of suspicion on attributional thinking and the correspondence bias. *Journal of Personality and Social Psychology, 70,* 1164–1184.

Feingold, A. (1988). Matching for attractiveness in romantic partners and same-sex friends: A meta-analysis and theoretical critique. *Psychological Bulletin, 104,* 226–235.

Feingold, A. (1992a). Gender differences in mate selection preferences: A test of the parental investment model. *Psychological Bulletin, 112,* 125–139.

Feingold, A. (1992b). Good-looking people are not what we think. *Psychological Bulletin, 111,* 304–341.

Feldman, P. J., Cohen, S., Doyle, W. J., Skoner, D. P., & Gwaltney, J. M., Jr. (1999). The impact of personality on the reporting of unfounded symptoms and illness. *Journal of Personality and Social Psychology, 77*(2), 370–378.

Feldman-Barrett, L., & Swim, J. K. (1998). Appraisals of prejudice and discrimination. In J. K. Swim & C. Stangor (Eds.), *Prejudice: The target's perspective.* New York, NY: Academic Press.

Feliciano, L., & Areán, P. A. (2007). Mood disorders: Depressive disorders. In M. Hersen, S. M. Turner, & D. C. Beidel (Eds.), *Adult psychopathology and diagnosis.* New York, NY: Wiley.

Felmlee, D. H., Hilton, K., & Orzechowicz, D. (2012). Romantic attraction and stereotypes of gender and sexuality. In M. A. Paludi (Ed.), *The psychology of love* (pp. 171-186). Santa Barbara, CA: Praeger/ABC-CLIO.

Felmlee, D. H., Sprecher, S., & Bassin, E. (1990). The dissolution of intimate relationships: A hazard model. *Social Psychology Quarterly,* 513–30.

Felson, R. B. (1989). Parents and the reflected appraisal process: A longitudinal analysis. *Journal of Personality and Social Psychology, 56,* 965–971.

Felson, R. B. (1992). Coming to see ourselves: Social sources of self-appraisals. *Advances in Group Processes, 9,* 185–205.

Feng, B., & MacGeorge, E. L. (2010). The influences of message and source factors on advice outcomes. *Communication Research, 37*(4), 553–575. doi:10.1177/0093650210368258

Feng, J., Spence, I., & Pratt, J. (2007). Playing an action video game reduces gender differences in spatial cognition. *Psychological Science, 18,* 850–855.

Ferguson, J. Bauld, L., Chesterson, J., & Judge, K. (2005). The English smoking treatment services: One-year outcomes. *Addiction, 100* (Suppl. 2), 59–69.

Ferrari, J. R. (1992). Psychometric validation of two adult measures of procrastination: Arousal and avoidance measures. *Journal of Psychopathology & Behavioral Assessment, 14,* 97–100.

Ferrari, J. R. (2001). Getting things done on time: Conquering procrastination. In C. R. Snyder (Ed.), *Coping with stress: Effective people and processes.* New York, NY: Oxford University Press.

Ferrari, J. R., Diaz-Morales, J. F., O'Callaghan, J., Diaz, K., & Argumedo, D. (2007). Frequent behavioral delay tendencies by adults: International prevalence rates of chronic procrastination. *Journal of Cross-Cultural Psychology, 38,* 458–464.

Ferrari, J. R., Johnson, J. L., & McCown, W. G. (1995). *Procrastination and task avoidance: Theory research and treatment.* New York, NY: Plenum Press.

Ferrer, R. A., Klein, W. P., Zajac, L. E., Sutton-Tyrrell, K., Muldoon, M. F., & Kamarck, T. W. (2012). Unrealistic optimism is associated with subclinical atherosclerosis. *Health Psychology, 31*(6), 815–820. doi:10.1037/a0027675

Festinger, L. (1954). A theory of social comparison processes. *Human Relations, 7,* 117–140.

Flfleld, J., Mcquillian, J., Armeli, S., Tennen, H., Reisine, S., & Affleck, G. (2004). Chronic strain, daily work stress and pain among workers with rheumatoid arthritis: Does job stress make a bad day worse? *Work and Stress, 18,* 275–291.

Figueredo, A. J., Gladden, P., Vásquez, G., Wolf, P. S. A., & Jones, D. N. (2009). Evolutionary theories of personality. In P. J. Corr & G. Matthews (Eds.), *The Cambridge handbook of personality psychology* (pp. 265–274). New York, NY: Cambridge University Press.

Figueredo, A. J., Sefcek, J. A., Vasquez, G., Brumbach, B. H., King, J. E., & Jacobs, W. J. (2005). Evolutionary personality psychology. In D. M. Buss (Ed.), *The handbook of evolutionary psychology.* New York, NY: Wiley.

Finan, P. H., Zautra, A. J., & Wershba, R. (2011). The Dynamics of emotion in adaptation to stress. In R. J. Contrada & A. Baum (Eds.), *The handbook of stress science: Biology, psychology, and health* (pp. 209-220). New York, NY: Springer.

Fincham, F. D. (2001). Attributions in close relationships: From Balkanization to integration. In G. J. O. Fletcher, & M. S. Clark (Eds.), *Blackwell handbook of social psychology: Vol. 2. Interpersonal processes.* Oxford: Blackwell.

Fincham, F. D. (2003). Marital conflict: Correlates, structure, and context. *Current Directions in Psychological Science, 12*(1), 23–27.

Fincham, F. D. (2009). Conflict, marital. In H. T. Reis & S. Sprecher (Eds.), *Encyclopedia of human relationships: Vol. 2* (pp. 298–303). Los Angeles: Sage Reference Publication.

Fincham, F. D., & Beach, S. R. H. (2006). Relationship satisfaction. In A. L. Vangelisti & D. Perlman (Eds.), *The Cambridge handbook of personal relationships.* New York, NY: Cambridge University Press.

Finder, A. (2006, June 11). For some, online persona undermines a resume. *New York Times.* Retrieved from http://www.nytimes.com/2006/06/11/us/11recruit.hyml

Fine, C. (2010). From scanner to sound bite: Issues in interpreting and reporting sex differences in the brain. *Current Directions in Psychological Science, 19*(5), 280–283. doi:10.1177/0963721410383248

Fingerhut, A. W. (2011). Straight allies: What predicts heterosexuals' alliance with the LGBT community? *Journal of Applied Social Psychology, 41*(9), 2230–2248. doi:10.1111/j.1559-1816.2011.00807.x

Fingerhut, A. W., Riggle, E. B., & Rostosky, S. (2011). Same-sex marriage: The social and psychological implications of policy and debates. *Journal of Social Issues, 67*(2), 225–241. doi:10.1111/j.1540-4560.2011.01695.x

Fink, M. F. (2009). Nonpharmacological somatic treatments: Electroconvulsive therapy. In M. C. Gelder, N. C. Andreasen, J. J. López-Ibor, Jr., & J. R. Geddes (Eds.), *New Oxford textbook of psychiatry* (2nd ed., Vol. 1). New York, NY: Oxford University Press.

Finkel, E. J., Eastwick, P. W., Karney, B. R., Reis, H. T., & Sprecher, S. (2012). Online dating: A critical analysis from the perspective of psychological science. *Psychological Science in the Public Interest, 13*(1), 3–66. doi:10.1177/1529100612436522

Finkelstein, E. A., Ruhm, C. J., & Kosa, K. M. (2005). Economic causes and consequences of obesity. *Annual Review of Public Health, 26*, 239–257.

Finkenauer, C., & Hazam, H. (2000). Disclosure and secrecy in marriage: Do both contribute to marital satisfaction? *Journal of Social and Personal Relationships, 17*(2), 245–263.

Finucane, M. L., Alhakami, A. S., Slovic, P. & Johnson, S. M. (2000). The affect heuristic in judgments of risks and benefits. *Journal of Behavioral Decision Making, 13*, 1–17.

First, M. B. (2008). Psychiatric classification. In A. Tasman, J. Kay, J. A. Lieberman, M. B. First, & M. Maj (Eds.), *Psychiatry* (3rd ed.). New York, NY: Wiley-Blackwell.

Fischer, P., Greitemeyer, T., & Pollozek, F. (2006). The unresponsive bystander: Are bystanders more responsive in dangerous emergencies? *European Journal of Social Psychology, 36*, 267–278.

Fischer, P., Krueger, J. I., Greitemeyer, T., Vogrincic, C., Kastenmüller, A., Frey, D., & . . . Kainbacher, M. (2011). The bystander-effect: A meta-analytic review on bystander intervention in dangerous and non-dangerous emergencies. *Psychological Bulletin, 137*(4), 517–537. doi:10.1037/a0023304

Fischer, R., Ferreira, M. C., Assmar, E., Redford, P., Harb, C., Glazer, S., Cheng, B.-S., Jiang, D.-Y., Wong, C. C., Kumar, N., Kärtner, J., Hofer, J., & Achoui, M. (2009). Individualism-collectivism as descriptive norms: Development of a subjective norm approach to cultural measurement. *Journal of Cross-Cultural Psychology, 40*(2), 187–213.

Fisher, D. A., Hill, D. L., Grube, J. W., Bersamine, M. M., Walker, S., & Gruber, E. L. (2009). Televised sexual content and parental mediation: Influences on adolescent sexuality. *Media Psychology, 12*, 121–147.

Fisher, T. D. (1990). Characteristics of mothers and fathers who talk to their adolescent children about sexuality. *Journals of Psychology & Human Sexuality, 3*, 53–70.

Fishman, D. B. (2007). Seeking an equal place at the therapy research table: An introduction to a series on the pragmatic case study method. *Pragmatic Case Studies in Psychotherapy, 3*(1), 1–5.

Fishman, D. B., Rego, S. A., & Muller, K. L. (2011). Behavioral theories of psychotherapy. In J. C. Norcross, G. R. Vandenbos, & D. K. Freedheim (Eds.), *History of psychotherapy: Continuity and change* (2nd ed.). Washington, DC: American Psychological Association.

Fiske, S. T. (1993). Social cognition and social perception. *Annual Review of Psychology, 44*, 155–194.

Fiske, S. T. (1998). Stereotyping, prejudice, and discrimination. In D. T. Gilbert, S. T. Fiske, & G. Lindzey (Eds.), *The handbook of social psychology.* New York, NY: McGraw-Hill.

Fiske, S. T. (2002). What we know now about bias and intergroup conflict, the problem of the century. *Current Directions in Psychological Science, 11*(4), 123–128.

Fiske, S. T. (2004). *Social beings: A core motives approach to social psychology.* New York, NY: Wiley.

Fiske, S. T., Harris, L. T., & Cuddy, A. J. C. (2004). Why ordinary people torture enemy prisoners. *Science, 36*, 1482–1483.

Fiske, S. T., & Ruscher, J. B. (1993). Negative interdependence and prejudice: Whence the affect? In D. M. Mackie & D. L. Hamilton (Eds.), *Affect, cognition, and stereotyping: Interactive processes in group perception.* New York, NY: Academic.

Fiske, S. T., & Taylor, S. E. (1991). *Social cognition.* New York, NY: McGraw-Hill.

Fitness, J., Fletcher, G., & Overall, N. (2007). Interpersonal attraction and intimate relationships. In M. A. Hogg & J. Cooper (Eds.), *The Sage handbook of social psychology.* Los Angeles: Sage.

Flaks, D. K., Ficher, I., Masterpasqua, M., & Joseph, G. (1995). Lesbians choosing motherhood: A comparative study of lesbians and heterosexual parents and their children. *Developmental Psychology, 31*, 105–114.

Fletcher, G. J. O. (2002). *The new science of intimate relationships.* Malden, MA: Blackwell. doi:10.1002/9780470773390

Fletcher, G. J. O., Overall, N. C., & Friesen, M. D. (2006). Social cognition in intimate relationships. In A. L. Vangelisti & D. Perlman (Eds.), *The Cambridge handbook of personal relationships.* New York, NY: Cambridge University Press.

Fletcher, G. J. O., Tither, J. M., O'Loughlin, C., Friesen, M., & Overall, N. (2004). Warm and homely or cold and beautiful? Sex differences in trading off traits in mate selection. *Personality and Social Psychology Bulletin, 30*, 659–672.

Fletcher, G. J. O., & Ward, C. (1988). Attribution theory and processes: A cross-cultural perspective. In M. H. Bond (Ed.), *The cross-cultural challenge to social psychology.* Newbury Park, CA: Sage.

Flett, G. L., Hewitt, P. L., & Martin, T. R. (1995). Dimensions of perfectionism and procrastination. In J. R. Ferrari, J. L. Johnson, & W. G. McCown (Eds.), *Procrastination and task avoidance: Theory, research, and treatment.* New York, NY: Plenum Press.

Floyd, F. J., & Bakeman, R. (2006). Coming-out across the life course: Implications of age and historical context. *Archives of Sexual Behavior, 35*, 287–297.

Floyd, K., Boren, J. P., Hannawa, A. F., Hesse, C., McEwan, B., & Veksler, A. E. (2009). Kissing in marital and cohabiting relationships: Effects on blood lipids, stress, and relationship satisfaction. *Western Journal of Communication, 73*, 113–133.

Floyd, M. (2003). Bibliotherapy as an adjunct to psychotherapy for depression in older adults. *Journal of Clinical Psychology, 59*(2), 187–195.

Flynn, B. S., Worden, J. K., Bunn, J., Connolly, S. W., & Dorwaldt, A. L. (2011). Evaluation of smoking prevention television messages based on the elaboration likelihood model. *Health Education Research, 26*(6), 976–987. doi:10.1093/her/cyr082

Flynn, F. J., Reagans, R. E., Amanatullah, E. T., & Ames, D. R. (2006). Helping one's way to the top: Self-monitors achieve status by helping others and knowing who helps whom. *Journal of Personality and Social Psychology, 91*, 1123–1137.

Foa, E. B. (1998). Rape and posttraumatic stress disorder. In E. A. Blechman & K. D. Brownell (Eds.), *Behavioral medicine and women: A comprehensive handbook.* New York, NY: Guilford Press.

Folkman, S. (2008). The case for positive emotions in the stress process. *Anxiety, Stress, Coping, 21*, 3–14.

Folkman, S. (2011). Stress, health, and coping: Synthesis, commentary, and future directions. In S. Folkman (Ed.). *The Oxford handbook of stress, health, & coping.* (pp. 453–462). New York, NY: Oxford University Press.

Folkman, S., Moskowitz, J. T., Ozer, E. M., & Park, C. L. (1997). Positive meaningful events and coping in the context of HIV/AIDS. In B. H. Gottlieb (Ed.), *Coping with chronic stress.* New York, NY: Plenum.

Follette, W. C., & Davis, D. (2009). Clinical practice and the issue of repressed memories on an ice patch on the slippery slope. In W. O'Donohue & S. R. Graybar (Eds.), *Handbook of contemporary psychotherapy: Toward an improved understanding of effective psychotherapy* (pp. 47–73). Thousand Oaks, CA: Sage.

Food and Agriculture Organization of the United Nations. (2006). Livestock's long shadow: Environmental issues and options. Retrieved from http://www.fao.org/docrep/010/a0701e/a0701e00.HTM

Foran, H., & O'Leary, K. (2008). Problem drinking, jealousy, and anger control: Variables predicting physical aggression against a partner. *Journal of Family Violence, 23*, 141–148.

Forest, A. L., & Wood, J. V. (2012). When social networking is not working: Individuals with low self-esteem recognize but do not reap the benefits of self-disclosure on Facebook. *Psychological Science, 23*(3), 295–302. doi:10.1177/0956797611429709

Forgas, J. P. (2011). Can negative affect eliminate the power of first impressions? Affective influences on primacy and recency effects in impression formation. *Journal of Experimental Social Psychology, 47*(2), 425-429. doi:10.1016/j.jesp.2010.11.005

Forgas, J. P., & Williams, K. D. (Eds.). (2002). *The social self: Cognitive, interpersonal, and intergroup perspectives.* New York, NY: Psychology Press.

Forgas, J. P., Baumeister, R. F., & Tice, D. M. (2009). The psychology of self-regulation: An introductory review. In J. P. Forgas, R. F. Baumeister, D. M. Tice (Eds.), *Psychology of self-regulation: Cognitive, affective, and motivational processes* (pp. 1–17). New York, NY: Psychology Press.

Forgeard, M. C. (2011). Happy people thrive on adversity: Pre-existing mood moderates the effect of emotion inductions on creative thinking. *Personality and Individual Differences, 51*(8), 904–909. doi:10.1016/j.paid.2011.07.015

Forsyth, D. R., Lawrence, N. K., Burnette, J. L., & Baumeister, R. F. (2007). Attempting to improve the academic performance of struggling college students by bolstering self-esteem: An intervention that backfired. *Journal of Social and Clinical Psychology, 26*, 447–459.

Forsyth, D. R., & Strong, S. R. (1986). The scientific study of counseling and psychotherapy: A unificationist view. *American Psychologist, 41*, 113–119.

Fortenberry, J. D., Schick, V., Herbenick, D., Sanders, S. A., Dodge, B., & Reece, M. (2010). Sexual behaviors and condom use at last vaginal intercourse: A national sample of adolescents ages 14 to 17 years. *Journal of Sexual Medicine, 7*(5), 305–314.

Fortune, E. E., & Goodie, A. S. (2010). The relationship between pathological gambling and sensation seeking: The role of subscale scores. *Journal of Gambling Studies, 26*, 331–346. doi:10.1007/s10899-009-9162-8

Fortune, J. L., & Newby-Clark, I. R. (2008). My friend is embarrassing me: Exploring the guilty by association effect. *Journal of Personality and Social Psychology, 95*(6), 1440–1449.

Fouad, N. A. (2007). Work and vocational psychology: Theory, Research, and applications. *Annual Review of Psychology, 58*, 543–564.

Fouad, N. A., & Mohler, C. J. (2004). Cultural validity of Holland's theory and the Strong Interest Inventory for five racial/ethnic groups. *Journal of Career Assessment, 12*, 423–439.

Fouad, N. A., & Walker, C. M. (2005). Cultural influences on responses to items on the Strong Interest Inventory. *Journal of Vocational Behavior, 66*(1), 104–123. doi:10.1016/j.jvb.2003.12.001

Fournier, J. C., DeRubeis, R. J., Hollon, S. D., Dimidjian, S., Amsterdam, J. D., Shelton, R. C., & Fawcett, J. (2010). Antidepressant drug effects and depression severity: A patient-level meta-analysis. *Journal of the American Medical Association, 303*(1), 47–53.

Fowers, B. J. (2000). *Beyond the myth of marital happiness: How embracing the virtues of loyalty, generosity, justice, and courage can strengthen your relationship.* San Francisco: Jossey-Bass.

Fowers, B. J., Applegate, B., Olson, D. H., & Pomerantz, B. (1994). Marital conventionalization as a measure of marital satisfaction: A confirmatory factor analysis. *Journal of Family Psychology, 8*, 98–103.

Fox, G. L., & Chancey, D. (1998). Sources of economic distress: Individual and family outcomes. *Journal of Family Issues, 19*, 725–749.

Fox, G. L., Bruce, C., & Combs-Orme, T. (2000). Parenting expectations and concerns of fathers and mothers of newborn infants. *Family Relations, 49*(2), 123–131.

Fraley, R. C. (2002). Attachment stability from infancy to adulthood: Meta-analysis and dynamic modeling of developmental mechanisms. *Personality and Social Psychology Review, 6*(2), 123–151.

Fraley, R., & Shaver, P. R. (2000). Adult romantic attachment: Theoretical developments, emerging controversies, and unanswered questions. *Review of General Psychology, 4*(2), 132–154. doi:10.1037/1089-2680.4.2.132

Frame, L. E., Mattson, R. E., & Johnson, M. D. (2009). Predicting success or failure of marital relationships. In H. T. Reis & S. Sprecher (Eds.), *Encyclopedia of human relationships: Vol. 3* (pp. 1275–1279). Los Angeles: Sage Reference Publication.

Francis, L. A., & Birch, L. L. (2005). Maternal influences on daughters' restrained eating behavior. *Health Psychology, 24*, 548–554.

Francoeur, R. T. (2007). Catholic culture and sexual health. In M. S. Tepper & A. F. Owens (Eds.), *Sexual health: Vol 3. Moral and cultural foundations* (pp. 43–77). Westport, CT: Praeger Publishers/Greenwood Publishing Group.

Frank, J. D. (1961). *Persuasion and healing.* Baltimore: John Hopkins University Press.

Frank, L. R. (1990). Electroshock: Death, brain damage, memory loss, and brainwashing. *The Journal of Mind and Behavior, 11*, 489–512.

Frank, M. G., & Ekman, P. (1997). The ability to detect deceit generalizes different types of high-stake lies. *Journal of Personality and Social Psychology, 72*, 1429–1439.

Franko, D. L., & Roehrig, J. P. (2011). African American body images. In T. F. Cash & L. Smolak (Eds.), *Body image: A handbook of science, practice, and prevention* (2nd ed., pp. 221–228). New York, NY: Guilford Press.

Franzoi, S. L., & Kern, K. (2009). Body image, relationship implications. In H. T. Reis & S. Sprecher (Eds.), *Encyclopedia of human relationships: Vol. 1* (pp. 181–183). Los Angeles: Sage Reference Publication.

Frazier, P. A. (2009). Rape. In H. T. Reis & S. Sprecher (Eds.), *Encyclopedia of human relationships: Vol. 3* (pp. 1325–1328). Los Angeles: Sage Reference Publication.

Frederick, S., & Loewenstein, G. (1999). Hedonic adaptation. In D. Kahneman, E. Diener, & N. Schwarz (Eds.), *Well-being: The foundations of hedonic psychology.* New York, NY: Sage.

Fredrickson, B. L. (1998). What good are positive emotions? *Review of General Psychology, 2*, 300–319.

Fredrickson, B. L. (2002). Positive emotions. In C. R. Snyder & S. J. Lopez (Eds.), *Handbook of positive psychology* (pp. 120–134). New York, NY: Oxford University Press.

Fredrickson, B. L. (2006). The broaden-and-build theory of positive emotions. In M. Csikszentmihalyi & I. S. Csikszentmihalyi (Eds.), *A life worth living: Contributions to positive psychology.* New York, NY: Oxford University Press.

Fredrickson, B. L. (2007). The broaden-and-build theory of positive emotions. In F. Huppert, N. Baylis, & B. Keverne (Eds.), *The science of well-being* (pp. 217–240). New York, NY: Oxford University Press.

Fredrickson, B. L., & Branigan, C. (2005). Positive emotions broaden the scope of attention and thought-action repertoires. *Cognition and Emotion, 19*, 313–332.

Fredrickson, B. L., & Joiner, T. (2002). Positive emotions trigger upward spirals toward emotional well-being. *Psychological Science, 13*, 172–175.

Fredrickson, B. L., & Levenson, R. (1998). Positive emotions speed recovery from the cardiovascular sequelae of negative emotions. *Cognition and Emotion, 12*, 191–220.

Fredrickson, B. L., & Losada, M. F. (2005). Positive affect and the complex dynamics of human flourishing. *American Psychologist, 60*, 678–686.

Fredrickson, B. L., Roberts, T., Noll, S. M., Quinn, D. M., & Twenge, J. M. (1998). That swimsuit becomes you: Sex differences in self-objectification, restrained eating, and math performance. *Journal of Personality and Social Psychology, 75*, 269–284.

Fredrickson, B. L., Tugade, M. M., Waugh, C. E., & Larkin, G. R. (2003). What good are positive emotions in crises? A prospective study of resilience and emotions following the terrorist attacks on the United States on September 11th, 2001. *Journal of Personality and Social Psychology, 84*(2), 365–376.

Freedberg, K., Losina, E., Weinstein, M., Paltiel, A., Cohen, C., Seage, G., Craven, D., Zhang, H., Kimmel, A., & Goldie, S. (2001). The cost effectiveness of combination antiretroviral therapy for HIV disease. *New England Journal of Medicine*, 824–831.

Freedman, J. L., & Fraser, S. C. (1966). Compliance without pressure: The foot-in-the-door technique. *Journal of Personality and Social Psychology, 4*, 195–202.

Freeman, D., Aquino, K., & McFerran, B. (2009). Overcoming beneficiary race as an impediment to charitable donations: Social Dominance Orientation, the experience of moral elevation, and donation behavior. *Personality and Social Psychology Bulletin, 35*(1), 72–84.

Freeman, N. K. (2007). Preschoolers' perceptions of gender appropriate toys and their parents' beliefs about genderized behaviors: Miscommunication, mixed messages, or hidden truths? *Early Childhood Education Journal, 34*, 357–366.

Fremouw, W. J., de Perczel, M., & Ellis, T. F. (1990). *Suicide risk: Assessment and response guidelines.* New York, NY: Pergamon.

French, S. A., Harnack, L., & Jeffrey, R. W. (2000). Fast food restaurant use among women in the Pound of Prevention study: Dietary, behavioral and demographic correlates. *International Journal of Obesity, 24*, 1353–1359.

Freud, A. (1936). *The ego and the mechanisms of defense.* London: Hogarth Press and Institute of Psycho-Analysis.

Freud, S. (1920/1924). *A general introduction to psychoanalysis.* New York: Boni and Liveright. (Original work published 1920)

Freud, S. (1923). The ego and the id. In J. Strachey (Ed., Trans.), *The standard edition of the complete psychological works of Sigmund Freud* (Vol. 19). London: Hogarth.

Freud, S. (1901/1960). *The psychopathology of everyday life* (Standard ed., Vol. 6.) London: Hogarth. (Original work published 1901)

Freud, S. (1910/1957). Leonardo da Vinci: A study in psychosexuality. In J. Strachey (Ed., Trans.), *The standard edition of the complete psychological works of Sigmund Freud* (Vol. 11). London: Hogarth Press. (First German edition, 1910)

Freud, S. (1961). The ego and the id. In J. Strachey (Ed., Trans.), *The standard edition of the complete psychological works of Sigmund Freud* (Volume 19, pp. 13–27). London: Hogarth Press and the Institute of Psychoanalysis. (Original work published 1923)

Frewen, P. A., Brinker, J., Martin, R. A., & Dozois, D. J. A. (2008). Humor styles and personality-vulnerability to depression. *Humor, 21*, 179–195.

Friedan, B. (1964). *The feminine mystique.* New York, NY: Dell.

Friedman, H. L., & Robbins, B. (2012). The negative shadow cast by positive psychology: Contrasting views and implications of humanistic and positive psychology on resiliency. *The Humanistic Psychologist, 40*(1), 87–102. doi:10.1080/08873267.2012.643720

Friedman, H. S. (1991). *The self-healing personality: Why some people achieve health and others succumb to illness.* New York, NY: Holt.

Friedman, H. S. (2007). Personality, disease, and self-healing. In H. S. Friedman & R. C. Silver (Eds.), *Foundations of health psychology.* New York, NY: Oxford University Press.

Friedman, H. S., & Adler, N. E. (2007). The history and background of health psychology. In H. S. Friedman & R. C. Silver (Eds.), *Foundations of health psychology.* New York, NY: Oxford University Press.

Friedman, H. S., & Martin, L. R. (2011). *The longevity project: Surprising discoveries for health and long life from the landmark eight-decade study.* New York, NY: Hudson Street Press/Penguin Group USA.

Friedman, H. S., & Silver, R. C. (Eds.). (2007). *Foundations of health psychology.* New York, NY: Oxford University Press.

Friedman, M. (1996). *Type A behavior: Its diagnosis and treatment.* New York, NY: Plenum Press.

Friedman, M., & Rosenman, R. F. (1974). *Type A behavior and your heart.* New York, NY: Knopf.

Frieze, I. H., & Ciccocioppo, M. (2009). Gender-role attitudes. In H. T. Reis & S. Sprecher (Eds.), *Encyclopedia of human relationships: Vol. 1* (pp. 751–754). Los Angeles: Sage Reference Publication.

Frieze, I. H., & Yu Li, M. (2010.) Gender, aggression, and prosocial behavior. In J. C. Chrisler & D. R. McCreary (Eds.), *Handbook of gender research in psychology* (Vol. 2, pp. 311–335). New York, NY: Springer.

Frijda, N. H. (1986). *The emotions.* Cambridge: Cambridge University Press.

Fritze, J. G., Blashki, G. A., Burke, S. and Wiseman, J. (2008). Hope, despair and transformation: Climate change and the promotion of mental health and well-being. *International Journal of Mental Health Systems, 2*.

Froh, J. J. (2009). Positive emotions. In S. J. Lopez (Ed.), *The encyclopedia of positive psychology* (Vol. II, pp. 711–717). Malden, MA: Wiley-Blackwell.

Fruhauf, C. A. (2009). Caregiver role. In H. T. Reis & S. Sprecher (Eds.), *Encyclopedia of human relationships: Vol. 2* (pp. 195–197). Los Angeles: Sage Reference Publication.

Frumkin, H. (2001). Beyond toxicity: Human health and the natural environment. *American Journal of Preventive Medicine, 20*, 234–240.

Fu, X., & Heaton, T. B. (2008). Racial and educational homogamy: 1980 to 2000. *Sociological Perspectives, 51*, 735–758.

Fuertes, J. N., Mislowack, A., Bennett, J., Paul, L., Gilbert, T. C., Fontan, G., et al. (2007). The physician-patient working alliance. *Patient Education and Counseling, 66*, 29–36.

Fuglestad, P. T., & Snyder, M. (2009). Self-monitoring. In M. R. Leary & R. H. Hoyle (Eds.), *Handbook of individual differences in social behavior* (pp. 574–591). New York, NY: Guilford Press.

Fuglestad, P. T., & Snyder, M. (2010). Status and the motivational foundations of self-monitoring. *Social and Personality Psychology Compass, 4*(11), 1031–1041. doi:10.1111/j.1751-9004.2010.00311.x

Fullana, M. A., Mataix-Cols, D., Caspi, A., Harrington, H., Grisham, J. R., Moffitt, T. E., & Poulton, R. (2009). Obsessions and compulsions in the community: Prevalence, interference, help-seeking, developmental stability, and co-occurring psychiatric conditions. *American Journal of Psychiatry, 166*(3), 329–336. doi:10.1176/appi.ajp.2008.08071006

Fuller-Rowell, T. E., Evans, G. W., & Ong, A. D. (2012). Poverty and health: The mediating role of social class discrimination. *Psychological Science, 23,* 734–739.

Funder, D. C. (2009). Persons, behaviors and situations: An agenda for personality psychology in the postwar era. *Journal of Research in Personality, 43,* 120–126. doi:10.1016/j.jrp.2008.12.041

Furnham, A., & Cheng, H. (2000). Perceived parental behavior, self-esteem and happiness. *Social Psychiatry and Psychiatric Epidemiology, 35*(10), 463–470.

Furnham, A., McManus, C., & Scott, D. (2004). Personality, empathy, and attitudes to animal welfare. *Anthrozoos, 16,* 135–146.

Furstenberg, F. F., Jr. (2001). The sociology of adolescence and youth in the 1990s: A critical commentary. In R. M. Milardo (Ed.), *Understanding families into the new millennium: A decade in review.* Minneapolis, MN: National Council on Family Relations.

Fyer, A. J. (2009). Anxiety disorders: Genetics. In B. J. Sadock, V. A. Sadock, & P. Ruiz (Eds.), *Kaplan & Sadock's comprehensive textbook of psychiatry* (pp. 1898–1905). Philadelphia: Lippincott Williams & Wilkins.

Gabbard, G. O. (1994). Reconsidering the American Psychological Association's policy on sex with former patients: Is it justifiable? *Professional Psychology: Research and Practice, 25,* 329–335.

Gable, S. L., Gonzaga, G. C., & Strachman, A. (2006). Will you be there for me when things go right? Supportive responses to positive event disclosures. *Journal of Personality and Social Psychology, 91,* 904–917.

Gable, S. L., Reis, H. T., Impett, E. A., & Asher, E. R. (2004). What do you do when things go right? The intrapersonal and interpersonal benefits of sharing positive events. *Journal of Personality and Social Psychology, 87,* 228–245.

Gabriel, S., & Gardner, W. L. (1999). Are there "his" and "hers" types of interdependence? The implications of gender differences in collective versus relational interdependence for affect, behavior, and cognition. *Journal of Personality and Social Psychology, 77*(3), 642–655.

Gaertner, S. L., & Dovidio, J. F. (2005). Understanding and addressing contemporary racism: From aversive racism to the common ingroup identity model. *Journal of Social Issues, 61,* 615–639.

Gage, F. H. (2002). Neurogenesis in the adult brain. *Journal of Neuroscience, 22,* 612–613.

Gailliot, M. T. (2008). Unlocking the energy dynamics of executive function: Linking executive functioning to brain glycogen. *Perspectives on Psychological Science, 3,* 245–263.

Gailliot, M. T., Baumeister, R. F., DeWall, C., Maner, J. K., Plant, E., Tice, D. M., & . . . Schmeichel, B. J. (2007). Self-control relies on glucose as a limited energy source: Willpower is more than a metaphor. *Journal of Personality and Social Psychology, 92*(2), 325–336. doi:10.1037/0022-3514.92.2.325

Gailliot, M. T., Peruche, B. M., Plant, E. A., & Baumeister, R. F. (2009). Stereotypes and prejudice in the blood: Sucrose drinks reduce prejudice and stereotyping. *Journal of Experimental Social Psychology, 45*(1), 288–290.

Gaines, S. O., Jr. (2009). Interracial and interethnic relationships. In T. Reis & S. Sprecher (Eds.), *Encyclopedia of human relationships: Vol. 1* (pp. 905–907). Los Angeles: Sage Reference Publication.

Gajendran, R. S., & Harrison, D. A. (2007). The good, the bad, and the unknown about telecommuting: Meta-analysis of psychological mediators and individual consequences. *Journal of Applied Psychology, 92*(6), 1524–1541.

Galdas, P. M., Cheater, F., & Marshall, P. (2005). Men and health-seeking behavior: Literature review. *Journal of Advanced Nursing, 49,* 616–623.

Galinsky, E., Bond, J. T., Kim, S. S., Backon, L., Brownfield, E., & Sakai, K. (2005). *Overwork in America.* New York, NY: Families and Work Institute.

Gallup. (2001). Most workers expect to continue to work after retirement age. Retrieved from http://www.gallup.com/poll/147866/Workers-Expect-Keep-Working-Retirement-Age.aspx

Gana, K., Alaphilippe, D., & Bailly, N. (2004). Positive illusions and mental and physical health in later life. *Aging and Mental Health, 8*(1), 58–64.

Ganahl, D. J., Prinsen, T. J., & Netzley, S. B. (2003). A content analysis of prime time commercials: A contextual framework of gender representation. *Sex Roles, 49,* 545–551.

Gangestad, S. W. (1993). Sexual selection and physical attractiveness: Implications for mating dynamics. *Human Nature, 4,* 205–235.

Gangestad, S. W., & Snyder, M. (2000). Self-monitoring appraisal and reappraisal. *Psychological Bulletin, 126*(4), 530–555.

Gangwisch, J. E., Malaspina, D., Boden-Albala, B., & Heymsfield, S. B. (2005). Inadequate sleep as a risk factor for obesity: Analyses of the NHANES I. *Sleep, 28,* 1289–1296.

Ganzach, Y. (1998). Intelligence and job satisfaction. *Academy of Management Journal, 41,* 526–539.

Gao, G. (2001). Intimacy, passion and commitment in Chinese and U.S. American romantic relationships. *International Journal of Intercultural Relations, 25*(3), 329–342.

Garb, H. N., Florio, C. M., & Grove, W. M. (1998). The validity of the Rorschach and the Minnesota Multiphasic Personality Inventory: Results from meta-analysis. *Psychological Science, 9,* 402–404.

García, F., & Gracia, E. (2009). Is always authoritative parenting the optimal parenting style? Evidence from Spanish families. *Adolescence, 44*(173), 101–131.

Garcia, S. M., & Tor, A. (2009). The N-effect: More competitors, less competition. *Psychological Science, 20*(7), 871–877.

Gardner, G., & Prugh, T. (2008). Seeding the sustainable economy. In L. Starke (Ed.), *2008 State of the World: Innovations for a sustainable economy* (pp. 3–17). New York, NY: Norton.

Gardner, G. T., & Stern, P. C. (2002). Human reactions to environmental hazards: Perceptual and cognitive processes. In *Environmental problems and human behavior* (2nd ed., pp. 205–252). Boston, MA: Allyn & Bacon.

Gardner, G. T., & Stern, P. C. (2008). The short list: The most effective actions U.S. households can take to curb climate change. *Environment, 50*(5), 12–24.

Garland, E. L., Fredrickson, B., Kring, A. M., Johnson, D. P., Meyer, P. S., & Penn, D. L. (2010). Upward spirals of positive emotions counter downward spirals of negativity: Insights from the broaden-and-build theory and affective neuroscience on the treatment of emotion dysfunctions and deficits in psychopathology. *Clinical Psychology Review, 30*(7), 849–864. doi:10.1016/j.cpr.2010.03.002.

Garland, E. L., Gaylord, S. A., & Fredrickson, B. L. (2011). Positive reappraisal mediates the stress-reductive effects of mindfulness: An upward spiral process. *Mindfulness, 2*(1), 59–67. doi:10.1007/s12671-011-0043-8

Garmezy, N. (1991). Resiliency and vulnerability of adverse developmental outcomes associated with poverty. *American Behavioral Scientist, 34,* 416–430.

Garnets, L. D., & Kimmel, D. C. (1991). Lesbian and gay male dimensions in the psychological study of human diversity. In J. D. Goodchilds (Ed.), *Psychological perspectives on human diversity in America.* Washington, DC: American Psychological Association.

Garnets, L. D., & Kimmel, D. C. (2003). Identity development and stigma management. In L. D. Garnets & D. C. Kimmel (Eds.), *Psychological perspectives on lesbian, gay, and bisexual experiences.* New York, NY: Columbia University Press.

Gartrell, N., Banks, A., Hamilton, J., Reed, N., Bishop, H., & Rodas, C. (1999). The national lesbian family study: Interviews with mothers of toddlers. *American Journal of Orthopsychiatry, 69,* 362–369.

Gates, G. (2011). How many people are lesbian, gay, bisexual, and transgender? The Williams Institute, UCLA School of Law. Retrieved from http://williamsinstitute.law.ucla.edu/wpcontent/uploads/Gates-How-Many-People-LGBTApr-2011.pdf

Gattig, A. & Hendricks, L. (2007). Judgmental discounting and environmental risk perception: Dimensional similarities, domain differences, and implications for sustainability. *Journal of Social Issues, 63,* 21–39.

Gawronski, B., Brochu, P. M., Sritharan, R., & Strack, F. (2012). Cognitive consistency in prejudice-related belief systems: Integrating old-fashioned, modern, aversive, and implicit forms of prejudice. In B. Gawronski & F. Strack (Eds.), *Cognitive consistency: A fundamental principle in social cognition* (pp. 369–389). New York, NY: Guilford Press.

Geary, D. C. (2007). An evolutionary perspective on sex differences in mathematics and the sciences. In S. J. Ceci & W. M. Williams (Eds.), *Why aren't more women in science?* (pp. 173–188). Washington, DC: American Psychological Association.

Gebhard, U., Nevers, P., & Billmann-Mahecha, E. (2003). Moralizing trees: Anthropomorphism and identity in children's relationships to nature. In S. Clayton & S. Opotow (Eds.), *Identity and the natural environment: The psychological significance of nature* (pp. 91–111). Cambridge, MA: MIT Press.

Gecas, V., & Seff, M. A. (1990). Families and adolescents: A review of the 1980s. *Journal of Marriage and the Family, 52,* 941–958.

Gee, T., Allen, K., & Powell, R. A. (2003). Questioning premorbid dissociative symptomatology in dissociative identity disorder. *Professional Psychology: Research & Practice, 34*(1), 114–116.

Geen, R. G. (1998). Aggression and antisocial behavior. In D. T. Gilbert, S. T. Fiske, & G. Lindzey (Eds.), *The handbook of social psychology* (4th ed., Vol. 2). Boston, MA: McGraw-Hill.

Geeraert, N. Y., Yzerbyt, V. Y., Corneille, O., & Wigboldus, D. (2004). The return of dispositionalism: On the linguistic consequences of dispositional suppression. *Journal of Experimental Social Psychology, 40,* 264–272.

Geller, E. S., Winett, R. A., & Everett, P. B. (1982). *Environmental preservation: New strategies for behavior change.* New York, NY: Pergamon Press.

Gentile, B., Grabe, S., Dolan-Pascoe, B., Wells, B. E., & Maitino, A. (2009). Gender differences in domain-specific self-esteem: A meta-analysis. *Review of General Psychology, 13*(1), 34–45.

George, L. K., Larson, D. B., Koenig, H. G., & McCullough, M. E. (2000). Spirituality and health: What we know, what we need to know. *Journal of Social and Clinical Psychology, 19,* 102–116.

Geraerts, E., Raymaekers, L., & Merckelbach, H. (2008). Recovered memories of childhood sexual abuse: Current findings and their legal implications. *Legal and Criminological Psychology, 13*(2), 165–176. doi:10.1348/135532508X298559

Geraerts, E., Schooler, J. W., Merckelbach, H., Jelicic, M., Hauer, B. A., & Ambadar, Z. (2007). The reality of recovered memories: Corroborating continuous and discontinuous memories of childhood sexual abuse. *Psychological Science, 18*(7), 564–568. doi:10.1111/j.1467-9280.2007.01940.x

Getzels, J. W., & Csikszentmihalyi, M. (1976). *The creative vision.* New York, NY: Wiley.

Ghani, J. A., & Deshpande, S. P. (1994). Task characteristics and the experience of optimal flow in human-computer interaction. *The Journal of Psychology, 128*(4), 381–391.

Giancola, P. R., Levinson, C. A., Corman, M. D., Godlaski, A. J., Morris, D. H., Philips, J. P., & Holt, J. C. D. (2009). Men and women, alcohol and aggression. *Experimental and Clinical Psychopharmacology, 17,* 154–164.

Giannantonio, C., & Hurley-Hanson, A. (2006). Applying image norms across Super's career development stages. *The Career Development Quarterly, 54*(4), 318–330.

Giannoglou, G., Chatzizisis, Y., Zamboulis, C., Parcharidis, G., Mikhailidis, D., & Louridas, G. (2008). Elevated heart rate and atherosclerosis: An overview of the pathogenic mechanisms. *International Journal of Cardiology, 126*(3), 302–312.

Gibbons, M. B. C., Crits-Christoph, P., & Hearon, B. (2008). The empirical status of psychodynamic therapies. *Annual Review of Clinical Psychology, 4,* 93–108.

Gibbons, R., D., Brown, C. H., Hur, K., Davis, J. M., & Mann, J. J. (2012). Suicidal thoughts and behavior with antidepressant treatment: Reanalysis of the randomized placebo-controlled studies of fluoxetine and venlafaxine. *Archives of General Psychiatry, 69,* 580–587. doi:10.1001/archgenpsychiatry.2011.2048

Gibbs, J. L., Ellison, N. B., & Heino, R. D. (2006). Self-presentation in online personals: The role of anticipated future interaction, self-disclosure, and perceived success in Internet dating. *Communication Research, 33*(2), 152–177.

Gierveld, J., van Tilburg, T., & Dykstra, P. A. (2006). Loneliness and social isolation. In A. L. Vangelisti & D. Perlman (Eds.) , *The Cambridge handbook of personal relationships* (pp. 485–499). New York, NY: Cambridge University Press.

Gifford, R. (2011). The role of nonverbal communication in interpersonal relations. In L. M. Horowitz & S. Strack (Eds.), *Handbook of interpersonal psychology: Theory, research, assessment, and therapeutic interventions* (pp. 171–190). Hoboken, NJ: Wiley.

Gilbert, D. T. (2006a, July 2). If only gay sex caused global warming. *Los Angeles Times.* Retrieved from http://articles.latimes.com/2006/jul/02/opinion/op-gilbert2

Gilbert, D. T. (2006b). *Stumbling on happiness.* New York, NY: Knopf.

Gilbert, D. T. (2008). Daniel Gilbert speaks about the psychology of global warming. Retrieved from http://www.youtube.com/watch?v=VTnkT2pcV3s&feature=related

Gilbert, D. T., Driver-Linn, E., & Wilson, T. D. (2002). The trouble with Vronsky: Impact bias in the forecasting of future affective states. In L. F. Barrett & P. Salovey (Eds.), *The wisdom in feelings: Psychological processes in emotional intelligence* (pp. 114–143). New York, NY: Guilford.

Gilbert, D. T., & Malone, P. S. (1995). The correspondence bias. *Psychological Bulletin, 117,* 21–38.

Gillham, J., & Reivich, K. (2007). Cultivating optimism in childhood and adolescence. In A. Monat, R. S. Lazarus, & G. Reevy (Eds.), *The Praeger handbook on stress and coping* (pp. 309–326). Westport, CT: Praeger Publishers.

Gillham, J., & Seligman, M. E. P. (1999). Footsteps on the road to positive psychology. *Behaviour Research and Therapy, 37,* S163–S173.

Gillham, J. E., Shatté, A. J., Reivich, K. J., & Seligman, M. E. P. (2001). Optimism, pessimism, and explanatory style. In E. C. Chang (Ed.), *Optimism & pessimism: Implications for theory, research, and practice.* Washington, DC: American Psychological Association.

Gill, D. S., Christensen, A., & Fincham, F. D. (1999). Predicting marital satisfaction from behavior: Do all roads really lead to Rome? *Personal Relationships, 6,* 369–387.

Gilovich, T., Kruger, J., & Medvec, V. H. (2002). The spotlight effect revisited: Overestimating the manifest variability of our actions and appearance. *Journal of Experimental Social Psychology, 38,* 93–99.

Gilovitch, T., Medvec, V. H., & Savitsky, K. (2000). The spotlight effect in social judgment: An egocentric bias in estimates of one's own actions and appearance. *Journal of Personality and Social Psychology, 78,* 211–222.

Giskes, K., Kunst, A. E., Benach, J., Borrell, C., Costa, G., Dahl, E., et al. (2005). Trends in smoking behaviour between 1985 and 2000 in nine European countries by education. *Journal of Epidemiology and Community Health, 59,* 595–401.

Gitlin, M. J. (2009). Pharmacotherapy and other somatic treatments for depression. In I. H. Gotlib & C. L. Hammen (Eds.), *Handbook of depression* (pp. 554–585). New York, NY: Guilford Press.

Glascock, J. (2001). Gender roles on prime-time network television: Demograhics and behaviors. *Journal of Broadcasting and Electronic Media, 45*(4), 656–669.

Glascock, J., & Preston-Schreck, C. (2004). Gender and racial stereotypes in daily newspaper comics: A time-honored tradition. *Sex Roles, 51,* 423–431.

Glass, C. R., & Arnkoff, D. B. (1992). Behavior therapy. In D. K. Freedheim (Ed.), *History of psychotherapy: A century of change.* Washington, DC: American Psychological Association.

Glass, R. M. (2001). Electroconvulsive therapy. *Journal of the American Medical Association, 285*(10), 1346–1348.

Glass, R. M. (2004). Treatment of adolescents with major depression: Contributions of a major trial. *Journal of the American Medical Association, 292*(7), 861–863.

Glassman, A., Maj, M., & Sartorius, N. (2011). *Depression and heart disease.* Hoboken, NJ: Wiley.

Glassman, A., Shapiro, P. A., Ford, D. E., Culpepper, L., Finkel, M. S., Swenson, J. R., Bigger, J. T., Rollman, B. L., & Wise, T. N. (2003). Cardiovascular health and depression. *Journal of Psychiatric Practice, 9*(6), 409–421.

Glavin, P., & Schieman, S. (2012). Work-family role blurring and work-family conflict: The moderating influence of job resources and job demands. *Work and Occupations, 39*(1), 71–98. doi:10.1177/0730888411406295

Gleaves, D. H., & Smith, S. M. (2004). False and recovered memories in the laboratory and clinic: A review of experimental and clinical evidence. *Clinical Psychology: Science and Practice, 11*(1), 2–28.

Glick, I. D., Ritvo, E. C., & Melnick, I. (2008). Couples and family therapy. In R. E. Hales, S. C. Yudofsky, & G. O. Gabbard (Eds.), *American Psychiatric Publishing textbook of psychiatry* (5th ed., pp. 1303–1327). Arlington, VA: American Psychiatric Publishing.

Glick, S., & Golden, M. R. (2010). Persistence of racial differences in attitudes toward homosexuality in the United States. *Journal of Acquired Immune Deficiency Syndromes, 55*(4), 516–523. doi:10.1097/QAI.0b013e3181f275e0

Gluck, M. E. (2006). Stress response and binge eating disorder. *Appetite, 46*(1), 26–30.

Gmel, G., & Rehm, J. (2003). Harmful alcohol use. *Alcohol Research & Health, 27,* 52–62.

Godlee, F., Smith, J., & Marcovitch, H. (2011). Wakefield's article linking MMR vaccine and autism was fraudulent. *BMJ, 342,* 64–66.

Goffman, E. (1959). *The presentation of self in everyday life.* Garden City, NJ: Doubleday.

Gold, M. S., & Jacobs, W. S. (2005). Cocaine and crack: Clinical aspects. In J. H. Lowinson, P. Ruiz, R. B. Millman, & J. G. Langrod (Eds.), *Substance abuse: A comprehensive textbook.* Philadelphia: Lippincott/Williams & Wilkins.

Gold, M. S., Miller, N. S., & Jonas, J. M. (1992). Cocaine (and crack): Neurobiology. In J. H. Lowinson, P. Ruiz, & R. B. Millman (Eds.), *Substance abuse: A comprehensive textbook* (2nd ed.). Baltimore: Williams & Wilkins.

Gold, R. (2008). Unrealistic optimism and event threat. *Psychology, Health, and Medicine, 13,* 193–201.

Goldberg, A. E. (2010a). Partners but not parents: Intimate relationships of lesbians and gay men. In *Lesbian and gay parents and their children: Research on the family life cycle* (pp. 15–48). Washington, DC: American Psychological Association. doi:10.1037/12055-002

Goldberg, A. E. (2010b). Children of lesbian and gay parents: Adjustment and experiences. In *Lesbian and gay parents and their children: Research on the family life cycle* (pp. 125–156). Washington, DC: American Psychological Association. doi:10.1037/12055-005

Goldberg, A. E., Kashy, D. A., & Smith, J. Z. (2012). Gender-typed play behavior in early childhood: Adopted children with lesbian, gay, and heterosexual parents. *Sex Roles, 67*(9–10), 503–515. doi:10.1007/s11199-012-0198-3

Goldberg, A. E., & Perry-Jenkins, M. (2004). Division of labor and working-class women's well-being across the transition to parenthood. *Journal of Family Psychology, 18*(1), 225–236.

Goldberg, C., & Zhang, L. (2004). Simple and joint effects of gender and self-esteem on responses to same-sex sexual harrassment. *Sex Roles, 50*(11/12), 823–833.

Goldberger, L. (1993). Sensory deprivation and overload. In L. Goldberger & S. Breznitz (Eds.), *Handbook of stress: Theoretical and clinical aspects* (2nd ed.). New York, NY: Free Press.

Goldenberg, I., Goldenberg, H., & Pelavin, E. G. (2011). Family therapy. In R. J. Corsini & D. Wedding (Eds.), *Current psychotherapies* (9th ed.). Belmont, CA: Brooks/Cole.

Goldhammer, D., & McCabe, M. P. (2012). Sexual dysfunction in intimate heterosexual relationships. In P. Noller & G. C. Karantzas (Eds.), *The Wiley-Blackwell handbook of couples and family relationships* (pp. 175–192). Malden, MA: Wiley-Blackwell.

Goldston, K., & Baillie, A. J. (2008). Depression and coronary heart disease: A review of the epidemiological evidence, explanatory mechanism and management approaches. *Clinical Psychology Review, 28,* 289–307.

Goldzweig, C. L., Balekian, T. M., Rolon, C., Yano, E. M., & Shekelle, P. G. (2006). The state of women veterans' health research: Results of a systematic literature review. *Journal of General Internal Medicine, 21*(Suppl 3), S82–S92.

Goleman, D. (2011). *Leadership: The power of social intelligence.* Florence, MA: More Than Sound.

Gonzaga, G. C. (2009). Similarity in ongoing relationships. In H. T. Reis & S. Sprecher (Eds.), *Encyclopedia of human relationships: Vol. 3* (pp. 1496–1499). Los Angeles: Sage Reference Publication.

Gonzaga, G. C., Campos, B, & Bradbury, T. (2007). Similarity, convergence, and relationship satisfaction in dating and married couples. *Journal of Personality and Social Psychology, 93,* 34–48.

González, H. M., Vega, W. A., Williams, D. R., Tarraf, W., West, B. T., & Neighbors, H. W. (2010). Depression care in the United States: Too little for too few. *Archives of General Psychiatry, 67*(1), 37–46.

Good, J. J., Woodzicka, J. A., & Wingfield, L. C. (2010). The effects of gender stereotypic and counter-stereotypic textbook images on science performance. *The Journal of Social Psychology, 150*(2), 132–147. doi:10.1080/00224540903366552

Goodall, I. (1972, November). Field report: Shapers at work. *Psychology Today,* pp. 53–63, 132–138.

Goode-Cross, D. T., & Good, G. E. (2008). African American men who have sex with men: Creating safe spaces through relationships. *Psychology of Men & Masculinity, 9,* 221–234.

Gooden, A. M., & Gooden, M. A. (2001). Gender representation in notable children's picture books: 1995–1999. *Sex Roles, 45*(1/2), 89–101.

Goodfriend, W. (2009). Proximity and attraction. In H. T. Reis & S. Sprecher (Eds.), *Encyclopedia of human relationships: Vol. 3* (pp. 1297–1299). Los Angeles: Sage Reference Publication.

Goodheart, C. D. (2006). Evidence, endeavor, and expertise in psychology practice. In C. D. Goodheart, A. E. Kazdin, & R. J. Sternberg (Eds.), *Evidence-based psychotherapy: Where practice and research meet* (pp. 37–62). Washington, DC: American Psychological Association.

Goodrick, G. K., Pendleton, V. R., Kimball, K. T., Poston, W. S., Carlos, R., Rebecca, S., & Foreyt, J. P. (1999). Binge eating severity, self-concept, dieting self-efficacy and social support during treatment of binge eating disorder. *International Journal of Eating Disorders, 26*(3), 295–300.

Goodwin, F. K. & Jamison, K. R. (2007). *Manic-depressive illness: Bipolar disorders and recurrent depression.* New York, NY: Oxford University Press.

Goodwin, G. (2009). Neurobiological aetiology of mood disorders. In M. C. Gelder, N. C. Andreasen, J. J. López-Ibor, Jr., & J. R. Geddes (Eds.), *New Oxford textbook of psychiatry* (2nd ed., Vol. 1). New York, NY: Oxford University Press.

Goodwin, R. (2009). Marriage, historical and cross-cultural trends. In H. T. Reis & S. Sprecher (Eds.), *Encyclopedia of human relationships: Vol. 1* (pp. 1048–1052). Los Angeles: Sage Reference Publication.

Goodwin, R. D., & Friedman, H. S. (2006). Health status and the five-factor personality traits in a nationally representative sample. *Journal of Health Psychology, 11,* 643–654.

Gorchoff, S. M., John, O. P., & Helson, R. (2008). Contextualizing change in marital satisfaction during middle age: An 18-year longitudinal study. *Psychological Science, 19*(11), 1194–1200. doi:10.1111/j.1467-9280.2008.02222.x

Gordon, P. A. (2003). The decision to remain single: Implications for women across cultures. *Journal of Mental Health Counseling, 25*(1), 33–44.

Gordon, R. A. (1996). Impact of ingratiation on judgments and evaluations: A meta-analytic investigation. *Journal of Personality and Social Psychology, 71*(1), 54–70.

Gordon, R. A. (2008). Attributional style and athletic performance: Strategic optimism and defensive pessimism. *Psychology of Sport and Exercise, 9*(3), 336–350.

Gordon, R. M. (2005). The doom and gloom of divorce research: Comment on Wallerstein and Lewis (2004). *Psychoanalytic Psychology, 22,* 450–451.

Gordon, V. M. (2006). *Career advising: An academic advisor's guide.* San Francisco: Jossey-Bass.

Gortner, E. M., Rude, S. S., & Pennebaker, J. W. (2006). Benefits of expressive writing in lowering rumination and depressive symptoms. *Behavior Therapy 37,* 292–303.

Gottdiener, J. S., Krantz, D. S., & Howell, R. H., Hecht, G. M., Klein, J., Falconer, J. J., & Rozanski, A. (1994). Induction of silent myocardial ischemia with mental stress testing: Relationship to the triggers of ischemia during daily life activities and to ischemic functional severity. *Journal of the American College of Cardiology, 24,* 1645–1651.

Gottesman, I. I. (2001). Psychopathology through a life span–genetic prism. *American Psychologist, 56,* 867–878.

Gottfried, A. E., & Gottfried, A. W. (2008). The upside of maternal and dual-earner employment: A focus on positive family adaptations, home environments, and child development in the Fullerton longitudinal study. In A. Marcus-Newhall, D. F. Halpern, & S. J. Tan (Eds.), *The changing realities of work and family* (pp. 25–42). Malden, MA: Wiley-Blackwell.

Gottman, J. M. (1994). *What predicts divorce?* Hillsdale, NJ: Erlbaum.

Gottman, J. M. (2011). *The science of trust: Emotional attunement for couples.* New York, NY: Norton.

Gottman, J. M., & Gottman, J. S. (2008). Gottman method couple therapy. In A. S. Gurman (Ed.), *Clinical handbook of couple therapy* (4th ed., pp. 138–164). New York, NY: Guilford Press.

Gottman, J. M., Gottman, J. S., & DeClaire, J. (2006). *Ten lessons to transform your marriage.* New York, NY: Three Rivers Press.

Gough, B., Weyman, N., Alderson, J., Butler, G., & Stoner, M. (2008). "They did not have a word": The parental quest to locate a "true sex" for their intersex children. *Psychology and Health, 23,* 493–507.

Gouin, J., Glaser, R., Malarkey, W. B., Beversdorf, D., & Kiecolt-Glaser, J. (2012). Chronic stress, daily stressors, and circulating inflammatory markers. *Health Psychology, 31*(2), 264–268. doi:10.1037/a0025536

Gourevitch, M. N., & Arnsten, J. H. (2005). Medical complications of drug use. In J. H. Lowinson, P. Ruiz, R. B. Millman, & J. G. Langrod (Eds.), *Substance abuse: A comprehensive textbook.* Philadelphia: Lippincott/Williams & Wilkins.

Gouzoulis-Mayfrank, E., Daumann, J., Tuchtenhagen, F., Pelz, S., Becker, S., Kunert, H.-J., Fimm, B., & Sass, H. (2000). Impaired cognitive performance in drug-free users of recreational ecstasy (MDMA). *Journal of Neurology, Neurosurgery, and Psychiatry, 68*(6), 719–725.

Grafanaki, S., Brennan, M., Holmes, S., Tang, K., & Alvarez, S. (2007). In search of flow in counseling and psychotherapy: Identifying the necessary ingredients of peak moments of therapy interaction. *Person-Centered and Experiential Psychotherapies, 6*(4), 240–255.

Graham, J. E., Christian, L. M., & Kiecolt-Glaser, J. K. (2006). Stress, age, and immune function: Toward a lifespan approach. *Journal of Behavioral Medicine, 29,* 389–400.

Graig, E. (1993). Stress as a consequence of the urban physical environment. In L. Goldberger & S. Breznitz (Eds.), *Handbook of stress: Theoretical and clinical aspects* (2nd ed.). New York, NY: Free Press.

Gray-Little, B., & Hafdahl, A. R. (2000). Factors influencing racial comparisons of self-esteem: A quantitative review. *Psychological Bulletin, 126,* 26–54.

Graziano, W. G. & Tobin, R. M. (2009). Agreeableness. In M. R. Leary & R. H. Hoyle (Eds.), *Handbook of individual differences in social behavior* (pp. 46–61). New York, NY: Guilford.

Grearson, J, & Smith, L. (2009). The luckiest girls in the world. In T. A. Karis & K. D. Killian, *Intercultural couples: Exploring diversity in intimate relationships* (pp. 71–87). New York, NY: Routledge/Taylor & Francis Group.

Green, J. D., Sedikides, C., Pinter, B., & Van Tongeren, D. R. (2009). Two sides to self-protection: Self-improvement strivings and feedback from close relationships eliminate mnemic neglect. *Self and Identity, 8*(2–3), 233–250.

Green, L. R., Richardson, D. S., Lago, T., & Schatten-Jones, E. C. (2001). Network correlates of social and emotional loneliness in young and older adults. *Personality and Social Psychology Bulletin, 27*(3), 281–288.

Greenberg, J., Kosloff, S., Solomon, S., Cohen, F., & Landau, M. (2010). Toward understanding the fame game: The effect of mortality salience on the appeal of fame. *Self and Identity, 9,* 1–18. doi:10.1080/15298860802391546

Greenberg, J., Landau, M., Kosloff, S., & Solomon, S. (2009). How our dreams of death transcendence breed prejudice, stereotyping, and conflict: Terror management theory. In T. D. Nelson (Ed.), *Handbook of prejudice, stereotyping, and discrimination* (pp. 309–332). New York, NY: Psychology Press.

Greenberg, J. S. (2002). *Comprehensive stress management: Health and human performance.* New York, NY: McGraw-Hill.

Greene, K., Derlega, V., & Mathews, A. (2006). Self-disclosure in personal relationships. In A. L. Vangelisti & D. Perlman (Eds.), *Cambridge handbook of personal relationships.* Cambridge, MA: Cambridge University Press.

Greene, R. L. (1992). *Human memory: Paradigms and paradoxes.* Hillsdale, NJ: Erlbaum.

Greenglass, E. R. (2007). Teaching and stress. In G. Fink (Ed.), *Encyclopedia of stress: Vols. 1–4* (2nd ed., pp. 713–717). San Diego, CA: Elsevier Academic Press.

Greenhaus, J. H. (2003). Career dynamics. In W. C. Borman, D. R. Ilgen, & R. J. Klimoski (Eds.), *Handbook of psychology: Vol. 12. Industrial and organizational psychology.* New York, NY: Wiley.

Greenhaus, J. H., & Powell, G. N. (2006). When work and family are allies: A theory of work-family enrichment. *Academy of Management Review, 31*(1), 72–92.

Greenland, P., Knoll, M. D., Stamler, J., Neaton, J. D., Dyer, A. R., Garside, D. B., & Wilson, P. W. (2003). Major risk factors as antecedents of fatal and nonfatal coronary heart disease events. *Journal of the American Medical Association, 290,* 891–897.

Greenson, R. R. (1967). *The technique and practice of psychoanalysis* (Vol. 1). New York, NY: International Universities Press.

Greenway, R. (1995). The wilderness effect and ecopsychology. In T. Roszak, M. E. Gomes, & A. D. Kanner (Eds.), *Eco-psychology: Restoring the earth, healing the mind* (pp. 122–135). San Francisco: Sierra Club Books.

Greenwood, D. N., & Lippman, J. R. (2010). Gender and media: Content, uses, and impact. In J. C. Chrisler & D. R. McCreary (Eds.), *Handbook of gender research in psychology* (Vol. 2, pp. 643-669). New York, NY: Springer.

Gregory, R. J., Schwer Canning, S., Lee, T. W., & Wise, J. C. (2004). Cognitive bibliotherapy for depression: A meta-analysis. *Professional Psychology: Research and Practice, 35*(3), 275–280.

Griffeth, R. W., Hom, P. W., & Gaertner, S. (2000). A meta-analysis of antecedents and correlates of employee turnover: Update, moderator tests, and research implications for the next millennium. *Journal of Management, 26,* 463–488.

Griffith, K. H., & Hebl, M. R. (2002). The disclosure dilemma for gay men and lesbians: "Coming out" at work. *Journal of Applied Psychology, 87*(6), 1191–1199.

Griffiths, M. (2011). Workaholism—a 21st-century addiction. *The Psychologist, 24* (10), 740–744.

Griner, D., & Smith, T. B. (2006). Culturally adapted mental health intervention: A meta-analytic review. *Psychotherapy: Theory, Research, Practice, Training, 43,* 531–548.

Grinspoon, L., Bakalar, J. B., & Russo, E. (2005). Marihuana: Clinical aspects. In J. H. Lowinson, P. Ruiz, R. B. Millman, & J. G. Langrod (Eds.), *Substance abuse: A comprehensive textbook.* Philadelphia: Lippincott/Williams & Wilkins.

Griskevicius, V., Tybur, J. M., & Van den Bergh, B. (2010). Going green to be seen: Status, reputation, and conspicuous conservation. *Journal of Personality and Social Psychology, 98*(3), 392-404. doi:10.1037/a0017346

Grob, C. S., & Poland, R. E. (2005). MDMA. In J. H. Lowinson, P. Ruiz, R. B. Millman, & J. G. Langrod (Eds.), *Substance abuse: A comprehensive textbook.* Philadelphia: Lippincott/Williams & Wilkins.

Groesz, L. M., Levine, M. P., & Murnen, S. K. (2002). The effect of experimental presentation of thin media images on body satisfaction: A meta-analytic review. *International Journal of Eating Disorders, 31,* 1–16.

Groleau, J. M., Calhoun, L. G., Cann, A., & Tedeschi, R. G. (2012). The role of centrality of events in posttraumatic distress and posttraumatic growth. *Psychological Trauma: Theory, Research, Practice, and Policy,* doi:10.1037/a0028809

Gross, J. J. (2001). Emotion regulation in adulthood: Timing is everything. *Current Directions in Psychological Science, 10,* 214–219.

Grossman, J. B., & Ruiz, P. (2004). Shall we make a leap-of-faith to disulfiram (Antabuse)? *Addictive Disorders & Their Treatment, 3*(3), 129–132.

Groth-Marnat, G. (1997). *Handbook of psychological assessment.* New York, NY: Wiley.

Grothues, C. A., & Marmion, S. L. (2006). Dismantling the myths about intimate violence against women. In P. K. Lundberg-Love & S. L. Marmion (Eds.), *"Intimate" violence against women: When spouses, partners, or lovers attack.* Westport, CT: Praeger Publishers.

Grunberg, N. E., Berger, S. S., & Hamilton, K. R. (2011). Stress and drug use. In R. J. Contrada & A. Baum (Eds.), *The handbook of stress science: Biology, psychology, and health* (pp. 286–300). New York, NY: Springer.

Grunberg, N. E., Faraday, M. M., & Rahman, M. A. (2001). The psychobiology of nicotine self-administration. In A. Baum, T. A. Revenson, & Singer, J. E. (Eds.), *Handbook of health psychology* (pp. 249–261). Mahwah, NJ: Erlbaum.

Grundy, E., & Henretta, J. C. (2006). Between elderly parents and adult children: A new look at the intergenerational care provided by the "sandwich generation." *Ageing & Society, 26,* 707–722.

Grzywacz, J. G., Almeida, D. M., Neupert, S. D., & Ettner, S. L. (2004). Socioeconomic status and health: A micro-level analysis of exposure and vulnerability to daily stressors. *Journal of Health and Social Behavior, 45,* 1–16.

Guarda, A. S., Pinto, A. M., Coughlin, J. W., Hussain, S., Haug, N. A., & Heinberg, L. J. (2007). Perceived coercion and change in perceived need for admission in patients hospitalized for eating disorders. *American Journal of Psychiatry, 164,* 108–114.

Guéguen, N. (2002). Status, apparel and touch: Their joint effects on compliance to a request. *North American Journal of Psychology, 4*(2), 279–286.

Guéguen, N. (2003). Fundraising on the web: The effect of an electronic door-in-the-face technique on compliance to a request. *CyberPsychology & Behavior, 6,* 189–193.

Guéguen, N., Fischer-Lokou, J., Lefebvre, L., & Lamy, L. (2008). Women's eye contact and men's later interest: Two field experiments. *Perceptual and Motor Skills, 106*(1), 63–66.

Guéguen, N., & Jacob, C. (2001). Fund-raising on the web: The effect of an electronic foot-in-the-door on donation. *Cyber Psychology and Behavior, 4,* 705–709.

Guéguen, N., Jacob, C., & Meineri, S. (2011). Effects of the door-in-the-face technique on restaurant customers' behavior. *International Journal of Hospitality Management, 30*(3), 759–761. doi:10.1016/j.ijhm.2010.12.010

Guiney, M. S., & Oberhauser, K. S. (2009). Conservation volunteers' connection to nature. *Ecopsychology, 1*(4), 187–197.

Günaydin, G., Zayas, V., Selcuk, E., & Hazan, C. (2012). I like you but I don't know why: Objective facial resemblance to significant others influences snap judgments. *Journal of Experimental Social Psychology, 48*(1), 350–353. doi:10.1016/j.jesp.2011.06.001

Gunter, C. (2009). Schizophrenia: missing heritability found? *Nature Reviews Neuroscience, 10*(8), 543. doi:10.1038/nrn2691

Gupta, G. R. (1992). Love, arranged marriage, and the Indian social structure. In J. J. Macionis & N. V. Benokraitis (Eds.), *Seeing ourselves: Classic, contemporary and cross-cultural reading in sociology.* Englewood Cliffs, NJ: Prentice-Hall.

Gupta, U., & Singh, P. (1982). Exploratory study of love and liking type of marriages. Indian *Journal of Applied Psychology, 19,* 92–97.

Gur, R. C., & Gur, R. E. (2007). Neural substrates for sex differences in cognition. In S. J. Ceci & W. M. Williams (Eds.), *Why aren't more women in science?* (pp. 189–198). Washington, DC: American Psychological Association.

Gutman, D. A., & Nemeroff, C. B. (2011). Stress and depression. In R. J. Contrada & A. Baum (Eds.), *The handbook of stress science: Biology, psychology, and health* (pp. 345–357). New York, NY: Springer.

Ha, T., Berg, J. M., Engels, R. E., & Lichtwarck-Aschoff, A. (2012). Effects of attractiveness and status in dating desire in homosexual and heterosexual men and women. *Archives of Sexual Behavior, 41*(3), 673–682. doi:10.1007/s10508-011-9855-9

Haas, L. (1999). Families and work. In M. B. Sussman, S. K. Steinmetz & G. W. Peterson *Handbook of marriage and the family.* New York, NY: Plenum Press.

Hadjikhani, N., Hoge, R., Snyder, J., & de Gelder, B. (2008). Pointing with the eyes: The role of gaze in communicating danger. *Brain and Cognition, 68*(1), 1–8.

Hadjistavropoulos, H., Dash, H., Hadjistavropoulos, T., & Sullivan, T. (2007). Recurrent pain among university students: Contributions of self-efficacy and perfectionism to the pain experience. *Personality and Individual Differences, 42,* 1081–1091.

Haeffel, G. J., Gibb, B. E., Metalsky, G. I., Alloy, L. B., Abramson, L. Y., Hankin, B. L., Joiner, T. E., Jr., & Swendsen, J. D. (2008). Measuring cognitive vulnerability to depression: Development and validation of the cognitive style questionnaire. *Clinical Psychology Review, 28,* 824–836.

Hafer, C. L. (2000). Do innocent victims threaten the belief in a just world? Evidence from a modified Stroop task. *Journal of Personality and Social Psychology, 79*(2), 165–173.

Hafer, C. L., & Bègue, L. (2005). Experimental research on just-world theory: Problems, developments, and future challenges. *Psychological Bulletin, 131*(1), 128–167.

Haggerty, G., Hilsenroth, M. J., & Vala-Stewart, R. (2009). Attachment and interpersonal distress: Examining the relationship between attachment styles and interpersonal problems in a clinical population. *Clinical Psychology and Psychotherapy, 16,* 1–9.

Haglund, K. A., & Fehring, R. J. (2010). The association of religiosity, sexual education, and parental factors with risky sexual behaviors among adolescents and young adults. *Journal of Religion and Health, 49*(4), 460–472. doi:10.1007/s10943-0099267-5

Haidt, J. (2006). *The happiness hypothesis: Finding modern truth in ancient wisdom.* New York, NY: Basic Books.

Haidt, J., & Keltner, D. (2004). Appreciation of beauty and excellence (awe, wonder, elevation). In C. Peterson & M. E. P. Seligman (Eds.), *Character strengths and virtues* (pp. 537–551). New York, NY: Oxford University Press.

Halim, M. L., & Ruble, D.. (2010). Gender identity and stereotyping in early and middle childhood. In J. C. Chrisler & D. R. McCreary (Eds.), *Handbook of gender research in psychology* (Vol. 1, pp. 495–525). New York, NY: Springer.

Hall, E. T. (1966) *The hidden dimension.* Garden City, NY: Doubleday.

Hall, E. T. (2008). Adumbration as a feature of intercultural communication. In C. D. Mortensen (Ed.), *Communication theory* (2nd ed., pp. 420–432). New Brunswick, NJ: Transaction Publishers.

Hall, E. T., & Whyte, W. (2008). Intercultural communication. In C. Mortensen (Ed.), *Communication theory* (2nd ed., pp. 403-419). Piscataway, NJ: Transaction Publishers.

Hall, J. A. (1990). *Nonverbal sex differences: Communication accuracy and expressive style* (2nd ed.). Baltimore: Johns Hopkins University Press.

Hall, J. A. (1998). How big are nonverbal sex differences? The case of smiling and sensitivity to nonverbal cues. In D. J. Canary & K. Dindia (Eds.), *Sex differences and similarities in communication: Critical essays and empirical investigations of sex and gender in interaction.* Mahwah, NJ: Erlbaum.

Hall, J. A. (2006a). How big are nonverbal sex differences? The case of smiling and nonverbal sensitivity. In K. Dindia & D. Canary (Eds.), *Sex differences and similarities in communication* (pp. 59–81). Mahwah, NJ: Erlbaum.

Hall, J. A. (2006b). Women's and men's nonverbal communication: Similarities, differences, stereotypes, and origins. In V. Manusov & M. L. Patterson (Eds.), *The Sage handbook of nonverbal communication* (pp. 201–218). Thousand Oaks, CA: Sage.

Hall, J. A., Coats, E., & Smith-LeBeau, L. (2005). Nonverbal behavior and the vertical dimension of social relations: A meta-analysis. *Psychological Bulletin, 131,* 898–924.

Hall, J. A., & Matsumoto, D. (2004). Gender differences in judgments of multiple emotions from facial expressions. *Emotion, 4*(2), 201–206.

Hall, J. A., & Veccia, E. M. (1990). More "touching" observations: New insights on men, women, and interpersonal touch. *Journal of Personality and Social Psychology, 59,* 1155–1162.

Hall, J. A., & Veccia, E. M. (1991). Touch asymmetry between the sexes. In C. L. Ridgeway (Ed.), *Gender, interaction, and inequality.* New York, NY: Springer-Verlag.

Hall, K., & Solis, H. L. (2011, December). *Women in the labor force: A data book.* Retrieved from www.bls.gov/CPS/WLF-databook-2011.pdf

Hall, P., West, J. H., & Hill, S. (2012). Sexualization in lyrics of popular music from 1959 to 2009: Implications for sexuality educators. *Sexuality and Culture: An Interdisciplinary Quarterly, 16*(2), 103–117. doi:10.1007/s12119-011-9103-4

Hallmayer, J., Cleveland, S., Torres, A., Phillips, J., Cohen, B., Torigoe, T., . . . Risch, N. (2011). Genetic heritability and shared environmental factors among twin pairs with autism. *Archives of General Psychiatry, 68,* 1095–1102. doi:10.1001/archgenpsychiatry.2011.76

Halmi, K. A. (2008). Eating disorders: Anorexia nervosa, bulimia nervosa, and obesity. In R. E. Hales, S. C. Yudofsky, & G. O. Gabbard (Eds.), *The American psychiatric publishing textbook of psychiatry* (pp. 971–998). Washington, DC: American Psychiatric Publishing.

Halpern, D. F. (1997). Sex differences in intelligence: Implications for education. *American Psychologist, 52,* 1091–1102.

Halpern, D. F. (2000). *Sex differences in cognitive abilities* (3rd ed.). Mahwah, NJ: Erlbaum.

Halpern, D. F. (2004). A cognitive-process taxonomy for sex differences in cognitive abilities. *Current Directions in Psychological Science, 13*(4), 135–139.

Halpern, D. F. (2005). Psychology at the intersection of work and family: Recommendations for employers, working families, and policymakers. *American Psychologist, 60,* 397–409.

Halpern, D. F. (2006). Girls and academic success: Changing patterns of academic achievement. In J. Worrell & C. D. Goodheart (Eds.), *Handbook of girls' and women's psychological health.* New York, NY: Oxford University Press.

Ham, J., & Vonk, R. (2011). Impressions of impression management: Evidence of spontaneous suspicion of ulterior motivation. *Journal of Experimental Social Psychology, 47*(2), 466–471. doi:10.1016/j.jesp.2010.12.008

Hamaideh, S. H. (2011). Stressors and reactions to stressors among university students. *International Journal of Social Psychiatry, 57*(1), 69–80. doi:10.1177/0020764010348442

Hamilton, A. (1999, February 15). You've got male! *Time, 83.*

Hamilton, J. C., Deemer, H. N., & Janata, J. W. (2003). Feeling sad but looking good: Sick role features that lead to favorable interpersonal judgments. *Journal of Social & Clinical Psychology, 22*(3), 253–274.

Hamilton, M. C., Anderson, D., Broaddus, M., & Young, K. (2006), Gender stereotyping and underrepresentation of female characters in 200 popular children's picture books: A twenty-first century update. *Sex Roles, 55,* 757–765.

Hammad, T. A., Laughren, T., & Racoosin, J. (2006). Suicidality in pediatric patients treated with antidepressant drugs. *Archives of General Psychiatry, 63,* 332–339.

Hammen, C. (2003). Mood disorders. In G. Stricker & T. A. Widiger (Eds.), *Handbook of psychology: Vol. 8. Clinical psychology.* New York, NY: Wiley.

Hammer, S. M., Saag, M. S., Schechter, M., Montaner, J. S. G., Schooley, R. T., Jacobsen, D. M., et al. (2006). Treatment for adult HIV infection: 2006 recommendations of the international AIDS society-USA panel. *Journal of the American Medical Association, 296,* 827–843.

Hampson, E., van Anders, S. M., & Mullin, L. I. (2006). A female advantage in the recognition of emotional facial expressions: Test of an evolutionary hypothesis. *Evolution and Human Behavior, 27,* 401–416.

Han, S. (1998). The relationship between life satisfaction and flow in elderly Korean immigrants. In M. Csikszentmihalyi & I. S. Csikszentmihalyi (Eds.), *Optimal experiences: Psychological studies of flow in consciousness* (pp. 138–149). New York, NY: Cambridge University Press

Hancock, K. A., & Greenspan, K. (2010). Emergence and development of the psychological study of lesbian, gay, bisexual, and transgender issues. In J. C. Chrisler & D. R. McCreary (Eds.), *Handbook of gender research in psychology* (Vol. 1, pp. 59–78). New York, NY: Springer.

Hancock, P. A., & Ganey, H. C. N. (2003). From the inverted-U to the extended-U: The evolution of a law of psychology. *Journal of Human Performance in Extreme Environment, 7*(1), 5–14.

Hanford, E. (2012). Angela Duckworth and the research on "Grit." Retrieved from http://americanradioworks.publicradio.org/features/tomorrows-college/grit/angeladuckworth-grit.html

Hanna, S. L., Suggett, R., & Radtke, D. (2008). *Person to person: Positive relationships don't just happen.* Upper Saddle River, NJ: Pearson/Prentice Hall.

Hans, J. D., & Kimberly, C. (2011). Abstinence, sex, and virginity: Do they mean what we think they mean? *American Journal of Sexuality Education, 6*(4), 329–342. doi:10.1080/15546128.2011.624475

Hans, J. D., Gillen, M., & Akande, K. (2010). Sex redefined: The reclassification of oral-genital contact. *Perspectives on Sexual and Reproductive Health, 42*(2), 74–78. doi:10.1363/4207410

Hansen, J. C. (2005). Assessment of interests. In S. D. Brown & R. W. Lent (Eds.), *Career development and counseling: Putting theory and research to work*. Hoboken, NJ: Wiley.

Hansen, P. E., Floderus, B., Fredrickson, K., & Johansen, C. B. (2005). Personality traits, health behavior, and risk for cancer: A prospective study of a twin cohort. *Cancer, 103*, 1082–1091.

Happonen, P., Voutilainen, S., & Salonen, J. T. (2004). Coffee drinking is dose dependently related to the risk of acute coronary events in middle-aged men. *Journal of Nutrition, 134*(9), 2381–2386.

Harari, Y. N. (2008). Combat flow: Military, political, and ethical dimensions of subjective well-being in war. *Review of General Psychology, 12*(3), 253–264.

Harasymchuk, C., & Fehr, B. (2010). A script analysis of relational boredom: Causes, feelings, and coping strategies. *Journal of Social and Clinical Psychology, 29*(9), 988–1019. doi:10.1521/jscp.2010.29.9.988

Harber, K. D., Zimbardo, P. G., & Boyd, J. N. (2003). Participant self-selection bias as a function of individual differences in time perspective. *Basic and Applied Social Psychology, 25*, 255–264.

Hardin, E. E., & Lakin, J. L. (2009). The Integrated Self-Discrepancy Index: A valid and reliable measure of self-discrepancies. *Journal of Personality Assessment, 91*(3), 245–253.

Hargie, O. (2011). *Skilled interpersonal communication: Research, theory, and practice* (5th ed.). New York, NY: Routedge/Taylor & Francis.

Haring, M., Hewitt, P. L., & Flett, G. L. (2003). Perfectionism, coping, and quality of intimate relationships. *Journal of Marriage & Family, 65*(1), 143–158.

Harpaz, I., & Snir, R. (2003). Workaholism: Its definition and nature. *Human Relations, 56*(3), 291–319.

Harper, S. (1995). The way of wilderness. In T. Roszak, M. E. Gomes, & A. D. Kanner (Eds.), *Ecopsychology: Restoring the Earth, Healing the Mind* (pp. 183–200). San Francisco, CA: Sierra Club Books.

Harrigan, J. A., Lucic, K. S., Kay, D., McLaney, A., & Rosenthal, R. (1991). Effect of expresser role and type of self-touching on observers' perceptions. *Journal of Applied Psychology, 21*, 585 609.

Harris, C. & Wagner, D. (2009, October 23). Business has grown for sweat-lodge guru: Cracks form in motivational mogul's empire. *The Arizona Republic*. Retrieved from http://www.azcentral.com/12news/news/articles/2009/10/23/20091023rayprofile1023-CP.html

Harris, J. B., Schwartz, S. M., & Thompson, B.(2008). Characteristics associated with self-identification as a regular smoker and desire to quit among college students who smoke cigarettes. *Nicotine and Tobacco Research, 10*, 69–76.

Harris, T. (1967). *I'm OK—You're OK*. New York, NY: HarperCollins.

Harrison, D. A., Kravitz, D. A., Mayer, D. M., Leslie, L. M., & Lev-Arey, D. (2006). Understanding attitudes towards affirmative action programs in employment: Summary and meta-analyses of 35 years of research. *Journal of Applied Psychology, 91*, 1013–1036.

Harrison, J. A., & Wells, R. B. (1991). Bystander effects on male helping behavior: Social comparison and diffusion of responsibility. *Representative Research in Social Psychology, 19*(1), 53–63.

Harter, J. K. (2008). Employee engagement: How great managing drives performance. In S. J. Lopez (Ed.), *Positive psychology: Exploring the best in people* (Vol. 4, pp. 99–110). Westport, CT: Praeger.

Harter, S. (1998). The development of self-representations. In N. Eisenberg (Ed.), *Handbook of child psychology: Vol. 3. Social, emotional, and personality development*. New York, NY: Wiley.

Harter, S. (2003). The development of self-representations during childhood and adolescence. In M. R. Leary & J. P. Tangney (Eds.), *Handbook of self and identity*. New York, NY: Guilford.

Harter, S. (2006). Developmental and individual difference perspectives on self-esteem. In D. K. Mroczek & T. D. Little (Eds.), *Handbook of personality development*. Mahwah, NJ: Erlbaum.

Harter, S. (2012). Emerging self-processes during childhood and adolescence. In M. R. Leary & J. P. Tangney (Eds.), *Handbook of self and identity* (2nd ed., pp. 680–715). New York, NY: Guilford.

Hartig, T., Evans, G. W., Jamner, L. D., Davis, D. S., & Gärling, T. (2003). Tracking restoration in natural and urban field settings. *Journal of Environmental Psychology, 23*, 109–123.

Hartup, W. W., & Stevens, N. (1999). Friendships and adaptation across the life span. *Current Directions in Psychological Science, 8*(3), 76–79.

Harvey, J. H., & Omarzu, J. (1997). Minding the close relationship. *Personality and Social Psychology Review, 1*(3), 224–240. doi:10.1207/s15327957pspr0103_3

Harvey, J. H., & Omarzu, J. (1999). *Minding the close relationship: A theory of relationship enhancement*. New York, NY: Cambridge University Press.

Harvey, J. H., & Pauwels, B. G. (2009). Relationship connection: A redux on the role of minding and the quality of feeling special in the enhancement of closeness. In S. J. Lopez & C. R. Snyder (Eds.), *Oxford handbook of positive psychology* (2nd ed., pp. 385–392). New York, NY: Oxford University Press.

Harvey, J. H., & Wenzel, A. (2006). Theoretical perspectives in the study of close relationships. In A. L. Vangelisti & D. Perlman (Eds.), *The Cambridge handbook of personal relationships*. New York, NY: Cambridge University Press.

Harvey, P. D. (2010). Cognitive functioning and disability in schizophrenia. *Current Directions in Psychological Science, 19*(4), 249–254. doi:10.1177/0963721410378033

Hasan, Y., Bègue, L., & Bushman, B. J. (2012). Viewing the world through "blood-red tinted glasses": The hostile expectation bias mediates the link between violent video game exposure and aggression. *Journal of Experimental Social Psychology, 48*(4), 953–956.

Haskell, W. L., Lee, I., Pate, R. R., Powell, K. E., Blair, S. N., Franklin, B. A., et al. (2007). Physical activity and public health: Updated recommendations from the American College of Sports Medicine and the American Heart Association. *Medical Science Sports Exercise, 39*, 1423–1434.

Hass, D. M., & Stafford, L. (1998). An initial examination of maintenance behaviors in gay and lesbian relationships. *Journal of Social and Personal Relationships, 15*(6), 846–855.

Hass, N. (2006. January 8). In your Facebook. Retrieved from http://www.nytimes.com/2006/01/08/education/edlife/facebooks.html?pagewanted=all&_r=0

Hatch, A. (2009). Alternative relationship lifestyles. In H. T. Reis & S. Sprecher (Eds.), *Encyclopedia of human relationships: Vol. 2* (pp. 85–88). Los Angeles: Sage Reference Publication.

Hatcher, R. A., Trussell, J., Stewart, F. H., Nelson, A. L., Cates, W. Jr., Guest, F., & Kowal, D. (2004). *Contraceptive Technology*. New York, NY: Ardent Media.

Hatfield, E., & Rapson, R. L. (1993). *Love, sex, and intimacy: Their psychology, biology, and history*. New York, NY: HarperCollins.

Hatfield, E., & Rapson, R. L. (2010). Culture, attachment style, and romantic relationships. In P. Erdman, K. Ng (Eds.), *Attachment: Expanding the cultural connections* (pp. 227–242). New York, NY: Routledge/Taylor & Francis Group.

Hatfield, E., & Sprecher, S. (2009). Matching hypothesis. In H. T. Reis & S. Sprecher (Eds.), *Encyclopedia of human relationships: Vol. 2* (pp. 1065–1067). Los Angeles: Sage Reference Publication.

Hatton, E., & Trautner, M. (2011). Equal opportunity objectification? The sexualization of men and women on the cover of *Rolling Stone*. *Sexuality & Culture: An Interdisciplinary Quarterly, 15*(3), 256–278. doi:10.1007/s12119-011-9093-2

Hatzenbuehler, M. L. (2009). How does sexual minority stigma "get under the skin"? A psychological mediation framework. *Psychological Bulletin, 135*, 707–730.

Hatzenbuehler, M. L., Hilt, L. M., & Nolen-Hoeksema, S. (2010). Gender, sexual orientation, and vulnerability to depression. In J. C. Chrisler & D. R.

McCreary (Eds.), *Handbook of gender research in psychology* (Vol. 2, pp. 133–151). New York, NY: Springer.

Havas, S., Dickinson, B. D., & Wilson, M. (2007). The urgent need to reduce sodium consumption. *Journal of the American Medical Association, 298*, 1439–1441.

Hawkins, D. N., & Booth, A. (2005). Unhappily ever after: Effects of long-term, low-quality marriages on well-being. *Social Forces, 84*, 451–471.

Hawkley, L. C., & Cacioppo, J. T. (2009). Loneliness. In H. T. Reis & S. Sprecher (Eds.), *Encyclopedia of human relationships: Vol. 2* (pp. 985–990). Los Angeles: Sage Reference Publication.

Hawkley, L. C., & Cacioppo, J. T. (2010). Loneliness matters: A theoretical and empirical review of consequences and mechanisms. *Annals of Behavioral Medicine, 40*(2), 218–227. doi:10.1007/s12160-010-9210-8

Haworth-Hoeppner, S. (2000). The critical shapes of body image: The role of culture and family in the production of eating disorders. *Journal of Marriage and the Family, 62*, 212–227.

Hawton, K., & Harriss, L. (2008). The changing gender ratio in occurrence of deliberate self-harm across the life cycle. *Crisis, 29*, 4–10.

Haynes, G. A., & Olson, J. M. (2006). Coping with threats to just-world beliefs: Derogate, blame, or help? *Journal of Applied Social Psychology, 36*(3), 664–682.

Hazan, C., & Shaver, P. (1986). *Parental caregiving style questionnaire*. Unpublished questionnaire.

Hazan, C., & Shaver, P. (1987). Romantic love conceptualized as an attachment process. *Journal of Personality and Social Psychology, 52*, 511–524.

Hazlett, H. C., Poe, M. D., Gerig, G., Styner, M., Chappell, C., Smith, R. G., . . . Piven, J. (2011). Early brain overgrowth in autism associated with an increase in cortical surface area before age 2 years. *Archives of General Psychiatry, 68*, 467–476. doi:10.1001/archgenpsychiatry.2011.39

Healy, D. (2004). *Let them eat Prozac: The unhealthy relationship between the pharmaceutical industry and depression*. New York, NY: NYU Press.

Healy, D., & Whitaker, C. (2003). Antidepressants and suicide: Risk-benefit conundrums. *Journal of Psychiatry & Neuroscience, 28*(5), 340–347.

Heatherton, T. F., & Polivy, J. (1991). Development and validation of a scale for measuring state self-esteem. *Journal of Personality and Social Psychology, 60*, 895–910.

Hebl, M. R., & Mannix, L. M. (2003). The weight of obesity in evaluating others: A mere proximity effect. *Personality and Social Psychology, 29*(1), 28–38.

Hegarty, P., & Buechel, C. (2006). Androcentric reporting of gender differences in APA journals: 1965–2004. *Review of General Psychology, 10*, 377–389.

Heider, F. (1958). *The psychology of interpersonal relations*. New York, NY: Wiley.

Heilman, M. E., & Okimoto, T. G. (2007). Why are women penalized for success at male tasks? The implied community deficit. *Journal of Applied Psychology, 92*, 81–92.

Heimpel, S. A., Wood, J. V., Marshall, M. A., & Brown, J. D. (2002). Do people with low self-esteem really want to feel better? Self-esteem differences in motivation to repair negative moods. *Journal of Personality and Social Psychology, 82*, 128–147.

Heine, S. J., Buchtel, E. E., & Norenzayan, A. (2008). What do cross-national comparisons of personality traits tell us? The case of conscientiousness. *Psychological Science, 19*(4), 309–313.

Heine, S. J., & Renshaw, K. (2002). Interjudge agreement, self-enhancement, and liking: Cross-cultural divergences. *Personality and Social Psychology Bulletin, 28*(5), 578–587.

Heinrichs, R. W. (2005). The primacy of cognition in schizophrenia. *American Psychologist, 60*, 229–242.

Heins, M., Simons, C., Lataster, T., Pfeifer, S., Versmissen, D., Lardinois, M., . . . Myin-Germeys, I. (2011). Childhood trauma and psychosis: A case-control and case-sibling comparison across different levels of genetic liability, psychopathology, and type of trauma. *The American Journal of Psychiatry, 168*, 1286–1294. doi:10.1176/appi.ajp.2011.10101531

Helgeson, V. S. (1994). Relation of agency and communion to well-being: Evidence and potential explanations. *Psychological Bulletin, 116,* 412–428.

Helgeson, V. S., & Mickelson, K. D. (1995). Motives for social comparison. *Personality and Social Psychology Bulletin, 21,* 1200–1209.

Helgeson, V. S., Reynolds, K. A., & Tomich, P. L. (2006). A meta-analytic review of benefit finding and growth. *Journal of Consulting and Clinical Psychology, 74*(5), 797–816. doi:10.1037/0022-006X.74.5.797

Helgeson, V. S., Snyder, P., & Seltman, H. (2004). Psychological and physical adjustment of breast cancer over 4 years: Identifying distinct trajectories of change. *Health Psychology, 23,* 3–15.

Helms, J. L., & Rogers, D. T. (2010). *Majoring in psychology: Achieving your educational and career goals.* Malden, MA: Wiley-Blackwell.

Helwig, A. (2008). From childhood to adulthood: A 15-year longitudinal career development study. *Career Development Quarterly, 57*(1), 38–50.

Helzer, J. E., Wittchen, H., Krueger, R. F., & Kraemer, H. C. (2008a). Dimensional options for DSM-V: The way forward. In J. E. Helzer, H. C. Kraemer, R. F. Krueger, H. Wittchen, P. J. Sirovatka, & D. A. Regier (Eds.), *Dimensional approaches in diagnostic classification: Refining the research agenda for DSM-V* (pp. 115–127). Washington, DC: American Psychiatric Association.

Helzer, J. E., Kraemer, H., Krueger, R., Wittchen, H., Sirovatka, P., & Regier, D. (Eds.). (2008b). *Dimensional approaches in diagnostic classification: Refining the research agenda for DSM-V.* Washington, DC: American Psychiatric Association.

Henderson, K. E., & Brownell, K. D. (2004). The toxic environment and obesity: Contribution and cure. In J. K. Thompson (Ed.), *Handbook of eating disorders and obesity.* New York, NY: Wiley.

Hendricks, N. J., Ortiz, C. W., Sugie, N., & Miller, J. (2007). Beyond the numbers: Hate crimes and cultural trauma within Arab American immigrant communities. *International Review of Victimology, 14*(1), 95–113.

Hendriks, H. F. J. (2007). Moderate alcohol consumption and insulin sensitivity: Observations and possible mechanisms. *Annals of Epidemiology, 17*(Suppl.), S40–S42.

Henley, N. M. (1986). *Body politics: Power, sex, and nonverbal communication* (2nd ed.). New York, NY: Simon & Schuster.

Henley, N. M., & Freeman, J. (1995). The sexual politics of interpersonal behavior. In J. Freeman (Ed.), *Women: A feminist perspective* (5th ed.). Mountain View, CA: Mayfield.

Henman, L. D. (2001). Humor as a coping mechanism: Lessons from POWs. *Humor, 14,* 83–94.

Henry, R. G., Miller, R. B., & Giarrusso, R. (2005). Difficulties, disagreements, and disappointments in late-life marriages. *International Journal of Aging and Human Development, 61,* 243–264.

Hepper, E. G., & Carnelley, K. B. (2012). Attachment and romantic relationships: The roles of working models of self and other. In M. A. Paludi (Ed.), *The psychology of love* (pp. 133–154). Santa Barbara, CA: Praeger/ABC-CLIO.

Heppner, P. P., & Lee, D. (2005). Problem-solving appraisal and psychological adjustment. In C. R. Snyder & S. J. Lopez (Eds.), *Handbook of positive psychology.* New York, NY: Oxford University Press.

Herbenick, D., Reece, M., Sanders, S., Dodge, B., Ghassemi, A., & Fortenberry, J. D. (2009). Prevalence and characteristics of vibrator use by women in the United States: Results from a nationally representative study. *Journal of Sexual Medicine, 6,* 1857–1866.

Herbenick, D., Reece, M., Schick, V., Sanders, S. A., Dodge, B., & Fortenberry, J. D. (2010a). An event-level analysis of the sexual characteristics and composition among adults ages 18 to 59: Results from a national probability sample in the United States. *Journal of Sexual Medicine, 7*(5), 346–361.

Herbenick, D., Reece, M., Schick, V., Sanders, S. A., Dodge, B., & Fortenberry, J. D. (2010b). Sexual behavior in the United States: Results from a national probability sample of men and women ages 14–94. *Journal of Sexual Medicine, 7*(5), 255–265.

Herbenick, D., Reece, M., Schick, V., Sanders, S. A., Dodge, B., & Fortenberry, J. D. (2010c). Sexual behaviors, relationships, and perceived health status among adult women in the United States: Results from a national probability sample. *Journal of Sexual Medicine, 7*(5), 277–290.

Herbenick, D., Reece, M., Sanders, S. A., Dodge, B., Ghassemi, A., & Fortenberry, J. (2010d). Women's vibrator use in sexual partnerships: Results from a nationally representative survey in the United States. *Journal of Sex & Marital Therapy, 36*(1), 49–65. doi:10.1080/00926230903375677

Herek, G. M. (2006). Legal recognition of same-sex relationships in the United States: A social science perspective. *American Psychologist, 61,* 607–621.

Herek, G. M. (2009a). Hate crimes and stigma-related experiences among sexual minority adults in the United States: Prevalence estimates from a national probability sample. *Journal of Interpersonal Violence, 24,* 54–74.

Herek, G. M. (2009b). Sexual prejudice. In T. D. Nelson (Ed.), *Handbook of prejudice, stereotyping, and discrimination* (pp. 441–467). New York, NY: Psychology Press.

Herek, G. M., & Capitanio, J. (1996). "Some of my best friends": Intergroup contact concealable stigma, and heterosexuals' attitudes toward gay men and lesbians. *Personality and Social Psychology Bulletin, 22,* 412–424.

Heres, S., Davis, J., Maino, K., Jetzinger, E., Kissling, W., & Leucht, S. (2006). Why olanzapine beats risperidone, risperidone beats quetiapine, and quetiapine beats olanzapine: An exploratory analysis of head-to-head comparison studies of second-generation antipsychotics. *American Journal of Psychiatry, 163,* 185–194.

Herman, C. P., & Polivy, J. (2010). Sex and gender differences in eating behavior. In J. C. Chrisler & D. R. McCreary (Eds.), *Handbook of gender research in psychology* (Vol. 1, pp. 455–469). New York, NY: Springer.

Herrmann, D., Raybeck, D., & Gruneberg, M. (2002). *Improving memory and study skills: Advances in theory and practice.* Ashland, OH: Hogrefe & Huber.

Hermann, R. C., Dorwart, R. A., Hoover, C. W., & Brody, J. (1995). Variation in ECT use in the United States. *American Journal of Psychiatry, 152,* 869–875.

Hermann, R. C., Ettner, S. L., Dorwart, R. A., Hoover, C. W., & Yeung, E. (1998). Characteristics of psychiatrists who perform ECT. *American Journal of Psychiatry, 155,* 889–894.

Hertenstein, M. J., Hansel, C. A., Butts, A. M., & Hile, S. N. (2009). Smile intensity in photographs predicts divorce later in life. *Motivation and Emotion, 33,* 99–105.

Hertenstein, M. J., Holmes, R., McCullough, M., & Keltner, D. (2009). The communication of emotion via touch. *Emotion, 9,* 566–573.

Hess, J. A. (2002). Distance regulation in personal relationships: The development of a conceptual model and a test of representational validity. *Journal of Social and Personal Relationships, 19*(5), 663–683. doi:10.1177/0265407502195007

Hess, J. A. (2003). Measuring distance in personal relationships: The Relationship Distance Index. *Personal Relationships, 10*(2), 197–215. doi:10.1111/1475-6811.00046

Hess, U., & Thibault, P. (2009). Darwin and emotion expression. *American Psychologist, 64,* 120–128.

Hetherington, E. M. (1993). An overview of the Virginia longitudinal study of divorce and remarriage with a focus on early adolescence. *Journal of Family Psychology, 7,* 1–18.

Hetherington, E. M. (1999). Should we stay together for the sake of the children? In E. M. Hetherington (Ed.), *Coping with divorce, single parenting, and remarriage: A risk and resiliency perspective.* Mahwah, NJ: Erlbaum.

Hetherington, E. M. (2003). Intimate pathways: Changing patterns in close personal relationships across time. *Family Relations: Interdisciplinary Journal of Applied Family Studies, 52*(4), 318–331.

Heymann, J., Earle, A., Simmons, S., Breslow, S., & Kuehnhoff, A. (2004). *The work, family, and equity index: Where does the United States stand globally?* Boston, MA: Harvard School of Public Health.

Hicks, T. V., & Leitenberg, H. (2001). Sexual fantasies about one's partner versus someone else: Gender differences in incidence and frequency. *Journal of Sex Research, 38*(1), 43–50.

Hidaka, B. H. (2012). Depression as a disease of modernity: Explanations for increasing prevalence. *Journal of Affective Disorders, 140,* 205–214. doi:10.1016/j.jad.2011.12.036

Higgins, E. T. (1987). Self-discrepancy: A theory relating self and affect. *Psychological Review, 94*(3), 319–340.

Higgins, E. T. (1999). When do self-descrepancies have specific relations to emotions? The second-generation question of Tangney, Niedenthal, Covert, and Barlow (1998). *Journal of Personality and Social Psychology, 77*(6), 1313–1317.

Higgins, E. T., Shah, J., & Friedman, R. (1997). Emotional responses to goal attainment: Strength of regulatory focus as a moderator. *Journal of Personality and Social Psychology, 72*(3), 515–525.

Hill, A. J. (2002). Prevalence and demographics of dieting. In C. G. Fairburn & K. D. Brownell (Eds.), *Eating disorders and obesity: A comprehensive handbook.* New York, NY: Guilford.

Hill, C. T., Rubin, Z., & Peplau, L. A. (1976). Break-ups before marriage: The end of 103 affairs. *Journal of Social Issues, 32,* 147–168.

Hill, J. J., Hokombe, C. C., Clark, L. L., Boothby, M., Hincks, A. A., Fisher, J. J., & . . . Salmon, P. P. (2011). Predictors of onset of depression and anxiety in the year after diagnosis of breast cancer. *Psychological Medicine, 41*(7), 1429–1436. doi:10.1017/S0033291710001868doi:10.1016/j.jesp.2011.12.019

Hill, J. O., & Wyatt, H. R. (2005). Role of physical activity in preventing and treating obesity. *Journal of Applied Physiology, 99,* 765–770.

Hill, P. C., & Pargament, K. I. (2003). Advances in the conceptualization and measurement of religion and spirituality. *American Psychologist, 58,* 64–74.

Hines, M. (1990). Gonadal hormones and human cognitive development. In J. Balthazart (Ed.), *Hormones, brain and behavior in vertebrates: 1. Sexual differentiation, neuroanatomical aspects, neurotransmitters and neuropeptides.* Basel: Karger.

Hines, M. (2010). Sex-related variation in human behavior and the brain. *Trends in Cognitive Sciences, 14*(10), 448–456. doi:10.1016/j.tics.2010.07.005

Hines, M. (2011). Gender development and the human brain. *Annual Review of Neuroscience, 34,* 69–88. doi:10.1146/annurev-neuro-061010-113654

Hinshaw, S. P. (2007). *The mark of shame: Stigma of mental illness and an agenda for change.* New York, NY: Oxford University Press.

Hinshaw, S. P., & Stier, A. (2008). Stigma as related to mental disorders. *Annual Review of Clinical Psychology, 4,* 367–393.

Hiroto, D. S., & Seligman, M. E. P. (1975). Generality of learned helplessness in man. *Journal of Personality and Social Psychology, 31,* 311–327.

Hirsch, J. K., Wolford, K., LaLonde, S. M., Brunk, L., & Parker-Morris, A. (2009). Optimistic explanatory style as a moderator of the association between negative life events and suicidal ideation. *Crisis, 30,* 48–53.

Hirschel, M. J., & Schulenberg, S. E. (2009). Hurricane Katrina's impact on the Mississippi Gulf Coast: General self-efficacy's relationship to PTSD prevalence and severity. *Psychological Services, 6*(4), 293–303. doi:10.1037/a0017467

Hirsh, J. B. (2010). Personality and environmental concern. *Journal of Environmental Psychology, 30*(2), 245–248.

Hirt, E. R., Zillman, D., Erikson, G. A., & Kennedy, C. (1992). Costs and benefits of allegiance: Changes in fans' self-ascribed competence after team victory versus defeat. *Journal of Personality and Social Psychology, 63,* 724–738.

Ho, A. K., Sidanius, J., Pratto, F., Levin, S., Thomsen, L., Kteily, N., & Sheehy-Skeffington, J. (2012). Social dominance orientation: Revisiting the structure and function of a variable predicting social and political attitudes. *Personality and Social Psychology Bulletin, 38*(5), 583–606. doi:10.1177/0146617211432765

Hochschild, A. R. (2003). *The managed heart: Commercialization of human feeling.* Berleley, CA: University of California Press.

Hock, M. F., Deshler, D. D., & Schumaker, J. B. (2006). Enhancing student motivation through the pursuit of possible selves. In C. Dunkel & J. Kerpelman (Eds.), *Possible selves: Theory, research, and applications.* Hauppauge, NY: Nova Science Publishers.

Hodge, B. (2002, March). PCs and the healthy office. *Smart Computing*, pp. 64–67.

Hodson, G., Dovidio, J. F., & Gaertner, S. L. (2010). The aversive form of racism. In J. Chin (Ed.), *The psychology of prejudice and discrimination: A revised and condensed edition* (pp. 1–13). Santa Barbara, CA: Praeger/ABC-CLIO.

Hoek, H. W. (2002). Distribution of eating disorders. In C. G. Fairburn & K. D. Brownell (Eds.), *Eating disorders and obesity: A comprehensive handbook.* New York, NY: Guilford.

Hoffnung, M. (2004). Wanting it all: Career, marriage, and motherhood during college-educated women's 20s. *Sex Roles, 50*(9/10), 711–723.

Hofmann, S. G., Sawyer, A. T., Witt, A. A., & Oh, D. (2010). The effect of mindfulness-based therapy on anxiety and depression: A meta-analytic review. *Journal of Consulting and Clinical Psychology, 78*(2), 169–183. doi:10.1037/a0018555

Hofstede, G. (1983). Dimensions of national cultures in fifty countries and three regions. In J. Deregowski, S. Dziurawiec, & R. Annis (Eds.), *Explications in cross-cultural psychology.* Lisse: Swets and Zeitlinger.

Hogan, B. F., & Linden, W. (2004). Anger response styles and blood pressure: At least don't ruminate about it! *Annals of Behavioral Medicine, 27,* 38–49.

Høglend, P., Bøgwald, K. –P., Amlo, S., Marble, A., Ulberg, R., Sjaastad, M. C., et al. (2008). Transference interpretations in dynamic psychotherapy: Do they really yield sustained effects? *American Journal of Psychiatry, 165,* 763–771.

Høglend, P., Hersoug, A., Bøgwald, K., Amlo, S., Marble, A., Sørbye, Ø., & . . . Crits-Christoph, P. (2011). Effects of transference work in the context of therapeutic alliance and quality of object relations. *Journal of Consulting and Clinical Psychology, 79*(5), 697–706. doi:10.1037/a0024863

Holahan, C. J., Moos, R. H., Holahan, C. K., Brennan, P. L., & Schutte, K. K. (2005). Stress generation, avoidance coping and depressive symptoms: A 10-year model. *Journal of Consulting and Clinical Psychology, 73,* 658–666.

Holden, C. (2004). FDA weighs suicide risk in children on antidepressants. *Science, 303,* 745.

Holen, A. (2007). Posttraumatic stress disorder, delayed. In G. Fink (Ed.), *Encyclopedia of stress: Vols. 1–4* (2nd ed., pp. 150–152). San Diego, CA: Elsevier Academic Press.

Holland, A. S., Fraley, R., & Roisman, G. I. (2012). Attachment styles in dating couples: Predicting relationship functioning over time. *Personal Relationships, 19*(2), 234-246.

Holland, J. C., & Lewis, S. (1993). Emotions and cancer: What do we really know? In D. Goleman & J. Gurin (Eds.), *Mind/body medicine: How to use your mind for better health.* Yonkers, NY: Consumer Reports Books.

Holland, J. L. (1985). *Making vocational choices: A theory of vocational personalities and work environments.* Englewood Cliffs, NJ: Prentice-Hall.

Holland, J. L. (1996). Exploring careers with a typology: What we have learned and some new directions. *American Psychologist, 51,* 397–406.

Holland, J. L. (1997). *Making vocational choices* (3rd ed.). Odessa, FL: Psychological Assessment Resources.

Holland, R. W., Roeder, U., van Baaren, R. B., Brandt, A. C., & Hannover, B. (2004). Don't stand so close to me: The effects of self-construal on interpersonal closeness. *Psychological Science, 15,* 237–242.

Hollander, E. & Simeon, D. (2008). Anxiety disorders. In R. E. Hales, S. C. Yudofsky, & G. O. Gabbard (Eds.), *The American psychiatric publishing textbook of psychiatry* (pp.505–608). Washington, DC: American Psychiatric Publishing.

Hollon, S. D., & DiGiuseppe, R. (2011). Cognitive theories of psychotherapy. In J. C. Norcross, G. R. Vandenbos, & D. K. Freedheim (Eds.), *History of psychotherapy: Continuity and change* (2nd ed.). Washington, DC: American Psychological Association.

Hollon, S. D., & Dimidjian, S. (2009). Cognitive and behavioral treatment of depression. In I. H. Gotlib & C. L. Hammen (eds.), *Handbook of depression* (pp. 586–603). New York, NY: Guilford.

Holmberg, D., & Blair, K. L. (2009). Sexual desire, communication, satisfaction, and preferences of men and women in same-sex versus mixed-sex relationships. *Journal of Sex Research, 46*(1), 57–66. doi:10.1080/00224490802645294

Holmes, T. H., & Rahe, R. H. (1967). The Social Readjustment Rating Scale. *Journal of Psychosomatic Research, 11,* 213–218.

Holt, T., Greene, L., & Davis, J. (2003). *National Survey of adolescents and young adults: Sexual health knowledge, attitudes, and experiences.* Menlo Park, CA: Henry J. Kaiser Family Foundation.

Holt-Lunstad J., Smith T. B., Layton J. B. (2010). Social relationships and mortality risk: A meta-analytic review. *PLoS Medicine, 7*(7): e1000316 doi:10.1371/journal.pmed.1000316

Homburg, A., & Stolberg, A. (2006). Explaining pro-environmental behavior with a cognitive theory of stress. *Journal of Environmental Psychology, 26,* 1–14.

Hong, G. K., Garcia, M., & Soriano, M. (2000). Responding to the challenge: Preparing mental health professionals for the new millennium. In I. Cuellar & F. A. Paniagua (Eds.), *Handbook of multicultural mental health: Assessment and treatment of diverse populations.* San Diego: Academic Press.

Honts, C. R., Raskin, D. C., & Kircher, J. C. (2002). The scientific status of research on polygraph testing. In D. L. Faigman, D. H. Kaye, M. J. Saks, & J. Sanders (Eds.), *Modern scientific evidence: The law and science of expert testimony* (Vol. 2). St. Paul, MN: West Publishing.

Hoobler, J. M., & Brass, D. J. (2006). Abusive supervision and family undermining as displaced aggression. *Journal of Applied Psychology, 91,* 1125–1133.

Hoobler, J. M., Lemmon, G., & Wayne, S. J. (2011). Women's underrepresentation in upper management: New insights on a persistent problem. *Organizational Dynamics, 40*(3), 151–156. doi:10.1016/j.orgdyn.2011.04.001

Hoobler, J. M., Wayne, S. J., & Lemmon, G. (2009). Bosses' perceptions of family-work conflict and women's promotability: Glass ceiling effects. *Academy of Management Journal, 52,* 939–957.

Hood, K. E., Draper, P., Crockett, L. J., & Petersen, A. C. (1987). The ontogeny and phylogeny of sexual differences in development: A biopsychosocial synthesis. In B. Carter (Ed.), *Current conceptions of sex roles and sex typing: Theory and research.* New York, NY: Praeger.

Hooley, J. M. (2004). Do psychiatric patients do better clinically if they live with certain kinds of families? *Current Directions in Psychological Science, 13*(5), 202–205.

Hooley, J. M. (2009). Schizophrenia: Interpersonal functioning. In P. H. Blaney & T. Millon (Eds.), *Oxford textbook of psychopathology* (pp. 333–360). New York, NY: Oxford University Press.

Hopper, K., Harrison, G., Janca, A., & Satorius, N. (2007). *Recovery from schizophrenia: An international perspective—A report from the WHO Collaborative Project, the international study of schizophrenia.* New York, NY: Oxford University Press.

Hopwood, C. J., & Wright, A. C. (2012). A comparison of passive-aggressive and negativistic personality disorders. *Journal of Personality Assessment, 94*(3), 296–303. doi:10.1080/00223891.2012.655819

Horvath, M., & Ryan, A. M. (2003). Antecedents and potential moderators of the relationship between attitudes and hiring discrimination on the basis of sexual orientation. *Sex Roles, 48*(3/4), 115–130.

Horvath, S., & Morf, C. C. (2010). To be grandiose or not to be worthless: Different routes to self-enhancement for narcissism and self-esteem. *Journal of Research in Personality, 44*(5), 585–592. doi:10.1016/j.jrp.2010.07.002

Horvath, T. L. (2005). The hardship of obesity: A soft-wired hypothalamus. *Nature Neuroscience, 8,* 561–565.

Horwitz, W. A. (1996). Developmental origins of environmental ethics. *Ethics and Behavior, 6*(1), 29-54.

Hovanesian, S., Isakov, I., & Cervellione, K. L. (2009). Defense mechanisms and suicide risk in major depression. *Archives of Suicide Research, 13,* 74–86.

Hovland, C. I., & Weiss, W. (1951). The influence of source credibility on communication effectiveness. *Public Opinion Quarterly, 15,* 635–650.

Howard, A. (Ed.). (1995). *The changing nature of work.* San Francisco, CA: Jossey-Bass.

Howes, O. D., & Kapur, S. (2009). The dopamine hypothesis of schizophrenia: Version III—The final common pathway. *Schizophrenia Bulletin, 35*(3), 549–562. doi:10.1093/schbul/sbp006

Hoyle, R., Fejfar, M. C., & Miller, J. D. (2000). Personality and sexual risk taking: A quantitative review. *Journal of Personality, 68,* 1203–1231.

Hsia, J. F., & Schweinle, W. E. (2012). Psychological definitions of love. In M. A. Paludi (Ed.), *The psychology of love* (pp. 15–17). Santa Barbara, CA: Praeger/ABC-CLIO.

Hsu, L. K. G. (1990). *Eating disorders.* New York, NY: Guilford Press.

Hu, F. B., & Willett, W. C. (2002). Optimal diets for prevention of coronary heart disease. *Journal of the American Medical Association, 288*(20), 2569–2578.

Hu, Y., Zhang, R., & Li, W. (2005). Relationships among jealousy, self-esteem and self-efficacy. *Chinese Journal of Clinical Psychology, 13*(2), 165–166, 172.

Huang, P. H., & Blumenthal, J. A. (2009). Positive institutions, law, and policy. In S. J. Lopez & C. R. Snyder (Eds.), *Oxford handbook of positive psychology* (2nd ed., pp. 589–597). New York, NY: Oxford University Press.

Hudson, J. I., Hiripi, E., Pope, H. G., & Kessler, R. C. (2007). The prevelance and correlates of eating disorders in the national comorbidity survey replication. *Biological Psychiatry, 61,* 348–358.

Huebner, E. S., & Gilman, R. (2006). Students who like and dislike school. *Applied Research in Quality of Life, 2,* 139–150.

Huebner, E. S., Gilman, R., Reschly, A. L., & Hall, R. (2009). Positive schools. In S. J. Lopez & C. R. Snyder (Eds.), *Oxford handbook of positive psychology* (2nd ed., pp. 561–568). New York, NY: Oxford.

Huffington Post. (2012). Fortune 500 list boasts more female CEOs than ever before. Retrieved from http://www.huffingtonpost.com/2012/05/07/fortune-500-female-ceos_n_1495734.html

Hughes, E., & Parkes, K. (2007). Work hours and well-being: The roles of work-time control and work-family interference. *Work & Stress, 21*(3), 264–278.

Hull, J. G., & Young, R. D. (1983). Self-consciousness, self-esteem, and success-failure as determinants of alcohol consumption in male social drinkers. *Journal of Personality and Social Psychology, 44,* 1097–1109.

Hull, J. G., Young, R. D. & Jouriles, E. (1986). Applications of the self-awareness model of alcohol consumption: Predicting patterns of use and abuse. *Journal of Personality and Social Psychology, 51,* 790–796.

Hulshoff, H. E., Hoek, H. W., Susser, E., Brown, A. S., Dingemans, A., Schnack, H. G., van Haren, N. E. M., Ramos, L. M. P., Gispen-de Wied, C. C., & Kahn, R. S. (2000). Prenatal exposure to famine and brain morphology in schizophrenia. *American Journal of Psychiatry, 157,* 1170–1172.

Hultin, M. (2003). Some take the glass escalator, some hit the glass ceiling? Career consequences of occupational sex segregation. *Work and Occupations, 30*(1), 30–61.

Human, L. J., Biesanz, J. C., Parisotto, K. L., & Dunn, E. W. (2012). Your best self helps reveal your true self: Positive self presentation leads to more accurate personality impressions. *Social Psychological and Personality Science, 3*(1), 23–30. doi:10.1177/1948550611407689

Hunsley, J., Lee, C. M., & Wood, J. M. (2003). Controversial and questionable assessment techniques. In S. O. Lilienfeld, S. J. Lynn, & J. M. Lohr (Eds.), *Science and pseudoscience in clinical psychology*. New York, NY: Guilford.

Hunter, E. (1998). Adolescent attraction to cults. *Adolescence, 33*, 709–714.

Hunter, J. E., & Hunter, R. F. (1984). Validity and utility of alternative predictors of job performance. *Psychological Bulletin, 96*(1), 72–98.

Hurley, D. B., & Kwon, P. (2012). Results of a study to increase savoring the moment: Differential impact on positive and negative outcomes. *Journal of Happiness Studies, 13*(4), 579–588. doi:10.1007/s10902-011-9280-8

Hust, S. J. T., Brown, J. D., & L'Engle, K. L. (2008). Boys will be boys and girls better be prepared: An analysis of the rare sexual health messages in young adolescents' media. *Mass Communication & Society, 11*, 3–23.

Huston, T. L., Niehuis, S., & Smith, S. E. (2001). The early marital roots of conjugal distress and divorce. *Current Directions in Psychological Science, 10*(4), 116–119.

Hutchinson, A. (2007, February). Watering holes: Las Vegas tries to prevent a water shortage. *Popular Mechanics*, p. 20.

Hyde, A. L., Conroy, D. E., Pincus, A. L., & Ram, N. (2011). Unpacking the feel-good effect of free-time physical activity: Between- and within-person associations with pleasant-activated feeling states. *Journal of Sport & Exercise Psychology, 33*(6), 884–902.

Hyde, J. S. (1994a). *Understanding human sexuality* (5th ed.). New York, NY: McGraw-Hill.

Hyde, J. S. (1994b). Can meta-analysis make feminist transformations in psychology? *Psychology of Women Quarterly, 18*, 451–462.

Hyde, J. S. (1996). Where are the gender differences? Where are the gender similarities? In D.M. Buss & N. M. Malamuth (Eds.), *Sex, power, conflict: Evolutionary and feminist perspectives*. New York, NY: Oxford University Press.

Hyde, J. S. (2004). *Half the human experience: The psychology of women*. Boston, MA: Houghton Mifflin.

Hyde, J. S. (2005). The gender similarities hypothesis. *American Psychologist, 60*, 581–592.

Hyde, J. S. (2007a) Women in science: Gender similarities in abilities and sociocultural forces. In S. J. Ceci & W. M. Williams (Eds.), *Why aren't more women in science?* (pp. 131–146). Washington, DC: American Psychological Association.

Hyde, J. S. (2007b). New directions in the study of gender similarities and differences. *Current Directions in Psychological Science, 16*, 259–263.

Hyde, J. S., & DeLamater, J. D. (2003). *Understanding human sexuality*. New York, NY: McGraw-Hill.

Hyde, J. S., & Frost, L. A. (1993). Meta-analysis in the psychology of women. In F. L. Denmark & M. A. Paludi (Eds.), *Psychology of women: A handbook of issue and theories*. Westport, CT: Greenwood Press.

Hyde, J. S., & Grabe, S. (2008). Meta-analysis in the psychology of women. In F. L. Denmark & M. A. Paludi (Eds.), *Psychology of Women: A Handbook of Issues and Theories* (2nd ed., pp. 142–173). Westport, CT: Praeger Publishers.

Hynes, K. H., & Clarkberg, M. (2005). Women's employment patterns during early parenthood: A group-based trajectory analysis. *Journal of Marriage and Family, 67*, 222–239.

Iaccino, J. F. (1996). A further examination of the bizarre imagery mnemonic: Its effectiveness with mixed context and delayed testing. *Perceptual & Motor Skills, 83*, 881–882.

Iacono, W. G. (2008). Accuracy of polygraph techniques: Problems using confessions to determine the truth. *Physiology & Behavior, 95*(1–2), 24–26.

Iacono, W. G. (2009). Psychophysiological detection of deception and guilty knowledge. In K. S. Douglas, J. L. Skeem, & S. O. Lilienfeld (Eds.), *Psychological science in the courtroom: Consensus and controversy* (pp. 224–241). New York, NY: Guilford.

Ickes, W., Patterson, M. L., Rajecki, D. W., & Tanford, S. (1982). Behavioral and cognitive consequences of reciprocal versus compensatory responses to preinteraction expectancies. *Social Cognition, 1*, 160–190.

Ickovics, J. R., Thayaparan, B., & Ethier, K. A. (2001). Women and AIDS: A contextual analysis. In A. Baum, T. A. Revenson, & J. E. Singer (Eds.), *Handbook of health psychology*. Mahwah, NJ: Erlbaum.

Ignatius, E., & Kokkonen, M. (2007). Factors contributing to verbal self-disclosure. *Nordic Psychology, 59*(4), 362–391.

Ilgen, D. R. (1990). Health issues at work: Opportunities for industrial/organization psychology. *American Psychologist, 45*, 252–261.

Ilies, R., Hauserman, N., Schwochau, S., & Stibal, J. (2003). Reported incidents of rates of work-related sexual harassment in the United States: Using meta-analysis to explain reported rate disparities. *Personnel Psychology, 56*, 607–631.

Imhoff, R., & Erb, H.-P. (2009). What motivates nonconformity? Uniqueness seeking blocks majority influence. *Personality and Social Psychology Bulletin, 35*(3), 309–320.

Impett, E. A., & Peplau, L. A. (2006). "His" and "her" relationships? A review of the empirical evidence. In A. L. Vangelisti & D. Perlman (Eds.), *The Cambridge handbook of personal relationships*. New York, NY: Cambridge University Press.

Impett, E. A., Peplau, L. A., & Gable, S. L. (2005). Approach and avoidance sexual motives: Implications for personal and interpersonal well-being. *Personal Relationships, 12*, 465–482.

Inagaki, K., & Hatano, G. (2004). Vitalistic causality in young children's naive biology. *Trends in Cognitive Sciences, 8*, 356–362.

Infante, J. R., Torres-Avisbal, M., Pinel, P., Vallejo. J. A., Peran, F., Gonzalez, F., Contreras, P., Pacheco, C., Roldan, A., & Latre, J. M. (2001). Catecholamine levels in practitioners of the transcendental meditation technique. *Physiology & Behavior, 72*(1-2), 141–146.

Inglehart, R., Foa, R., Peterson, C., & Welzel, C. (2008). Development, freedom, and rising happiness: A global perspective (1981–2007). *Perspectives on Psychological Science, 3* (4), 264–285.

Ingram, R. E., Scott, W. D., & Hamill, S. (2009). Depression: Social and cognitive aspects. In P. H. Blaney & T. Millon (Eds.), *Oxford textbook of psychopathology* (pp. 230–252). New York, NY: Oxford University Press.

Insel, T. R. (2010). Psychiatrists' relationships with pharmaceutical companies: Part of the problem or part of the solution? *Journal of the American Medical Association, 303*(12), 1192–1193. doi:10.1001/jama.2010.317

Insko, C. A., Smith, R. H., Alicke, M. D., Wade, J., & Taylor, S. (1985). Conformity and group size: The concern with being right and the concern with being liked. *Personality and Social Psychology Bulletin, 11*, 41–50.

Institute of Physics. (2013, May 15). Scientific consensus on anthropogenic climate change. *ScienceDaily*. Retrieved from http://www.sciencedaily.com /releases/2013/05/130515203048.htm

Institute for Women's Policy Research. (2012). The gender wage gap by occupation. Retrieved from http://www.iwpr.org/publications/pubs/the-gender-wage-gap-by-occupation-1

Intergovernmental Panel on Climate Change. (2007). *Climate change 2007: Synthesis report*. Retrieved from http://www.ipcc.ch/pdf/assessment-report/ar4/syr/ar4_syr.pdf

International Labour Office. (2002). *Key indicators of the labour market, 2001–2002*. Geneva: United Nations International Labour Office.

Internet World Stats. (2011). *Internet usage statistics—the Internet big picture*. Retrieved from http://www.internetworldstats.com/stats.htm

Ippolito, J., Adler, A. B., Thomas, J. L., Litz, B. T., & Holzl, R. (2005). Extending and applying the demand-control model: The role of soldier's coping on a peacekeeping deployment. *Journal of Occupational Health Psychology, 10*, 452–464.

Iribarren, C., Sidney, S., Bild, D. E., Liu, K., Markovitz, J. H., Roseman, J. M., & Matthews, K. (2000). Association of hostility with coronary artery calcification in young adults: The CARDIA study. *Journal of the American Medical Association, 283*(19), 2546–2551.

Isacsson, G. G., Holmgren, A. A., Ösby, U. U., & Ahlner, J. J. (2009). Decrease in suicide among the individuals treated with antidepressants: A controlled study of antidepressants in suicide, Sweden 1995–2005. *Acta Psychiatrica Scandinavica, 120*(1), 37–44. doi:10.1111/j.1600-0447.2009.01344.x

Isen, A. M. (1987). Positive affect, cognitive processes, and social behavior. In L. Berkowitz (Ed.), *Advances in experimental social psychology* (Vol. 20, pp. 203–253). San Diego, CA: Academic Press.

Isen, A. M. (2002). A role for neuropsychology in understanding the facilitating influence of positive affect on social behavior and cognitive processes. In C. R. Snyder & S. J. Lopez (Eds.), *Handbook of positive psychology* (pp. 528–540). New York, NY: Oxford University Press.

Isen, A. M. (2004). Some perspectives on positive feelings and emotions: Positive affect facilitates thinking and problem solving. In A. S. R. Manstead, N. Frijda, & A. Fischer (Ed.), *Feelings and emotions: The Amsterdam symposium* (pp. 263–281). New York, NY: Cambridge University Press.

Isen, A. M., Daubman, K. A., & Nowicki, G. P. (1987). Positive affect facilitates creative problem solving. *Journal of Personality and Social Psychology, 52*, 1121–1131.

Islam, G., & Zyphur, M. (2009). Concepts and directions in critical industrial/organizational psychology. In D. Fox, I. Prilleltensky, & S. Austin (Eds.), *Critical psychology: An introduction* (2nd ed., pp. 110–125). Thousand Oaks, CA: Sage Publications Ltd.

Isley, M. M., Edelman, A., Kaneshiro, B., Peters, D., Nichols, M. D., & Jensen, J. T. (2010). Sex education and contraceptive use at coital debut in the United States: results from Cycle 6 of the National Survey of Family Growth. *Contraception, 82*(3), 236–242.

Ito, T. A. (2011). Perceiving social category information from faces: Using ERPs to study person perception. In A. Todorov, S. T. Fiske, & D. A. Prentice (Eds.), *Social neuroscience: Toward understanding the underpinnings of the social mind* (pp. 85–100). New York, NY: Oxford University Press.

Ito, T. A., Chiao, K. W., Devine, P. G., Lorig, T., & Cacioppo, J. T. (2006). The influence of facial feedback on race bias. *Psychological Science, 17*, 256–261.

Ivancevich, J. M., Matteson, M. T., Freedman, S. M., & Phillips, J. S. (1990). Worksite stress management interventions. *American Psychologist, 45*, 252–261.

Iwao, S. (1993). *The Japanese woman: Traditional image and changing reality*. New York, NY: Free Press.

Iwasaki, Y., Mackay, K. J., Mactavish, J. B., Ristock, J., & Bartlett, J. (2006). Voices from the margins: Stress, active living, and leisure as a contributor to coping with stress. *Leisure Sciences, 28*, 163–180.

Iwasaki, Y., & Ristock, J. L. (2007). The nature of stress experienced by lesbians and gay men. *Anxiety, Stress, & Coping, 20*, 299–319.

Izard, C., Fine, S., Schultz, D., Mostow, A., Ackerman, B., & Youngstrom, E. (2001). Emotion knowledge as a predictor of social behavior and academic competence in children at risk. *Psychological Science, 12*(1), 18–23.

Jablensky, A. (2009). Course and outcome of schizophrenia and their prediction. In M. C. Gelder, N. C. Andreasen, J. J. López-Ibor, Jr., & J. R. Geddes (Eds.), *New Oxford textbook of psychiatry* (2nd ed., Vol. 1). New York, NY: Oxford University Press.

Jackson, L. A., Hunter, J. E., & Hodge, C. N. (1995). Physical attractiveness and intellectual competence: A meta-analytic review. *Social Psychology Quarterly, 58*, 108–122.

Jackson, M. (2005). The limits of connectivity: Technology and 21st-century life. In D. F. Halpern & S. E. Murphy (Eds.), *From work-family balance to work-family interaction: Changing the metaphor*. Mahwah, NJ: Erlbaum.

Jackson, T., Fritch, A., Nagasaka, T., & Gunderson, J. (2002). Towards explaining the association between shyness and loneliness: A path analysis with American college students. *Social Behavior and Personality, 30*(3), 263–270.

Jacobs, B. L. (2004). Depression: The brain finally gets into the act. *Current Directions in Psychological Science, 13*(3), 103–106.

Jacques, P. J., Dunlap, R. E., & Freeman, M. (2008). The organization of denial: Conservative think tanks and environmental skepticism. *Environmental Politics, 17*, 349–385.

Jacques, R. (1997). The unbearable whiteness of being: Reflections of a pale, stale male. In P. Prasad, A. Mills, M. Elmes, & A. Prasad (Eds.), *Managing the organizational melting pot: Dilemmas of workplace diversity*. Thousand Oaks, CA: Sage.

Jaffe, H. W., Valdiserri, R. O., & De Cock, K. M. (2007). The reemerging HIV/AIDS epidemic in men who have sex with men. *Journal of the American Medical Association, 298*, 2412–2414.

Jain, S., Shapiro, S. L., Swanick, S., Roesch, S. C., Mills, P. J., Bell, I., & Schwartz, G. E. R. (2007). A randomized controlled trial of mindfulness meditation versus relaxation training: Effects on distress, positive states of mind, rumination, and distraction. *Annals of Behavioral Medicine, 33*, 11–21.

Jakicic, J. M., & Gallagher, K. I. (2002). Physical activity considerations for management of body weight. In D. H. Bessesen, & R. Kushner (Eds.), *Evaluation & Management of Obesity*. Philadelphia: Hanley & Belfus.

Jakicic, J. M., & Otto, A. D. (2005). Physical activity considerations for the treatment and prevention of obesity. *American Journal of Clinical Nutrition, 82*(Suppl. 1), 226S–229S.

Jakupcak, M., Salters, K., Gratz, K. L., & Roemer, L. (2003). Masculinity and emotionality: An investigation of men's primary and secondary emotional responding. *Sex Roles, 49*(3/4), 111–120.

James, J. E. (2004). Critical review of dietary caffeine and blood pressure: A relationship that should be taken more seriously. *Psychosomatic Medicine, 66*(1), 63–71.

Janis, I. L. (1958). *Psychological stress*. New York, NY: Wiley.

Janis, I. L. (1993). Decision making under stress. In L. Goldberger & S. Breznitz (Eds.), *Handbook of stress: Theoretical and clinical aspects* (2nd ed.). New York, NY: Free Press.

Janiszewski, P. M., Janssen, I., & Ross, R. (2009). Abdominal obesity and physical inactivity are associated with erectile dysfunction independent of body mass index. *Journal of Sexual Medicine, 6*, 1990–1998.

Jansz, J. (2000). Masculine identity and restrictive emotionality. In A. H. Fischer (Ed.), *Gender and emotion: Social psychological perspectives*. Cambridge, UK: Cambridge University Press.

Jawahar, I. M., Stone, T. H., & Kisamore, J. L. (2007). Role conflict and burnout: The direct and moderating effects of political skill and perceived organizational support on burnout dimensions. *International Journal of Stress Management, 14*, 142–159.

Jayaratne, T. E., Gelman, S. A., Feldbaum, M., Sheldon, J. P., Petty, E. M., & Kardia, S. L. R. (2009). The perennial debate: Nature, nurture, or choice? Black and white Americans' explanations for individual differences. *Review of General Psychology, 13*, 24–33.

Jefferson, J. W. & Greist, J. H. (2009). Lithium. In B. J. Sadock, V. A. Sadock, & P. Ruiz (Eds.), *Kaplan & Sadock's comprehensive textbook of psychiatry* (pp. 3132–3144). Philadelphia: Lippincott Williams & Wilkins.

Jeffery, R. W., Epstein, L. H., Wilson, G. T., Drewnowski, A., Stunkard, A. J., Wing, R. R., & Hill, D. R. (2000). Long-term maintenance of weight loss: Current status. *Health Psychology, 19*(1), 5–16.

Jeffery, R. W., Kelly, K. M., Rothman, A. J., Sherwood, N. E., & Boutelle, K. N. (2004). The weight–loss experience: A descriptive analysis. *Annals of Behavioral Medicine, 27*, 100–106.

Jemmott, J. B., III, & Magloire, K. (1988). Academic stress, social support, and secretory Immunoglobin A. *Journal of Personality and Social Psychology, 55*, 803–810.

Jenks, R. A., & Higgs, S. (2007). Associations between dieting and smoking-related behaviors in young women. *Drug and Alcohol Dependence, 88*, 291–299.

Jenness, V., & Geis, G. (2011). Transgender lives and lifestyles. In C. D. Bryant (Ed.), *The Routledge handbook of deviant behavior*. New York, NY: Routledge/Taylor & Francis Group.

Jex, S. M., Bliese, P. D., Buzzell, S., & Primeau, J. (2001). The impact of self-efficacy on stressor-strain relations: Coping style as an explanatory mechanism. *Journal of Applied Psychology, 86*, 401–409.

Jeynes, W. H. (2006). The impact of parental remarriage on children: A meta-analysis. *Marriage & Family Review, 40*, 75–102.

Jick, H., & Kaye, J. A. (2004). Autism and DPT vaccination in the United Kingdom. *New England Journal of Medicine, 350*(26), 2722–2723.

Johansen, C. (2010). Psychosocial factors. In J. C. Holland, W. S. Breitbart, P. B. Jacobsen, M. S. Lederberg, M. J. Loscalzo, & R. McCorkle (Eds.), *Psycho-oncology* (2nd ed., pp. 57–61). New York, NY: Oxford University Press.

John, O. P., Naumann, L. P., & Soto, C. J. (2008). Paradigm shift to the integrative big five trait taxonomy: History, measurement, and conceptual issues. In O. P. John, R. W. Robins, & L. A. Pervin (Eds.), *Handbook of personality: Theory and research* (pp. 114–158). New York, NY: Guilford.

Johnson, A. J., Haigh, M. M., Becker, J. A. H., Craig, E. A., & Wigley, S. (2008). College students' use of relational maintenance strategies in email in long-distance and geographically close relationships. *Journal of Computer-Mediated Communication, 13*, 381–404.

Johnson, B. A., & Ait-Dauod, N. (2005). Alcohol: Clinical aspects. In J. H. Lowinson, P. Ruiz, R. B. Millman, & J. G. Langrod (Eds.), *Substance abuse: A comprehensive textbook*. Philadelphia: Lippincott/Williams & Wilkins.

Johnson, M. P., & Ferraro, K. J. (2001). Research on domestic violence in the 1990's: Making distinctions. In R. M. Milardo (Ed.), *Understanding families into the new millennium: A decade in review*. Minneapolis, MN: National Council on Family Relations.

Johnson, S. (2007). Promoting easy sex without genuine intimacy: *Maxim* and *Cosmopolitan* cover lines and cover images. In M. Galician, & D. L. Merskin (Eds.), *Critical thinking about sex, love, and romance in the mass media* (pp. 55–74). Mahwah, NJ: Erlbaum.

Johnson, S. B., & Carlson, D. N. (2004). Medical regimen adherence: Concepts, assessment, and interventions. In J. M. Raczynski & L. C. Leviton (Eds.), *Handbook of clinical health psychology: Vol. 2. Disorders of behavior and health*. Washington, DC: American Psychological Association.

Johnson, S. L., Joormann, J., Lemoult, J., & Miller, C. (2009). Mood disorders: Biological bases. In P. H. Blaney & T. Millon (Eds.), *Oxford textbook of psychopathology* (pp. 198–229). New York, NY: Oxford University Press.

Johnson, W. (2010). Understanding the genetics of intelligence: Can height help? Can corn oil? *Current Directions in Psychological Science, 19*, 177–182. doi:10.1177/0963721410370136

Johnson, W., & Krueger, R. F. (2006). How money buys happiness: Genetic and environmental processes linking finances and life satisfaction. *Journal of Personality and Social Psychology, 90*, 680–691.

Johnston, L. D., O'Malley, P. M., Bachman, J. G., &n Schulenberg, J. E. (2007). *Monitoring the future: National survey results on drug use, 1975–2006: Vol. 2. College students and adults ages 19–45* (NIH Publication No. 07–6206). Bethesda, MD: National Institute on Drug Abuse.

Johnston, L. D., O'Malley, P. M., Bachman, J. G., &n Schulenberg, J. E. (2008). *Monitoring the future: National results on adolescent drug use: Overview of key findings* (NIH Publication No. 08–6418). Bethesda, MD: National Institute on Drug Abuse.

Johnston, L. D., O'Malley, P. M., Bachman, J. G., & Schulenberg, J. E. (2009). *Monitoring the future: National survey on drug use, 1975–2008: Vol. 2, College students and adults ages 19–50* (NIH Publication No. 09-7403). Bethesda, MD: National Institute on Drug Abuse.

Joiner, T. E., & Timmons, K. A. (2009). Depression in its interpersonal context. In I. H. Gotlib & C. L. Hammen (Eds.), *Handbook of depression* (pp. 322–339). New York, NY: Guilford.

Joiner, T. E., van Orden, K. A., Witte, T. K., & Rudd, M. D. (2009). *The interpersonal theory of suicide: guidance for working with suicidal patients*. Washington, DC: American Psychological Association.

Jonas, S., Bebbington, P., McManus, S., Meltzer, H., Jenkins, R., Kuipers, E., . . . Brugha, T. (2011). Sexual abuse and psychiatric disorder in England: Results from the 2007 Adult Psychiatric Morbidity Survey. *Psychological Medicine, 41*, 709–719. doi:10.1017/s003329171000111x

Jones, D. (1995). Sexual selection, physical attractiveness, and facial neotony: Cross-cultural evidence and implications. *Current Anthropology, 36*, 723–748.

Jones, E. E. (1990). *Interpersonal perception*. New York, NY: Freeman.

Jones, E. E., & Davis, K. (1965). From acts to dispositions: The attribution process in person perception. In L. Berkowitz (Ed.), *Advances in experimental social psychology* (Vol. 2). New York, NY: Academic Press.

Jones, E. E., Kanouse, D. E., Kelley, H. H., Nisbett, R. E., Valins, S., & Weiner, B. (1972). *Attribution: Perceiving the causes of behavior*. Morristown, NJ: General Learning Press.

Jones, R. A., & Brehm, J. W. (1970). Persuasiveness of one- and two-sided communications as a function of awareness there are two sides. *Journal of Experimental Social Psychology, 6*, 47–56.

Jordan, M., & Marshall, H. (2010). Taking counseling and psychotherapy outside: Destruction or enrichment of the therapeutic frame? *European Journal of Psychotherapy & Counseling, 12*(4), 345–359.

Jorgensen, R. S., & Kolodziej, M. E. (2007). Suppressed anger, evaluative threat, and cardiovascular reactivity: A tripartite profile approach. *International Journal of Psychophysiology, 66*, 102–108.

Jorgensen, R. S., Johnson, B. T., Kolodziej, M. E., & Schreer, G. E. (1996). Elevated blood pressure and personality: A meta-analytic review. *Psychological Bulletin, 120*, 293–320.

Jose, A., O'Leary, K. K., & Moyer, A. (2010). Does premarital cohabitation predict subsequent marital stability and marital quality? A meta-analysis. *Journal of Marriage and Family, 72*(1), 105–116. doi:10.1111/j.1741-3737.2009.00686.x

Jose, P. E., Lim, B. T., & Bryant, F. B. (2012). Does savoring increase happiness? A daily diary study. *The Journal of Positive Psychology, 7*(3), 176–187. doi:10.1080/17439760.2012.671345

Jovanović, D., Stanojević, P., & Stanojević, D. (2011). Motives for, and attitudes about, driving-related anger and aggressive driving. *Social Behavior and Personality, 39*(6), 755–764. doi:10.2224/sbp.2011.39.6.755

Joyner, T. (1999, November 14). All-work is American way: Atlanta poll finds 21 percent work 50-plus hours a week. *The Atlanta Journal-Constitution*, pp. R1, R5.

Joyner, T. (2001, May 27). Why can't we enjoy a vacation? Americans getting tired, and it shows at work. *The Atlanta Journal-Constitution*, pp. D1, D3.

Judge, T. A., & Klinger, R. (2008). Job satisfaction: Subjective well-being at work. In M. Eid & R. J. Larsen (Eds.), *The science of subjective well-being* (pp. 393–413). New York, NY: Guilford.

Judge, T. A., Livingston, B. A., & Hurst, C. (2012). Do nice guys—and gals—really finish last? The joint effects of sex and agreeableness on income. *Journal of Personality and Social Psychology, 102,* 390–407. doi:10.1037/a0026021

Julien, R. M. (2008). *A primer of drug action* (11th ed.). New York, NY: Worth.

Jung, C. G. (1921). Psychological types. In *Collected Works* (Vol. 6). Princeton, NJ: Princeton University Press.

Jung, C. G. (1933). *Modern man in search of a soul.* New York, NY: Harcourt, Brace & World.

Jussim, L. (2012). *Social perception and social reality: Why accuracy dominates bias and self-fulfilling prophecy.* New York, NY: Oxford University Press.

Justman, S. (2005). *Fool's paradise: The unreal world of pop psychology.* Chicago: Ivan R. Dee.

Kabat-Zinn, J. (1982). An outpatient program in behavioral medicine for chronic pain patients based on the practice of mindfulness meditation: Theoretical considerations and preliminary results. *General Hospital Psychiatry, 4,* 33–47.

Kabat-Zinn, J. (1990). *Full catastrophe living.* New York, NY: Dell.

Kabat-Zinn, J. (1993). Mindfulness meditation: Health benefits of an ancient Buddhist practice. In D. Goleman & J. Gurin (Eds.), *Mind/body medicine: How to use your mind for better health* (pp. 259–275). Yonkers, NY: Consumer Report Books.

Kaestle, C. E., Halpern, C. T., & Brown J. D. (2007). Music videos, pro wrestling, and acceptance of date rape among middle school males and females: An exploratory analysis. *Journal of Adolescent Health Care, 40,* 185–187.

Kafetsios, K., Maridaki-Kassotaki, A., Zammuner, V. L., Zampetakis, L. A., & Vouzas, F. (2009). Emotional intelligence abilities and traits in different career paths. *Journal of Career Assessment, 17*(4), 367–383. doi:10.1177/1069072709334233

Kagan, J., Snidman, N., & Arcus, D. M. (1992). Initial reactions to unfamiliarity. *Current Directions in Psychological Science, 1*(6), 171–174.

Kahlenberg, S. G., & Hein, M. M. (2010). Progression on Nickelodeon? Gender-role stereotypes in toy commercials. *Sex Roles, 62*(11–12), 830–847. doi:10.1007/s11199-009-9653-1

Kahn, A. S., & Andreoli Mathie, V. (1999). Sexuality, society, and feminism: Psychological perspectives on women. In C. B. Travis & J. W. White (Eds.), *Sexuality, society, and feminism: Psychological perspectives on women.* Washington, DC: American Psychological Association.

Kahn, K., Ho, A. K., Sidanius, J., & Pratto, F. (2009). The space between us and them: Perceptions of status differences. *Group Processes & Intergroup Relations, 12*(5), 591–604.

Kahn, P. H., Jr. (2003). The development of environmental moral identity. In S. Clayton & S. Opotow (Eds.), *Identity and the natural environment: The psychological significance of nature* (pp. 113–134). Cambridge, MA: MIT Press.

Kahn, P. H., Jr. (2007). The child's environmental amnesia—it's ours. *Children, Youth and Environments 17,* 199–207.

Kahn, P. H., Jr., & Kellert, S. R. (2002). *Children and nature: Psychological, sociocultural, and evolutionary investigations.* Cambridge MA: MIT Press.

Kahneman, D. (1999). Objective happiness. In D. Kahneman, E. Diener, & N. Schwarz (Eds.), *Well-being: The foundations of hedonic psychology.* New York, NY: Sage.

Kahneman, D. (2011). *Thinking, fast and slow.* New York, NY: Farrar, Straus, & Giroux.

Kahneman, D., & Deaton, A. (2010). High income improves evaluation of life but not emotional well-being. *Proceedings of the National Academy of Sciences of the United States of America, 107*(38), 16489–16493. doi:10.1073/pnas.1011492107

Kahneman, D., Krueger, A. B., Schkade, D., Schwarz, N., & Stone, A. A. (2006). Would you be happier if you were richer? A focusing illusion. *Science, 312,* 1908–1910.

Kahr, B. (2008). *Who's been sleeping in your head? The secret world of sexual fantasies.* New York, NY: Basic Books.

Kaiser, A., Haller, S., Schmitz, S., & Nitsch, C. (2009). On sex/gender related similarities and differences in fMRI language research. *Brain Research Reviews, 61,* 49–59.

Kaiser, A., Kuenzli, E., Zappatore, D., & Nitsch, C. (2007). On females' lateral and males' bilateral activation during language production: A fMRI study. *International Journal of Psychophysiology, 63*(2), 192–198. doi:10.1016/j.ijpsycho.2006.03.008

Kaiser Family Foundation (2012a). HIV/AIDS policy fact sheet: Black Americans and HIV/AIDS. Retrieved from http://www.kff.org/hivaids/6007.cfm

Kaiser Family Foundation (2012b). HIV/AIDS policy fact sheet: Latinos and HIV/AIDS. Retrieved from http://www.kff.org/hivaids/6007.cfm

Kaiser Family Foundation, Holt, T., Greene, L., & Davis, J. (2003). *National Survey of adolescents and young adults: Sexual health knowledge, attitudes, and experiences.* Menlo Park, CA: Henry J. Kaiser Family Foundation.

Kalant, H. (2004). Adverse effects of cannabis on health: An update of the literature since 1966. *Progress in Neuro-Psychopharmocology and Biological Psychiatry, 28,* 849–863.

Kalant, H., & Kalant, O. J. (1979). Death in amphetamine users: Causes and rates. In D. E. Smith (Ed.), *Amphetamine use, misuse and abuse.* Boston, MA: G. K. Hall.

Kalichman, S. C. (1995). *Understanding AIDS: A guide for mental health professionals.* Washington, DC: American Psychological Association.

Kalichman, S. C., Eaton, L., Cain, D., Cherry, C., Fuhrel, A., Kaufman, M., & Pope, H. (2007). Changes in HIV treatment beliefs and sexual risk behaviors among gay and bisexual men, 1997–2005. *Health Psychology, 26,* 650–656.

Kalichman, S. C., Eaton, L., & Cherry, C. (2010). 'There is no proof that HIV causes AIDS': AIDS denialism beliefs among people living with HIV/AIDS. *Journal of Behavioral Medicine, 33*(6), 432–440. doi:10.1007/s10865-010-9275-7

Kalichman, S. C., Roffman, R. A., Picciano, J. F., & Bolan, M. (1998). Risk for HIV infection among bisexual men seeking HIV-prevention services and risks posed to their female partners. *Health Psychology, 17,* 320–327.

Kals, E., & Ittner, H. (2003). Children's environmental identity: Indicators and behavioral impacts. In S. Clayton & S. Opotow (Eds.), *Identity and the natural environment: The psychological significance of nature* (pp. 135–157). Cambridge, MA: MIT Press.

Kamp Dush, C. M., & Taylor, M. G. (2012). Trajectories of marital conflict across the life course: Predictors and interactions with marital happiness trajectories. *Journal of Family Issues, 33*(3), 341–368. doi:10.1177/0192513X11409684

Kamp Dush, C. M., Cohan, C. L., & Amato, P. R. (2003). The relationship between cohabitation and marital quality and stability: Change across cohorts? *Journal of Marriage and Family, 65,* 539–549.

Kane, E. W. (2000). Racial and ethnic variations in gender-related attitudes. *Annual review of sociology, 26,* 419–439.

Kane, J. M., Stroup, T. S., & Marder, S. R. (2009). Schizophrenia: Pharmacological treatment. In B. J. Sadock, V. A. Sadock, & P. Ruiz (Eds.), *Kaplan & Sadock's comprehensive textbook of psychiatry* (pp. 1547–1555). Philadelphia: Lippincott Williams & Wilkins.

Kant, A. K., Schatzkin, A., Graubard, B. I., & Schairer, C. (2000). A prospective study of diet quality and mortality in women. *Journal of the American Medical Association, 283,* 2109–02115.

Kantamneni, N., & Fouad, N. (2011). Structure of vocational interests for diverse groups on the 2005 Strong Interest Inventory. *Journal of Vocational Behavior, 78*(2), 193–201. doi:10.1016/j.jvb.2010.06.003

Kapinus, C. A., & Johnson, M. P. (2003). The utility of family life cycle as a theoretical and empirical tool: Commitment and family life-cycle stage. *Journal of Family Issues, 24,* 155–184.

Kaplan, D. S., Liu, R. X., & Kaplan, H. B. (2005). School-related stress in early adolescence and academic performance three years later: The conditional influence of self expectation. *Social Psychology of Education, 8,* 3–17.

Kaplan, H. S. (1979). *Disorders of sexual desire.* New York, NY: Simon & Schuster.

Kaplan, R. (2001). The nature of the view from home: Psychological benefits. *Environment and Behavior, 33*(4), 507–542.

Kaplan, R., & Kaplan, S. (1989). *The experience of nature: A psychological perspective.* Cambridge, MA: Cambridge University Press.

Kaplan, S. (2001). Meditation, restoration, and the management of mental fatigue. *Environment and Behavior, 33,* 480–506.

Karam, E., Kypri, K., & Salamoun M. (2007). Alcohol use among college students: An international perspective. *Current Opinion in Psychiatry, 20,* 213–221.

Karasek, R. A., Jr. (1979). Job demands, job decision latitude, and mental strain: Implications for job redesign. *Administrative Science Quarterly, 24,* 285–308.

Karasek, R. A., Jr., Baker, D., Marxer, F., Ahlbom, A., & Theorell, T. (1981). Job decision latitude, job demands, and cardiovascular disease: A prospective study of Swedish men. *American Journal of Public Health, 71,* 694–705.

Karasek, R. A., Jr., & Theorell, T. (1990). *Healthy work: Stress, productivity, and the reconstruction of working life.* New York, NY: Basic Books.

Karlsen, E., Dybdahl, R., & Vitterso, J. (2006). The possible benefits of difficulty: How stress can increase and decrease subjective well-being. *Scandinavian Journal of Psychology, 47,* 411–417.

Karpicke, J. D., & Blunt, J. R. (2011). Retrieval practice produces more learning than elaborate studying with concept mapping. *Science, 331,* 772–775. doi:10.1126/science.1199327

Karpicke, J. D., Butler, A. C., & Roediger, H. (2009). Metacognitive strategies in student learning: Do students practise retrieval when they study on their own? *Memory, 17*(4), 471–479. doi:10.1080/09658210802647009

Karpicke, J. D., & Roediger III, H. L. (2003).The critical importance of retrieval for learning. *Science, 319,* 966–968.

Kasser, T. (2002). *The high price of materialism.* Cambridge, MA: MIT Press.

Kasser, T., & Kanner, A. D. (2004). *Psychology and consumer culture: The struggle for a good life in a materialistic world.* Washington DC: American Psychological Association.

Kasser, T., Ryan, R. M., Couchman, C. E., & Sheldon, K. M. (2004). Materialistic values: Their causes and consequences. In T. Kasser & A. D. Kanner (Eds.), *Psychology and consumer culture: The struggle for a good life in a materialistic world.* Washington, DC: American Psychological Association.

Kassin, S. M., Fein, S., & Markus, H. (2011). *Social psychology* (8th ed.). Belmont, CA: Wadsworth/Cengage.

Kath, L., Swody, C., Magley, V., Bunk, J., & Gallus, J. (2009). Cross-level, three-way interactions among work-group climate, gender, and frequency of harassment on morale and withdrawal outcomes of sexual harassment. *Journal of Occupational & Organizational Psychology, 82*(1), 159–182.

Kato, T. (2012). Development of the Coping Flexibility Scale: Evidence for the coping flexibility hypothesis. *Journal of Counseling Psychology, 59*(2), 262–273. doi:10.1037/a0027770

Katz, J., & Tirone, V. (2009). Women's sexual compliance with male dating partners: Associations with investments in ideal womanhood and romantic well-being. *Sex Roles, 60,* 347–356.

Katz, L. S., & Epstein, S. (2005). The relation of cancer-prone personality to exceptional recovery from cancer: A preliminary study. *Advances in Mind-Body Medicine, 21,* 6–20.

Kavesh, L., & Lavin, C. (1988). *Tales from the front.* New York, NY: Doubleday.

Kawachi, I., Colditz, G. A., Stampfer, M. J., Willett, W. C., Manson, J. E., Rosner, B., & et al. (1994). Smoking cessation and time course of decreased risks of coronary heart disease in middle-aged women. *Archives of Internal Medicine, 154,* 169–175.

Kay, J., & Kay, R. L. (2008). Individual psychoanalytic psychotherapy. In A. Tasman, J. Kay, J. A. Lieberman, M. B. First, & M. Maj (Eds.), *Psychiatry* (3rd ed.). New York, NY: Wiley-Blackwell.

Kazdin, A. E. (1994). Methodology, design, and evaluation in psychotherapy research. In A. E. Bergin & S. L. Garfield (Eds.), *Handbook of psychotherapy and behavior change* (4th ed.). New York, NY: Wiley.

Kazdin, A. E. (2001). *Behavior modification in applied settings.* Belmont, CA: Wadsworth.

Kazdin, A. E. (2007). Mediators and mechanisms of change in psychotherapy research. *Annual Review of Clinical Psychology, 3,* 1–27.

Kazdin, A. E., & Blase, S. L. (2011). Rebooting psychotherapy research and practice to reduce the burden of mental illness. *Perspectives on Psychological Science, 6,* 21–37. doi:10.1177/1745691610393527

Keesey, R. E. (1993). Physiological regulation of body energy: Implications for obesity. In A. J. Stunkard & T. A. Wadden (Eds.), *Obesity: Theory and therapy.* New York, NY: Raven Press.

Keesey, R. E. (1995). A set-point model of body weight regulation. In K. D. Brownell & C. G. Fairburn (Eds.), *Eating disorders and obesity: A comprehensive handbook.* New York, NY: Guilford Press.

Kegan, R. (1994). *In over our heads: The mental demands of modern life.* Cambridge, MA: Harvard University Press.

Keinan, G. (1987). Decision making under stress: Scanning of alternatives under controllable and uncontrollable threats. *Journal of Personality and Social Psychology, 52,* 639–644.

Keita, G. P., & Hurrell, J. J., Jr. (1994). *Job stress in a changing workforce.* Washington, DC: American Psychological Association.

Kelleher, E. (2007). In dual-earner couples, family roles are changing in U.S. Retrieved from http://www.america.gov/st/washfile-english/2007/March-2007032116291berehellek0.6708338.html

Kellert, S. R. (2002). Experiencing nature: Affective, cognitive, and evaluative development in children. In P. H. Kahn, Jr. & S. R. Kellert (Eds.), *Children and nature: Psychological, sociocultural, and evolutionary investigations* (pp. 117–151). Cambridge MA: MIT Press.

Kelley, H. H. (1950). The warm-cold dimension in first impressions of persons. *Journal of Personality, 18,* 431–439.

Kelley, H. H. (1967). Attribution theory in social psychology. In D. Levine (Ed.), *Nebraska Symposium on Motivation* (Vol. 15). Lincoln: University of Nebraska Press.

Kelley, H. H., & Thibaut, J. W. (1978). *Interpersonal relations: A theory of interdependence.* New York, NY: Wiley-Interscience.

Kellner, C. H., Greenberg, R. M., Murrough, J. W., Bryson, E. O., Briggs, M. C., & Pasculli, R. M. (2012). ECT in treatment-resistant depression. *American Journal of Psychiatry, 169,* 1238–1244.

Kellogg, S. H., & Young, J. E. (2008). Cognitive therapy. In J. L. Lebow (Ed.), *Twenty-first century psychotherapies: Contemporary approaches to theory and practice.* New York, NY: Wiley.

Kelly, J. B., & Emery, R. E. (2003). Children's adjustment following divorce: Risk and resilience perspectives. *Family Relations: Interdisciplinary Journal of Applied Family Studies, 52*(4), 352–362.

Kelman, H. C., & Hamilton, V. L. (1989). *Crimes of obedience: Toward a social psychology of authority and responsibility.* New Haven, CT: Yale University Press.

Kelsoe, J. R. (2009). Mood disorders: Genetics. In B. J. Sadock, V. A. Sadock, & P. Ruiz (Eds.), *Kaplan & Sadock's comprehensive textbook of psychiatry* (pp. 1653–1663). Philadelphia: Lippincott Williams & Wilkins.

Keltner, D. (2009). *Born to be good: The science of a meaningful life.* New York, NY: Norton.

Keltner, D., & Haidt, J. (2003). Approaching awe, a moral, spiritual, and aesthetic emotion. *Cognition and Emotion, 17,* 297–314.

Kemeny, M. E. (2003). The psychobiology of stress. *Current Directions in Psychological Science, 12*(4), 124–129.

Kempton, M. J., Salvador, Z., Munafò, M. R., Geddes, J. R., Simmons, A., Frangou, S., & Williams, S. C. R. (2011). Structural neuroimaging studies in major depressive disorder: Meta-analysis and comparison with bipolar disorder. *Archives of General Psychiatry, 68,* 675–690. doi:10.1001/archgenpsychiatry.2011.60

Kendler, K. S., Myers, J., & Prescott, C. A. (2005). Sex differences in the relationship between social support and risk for major depression: A longitudinal study of opposite-sex twin pairs. *American Journal of Psychiatry, 162,* 250–256.

Kenfield, S. A., Stampfer, M. J., Rosner, B. A., & Colditz, G. A. (2008). Smoking and smoking cessation in relation to mortality in women. *Journal of the American Medical Association, 299,* 2037–2047.

Kennedy, K. A., & Pronin, E. (2008). When disagreement gets ugly: Perceptions of bias and the escalation of conflict. *Personality and Social Psychology Bulletin, 34*(6), 833–848. doi:10.1177/0146167208315158

Kennedy, S. (2007). Psychological factors and immunity in HIV infections: Stress, coping, social support, and intervention outcomes. In A. Monat, R. S. Lazarus, & G. Reevy (Eds.), *The Praeger handbook on stress and coping* (pp. 199–215). Westport, CT: Praeger Publishers.

Kenrick, D. T., Griskevicius, V., Neuberg, S. L., & Schaller, M. (2010). Renovating the pyramid of needs: Contemporary extensions built upon ancient foundations. *Perspectives on Psychological Science, 5*(3), 292–314. doi:10.1177/1745691610369469

Kenrick, D. T., & Trost, M. R. (1993). The evolutionary perspective. In A. E. Beall & R. J. Sternberg (Eds.), *The psychology of gender.* New York, NY: Guilford Press.

Kenrick, D. T., Trost, M. R., & Sundie, J. M. (2004). Sex roles as adaptations: An evolutionary perspective on gender differences and similarities. In A. H. Eagly, A. E. Beall, & R. J. Sternberg (Eds.), *The psychology of gender.* New York, NY: Guilford Press.

Kern, M. L., & Friedman, H. S. (2008). Do conscientious individuals live longer? A quantitative review. *Health Psychology, 27*(5), 505–512. doi:10.1037/0278-6133.27.5.505

Kern, M. L., & Friedman, H. S. (2011a). Personality and pathways of influence on physical health. *Social and Personality Psychology Compass, 5*(1), 76–87. doi:10.1111/j.1751-9004.2010.00331.x

Kern, M. L., & Friedman, H. S. (2011b). Personality and differences in health and longevity. In T. Chamorro-Premuzic, S. von Stumm, & A. Furnham (Eds.), *The Wiley-Blackwell handbook of individual differences* (pp. 461–489). Wiley-Blackwell.

Kernis, M. H. (2003a). Optimal self-esteem and authenticity: Separating fantasy from reality. *Psychological Inquiry, 14*(1), 83–89.

Kernis, M. H. (2003b). Toward a conceptualization of optimal self-esteem. *Psychological Inquiry, 14*(1), 1–26.

Kernis, M. H., & Goldman, B. M. (2003). Stability and variability in self-concept and self-esteem. In M. R. Leary and J. P. Tangney (Eds.), *Handbook of self and identity.* New York, NY: Guilford.

Kesebir, S., Graham, J., & Oishi, S. (2010). A theory of human needs should be human-centered, not animal-centered: Commentary on Kenrick et al. (2010). *Perspectives on Psychological Science, 5*(3), 315–319. doi:10.1177/1745691610369470

Kessler, R. C., Berglund, P., Demler, O., Jin, R., & Walters, E. E. (2005a). Lifetime prevalence and age-of-onset distributions of DSM-IV disorders in the national comorbidity survey replication. *Archives of General Psychiatry, 62,* 593–602.

Kessler, R. C., Berglund, P., Demler, O., Jin, R., Koretz, D., Merikangas, K. R., Rush, A. J., Walters, E. E., & Wang, P. S. (2003). The epidemiology of major depressive disorder: Results from the national comorbidity survey replication (NCS-R). *The Journal of the American Medical Association, 289*(23), 3095–3105.

Kessler, R. C., Demler, O., Frank, R. G., Olfson, M., Pincus, H. A., Walters, E. E., Wang, P., Wells, K. B., & Zaslavsky, A. M. (2005b). Prevalence and treatment of mental disorders. 1990–2003. *New England Journal of Medicine, 352,* 2515–2523.

Kessler, R. C., & Zhao, S. (1999). The prevalence of mental illness. In A. V. Horvitz & T. L. Scheid (Eds.), *A handbook for the study of mental health: Social contexts, theories, and systems.* New York, NY: Cambridge University Press.

Keyes, C. M. (2009). Toward a science of mental health. In S. J. Lopez & C. R. Snyder (Eds.), *Oxford handbook of positive psychology* (2nd ed., pp. 89–95). New York, NY: Oxford University Press.

Keyes, C. M., & Haidt, J. (Eds.). (2003). *Flourishing: Positive psychology and the life well-lived.* Washington, DC: American Psychological Association.

Keyes, C. M., & Lopez, S. J. (2002). Toward a science of mental health: Positive directions in diagnosis and interventions. In C. R. Snyder, S. J. Lopez (Eds.), *Handbook of positive psychology* (pp. 45–59). New York, NY: Oxford University Press.

Keysar, B., & Henly, A. S. (2002). Speakers' overestimation of their effectiveness. *Psychological Science, 13,* 207–212.

Khot, U. N., Khot, M. B., Bajzer, C. T., Sapp, S. K., Ohman, E. M., Brener, S. J., Ellis, S. G., Lincoff, M. A., & Topol, E. J. (2003). Prevalence of conventional risk factors in patients with coronary heart disease. *Journal of the American Medical Association, 290,* 898–904.

Kiecolt-Glaser, J. K. (2009). Psychoneuroimmunology: Psychology's gateway to biomedical future. *Perspectives On Psychological Science, 4*(4), 367–369. doi:10.1111/j.1745-6924.2009.01139.x

Kiecolt-Glaser, J. K., Garner, W., Speicher, C., Penn, G. M., Holliday, J., & Glaser, R. (1984). Psychosocial modifiers of immunocompetence in medical students. *Psychosomatic Medicine, 46,* 7–14.

Kiecolt-Glaser, J. K., & Glaser, R. (1995). Measurement of immune response. In S. Cohen, R. C. Kessler, & L. U. Gordon (Eds.), *Measuring stress: A guide for health and social scientists.* New York, NY: Oxford University Press.

Kieffer, K. M., Cronin, C., & Gawet, D. L. (2006). Test and study worry and emotionality in the prediction of college students' reason for drinking: An exploratory investigation. *Journal of Alcohol and Drug Addiction, 50*(1), 57–81.

Kiernan, K. (2004). Redrawing the boundaries of marriage. *Journal of Marriage and Family, 66,* 980–987.

Kiesler, D. J. (1999). *Beyond the disease model of mental disorders.* New York, NY: Praeger.

Kihlstrom, J. F. (2001). Dissociative disorders. In P. B. Sutker & H. E. Adams (Eds.), *Comprehensive handbook of psychopathology* (3rd ed.). New York, NY: Kluwer Academic/Plenum Publishers.

Kihlstrom, J. F. (2004). An unbalanced balancing act: Blocked, recovered, and false memories in the laboratory and clinic. *Clinical Psychology: Science & Practice, 11*(1), 34–41.

Kihlstrom, J. F. (2005). Dissociative disorders. *Annual Review of Clinical Psychology, 1,* 227–253.

Kihlstrom, J. F., Glisky, M. L., & Angiulo, M. J. (1994). Dissociative tendencies and dissociative disorders. *Journal of Abnormal Psychology, 103,* 117–124.

Kilmartin, C. T. (2000). *The masculine self* (2nd ed.). Boston, MA: McGraw-Hill.

Kilmartin, C. T. (2007). *The masculine self.* Cornwall-on-Hudson, NY: Sloan Publishing.

Kiluk, B. D., Sugarman, D. E., Nich, C., Gibbons, C. J., Martino, S., Rounsaville, B. J., & Carroll, K. M. (2011). A methodological analysis of randomized clinical trials of computer-assisted therapies for psychiatric disorders: Toward improved standards for an emerging field. *The American Journal of Psychiatry, 168,* 790–799. doi:10.1176/appi.ajp.2011.10101443

Kim, H., & Markus, H. R. (1999). Deviance or uniqueness, harmony or conformity? A cultural analysis. *Journal of Personality and Social Psychology, 77*(4), 785–800.

Kim, H. S., Sherman, D. K., Ko, D., & Taylor, S. E. (2006). Pursuit of comfort and pursuit of harmony: Culture, relationships, and social support seeking. *Personality and Social Psychology Bulletin, 32*,1595–1607.

Kim, H. S., Sherman, D. K., & Taylor, S. E. (2008). Culture and social support. *American Psychologist, 63*, 518–526.

Kim, J., & Gray, K. (2008). Leave or stay? Battered women's decision after intimate partner violence. *Journal of Interpersonal Violence, 23*, 1465–1482.

Kim, J. L., & Ward, L. M. (2007). Silence speaks volumes: Parental sexual communication among Asian American emerging adults. *Journals of Adolescent Research, 22*, 3–31.

Kimiecik, J. C., & Stein, G. L. (1992). Examining flow in sports contexts: Conceptual issues and methodological concerns. *Journal of Applied Sport Psychology, 4*, 144–160.

Kim-Jo, T., Benet-Martínez, V., & Ozer, D. J. (2010). Culture and interpersonal conflict resolution styles: Role of acculturation. *Journal of Cross-Cultural Psychology, 41*(2), 264–269. doi:10.1177/0022022109354643

King, B. M. (2005). *Human sexuality today*. Upper Saddle River, NJ: Pearson Prentice Hall.

King, E. B., Hebl, M. R., George, J. M., & Matusik, S. F. (2010). Understanding tokenism: Antecedents and consequences of a psychological climate of gender inequity. *Journal of Management, 36*(2), 482–510. doi:10.1177/0149206308328508

King, G. R., & Ellinwood Jr., E. H. (2005). Amphetamines and other stimulants. In J. H. Lowinson, P. Ruiz, R. B. Millman, & J. G. Langrod (Eds.), *Substance abuse: A comprehensive textbook*. Philadelphia: Lippincott/Williams & Wilkins.

King, L. A., & Emmons, R. A. (1990). Conflict over emotional expression: Psychological and physical correlates. *Journal of Personality and Social Psychology, 58*, 864–877.

King, L. A., & Emmons, R. A. (1991). Psychological, physical, and interpersonal correlates of emotional expressiveness, conflict and control. *European Journal of Personality, 5*, 131–150.

King, L. A., King, D. W., Fairbank, J. A., Keane, T. M., & Adams, G. A. (1998). Resilience-recovery factors in post-traumatic stress disorder among female and male Vietnam veterans: Hardiness, postwar social support, and additional stressful life events. *Journal of Personality and Social Psychology, 74*, 420–434.

King, S., St-Hilaire, A., & Heidkamp, D. (2010). Prenatal factors in schizophrenia. *Current Directions in Psychological Science, 19*(4), 209–213. doi:10.1177/0963721410378360

Kinsey, A. C., Pomeroy, W. B., & Martin, C. E. (1948). *Sexual behavior in the human male*. Philadelphia: Saunders.

Kinsey, A. C., Pomeroy, W. B., Martin, C. E., & Gebhard, P. H. (1953). *Sexual behavior in the human female*. Philadelphia: Saunders.

Kirby, D. (2005). *Evidence of harm: Mercury in vaccines and the autism epidemic: A medical controversy*. New York, NY: St. Martin's Press.

Kirov, G., & Owen, M. J. (2009). Genetics of schizophrenia. In B. J. Sadock, V. A. Sadock, & P. Ruiz (Eds.), *Kaplan & Sadock's comprehensive textbook of psychiatry* (pp. 1462–1474). Philadelphia: Lippincott Williams & Wilkins.

Kirsch, I. (2010). *The emperor's new drugs: Exploding the antidepressant myth*. New York, NY: Basic Books.

Kistler, M. E., & Lee, M. J. (2010). Does exposure to sexual hip-hop music videos influence the sexual attitudes of college students? *Mass Communication and Society, 13*(1), 67–86. doi:10.1080/15205430902865336

Kitayama, S. (1996). *The mutual constitution of culture and the self: Implications for emotions*. Paper presented at the Annual Meeting of the American Psychological Society.

Kite, M. E. (2001). Gender stereotypes. In J. Worell (Ed.), *Encyclopedia of women and gender: Sex similarities and differences and the impact of society on gender* (Vol. 1, pp. 561–570). San Diego, CA: Academic Press.

Kito, M. (2005). Self-disclosure in romantic relationships and friendships among American and Japanese college students. *Journal of Social Psychology, 145*(2), 127–140.

Kitzes, J., Wackernagel, M., Loh, J., Peller, A., Goldfinger, S., Cheng, D., & Tea, K. (2008). Shrink and share: Humanity's present and future ecological footprint. *Philosophical Transactions of the Royal Society of London*, Series B, Biological Sciences, *363*, 467–475.

Klassen, M. (1987). How to get the most out of your time. In A. D. Timpe (Ed.), *The management of time*. New York, NY: Facts on File.

Klatsky, A. L. (2008). Alcohol, wine, and vascular diseases: An abundance of paradoxes. *American Journal of Physiology: Heart and Circulatory Physiology, 63*, 582–583.

Klein, D. N. (2010). Chronic depression: Diagnosis and classification. *Current Directions in Psychological Science, 19*(2), 96–100. doi:10.1177/0963721410366007

Klein, O., Snyder, M., & Livingston, R. W. (2004). Prejudice on the stage: Self-monitoring and the public expression of group attitudes. *British Journal of Social Psychology, 43*(2), 299–314. doi:10.1348/0144666041501697

Kleinke, C. L. (1986). Gaze and eye contact: A research review. *Psychological Bulletin, 100*, 78–100.

Kleinke, C. L. (2007). What does it mean to cope? In A. Monat, R. S. Lazarus, & G. Reevy (Eds.), *The Praeger handbook on stress and coping* (pp. 289–308). Westport, CT: Praeger Publishers.

Kleinmuntz, B. (1980). *Essentials of abnormal psychology*. San Francisco: Harper & Row.

Kline, G. H., Pleasant, N. D., Whitton, S. W., & Markman, H. J. (2006). Understanding couple conflict. In A. L. Vangelisti & D. Perlman (Eds.), *The Cambridge handbook of personal relationships*. New York, NY: Cambridge University Press.

Kline, P. (1995). A critical review of the measurement of personality and intelligence. In D. H. Saklofske & M. Zeidner (Eds.), *International handbook of personality and intelligence*. New York, NY: Plenum Press.

Klinesmith, J., Kasser, T., & McAndrew, F. T. (2006). Guns, testosterone, and aggression: An experimental test of a mediational hypothesis. *Psychological Science, 17*, 568–571.

Kling, K. C., Hyde, J. S., Showers, C. J., & Buswell, B. N. (1999). Gender differences in self-esteem: A meta-analysis. *Psychological Bulletin, 125*(4), 470–500.

Kloth, N., Altmann, C. S., & Schweinberger, S. R. (2011). Facial attractiveness biases the perception of eye contact. *The Quarterly Journal of Experimental Psychology, 64*(10), 1906–1918. doi:10.1080/17470218 .2011.587254

Kluft, R. P. (1996). Dissociative identity disorder. In L. K. Michelson & W. J. Ray (Eds.), *Handbook of dissociation: Theoretical, empirical, and clinical perspectives*. New York, NY: Plenum.

Kluger, R. (1996). *Ashes to ashes: America's hundred-year cigarette war, the public health and the unabashed triumph of Philip Morris*. New York, NY: Knopf.

Knapp, C. M., Ciraulo, D. A., & Jaffe, J. (2005). Opiates: Clinical aspects. In J. H. Lowinson, P. Ruiz, R. B. Millman, & J. G. Langrod (Eds.), *Substance abuse: A comprehensive textbook*. Philadelphia: Lippincott/Williams & Wilkins.

Knapp, D. E., Faley, R. H., Ekeberg, W. C., & Dubois, C. L. Z. (1997). Determinants of target responses to sexual harassment: A conceptual framework. *Academy of Management Review, 22*(3), 687–729.

Knapp, M. L., & Hall, J. A. (2006). *Nonverbal communication in human interaction*. Belmont, CA: Thompson/Wadsworth.

Knaus, W. (2000). Procrastination, blame, and change. *Journal of Social Behavior and Personality, 15*, 153–166.

Knauss, W. (2005). Group psychotherapy. In G. O. Gabbard, J. S. Beck, & J. Holmes (Eds.), *Oxford textbook of psychotherapy*. New York, NY: Oxford University Press.

Knox, D. (2000). *The divorced dad's survival book: How to stay connected to your kids*. New York, NY: Perseus.

Knox, D., Vail-Smith, K., & Zusman, M. (2007). The lonely college male. *International Journal of Men's Health, 6*(3), 273–279. doi:10.3149/jmh.0603.273

Knox, D., Vail-Smith, K., & Zusman, M. (2008). "Men are dogs": Is the stereotype justified? Data on the cheating college male. *College Student Journal, 42*, 1015–1022.

Knox, D., Zusman, M., & McNeely, A. (2008). University student beliefs about sex: Men vs. women. *College Student Journal, 42*, 181–185.

Knutson, K. L., & Van Cauter, E. (2008). Associations between sleep loss and increased risk of obesity and diabetes. *Annals of the New York Academy of Sciences, 1129*(Suppl. 1), 287–304.

Kobasa, S. C. (1979). Stressful life events, personality, and health: An inquiry into hardiness. *Journal of Personality and Social Psychology, 37*, 1–11.

Kobasa, S. C. (1984, September). How much stress can you survive? *American Health*, pp. 64–77.

Kobrin, J. L., Patterson, B. F., Shaw, E. J., Mattern, K. D., & Barbuti, S. M. (2008). *Validity of the SAT for predicting first-year college grade point average* (College Board research report no. 2008–5). New York, NY: College Board.

Koc, E. W. (2007, December). Attracting the recent college graduate: The question of location. *NACE Journal*, pp. 17–20.

Kock, N. (2012). Media naturalness theory: Human evolution and behaviour towards electronic communication technologies. In S. Roberts (Ed.), *Applied evolutionary psychology* (pp. 381–398). New York, NY: Oxford University Press.

Koenig, H. G. (2004). Religion, spirituality, and medicine: Research findings and implications for clinical practice. *South Medical Journal, 97*, 1194 –1200.

Koenig, H. G. (2010). Spirituality and mental health. *International Journal of Applied Psychoanalytic Studies, 7*(2), 116–122.

Koenig, H. G., & Cohen, H. J. (Eds.). (2002). *The link between religion and health: Psychoneuroimmunology and the faith factor*. New York, NY: Oxford University Press.

Koenig, H. G., McCullough, M. E., & Larson, D. B. (2001). *Handbook of religion and health*. London: Oxford University Press.

Koger, S. M., Schettler, T., & Weiss, B. (2005). Environmental toxicants and developmental disabilities: A challenge for psychologists. *American Psychologist, 60*, 243–255.

Koger, S. M., & Winter, D. D. (2010). *The psychology of environmental problems: psychology for sustainability* (3rd ed.). New York, NY: Taylor & Francis: Psychology Press.

Kollmuss, A., & Agyeman, J. (2002). Mind the gap: Why do people act environmentally and what are the barriers to pro-environmental behaviour? *Environmental Education Research, 8*, 239–260.

Koopmann-Holm, B., & Matsumoto, D. (2011). Values and display rules for specific emotions. *Journal of Cross-Cultural Psychology, 42*(3), 355–371. doi:10.1177/0022022110362753

Koopmans, G. T., & Lamers, L. M. (2007). Gender and health care utilization: The role of mental distress and help-seeking propensity. *Social Science & Medicine, 64*, 1216–1230.

Koriat, A., & Bjork, R. A. (2005). Illusions of competence in monitoring one's knowledge during study. *Journal of Experimental Psychology: Learning, Memory, and Cognition, 31*, 187–194.

Kornell, N., Castel, A. D., Eich, T. S., & Bjork, R. A. (2010). Spacing as the friend of both memory and induction in young and older adults. *Psychology and Aging, 25*(2), 498–503. doi:10.1037/a0017807

Kornell, N., Hays, M., & Bjork, R. A. (2009). Unsuccessful retrieval attempts enhance subsequent learning. *Journal of Experimental Psychology: Learning, Memory, and Cognition, 35*(4), 989–998. doi:10.1037/ a0015729

Kornell, N., Rhodes, M. G., Castel, A. D., & Tauber, S. K. (2011). The ease-of-processing heuristic and the stability bias: Dissociating memory, memory beliefs, and memory judgments. *Psychological Science, 22,* 787–794. doi:10.1177/0956797611407929

Kornspan, A. S., & Etzel, E. F. (2001). The relationship of demographic and psychological variables to career maturity of junior college student-athletes. *Journal of College Student Development, 42*(2), 122–132.

Korotkov, D., Perunovic, M., Claybourn, M., Fraser, I., Houlihan, M., Macdonald, M., & Korotkov, K. (2011). The Type B behavior pattern as a moderating variable of the relationship between stressor chronicity and health behavior. *Journal of Health Psychology, 16*(3), 397–409. doi:10.1177/1359105310380082

Koslowsky, M., & Pindek, S. (2011). Impression management: Influencing perceptions of self. In D. Chadee (Ed.), *Theories in social psychology* (pp. 280–296). Wiley-Blackwell.

Kowalski, R. M. (1993). Inferring sexual interest from behavioral cues: Effects of gender and sexually relevant attitudes. *Sex Roles, 29,* 13–36.

Kozlowski, S. W. J., & Bell, B. S. (2003). Work groups and teams in organizations. In W. C. Borman, D. R. Ilgen, & R. J. Klimoski (Eds.), *Handbook of psychology: Vol. 12. Industrial and organizational psychology.* New York, NY: Wiley.

Kraaij, V., & Garnefski, N. (2006). The role of intrusion, avoidance, and cognitive coping strategies more then 50 years after war. *Anxiety, Stress, & Coping, 19*(1), 1–14.

Kraaij, V., Garnefski, N., & Vlietstra, A. (2008). Cognitive coping and depressive symptoms in definitive infertility: A prospective study. *Journal of Psychosomatic Obstetrics & Gynecology, 29,* 9–16.

Kraemer, H. C. (2008). DSM categories and dimensions in clinical and research contexts. Dimensional approaches in diagnostic classification: Refining the research agenda for DSM-V. In J. E Helzer, H. C. Wittchen, R. F. Krueger, & H. C.Kraemer (Eds.), *Dimensional approaches in diagnostic classification: refining the research agenda for DSM-V* (pp. 5–17). Washington, DC: American Psychiatric Association.

Kraft, S. (2009, October 22). Sweat lodge deaths a new test for self-help guru. *LA Times.* Retrieved from http://www.latimes.com/news/nationworld/nation/la-na-guru22-2009oct22,0,6180058.story

Kramer, P. D. (2006). *Freud: Inventor of the modern mind.* New York, NY: HarperCollins.

Kramer, U. (2010). Coping and defence mechanisms: What's the difference? Second act. *Psychology and Psychotherapy: Theory, Research and Practice, 83*(2), 207–221. doi:10.1348/147608309X475989

Kreider, R. M. (2005). *Number, timing, and duration of marriages and divorces: 2001. U.S. Census Bureau, Household Economic Studies.* Washington DC: Department of Commerce.

Kreith, M. (1991). Water inputs in California food production. University of California Agricultural Issues Center. Retrieved from http://www.sakia.org/cms/fileadmin/content/irrig/general/kreith_1991_water_inputs_in_ca_food_production-excerpt.pdf

Kring, A. M., & Gordon, A. H. (1998). Sex differences in emotion: Expression, experience, and physiology. *Journal of Personality and Social Psychology, 74*(3), 686–703.

Kristof-Brown, A. L., Zimmerman, R. D., & Johnson, E. C. (2005). Consequences of individuals' fit a work: A meta-analysis of person-job, person-organization, person-group, and person-supervisor fit. *Personnel Psychology, 58,* 281–342.

Krueger, J. I., Vohs, K. D., & Baumeister, R. F. (2009). Is the allure of self-esteem a mirage after all? *American Psychologist, 63,* 64–65.

Krueger, R. F. & Johnson, W. (2008). Behavioral genetics and personality: A new look at the integration of nature and nurture. In O. P. John, R. W. Robins, & L. A. Pervin (Eds.), *Handbook of personality: Theory and research* (pp. 287–310). New York, NY: Guilford.

Krueger, W. C. F. (1929). The effect of overlearning on retention. *Journal of Experimental Psychology, 12,* 71–78.

Kruger, J., Galuska, D. A, Serdula, M. K., & Jones, D. A. (2004). Attempting to lose weight: Specific prac-

tices among U.S. adults. *American Journal of Preventive Medicine, 26,* 402–406.

Krumrei, E, Coit, C., Martin, S., Fogo, W., & Mahoney, A. (2007). Post-divorce adjustment and social relationships: A meta-analytic review. *Journal of Divorce & Remarriage, 46,* 145–166.

Krusemark, E. A., Campbell, W. K., & Clementz, B. A. (2008). Attributions, deception, and event related potentials: An investigation of the self-serving bias. *Psychophysiology, 45*(4), 511–515.

Kteily, N., Ho, A. K., & Sidanius, J. (2012). Hierarchy in the mind: The predictive power of social dominance orientation across social contexts and domains. *Journal of Experimental Social Psychology, 48*(2), 543–549. doi:10.1016/j.jesp.2011.11.007

Kuepper, R., Morrison, P. D., van Os, J., Murray, R. M., Kenis, G., & Henquet, C. (2010). Does dopamine mediate the psychosis-inducing effects of cannabis? A review and integration of findings across disciplines. *Schizophrenia Research, 121*(1–3), 107–117. doi:10.1016/j.schres.2010.05.031

Kuepper, R., van Os, J., Lieb, R., Wittchen, H., Höfler, M., & Henquet, C. (2011). Continued cannabis use and risk of incidence and persistence of psychotic symptoms: 10-year follow-up cohort study. *BMJ: British Medical Journal, 342*(7796). Retrieved from http://www.bmj.com/content/342/bmj.d738.full

Kuiper, N., Martin, R, & Olinger, L. J. (1993). Coping humour, stress, and cognitive appraisals. *Canadian Journal of Behavioural Science, 25,* 81–96.

Kulick, A. R., Pope, H. G., & Keck, P. E. (1990). Lycanthropy and self-identification. *Journal of Nervous and Mental Disease, 178,* 134–137.

Kulik, L. (2000). Jobless men and women: A comparative analysis of job search intensity, attitudes toward unemployment and related responses. *Journal of Occupational and Behavioral Psychology, 73*(4), 487–500.

Kung, H. C., Hoyert, D. L., Xu, J. Q., & Murphy, S. L. (2008). Deaths: Final data for 2005. *National Vital Statistics Reports, 56*(10), 1–66.

Kunkel, D., Eyal, K., Donnerstein, E., Farrar, K. M., Biely, E., & Rideout, V. (2007). Sexual socialization messages on entertainment television: Comparing content trends 1997–2002. *Media Psychology, 9*(3), 595–622. doi:10.1080/15213260701283210

Kunkel, D., Farrar, K. M., Eyal, K., Biely, E., Donnerstein, E., & Rideout, V. (2007). Sexual socialization messages on entertainment television: Comparing content trends, 1997–2002. *Media Psychology, 10,* 595–622.

Kunstler, J. H. (2005). *The long emergency: Surviving the end of oil, climate change, and other converging catastrophes of the twenty-first century.* New York, NY: Grove Press.

Kuo, F. E., & Sullivan, W. C. (2001). Aggression and violence in the inner city: Effects of environment via mental fatigue. *Environment and Behavior, 33*(4), 543–571.

Kurdek, L. A. (1994). The nature and correlates of relationship quality in gay, lesbian, and heterosexual cohabiting couples. In B. Greene & G. M. Herek (Eds.), *Lesbian and gay psychology.* Thousand Oaks, CA: Sage.

Kurdek, L. A. (1998). Relationship outcomes and their predictors: Longitudinal evidence from heterosexual married, gay cohabiting, and lesbian cohabiting couples. *Journal of Marriage and the Family, 30,* 553–568.

Kurdek, L. A. (2004). Gay men and lesbians: The family context. In M. Coleman & L. H. Ganong (Eds.), *Handbook of contemporary families: Considering the past, contemplating the future.* Thousand Oaks, CA: Sage.

Kurdek, L. A. (2005). What do we know about gay and lesbian couples? *Current Directions in Psychological Science, 14*(5), 251–254.

Kurdek, L. A., & Schmitt, J. P. (1986a). Early development of relationship quality in heterosexual married, heterosexual cohabiting, gay, and lesbian couples. *Developmental Psychology, 22,* 305–309.

Kurdek, L. A., & Schmitt, J. P. (1986b). Interaction of sex role self-concept with relationship quality and relationship beliefs in married, heterosexual cohabiting, gay, and lesbian couples. *Journal of Personality and Social Psychology, 51,* 365–370.

Kuroki, T., Ohta, A., Sherriff-Tadano, R., Matsuura, E., Takashima, T., Iwakiri, R., & Fujimoto, K. (2011). Imbalance in the stress-adaptation system in patients with inflammatory bowel disease. *Biological Research for Nursing, 13,* 391–398.

Kurtz, M. M., & Mueser, K. T. (2008). A meta-analysis of controlled research on social skills training for schizophrenia. *Journal of Consulting and Clinical Psychology, 76*(3), 491–504. doi:10.1037/0022-006X.76.3.491

Kutchins, H., & Kirk, S. A. (1997). *Making us crazy: DSM—The psychiatric Bible and the creation of mental disorders.* New York, NY: Free Press.

Kuther, T. L., & Morgan, R. D. (2012). *Careers in psychology: Opportunities in a changing world.* Belmont, CA: Wadsworth.

Kuyper, H., & Dijkstra, P. (2009). Better-than-average effects in secondary education: A 3-year follow-up. *Educational Research and Evaluation, 15*(2), 167–184.

Labbé, E., Schmidt, N., Babin, J., & Pharr, M. (2007). Coping with stress: The effectiveness of different types of music. *Applied Psychophysiology and Biofeedback, 32*(3–4), 163–168. doi:10.1007/s10484-007-9043-9

Ladd, G. W., Buhs, E. S., & Seid, M. (2000). Children's initial sentiments about kindergarten: Is liking school an antecedent of early classroom participation and achievement? *Merrill-Palmer Quarterly, 46,* 255–278.

LaFrance, M., Hecht, M. A., & Paluck, E. L. (2003). The contingent smile: A meta-analysis of sex differences in smiling. *Psychological Bulletin, 129,* 305–334.

La Greca, A. M. (2007). Posttraumatic stress disorder in children. In G. Fink (Ed.), *Encyclopedia of stress: Vols. 1–4* (2nd ed., pp. 145–149). San Diego, CA: Elsevier Academic Press.

Lahey, B. B. (2009). Public health significance of neuroticism. *American Psychologist, 64*(4), 241–256. doi:10.1037/a0015309

Lakein, A. (1996). *How to get control of your time and your life.* New York, NY: New American Library.

Lakey, B., & Cronin, A. (2008). Low social support and major depression: Research, theory and methodological issues. In K. S. Dobson & D. A. Dozois (Eds.), *Risk factors in depression* (pp. 385–408). San Diego, CA: Academic Press. doi:10.1016/B978-0-08-045078-0.00017-4

Lakoff, R. (1973). Language and woman's place. *Language in Society, 1*(2), 45–80. doi:10.1017/S0047404500000051

Lambert, A. J., Burroughs, T., & Nguyen, T. (1999). Perceptions of risk and the buffering hypothesis: The role of just world beliefs and right wing authoritarianism. *Personality and Social Psychology Bulletin, 25,* 643–656.

Lambert, M. J. (2011). Psychotherapy research and its achievements. In J. C. Norcross, G. R. Vandenbos, & D. K. Freedheim (Eds.), *History of psychotherapy: Continuity and change* (2nd ed.). Washington, DC: American Psychological Association.

Lambert, M. J., Bergin, A. E., & Garfield, S. L. (2004). Introduction and historical overview. In M. J. Lambert (Ed.), *Bergin and Garfield's handbook of psychotherapy and behavior change.* New York, NY: Wiley.

Lambert, M. J., & Erekson, D. M. (2008). Positive psychology and the humanistic tradition. *Journal of Psychotherapy Integration, 18*(2), 222–232. doi:10.1037/1053-0479.18.2.222

Lambert, M. J., Hansen, N. B., & Finch, A. E. (2001). Patient-focused research: Using patient outcome data to enhance treatment effects. *Journal of Consulting and Clinical Psychology, 69,* 159–172.

Lambert, M. J., & Ogles, B. M. (2004). The efficacy and effectiveness of psychotherapy. In M. J. Lambert (Ed.), *Bergin and Garfield's handbook of psychotherapy and behavior change.* New York, NY: Wiley.

Lambrecht, L., Kreifelts, B., & Wildgruber, D. (2012). Age-related decrease in recognition of emotional facial and prosodic expressions. *Emotion, 12*(3), 529–539. doi:10.1037/a0026827

Landabaso, M. A., Iraurgi, I., Sanz, J., Calle, R., Ruiz de Apodaka, J., Jimenez-Lerma, J. M., & Guticrrez-Fraile, M. (1999). Naltrexone in the treatment of alcoholism. Two-year follow up results. *European Journal of Psychiatry, 13*, 97–105.

Landers, D. M. (2007). The arousal-performance relationship revisited. In D. Smith & M. Bar-Eli (Eds.), *Essential Readings in Sport and Exercise Psychology* (pp. 211–218). Champaign, IL: Human Kinetics.

Landrine, H., & Klonoff, E. A. (2001). Cultural diversity and health psychology. In A. Baum, T. A. Revenson, & J. E. Singer (Eds.), *Handbook of health psychology* (pp. 851–891). Mahwah, NJ: Erlbaum.

Landrum, R. E. (2009). *Finding jobs with a psychology bachelor's degree: Expert advice for launching your career.* Washington, DC: American Psychological Association.

Lane S. D., Cherek, D. R., Tcheremissine, O. V., Lieving, L. M., & Pietras, C. J. (2005). Acute marijuana effects on human risk taking. *Neuropsychopharmocology, 30*, 800–809.

Lane, J. M., & Addis, M. E. (2005). Male gender role conflict and patterns of help seeking in Costa Rica and the United States. *Psychology of Men & Masculinity, 6*, 155–168.

Langbein, L., & Yost, M. A. (2009). Same-sex marriage and negative externalities. *Social Science Quarterly, 90*, 292–308.

Langer, E. J. (1975). The illusion of control. *Journal of Personality and Social Psychology, 32*(2), 311–328.

Langer, E. J. (1989). *Mindfulness.* New York, NY: Addison-Wesley.

Langer, E. J. (1990). *Mindfulness.* Cambridge, MA: Da Capo Press.

Langer, E. J. (1998). *The power of mindful learning.* Cambridge, MA: Da Capo Press.

Langer, E. J. (2002). Well-being: Mindfulness versus positive evaluation. In C. R. Snyder & S. J. Lopez (Eds.), *The handbook of positive psychology* (pp. 214–230). New York, NY: Oxford.

Langer, E. J. (2009a). Mindfulness. In S. J. Lopez (Ed.), *The encyclopedia of positive psychology* (Vol. II, pp. 618–622). Malden, MA: Wiley-Blackwell.

Langer, E. J. (2009b). *Counterclockwise: Mindful health and the power of possibility.* New York, NY: Ballantine Books.

Langer, E. J., Russell, T., & Eisenkraft, N. (2009). Orchestral performance and the footprint of mindfulness. *Psychology of Music, 37*(2), 125–136.

Langlois, J. H., Kalakanis, L., Rubenstein, A. J., Larson, A., Hallam, M., & Smoot, M. (2000). Maxims or myths of beauty? A meta-analytic and theoretical review. *Psychological Bulletin, 126*(3), 390–423.

Lansford, J. E. (2009). Parental divorce and children's adjustment. *Perspectives on Psychological Science, 4*, 140–152.

LaPiere, R. T. (1934). Attitudes vs. actions. *Social Forces, 13*, 230–237.

Large, M., Sharma, S., Compton, M. T., Slade, T., & Nielssen, O. (2011). Cannabis use and earlier onset of psychosis: A systematic meta-analysis. *Archives of General Psychiatry, 68*, 555–561. doi:10.1001/archgenpsychiatry.2011.5

Larkin, K. T., Frazer, N. L., & Wheat, A. L. (2011). Responses to interpersonal conflict among young adults: Influence of family of origin. *Personal Relationships, 18*(4), 657–667. doi:10.1111/j.1475-6811.2010.01334.x

Larkin, W., & Read, J. (2008). Childhood trauma and psychosis: Evidence, pathways, and implications. *Journal of Postgraduate Medicine, 54*, 287–293.

LaRose, R., & Rifon, N. A. (2007). Promoting *i*-safety: Effects of privacy warnings and privacy seals on risk assessment and online privacy behavior. *The Journal of Consumer Affairs, 41*(1), 127–149.

Larsen, R. J., & Prizmic, Z. (2008). Regulation of emotional well-being: Overcoming the hedonic treadmill. In M. Eid & R. J. Larsen (Eds.), *The science of subjective well-being* (pp. 258–289). New York, NY: Guilford.

Larson, R., & Pleck, J. (1998). Hidden feelings: Emotionality in boys and men. In *Gender and motivation* (Vol. 45). Lincoln: University of Nebraska Press.

Laskoff, M. B. (2004). *Landing on the right side of your ass: A survival guide for the recently unemployed.* New York, NY: Three Rivers Press.

Las Vegas Valley Water District. (2013). Drought & restrictions. Retrieved from http://www.lvvwd.com/conservation/drought.html

Latzer, Y., Tzichinsky, O., & Roer, S. (2007). Sleep-wake cycles in obese children with and without binge eating episodes. *Appetite, 49*, 306.

Lauer, J., & Lauer, R. (1985, June). Marriages made to last. *Psychology Today*, pp. 22–26.

Laughlin, H. (1967). *The neuroses.* Washington, DC: Butterworth.

Laughlin, H. (1979). *The ego and its defenses.* New York, NY: Aronson.

Laumann, E. O., Glasser, D. B., Neves, R. C. S., & Moreira, E. D. (2009). A population-based survey of sexual activity, sexual problems and associated help-seeking behavior patterns in mature adults in the United States of America. *International Journal of Impotence Research, 21*, 171–178.

Laumann, E. O., Mahay, J., & Youm, Y. (2007). Sex, intimacy, and family life in the United States. In M. Kimmel (Ed.), *The sexual self: The construction of sexual scripts* (pp. 165–190). Nashville, TN: Vanderbilt University Press.

Laurenceau, J. P., Barrett, L. F., & Rovine, M. J. (2005). The interpersonal process model of intimacy in marriage: A daily-diary and multilevel modeling approach. *Journal of Family Psychology, 19*, 314–323.

Laurenceau, J. P., & Kleinman, B. M. (2006). Intimacy in personal relationships. In A. L. Vangelisti & D. Perlman (Eds.), *The Cambridge handbook of personal relationships.* New York, NY: Cambridge University Press.

Lauriello, J., Bustillo, J. R., & Keith, S. J. (2005). Schizophrenia: Scope of the problem. In B. J. Sadock & V. A. Sadock (Eds.), *Kaplan & Sadock's comprehensive textbook of psychiatry.* Philadelphia: Lippincott Williams & Wilkins.

Lautsch, B. A., Kossek, B. A., & Ernst, E. (2011). Managing a blended workforce: Telecommuters and non-telecommuters. *Organizational Dynamics, 40* (1), 10–17. doi:10.1016/j.orgdyn.2010.10.005

Lavee, Y., & Ben-Ari, A. (2007). Relationship of dyadic closeness with work-related stress: A daily diary study. *Journal of Marriage and Family, 69*, 1021–1035.

Lawrence, E., Rothman, A. D., Cobb, R. J., Rothman, M. T., & Bradbury, T. N. (2008). Marital satisfaction across the transition to parenthood. *Journal of Family Psychology, 22*, 41–50.

Lawton, C. A. (2010). Gender, spatial abilities, and wayfinding. In J. C. Chrisler & D. R. McCreary (Eds.), *Handbook of gender research in psychology* (Vol. 1, pp. 317–341). New York, NY: Springer.

Lay, C. H. (1995). Trait procrastination, agitation, dejection, and self-discrepancy. In J. R. Ferrari, J. L. Johnson, & W. G. McCown (Eds.), *Procrastination and task avoidance: Theory, research, and treatment.* New York, NY: Plenum.

Lazarus, A. A. (1989). Multimodal therapy. In R. J. Corsini & D. Wedding (Eds.), *Current psychotherapies.* Itasca, IL: F. E. Peacock.

Lazarus, A. A. (1995). Different types of eclecticism and integration: Let's be aware of the dangers. *Journal of Psychotherapy Integration, 5*, 27–39.

Lazarus, A. A. (2008). Technical eclecticism and multimodal therapy. In J. L. Lebow (Ed.), *Twenty-first century psychotherapies: Contemporary approaches to theory and practice.* New York, NY: Wiley.

Lazarus, R. S. (1991). *Emotion and adaptation.* New York, NY: Oxford.

Lazarus, R. S. (1993). Why we should think of stress as a subset of emotion. In L. Goldberger & S. Breznitz (Eds.), *Handbook of stress: Theoretical and clinical aspects* (2nd ed.). New York, NY: Free Press.

Lazarus, R. S. (2003a). Does the positive psychology movement have legs? *Psychological Inquiry, 14*, 93–109.

Lazarus, R. S. (2003b). The Lazarus manifesto for positive psychology and psychology in general. *Psychological Inquiry, 14*, 173–189.

Lazarus, R. S. (2006). Emotions and interpersonal relationships: Toward a person-centered conceptualization of emotions and coping. *Journal of Personality, 71*, 9–46.

Lazarus, R. S., & Folkman, S. (1984). *Stress, appraisal and coping.* New York, NY: Springer.

Le, B. (2009). Familiarity principle of attraction. In H. T. Reis & S. Sprecher (Eds.), *Encyclopedia of human relationships: Vol. 1* (pp. 596–597). Los Angeles: Sage Reference Publication.

Le, B., & Agnew, C. R. (2003). Commitment and its theorized determinants: A meta-analysis of the investment model. *Personal Relationships, 10*(1), 37–57.

Le, B., Dove, N. L., Agnew, C. R., Korn, M. S., & Mutso, A. A. (2010). Predicting nonmarital romantic relationship dissolution: A meta-analytic synthesis. *Personal Relationships, 17*(3), 377–390. doi:10.1111/j.1475-6811.2010.01285.x

Leal, S., & Vrij, A. (2008). Blinking during and after lying. *Journal of Nonverbal Behavior, 32*, pp. 187–194.

Leana, C. R., & Feldman, D. C. (1991). Gender differences in responses to unemployment. *Journal of Vocational Behavior, 38*, 65–77.

Leaper, C. R., Breed, L., Hoffman, L., & Perlman, C. A. (2002). Variations in the gender-stereotyped content of children's television cartoons across genres. *Journal of Applied Social Psychology, 32*, 1653–1662.

Leaper, C., & Robnett, R. D. (2011). Women are more likely than men to use tentative language, aren't they? A meta-analysis testing for gender differences and moderators. *Psychology of Women Quarterly, 35*(1), 129–142. doi:10.1177/0361684310392728

Leary, M. R. (2004a). The function of self-esteem in terror management theory and sociometer theory: Comment on Pyszczynski et al. (2004). *Psychological Bulletin, 130*(3), 478–482.

Leary, M. R. (2004b). The sociometer, self-esteem, and the regulation of interpersonal behavior. In K. D.Vohs & R. F. Baumeister (Eds.), *Handbook of self-regulation: Research, theory, and applications* (pp. 373–391). New York, NY: Guilford Press.

Leary, M. R., & Baumeister, R. F. (2000). The nature and function of self-esteem: Sociometer theory. In M. P. Zanna (Ed.), *Advances in experimental social psychology* (Vol. 32). San Diego, CA: Academic Press.

Leavitt, F. (1995). *Drugs and behavior* (3rd ed.). Thousand Oaks, CA: Sage.

Lebow, J. L. (2008). Couple and family therapy. In J. L Lebow (Ed.), *Twenty-first century psychotherapies: Contemporary approaches to theory and practice* (pp. 307–346). New York, NY: Wiley.

Lebowitz, F. (1982). *Social studies.* New York, NY: Pocket Books.

Lechner, S. C., Tennen, H., & Affleck G. (2009). Benefit-finding and growth. In S. J. Lopez & C. R. Snyder (Eds.), *Oxford handbook of positive psychology* (2nd ed., pp. 633–640). New York, NY: Oxford.

Ledbetter, A. M. (2009). Family communication patterns and relational maintenance behavior: Direct and mediated associations with friendship closeness. *Human Communication Research, 35*(1), 130–147. doi:10.1111/j.1468-2958.2008.01341.x

Ledbetter, A. M., Griffin, E., & Sparks, G. G. (2007). Forecasting "friends forever": A longitudinal investigation of sustained closeness between best friends. *Personal Relationships, 14*, 343–350.

Ledbetter, A. M., Mazer, J. P., DeGroot, J. M., Meyer, K. R., Mao, Y., & Swafford, B. (2011). Attitudes toward online social connection and self-disclosure as predictors of Facebook communication and relational closeness. *Communication Research, 38*(1), 27–53. doi:10.1177/0093650210365537

Ledermann, T., Bodenmann, G., Rudaz, M., & Bradbury, T. N. (2010). Stress, communication, and marital quality in couples. *Family Relations: An Interdisciplinary Journal of Applied Family Studies, 59*(2), 195–206.

Lee, I.-M., & Skerrett, P. J. (2001). Physical activity and all-cause mortality. What is the dose-response relation? *Medicine and Science in Sports and Exercise, 33*, S459–S471.

Lee, K., & Ashton, M. C. (2008). The HEXACO personality factors in the indigenous personality lexicons of English and 11 other languages. *Journal of Personality, 76*(5), 1001–1053. doi:10.1111/j.1467-6494.2008.00512.x

Lee, S., & Oyserman, D. (2009). Expecting to work, fearing homelessness: The possible selves of low-income mothers. *Journal of Applied Social Psychology, 39*(6), 1334–1355.

Leeds, E. M., & Maurer, R. A. (2009). Using digital video technology to reduce communication apprehension in business education. *INFORMS Transactions on Education, 9*(2), 84–92. doi:10.1287/ited.1090.0023

Lefcourt, H. M. (2005). Humor. In C. R. Snyder & S. J. Lopez (Eds.), *Handbook of positive psychology.* New York, NY: Oxford University Press.

Lefcourt, H. M., Davidson, K., Shepherd, R., Phillips, M., Prkachin, K., & Mills, D. (1995). Perspective-taking humor: Accounting for stress moderation. *Journal of Social and Clinical Psychology, 14,* 373–391.

Leff, J., & Vaughn, C. (1985). *Expressed emotion in families.* New York, NY: Guilford Press.

Legault, E., & Laurence, J.-R. (2007). Recovered memories of childhood sexual abuse: Social worker, psychologist, and psychiatrist reports of beliefs, practices, and cases. *Australian Journal of Clinical & Experimental Hypnosis, 35,* 111–133.

Lehman, P. K., & Geller, E. S. (2004). Behavior analysis and environmental protection: Accomplishments and potential for more. *Behavior and Social Issues, 13,* 13–32.

Leibel, R. L., Rosenbaum, M., & Hirsch, J. (1995). Changes in energy expenditure resulting from altered body weight. *New England Journal of Medicine, 332,* 621–629.

Leising, D., & Borkenau, P. (2011). Person perception, dispositional inferences, and social judgment. In L. M. Horowitz & S. Strack (Eds.), *Handbook of interpersonal psychology: Theory, research, assessment, and therapeutic interventions* (pp. 157–170). Hoboken, NJ: Wiley.

Leitenberg, H., Detzer, M. J., & Srebnik, D. (1993). Gender differences in masturbation and the relation of masturbation experience in preadolescence and/or early adolescence to sexual behavior and sexual adjustment in young adulthood. *Archives of Sexual Behavior, 22,* 87–98.

Lengua, L. J., Long, A. C., & Meltzoff, A. N. (2006). Pre-attack stress-load, appraisals, and coping in children's responses to the 9/11 terrorist attacks. *Journal of Child Psychology and Psychiatry, 47,* 1219–1227.

Leonard, N. H., & Harvey, M. (2008). Negative perfectionism: Examining negative excessive behavior in the workplace. *Journal of Applied Social Psychology, 38,* 585–610.

Leondari, A., & Gonida, E. N. (2008). Adolescents' possible selves, achievement goal orientations, and academic achievement. *Hellenic Journal of Psychology, 5*(2), 179–198.

Lepore, S. J., Revenson, T. A., Weinberger, S. L., Weston, P., Frisina, P. G., Robertson, R., et al. (2006). Effects of social stressors on cardiovascular reactivity in black and white women. *Annals of Behavioral Medicine, 31,* 120–127.

Lerman, H. (1986). *A mote in Freud's eye: From psychoanalysis to the psychology of women.* New York, NY: Springer.

Lerner, M. J. (1998). The two forms of belief in a just world: Some thoughts on why and how people care about justice. In L. Montada & M. J. Lerner (Eds.), *Responses to victimizations and belief in a just world: Critical issues in social justice.* New York, NY: Plenum Press.

Leslie, L. A., & Letiecq, B. L. (2004). Marital quality of African American and white partners in interracial couples. *Personal Relationships, 11,* 559–574.

Lett, H. S., Blumenthal, J. A., Babyak, M. A., Sherwood, A., Strauman, T., Robins, C., & Newman, M. F. (2004). Depression as a risk factor for coronary artery disease: Evidence, mechanisms, and treatment. *Psychosomatic Medicine, 66*(3), 305–315.

Leung, L. (2007). Stressful life events, motives for Internet use, and social support among digital kids. *CyberPsychology & Behavior, 10,* 204–214.

Levant, R. F. (1996). The new psychology of men. *Professional Psychology: Research and Practice, 27,* 259–265.

Levant, R. F. (2003, Fall). Why study boys and men? *Nova Southeastern University Center for Psychological Studies Newsletter,* pp. 12–13.

Levant, R. F. (2011). Research in the psychology of men and masculinity using the gender role strain paradigm as a framework. *American Psychologist, 66*(8), 765–776. doi:10.1037/a0025034

Levant, R. F., & Richmond, K. (2007). A review of research on masculinity ideologies using the Male Role Norms Inventory. *The Journal of Men's Studies, 15,* 130–146.

Levenson, R. W., Carstensen, L. L., & Gottman, J. M. (1993). Long-term marriage: Age, gender, and satisfaction. *Psychology and Aging, 8,* 301–313.

Levenstein, S. (2002). Psychosocial factors in peptic ulcer and inflammatory bowel disease. *Journal of Consulting & Clinical Psychology, 70*(3), 739–750.

Leventhal, H., Cameron, L., & Leventhal, E. A. (2005). Do messages from your body, your friends, your doctor, or the media shape your health behavior? In T. C. Brock & M. C. Green (Eds.), *Persuassion: Psychological insights and perspectives.* Thousand Oaks, CA: Sage.

Leventhal, H., Musumeci, T., & Leventhal, E. (2006). Psychological approaches to the connection of health and behavior. *South African Journal of Psychology, 36,* 666–682.

Lever, J. (1994, August 24). Sexual revelations. *The Advocate,* 17–24.

Levine, M. P., & Harrison, K. (2004). Media's role in the perpetuation and prevention of negative body image and disordered eating. In J. K. Thompson (Ed.), *Handbook of eating disorders and obesity.* New York, NY: Wiley.

Levine, M. P., & Smolak, L. (2010). Cultural influences on body image and the eating disorders. In W. Agras (Ed.), *The Oxford handbook of eating disorders* (pp. 223–246). New York, NY: Oxford University Press.

Levine, R. V., Martinez, T. S., Brase, G., & Sorenson, K. (1994). Helping in 36 U.S. cities. *Journal of Personality and Social Psychology, 67*(1), 69–82.

Levine, R. V., Sato, S., Hashimoto, T., & Verma, J. (1995). Love and marriage in eleven cultures. *Journal of Cross-Cultural Psychology, 26*(5), 554–571.

Levinson, D. F. (2009). Genetics of major depression. In I. H. Gotlib & C. L. Hammen (Eds.), *Handbook of Depression* (pp. 165–186). New York, NY: Guilford.

Levinthal, C. F. (2008). *Drugs, behavior, and modern society.* Boston, MA: Pearson.

Levis, D. J. (1989). The case for a return to a two-factor theory of avoidance: The failure of non-fear interpretations. In S. B. Klein & R. R. Bowrer (Eds.), *Contemporary learning theories: Pavlovian conditioning and the status of traditional learning theory.* Hillsdale, NJ: Erlbaum.

Levitt, J. G. (2006). *Your career: How to make it happen.* Mason, OH: South-Western.

Levy, K. N., Ellison, W. D., & Reynoso, J. S. (2011). A historical review of narcissism and narcissistic personality. In W. K. Campbell & J. D. Miller (Eds.), *The handbook of narcissism and narcissistic personality disorder: Theoretical approaches, empirical findings, and treatments* (pp. 3–13). New York, NY: Wiley.

Levy, S. R., Stroessner, S. J., & Dweck, C. S. (1998). Stereotype formation and endorsement: The role of implicit theories. *Journal of Personality and Social Psychology, 74*(6), 1421–1436.

Lewandowski, C. A. (2003). Organizational factors contributing to worker frustration: The precursor to burnout. *Journal of Sociology and Social Welfare, 30*(4), 175–185.

Lewandowski, G. R., Aron, A., & Gee, J. (2007). Personality goes a long way: The malleability of opposite-sex physical attractiveness. *Personal Relationships, 14*(4), 571–585. doi:10.1111/j.1475-6811.2007.00172.x

Lewin, K. (1935). *A dynamic theory of personality.* New York, NY: McGraw-Hill.

Lewis, K., Kaufman, J., & Christakis, N. (2008). The taste for privacy: An analysis of college student privacy settings in an online social network. *Journal of Computer-Mediated Communication, 14,* 79–100.

Lewis, R. J., Derlega, V. J., Clarke, E. G., & Kuang, J. C. (2006). Stigma consciousness, social constraints, and lesbian well-being. *Journal of Counseling Psychology, 53,* 48–56.

Lewis, S., Escalona, P. R., & Keith, S. J. (2009). Phenomenology of schizophrenia. In B. J. Sadock, V. A. Sadock, & P. Ruiz (Eds.), *Kaplan & Sadock's comprehensive textbook of psychiatry* (pp. 1433–1450). Philadelphia: Lippincott Williams & Wilkins.

Li, N. P., & Tausczik, Y. R. (2009). Mate preferences. In H. T. Reis & S. Sprecher (Eds.), *Encyclopedia of human relationships: Vol. 2* (pp. 1070–1075). Los Angeles: Sage Reference Publication.

Li, S., & Li, Y-M. (2007). How far is enough? A measure of information privacy in terms of interpersonal distance. *Environment and Behavior, 39,* 317–331.

Li, Y., Johnson, K. A., Cohen, A. B., Williams, M. J., Knowles, E. D., & Chen, Z. (2012). Fundamental(ist) attribution error: Protestants are dispositionally focused. *Journal of Personality and Social Psychology, 102*(2), 281–290. doi:10.1037/a0026294

Libby, P., Ridker, P. M., & Maseri, A. (2002). Inflammation and atherosclerosis. *Circulation, 105,* 1135–1143.

Liberman, R. P., & Kopelowicz, A. (2005). Recovery from schizophrenia: A concept in search of research. *Psychiatric Services, 56,* 735–742.

Liberman, R. P., Kopelowicz, A., Ventura, J., & Gutkind, D. (2002). Operational criteria and factors related to recovery from schizophrenia. *International Review of Psychiatry, 14*(4), 256–272.

Lichter, D. T., Batson, C. D., & Brown, J. B. (2004). Welfare reform and marriage promotion: The marital expectations and desires of single and cohabiting mothers. *Social Service Review, 78*(1), 2–25.

Lichter, D. T., & Crowley, M. L. (2004). Welfare reform and child poverty: Effects of maternal employment, marriage, and cohabitation. *Social Science Research, 33,* 385–408.

Liddle, P. F. (2009). Descriptive clinical features of schizophrenia. In M. C. Gelder, N. C. Andreasen, J. J. López-Ibor, Jr., & J. R. Geddes (Eds.), *New Oxford textbook of psychiatry* (2nd ed., Vol. 1). New York, NY: Oxford University Press.

Lieberman, M. D., Gaunt, R., Gilbert, D. T., & Trope, Y. (2004). Reflection and reflexion: A social cognitive neuroscience approach to attributional inference. In M. P. Zanna (Ed.), *Advances in experimental social psychology* (Vol. 34). San Diego, CA: Academic Press.

Liebert, R. M., & Liebert, L. L. (1998). *Liebert & Spiegler's personality strategies and issues.* Pacific Grove: Brooks/Cole.

Lievens, F., & Chan, D. (2010). Practical intelligence, emotional intelligence, and social intelligence. In J. L. Farr, N. T. Tippins (Eds.), *Handbook of employee selection* (pp. 339–359). New York, NY: Routledge/Taylor & Francis Group.

Liewer, L., Mains, D., Lykens, K., & René, A. (2008). Barriers to women's cardiovascular risk knowledge. *Health Care for Women International, 29*(1), 23–38.

Lilienfeld, S. O. (2007). Psychological treatments that cause harm. *Perspectives on Psychological Science, 2,* 53–70.

Lilienfeld, S. O., & Arkowitz, H. (2011, September/October). Can people have multiple personalities? Although many therapists think it is possible, research raises doubts. *Scientific American Mind,* 64–65.

Lilienfeld, S. O., & Landfield, K. (2008a). Issues in diagnosis: Categorical vs. dimensional. In W. E. Craighead, D. J. Miklowitz, & L. W. Craighead (Eds.), *Psychopathology: History, diagnosis, and empirical foundations.* New York, NY: Wiley.

Lilienfeld, S. O., & Landfield, K. (2008b). Science and pseudoscience in law enforcement: A user-friendly primer. *Criminal Justice and Behavior, 35*(10), 1215–1230.

Lilienfeld, S. O., & Lynn, S. J. (2003). Dissociative identity disorder: Multiple personalities, multiple controversies. In S. O. Lilienfeld, S. Lynn, S. Jay, & J. M. Lohr (Eds.), *Science and pseudoscience in clinical psychology.* New York, NY: Guilford Press.

Lilienfeld, S. O., Lynn, S. J., Kirsch, I., Chaves, J. F., Sarbin, T. R., Ganaway, G. K., & Powell, R. A. (1999). Dissociative identity disorder and the sociocognitive model: Recalling the lessons of the past. *Psychological Bulletin, 125*(5), 507–523.

Lilienfeld, S. O., Wood, J. M., & Garb, H. N. (2000). The scientific status of projective tests. *Psychological Science in the Public Interest, 1*(2), 27–66.

Lima, M. L. (2004). On the influence of risk perception on mental health: living near an incinerator. *Journal of Environmental Psychology, 24*, 71–84.

Lin, Y., & Huang, C. (2006). The process of transforming daily social interactions to relationship intimacy: A longitudinal study. *Chinese Journal of Psychology, 48*(1), 35–52.

Lindau, M., Almkvist, O., & Mohammed, A. H. (2007). Learning and memory, effects of stress on. In G. Fink (Ed.), *Encyclopedia of stress: Vols. 1–4* (2nd ed., pp. 571–576). San Diego, CA: Elsevier Academic Press.

Lindau, S. T., Schumm, L. P., Laumann, E. O., Levinson, W., O'Muircheartaigh, C. A., & Waite, L. J. (2007). A study of sexuality and health among older adults in the United States. *The New England Journal of Medicine, 357*, 762–775.

Lindberg, S. M., Hyde, J., Petersen, J. L., & Linn, M. C. (2010). New trends in gender and mathematics performance: A meta-analysis. *Psychological Bulletin, 136*(6), 1123–1135. doi:10.1037/a0021276

Linde, J. A., Rothman, A. J., Baldwin, A. S., & Jeffery, R. W. (2006). The impact of self-efficacy on behavior change and weight change among overweight participants in a weight loss trial. *Health Psychology, 25*, 282–291.

Lindgren, H. C. (1969). *The psychology of college success: A dynamic approach.* New York, NY: Wiley.

Lindsay, D. S., Hagen, L., Read, J. D., Wade, K. A., & Garry, M. (2004). True photographs and false memories. *Psychological Science, 15*(3), 149–154.

Lindsay, D. S., & Read, J. D. (1994). Psychotherapy and memories of childhood sexual abuse: A cognitive perspective. *Applied Cognitive Psychology, 8*, 281–338.

Linley, P. A. (2009). Positive psychology (history). In S. J. Lopez (Ed.), *The encyclopedia of positive psychology* (Vol. II, pp. 742–746). Malden, MA: Wiley-Blackwell.

Linley, P. A., & Joseph, S. (2004a). Preface. In P. A. Linley & S. Joseph (Eds.), *Positive psychology in practice* (pp. xv–xvi). Hoboken, NJ: Wiley.

Linley, P. A., & Joseph, S. (2004b). Positive change following trauma and adversity: A review. *Journal of Traumatic Stress, 17*(1), 11–21.

Linn, S. (2008). Commercializing childhood: The corporate takeover of kids' lives. (interview by the Multinational Monitor). Retrieved from http://towardfreedom.com/home/content/view/1389/1/

Lipkus, I. M., Dalbert, C., & Siegler, I. C. (1996). The importance of distinguishing the belief in a just world for self versus for others: Implications for psychological well-being. *Personality and Social Psychology Bulletin, 22*, 666–677.

Lippa, R. A. (2005). *Gender, nature, and nurture.* Mahwah, NJ: Erlbaum.

Lippa, R. A. (2006). The gender reality hypothesis. *American Psychologist, 61*, 639–640.

Lippa, R. A. (2007). The preferred traits of mates in a cross-national study of heterosexual and homosexual men and women: An examination of biological and cultural influences. *Archives of Sexual Behavior 36*, 193–208.

Lippa, R. A. (2010). Sex differences in personality traits and gender-related occupational preferences across 53 nations: Testing evolutionary and social-environmental theories. *Archives of Sexual Behavior, 39*(3), 619–636. doi:10.1007/s10508-008-9380-7

Lishner, D. A., Nguyen, S., Stocks, E. L., & Zillmer, E. J. (2008). Are sexual and emotional infidelity equally upsetting to men and women? Making sense of forced-choice responses. *Evolutionary Psychology, 6*, 667–675.

Liston, C. C., McEwen, B. S., & Casey, B. J. (2009). Psychosocial stress reversibly disrupts prefrontal processing and attentional control. *PNAS Proceedings of the National Academy of Sciences of the United States of America, 106*(3), 912–917. doi:10.1073/pnas.0807041106

Littlefield, M. B. (2003). Gender role identity and stress in African American women. *Journal of Human Behavior in the Social Environment, 8*(4), 93–104.

Litzinger, S., & Gordon, K. C. (2005). Exploring relationships among communication, sexual satisfaction, and marital satisfaction. *Journal of Sex & Marital Therapy, 31*, 409–424.

Liu, H., & Wang H. (2009). Relationship between loneliness, friendship quality and peer acceptance in 209 primary school children. *Chinese Mental Health Journal, 23*, 44–47.

Liverant, G. I., Hofmann, S. G., & Litz, B. T. (2004). Coping and anxiety in college students after the September 11th terrorists attacks. *Anxiety, Stress, & Coping, 17*(2), 127–139.

Livesay, C., & Duck, S. (2009). Personal relationships, defining characteristics. In H. T. Reis & S. Sprecher (Eds.), *Encyclopedia of human relationships: Vol. 3* (pp. 1220–1224). Los Angeles: Sage Reference Publication.

Llorca, P. (2008). Monitoring patients to improve physical health and treatment outcome. *European Neuropsychopharmacology, 18*, S140–S145.

Lock, R. D. (2005a). *Taking charge of your career direction: Career planning guide, Book 1.* Belmont, CA: Wadsworth.

Lock, R. D. (2005b). *Job Search: Career Planning Guide, Book 2.* Belmont, CA: Wadsworth.

Lockwood, P. (2002). Could it happen to you? Predicting the impact of downward social comparisons on the self. *Journal of Personality and Social Psychology, 82*, 343–358.

Loewenstein, G., O'Donoghue, T., & Rabin, M. (2003). Projection bias in predicting future utility. *Quarterly Journal of Economics, 118*(4), 1209–1248.

Lofquist, D. (2011). Same-sex couple households. Retrieved from http://www.census.gov/prod/2011pubs/acsbr10-03.pdf

Lofquist, D., Lugaila, T., O'Connell, M., & Feliz, S. (2012). Households and families: 2010. *2010 Census briefs.* Retrieved from http://www.census.gov/prod/cen2010/briefs/c2010br-14.pdf

Loftus, E. F. (1994). The repressed memory controversy. *American Psychologist, 49*, 443–445.

Loftus, E. F. (2003). Make believe memories. *American Psychologist, 58*, 864–873.

Loftus, E. F., & Cahill, L. (2007). Memory distortion: From misinformation to rich false memory. In J. S. Nairne (Ed.), *The foundations of remembering: Essays in honor of Henry L. Roediger III.* New York, NY: Psychology Press.

Loftus, E. F., & Davis, D. (2006). Recovered memories. *Annual Review of Clinical Psychology, 2*, 469–498.

Lohmer, M. (2012). Different organizations—different burnouts: Burnout as interplay between personality pattern and organizational structure. In H. Brunning (Ed.), *Psychoanalytic reflections on a changing world* (pp. 51–65). London England: Karnac Books.

Lohoff, F. W. & Berrettini, W. H. (2009). Genetics of mood disorders. In D. S. Charney & E. J. Nestler (Eds.), *Neurobiology of mental illness* (pp. 360–377). New York: Oxford University Press.

Lohr, J. M., Olatunji, B. O., Baumeister, R. F., & Bushman, B. J. (2007). The psychology of anger venting and empirically supported alternatives that do no harm. *The Scientific Review of Mental Health Practice, 5*, 53–64.

Lonsdale, A. J., & North, A. C. (2009). Musical taste and ingroup favouritism. *Group Processes & Intergroup Relations, 12*(3), 319–327.

Lopes, P. N., Brackett, M. A., Nezlek, J. B., Schutz, A., Sellin, I., & Salovey, P. (2004). Emotional intelligence and social interaction. *Personality and Social Psychology Bulletin, 30*(8), 1018–1034.

Lopez, S. J., & Snyder, C. R. (Eds.). (2009). *Oxford handbook of positive psychology* (2nd ed.). New York, NY: Oxford.

Loth, K., van den Berg, P., Eisenberg, M., & Neumark-Sztainer, D. (2008). Stressful life events and disordered eating behaviors: Findings from Project EAT. *Journal of Adolescent Health, 43*, 514–516.

Louv, R. (2005). *Last child in the woods: Saving our children from nature-deficit disorder.* Chapel Hill, NC: Algonquin Books.

Lovejoy, T. E., & Hannah, L. (2005). *Climate change and biodiversity.* New Haven, CT: Yale University Press.

Lowinson, J. H., Ruiz, P., Millman, R. B., & Langrod, J. G. (2005). *Substance abuse: A comprehensive textbook.* Philadelphia: Lippincott/Williams & Wilkins.

Lozano, B. E., Stephens, R. S., & Roffman, R. A. (2006). Abstinence and moderate use goals in the treatment of marijuana dependence. *Addiction, 101*, 1589–1597.

Luborsky, E. B., O'Reilly-Landry, M., & Arlow, J. A. (2011). Psychoanalysis. In R. J. Corsini & D. Wedding (Eds.), *Current psychotherapies* (9th ed.). Belmont, CA: Brooks/Cole.

Luborsky, L., Diguer, L., Seligman, D. A., Rosenthal, R., Krause, E. D., Johnson, S., . . . & Schweizer, E. (1999). The researcher's own therapy allegiance: A "wild card" in comparisons of treatment efficacy. *Clinical Psychology: Science & Practice, 6*(1), 95–106.

Luborsky, L., Rosenthal, R., Diguer, L., Andrusyna, T. P., Berman, J. S., Levitt, J. T., Seligman, D. A., & Krause, E. D. (2002). The dodo bird verdict is alive and well—mostly. *Clinical Psychology: Science & Practice, 9*, 2–12.

Luborsky, L., Singer, B., & Luborsky, L. (1975). Comparative studies of psychotherapies: Is it true that everyone has won and all must have prizes? *Archives of General Psychiatry, 32*, 995–1008.

Lucas, A. R., Beard, C. M., O'Fallon, W. M., & Kurland, L. T. (1991). 50-year trends in the incidence of anorexia nervosa in Rochester, Minn.: A population-based study. *American Journal of Psychiatry, 148*, 917–922.

Lucas, J. W., & Lovaglia, M. J. (2005). Self-handicapping: Gender, race, and status. *Current Research in Social Psychology, 10*(16). http://www.uiowa.edu/~grpproc/crisp/crisp.10.16.html

Lucas, R. E. (2007). Adaptation and the set-point model of subjective well-being: Does happiness change after major life events? *Current Directions in Psychological Science, 16*, 75–79.

Lucas, R. E., & Diener, E. (2008). Personality and subjective well-being. In O. P. John, R. W. Robins, & L. A. Pervin (Eds.), *Handbook of personality: Theory and research* (pp. 795–814). New York, NY: Guilford.

Lucas, R. E., Clark, A. E., Georgellis, Y., & Diener, E. (2004). Unemployment alters the set point for life satisfaction. *Psychological Science, 15*(1), 8–13.

Lucas-Thompson, R. G., Goldberg, W. A., & Prause, J. (2010). Maternal work early in the lives of children and its distal associations with achievement and behavior problems: A meta-analysis. *Psychological Bulletin, 136*(6), 915–942. doi:10.1037/a0020875

Lukaszewski, A. W., & Roney, J. R. (2011). The origins of extraversion: Joint effects of facultative calibration and genetic polymorphism. *Personality and Social Psychology Bulletin, 37*, 409–421. doi:10.1177/0146167210397209

Lulofs, R. S. (1994). *Conflict: From theory to action.* Scottsdale, AZ: Gorsuch Scarisbuck Publishers.

Lulofs, R. S., & Cahn, D. D. (2000). *Conflict: From theory to action* (2nd ed.). Boston, MA: Allyn & Bacon.

Lumley, M. A., & Provenzano, K. M. (2003). Stress management through written emotional disclosure improves academic performance among college students with physical symptoms. *Journal of Educational Psychology, 95,* 641–649.

Lund, O. C. H., Tamnes, C. K., Moestue, C., Buss, D. M., & Vollrath, M. (2007). Tactics of hierarchy negotiation. *Journal of Research in Personality, 41,* 25–44.

Lundberg, A. (1998). Environmental change and human health. In A. Lundberg (Ed.), *The Environment and Mental Health: A Guide for Clinicians* (pp. 5–23). Mahwah, NJ: Erlbaum.

Lundberg, U. (2007). Workplace stress. In G. Fink (Ed.), *Encyclopedia of stress: Vols. 1–4* (2nd ed., pp. 871–878). San Diego, CA: Elsevier Academic Press.

Lundberg, U. (2011). Neuroendocrine measures. In R. J. Contrada & A. Baum (Eds.), *The handbook of stress science: Biology, psychology, and health* (pp. 531–542). New York, NY: Springer.

Lundberg-Love, P. K., & Wilkerson, D. K. (2006). Battered women. In P. K. Lundberg-Love & S. L. Marmion (Eds.), *"Intimate" violence against women; When spouses, partners, or lovers attack.* Westport, CT: Praeger.

Luo, S., & Klohnen, E. C. (2005). Assortative mating and marital quality in newlyweds: A couple-centered approach. *Journal of Personality and Social Psychology, 88,* 304–326.

Luthans, F., & Youssef, C. M. (2009). Positive workplaces. In S. J. Lopez & C. R. Snyder (Eds.), *Oxford handbook of positive psychology* (2nd ed., pp. 579–588). New York, NY: Oxford University Press.

Luthans, F., Youssef, C. M., & Avolio, B. J. (2007). *Psychological capital: Developing the human competitive edge.* Oxford, UK: Oxford University Press.

Lutz, C. J., & Ross, S. R. (2003). Elaboration versus fragmentation: Distinguishing between self-complexity and self-concept differentiation. *Journal of Social and Clinical Psychology, 22*(5), 537–559.

Lykken, D. (1999). *Happiness: The nature and nurture of joy and contentment.* New York, NY: St. Martin's.

Lyness, K. S., & Heilman, M. E. (2006). When fit is fundamental: Performance evaluations and promotions of upper-level female and male managers. *Journal of Applied Psychology, 91,* 777–785.

Lynn, D. J., & Vaillant, G. E. (1998). Anonymity, neutrality, and confidentiality in the actual methods of Sigmund Freud: A review of 43 cases, 1907–1939. *American Journal of Psychiatry, 155,* 163–171.

Lynn, M., & Shurgot, B. A. (1984). Responses to lonely hearts advertisements: Effects of reported physical attractiveness, physique, and coloration. *Personality and Social Psychology Bulletin, 10,* 349–357.

Lyons, H., Giordano, P. C., Manning, W. D., & Longmore, M. A. (2011). Identity, peer relationships, and adolescent girls' sexual behavior: An exploration of the contemporary double standard. *Journal of Sex Research, 48*(5), 437–449. doi:10.1080/00224499.2010.506679

Lytton, H., & Romney, D. M. (1991). Parents' differential socialization of boys and girls: A meta-analysis. *Psychological Bulletin, 109,* 267–296.

Lyubomirsky, S., King, L., & Diener, E. (2005). The benefits of frequent positive affect: Does happiness lead to success? *Psychological Bulletin, 131,* 803–855.

Lyubomirsky, S., Sheldon, K. M., & Schkade, D. (2005). Pursuing happiness: The architecture of sustainable change. *Review of General Psychology, 9*(2), 111–131.

Lyubomirsky, S., Tkach, C., & DiMatteo, R. (2006). What are the differences between happiness and self-esteem? *Social Indicators Research, 78*(3), 363–404. doi:10.1007/s11205-005-0213-y

Maatta, S., Nurmi, J., & Stattin, H. (2007). Achievement orientations, school adjustment, and well-being: A longitudinal study. *Journal of Research on Adolescence, 17,* 789–812.

MacCann, C., & Roberts, R. D. (2010). Do time management, grit, and self-control relate to academic achievement independently of conscientiousness? In R. E. Hicks (Ed.), *Personality and individual differences: Current directions* (pp. 79–90). Bowen Hills, QLD Australia: Australian Academic Press.

Maccoby, E. E. (1990). Gender and relationships: A developmental account. *American Psychologist, 45,* 513–520.

Maccoby, E. E. (1998). *The two sexes: Growing up apart, coming together.* Cambridge, MA: Belknap Press.

Maccoby, E. E. (2002). Gender and group processes: A developmental perspective. *Current Direction in Psychological Science, 11*(2), 54–58.

Maccoby, E. E., & Martin, J. A. (1983). Socialization in the context of the family: Parent-child interaction. In P. H. Mussen (Series Ed.) & E. M. Hetherington (Vol. Ed.), *Handbook of child psychology: Vol. 4. Socialization, personality, and social development.* New York, NY: Wiley.

MacDonald, G., Saltzman, J. L., & Leary, M. R. (2003). Social approval and trait self-esteem. *Journal of Research in Personality, 37*(2), 23–40.

MacGeorge, E. L., Graves, A. R., Feng, B., Gillihan, S. J., & Burleson, B. R. (2004). The myth of gender cultures: Similarities outweigh differences in men's and women's provision of and responses to supportive communication. *Sex Roles, 50*(3/4), 143–175.

MacGregor, J. D., & Holmes, J. G. (2011). Rain on my parade: Perceiving low self-esteem in close others hinders positive self-disclosure. *Social Psychological and Personality Science, 2*(5), 523–530. doi:10.1177/1948550611400098

Mack, A. H., Franklin Jr., J. E., & Frances, R. J. (2003). Substance use disorders. In R. E. Hales & S. C. Yudofsky (Eds.), *Textbook of clinical psychiatry.* Washington, DC: American Psychiatric Publishing.

MacKellar, D. A., Valleroy, L. A., Secura, G. M., Behel, S., Bingham, T., Celentano, D. D., . . . & Janssen, R. S., & Young Men's Survey Study Group. (2005). Unrecognized HIV infection, risk behaviors, and perceptions of risk among young men who have sex with men: Opportunities for advancing HIV prevention in the third decade of HIV/AIDS. *Journal of Acquired Immune Deficiency Syndrome, 38,* 603–614.

Mackenzie, R. A. (1997). *The time trap.* New York, NY: AMACOM.

Mackie, D. M., Worth, L. T., & Asuncion, A. G. (1990). Processing of persuasive in-group messages. *Journal of Personality and Social Psychology, 58,* 812–822.

MacMillan, H. L., Fleming, J. E., Streiner, D. L., Lin, E., Boyle, M. H., Jamieson, E., Duku, E. K., Walsh, C. A., Wong, M. Y. Y., & Beardslee, W. R. (2001). Childhood abuse and lifetime psychopathology in a community sample. *American Journal of Psychiatry, 158,* 1878–1883.

Macrae, C. N., & Bodenhausen, G. V. (2001). Social cognition: Categorical person perception. *British Journal of Social Psychology, 92,* 239–255.

Macrae, C. N., Milne, A. B., & Bodenhausen, G. V. (1994). Stereotypes as energy-saving devices: A peek inside the cognitive toolbox. *Journal of Personality and Social Psychology, 66,* 37–47.

Macy, J. R. (1995). Working through environmental despair. In T. Roszak, M. E. Gomes, & A. D. Kanner (Eds.), *Ecopsychology: Restoring the earth, healing the mind* (pp. 240–259). San Francisco, CA: Sierra Club.

Madathil, J., & Benshoff, J. M. (2008). Importance of marital characteristics and marital satisfaction: A comparison of Asian Indians in arranged marriages and Americans in marriages of choice. *The Family Journal, 16,* 222–230.

Madden, M., & Lenhart, A. (2006). *Online dating.* Retrieved April 29, 2007 from http://www.pewinternet.org/pdfs/PIP_Online_Dating.pdf.

Maddi, S. R. (2007). The story of hardiness: Twenty years of theorizing, research, and practice. In A. Monat, R. S. Lazarus, & G. Reevy (Eds.), *The Praeger handbook on stress and coping* (pp. 327–340). Westport, CT: Praeger Publishers.

Maddi, S. R., Matthews, M. D., Kelly, D. R., Villarreal, B., & White, M. (2012). The role of hardiness and grit in predicting performance and retention of USMA cadets. *Military Psychology, 24*(1), 19–28. doi:10.1080/08995605.2012.639672

Maddux, J. E. (2002). Stopping the "madness": Positive psychology and deconstructing the illness ideology and the DSM. In S. J. Lopez & C. R. Snyder (Eds.), *Oxford handbook of positive psychology* (2nd ed., pp. 61–69). New York, NY: Oxford University Press.

Maddux, J. E. (2009). Stopping the "madness": Positive psychology and deconstructing the illness ideology and the DSM. In S. J. Lopez, C. R. Snyder (Eds.), *Oxford handbook of positive psychology* (2nd ed., pp. 61–69). New York, NY: Oxford University Press.

Maddux, J. E., & Gosselin, J. T. (2003). Self-efficacy. In M. R. Leary & J. P. Tangney (Eds.), *Handbook of self and identity.* New York, NY: Guilford.

Madey, S. F., & Rodgers L. (2009). The effect of attachment and Sternberg's triangular theory of love on relationship satisfaction. *Individual Differences Research, 7,* 76–84.

Madon, S., Willard, J., Guyll, M., & Scherr, K. C. (2011). Self-fulfilling prophecies: Mechanisms, power, and links to social problems. *Social and Personality Psychology Compass, 5*(8), 578–590. doi:10.1111/j.1751-9004.2011.00375.x

Madsen, K. M., Hviid, A., Vestergaard, M., Schendel, D., Wohlfahrt, J., Thorsen, P., et al. (2002). A population-based study of measles, mumps, and rubella vaccination and autism. *New England Journal of Medicine, 347,* 1477–1482.

Magnavita, J. J. (2008). Psychoanalytic psychotherapy. In J. L. Lebow (Ed.), *Twenty-first century psychotherapies: Contemporary approaches to theory and practice.* New York, NY: Wiley.

Magnavita, N., Elovaino, M., Heponiemi, T., Magnavita, A. M., & Bergamaschi, A. (2011). Are skin disorders related to work strain in hospital workers? A cross-sectional study. *BMC Public Health, 11,* 600. Retrieved from http:www.biomedcentral.com/1471-2458/11/600

Maher, B. A. (2001). Delusions. In P. B. Sutker & H. E. Adams (Eds.), *Comprehensive handbook of psychopathology* (3rd ed.). New York, NY: Kluwer Academic/Plenum Publishers.

Mahoney, M. J. (1974). *Cognition and behavior modification.* Cambridge, MA: Ballinger.

Mahoney, M. J. (1979). *Self-change: Strategies for solving personal problems.* New York, NY: Norton.

Maisel, N. C., Gable, S. L., & Strachman, A. (2008). Responsive behaviors in good times and in bad. *Personal Relationships, 15,* 317–338.

Major, B., Barr, L., Zubeck, J., & Babey, S. H. (1999). Gender and self-esteem: A meta-analysis. In W. B. Swann, Jr., J. H. Langlois, & L. A. Gilbert (Eds.), *Sexism and stereotypes in modern society: The gender science of Janet Taylor Spence.* Washington, DC: American Psychological Association.

Major, B., Schmidlin, A. M., & Williams, L. (1990). Gender patterns in social touch: The impact of setting and age. *Journal of Personality and Social Psychology, 58,* 634–643.

Major, D. A., & Morganson, V. J. (2011). Applying industrial-organizational psychology to help organizations and individuals balance work and family. *Industrial and Organizational Psychology: Perspectives on Science and Practice, 4*(3), 398–401. doi:10.1111/j.1754-9434.2011.01360.x

Maki, K., Vahtera, M., Virtanen, M., Elovainio, M., Keltikangas-Jarvinen, L., & Kivmaki, M. (2007). Work stress and new-onset migraine in a femal employee population. *Cephalagia, 28,* 18–25.

Mäki, N., & Martikainen, P. (2012). A register-based study on excess suicide mortality among unemployed men and women during different levels of unemployment in Finland. *Journal of Epidemiology and Community Health, 66*(4), 302–307. doi:10.1136/jech.2009.105908

Malaspina, D., Kleinhaus, K. R., Perrin, M. C., Fennig, S., Nahon, D., Friedlander, Y, et al. (2008). Acute material stress in pregnancy and schizophrenia in offspring: A cohort prospective study. *BMC Psychiatry, 8,* ArtID 71.

Maldonado, J. R. & Spiegel, D. (2008). Dissociative disorders. In R. E. Hales, S. C. Yudofsky, & G. O. Gabbard (Eds.), *The American psychiatric publishing textbook of psychiatry* (pp. 665–710). Washington, DC: American Psychiatric Publishing.

Maletzky, B. M. (2002). The paraphilias: Research and treatment. In P. E. Nathan & J. M. Gorman (Eds), *A guide to treatments that work*. London: Oxford University Press.

Malle, B. F. (2004). *How the mind explains behavior: Folk explanations, meaning, and social interaction*. Cambridge, MA: MIT Press.

Malle, B. F. (2006). *How the mind explains behavior: Folk explanations, meaning, and social interaction*. Cambridge, MA: MIT Press.

Malle, B. F. (2011). Attribution theories: How people make sense of behavior. In D. Chadee (Ed.), *Theories in social psychology* (pp. 72–95). Wiley-Blackwell.

Malle, B. F., & Knobe, J. (1997). Which behaviors do people explain? A basic actor-observer asymmetry. *Journal of Personality and Social Psychology, 72*, 288–304.

Mallen, M. J., Day, S. X., & Green, M. A. (2003). Online versus face-to-face conversations: An examination of relational and discourse variable. *Psychotherapy: Theory, Research, Practice, Training, 40*(1–2), 155–163.

Maltz, D. N., & Borker, R. A. (1983). A cultural approach to male-female miscommunication. In J. A. Gumperz (Ed.), *Language and social identity*. New York, NY: Cambridge University Press.

Mandel, H. & Young, J. (2009). *Here's the deal: Don't touch me*. New York, NY: Bantam Books.

Mandler, G. (1993). Thought, memory, and learning: Effects of emotional stress. In L. Goldberger & S. Breznitz (Eds.), *Handbook of stress: Theoretical and clinical aspects* (2nd ed.). New York, NY: Free Press.

Mann, J. J., & Currier, D. (2006). Understanding and preventing suicide. In D. J. Stein, D. J. Kupfer, & A. F. Schatzberg (Eds.), *Textbook of mood disorders*. Washington, DC: American Psychiatric Publishing.

Manning, W. D. (2004). Children and the stability of cohabiting couples. *Journal of Mariage and Family, 66*, 674–689.

Manning, W. D., & Cohen, J. A. (2012). Premarital cohabitation and marital dissolution: An examination of recent marriages. *Journal of Marriage and Family, 74*(2), 377–387. doi:10.1111/j.1741-3737.2012.00960.x

Manning, W. D., Longmore, M. A., & Giordano, P. C. (2007). The changing institution of marriage: Adolescents' expectations to cohabit and to marry. *Journal of Marriage and Family, 69*, 559–575.

Manson, J. E., Skerrett, P. J., Greenland, P., & VanItallie, T. B. (2004). The escalating pandemics of obesity and sedentary lifestyles: A call to action for clinicians. *Archives of Internal Medicine, 164*, 249–258.

Manson, J. E., Skerrett, P. J., & Willett, W. C. (2002). Epidemiology of health risks associated with obesity. In C. G. Fairburn & K. D. Brownell (Eds.), *Eating disorders and obesity: A comprehensive handbook*. New York, NY: Guilford.

Mantell, J. E., Stein, Z. A., & Susser, I. (2008). Women in the time of AIDS: Barriers, bargains, and benefits. *AIDS Education and Prevention, 20*, 91–106.

Marchand, W. R. (2012). Mindfulness-based stress reduction, mindfulness-based cognitive therapy, and Zen mediation for depression, anxiety, pain, and psychological distress. *Journal of Psychiatric Practice, 18*(4), 233–252. doi:10.1097/01.pra.0000416014.53215.86

Marder, S. R., Hurford, I. M., & van Kammen, D. P. (2009). Second–generation antipsychotics. In B. J. Sadock, V. A. Sadock, & P. Ruiz (Eds.), *Kaplan & Sadock's comprehensive textbook of psychiatry* (pp. 3206–3240). Philadelphia, PA: Lippincott Williams & Wilkins.

Margolin, G., & Gordis, E. B. (2004). Children's exposure to violence in the family and community. *Current Directions in Psychological Science, 13*, 152–155.

Mariani, M. (2001, Summer). Distance learning in post-secondary education. *Occupational Outlook Quarterly*, pp. 2–10.

Maricchiolo, F., Gnisci, A., Bonaiuto, M., & Ficca, G. (2009). Effects of different types of hand gestures in persuasive speech on receivers' evaluations. *Language and Cognitive Processes, 24*(2), 239–266.

Mark, K. P., Janssen, E., & Milhausen, R. R. (2011). Infidelity in heterosexual couples: Demographic, interpersonal, and personality-related predictors of extradyadic sex. *Archives of Sexual Behavior, 40*(5), 971–982. doi:10.1007/s10508-011-9771-z

Marker, N. F. (1996). Flying solo at midlife: Gender, marital status, and psychological well-being. *Journal of Marriage and the Family, 58*, 917–932.

Markey, P. M., Wells, S. M., & Markey, C. N. (2001). Personality and social psychology in the culture of cyberspace. In S. P. Shohov (Ed.). *Advances in psychology research* (Vol. 9, pp. 103–124). Hauppauge, NY: Nova Science Publishers, Inc.

Markey, P. M., Wells, S. M., & Markey, C. N. (2002). Social and personality psychology in the culture of cyberspace. In S. P. Shohov (Ed.), *Advances in psychology research, Vol. 9* (pp. 94–113). Hauppauge, NY: Nova Science Publishers.

Markman, A. B., & Maddox, W. T. (2006). Choking and excelling under pressure. *Psychological Science, 17*, 944–948.

Markman, H. J., Rhoades, G. K., Stanley, S. M., Ragan, E. P., & Whitton, S. W. (2010). The premarital communication roots of marital distress and divorce: The first five years of marriage. *Journal of Family Psychology, 24*(3), 289–298. doi:10.1037/a0019481

Markowitz, E. M., Goldberg, L. R., Ashton, M. C., & Lee, K. (2012). Profiling the "pro-environmental individual": A personality perspective. *Journal of Personality, 80*, 81–111.

Marks, M. J., & Fraley, R. C. (2006). Confirmation bias and the sexual double standard. *Sex Roles, 54*, 19–26.

Marks, M. L., & De Meuse, K. P. (2005). Resizing the organization: maximizing the gain while minimizing the pain of layoffs, divestitures, and closings. *Organizational Dynamics, 34*(1), 19–35.

Markus, H., & Cross, S. (1990). The interpersonal self. In L. A. Pervin (Ed.), *Handbook of personality: Theory and research* (pp. 576–608). New York, NY: Guilford.

Markus, H., & Kitayama, S. (2004). Models of agency: Sociocultural diversity in the construction of action. In V. Murphy-Berman & J. Berman (Eds.), *Nebraska Symposium on Motivation. Cross-cultural differences in perspectives on the self*. Lincoln: University of Nebraska Press.

Markus, H., & Nurius, P. (1986). Possible selves. *American Psychologist, 41*, 954–969.

Markus, H., & Wurf, E. (1987). The dynamic self-concept: A social psychological perspective. *Annual Review of Psychology, 38*, 299–337.

Marques, L., Alegria, M., Becker, A. E., Chen, C., Fang, A., Chosak, A., & Diniz, J. (2011). Comparative prevalence, correlates of impairment, and service utilization for eating disorders across US ethnic groups: Implications for reducing ethnic disparities in health care access for eating disorders. *International Journal of Eating Disorders, 44*(5), 412–420. doi:10.1002/eat.20787

Marsh, H. W., & O'Mara, A. (2008). Reciprocal effects between academic self-concept, self-esteem, achievement, and attainment over seven adolescent years: Unidimensional and multidimensional perspectives of self-concept. *Personality and Social Psychology Bulletin, 34*, 542–552.

Marsh, H. W., Kong, C-K., & Hau, K-T. (2000). Longitudinal multilevel models of the big-fish-little-pond effect in academic self-concept: Counterbalancing contrast and reflected-glory effects in Hong Kong schools. *Journal of Personality and Social Psychology, 78*, 337–349.

Marshall, L. (2005, February 25). Sex, romance and a patch. *Statesboro Herald*, p. 6A.

Marshall, S. J., Gorely, T., & Biddle, S. H. (2006). A descriptive epidemiology of screen-based media use in youth: A review and critique. *Journal Of Adolescence, 29*(3), 333–349. doi:10.1016/j.adolescence.2005.08.016

Marshall, T. C. (2010). Gender, peer relations, and intimate romantic relationships. In J. C. Chrisler & D. R.

McCreary (Eds.), *Handbook of gender research in psychology* (Vol. 2, pp. 281–310). New York, NY: Springer.

Martin, A. J., Marsh, H. W., Williamson, A., & Debus, R. L. (2003). Self-handicapping, defensive pessimism, and goal orientation: A qualitative study of university students. *Journal of Educational Psychology, 95*, 617–628.

Martin, B. S. (2012). A stranger's touch: Effects of accidental interpersonal touch on consumer evaluations and shopping time. *Journal of Consumer Research, 39*(1), 174–184. doi:10.1086/662038

Martin, C. L., Ruble, D., & Szkrybalo, J. (2002). Cognitive theories of early gender development. *Psychological Bulletin, 128*(6), 903–933.

Martin, L. R., Haskard-Zolnierek, K. B., & DiMatteo, M. R. (2010). *Health behavior change and treatment adherence: Evidence-based guidelines for improving health care*. New York, NY: Oxford University Press.

Martin, R., & Leventhal, H. (2004). Symptom perception and health care–seeking behavior. In J. M. Raczynski & L. C. Leviton (Eds.), *Handbook of clinical health psychology: Vol. 2. Disorders of behavior and health*. Washington, DC: American Psychological Association.

Martin, R. A. (2002). Is laughter the best medicine? Humor, laughter, and physical health. *Current Directions in Psychological Science, 11*(6), 216–220.

Martin, R. A., & Lefcourt, H. M. (1983). Sense of humor as a moderator of the relation between stressors and moods. *Journal of Personality and Social Psychology, 45*, 1313–1324.

Martinez, E. (2009, October 27). James Ray gives "laughable" 50 percent refund to Sweat Lodge victim's family. *CBS News*, Retrieved from http://www.cbsnews.com/blogs/2009/08/28/crimesider/entry5271390.shtml

Martinez, G., Abma, J. & Casey, C. (2010). Educating teenagers about sex in the United States. *NCHS Data Brief*, No. 44.

Martinez, G., Copen, C. E., & Abma, J. C. (2011). Teenagers in the United States: Sexual activity, contraceptive use, and childbearing, 2006–2010, *Vital and Health Statistics, Series 23, No. 31*.

Martinez, M., Marangell, L. B., & Martinez, J. M. (2008). Psychopharmacology. In R. E. Hales, S. C. Yudofsky, & G. O. Gabbard (Eds.), *The American psychiatric publishing textbook of psychiatry* (pp. 1053–1132). Washington, DC: American Psychiatric Publishing, Inc.

Martino, S. C., Collins, R. L., Elliott, M. N., Strachman, A., Kanouse, D. E., & Berry, S. H. (2006). Exposure to degrading versus nondegrading music lyrics and sexual behavior among youth. *Pediatrics, 118*, e430–e441.

Martins, A., Ramalho, N., & Morin, E. (2010). A comprehensive meta-analysis of the relationship between emotional intelligence and health. *Personality and Individual Differences, 49*(6), 554–564. doi:10.1016/j.paid.2010.05.029

Martins, Y., Tiggemann, M., & Churchett, L. (2008). The shape of things to come: Gay men's satisfaction with specific body parts. *Psychology of Men & Masculinity, 9*, 248–256.

Martins, Y., Tiggemann, M., & Kirkbride, A. (2007). Those speedos become them: The role of self-objectification in gay and heterosexual men's body image. *Personality and Social Psychology Bulletin, 33*, 634–647.

Maslach, C. (2003). Job burnout: New directions in research and intervention. *Current Directions in Psychological Science, 12*(5), 189–192.

Maslach, C. (2005). Understanding burnout: Work and family issues. In D. F. Halpern & S. E. Murphy (Eds.), *From work-family balance to work-family interaction: Changing the metaphor*. Mahwah, NJ: Erlbaum.

Maslach, C., & Leiter, M. P. (1997). *The truth about burnout*. San Francisco: Jossey-Bass.

Maslach, C., & Leiter, M. P. (2007). Burnout. In G. Fink (Ed.), *Encyclopedia of stress: Vols. 1–4* (2nd ed., pp. 368–371). San Diego, CA: Elsevier Academic Press.

Maslow, A. H. (1968). *Toward a psychology of being.* New York, NY: Van Nostrand.

Maslow, A. H. (1970). *Motivation and personality.* New York, NY: Harper & Row.

Maslow, A. H. (1973). Self-actualizing people: A study of psychological health. In R. J. Lowry (Ed.), *Dominance, self-esteem, self-actualization: Germinal papers of A. H. Maslow* (pp. 177–201). Monterey, CA: Brooks/Cole. (Original work published 1950)

Massen, C., & Vaterrodt-Plünnecke, B. (2006). The role of proactive interference in mnemonic techniques. *Memory, 14,* 189–196.

Massen, C., Vaterrodt-Plünnecke, B., Krings, L., & Hilbig, B. E. (2009). Effects of instruction on learners' ability to generate an effective pathway in the method of loci. *Memory, 17*(7), 724–731. doi:10.1080/09658210903012442

Mast, M., & Sczesny, S. (2010). Gender, power, and nonverbal behavior. In J. C. Chrisler & D. R. McCreary (Eds.), *Handbook of gender research in psychology, Vol 1: Gender research in general and experimental psychology* (pp. 411–425). New York, NY: Springer Science + Business Media.

Masten, A. S. (2001). Ordinary magic: Resilience processes in development. *American Psychologist, 56,* 227–238.

Masten, A. S., & Coatsworth, J. D. (1998). The development of competence in favorable and unfavorable environments: Lessons from research on successful children. *American Psychologist, 53,* 205–220.

Masten, A. S., & Reed, M. J. (2002). Resilience in development. In C. R. Snyder & S. J. Lopez (Eds.), *Handbook of positive psychology* (pp. 74–88). New York, NY: Oxford University Press.

Masters, W. H., & Johnson, V. E. (1966). *Human sexual response.* Boston, MA: Little, Brown.

Masters, W. H., & Johnson, V. E. (1970). *Human sexual inadequacy.* Boston, MA: Little, Brown.

Masuda, T., & Nisbett, R. E. (2006). Culture and change blindness. *Cognitive Science, 30,* 381–399.

Mathew, S. J., Hoffman, E. J., Charney, D. S. (2009). Pharmacotherapy of anxiety disorders. In D. S. Charney & E. J. Nestler (Eds.), *Neurobiology of mental illness* (p. 731). New York, NY: Guilford.

Mathews, C. A., & Reus, V. I. (2001). Assortative mating in the affective disorders: A systematic review and meta-analysis. *Comprehensive Psychiatry, 42*(4), 257–262.

Mathews, S., & Herzog, H. A. (1997). Personality and attitudes toward the treatment of animals. *Society and Animals, 5,* 169–175.

Matlin, M. W. (2004). *The psychology of women* (5th ed.). Belmont, CA: Wadsworth.

Matsumoto, D. (2006). Culture and nonverbal behavior. In V. Manusov & M. L. Patterson (Ed.), *The Sage handbook of nonverbal communication* (pp. 219–235). Thousand Oaks, CA: Sage.

Matsumoto, D., & Yoo, S. (2005). Culture and applied nonverbal communication. In R. E. Riggio & R. S. Feldman (Eds.), *Applications of nonverbal communication* (pp. 255–277). Mahwah, NJ: Lawrence Erlbaum Associates Publishers.

Mattar, C., Harharahm, L., Su, L., Agarwal, A., Wong, P., & Choolani, M. (2008). Menopause, hormone therapy and cardiovascular and cerebrovascular disease. *Annals of the Academy of Medicine Singapore, 37*(1), 54–62.

Matthews, G., Emo, A. K., Funke, G., Zeidner, M., Roberts, R. D., Costa Jr., P. T., & Schulze, R. (2006). Emotional intelligence, personality, and task-induced stress. *Journal of Experimental Psychology: Applied, 12,* 96–107.

Mayer, F. S., & Frantz, C. M. (2004). The connectedness to nature scale: A measure of individuals' feeling in community with nature. *Journal of Environmental Psychology, 24,* 503–515.

Mayer, J. D., Perkins, D. M., Caruso, D. R., & Salovey, P. (2001). Emotional intelligence and giftedness. *Roeper Review, 23,* 131–137.

Mayer, J. D., Salovey, P., & Caruso, D. R. (2002). *Mayer-Salovey-Caruso Emotional Intelligence Test (MSCEIT): User's manual.* Toronto, Canada: Multi-Health Systems.

Mayer, J. D., Salovey, P., & Caruso, D. R. (2008). Emotional Intelligence: New ability or eclectic traits, *American Psychologist, 63,* 503–517.

Mayes, F. (1996). *Under the Tuscan sun: At home in Italy.* New York, NY: Chronicle Books.

Maynard, D. C., & Feldman, D. C. (2011). *Underemployment: Psychological, economic, and social challenges.* New York, NY: Springer Science + Business Media.

Mayo Clinic. (2009). *Premature ejaculation.* Retrieved from http://www.mayoclinic.com/health/premature-ejaculation/DS00578

Mayo Clinic. (2011). Premature ejaculation. Retrieved from http://www.mayoclinic.com/health/premature-ejaculation/DS00578

Maysent, M., & Spera, S. (1995). Coping with job loss and career stress: Effectiveness of stress management training with outplaced employees. In L. R. Murphy, J. J. Hurrell, Jr., S. L. Sauter, & G. P. Keita (Eds.), *Job stress interventions* (pp. 159–170). Washington, DC: American Psychological Association.

Mazzoni, G., Heap, M., & Scoboria, A. (2010). Hypnosis and memory: Theory, laboratory research, and applications. In S. Lynn, J. W. Rhue, & I. Kirsch (Eds.), *Handbook of clinical hypnosis* (2nd ed., pp. 709–741). Washington, DC: American Psychological Association.

McAndrew, F. T., & De Jonge, C. (2011). Electronic person perception: What do we infer about people from the style of their e-mail messages? *Social Psychological and Personality Science, 2*(4), 403–407. doi:10.1177/1948550610393988

McBride, D. L. & Korell, G. (2005). Wilderness therapy for abused women. *Canadian Journal of Counseling, 39,* 3–14.

McCabe, R. E., & Antony, M. M. (2008). Anxiety disorders: Social and specific phobias. In A. Tasman, J. Kay, J. A. Lieberman, M. B. First, & M. Maj (Eds.), *Psychiatry* (3rd ed.). New York, NY: Wiley-Blackwell.

McCallum, E. B., & Peterson, Z. D. (2012). Investigating the impact of inquiry mode on self-reported sexual behavior: Theoretical considerations and review of the literature. *Journal of Sex Research, 49*(2–3), 212–226. doi:10.1080/00224499.2012.658923

McCarthy, B. W., Bodnar, L. E., & Handal, M. (2004). Integrating sex therapy and couple therapy. In J. H. Harvey, A. Wenzel, & S. Sprecher (Eds.), *The handbook of sexuality in close relationships.* Mahwah, NJ: Lawrence Erlbaum.

McCave, E. L. (2007). Comprehensive sexuality education vs. abstinence-only sexuality education: The need for evidence-based research and practice. *School Social Work Journal, 32,* 14–28.

McClernon, F. J., & Gilbert, D. G. (2007). Smoking and stress. In G. Fink (Ed.), *Encyclopedia of stress: Vols. 1–4* (2nd ed., pp. 515–520). San Diego, CA: Elsevier Academic Press.

McClure-Tone, E. B. & Pine, D. S. (2009). Clinical features of the anxiety disorders. In B. J. Sadock, V. A. Sadock, & P. Ruiz (Eds.), *Kaplan & Sadock's comprehensive textbook of psychiatry* (pp. 1844–1555). Philadelphia: Lippincott Williams & Wilkins.

McCormack, S. A., & Levine, T. R. (1990). When lovers become leery: The relationship between suspiciousness and accuracy in detecting deception. *Communication Monographs, 57,* 219–230.

McCoy, S. K., & Major, B. (2003). Group identification moderates emotional responses to perceived prejudice. *Personality and Social Psychology Bulletin, 29,* 1005–1017.

McCrae, R. R. (2005). Personality structure. In V. A. Derlega, B. A. Winstead, & W. H. Jones (Eds.), *Personality: Contemporary theory and research.* Belmont, CA: Wadsworth.

McCrae, R. R., & Costa, P. T., Jr. (1987). Validation of the five-factor model of personality across instruments and observers. *Journal of Personality and Social Psychology, 52,* 81–90.

McCrae, R. R., & Costa, P. T., Jr. (1997). Personality trait structure as a human universal. *American Psychologist, 52,* 509–516.

McCrae, R. R., & Costa, P. T., Jr. (2003). *Personality in adulthood: A five-factor theory perspective.* New York, NY: Guilford.

McCrae, R. R., & Costa, P. T., Jr. (2008a). Empirical and theoretical status of the five-factor model of personality traits. In G. J. Boyle, G. Matthews, D. H. Saklofske (Eds.), *The Sage handbook of personality theory and assessment* (pp. 273–294). Los Angeles: Sage.

McCrae, R. R., & Costa, P. T., Jr. (2008b). The five-factor theory of personality. In O. P. John, R. W. Robins, & L. A. Pervin (Eds.), *Handbook of personality: Theory and research* (pp. 159–181). New York, NY: Guilford.

McCrae, R. R., & Sutin, A. R. (2009). Openness to experience. In M. R. Leary & R. H. Hoyle (Eds.), *Handbook of individual differences in social behavior* (pp. 257–274). New York, NY: Guilford.

McCrae, R. R., & Terracciano, A. (2006). National character and personality. *Current Direction in Psychological Science, 15*(4), 156–161.

McCrae, R. R., Terracciano, A., & 78 members of the Personality Profiles of Cultures Project. (2005). Universal features of personality traits from the observer's perspective: Data from 50 cultures. *Journal of Personality and Social Psychology, 88,* 547–561.

McCrea, S. M., Hirt, E. R., Hendrix, K. L., Milner, B. J., Steele, N. L.(2008). The worker scale: Developing a measure to explain gender differences in behavioral self-handicapping. *Journal of Research in Personality, 42*(4), 949–970.

McCreary, D. R., & Chrisler, J. C. (2010). Introduction. In J. C. Chrisler & D. R. McCreary (Eds.), *Handbook of gender research in psychology* (Vol. 1, pp. 1–16). New York, NY: Springer.

McCroskey, J. C. (1982). Oral communication apprehension: A reconceptualization. In M. Burgoon (Ed.), *Communication Yearbook 6* (pp. 136–170). Beverly Hills, CA: Sage.

McCullough, M. E. (2001). Forgiving. In C. R. Snyder (Ed.), *Coping with stress. Effective people and processes.* New York, NY: Oxford University Press.

McCullough, M. E., Bellah, C. G., Kilpatrick, S. D., & Johnson, J. L. (2001). Vengefulness: Relationships with forgiveness, rumination, well-being, and the Big Five. *Personality and Social Psychology Bulletin, 27*(5), 601–610.

McCullough, M. E., & Witvliet, C. V. (2005). The psychology of forgiveness. In C. R. Snyder & S. J. Lopez (Eds.), *Handbook of positive psychology.* New York, NY: Oxford University Press.

McDaniel, E., & Quasha, S. (2000). The communicative aspects of doing business in Japan. In L. Samovar & R. Porter (Eds.), *Intercultural communication: A reader* (9th ed., pp. 312–324). Belmont, CA: Wadsworth.

McDaniel, M. A., Agarwal, P. K., Huelser, B. J., McDermott, K. B., & Roediger, H. L. III. (2011). Test-enhanced learning in a middle school science classroom: The effects of quiz frequency and placement. *Journal of Educational Psychology, 103,* 399–414. doi:10.1037/a0021782

McDaniel, M. A., Waddill, P. J., & Shakesby, P. S. (1996). Study strategies, interest, and learning from text: The application of material appropriate processing. In D. J. Herrmann, C. McEvoy, C. Hertzog, P. Hertel, & M. K. Johnson (Eds.), *Basic and applied memory research: Theory in context* (Vol. 1). Mahwah, NJ: Erlbaum.

McDonald, P. (2012). Workplace sexual harassment 30 years on: A review of the literature. *International Journal of Management Reviews, 14*(1), 1–17. doi:10.1111/j.1468-2370.2011.00300.x

McDonald, W. M., Thompson, T. R., McCall W. V., & Zormuski, C. F. (2004). In A. F. Schatzberg, & C. B. Nemeroff (Eds.), *Textbook of psychopharmacology.* Washington, DC: American Psychiatric Publishing.

McDougle, L. G. (1987). Time management: Making every minute count. In A. D. Timpe (Ed.), *The management of time.* New York, NY: Facts on File.

McElwee, R. O., & Haugh, J. A. (2010). Thinking clearly versus frequently about the future self: Exploring this distinction and its relation to possible selves. *Self and Identity, 9*(3), 298–321. doi:10.1080/15298860903054290

McGee, M. (2005). *Self-help, Inc.: Makeover culture in American life.* New York, NY: Oxford University Press.

McGlashan, T. H., & Hoffman, R. E. (2000). Schizophrenia: Psychodynamic to neurodynamic theories. In B. J. Sadock & V. A. Sadock (Eds.), *Kaplan and Sadock's comprehensive textbook of psychiatry* (7th ed., Vol. 1). Philadelphia: Lippincott/Williams & Wilkins.

McGoldrick, M., & Carter, B. (2003). The family life cycle. In F. Walsh (Ed.), *Normal family processes: Growing diversity and complexity* (3rd ed.) (pp. 375–398). New York, NY: Guilford Press.

McGrath, J., Welham, J., Scott, J., Varghese, D., Degenhardt, L., Hayatbakhsh, M., et al. (2010). Association between cannabis use and psychosis-related outcomes using sibling pair analysis in a cohort of young adults. *Archives of General Psychiatry, 67*(5), 440–447. doi:10.1001/archgenpsychiatry.2010.6

McGraw, L. A., & Walker, A. J. (2004). The more things change, the more they stay the same. In M. Coleman & L. H. Ganong (Eds.), *Handbook of contemporary families: Considering the past, contemplating the future.* Thousand Oaks, CA: Sage.

McHugh, M. C., & Hambaugh, J. (2010.) She said, he said: Gender, language and power. In J. C. Chrisler & D. R. McCreary (Eds.), *Handbook of gender research in psychology* (Vol. 2, pp. 379–410). New York, NY: Springer.

McHugh, P. R. (1995). Dissociative identity disorder as a socially constructed artifact. *Journal of Practical Psychiatry and Behavioral Health, 1,* 158–166.

McHugh, P. R., Lief, H. I., Freyd, P. P., & Fetkewicz, J. M. (2004). From refusal to reconciliation: Family relationships after an accusation based on recovered memories. *Journal of Nervous and Mental Disease, 192,* 525–531.

McIntyre, K. P., Korn, J. H., & Matsuo, H. (2008). Sweating the small stuff: How different types of hassles result in the experience of stress. *Stress and Health, 24,* 383–392.

McKay, M., & Fanning, P. (2000). *Self-esteem* (3rd ed.). Oakland, CA: New Harbinger.

McKay, M., Davis, M., & Fanning, P. (1995). *Messages: The communication skills book.* Oakland, CA: New Harbinger.

McKee-Ryan, F. M., & Harvey, J. (2011). "I have a job, but . . .": A review of underemployment. *Journal of Management, 37*(4), 962–996. doi:10.1177/0149206311398134

McKeever, V. M., & Huff, M. E. (2003). A diathesis-stress model of posttraumatic stress disorder: Ecological, biological and residual stress pathways. *Review of General Psychology, 7*(3), 237–250.

McKenna, K. Y. A. (2009). Internet, attraction on. In H. T. Reis & S. Sprecher (Eds.), *Encyclopedia of human relationships: Vol. 2* (pp. 881–884). Los Angeles: Sage Reference Publication.

McKenna, K. Y. A., & Bargh, J. A. (2000). Plan 9 from cyberspace: The implications of the Internet for personality and social psychology. *Personality and Social Psychology Review, 4*(1), 57–75.

McKenna, K. Y. A., Green, A., & Gleason, M. (2002). Relationship formation on the Internet: What's the big attraction? *Journal of Social Issues, 58,* 9–31.

McKenna, M. C., Zevon, M. A., Corn, B., & Rounds, J. (1999). Psychosocial factors and the development of breast cancer: A meta-analysis. *Health Psychology, 18*(5), 520–531.

McLaughlin, K. A., Nandi, A., Keyes, K. M., Uddin, M., Aiello, A. E., Galea, S., & Koenen, K. C. (2012). Home foreclosure and risk of psychiatric morbidity during the recent financial crisis. *Psychological Medicine, 42,* 1441–1448. doi:10.1017/S0033291711002613

McLean, D. E., & Link, B. G. (1994). Unraveling complexity: Strategies to refine concepts, measures,

and research designs in the study of life events and mental health. In W. R. Avison & I. H. Gotlib (Eds.), *Stress and mental health: Contemporary issues and prospects for the future.* New York, NY: Plenum Press.

McManus, P. A., & DiPrete, T. (2001). Losers and winners: Financial consequences of separation and divorce for men. *American Sociological Review, 66,* 246–268.

McNally, R. J. (1996). *Panic disorder: A critical analysis.* New York, NY: Guilford Press.

McNally, R. J. (2007). Betrayal trauma theory: A critical appraisal. *Memory, 15,* 280–294.

McNally, R. J., & Geraerts, E. (2009). A new solution to the recovered memory debate. *Perspectives on Psychological Science, 4*(2), 126–134. doi:10.1111/j.1745-6924.2009.01112.x

McNulty, J. K. (2011). The dark side of forgiveness: The tendency to forgive predicts continued psychological and physical aggression in marriage. *Personality and Social Psychology Bulletin, 37*(6), 770–783. doi:10.1177/0146167211407077

McPherson, M., Smith-Lovin, L., & Brashears, M. E. (2006). Social isolation in America: Changes in core discussion networks over two decades. *American Sociological Review, 71,* 353–375.

McPherson, M., Smith-Lovin, L., & Cook, J. M. (2001). Birds of a feather: Homophily in social networks. *Annual Review Of Sociology, 27* 415–444. doi:10.1146/annurev.soc.27.1.415

McQuillan, J., & Conde, G. (1996). The conditions of flow in reading: Two studies of optimal experience. *Reading Psychology: An International Quarterly, 17,* 109–135.

McQuillan, J., Greil, A. L., Shreffler, K. M., Wonch-Hill, P. A., Gentzler, K. C., & Hathcoat, J. D. (2012). Does the reason matter? Variations in childlessness concerns among U.S. women. *Journal of Marriage and Family, 74*(5), 1166–1181.

McWhirter, B. T. (1990). Loneliness: A review of current literature, with implications for counseling and research. *Journal of Counseling and Development, 68,* 417–422.

McWhorter, K. T., & Sember, B. M. (2013). *College reading and study skills.* Upper Saddle River, NJ: Longman.

McWilliams, L. A., Becker, E. S., Margraf, J., Clara, I. P., & Vriends, N. (2007). Anxiety disorders specificity of anxiety sensitivity in a community sample of young women. *Personality and Individual Differences, 42,* 345–354.

Mead, M. (1950). *Sex and temperament in three primitive societies.* New York, NY: Mentor Books.

Mechanic, D. (1999). Mental health and mental illness. In A. V. Horvitz & T. L. Scheid (Eds.), *A handbook for the study of mental health: Social contexts, theories, and systems.* New York, NY: Cambridge University Press.

Medina, K. L., Shear, P. K., & Corcoran, K. (2005). Ecstasy (MDMA) exposure and neuropsychological functioning: A polydrug perspective. *Journal of the International Neuropsychological Society, 11*(6), 1–13.

Medlock, G. (2012). The evolving ethic of authenticity: From humanistic to positive psychology. *The Humanistic Psychologist, 40*(1), 38–57. doi:10.1080/08873267.2012.643687

Mednick, S. A., Machon, R. A., Huttunen, M. O., & Bonett, D. (1988). Adult schizophrenia following prenatal exposure to an influenza epidemic. *Archives of General Psychiatry, 45,* 189–192.

Meece, J. L., & Scantlebury, K. (2006). Gender and schooling: Progress and persistent barriers. In J. Worrell & C. D. Goodheart (Eds.), *Handbook of girls' and women's psychological health.* New York, NY: Oxford University Press.

Mehdizadeh, S. (2010). Self-presentation 2.0: Narcissism and self-esteem on Facebook. *Cyberpsychology, Behavior, and Social Networking, 13*(4), 357–364. doi:10.1089/cyber.2009.0257

Mehl, M. R. (2007). Eavesdropping on health: A naturalistic observation approach for social health research.

Social and Personality Psychology Compass, 1(1), 359–380. doi:10.1111/j.1751-9004.2007.00034.x.

Mehl, M. R., Vazire, S., Holleran, S. E., & Clark, C. (2010). Eavesdropping on happiness: Well-being is related to having less small talk and more substantive conversations. *Psychological Science, 21*(4), 539–541.

Meichenbaum, D. (1977). *Cognitive-behavior modification.* New York, NY: Plenum.

Meichenbaum, D. (1993). Stress inoculation training: A 20-year update. In P. M. Lehrer & R. L. Woolfolk (Eds.), *Principles and practice of stress management* (2nd ed.). New York, NY: Guilford Press.

Meijer, A. M., & van den Wittenboer, G. L. H. (2007). Contribution of infants' sleep and crying to marital relationship of first-time parent couples in the 1st year after childbirth. *Journal of Family Psychology, 21,* 49–57.

Meissner, C. A., & Brigham, J. C. (2001). Thirty years of investigating the own-race bias in memory for faces: A meta-analytic review. *Psychology, Public Policy, and Law, 7,* 3–35.

Melanson, K. J. (2007). Dietary factors in reducing risk of cardiovascular diseases. *American Journal of Lifestyle Medicine, 1*(1), 24–28.

Melchior, M., Caspi, A., Milne, B. J., Danese, A., Poulton, R., & Moffitt, T. E. (2007). Work stress precipitates depression and anxiety in young working men and women. *Psychological Medicine, 37,* 1119–1129.

Mellers, B. A., Richards, V., & Birnbaum, M. H. (1992). Distributional theories of impression formation. *Organizational Behavior and Human Decision Processes, 51,* 313–343.

Melson, G. F. (2001). *Why the wild things are: Animals in the lives of children.* Cambridge, MA: Harvard University Press.

Melson, G. F. (2003). Child development and the human-companion animal bond. *American Behavioral Scientist, 47,* 31–39.

Meltzer, H. Y., & Bobo, W. V. (2009). Antipsychotic and anticholinergic drugs. In M. C. Gelder, N. C. Andreasen, J. J. López-Ibor, Jr., & J. R. Geddes (Eds.), *New Oxford textbook of psychiatry* (2nd ed., Vol. 1). New York, NY: Oxford University Press.

Melvin, G. A., Posner, K., Standley, B. H., & Oquendo, M. A. (2008). Management of the suicidal patient. In A. Tasman, J. Kay, J. A. Lieberman, M. B. First, & M. Maj (Eds.), *Psychiatry* (3rd ed.). New York, NY: Wiley-Blackwell.

Mendoza-Denton, R., Park, S. H., & O'Connor, A. (2008). Gender stereotypes as situation-behavior profiles. *Journal of Experimental Social Psychology, 44*(4), 971–982.

Merali, N. (2012). Arranged and forced marriage. In M. A. Paludi (Ed.), *The psychology of love* (pp. 143–168). Santa Barbara, CA: Praeger/ABC-CLIO.

Meredith, P., Merson, K., & Strong, J. (2007). Differences in adult attachment style, career choice and career satisfaction for occupational therapy and commerce students. *The British Journal of Occupational Therapy, 70*(6), 235–242.

Merikangas, K. R., & Pato, M. (2009). Recent developments in the epidemiology of bipolar disorder in adults and children: Magnitude, correlates, and future directions. *Clinical Psychology: Science and Practice, 16*(2), 121–133. doi:10.1111/j.1468-2850.2009.01152.x

Merikangas, K. R., Ames, M., Cui, L., Stang, P. E., Ustun, T. B., Von Korff, M., et al. (2007). The impact of comorbidity of mental and physical conditions on role disability in the U.S. adult household population. *Archive of General Psychiatry, 64,* 1180–1188.

Merritt, M. M., Bennett, G. G., Williams, R. B., Sollers, J. J., III, & Thayer, J. F. (2004). Low educational attainment, John Henryism, and cardiovascular reactivity to and recovery from personally relevant stress. *Psychosomatic Medicine, 66,* 49–55.

Merton, R. (1948). The self-fulfilling prophecy. *Antioch Review, 8,* 193–210.

Merz, C. J., Wolf, O. T., & Hennig, J. (2010). Stress impairs retrieval of socially relevant information. *Behavioral Neuroscience, 124*(2), 288–293. doi:10.1037/a0018942

Mesagno, C., Harvey, J. T., & Janelle, C. M. (2012). Choking under pressure: The role of fear of negative evaluation. *Psychology of Sport and Exercise, 13*(1), 60–68. doi:10.1016/j.psychsport.2011.07.007

Mesch, G. S., & Talmud, I. (2007). Similarity and the quality of online and offline social relationships among adolescents in Israel. *Journal of Research on Adolescence, 17,* 455–466.

Mesmer-Magnus, J., Glew, D. J., & Viswesvaran, C. (2012). A meta-analysis of positive humor in the workplace. *Journal of Managerial Psychology, 27*(2), 155–190. doi:10.1108/02683941211199554

Messineo, M. J. (2008). Does advertising on Black Entertainment Television portray more positive gender representation compared to broadcast networks? *Sex Roles, 59,* 752–764.

Meyer, P. S., Johnson, D. P., Parks, A., Iwanski, C., & Penn, D. L. (2012). Positive living: A pilot study of group positive psychotherapy for people with schizophrenia. *The Journal of Positive Psychology, 7,* 239–248. doi:10.1080/17439760.2012.677467

Meyerbröker, K., & Emmelkamp, P. G. (2010). Virtual reality exposure therapy in anxiety disorders: A systematic review of process-and-outcome studies. *Depression and Anxiety, 27*(10), 933–944. doi:10.1002/da.20734

Meyer-Griffith, K., Reardon, R. C., & Hartley, S. (2009). An examination of the relationship between career thoughts and communication apprehension. *The Career Development Quarterly, 58*(2), 171–180.

Mezulis, A. H., Abramson, L. Y., Hyde, J. S., & Hankin, B. L. (2004). Is there a universal positivity bias in attributions? A meta-analytic review of individual, developmental, and cultural differences in the self-serving attributional bias. *Psychological Bulletin, 130,* 711–747.

Mickelson, K. D., Kessler, R. C., & Shaver, P. R. (1997). Adult attachment in a nationally representative sample. *Journal of Personality and Social Psychology, 73,* 1092–1106.

Miklowitz, D. J., & Johnson, S. L. (2007). Bipolar disorders. In M. Hersen, S. M. Turner, & D. C. Beidel (Eds.), *Adult psychopathology and diagnosis.* New York, NY: Wiley.

Mikulincer, M., & Shaver, P. R. (2003). The attachment behavioral system in adulthood: Activation, psychodynamics, and interpersonal processes. In Mark P. Zanna (Ed.), *Advances in Experimental Social Psychology* (Vol. 35). San Diego: Academic Press.

Mikulincer, M., & Shaver, P. R. (2011). An attachment perspective on interpersonal and intergroup conflict. In J. P. Forgas, A. W. Kruglanski, & K. D. Williams (Eds.), *The psychology of social conflict and aggression* (pp. 19–35). New York, NY: Psychology Press.

Milfont, T. L., & Sibley, C. G. (2012). The Big Five personality traits and environmental engagement: Associations at the individual and societal level. *Journal of Environmental Psychology, 32,* 187–195.

Milgram, N., Marshevsky, S., & Sadeh, C. (1995). Correlates of academic procrastination: Discomfort, task aversiveness, and task capability. *Journal of Psychology, 129,* 145–155.

Milgram, S. (1963). Behavioral study of obedience. *Journal of Abnormal and Social Psychology, 67,* 371–378.

Milgram, S. (1974). *Obedience to authority.* New York, NY: Harper & Row.

Milinski, M., Sommerfeld, R. D., Krambeck, H. J., Reed, F. A., & Marotzke, J. (2008). The collective-risk social dilemma and the prevention of simulated dangerous climate change. *Proceedings of the National Academy of Sciences, 105,* 2291–2294.

Miller, B. K., Rutherford, M. A., & Kolodinsky, R. W. (2008). Perceptions of organizational politics: A meta-analysis of outcomes. *Journal of Business and Psychology, 22,* 209–222.

Miller, C. B. (2009). Yes we did! Basking in reflected glory and cutting off reflected failure in the 2008 presidential election. *Analyses of Social Issues and Public Policy (ASAP), 9*(1), 283–296. doi:10.1111/j.1530-2415.2009.01194.x

Miller, G. E., & Blackwell, E. (2006). Turning up the heat: Inflammation as a mechanism linking chronic stress, depression, and heart disease. *Current Directions in Psychological Science, 15,* 269–272.

Miller, G. P. (1978). *Life choices: How to make the critical decisions—about your education, career, marriage, family, life style.* New York, NY: Thomas Y. Crowell.

Miller, G. T. (2007). *Living in the environment: Principles, connections and solutions* (14th ed.). Belmont, CA: Wadsworth/Thompson Learning.

Miller, J. G. (1984). Culture and the development of everyday social explanation. *Journal of Personality and Social Psychology, 46,* 961–978.

Miller, N. E. (1944). Experimental studies of conflict. In J. McV. Hunt (Ed.), *Personality and the behavior disorders* (Vol. 1). New York, NY: Ronald.

Miller, N. E. (1959). Liberalization of basic S-R concepts: Extension to conflict behavior, motivation, and social learning. In S. Koch (Ed.), *Psychology: A study of a science.* (Vol. 2). New York, NY: McGraw-Hill.

Miller, R. S. (2008). Attending to temptation: The operation (and perils) of attention to alternatives in close relationships. In J. P. Forgas & J. Fitness (Eds.), *Social relationships: Cognitive, affective, and motivational processes* (pp. 321–337). New York, NY: Psychology Press.

Miller, R. S., Perlman, D., & Brehm, S. S. (2007). *Intimate relationships.* Boston, MA: McGraw-Hill.

Miller, S. L., & Maner, J. K. (2008). Coping with romantic betrayal: Sex differences in responses to partner infidelity. *Evolutionary Psychology, 6,* 413–426.

Miller, T. W. (2007). Trauma, change, and psychological health in the 21st century. *American Psychologist, 62,* 889–898.

Miller Burke, J., & Attridge, M. (2011). Pathways to career and leadership success: Part 1—A psychosocial profile of $100k professionals. *Journal of Workplace Behavioral Health, 26,* 175–206. doi:10.1080/1555524 0.2011.589718

Millett, K. (1970). *Sexual politics.* Garden City, NY: Doubleday.

Millman, R. B., & Beeder, A. B. (1994). The new psychedelic culture: LSD, ecstasy, "rave" parties and the Grateful Dead. *Psychiatric Annals, 24*(3), 148–150.

Mineka, S., & Öhman, A. (2002). Phobias and preparedness: The selective, automatic and encapsulated nature of fear. *Biological Psychiatry, 52,* 927–937.

Mineka, S., & Zinbarg, S. (2006). A contemporary learning theory perspective on the etiology of anxiety disorders: It's not what you thought it was. *American Psychologist, 61,* 10–26.

Minzenberg, M. J., Yoon, J. H., & Carter, C. S. (2008). Schizophrenia. In R. E. Hales, S. C. Yudofsky, & G. O. Gabbard (Eds.), *The American psychiatric publishing textbook of psychiatry* (pp. 407–456). Washington, DC: American Psychiatric Publishing.

Miranda, J., Bernal, G., Lau, A., Kohn, L., Hwang, W., & LaFromboise, T. (2005). State of the science on psychosocial interventions for ethnic minorities. *Annual Review of Clinical Psychology, 1,* 113–142.

Mischel, W. (1973). Toward a cognitive social learning conceptualization of personality. *Psychological Review, 80,* 252–283.

Mischel, W. (1990). Personality dispositions revisited and revised: A view after three decades. In L. A. Pervin (Ed.), *Handbook of personality: Theory and research.* New York, NY: Guilford Press.

Mischel, W., Shoda, Y., & Peake, P. K. (1988). The nature of adolescent competencies predicted by preschool delay of gratification. *Journal of Personality and Social Psychology, 54,* 687–696.

Mitchell, A. E., Castellani, A. M., Herrington, R. L., Joseph, J. I., Doss, B. D., & Snyder, D. K. (2008). Predictors of intimacy in couples' discussions of relationship injuries: An observational study. *Journal of Family Psychology, 22,* 21–29.

Mitchell, V. F. (1987). Rx for improving staff effectiveness. In A. D. Timpe (Ed.), *The management of time.* New York, NY: Facts on File.

Miyamoto, Y., & Kitayama, S. (2002). Cultural variation in correspondence bias: The critical role of attitude diagnosticity of socially constrained behavior. *Journal of Personality and Social Psychology, 83*(5), 1239–1248.

Miyamoto, Y., Nisbett, R. E., & Masuda, T. (2006). Culture and the physical environment: Holistic versus analytic perceptual affordances. *Psychological Science, 17,* 113–119.

Moak, D. H., & Anton, R. F. (1999). Alcohol. In B. S. McCrady & E. E. Epstein (Eds.), *Addictions: A comprehensive guidebook.* New York, NY: Oxford University Press.

Modestin, J. (1992). Multiple personality disorder in Switzerland. *American Journal of Psychiatry, 149,* 88–92.

Mohr, D. C., Vella, L., Hart, S., Heckman, T., & Simon, G. (2008). The effect of telephone-administered psychotherapy on symptoms of depression and attrition: A meta-analysis. *Clinical Psychology: Science and Practice, 15,* 243–253. doi:10.1111/j.1468-2850 .2008.00134.x

Mohren, D. C. L., Swaen, G. M. H., Kant, I., van Schayck, C. P., & Galama, J. M. D. (2005). Fatigue and job stress as predictors for sickness absence during common infections. *International Journal of Behavioral Medicine, 12*(1), 11–20.

Mojtabai, R., & Olfson, M. (2008). National trends in psychotherapy by office-based psychiatrists. *Archives of General Psychiatry, 65,* 962–970.

Mojtabai, R., & Olfson, M. (2010). National trends in psychotropic medication polypharmacy in office-based psychiatry. *Archives of General Psychiatry, 67*(1), 26–36.

Mokdad, A. H., Marks, J. S., Stroup, D. F., & Gerberding, J. L. (2004). Actual causes of death in the United States, 2000. *Journal of the American Medical Association, 291,* 1238–1245.

Monastra, V. J. (2008). Social skills training for children and teens with ADHD: The neuroeducational life skills program. In V. J. Monastra (Ed.), *Unlocking the potential of patients with ADHD: A model for clinical practice.* Washington, DC: American Psychological Association.

Mongrain, M., & Anselmo-Matthews, T. (2012). Do positive psychology exercises work? A replication of Seligman et al. (2005). *Journal of Clinical Psychology, 68*(4), 382–389. doi:10.1002/jclp.21839

Monroe, S. M., & Hadjiyannakis, K. (2002). The social environment and depression: Focusing on severe life stress. In I. H. Gotlib & C. L. Hammen (Eds.), *Handbook of depression.* New York, NY: Guilford.

Monroe, S. M., & Reid, M. W. (2009). Life stress and major depression. *Current Directions in Psychological Science, 18*(2), 68–72. doi:10.1111/j.1467-8721.2009.01611.x

Monroe, S. M., Slavich, G. M., & Georgiades, K. (2009).The social environment and life stress in depression. In I. H. Gotlib & C. L. Hammen (Eds.), *Handbook of depression* (pp. 340–360). New York, NY: Guilford.

Montepare, J. M. (2010). "Cue, view, action": An ecological approach to person perception. In E. Balcetis & G. Lassiter (Eds.), *Social psychology of visual perception* (pp. 299–323). New York, NY: Psychology Press.

Montesi, J. L., Fauber, R. L., Gordon, E. A., & Heimberg, R. G. (2011). The specific importance of communicating about sex to couples' sexual and overall relationship satisfaction. *Journal of Social and Personal Relationships, 28*(5), 591–609. doi:10.1177/0265407510386833

Montoya, R., & Horton, R. S. (2012). The reciprocity of liking effect. In M. A. Paludi (Ed.), *The psychology of love* (pp. 39–57). Santa Barbara, CA: Praeger/ABC-CLIO.

Montoya, R., Horton, R. S., & Kirchner, J. (2008). Is actual similarity necessary for attraction? A meta-analysis of actual and perceived similarity. *Journal of Social and Personal Relationships, 25*(6), 889–922. doi:10.1177/0265407508096700

Moore, D. S., & Johnson, S. P. (2008). Mental rotation in human infants. *Psychological Science, 19,* 1063–1066.

Moore, D. W. (2001, August 31). Most American workers satisfied with their job: One-third would be happier in another job. Available: www.gallup.com/poll/releases/pr010831.asp. Retrieved 1/19/2002.

Moore, D. W. (2003, January 3). Family, health most important aspects of life. Retrieved from http://www.Gallup.Com/Poll/Content/?Ci−7504.

Moore, R. L., & Wei, L. (2012). Modern love in China. In M. A. Paludi (Ed.), *The psychology of love* (pp. 27–42). Santa Barbara, CA: Praeger/ABC-CLIO.

Moos, R. H., & Billings, A. G. (1982). Conceptualizing and measuring coping resources and processes. In L. Goldberger & S. Breznitz (Eds.), *Handbook of stress: Theoretical and clinical aspects.* New York, NY: Free Press.

Moradi, B., & Risco, C. (2006). Perceived discrimination experiences and mental health of Latina/o American persons. *Journal of Counseling Psychology, 53,* 411–421.

Morahan-Martin, J., & Schumacher, P. (2003). Loneliness and social uses of the Internet. *Computers in Human Behavior, 19*(6), 659–671.

Moretti, M. M., & Higgins, E. T. (1990). Relating self-discrepancy to self-esteem: The contribution of discrepancy beyond actual-self ratings. *Journal of Experimental Social Psychology, 26,* 108–123.

Morgan, H. J., & Janoff-Bulman, R. (1994). Victims' responses to traumatic life events: An unjust world or an uncaring world? *Social Justice Research, 7,* 47–68.

Morgan, M. J. (2000). Ecstasy (MDMA): A review of its possible persistent psychological effects. *Psychopharmacology, 152*(3), 230–248.

Morgan, R. D., & Cohen, L. M. (2008). Clinical and counseling psychology: Can differences be gleaned from printed recruiting materials? *Training and Education in Professional Psychology, 2*(3), 156–164.

Morgenstern, J. (2000). *Time management from the inside out.* New York, NY: Holt.

Mori, K., & Arai, M. (2010). No need to fake it: Reproduction of the Asch experiment without confederates. *International Journal of Psychology, 45*(5), 390–397. doi:10.1080/00207591003774485

Morris, M. W., & Peng, K. (1994). Culture and cause: American and Chinese attributions for social and physical events. *Journal of Personality and Social Psychology, 67,* 949–971.

Morris, W. L., & DePaulo, B. M. (2009). Singlehood. In H. T. Reis & S. Sprecher (Eds.), *Encyclopedia of human relationships: Vol. 3* (pp. 1504–1507). Los Angeles: Sage Reference Publication.

Morris, W. N. (1999). The mood system. In D. Kahneman, E. Diener, & N. Schwartz (Eds.), *Well-being: The foundations of hedonic psychology* (pp. 169–189). New York, NY: Russell Sage Foundation.

Morrison, C. M., & Gore, H. (2010). The relationship between excessive Internet use and depression: A questionnaire-based study of 1,319 young people and adults. *Psychopathology, 43*(2), 121–126. doi:10.1159/000277001

Morrison, T. G., Morrison, M. A., & Hopkins, C. (2003). Striving for bodily perfection? An exploration of the drive for masculinity in Canadian men. *Psychology of Men and Masculinity, 4*(2), 111–120.

Morrow, G. D. (2009). Exchange processes. In H. T. Reis & S. Sprecher (Eds.), *Encyclopedia of human relationships: Vol. 1* (pp. 551–555). Los Angeles: Sage Reference Publication.

Morry, M. M. (2007). The attraction-similarity hypothesis among cross-sex friends: Relationship satisfactions, perceived similarities, and self-serving perceptions. *Journal of Social and Personal Relationships, 24,* 117–138.

Morry, M. M. (2009). Similarity principle of attraction. In H. T. Reis & S. Sprecher (Eds.), *Encyclopedia of human relationships: Vol. 3* (pp. 1500–1504). Los Angeles: Sage Reference Publication.

Mortenson, S. T. (2006). Cultural differences and similarities in seeking support as a response to academic failure: A comparison of American and Chinese college students. *Communication Education, 55*(2), 127–146.

Mosher, D. L. (1991). Macho men, machismo, and sexuality. *Annual Review of Sex Research, 2,* 199–248.

Mosher, W. D., Chandra, A., & Jones, J. (2005). *Sexual behavior and selected health measures: Men and women 15–44 years of age, United States, 2002.* Hyattsville, MD: National Center for Health Statistics.

Mosher, W. D., Jones, J., & Abma, J. C. (2012). *Intended and unintended births in the United States: 1982–2010.* Hyattsville, MD: National Center for Health Statistics.

Moskowitz, D. S. (1994). Cross-situational generality and the interpersonal circumplex. *Journal of Personality and Social Psychology, 66,* 921–933.

Moskowitz, J. T. (2003). Positive affect predicts lower risk of AIDS mortality. *Psychosomatic Medicine, 65,* 620–626.

Motivala, S. J., Khanna, D., FitzGerald, J., & Irwin, M. R. (2008). Stress activation of cellular markers of inflammation in rheumatoid arthritis: Protective effects of tumor necrosis factor a antagonists. *Arthritis & Rheumatism, 58,* 376–383.

Mott, S. L., Schiller, C., Richards, J., O'Hara, M. W., & Stuart, S. (2011). Depression and anxiety among postpartum and adoptive mothers. *Archives of Women's Mental Health, 14*(4), 335–343. doi:10.1007/s00737-011-0227-1

Mowrer, O. H. (1947). On the dual nature of learning: A reinterpretaton of "conditioning" and "problem-solving." *Harvard Educational Review, 17,* 102–150.

Moynihan, J. A., & Ader, R. (1996). Psychoneuroimmunology: Animal models of disease. *Psychosomatic Medicine, 58,* 546–558.

Mroczek, D. K., & Almeida, D. M. (2004). The effect of daily stress, personality, and age on daily negative affect. *Journal of Personality, 72,* 355–378.

Muehlenhard, C. L. (2011). Examining stereotypes about token resistance to sex. *Psychology of Women Quarterly, 35*(4), 676–683. doi:10.1177/0361684311426689

Muehlenhard, C. L., & Peterson, Z. D. (2011). Distinguishing between sex and gender: History, current conceptualizations, and implications. *Sex Roles, 64*(11–12), 791–803. doi:10.1007/s11199-011-9932-5

Muehlenhard, C. L., & Shippee, S. K. (2010). Men's and women's reports of pretending orgasm. *Journal of Sex Research, 47*(6), 552–567. doi:10.1080/00224490903171794

Muench, J., & Hamer, A. M. (2010). Adverse effects of antipsychotic medications. *American Family Physician, 81*(5), 617–622.

Mukamal, K. J., Conigrave, K. M., Mittleman, M. A., Camargo, C. A., Stampfer, M. J., Willet, W. C., & Rimm, E. B. (2003). Roles of drinking pattern and type of alcohol consumed in coronary heart disease in men. *New England Journal of Medicine, 348*(2), 109–118.

Mulhall, J., King, R., Glina, S., & Hvidsten, K. (2008). Importance of and satisfaction with sex among men and women worldwide: Results of the Global Better Sex Survey. *Journal of Sexual Medicine, 5,* 788–795.

Munafò, M. R., Yalcin, B., Willis-Owen, S. A., & Flint, J. (2008). Association of the dopamine D4 receptor (DRD4) gene and approach-related personality traits: Meta-analysis and new data. *Biological Psychiatry, 63*(2), 197–206. doi:10.1016/j.biopsych.2007.04.006

Mund, M., & Mitte, K. (2012). The costs of repression: A meta-analysis on the relation between repressive coping and somatic diseases. *Health Psychology, 31*(5), 640–649. doi:10.1037/a0026257

Munsey, C. (2008a). DoD allocates $25 million to study PTSD. *Monitor on Psychology, 39*(7), p. 16–17.

Munsey, C. (2008b). Prescriptive authority in the states: A look at which states allow RxP and which have considered it. *Monitor on Psychology, 39*(2).

Muris, P. (2002). Relationships between self-efficacy and symptoms of anxiety disorders and depression in a normal adolescent sample. *Personality and Individual Differences, 32,* 337–348.

Murnen, S. K., & Smolak, L. (2010). Quantitative approaches to the study of gender. In J. C. Chrisler & D. R. McCreary (Eds.), *Handbook of gender research in psychology* (Vol. 1, pp. 81–101). New York, NY: Springer.

Murphy, N. A. (2012). Nonverbal perception. In S. T. Fiske & C. N. Macrae (Eds.), *The Sage handbook of social cognition* (pp. 191–210). Thousand Oaks, CA: Sage.

Murphy, S. F., & Zagorski, D. A. (2005). Enhancing work-family and work-life interaction: The role of management. In D. F. Halpern & S. E. Murphy (Eds.), *From work-family balance to work-family interaction: Changing the metaphor.* Mahwah, NJ: Erlbaum.

Murray, R. M., & Bramon, E. (2005). Developmental model of schizophrenia. In B. J. Sadock & V. A. Sadock (Eds.), *Kaplan & Sadock's comprehensive textbook of psychiatry.* Philadelphia: Lippincott Williams & Wilkins.

Murray, S. L., Holmes, J. G., & Griffin, D. W. (1996). The self-fulfilling nature of positive illusions in romantic relationships: Love is not blind, but prescient. *Journal of Personality and Social Psychology, 71,* 1155–1180.

Murrell, A. J., & James, E. H. (2001). Gender and diversity in organizations: Past, present, and future directions. *Sex Roles, 45*(5/6), 243–257.

Murrell, A. J., Dietz-Uhler, B. L., Dovidio, J. F., Gaertner, S. L., & Drout, E. (1994). Aversive racism and resistance to affirmative action: Perceptions of justice are not necessarily color blind. *Basic and Applied Social Psychology, 17*(1–2), 71–86.

Musick, K., & Bumpass, L. (2012). Reexamining the case for marriage: Union formation and changes in well-being. *Journal of Marriage and Family, 74,* 1–18. doi:10.1111/j.1741-3737.2011.00873.x

Mussweiler, T., & Rütter, K. (2003). What friends are for! The use of routine standards in social comparison. *Journal of Personality and Social Psychology, 85,* 467–481.

Mussweiler, T., Rütter, K., & Epstude, K. (2004). The man who wasn't there: Subliminal social comparison standards influence self-evaluation. *Journal of Experimental Social Psychology, 40,* 689–696.

Muzina, D. J., Kemp, D. E., & Calabrese, J. R. (2008). Mood stabilizers. In A. Tasman, J. Kay, J. A. Lieberman, M. B. First, & M. Maj (Eds.), *Psychiatry* (3rd ed.). New York, NY: Wiley-Blackwell.

Myers, D. G. (1980). *Inflated self: Human illusions and the biblical call to hope.* New York, NY: Seabury Press.

Myers, D. G. (1992). *The pursuit of happiness: Who is happy—and why.* New York, NY: Morrow.

Myers, D. G. (1999). Close relationships and quality of life. In D. Kahneman, E. Diener, & N. Schwarz (Eds.), *Well-being: The foundations of hedonic psychology.* New York, NY: Sage.

Myers, D. G. (2000a). The funds, friends, and faith of happy people. *American Psychologist, 55,* 56–67.

Myers, D. G. (2000b). *The American paradox: Spiritual hunger in an age of plenty.* New Haven, CT: Yale University Press.

Myers, D. G. (2008). Religion and human flourishing. In M. Eid & R. J. Larsen (Eds.), *The science of subjective well-being* (pp. 323–346). New York, NY: Guilford.

Myers, D. G., & Diener, E. (1995). Who is happy? *Psychological Science, 6,* 10–19.

Myers, D. G., & Diener, E. (1997). The pursuit of happiness. *Scientific American, Special Issue 7,* 40–43.

Myers, G. (2007). *The significance of children and animals: Social development and our connections to other species.* West Lafayette, IN: Purdue University Press.

Myers, L. B. (2010). The importance of repressive coping style: Findings from 30 years of research. *Anxiety, Stress, & Coping, 23,* 3–17. doi:10.1080/10615800903366945

Myers, L. B., Burns, J. W., Derakshan, N., Elfant, E., Eysenck, M.W., & Phipps, S. (2007). Current issues in repressive coping and health. In J. Denollet, I. Nyklicek, & A. Vingerhoets (Eds.), *Emotion regulation: Conceptual and clinical issues* (pp. 69–86). New York, NY: Springer.

Myrtek, M. (2007). Type A behavior and hostility as independent risk factors for coronary heart disease. In J. Jochen, B. Barde, & A. M. Zeiher (Eds.), *Contributions toward evidence-based psychocardiology: A systematic review of the literature.* Washington, DC: American Psychological Association.

Nadal, K. L. (2008). Preventing racial, ethnic, gender, sexual minority, disability, and religious microaggressions: Recommendations for promoting positive mental health. *Prevention in Counseling Psychology: Theory, Research, Practice and Training, 2,* 22–27.

Nadal, K. L. (2011). Responding to racial, gender, and sexual orientation microaggressions in the workplace. In M. A. Paludi, C. r. Paludi, E. R. DeSouza (Eds.), *Praeger handbook on understanding and preventing workplace discrimination* (pp. 23–32). Santa Barbara, CA: Praeger/ABC-CLIO.

Nadal, K. L., & Haynes, K. (2012). The effects of sexism, gender microaggressions, and other forms of discrimination on women's mental health and development. In P. K. Lundberg-Love, K. L. Nadal, & M. A. Paludi (Eds.), *Women and mental disorders* (pp. 87–101). Santa Barbara, CA: Praeger/ABC-CLIO.

Nadelson, C. C., Notman, M. T., & McCarthy, M. K. (2005). Gender issues in psychotherapy. In G. O. Gabbard, J. S. Beck, & J. Holmes (Eds.), *Oxford textbook of psychotherapy.* New York, NY: Oxford University Press.

Nakamura, J., & Csikszentmihalyi, M. (2009). Flow theory and research. In C. R. Snyder & S. Lopez (Eds)., *Oxford handbook of positive psychology* (2nd ed., pp. 195–206). New York, NY: Oxford University Press.

Nardi, P. M. (2007). Friendship, sex, and masculinity. In M. Kimmel (Ed.), *The sexual self: The construction of sexual scripts* (pp. 49–57). Nashville, TN: Vanderbilt University Press.

National Association of Women Business Owners. (2010). New census data reinforces the economic power of women owned businesses in the U.S. says NAWBO. Retrieved from http://http://nawbo.org/content_11800.cfm

National Center for Health Statistics. (2006). *Chartbook on trends in the health of Americans. Health, United States, 2006.* Hyattsville, MD: Public Health Service.

National Institute of Child Health and Human Development (NICHD). Early Child Care Research Network. (1997). The effects of infant child care on infant-mother attachment security: Results of the NICHD Study of Early Child Care. *Child Development, 68,* 860–879.

National Institute of Justice & Centers for Disease Control & Prevention (1998). Prevalence, incidence and consequences of violence against women survey.

National Oceanic and Atmospheric Administration (NOAA). (2012). State of the climate: Global analysis for annual 2012. Retrieved from http://www.ncdc.noaa.gov/sotc/global/2012/13

Naumann, L. P., Vazire, S., Rentfrow, P. J., & Gosling, S. D. (2009). Personality judgments based on physical appearance. *Personality and Social Psychology Bulletin, 35*(12), 1661–1671. doi:10.1177/0146167209346309

Neff, L. A. (2012). Putting marriage in its context: The influence of external stress on early marital development. In L. Campbell & T. J. Loving (Eds.), *Interdisciplinary research on close relationships: The case for integration* (pp. 179–203). Washington, DC: American Psychological Association. doi:10.1037/13486-008

Negy, C., Schwartz, S., & Reig-Ferrer, A. (2009). Violated expectations and acculturative stress among U.S. Hispanic immigrants. *Cultural Diversity and Ethnic Minority Psychology, 15,* 255–264.

Neighbors, H. W., Caldwell, C., Williams, D. R., Nesse, R., Taylor, R. J., Bullard, K. M., et al. (2007). Race, ethnicity, and the use of services for mental disorders: Results from the National Survey of American Life. *Archives of General Psychiatry, 64,* 485–494.

Nelson, C., & Demas, G. E. (2004). Seasonal patterns of stress, disease, and sickness responses. *Current Directions in Psychological Science, 13,* 198–201.

Nelson, D. L., & Cooper, C. L. (Eds.), (2007). *Positive organizational behavior.* London: Sage.

Nelson, E. L., Wenzel, L., Osann, K., Dogan-Ates, A., Chantana, N., Reina-Patton, A., et al. (2008). Stress, immunity, and cervical cancer: biobehavioral

outcomes of a randomized clinical trial. *Clinical Cancer Research, 14,* 2111–2118.

Nelson, L. J., & Miller, D. T. (1995). The distinctiveness effect in social categorization: You are what makes you unusual. *Psychological Science, 6,* 246.

Nelson, R. J., Franks, S., & Brose, A. (2005). The influence of hostility and family history of cardiovascular disease on autonomic activation in response to controllable versus uncontrollable stress, anger imagery reduction, and relaxation therapy. *Journal of Behavioral Medicine, 28,* 213–221.

Neria, Y., DiGrande, L., & Adams, B. G. (2011). Posttraumatic stress disorder following the September 11, 2001, terrorist attacks: A review of the literature among highly exposed populations. *American Psychologist, 66*(6), 429–446. doi:10.1037/a0024791

Nesdale, D., De Vries Robbé, M., & Van Oudenhoven, J. (2012). Intercultural effectiveness, authoritarianism, and ethnic prejudice. *Journal of Applied Social Psychology, 42*(5), 1173–1191. doi:10.1111/j.1559-1816.2011.00882.x

Nettelhorst, S. C., & Brannon, L. A. (2012). The effect of advertisement choice, sex, and need for cognition on attention. *Computers in Human Behavior, 28*(4), 1315–1320. doi:10.1016/j.chb.2012.02.015

Nettle, D. (2006). The evolution of personality variation in humans and other animals. *American Psychologist, 61*(6), 622–631.

New Freedom Commission on Mental Health. (2003). *Achieving the promise: Transforming mental health care in America.* Rockville, MD: DHHS Pub. No. SMA-03-3831.

New Media Trend Watch. (2012) *Demographics.* Retrieved from http://www.newmediatrendwatch.com/markets-by-country/17-usa/123-demographics

Newcombe, N. S. (2007). Taking science seriously: Straight thinking about spatial sex differences. In S. J. Ceci & W. M. Williams (Eds.), *Why aren't more women in science?* (pp. 69–78). Washington, DC: American Psychological Association.

Newcombe, N. S. (2010). On tending our scientific knitting: Thinking about gender in the context of evolution. In J. C. Chrisler & D. R. McCreary (Eds.), *Handbook of gender research in psychology* (Vol. 1, pp. 259–274). New York, NY: Springer.

Newmahr, S. (2011). Homosexuality. In C. D. Bryant (Ed.), *The Routledge handbook of deviant behavior* (pp. 253–259). New York, NY: Routledge/Taylor & Francis Group.

Newman, C. F. & Beck, A. T. (2009). Cognitive therapy. In B. J. Sadock, V. A. Sadock, & P. Ruiz (Eds.), *Kaplan & Sadock's comprehensive textbook of psychiatry* (pp. 2857–2872). Philadelphia: Lippincott Williams & Wilkins.

Newport, F. (2012). Half of Americans support legal gay marriage. Retrieved from http://www.gallup.com/poll/154529/half-americans-support-legal-gay-marriage.aspx

Newschaffer, C. J., Croen, L. A., Daniels, J., Giarelli, E., Grether, J. K., Levy, S. E., et al. (2007). The epidemiology of autism spectrum disorders. *Annual Review of Public Health, 28,* 235–258.

Nezu, A. M., Nezu, C. M., Felgoise, S. H., & Zwick, M. L. (2003). Psychosocial oncology. In A. M. Nezu, C. M. Nezu, & P. A. Geller (Eds.), *Handbook of psychology: Vol. 9. Health psychology.* New York, NY: Wiley.

Ng, T. W., & Feldman, D. C. (2009). How broadly does education contribute to job performance? *Personnel Psychology, 62,* 89–134.

Ng, T. W., Sorenson, K. L., & Feldman, D. C. (2007). Dimensions, antecedents, and consequences of workaholism: A conceptual integration and extension. *Journal of Organizational Behavior, 28,* 111–136.

Nguyen, M., Bin, Y., & Campbell, A. (2012). Comparing online and offline self-disclosure: A systematic review. *Cyberpsychology, Behavior, and Social Networking, 15*(2), 103–111. doi:10.1089/cyber.2011.0277

Niaura, R., & Abrams, D. B. (2002). Smoking cessation: Progress, priorities, and prospectus. *Journal of Consulting & Clinical Psychology, 70*(3), 494–509.

Nicholson, C. (2006). Freedom and choice, culture, and class. *APS Observer, 19*(8), 31, 45.

Nicholson, I. (2011). "Torture at Yale": Experimental subjects, laboratory torment and the "rehabilitation" of Milgram's "Obedience to Authority." *Theory & Psychology, 21*(6), 737–761. doi:10.1177/0959354311420199

Nickerson, C., Schwarz, N., Diener, E., & Kahneman, D. (2003). Zeroing in on the dark side of the American dream: A closer look at the negative consequences of the goal for financial success. *Psychological Science, 14*(6), 531–536.

Nickerson, R. S. (1998). Confirmation bias: A ubiquitous phenomenon in many guises. *Review of General Psychology, 2,* 175–220.

Nie, N. H., & Erbring, L. (2002). Internet and society: A preliminary report. *IT & Society, 1*(1), 275–283.

Niedenthal, P. M., Setterlund, M. B., & Wherry, M. B. (1992). Possible self-complexity and affective reactions to goal-relevant evaluation. *Journal of Personality and Social Psychology, 63,* 5–16.

Niederhoffer, K. G., & Pennebaker, J. W. (2005). Sharing one's story: On the benefits of writing or talking about emotional experience. In C. R. Snyder & S. J. Lopez (Eds.), *Handbook of positive psychology.* New York, NY: Oxford University Press.

Nielsen, M. B., & Einarsen, S. S. (2012). Prospective relationships between workplace sexual harassment and psychological distress. *Occupational Medicine, 62*(3), 226–228. doi:10.1093/occmed/kqs010

Nielsen Media Research. (2012). The cross-platform report: How and where content is watched. Retrieved from http://blog.nielsen.com/nielsenwire/media_entertainment/the-cross-platform-report-how-and-where-content-is-watched/

Niessen, C., Heinrichs, N., & Dorr, S. (2009). Pursuit and adjustment of goals during unemployment: The role of age. *International Journal of Stress Management, 16*(2), 102–123.

Nisbett, R. E. (2004). *The geography of thought: How Asians and Westerners think differently . . . and why.* New York, NY: Free Press.

Nisbett, R. E., & Miyamoto, Y. (2005). The influence of culture: Holistic versus analytic perception. *Trends in Cognitive Science, 9,* 467–473.

Nisbett, R. E., Peng, K., Choi, I., & Norenzayan, A. (2001). Culture and systems of thought: Holistic versus analytic cognition. *Psychological Review, 108*(2), 291–310.

Nobler, M. S., & Sackeim, H. A. (2006). Electroconvulsive therapy and transcranial magnetic stimulation. In D. J. Stein, D. J. Kupfer, & A. F. Schatzberg (Eds.), *Textbook of mood disorders.* Washington, DC: American Psychiatric Publishing.

Noftle, E. E., & Robins, R. W. (2007). Personality predictors of academic outcomes: Big Five correlates of GPA and SAT scores. *Journal of Personality and Social Psychology, 93,* 116–130.

Nolen-Hoeksema, S. (1991). Responses to depression and their effects on the duration of depressive episodes. *Journal of Abnormal Psychology, 100,* 569–582.

Nolen-Hoeksema, S. (2000). The role of rumination in depressive disorders and mixed anxiety/depressive symptoms. *Journal of Abnormal Psychology, 109*(3), 504–511.

Nolen-Hoeksema, S. (2001). Gender differences in depression. *Current Directions in Psychological Science, 10,* 173–176.

Nolen-Hoeksema, S. (2002). Gender differences in depression. In I. H. Gotlib & C. L. Hammen (Eds.), *Handbook of depression.* New York, NY: Guilford.

Nolen-Hoeksema, S. (2012). Emotion regulation and psychopathology: The role of gender. *Annual Review of Clinical Psychology,* 861–887. doi:10.1146/annurev-clinpsy-032511-143109

Nolen-Hoeksema, S., & Davis, C. G. (2005). Positive responses to loss: Perceiving benefits and growth. In C. R. Snyder & S. J. Lopez (Eds.), *Handbook of positive psychology.* New York, NY: Oxford University Press.

Nolen-Hoeksema, S., & Hilt, L. M. (2009). Gender differences in depression. In I. H. Gotlib & C. L. Hammen (Eds.), *Handbook of depression* (pp. 386–404). New York, NY: Guilford.

Nolen-Hoeksema, S., & Keita, G. P. (2003). Women and depression: An introduction. *Psychology of Women Quarterly, 27,* 89–90.

Nolen-Hoeksema, S., Wisco, B. E., & Lybomirsky, S. (2008). Rethinking rumination. *Perspectives on Psychological Science, 3,* 400–424.

Noller, P. (1985). Negative communications in marriage. *Journal of Social and Personal Relationships, 2,* 289–301.

Noller, P. (1987). Nonverbal communication in marriage. In D. Perlman & S. Duck (Eds.), *Intimate relationships: Development, dynamics, and deterioration.* Newbury Park, CA: Sage.

Noller, P., & Fitzpatrick, M. A. (1990). Marital communication in the eighties. *Journal of Marriage and the Family, 52,* 832–843.

Noller, P., & Gallois, C. (1988). Understanding and misunderstanding in marriage: Sex and marital adjustment differences in structured and free interaction. In P. Noller & M. A. Fitzpatrick (Eds.), *Perspectives on marital interaction.* Clevedon, England: Multilingual Matters.

Nomaguchi, K. M. (2006). Maternal employment, nonparental care, mother-child interactions and child outcomes during preschool years. *Journal of Marriage and Family, 68,* 1341–1369.

Nomaguchi, K. M., & Milkie, M. A. (2003). Costs and rewards of children: The effects of becoming a parent on adults' lives. *Journal of Marriage and Family, 65,* 356–374.

Norcross, J. C., Hedges, M., & Castle, P. H. (2002). Psychologists conducting psychotherapy in 2001: A study of the Division 29 membership. *Psychotherapy: Theory, Research, Practice, Training, 39,* 97–102.

Norcross, J. C., Santrock, J. W., Campbell, L. F., Smith, T. P., Sommer, R., & Zuckerman, E. L. (2003). *Authoritative guide to self-help resources in mental health.* New York: Guilford.

Norem, J. K. (2008). Defensive pessimism, anxiety, and the complexity of evaluating self-regulation. *Social and Personality Psychology Compass, 2*(1), 121–134.

Norem, J. K. (2009). Psychological defensiveness: Repression, blunting, and defensive pessimism. In M. R. Leary & R. H. Hoyle (Eds.), *Handbook of individual differences in social behavior* (pp. 480–492). New York, NY: Guilford Press.

Norem, J. K., & Smith, S. (2006). Defensive pessimism: Positive past, anxious present, and pessimistic future. In L. J. Sanna & E. C. Chang (Eds.), *Judgments over time: The interplay of thoughts, feelings, and behaviors.* New York, NY: Oxford University Press.

Norenzayan, A., Choi, I., & Nisbett, R. E. (2002). Cultural similarities and differences in social inference: Evidence from behavioral predictions and lay theories of behavior. *Personality and Social Psychology Bulletin, 28,* 109–120.

Norris, I. J., & Larsen, J. T. (2011). Wanting more than you have and its consequences for well-being. *Journal of Happiness Studies, 12,* 877–885. doi:10.1007/s10902-010-09232-8

North, R. J., & Swann, W. B., Jr. (2009a). Self-verification 360°: Illuminating the light and dark sides. *Self and Identity, 8*(2–3), 131–146.

North, R. J., & Swann, W. B., Jr. (2009b). What's positive about self-verification? In S. J. Lopez & C. R. Snyder (Eds.), *Oxford handbook of positive psychology* (2nd ed., pp. 464–474). New York, NY: Oxford University Press.

Norton, P. G. W. (2004, February 1). Low-fat foods helped fuel obesity epidemic. *Family Practice News,* p. 22.

Norton, S. (2002). Women exposed: Sexual harrassment and female vulnerability. In L. Diamant & J. Lee (Eds.), *The psychology of sex, gender, and jobs.* Westport, CT: Praeger.

Norwood, K., & Duck, S. (2009). Dissolution of relationships, processes. In H. T. Reis & S. Sprecher (Eds.), *Encyclopedia of human relationships: Vol. 2* (pp. 445–449). Los Angeles: Sage Reference Publication.

Nouri, M., Hill, L. G., & Orrell-Valente, J. K. (2011). Media exposure, internalization of the thin ideal, and body dissatisfaction: Comparing Asian American and European American college females. *Body Image, 8*(4), 366–372. doi:10.1016/j.bodyim.2011.05.008

Novelli, D., Drury, J., & Reicher, S. (2010). Come together: Two studies concerning the impact of group relations on "personal space." *British Journal of Social Psychology, 49*(2), 223–236. doi:10.1348/014466609X449377

Novotney, A. (2009). Yoga as a pratice tool. *Monitor on Psychology, 40*(10), 38–42.

Nurnberger, J. I., & Zimmerman, J. (1970). Applied analysis of human behavior: An alternative to conventional motivational inferences and unconscious determination in therapeutic programming. *Behavior Therapy, 1,* 59–69.

Nye, C. D., Su, R., Rounds, J., & Drasgow, F. (2011). *Vocational interests and performance: A quantitative summary of 60 years of research.* Paper presented at the annual meeting of the International Personnel Assessment Council, Washington, DC.

Oakes, P. (2001). The root of all evil in intergroup relations? Unearthing the categorization process. In R. Brown & S. L. Gaertner (Eds.), *Blackwell handbook of social psychology: Intergroup processes.* London: Blackwell.

Oaten, M., & Cheng, K. (2005). Academic examination stress impairs self-control. *Journal of Social and Clinical Psychology, 24,* 254–279.

Oaten, M., & Cheng, K. (2006). Longitudinal gains in self-regulation from regular physical exercise. *British Journal of Health Psychology, 11,* 717–733.

Oattes, M. K., & Offman, A. (2007). Global self-esteem and sexual self-esteem as predictors of sexual communication in intimate relationships. *The Canadian Journal of Human Sexuality, 16,* 89–100.

O'Brien, S. J., & Vertinsky, P. A. (1991). Unfit survivors: Exercise as a resource for aging women. *The Gerontologist, 31,* 347–357.

O'Callahan, M., Andrews, A. M., & Krantz, D. S. (2003). Coronary heart disease and hypertension. In A. M. Nezu, C. M. Nezu, & P. A. Geller (Eds.), *Handbook of psychology: Vol. 9. Health psychology.* New York, NY: Wiley.

Ocon, R. (2006). *Issues on gender and diversity in management.* Lanham, MD: University Press of America.

O'Connor, A. (2012, June 12). Really? Quitting smoking is harder for women. *The New York Times,* D5.

O'Connor, D. B., & Conner, M.. (2011). Effects of stress on eating behavior. In R. J. Contrada & A. Baum (Eds.), *The handbook of stress science: Biology, psychology, and health* (pp. 275–286). New York, NY: Springer.

O'Connor, R. J., McNeill, A., Borland, R., Hammond, D., King, B., Boudreau, C., et al. (2007). Smokers' beliefs about the relative safety of other tobacco products: Findings from the ITC collaboration. *Nicotine and Tobacco Research, 9,* 1033–1042.

O'Connell, M., & Feliz, S. (2011) Same-sex couple household statistics from the 2010 census. *SEHSD Working Paper Number 2011-26.* Released September 27, 2011. http://www.census.gov/hhes/files/ss-report.doc

Odle-Dusseau, H. N., Britt, T. W., & Greene-Shortridge, T. M. (2012). Organizational work-family resources as predictors of job performance and attitudes: The process of work-family conflict and enrichment. *Journal of Occupational Health Psychology, 17*(1), 28–40. doi:10.1037/a0026428

Oesterman, K., Bjoerkqvist, K., Lagerspetz, K. M. J., Kaukiainen, A., Landau, S. F., Fraczek, A., & Caprara, G. V. (1998). Cross-cultural evidence of female indirect aggression. *Aggressive Behavior, 24*(1), 1–80.

Oettingen, G., & Gollwitzer, P. M. (2001). Goal setting and goal striving. In A. Tesser & N. Schwarz. (Eds.), *Blackwell handbook of social psychology: Intra-individual processes.* Malden, MA: Blackwell.

Ogden, C. L., Carroll, M. D., & Flegal, K. M. (2008). High body mass index for age among US children and adolescents, 2003–2006. *Journal of the American Medical Association, 299,* 2401–2405.

O'Hara, M. W. (2009). Postpartum depression: What we know. *Journal of Clinical Psychology, 65,* 1258–1269.

Öhman, A., & Mineka, S. (2001). Fears, phobias, and preparedness: Toward an evolved module of fear and fear learning. *Psychological Review, 108,* 483–522.

Oishi, S., Kesebir, S., & Diener, E. (2011). Income inequality and happiness. *Psychological Science, 22,* 1095–1100. doi:10.1177/0956797611417262

O'Keefe, D. (2002). *Persuasion: Theory and research* (2nd ed.). Newbury Park, CA: Sage.

O'Keefe, D. J., & Hale, S. L. (2001). An odds-ratio based meta-analysis of research on the door-in-the-face influence strategy. *Communication Reports, 14*(1), 31–38.

Olds, J., & Schwartz, R. S. (2009). *The lonely American: Drifting apart in the twenty-first century.* Boston, MA: Beacon Press.

O'Leary, K., Acevedo, B. P., Aron, A., Huddy, L., & Mashek, D. (2012). Is long-term love more than a rare phenomenon? If so, what are its correlates?. *Social Psychological And Personality Science, 3*(2), 241–249. doi:10.1177/1948550611417015

O'Leary-Kelly, A. M., Bowes-Sperry, L., Bates, C. A., & Lean, E. R. (2009). Sexual harassment at work: A decade (plus) of progress. *Journal of Management, 35*(3), 503–536.

Olfson, M. & Marcus, S. C. (2009). National patterns in antidepressant medication treatment. *Archives of General Psychiatry, 66,* 848–856.

Olfson, M., & Marcus, S. C. (2010). National trends in outpatient psychotherapy. *The American Journal of Psychiatry, 167*(12), 1456–1463. doi:10.1176/appi.ajp.2010.10040570

Olfson, M., Cherry, D. K., & Lewis-Fernández, R. (2009). Racial differences in visit duration of outpatient psychiatric visits. *Archives of General Psychiatry, 66,* 214–221.

Olivardia, R., Pope, H. G., & Phillips, K. A. (2000). *The Adonis complex: The secret crisis of male body obsession.* New York, NY: Free Press.

Oliver, M. B., & Hyde, J. S. (1993). Gender differences in sexuality: A meta-analysis. *Psychological Bulletin, 114,* 29–51.

Olivola, C. Y., & Todorov, A. (2010). Fooled by first impressions? Reexamining the diagnostic value of appearance-based inferences. *Journal of Experimental Social Psychology, 46*(2), 315–324. doi:10.1016/j.jesp.2009.12.002

Ollendick, T. H., Öst, L.-G., Reuterskiöld, L., Costa, N., Cederlund, R., Sirbu, C., et al. (2009). One-session treatment of specific phobias in youth: A randomized clinical trial in the United States and Sweden. *Journal of Consulting and Clinical Psychology, 77,* 504–516.

Olson, K. R., Dunham, Y., Dweck, C. S., Spelke, E. S., & Banaji, M. R. (2008). Judgments of the lucky across development and culture. *Journal of Personality and Social Psychology, 94,* 757–776.

Oman, D., & Thoresen, C. E. (2005). Do religion and spirituality influence health? In R. F. Paloutzian & C. L. Park (Eds.), *Handbook of the psychology of religion and spirituality* (pp. 435–459). New York, NY: Guilford Press.

O'Mara, E. M., McNulty, J. K., & Karney, B. R. (2011). Positively biased appraisals in everyday life: When do they benefit mental health and when do they harm it? *Journal of Personality and Social Psychology, 101*(3), 415-432. doi:10.1037/a0023332

Omarzu, J. (2009). Minding the relationship. In H. T. Reis & S. Sprecher (Eds.), *Encyclopedia of human relationships: Vol. 2* (pp. 1107–1108). Los Angeles: Sage Reference Publication.

O'Neil, J. M., & Egan, J. (1992). Men's and women's gender role journeys: A metaphor for healing, transition, and transformation. In B. Wainrib (Ed.), *Gender issues across the life cycle.* New York, NY: Springer.

O'Neill, N., & O'Neill, G. (1972). *Open marriage.* New York, NY: Evans.

Ong, A. D. (2010). Pathways linking positive emotion and health in later life. *Current Directions in Psychological Science, 19*(6), 358–362. doi:10.1177/0963721410388805

Ono, H. (1998). Husbands' and wives' resources and marital dissolution. *Journal of Marriage and the Family, 60,* 674–689.

Ono, H. (2006). Homogamy among the divorced and never married on marital history in recent decades: Evidence from vital statistics data. *Social Science Research, 35,* 356–383.

Opotow, S., & Weiss, L. (2000). Denial and the process of moral exclusion in environmental conflict. *Journal of Social Issues, 56,* 475–490.

Oppliger, P. A. (2007). Effects of gender stereotyping on socialization. In R. W. Preiss, B. M. Gayle, N. Burrell, M. Allen, & J. Bryant (Eds.), *Mass media effects research: Advances through meta-analysis* (pp. 199–214). Mahwah, NJ: Erlbaum.

Opris, D., Pintea, S., Garcia-Palacios, A., Botella, C., Szamosközi, S., & David, D. (2012). Virtual reality exposure therapy in anxiety disorders: A quantitative meta-analysis. *Depression and Anxiety, 29,* 85–93. doi:10.1002/da.20910

Oringher, J., & Samuelson, K. W. (2011). Intimate partner violence and the role of masculinity in male same-sex relationships. *Traumatology, 17*(2), 68–74. doi:10.1177/1534765610395620

Orth, U., Robins, R. W., & Widaman, K. F. (2012). Life-span development of self-esteem and its effects on important life outcomes. *Journal of Personality and Social Psychology, 102*(6), 1271–1288. doi:10.1037/a0025558

Orth, U., Robins, R. W., Meier, L. L. (2009b). Disentangling the effects of low self-esteem and stressful events on depression: Findings from three longitudinal studies. *Journal of Personality and Social Psychology, 97*(2), 307–321.

Orth, U., Robins, R. W., Trzesniewski, K. H., Maes, J., & Schmitt, M. (2009a). Low self-esteem is a risk factor for depressive symptoms from young adulthood to old age. *Journal of Abnormal Psychology, 118,* 472–478.

Orth-Gomer, K., Wamala, S. P., Horsten, M., Schenck-Gustafsson, K., Schneiderman, N., & Mittleman, M. A. (2000). Marital stress worsens prognosis in women with coronary heart disease: The Stockholm female coronary risk study. *Journal of the American Medical Association, 284*(23), 3008–3014.

Osbaldiston, R., & Sheldon, K. M. (2002). Social dilemmas and sustainability: Promoting peoples' motivation to "cooperate with the future." In P. Schmuck & W. P. Schultz (Eds.), *Psychology of sustainable development* (pp. 37–58). Boston, MA: Kluwer Academic Press.

Ost, J. (2006). Recovered memories. In T. Williamson (Ed.), *Investigative interviewing: Rights, research, regulation* (pp. 259–291). Devon, United Kingdom: Willan Publishing.

Ost, J. (2009). Recovered memories. In R. Bull, T. Valentine, T. Williamson, & R. Bull (Eds.), *Handbook of psychology of investigative interviewing: Current developments and future directions* (pp. 181–204). Wiley-Blackwell. doi:10.1002/9780470747599.ch11

Öst, L.-G. (1997). Rapid treatment of specific phobias. In G. C. L. Davey (Ed.), *Phobias: A handbook of theory, research and treatment* (pp. 227–247). Oxford, England: Wiley.

Öst, L.-G., Svensson, L., Hellström, K., & Lindwall, R. (2001). One-session treatment of specific phobias in youths: A randomized clinical trial. *Journal of Consulting and Clinical Psychology, 69,* 814–824.

Osteen, J. (2009). *Become a better you: 7 keys to improving your life every day.* New York, NY: Free Press.

Ostrom, T. M., & Sedikides, C. (1992). Out-group homogeneity effects in natural and minimal groups. *Psychological Bulletin, 112,* 536–552.

Overstreet, S. (2000). Exposure to community violence: Defining the problem and understanding the consequences. *Journal of Child and Family Studies, 9,* 7–25.

Overton, S. L. & Medina, S. L. (2008). The stigma of mental illness. *Journal of Counseling & Development, 86*(2), 143–151.

Owen, J., & Fincham, F. D. (2011). Effects of gender and psychosocial factors on "friends with benefits" relationships among young adults. *Archives of Sexual Behavior, 40*(2), 311–320. doi:10.1007/s10508-010-9611-6

Owen, J. J., Rhoades, G. K., Stanley, S. M., & Fincham, F. D. (2010). "Hooking up" among college students: Demographic and psychosocial correlates. *Archives of Sexual Behavior, 39*(3), 653–663. doi:10.1007/s10508-008-9414-1

Oyserman, D., Bybee, D., & Terry, K. (2006). Possible selves and academic outcomes: How and when possible selves impel action. *Journal of Personality and Social Psychology, 91,* 188–204.

Oyserman, D., Elmore, K., & Smith, G. (2012). Self, self-concept, and identity. In M. R. Leary & J. P. Tangney (Eds.), *Handbook of self and identity* (2nd ed., pp. 69–104). New York, NY: Guilford.

Ozer, E. M., & Bandura, A. (1990). Mechanisms governing empowerment effects: A self-efficacy analysis. *Journal of Personality and Social Psychology, 58,* 472–486.

Ozer, D. J., & Reise, S. P. (1994). Personality assessment. *Annual Review of Psychology, 45,* 357–388.

Ozer, E. J., Best, S. R., Lipsey, T. L., & Weiss, D. S. (2003). Predictors of posttraumatic stress disorder and symptoms in adults: A meta-analysis. *Psychological Bulletin, 129*(1), 52–73.

Pachter, W. S., Fox, R. E., Zimbardo, P., & Antonuccio, D. O. (2007). Corporate funding and conflicts of interest: A primer for psychologists. *American Psychologist, 62*(9), 1005–1015.

Pahl, S., Etser, J. R., & White, M. P. (2009). Boundaries of self-positivity: The effect of comparison focus in self-friend comparisons. *The Journal of Social Psychology, 149*(4), 413–424.

Pahl, S., Harris, P. R., Todd, H. A., & Rutter, D. R. (2005). Comparative optimism for environmental risks. *Journal of Environmental Psychology, 25,* 1–11.

Palomares, N. A. (2009). Women are sort of more tentative than men, aren't they? How men and women use tentative language differently, similarly, and counterstereotypically as a function of gender salience. *Communication Research, 36,* 538–560.

Pandey, A., Quick, J. C., Rossi, A. M., Nelson, D. L., & Martin, W. (2011). Stress and the workplace: 10 years of science, 1997–2007. In R. J. Contrada & A. Baum (Eds.), *The handbook of stress science: Biology, psychology, and health* (pp. 137–149). New York, NY: Springer.

Pang, M., Chua, B., & Chu, C. (2008). Learning to stay ahead in an uncertain environment. *International Journal of Human Resource Management, 19*(7), 1383–1394.

Papaharitou, S., Nakopoulou, E., Kirana, P., Giaglis, G., Moraitou, M., & Hatzichristou, D. (2008). Factors associated with sexuality in later life: An exploratory study in a group of Greek married older adults. *Archives of Gerontology and Geriatrics, 46,* 191–201.

Papas, R. K., Belar, C. D., & Rozensky, R. H. (2004). The practice of clinical health psychology: Professional issues. In R. G. Frank, A. Baum, & J. L. Wallander (Eds.), *Handbook of clinical health psychology* (Vol. 3, pp. 293–319). Washington, DC: American Psychological Association.

Papernow, P. L. (1993). *Becoming a stepfamily: Patterns of development in remarried families.* San Francisco, CA: Jossey-Bass.

Papp, L. M., Cummings, E. M., & Schermerhorn, A. C. (2004). Pathways among marital distress, parental symptomatology, and child adjustment. *Journal of Marriage and Family, 66,* 368–384.

Pargament, K. I. (2011). Religion and coping: The current state of knowledge. In S. Folkman (Ed.), *The Oxford handbook of stress, health, and coping* (pp. 269–288). New York, NY: Oxford University Press.

Pargament, K. I., & Mahoney, A. (2002). Spirituality: Discovering and conserving the sacred. In C. R. Snyder & S. J. Lopez (Eds.), *Handbook of positive psychology* (pp. 646–659). New York, NY: Oxford.

Pargament, K. I., & Mahoney, A. (2009). Spirituality: The search for the sacred. In S. J. Lopez & C. R. Snyder (Eds.), *Handbook of positive psychology* (2nd ed., pp. 611–619). New York, NY: Oxford.

Park, C. L. (1998). Implications of posttraumatic growth for individuals. In R. G. Tedeschi, C. L. Park, & L. G. Calhoun (Eds.), *Posttraumatic growth: Positive changes in the aftermath of crisis* (pp. 153–178). Mahwah, NJ: Erlbaum.

Park, C. L., Bharadwaj, A. K., & Blank, T. O. (2011). Illness centrality, disclosure, and well-being in younger and middle-aged adult cancer survivors. *British Journal of Health Psychology, 16*(4), 880–889. doi:10.1111/j.2044-8287.2011.02024.x

Park, C. L., & Folkman, S. (1997). Meaning in the context of stress and coping. *Review of General Psychology, 1,* 115–144.

Park, C. W., & Young, S. M. (1986). Consumer response to television commercials: The impact of involvement and background music on brand attitude formation. *Journal of Marketing Research, 23* 11–24.

Park, K. (2005). Choosing childlessness: Weber's typology of action and motives of the voluntarily childless. *Sociological Inquiry, 75,* 372–402.

Park, N., & Peterson, C. (2009). Achieving and sustaining a good life. *Perspectives on Psychological Science, 4,* 422–428.

Park, N., Peterson, C., & Seligman, M. E. P. (2004). Strengths of character and well-being. *Journal of Social and Clinical Psychology, 23,* 603–619.

Parker, R. (2000). Health literacy: A challenge for American patients and their health care providers. *Health Promotion International, 15,* 277–283.

Parrott, A. C. (2000). Human research on MDMA (3,4-Methylenedioxymethamphetamine) neurotoxicity: Cognitive and behavioural indices of change. *Neuropsychobiology, 42*(1), 17–24.

Parrott, D. J., Peterson, J. L., Vincent, W., & Bakeman, R. (2008). Correlates of anger in response to gay men: Effects of male gender role beliefs, sexual prejudice, and masculine gender role stress. *Psychology of Men & Masculinity, 9,* 167–178.

Parrott, L. (2012). *You're stronger than you think: The power to do what you feel you can't.* Carol Stream, IL: Tyndale House.

Pashang, B., & Singh, M. (2008). Emotional intelligence and use of coping strategies. *Psychological Studies, 53,* 81–82.

Pasley, K., & Moorefield, B. S. (2004). Stepfamilies: Changes and challenges. In M. Coleman, & L. H. Ganong (Eds.), *Handbook of contemporary families: Considering the past, contemplating the future.* Thousand Oaks, CA: Sage.

Pasupathi, M. (2009). Arranged marriages. In H. T. Reis & S. Sprecher (Eds.), *Encyclopedia of human relationships: Vol. 2* (pp. 113–115). Los Angeles: Sage Reference Publication.

Pasupathi, M., McLean, K. C., & Weeks, T. (2009). To tell or not to tell: Disclosure and the narrative self. *Journal of Personality, 77,* 89–124.

Patel, J. K., Pinals, D. A., & Breier, A. (2003). Schizophrenia and other psychoses. In A. Tasman, J. Kay, & J. A. Lieberman (Eds.), *Psychiatry.* New York, NY: Wiley.

Patel, J. K., Pinals, D. A., & Breier, A. (2008). Schizophrenia and other psychoses. In A. Tasman, J. Kay, J. A. Lieberman, M. B. First, & M. Maj (Eds.), *Psychiatry* (3rd ed.). New York, NY: Wiley-Blackwell.

Pato, M. T., Fanous, A., Eisen, J. L., & Phillips, K. A. (2008). Anxiety disorders: Obsessive-compulsive disorder. In A. Tasman, J. Kay, J. A. Lieberman, M. B. First, & M. Maj (Eds.), *Psychiatry* (3rd ed.). New York, NY: Wiley-Blackwell.

Patterson, C. J. (2001). Family relationships of lesbians and gay men. In R. M. Milardo (Ed.), *Understanding families into the new millennium: A decade in review.* Minneapolis: National Council on Family Relations.

Patterson, C. J. (2003). Children of lesbian and gay parents. In L. D. Garnets & D. C. Kimmel (Eds.), *Psychological perspectives on lesbian, gay, and bisexual experiences*. New York, NY: Columbia University Press.

Patterson, C. J. (2006). Children of lesbian and gay parents. *Current Directions in Psychological Science, 15*, 241–254.

Patterson, C. J. (2009). Lesbian and gay parents and their children: A social science perspective. In D. A. Hope (Ed.), *Contemporary perspectives on lesbian, gay, and bisexual identities* (pp. 141–182). New York, NY: Springer Science and Business Media.

Patterson, M. L. (1988). Functions of nonverbal behavior in close relationships. In S. Duck (Ed.), *Handbook of personal relationships: Theory, research, and interventions*. New York, NY: Wiley.

Patton, W., & Lokan, J. (2001). Perspectives on Donald Super's construct of career maturity. *International Journal for Educational and Vocational Guidance, 1*(1–2), 31–48. doi:10.1023/A:1016964629452

Paul, A. M. (2001). Self-help: Shattering the myths. *Psychology Today, 34*(2), 60.

Paul, E. L., Wenzel, A., & Harvey J. (2008). Hookups: A facilitator or a barrier to relationship initiation and intimacy development? In S. Sprecher, A. Wenzel, & J. Harvey (Eds.), *Handbook of Relationship Initiation* (pp. 375–388). New York, NY: Psychology Press.

Paul, K. I., & Moser, K. (2009). Unemployment impairs mental health: Meta-analyses. *Journal of Vocational Behavior, 74*(3), 264–282.

Paul, R. (2009). Parents ask: Am I risking autism if I vaccinate my children? *Journal of Autism and Developmental Disorders, 39*(6), 962–963.

Paulhus, D. L., Fridhandler, B., & Hayes, S. (1997). Psychological defense: Contemporary theory and research. In R. Hogan, J. Johnson, & S. Briggs (Eds), *Handbook of personality psychology*. San Diego: Academic Press.

Paullay, I. M., Alliger, G. M., & Stone-Romero, E. F. (1994). Construct validation of two instruments designed to measure job involvement and work centrality. *Journal of Applied Psychology, 7*, 224–228.

Paulsen, N., Callan, V. J., Grice, T. A., Rooney, D., Gallois, C., Jones, E., et al. (2005). Job uncertainty and personal control during downsizing: A comparison of survivors & victims. *Human Relations, 58*, 463–496.

Pavlov, I. P. (1906). The scientific investigation of psychical faculties or processes in the higher animals. *Science, 24*, 613–619.

Paxton, S. J., Norris, M., Wertheim, E. H., Durkin, S. J., & Anderson, J. (2005). Body dissatisfaction, dating, and importance of thinness to attractiveness in adolescent girls. *Sex Roles, 53*, 663–675.

Payne, B. K. (2006). Weapon bias: Split-second decisions and unintended sterotyping. *Current Directions in Psychological Science, 15*, 287–291.

Pechnick, R. N., & Ungerleider, T. J. (2005). Hallucinogens. In J. H. Lowinson, P. Ruiz, R. B. Millman, & J. G. Langrod (Eds.), *Substance abuse: A comprehensive textbook*. Philadelphia: Lippincott/Williams & Wilkins.

Pedersen, P. (1994). A culture-centered approach to counseling. In W. J. Lonner & R. Malpass (Eds.), *Psychology and culture*. Boston, MA: Allyn & Bacon.

Pedersen, S., Vitaro, F., Barker, E. D., & Borge, A. I. H. (2007). The timing of middle-childhood peer rejection and friendship: Linking early behavior to early-adolescent adjustment. *Child Development, 78*, 1037–1051.

Pedersen, W., & Skrondal, A. (1999). Ecstasy and new patterns of drug use: A normal population study. *Addiction, 94*(11), 1695–1706.

Pelham, W. E., Jr. (2001). ADHD and behavioral modification. *Drug Benefit Trends, 13*, 11–14.

Pennebaker, J. W. (Ed.). (2002). *Emotion, disclosure, and health*. Washington, DC: American Psychological Association.

Pennebaker, J. W., Colder, M., & Sharp, L. K. (1990). Accelerating the coping process. *Journal of Personality and Social Psychology, 58*, 528–537.

Penner, L. A., Dovidio, J. F., West, T. V., Gaertner, S. L., Albrecht, T. L., Dailey, R. K., & Markova, T. (2010). Aversive racism and medical interactions with black patients: A field study. *Journal of Experimental Social Psychology, 46*(2), 436–440. doi:10.1016/j.jesp.2009.11.004

Peplau, L. A. (1991). Lesbian and gay relationships. In J. C. Gonsiorek & J. D. Weinrich (Eds.), *Homosexuality: Research implications for public policy*. Newbury Park, CA: Sage.

Peplau, L. A., & Fingerhut, A. W. (2007). The close relationships of lesbians and gay men. *Annual Review of Psychology, 58*, 405–424. doi:10.1146/annurev.psych.58.110405.085701

Peplau, L. A., Fingerhut, A., & Beals, K. P. (2004). Sexuality in the relationships of lesbians and gay men. In J. H. Harvey, A. Wenzel, & S. Sprecher (Eds.), *The handbook of sexuality in close relationships*. Mahwah, NJ: Lawrence Erlbaum.

Peplau, L. A., & Ghavami, N. (2009). Gay, lesbian, and bisexual relationships. In H. T. Reis & S. Sprecher (Eds.), *Encyclopedia of human relationships: Vol. 1* (pp. 746–751). Los Angeles: Sage Reference Publication.

Peplau, L. A., & Gordon, S. L. (1985). Women and men in love: Gender differences in close heterosexual relationships. In V. E. O'Leary, R. K. Unger, & B. S. Wallston (Eds.), *Women, gender, and social psychology*. Hillsdale, NJ: Erlbaum.

Peplau, L. A., Hill, C. T., & Rubin, Z. (1993). Sex role attitudes in dating and marriage: A 15-year follow-up of the Boston couples study. *Journal of Social Issues, 49*, 31–52.

Peplau, L. A., & Spalding, L. R. (2000). The close relationships of lesbians, gay men, and bisexuals. In C. Hendrick & S. S. Hendrick (Eds.), *Close relationships: A sourcebook*. Thousand Oaks, CA: Sage.

Peplau, L. A., & Spalding, L. R. (2003). The close relationships of lesbians, gay men, and bisexuals. In L. D. Garnets & D. C. Kimmel (Eds.), *Psychological perspectives on lesbian, gay, and bisexual experiences*. New York, NY: Columbia University Press.

Pereira, M. A., Kartshov, A. I., Ebbeling, C. B., Van Horn, L., Slattery, M. L., Jacobs, D. R., Jr. et al. (2005). Fast food habits, weight gain, and insulin resistance (the CARDIA Study): 15-year prospective analysis. *Lancet, 365*, 36–42.

Peretti, P. O., & Abplanalp, R. R., Jr. (2004). Chemistry in the college dating process: Structure and function. *Social Behavior and Personality, 32*(2), 147–154.

Perez, G. K., Cruess, D. G., & Kalichman, S. C. (2010). Effects of stress on health in HIV/AIDS. In R. Contrada & A. Baum (Eds.), *The handbook of stress science: Biology, psychology, & health* (pp. 447–460). New York, NY: Springer.

Perkins, A. M., Inchley-Mort, S. L., Pickering, A. D., Corr, P. J., & Burgess, A. P. (2012). A facial expression for anxiety. *Journal of Personality and Social Psychology, 102*(5), 910–924. doi:10.1037/a0026825

Perkins, D. O., Miller-Anderson, L., & Lieberman, J. A. (2006). Natural history and predictors of clinical course. In J. A. Lieberman, T. S. Stroup, & D. O. Perkins (Eds.), *Textbook of schizophrenia* (pp. 289–302). Washington, DC: American Psychiatric Publishing.

Perlis, R. H., Perlis, C. S., Wu, Y., Hwang, C., Joseph, M., & Nierenberg, A. A. (2005). Industry sponsorship and financial conflict of interest in the reporting of clinical trials in psychiatry. *American Journal of Psychiatry, 162*, 1957–1960.

Perlman, D. (2007). The best of times, the worst of times: The place of close relationships in psychology and our daily lives. *Canadian Psychology/Psychologie Canadienne, 48*, 7–18.

Perlman, D., & Carcedo, R. J. (2011). Overview of the dark side of relationships research. In W. R. Cupach, B. H. Spitzberg (Eds.), *The dark side of close relationships II* (pp. 1–37). New York, NY: Routledge/Taylor & Francis Group.

Perloff, R. M. (1993). *The dynamics of persuasion*. Hillsdale, NJ: Erlbaum.

Perreault, S., & Bourhis, R. Y. (1999). Ethnocentrism, social identification, and discrimination. *Personality and Social Psychology Bulletin, 25*(1), 92–103.

Perrett, D. I., Lee, K. J., Penton-Voak, I., Rowland, D., Yoshikawa, S., Burt, D. M., Henzi, S. P., Castles, D. L., & Akamatsu, S. (1998). Effects of sexual dimorphism on facial attractiveness. *Nature, 394*, 884–887.

Perri, M. G., Anton, S. D., Durning, P. E., Ketterson, T. U., Sydeman, S. J., Berlant, N. E., Kanasky Jr., W. F., Newton Jr., R. L., Llimacher, M. C., & Martin, A. D. (2002). Adherence to exercise prescriptions: Effects of prescribing moderate versus higher levels of intensity and frequency. *Health Psychology, 21*(5), 452–458.

Perry-Jenkins, M., Repetti, R. L., & Crouter, A. C. (2001). Work and family in the 1990s. In R. M. Milardo (Ed.), *Understanding families into the new millennium: A decade in review*. Minneapolis, MN: National Council on Family Relations.

Person, E. S. (1990). The influence of values in psychoanalysis: The case of female psychology. In C. Zanardi (Ed.), *Essential papers in psychoanalysis*. New York, NY: New York University Press.

Pervin, L. A., & John, O. P. (2001). *Personality: Theory and research*. New York, NY: Wiley.

Pescosolido, B. A., Martin, J. K., Long, J., Medina, T. R., Phelan, J. C., & Link, B. G. (2010). "A disease like any other"? A decade of change in public reactions to schizophrenia, depression, and alcohol dependence. *American Journal of Psychiatry, 167*(11), 1321–1330. doi:10.1176/appi.ajp.2010.09121743

Petersen, J. L., & Hyde, J. (2010a). Gender differences in sexuality. In J. C. Chrisler & D. R. McCreary (Eds.), *Handbook of gender research in psychology, Vol 1: Gender research in general and experimental psychology* (pp. 471–491). New York, NY: Springer Science + Business Media.

Petersen, J. L., & Hyde, J. (2010b). A meta-analytic review of research on gender differences in sexuality, 1993–2007. *Psychological Bulletin, 136*(1), 21–38. doi:10.1037/a0017504

Petersen, J. L., & Hyde, J. (2011). Gender differences in sexual attitudes and behaviors: A review of meta-analytic results and large datasets. *Journal of Sex Research, 48*(2–3), 149–165. doi:10.1080/00224499.2011.551851

Peterson, C. (2006). *A primer in positive psychology*. New York, NY: Oxford University Press.

Peterson, C., & Park, N. (2009). Positive psychology. In B. J. Sadock, V. A. Sadock, & P. Ruiz (Eds.), *Kaplan & Sadock's comprehensive textbook of psychiatry* (pp. 2939–2951). Philadelphia: Lippincott Williams & Wilkins.

Peterson, C., & Park, N. (2010). What happened to self-actualization? Commentary on Kenrick et al. (2010). *Perspectives on Psychological Science, 5*(3), 320–322. doi:10.1177/1745691610369471

Peterson, C., & Seligman, M. E. P. (2003). Positive organizational studies: Thirteen lessons from positive psychology. In K. S. Cameron, J. E. Dutton, & R. E. Quinn (Eds.), *Positive organizational scholarship: Foundations of a new discipline* (pp. 14–27). San Francisco: Berrett-Koehler.

Peterson, C., & Seligman, M. E. P. (2004). *Character strengths and virtues: A handbook and classification*. New York, NY: Oxford University Press/Washington, DC: American Psychological Association.

Peterson, C., & Steen, T. A. (2009). Optimistic explanatory style. In S. J. Lopez & C. R. Snyder (Eds.), *Oxford handbook of positive psychology* (2nd ed., pp. 313–321). New York, NY: Oxford University Press.

Peterson, C., & Vaidya, R. S. (2001). Explanatory style, expectations, and depressive symptoms. *Personality and Individual Differences, 31*, 1217–1223.

Peterson, C., Maier, S. F., & Seligman, M. E. P. (1993). *Learned helplessness: A theory for the age of personal control*. New York, NY: Oxford University Press.

Peterson, C., Seligman, M. E. P., & Vaillant, G. E. (1988). Pessimistic explanatory style is a risk factor for physical illness: A thirty-five-year longitudinal study. *Journal of Personality and Social Psychology, 55*, 23–27.

Peterson, C., Seligman, M. E. P., Yurko, K. H., Martin, L. R., & Friedman, H. S. (1998). Castastrophizing and untimely death. *Psychological Science, 9*, 127–130.

Peterson, J. L., & Bakeman, R. (2006). Impact of beliefs about HIV treatment and peer condom norms on risky sexual behavior among gay and bisexual men. *Journal of Community Psychology, 34*(1), 37–46.

Peterson, S. H., Wingood, G. M., DiClemente, R. J., Davies, S., & Harrington, K. (2007). Images of sexual stereotypes in rap videos and the health of African American female adolescents. *Journal of Women's Health, 16,* 1157–1164.

Petit, J. W., & Joiner, T. E. (2006). *Chronic depression: Interpersonal sources, therapeutic solutions.* Washington, DC: American Psychological Association.

Petrill, S. A. (2005). Behavioral genetics and intelligence. In O. Wilhelm & R. W. Engle (Eds.), *Handbook of understanding and measuring intelligence.* Thousand Oaks, CA: Sage Publications.

Petry, N. M. (2010). Pathological gambling and the DSM-V. *International Gambling Studies, 10*(2), 113–115. doi:10.1080/14459795.2010.501086

Pettigrew, T. F. (2001). The ultimate attribution error: Extending Allport's cognitive analysis of prejudice. In M. A. Hogg & D. Abrams (Eds.), *Intergroup relations: Essential readings.* New York, NY: Psychology Press.

Pettigrew, T. F., & Tropp, L. R. (2006). A meta-analytic test of intergroup contact theory. *Journal of Personality and Social Psychology, 90,* 751–783.

Petty, R. E., Barden, J., & Wheeler, S. (2009). The Elaboration Likelihood Model of persuasion: Developing health promotions for sustained behavioral change. In R. J. DiClemente, R. A. Crosby, & M. C. Kegler (Eds.), *Emerging theories in health promotion practice and research* (2nd ed., pp. 185–214). San Francisco, CA: Jossey-Bass.

Petty, R. E., & Briñol, P. (2012). The elaboration likelihood model. In P. M. Van Lange, A. W. Kruglanski, & E. Higgins (Eds.), *Handbook of theories of social psychology* (Vol 1, pp. 224–245). Thousand Oaks, CA: Sage Publications Ltd.

Petty, R. E., & Cacioppo, J. T. (1986). The elaboration likelihood model of persuasion. In L. Berkowitz (Ed.), *Advances in experimental social psychology* (Vol. 19). Orlando, FL: Academic Press.

Petty, R. E., & Cacioppo, J. T. (1990). Involvement and persuasion: Tradition versus integration. *Psychological Bulletin, 107,* 367–374.

Petty, R. E., Cacioppo, J. T., Strathman, A. J., Priester, J. R. (2005). To think or not to think: Exploring two routes to persuasion. In T. C. Brock & M. C. Green (Eds.), *Persuasion: Psychological insights and perspectives* (2nd ed., pp. 81–116). Thousand Oaks, CA: Sage Publications.

Petty, R. E., Fleming, M. A., Priester, J. R., & Feinstein, A. H. (2001). Individual versus group interest violation: Surprise as a determinant of argument scrutiny and persuasion. *Social Cognition, 19*(4), 418–442.

Petty, R. E., & Fazio, R. H. (Eds.). (2008). *Attitudes: Insights from the new implicit measures.* New York, NY: Psychology Press.

Petty, R. E., Priester, J. R., & Wegener, D. T. (1994). Cognitive processes in attitude change. In R. S. Wyer & T. K. Srull (Eds.), *Handbook of social cognition* (Vol. 2). Hillsdale, NJ: Erlbaum.

Petty, S. C., Sachs-Ericsson, N., & Joiner, T. E., Jr. (2004). Interpersonal functioning deficits: Temporary or stable characteristics of depressed individuals. *Journal of Affective Disorders, 81*(2), 115–122.

Petty, R. E., & Wegener, D. T. (1998). Attitude change: Multiple roles for persuasion variables. In D. T. Gilbert, S. T. Fiske, & G. Lindzey (Eds.), *The handbook of social psychology* (4th ed., Vol. 1). New York, NY: McGraw-Hill.

Petty, R. E., Wegener, D. T., & Fabrigar, L. R. (1997). Attitudes and attitude change. *Annual Review of Psychology, 48,* 609–647.

Pew Research Center. (2010). Childlessness up among all women; down among women with advanced degrees. Retrieved from http://www.pewsocialtrends.org/2010/06/25/childlessness-up-among-all-women-down-among-women-with-advanced-degrees/

Phillips. A. G., & Silvia, P. J. (2010). Individual differences in self-discrepancies and emotional experience: Do distinct discrepancies predict distinct emotions? *Personality and Individual Differences, 49,* 148–151.

Phillips, W. T., Kiernan, M., & King, A. C. (2001). The effects of physical activity on physical and psychological health. In A. Baum, T. A. Revenson, & J. E. Singer (Eds.), *Handbook of health psychology.* Mahwah, NJ: Erlbaum.

Pierce, J. P., Distefan, J. M., Kaplan, R. M., & Gilpin, E. A. (2005). The role of curiosity in smoking initiation. *Addictive Behaviors, 30,* 685–696.

Pies, R. (2009). Should DSM-V designate "Internet addiction" a mental disorder? *Psychiatry, 6*(2), 31–37.

Piferi, R. L., & Lawler, K. A. (2006). Social support and ambulatory blood pressure: An examination of both receiving and giving. *International Journal of Psychophysiology, 62,* 328–336.

Piko, B. F., & Balázs, M. Á. (2012). Authoritative parenting style and adolescent smoking and drinking. *Addictive Behaviors, 37*(3), 353–356. doi:10.1016/j.addbeh.2011.11.022

Pilote, L., Dasgupta, K., Guru, V., Humphries, K. H., McGrath, J., Norris, C., et al. (2007). A comprehensive review of sex-specific issues related to cardiovascular disease. *Canadian Medical Association Journal, 176*(6), S1–S44.

Pinel, J. P. J., Assanand, S., & Lehman, D. R. (2000). Hunger, eating, and ill health. *American Psychologist, 55,* 1105–1116.

Pink, D. H. (2001). *Free agent nation: The future of working for yourself.* New York, NY: Warner Business Books.

Pinquart, M. (2003). Loneliness in married, widowed, divorced, and never-married older adults. *Journal of Social and Personal Relationships, 20*(1), 31–53.

Pipher, M. (1994). *Reviving Ophelia: Saving the selves of adolescent girls.* New York, NY: Ballantine.

Pirog, R., & Benjamin, A. (2003). *Checking the food odometer: Comparing food miles for local versus conventional produce sales to Iowa institutions.* Ames: Leopold Center for Sustainable Agriculture, Iowa State University.

Pi-Sunyer, F. X. (2002). Medical complications of obesity in adults. In C. G. Fairburn & K. D. Brownell (Eds.), *Eating disorders and obesity: A comprehensive handbook.* New York, NY: Guilford.

Pitt, R. N., & Borland, E. (2008). Bachelorhood and men's attitudes about gender roles. *The Journal of Men's Studies, 16,* 140–158.

Pittman, F., III. (1994, January/February). A buyer's guide to psychotherapy. *Psychology Today,* pp. 50–53, 74–81.

Piver, S. (2000). *The hard questions: 100 questions to ask before you say "I do."* New York, NY: Jeremy P. Tarcher/Putnam.

Planalp, S., Fitness, J., & Fehr, B. (2006). Emotion in theories of close relationships. In A. L. Vangelisti & D. Perlman (Eds.), *The Cambridge handbook of personal relationships.* New York, NY: Cambridge University Press.

Planned Parenthood Federation of America (2012a). The abortion pill (medication abortion). Retrieved from http://www.plannedparenthood.org/health-topics/abortion/abortion-pillmedication-abortion-4354.asp

Planned Parenthood Federation of America (2012b). Morning-after pill (emergency contraception). Retrieved from http://www.plannedparenthood.org/health-topics/emergencycontraception-morning-after-pill-4363.asp

Plante, T. G., Caputo, D., & Chizmar, L. (2000). Perceived fitness and responses to laboratory induced stress. *International Journal of Stress Management, 7*(1), 61–73.

Pleck, J. H. (1981). *The myth of masculinity.* Cambridge, MA: MIT Press.

Pleck, J. H. (1995). The gender role strain paradigm: An update. In R. F. Levant & W. S. Pollack (Eds.), *A new psychology of men.* New York, NY: Basic Books.

Plomin, R., DeFries, J. C., McClearn, G. E., & McGuffin, P. (2008). *Behavioral genetics.* New York, NY: Worth.

Pogue-Geile, M. F., & Yokley, J. L. (2010). Current research on the genetic contributors to schizophrenia. *Current Directions in Psychological Science, 19*(4), 214–219. doi:10.1177/0963721410378490

Polivy, J., & Herman, C. P. (2002). Causes of eating disorder. *Annual Review of Psychology, 53,* 187–213.

Pollack, C. E., & Lynch, J. (2009). Health status of people undergoing foreclosure in the Philadelphia region. *American Journal of Public Health, 99,* 1833–1839.

Pollak, L. (2007). *Getting from college to career: 90 things to do before you join the real world.* New York, NY: HarperCollins.

Pope, H. G., Barry, S., Bodkin, A., & Hudson, J. I. (2006). Tracking scientific interest in the dissociative disorders: A study of scientific publication output 1984–2003. *Psychotherapy and Psychosomatics, 75,* 19–24.

Pope, H. G., Gruber, A. J., & Yurgelun-Todd, D. (2001). Residual neuropsychologic effects of cannabis. *Current Psychiatry Report, 3,* 507–512.

Pope, H. G., Oliva, P. S., Hudson, J. I., Bodkin, J. A., & Gruber, A. J. (1999). Attitudes toward DSM-IV dissociative disorders diagnoses among board-certified American psychiatrists. *American Journal of Psychiatry, 156*(2), 321–323.

Pope, J. (2012). Forgiveness is freedom, says holocaust survivor. *The Times-Picayune,* September 6.

Pope, K. S., Keith-Spiegel, P., & Tabachnick, B. G. (1986). Sexual attraction to clients. *American Psychologist, 41,* 147–158.

Porcerelli, J. H., Cogan, R., Kamoo, R., & Miller, K. (2010). Convergent validity of the Defense Mechanisms Manual and the Defensive Functioning Scale. *Journal of Personality Assessment, 92*(5), 432–438. doi:10.1080/00223891.2010.497421

Porter, S., ten Brinke, L., & Wallace, B. (2012). Secrets and lies: Involuntary leakage in deceptive facial expressions as a function of emotional intensity. *Journal of Nonverbal Behavior, 36*(1), 23–37. doi:10.1007/s10919-011-0120-7

Post, J. M. (2011). Crimes of obedience: "Groupthink" at Abu Ghraib. *International Journal of Group Psychotherapy, 61*(1), 49–66. doi:10.1521/ijgp.2011.61.1.48

Post, R. M. & Altshuler, L. L. (2009). Mood disorders: Treatment of bipolar disorders. In B. J. Sadock, V. A. Sadock, & P. Ruiz (Eds.), *Kaplan & Sadock's comprehensive textbook of psychiatry* (pp. 1743–1812). Philadelphia: Lippincott Williams & Wilkins.

Powell, D. E., & Fine, M. A. (2009). Dissolution of relationships, causes. In H. T. Reis & S. Sprecher (Eds.), *Encyclopedia of human relationships: Vol. 1* (pp. 436–440). Los Angeles: Sage Reference Publication.

Powell, J. L., & Drucker, A. D. (1997). The role of peer conformity in the decision to ride with an intoxicated driver. *Journal of Alcohol and Drug Education, 43*(1), 1–7.

Powell, R. A., & Gee, T. L. (1999). The effects of hypnosis on dissociative identity disorder: A reexamination of the evidence. *Canadian Journal of Psychiatry, 44,* 914–916.

Prati, G., & Pietrantoni, L. (2009). Optimism, social support, and coping strategies as factors contributing to posttraumatic growth: A meta-analysis. *Journal of Loss and Trauma, 1,* 364–388.

Pratkanis, A. R., & Aronson, E. (2000). *Age of propaganda: The everyday use and abuse of persuasion.* New York, NY: Freeman.

Prat-Sala, M., & Redford, P. (2010). The interplay between motivation, self-efficacy, and approaches to studying. *British Journal of Educational Psychology, 80*(2), 283–305. doi:10.1348/000709909X480563

Prat-Sala, M., & Redford, P. (2012). Writing essays: Does self-efficacy matter? The relationship between self-efficacy in reading and in writing and undergraduate students' performance in essay writing. *Educational Psychology, 32*(1), 9–20. doi:10.1080/01443410.2011.621411

Pratt, L. A., Ford, D. E., Crum, R. M., Armenian, H. K., Gallo, J. J., & Eaton, W. W. (1996). Depression, psychotropic medication, and risk of myocardial infarction: Prospective data from the Baltimore ECA follow-up. *Archives of Internal Medicine, 94,* 3123–3129.

Pratto, F., & Walker, A. (2004). The bases of gendered power. In A. H. Eagly, A. E. Beall, & R. J. Sternberg (Eds.), *The psychology of gender.* New York, NY: Guilford Press.

Presser, H. B. (2000). Nonstandard work schedules and marital instability. *Journal of Marriage and the Family, 62,* 93–110.

Pressman, S. (1993). *Outrageous betrayal: The real story of Werner Erhard, EST and the Forum.* New York, NY: St. Martin's Press.

Preuper, H. R. S., Boonstra, A. M., Wever, D., Heuts, P. H. T. G., Dekker, J. H. M., Smeets, R. J. E. M., Brouwer, S., Geertzen, J. H. B., & Reneman, M. F. (2011). Differences in the relationship between psychosocial distress and self-reported disability in patients with chronic low back pain in six pain rehabilitation centers in the Netherlands. *Spine, 36,* 969–976.

Price, M. (2008a). Div. 55's drive for RxP: The American Society for the Advancement of Pharmacotherapy pushes for prescriptive authority. *Monitor on Psychology, 39*(2).

Price, M. (2008b). Research roundup: Get out of town. *gradPSYCH, 6*(3), 10.

Priess, H. A., & Hyde, J. S. (2010). Gender and academic abilities and preferences. In J. C. Chrisler & D. R. McCreary (Eds.), *Handbook of gender research in psychology* (Vol. 1, pp. 297–316). New York, NY: Springer.

Primack, B. A., Douglas, E. L., Fine, M. J., & Dalton, M. A. (2009). Exposure to sexual lyrics and sexual experience among urban adolescents. *American Journal of Preventive Medicine, 36*(4), 317–323. doi:10.1016/j.amepre.2008.11.011

Pritchard, J. (2010). Virtual rewards for driving green. *The Behavior Analyst, 33,* 185-187.

Pronin, E., Berger, J., & Moluki, S. (2007). Alone in a crowd of sheep: Asymmetric perceptions of conformity and their roots in an introspection illusion. *Journal of Personality and Social Psychology, 92,* 585–595.

Pronin, E., Fleming, J. J., & Steffel, M. (2008). Value revelations: Disclosure is in the eye of the beholder. *Journal of Personality and Social Psychology, 95,* 795–809.

Pronin, E., Gilovich, T., & Ross, L. (2004). Objectivity in the eye of the beholder: Divergent perceptions of bias in self versus others. *Psychological Review, 111*(3), 781–799. doi:10.1037/0033-295X.111.3.781

Pronin, E., & Jacobs, E. (2008). Thought speed, mood, and the experience of mental motion. *Perspectives on Psychological Science, 3,* 461–485.

Pronin, E., Jacobs, E., & Wegner, D. M. (2008). Psychological effects of thought acceleration. *Emotion, 8,* 597–612.

Pronin, E., Lin, D. Y., & Ross, L. (2002). The bias blind spot: Perceptions of bias in self versus others. *Personality and Social Psychology Bulletin, 28*(3), 369–381. doi:10.1177/0146167202286008

Pronin, E., & Ross, L. (2006). Temporal differences in trait self-ascription: When the self is seen as an other. *Journal of Personality and Social Psychology, 90*(2), 197–209. doi:10.1037/0022-3514.90.2.197

Pronin, E., & Wegner, D. M. (2006). Independent effects of thought speed and thought content on mood. *Psychological Science, 17,* 807–813.

Proulx, C. M., Helms, H. M., & Buehler, B. (2007). Marital quality and personal well-being: A meta-analysis. *Journal of Marriage and Family, 69,* 576–593.

Prudic, J. (2009). Electroconvulsive therapy. In B. J. Sadock, V. A. Sadock, & P. Ruiz (Eds.), *Kaplan & Sadock's comprehensive textbook of psychiatry* (pp. 3285–3300). Philadelphia: Lippincott Williams & Wilkins.

Prudic, J., Olfson, M., Marcus, S. C., Fuller, R. B., & Sackeim, H. A. (2004). Effectiveness of electroconvulsive therapy in community settings. *Biological Psychiatry, 55,* 301–312.

Pryor, B., Butler, J., & Boehringer, K. (2005). Communication apprehension and cultural context: A comparison of communication apprehension in Japanese and American students. *North American Journal of Psychology, 7*(2), 247–252.

Pryor, F. L., & Schaffer, D. (1997, July). Wages and the university educated: A paradox resolved. *Monthly Labor Review,* 3–14.

Pryor, J. B., Giedd, J. L., & Williams, K. B. (1995). A social psychological model for predicting sexual harassment. *Journal of Social Issues, 51,* 69–84.

Pseekos, A., Bullock-Yowell, E., & Dahlen, E. R. (2011). Examining Holland's person-environment fit, workplace aggression, interpersonal conflict, and job satisfaction. *Journal of Employment Counseling, 48*(2), 63–71. doi:10.1002/j.2161-1920.2011.tb00115.x

Puentes, J., Knox, D., & Zusman, M. E. (2008). Participants in "friends with benefits" relationships. *College Student Journal, 42,* 176–180.

Puetz, T. W., O'Connor, P. J., & Dishman, R. K. (2006). Effects of chronic exercise on feelings of energy and fatigue: A quantitative synthesis. *Psychological Bulletin, 132,* 866–876.

Pugh, S., Dietz, J., Brief, A., & Wiley, J. (2008). Looking inside and out: The impact of employee and community demographic composition on organizational diversity climate. *Journal of Applied Psychology, 93,* 1422–1428.

Pujols, Y., Meston, C. M., & Seal, B. N. (2010). The association between sexual satisfaction and body image in women. *Journal of Sexual Medicine, 7*(2), 905–916. doi:10.1111/j.1743-6109.2009.01604.x

Pulay, A. J., Goldstein, R. B., & Grant, B. F. (2011). Sociodemographic correlates of DSM-IV narcissistic personality disorder: Results from the Wave 2 National Epidemiologic Survey on Alcohol and Related Conditions. In W. K. Campbell & J. D. Miller (Eds.), *The handbook of narcissism and narcissistic personality disorder: Theoretical approaches, empirical findings, and treatments* (pp. 167–180). New York, NY: John Wiley & Sons, Inc.

Pyszczynski, T., Greenberg, J., Solomon, S., Arndt, J., & Schimel, J. (2004). Why do people need self-esteem? A theoretical and empirical review. *Psychological Bulletin, 130*(3), 435–468.

Pyszczynski, T., Solomon, S., & Greenberg, J. (2003a). Giving peace a chance. In T. Pyszczynski, S. Solomon, & J. Greenberg (Eds.), *In the wake of 9/11: The psychology of terror.* Washington, DC: American Psychological Association.

Pyszczynski, T., Solomon, S., & Greenberg, J. (2003b). *In the wake of 9/11: The psychology of terror.* Washington, DC: American Psychological Association.

Quinn, K. A., Macrae, C. N., & Bodenhausen, G. V. (2003). Stereotyping and impression formation: How categorical thinking shapes person perception. In M. A. Hogg & J. Cooper (Eds.), *The Sage handbook of social psychology.* Thousand Oaks, CA: Sage Publications.

Quoidbach, J., Dunn, E. W., Petrides, K. V., & Mikolajczak, M. (2010). Money giveth, money taketh away: The dual effect of wealth on happiness. *Psychological Science, 21*(6), 759–763.

Raacke, J., & Bonds-Raacke, J. (2008). Myspace and Facebook: Applying the uses and gratifications theory to exploring friend-networking sites. *CyberPsychology & Behavior 11,* 169–174.

Rachman, S. J. (1992). Behavior therapy. In L. R. Squire (Ed.), *Encyclopedia of learning and memory.* New York, NY: Macmillan.

Rachman, S. J. (2009). Psychological treatment of anxiety: The evolution of behavior therapy and cognitive behavior therapy. *Annual Review of Clinical Psychology, 5,* 97–119.

Ragins, B. R., Cornwell, J. M., & Miller, J. S. (2003). Heterosexism in the workplace: Do race and gender matter? *Group & Organization Management, 28*(1), 45–74.

Rahe, R. H., & Arthur, R. H. (1978). Life change and illness studies. *Journal of Human Stress, 4,* 3–15.

Rahim, M. A., & Magner, N. R. (1995). Confirmatory factor analysis of the styles of handling interpersonal conflict: First-order factor model and its invariance across groups. *Journal of Applied Psychology, 80,* 122–132.

Raikes, H. A., & Thompson R. A. (2008). Attachment security and parenting quality predict children's problem-solving, attributions, and loneliness with peers. *Attachment & Human Development, 10,* 319–344.

Raiya, H., Pargament, K. I., & Magyar-Russell, G. (2010). When religion goes awry: Religious risk factors for poorer health and well-being. In P. J. Verhagen, H. M. van Praag, J. R. López-Ibor, J. L. Cox, & D. Moussaoui (Eds.), *Religion and psychiatry: Beyond boundaries* (pp. 389–411). Wiley-Blackwell. doi:10.1002/9780470682203.ch22

Raj, A., & Sheehan, D. (2004). Benzodiazepines. In A. F. Schatzberg & C. B. Nemeroff (Eds.), *Textbook of psychopharmacology.* Washington, DC: American Psychiatric Publishing.

Ramaekers, J. G., Robbe, H. W. J., & O'Hanlon, J. F. (2000). Marijuana, alcohol and actual driving performance. *Human Psychopharmacology Clinical & Experimental, 15*(7), 551–558.

Ramanathan, S., & Williams, P. (2007). Immediate and delayed emotional consequences of indulgence: The moderating influence of personality type on mixed emotions. *Journal of Consumer Research, 34,* 212–223.

Ramirez-Esparza, N., Mehl, M. R., Alvarez-Bermudez, J., & Pennebaker, J. W. (2009). Are Mexicans more or less sociable than Americans? Insights from a naturalistic observation study. *Journal of Research in Personality, 43*(1), 1–7. doi:doi:10.1016/j.jrp.2008.09.002.

Rand, K. L., & Cheavens, J. S. (2009). Hope theory. In S. J. Lopez, C. R. Snyder (Eds.), *Oxford handbook of positive psychology* (2nd ed., pp. 323–333). New York, NY: Oxford University Press.

Rapee, R. M., & Barlow, D. H. (2001). Generalized anxiety disorders, panic disorders, and phobias. In P. B. Sutker & H. E. Adams (Eds.), *Comprehensive handbook of psychopathology* (3rd ed., pp. 131–154). New York, NY: Kluwer Academic/Plenum Publishers.

Rashid, T., & Anjum, A. (2008). Positive psychotherapy for young adults and children. In J. Z. Abela & B. L. Hankin (Eds.), *Handbook of depression in children and adolescents* (pp. 250–287). New York, NY: Guilford Press.

Raskin, N. J., Rogers, C. R., & Witty, M. C. (2011). Client-centered therapy. In R. J. Corsini & D. Wedding (Eds.), *Current psychotherapies* (9th ed.). Belmont, CA: Brooks/Cole.

Raskin, R., & Hall, C. S. (1979). A narcissistic personality inventory. *Psychological Reports, 40,* 590.

Raskin, R., & Hall, C. S. (1981). The Narcissistic Personality Inventory: Alternate form reliability and further evidence of construct validity. *Journal of Personality Assessment, 45,* 159–162.

Raskin, R., & Terry, H. (1988). A principal-components analysis of the Narcissistic Personality Inventory and further evidence of its construct validity. *Journal of Personality and Social Psychology, 54,* 890–902.

Rassin, E. (2008). Individual differences in susceptibility to conformation bias. *Netherlands Journal of Psychology, 64*(2), 87–93.

Rathunde, K. (1988). Optimal experience and the family context. In M. Csikszentmihalyi & I. S. Csikszentmihalyi (Eds.), *Optimal experience* (pp. 342–363). Cambridge, UK: Cambridge University Press.

Raub, S., & Liao, H. (2012). Doing the right thing without being told: Joint effects of initiative climate and general self-efficacy on employee proactive customer service performance. *Journal of Applied Psychology, 97,* 651–667. doi:10.1037/a0026736

Ravindran, L. N., & Stein, M. B. (2009). Anxiety disorders: Somatic treatment. In B. J. Sadock, V. A. Sadock, & P. Ruiz (Eds.), *Kaplan & Sadock's comprehensive textbook of psychiatry* (pp. 1906–1914). Philadelphia: Lippincott Williams & Wilkins.

Ray, G. E., Cohen, R., Secrist, M. E., & Duncan, M. K. (1997). Relating aggressive and victimization behaviors to children's sociometric status and friendships. *Journal of Social and Personal Relationships, 14*(1), 95–108.

Reardon, R. C., Lenz, J. G., Sampson, J. P., Jr., & Peterson, G. W. (2009). *Career development and planning: A comprehensive approach.* Belmont, CA: Cengage.

Reece, M., Herbenick, D., Sanders, S. A., Dodge, B., Ghassemi, A., & Fortenberry, J. D. (2009). Prevalence and characteristics of vibrator use by men in the United States. *Journal of Sexual Medicine, 6,* 1867–1874.

Reece, M., Herbenick, D., Schick, V., Sanders, S. A., Dodge, B., & Fortenberry, J. D. (2010). Sexual behaviors, relationships, and perceived health among adult men in the United States: Results from a national probability sample. *Journal of Sexual Medicine, 7*(5), 291–304.

Reed, G. M., Kemeny, M. E., Taylor, S. E., & Visscher, B. R. (1999). Negative HIV-specific expectancies and AIDS-related bereavement as predictors of symptom onset in asymptomatic HIV-positive gay men. *Health Psychology, 18,* 354–363.

Rees, C. J., & Metcalfe, B. (2003). The faking of personality questionnaire results: Who's kidding whom. *Journal of Managerial Psychology, 18,* 156–165.

Regan, P. C., & Berscheid, E. (1997). Gender differences in characteristics desired in potential sexual and marriage partners. *Journal of Psychology and Human Sexuality, 9*(1), 25–37.

Reger, G. M., Holloway, K. M., Candy, C., Rothbaum, B. O., Difede, J., Rizzo, A. A., & Gahm, G. A. (2011). Effectiveness of virtual reality exposure therapy for active duty soldiers in a military mental health clinic. *Journal of Traumatic Stress, 24*(1), 93–96. doi:10.1002/jts.20574

Regier, D. A., & Burke, J. D. (2000). Epidemiology. In B. J. Sadock & V. A. Sadock (Eds.), *Kaplan and Sadock's comprehensive textbook of psychiatry.* Philadelphia: Lippincott/Williams & Wilkins.

Regier, D. A., & Kaelber, C. T. (1995). The epidemiologic catchment area (ECA) program: Studying the prevalence and incidence of psychopathology. In M. T. Tsuang, M. Tohen, & G. E. P. Zahner (Eds.), *Textbook in psychiatric epidemiology.* New York, NY: Wiley.

Regier, D. A., Narrow, W. E., Kuhl, E. A., & Kupfer, D. J. (2009). The conceptual development of DSM-V. *American Journal of Psychiatry, 166*(6), 645–650. doi:10.1176/appi.ajp.2009.09020279

Regnerus, M. D. (2007). *Forbidden fruit: Sex and religion in the lives of American teenagers.* New York, NY: Oxford Press.

Rehman, U. S., & Holtzworth-Munroe, A. (2007). A cross-cultural examination of the relation of marital communication behavior to marital satisfaction. *Journal of Family Psychology, 21,* 759–763.

Reibel, D. K., Greeson, J. M., Brainard, G. C., & Rosenzweig, S. (2001). Mindfulness-based stress reduction and health-related quality of life in a heterogeneous patient population. *General Hospital Psychiatry, 23*(4), 183–192.

Reich, M., Lesur, A., & Perdrizet-Chevallier, C. (2008). Depression, quality of life and breast cancer: A review of the literature. *Breast Cancer Research and Treatment, 110*(1), 9–17.

Reid, M., Miller, W., & Kerr, B. (2004). Sex-based glass ceilings in U.S. state-level bureaucracies, 1987–1997. *Administration and Society, 36,* 377–405.

Reidy, D. E., Foster, J. D., & Zeichner, A. (2010). Narcissism and unprovoked aggression. *Aggressive Behavior, 36*(6), 414–422. doi:10.1002/ab.20356

Reis, H. T., & Holmes, J. G. (2012). Perspectives on the situation. In K. Deaux, & M. Snyder (Eds.), *The Oxford handbook of personality and social psychology* (pp. 64–92). New York, NY: Oxford University Press.

Reis, H. T., Maniaci, M. R., Caprariello, P. A., Eastwick, P. W., & Finkel, E. J. (2011). Familiarity does indeed promote attraction in live interaction. *Journal of Personality and Social Psychology, 101*(3), 557–570. doi:10.1037/a0022885

Reis, H. T., & Patrick. B. C. (1996). Attachment and intimacy: Component processes. In E. T. Higgins & A. Kruglanski (Eds.), *Social psychology: Handbook of basic principles.* New York, NY: Guilford.

Reis, H. T., & Shaver, P. (1988). Intimacy as an interpersonal process. In S. W. Duck (Ed.), *Handbook of personal relationships.* New York, NY: Wiley.

Reis, H. T., Snyder, D. K., & Roberts, L. J. (2009). Repairing relationships. In H. T. Reis & S. Sprecher (Eds.), *Encyclopedia of human relationships: Vol. 3* (pp. 1363–1367). Los Angeles: Sage Reference Publication.

Reis, H. T., & Wheeler, L. (1991). Studying social interaction with the Rochester Interaction Record. *Advances in Experimental Social Psychology, 24,* 269–318.

Reis, T. J., Gerrard, M., & Gibbons, F. X. (1993). Social comparison and the pill: Reactions to upward and downward comparison of contraceptive behavior. *Personality and Social Psychology Bulletin, 19,* 13–21.

Reissman, C., Aron, A., & Bergen, M. R. (1993). Shared activities and marital satisfaction: Causal direction and self-expansion versus boredom. *Journal of Social and Personal Relationships, 10,* 243–254.

Reissner, S. C. (2010). Change, meaning and identity at the workplace. *Journal of Organizational Change Management, 23*(3), 287–299. doi:10.1108/09534811011049617

Reivich, K. J., Seligman, M. P., & McBride, S. (2011). Master resilience training in the U.S. Army. *American Psychologist, 66*(1), 25–34. doi:10.1037/a0021897

Rendi, M., Szarbo, A., Szabo, T., Velenczei, A., & Kovacs, A. (2008). Acute psychological benefits of aerobic exercise: A field study into the effects of exercise characteristics. *Psychology, Health & Medicine, 13,* 180–184.

Reners, M., & Brecx, M. (2007). Stress and periodontal disease. *International Journal of Dental Hygiene, 5,* 199–204.

Rennie, D. L. (2012). Occluded humanistic qualitative research: Implications for positive psychology. *The Humanistic Psychologist, 40*(2), 166–178. doi:10.1080/08873267.2012.643692

Rennison, C. M., & Welchans, S. (2000). *Intimate partner violence.* Washington, DC: U.S. Department of Justice, Office of Justice Programs, Bureau of Justice Statistics.

Repetti, R. L., & Wang, S. (2009). Work-family spillover. In H. T. Reis & S. Sprecher (Eds.), *Encyclopedia of human relationships: Vol. 3* (pp. 1694–1697). Los Angeles: Sage Reference Publication.

Repetto, M., & Gold, M. S. (2005). Cocaine and crack: Neurobiology. In J. H. Lowinson, P. Ruiz, R. B. Millman, & J. G. Langrod (Eds.), *Substance abuse: A comprehensive textbook.* Philadelphia: Lippincott/Williams & Wilkins.

Reuters. (2012, April 30). What's the value of a college degree? Retrieved from http://www.reuters.com/article/2012/04/30/us-personalfinance-grad-qa-idUSBRE83T0WK20120430

Revollo, H., Qureshi, A., Collazos, F., Valero, S., & Casas, M. (2011). Acculturative stress as a risk factor of depression and anxiety in the Latin American immigrant population. *International Review of Psychiatry, 23*(1), 84–92. doi:10.3109/09540261.2010.545988

Reynolds, E. K., & Lejuez, C. W. (2011). Narcissism in the DSM. In W. K. Campbell & J. D. Miller (Eds.), *The handbook of narcissism and narcissistic personality disorder: Theoretical approaches, empirical findings, and treatments* (pp. 14–21). New York, NY: John Wiley & Sons, Inc.

Reynolds, G. (2012, June 12). An argument for the slow-but-steady approach. *The New York Times,* D5.

Rhoades, G. K., Stanley, S. M., Markman, H. J., & Ragan, E. P. (2012). Parents' marital status, conflict, and role modeling: Links with adult romantic relationship quality. *Journal of Divorce and Remarriage, 53*(5), 348–367. doi:10.1080/10502556.2012.675838

Rhodewalt, F., & Peterson, B. (2009). Narcissism. In M. R. Leary & R. H. Hoyle (Eds.), Handbook of individual differences in social behavior (pp. 547–560). New York, NY: Guilford.

Rhodewalt, F., Tragakis, M. W., & Finnerty, J. (2006). Narcissism and self-handicapping: Linking self-aggrandizement to behavior. *Journal of Research in Personality, 40,* 573–597.

Riccardi, N. (2011, June 22). Self-help guru convicted in Arizona sweat lodge deaths. *Los Angeles Times.* Retrieved from http://articles.latimes.com/2011/jun/22/nation/la-na-sweat-lodge-trial-20110623

Rice, J. K., & Else-Quest, N. (2006). The mixed messages of motherhood. In J. Worrell & C. D. Goodheart (Eds.), *Handbook of girls' and women's psychological health.* New York, NY: Oxford University Press.

Rice, K. G., Richardson, C. E., & Clark, D. (2012). Perfectionism, procrastination, and psychological distress. *Journal of Counseling Psychology, 59*(2), 288–302. doi:10.1037/a0026643

Richard, N. T., & Wright, S. C. (2010). Advantaged group members' reactions to tokenism. *Group Processes & Intergroup Relations, 13*(5), 559–569. doi:10.1177/1368430210362227

Richards, Z., & Hewstone, M. (2001). Subtyping and subgrouping: Processes for the prevention and promotion of stereotype change. *Personality and Social Psychology Review, 5,* 52–73.

Richardson, C. R., Kriska, A. M., Lantz, P. M., & Hayword, R. A. (2004). Physical activity and mortality across cardiovascular disease risk groups. *Medicine and Science in Sports and Exercise, 36*(11), 1923–1929.

Richardson, F. C., & Guignon, C. B. (2008). Positive psychology and philosophy of social science. *Theory & Psychology, 18,* 605–627.

Richardson, J. T. & Introvigne, M. (2001). "Brainwashing" theories in European parliamentary and administrative reports on "cults" and "sects." *Journal for the Scientific Study of Religion, 40* (2), 143–168.

Richeson, J. A., & Shelton, J. N. (2003). When prejudice doesn't pay: Effects of interracial contact on executive function. *Psychological Science, 14,* 287–290.

Richeson, J. A., Trawalter, S., & Shelton, J. N. (2005). African Americans' implicit racial attitudes and the depletion of executive function after interracial interactions. *Social Cognition, 23,* 336–352.

Richey, E., Knox, D., & Zusman, M. (2009). Sexual values of 783 undergraduates. *College Student Journal, 43,* 175–180.

Richmond, V. P., & McCroskey, J. C. (1995). *Communication: Apprehension, avoidance, and effectiveness* (5th ed.). Boston, MA: Allyn & Bacon.

Richter, H. (2007, May 7). Lights, camera, hired! *Newsweek,* p. 65.

Rick, S. I., Small, D. A., & Finkel, E. J. (2011). Fatal (fiscal) attraction: Spendthrifts and tightwads in marriage. *Journal of Marketing Research, 48*(2), 228–237. doi:10.1509/jmkr.48.2.228

Ridge, S. R., & Feeney, J. A. (1998). Relationship history and relationship attitudes in gay males and lesbians: Attachment style and gender differences. *Australian and New Zealand Journal of Psychiatry, 32*(6), 848–859.

Ridgeway, C. L., & Bourg, C. (2004). Gender as status: An expectation states theory approach. In A. H. Eagly, A. E. Beall, & R. J. Sternberg (Eds.), *The psychology of gender.* New York, NY: Guilford Press.

Ridker, P. M. (2001). High-sensitivity C-reactive protein: Potential adjunct for global risk assessment in the primary prevention of cardiovascular disease. *Circulation, 103,* 1813–1818.

Riegle-Crumb, C., & Humphries, M. (2012). Exploring bias in math teachers' perceptions of students' ability by gender and race/ethnicity. *Gender and Society, 26*(2), 290–322. doi:10.1177/0891243211434614

Riek, B. M., & Mania, E. W. (2012). The antecedents and consequences of interpersonal forgiveness: A meta-analytic review. *Personal Relationships, 19*(2), 304–325.

Rihmer, Z., & Angst, J. (2005). Mood disorders: Epidemiology. In B. J. Sadock & V. A. Sadock (Eds.), *Kaplan & Sadock's comprehensive textbook of psychiatry.* Philadelphia: Lippicott Williams & Wilkins.

Riis, J., Loewenstein, G., Baron, J., Jepson, C., Fagerlin, A., & Ubel, P. A. (2005). Ignorance of hedonic adaptation to hemodialysis: A study using ecological momentary assessment. *Journal of Experimental Psychology: General, 134,* 3–9.

Riise, T., Mohr, D. C., Munger, K. L., Rich-Edwards, J. W., Kawachi, I., & Ascherio, A. (2011). Stress and the risk of multiple sclerosis. *Neurology, 76,* 1866–1871.

Riley, L. D., & Bowen, C. (2005). The sandwich generation: Challenges and coping strategies of multigenerational families. *Family Journal: Counseling and Therapy for Couples and Families, 13,* 52–58.

Ringström, G., Abrahamsson, H., Strid, H., & Simrén, M. (2007). Why do subjects with irritable bowel syndrome seek health care for their symptoms? *Scandinavian Journal of Gastroenterology, 42,* 1194–1203.

Rising, K., Bacchetti, & Bero, L. (2008). Reporting bias in drug trials submitted to the Food and Drug Administration: Review of publication and presentation. *PLoS Medicine, 5*(11), e217.

Riskey, D. R., & Birnbaum, M. H. (1974). Compensatory effects in moral judgment: Two rights don't make up for a wrong. *Journal of Experimental Psychology, 103,* 171–173.

Riskind, J. H. (2005). Cognitive mechanisms in generalized anxiety disorder: A second generation of theoretical perspectives. *Cognitive Therapy & Research, 29*(1), 1–5.

Riso, L. P., du Toit, P. L., Blandino, J. A., Penna, S., Dacey, S., Duin, J. S., Pacoe, E. M., Grant, M. M., & Ulmer, C. S. (2003). Cognitive aspects of chronic depression. *Journal of Abnormal Psychology, 112*(1), 72–80.

Ritchart, R., & Perkins, D. N. (2002). Life in the mindful classroom: Nurturing the disposition of mindfulness. *Journal of Social Issues, 56*(1), 27–47.

Ritvo, E., Glick, I. D., & Berman, E. (2008). Couples therapy. In A. Tasman, J. Kay, J. A. Lieberman, M. B. First, & M. Maj (Eds.), *Psychiatry* (3rd ed.). New York, NY: Wiley-Blackwell.

Robbins, B. D. (2008). What is the good life? Positive psychology and the renaissance of humanistic psychology. *The Humanistic Psychologist, 36,* 96–112.

Robelia, B. A., Greenhow, C., & Burton, L. (2011). Environmental learning in online social networks: Adopting environmentally responsible behaviors. *Environmental Education Research, 17,* 553-575. doi: 10.1080/13504622.2011.565118

Robert, A. C., & Sonenstein, F. L. (2010). Adolescents' reports of communication with their parents about sexually transmitted diseases and birth control: 1988, 1995, and 2002. *Journal of Adolescent Health,* 1–6.

Roberts, B. W., Caspi, A., & Moffitt, T. (2003). Work experiences and personality development in young adulthood. *Journal of Personality and Social Psychology, 84,* 582–593.

Roberts, B. W., Jackson, J. J., Fayard, J. V., Edmonds, G., & Meints, J. (2009). Conscientiousness. In M. R. Leary & R. H. Hoyle (Eds.), *Handbook of individual differences in social behavior* (pp. 369–381). New York, NY: Guilford.

Roberts, B. W., Kuncel, N. R., Shiner, R., Caspi, A., & Goldberg, L. R. (2007). The power of personality: The comparative validity of personality traits, socioeconomic status, and cognitive ability for predicting important life outcomes. *Perspectives on Psychological Science, 2,* 313–345.

Roberts, D. F., Foehr, U. G., & Rideout, V. (2005). Generation M: Media in the lives of 8–18 year olds (Publication No. 7251). Menlo Park, CA: Henry J. Kaiser Family Foundation.

Roberts, S. (2006, October 15). It's official: To be married means to be outnumbered. *New York Times.*

Robins, R. W., Mendelsohn, G. A., Connell, J. B., & Kwan, V. S. Y. (2004). Do people agree about the causes of behavior? A social relations analysis of behavior ratings and causal attribution. *Journal of Personality and Social Psychology, 86,* 334–344.

Robins, R. W., & Trzesniewski, K. H. (2005). Self-esteem development across the lifespan. *Current Direction in Psychological Science, 14,* 158–162.

Robinson, B., Frye, E. M., & Bradley, L. J. (1997). Cult affiliation and disaffiliation: Implications for counseling. *Counseling and Values, 41,* 166–173.

Robinson, B. E., Flowers, C., & Ng, K. (2006). The relationship between workaholism and marital disaffection: Husband's perspective. *Family Journal: Counseling and Therapy for Couples and Families, 14,* 213–220.

Robinson, E. B., Koenen, K. C., McCormick, M. C., Munir, K., Hallett, V., Happé, F., . . . Ronald, A. (2011). Evidence that autistic traits show the same etiology in the general population and at the quantitative extremes (5%, 2.5%, and 1%). *Archives of General Psychiatry, 68,* 1113–1121. doi:10.1001/archgenpsychiatry.2011.119

Robinson, M. D., Johnson, J. T., & Shields, S. A. (1995). On the advantages of modesty: The benefits of a balanced self-presentation. *Communication Research, 22,* 575–591.

Robinson, O., & Griffiths, A. (2005). Coping with the stress of transformational change in a government department. *Journal of Applied Behavioral Science, 41*(2), 203–221.

Rock, V. J., Malarcher, A., Kahende, J. W., Asman, K., Husten, C., & Caraballo, R. (2007). Cigarette smoking among adults—United States, 2006. *Morbidity and Mortality Weekly Reports, 56,* 1157–1161.

Rodin, J., Schank, D., & Striegel-Moore, R. H. (1989). Psychological features of obesity. *Medical Clinics of North America, 73,* 47–66.

Rodrigues, A. E., Hall, J. H., & Fincham, F. D. (2006). What predicts divorce and relationship dissolution. In M. A. Fine & J. H. Harvey (Eds.), *Handbook of divorce and relationship resolution.* Mahwah, NJ: Erlbaum.

Roediger, H., L., III, Agarwal, P. K., Kang, S. K., & Marsh, E. J. (2010). Benefits of testing memory: Best practices and boundary conditions. In G. M. Davies & D. B. Wright, (Eds.), *Current issues in applied memory research* (pp. 13–49). New York, NY: Psychology Press.

Roediger, H. L., III, Agarwal, P. K., McDaniel, M. A., & McDermott, K. B. (2011). Test-enhanced learning in the classroom: Long-term improvements from quizzing. *Journal of Experimental Psychology: Applied, 17,* 382–395. doi:10.1037/a0026252

Roediger, H. L., III, & Butler, A. C. (2011). The critical role of retrieval practice in long-term retention. *Trends in Cognitive Sciences, 15,* 20–27. doi:10.1016/j.tics/2010.09.003

Roediger, H. L., III, & Karpicke, J. D. (2006a). Test-enhanced learning: Taking memory tests improves long-term retention. *Psychological Science, 17,* 249–255.

Roediger, H. L., III, & Karpicke, J. D. (2006b). The power of testing memory: Basic research and implications for educational practice. *Perspectives on Psychological Science, 1*(3), 181–210.

Rogers, C. J., Colbert, L. H., Greiner, J. W., Perkins, S. N., & Hursting, S. D. (2008). Physical activity and cancer prevention: Pathways and targets for intervention. *Sports Medicine, 38,* 271–296.

Rogers, C. R. (1951). *Client-centered therapy: Its current practice, implications, and theory.* Boston, MA: Houghton Mifflin.

Rogers, C. R. (1961). *On becoming a person: A therapist's view of psychotherapy.* Boston, MA: Houghton Mifflin.

Rogers, C. R. (1977). *Carl Rogers on personal power.* New York, NY: Delacorte.

Rogers, C. R. (1986). Client-centered therapy. In I. L. Kutash & A. Wolf (Eds.), *Psychotherapist's casebook.* San Francisco: Jossey-Bass.

Rohner, J., & Rasmussen, A. (2012). Recognition bias and the physical attractiveness stereotype. *Scandinavian Journal of Psychology, 53*(3), 239–246. doi:10.1111/j.1467-9450.2012.00939.x

Rohner, R. P., & Veneziano, R. A. (2001). The importance of father love: History and contemporary evidence. *Review of General Psychology, 5*(4), 382–405.

Rohrer, D., & Pashler, H. (2010). Recent research on human learning challenges conventional instructional strategies. *Educational Researcher, 39,* 406–412. doi:10.3102/0013189X10374770

Rohrer, D., Taylor, K., Pashler, H., Wixted, J. T., & Capeda, N. J. (2005). The effect of overlearning on long-term retention. *Applied Cognitive Psychology, 19,* 361–374.

Rojewski, J. W. (2005). Occupational aspirations: Constructs, meanings, and application. In S. D. Brown & R. W. Lent (Eds.), *Career development and counseling: Putting theory and research to work.* New York, NY: Wiley.

Rollie, S. S., & Duck, S. (2006). Divorce and dissolution of romantic relationships. In M. A. Fine & J. H. Harvey (Eds.), *Handbook of divorce and relationship resolution.* Mahwah, NJ: Erlbaum.

Rook, K. S. (1998). Investigating the positive and negative sides of personal relationships: Through a lens darkly? In B. H. Spitzberg & W. R. Cupach (Eds.), *The dark side of close relationships.* Mahwah, NJ: Lawrence Erlbaum.

Rook, K. S., August, K. J., & Sorkin, D. H. (2011). Social network functions and health. In R. J. Contrada & A. Baum (Eds.), *The handbook of stress science: Biology, psychology, and health* (pp. 123–135). New York, NY: Springer.

Rose, D., Wykes, T., Leese, M., Bindman, J., & Fleischmann, P. (2003). Patient's perspectives on electroconvulsive therapy: Systematic review. *British Medical Journal, 326,* 1363–1365.

Rose, D. P. (1997). Dietary fatty acids and cancer. *American Journal of Clinical Nutrition, 66*(4), 998S–1003S.

Rosen, G. M. (1993). Self-help or hype? Comments on psychology's failure to advance self-care. *Professional Psychology: Research and Practice, 24,* 340–345.

Rosen, G. M., Glasgow, R. E., & Moore, T. E. (2003). Self-help therapy: The science and business of giving psychology away. In S. O. Lilienfeld, S. J. Lynn, & J. M. Lohr (Eds.), *Science and pseudoscience in clinical psychology.* New York, NY: Guilford Press.

Rosen, R. D. (1977). *Psychobabble.* New York, NY: Atheneum.

Rosenbaum, J. E. (2009). Patient teenagers? A comparison of the sexual behavior of virginity pledgers and matched nonpledgers. *Pediatrics, 123,* 110–120.

Rosenfarb, I. S., Goldstein, M. J., Mintz, J., & Nuechterlein, K. H. (1995). Expressed emotion and subclinical psychopathology observable within the transactions between schizophrenic patients and their family members. *Journal of Abnormal Psychology, 104,* 259–267.

Rosenman, R. H. (1993). Relationships of the Type A behavior pattern with coronary heart disease. In L. Goldberger & S. Breznitz (Eds.), *Handbook of stress: Theoretical and clinical aspects* (2nd ed.). New York, NY: Free Press.

Rosenman, R. H., Brand, R. J., Jenkins, C. D., Friedman, M., Straus, R., & Wurm, M. (1975). Coronary heart disease in the Western Collaborative Group Study: Final follow-up of 8½ years. *Journal of the American Medical Association, 233,* 872–877.

Rosenthal, H. (1988). *Not with my life I don't: Preventing suicide and that of others.* Muncie, IN: Accelerated Development.

Rosenthal, R. (1985). From unconscious experimenter bias to teacher expectancy effects. In J. B. Dusek, V. C. Hall & W. J. Meyer (Eds.), *Teacher expectancies.* Hillsdale, NJ: Erlbaum.

Rosenthal, R. (2002). The Pygmalion effect and its mediating mechanisms. In J. Aronson (Ed.), *Improving academic achievement: Impact of psychological factors on education* (pp. 25–36). San Diego, CA: Academic Press.

Rospenda, K. M., Fujishiro, K., Shannon, C. A., & Richman, J. A. (2008). Workplace harassment, stress, and drinking behavior over time: Gender differences in a national sample. *Addictive Behaviors, 33*(7), 964–967.

Rospenda, K. M., Richman, J. A., Shannon, C. A. (2009). Prevalence and mental health correlates of harassment and discrimination in the workplace: Results from a national study. *Journal of Interpersonal Violence, 24*(5), 819–843.

Ross, C. E., & Van Willigen, M. (1997). Education and the subjective quality of life. *Journal of Health & Social Behavior, 38,* 275–297.

Ross, L., & Ward, A. (1996). Naive realism: Implications for social conflict and misunderstanding. In T. Brown, E. Reed, & E. Turiel (Eds.), *Values and knowledge.* Hillsdale, NJ: Erlbaum.

Ross, L. D. (1977). The intuitive psychologist and his shortcomings: Distortions in the attribution process. In L. Berkowitz (Ed.), *Advances in experimental social psychology* (Vol. 10). New York, NY: Academic Press.

Ross, M., & Conway, M. (1986). Remembering one's own past: The construction of personal histories. In R. M. Sorrentino & E. T. Higgins (Eds.), *Handbook of* motivation and cognition: Foundations of social behavior. New York, NY: Guilford Press.

Ross, M., & Wilson, A. E. (2002). It feels like yesterday: Self-esteem, valence of personal past experiences, and judgments of subjective distance. *Journal of Personality and Social Psychology, 82*, 792–803.

Rossow, L., Grøholt, B., & Wichstrøm, L. (2005). Intoxicants and suicidal behavior among adolescents: Changes in levels and associations from 1992 to 2002. *Addiction, 100*, 79–88.

Roszak, T. (1992). *The voice of the earth: An exploration of eco-psychology.* New York, NY: Simon & Schuster.

Roth, P. L., BeVier, C. A., Switzer, F. S., & Schippmann, J. S. (1996). Meta-analyzing the relationship between grades and job performance. *Journal of Applied Psychology, 81*(5), 548–556.

Roth, P. L., & Clarke, R. L. (1998). Meta-analyzing the relationship between grades and salary. *Journal of Vocational Behavior, 53*, 386–400.

Roughton, B. (2001, May 27). In Europe, workers time off adds up. *The Atlanta Journal-Constitution,* pp. D1–D2.

Rounding, K., Lee, A., Jacobson, J. A., & Ji, L. (2012). Religion replenishes self-control. *Psychological Science, 23*(6), 635–642. doi:10.1177/0956797611431987

Rowa, K., & Antony, M. M. (2008). Generalized anxiety disorders. In W. E. Craighead, D. J. Miklowitz, & L. W. Craighead (Eds.), *Psychopathology: History, diagnosis, and empirical foundations.* New York, NY: Wiley.

Rowe, D., & van den Oord, E. J. C. G. (2005). Genetic and environmental influences. In V. A. Derlega, B. A. Winstead, & W. H. Jones (Eds.), *Personality: Contemporary theory and research.* Belmont, CA: Wadsworth.

Rowny, S., & Lisanby, S. H. (2008). Brain stimulation in psychiatry. In A. Tasman, J. Kay, J. A. Lieberman, M. B. First, & M. Maj (Eds.), *Psychiatry* (3rd ed.). New York, NY: Wiley-Blackwell.

Rozanski, A., Blumenthal, J. A., & Kaplan, J. (1999). Impact of psychological factors on the pathogenesis of cardiovascular disease and implications for therapy. *Circulation, 99*(16), 2192–2197.

Rubenstein, C. M., & Shaver, P. (1982). The experience of loneliness. In L. A. Peplau & D. Perlman (Eds.), *Loneliness: A sourcebook of current theory, research and therapy.* New York, NY: Wiley.

Rubin, R. H. (2001). Alternative lifestyles revisited, or whatever happened to swingers, group marriages, and communes? *Journal of Family Issues, 22*, 711–726.

Rubin, Z., Peplau, L. A., & Hill, C. T. (1981). Loving and leaving: Sex differences in romantic attachments. *Sex Roles, 7*, 821–835.

Rudisch, B., & Nemeroff, C. B. (2003). Epidemiology of comorbid coronary artery disease and depression. *Biological Psychiatry, 54*(3), 227–240.

Ruff, E. A., Reardon, R. C., & Bertoch, S. C. (2008, June). Holland's RIASEC theory and applications: Exploring a comprehensive bibliography. *Career Convergence.* Retrieved from TCSLINKTONEWS[5483,ncda.org,layout_details]

Ruini, C., & Fava, G. A. (2004). Clinical application of well-being therapy. In P. A. Linley & S. Joseph (Eds.), *Positive psychology in practice.* Hoboken, NJ: Wiley.

Ruiz, P., & Strain, E. C. (Eds.). (2011). *Lowinson and Ruiz's substance abuse: A comprehensive textbook* (5th ed.). Philadelphia, PA: Lippincott Williams & Wilkins.

Rupp, H. A., & Wallen, K. (2009). Sex-specific content preferences for visual sexual stimuli. *Archives of Sexual Behavior, 38*, 417–426.

Rusbult, C. E., Agnew, C. R., & Arriaga, X. B. (2012). The investment model of commitment processes. In P. M. Van Lange, A. W. Kruglanski, E. Higgins (Eds.), *Handbook of theories of social psychology* (Vol. 2, pp. 218–231). Thousand Oaks, CA: Sage Publications Ltd.

Rusbult, C. E., Finkel, E. J., & Kumashiro, M. (2009). The Michelangelo phenomenon. *Current Directions in Psychological Science, 18*, 305–309.

Rush, A. J. (1984). Cognitive therapy. In T. B. Karasu (Ed.), *The psychiatric therapies.* Washington, DC: American Psychiatric Association.

Russell, G. F. M. (2009). Anorexia nervosa. In M. C. Gelder, N. C. Andreasen, J. J. López-Ibor, Jr., & J. R. Geddes (Eds.), *New Oxford textbook of psychiatry* (2nd ed., Vol. 1). New York, NY: Oxford University Press.

Russell, K. C. (2005). Two years later: A qualitative assessment of youth well-being and the role of aftercare in outdoor behavioral healthcare treatment. *Child and Youth Care Forum, 34*(3), 209–239.

Rutkowski, E. M., & Connelly, C. D. (2012). Self-efficacy and physical activity in adolescent and parent dyads. *Journal for Specialists in Pediatric Nursing, 17*, 51–60. doi:10.1111/j.1744-6155.2011.00314.x

Rutter, M. (2007). Gene-environment interdependence. *Developmental Science, 10*, 12–18.

Ruz, M., & Tudela, P. (2011). Emotional conflict in interpersonal interactions. *Neuroimage, 54*(2), 1685–1691. doi:10.1016/j.neuroimage.2010.08.039

Ryan, A., & Wessel, J. (2012). Sexual orientation harassment in the workplace: When do observers intervene? *Journal of Organizational Behavior, 33*(4), 488–509. doi:10.1002/job.765

Ryan, C., & Futterman, D. (1997). Lesbian and gay youth: Care and counseling. *Adolescent Medicine, 8*, 221.

Ryan, M. P. (2008). The antidepressant effects of physical activity: Mediating self-esteem and self-efficacy mechanisms. *Psychology and Health, 23*, 279–307.

Rye, M. S., Folck, C. D., Heim, T. A., Olszewski, B. T., & Traina, E. (2004). Forgiveness of an ex-spouse: How does it relate to mental health following a divorce? *Journal of Divorce and Remarriage, 41*, 31–51.

Ryff, C. D., & Singer, B. (2003). Flourishing under fire: Resilience as a prototype of challenged thriving. In C. L. M. Keyes & J. Haidt (Eds.), *Flourishing: Positive psychology and the life well-lived* (pp. 15–36). Washington, DC: American Psychological Association.

Saad, L. (1999, September 3). American workers generally satisfied, but indicate their jobs leave much to be desired. Princeton, NJ: Gallup News Service.

Saad, L. (2007). Americans rate the morality of 16 social issues. Retrieved June 23, 2007 from http://www.galluppoll.com/content/?ci=27757&p=1.

Sackeim, H. A., Dillingham, E. M., Prudic, J., Cooper, T., McCall, W. V., Rosenquist, P., et al. (2009). Effect of concomitant pharmacotherapy on electroconvulsive therapy outcomes: Short-term efficacy and adverse effects. *Archives of General Psychiatry, 66*(7), 729–737.

Sadler, J. Z. (2005). *Values and psychiatric diagnosis.* New York, NY: Oxford University Press.

Safron, A., Barch, B., Bailey, J. M., Gitelman, D. R., Parrish, T., & Reber, P. (2007). Neural correlates of sexual arousal in homosexual and heterosexual men. *Behavioral Neuroscience, 121*, 237–248.

Sagiv, L., Roccas, S., & Hazan, O. (2004). Value pathways to well-being: Healthy values, valued goal attainment, and environmental congruence. In P. A. Linley & S. Joseph (Eds.), *Positive psychology in practice.* New York, NY: Wiley.

Sagrestano, L. M., Heavey, C. L., & Christensen, A. (2006). Individual differences versus social structural approaches to explaining demand-withdraw and social influence behaviors. In K. Dindia, & D. J. Canary (Eds.), *Sex differences and similarities in communication.* Mahwah, NJ: Erlbaum.

Saint-Bauzel, R., & Fointiat, V. (2012). The sweet smell of the requester: Vanilla, camphor, and foot-in-the-door. *Social Behavior and Personality, 40*(3), 369–374. doi:10.2224/sbp.2012.40.3.369

Saks, A. M. (2006). Multiple predictions and criteria of job search success. *Journal of Vocational Behavior, 68*, 400–415.

Salerno, S. (2005). *Sham: How the self-help movement made America helpless.* New York, NY: Crown Publishers.

Salovey, P., & Mayer, J. D. (1990). Emotional intelligence. *Imagination, Cognition, and Personality, 9*, 185–211.

Salvatore, J., & Shelton, J. N. (2007). Cognitive costs of exposure to racial prejudice. *Psychological Science, 18*, 810–815.

Samberg, E., & Marcus, E. R. (2005). Process, resistance, and interpretation. In E. S. Person, A. M. Cooper, & G. O. Gabbard (Eds.), *Textbook of psychoanalysis.* Washington, DC: American Psychiatric Publishing.

Samnaliev, M. & Clark, R. E. (2008) The economics of schizophrenia. In K. T. Mueser & D. V. Jeste (Eds.), *Clinical handbook of schizophrenia* (pp. 507–515). New York, NY: Guilford.

Samovar, L. A., & Porter, R. E. (2004). *Communication between cultures.* Belmont, CA: Wadsworth.

Samovar, L. A., Porter, R. E., & McDaniel, E. R. (2007). *Communication between cultures.* Belmont, CA: Wadsworth.

Samovar, L. A., Porter, R. E., & Stefani, L. A. (1998). *Communication between cultures* (2nd ed.). Belmont, CA: Wadsworth.

Sanchez, D. T., Fetterolf, J. C., & Rudman, L. A. (2012). Eroticizing inequality in the United States: The consequences and determinants of traditional gender role adherence in intimate relationships. *Journal of Sex Research, 49*(2–3), 168–183.

Sanchez, L. (2009). Covenant marriage. In H. T. Reis & S. Sprecher (Eds.), *Encyclopedia of human relationships: Vol. 2* (pp. 363–365). Los Angeles: Sage Reference Publication.

Sanders, G. (2000). Men together: Working with gay couples in contemporary times. In P. Papp (Ed.), *Couples on the fault line.* New York, NY: Guilford Press.

Sanderson, C. A. Wallier, J. M., Stockdale, J. E., & Yopyk, D. J. A. (2008). Who feels discrepant and how does feeling discrepant matter? Examining the presence and consequences of feeling discrepant from personal and social norms related to thinness in American and British high school girls. *Journal of Social and Clinical Psychology, 27*, 995–1020.

Sanjuán, P., Magallares, A., & Gordillo, R. (2011). Self-serving attributional bias and hedonic and eudaimonic aspects of well-being. In I. Brdar (Ed.), *The human pursuit of well-being: A cultural approach* (pp. 15–26). New York, NY: Springer.

Sansone, R. A., & Sansone, L. A. (2010). Road rage: What's driving it? *Psychiatry, 7*(7), 14–18.

Sapolsky, R. M. (2004). *Why zebras don't get ulcers: The acclaimed guide to stress, stress-related diseases, and coping.* New York, NY: Holt.

Sarwer, D. B., Foster, G. D., & Wadden, T. A. (2004). Treatment of obesity I: Adult obesity. In J. K. Thompson (Ed.), *Handbook of eating disorders and obesity.* New York, NY: Wiley.

Sassler, S., & Miller, A. J. (2011). Class differences in cohabitation processes. *Family Relations: An Interdisciplinary Journal of Applied Family Studies, 60*(2), 163–177. doi:10.1111/j.1741-3729.2010.00640.x

Saucier, D., & Ehresman, C. (2010). The physiology of sex differences. In J. C. Chrisler & D. R. McCreary (Eds.), *Handbook of gender research in psychology* (Vol. 1, pp. 215–233). New York, NY: Springer.

Saunders, C. D. (2003). The emerging field of conservation psychology. *Human Ecology Review, 10*, 137–149.

Saunders, C. D., & Myers, O. E. (Eds.) (2003). Conservation psychology [Special issue]. *Human Ecology Review, 10*(2).

Savin-Williams, R. C. (2001). *Mom, dad. I'm gay.* Washington, D. C.: American Psychological Association.

Savin-Williams, R. C. (2009). How many gays are there? It depends. In D. A. Hope (Ed.), *Contemporary perspectives on lesbian, gay, and bisexual identities* (pp. 5–42). New York, NY: Springer Science and Business Media.

Savin-Williams, R. C., Pardo, S. T., Vrangalova, Z., Mitchell, R. S., & Cohen, K. M. (2010). Sexual and gender prejudice. In J. C. Chrisler & D. R. McCreary (Eds.), *Handbook of gender research in psychology, Vol 2: Gender research in social and applied psychology* (pp. 359–376). New York, NY: Springer Science + Business Media. doi:10.1007/978-1-4419-1467-5_15

Sawdon, A. M., Cooper, M., & Seabrook, R. (2007). The relationship between self-discrepancies, eating disorder, and depressive symptoms in women. *European Eating Disorders Review, 15*(3), 207–212.

Sawyer, N. T., & Escayg, A. (2010). Stress and epilepsy: Multiple models, multiple outcomes. *Journal of Clinical Neurophysiology, 27,* 445–452.

Sayer, L. C. (2005). Gender, time, and inequality: Trends in women's and men's paid work, unpaid work, and free time. *Social Forces, 84,* 285–303.

Sayers, S. L. (2004). Depression and heart disease: The interrelationship between these two common disorders is complex and requires careful diagnostic and treatment methods. *Psychiatric Annals, 34*(4), 282–288.

Sazant, S. (2010). Building self-esteem using assertiveness training and props. In S. Fehr (Ed.), *101 interventions in group therapy* (Rev. ed., pp. 303–306). New York, NY: Routledge/Taylor & Francis Group.

Sbarra, D. A., Law, R. W., & Portley, R. M. (2011). Divorce and death: A meta-analysis and research agenda for clinical, social, and health psychology. *Perspectives on Psychological Science, 6*(5), 454–474. doi:10.1177/1745691611414724

Sbarra, D. A., Smith, H. L., & Mehl, M. R. (2012). When leaving your ex, love yourself: Observational ratings of self-compassion predict the course of emotional recovery following marital separation. *Psychological Science, 23*(3), 261–269. doi:10.1177/0956797611429466

Schachner, D. A., Shaver, P. R., & Mikulincer, M. (2005). Patterns of nonverbal behavior and sensitivity in the context of attachment relations. *Journal of Nonverbal Behavior, 29*(3), 141–169.

Schachter, R. (2011). Using the group in cognitive group therapy. *Group, 35*(2), 135–149.

Schachter, S. (1959). *The psychology of affiliation.* Stanford, CA: Stanford University Press.

Schachter, S. (1982). Recidivism and self-cure of smoking and obesity. *American Psychologist, 37,* 436–444.

Schaffer, A. (2008, August 11). Prescriptions for health, the environmental kind. *New York Times,* Health section.

Schaffer, M., Jeglic, E. L., & Stanley, B. (2008). The relationship between suicidal behavior, ideation, and binge drinking among college students. *Archives of Suicide Research, 12,* 124–132.

Schaninger, C. M., & Buss, W. C. (1986). A longitudinal comparison of consumption and finance handling between happily married and divorced couples. *Journal of Marriage and the Family, 48,* 129–136.

Schaufeli, W. B., Leiter, M. P., & Maslach, C. (2009). Burnout: 35 years of research and practice. *The Career Development International, 14*(3), 204–220. doi:10.1108/13620430910966406

Scheier, M. F., & Carver, C. S. (1985). Optimism, coping, and health: Assessment and implications of generalized outcome expectancies. *Health Psychology, 4,* 219–247.

Scheier, M. F., & Carver, C. S. (2007). Optimism, pessimism, and stress. In G. Fink (Ed.), *Encyclopedia of stress: Vols. 1–4* (2nd ed., pp. 26–29). San Diego, CA: Elsevier Academic Press.

Scheier, M. F., Matthews, K. A., Owens, J. F., Magovern, G. J., Sr., Lefebvre, R. C., Abbott, R. A., & Carver, C. S. (1989). Dispositional optimism and recovery from coronary artery bypass surgery: The beneficial effects on physical and psychological well-being. *Journal of Personality and Social Psychology, 57,* 1024–1040.

Schick, V., Herbenick, D., Reece, M., Sanders, S. A., Dodge, B., Middlestat, S. E., & Fortenberry, J. D. (2010). Sexual behaviors, condom use, and sexual health of Americans over 50: Implications for sexual health promotion for older adults. *Journal of Sexual Medicine, 7*(5), 315–329.

Schietroma, M., Piccione, F., Carlei, F., Clementi, M., Bianchi, Z., De Vita, F., & Amicucci, G. (2012). Peritonitis from perforated appendicitis: Stress response after laproscopic or open treatment. *The American Surgeon, 78,* 582–590.

Schiffman, J., Ekstrom, M., LaBrie, J., Schulsinger, F., Sorenson, H., & Mednick, S. (2002). Minor physical anomalies and schizophrenia spectrum disorders: A prospective investigation. *American Journal of Psychiatry, 159,* 238–243.

Schilit, W. K. (1987). Thinking about managing your time. In A. D. Timpe (Ed.), *The management of time.* New York, NY: Facts On File.

Schimmel, S. (2000). Vices, virtues and sources of human strength in historical perspective. *Journal of Social and Clinical Psychology, 19*(1), 137–150. doi:10.1521/jscp.2000.19.1.137

Schkade, D. A., & Kahneman, D. (1998). Does living in California make people happy? A focusing illusion in judgments of life satisfaction. *Psychological Science, 9,* 340–346.

Schlapobersky, J., & Pines, M. (2009). Group methods in adult psychiatry. In M. C. Gelder, N. C. Andreasen, J. J. López-Ibor, Jr., & J. R. Geddes (Eds.), *New Oxford textbook of psychiatry* (2nd ed., Vol. 1). New York, NY: Oxford University Press.

Schlenger, W. E., Kulka, R. A., Fairbank, J. A., Hough, R. L., et al. (1992). The prevalence of posttraumatic stress disorder in the Vietnam generation: A multimethod, multisource assessment of psychiatric disorder. *Journal of Traumatic Stress, 5,* 333–363.

Schlenker, B. R. (2003). Self-presentation. In M.R. Leary & J. P. Tangney (Eds.), *Handbook of self and identity.* New York, NY: Guilford.

Schlenker, B. R., & Pontari, B. A. (2000). The strategic control of information: Impression management and self-presentation in daily life. In A. Tesser, R. B. Felson, & J. M. Suls (Eds.), *Psychological perspectives on self and identity.* Washington, DC: American Psychological Association.

Schlicht, W., Kanning, M., & Bös, K. (2007). Psychosocial interventions to influence physical inactivity as a risk factor: Theoretical models and practical evidence. In J. Dordan, B. Bardé, & A. M. Zeiher, (Eds.), *Contributions toward evidence-based psychocardiology: A systematic review of the literature* (pp. 107–123). Washington, DC: American Psychological Association.

Schmeichel, B. J., Gailliot, M. T., Filardo, E., McGregor, I., Gitter, S., & Baumeister, R. F. (2009). Terror management theory and self-esteem revisited: The roles of implicit and explicit self-esteem in mortality salience effects. *Journal of Personality and Social Psychology, 96*(5), 1077–1087. doi:10.1037/a0015091

Schmitz, J. M., & DeLaune, K. A. (2005). Nicotine. In J. H. Lowinson, P. Ruiz, R. B. Millman, & J. G. Langrod (Eds.), *Substance abuse: A comprehensive textbook.* Philadelphia: Lippincott/Williams & Wilkins.

Schmuck, P., & Schultz, P. W. (2002). Sustainable development as a challenge for psychology. In P. Schmuck & P. W. Schultz (Eds.), *Psychology of Sustainable Development* (pp. 3–17). Boston, MA: Kluwer Academic Publishers.

Schneider, D. J. (2004). *The psychology of stereotyping.* New York, NY: Guilford.

Schneider, T. R. (2008). Evaluations of stressful transactions: What's in an appraisal? *Stress and Health, 24,* 151–158.

Schneider, T. R., Rench, T. A., Lyons, J. B., & Riffle, R. R. (2012). The influence of neuroticism, extraversion and openness on stress responses. *Stress and Health: Journal of the International Society for the Investigation of Stress, 28*(2), 102–110. doi:10.1002/smi.1409

Schnittker, J. (2007). Look (closely) at all the lonely people: Age and the social psychology of social support. *Journal of Aging Health, 19,* 659–682.

Schnittker, J. (2008). An uncertain revolution: Why the rise of a genetic model of mental illness has not increased tolerance. *Social Science & Medicine, 67*(9), 1370–1381. doi:10.1016/j.socscimed.2008.07.007

Schnoll, R., Martinez, E., Tatum, K., Glass, M., Bernath, A., Ferris, D., & Reynolds, P. (2011). Increased self-efficacy to quit and perceived control over withdrawal symptoms predict smoking cessation following nicotine dependence treatment. *Addictive Behaviors, 36*(1–2), 144–147.

Schoen, R., & Canudas-Romo, V. (2006). Timing effects on divorce: 20th century experience in the United States. *Journal of Marriage and Family, 68*(3), 749–758. doi:10.1111/j.1741-3737.2006.00287.x

Schoon, I., & Parsons, S. (2002). Teenage aspirations for future careers and occupational outcomes. *Journal of Vocational Behavior, 60*(2), 262–288.

Schopler, J., & Insko, C. A. (1992). The discontinuity effect in interpersonal and intergroup relations: Generality and mediation. *European Review of Social Psychology, 3,* 121–151.

Schramm, D. G., Marshall, J. P., Harris, V. W., & Lee, T. R. (2005). After "I do": The newlywed transition. *Marriage & Family Review, 38,* 45–67.

Schramm, W. (1955). *The process and effects of mass communication.* Urbana: University of Illinois Press.

Schraw, G., Wadkins, T., & Olafson, L. (2007). Doing the things we do: A grounded theory of academic procrastination. *Journal of Educational Psychology, 99*(1), 12–25.

Schreiber, F. R. (1973). *Sybil.* New York, NY: Warner.

Schreiner-Engel, P., Schiavi, R. C., White, D., & Ghizzani, A. (1989). Low sexual desire in women: The role of reproductive hormones. *Hormones and Behavior, 23,* 221–234.

Schrijvers, D. L., Bollen, J., & Sabbe, B. C. (2012). The gender paradox in suicidal behavior and its impact on the suicidal process. *Journal of Affective Disorders, 138*(1-2), 19–26. doi:10.1016/j.jad.2011.03.050

Schrock, D., & Schwalbe, M. (2009). Men, masculinity, and manhood acts. *Annual Review of Sociology, 35,* 277–259.

Schuckit, M. A. (2000). Alcohol-related disorders. In B. J. Sadock & V. A. Sadock (Eds.), *Kaplan and Sadock's comprehensive textbook of psychiatry* (7th ed.). Philadelphia: Lippincott/Williams & Wilkins.

Schug, J., Yuki, M., & Maddux, W. (2010). Relational mobility explains between- and within-culture differences in self-disclosure to close friends. *Psychological Science, 21*(10), 1471–1478. doi:10.1177/0956797610382786

Schultz, P. W. (2001). The structure of environmental concern: Concern for self, other people, and the biosphere. *Journal of Environmental Psychology, 21,* 1–13.

Schultz, P. W., Gouveia, V. V., Cameron, L. D., Tankha, G., Schmuck, P., & Franek, M. (2005). Values and their relationship to environmental concern and conservation behavior. *Journal of Cross-Cultural Psychology, 36,* 457–475.

Schumann, C. M., Bloss, C. S., Barnes, C. C., Wideman, G. M., Carper, R. A., Akschoomoff, N., . . . Courchesne, E. (2010). Longitudinal magnetic resonance imaging study of cortical development through early childhood in autism. *Journal of Neuroscience, 30,* 4419–4427.

Schurtz, D. R., Blincoe, S., Smith, R. H., Powell, C. J., Combs, D. Y., & Kim, S. (2012). Exploring the social aspects of goose bumps and their role in awe and envy. *Motivation and Emotion, 36*(2), 205–217. doi:10.1007/s11031-011-9243-8

Schutte, N. S., Malouff, J. M., Thorsteinsson, E. B., Bhullar, N., & Rooke, S. E. (2007). A meta-analytic investigation of the relationship between emotional intelligence and health. *Personality and Individual Differences, 42,* 921–933.

Schwartz, B. (2004). *The paradox of choice: Why more is less.* New York, NY: Ecco.

Schwartz, J. E., Neale, J., Marco, C., Shiffman, S. S., & Stone, A. A. (1999). Does trait coping exist? A momentary assessment approach to the evaluation of traits. *Journal of Personality and Social Psychology, 77*(2), 360–369.

Schwartz, P., & Young, L. (2009). Sexual satisfaction in committed relationships. *Sexuality Research & Social Policy: A Journal of the NSRC, 6*(1), 1–17.

Schwartz, S. J., Unger, J. B., Zamboanga, B. L., & Szapocznik, J. (2010). Rethinking the concept of acculturation: Implications for theory and research. *American Psychologist, 65*(4), 237–251. doi:10.1037/a0019330

Schwarz, N., & Strack, F. (1999). Reports of subjective well-being: Judgmental processes and their methodological implications. In D. Kahneman, E. Diener, & N. Schwarz (Eds.), *Well-being: The foundations of hedonic psychology.* New York, NY: Russell Sage Foundation.

Schwarzer, R., & Schulz, U. (2003). Stressful life events. In A. M. Nezu, C. M. Nezu, & P. A. Geller (Eds.), *Handbook of psychology: Vol. 9. Health psychology.* New York, NY: Wiley.

Schwind, C., Buder, J., Cress, U., & Hesse, F. W. (2012). Preference-inconsistent recommendations: An effective approach for reducing confirmation bias and stimulating divergent thinking? *Computers & Education, 58*(2), 787–796. doi:10.1016/j.compedu.2011.10.003

Scott, D. L., & Levine, S. B. (2010). Understanding gay and lesbian life. In S. B. Levine (Ed.), *Handbook of clinical sexuality for mental health professionals* (2nd ed., pp. 351–368). New York, NY: Routledge/Taylor & Francis Group.

Scully, J. A., Tosi, H., & Banning, K. (2000). Life event checklists: Revisiting the social readjustment rating scale after 30 years. *Educational & Psychological Measurement, 60*(6), 864–876.

Seccombe, K. (2001). Families in poverty in the 1990s: Trends, causes, consequences, and lessons learned. In R. M. Milardo (Ed.), *Understanding families into the new millennium: A decade in review.* Minneapolis: National Council on Family Relations.

Sedikides, C., & Alicke, M. D. (2012). Self-enhancement and self-protection motives. In R. M. Ryan (Ed.), *The Oxford handbook of human motivation* (pp. 303–322). New York, NY: Oxford University Press.

Sedikides, C., & Hepper, E. D. (2009). Self-improvement. *Social and Personality Psychology Compass, 3*(6), 899–917. doi:10.1111/j.1751-9004.2009.00231.x

Sedlmeier, P., Eberth, J., Schwarz, M., Zimmermann, D., Haarig, F., Jaeger, S., & Kunze, S. (2012). The psychological effects of meditation: A meta-analysis. *Psychological Bulletin, 138*(6), 1139–1171. doi:10.1037/a0028168

See, Y. H. M., Petty, R. E., Evans, L. M. (2009). The impact of perceived message complexity and need for cognition on information processing and attitudes. *Journal of Research in Personality, 43*(5), 880–889.

Seery, M. D. (2011). Resilience: A silver lining to experiencing adverse life events? *Current Directions in Psychological Science, 20*(6), 390–394. doi:10.1177/0963721411424740

Segal, M. W. (1974). Alphabet and attraction: An unobtrusive measure of the effect of propinquity in a field setting. *Journal of Personality and Social Psychology, 30,* 654–657.

Segall, A. (1997). Sick role concepts and health behavior. In D. S. Gochman (Ed.), *Handbook of health behavior research I: Personal and social determinants.* New York : Plenum Press.

Segerstrom, S. C., & Miller, G. E. (2004). Psychological stress and the human immune system: A meta-analytic study of 30 years of inquiry. *Psychological Bulletin, 130,* 601–630.

Segerstrom, S. C., & O'Connor, D. B. (2012). Stress, health and illness: Four challenges for the future. *Psychology and Health, 27*(2), 128–140. doi:10.1080/08870446.2012.659516

Seiter, J. S. (2007). Ingratiation and gratuity: The effect of complimenting customers on tipping behavior in restaurants. *Journal of Applied Social Psychology, 37*(3), 478–485.

Sekerka, L. E., Vacharkulksemsuk, T., & Fredrickson, B. L. (2012). Positive emotions. In K. S. Cameron & G. M. Spreitzer (Eds.), *The Oxford handbook of positive organizational scholarship* (pp. 168–177). New York, NY: Oxford University Press.

Selfhout, M., Denissen, J., Branje, S., & Meeus, W. (2009). In the eye of the beholder: Perceived, actual, and peer-rated similarity in personality, communication, and friendship intensity during the acquaintanceship process. *Journal of Personality and Social Psychology, 96,* 1152–1165.

Seligman, M. E. P. (1971). Phobias and preparedness. *Behavior Therapy, 2,* 307–321.

Seligman, M. E. P. (1974). Depression and learned helplessness. In R. J. Friedman & M. M. Katz (Eds.), *The psychology of depression: Contemporary theory and research.* New York, NY: Wiley.

Seligman, M. E. P. (1990). *Learned optimism: How to change your mind and your life.* New York, NY: Pocket Books.

Seligman, M. E. P. (1991). *Learned optimism.* New York, NY: Alfred A. Knopf.

Seligman, M. E. P. (1992). *Helplessness: On depression, development, and death.* New York, NY: Freeman.

Seligman, M. E. P. (1994). *What you can change and what you can't.* New York, NY: Knopf.

Seligman, M. E. P. (1995). The effectiveness of psychotherapy. *American Psychologist, 50,* 965–974.

Seligman, M. E. P. (1998). Positive social science. *APA Monitor Online, 29*(4).

Seligman, M. E. P. (1999). The president's address. *American Psychologist, 54,* 559–562.

Seligman, M. E. P. (2002). Positive psychology, prevention, and positive therapy. In C. R. Snyder & S. J. Lopez (Eds.), *Handbook of positive psychology* (pp. 3–13). New York, NY: Oxford University Press.

Seligman, M. E. P. (2003a). The past and future of positive psychology. In C. L. M. Keyes & J. Haidt (Eds.), *Flourishing: Positive psychology and the life well-lived.* Washington, DC: American Psychological Association.

Seligman, M. E. P. (2003b). *Authentic happiness: Using the new positive psychology to realize your potential for lasting fulfillment.* New York, NY: Free Press.

Seligman, M. E. P. (2011). *Flourish: A visionary new understanding of happiness and well-being.* New York, NY: Free Press.

Seligman, M. E. P., & Csikszentmihalyi, M. (2000). Positive psychology: An introduction. *American Psychologist, 55*(1), 5–14.

Seligman, M. E. P., Rashid, T., & Parks, A. C. (2006). Positive psychotherapy. *American Psychologist, 61,* 774–788.

Seligman, M. E. P., Schulman, P., & Tryon, A. M. (2007). Group prevention of depression and anxiety symptoms. *Behaviour Research and Therapy, 45,* 1111–1126.

Seligman, M. E. P., Schulman, P., DeRubeis, R. J., & Hollon, S. D. (1999). The prevention of depression and anxiety. *Prevention and Treatment,* http://journals.apa.org/prevention/volume2/pre0020008a.html

Seligman, M. E. P., Steen, T. A., Park, N., & Peterson, C. (2005). Positive psychology progress: Empirical validation of interventions. *American Psychologist, 60,* 410–421.

Seltzer, J. A. (2001). Families formed outside of marriage. In R. M. Milardo (Ed.), *Understanding families into the new millennium: A decade in review.* Minneapolis: National Council on Family Relations.

Seltzer, J. A. (2004). Cohabitation and family change. In M. Coleman & L. H. Ganong (Eds.), *Handbook of contemporary families: Considering the past, contemplating the future.* Thousand Oaks, CA: Sage.

Selye, H. (1936). A syndrome produced by diverse nocuous agents. *Nature, 138,* 32.

Selye, H. (1956). *The stress of life.* New York, NY: McGraw-Hill.

Selye, H. (1974). *Stress without distress.* New York, NY: Lippincott.

Selye, H. (1982). History and present status of the stress concept. In L. Goldberger & S. Breznitz (Eds.), *Handbook of stress: Theoretical and clinical aspects.* New York, NY: Free Press.

Semans, J. H. (1956). Premature ejaculation: A new approach. *Journal of Southern Medicine, 79,* 353–361.

Sen, S., Burmeister, M., & Ghosh, D. (2004). Meta-analysis of the association between a serotonin transporter promoter polymorphism (5-HTTLPR) and anxiety-related personality traits. *American Journal of Medical Genetics, 127B*(1), 85–89.

Senecal, C., Lavoie, K., & Koestner, R. (1997). Trait and situational factors in procrastination: An interactional model. *Journal of Social Behavior and Personality, 12,* 889–903.

Serido, J., Almeida, D. M., & Wethington, E. (2004). Chronic stressors and daily hassles: Unique and inter-active relationships with psychological distress. *Journal of Health and Social Behavior, 45,* 17–33.

Sesso, H. D., Buring, J. E., Rifai, N., Blake, G. J., Gaziano, J. M., & Ridker, P. M. (2003). C-reactive protein and the risk of developing hypertension. *Journal of the American Medical Association, 290*(22), 2945–2951.

Seta, J. J., Seta, C. E., & McElroy, T. (2002). Strategies for reducing the stress of negative life experiences: An averaging/summation analysis. *Personality and Social Psychology Bulletin, 28*(11), 1574–1585.

Settles, I. H., Cortina, L. M., Malley, J., & Stewart, A. J. (2006). The climate for women in academic science: The good, the bad, and changeable. *Psychology of Women Quarterly, 30,* 47–58.

Shaffer, D. R. (1989). *Developmental psychology: Childhood and adolescence.* Pacific Grove, CA: Brooks/Cole.

Shah, J., & Higgins, E. T. (2001). Regulatory concerns and appraisal efficiency: The general impact of promotion and prevention. *Journal of Personality and Social Psychology, 80,* 693–705.

Shapiro, A. F., Gottman, J. M., & Carrère, S. (2000). The baby and marriage: Identifying factors that buffer against decline in marital satisfaction after the first baby arrives. *Journal of Family Psychology, 14*(1), 59–70.

Shapiro, D. H., Jr. (1984). Overview: Clinical and physiological comparison of meditation with other self-control strategies. In D. H. Shapiro, Jr. & R. N. Walsh (Eds.), *Meditation: Classic and contemporary perspectives.* New York, NY: Aldine.

Shapiro, J. R., & Neuberg, S. L. (2007). From stereotype threat to stereotype threats: Implications of a multi-threat framework for causes, moderators, mediators, consequences, and interventions. *Personality & Social Psychology Review, 11,* 107–130.

Shapiro, S. L., Astin, J. A., Bishop, S. R., & Cordova, M. (2005). Mindfulness-based stress reduction for health care professionals: Results from a randomized trial. *International Journal of Stress Management, 12,* 164–176.

Shapiro, S. L., & Carlson, L. E. (2009). *The art and science of mindfulness: Integrating mindfulness into psychology and the helping professions.* Washington, DC: American Psychological Association.

Shapiro, S. L., Schwartz, G. E. R., & Bonner, G. (1998). The effects of mindfulness-based stress reduction on medical and pre-medical students. *Journal of Behavioral Medicine, 21,* 581–599.

Shapiro, S. L., Schwartz, G. E. R., & Santerre, C. (2005). Meditation and positive psychology. In C. R. Snyder & S. J. Lopez (Eds.), *Handbook of positive psychology.* New York, NY: Oxford University Press.

Sharot, T., Korn, C. W., & Dolan, R. J. (2011). How unrealistic optimism is maintained in the face of reality. *Nature Neuroscience, 14*(11), 1475–1479. doi:10.1038/nn.2949

Sharp, E. A., & Ganong, L. (2011). "I'm a loser, I'm not married, let's just all look at me": Ever-single women's perceptions of their social environment. *Journal of Family Issues, 32*(7), 956–980. doi:10.1177/0192513X10392537

Shattuck, P. T. (2006). The contribution of diagnostic substitution to the growing administrative prevalence of autism in U.S. special education. *Pediatrics, 117,* 1028–1037.

Shavelson, R. J., Hubner, J. J., & Stanton, G. C. (1976). Self-concept: Validation of construct interpretations. *Review of Educational Research, 46,* 407–411.

Shaver, P. R., & Brennan, K. A. (1992). Attachment styles and the "Big Five" personality traits: Their connections with each other and with romantic relationship outcomes. *Personality and Social Psychology Bulletin, 18,* 536–545.

Shaver, P. R., & Hazan, C. (1993). Adult attachment: Theory and research. In W. Jones & D. Perlman (Eds.), *Advances in personal relationships* (Vol. 4). London: Jessica Kingsley.

Shaver, P. R., & Mikulincer, M. (2006). Attachment theory, individual psychodynamics, and relationship functioning. In A. L. Vangelisti & D. Perlman (Eds.), *The Cambridge handbook of personal relationships.* New York, NY: Cambridge University Press.

Shaver, P. R., & Mikulincer, M. (2008). Augmenting the sense of security in romantic, leader-follower, therapeutic, and group relationships: A relational model of psychological change. In J. P. Forgas & J. Fitness (Eds.) *Social relationships: Cognitive, affective, and motivational processes* (pp. 55–74). New York, NY: Psychology Press.

Shaver, P. R., & Mikulincer, M. (2012). Attachment theory. In P. M. Van Lange, A. W. Kruglanski, & E. Higgins (Eds.), *Handbook of theories of social psychology* (Vol. 2, pp. 160–179). Thousand Oaks, CA: Sage Publications Ltd.

Shaw, L. H., & Gant, L. M. (2002). In defense of the Internet: The relationship between Internet communication and depression, loneliness, self-esteem, and perceived social support. *CyberPsychology, 5*(2), 157–171.

Shaw, R. (2011). Women's experiential journey toward voluntary childlessness: An interpretative phenomenological analysis. *Journal of Community and Applied Social Psychology, 21*(2), 151–163. doi:10.1002/casp.1072

Shedler, J. (2010). The efficacy of psychodynamic psychotherapy. *American Psychologist, 65*(2), 98–109. doi:10.1037/a0018378

Sheehan, S. (1982). *Is there no place on earth for me?* Boston, MA: Houghton Mifflin.

Shelby, R. A., Crespin, T. R., Wells-Di Gregorio, S. M., Siegel, J. E., Taylor, K. L., & Lamdan, R. M. (2008). Optimism, social support, and adjustment in African American women with breast cancer. *Journal of Behavioral Medicine, 31*, 433–444.

Sheldon, J. P. (2004). Gender stereotypes in educational software for young children. *Sex Roles, 51*, 433–444.

Sheldon, K. M., & Kasser, T. (2001a). Getting older, getting better? Personal strivings and psychological maturity across the life span. *Developmental Psychology, 37*(4), 491–501.

Sheldon, K. M., & Kasser, T. (2001b). Goals, congruence, and positive well-being: New empirical support for humanistic theories. *Journal of Humanistic Psychology, 41*(1), 30–50.

Sheldon, K. M., & Lyubomirsky, S. (2006). How to increase and sustain positive emotion: The effects of expressing gratitude and visualizing best possible selves. *The Journal of Positive Psychology, 1*, 73–82.

Shelton, K. H., & Harold, G. T. (2007). Marital conflict and children's adjustment: The mediating and moderating role of children's coping strategies. *Social Development, 16*, 497–511.

Shen, L., & Dillard, J. P. (2007). Reactance proneness assessment. In R. A. Reynolds, R. Woods, & J. D. Baker (Eds.), *Handbook of research on electronic surveys and measurements* (pp. 323–329). Hershey, PA: Idea Group Reference/IGI Global.

Shenton, M. E. & Kubicki, M. (2009). Structural brain imaging in schizophrenia. In B. J. Sadock, V. A. Sadock, & P. Ruiz (Eds.), *Kaplan & Sadock's comprehensive textbook of psychiatry* (pp. 1494–1506). Philadelphia: Lippincott Williams & Wilkins.

Shepperd, J., Malone, W., & Sweeny, K. (2008). Exploring causes of the self-serving bias. *Social and Personality Psychology Compass, 2*(2), 895–908.

Shepperd, J., & Taylor, K. M. (1999). Ascribing advantages to social comparison targets. *Basic and Applied Social Psychology, 21*, 103–117.

Sher, T. G., & Baucom, D. H. (1993). Marital communication: Differences among maritally distressed, depressed, and nondistressed-nondepressed couples. *Journal of Family Psychology, 7*, 148–153.

Sherif, M., Harvey, O., White, B., Hood, W., & Sherif, C. (1961). *Intergroup conflict and cooperation: The Robber's Cave experiment.* Norman: University of Oklahoma, Institute of Group Behavior.

Sherman, G. D., Lee, J. J., Cuddy, A. J. C., Renshon, J., Oveis, C., Grosse, J. J., & Lerner, J. S. (2012). Leadership is associated with lower levels of stress. *Proceedings of the National Academy of Sciences.* doi:10.1073/pnas.1207042109

Shiffman, S., Brockwell, S. E., Pillitteri, J. L., & Gitchell, J. G. (2008). Use of smoking-cessation treatments in the United States. *American Journal of Preventive Medicine, 34*, 102–111.

Shifron, R., & Reysen, R. R. (2011). Workaholism: Addiction to work. *The Journal of Individual Psychology, 67*(2), 136–146.

Shike, M. (1999). Diet and lifestyle in the prevention of colorectal cancer: An overview. *American Journal of Medicine, 106*(1A), 11S–15S, 50S–51S.

Shin, N. (2006). Online learner's "flow" experience: An empirical study. *British Journal of Education Technology, 37*(5), 705–720.

Shiota, M. N. (2006). Silver linings and candles in the dark: Differences among positive coping strategies in predicting subjective well-being. *Emotion, 6*, 335–339.

Shiovitz-Ezra, S., & Leitsch, S. A. (2010). The role of social relationships in predicting loneliness: The National Social Life, Health, and Aging Project. *Social Work Research, 34*(3), 157–167. doi:10.1093/swr/34.3.157

Shneidman, E. S., Farberow, N. L., & Litman, R. E. (1994). *The psychology of suicide: A clinician's guide to evaluation and treatment.* Northvale, NJ: J. Aronson.

Shobe, K. K., & Schooler, J. W. (2001). Discovering fact and fiction: Case-based analyses of authentic and fabricated discovered memories of abuse. In G. M. Davies & T. Dalgleish (Eds.), *Recovered memories: Seeking the middle ground.* Chichester, England: Wiley.

Shoda, Y., Mischel, W., & Peake, P. K. (1990). Predicting adolescent cognitive and self-regulatory competencies from preschool delay of gratification: Identifying diagnostic conditions. *Developmental Psychology, 26*, 978–986.

Shook, N. J., & Fazio, R. H. (2008). Interracial roommate relationships: An experimental field test of the contact hypothesis. *Psychological Science, 19*, 717–723.

Shors, T. J. (2004). Learning during stressful times. *Learning and Memory, 11*(2), 137–144.

Showers. C. J., & Zeigler-Hill, V. (2012). Organization of self-knowledge: Features, functions, and flexibility. In M. R. Leary & J. P. Tangney (Eds.), *Handbook of self and identity* (2nd ed., pp. 105–123). New York, NY: Guilford.

Shu, S. B., & Gneezy, A. (2010). Procrastination of enjoyable experiences. *Journal of Marketing Research, 47*(5), 933–944. doi:10.1509/jmkr.47.5.933

Sibley, C. G., & Duckitt, J. (2008). Personality and prejudice: A meta-analytic and theoretical review. *Personality and Social Psychology Review, 12*(3), 248–279.

Sidanius, J., & Pratto, P. (1999). *Social dominance: An intergroup theory of social hierarchy and oppression.* New York, NY: Cambridge University Press.

Sidanius, J., Van Laar, C., Levin, S., & Sinclair, S. (2004). Ethnic enclaves and the dynamics of social identity on the college campus: The good, the bad, and the ugly. *Journal of Personality and Social Psychology, 87*, 96–110.

Siddiqui, R. N., & Pandey, J. (2003). Coping with environmental stressors by urban slum dwellers. *Enviroment and Behavior, 35*, 589–604.

Siebert, A., & Karr, M. (2008). *The adult student's guide to survival & success.* Portland, OR: Practical Psychology Press.

Siegel, K., Schrimshaw, E. W., Lekas, H., & Parsons, J. T. (2008). Sexual behaviors of non-gay identified non-disclosing men who have sex with men and women. *Archives of Sexual Behavior, 37*, 720–735.

Siegel, M. (2007, August, 28). New Orleans still facing a psychiatric emergency. *The Globe and Mail* (Canada), A17.

Siegler, I. C., Peterson, B. L., Barefoot, J. C., & Williams, R. B. (1992). Hostility during late adolescence predicts coronary risk factors at mid-life. *American Journal of Epidemiology, 136*(2), 146–154.

Siegman, A. W. (1994). From Type A to hostility to anger: Reflections on the history of coronary-prone behavior. In A. W. Siegman & T. W. Smith (Eds.), *Anger, hostility, and the heart* (pp. 1–21). Hillsdale, NJ: Erlbaum.

Silverstein, M., & Ruiz, S. (2009). Intergenerational relationships in families,. In H. T. Reis & S. Sprecher (Eds.), *Encyclopedia of human relationships: Vol. 1* (pp. 606–610). Los Angeles: Sage Reference Publication.

Silvia, P. J., & Duval, T. S. (2001). Objective self-awareness theory: Recent progress and enduring problems. *Personality and Social Psychology Review, 5*, 230–241.

Silvia, P. J., & Eddington, K. M. (2012). Self and emotion. In M. R. Leary & J. P. Tangney (Eds.), *Handbook of self and identity* (2nd ed., pp. 425–445). New York, NY: Guilford.

Silvia, P. J., & Gendolla, G. H. E. (2001). On introspection and self-perception: Does self-focused attention enable accurate self-knowledge? *Review of General Psychology, 5*, 241–269.

Simeon, D. & Loewenstein, R. J. (2009). Dissociative disorders. In B. J. Sadock, V. A. Sadock, & P. Ruiz (Eds.), *Kaplan & Sadock's comprehensive textbook of psychiatry* (pp. 1965–2026). Philadelphia: Lippincott Williams & Wilkins.

Simon, G. E., & Savarino, J. (2007). Suicide attempts among patients starting depression treatment with medications or psychotherapy. *American Journal of Psychiatry, 164*, 1029–1034.

Simon, G. E., Savarino, J., Operskalski, B., & Wang, P. S. (2006). Suicide risk during antidepressant treatment. *American Journal of Psychiatry, 163*, 41–47.

Simon, R. I. (2011). *Preventing patient suicide: Clinical assessment and management.* Washington, DC: American Psychiatric Publishing.

Simpson, J. A. (1987). The dissolution of romantic relationships: Factors involved in relationship stability and emotional distress. *Journal of Personality and Social Psychology, 53*, 683–692.

Simpson, J. A., Collins, W., & Salvatore, J. E. (2011). The impact of early interpersonal experience on adult romantic relationship functioning: Recent findings from the Minnesota longitudinal study of risk and adaptation. *Current Directions in Psychological Science, 20*(6), 355–359. doi:10.1177/0963721411418468

Simpson, J. R. (2008). Functional MRI lie detection: Too good to be true? *Journal of the American Academy of Psychiatry and the Law, 36*, 491–498.

Sinclair, R. C., Mark, M. M., & Clore, G. L. (1994). Mood-related persuasion depends on (mis)attributions. *Social Cognition, 12*, 309–326.

Singer, A. R., Cassin, S. E., & Dobson, K. S. (2005). The role of gender in the career aspirations of professional psychology graduates: Are there more similarities than differences? *Canadian Psychology, 46*(4), 215–222.

Singer, M. T. (2003). *Cults in our midst.* San Francisco: Jossey-Bass.

Singh, D. (1993). Adaptive significance of female physical attractiveness: Role of waist-to-hip ratio. *Journal of Personality and Social Psychology, 65*, 293–307.

Singh, D. (1995). Female judgment of male attractiveness and desirability for relationships: Role of waist-to-hip ratio and financial status. *Journal of Personality and Social Psychology, 69*, 1089–1101.

Singleton, R, A., Jr., & Vacca, J. (2007). Interpersonal competition in friendships. *Sex Roles, 57*, 617–627.

Sinke, C. A., Kret, M. E., & de Gelder, B. (2012). Body language: Embodied perception of emotion. In B. Berglund, G. B. Rossi, J. T. Townsend, & L. R. Pendrill (Eds.), *Measurement with persons: Theory, methods, and implementation areas* (pp. 335–352). New York, NY: Psychology Press.

Skinner, B. F. (1953). *Science and human behavior.* New York, NY: Macmillan.

Skinner, B. F. (1974). *About behaviorism.* New York, NY: Knopf.

Skinner, B. F. (1990). Can psychology be a science of mind? *American Psychologist, 45*, 1206–1210.

Skinner, B. F. (1991). Why we are not acting to save the world. In W. Ishaq (Ed.), *Human behavior in today's world* (pp. 19–29). New York, NY: Praeger.

Skinner, E. A., Edge, K., Altman, J., & Sherwood, H. (2003). Searching for the structure of coping: A review and critique of category systems for classifying ways of coping. *Psychological Bulletin, 129*, 216–269.

Skinner, P. H., & Shelton, R. L. (1985). *Speech, language, and hearing: Normal processes and disorders* (2nd ed.). New York, NY: Wiley.

Skowronski, J. J., & Carlston, D. E. (1992). Caught in the act: When impressions are based on highly diagnostic information behaviours are resistant to contradiction. *European Journal of Social Psychology, 22*, 435–452.

Slashinki, M. J., Coker, A. L., & Davis, K. E. (2003). Physical aggression, forced sex, and stalking victimization by a dating partner: An analysis of the National Violence Against Women Survey. *Violence & Victims, 18*(6), 595–617.

Sloan Work and Family Research Network. (2009). Questions and answers about women in the workforce. *A Sloan Work and Family Research Network Fact Sheet.* Retrieved from http://wfnetwork.bc.edu/statistics.php

Slonim-Nevo, V., & Al-Krenawi, A. (2006). Success and failure among polygamous families: The experience of wives, husbands, and children. *Family Process, 45*, 311–330.

Slovic, P., Finucane, M. L., Peters, E., & MacGregor, D. G. (2004). Risk as analysis and risk as feelings: Some thoughts about affect, reason, risk, and rationality. *Risk Analysis, 24*, 311–322.

Slowinski, J. (2007). Sexual problems and dysfunctions in men. In A. F. Owens & M. S. Tepper (Eds.), *Sexual Health: Vol. 4. State-of-the-art treatments and research* (pp. 1–14). Westport, CT: Praeger Publishers/Greenwood Publishing Group.

Small, D. A., Gelfand, M., Babcock, L., & Gettman, H. (2007). Who goes to the bargaining table? The influence of gender and framing on the initiation of negotiation. *Journal of Personality and Social Psychology, 93*, 600–613.

Smetana, J. G. (2009). Parent-adolescent communication. In H. T. Reis & S. Sprecher (Eds.), *Encyclopedia of human relationships: Vol. 3* (pp. 1189–1193). Los Angeles: Sage Reference Publication.

Smiler, A. P. (2004). Thirty years after the discovery of gender: Psychological concepts and measures of masculinity. *Sex Roles, 50*(1–2), 15–26.

Smith, A. K. (2000, November 6). Charting your own course. *U.S. News & World Report*, 56–60, 62, 64–65.

Smith, C. A., Johnston-Robledo, I, McHugh, M. C., & Chrisler, J. C. (2010). Words matter: The language of gender. In J. C. Chrisler & D. R. McCreary (Eds.), *Handbook of gender research in psychology* (Vol. 1, pp. 361–377). New York, NY: Springer.

Smith, G. S., Branas, C. C., & Miller, T. R. (1999). Fatal nontraffic injuries involving alcohol: A meta-analysis. *Annals of Emergency Medicine, 33*(6), 659–668.

Smith, J. A., McPherson, M., & Smith-Lovin, L. (2009). Social isolation. In H. T. Reis & S. Sprecher (Eds.), *Encyclopedia of human relationships: Vol. 3* (pp. 1529–1531). Los Angeles: Sage Reference Publication.

Smith, J. L., Hardy, T., & Arkin, R. (2009). When practice doesn't make perfect: Effort expenditure as an active behavioral self-handicapping strategy. *Journal of Research in Personality, 43*(1), 95–98.

Smith, M. (2003, January). Employee health affects more than the bottom line. *IPMA News*, pp. 8–10.

Smith, M., & Pazder, L. (1980). *Michelle remembers.* New York, NY: Pocket Books.

Smith, M. L., & Glass, G. V. (1977). Meta-analysis of psychotherapy outcome studies. *American Psychologist, 32*, 752–760.

Smith, R. E. (1989). Effects of coping skills training on generalized self-efficacy and locus of control. *Journal of Personality and Social Psychology, 56*, 228–233.

Smith, S. M., & Caprariello, P. A. (2009). Liking. In H. T. Reis & S. Sprecher (Eds.), *Encyclopedia of human relationships: Vol. 2* (pp. 978–982). Los Angeles: Sage Reference Publication.

Smith, S. M., & Gleaves, D. H. (2007). Recovered memories. In M. P. Toglia, J. D. Read, D. F. Ross, & R. C. L. Lindsay (Eds.), *Handbook of eyewitness psychology: Volume 1. Memory for events.* Mahwah, NJ: Erlbaum.

Smith, S. W., & Wilson, S. R. (2010). *New directions in interpersonal communication research.* Thousand Oaks, CA: Sage.

Smith, T. W. (2003). Hostility and health: Current status of a psychosomatic hypothesis. In P. Salovey & A. J. Rothman (Eds.), *Social psychology of health.* New York, NY: Psychology Press.

Smith, T. W. (2006). Personality as risk and resilience in physical health. *Current Directions in Psychological Science, 15*, 227–231.

Smith, T. W., & Gallo, L. C. (1999). Hostility and cardiovascular reactivity during marital interaction. *Psychosomatic Medicine, 61*, 436–445.

Smith, T. W., & Gallo, L. C. (2001). Personality traits as risk factors for physical illness. In A. Baum, T. A. Revenson, & J. E. Singer (Eds.), *Handbook of health psychology.* Mahwah, NJ: Erlbaum.

Smith, T. W., Glazer, K., & Ruiz, J. M. (2004). Hostility, anger, aggressiveness, and coronary heart disease: An interpersonal perspective on personality, emotion, and health. *Journal of Personality, 72*, 1217–1270.

Smith, T. W., Pope, M. K., Sanders, J. D., Allred, K. D., & O'Keefe, J. L. (1988). Cynical hostility at home and work: Psychosocial vulnerability across domains. *Journal of Research in Personality, 22*, 525–548.

Smith, W. P., Compton, W. C., & West, W. B. (1995). Meditation as an adjunct to a happiness enhancement program. *Journal of Clinical Psychology, 51*, 269–273.

Smock, P. J., Manning, W. D., & Gupta, S. (1999). The effect of marriage and divorce on women's economic well-being. *American Sociological Review, 64*, 794–812.

Smolak, L. (2006). Body image. In J. Worrell & C. D. Goodheart (Eds.), *Handbook of girls' and women's psychological health.* New York, NY: Oxford University Press.

Smyth, J., Litcher, L., Hurewitz, A., & Stone, A. (2001). Relaxation training and cortisol secretion in adult asthmatics. *Journal of Health Psychology, 6*(2), 217–227.

Smyth, J. M., & Pennebaker, J. W. (1999). Sharing one's story: Translating emotional experiences into words as a coping tool. In C. R. Snyder (Ed.), *Coping: The psychology of what works.* New York, NY: Oxford University Press.

Smyth, J. M., & Pennebaker, J. W. (2001). What are the health effects of disclosure? In A. Baum, T. A. Revenson, & J. E. Singer (Eds.), *Handbook of health psychology.* Mahwah, NJ: Erlbaum.

Smyth, J. M., Pennebaker, J. W., & Arigo, D. (2012). What are the health effects of disclosure? In A. Baum, T. A. Revenson, J. Singer (Eds.), *Handbook of health psychology* (2nd ed., pp. 175–191). New York, NY: Psychology Press.

Snell, J. C., & Marsh, M. (2008). Life cycle loneliness curve. *Psychology and Education: An Interdisciplinary Journal, 45*, 26–28.

Snowden, L. R., & Yamada, A. (2005). Cultural differences in access to care. *Annual Review of Clinical Psychology, 1*, 143–166.

Snyder, C. R. (1994/2000). *The psychology of hope: You can get there from here.* New York, NY: Free Press.

Snyder, C. R. (2002). Hope theory: Rainbows of the mind. *Psychological Inquiry, 13*, 249–275.

Snyder, C. R., Harris, C., Anderson, J. R., Holeran, S. A., Irving, L. M., Sigmon, S. T., . . . & Harney, P. (1991). The will and the ways: Development and validation of an individual-differences measure of hope. *Journal of Personality and Social Psychology, 60*, 570–585.

Snyder, C. R., Hoza, B., Pelham, W. E., Rapoff, M., Ware, L., Danovsky, M., Highberger, L., Rubenstein, H., & Stahl, K. J. (1997). The development and validation of the Children's Hope Scale. *Journal of Pediatric Psychology, 22*, 399–421.

Snyder, C. R., & Lopez, S. J. (2007). *Positive psychology: The scientific and practical exploration of human strengths.* Thousand Oaks, CA: Sage.

Snyder, C. R., Rand, K. L., & Sigmon, D. R. (2002). Hope theory: A member of the positive psychology family. In C. R. Snyder & S. J. Lopez (Eds.), *Handbook of positive psychology* (pp. 257–276). New York, NY: Oxford.

Snyder, C. R., Sympson, S. C., Ybasco, F. C., Borders, T. F., Babyak, M. A., & Higgins, R. L. (1996). Development and validation of the State Hope Scale. *Journal of Personality and Social Psychology, 70*, 321–335.

Snyder, M. (1986). *Public appearances/Private realities: The psychology of self-monitoring.* New York, NY: Freeman.

Society for Human Resource Management (SHRM). (2011). *2011 Employee benefits: Examining employee benefits amidst uncertainty.* Alexandria, VA: Society for Human Resource Management.

Solberg, E. C., Diener, E., Wirtz, D., Lucas, R. E., & Oishi, S. (2002). Wanting, having, and satisfaction: Examining the role of desire discrepancies in satisfaction with income. *Journal of Personality and Social Psychology, 83*(3), 725–734.

Solomon, S., Greenberg, J. L., & Pyszczynski, T. (1991). A terror management theory of social behavior: The psychological functions of self-esteem and cultural worldviews. In M. Zanna (Ed.), *Advances in experimental social psychology* (Vol. 24). Orlando, FL: Academic Press.

Solomon, S., Greenberg, J., & Pyszczynski, T. (2004a). The cultural animal: Twenty years of terror management. In J. Greenberg, S. L. Koole, & T. Pyszczynski (Eds.), *Handbook of experimental existential psychology.* New York, NY: Guilford Press.

Solomon, S., Greenberg, J., & Pyszczynski, T. (2004b). Lethal consumption: Death-denying materialism. In T. Kasser, & A. D. Kanner (Eds.), *Psychology and consumer culture: The struggle for a good life in a materialistic world.* Washington, DC: American Psychological Association.

Solomon, S. E., Rothblum, E. D., & Balsam, K. F. (2004). Pioneers in partnership: Lesbian and gay male couples in civil unions compared with those not in civil unions and married heterosexual siblings. *Journal of Family Psychology, 18*, 275–286.

Solowij, N., Stephens, R. S., Roffman, R. A., Babor, T., Kadden, R., Miller, M., Christiansen. K., McRee, B., & Vendetti, J. (2002). Cognitive functioning of long-term heavy cannabis users seeking treatment. *Journal of the American Medical Association, 287*, 1123–1131.

Son Hing, L. S., Bobocel, D. R., & Zanna, M. P. (2007). Authoritarian dynamics and unethical decision making: High social dominance orientation leaders and high right wing authoritarianism followers. *Journal of Personality and Social Psychology, 92*, 67–81.

Son Hing, L. S., Li, W., & Zanna, M. P. (2002). Inducing hypocrisy to reduce prejudicial responses among aversive racists. *Journal of Experimental Social Psychology, 38*, 71–78.

Song, Z., & Chon, K. (2012). General self-efficacy's effect on career choice goals via vocational interests and person–job fit: A mediation model. *International Journal of Hospitality Management, 31*(3), 798–808. doi:10.1016/j.ijhm.2011.09.016

Sonnentag, S. (2012). Psychological detachment from work during leisure time: The benefits of mentally disengaging from work. *Current Directions in Psychological Science, 21*(2), 114–118. doi:10.1177/0963721411434979

Sonnentag, S., & Frese, M. (2003). Stress in organizations. In W. C. Borman, D. R. Ilgen, & R. J. Klimoski (Eds.), *Handbook of psychology: Vol. 12. Industrial and organizational psychology.* New York, NY: Wiley.

South, S. J., Bose, S., & Trent, K. (2004). Anticipating divorce: Spousal agreement, predictive accuracy, and effects on labor supply and fertility. *Journal of Divorce and Remarriage, 40*(3–4), 1–22.

Souza, R., Bernatsky, S., Reyes, R., & de Jong, K. (2007). Mental health status of vulnerable tsunami-affected communities: A survey in Aceh Province, Indonesia. *Journal of Traumatic Stress, 20*, 263–269.

Spanos, N. P. (1996). *Multiple identities and false memories.* Washington, DC: American Psychological Association.

Sparrevohn, R. M., & Rapee, R. M. (2009). Self-disclosure, emotional expression and intimacy within romantic relationships of people with social phobia. *Behaviour Research and Therapy, 47*(12), 1074–1078. doi:10.1016/j.brat.2009.07.016

Special, W. P., & Li-Barber, K. T. (2012). Self-disclosure and student satisfaction with Facebook. *Computers In Human Behavior, 28*(2), 624–630. doi:10.1016/j.chb.2011.11.008

Spelke, E. S. (2005). Sex differences in intrinsic aptitude for mathematics and science? *American Psychologist, 60,* 950–958.

Spence, I., Yu, J. J., Feng, J., & Marshman, J. (2009). Women match men when learning a spatial skill. *Journal of Experimental Psychology, 35,* 1097–1103.

Spence, J. T. (1983). Comment on Lubinski, Tellegen, and Butcher's "Masculinity, femininity, and androgyny viewed and assessed as distinct concepts." *Journal of Personality and Social Psychology, 44,* 440–446.

Spencer, P. T. (1990). Exercise as psychotherapy. *Counseling Psychology Quarterly, 3*(3), 291–293.

Spencer, S. J., Steele, C. M., & Quinn, D. M. (1999). Stereotype threat and women's math performance. *Journal of Experimental Social Psychology, 35*(1), 4–28.

Sperry, L. (2006). *Psychological treatment of chronic illness: The biopsychosocial therapy approach.* Washington, DC: American Psychological Association.

Sperry, R. W. (1982). Some effects of disconnecting the cerebral hemispheres. *Science, 217,* 1223–1226, 1250.

Spiegler, M. D., & Guevremont, D. C. (2010). *Contemporary behavior therapy* (5th ed.). Belmont, CA: Wadsworth.

Spinda, J. W. (2011). The development of basking in reflected glory (BIRGing) and cutting off reflected failure (CORFing) measures. *Journal of Sport Behavior, 34*(4), 392–420.

Spitz, H. I. (2009). Group psychotherapy. In B. J. Sadock, V. A. Sadock, & P. Ruiz (Eds.), *Kaplan & Sadock's comprehensive textbook of psychiatry* (pp. 2832–2856). Philadelphia: Lippincott Williams & Wilkins.

Spitz, H. I., & Spitz, S. (2009). Family and couple therapy. In B. J. Sadock, V. A. Sadock, & P. Ruiz (Eds.), *Kaplan & Sadock's comprehensive textbook of psychiatry* (pp. 2845–2856). Philadelphia, PA: Lippincott, Williams & Wilkins.

Spitzberg, B. H. (2011). Intimate partner violence and aggression: Seeing the light in a dark place. In W. R. Cupach & B. H. Spitzberg (Eds.), *The dark side of close relationships II.* (pp. 327–380). New York, NY: Routledge.

Spokane, A. R., & Cruza-Guet, M. C. (2005). Holland's theory of vocational personalities in work environments. In S. D. Brown & R. W. Lent (Eds.), *Career development and counseling: Putting theory and research to work.* Hoboken, NJ: Wiley.

Sporer, S. L., & Schwandt, B. (2007). Moderators of nonverbal indicators of deception: A meta-analytic synthesis. *Psychology, Public Policy, and Law, 13,* 1–34.

Sprecher, S. (1994). Two sides to the breakup of dating relationships. *Personal Relationships, 1,* 199–222.

Sprecher, S. (2002). Sexual satisfaction in premarital relationships: Associations with satisfaction, love, commitment, and stability. *The Journal of Sex Research, 39*(3), 190–196.

Sprecher, S. (2011). Internet mathing services: The good, the bad, and the ugly (disguised as attractive). In W. R. Cupach & B. H. Spitzberg (Eds.), *The dark side of close relationships II* (pp. 119–143). New York, NY: Routledge.

Sprecher, S., & Cate, R. M. (2004). Sexual satisfaction and sexual expression as predictors of relationship satisfaction and stability. In J. H. Harvey, A. Wenzel, & S. Sprecher (Eds.), *The handbook of sexuality and close relationships.* Mahwah, NJ: Lawrence Erlbaum.

Sprecher, S., Christopher, F. S., & Cate, R. (2006). Sexuality in close relationships. In A. L. Vangelisti & D. Perlman (Eds.), *The Cambridge handbook of personal relationships.* New York, NY: Cambridge University Press.

Sprecher, S., & Felmlee, D. (2008). Insider perspectives on attraction. In S. Sprecher, A. Wenzel, & J. Harvey (Eds.), *Handbook of relationship initiation* (pp. 297–314). New York, NY: Psychology Press.

Sprecher, S., Sullivan, Q., & Hatfield, E. (1994). Mate selection preferences: Gender differences examined in a national sample. *Journal of Personality and Social Psychology, 66,* 1074–1080.

Sprecher, S., Zimmerman, C., & Abrahams, E. M. (2010). Choosing compassionate strategies to end a relationship: Effects of compassionate love for partner and the reason for the breakup. *Social Psychology, 41*(2), 66–75. doi:10.1027/1864-9335/a000010

Springer, S. P., & Deutsch, G. (1998). *Left brain, right brain.* New York: Freeman.

Stafford, L. (2010). Geographic distance and communication during courtship. *Communication Research, 37*(2), 275–297. doi:10.1177/0093650209356390

Stafford, L., & Canary, D. J. (1991). Maintenance strategies and romantic relationship type, gender and relational characteristics. *Journal of Social and Personal Relationships, 8,* 217–242.

Stafford, L., & Canary, D. J. (2006). Equity and interdependence as predictors of relational maintenance strategies. *The Journal of Family Communication, 6,* 227–254.

Staines, G. L. (2008). The relative efficacy of psychotherapy: Reassessing the methods-based paradigm. *Review of General Psychology, 12*(4), 330–343.

Staines, G. L., & Cleland, C. M. (2007). Bias in meta-analytic estimates of the absolute efficacy of psychotherapy. *Review of General Psychology, 11*(4), 329–347.

Stajkovic, A. D., & Luthans, F. (1998). Self-efficacy and work-related performance: A meta-analysis. *Psychological Bulletin, 124*(2), 240–261.

Stake, J. E. & Eisele, H. (2010). Gender and personality. In J. C. Chrisler & D. R. McCreary (Eds.), *Handbook of gender research in psychology* (Vol. 2, pp. 19–40). New York, NY: Springer.

Stalder, D. R. (2009). Competing roles for the subfactors of need for closure in committing the fundamental attribution error. *Personality and Individual Differences, 47*(7), 701–705.

Stamatakis, E., Hillsdon, M., Mishra, G., Hamer, M., & Marmot, M. (2009). Television viewing and other screen-based entertainment in relation to multiple socioeconomic status indicators and area deprivation: The Scottish Health Survey 2003. *Journal of Epidemiology and Community Health, 63,* 734–740. doi:10.1136/jech.2008.085902

Stambush, M. A., & Mattingly, B. A. (2010). When being liked makes us dislike ourselves: Self-rated attractiveness as influenced by an attractive or unattractive other's romantic interest in the self. *North American Journal of Psychology, 12*(2), 341–354.

Stamler, J., Daviglus, M. L., Garside, D. B., Dyer, A. R., Greenland, P., & Neaton, J. D. (2000). Relationship of baseline serum cholesterol levels in 3 large cohorts of younger men to long-term coronary, cardiovascular, and all-cause mortality and to longevity. *Journal of the American Medical Association, 284,* 311–318.

Stanley, M. A. & Beidel, D. C. (2009). Behavior therapy. In B. J. Sadock, V. A. Sadock, & P. Ruiz (Eds.), *Kaplan & Sadock's comprehensive textbook of psychiatry* (pp. 2781–2803). Philadelphia: Lippincott Williams & Wilkins.

Stanley, S. M., & Rhoades, G. K. (2009). Cohabitation. In H. T. Reis & S. Sprecher (Eds.), *Encyclopedia of human relationships: Vol. 2* (pp. 229–231). Los Angeles: Sage Reference Publication.

Stanley, S. M., Rhoades, G. K., Amato, P. R., Markman, H. J., & Johnson, C. A. (2010). The timing of cohabitation and engagement: Impact on first and second marriages. *Journal of Marriage and Family, 72*(4), 906–918. doi:10.1111/j.1741-3737 .2010.00738.x

Stanley, S. M., Whitton, S. W., & Markman, H. J. (2004). Maybe I do? Interpersonal commitment and premarital or nonmarital cohabitation. *Journal of Family Issues, 25,* 496–519.

Stanton, A. L. (2011). Regulating emotions during stressful experiences: The adaptive utility of coping through emotional approach. In S. Folkman (Ed.). *The Oxford handbook of stress, health, & coping* (pp. 369–386). New York, NY: Oxford University Press.

Stanton, A. L., Lobel, M., Sears, S., & DeLuca, R. S. (2002). Psychosocial aspects of selected issues in women's reproductive health: Current status and future directions. *Journal of Consulting & Clinical Psychology, 70*(3), 751–770.

Stapel, D. A., & Suls, J. (2004). Method matters: Effects of explicit versus implicit social comparisons on activation, behavior, and self-views. *Journal of Personality and Social Psychology, 87,* 860–875.

Starker, S. (1992). Characteristics of self-help book readers among VA medical outpatients. *Medical Psychotherapy: An International Journal, 5,* 89–93.

Stead, L. F., Perera, R., Bullen, C., Mant, D., & Lancaster, T. (2008). Nicotine replacement therapy for smoking cessation. *Cochrane Database of Systematic Reviews,* Cochrane AN: CD000146.

Steel, P. (2007). The nature of procrastination: A meta-analytic and theoretical review of quintessential self-regulatory failure. *Psychological Bulletin, 133*(1), 65–94.

Steel, P., Schmidt, J., & Shultz, J. (2008). Refining the relationship between personality and subjective well-being. *Psychological Bulletin, 134,* 138–161. doi:10.1037/0033-2909.134.1.138

Steele, C. M. (1992, April). Race and the schooling of black Americans. *The Atlantic Monthly,* 68–78.

Steele, C. M. (1997). A threat in the air: How stereotypes shape intellectual identity and performance. *American Psychologist, 52,* 613–629.

Steele, C. M. (2011). *Whistling Vivaldi: How stereotypes affect us and what we can do.* New York, NY: Norton.

Steele, C. M., & Aronson, J. (1995). Stereotype threat and the intellectual test performance of African Americans. *Journal of Personality and Social Psychology, 69,* 797–811.

Steele, C. M., Spencer, S. J., & Lynch, M. (1993). Self-image resilience and dissonance: The role of affirmational resources. *Journal of Personality and Social Psychology, 64,* 885–896.

Steiger, H., & Bruce, K. R. (2009). Eating disorders. In P. H. Blaney & T. Millon (Eds.), *Oxford textbook of psychopathology* (pp. 431–451). New York, NY: Oxford University Press.

Steiger, H., Bruce, K. R., & Israël, M. (2003). Eating disorders. In G. Stricker & T. A. Widiger (Eds.), *Handbook of psychology: Vol. 8. Clinical psychology.* New York, NY: Wiley.

Steil, J. M. (2009). Dual-earner couples. In H. T. Reis & S. Sprecher (Eds.), *Encyclopedia of human relationships: Vol. 2* (pp. 469–471). Los Angeles: Sage Reference Publication.

Steinberg, L., & Monahan, K. C. (2011). Adolescents' exposure to sexy media does not hasten the initiation of sexual intercourse. *Developmental Psychology, 47*(2), 562–576. doi:10.1037/a0020613

Steinbrook, R. (2004). The AIDS epidemic in 2004. *New England Journal of Medicine, 351,* 115–117.

Steiner, H., Erickson, S. J., MacLean, P., Medic, S., Plattner, B., & Koopman, C. (2007). Relationship between defenses, personality, and affect during a stress task in normal adolescents. *Child Psychiatry Human Development, 38,* 107–119.

Steinfeldt, J. A., Vaughan, E. L., LaFollette, J. R., & Steinfeldt, M. C. (2012). Bullying among adolescent football players: Role of masculinity and moral atmosphere. *Psychology of Men and Masculinity, 13*(4), 340–353.

Steinhausen, H. (2002). The outcome of anorexia nervosa in the 20th century. *American Journal of Psychiatry, 159,* 1284–1293.

Stelmack, R. M. & Rammsayer, T. H. (2008). Psychophysiological and biochemical correlates of personality. In G. J. Boyle, G. Matthews, D. H. Saklofske (Eds.), *The sage handbook of personality theory and assessment* (pp. 33–55). Los Angeles: Sage.

Stephens, N. M., Markus, H. R., & Townsend, S. S. M. (2007). Choice as an act of meaning: The case of social class. *Journal of Personality and Social Psychology, 93,* 814–830.

Sternberg, R. J. (1986). A triangular theory of love. *Psychological Review, 93,* 119–135.

Sternberg, R. J. (1988). Triangulating love. In R. J. Sternberg & M. L. Barnes (Eds.), *The psychology of love.* New Haven, CT: Yale University Press.

Sternberg, R. J. (2006). A duplex theory of love. In R. J. Sternberg & K. Weis (Eds.), *The New Psychology of Love* (pp. 184–199). New Haven, CT: Yale University Press.

Stets, J. E., & Burke, P. J. (2003). A sociological approach to self and identity. In M. R. Leary & J. P. Tangney (Eds.), *Handbook of self and identity* (pp. 128–152). New York, NY: Guilford.

Stevens, C., & Bavelier, D. (2012). The role of selective attention on academic foundations: A cognitive neuroscience perspective. *Developmental Cognitive Neuroscience, 2*(Suppl 1), S30–S48. doi:10.1016/j.dcn.2011.11.001

Stevens, D. P., Minnotte, K. L., Mannon, S. E., & Kiger, G. (2007). Examining the "neglected side of the work-family interface": Antecedents of positive and negative family-to-work spillover. *Journal of Family Issues, 28,* 242–262.

Stewart-Knox, B. J., Sittlington, J., Rugkasa, J., Harrisson, S., Treacy, M. & Abauza, P. S. (2005). Smoking and peer groups: Results from a longitudinal qualitative study of young people in Northern Ireland. *British Journal of Social Psychology, 44,* 397–414.

Stinson, D., Cameron, J. J., Wood, J. V., Gaucher, D., & Holmes, J. G. (2009). Deconstructing the "reign of error": Interpersonal warmth explains the self-fulfilling prophecy of anticipated acceptance. *Personality and Social Psychology Bulletin, 35*(9), 1165–1178. doi:10.1177/0146167209338629

Stith, S. M., Rosen, K. H., Middleton, K. A., Busch, A. L., Lundeberg, K., & Carlton, R. P. (2000). The intergenerational transmission of spouse abuse: A meta-analysis. *Journal of Marriage and the Family, 62,* 640–654.

Stith, S. M., Smith, D. B., Penn, C. E., Ward, D. B., & Tritt, D. (2004). Intimate partner physical abuse perpetration and victimization risk factors: A meta-analytic review. *Aggression and Violent Behavior, 10,* 65–98.

Stokstad, E. (2009, November 25). Americans' eating habits more wasteful than ever. *ScienceNOW.* Retrieved from http://news.sciencemag.org/sciencenow/2009/11/25-01.html?ref=hp

Stoll, B. M., Arnaut, G. L., Fromme, D. K., & Felker-Thayer, J. A. (2005). Adolescents in stepfamilies: A qualitative analysis. *Journal of Divorce & Remarriage, 44,* 177–189.

Stone, A. A., Schwartz, J. E., Broderick, J. E., & Deaton, A. (2010). A snapshot of the age distribution of psychological well-being in the United States. *PNAS: Proceedings for the National Academy of Sciences, 107,* 9985–9990. doi:10.1073/pnas.1003744107

Stone, J., & McWhinnie, C. (2008). Evidence that blatant versus subtle stereotype threat cues impact performance through dual processes. *Journal of Experimental Social Psychology, 44*(2), 445–452.

Stone, P., & Lovejoy, M. (2004, November). Fast-track women and the "choice" to stay home. *Annals of the American Academy of Political and Social Science, 596,* 62–83.

Stone, W. N. (2008). Group psychotherapy. In A. Tasman, J. Kay, J. A. Lieberman, M. B. First, & M. Maj (Eds.), *Psychiatry* (3rd ed.). New York, NY: Wiley-Blackwell.

Stoney, C. M. (2003). Gender and cardiovascular disease: A psychobiological and integrative approach. *Current Directions in Psychological Science, 12*(4), 129–133.

Strahan, E. J., Lafrance, A., Wilson, A. E., Ethier, N., Spencer, S. J., & Zanna, M. P. (2008). Victoria's dirty secret: How sociocultural norms influence adolescent girls and women. *Personality and Social Psychology Bulletin, 34*(2), 288–301.

Strauss, B. & Kopp, R.. (2012). Rising Seas, Vanishing Coastlines. *New York Times* 25 Nov. 2012: 6(L).

Streeck, J., Goodwin, C., & LeBaron, C. (2011). *Embodied interaction: Language and body in the material world.* New York, NY: Cambridge University Press.

Striegel-Moore, R. H., & Bulik, C. M. (2007). Risk factors for eating disorders. *American Psychologist, 62,* 181–198.

Stroebe, K., Lodewijkx, H. F. M., & Spears, R. (2005). Do unto others as they do unto you: Reciprocity and social identification as determinants of ingroup favoritism. *Personality and Social Psychology Bulletin, 31,* 831–845.

Strother, E., Lemberg, R., Stanford, S., & Turberville, D. (2012). Eating disorders in men: Underdiagnosed, undertreated, and misunderstood. *Eating Disorders: The Journal of Treatment and Prevention, 20*(5), 346–355. doi:10.1080/10640266.2012.715512

Stunkard, A. J., Allison, K. C., Geliebter, A., Lundgren, J. D., Gluck, M. E., O'Reardon, J. P. (2009). Development of criteria for a diagnosis: Lessons from the night eating syndrome. *Comprehensive Psychiatry, 50*(5), 391–399.

Stunkard, A. J., Harris, J. R., Pederson, N. L., & McClearn, G. E. (1990). The body-mass index of twins who have been reared apart. *New England Journal of Medicine, 322,* 1483–1487.

Stunkard, A. J., Sorensen, T., Hanis, C., Teasdale, T. W., Chakraborty, R., Schull, W. J., & Schulsinger, F. (1986). An adoption study of human obesity. *New England Journal of Medicine, 314,* 193–198.

Suarez, E. C. (2004). C-reactive protein is associated with psychological risk factors of cardiovascular disease in apparently healthy adults. *Psychosomatic Medicine, 66*(5), 684–691.

Suarez, E. C., Saab, P. G., Llabre, M. M., Kuhn, C. M., & Zimmerman, E. (2004). Ethnicity, gender, and age effects on adrenoceptors and physiological responses to emotional stress. *Psychophysiology, 41,* 450–460.

Subotnik, K. L., Nuechterlein, K. H., Ventura, J., Gitlin, M. J., Marder, S., Mintz, J., et al. (2011). Risperidone nonadherence and return of positive symptoms in the early course of schizophrenia. *American Journal of Psychiatry, 168*(3), 286–292.

Substance Abuse and Mental Health Services Administration. (2011). Results from the 2010 National Survey on Drug Use and Health: Summary of National Findings, NSDUH Series H-41, HHS Publication No. (SMA) 11-4658. Rockville, MD: Substance Abuse and Mental Health Services Administration.

Sudak, H. S. (2005). Suicide. In B. J. Sadock & V. A. Sadock (Eds.), *Kaplan & Sadock's comprehensive textbook of psychiatry.* Philadelphia: Lippincott Williams & Wilkins.

Sudak, H. S. (2009). Suicide. In B. J. Sadock, V. A. Sadock, & P. Ruiz (Eds.), *Kaplan & Sadock's comprehensive textbook of psychiatry* (pp. 2717–2731). Philadelphia: Lippincott Williams & Wilkins.

Sue, D., Capodilupo, C. M., Nadal, K. L., & Torino, G. C. (2008). Racial microaggressions and the power to define reality. *American Psychologist, 63*(4), 277–279. doi:10.1037/0003-066X.63.4.277

Sue, S., Zane, N., Hall, G., & Berger, L. K. (2009). The case for cultural competency in psychotherapeutic interventions. *Annual Review of Psychology, 60,* 525–548. doi:10.1146/annurev.psych.60.110707.163651

Sue, S., Zane, N., & Young, K. (1994). Research on psychotherapy with culturally diverse populations. In A. E. Bergin & S. L. Garfield (Eds.), *Handbook of psychotherapy and behavior change* (4th ed.). New York, NY: John Wiley.

Sulloway, F. J. (1991). Reassessing Freud's case histories: The social construction of psychoanalysis. *ISIS, 82,* 245–275.

Sullum, J., Clark, M. M., & King, T. K. (2000). Predictors of exercise relapse in a college population. *Journal of American College Health, 48,* 175–180.

Suls, J., & Bunde, J. (2005). Anger, anxiety, and depression as risk factors for cardiovascular disease: The problems and implications of overlapping affective dispositions. *Psychological Bulletin, 131,* 260–300.

Sulsky, L., & Smith, C. (2005). *Work stress.* Belmont, CA: Wadsworth.

Sulsky, L., & Smith, C. (2007). Work stress: Macro-level work stressors. In A. Monat, R. S. Lazarus, & G. Reevy (Eds.), *The Praeger handbook on stress and coping* (pp. 53–86). Westport, CT: Praeger Publishers.

Summers, G., & Feldman, N. S. (1984). Blaming the perpetrator: An attributional analysis of spouse abuse. *Journal of Social and Clinical Psychology, 2,* 339–347.

Summers, L. (2005, January 14). Full transcript: President Summers' remarks at the National Bureau of Economic Research. *Harvard Crimson,* Retrieved April 26, 2007 from http://www.thecrimson.com/article.aspx?ref=505844.

Super, D. E. (1988). Vocational adjustment: Implementing a self-concept. *The Career Development Quarterly, 36,* 351–357.

Super, D. E. (1990). A life-span, life-space approach to career development. In D. Brown & L. Brooks (Eds.), *Career choice and development* (2nd ed., pp. 197–261). San Francisco, CA: Jossey-Bass.

Surra, C. A., Gray, C. R., Boettcher, T. M. J., Cottle, N. R., & West, A. R. (2006). From courtship to universal properties: Research on dating and mate selection, 1950 to 2003. In A. L. Vangelisti & D. Perlman (Eds.), *The Cambridge handbook of personal relationships.* New York, NY: Cambridge University Press.

Surtees, P. G., Wainwright, N. W., J., Luben, R., Day, N. E., & Khaw, K.-T. (2005). Prospective cohort study of hostility and the risk of cardiovascular disease mortality. *International Journal of Cardiology, 100,* 155–161.

Suschinsky, K. D., Lalumiere, M. L., & Chivers, M. L. (2009). Sex differences in patterns of genital sexual arousal: Measurement artifacts of true phenomena? *Archives of Sexual Behavior, 38,* 559–574.

Susman, E. J., Dorn, L. D., & Schiefelbein, V. L. (2003). Puberty, sexuality, and health. In R. M. Lerner, M.A. Easterbrooks, & J. Mistry (Eds.), *Handbook of psychology: Vol. 6. Developmental psychology.* New York, NY: Wiley.

Susser, E., Neugebauer, R., Hoek, H. W., Brown, A. S., Lin, S., Labovitz, D., & Gorman, J. M. (1996). Schizophrenia after prenatal famine: Further evidence. *Archives of General Psychiatry, 53,* 25–31.

Sussman, N. (2009). Selective serotonin reuptake inhibitors. In B. J. Sadock, V. A. Sadock, & P. Ruiz (Eds.), *Kaplan & Sadock's comprehensive textbook of psychiatry* (pp. 3190–3205). Philadelphia: Lippincott Williams & Wilkins.

Sutherland, V. J. (2000). Understimulation/boredom. In G. Fink (Ed.), *Encyclopedia of stress* (Vol. 3). San Diego: Academic Press.

Sutin, A. R., Ferrucci, L., Zonderman, A. B., & Terracciano, A. (2011). Personality and obesity across the adult life span. *Journal of Personality and Social Psychology, 101*(3), 579–592.

Swan, G. E., Hudmon, K. S., & Khroyan, T. V. (2003). Tobacco dependence. In A. M. Nezu, C. M. Nezu, & P. A. Geller (Eds.), *Handbook of psychology: Vol. 9. Health psychology.* New York, NY: Wiley.

Swank, J. M., & Daire, A. P. (2010). Multiple family adventure-based therapy groups: An innovative integration of two approaches. *The Family Journal: Counseling and Therapy for Couples and Families, 18*(3), 241–247.

Swann, W. B., Jr. (2012). Self-verification theory. In P. M. Van Lange, A. W. Kruglanski, E. Higgins (Eds.), *Handbook of theories of social psychology* (Vol 2, pp. 23–42). Thousand Oaks, CA: Sage Publications Ltd.

Swann, W. B., Jr., Chang-Schneider, C., & McClarty, K. L. (2007). Do people's self–views matter? Self-concept and self-esteem in everyday life. *American Psychologist, 62,* 84–94.

Swann, W. B., Jr., Rentfrow, P. J., & Guinn, J. S. (2003). Self-verification: The search for coherence. In M. R. Leary & J. P. Tangney (Eds.), *Handbook of self and identity.* New York, NY: Guilford.

Swann, W. B., Jr., Stein-Seroussi, A., & Giesler, R. (1992). Why people self-verify. *Journal of Personality and Social Psychology, 62*(3), 392–401. doi:10.1037/0022-3514.62.3.392

Swann, W. B., Jr., Stein-Seroussi, A., & McNulty, S. E. (1992). Outcasts in a white-lie society: The enigmatic worlds of people with negative self-conceptions. *Journal of Personality and Social Psychology, 62,* 618–624.

Swanson, J. L., & D'Achiardi, C. (2005). Beyond interests, needs/values, and abilities: Assessing other important career constructs over the life span. In S. D. Brown & R. W. Lent (Eds.), *Career development and counseling: Putting theory and research to work.* New York, NY: Wiley.

Swanson, S. A., Crow, S. J., Le Grange, D., Swendsen, J., & Merikangas, K. R. (2011). Prevalence and correlates of eating disorders in adolescents: Results from the national comorbidity survey replication adolescent supplement. *Archives of General Psychiatry, 68,* 714–723. doi:10.1001/archgenpsychiatry.2011.22

Sweeney, M. M., Wang, H., & Videon, T. M. (2009). Reconsidering the association between stepfather families and adolescent well-being. In H. E. Peters & C. M. K. Dush (Eds.), *Marriage and family: Perspectives and complexities* (pp. 177–225). New York, NY: Columbia University Press.

Swendsen, J., Burstein, M., Case, B., Conway, K. P., Dierker, L., He, J., & Merikangas, K. R. (2012). Use and abuse of alcohol and illicit drugs in US adolescents: Results of the National Comorbidity Survey-Adolescent Supplement. *Archives of General Psychiatry, 69*(4), 390–398. doi:10.1001/archgenpsychiatry.2011.1503

Swim, J. K., Johnston, K., & Pearson, N. B. (2009). Daily experiences with heterosexism: Relations between heterosexist hassles and psychological well-being. *Journal of Social and Clinical Psychology, 28,* 597–629.

Szasz, T. S. (1974). *The myth of mental illness.* New York, NY: HarperCollins.

Szasz, T. S. (1993). *A lexicon of lunacy: Metaphoric malady, moral responsibility, and psychiatry.* New Brunswick, NJ: Transaction.

Szigethy, E. M. & Friedman, E. S. (2009). Combined psychotherapy and pharmacology. In B. J. Sadock, V. A. Sadock, & P. Ruiz (Eds.), *Kaplan & Sadock's comprehensive textbook of psychiatry* (pp. 2923–2931). Philadelphia: Lippincott Williams & Wilkins.

Szlemko, W. J., Benfield, J. A., Bell, P. A., Deffenbacher, J. L., & Troup, L. (2008). Territorial markings as a predictor of driver aggression and road rage. *Journal of Applied Social Psychology, 38,* 1664–1688.

Tabi, M. M., Doster, C. C., & Cheney, T. T. (2010). A qualitative study of women in polygynous marriages. *International Nursing Review, 57*(1), 121–127. doi:10.1111/j.1466-7657.2009.00762.x

Tajfel, H. (1982). *Social identity and intergroup relations.* London: Cambridge University Press.

Takarangi, M. T., Polaschek, D. L., Garry, M., & Loftus, E. F. (2008). Psychological science, victim advocates, and the problem of recovered memories. *International Review of Victimology, 15*(2), 147–163.

Tal-Or, N. (2010). Direct and indirect self-promotion in the eyes of the perceivers. *Social Influence, 5*(2), 87–100. doi:10.1080/15534510903306489

Tam, C. S., Garnett, S. P., Cowell, C. T., Campbell, K., Cabrera, G., & Baur, L. A. (2006). Soft drink consumption and excess weight gain in Australian school students: Results from the Nepean study. *International Journal of Obesity, 30,* 1091–1093.

Tamborski, M., & Brown, R. P. (2011). The measurement of trait narcissism in social-personality research. In W. K. Campbell & J. D. Miller (Eds.), *The handbook of narcissism and narcissistic personality disorder: Theoretical approaches, empirical findings, and treatments* (pp. 133–140). New York, NY: John Wiley & Sons, Inc.

Tamir, M. (2009). What do people want to feel and why?: Pleasure and utility in emotion regulation. *Current Directions in Psychological Science, 18,* 101–105.

Tang, M. (2002). A comparison of Asian American, Caucasian American, and Chinese college students: An initial report. *Journal of Multicultural Counseling and Development, 30*(2), 124–134.

Tannen, D. (1990). *You just don't understand: Women and men in conversation.* New York, NY: Ballantine.

Tardy, C. H., & Dindia, K. (2006). Self-disclosure: Strategic revelation of information in personal and professional relationships. In O. Hargie (Ed.), *The handbook of communication skills* (3rd ed., pp. 229–266). New York, NY: Routledge.

Tashiro, T., Frazier, P., & Berman, M. (2006). Stress-related growth following divorce and relationship dissolution. In M. A. Fine & J. H. Harvey (Eds.), *Handbook of divorce and relationship resolution.* Mahwah, NJ: Erlbaum.

Tasker, F. (2005). Lesbian mothers, gay fathers, and their children: A review. *Journal of Developmental & Behavioral Pediatrics, 26,* 224–240.

Tavris, C. (1982). *Anger: The misunderstood emotion.* New York, NY: Simon & Schuster.

Tavris, C. (1989). *Anger: The misunderstood emotion* (2nd ed.). New York, NY: Simon & Schuster.

Taylor, D. A., & Altman, I. (1987). Communication in interpersonal relationships: Social penetration processes. In M. E. Roloff & G. R. Miller (Eds.), *Interpersonal processes: New directions in communication research.* Newbury Park, CA: Sage.

Taylor, E. (2001). Positive psychology and humanistic psychology: A reply to Seligman. *Journal of Humanistic Psychology, 41*(1), 13–29.

Taylor, L., Fiore, A. T., Mendelsohn, G. A., & Cheshire, C. (2011). "Out of my league": A real-world test of the matching hypothesis. *Personality and Social Psychology Bulletin, 37*(7), 942–954. doi:10.1177/0146167211409947

Taylor, M. C. (1995). White backlash to workplace affirmative action: Peril or myth? *Social Forces, 73,* 1385–1414.

Taylor, S. E. (1981). The interface of cognitive and social psychology. In J. Harvey (Ed.), *Cognition, social behavior, and the environment* (pp. 189–211). Hillsdale, NJ: Lawrence Erlbaum.

Taylor, S. E. (2007). Social support. In H. S. Friedman & R. C. Silver (Eds.), *Foundations of health psychology.* New York, NY: Oxford University Press.

Taylor, S. E. (2011a). Affiliation and stress. In S. Folkman (Ed.). *The Oxford handbook of stress, health, & coping* (pp. 86–100). New York, NY: Oxford University Press.

Taylor, S. E. (2011b). Positive illusions: How ordinary people become extraordinary. In M. Gernsbacher, R. W. Pew, L. M. Hough, & J. R. Pomerantz (Eds.), *Psychology and the real world: Essays illustrating fundamental contributions to society* (pp. 224–228). New York, NY: Worth Publishers.

Taylor, S. E., & Brown, J. D. (1988). Illusion and well-being: A social psychological perspective on mental health. *Psychological Bulletin, 103,* 193–210.

Taylor, S. E., & Brown, J. D. (1994). Positive illusions and well-being revisited: Separating fact from fiction. *Psychological Bulletin, 116,* 21–27.

Taylor, S. E., Cox, B. J., & Asmundson, J. G. (2009). Anxiety disorders: Panic and phobias. In P. H. Blaney & T. Millon (Eds.), *Oxford textbook of psychopathology* (pp. 119–145). New York, NY: Oxford University Press.

Taylor, S. E., Lerner, J. S., Sherman, D. K., Sage, R. M., & McDowell, N. K. (2003). Are self-enhancing cognitions associated with healthy or unhealthy biological profiles? *Journal of Personality and Social Psychology, 85*(4), 605–615.

Taylor, S. E., & Master, S. L. (2011). Social responses to stress: The tend-and-befriend model. In R. J. Contrada & A. Baum (Eds.), *The handbook of stress science: Biology, psychology, and health* (pp. 101–109). New York, NY: Springer.

Taylor, S. E., Sherman, D. K., Kim, H. S., Jarcho, J., Takagi, K., & Dunagan, M. S. (2004). Culture and social support: Who seeks it and why? *Journal of Personality, 87,* 354–362.

Taylor, S. E., & Stanton, A. L. (2007). Coping resources, coping processes, and mental health. *Annual Review of Clinical Psychology, 3,* 377–401. doi:10.1146/annurev.clinpsy.3.022806.091520

Teachman, J. D. (2003). Premarital sex, premarital cohabitation, and the risk of subsequent marital dissolution among women. *Journal of Marriage and Family, 65,* 444–445.

Teachman, J. D. (2009). Divorce, prevalence and trends. In H. T. Reis & S. Sprecher (Eds.), *Encyclopedia of human relationships: Vol. 2* (pp. 461–464). Los Angeles: Sage Reference Publication.

Tedeschi, R. G., & Calhoun, L. G. (1996). The traumatic growth inventory: Measuring the positive legacy of trauma. *Journal of Traumatic Stress, 9,* 455–471.

Tedeschi, R. G., & Calhoun, L. G. (2004). Posttraumatic growth: Conceptual foundations and empirical evidence. *Psychological Inquiry, 15*(1), 1–18.

Tedeschi, R. G., Park, C. L., & Calhoun, L. G. (Eds.). (1998). *Posttraumatic growth: Positive changes in the aftermath of crisis.* Mahwah, NJ: Erlbaum.

Teich, N. M. (2012). *Transgender 101: A simple guide to a complex issue.* New York, NY: Columbia University Press.

Tellegen, A., Lykken, D. T., Bouchard, T. J., Jr., Wilcox, K. J., Segal, N. L., & Rich, S. (1988). Personality similarity in twins reared apart and together. *Journal of Personality and Social Psychology, 54,* 1031–1039.

Temoshok, L. R. (2004). Type C coping/behavior pattern. In A. J. Christensen, R. Martin, & J. Morrision Smyth (Eds.), *Encyclopedia of health psychology* (pp. 332–333). New York, NY: Kluwer Academic/Plenum.

ten Brinke, L., MacDonald, S., Porter, S., & O'Connor, B. (2012). Crocodile tears: Facial, verbal and body language behaviours associated with genuine and fabricated remorse. *Law and Human Behavior, 36*(1), 51–59. doi:10.1037/h0093950

Teng, C. (2011). Who are likely to experience flow? Impact of temperament and character on flow. *Personality and Individual Differences, 50*(6), 863–868. doi:10.1016/j.paid.2011.01.012

Tennessen, C. M., & Cimprich, B. (1995). Views to nature: Effects on attention. *Journal of Environmental Psychology, 15,* 77–85.

Terracciano, A., Abdel-Khalak, A. M., Adam, N., Adamovova, L., Ahn, C. K., Ahn, H. N., et al. (2005). National character does not reflect mean personality trait levels in 49 cultures. *Science, 310,* 96–100.

Tesdeschi, R. G., & Calhoun, L. G. (Eds.). (1995). *Trauma and transformation: Growing in the aftermath of suffering.* Thousand Oaks, CA: Sage.

Tesser, A., Wood, J. V., & Stapel, D. A. (Eds.). (2005). *On building, defending, and regulating the self: A psychological perspective.* New York, NY: Psychology Press.

Testa, M., Vazile-Tamsen, C., & Livingston, J. A. (2004). The role of victim and perpetrator intoxication in sexual assault outcomes. *Journal of Studies on Alcohol, 65,* 320–329.

Tetlie, T., Eik-Nes, N., Palmstierna, T. Nottestad, J. A., & Callaghan, P. (2008). The effect of exercise on psychological & physical health outcomes: Preliminary results from a Norwegian forensic hospital. *Journal of Psychosocial Nursing & Mental Health Services, 46*(7), 39–43.

Tez, M., & Tez, S. (2008). Is cancer an adaptation mechanism to stress? *Cell Biology International, 32*(6), 713.

Thase, M. E. (2009). Neurobiological aspects of depression. In I. H. Gotlib & C. L. Hammen (Eds.), *Handbook of depression* (2nd ed., pp. 187–217). New York, NY: Guilford Press.

Thase, M. E., & Denko, T. (2008). Pharmacotherapy of mood disorders. *Annual Review of Clinical Psychology, 4,* 53–91.

Thayer, A., & Lynn, S. J. (2006). Guided imagery and recovered memory therapy: Considerations and cautions. *Journal of Forensic Psychology Practice, 6,* 63–73.

Thibaut, J. W., & Kelley, H. H. (1959). *The social psychology of groups.* New York, NY: Wiley.

Thobaben, M. (2005). Defense mechanisms and defense levels. *Home Health Care Management & Practice, 17,* 330–332.

Thomaes, S., & Bushman, B. J. (2011). Mirror, mirror, on the wall, who's the most aggressive of them all? Narcissism, self-esteem, and aggression. In P. R. Shaver & M. Mikulincer (Eds.), *Human aggression and violence: Causes, manifestations, and consequences* (pp. 203–219). Washington, DC: American Psychological Association. doi:10.1037/12346-011

Thomas, K. M. (2005). *Diversity dynamics in the workplace.* Belmont, CA: Wadsworth.

Thomas, S. P. (2011). In defense of defensive pessimism. *Issues in Mental Health Nursing, 32*(1), doi:10.3109/01612840.2011.535350

Thompson, J. K., & Kinder, B. (2003). Easting disorders. In M. Hersen & S. Turner (Eds.), *Handbook of adult psychopathology.* New York, NY: Plenum Press.

Thompson, J. K., & Stice, E. (2001). Thin-ideal internalization: Mounting evidence for a new risk factor for body-image disturbance and eating pathology. *Current Directions in Psychological Science, 10*(5), 181–183.

Thompson, J. K., Roehrig, M., & Kinder, B. N. (2007). Eating disorders. In M. Hersen, S. M. Turner, & D. C. Beidel (Eds.), *Adult psychopathology and diagnosis.* New York, NY: Wiley.

Thompson, N. J., Walker, E. R., Obolensky, N., Winning, A., Barmon, C., Dilorio, C., & Compton, M. T. (2010). Distance delivery of mindfulness-based cognitive therapy for depression: Project UPLIFT. *Epilepsy & Behavior, 19,* 247–254. doi:10.1016/j.yebeh.2010.07.031

Thornton, L. M., Mazzeo, S. E., & Bulik, C. M. (2011). The heritability of eating disorders: Methods and current findings. In R. H. Adan & W. H. Kaye (Eds.), *Behavioral neurobiology of eating disorders* (pp. 141–156). New York, NY: Springer-Verlag.

Thune, I., & Furberg, A. (2001). Physical activity and cancer risk: Dose-response and cancer, all sites and site specific. *Medicine and Science in Sports and Exercise, 33*(6), S530–S550.

Tice, D. M., & Baumeister, R. F. (1997). Longitudinal study of procrastination, performance, stress, and health: The cost and benefits of dawdling. *Psychological Science, 8,* 454–458.

Tice, D. M., Baumeister, R. F., Shmueli, D., & Muraven, M. (2007). Restoring the self: Positive affect helps improve self-regulation following ego depletion. *Journal of Experimental Social Psychology, 43*(3), 379–384.

Tice, D. M., Butler, J. L., Muraven M. B., & Stillwell A. M. (1995). When modesty prevails: Differential favorability of self-presentation to friends and strangers. *Journal of Personality and Social Psychology, 69,* 1120–1138.

Tice, D. M., & Wallace, H. M. (2003). The reflected self: Creating yourself as (you think) others see you. In M. R. Leary & J. P. Tangney (Eds.), *Handbook of self and identity.* New York, NY: Guilford.

Tiggemann, M., Martins, Y., & Kirkbride, A. (2007). Oh to be lean and muscular: Body image ideals in gay and heterosexual men. *Psychology of Men & Masculinity, 8,* 15–24.

Timm, D. A., & Slavin, J. L. (2008). Dietary fiber and the relationship to chronic diseases. *American Journal of Lifestyle Medicine, 2,* 233–240.

Titsworth, B. S., & Kiewra, K. A. (2004). Spoken organizational lecture cues and student notetaking as facilitators of student learning. *Contemporary Educational Psychology, 29,* 447–461.

To, M. L., Fisher, C. D., Ashkanasy, N. M., & Rowe, P. A. (2012). Within-person relationships between mood and creativity. *Journal of Applied Psychology, 97*(3), 599–612. doi:10.1037/a0026097

Toffler, A. (1980). *The third wave.* New York, NY: Bantam Books.

Tolin, D. F., & Foa, E. B. (2006). Sex differences in trauma and posttraumatic stress disorder: A quantitative review of 25 years of research. *Psychological Bulletin, 132,* 959–992.

Toma, C. L., & Hancock, J. T. (2010). Looks and lies: The role of physical attractiveness in online dating self-presentation and deception. *Communication Research, 37*(3), 335–351. doi:10.1177/0093650209356437

Tomfohr, L. M., Martin, T. M., & Miller, G. E. (2008). Symptoms of depression and impaired endothelial function in healthy adolescent women. *Journal of Behavioral Medicine, 31,* 137–143.

Toossi, M. (2007, November). Labor force projections to 2016: More workers in their golden years. *Monthly Labor Review,* 33–52.

Toossi, M. (2009, November). Labor force projections in 2018: Older workers staying more active. *Monthly Labor Review,* 30–51.

Torres, A. R., Prince, M. J., Bebbington, P. E., Bhugra, D., Brugha, T. S., Farrell, M., Jenkins, R., Lewis, G., Meltzer, H., & Singleton, N. (2006). Obsessive-compulsive disorder: Prevalence, comorbidity, impact, and help-seeking in the British national psychiatric morbidity survey of 2000. *American Journal of Psychiatry, 163,* 1978–1985.

Torres, L., & Saunders, S. M. (2009). Evaluation of psychotherapy. In B. J. Sadock, V. A. Sadock, & P. Ruiz (Eds.), *Kaplan & Sadock's comprehensive textbook of psychiatry* (9th ed.). Philadelphia, PA: Lippincott, Williams & Wilkins.

Torrey, E. F. (1992). *Freudian fraud: The malignant effect of Freud's theory on American thought and culture.* New York, NY: Harper Perennial.

Tortolero, S. R., Johnson, K., Peskin, M., Cuccaro, P. M., Markham, C., Hernandez, B. F., Addy, R. C., Shegog, R., & Li, D. H. (2011). Dispelling the myth: What parents really think about sex education in schools. *Journal of Applied Research on Children: Informing Policy for Children at Risk, 2*(2).

Tough, P. (2012). *How children succeed: Grit, curiosity, and the hidden power of character.* Boston, MA: Houghton Mifflin Harcourt.

Tov, W., & Diener, E. (2007). Culture and subjective well-being. In S. Kitayama & D. Cohen (Eds.), *Handbook of cultural psychology* (pp. 691–713). New York, NY: Guilford.

Trachtenberg, J. D., & Sande, M. A. (2002). Emerging resistance to nonnucleoside reverse transcriptase inhibitors: A warning and a challenge. *Journal of the American Medical Association, 288*(2), 239–241.

Tracy, E. (2006). *The student's guide to exam success* (2nd ed.). New York, NY: McGraw Hill.

Traut-Mattausch, E., Jones, E., Frey, D., & Zanna, M. P. (2011). Are there "his" and "her" types of decisions? Exploring gender differences in the confirmation bias. *Sex Roles, 65,* 223–233. doi:10.1007/s11199-011-0009-2

Travis, F. (2001). Autonomic and EEG patterns distinguish transcending from other experiences during Transcendental Meditation practice. *International Journal of Psychophysiology, 42,* 1–9.

Travis, L. A., Bliwise, N. G., Binder, J. L., & Horne-Moyer, H. L. (2001). Changes in clients' attachment style over the course of time-limited dynamic psychotherapy. *Psychotherapy: Theory, Research, Practice, Training, 38*(2), 149–159.

Treas, J., & Giesen, D. (2000). Sexual infidelity among married and cohabiting Americans. *Journal of Marriage and the Family, 62,* 48–60.

Trevithick, P., & Wengraf, T. (2011). Special issue: Defences and defensiveness. *Journal of Social Work Practice, 25*(4), 383–387. doi:10.1080/02650533.2011.626641

Triandis, H. C. (1994). *Culture and social behavior.* New York, NY: McGraw-Hill.

Triandis, H. C. (1995). *Individualism and collectivism.* Boulder, CO: Westview.

Triandis, H. C. (2001). Individualism-collectivism and personality. *Journal of Personality, 69*(6), 907–924.

Trope, Y. (1986). Self-enhancement and self-assessment in achievement behavior. In R. Sorrentino & E. T. Higgins (Eds.), *Handbook of motivation and cognition* (Vol. 2). New York, NY: Guilford Press.

Trope, Y., & Gaunt, R. (2003). Attribution and person perception. In M. A. Hogg & J. Cooper (Eds.), *The Sage handbook of social psychology.* Thousand Oaks, CA: Sage Publications.

Tropp, L. R., & Molina, L. E. (2012). Intergroup processes: From prejudice to positive relations between groups. In K. Deaux & M. Snyder (Eds.), *The Oxford handbook of personality and social psychology* (pp. 545–570). New York, NY: Oxford University Press.

Trotter, P. B. (2009). Divorce, effects on adults. In H. T. Reis & S. Sprecher (Eds.), *Encyclopedia of human relationships: Vol. 2* (pp. 458–461). Los Angeles: Sage Reference Publication.

Troy, A. B., Lewis-Smith, J., & Laurenceau, J. (2006). Interracial and intraracial romantic relationships: The search for differences in satisfaction, conflict, and attachment style. *Journal of Social & Personal Relationships, 23,* 65–80.

Trussell, J. (2004). Contraceptive efficacy. In R. A. Hatcher, J. Trussell, F. H. Stewart, A. L. Nelson, W. Cates Jr., F. Guest, & D. Kowal *Contraceptive technology.* New York, NY: Ardent Media.

Trzesniewski, K. H., Donnellan, M. B., & Robins, R. W. (2003). Stability of self-esteem across the life span. *Journal of Personality and Social Psychology, 84*(1), 205–220.

Tsutsumi, A., Kayaba, K., & Ishikawa, S. (2011). Impact of occupational stress on stroke across occupational classes and genders. *Social Science & Medicine, 72,* 1652–1658.

Tucker, O. N., Szomstein, S., & Rosenthal, R. J. (2007). Nutritional consequences of weight loss surgery. *Medical Clinics of North America, 91,* 499–513.

Tuerk, P. W., Yoder, M., Ruggiero, K. J., Gros, D. F., & Acierno, R. (2010). A pilot study for prolonged exposure therapy for posttraumatic stress disorder delivered via telehealth technology. *Journal of Traumatic Stress, 23,* 116–123. doi:10.1002/jts.20494

Tufekci, Z. (2008). Grooming, gossip, Facebook, and Myspace. What can we learn about these sites from those who won't assimilate? *Information, Communication, & Society, 11,* 544–564.

Tugade, M. M. (2011). Positive emotions and coping: Examining dual-process models of resilience. In S. Folkman (Ed.). *The Oxford handbook of stress, health, & coping* (pp. 186–199). New York, NY: Oxford University Press.

Turkle, S. (2011). *Alone together: Why we expect more from technology and less from each other.* New York, NY: Basic Books.

Turner, E. H., Matthews, A. M., Linardos, E., Tell, R. A., & Rosenthal, R. (2008). Selective publication of antidepressant trials and its influence on apparent efficacy. *The New England Journal of Medicine, 358,* 252–260.

Turner, J. C. (1987). *Rediscovering the social group: A self-categorization theory.* Oxford, England: Basil Blackwell.

Turner, J. C., & Reynolds, K. J. (2004). The social identity perspective in intergroup relations: Theories, themes, and controversies. In M. B. Brewer & M. Hewstone (Eds.), *Self and social identity.* Malden, MA: Blackwell.

Turner, J. R., & Wheaton, B. (1995). Checklist measurement of stressful life events. In S. Cohen, R. C. Kessler, & L. U. Gordon (Eds.), *Measuring stress: A guide for health and social scientists.* New York, NY: Oxford University Press.

Turner, J. S. (2011). Sex and the spectacle of music videos: An examination of the portrayal of race and sexuality in music videos. *Sex Roles, 64*(3–4), 173–191. doi:10.1007/s11199-010-9766-6

Turner-Bowker, D. M. (2001). How can you pull yourself up by your bootstraps if you don't have boots? Work appropriate clothing for women. *Journal of Social Issues, 57,* 311–322.

Twenge, J. M. (2000). The age of anxiety? Birth cohort change in anxiety and neuroticism, 1952–1993. *Journal of Personality and Social Psychology, 79*(6), 1007–1021.

Twenge, J. M. (2008). Social exclusion, motivation, and self-defeating behavior: Why breakups lead to drunkenness and ice cream. In J. Y. Shah & W. L. Gardner (Eds.), *Handbook of motivation science* (pp. 508–517). New York, NY: Guilford Press.

Twenge, J. M. (2011). Generational differences in mental health: Are children and adolescents suffering more, or less? *American Journal of Orthopsychiatry, 81*, 469–472. doi:10.1111/j.1939-0025.2011.01115.x

Twenge, J. M., & Campbell W. K. (2003). Isn't it fun to get the respect that we're going to deserve? Narcissism, social rejection, and aggression. *Personality and Social Psychology, 29*(2), 261–272.

Twenge, J. M., & Campbell, W. K. (2009). *The narcissism epidemic: Living in the age of entitlement.* New York, NY: Free Press.

Twenge, J. M., Campbell, W. K., & Foster, C. A. (2003). Parenthood and marital satisfaction: A meta-analytic review. *Journal of Marriage and Family, 65*, 574–83.

Twenge, J. M., Catanese, K. R., & Baumeister, R. F. (2002). Social exclusion causes self-defeating behavior. *Journal of Personality and Social Psychology, 83*(3), 606–615. doi:10.1037/0022-3514.83.3.606

Twenge, J. M., & Crocker, J. (2002). Race and self-esteem: Meta-analyses comparing whites, blacks, Hispanics, Asians, and American Indians and comment on Gray-Little and Hafdahl (2000). *Psychological Bulletin, 128*(3), 371–408.

Twenge, J. M., & Foster, J. D. (2010). Birth cohort increases in narcissistic personality traits among American college students, 1982–2009. *Social Psychological and Personality Science, 1*, 99–106.

Twenge, J. M., Konrath, S., Foster, J. D., Campbell, W. K., & Bushman, B. J. (2008). Egos inflating over time: A cross-temporal meta-analysis of the Narcissistic Personality Inventory. *Journal of Personality, 76*, 903–917.

Uchino, B. N., & Birmingham, W. (2011). Stress and support processes. In R. J. Contrada & A. Baum (Eds.), *The handbook of stress science: Biology, psychology, and health* (pp. 111–121). New York, NY: Springer.

Uchino, B. N., Cacioppo, J. T., & Kiecolt-Glaser, J. K. (1996). The relationship between social support and physiological processes: A review with emphasis on underlying mechanisms and implications for health. *Psychological Bulletin, 119*, 488–531.

Uleman, J. S., & Saribay, S. A. (2012). Initial impressions of others. In K. Deaux & M. Snyder (Eds.), *The Oxford handbook of personality and social psychology* (pp. 337–366). New York, NY: Oxford University Press.

Uleman, J. S., Hon, A., Roman, R. J., & Moskowitz, G. B. (1996). Online evidence for spontaneous trait inferences at encoding. *Personality and Psychology Bulletin, 22*(4), 377–394.

Ullman, S. E. (2004). Sexual assault victimization and suicidal behavior in women: A review of the literature. *Aggression and Violent Behavior, 9*(4), 331–351.

Ullman, S. E., Filipas, H. H., Townsend, S. M., & Starzynski, L. L. (2007). Psychosocial correlates of PTSD symptom severity in sexual assault survivors. *Journal of Traumatic Stress, 20*, 821–831.

Umberson, D., Pudrovska, T., & Reczek, C. (2010). Parenthood, childlessness, and well-being: A life course perspective. *Journal of Marriage and Family, 72*(3), 612–629. doi:10.1111/j.1741-3737.2010.00721.x

UNAIDS. (2005). *AIDS epidemic.* Retrieved from http://www.unaids.org/Epi2005/doc/EPIupdate2005_html_en/epi05_03

UNAIDS. (2007). *AIDS epidemic update, 2007.* Geneva: Joint United Nations Program on HIV/AIDS.

UNAIDS. (2008). *Toward universal access: Scaling up priority HIV/AIDS interventions in the health sector: A progress report 2008.* Geneva: World Health Organization.

Urbán, R. (2010). Smoking outcome expectancies mediate the association between sensation seeking, peer smoking, and smoking among young adolescents. *Nicotine & Tobacco Research, 12*, 59–68. doi:10.1093/ntr/ntp174

Ursano, A. M., Kartheiser, P. H., & Barnhill, L. J. (2008). Disorders usually first diagnosed in infancy, childhood, or adolescence. In R. E. Hales, S. C. Yudofsky, & G. O. Gabbard (Eds.), *The American Psychiatric Publishing Textbook of Psychiatry* (5th ed., pp. 861–920). Washington, DC: American Psychiatric Publishing, Inc.

Ursano, R. J., Sonnenberg, S. M., & Lazar, S. G. (2008). Psychodynamic psychotherapy. In R. E. Hales, S. C. Yudofsky, & G. O. Gabbard (Eds.), *The American Psychiatric Publishing textbook of psychiatry* (pp. 1171–1190). Washington, DC: American Psychiatric Publishing.

U.S. Bureau of Labor Statistics. (2004). *Occupational outlook handbook: 2004–2005.* Washington, DC: U.S. Government Printing Office.

U.S. Bureau of Labor Statistics. (2006). *Occupational outlook handbook, 2006–2007 edition.* Washington, D.C.: U.S. Government Printing Office.

U.S. Bureau of Labor Statistics. (2009). *Employment and earnings online.* Retrieved from http://www.bls.gov/opub/ee/home.htm; *Monthly Labor Review,* November 2007; and http://www.bls.gov/emp/emplab1.htm

U.S. Bureau of Labor Statistics. (2009). *Vacations, holidays, and personal leave: Access, quantity, costs, and trends.* Retrieved from www.bls.gov/opub/perspectives/issue2.pdf

U.S. Bureau of Labor Statistics. (2012a, Summer). High wages after high school without a bachelor's degree. *Occupational Outlook Quarterly.* Retrieved from www.bls.gov/opub/OOQ/2012/Summer/art03.pdf

U.S. Bureau of Labor Statistics. (2012b). *Unemployed persons by duration of unemployment.* Retrieved from http://www.bls.gov/news.release/empsit.t12.htm

U.S. Bureau of Labor Statistics. (2012c). Labor force statistics from the current population survey. Retrieved from data.bls.gov/timeseries/LNS14000000

U.S. Bureau of the Census. (1975). *Historical statistics of the United States: Colonial times to 1970: Part I.* Washington, DC: U.S. Government Printing Office.

U.S. Bureau of the Census. (2006a). Americans marrying older, living alone more, see households shrinking, *Census Bureau reports* (CB06-83). Retrieved from http://www.census.gov/Press-Release/www/releases/archives/families_households/006840.html.

U.S. Bureau of the Census. (2006b). *Statistical abstract of the United States: 2007.* Washington, DC: U.S. Government Printing Office.

U.S. Bureau of the Census. (2007). *Statistical abstract of the United States: 2008.* Washington, DC: U.S. Government Printing Office.

U.S. Bureau of the Census. (2010). U.S. Census Bureau reports men and women wait longer to marry. Retrieved from http://www.census.gov/newsroom/releases/archives/families_households/cb10-174.html

U.S. Bureau of the Census. (2011a). More young adults are living in their parents' home, Census Bureau reports. Retrieved from http://www.census.gov/newsroom/releases/archives/families_households/cb11-183.html

U.S. Bureau of the Census. (2011b). One-third of fathers with working wives regularly care for their children, Census Bureau reports. Retrieved from http://www.census.gov/newsroom/releases/archives/children/cb11-198.html

U.S. Bureau of the Census. (2012a). Labor force participation rates by marital status, sex, and age: 1970 to 2010. *Statistical Abstract of the United States:2012.* Retrieved from www.census.gov/compendia/statab/2012/tables/12s0598.pdf

U.S. Bureau of the Census. (2012b). Labor force participation rates for wives, husband present, by age of own youngest child: 1990 to 2009. *Statistical Abstract of the United States: 2012.* Retrieved from www.census.gov/compendia/Statab/2012/tables/12s0599.pdf

U.S. Bureau of the Census. (2012c). 2010 Census shows interracial and interethnic married couples grew by 28 percent over decade. http://www.census.gov/newsroom/releases/archives/2010_census/cb12-68.html

U.S. Department of Health and Human Services. (1990). *The health benefits of smoking cessation: A report of the surgeon general.* Washington, DC: U.S. Government Printing Office.

U.S. Department of Health and Human Services. (1995). *Healthy people 2000 review, 1994.* Washington, DC: U.S. Government Printing Office.

U.S. Department of Health and Human Services. (2000). *Healthy people 2010: Understanding and improving health* (2nd ed.). Washington, DC: U.S. Government Printing Office.

U.S. Department of Health and Human Services. (2004). *The health consequences of smoking: A report of the Surgeon General.* Atlanta, GA: DHHS.

U.S. Department of Health and Human Services. (2007). *Impacts of four Title V, Section 510 abstinence education programs, final report.* Retrieved from http://aspe.hhs.gov/hsp/abstinence07/index.htm.

U.S. Department of Labor. (1992). *Pipelines of progress: An update on the glass ceiling initiative.* Washington, DC: U.S. Government Printing Office.

U.S. Department of Labor. (2000, Summer). Futurework: Trends and challenges for work in the 21st century. *Occupational Outlook Quarterly,* pp. 31–36.

U.S. Department of Labor. (2003). *Facts on women workers.* Washington, DC: U.S. Government Printing Office.

U.S. Energy Information Administration. (2013). Overview data for the United States. Retrieved from http://www.eia.doe.gov/iea/wec.html

U.S. Environmental Protection Agency. (2012). Toxic air pollutants. Retrieved from http://www.epa.gov/air/toxicair/newtoxics.html

U.S. Environmental Protection Agency. (2013). Food waste basics. Retrieved from http://www.epa.gov/foodrecovery/

Uysal, A., & Knee, C. (2012). Low trait self-control predicts self-handicapping. *Journal of Personality, 80*(1), 59–79. doi:10.1111/j.1467-6494.2011.00715.x

Väänänen, A. (2010). Psychosocial work environment and risk of ischaemic heart disease in women. *Occupational & Environmental Medicine, 67*(5), 291–292.

Valkenburg, P. M., & Peter, J. (2007). Preadolescents' and adolescents' online communication and their closeness to friends. *Developmental Psychology, 43*, 267–277.

Vallone, R. P., Ross, L., & Lepper, M. R. (1985). The hostile media phenomenon: Biased perception and perceptions of bias in coverage of the Beirut massacre. *Journal of Personality and Social Psychology, 50*, 482–491.

Van Blerkom, D. L. (2012). *College study skills: Becoming a strategic learner.* Belmont, CA: Wadsworth.

van Bommel, M., van Prooijen, J., Elffers, H., & Van Lange, P. M. (2012). Be aware to care: Public self-awareness leads to a reversal of the bystander effect. *Journal of Experimental Social Psychology,* doi:10.1016/j.jesp.2012.02.011

Van Boven, L. (2005). Experientialism, materialism, and the pursuit of happiness. *Review of General Psychology, 9*(2), 132–142.

Vandello, J. A., Bosson, J. K., Cohen, D., Burnaford, R. M., & Weaver, J. R. (2008). Precarious manhood. *Journal of Personality and Social Psychology, 95*, 1325–1339.

van den Berg, A. E., Hartig, T., Staats, H. (2007). Preference for nature in urbanized societies: Stress, restoration, and the pursuit of sustainability. *Journal of Social Issues, 63*, 79–96.

van den Berg, A. E., & van den Berg C. G. (2011). A comparison of children with ADHD in a natural and built setting. *Child Care, Health and Development, 37*, 430–439. doi:10.1111/j.1365-2214.2010.01172.x

Vandenberg, S. G. (1987). Sex differences in mental retardation and their implications for sex differences in ability. In J. M. Reinisch, L. A. Rosenblum, & S. A. Sanders (Eds.), *Masculinity/Femininity: Basic perspectives.* New York, NY: Oxford University Press.

Vandenbroucke, J. P., & Psaty, B. M. (2008). Benefits and risks of drug treatments: How to combine the best evidence on benefits with the best data about adverse effects. *Journal of the American Medical Association, 300*(20), 2417–2419.

Vandereycken, W. (2002). History of anorexia nervosa and bulimia nervosa. In C. G. Fairburn & K. D. Brownell (Eds.), *Eating disorders and obesity.* New York, NY: Guilford Press.

Van der Hart, O. & Nijenhuis, E. R. S. (2009). Dissociative disorders. In P. H. Blaney & T. Millon (Eds.), *Oxford textbook of psychopathology* (pp. 452–481). New York, NY: Oxford University Press.

Vandewater, E. A., Bickham, D. S., Lee, J. H., Cummings, H. M., Wartella, E. A., & Rideout, V. J. (2005). When the television is always on. *American Behavioral Scientist, 48,* 562–577.

van Kammen, D. P., Hurford, I., & Marder, S. R. (2009). First-generation antipsychotics. In B. J. Sadock, V. A. Sadock, & P. Ruiz (Eds.), *Kaplan & Sadock's comprehensive textbook of psychiatry* (pp. 3105–3126). Philadelphia: Lippincott Williams & Wilkins.

van Kesteren, N. M. C., Hospers, H. J., & Kok, G. (2007). Sexual risk behavior among HIV-positive men who have sex with men: A literature review. *Patient Education and Counseling, 65,* 5–20.

Van Kleef, G. A., De Dreu, C. W., & Manstead, A. R. (2006). Supplication and appeasement in conflict and negotiation: The interpersonal effects of disappointment, worry, guilt, and regret. *Journal of Personality and Social Psychology, 91*(1), 124–142. doi:10.1037/0022-3514.91.1.124

Van Volkmon, M. (2008). Attitudes toward cigarette smoking among college students. *College Student Journal, 42,* 294–304.

Van Vugt, M. (2002). Central, individual, or collective control? Social dilemma strategies for natural resource management. *American Behavioral Scientist, 45,* 783–800.

Vanwesenbeeck, I. (2009). Doing gender in sex and sex research. *Archives of Sexual Behavior, 38*(6), 883–898. doi:10.1007/s10508-009-9565-8

Vartanian, L. R., Giant, C. L., & Passino, R. M. (2001). "Ally McBeal vs. Arnold Schwarzenegger": Comparing mass media, interpersonal feedback and gender as predictors of satisfaction with body thinness and masculinity. *Social Behavior and Personality, 29*(7), 711–723.

Vazire, S., & Funder, D. C. (2006). Impulsivity and the self-defeating behavior of narcissists. *Personality and Social Psychology Review, 10*(2), 154–165. doi:10.1207/s15327957pspr1002_4

Vazquez, C., Cervellon, P., Perez-Sales, P., Vidales, D., & Gaborit, M. (2005). Positive emotions in earthquake survivors in El Salvador (2001). *Journal of Anxiety Disorders, 19,* 313–328.

Veenhoven, R. (1993). *Happiness in nations.* Rotterdam, Netherlands: Risbo.

Veenhoven, R. (2008). Healthy happiness: Effects of happiness on physical health and the consequences for preventive care. *Journal of Happiness Studies, 9*(3), 449–469.

Veevers, J. E., Gee, E. M., & Wister, A. V. (1996). Homeleaving age norms: Conflict or consensus? *International Journal of Aging and Human Development, 43*(4), 277–295.

Ventura, S. J., & Hamilton, B. E. (2011). U.S. teenage birth rate resumes decline. *NCHS data brief, no. 58.* Hyattsville, MD: National Center for Health Statistics.

Verderber, K. S., Verderber, R. F., & Berryman-Fink, C. (2007). *Inter-act: Interpersonal communication concepts, skills, and contexts.* New York, NY: Oxford University Press.

Verderber, R. F., & Verderber, K. S. (2004). *Interact: Interpersonal communication concepts, skills, and contexts.* New York, NY: Oxford University Press.

Verderber, R. F., Verderber, K. S., & Berryman-Fink, C. (2008). *Communicate.* Belmont, CA: Wadsworth.

Verona, E., & Curtin, J. J. (2006). Gender differences in the negative affective priming of aggressive behavior. *Emotion, 6*(1), 115–124.

Verschuere, B., Crombez, G., Degroote, T., & Rosseel, Y. (2010). Detecting concealed information with reaction times: Validity and comparison with the polygraph. *Applied Cognitive Psychology, 24*(7), 991–1002. doi:10.1002/acp.1601

Vetter, M. L., Dumon, K. R., & Williams, N. N. (2011). Surgical treatments for obesity. *Psychiatric*

Clinics of North America, 34(4), 881–893. doi:10.1016/j.psc.2011.08.012

Vida, M. D., & Maurer, D. (2012). The development of fine-grained sensitivity to eye contact after 6 years of age. *Journal of Experimental Child Psychology, 112*(2), 243–256. doi:10.1016/j.jecp.2012.02.002

Vidal, M. E., & Petrak, J. (2007). Shame and adult sexual assault: A study with a group of female survivors recruited from an east London population. *Sexual and Relationship Therapy, 22,* 159–171.

Videbech, P. (2006). Hippocampus and unipolar depression. *Directions in Psychiatry, 26*(3), 183–194.

Videbech, P., & Ravnkilde, B. (2004). Hippocampal volume and depression: A meta-analysis of MRI studies. *American Journal of Psychiatry, 161,* 1957–1966.

Viglione, D. J., & Rivera, B. (2003). Assessing personality and psychopathology with projective methods. In J. R. Graham, & J. A. Naglieri (Eds.), *Handbook of psychology: Vol. 10. Assessment psychology.* New York, NY: Wiley.

Vignoles, V. L., Manzi, C., Regalia, C., Jemmolo, S., & Scabini, E. (2008). Identity motives underlying desired and feared possible future selves. *Journal of Personality, 76,* 1165–1200.

Vilain, E. (2000). Genetics of sexual development. *Annual Review of Sex Research, 11,* 1–25.

Vittengl, J. R., & Holt, C. S. (2000). Getting acquainted: The relationship of self-disclosure and social attraction to positive affect. *Journal of Social and Personal Relationships, 17*(1), 53–56.

Vlek, C., & Steg, L. (2007). Human behavior and environmental sustainability: Problems, driving forces, and research topics. *Journal of Social Issues, 63,* 1–19.

Voas, R. B., Roman, T. E., Tippetts, A. S., & Durr-Holden, C. (2006). Drinking status and fatal crashes: Which drinkers contribute most to the problem? *Journal of Studies on Alcohol, 67,* 722–729.

Vohs, K. D., & Baumeister, R. F. (Eds.). (2011). *Handbook of self-regulation: Research, theory, and applications* (2nd ed.). New York, NY: Guilford Press.

Vohs, K. D., Baumeister, R. F., & Ciarocco, N. J. (2005). Self-regulation and self-presentation: Regulatory resource depletion impairs impression management and effortful self-presentation depletes regulatory resources. *Journal of Personality and Social Psychology, 88,* 632–657.

Vohs, K. D., Baumeister, R. F., Schmeichel, B. J., Twenge, J. M., Nelson, N. M., & Tice, D. M. (2008). Making choices impairs subsequent self-control: A limited-resource account of decision making, self-regulation, and active initiative. *Journal of Personality and Social Psychology, 94*(5), 883–898. doi:10.1037/0022-3514.94.5.883

Vohs, K. D., Baumeister, R. F., & Tice, D. M. (2008). Self-regulation: Goals, consumption, choices. In C. P. Haugtvedt, P. M. Herr, & F. R. Kardes (Eds.), *Handbook of consumer psychology* (pp. 349–366). New York, NY: Taylor & Francis Group/Lawrence Erlbaum Associates.

Volkmar, F. R., Klin, A., Schultz, R. T., & State, M. W. (2009). Pervasive developmental disorders. In B. J. Sadock, V. A. Sadock, & P. Ruiz (Eds.), *Kaplan & Sadock's comprehensive textbook of psychiatry* (9th ed., pp. 3540–3559). Philadelphia: Lippincott Williams & Wilkins.

Von Baeyer, C. L., Sherk, D. L., & Zanna, M. P. (1981). Impression management in the job interview: When the female applicant meets the male (chauvinist) interviewer. *Personality and Social Psychology Bulletin, 7,* 45–51.

Vonk, R. (1993). The negativity effect in trait rating and in open-ended descriptions of persons. *Personality and Social Psychology Bulletin, 19,* 269–278.

Vorauer, J. D., Cameron, J. J., Holmes, J. G., & Pearce, D. G. (2003). Invisible overtures: Fears of rejection and the signal amplification bias. *Journal of Personality and Social Psychology, 84*(4), 793–812.

Voydanoff, P. (2005). Consequences of boundary-spanning demands and resources for work-to-family

conflict and perceived stress. *Journal of Occupational Health Psychology, 10,* 491–503.

Voydanoff, P., & Donnelly, B. W. (1999). Multiple roles and psychological distress: The intersection of the paid worker, spouse, and parent roles with the role of the adult child. *Journal of Marriage and the Family, 61,* 725–738.

Vrugt, A., & Luyerink, M. (2000). The contribution of bodily posture to gender stereotypical impressions. *Social Behavior and Personality, 28*(1), 91–103.

Waelde, L. C., Uddo, M., Marquett, R., Ropelato, M., Freightman, S., Pardo, A., & Salazar, J. (2008). A pilot study of meditation for mental health workers following Hurricane Katrina. *Journal of Traumatic Stress, 21,* 497–500.

Waggoner, A. S., Smith, E. R., & Collins, E. C. (2009). Person perception by active versus passive perceivers. *Journal of Experimental Social Psychology, 45*(4), 1028–1031.

Wagner, B. C., & Petty, R. E. (2011). The elaboration likelihood model of persuasion: Thoughtful and non-thoughtful social influence. In D. Chadee (Ed.), *Theories in social psychology* (pp. 96–116). Wiley-Blackwell.

Wagner, D. M. (1998, Feb 1). Divorce reform: New directions. *Current,* pp. 7–10.

Wai, J., Putallaz, M., & Makel, M. C. (2012). Studying intellectual outliers: Are there sex differences, and are the smart getting smarter? *Current Directions in Psychological Science, 21*(6), 382–390. doi:10.1177/0963721412455052

Waite, L. J. (1995). Does marriage matter? *Demography, 32,* 483–507.

Waite, L. J. (2000). Trends in men's and women's well-being in marriage. In L. J. Waite (Ed.), *The ties that bind.* New York, NY: Aldine de Gruyter.

Wakefield, J. C. (1999). The measurement of mental disorder. In A. V. Horvitz & T. L. Scheid (Eds.), *A handbook for the study of mental health: Social contexts, theories, and systems.* New York, NY: Cambridge University Press.

Wakefield, J. C., & Spitzer, R. L. (2002). Lowered estimates—but of what? *Archives of General Psychiatry, 59*(2), 129–130.

Wakslak, C. J., & Trope, Y. (2009). Cognitive consequences of affirming the self: The relationship between self-affirmation and object construal. *Journal of Experimental Social Psychology, 45,* 927–932.

Walker, E., Kestler, L., Bollini, A., & Hochman, K. M. (2004). Schizophrenia: Etiology and course. *Annual Review of Psychology, 55,* 401–30.

Walker, E., Mittal, V., & Tessner, K. (2008). Stress and the hypothalamic pituitary adrenal axis in the developmental course of schizophrenia. *Annual Review of Clinical Psychology, 4,* 189–216.

Walker, E., & Tessner, K. (2008). Schizophrenia. *Perspectives on Psychological Science, 3,* 30–37.

Walker, K. (1994). Men, women, and friendship: What they say, what they do. *Gender & Society, 8,* 246–265.

Walker, L. S., Claar, R. L., & Garber, J. (2002). Social consequences of children's pain: When do they encourage symptoms of maintenance? *Journal of Pediatric Psychology, 27*(8), 689–698.

Wallace, H. M., Baumeister, R. F., & Vohs, K. D. (2005). Audience support and choking under pressure: A home disadvantage? *Journal of Sports Sciences, 23,* 429–438.

Waller, R., & Gilbody, S. (2009). Barriers to the uptake of computerized cognitive behavioural therapy: A systematic review of the quantitative and qualitative evidence. *Psychological Medicine, 39,* 705–712. doi:10.1017/s0033291708004244

Wallerstein, J. S. (2005). Growing up in the divorced family. *Clinical Social Work Journal, 33,* 401–418.

Wallerstein, J. S., & Blakeslee, S. (1989). *Second chances: Men, women, and children a decade after divorce.* Boston, MA: Houghton Mifflin.

Wallerstein, J. S., & Lewis, J. M. (2004). The unexpected legacy of divorce: Report of a 25-year study. *Psychoanalytic Psychology, 21,* 353–370.

Wallerstein, J. S., & Lewis, J. M. (2007). Sibling outcomes and disparate parenting and stepparenting after divorce: Report from a 10-year longitudinal study. *Psychoanalytic Psychology, 24,* 445–458.

Wallerstein, J. S., Lewis, J. M., & Blakeslee, S. (2000). *The unexpected legacy of divorce: A 25-year landmark study.* New York, NY: Hyperion.

Wallis, C. (2004, March 22). The case for staying home. *Time,* pp. 51–59.

Walsh, B. (2008, September 10). Meat: Making global warming worse. *Time: Health & Family.* Retrieved from http://www.time.com/time/health/article/0%2C8599%2C1839995%2C00.html

Walsh, F. (1999). Families in later life: Challenges and opportunities. In B. Carter & M. McGoldrick (Eds.), *The expanded family life cycle: Individual, family, and social perspectives* (3rd ed.). Boston, MA: Allyn & Bacon.

Walsh, J. K., Dement, W. C., & Dinges, D. F. (2011). Sleep medicine, public policy, and public health. In M. H. Kryger, T. Roth, & W. C. Dement (Eds.), *Principles and practice of sleep medicine.* Philadelphia, PA: Elsevier Saunders.

Walsh, R. (2011). Lifestyle and mental health. *American Psychologist, 66*(7), 579–592. doi:10.1037/a0021769

Waltenbaugh, A. W., & Zagummy, M. J. (2004). Optimistic bias and perceived control among cigarette smokers. *Journal of Alcohol and Drug Education, 47,* 20–33.

Wanberg, C. R. (2012). The individual experience of unemployment. *Annual Review of Psychology, 63,* 369–396. doi:10.1146/annurev-psych-120710-100500

Wang, H., & Amato, P. R. (2000). Predictors of divorce adjustment: Stressors, resources, and definitions. *Journal of Marriage and the Family, 62,* 655–668.

Wang, P. S., Berglund, P., Olfson, M., Pincus, H. A., Wells, K. B., & Kessler, R. C. (2005a). Failure and delay in initial treatment contact after first onset of mental disorders in the National Comorbidity Survey Replication. *Archives of General Psychiatry, 62,* 603–613.

Wang, P. S., Lane, M., Olfson, M., Pincus, H. A., Wells, K. B., & Kessler, R. C. (2005b). Twelve-month use of mental health services in the United States: Results from the National Comorbidity Survey Replication. *Archives of General Psychiatry, 62,* 629–640.

Wang, P. S., Tohen, M., Bromet, E. J., Angst, J., & Kessler, R. C. (2008). Psychiatric epidemiology. In A. Tasman, J. Kay, J. A. Lieberman, M. B. First, & M. Maj (Eds.), *Psychiatry* (3rd ed.). New York, NY: Wiley-Blackwell.

Wang, Q., Fink, E. L., & Cai, D. A. (2012). The effect of conflict goals on avoidance strategies: What does not communicating communicate? *Human Communication Research, 38*(2), 222–252. doi:10.1111/j.1468-2958.2011.01421.x

Ward, A., & Brenner, L. (2006). Accentuate the negative: The positive effects of negative acknowledgement. *Psychological Science, 17,* 959–962.

Wareham, J., Boots, D. P., & Chavez, J. M. (2009). A test of social learning and intergenerational transmission among batterers. *Journal of Criminal Justice, 37,* 163–173.

Warr, P. (2007). *Work, happiness, and unhappiness.* Mahwah, NJ: Erlbaum.

Warren, R. (2002). *The purpose driven life: What on Earth am I here for?* Grand Rapids, MI: Zondervan.

Waters, E., Merrick, S., Treboux, D., Crowell, J., & Albersheim, L. (2000). Attachment security in infancy and early adulthood: A twenty-year longitudinal study. *Child Development, 71*(3), 684–689.

Waters, E. A., Klein, W. M. P., Moser, R. P., Yu, M., Waldron, W. R., McNeel, T. S., & Freedman, A. N. (2011). Correlates of unrealistic optimism in a nationally representative sample. *Journal of Behavioral Medicine, 34*(3), 225–235.

Watkins, P. C., Van Gelder, M., & Frias, A. (2009). Furthering the science of gratitude. In S. J. Lopez, C. R. Snyder (Eds.), *Oxford handbook of positive psychology* (2nd ed., pp. 437–445). New York, NY: Oxford University Press.

Watkins, P. C., Woodward, K., Stone, T., & Russell, L. (2003). Gratitude and happiness: Development of a measure of gratitude and relationships with subjective well-being. *Social Behavior and Personality, 31,* 431–452.

Watson, D. (2002). Positive affectivity: The disposition to experience pleasurable emotional states. In C. R. Snyder & S. J. Lopez (Eds.), *Handbook of positive psychology* (pp. 106–119). New York, NY: Oxford.

Watson, D., & Clark, L. A. (1984). Negative affectivity: The disposition to experience aversive emotional states. *Psychological Bulletin, 96,* 465–490.

Watson, D., Klohnen, E. C., Casillas, A., Nus Simms, E., Haig, J., & Berry, D. S. (2004). Match makers and deal breakers: Analyses of assortative mating in newlywed couples. *Journal of Personality, 72,* 1029–1068.

Watson, D., & Naragon, K. (2009). Positive affectivity: The disposition to experience positive affect. In C. R. Snyder & S. J. Lopez (Eds.), *Oxford handbook of positive psychology* (2nd ed., pp. 207–216). New York, NY: Oxford University Press.

Watson, D., & Pennebaker, J. W. (1989). Health complaints, stress, and distress: Exploring the central role of negative affectivity. *Psychological Review, 96,* 234–254.

Watson, D. L., & Tharp, R. G. (2007). *Self-directed behavior: Self-modification for personal adjustment.* Belmont, CA: Wadsworth.

Watson, J. B. (1913). Psychology as the behaviorist views it. *Psychological Review, 20,* 158–177.

Watt, H. G., Shapka, J. D., Morris, Z. A., Durik, A. M., Keating, D. P., & Eccles, J. S. (2012). Gendered motivational processes affecting high school mathematics participation, educational aspirations, and career plans: A comparison of samples from Australia, Canada, and the United States. *Developmental Psychology, 48*(6), 1594–1611. doi:10.1037/a0027838

Way, N. (2011). *Deep secrets: Boys' friendships and the crisis of connection.* Cambridge, MA: Harvard University Press.

Wayment, H. A., & O'Mara, E. M. (2008). The collective and compassionate consequences of downward social comparisons. In H. A. Wayment & J. J. Bauer (Eds.), *Transcending self-interest: Psychological explorations of the quiet ego* (pp. 159–169). Washington, DC: American Psychological Association.

Weaver, J. (2007) Many cheat for a thrill, more stay true for love. Retrieved from http://www.msnbc.msn.com/id/17951664/ns/health-sexual_health/t/many-cheat-thrillmore-stay-true-love/#.UEycdBi9VT4

Webb, T. E., Wery, K. D., & Krill, C. E., Jr. (2001). Childhood hemophilia: Application of a measure of self-reported psychosocial distress. *The Journal of Genetic Psychology, 146,* 281–282.

Weber, L. J. (2006). *Profits before people?* Bloomington, IN: Indiana University Press.

Webster, D. M. (1993). Motivated augmentation and reduction of the overattribution bias. *Journal of Personality and Social Psychology, 65,* 261–271.

Webster, D. M., Richter, L., & Kruglanski, A. W. (1996). On leaping to conclusions when feeling tired: Mental fatigue effects on impressional primacy. *Journal of Experimental Social Psychology, 32,* 181–195.

Webster, G. D. (2009). Parental investment theory. In H. T. Reis & S. Sprecher (Eds.), *Encyclopedia of human relationships: Vol. 3* (pp. 1194–1197). Los Angeles: Sage Reference Publication.

Wechsler, H., Lee, J. E., Kuo, M., Seibring, M., Nelson, T. F., & Lee, H. (2002). Trends in college binge drinking during a period of increased prevention efforts. *Journal of American College Health, 50*(5), 203–217.

Wegener, D. T., & Petty, R. E. (1994). Mood management across affective states: The hedonic contingency hypothesis. *Journal of Personality and Social Psychology, 66,* 1034–1048.

Weinberger, D. A. (1990). The construct validity of the repressive coping style. In J. L. Singer (Ed.), *Repression and dissociation.* Chicago: University of Chicago Press.

Weiner, B. (Ed.). (1974). *Achievement motivation and attribution theory.* Morristown, NJ: General Learning Press.

Weiner, B. (1994). Integrating social and personal theories of achievement striving. *Review of Educational Research, 64,* 557–573.

Weiner, B. (2006). *Social motivation, justice, and the moral emotions: An attributional approach.* Mahwah, NJ: Erlbaum.

Weiner, B. (2012). An attribution theory of motivation. In P. M. Van Lange, A. W. Kruglanski, & E. Higgins (Eds.), *Handbook of theories of social psychology* (Vol. 1, pp. 135–155). Thousand Oaks, CA: Sage Publications Ltd.

Weinstein, A., & Lejoyeux, M. (2010). Internet addiction or excessive Internet use. *The American Journal of Drug and Alcohol Abuse, 36*(5), 277–283. doi:10.3109/00952990.2010.491880

Weinstein, N., Ryan, W. S., DeHaan, C. R., Przybylski, A. K., Legate, N., & Ryan, R. M. (2012). Parental autonomy support and discrepancies between implicit and explicit sexual identities: Dynamics of self-acceptance and defense. *Journal of Personality and Social Psychology, 102,* 815–832. doi:10.1037/a0026854

Weinstein, N. D. (2003). Exploring the links between risk perceptions and preventive health behavior. In J. Suls & K. A. Wallston (Eds.), *Social psychological foundations of health and illness.* Malden, MA: Blackwell Publishing.

Weinstein, N. D., Slovic, P., & Gibson, G. (2004). Accuracy and optimism in smokers' beliefs about quitting. *Nicotine & Tobacco Research, 6*(Suppl3), 375–380.

Weinstein, Y., McDermott, K. B., & Roediger, H. L., III. (2010). A comparison of study strategies for passages: Rereading, answering questions, and generating questions. *Journal of Experimental Psychology: Applied, 16,* 308–316. doi:10.1037/a0020992

Weintraub, K. (2011).Autism counts. *Nature, 479*(7371), 22–24. doi:10.1038/479022a

Weisbuch, M., & Ambady, N. (2008). Nonconscious routes to building culture: Nonverbal components of socialization. *Journal of Consciousness Studies, 15,* 159–183.

Weiser, D. A., & Riggio, H. R. (2010). Family background and academic achievement: Does self-efficacy mediate outcomes? *Social Psychology of Education, 13*(3), 367–383. doi:10.1007/s11218-010-9115-1

Weiss, J. L., Overpeck, J. T., & Strauss, B. (2011). Implications of recent sea level rise science for low-elevation areas in coastal cities of the conterminous U.S.A. *Climatic Change 105,* 635–645.

Weiss, R. (1973). *Loneliness: The experience of emotional and social isolation.* Cambridge, MA: MIT Press.

Weiss, R. S. (1975). *Marital separation.* New York, NY: Basic Books.

Weisz, J. R., Rothbaum, F., & Blackburn, T. F. (1984). Standing out and standing in: The psychology of control in the U.S. and Japan. *American Psychologist, 39,* 955–969.

Weiten, W. (1988). Pressure as a form of stress and its relationship to psychological symptomatology. *Journal of Social and Clinical Psychology, 6,* 127–139.

Weiten, W. (1998). Pressure, major life events, and psychological symptoms. *Journal of Social Behavior and Personality, 13,* 51–68.

Weiten, W., Guadagno, R. E., & Beck, C. A. (1996). Students' perceptions of textbook pedagogical aids. *Teaching of Psychology, 23,* 105–107.

Weitzman, L. (1996). The economic consequences of divorce are still unequal: Comment on Peterson. *American Sociological Review, 61,* 537–538.

Wells, N. M., & Evans, G. W. (2003). Nearby nature: A buffer of life stress among rural children. *Environment and Behavior, 35,* 311–330.

Wener, R. E., & Evans, G. W. (2011). Comparing stress of car and train commuters. *Transportation Research Part F: Traffic Psychology and Behaviour, 14*(2), 111–116. doi:10.1016/j.trf.2010.11.008

Wesson, D. R., Smith, D. E., Ling, W., & Seymour, R. B. (2005). Sedatives–hypnotics. In J. H. Lowinson, P. Ruiz, R. B. Millman, & J. G. Langrod (Eds.), *Substance abuse: A comprehensive textbook* . Philadelphia: Lippincott/Williams & Wilkins.

West, D. S., Harvey-Berino, J., & Raczynski, J. M. (2004). Behavioral aspects of obesity, dietary intake, and chronic disease. In J. M. Raczynski & L. C. Leviton (Eds.), *Handbook of clinical health psychology: Vol. 2. Disorders of behavior and health.* Washington, DC: American Psychological Association.

Westefeld, J. S., Maples, M. R., Buford, B., & Taylor, S. (2001). Gay, lesbian, and bisexual college students: The relationship between sexual orientation and depression, loneliness and suicide. *Journal of College Student Psychotherapy, 15*(3), 71–82.

Westen, D., Gabbard, G. O., & Ortigo, K. M. (2008). Psychoanalytic approaches to personality. In O. P. John, R. W. Robins, & L. A. Pervin (Eds.), *Handbook of personality: Theory and research* (pp. 61–113). New York, NY: The Guilford Press.

Wetherby, A. M., & Prizant, B. M. (2005). Enhancing language and communication development in autism spectrum disorders: Assessment and intervention guidelines. In D. Zager (Ed.), *Autism spectrum disorders: Identification, education, and treatment* (3rd ed., pp. 327–365). Hillside, NJ: Lawrence Erlbaum Associates.

Wetter, D. W., Cofta-Gunn, L., Fouladi, R. T., Irvin, J. E., Daza, P. Mazas, C., et al. (2005). Understanding the association among education, employment characteristics, and smoking. *Addictive Behaviors, 30,* 905–914.

Whatley, M. A., Webster, J. M., Smith, R. H., & Rhodes, A. (1999). The effect of a favor on public and private compliance: How internalized is the norm of reciprocity? *Basic and Applied Social Psychology, 21,* 251–261.

Wheeler, L., & Kim, Y. (1997). What is beautiful is culturally good: The physical attractiveness stereotype has different content in collectivistic cultures. *Personality and Social Psychology Bulletin, 23,* 795–802.

Wheeler, L., Koestner, R., & Driver, R. (1982). Related attributes in the choice of comparison others: It's there, but it isn't all there is. *Journal of Experimental Social Psychology, 18,* 489–500.

Wheeler, L., & Suls, J. (2005). Social comparison and self-evaluations of competence. In A. J. Elliot & C. S. Dweck (Eds.), *Handbook of competence and motivation.* New York, NY: Guilford.

Whelan, C. B. (2009, October 25). For these "spiritual warriors," the casualties were real. *The Washington Post.* Retrieved from http://www.washigtonpost.com/wp-dyn/content/article/2009/10/23//AR2009102302411.html

Whiston, S. C., & Keller, B. K. (2004). The influences of the family of origin on career development: A review and analysis. *Counseling Psychologist, 32*(4), 493–568.

Whitbourne, S. K. (1996). *The aging individual: Physical and psychological perspectives.* New York, NY: Springer.

White, C. M., & Hoffrage, U. (2009). Testing the tyranny of too much choice against the allure of more choice. *Psychology & Marketing, 26*(3), 280–298. doi:10.1002/mar.20273

White, L. K., & Rogers, S. J. (2001). Economic circumstances and family outcomes: A review of the 1990s. In R. M. Milardo (Ed.), *Understanding families into the new millennium: A decade in review.* Minneapolis: National Council on Family Relations.

White, R., & Heerwagen, J. (1998). Nature and mental health: Biophilia and biophobia. In A. Lundberg (Ed.), *The environment and mental health: A guide for clinicians* (pp. 175–192). Mahwah, NJ: Erlbaum.

Whitehead, B. D., & Popenoe, D. (2001). *The state of our unions: The social health of marriage in America, 2001.* Piscataway, NJ: The National Marriage Project.

Whitehouse, W. G., Orne, E. C., & Orne, M. T. (2007). Relaxation techniques. In G. Fink (Ed.), *Encyclopedia of stress: Vols. 1–4* (2nd ed., pp. 345–350). San Diego, CA: Elsevier Academic Press.

Whiteman, S. D., McHale, S. M., & Crouter, A. C. (2003). What parents learn from experience: The first child as a first draft? *Journal of Marriage and Family, 65,* 608–621.

Whitley, B. E. (1983). Sex role orientation and self-esteem: A critical meta-analytic review. *Journal of Personality and Social Psychology, 44,* 765–778.

Whitley, B. E., & Kite, M. E. (2006). *The psychology of prejudice and discrimination.* Belmont, CA: Wadsworth.

Whitton, S. W., Waldinger, R. J., Schulz, M. S., Allen, J. P., Crowell, J. A., & Hauser, S. T. (2008). Prospective associations from family-of-origin interactions to adult marital interactions and relationship adjustment. *Journal of Family Psychology, 22,* 274–286.

Whybrow, P. C. (2005). *American mania: When more is not enough.* New York, NY: Norton.

Wickrama, K. A. S., Lorenz, F. O., Conger, R. D., & Elder, G. H. (1997). Marital quality and physical illness: A latent growth curve analysis. *Journal of Marriage and Family, 59,* 143–155.

Widiger, T. A. (2009). Neuroticism. In M. R. Leary & R. H. Hoyle (Eds.), *Handbook of individual differences in social behavior* (pp. 129–146). New York, NY: The Guilford Press.

Widiger, T. A., & Trull, T. J. (2007). Plate tectonics in the classification of personality disorder: Shifting to a dimensional model. *American Psychologist, 62*(2), 71–83.

Wiederman, M. W. (1993). Evolved gender differences in mate preferences: Evidence from personal advertisements. *Ethology and Sociobiology, 14,* 331–352.

Wiederman, M. W. (2004). Methodological issues in studying sexuality in close relationships. In J. H. Harvey, A. Wenzel, & S. Sprecher (Eds.), *The handbook of sexuality in close relationships.* Mahwah, NJ: Lawrence Erlbaum.

Wijlaars, L. P. M. M., Nazareth, I., & Petersen, I. (2012). Trends in depression and antidepressant prescribing in children and adolescents: A cohort study in the Health Improvement Network (THIN). *PLoS ONE, 7*(3), 1–8. doi:10.1371/journal.pone.0033181

Wilfong, J. D. (2006). Computer anxiety and anger: The impact of computer use, computer experience, and self–efficacy beliefs. *Computers in Human Behavior, 22,* 1001–1011.

Wilgosh, L. (2001). Enhancing gifts and talents of women and girls. *High Ability Studies, 12*(1), 45–59.

Willets, M. C., Sprecher, S., & Beck, F. D. (2004). Overview of sexual practices and attitudes within relationship contexts. In J. H. Harvey, A. Wenzel, & S. Sprecher (Eds.), *The handbook of sexuality in close relationships.* Mahwah, NJ: Lawrence Erlbaum.

Willett, W. C., & Stampfer, W. J. (2003). Rebuilding the food pyramid. *Scientific American, 288*(1), 64–71.

Williams, C. G., Gagne, M., Ryan, R. M., & Deci, E. L. (2002). Facilitating autonomous motivation for smoking cessation. *Health Psychology, 21,* 40–50.

Williams, D. F., Wener, D., Core, C., Adler, R. K., Saul, R., Danesh, A. A., & . . . Cheng, L. (2012). *Communication sciences and disorders: An introduction to the professions.* New York, NY: Psychology Press.

Williams, D. R., & Mohammed, S. A. (2007). Racial harassment/discrimination. In G. Fink (Ed.), *Encyclopedia of stress: Vols. 1–4* (2nd ed., pp. 321–326). San Diego, CA: Elsevier Academic Press.

Williams, J. A., Burns, E. L., & Harmon, E. A. (2009). Insincere utterances and gaze: Eye contact during sarcastic statements. *Perceptual and Motor Skills, 108*(2), 565–572.

Williams, J. E., Paton, C. C., Siegler, I. C., Eigenbrodt, M. L., Neito, F. J., & Tyroler, H. A. (2000). Anger proneness predicts coronary heart disease risk. *Circulation, 101,* 2034–2039.

Williams, J. E., Satterwhite, R. C., & Best, D. L. (1999). Pancultural gender stereotypes revisited: The five-factor model. *Sex Roles, 40,* 513–526.

Williams, K. B., Radefeld, P. S., Binning, J. F., & Sudak, J. R. (1993). When job candidates are "hard-" versus "easy-to-get": Effects of candidate availability on employment decisions. *Journal of Applied Social Psychology, 23*(3), 169–198.

Williams, N. A., & Deffenbacher, J. L. (1983). Life stress and chronic yeast infections. *Journal of Human Stress, 9,* 26–31.

Williams, P. (2005). What is psychoanalysis? What is a psychoanalyst? In E. S. Person, A. M. Cooper, & G. O. Gabbard (Eds.), *Textbook of psychoanalysis.* Washington, DC: American Psychiatric Publishing.

Williams, R. B. (1989). *The trusting heart: Great news about Type A behavior.* New York, NY: Times Books.

Williams, R. B. (1996). Hostility and the heart. In D. Goleman & J. Gurin (Eds.), *Mind-body medicine: How to use your mind for better health.* Yonkers, NY: Consumer Reports Books.

Williams, S. L. (1995). Self-efficacy, anxiety, and phobic disorders. In J. E. Maddux (Ed.), *Self-efficacy, adaptation, and adjustment: Theory, research, and application.* New York, NY: Plenum Press.

Williamson, D. A., Zucker, N. L., Martin, C. K., & Smeets, M. A. M. (2001). Etiology and management of eating disorders. In P. B. Sutker & H. E. Adams (Eds.), *Comprehensive handbook of psychopathology* (3rd ed.). New York, NY: Kluwer Academic/Plenum.

Williamson, I., & Gonzales, M. H. (2007). The subjective experience of forgiveness: Positive construals of the forgiveness experience. *Journal of Social and Clinical Psychology, 26,* 407–446.

Willness, C. R., Steel, P., & Lee, K. (2007). A meta-analysis of antecedents and consequences of workplace sexual harassment. *Personnel Psychology, 60*(1), 127–162.

Wills, T. A., & Sandy, J. M. (2001). Comparing favorably: A cognitive approach to coping through comparison with other persons. In C. R. Snyder (Ed.), *Coping with stress: Effective people and processes* (pp. 154–177). New York, NY: Oxford University Press.

Wilmot, W., & Hocker, J. (2006). *Interpersonal conflict* (7th ed.). New York, NY: McGraw-Hill.

Wilson, E. K., Dalberth, B. T., Koo, H. P., & Gard, J. C. (2010). Parents' perspectives on talking to preteenage children about sex. *Perspectives on Sexual and Reproductive Health, 42,* 56–63. doi:10.1363/4205610

Wilson, G. T. (2011). Behavior therapy. In R. J. Corsini & D. Wedding (Eds.), *Current psychotherapies* (9th ed.). Belmont, CA: Brooks/Cole.

Wilson, L. C., & Scarpa, A. (2011). The link between sensation seeking and aggression: A meta-analytic review. *Aggressive Behavior, 37,* 81–90. doi:10.1002/ab.20369

Wilson, T. D. (2002). *Strangers to ourselves: Discovering the adaptive unconscious.* Cambridge: Belknap Press.

Wilson, T. D. (2011). *Redirect: The surprising new science of psychological change.* New York, NY: Little, Brown and Company.

Wilson, T. D., & Gilbert, D. T. (2003). Affective forecasting. In M. P. Zanna (Ed.), *Advances in experimental social psychology* (pp. 345–411). San Diego, CA: Elsevier Academic Press. doi:10.1016/S0065-2601(03)01006-2

Wilson, T. D., & Gilbert, D. T. (2005). Affective forecasting: Knowing what to want. *Current Directions in Psychological Science, 14*(3), 131–134.

Wilson, T. D., Wheatley, T. P., Meyers, J. M., Gilbert, D. T., & Axsom, D. (2000). Focalism: A source of durability bias in affective forecasting. *Journal of Personality and Social Psychology, 78,* 821–836.

Wilt, J. & Revelle, W. (2009). Extraversion. In M. R. Leary & R. H. Hoyle (Eds.), *Handbook of individual differences in social behavior* (pp. 27–45). New York, NY: Guilford.

Wiltermuth, S. (2012). Synchrony and destructive obedience. *Social Influence, 7*(2), 78–89. doi:10.1080/15534510.2012.658653

Winett, R. A., Hatcher, J. W., Fort, T. R., Leckliter, I. N., Love, S. Q., Riley, A. W., & Fishback, J. F. (1982). The effects of videotape modeling and daily feedback on residential electricity conservation, home temperature and humidity, perceived comfort, and clothing worn: Winter and summer. *Journal of Applied Behavior Analysis, 15,* 381–402.

Wing, J. F., Schutte, N. S., & Byrne, B. (2006). The effect of positive writing on emotional intelligence and life satisfaction. *Journal of Clinical Psychology, 62,* 1291–1302.

Wing, L., & Potter, D. (2009). The epidemiology of autism spectrum disorders: Is the prevalence rising? In S. Goldstein, J. A. Naglieri, & S. Ozonoff (Eds.), *Assessment of autism spectrum disorders* (pp. 18–54). New York, NY: The Guilford Press.

Wing, R. R., & Polley, B. A. (2001). Obesity. In A. Baum, T. A. Revenson, & J. E. Singer (Eds.), *Handbook of health psychology.* Mahwah, NJ: Erlbaum.

Winick, C., & Norman, R. L. (2005). Epidemiology. In J. H. Lowinson, P. Ruiz, R. B. Millman, & J. G. Langrod (Eds.), *Substance abuse: A comprehensive textbook.* Philadelphia: Lippincott/Williams & Wilkins.

Winstead, Z. A. (2009). Friendships, sex differences and similarities. In H. T. Reis & S. Sprecher (Eds.), *Encyclopedia of human relationships: Vol. 2* (pp. 713–716). Los Angeles: Sage Reference Publication.

Winter, D. D., & Cava, M. M. (2006) The psychoecology of armed conflict. *Journal of Social Issues, 62,* 19–40.

Wipfli, B. M., Rethorst, C. D., & Landers, D. M. (2008). The anxiolytic effect of exercise: A meta-analysis of randomized trials and dose-response analysis. *Journal of Sport and Exercise Psychology, 30,* 392–410.

Wise, D., & Rosqvist, J. (2006). Explanatory style and well-being. In J. C. Thomas, D. L. Segal, & M. Hersen (Eds.), *Comprehensive handbook of personality and psychopathology: Personality and everyday functioning.* Hoboken, NJ: Wiley.

Wissink, I. B., Dekovic, M., & Meijer, A. M. (2006). Parenting behavior, quality of the parent-adolescent functioning in four ethnic groups. *Journal of Early Adolescence, 26,* 133–159.

Wittenbrink, B., & Schwartz, N. (Eds.). (2007). *Implicit measures of attitudes.* New York, NY: Guilford.

Witvliet, C., Ludwig, T. E., & Vander Laan, K. L. (2001). Granting forgiveness or harboring grudges: Implications for emotion, physiology, and health. *Psychological Science, 121*(2), 117–123.

Wohl, M. J. A., & Enzle, M. E. (2002). The deployment of personal luck: Sympathetic magic and illusory control in games of pure chance. *Personality and Social Psychology Bulletin, 28,* 1388–1397.

Wolfinger, N. H. (2005). *Understanding the divorce cycle: The children of divorce in their own marriages.* New York, NY: Cambridge University Press.

Wolinsky, F. D. (1988). Sick role legitimation. In D. S. Gochman (Ed.), *Health behavior: Emerging research perspectives.* New York, NY: Plenum Press.

Wolitzky, D. L. (2006). Psychodynamic theories. In J. C. Thomas & D. L. Segal (Eds.), *Comprehensive handbook of personality and psychopathology.* New York, NY: Wiley.

Woloshin, S., Schwartz L.M., & Welch H. G. (2002). Risk charts: Putting cancer in context. *Journal of the National Cancer Institute, 94,* 803.

Wolpe, J. (1958). *Psychotherapy by reciprocal inhibition.* Stanford, CA: Stanford University Press.

Wolpe, J. (1987). The promotion of scientific therapy: A long voyage. In J. K. Zeig (Ed.), *The evolution of psychotherapy.* New York, NY: Brunner/Mazel.

Wonderlich, S. A. (2002). Personality and eating disorders. In C. G. Fairburn & K. D. Brownell (Eds.), *Eating disorders and obesity: A comprehensive handbook.* New York, NY: Guilford.

Wong, L. A. (2012) *Essential study skills.* Belmont, CA: Wadsworth.

Wong, P. T. P. (2006). Existential and humanistic theories. In J. C. Thomas & D. L. Segal (Eds.), *Comprehensive handbook of personality and psychopathology.* New York, NY: Wiley.

Wood, A. M., Froh, J. J., & Geraghty, A. A. (2010). Gratitude and well-being: A review and theoretical integration. *Clinical Psychology Review, 30*(7), 890–905. doi:10.1016/j.cpr.2010.03.005

Wood, E., Desmarais, S., & Gugula, S. (2002). The impact of parenting experience on gender stereotyped toy play of children. *Sex Roles, 47*(1–2), 39–49,

Wood, J. T. (2006) Chopping the carrots: Creating intimacy moment by moment. In J. T. Wood & S. W. Duck (Eds.), *Composing relationships: Communication in everyday life* (pp. 24–35). Belmont, CA: Thompson/Wadsworth.

Wood, J. T. (2010). *Interpersonal communication: Everyday encounters* (6th ed.). Belmont, CA: Wadsworth/Cengage.

Wood, J. V. (1989). Theory and research concerning social comparisons of personal attributes. *Psychological Bulletin, 106,* 231–248.

Wood, J. V., & Wilson, A. E. (2003). How important is social comparison? In M. R. Leary, & J. P. Tangney (Eds.), *Handbook of self and identity.* New York, NY: Guilford.

Wood, M. D., Britt, T. W., Thomas, J. L., Klocko, R. P., & Bliese, P. D. (2011). Buffering effects of benefit finding in a war environment. *Military Psychology, 23*(2), 202–219. doi:10.1080/08995605.2010.521732

Wood, M. D., Britt, T. W., Wright, K. M., Thomas, J. L., & Bliese, P. D. (2012). Benefit finding at war: A matter of time. *Journal of Traumatic Stress, 25*(3), 307–314. doi:10.1002/jts.21701

Wood, M. D., Vinson, D. C., & Sher, K. J. (2001). Alcohol use and misuse. In A. Baum, T. A. Revenson, & J. E. Singer (Eds.), *Handbook of health psychology.* Mahwah, NJ: Erlbaum.

Wood, N., & Cowan, N. (1995). The cocktail party phenomenon revisited: How frequent are attention shifts to one's name in an irrelevant auditory channel? *Journal of Experimental Psychology: Learning, Memory, and Cognition, 21,* 255–260.

Wood, R. T. A., & Griffiths, M. D. (2007). A qualitative investigation of problem gambling as an escape-based coping strategy. *Psychology and Psychotherapy: Theory, Research, and Practice, 80,* 107–125.

Wood, W., & Quinn, J. M. (2003). Forewarned and forearmed? Two meta-analytic syntheses of forewarnings of influence appeals. *Psychological Bulletin, 129*(1), 119–138.

Wood, W., Conway, M., Pushkar, D., & Dugas, M. J. (2005). People's perceptions of women's and men's worry about life issues: Worrying about love, accomplishment, or money? *Sex Roles, 53,* 545–551.

Woodhill, B. M., & Samuels, C. A. (2003). Positive and negative androgyny and their relationship with psychological health and well-being. *Sex Roles, 48,* 555–565.

Woodhouse, S. S., Dykas, M. J., & Cassidy, J. (2012). Loneliness and peer relations in adolescence. *Social Development, 21*(2), 273–293. doi:10.1111/j.1467-9507.2011.00611.x

Woods Hole Research Center. (2009). Retrieved from http://whrc.org/

Woodzicka, J. A., & LaFrance, M. (2005). The effects of subtle sexual harassment on women's performance in a job interview. *Sex Roles, 53,* 67–77.

Woolfolk, R. L. (2002). The power of negative thinking: Truth, melancholia, and the tragic sense of life. *Journal of Theoretical and Philosophical Psychology, 22*(1), 19–27. doi:10.1037/h0091192

World Resources Institute. (2001). *Facts and figures: Environmental data tables, energy and resource use.* Table ERC.5: Resource Consumption. [Data file]. Retrieved from http://www.wri.org/trends/index.html

Worthington, R. L., Flores, L. Y., & Navarro, R. L. (2005). Career development in context: Research with people of color. In S. D. Brown & R. W. Lent (Eds.), *Career development and counseling: Putting theory and research to work.* New York, NY: Wiley.

Worthington, R. L., & Reynolds, A. L. (2009). Within-group differences in sexual orientation and identity. *Journal of Counseling Psychology, 56,* 44–55.

Worthington, R. L., Soth-McNett, A. M., & Moreno, M. V. (2007). Multicultural counseling competencies research: A 20-year content analysis. *Journal of Counseling Psychology, 54,* 351–361.

Wright, C. E., O'Donnell, K., Brydon, L., Wardle, J., & Steptoe, A. (2007). Family history of cardiovascular disease is associated with cardiovascular responses to stress in healthy young men and women. *International Journal of Psychophysiology, 63,* 275–282.

Wright, P. H. (2006). Toward an expanded orientation to the comparative study of women's and men's same-sex friendships. In K. Dindia & D. J. Canary (Eds.), *Sex differences and similarities in communication.* Mahwah, NJ: Erlbaum.

Wright, S. C., & Taylor, D. M. (2003). The social psychology of cultural diversity: Social stereotyping, prejudice, and discrimination. In M. A. Hogg & J. Cooper (Eds.), *The Sage handbook of social psychology.* Thousand Oaks, CA: Sage Publications.

Wright, T. A. (2003). Positive organizational behavior: An idea whose time has truly come. *Journal of Organizational Behavior, 24,* 437–442.

Wrosch, C. (2011). Self-regulation of unattainable goals and pathways to quality of life. In S. Folkman (Ed.). *The Oxford handbook of stress, health, & coping* (pp. 319–333). New York, NY: Oxford University Press.

Wrosch, C., Miller, G. E., Scheier, M. F., & de Pontet, S. (2007). Giving up on unattainable goals: benefits for health? *Personality and Social Psychology Bulletin, 33*(2), 251–265. doi:10.1177/0146167206294905

Wrzesniewski, A., McCauly, C., Rozin, P., & Schwartz, B. (1997). Jobs, careers, and callings: People's relations to their work. *Journal of Research in Personality, 31,* 21–33.

Wynder, E. L., Cohen, L. A., Muscat, J. E., Winters, B., Dwyer, J. T., & Blackburn, G. (1997). Breast cancer: Weighing the evidence for a promoting role of dietary fat. *Journal of the National Cancer Institute, 89*(11), 766–775.

Xiaohe, X., & Whyte, M. K. (1990). Love matches and arranged marriages: A Chinese replication. *Journal of Marriage and the Family, 52,* 709–722.

Xie, J. (2011). Relationship between emotional intelligence, job burnout and job satisfaction. *Chinese Journal of Clinical Psychology, 19*(3), 372–373.

Xu, J., & Roberts, R. E. (2010). The power of positive emotions: It's a matter of life or death—Subjective well-being and longevity over 28 years in a general population. *Health Psychology, 29*(1), 9–19. doi:10.1037/a0016767

Yalom, I. D. (1980). *Existential psychotherapy.* New York, NY: Basic Books.

Yang, A. C., Tsai, S-J., & Huang, N. E. (2011). Decomposing the association of completed suicide with air pollution, weather, and unemployment data at different time scales. *Journal of Affective Disorders, 129*(1–3), 275–281. doi:10.1016/j.jad.2010.08.010

Yang, H., Liu, T., & Zang, D. (2000). A study of stressful life events before the onset of hypothyroidism. *Chinese Mental Health Journal, 14*(3), 201–202.

Yate, M. (2006). *Knock 'em dead: The ultimate job search guide.* Avon, MA: Adams Media.

Ybema, J. F., Smulders, P. G. W., & Bongers, P. M. (2010). Antecedents and consequences of employee absenteeism: A longitudinal perspective on the role of job satisfaction and burnout. *European Journal of Work and Organizational Psychology, 19,* 102–124.

Yehuda, R., & Wong, C. M. (2007). Acute stress disorder and posttraumatic stress disorder. In G. Fink (Ed.), *Encyclopedia of stress: Vols. 1–4* (2nd ed., pp. 2–6). San Diego, CA: Elsevier Academic Press.

Yi, H., Stinson, F. S., Williams, G. D., & Dufour, M. C. (1999). *Surveillance report #53: Trends in alcohol-related fatal traffic crashes, United States, 1977–1998.* Rockville, MD: National Institute on Alcohol Abuse and Alcoholism.

Yoder, J. D., & Kahn, A. S. (2003). Making gender comparisons more meaningful: A call for more attention to social context. *Psychology of Women Quarterly, 27,* 281–290.

Young, J. E. (1982). Loneliness, depression and cognitive therapy: Theory and application. In L. A. Peplau & D. Perlman (Eds.), *Loneliness: A sourcebook of current theory, research and therapy*. New York, NY: Wiley.

Young, K. S. (1998). *Caught in the net: How to recognize the signs of Internet addiction—and a winning strategy for recovery*. New York, NY: Wiley.

Young, K. S. (2009). Assessment and treatment of Internet addiction. In A. Browne-Miller (Ed.), *The Praeger international collection on addictions, Vol 4: Behavioral addictions from concept to compulsion* (pp. 217–234). Santa Barbara, CA: Praeger/ABC-CLIO.

Young, L. R., & Nestle, M. (2002). The contribution of expanding portion sizes to the US obesity epidemic. *American Journal of Public Health, 92*, 246–249.

Young, R., & Sweeting, H. (2004). Adolescent bullying, relationships, psychological well-being, and gender-atypical behavior: A gender diagnosticity approach. *Sex Roles, 50*, 525–537.

Zagorsky, J. L. (2004). The wealth effects of smoking. *Tobacco control, 13*, 370–374.

Zahn, B. (2012). Yes, we do. Even at our age. In M. A. Paludi (Ed.), *The Psychology of love* (pp. 1–2). Santa Barbara, CA: Praeger/ABC-CLIO.

Zajonc, R. B. (1968). Attitudinal effects of mere exposure. *Journal of Personality and Social Psychology, 9*, 1–27.

Zakzanis, K. K., & Young, D. A. (2001). Memory impairment in abstinent MDMA ("Ecstasy") users: A longitudinal investigation. *Neurology, 56*, 966–969.

Zane, N., Hall, G. C. N., Sue, S., Young, K., & Nunez, J. (2004). Research on psychotherapy with culturally diverse populations. In M. J. Lambert (Ed.), *Bergin and Garfield's handbook of psychotherapy and behavior change*. New York, NY: Wiley.

Zautra, A. J., & Reich, J. W. (2011). Resilience: The meanings, methods, and measures of a fundamental characteristic of human adaptation. In S. Folkman (Ed.). *The Oxford handbook of stress, health, & coping* (pp. 173–185). New York, NY: Oxford University Press.

Zebrowitz, L. A., & Montepare, J. M. (2008). First impressions from facial appearance cues. In N. Ambady & J. J. Skowronski (Eds.), *First impressions* (pp. 171–204). New York, NY: Guilford Publications.

Zedek, S. (Ed.). (2011). *APA handbook of industrial and organizational psychology* (2 vols). Washington, DC: American Psychological Association.

Zeig, J. K. (1987). Introduction: The evolution of psychotherapy—Fundamental issues. In J. K. Zeig (Ed.), *The evolution of psychotherapy*. New York, NY: Brunner/Mazel.

Zhang, J. W., & Howell, R. T. (2011). Do time perspectives predict unique variance in life satisfaction beyond personality traits? *Personality and Individual Differences, 50*, 1261–1266. doi:10.1016/j.paid.2011.02.021

Zhang, L., Amos, C., & McDowell, W. C. (2008). A comparative study of Internet addiction between the United States and China. *CyberPsychology & Behavior, 11*, 727–729.

Zhang, Y. B., Harwood, J., & Hummert, M. (2005). Perceptions of conflict management styles in Chinese intergenerational dyads. *Communication Monographs, 72*, 71–91.

Zimbardo, P. G. (1977). *Shyness: What it is, what to do about it*. Reading, MA: Addison-Wesley.

Zimbardo, P. G. (1990). *Shyness*. Reading, MA: Addison-Wesley.

Zimbardo, P. G. (1992). Cults in everyday life: Dependency and power. *Contemporary Psychology, 37*, 1187–1189.

Zimbardo, P. G. (2002). Mind control: Psychological reality or mindless rhetoric. *Cultic Studies Review, 1*, 309–311.

Zimmerman, M., & Spitzer, R. L. (2009). Psychiatric classification. In B. J. Sadock, V. A. Sadock, & P. Ruiz (Eds.), *Kaplan & Sadock's comprehensive textbook of psychiatry* (pp. 1108–1138). Philadelphia: Lippincott Williams & Wilkins.

Zinbarg, R. E., & Griffith, J. W. (2008). Behavior therapy. In J. L. Lebow (Ed.), *Twenty-first century psychotherapies: Contemporary approaches to theory and practice*. New York, NY: Wiley.

Zinnebauer, B. J., & Pargament, K. I. (2005). Religiousness and spirituality. In R. F. Pargament & C. L. Park (Eds.), *Handbook of the psychology of religion and spirituality* (pp. 21–42). New York, NY: Guilford.

Zinnebauer, B. J., Pargament, K. I., Cole, B., Rye, M. S., Butter, E. M., Belavich, T. G., et al. (1997). Religion and spirituality: Unfuzzying the fuzzy. *Journal of the Scientific Study of Religion, 36*, 549–564.

Zinnebauer, B. J., Pargament, K. I., & Scott, A. B. (1999). The emerging meanings of religiousness and spirituality: Problems and prospects. *Journal of Personality, 67*, 889–920.

Zisook, S., Lesser, I., Stewart, J. W., Wisniewski, S. R., Balasubramani, G. K., Fava, M., et al. (2007). Effect of age at onset on the course of major depressive disorder. *American Journal of Psychiatry, 164*, 1539–1546.

Zohar, J., Fostick, L., & Juven-Wetzler, E. (2009). Obsessive-compulsive disorder. In M. C. Gelder, N. C. Andreasen, J. J. López-Ibor, Jr., & J. R. Geddes (Eds.), *New Oxford textbook of psychiatry* (2nd ed., Vol. 1). New York, NY: Oxford University Press.

Zuckerman, M. (1979). *Sensation seeking: Beyond the optimal level of arousal*. Hillsdale, NJ: Erlbaum.

Zuckerman, M. (1984). Experience and desire: A new format for sensation seeking scales. *Journal of Behavioral Assessment, 6*, 101–114.

Zuckerman, M. (1996). The psychobiological model for impulsive unsocialized sensation seeking: A comparative approach. *Neuropsychobiology, 34*, 125–129.

Zuckerman, M. (2006). Sensation seeking in entertainment. In J. Bryant & P. Vorderer (Eds.), *Psychology of Entertainment* (pp. 367–387). Mahwah, NJ: Erlbaum.

Zuckerman, M. (2007). *Sensation seeking and risky behavior*. Washington, DC: American Psychological Association.

Zuckerman, M. (2008). Personality and sensation seeking. In G. J. Boyle, G. Matthews, D. H. Saklofske (Eds.), *The Sage handbook of personality theory and assessment* (pp. 379–398). Los Angeles: Sage.

Zuckerman, M. (2009). Sensation seeking. In M. R. Leary & R. H. Hoyle (Eds.), *Handbook of individual differences in social behavior* (pp. 455–465). New York, NY: The Guilford Press.

Zuckerman, M., Kieffer, S. C., & Knee, C. R. (1998). Consequences of self-handicapping: Effects of coping, academic performance, and adjustment. *Journal of Personality and Social Psychology, 74*(6), 1619–1628.

Zuckerman, M., & Tsai, F. (2005). Costs of self-handicapping. *Journal of Social Psychology, 73*, 411–442.

Zvonkovic, A. M., Solomon, C. R., Humble, A. M., & Monoogian, M. (2005). Family work and relationships: Lessons from families of men whose jobs require travel. *Family Relations, 54*, 411–422.

Zytowski, D. G., & Kuder, F. (1999). *Kuder Career Search with Person Match*. Adel, IA: National Career Assessment Services, Inc.

NAME INDEX

Beddoe, R., A-5
Beeder, A. B., 162
Bègue, L., 103, 208
Behar, R., 4
Beidel, D. C., 430, 465, 469
Beilock, S., 85
Beisecker, A. E., 156
Bekelman, J. E., 473
Bekkouche, N. S., 88
Belar, C. D., 129, 130
Belger, A., 443
Bell, A. P., 362
Bell, B. S., 388
Bell, J. E., 153
Belland, J. C., 104
Belmore, S. M., 209
Belsky, J., 301
Beltz, A. M., 331
Bem, D., 225
Bem, S. L., 335, 345, 346
Ben-Ari, A., 299
Ben-Ari, R., 253
Bendall, S., 445
Bender, D. S., 476
Benet-Martínez, V., 253
Ben-Ezra, M. 77
Benjamin, A., A-6
Bennett, K. M., 267
Benoit, M., A-10
Benoit, P. J., 218
Benoit, W. L., 218
Ben-Porath, Y. S., 63
Benshoff, J. M., 296
Benson, H., 119
Benson, P. L., 503
Bentall, R. P., 445, 473
Berdahl, J. L., 343
Berenbaum, S. A., 331, 332
Bergen, M. R., 282
Berger, J., 220
Berger, S. S., 103, 86
Bergin, A. E., 463
Berkowitz, L., 102
Berman, M., 309
Berman, M. G., 496, 497, A-2, A-13
Berman, R. M., 472
Bernache-Assollant, I., 185
Bernieri, F. J., 200
Bero, L., 473
Berrettini, W. H., 435
Berry, D., 92
Berryman-Fink, C., 232
Berscheid, E., 206, 263, 297
Berthoud, H., 146
Berto, R., 497
Bertoch, S. C., 393
Berzon, B., 380
Best, D. L., 323
Bettelheim, B., 446
Bettmann, J. E., A-13
Betz, N. E., 189, 343, 395, 396, 404
Beusterien, K. M., 153
Beutler, L. E., 478, 479, 480
Bevan, J. L., 251
Bevans, K., 70
Bhagwagar, Z., 436
Bharadwaj, A. K., 247
Bhasin, T., 446
Bhattachary, S., 163
Bianchi, S. M., 304, 314
Biblarz, T. J., 304
Biddle, S. J. H., 337

Biernat, M., 182
Billings, A. G., 103, 107
Billings, L. S., 182
Bilmann-Mahecha, E., A-11
Bin, Y., 248
Binder, J., 215
Bini, L., 474
Bin Kassim, M. A., 79
Birch, L. L., 449
Birmingham, W., 90, 114
Birnbaum, M. H., 200, 209
Biron, C., 156
Biswas-Diener, R., 392, 488, 493
Bittman, M., A-6
Bivona, J. M., 368
Bjork, R. A., 25, 26
Bjorklund, D. F., 464
Björntorp, P., 144
Blackburn, T. C., 208
Blackwell, E., 131
Blaine, B., 174
Blair, C., 70
Blair, K. L., 367
Blair, S. N., 150, 151
Blair-Loy, M., 396
Blais, J. J., 284
Blakemore, E. R., 406
Blakemore, J. E. O., 331, 336
Blakeslee, S., 309–310
Blank, T. O., 247
Blankenship, K. L., 219
Blanton, H., 171
Blasé, S., 476
Blass, T., 222, 223, 224
Blau, F. D., 398
Bleakley, A., 358, 359
Bleuler, E., 439
Blieszner, R., 302
Bliss-Moreau, E., 201
Bloch, S., 463
Block, J., 106
Block, J. H., 347
Bloor, M., 156
Blume, B. D., 251
Blumenthal, J. A., 117, 132, 134, 504
Blumstein, P., 299, 303
Blunt, J. R., 24
Boase, J., 234, 284
Bobek, B. L., 408, 409
Bobo, W. V., 442, 471
Bobocel, D. R., 211
Bodenhausen, G. V., 203, 206, 207, 212
Bodenmann, G., 299, 306
Bodnar, L. E., 382
Boehringer, K., 251
Boen, F., 185, 186
Boeree, C. G., 49
Bögels, S. M., 468
Bogle, K., 371
Bohnert, A. M., 288
Boland, R. J., 433, 472
Boles, D. B., 333
Bolger, N., 106
Bolino, M. C., 405
Bollen, J., 330
Bolles, R. N., 414
Bonanno, G. A., 500
Bond, C. F., Jr., 243
Bond, J. T., 397
Bonebright, C. A., 410

Bonetti, L., 288
Bongar, B., 478
Bongers, P. M., 406
Bonneau, R. H.. 135
Bonner, G., 496
Bono, G., 502
Bookwala, J., 303
Booth, A., 308
Boots, D. P., 317
Bordnick, P., 468
Borkenau, P., 199
Borker, R. A., 348
Borland, E., 316
Bornstein, R. F., 41
Borys, S., 286
Bös, K., 150
Bose, S., 308
Bosson, J. K., 338
Bouchard, C., 146
Bourg, C., 324
Bourgeois, J. A., 435
Bourhis, J., 251
Bourhis, R., 213
Bovornusvakool, W., 410
Bowen, C., 302
Bower, G. H., 27, 256, 257, 258, 259
Bower, S. A., 256, 257, 258, 259
Bowers, K., 456, 486
Bowes-Sperry, L., 408
Bowins, B., 105
Bowlby, J., 277
Boyce, C. J., 21
Boyd, J. N., 114
Boyle, G. J., 33
Boyle, M., 422
Bradbury, T. N., 270, 299, 345
Braddock, J. H., 185
Bradley, L. J., 5
Brady-Amoon, P., 189
Bragg, E. A., A-9
Brainerd, C. J., 464
Brajša-Žganec, A., 412
Brambilla, M., 207
Bramlett, M. D., 298
Bramon, E., 444
Branaman, T. F., 244
Branas, C. C., 143
Brandes, D., 85
Brandt, M. J., 342
Branigan, C., 492
Brannon, L., 402
Brannon, L. A., 218
Brannon, R., 338
Branscombe, N. R., 402
Brashears, M. E., 286
Brass, D. J., 102
Brassard, A., 279
Bratko, D., 57
Bray, J. H., 311
Brecx, M., 135
Bredt, B. M., 162
Breggin, P. R., 473, 475
Brehm, J. W., 217
Brehm, S. S., 177, 227, 246, 272, 278
Breier, A., 442
Brenes, G. A., 477
Brennan, K. A., 278, 279
Brenner, L., 192
Breslin, F. C., 408
Brewer, M. B., 205, 213, 215

Brewin, C. R., 464
Brickman, P., 20
Bridge, J. A., 472
Bridges, K. R., 123
Brigham, J. C., 205
Brink, E. 47
Briñol, P., 216
Brinthaupt, T. M., 495
Brissette, I., 273
Briton, N. J., 240
Britt, T. W., 387
Britton, B. K, 123
Brodsky, J. B., 400
Brody, C., 508
Brody, L. R., 329, 347
Brody, S., 369
Broida, J., A-9
Bromley, M., 302
Brondolo, E., 70
Brookes, R., 356
Brooks, G., 339
Brooks, M. L., 184, 235
Brooks-Gunn, J., 355
Broomhall, H. S., 409
Brose, A., 132
Brotherridge, C. M., 406
Brotto, L. A., 382
Brown, A. S., 443
Brown, D., 390
Brown, E. J. P., 430
Brown, G. A., 21
Brown, J., 106
Brown, J. B., 315
Brown, J. D., 171, 175, 359
Brown, J. M., 134
Brown, K., 486
Brown, R. D., 464
Brown, R. J., 205, 215
Brown, R. P., 58
Brown, S., 311
Brown, S. L., 90
Brown, T. A., 426
Brown, T. T., 162
Browne, A., 318
Brownell, K. D., 144, 145, 146
Bruce, C., 301
Bruce, K. R., 448, 449
Brugha, T. S., 446
Brumbaugh, C. C., 279
Brunell, A. B., 58
Brunet, P. M., 287
Bryant, F. B., 497–498
Bryant, R. A., 108
Buchanan, C. M., 205
Buchanan, R. W., 439
Buchtel, E. E., 60
Buckingham, J. T., 184
Buckman, R., 156
Buechel, C., 324
Buehler, C., 19
Buehlman, K. T., 306
Buffardi, L. E., 58
Buhs, E. S., 506
Bulcroft, R., 294
Bulik, C. M., 447, 449
Bullinger, M., 69
Bullock-Yowell, E., 393
Bumpass, L., 20, 314
Bunde, J., 132
Burger, J. M., 53, 224, 225
Burgess, C., 163
Burgoon, J. K., 243

Burhans, K. K., 172
Burke, B. L., 59
Burke, J. D., 425
Burke, M. E., 398
Burke, P. J., 167
Burke, R. J., 410, 411
Burke, W. W., 396
Burlingame, G. M., 461
Burmeister, M., 55
Burn, S. M., 345
Burns, A. B., 438
Burns, E. L., 239
Burpee, L., 495
Burroughs, T., 208
Burrows, L., 210
Burton, L., A-10
Bushman, B. C., 417
Bushman, B. J., 102, 103, 178, 190,
191, 193
Buss, D., 55, 176, 266, 268–269,
280, 297, 298, 331, 347
Buss, W. C., 306
Bussey, K., 334
Bustillo, J. R., 439
Butkovic, A., 57
Butler, A. C., 26
Butler, E. A., 116
Butler, J., 251
Butler, J. L., 85
Buunk, A. P., 171, 212, 372
Buxton, M. N., 135
Buzzell, L. A-2
Bybee, D., 169
Byers, E., 364
Byne, W., 362
Byrm, R. J., 283, 284
Byrne, B., 115
Byrne, D., 270
Byrne, R., 6

C

Cabral, G. A., 162
Cacioppo, J. T., 90, 218, 286, 287,
288, 289
Caddy, A. J. C., 224
Cadinu, M., 214
Caggiula, A., 141
Cahill, L., 464
Cahn, D. D., 254, 274
Cai, D. A., 254
Calabrese, J. R., 472
Calasanti, T., 304
Calhoun, L. G., 88, 500, 501
Callander, J. C., 202
Calogero, R. M., 330
Caltabiano, N. J., 109
Cameron, D., 330, 347, 349
Cameron, K. D., 504
Cameron, L., 129, 155
Campbell, A., 248
Campbell, J. D., 168, 174, 175
Campbell, K., 296, 308
Campbell, L., 279
Campbell, L. F., 7
Campbell, M., 288
Campbell, S. M., 345
Campbell, W. K., 8, 58, 177, 185,
301
Campos, B., 270
Canary, D. J., 270, 271
Cancro, R., 441

Canetto, S. S., 330
Canli, T., 55
Cannon, W., 80
Cantor, J. R., 218
Canudas-Romo, V., 307
Capitanio, J., 363
Cappadocia, M., 468
Caprariello, P. A., 270
Caputo, D., 151
Carbonell, D. M., 100
Carcedo, R. J., 263
Cardena, E., 118, 430
Carducci, B., 246
Carey, M. P., 153
Carlson, D. N., 156
Carlson, E. N., 58, 173
Carlson, L., 135
Carlson, L. E., 496
Carlson, R., 6
Carlston, D. E., 200
Carmody, J., 180
Carnagey, N. L., 103
Carney, S., 474
Carpenter, C. J., 58
Carpenter, J. M., 235
Carpenter, W. T., 439, 441, 473
Carr, A., 486
Carrère, 302
Carroll, J. L., 376
Carroll, J. S., 306
Carroll, M. D, 144
Carroll-Ghosh, T., 435
Carson, E. A., 329
Carson, S. H., 180
Carstersen, L. L., 303
Carter, B., 299, 300
Carter, C. S., 440
Carter, T. J., 183
Carter-Sowell, A. R., 227
Carton, J. S., 246
Caruso, D. R., 115, 388
Carvalho, J., 382
Carver, C. S., 83, 91, 99, 101, 103,
107, 273
Case, B. G., 474
Casey, B. J., 85
Casey, C., 356, 357
Cashdan, E., 240
Casper. L. M., 314
Caspi, A., 33
Cassel, R. N., 49
Cassidy, J., 287
Cassin, S. E., 342
Castano, E., 213
Castle, D., 442
Castle, P. H., 475
Castonguay, L. G., 475
Catalano, S., 318
Cate, R. M., 298, 356, 371
Cattell, R. B., 32, 62, 63
Cava, M. M., A-6
Caverly, D. C., 24
Ceci, S. J., 326
Ceja, L., 493
Cepeda, N. J., 26
Cerbone, A., 70
Cerletti, U., 474
Cervellione, K. L., 106
Cetron, M. J., 396
Chadee, D., 226
Chaiken, S., 216, 217
Chalquist, C., A-2, A-13

Chamberlin, C. M., 411
Chamberlin, J., 415
Chamorro-Premuzic, T., 276
Chan, D., 388
Chan, M., 234
Chancey, D., 306
Chandler, J. J., 491
Chandola, T., 70
Chandra, A., 355, 369, 379
Chang, C. H., 404
Chang, R. Y., 113
Chang-Schneider, C., 176
Chaplin, T. M., 335
Chaplin, W. F., 417
Chapman, B., 32
Charlesworth, W. R., 348
Charney, D. S., 472
Chavez, J. M., 317
Chawla, L., A-12
Cheater, F., 155
Cheavens, J. S., 499
Chen, E., 135
Chen, G., 110
Chen, M., 210
Chen, S., 168, 202
Chen, Y. Y., 133
Chen, Z., 227
Cheng, C., 99
Cheng, H., 178
Cheng, K., 79, 117
Cheng, Y., 150
Cherlin, A. J., 293, 295, 310
Cherry, C., 153
Cherry, D. K., 476
Cheung, M. W. L., 100
Chew, B., 175
Chia, R. C., 335
Chiapelli, F., 136
Chida, Y., 134
Chin, H. B., 357
Chin, S., 132
Chiu, C.-Y., 60
Chivers, M. L., 366
Chizmar, L., 151
Choi, I., 208
Choi, L., 207
Choi, Y., 495
Chon, K., 388
Chopra, D., 6
Chopra, S. S., 473
Chou, C., 104
Chou, F., 153
Chow, H. H., 123
Chow, S., 486
Chrisler, J. C., 323
Christakis, N., 235
Christensen, A. J., 157
Christian, L. M., 136
Christiansen, A., 281
Christopher, F. S., 356
Chu, A. T., 104
Chu, C., 394
Chua, B., 394
Chua, H. F., 208
Chudzikowski, K., 392
Church, A. T., 59, 60
Church, M. A., 186
Churchett, L., 267
Cialdini, R. B., 185, 222, 225, 226,
227, A-8
Ciarocco, N. J., 243
Ciarrochi, J., 86

Ciccocioppo, M., 304, 340
Cimprich, B., 497
Ciraulo, D. A., 159
Claar, R. L., 156
Claidière, N., 220
Clark, A. J., 251
Clark, C. L., 278
Clark, D., 123
Clark, L. A., 491
Clark, M. A., 410
Clark, M. M., 118
Clark, M. S., 254, 272
Clark, R., 133
Clark, R. E., 439
Clarkberg, M., 396
Clarke, R. L., 390
Clarke, V. A., 91
Classen, T. J., 86, 408
Clay, D. L., 410
Clayton, S., A-2, A-9
Cleary, P. D., 140
Cleek, M. G., 306
Cleland, C. M., 463
Clemans, K. H., 336
Clements, A. M., 332
Clements, M. L., 299
Clementz, B. A., 185
Cleveland, J. N., 410
Clifford, S., 156
Clinebell, H., A-2
Clore, G. L., 219, 270
Coates, D. D., 5, 20
Coates, L., 239
Coates, T. J., 154
Coats, E. J., 246
Coatsworth, J. D., 500
Cochran, S. D., 364
Cocomazzi, D., 239
Coelho, C., 429
Cohan, C. L., 299, 315
Cohen, C. E., 202
Cohen, G., 171
Cohen, H. J., 503
Cohen, L. M., 456
Cohen, M. J. M., 134
Cohen, P., 390
Cohen, S., 69, 78, 83, 90, 135, 136,
137, 140
Cohn, V., 293, 316
Coker, A. L., 318
Colder, M., 116
Cole, E., A-13
Cole, P. M., 335
Coleman, L. J., 495
Coles, M. E., 428
Collaer, M. L., 333
Colley, A., 273
Colligan, T. W., 405
Collins, C., 154
Collins, E. C., 199
Collins, R. L., 337
Collins, W. A., 273, 279
Coltrane, S., 303, 304, 308
Colvin, C. R., 106
Comas-Diaz, L., 335
Combs, D. R., 440, 441
Combs-Orme, T., 301
Compton, M. T., 162
Compton, W. C., 118, 503
Conde, G., 495
Condron, L., 104
Confer, J. C., 266

G

Gabbard, G. O., 41, 479
Gable, S. L., 248, 299, 364
Gable, S., 510
Gabriel, S., 174
Gaertner, S. L., 70, 210, 211, 388
Gage, F. H., 436
Gailliot, M. T., 188, 206
Gaines, S. O., JR., 297
Gajendran, R. S., 396
Galdas, P. M., 155
Galinsky, E., 403, 411
Gallagher, K. I., 152
Gallagher, S., 172, 244
Gallo, L. C., 132, 136
Gallois, C., 306
Gana, K., 106
Ganahl, D. J., 337
Ganey, H. C. N., 80
Gangestad, S. W., 193, 239, 269
Gangwisch, J. E., 147
Ganong, L., 315, 340
Gant, L. M., 288
Ganzach, Y., 388
Gao, G., 276
Garb, H. N., 63
Garber, J., 156
Garcia, F., 178
Garcia, M., 476
Garcia, S. M., 171
Gardner, G., A-4, A-8, A-10, A-14
Gardner, W. L., 174
Garfield, S. L., 463
Garland, E. L., 118, 492
Garlow, S. H., 436
Garmezy, N., 500
Garnefski, N., 104
Garnets, L. D., 312, 362
Gartrell, N., 314
Gates, G., 360
Gattig, A., A-3
Gaunt, R., 200, 202, 208
Gawet, D. L., 76
Gawronski, B., 210, 211
Geary, D. C., 331
Gebhard, U., A-11, A-11
Gecas, V., 302
Geddes, J., 474
Gee, C. B., 306
Gee, E. M., 302
Gee, J., 266
Gee, T. L., 431
Geeraert, N. Y., 208
Geis, G., 354
Geisler, R. B., 184
Geller, E. S., A-10
Gençöz, T., 235
Gendolla, G. H., E., 170
Gentile, B., 179, 328
George, L. K., 503
Georgiades, K., 438
Geraerts, E., 464, 465
Geraghty, A. A., 502
Gerard, H. B., 221
German, S. T., 400
Gerrard, M., 184
Getzels, J. W., 495
Ghani, J. A., 495
Ghavami, N., 275, 313
Ghosh, D., 55
Gianciola, P. R., 329
Giannantonio, C., 394

Giannoglou, G., 131
Giant, C. L., 267
Giarrusso, R., 303
Gibbons, F. X., 171, 184
Gibbons, M. B. C., 463, 459
Gibbons, R. D., 472
Gibbs, J. L., 283, 284
Gibson, G., 139
Giedd, J. L., 408
Gierveld, J., 287
Giesen, D., 373
Gifford, R., 236
Gilbert, D. G., 103
Gilbert, D. T., 21, 183, 207, 356, 488, 511, A-5
Gilbody, S., 477
Gill, M., 163
Gillen, M., 369
Gillham, J., 91
Gillham, J. E., 488
Gilligan, S., 133
Gilman, R., 506
Gilmore, L., 288
Gilovich, T., 180, 185, 191
Giordano, P. C., 314
Giskes, K., 139
Gitlin, M., 472
Glascock, J., 337, 338
Glaser, R., 135, 136
Glasgow, R. E., 7
Glass, G. V., 479, 480
Glass, R. M., 475
Glassman, A., 134
Glavin, P., 387
Glazer, K., 133
Gleason, M. E. J., 283, 284
Gleaves, D. H., 430, 464
Glew, D. J., 110
Glick, I. D., 463
Glick, S., 363
Glisky, M. L., 431
Gluck, M. E., 448
Gmel, G., 143
Gneezy, A., 122
Godlee, F., 446
Goffman, E., 191
Gold, M. S., 160
Gold, R., 138
Goldberg, A. E., 312, 314, 335, 342
Goldberg, C., 407
Goldberg, W. A., 305
Goldberger, L., 88
Golden-Kreutz, D. M., 135
Golden, M. R., 363
Goldenberg, H., 462
Goldenberg, I., 462
Goldhammer, D., 382
Goldman, B. M., 175
Goldstein, E., 464
Goldstein, R. B., 58
Goldston, K., 134
Goldzweig, C. L., 407
Goleman, D., 115
Gollwitzer, P. M., 183
Gonida, E. N, 169
Gonzaga, G. C., 270, 297, 299
Gonzales, M. H., 117
González, H. M., 476
Good, G. E., 274
Good, J. J., 336
Goodall, K., 92

Goode-Cross, D. T., 274
Gooden, A. M., 335
Gooden, M. A., 335
Goodfriend, W., 265
Goodrick, G. K., 189
Goodwin, C., 240
Goodwin, F. K., 434, 437
Goodwin, R. D., 155
Gorchoff, S. M., 302, 303
Gordillo, R., 184
Gordis, E. B., 70
Gordon, A. H., 329
Gordon, K. C., 306
Gordon, L. U., 137
Gordon, R. A., 182, 192
Gordon, R. M., 310
Gordon, V. M., 390
Gore, H., 104
Gore, J. S., 173
Gorely, T., 337
Gosselin, J. T., 189
Gottdiener, J. S., 133
Gottesman, I. I., 442
Gottfried, A. E., 305
Gottfried, A. W., 305
Gottman, J., 355
Gottman, J. M., 299, 302, 303, 306, 307
Gottman, J. S., 307
Gough, B., 355
Gouin, J., 83, 136
Goulding, S. M., 162
Gourevitch, M. N., 160
Gouzoulis-Mayfrank, E., 163
Graber, J. A., 355
Gracia, E., 178
Grafanaki, S., 495
Graham, J., 52, 297
Graham, J. E., 136
Graig, E., 72
Grandey, A. A., 406
Grant, B. F., 58
Gray, J. R., 55
Gray, K., 318
Gray-Little, B., 179
Graziano, W. G., 32
Grearson, J, 296
Green, A. S., 283, 284
Green, C. R., 139
Green, J. D., 173
Green, L. R., 285
Green, M., 3
Green, M. A., 283
Greenberg, J. L., 58–59
Greenberg, J. S., 152
Greenberg, M., 27
Greene, K., 247, 248
Greene, R. L., 25
Greene-Shortridge, T. M., 387
Greenglass, E. R., 90
Greenhaus, J. H., 387, 395
Greenhow, C., A-10
Greenland, P., 131
Greenson, R. R., 457
Greenspan, K., 364
Greenway, R., A-2, A-13
Greenwood, D. N., 338
Gregory, R. J., 7
Greitmeyer, T., 222
Griest, J. H., 472
Griffeth, R. W., 388

Griffin, D. W., 281
Griffin, E., 270
Griffith, J. W., 469
Griffith, K. H., 400
Griffiths, A., 405
Griffiths, M., 410
Griffiths, M. D., 103
Griner, D., 476
Grinspoon, L., 161, 162
Griskevicius, V., 275, A-10
Grob, C. S., 163
Groesz, L. M., 267
Grohol, J., 478
Grøholt, B., 143
Groleau, J., M., 500
Gross, C. P., 473
Gross, J. J., 116
Grossman, J. B., 468
Grote, N. K., 254
Groth-Marnat, G., 63
Grothues, C. A., 318
Grove, W. M., 63
Gruber, A. J., 162
Grunberg, N. E., 86, 88, 103, 140
Grundy, E., 302
Grzywacz, J. G., 155
Guadagno, R. E., 225
Guarda, A. S., 448
Guardiani, J. M., 381
Guéguen, N., 225, 226, 239, 241
Guevremont, D. C., 466
Gugula, S., 335
Guignon, C. B., 507
Guiney, M. S., A-12
Guinn, I. S., 184
Günaydin, G., 200
Gunnoe, J., 241
Gunter, C., 442
Gupta, G. R., 295
Gupta, S., 309
Gupta. U., 296
Gur, R. A., 332
Gur, R. C., 332
Gute, G., 370
Guthrie, R. M., 108
Gutman, D. A., 86
Guyker, W., 477

H

Ha, T., 266
Haas, E., 348
Haas, L., 304, 305
Hadjikhani, N., 240
Hadjistavropoulos, H., 47
Hadjiyannakis, K., 438
Haeffel, G. J., 182
Hafdahl, A. R., 179
Hafer, C. L., 208
Hagan, H., 160
Haggerty, G., 279
Haglund, K. A., 357
Haidt, J., 170, 485, 487, 488, 503
Hale, S. L., 227
Halim, M. L., 335
Hall, A. H., 316
Hall, A. J., 200
Hall, C. S., 58
Hall, E. T., 237
Hall, J. A., 237, 240, 241, 246, 329, 347
Hall, K., 395

Opris, D., 477
O'Reilly-Landry, M., 457
Oringher, J., 345
Orlando, V. P., 24
Orne, E. C., 118
Orne, M. T., 118
Orrell-Valente, J. K., 267
Orth, U., 175, 178
Orth-Gomer, K., 135
Ortigo, K. M., 41
Orzechowicz, D., 275
Osbaldiston, R., A-8
Ost, J., 464
Öst, L.-G., 466, 467
Osteen, J., 6
Ostrom, T. M., 205
O'Sullivan, M., 243
Otto, A. D., 150
Oulette, S., 90
Overall, N. C., 266, 268
Overpeck, J. T., A-4
Overstreet, S., 70
Owen, J., 370
Owen, M. J., 442
Oyserman, D., 167, 168
Özdemir, M., 273
Ozer, D. J., 34, 33, 253
Ozer, E. J., 87
Ozer, E. M., 189

P

Pahl, S., 171, A-10
Pallanti, S P., 430
Palomares, N. A., 347
Paluck, E. L., 239
Pandey, A., 122
Pandey, J., 69
Pang, M., 394
Papaharitou, S., 372
Papas, R. K., 129
Pape, C. L., 246
Papernow, P. L., 311
Papp, L. M., 310
Pargament, K. I., 120, 502, 503
Park, C. L., 247, 500, 501, 503
Park, C. W., 218
Park, K. 301
Park, L. E., 177
Park, N., 51–52, 461, 508, 509
Parker, R., 156
Parker, S. H., 201
Parkes, K., 411
Parks, A. C., 461
Parrott, A. C., 163
Parrott, D. J., 340
Parrott, L., 6
Parsons, S., 389
Pashang, B., 115
Pashler, H., 26
Pasley, K., 311
Passino, R. M., 267
Pasupathi, M., 248, 296
Patel, J. K., 442
Pato, M. T., 427, 428, 434
Patrick, B. C., 248
Patrick, W., 286, 289
Patterson, C. J., 314, 362
Patterson, M. L., 239
Patton, W., 394, 395
Paul, A. M., 7
Paul, E. L., 370

Paul, K. I., 408, 409
Paul, R., 446
Paulhus, D. L., 37
Paullay, I. M., 410
Paulsen, N., 408
Pauwels, B. G., 281
Pavlov, I., 42–43, 47
Paxton, S. J., 267
Payne, B. K., 206
Pazder, L., 431
Peake, P. K., 188
Pearson, A. R., 210
Pearson, N. B., 71
Pearson, T. A., 306
Pechnick, R. N., 161
Pedersen, R., 476
Pedersen, S., 286
Pederson, W., 163
Pelavin, E. G., 462
Pelham, W. E., Jr., 92
Peng, K., 208
Pennebaker, J. W., 116, 133, 136
Penner, L. A., 211
Peplau, L. A., 264, 266, 272, 274, 275, 313, 314, 364, 367, 368, 371, 372
Perdrizet-Chevalier, C., 135
Peretti, P. O., 297
Perez, G. K., 135
Periera, M. A., 146
Perilloux, C., 266
Perkins, A., M., 239
Perkins, D. N., 495
Perkins, D. O., 441
Perkins, K., 141
Perlis, R. H., 473
Perlman, D., 246, 263, 278, 286
Perloff, R. M., 217
Perreault, S., 213
Perrett, D. L., 266
Perri, M. G., 144, 152
Perry, N. W., Jr., 130
Perry-Jenkins, M., 305, 342
Persky, I., 477
Person, E. S., 41
Pescosolido, B. A., 422
Peter, J., 284
Petersen, I., 433
Petersen, J. L., 329, 333, 342, 356, 359
Peterson, B., 57, 58
Peterson, C., 51–52, 88, 91, 182, 461, 486, 499, 502, 506, 507, 508–509
Peterson, J. L., 378
Peterson, R. F., 215
Peterson, S. H., 359
Peterson, Z. D., 323, 353
Petit, D. A. D., 162
Petrak, J., 104
Petrill, S. A., 54
Pettigrew, T. F., 212, 215
Petty, K. N., 200
Petty, R. E., 209, 216, 217, 218, 219
Petty, S. C., 438
Phillips, K. A., 330
Phillips, W. T., 151, 152
Phillips. A. G., 169
Pierce, J. P., 139
Pies, R., 104
Pietrantoni, L., 90
Pietrefesa, A. S., 428

Piferi, R. L., 90
Pike, C. L., 266
Piko, B. F., 179
Pillard, R. C., 362
Pilote, L., 131
Pinals, D. A., 442
Pindek, S., 191
Pine, D. S., 417
Pineda, A. S., 104
Pinel, J. P. J., 145, 146
Pines, M., 461
Pink, D. H., 397
Pinquart, M., 286
Piotrowski, N. A., 189
Pipher, M., 179
Pirog, R., A-6
Pirson, M., 495
Pi-Sunyer, F. X., 145
Pitt, R. N., 316
Pittman, F., III, 478
Piver, S., 281
Pizzagalli, D. A., 436
Planalp, S., 248
Plante, G. G., 151
Pleck, J. H., 338–339, 344, 347
Plomin, R., 54
Pogue-Geile, M. F., 442
Polan, H. J., 436
Poland, R. E., 163
Polivy, J., 175, 330
Pollack, C. E., 86
Pollack, L., 392, 416
Polley, B. A., 146
Pollozek, F., 222
Pontari, B. A., 183
Pope, H. G., 162, 330, 431, 439
Pope, J., 116
Pope, K. S., 479
Popenoe, D., 293
Porcerelli, J. H., 41
Porter, R. E., 236, 240
Porter, S., 239
Post, J. M., 224
Post, R. M., 472
Potter, D., 446
Powell, D. E., 280
Powell, G. N., 387
Powell, J. A., 224
Powell, J. H., 163
Powell, R. A., 431
Prati, G., 90
Pratkanis, A. R., 216
Prat-Sala, M., 47
Pratt, L. A., 134
Pratto, F., 211, 343
Prause, J., 305
Prescott, C. A., 330
Presser, H. B., 305
Pressman, S., 4
Pressman, S. D., 78
Preston-Schreck, C., 338
Preuper, H. R. S., 135
Previti, D., 308
Price, M., 454, 497
Prideaux, L., 395
Priess, H. A., 326
Priester, J. R., 219
Primack, B. A., 358
Prislin, R., 216
Pritchard, J., A-10
Prizant, B. M., 446
Prizmic, Z., 502

Pronin, E., 185, 220, 248, 490, 491
Proulx, C. M., 19
Provenzano, K. M., 116
Prudic, J., 474
Prugh, T., A-4
Pryor, B., 251
Pryor, F. L., 398
Pryor, J. B., 408
Psaty, B. M., 473
Pseekos, A., 393
Pudrovska, T., 301
Puentes, J., 371
Puetz, T. W., 117
Pugh, S., 402
Pulay, A. J., 58
Purkis, H., 429
Pyszczynski, T. A., 58–59

Q

Quasha, S., 254
Quidback, J., 18
Quilitch, H. R., 215
Quinn, D. M., 214
Quinn, J. M., 218
Quinn, K. A., 207
Quinn, P. D., 501
Quinn, R. E., 504

R

Rabin, M., 183
Rachman, S. J., 92, 466, 468
Racoosin, J., 472
Raczynski, J. M, 144
Radel, J., 251
Radtke, D., 249
Ragins, B. R., 400
Rahe, R. H., 73–74, 90
Rahim, M. A., 254
Rahman, M. A., 140
Raikes, H. A., 286
Raiya, H., 503
Raj, A., 470
Raley, S. B., 314
Ramaekers, J. G., 162
Ramalho, N., 115
Ramanthan, S., 104
Ramirez-Esparza, N., 14
Rammsayer, T. H., 54
Ramsey, M. W., 152
Rand, K. L., 499, 500
Rapee, R. M., 248, 287, 426
Rapson, E., 274, 278
Rapson, R. L., 295
Rashid, T., 461
Raskin, D. C., 244
Raskin, N. J., 460
Raskin, R., 58
Rasmussen, A., 206
Rassin, E., 202
Rathunde, K., 495
Raub, S., 47
Ravenna, M., 207
Ravindran, L. N., 472
Ravnkilde, B., 436
Ray, G. E., 286
Raybeck, D., 27
Raymaekers, L., 464
Read, J., 445
Read, J. D., 464
Reardon, R. C., 251, 392, 393

SUBJECT INDEX

A

ability-achievement gap, 340
abnormal behavior
  criteria of, 422–423
  medical model of, 421–422
  see also psychological disorders
abstinence, 378
abstinence-only programs, 357
abstinence pledges, 357
abstinence syndrome, 158
Abu Ghraib incident, 224
academic performance
  emotional disclosure and, 116
  improving, 22–27
  pressure and, 76
  self-efficacy and, 47
  self-esteem and, 176
  stress and, 86
  teachers' expectations of, 205
academic success
  N-effect in, 171
  occupation and, 388
  self-efficacy and, 189
acceptance
  meditation and, 496
  by therapist, 460
accidents
  drunk driving, 143
  motor vehicle, 137
  sedative use and, 160
accommodating style, 254
acculturation, 71
achievement, self-esteem and, 176
acquired immune deficiency syndrome. *See* AIDS
acronyms, 27
acrophobia, 426
acrostics, 26–27
ACTH, 82
action tendencies, 492
active listening, 24–25, 250
activity schedule, 23
actual self, 169–171
acute stressors, 71
adaptation, adjustment and, 10
adaptational outcomes, 84
addiction
  heroin, 159
  Internet surfing as, 103–104
  studies of, 141
adjustment, defined, 10
adolescents
  development of self-esteem in, 178, 179
  eating disorders in, 449
  homosexual, 286
  obesity in, 144
  occupational choices of, 394
  parenting of, 302
  pregnancy in, 373
  self-concept of, 172
  sexual socialization in, 356, 357, 358
  suicide by, 435
adrenal glands, 82
adultery, 372–373
advertising, 217
  gender stereotypes in, 337
  scarcity principle in, 227

aerobic exercise, 118
aesthetic needs, 51
affect, negative, 502
affective forecasting, 21, 183
affiliation, need for, 12, 13, 81
affirmative action, 210, 403
affluence. *See* wealth
affluenza, A-6
African Americans
  attitudes toward homosexuality among, 363
  divorce rates for, 308
  eye contact by, 240
  gender-role socialization of, 335
  heart disease in, 132, 133
  male role among, 339
  mental health services use by, 476
  preferred body types of, 266
  self-esteem in, 179
  sexual socialization of, 359
  stereotype threat and, 214, 327
  stereotypes of, 206, 324
  stresses for, 70
  TV viewing habits of, 337
  in workforce, 399, 400
age
  facial expression recognition and, 239
  happiness and, 18
  at marriage, 298, 300
  medical care seeking and, 155
agency, 499
aggression
  alcohol consumption and, 143
  as aspect of masculinity, 338
  as coping response, 101–102
  authoritarian, 211
  evolutionary origin of, 331
  Freud's view of, 36
  gender differences in, 328–329
  indirect, 328
  narcissism and, 58, 177–178
  relational, 316–318, 328
  sexual, 318–319
  terror management and, 59
  testosterone and, 333
  toward females, 343
  workaholism and, 410
aggressive communication, 257, 258
aging
  exercise and, 152
  immune system and, 136
  sexual behavior and, 372
aging parents, care of, 302
agoraphobia, 426–427
agreeableness, 32, 35, 33, 55, 56, 276
AIDS (acquired immune deficiency syndrome), 152–154, 377, 378
  IV drug use and, 160
  misconceptions about, 153–154
  partners of men with, 78
  positive illusions and, 106
  prevention of, 154
  symptoms of, 153
  transmission of, 153
  treatment for, 153
alarm reaction, 81, 82
Alba, Jessica, 421

alcohol
  consumption patterns for, 142
  date rape and, 318
  dependence on, 144
  use of, 142–144
alcohol abuse, 190
  health effects of, 144, 145
  mortality and, 137
  self-awareness and, 170
alcoholism, 144
  aversion therapy for, 466–467
alprazolam, 470
alternatives, evaluating, 113
ambient stress, 69
ambivalent/inconsistent style, 277
ambushing, 252
amenorrhea, 447
American Academy of Child and Adolescent Psychiatry (AACAP), 301
American Association of Sex Educators, Counselors, and Therapists, 382
American Civil Liberties Union, 212
American Institute of Stress, 81
American Psychiatric Association, 424
American Psychological Association (APA), 16, 390, 486
amnesia, dissociative, 430, 431
amphetamines, 158, 160
Amway Corporation, 227
amygdala, 401
anal sex, 154, 368, 369, 379
anal stage, 38
analytic approach, 208
analytical psychology, 39–40
androcentrism, 324
androgens, 333, 354, 355, 356
androgyny, 345–346
anger, 77
  benefits of, 103
  displaced, 37
  expressing, 115–116
  heart disease and, 132
  managing, 116–117
  venting, 102
angina, 131, 133
anhedonia, 432
animal research, 10, 48
animals, children's relationship with, A-11
annoyance, 77
anorexia nervosa, 447–449
antecedents, 92
  control of, 94–95
anthropocentric thinking, A-11
antianxiety drugs, 428, 470–471
antibodies, stress and, 83
anticipatory stressors, 71–72, 85
antidepressant drugs, 436, 472
anti-femininity, 338
antipsychotic drugs, 470, 471
anxiety, 78
  affiliation need and, 12, 13
  avoidance behavior and, 45
  as basic emotion, 238–239
  choice overload and, 2
  conditioned, 43–44
  coping strategies and, 101

bulimia nervosa, 447–449
burnout, 72, 85–86, 90, 115, 302, 405–406, 411
bystander effect, 222

C

caffeine, 148, 160
calling, work as, 505–506
calories, 147
cancer, 129
    alcohol abuse and, 144
    diet and, 148
    exercise and, 150–151
    HPV and, 378
    obesity and, 145
    oral contraceptives and, 374
    smoking and, 139
    stress and, 134–135
cannabis, 158, 159, 161
capitalization, 510
carbohydrates, 149
carbon dioxide trends, A-3
cardiovascular disease
    diet and, 148
    negative emotions and, 116
    smoking and, 139
    TV viewing and, 15
    see also heart disease
cardiovascular fitness, 150
career choice, 388–392
    models of, 392–396
career counseling, gender bias in, 336
career success, Big Five traits and, 33
careers
    positive workplaces and, 504–506
    for women, 304, 340, 343
    see also occupations
caregiving, for elderly parents, 302
carrying capacity, A-5–A-6
cartoons, gender stereotypes in, 337
case studies, 15
catastrophic thinking, 104, 108–109, 182, 469
catatonic schizophrenia, 440
catecholamines, 82, 83
categorization, social, 205
catharsis, 102
causation
    correlation and, 16
    experimental method and, 12
cell phones, 234
cellular immune response, 136
Centers for Disease Control and Prevention, 136
cerebral hemispheres, 332–333
cerebrospinal fluid, 443
cervical cap, 375
challenges, skills and, 494
change
    Buddhist view of, 503–504
    as source of stress, 73–75
channels
    for messages, 216, 232
    for nonverbal communication, 236
Chantix, 141
charitable donations, 511
chat rooms, 233. 234, 282
chemicals, harmful, A-12
child abuse
    dissociative disorders and, 431
    recovered memories of, 464–465
child care, 342

childlessness, 294, 301
children
    autism in, 445–446
    delaying having, 294
    development of self-esteem in, 178
    environment and, A-11–A-18
    environmental stresses on, 69, 70
    of gay parents, 314
    happiness and, 18
    launching into adult world, 302
    obesity in, 144
    observational learning by, 47
    occupational choices of, 394
    parents' work and, 305
    psychosexual stages in, 38–39
    PTSD in, 87
    remarriage and, 310–311
    self-concept in, 49, 172
    sexual identity in, 362
    sexual socialization of, 356–359
    therapy for, 462–463
    young, 301
    see also adolescents
children's books, 335
China, 104, 295
chlamydia, 377
chlorpromazine, 470, 471
choices, increase in, 1–2
choking under pressure, 85
cholesterol, 131, 148, 149
chronic diseases, 129
    stress and, 135
chronic stressors, 71, 81, 86
Cialis, 382
cigar smoking, 139
cigarette smoking, 139–142
clarification, in client-centered therapy, 460
clarifying, 250
classical conditioning, 42–43
    of anxiety, 428, 429, 465
    for aversion therapy, 466–467
claustrophobia, 426
client-centered therapy, 475, 480
climate change, A-4–A-5
clinical psychologists, 454–455
clinical psychology, 10, 486
Clinton, Bill, 407
clitoris, 367
close relationships, 263–289
    development of, 264–272
    homosexual, 274–275, 311–314
    Internet and, 282–285
    see also friendship; marriage; romantic relationships
clothing, person perception and, 200
clozapine, 471
clutter, 122
cocaine, 158, 160
cocktail party effect, 180
coefficient of determination, 14
cognition, 46
    positive emotions and, 492
    school satisfaction and, 506
cognitive abilities, gender differences in, 326–328
cognitive behavioral therapy, 475
cognitive consistency, 209
cognitive dissonance, A-8
cognitive distortions, 205–208, 212–213
cognitive misers, 180, 207
cognitive needs, 51
cognitive processes, self-esteem and, 180

cognitive psychology, applied to environmental behavior, A-10–A-11
cognitive therapy, 289, 479
cognitive-behavioral therapy, 182
cohabitation, 20, 293, 308, 314–315
cohabitation effect, 315
coitus, 369
cold/rejecting style, 277
collaborating, 255
collective self, 213
collective unconscious, 39, 40
collectivism, 179, 249
    attribution errors and, 208
    conflict and, 253
    marriage in, 295–296
    self-concept and, 173–174
    social support and, 114
college admission tests, 22
college degree
    earnings and, 398
    jobs and, 390
college grades, admissions tests and, 22
college students
    drinking by, 142
    loneliness in, 286
    narcissism in, 58
    sexual activity of, 370
    smoking among, 139
comic strips, gender bias in, 338
commitment
    love and, 276, 279
    in marriage, 293
    premature, 280
    relationship satisfaction and, 271–272
common cold, stress and, 135
commons dilemma, A-8
communal relationships, 272
communication
    adjustment and, 235
    aggressive, 257, 258
    assertive, 256–259
    defined, 231
    electronically mediated, 233–234
    face-to-face, 234
    with health providers, 156, 476
    ineffective, 280
    in marriage, 306–307
    online, 282–285
    problems in, 250–252
    in romantic relationships, 280
    sexual, 364–365, 380
    submissive, 256, 258
    tips for improving, 349
    see also interpersonal communication; nonverbal communication
communication apprehension, 250–252
communication process, 232–233
communication style, gender differences in, 330, 346–347
community mental health centers, 479
comorbidity, 424
companionate love, 276
comparative optimism, A-10
comparison level, 271–272
comparison level for alternatives, 272
compensation, 40
competition, effects of, 213
competitive style, for dealing with conflict, 254
compliance, 221–222, 225
    with medical advice, 156–157
compliments, giving, 192
compromising, 254–255

choice overload and, 2
exercise and, 151
hopelessness and, 437
Internet addiction and, 104
learned helplessness and, 101
low self-esteem and, 175
meditation and, 496
negative thinking and, 437–438
pessimistic style and, 182
postpartum, 301
self-blame and, 104
self-discrepancies and, 169
stress and, 86
suicide and, 435, 472
unemployment and, 409
depressive disorders, 431–438
computerized treatment of, 477
biological causes of, 436–437
cognitive factors in, 437
cognitive therapy for, 468–469
drug therapy for, 472
electroconvulsive therapy for, 474–475
etiology of, 435–438
gender differences in, 330
heart disease and, 134
interpersonal roots of, 438
positive psychotherapy for, 461
prevalence of, 425, 433
stress and, 438
descriptive norms, A-8
desensitization, 102
detachment, as skill, 504
developmental psychology, applied to
environmental behavior, A-11–A-12
developmental stages, for stepfamilies, 311
developmental tasks, in family life cycle, 301
deviance, 423
diabetes, 131
obesity and, 145
TV viewing and, 15
diagnosis, 422
*Diagnostic and Statistical Manual of Mental
Disorders* (DSM), 423–424
diaphragm, 375
diazepam, 470
dichotomous thinking, 469
diet, health and, 148–150
dieting, 147
diligence, 32
direction, search for sense of, 4–9
disasters, 69–70, 77, 87
discipline, using punishment for, 46
disclosure. *See* self-disclosure
disconfirmation bias, 218
discrimination, 205, 209–211
employment, 400
against gays and lesbians, 362–363
gender-based, 342–343
ingroups and, 213–214
modern, 210–211
as source of stress, 70–71
subjective perception of, 71
in workplace, 404
disease. *See* illness; specific diseases
disengagement coping, 100
disengagement, behavioral, 101
disobedience, to authority, 222, 224
disorganized schizophrenia, 440
displaced workers, 408
displacement, 37, 102
display rules, 239
dissociative amnesia, 430, 431

dissociative disorders, 430–431
prevalence of, 425, 430
dissociative experiences, in posttraumatic stress
disorder, 87
dissociative identity disorder (DID), 430–431
distance, interpersonal, 236–238
distance education, 397
distinctiveness, personality and, 31
distributed practice, 26
diversity, in workforce, 399–402
diversity training, 403
division of labor
gender roles and, 344
in marriage, 304
divorce, 307–311
adjusting to, 309
cohabitation and, 315
deciding to, 308–309
effects on children, 309–310
factors in, 298
forgiveness and, 117
happiness and, 19
infidelity and, 373
loneliness and, 286
personality and, 33
prediction of, 306
divorce rates, 293, 307–308, 310, 395
domestic violence, 316–318
door-in-the-face technique, 226–227
dopamine, 442
double standard, sexual, 203, 318–319, 354, 359
downsizing, 397, 404, 405, 408
"down low," 378
downward social comparison, 171, 184
Dr. Laura, 5–6
Dr. Phil, 4
dream analysis, 39, 457
drinking, 142–144
drinking water, A-6
drives, basic, 51
driving, 102
drunk, 143
marijuana use and, 162
drug abuse, 157–163
mortality and, 137
stress and, 86
drug companies, 474
drug therapy, 436, 454, 456, 470–475
effectiveness of, 473–474
drugs
dependence on, 158, 159, 160
effects of, 158
overdose potential of, 159, 160
recreational use of, 157–163
risks of, 158, 159, 160, 161
tolerance for, 158, 159
drunk driving, 143
DSM-IV, 423, 424
DSM-5, 424, 440–441, 446
dual-career couples, 305, 397, 411
dyslexia, 326

E

eating
oral fixation and, 38
stress-induced, 103
eating disorders, 86, 267, 330, 447–449
eating habits, 147–150
echolalia, 446
eclecticism, in therapy, 475
ecological dilemma, A-8

ecological footprint, A-5–A-6
ecologically connected self, A-9
economy, unpredictability of, 405
ecopsychology, A-2
ecosystems, A-5
ecstasy, 162–163
education
occupational earnings and, 398
smoking and, 139
see also schools
educational attainment, happiness and, 19
effectiveness, time management and, 123
efficiency
in person perception, 208–209
time management and, 123, 125
ego, 34, 35
ego depletion, 79
ego-depletion model, 187–188
ego threats, 177
egocentric values, A-8
ejaculation, 355, 366
premature, 381–382, 383
elaboration likelihood model, 218–219
Elavil, 472
electroconvulsive therapy (ECT), 474–475
electronically activated recorder (ERA), 14
electronically mediated communication, 233–234
email, 200, 233, 234, 242
emetic drugs, 466
emoticons, 242
emotion-focused coping, 100
emotional arousal, interpretation of, 190
emotional expression, gender differences in, 329
emotional intelligence, 115
Emotional Intelligence (Goleman), 115
emotional loneliness, 285
Emotional Reactions to Rejection, 265
emotions
agitation-related, 169
arousal of, 78–79
basic, 238–239
conditioning of, 43–44
conveyed through touch, 242
defined, 77, 491
dejection-related, 169
Ellis's view of, 108–109
expressing, 115
facial expression of, 238–239
heart disease and, 132–134
masculinity and, 339
moods and, 489
negative, 68, 77–78, 115–117, 132–134, 169,
170, 491
nonverbal communication of, 236
paralanguage and, 242
physiological indicators of, 243
positive, 78, 79, 110, 491–493
release of, 102
in schizophrenic disorders, 440
suppression of, 11, 133–134, 339–340
Emotions, Cortisol, and Immune Response, 83
empathy, 32, 117
in interpersonal communication, 255
meditation and, 496
in therapy, 460
empiricism, 11
employees
job stress and, 403–406
sexual harassment of, 407
employers
background checks by, 415
researching, 416

heredity *(continued)*
  in obesity, 146
  personality and, 53
  see also genetics
heritability ratios, 54
hermaphrodites, 355
heroin, 158, 159
herpes, genital, 377
heterosexism, 274–275, 400
heterosexuals, 274, 353
hierarchy of needs, Maslow's, 51
highlighting, in textbooks, 24
highly active antiretroviral therapy, 153
Hill, Anita, 407
hindsight bias, 56
hippocampus, 436
Hispanic Americans
  divorce rates for, 308
  male role among, 339
  self-esteem in, 179
  stresses for, 70
  in workforce, 400
Hitler, Adolf, 222
HIV infection, 369, 378
hoarding, 427
hobbies, 412
holistic approach, 208
homogamy, 297
homophobia, 37–38, 273, 340, 362–363
homosexuality, 360–364
  AIDS and, 153, 378
  attitudes toward, 312, 313, 362–363
  marriage and, 312, 313, 362, 363
  origins of, 361–362
  prevalence of, 360
  reaction formation and, 37
homosexuals, 274, 353–354
  children of, 363
  dating challenges of, 264
  friendships and, 274
  loneliness and, 286
  parents of, 363
  relationships of, 311–314, 372
  sexual activity of, 370
  sexual socialization of, 360
  in workforce, 399–400
honesty, in interpersonal communication, 255
"hooking up," 370
hope, 499–500
Hope Scale, 499
hopelessness, 433
hopelessness theory, 437
hormone-based contraceptives, 374, 375
hormones, 333
  depressive disorders and, 437
  homosexuality and, 362
  sex, 354–355, 356
  stress, 69, 82–83, 118
hostile work environment, 343, 407
hostility
  heart disease and, 132
  managing, 116–117
  narcissism and, 177
household chores, 304, 342
Hughes, Howard, 427
human immunodeficiency virus (HIV), 153
human nature, 49, 50
human papillomavirus (HPV), 377, 378
human potential movement, 49
humanism, 48

humanistic psychology, 487
humanistic theories
  evaluation of, 52–53
  Maslow's, 50–52
  Rogers's, 49–50
humor
  as stress reducer, 109–110
  self-defeating, 110
humoral immune response, 136
hunting-and-gathering societies, 331–332, 344
Hurricane Katrina, 109, 110, A-12
hydrophobia, 426
hypertension, 131
  alcohol and, 144
  caffeine and, 148
  obesity and, 145
  salt and, 148
hypnosis, for recovering repressed memories, 464
hypoactive sexual desire, 382, 383
hypodermic needles, 159
hypothalamic-pituitary-adrenocortical (HPA) axis, 437
hypothalamus, 437, 82
hypothesis, 12, 13

I

id, 34, 35
ideal self, 169–171, 284
identical twins, 54
identification, 37, A-9
Identifying Early Signs of Schizophrenia, 444
identity
  culture and, 173
  gender-role, 344–345
  loss of, 430
  possible selves and, 168
  sexual, 353–354
illness
  Big Five traits and, 33
  job stress and, 406
  life changes and, 74–75
  obesity and, 145
  reactions to, 155–157
  stress and, 82, 88, 135
illusion of control, 184
illusions, positive, 106
imitation
  of gender roles, 334
  in observational learning, 47
immigration, 71
immune functioning
  AIDS and, 153
  loneliness and, 287
  marijuana use and, 162
  optimism and, 91
  positive emotional style and, 78
  social support and, 89–90
  stress and, 83–84, 136
impact bias, 183
impatience, 131
Implanon, 375
Implicit Association Test, 210, 401
impotence, 381
  marijuana use and, 162
impression formation, 199–209
  in job interviews, 416–417
  see also person perception
impression management, 191–193
impulsivity, 191

incentives, A-10
income
  education and, 398
  happiness and, 17–18
  marriage and, 306
incongruence, 49, 50, 459–460
independent variables, 12, 13
independent view of self, 174
India, 69, 295, 296
individualism, 179, 248–249
  attribution errors and, 208
  conflict and, 253
  marriage and, 295–296
  self-concept and, 173–174
  self-serving bias and, 185
  social support and, 114
indulgence, as coping strategy, 103–104
industrial/organizational (I/O) psychology, 387
infantile autism, 445
infants
  attachment styles in, 277, 305
  responses to threats of, 81
infectious diseases, 129
inferiority complex, 40
infidelity, 372–373
inflammation
  chronic, 84
  heart disease and, 131
information, retention of, 25
information influence, 222
ingratiation, 192
ingroup favoritism, 213, 214
ingroups, 205, 211
inhibitions
  alcohol and, 143
  sexual, 359–360
injunctive norms, A-8
inkblots test, 63
insecurity, 279, 298
insight therapies, 453, 456–465
  client-centered, 459–460
  effectiveness of, 463, 480
  psychoanalysis, 457–458
insomnia, stress and, 86
instant messaging (IM), 3, 233, 234
institutions
  positive, 504–507
  virtuous, 506–507
instrumental style, 346
instrumentality, 324
intellectualization, 105
intelligence
  emotional, 115
  happiness and, 19
  heritability of, 54
  occupation and, 388
intercourse, sexual, 367, 368, 369–370
interdependence theory, 271–272
interdependent view of self, 174
interest inventories, 390–391
Intergovernmental Panel on Climate Change (IPCC), A-4
Internet
  close relationships and, 282–285
  communicating via, 233–235
  conducting therapy via, 477
  increasing use of, 3
  for overcoming loneliness, 288
  sexual content on, 359
  surfing, 412
Internet addiction, 103–104

interpersonal communication
  barriers to, 252
  defined, 231
  improving, 246–250
  in marriage, 306–307
  premarital, 299
  problems in, 250–252
  about sex, 364–365
  technology and, 233–235
interpersonal psychotherapy (IP), 15
interpersonal relationships. *See* close relationships
interpretation
  of aversive events, 101
  in psychoanalysis, 457–458
interruptions, 122, 125
intersex individuals, 355
interviews, job, 416–417
intimacy
  in friendships, 273
  in online communication, 235, 283
  love and, 275, 276, 279
  self-disclosure and, 248
  sex and, 340, 360
  touch and, 241
intimate violence, 316–319
intimidation, 192
intrauterine device (IUD), 375
intravenous drug use, 153, 159
introducing oneself, 247
introversion, 40, 53
inverted-U hypothesis, 79–80
investments, in relationships, 272
irrational assumptions, 104
irrational thinking, 195, 288, 439–440
irritable bowel syndrome, 251
ischemia, 131

J

Japan, 185, 253, 295
jealousy, 47, 317
job interviews, 416–417
job loss, 405, 408–409
job performance
  self-efficacy and, 189
  self-esteem and, 176
job satisfaction, 20, 305
  career choice and, 388
  flow and, 495
  interest inventories and, 390
  personality fit and, 393
job search, 413–417
job security, 396
job sharing, 398
job skills, 397
job stress, 403–406
  demand-control model of, 405
  effects of, 405–406
jobs
  information about, 389–390
  positive workplaces and, 504–506
  see also work
Johnson, Lyndon B., 241
joy, 492
judgments, snap vs. systematic, 200–201, 218

K

Kaiser Family Foundation, 369
kindness, meditation and, 496
kinesics, 240
kissing, 368

Koreans, 206
Kuder Career Search with Placement Match, 390

L

labeling, of mentally ill, 422
labor, division of, 331–332, 410
labor force, changing, 399–403
language, 232
  gender differences in, 347–349
Las Vegas, A-6
Last Children in the Woods (Louv), A-11
latency stage, 38, 39
lateralization, hemispheric, 332–333
learned helplessness, 101, 182, 437
learning
  behaviorist view of, 465
  via classical conditioning, 42–43
  lifelong, 397
  observational, 46–47
  via operant conditioning, 44–46
Lebowitz, Fran, 510
lectures, getting more from, 24–25
leisure, 18, 412–413
lesbians, 274, 311–314, 354, 360–364
  friendships and, 274
  sexual activity of, 367
  sexual satisfaction of, 372
letting go, 504
Levitra, 382
LGBT, 354
liberals, 211
lice, pubic, 377
lie detector, 243–245
life changes, 73–75
life expectancy
  smoking and, 139
  social support and, 90
lifelong learning, 397
lifestyles, environmentally responsible,
  A-14–A15
likability, of source, 217
link method, 27
liquor, 142
listening, 232
  during lectures, 24–25
  effective, 249–250
  gaze and, 239
  to good news, 510
lithium, 472
littering, A-8
liver, alcohol and, 144, 145
loneliness, 285–289
  causes of, 286
  overcoming, 287–288
  prevalence of, 286
  shyness and, 298
  stress and, 83
Loneliness (Cacioppo & Patrick), 289
longevity
  optimism and, 91
  physical fitness and, 150
  positive emotional style and, 78, 79
loss
  of job, 408–409
  resilience and, 500
  as source of stress, 72
love
  as attachment, 276–279
  course of, 279–281
  happiness and, 19
  romantic, 274–282

triangular theory of, 275–276, 279
  unconditional, 50
lowball technique, 225–226
LSD, 158, 161
luck, 208
lung cancer
  marijuana use and, 162
  smoking and, 139
lying, 242–245, 284

M

macho sexual image, 340
magazines, gender stereotypes in, 358
major depressive disorder, 432–434
makeover culture, 2
Making Sense of People (Barondes), 56
maladaptive behavior, 423
male role, 339–340
malnutrition, prenatal, 443–444
Mandel, Howie, 421
manhood, 338
mania, 432, 433, 434
manipulation, 256
Mann, Aimee, 109
MAO inhibitors, 472
marijuana, 158, 161–162, 442
marital satisfaction, 19–20
  in early years, 300–301
  in later years, 303
  nonverbal sensitivity and, 246
  optimism and, 91
  predictors of, 270–271
  sexual satisfaction and, 371
  work and, 304–305
  of working women, 411
marital status, happiness and, 19–20
marital success, predictors of, 298–299
marital therapy, 462–463
marriage, 293
  abuse in, 316–318
  age at first, 293, 294
  alternatives to, 311–316
  arranged, 295–296
  communication in, 306–307
  conflict in, 303
  cultural influences on, 295–296
  deciding on, 281
  decision about, 295–299
  division of labor in, 304
  financial problems in, 306
  infidelity in, 372–373
  interracial, 297
  motivation for, 295, 296
  open, 372
  same-sex, 312–313, 362, 363
  sexual activity in, 371–372
  trends in, 293–294
  vulnerable areas in, 303–307
  see also divorce
marriage and family therapists, 455, 456
Marriage-Go-Round, The (Cherlin), 295
marriage mandate, 340
marriage partner, desired characteristics in, 266
masculinity, 324, 338–339, 344–345
masculinity crisis, 339
massed practice, 26
masturbation, 355, 368–369
matching hypothesis, 268
mate selection, 266, 297–299
materialism, 2, 18, 59, A-7, A-8
mathematical abilities, gender differences in, 326

maturation, sexual, 355
Mayer-Salovey-Caruso Emotional Intelligence
    Test, 115
MDMA, 162–163
"me first" philosophy, 8, 58
meaning, search for, 3, 503
meaning-focused coping, 100
meat consumption, A-6
media
    eating disorders and, 449
    health information in, 138
    for messages, 216
    sexual content of, 358–360
    as source of gender-role socialization, 337–338
    violence in, 102
medical advice, adherence to, 156–157
Medical College Admissions Test (MCAT), 106
medical treatment, seeking, 155
meditation, 118–119, 496
Mellaril, 471
memories
    pleasant, 488
    recovered, 464–465
memorization, 25
memory
    emotional arousal and, 79
    facial identification and, 239
    improving, 25–27
    loss of, 430
    marijuana use and, 162
    stress and, 85
menarche, 355
menopause, 131
menstruation, 355
mental ability tests, 61
mental disorders, Big Five traits and, 33
mental health professions, 454–456
mental health services, technology for, 476–477
mental hospitals, declining populations in, 470
mental illness. *See* psychological disorders
mental motion, 490–491
mental processes
    behavioral perspective on, 41
    study of, 10
mental rotation, 328
mercury, in vaccines, 446
mere exposure effect, 265–266
mescaline, 158, 161
messages, 232
    persuasive, 216–218
Messages: The Communication Skills Book
    (McKay, Davis, and Fanning), 246
meta-analysis, 325
metabolism, obesity and, 146
methamphetamine, 160
method of loci, 27
Mexicans, stereotypes of, 14
Michelangelo phenomenon, 172
Michelle Remembers (Smith and Pazder), 431
mifepristone, 376
mind control, 5
mindfulness, 118, 180, 215, 495–497
minding, of relationships, 271
Mindless Eating (Wansink), 148
mindlessness, 180, 215, 218, 495
minerals, 149
Minnesota Multiphasic Personality Inventory
    (MMPI), 62
minority groups
    discrimination against, 210
    self-esteem in, 179
    stresses for, 70–71

therapeutic services for, 454, 455, 475–476
    in workforce, 399–420
    see also specific minority groups
"miracle on the Hudson," 485
miscarriage, 376
miscommunication, 232
missionary position, 370
mnemonics, 26–27
modal personality, 60
models/ modeling, 189
    of assertive communication, 259
    of gender roles, 334
    in observational learning, 46–47
    in social skills training, 468
    for sustainable lifestyles, A-10
modesty, 509
    false, 192
money
    as marital problem, 306
    happiness and, 17–18
monogamy, 297
Monroe, Marilyn, 41
mood disorders, 330, 431
mood stabilizers, 472
moods
    gratitude and, 502
    positive, 489–490
Mormon Church, 297
"morning after pill," 376
morphine, 158, 159
mortality
    Big Five traits and, 33
    from health-impairing behaviors, 137
    obesity and, 145
    physical fitness and, 150
    smoking and, 139
mortality rates, for diseases, 129
mortality salience, 59
motherhood mandate, 340
motivation, persuasion and, 219
motivational distortion, 252
motives
    guiding self-understanding, 182–183
    sexual, 364
motor vehicle accidents, 137
Mozes, Eva, 116
multiaxial system of classification, 423, 424
Multicultural Manners (Dresser), 232, 233
multiple-personality disorder, 430–431
Mundugumor, 334
musculoskeletal pain, obesity and, 145
music videos, 338, 358–359
My Lai incident, 224
myocardial infarction, 131
myocardial ischemia, 131, 133
Myths of Happiness, The (Lyubomirsky), 506

N

narcissism, 7–8, 57–58, 177–178, 187, 191
narcissistic entitlement, 117
narcissistic personality disorder (NPD), 57
Narcissistic Personality Inventory, 58
narcotics, 158, 159
Nardil, 472
narrative identity, 248
Nash, John, 441
National Alliance for the Mentally Ill, 424
national character, 60
National Institute on Drug Abuse, 157
nations, subjective well-being of, 17
natural resources, depletion of, 2

natural selection, 55, 331
naturalistic observation, 14
nature, experiences in, 496–497, A-11–A-12
Nazi war crimes, 222
needs
    gratification of, 38
    hierarchy of, 51
N-effect, 171
negative acknowledgment, 192–193
negative reinforcement, 45, 46
negative self, 168
negative thinking, 468–469
    depression and, 437–438
neglectful parenting, 178
negotiation, cultural differences in, 253
NEO Personality Inventory, 62
neonate qualities, attractiveness and, 266
netlingo, 233
neurodevelopmental hypothesis, 443–444
neurogenesis, suppression of, 436–437
neuroses, 457
neuroticism, 32, 33, 55
    cancer and, 134
    happiness and, 20
neurotransmitters, 428, 436, 442
newlyweds, 300–301
Nickelodeon, 337
nicotine, 160
nicotine substitutes, 140–142
no, inability to say, 121
noise
    in communication process, 232
    as stressful, 69
nonverbal communication, 232, 236–246
    elements of, 236–238
    gender differences in, 347
    in job interviews, 416
    lying and, 243, 244
    in person perception, 200
    in self-disclosure, 247
    significance of, 246
nonverbal cues, in effective listening, 250
nonverbal sensitivity, 246
Nordyke, Robert, 307
norepinephrine, 436
normality, 422, 424
normative influences, 222
norms
    group, 208
    test, 61
    see also social norms
note taking, from lectures, 24
nuclear family, 294
nutrients, essential, 149
nutrition, 147–150
Nuvaring, 375

O

obedience, 222–224
obesity, 144–147, 266
    exercise and, 150
    TV viewing and, 15
observation, naturalistic, 14
observational learning, 46–47
    gender-role socialization, 334
    of social skills, 468
obsession, 280, 427
obsessive-compulsive disorder (OCD), 421,
    427–428, 479
    computerized treatment of, 477
    drug therapy for, 472

occupational development, 394–395
occupational interest inventories, 390–391
Occupational Outlook Handbook, 389
occupations
 choosing, 388–392
 high growth, 398
 researching, 389–390
 for women, 343
Oedipal complex, 39, 361, 458
olanzapine, 471
omega 3 fatty acids, 148
one-session treatment (OST), 466, 467
online privacy, 235
Online Relationships, 3
open marriage, 372
openness to experience, 32, 33, 55
 meditation and, 496
operant conditioning, 44–46
 of anxiety disorders, 428, 429
 of gender roles, 334
 for self-modification programs, 93–95
opiates, 158, 159
optimal experience, 493
optimal level of arousal, 79–80
optimal margin of illusion, 106
optimism, 68, 91, 186, 218, 499
 comparative, A-10
 religious faith and, 503
 unrealistic, 106, 138, 140
optimistic explanatory style, 91, 182
oral contraceptives, 374, 375
oral presentations, 251
oral sex, 367, 368
oral stage, 38
orgasm, 366
 faking, 367
orgasmic difficulties, 382, 383
osteoporosis, 447
ought self, 169–171
outcome studies, of insight therapies, 463
outcomes, in social exchanges, 272
Outdoor Behavioral Health Industry Council,
 A-13
outgroup derogation, 213
outgroup homogeneity effect, 205
outgroups, 205, 207, 211
outlining, 26
outsourcing, 397
overcommunication, 251
overcompensation, 40, 105
overconsumption, 2, A-6–A-7
overdose, alcohol, 143
overeating, 94, 144–147, 190
overlearning, 25
Oxycontin, 159
oxytocin, 81

P

pack rats, 122
pain, self-efficacy and, 47
pain tolerance, 503
panic attacks, with hallucinogens, 161
panic disorder, 426–427, 472, 479
paradox of close relationships, 263
paralanguage, 242
paralysis of perfection, 122
paranoia, drug, 161
paranoid schizophrenia, 440
paraphrasing, 250
parasympathetic nervous system, 80–81, A-12
parental investment theory, 268–269

parenthood/parenting, 301–303
 expectations for, 301
 happiness and, 18
 inferiority complex and, 40
 self-esteem development and, 178
 in stepfamilies, 311
parenting styles, 178
 attachment and, 277
 occupation and 389
parents
 adult children living with, 302
 feedback from, 172
 gay, 314
 of gay children, 363
 as influence on children's sexual identity, 356
 loneliness and, 286
 punishment by, 46
 as source of gender-role socialization, 334,
  335–336
 unconditional love from, 50
paroxetine, 472
partner abuse, 178, 316–318
passion, 275–276, 279
passive aggression, 256
pathways, 499
patience, meditation and, 496
peak experiences, 52
peak performance, 80
peers
 adolescents' influence by, 302
 as source of gender-role socialization, 336
 sex information from, 356–357
penis, 365–367, 369
penis envy, 39, 41
perception
 distorted, 440
 stress and, 69
 see also person perception
perfectionism, 122, 298, 449
performance pressure, 75, 76, 85, 402, 404
permissive parenting, 178
persecution, delusions of, 440
person-centered theory, Rogers's, 49–50
person-centered therapy, 459
person-environment fit model, 392–394
person perception, 199–209
 attribution processes in, 201
 cognitive distortions in, 205–208
 expectations and, 202–205
 key themes in, 208–209
 sources of information for, 199–200
personal growth, 9
personal space, 26–238
personal unconscious, 39
personality
 Adler's view of, 40
 authoritarian, 211
 Bandura's view of, 47
 behavioral perspectives on, 41–48
 biological perspectives on, 53–56
 cancer and, 134
 career choice and, 389
 choking under pressure and, 85
 consistency in, 47
 culture and, 59–60, 173
 defined, 31
 eating disorders and, 449
 evolutionary perspective on, 55
 Eysenck's view of, 53
 as factor in attraction, 270
 five-factor model of, 32–33
 flow and, 495

 Freud's theory of, 34–39
 gender differences in, 328–329
 happiness and, 20
 healthy, 52
 heart disease and, 130–134
 heritability of, 54
 humanistic theories of, 49–53
 Jung's view of, 39–40
 marital success and, 298
 Maslow's view of, 50–52
 obesity and, 146
 person perception and, 200
 psychodynamic perspectives on, 33–41
 self-monitoring and, 193
 Skinner's view of, 45, 46
 social class and, 32, 33
personality development
 Adler's view of, 40
 behavioral perspectives on, 42
 Freud's psychosexual stages of, 38–39
 Rogers's view of, 49–50
 Skinner's view of, 45
personality signatures, 48
Personality, Situations, and Emotion, 48
personality structure
 Eysenck's view of, 53, 54
 Freud's view of, 34–35
 Rogers's view of, 49, 50
personality tests, 55, 61–63
personality traits, 31–32
 cultural differences in, 60
 gender-typed, 345–346
 hierarchy of, 53, 54
 love and, 276
 positive, 498–504
 testing of, 62–63
personality types, career choice and, 392–394
persuasion, 216–219
 defined, 216
 peripheral vs. central routes to, 219
 process of, 216–218
pessimism, defensive, 186
pessimistic explanatory style, 91, 101, 182, 437
pessimists, 218
pesticides, A-14
peyote, 161
phallic stage, 38, 39
pharmaceutical industry, 474
phobias, 479
 common, 426
 conditioning of, 43–44, 428–429
 treatment of, 466, 467, 477
phobic disorder, 426
physical appearance, in person perception,
 199–200
physical attractiveness
 evolutionary perspective on, 268–269
 eating disorders and, 448
 extraversion and, 56
 as factor in attraction, 266–269
 happiness and, 19
 narcissism and, 58
 of persuader, 217
 stereotypes of, 206
physical fitness, heart disease and, 133
physique, desirable, 266
Pink, 217
pituitary gland, 82
Plan B pills, 376
plastics, A-25
play activities, gender roles and, 335, 336
pleasure, 497

pleasure principle, 34
plural marriage, 297
poker face, 239
polarization, false, A-11
politics
  authoritarianism and, 211
  terror management and, 59
pollution, A-6
polygamy, 297
polygraph, 243–245
polyunsaturated fats, 150
positive approach, in relationships, 281
positive emotions, 299
  generating, 218
Positive Institutions and Volunteering, 505
positive organizational behavior (POB), 504–506
positive outlook, 195
Positive Power of Negative Thinking, The
  (Norem), 186
positive psychology, 461, 485–511
  criticism of, 507–508
  defined, 486
  future of, 508
  history of, 486–487
  scope of, 485–488
positive psychology movement, 52, 88
positive psychotherapy, 461
positive regard, unconditional, 460
positive reinforcement, 44–45
positive reinterpretation, 111, 252
positive self, 168
postpartum distress, 301
posttraumatic growth, 88, 90, 500–501
posttraumatic stress disorder (PTSD), 78, 87, A-12
  benefit finding and, 111
  catastrophic thinking and, 108
  following rape, 318
  gender differences in, 330
  reducing effects of, 90
  self-blame and, 104
  self-efficacy and, 47
posture, 240
poverty, 17, 70
preconscious, 35
prefrontal cortex, 85
pregnancy, 355
  fear of, 359–360
  influenza during, 443
  planning for, 301
  preventing, 373–376
  stress during, 444
pregnancy rates, 373
prejudice, 205, 209–215
  causes of, 211–214
  competition and, 213
  reducing, 206, 214–215
  as source of stress, 70–71
  terror management and, 59
  in workplace, 401, 402
prenatal development
  gender differentiation in, 333
  homosexuality and, 362
  schizophrenic disorders and, 443–445
  sexual differentiation in, 354–355
preparedness, 429
present orientation, 114
pressure
  to conform, 221
  to perform, 85
  to succeed, 339
  as source of stress, 75–76
primacy effect, 209

primary appraisal, 69
primary process thinking, 34
primary sex characteristics, 355
priorities, sticking to, 121
privacy
  online, 235
  self-disclosure and, 248
proactive coping, 100
problem drinking, 144
problem-focused coping, 100, A-12
problem solving
  positive moods and, 489
  systematic, 113
problems in living, 422
procrastination, 47, 122–123, 190
  in seeking treatment, 155
professional occupations, 397
progesterone, 374
prognosis, 422
progress, paradox of, 1–3
projection, 37, A-9
projective tests, 63
promiscuity, 203
prompts, A-10
prosocial spending, 510–511
protein, 149
proxemics, 236–237
proximity, as factor in attraction, 264
Prozac, 472
pseudolistening, 252
psilocybin, 158, 161
psychiatric nurses, 455, 456
psychiatrists, 454, 455–456
psychoanalysis, 34, 457–458
psychoanalytic theory, 34–39
  applied to environmental behavior, A-9
psychobabble, 7
psychodiagnosis, 423–424
psychodynamic theories
  Adler's 40
  evaluation of, 40–41
  Freud's, 34–39
  Jung's, 39–40
psychodynamic therapy, 475, 480
psychological disorders
  classification of, 423–424
  Freud's view of, 39
  gender differences in, 330
  prevalence of, 424–425
  Rogers's view of, 50
  stress and, 86
psychological tests, 61–63
  for career decisions, 390–391
psychologists, 454–455
  environmental, A-2
psychology
  careers in, 390
  defined, 10
  environmentally responsible behavior and,
    A-8–A-13
  as profession, 10
  as science, 10
psychopathology, 421
psychopharmacotherapy, 470
psychosexual stages, 38–39
psychosomatic diseases, 88
psychotherapy. *See* therapy
PTSD. *See* posttraumatic stress disorder
puberty, 39, 355
pubic lice, 377
public goods dilemma, A-8
public self, 191

public speaking, 250–252
pulmonary diseases, smoking and, 139
punishment
  disciplinary, 46
  in gender-role socialization, 334
  in operant conditioning, 45–46
  in self-modification, 95
purity rings, 357
putdowns, responding to, 259
puzzle solving, 413

Q

Quaalude, 158
queer, 354
questionnaires, 15
quetiapine, 471

R

racial profiling, 212
racial stereotypes, 206, 214
racism, 210–211
  as source of stress, 70–71
  in workplace, 404
rage, 77
rap music, 359
rape, 317
  date, 318–319
  drinking and, 143
Rape, Abuse, and Incest National Network
  (RAINN), 316
rape acceptance, music videos and, 359
rational-emotive behavior therapy, 108, 468, 480
rational thinking, as coping strategy, 108–109
rationalization, 36, 37, A-9
Ray, James, 4–5
Ray, Rachel, 217
reaction formation, 37
reaction time, 245
reading
  methods for improving, 24
  for pleasure, 412, 495
reality principle, 34
receiver, of message, 216, 218, 232
receptivity, of audience, 218
reciprocal liking, 269–270
reciprocity, in self-disclosure, 248
reciprocity principle, 226–227
recovered memories controversy, 464–465
recreational activities, 412–413
recycling, A-7
reference groups, 171
reflexes, learned, 42
refractory period, 366
regression, 38, 37
rehearsal
  of assertive communication, 259
  in memorization, 25
reinforcement, 44–45
  of gender roles, 334
  negative, 428, 429
  positive, 93–94
  in relationships, 271
rejection, 265, 286
rejection anxiety, 287
relational aggression, 328
relationship maintenance, 270–271
relationship problems, therapy for, 462–463
relationship satisfaction
  commitment and, 271–272
  sexual satisfaction and, 16

relationships. *See* close relationships
relaxation procedures, 118–119
relaxation training, 466
reliability, of psychological tests, 61–62
religion
  happiness and, 19
  sexual identity and, 357
  spirituality and, 502–503
  stress and, 119
religious groups, unorthodox, 5
religious rituals, 495
remarriage, 310–311
repression, 37
repressive coping style, 37
reproach, 253
reproductive fitness, 52, 55, 331
reputation, damage to, 200
research methods, 11–16
resignation, 101
resilience, 68, 78, 88, 112, 500–501
Resilience in Children, 112
resistance, in psychoanalysis, 458
resistance stage, of general adaptation syndrome, 81, 82
resource consumption, A-14
resource exchange, in dating, 268
response tendencies, 42, 45
responsibility, delegating, 121
résumé, preparing, 414–416
retention, in learning, 25
retirement, 394–395
retrieval practice approach, 24
revenge, 117
reward
  alternative, 103
  intrinsic, 494
  as reinforcement, 45
  in relationships, 271
  for studying, 23
rhymes, as mnemonics, 27
rhythm method, 375
right-wing authoritarianism (RWA), 211
Rihanna, 317
risk dilemma, A-8
risk taking, 57, 491
  personality and, 56
  in sexual behavior, 373
  stress and, 88
risks, underestimating, 138
rituals, compulsive, 427
road rage, 72, 101, 102, 240
Robbers' Cave, 213, 215
Robbins, Tony, 4
rohypnol, 318
role expectations, in marriage, 294, 303–304
  see also gender-role expectations
role models, 46–47, 189, 334
role playing, 259
roles, multiple, 340–341, 411
romantic love, 274–282
romantic relationships
  attraction in, 264–270
  breakup of, 280–281
  course of, 279–281
  long-distance, 270–271
  maintaining, 281–282
  nonverbal sensitivity and, 246
  self-disclosure in, 248
  self-esteem and, 177
Rorschach test, 63
Rosenberg Self-Esteem Scale, 176
RU 486, 376

rumination, 117, 490
  depression and, 433–434, 437
  frustration and, 102
  heart disease and, 134
Rutues, Annette, 112

S

sadness, 78, 101, 169
safe sex practices, 154, 378–379
safety and security needs, 51
salary
  education and, 398
  gender gap in, 343
  negotiating, 417
salary considerations, in career choice, 392
salespeople, tactics of, 225–227
salivation response, 42
salt, in diet, 148, 149–150
sampling, in psychological testing, 61
sandwich generation, 302
saturated fats, 149
saving face, 186
savoring, 497–498
scarcity principle, 227
schedules, making, 23, 124
schizophrenic disorders, 439–445
  biological causes of, 442–444
  course and outcome of, 441–442
  drug therapy for, 471
  etiology of, 442–445
  expressed emotion and, 444
  marijuana use and, 162
  neurodevelopmental hypothesis of, 443–444
  positive vs. negative symptoms in, 441
  prevalence of, 425, 439
  prognosis for, 441
  stress and, 86, 444
  subtypes of, 440
  symptoms of, 439–440
  vulnerability to, 444
Schlessinger, Laura, 5–6
school satisfaction, 506
schools
  as source of gender-role socialization, 336
  positive, 506
  sex education in, 357
scientific approach, 11–16
Scientology, 4
Seconal, 158
secondary appraisal, 69
secondary process thinking, 34
secondary sex characteristics, 355
secure attachment style, 277, 278
  career choice and, 388
sedatives, 158, 159, 160
sedentary behavior, health consequences of, 15
Sedona, Arizona, 4
segregation, job, 400–401
selective attention, 180, 252
selective serotonin reuptake inhibitors (SSRIs), 472
selectivity, in person perception, 209
self
  collective, 213
  ecologically connected, A-9
  independent vs. interdependent view of, 174
  public, 191
self-acceptance, 180
self-actualization, need for, 51–52
self-affirmation, 170–171
self-assessment motive, 182–183
self-attributions, 180–181

self-awareness, self-discrepancies and, 170
self-beliefs, 169, 170
self-blame, 77, 104, 177
self-compassion, 309
self-concept, 167–174
  culture and, 173–174
  defense mechanisms and, 106
  factors shaping, 171–174
  narcissism and, 58
  occupational development and, 394
  Rogers's view of, 49–50, 460
  stress and, 88
self-concept confusion, 175
self-consciousness, 85
self-consistency, 183–184
self-control, 102, 187, 188
  reducing prejudice using, 206
  religion and, 119
  stress reduction and, 91–95
self-deception, 105–106
  defense mechanisms and, 37
self-defeating attributional style, 287, 288
self-defeating behavior, 186, 190–191
self-deprecation, 192
self-destruction, deliberate, 190
self-destructive habits, 137–154
Self-Directed Search (SDS), 390
self-disclosure, 247–249
  emotional, 116, 248
  in friendships, 273
  in maintaining relationships, 281
  in marriage, 299, 306
  in online relationships, 283, 284
  in relationship maintenance, 271
  of sexual orientation, 363–364
self-discrepancies, 169–171
self-effacing bias, 185
self-efficacy, 47, 189–190
  burnout and, 86
  exercise and, 118
self-enhancement, 184–187
self-esteem, 174–179
  depression and, 433
  development of, 178–179
  divorce and, 309
  domain-specific, 175–176
  ethnicity and, 179
  exercise and, 117, 151
  fragile, 177
  gender differences in, 328
  gender roles and, 335
  identification and, 37
  importance of, 176–178
  improving, 194–195
  measurement of, 176
  narcissism and, 58
  self-discrepancies and, 169
  sexual, 365
  social identity and, 213
  structure of, 174, 175
  terror management and, 58–59
  threats to, 105, 213
  trait vs. state, 175
self-fulfilling prophecies, 203–205, 207, 270, 346
Self-Fulfilling Prophecies and School Performance, 204
self-handicapping, 186–187, 190
self-help books, 6–9
self-help gurus, 4–6
self-image, distortions in, 171, 172
self-improvement, 194–195
self-indulgence, 103–104

Personal Explorations Workbook

PERSONAL EXPLORATIONS WORKBOOK CONTENTS

INTRODUCTION

In your textbook, *Psychology Applied to Modern Life,* the value of developing an accurate self-concept is emphasized repeatedly. A little self-deception may occasionally be adaptive (see Chapter 4), but most theories of psychological health endorse the importance of forming a realistic picture of one's personal qualities and capabilities. This *Personal Explorations Workbook* contains two types of exercises intended to help you achieve this goal. They are (1) a series of *Self-Assessments,* or self-scoring psychological scales, intended to help you gain insight into your attitudes and personality traits, and (2) a series of *Self-Reflections* intended to help you systematically analyze various aspects of your life in relation to adjustment issues.

How you use these personal exploration exercises will depend, in large part, on your instructor. Some instructors will formally assign some of these exercises and then collect them for individual scrutiny or class discussion. That is why the pages of this workbook are perforated—to make it convenient for those instructors who like to assign the exercises as homework. Other instructors may simply encourage students to complete the exercises that they find intriguing. We believe that, even if the exercises are not assigned, you will find many of them very interesting and we encourage you to complete them on your own. Let's briefly take a closer look at these exercises.

Self-Assessments

The Self-Assessments are a collection of attitude scales and personality tests that psychologists have used in their research. One Self-Assessment questionnaire has been selected for each chapter in your text. Instructions are provided so that you can administer these scales to yourself and then compute your score. Each Self-Assessment also includes an explanation of what the scale measures followed by a brief review of the research on the scale. These reviews discuss the evidence on the reliability, validity, and behavioral correlates of each scale. The final section of each Self-Assessment provides information which allows you to interpret the meaning of your score. Test norms are supplied to indicate what represents a high, intermediate, or low score on the scale. We hope you may gain some useful insights about yourself by responding to these scales.

However, you should be careful about attributing too much significance to your scores. As explained in Chapter 2 in your text, the results of psychological tests can be misleading, and caution is always in order when interpreting test scores. It is probably best to view your scores as interesting "food for thought" rather than as definitive statements about your personal traits or abilities.

Most of the scales included in this book are self-report inventories. Your scores on such tests are only as accurate as the information that you provide in your responses. Hence, we hasten to emphasize that the Self-Assessments will only be as valuable as you make them by striving to respond honestly. Usually, people taking a scale do not know what the scale measures. The conventional approach is to put some sort of vague or misleading title, such as "Biographical Inventory," at the top of the scale. We have not adhered to this practice because you could easily find out what any scale measures simply by reading ahead a little. Thus, you will be taking each scale with some idea (based on the title) of what the scale measures. Bear in mind, however, that these scales are intended to satisfy your curiosity. There is no reason to try to impress or mislead anyone—including yourself. Your test scores will be accurate and meaningful only if you try very hard to respond in a candid manner.

Self-Reflections

The Self-Reflections consist of sets of questions designed to make you think about yourself and your personal experiences in relation to specific issues and topics raised in your text. They involve systematic inquiries into how you behave in certain situations, how your behavior has been shaped by past events, how you feel about certain issues, how you might improve yourself in some areas, how you anticipate behaving under certain circumstances in the future, and so forth. There is one Self-Reflection for each of the sixteen chapters in your textbook. The aspects of life probed by these inquiries are, of course, tied to the content of the chapters in your text. You will probably derive the most benefit from them if you read the corresponding text chapter before completing the Self-Reflections.

Wayne Weiten
Dana S. Dunn
Elizabeth Yost Hammer

REFERENCES

Ames, D. R., Rose, P., & Anderson, C. P. (2006). The NPI-16 as a short measure of narcissism. *Journal of Research in Personality, 40,* 440–450.

Ames, S. C., Jones, G. N., Howe, J. T., & Brantley, P. J. (2001). A prospective study of the impact of stress on quality of life: An investigation of low-income individuals with hypertension. *Annals of Behavioral Medicine, 23*(2), 112–119.

Anderson, N. H. (1968). Likableness ratings of 555 personality trait words. *Journal of Personality and Social Psychology, 9,* 272–279.

Arnaut, G. L. Y. (2006). Sensation seeking, risk taking, and fearlessness. In J. C. Thomas & D. L. Segal (Eds.), *Comprehensive handbook of personality and psychopathology, Vol 1: Personality and everyday functioning* (pp. 322–344). New York: Wiley.

Barnes, G. E., & Vulcano, B. A. (1982). Measuring rationality independent of social desirability. *Personality and Individual Differences, 3,* 303–309.

Baumeister, R. F., & Vohs, K. D. (2001). Narcissism as addiction to esteem. *Psychological Inquiry, 12,* 206–210.

Becker, H. A. (1980). The Assertive Job-Hunting Survey. *Measurement and Evaluation in Guidance, 13,* 43–48.

Compton, W. C. (2005). *An introduction to positive psychology.* Belmont, CA: Thompson/Wadsworth.

Denisoff, E., & Endler, N. S. (2000). Life experiences, coping, and weight preoccupation in young adult women. *Canadian Journal of Behavioural Science, 32*(2), 97–103.

Egan, G. (1977). *You and me: The skills of communicating and relating to others.* Pacific Grove, CA: Brooks/Cole.

Ellis, A. (1962). *Reason and emotion in psychotherapy.* Secaucus, NJ: Lyle Stuart.

Fischer, E. H., & Turner, J. L. (1970). Orientations to seeking professional help: Development and research utility of an attitude scale. *Journal of Consulting and Clinical Psychology, 35,* 82–83.

Hatfield, E., & Sprecher, S. (1986). Measuring passionate love in intimate relationships. *Journal of Adolescence, 9,* 383–410.

Ickes, W., & Barnes, R. D. (1977). The role of sex and self-monitoring in unstructured dyadic interactions. *Journal of Personality and Social Psychology, 35,* 315–330.

Infante, D. A., & Rancer, A. S. (1982). A conceptualization and measure of argumentativeness. *Journal of Personality Assessment, 46,* 72–80.

Malefo, V. (2000). Psycho-social factors and academic performance among African women students at a predominantly white university in South Africa. *South African Journal of Psychology, 30*(4), 40–45.

Miller, L. C., Berg, J. H., & Archer, R. L. (1983). Openers: Individuals who elicit intimate self-disclosure. *Journal of Personality and Social Psychology, 44,* 1234–1244.

Peterson, C. (2006). *A primer in positive psychology.* New York: Oxford University Press.

Peterson, C., Park, N., & Seligman, M. E. P. (2005). Orientations to happiness and life satisfaction: The full life versus the empty life. *Journal of Happiness Studies, 6,* 25–41.

Raskin, R., & Terry, H. (1988). A principal-components analysis of the Narcissistic Personality Inventory and further evidence of its construct validity. *Journal of Personality and Social Psychology, 54,* 890–902.

Rhodewalt, F. & Peterson, B. (2009). Narcissism. In M. R. Leary & R. H. Hoyle (Eds.), *Handbook of individual differences in social behavior* (pp. 547–560). New York: Guilford.

Rhodewalt, F., & Morf, C. C. (2005). Reflections in troubled waters: Narcissism and the vicissitudes of an interpersonality contextualized self. In A. Tesser, J. V. Wood, & D. A. Staper (Eds.), *On Building, defending, and regulating the self* (pp. 127–152). New York: Psychology Press.

Rotter, J. B. (1966). Generalized expectancies for internal versus external control of reinforcement. *Psychological Monographs, 80* (Whole No. 609).

Sarason, I. G., Johnson, J. H., & Siegel, J. M. (1978). Assessing the impact of life changes: Development of the Life Experiences Survey. *Journal of Consulting and Clinical Psychology, 46,* 932–946.

Snell, W. E., Jr., & Papini, D. R. (1989). The sexuality scale: An instrument to measure sexual-esteem, sexual-depression, and sexual-preoccupation. *Journal of Sex Research, 26,* 256–263.

Snyder, M. (1974). Self-monitoring of expressive behavior. *Journal of Personality and Social Psychology, 30,* 526–537.

Spence, J. T., & Helmreich, R. L. (1978). *Masculinity and femininity: Their psychological dimensions, correlates, and antecedents.* Austin: University of Texas Press.

Suinn, R. M. (1968). Removal of social desirability and response set items from the Manifest Anxiety Scale. *Educational and Psychological Measurement, 28,* 1189–1192.

Taylor, J. A. (1953). A personality scale of manifest anxiety. *Journal of Abnormal and Social Psychology, 48,* 285–290.

Twenge, J. M., & Campbell, W. K. (2009). *The narcissism epidemic: Living in the age of entitlement.* New York: Free Press.

Twenge, J. M., Konrath, S., Foster, J. D., Campbell, W. K., & Bushman, B. J. (2008). Egos inflating over time: A cross-temporal meta-analysis of the Narcissistic Personality Inventory. *Journal of Personality, 76*(4), 903–917.

U.S. Department of Health and Human Services. (1981). *Health style: A self-test.* Washington, DC: Department of Health and Human Services, Public Health Service, PHS 81–50155.

Wallston, K. A. (2005). The validity of the Multidimensional Health Locus of Control Scales. *Journal of Health Psychology, 10,* 623–631.

Wallston, K. A., Wallston, B. S., & DeVellis, R. (1978). Development of the Multidimensional Health Locus of Control (MHLC) Scales. *Health Education Monographs, 6,* 160–170.

Watson, D. L., & Friend, R. (1969). Measurement of social-evaluative anxiety. *Journal of Consulting and Clinical Psychology, 33,* 448–457.

Zuckerman, M. (1979). *Sensation seeking: Beyond the optimal level of arousal.* Hillsdale, NJ: Erlbaum.

Zuckerman, M. (1994). *Behavioral expressions and biosocial bases of sensation seeking.* New York: Cambridge University Press.

Zuckerman, M. (2007). *Sensation seeking and risky behavior.* Washington, DC: American Psychological Association.

EXERCISE 1.1 *Self-Assessment:* Narcissistic Personality Inventory

INSTRUCTIONS

Read each pair of statements below and place an "X" by the one that comes closest to describing your feelings and beliefs about yourself. You may feel that neither statement describes you well, but pick the one that comes closest. **Please complete all pairs.**

The Scale

1. _____ A. When people compliment me I sometimes get embarrassed.

   _____ B. I know that I am good because everybody keeps telling me so.

2. _____ A. I prefer to blend in with the crowd.

   _____ B. I like to be the center of attention.

3. _____ A. I am no better or worse than most people.

   _____ B. I think I am a special person.

4. _____ A. I like to have authority over other people.

   _____ B. I don't mind following orders.

5. _____ A. I find it easy to manipulate people.

   _____ B. I don't like it when I find myself manipulating people.

6. _____ A. I insist upon getting the respect that is due me.

   _____ B. I usually get the respect that I deserve.

7. _____ A. I try not to be a show off.

   _____ B. I will usually show off if I get the chance.

8. _____ A. I always know what I am doing.

   _____ B. Sometimes I am not sure of what I am doing.

9. _____ A. Sometimes I tell good stories.

   _____ B. Everybody likes to hear my stories.

10. _____ A. I expect a great deal from other people.

    _____ B. I like to do things for other people.

11. _____ A. I really like to be the center of attention.

    _____ B. It makes me uncomfortable to be the center of attention.

12. _____ A. Being an authority doesn't mean that much to me.

    _____ B. People always seem to recognize my authority.

13. _____ A. I am going to be a great person.

    _____ B. I hope I am going to be successful.

14. _____ A. People sometimes believe what I tell them.

    _____ B. I can make anybody believe anything I want them to.

15. _____ A. I am more capable than other people.

    _____ B. There is a lot that I can learn from other people.

16. _____ A. I am much like everybody else.

    _____ B. I am an extraordinary person.

Scoring the Scale

The scoring key is reproduced below. You should circle your response of A or B each time it corresponds to the keyed response below. Add up the number of responses you circled. This total is your score on the Narcissistic Personality Inventory. Record your score below.

1. B	5. A	9. B	13. A
2. B	6. A	10. A	14. B
3. B	7. B	11. A	15. A
4. A	8. A	12. B	16. B

My score _____

What the Scale Measures

As noted briefly in Chapter 1, *narcissism* is a personality trait marked by an inflated sense of importance, a need for attention and admiration, a sense of entitlement, and a tendency to exploit others. Those who score high in narcissism tend to exhibit feelings of superiority, although their feelings of self-esteem are actually quite fragile and constantly require validation (Rhodewalt & Morf, 2005). This insecurity creates an insatiable need for expressions of admiration from others that leads to grandiose self-presentations (Rhodewalt & Peterson, 2009). Baumeister and Vohs (2001) compare narcissists' craving for approval and admiration to an addiction. Twenge and Campbell (2009) emphasize narcissists' sense of entitlement—the expectation that everything should revolve around them and that they should receive special favors and treatment.

The Narcissistic Personality Inventory (NPI) was developed by Robert Raskin and colleagues (Raskin & Hall, 1979, 1981; Raskin & Terry, 1988) to assess normal levels of narcissism on a continuum. The original 54-item measure was reduced to a 40-item scale in 1988. The assessment you took here is a 16-item version devised and validated by Ames, Rose, and Anderson (2006). There is extensive evidence that the various versions of the NPI accurately measure what they set out to measure.

Interpreting Your Score

Our norms are based on data from five studies reported by Ames, Rose, and Anderson (2006). Our high and low scores are basically ¾ of a standard deviation above and below the mean, with a little rounding (the standard deviation is an index of how much variability there tends to be on a measure). Roughly speaking, that means high scorers fall in the upper 25% on this trait, medium scorers in the middle 50%, and low scorers in the bottom 25%. There are some small gender differences on the NPI-16, so norms are reported separately for males and females.

Norms

	Males	Females
High score:	9–16	7–16
Medium score:	4–8	3–6
Low score:	0–3	0–2

Source: From Ames, D. R., Rose, P., & Anderson, C. P. (2006). The NPI-16 as a short measure of narcissism. *Journal of Research in Personality, 40*(4), 440–450. Appendix A. Reprinted with permission from Elsevier.

EXERCISE 1.2 *Self-Reflection:* What Are Your Study Habits Like?

Do you usually complete your class assignments on time?   YES   NO

Do you usually find time to prepare adequately for your exams?   YES   NO

Do you frequently delay schoolwork until the last minute?   YES   NO

When do you usually study (mornings, evenings, weekends, etc.)?

Do you write out and follow a study schedule?   YES   NO

Are your study times planned for when you're likely to be alert?   YES   NO

Do you allow time for brief study breaks?   YES   NO

Where do you usually study (library, kitchen, bedroom, etc.)?

Do you have a special place set up for studying and nothing else?   YES   NO

What types of auditory, visual, and social distractions are present in your study areas?

Can you suggest any changes to reduce distractions in your study areas?

Source: © Cengage Learning

EXERCISE 2.1 *Self-Assessment:* Sensation-Seeking Scale

INSTRUCTIONS

Each of the items below contains two choices, A and B. Please indicate in the spaces provided on the left which of the choices most describes your likes or the way you feel. It is important that you respond to all items with only one choice, A or B. In some cases you may find that both choices describe your likes or the way you feel. Please choose the one that better describes your likes or feelings. In some cases you may not like either choice. In these cases mark the choice you dislike least. We are interested only in your likes or feelings, not in how others feel about these things or how one is supposed to feel. There are no right or wrong answers. Be frank and give your honest appraisal of yourself.

The Scale

_____ 1. A. I would like a job that would require a lot of traveling.

B. I would prefer a job in one location.

_____ 2. A. I am invigorated by a brisk, cold day.

B. I can't wait to get indoors on a cold day.

_____ 3. A. I find a certain pleasure in routine kinds of work.

B. Although it is sometimes necessary, I usually dislike routine kinds of work.

_____ 4. A. I often wish I could be a mountain climber.

B. I can't understand people who risk their necks climbing mountains.

_____ 5. A. I dislike all body odors.

B. I like some of the earthy body smells.

_____ 6. A. I get bored seeing the same old faces.

B. I like the comfortable familiarity of everyday friends.

_____ 7. A. I like to explore a strange city or section of town by myself, even if it means getting lost.

B. I prefer a guide when I am in a place I don't know well.

_____ 8. A. I find the quickest and easiest route to a place and stick to it.

B. I sometimes take different routes to a place I often go, just for variety's sake.

_____ 9. A. I would not like to try any drug that might produce strange and dangerous effects on me.

B. I would like to try some of the new drugs that produce hallucinations.

_____ 10. A. I would prefer living in an ideal society where everyone is safe, secure, and happy.

B. I would have preferred living in the unsettled days of our history.

_____ 11. A. I sometimes like to do things that are a little frightening.

B. A sensible person avoids activities that are dangerous.

_____ 12. A. I order dishes with which I am familiar, so as to avoid disappointment and unpleasantness.

B. I like to try new foods that I have never tasted before.

_____ 13. A. I can't stand riding with a person who likes to speed.

B. I sometimes like to drive very fast because I find it exciting.

_____ 14. A. If I were a salesperson, I would prefer a straight salary rather than the risk of making little or nothing on a commission basis.

B. If I were a salesperson, I would prefer working on a commission if I had a chance to make more money than I could on a salary.

_____ 15. A. I would like to take up the sport of water skiing.

B. I would not like to take up the sport of water skiing.

_____ 16. A. I don't like to argue with people whose beliefs are sharply divergent from mine, since such arguments are never resolved.

B. I find people who disagree with my beliefs more stimulating than people who agree with me.

_____ 17. A. When I go on a trip, I like to plan my route and time-table fairly carefully.

B. I would like to take off on a trip with no pre-planned or definite routes or timetables.

_____ 18. A. I enjoy the thrills of watching car races.

B. I find car races unpleasant.

_____ 19. A. Most people spend entirely too much money on life insurance.

B. Life insurance is something that no one can afford to be without.

_____ 20. A. I would like to learn to fly an airplane.

B. I would not like to learn to fly an airplane.

_____ 21. A. I would not like to be hypnotized.

B. I would like to have the experience of being hypnotized.

_____ 22. A. The most important goal of life is to live it to the fullest and experience as much of it as you can.

B. The most important goal of life is to find peace and happiness.

_____ 23. A. I would like to try parachute jumping.

B. I would never want to try jumping out of a plane, with or without a parachute.

_____ 24. A. I enter cold water gradually, giving myself time to get used to it.

B. I like to dive or jump right into the ocean or a cold pool.

_____ 25. A. I do not like the irregularity and discord of most modern music.

B. I like to listen to new and unusual kinds of music.

(continued)

_____ 26. A. I prefer friends who are excitingly unpredictable.

B. I prefer friends who are reliable and predictable.

_____ 27. A. When I go on a vacation, I prefer the comfort of a good room and bed.

B. When I go on a vacation, I prefer the change of camping out.

_____ 28. A. The essence of good art is in its clarity, symmetry of form, and harmony of colors.

B. I often find beauty in the "clashing" colors and irregular forms of modern paintings.

_____ 29. A. The worst social sin is to be rude.

B. The worst social sin is to be a bore.

_____ 30. A. I look forward to a good night of rest after a long day.

B. I wish I didn't have to waste so much of a day sleeping.

_____ 31. A. I prefer people who are emotionally expressive even if they are a bit unstable.

B. I prefer people who are calm and even-tempered.

_____ 32. A. A good painting should shock or jolt the senses.

B. A good painting should give one a feeling of peace and security.

_____ 33. A. When I feel discouraged, I recover by relaxing and having some soothing diversion.

B. When I feel discouraged, I recover by going out and doing something new and exciting.

_____ 34. A. People who ride motorcycles must have some kind of an unconscious need to hurt themselves.

B. I would like to drive or ride on a motorcycle.

Scoring the Scale

The scoring key is reproduced below. You should circle your response of A or B each time it corresponds to the keyed response below. Add up the number of responses you circled. This total is your score on the Sensation-Seeking Scale. Record your score below.

1. A	8. B	15. A	22. A	29. B
2. A	9. B	16. B	23. A	30. B
3. B	10. B	17. B	24. B	31. A
4. A	11. A	18. A	25. B	32. A
5. B	12. B	19. A	26. A	33. B
6. A	13. B	20. A	27. B	34. B
7. A	14. B	21. B	28. B	

My score _____

What the Scale Measures

As its name implies, the Sensation-Seeking Scale (SSS) measures one's need for a high level of stimulation. Sensation seeking involves the active pursuit of experiences that many people would find very stressful. As discussed in the chapter, Marvin Zuckerman (1994, 2007) believes that this thirst for sensation is a highly heritable personality trait that leads people to seek thrills, adventures, and new experiences.

The scale you have just responded to is the second version of the SSS (Zuckerman, 1979), but it shares a great deal of overlap with the current version (Arnaut, 2006). Sensation seeking is distributed along a continuum, and many people fall in the middle. Factor analyses indicate that the personality trait of sensation seeking consists of four related components. When compared to low sensation seekers, those high in sensation seeking display the following four sets of characteristics (Arnaut, 2006; Zuckerman, 1994):

- *Thrill and adventure seeking.* They're more willing to engage in activities that may involve a physical risk. Thus, they're more likely to go mountain climbing, skydiving, surfing, and scuba diving.
- *Experience seeking.* They're more willing to volunteer for unusual experiments or activities that they may know little about. They tend to relish extensive travel, provocative art, wild parties, and unusual friends.
- *Disinhibition.* They are relatively uninhibited. Hence, they are prone to engage in heavy drinking, recreational drug use, gambling, and sexual experimentation.
- *Susceptibility to boredom.* Their chief foe is monotony. They have a low tolerance for routine and repetition, and they quickly and easily become bored.

Test-retest reliabilities are quite respectable and there is ample evidence to support the scale's predictive validity. For example, studies show that high sensation seekers appraise hypothetical situations as less risky than low sensation seekers do and are more willing to volunteer for an experiment in which they will be hypnotized. The scale also shows robust positive correlations with measures of change seeking, novelty seeking, and impulsiveness. Interestingly, SSS scores tend to decline with age.

Interpreting Your Score

Our norms are based on percentiles reported by Zuckerman and colleagues for a sample of 62 undergraduates. Although males generally tend to score a bit higher than females on the SSS, the differences are small enough to report one set of (averaged) norms. Remember, sensation-seeking scores tend to decline with age. So, if you're not in the modal college student age range (17–23), these norms may be a bit high.

Norms

High score:	**21–34**
Intermediate score:	**11–20**
Low score:	**0–10**

Source: From Zuckerman, M. (1979). *Sensation seeking: Beyond the optimal level of arousal* (pp. 385–387). Hillsdale, NJ: Lawrence Erlbaum Associates. Reprinted with permission of Taylor & Francis Group LLC.

EXERCISE 2.2 *Self-Reflection:* Who Are You?

Below you will find 75 personality trait words taken from an influential list assembled by Anderson (1968). Try to select the 20 traits (20 only!) that describe you best. Check them.

sincere	forgetful	truthful	imaginative	outgoing
pessimistic	crafty	mature	impolite	dependable
open-minded	methodical	skeptical	diligent	persistent
suspicious	sly	efficient	prideful	orderly
patient	headstrong	resourceful	optimistic	energetic
tense	naive	perceptive	considerate	modest
cooperative	sloppy	punctual	courteous	smart
neat	grouchy	prejudiced	candid	kind
logical	ethical	friendly	idealistic	good-humored
vain	persuasive	gracious	warm	unselfish
sociable	nervous	shy	versatile	cordial
scornful	clumsy	short-tempered	courageous	wholesome
cheerful	rebellious	compulsive	tactful	generous
honest	studious	sarcastic	loyal	boastful
reasonable	understanding	respectful	reliable	daring

Review the 20 traits that you chose. Overall, is it a favorable or unfavorable picture that you have sketched?

Considering Carl Rogers's point that we often distort reality and construct an overly favorable self-concept, do you feel that you were objective?

What characteristics make you unique?

What are your greatest strengths?

What are your greatest weaknesses?

Source: © Cengage Learning

CHAPTER 3 STRESS AND ITS EFFECTS

EXERCISE 3.1 *Self-Assessment:* The Life Experiences Survey (LES)

INSTRUCTIONS

Listed below are a number of events that sometimes bring about change in the lives of those who experience them and that necessitate social readjustment. Examine each event on the list, and if that event has occurred in your life during the past year please indicate the extent to which you viewed the event as having either a positive or negative impact on your life at the time it occurred. That is, circle a number on the appropriate line to indicate the type and extent of impact that the event had. A rating of −3 would indicate an extremely negative impact. A rating of 0 suggests no impact, either positive or negative. A rating of +3 would indicate an extremely positive impact.

The Scale

	Extremely negative	Moderately negative	Slightly negative	No impact	Slightly positive	Moderately positive	Extremely positive
Section 1							
1. Marriage	−3	−2	−1	0	+1	+2	+3
2. Detention in jail or comparable institution	−3	−2	−1	0	+1	+2	+3
3. Death of spouse	−3	−2	−1	0	+1	+2	+3
4. Major change in sleeping habits	−3	−2	−1	0	+1	+2	+3
5. Death of a close family member	−3	−2	−1	0	+1	+2	+3
a. Mother	−3	−2	−1	0	+1	+2	+3
b. Father	−3	−2	−1	0	+1	+2	+3
c. Brother	−3	−2	−1	0	+1	+2	+3
d. Sister	−3	−2	−1	0	+1	+2	+3
e. Grandmother	−3	−2	−1	0	+1	+2	+3
f. Grandfather	−3	−2	−1	0	+1	+2	+3
g. Other (specify)	−3	−2	−1	0	+1	+2	+3
6. Major change in eating habits (much more or much less food intake)	−3	−2	−1	0	+1	+2	+3
7. Foreclosure on mortgage or loan	−3	−2	−1	0	+1	+2	+3
8. Death of a close friend	−3	−2	−1	0	+1	+2	+3
9. Outstanding personal achievement	−3	−2	−1	0	+1	+2	+3
10. Minor law violations	−3	−2	−1	0	+1	+2	+3
11. Male: Wife/girlfriend's pregnancy	−3	−2	−1	0	+1	+2	+3
12. Female: Pregnancy	−3	−2	−1	0	+1	+2	+3
13. Changed work situation (different work responsibility, major change in working conditions, working hours, etc.)	−3	−2	−1	0	+1	+2	+3
14. New job	−3	−2	−1	0	+1	+2	+3
15. Serious illness or injury of close family member:	−3	−2	−1	0	+1	+2	+3
a. Mother	−3	−2	−1	0	+1	+2	+3
b. Father	−3	−2	−1	0	+1	+2	+3
c. Brother	−3	−2	−1	0	+1	+2	+3
d. Sister	−3	−2	−1	0	+1	+2	+3
e. Grandmother	−3	−2	−1	0	+1	+2	+3
f. Grandfather	−3	−2	−1	0	+1	+2	+3
g. Spouse	−3	−2	−1	0	+1	+2	+3
h. Other (specify)	−3	−2	−1	0	+1	+2	+3
16. Sexual difficulties	−3	−2	−1	0	+1	+2	+3
17. Trouble with employer (in danger of losing job, being suspended, being demoted, etc.)	−3	−2	−1	0	+1	+2	+3
18. Trouble with in-laws	−3	−2	−1	0	+1	+2	+3
19. Major change in financial status (a lot better off or a lot worse off)	−3	−2	−1	0	+1	+2	+3
20. Major change in closeness of family members (increased or decreased closeness)	−3	−2	−1	0	+1	+2	+3

	Extremely negative	Moderately negative	Slightly negative	No impact	Slightly positive	Moderately positive	Extremely positive
21. Gaining a new family member (through birth, adoption, family member moving in, etc.)	−3	−2	−1	0	+1	+2	+3
22. Change in residence	−3	−2	−1	0	+1	+2	+3
23. Marital separation from mate (due to conflict)	−3	−2	−1	0	+1	+2	+3
24. Major change in church activities (increased or decreased attendance)	−3	−2	−1	0	+1	+2	+3
25. Marital reconciliation with mate	−3	−2	−1	0	+1	+2	+3
26. Major change in number of arguments with spouse (a lot more or a lot fewer)	−3	−2	−1	0	+1	+2	+3
27. Married male: Change in wife's work outside the home (beginning work, ceasing work, changing to a new job, etc.)	−3	−2	−1	0	+1	+2	+3
28. Married female: Change in husband's work (loss of job, beginning new job, retirement, etc.)	−3	−2	−1	0	+1	+2	+3
29. Major change in usual type and/or amount of recreation	−3	−2	−1	0	+1	+2	+3
30. Borrowing for a major purchase (buying a home, business, etc.)	−3	−2	−1	0	+1	+2	+3
31. Borrowing for a smaller purchase (buying a car or TV, getting school loan, etc.)	−3	−2	−1	0	+1	+2	+3
32. Being fired from job	−3	−2	−1	0	+1	+2	+3
33. Male: Wife/girlfriend having an abortion	−3	−2	−1	0	+1	+2	+3
34. Female: Having an abortion	−3	−2	−1	0	+1	+2	+3
35. Major personal illness or injury	−3	−2	−1	0	+1	+2	+3
36. Major change in social activities, e.g., parties, movies, visiting (increased or decreased participation)	−3	−2	−1	0	+1	+2	+3
37. Major change in living conditions of family (building new home, remodeling, deterioration of home or neighborhood, etc.)	−3	−2	−1	0	+1	+2	+3
38. Divorce	−3	−2	−1	0	+1	+2	+3
39. Serious injury or illness of close friend	−3	−2	−1	0	+1	+2	+3
40. Retirement from work	−3	−2	−1	0	+1	+2	+3
41. Son or daughter leaving home (due to marriage, college, etc.)	−3	−2	−1	0	+1	+2	+3
42. End of formal schooling	−3	−2	−1	0	+1	+2	+3
43. Separation from spouse (due to work, travel, etc.)	−3	−2	−1	0	+1	+2	+3
44. Engagement	−3	−2	−1	0	+1	+2	+3
45. Breaking up with boyfriend/girlfriend	−3	−2	−1	0	+1	+2	+3
46. Leaving home for the first time	−3	−2	−1	0	+1	+2	+3
47. Reconciliation with boyfriend/girlfriend	−3	−2	−1	0	+1	+2	+3

Other recent experiences that have had an impact on your life. List and rate.

	Extremely negative	Moderately negative	Slightly negative	No impact	Slightly positive	Moderately positive	Extremely positive
48. _____	−3	−2	−1	0	+1	+2	+3
49. _____	−3	−2	−1	0	+1	+2	+3
50. _____	−3	−2	−1	0	+1	+2	+3

Section 2. Students only

	Extremely negative	Moderately negative	Slightly negative	No impact	Slightly positive	Moderately positive	Extremely positive
51. Beginning a new school experience at a higher academic level (college, graduate school, professional school)	−3	−2	−1	0	+1	+2	+3
52. Changing to a new school at the same academic level (undergraduate, graduate, etc.)	−3	−2	−1	0	+1	+2	+3
53. Academic probation	−3	−2	−1	0	+1	+2	+3
54. Being dismissed from dormitory or other residence	−3	−2	−1	0	+1	+2	+3
55. Failing an important exam	−3	−2	−1	0	+1	+2	+3
56. Changing a major	−3	−2	−1	0	+1	+2	+3
57. Failing a course	−3	−2	−1	0	+1	+2	+3
58. Dropping a course	−3	−2	−1	0	+1	+2	+3
59. Joining a fraternity/sorority	−3	−2	−1	0	+1	+2	+3
60. Financial problems concerning school (in danger of not having sufficient money to continue)	−3	−2	−1	0	+1	+2	+3

Scoring the Scale

Arriving at your scores on the LES is very simple. Add up all the positive impact ratings on the right side. The total is your positive change score. Your negative change score is the sum of all of the negative impact ratings that you made on the left side. Adding these two values yields your total change score. Record your scores below.

My positive change score _____

My negative change score _____

My total change score _____

What the Scale Measures

The Life Experiences Survey (LES), assembled by Irwin Sarason and colleagues (1978), has become a widely used measure of stress in contemporary research (for examples see Ames et al., 2001; Denisoff & Endler, 2000; Malefo, 2000). The LES recognizes that stress involves more than mere change and asks respondents to indicate whether events had a positive or negative impact on them. This strategy helps researchers gain much more insight into which facets of stress are most crucial. The LES also takes into consideration differences among people in their appraisal of stress, by dropping the normative weights and replacing them with personally assigned weightings of the impact of relevant events. The LES allows the respondent to write in personally important events that are not included on the scale. Finally, the LES has an extra section just for students.

Interpreting Your Score

Approximate norms for all three of the scores are listed below so that you can get some idea of what your score means. Research to date suggests that the negative change score is the crucial one; positive change has not been found to be a good predictor of adaptational outcomes. Thus far, research has shown that negative change scores are related to a variety of negative adaptational outcomes.

There is merit in getting an estimate of how much stress you have experienced lately, but scores on the LES should be interpreted with caution. You need not panic if you add up your negative change score and find that it falls in the "high" category. For one thing, the strength of the association between stress and adaptational problems is modest. Second, stress interacts with many other factors, such as lifestyle, coping skills, social support, hardiness, and genetic inheritance, in influencing one's mental and physical health.

Norms for LES

Score change	Negative change	Positive change	Total change
High	14 and above	16 and above	28 and above
Medium	4–13	7–15	12–27
Low	0–3	0–6	0–11

Source: From Sarason, I. G., Johnson, J. H., & Siegel, J. M. (1978). Assessing the impact of life changes: Development of the life experiences survey. *Journal of Consulting and Clinical Psychology, 46,* 943–946. © American Psychological Association. Adapted with permission of the publisher and Irwin G. Sarason. No further reproduction or distribution is permitted without written permission from the American Psychological Association.

EXERCISE 3.2 *Self-Reflection:* Stress—How Do You Control It?

1. Do modern lifestyles create more stress than in the past? How so?

2. How do *you* create stress in your own life?

3. How could you change the nature of our society to make it less stressful?

4. It could be said that some stress comes from leading "out-of-balance" lives. What can people do to "keep it simple"? Furthermore, in what ways can individuals control the stressors they will encounter beforehand?

5. How could you change the way in which you interact with your school demands or your work demands to change the amount of stress that you feel?

CHAPTER 4 COPING PROCESSES

EXERCISE 4.1 *Self-Assessment:* Barnes-Vulcano Rationality Test

INSTRUCTIONS

For each of the following statements, please indicate the degree to which you tend to either agree or disagree with the statement according to the following five-point scale:

1	2	3	4	5
Agree Strongly	Agree	Neither Agree nor Disagree	Disagree	Disagree Strongly

The Scale

_____ 1. I do not need to feel that everyone I meet likes me.

_____ 2. I frequently worry about things over which I have no control.

_____ 3. I find it easy to overcome irrational fears.

_____ 4. I can usually shut off thoughts that are causing me to feel anxious.

_____ 5. Life is a ceaseless battle against irrational worries.

_____ 6. I frequently worry about death.

_____ 7. Crowds make me nervous.

_____ 8. I frequently worry about the state of my health.

_____ 9. I tend to worry about things before they actually happen.

_____ 10. If I were told that someone had a criminal record I would not hire him or her to work for me.

_____ 11. When I make a mistake I feel worthless and inadequate.

_____ 12. When someone is wrong I sure let them know.

_____ 13. When I am frustrated the first thing I do is ask myself whether there is anything I can do to change it now.

_____ 14. Whenever something goes wrong I ask myself, "Why did this have to happen to me?"

_____ 15. Whenever things go wrong I say to myself, "I don't like this, I can't stand it."

_____ 16. I usually find a cure for my own depression when it occurs.

_____ 17. Once I am depressed it takes me a long while to recover.

_____ 18. I feel that when I become depressed or unhappy it is caused by other people or the events that happen.

_____ 19. People have little or no ability to control their sorrows or rid themselves of their negative feelings.

_____ 20. When I become angry I usually control my anger.

_____ 21. I can usually control my appetite for food and alcohol.

_____ 22. The value of a human being is directly proportionate to her/his accomplishments; if s/he is not thoroughly competent and adequate in achieving, s/he might as well curl up and die.

_____ 23. The important part of playing the game is that you succeed.

_____ 24. I feel bad when my achievement level is lower than others'.

_____ 25. I feel that I must succeed at everything I undertake.

_____ 26. When I feel doubts about potential success, I avoid participating and risking the chance of failure.

_____ 27. When I set out to accomplish a task I stick with it to the end.

_____ 28. If I find difficulties in life, I discipline myself to face them.

_____ 29. If I try to do something and encounter problems, I give up easily.

_____ 30. I find it difficult to work at tasks that have a long-range payoff.

_____ 31. I usually like to face my problems head on.

_____ 32. A person never learns from his/her mistakes.

_____ 33. Life is what you make of it.

_____ 34. Unhappy childhoods inevitably lead to problems in adult life.

_____ 35. I try not to brood over past mistakes.

_____ 36. People who are selfish make me mad because they really should not be that way.

_____ 37. If I had to nag someone to get what I wanted I would not think it was worth the trouble.

_____ 38. I frequently find that life is boring.

_____ 39. I often wish that something new and exciting would happen.

_____ 40. I experience life as just the same old thing from day to day.

_____ 41. I often wish life were more stimulating.

_____ 42. I often feel that everything is tiresome and dull.

_____ 43. I wish I could change places with someone who lives an exciting life.

_____ 44. I often wish life were different than it is.

Scoring the Scale

To score this scale, you must reverse the numbers you entered for 12 of the items. The responses to be reversed are those for items 1, 3, 4, 13, 16, 20, 21, 27, 28, 31, 33, and 35. For each of these items, make the following conversions: If you chose 1, change it to 5. If you chose 2, change it to 4. If you chose 3, leave it unchanged. If you chose 4, change it to 2. If you chose 5, change it to 1.

Now add up the numbers for all 44 items, using the new numbers for the reversed items. This sum, which should fall somewhere between 44 and 220, is your score on the Barnes-Vulcano Rationality Test. Enter it below.

My score _____

What the Scale Measures

Devised by Gordon Barnes and Brent Vulcano (1982), the Barnes-Vulcano Rationality Test (BVRT) measures the degree to which people do or do not subscribe to the irrational assumptions described by Albert Ellis (1973). As Chapter 4 in your text explains, Ellis believes that troublesome emotions and overreactions to stress are caused by negative self-talk or catastrophic thinking. Such thinking is thought to be derived from irrational assumptions that people hold. The items on the BVRT are based on 10 of the irrational assumptions described by Ellis, such as the idea that one must receive love and affection from certain people, or the idea that one must be thoroughly competent in all endeavors.

The scale is set up so that high scores indicate that one tends to think relatively rationally, whereas low scores indicate that one is prone to the irrational thinking described by Ellis. The BVRT has excellent reliability, and the authors took steps to minimize contamination from social desirability bias. Evidence regarding the test's validity can be gleaned from various correlational analyses. For example, high scores on the BVRT have been found to correlate negatively with measures of neuroticism ($-.50$), depression ($-.55$), and fear ($-.31$), indicating that respondents who score high on the test tend to be less neurotic, depressed, or fearful than those who score lower.

Interpreting Your Score

Our norms, which are shown below, are based on combined data from two sets of adults studied by Barnes and Vulcano (1982). The first sample consisted of 172 subjects (with a mean age of 22), and the second included 177 subjects (with a mean age of 27).

Norms

High score:	166–220
Medium score:	136–165
Low score:	44–135

Source: From Barnes, G. E., & Vulcano, B. A. (1982). Measuring rationality independent of social desirability. *Personality and Individual Differences, 3,* 303–309. Reprinted with permission from Elsevier and Brent Vulcano.

EXERCISE 4.2 *Self-Reflection:* Analyzing Coping Strategies

1. You just generally feel "lousy" but are unsure as to what might be causing it. How would you go about figuring out what is wrong? What questions would you ask yourself to ensure that you come to an accurate conclusion?

2. What are some of the phrases that a person might use who is operating in the mode of "learned helplessness"? How could you help individuals tell the difference between something they have control over and something they do not?

3. Rationalization is a mechanism fraught with consequences. List some negative consequences of rationalization in the following areas: school, work, home, and relationships.

4. Discuss the issue of deadlines as they apply to any area of your life. How do you react to deadline pressures? What are some positive and negative coping strategies you have used in dealing with deadlines?

5. How do you explain negative events that occur in your life? What is your explanatory style?

EXERCISE 5.1 *Self-Assessment:* Multidimensional Health Locus of Control Scales

INSTRUCTIONS

Each item below is a belief statement with which you may agree or disagree. Beside each statement is a scale that ranges from strongly disagree (1) to strongly agree (6). For each item we would like you to circle the number that represents the extent to which you agree or disagree with that statement. The more you agree with a statement, the higher will be the number you circle. The more you disagree with a statement, the lower will be the number you circle. Please make sure that you answer *every item* and that you circle *only one* number per item. This is a measure of your personal beliefs; obviously, there are no right or wrong answers. The scale for responding is shown below.

1	2	3	4	5	6
Strongly disagree	Moderately disagree	Slightly disagree	Slightly agree	Moderately agree	Strongly agree

The Scale

1. If I become sick, I have the power to make myself well again.
   1   2   3   4   5   6

2. Often I feel that no matter what I do, if I am going to get sick, I will get sick.
   1   2   3   4   5   6

3. If I see an excellent doctor regularly, I am less likely to have health problems.
   1   2   3   4   5   6

4. It seems that my health is greatly influenced by accidental happenings.
   1   2   3   4   5   6

5. I can only maintain my health by consulting health professionals.
   1   2   3   4   5   6

6. I am directly responsible for my health.
   1   2   3   4   5   6

7. Other people play a big part in whether I stay healthy or become sick.
   1   2   3   4   5   6

8. Whatever goes wrong with my health is my own fault.
   1   2   3   4   5   6

9. When I am sick, I just have to let nature run its course.
   1   2   3   4   5   6

10. Health professionals keep me healthy.
    1   2   3   4   5   6

11. When I stay healthy, I'm just plain lucky.
    1   2   3   4   5   6

12. My physical well-being depends on how well I take care of myself.
    1   2   3   4   5   6

13. When I feel ill, I know it is because I have not been taking care of myself properly.
    1   2   3   4   5   6

14. The type of care I receive from other people is what is responsible for how well I recover from an illness.
    1   2   3   4   5   6

15. Even when I take care of myself, it's easy to get sick.
    1   2   3   4   5   6

16. When I become ill, it's a matter of fate.
    1   2   3   4   5   6

17. I can pretty much stay healthy by taking good care of myself.
    1   2   3   4   5   6

18. Following doctor's orders to the letter is the best way for me to stay healthy.
    1   2   3   4   5   6

Scoring the Scale

This assessment instrument actually consists of three subscales that measure health-related attitudes and beliefs. In the blanks below record the numbers you circled for the indicated items. Then add up the numbers in each column to calculate your score on each subscale. Record your score for each scale in the Total space at the bottom of each column.

IHLC Scale	PHLC Scale	CHLC Scale
1. _____	3. _____	2. _____
6. _____	5. _____	4. _____
8. _____	7. _____	9. _____
12. _____	10. _____	11. _____
13. _____	14. _____	15. _____
17. _____	18. _____	16. _____
Total _____	Total _____	Total _____

What the Scale Measures

These scales all relate to a personality dimension called *locus of control* originally described by Julian Rotter (1966). Locus of control is a generalized expectancy about the degree to which individuals control their outcomes. Individuals with an *external locus of control* believe that their successes and failures are governed by external factors such as fate, luck, and chance. They feel that their outcomes are largely beyond their control—that they're pawns of fate. In contrast, individuals with an *internal locus of control* believe that their successes and failures are determined by their actions and abilities (internal, or personal, factors). They consequently feel that they have more influence over their outcomes than people with an external locus of control. Of course, locus of control is not an either-or proposition. Like any other dimension of personality, it should be thought of as occurring on a continuum. Some people are very external, some are very internal, but most people fall somewhere in between.

Developed by Wallston, Wallston, and DeVellis (1978), the *Multidimensional Health Locus of Control Scales* assess individuals' locus of control in relation to health concerns. The *Internal Health Locus of Control Scale* (*IHLC*) measures internality in the realm of health. The other two scales measure different aspects of externality. The *Powerful Others Health Locus of Control Scale* (*PHLC*) measures a form of externality marked by the belief that one's health rests in the hands of medical personnel. The *Chance Health Locus of Control Scale* (*CHLC*) assesses a form of externality marked by the belief that one's health is a matter of chance and luck. The assumption underlying these scales is that people's scores should predict health-related behaviors, such as seeking information related to health issues, engaging in preventive measures to maintain good health, and adherence to medical advice. Some studies have provided support for this assumption, although the findings have been a mixed bag and the observed correlations have generally been rather modest (Wallston, 2005).

Interpreting Your Score

Our norms are based on data from Wallston, Wallston, and DeVellis (1978). Our cutoffs for high and low scores are based on being one standard deviation above or below the mean.

Norms

	IHLC	PHLC	CHLC
High score:	30–36	27–36	21–36
Intermediate score:	21–29	15–26	10–20
Low score:	0–20	0–15	0–9

Source: Scale reproduced with permission of Kenneth A. Wallston, Ph.D.

EXERCISE 5.2 *Self-Reflection:* How Do Your Health Habits Rate?

	Almost Always	Sometimes	Almost Never
Eating Habits			
1. I eat a variety of foods each day, such as fruits and vegetables, whole-grain breads and cereals, lean meats, dairy products, dry peas and beans, and nuts and seeds.	4	1	0
2. I limit the amount of fat, saturated fat, and cholesterol I eat (including fat on meats, eggs, butter, cream, shortenings, and organ meats such as liver).	2	1	0
3. I limit the amount of salt I eat by cooking with only small amounts, not adding salt at the table, and avoiding salty snacks.	2	1	0
4. I avoid eating too much sugar (especially frequent snacks of sticky candy or soft drinks).	2	1	0

Eating Habits Score: _____

	Almost Always	Sometimes	Almost Never
Exercise/Fitness			
1. I maintain a desired weight, avoiding overweight and underweight.	3	1	0
2. I do vigorous exercises for 15 to 30 minutes at least three times a week (examples include running, swimming, and brisk walking).	3	1	0
3. I do exercises that enhance my muscle tone for 15 to 30 minutes at least three times a week (examples include yoga and calisthenics).	2	1	0
4. I use part of my leisure time participating in individual, family, or team activities that increase my level of fitness (such as gardening, bowling, golf, and baseball).	2	1	0

Exercise/Fitness Score: _____

	Almost Always	Sometimes	Almost Never
Alcohol and Drugs			
1. I avoid drinking alcoholic beverages or I drink no more than one or two drinks a day.	4	1	0
2. I avoid using alcohol or other drugs (especially illegal drugs) as a way of handling stressful situations or the problems in my life.	2	1	0
3. I am careful not to drink alcohol when taking certain medicines (for example, medicine for sleeping, pain, colds, and allergies).	2	1	0
4. I read and follow the label directions when using prescribed and over-the-counter drugs.	2	1	0

Alcohol and Drugs Score: _____

What Your Scores Mean:

9–10	**Excellent**
6–8	**Good**
3–5	**Mediocre**
0–2	**Poor**

Do any of your scores surprise you? Why?

Source: © Cengage Learning

EXERCISE 6.1 *Self-Assessment:* Self-Monitoring Scale

INSTRUCTIONS

The statements below concern your personal reactions to a number of situations. No two statements are exactly alike, so consider each statement carefully before answering. If a statement is true or mostly true as applied to you, mark T as your answer. If a statement is false or not usually true as applied to you, mark F as your answer. It is important that you answer as frankly and as honestly as you can. Record your responses in the spaces provided on the left.

The Scale

_____ 1. I find it hard to imitate the behavior of other people.

_____ 2. My behavior is usually an expression of my true inner feelings, attitudes, and beliefs.

_____ 3. At parties and social gatherings, I do not attempt to do or say things that others will like.

_____ 4. I can only argue for ideas I already believe.

_____ 5. I can make impromptu speeches even on topics about which I have almost no information.

_____ 6. I guess I put on a show to impress or entertain people.

_____ 7. When I am uncertain how to act in a social situation, I look to the behavior of others for cues.

_____ 8. I would probably make a good actor.

_____ 9. I rarely need the advice of my friends to choose movies, books, or music.

_____ 10. I sometimes appear to others to be experiencing deeper emotions than I actually am.

_____ 11. I laugh more when I watch a comedy with others than when alone.

_____ 12. In a group of people I am rarely the center of attention.

_____ 13. In different situations and with different people, I often act like very different persons.

_____ 14. I am not particularly good at making other people like me.

_____ 15. Even if I am not enjoying myself, I often pretend to be having a good time.

_____ 16. I'm not always the person I appear to be.

_____ 17. I would not change my opinions (or the way I do things) in order to please someone else or win their favor.

_____ 18. I have considered being an entertainer.

_____ 19. In order to get along and be liked, I tend to be what people expect me to be rather than anything else.

_____ 20. I have never been good at games like charades or improvisational acting.

_____ 21. I have trouble changing my behavior to suit different people and different situations.

_____ 22. At a party, I let others keep the jokes and stories going.

_____ 23. I feel a bit awkward in company and do not show up quite so well as I should.

_____ 24. I can look anyone in the eye and tell a lie with a straight face (if for a right end).

_____ 25. I may deceive people by being friendly when I really dislike them.

Scoring the Scale

The scoring key is reproduced below. You should circle your response of true or false each time it corresponds to the keyed response below. Add up the number of responses you circle. This total is your score on the Self-Monitoring Scale. Record your score below.

1. False	6. True	11. True	16. True	21. False
2. False	7. True	12. False	17. False	22. False
3. False	8. True	13. True	18. True	23. False
4. False	9. False	14. False	19. True	24. True
5. True	10. True	15. True	20. False	25. True

My Score _____

What the Scale Measures

Developed by Mark Snyder (1974), the Self-Monitoring (SM) Scale measures the extent to which you consciously use impression management strategies in social interactions. Basically, the scale assesses the degree to which you manipulate the nonverbal signals that you send to others and the degree to which you adjust your behavior to situational demands. Research shows that some people work harder at managing their public images than others do.

In his original study, Snyder (1974) reported very reasonable test-retest reliability (.83 for one month) and, for an initial study, provided ample evidence regarding the scale's validity. In assessing the validity of the scale, he found that in comparison to low SM subjects, high SM subjects were rated by peers as being better at emotional self-control and better at figuring out how to behave appropriately in new social situations. Furthermore, Snyder found that stage actors tended to score higher on the scale than undergraduates, as one would expect. Additionally, Ickes and Barnes (1977) summarize evidence that high SM people are (1) very sensitive to situational cues, (2) particularly skilled at detecting deception on the part of others, and (3) especially insightful about how to influence the emotions of others.

Interpreting Your Score

Our norms are based on guidelines provided by Ickes and Barnes (1977). The divisions are based on data from 207 undergraduate subjects.

Norms

High score:	15–22
Intermediate score:	9–14
Low score:	0–8

Source: From Snyder, M. (1974). Self-monitoring of expressive behavior. *Journal of Personality and Social Psychology, 330,* 526–537. Table 1, p. 531 (adapted). Copyright © 1974 by the American Psychological Association. Adapted with permission of the publisher and Mark Snyder. No further reproduction or distribution is permitted without written permission from the American Psychological Association.

Below you will find a list of 15 traits, each portrayed on a 9-point continuum. Mark with an X where you think you fall on each trait. Try to be candid and accurate; these marks will collectively describe a portion of your self-concept. When you are finished, go back and circle where you *wish* you could be on each dimension. These marks describe your self-ideal. Finally, in the spaces on the right, indicate the size of the discrepancy between self-concept and self-ideal for each trait (subtract one score from the other).

1. Decisive   Indecisive   _____
   9   8   7   6   5   4   3   2   1

2. Anxious   Relaxed   _____
   9   8   7   6   5   4   3   2   1

3. Easily influenced   Independent thinker   _____
   9   8   7   6   5   4   3   2   1

4. Very intelligent   Less intelligent   _____
   9   8   7   6   5   4   3   2   1

5. In good physical shape   In poor physical shape   _____
   9   8   7   6   5   4   3   2   1

6. Undependable   Dependable   _____
   9   8   7   6   5   4   3   2   1

7. Deceitful   Honest   _____
   9   8   7   6   5   4   3   2   1

8. A leader   A follower   _____
   9   8   7   6   5   4   3   2   1

9. Unambitious   Ambitious   _____
   9   8   7   6   5   4   3   2   1

10. Self-confident   Insecure   _____
    9   8   7   6   5   4   3   2   1

11. Conservative   Adventurous   _____
    9   8   7   6   5   4   3   2   1

12. Extraverted   Introverted   _____
    9   8   7   6   5   4   3   2   1

13. Physically attractive   Physically unattractive   _____
    9   8   7   6   5   4   3   2   1

14. Lazy   Hardworking   _____
    9   8   7   6   5   4   3   2   1

15. Funny   Little sense of humor   _____
    9   8   7   6   5   4   3   2   1

Overall, how would you describe the discrepancy between your self-concept and your self-ideal (large, moderate, small, large on a few dimensions)?

How do sizable gaps on any of the traits affect your self-esteem?

Do you feel that any of the gaps exist because you have had others' ideals imposed on you or because you have thoughtlessly accepted others' ideals?

Source: © Cengage Learning

EXERCISE 7.1 *Self-Assessment:* Argumentativeness Scale

INSTRUCTIONS

This questionnaire contains statements about arguing controversial issues. Indicate how often each statement is true for you personally by placing the appropriate number in the blank to the left of the statement:

1	2	3	4	5
Almost Never True	Rarely True	Occasionally True	Often True	Almost Always True

The Scale

_____ 1. While in an argument, I worry that the person I am arguing with will form a negative impression of me.

_____ 2. Arguing over controversial issues improves my intelligence.

_____ 3. I enjoy avoiding arguments.

_____ 4. I am energetic and enthusiastic when I argue.

_____ 5. Once I finish an argument I promise myself that I will not get into another.

_____ 6. Arguing with a person creates more problems for me than it solves.

_____ 7. I have a pleasant, good feeling when I win a point in an argument.

_____ 8. When I finish arguing with someone I feel nervous and upset.

_____ 9. I enjoy a good argument over a controversial issue.

_____ 10. I get an unpleasant feeling when I realize I am about to get into an argument.

_____ 11. I enjoy defending my point of view on an issue.

_____ 12. I am happy when I keep an argument from happening.

_____ 13. I do not like to miss the opportunity to argue a controversial issue.

_____ 14. I prefer being with people who rarely disagree with me.

_____ 15. I consider an argument an exciting intellectual challenge.

_____ 16. I find myself unable to think of effective points during an argument.

_____ 17. I feel refreshed and satisfied after an argument on a controversial issue.

_____ 18. I have the ability to do well in an argument.

_____ 19. I try to avoid getting into arguments.

_____ 20. I feel excitement when I expect that a conversation I am in is leading to an argument.

Scoring the Scale

Add up the numbers that you have recorded for items 2, 4, 7, 9, 11, 13, 15, 17, 18, and 20. This total reflects your tendency to approach argumentative situations. Next, add up the numbers that you have recorded for items 1, 3, 5, 6, 8, 10, 12, 14, 16, and 19. This total reflects your tendency to avoid getting into arguments. Record these subtotals in the spaces below. Subtract your avoidance score from your approach score to arrive at your overall score.

_____	−	_____	=	_____
Approach score		**Avoidance score**		**Total score**

What the Scale Measures

This questionnaire measures an aspect of your social influence behavior. Specifically, it assesses your tendency to argue with others in persuasive efforts. Persons who score high on this scale are not bashful about tackling controversial issues, are willing to attack others verbally to make their points, and are less compliant than the average person. Developed by Infante and Rancer (1982), this scale has high test-retest reliability (.91 for a period of one week). Examinations of the scale's validity show that it correlates well with other measures of communication tendencies and with friends' ratings of subjects' argumentativeness.

Interpreting Your Score

Our norms are based on the responses of over 800 undergraduate subjects studied by Infante and Rancer (1982).

Norms
High score:	**16 and above**
Intermediate score:	**6 to 15**
Low score:	**7 and below**

Source: From Infante, D. A., & Rancer, A. S. (1982). A Conceptualization and measure of argumentativeness. *Journal of Personality Assessment, 46,* 72–80. Copyright © Lawrence Erlbaum Associates, Inc. Reprinted by permission of Taylor & Francis, and Dominic Infante.

EXERCISE 7.2 *Self-Reflection:* Can You Identify Your Prejudicial Stereotypes?

1. List and briefly describe examples of three prejudicial stereotypes that you hold or have held at one time.

   Example 1:

   Example 2:

   Example 3:

2. Try to identify the sources (family, friends, media, etc.) of each of these stereotypes.

   Example 1:

   Example 2:

   Example 3:

3. For each stereotype, how much actual interaction have you had with the stereotyped group, and has this interaction affected your views?

   Example 1:

   Example 2:

   Example 3:

4. Can you think of any ways in which the fundamental attribution error or defensive attribution has contributed to these stereotypes?

   Fundamental attribution error:

   Defensive attribution:

Source: © Cengage Learning

EXERCISE 8.1 *Self-Assessment:* Opener Scale

INSTRUCTIONS

For each statement, indicate your degree of agreement or disagreement, using the scale shown below. Record your responses in the spaces on the left.

4 = I strongly agree
3 = I slightly agree
2 = I am certain
1 = I slightly disagree
0 = I strongly disagree

The Scale

_____ 1. People frequently tell me about themselves.

_____ 2. I've been told that I'm a good listener.

_____ 3. I'm very accepting of others.

_____ 4. People trust me with their secrets.

_____ 5. I easily get people to "open up."

_____ 6. People feel relaxed around me.

_____ 7. I enjoy listening to people.

_____ 8. I'm sympathetic to people's problems.

_____ 9. I encourage people to tell me how they are feeling.

_____ 10. I can keep people talking about themselves.

Scoring the Scale

This scale is easy to score! Simply add up the numbers that you have recorded in the spaces on the left. This total is your score on the Opener Scale.

My Score _____

What the Scale Measures

Devised by Lynn Miller, John Berg, and Richard Archer (1983), the Opener Scale is intended to measure your perception of your ability to get others to "open up" around you. In other words, the scale assesses your tendency to elicit intimate self-disclosure from people.

The items assess your perceptions of (a) others' reactions to you ("People feel relaxed around me"), (b) your interest in listening ("I enjoy listening to people"), and (c) your interpersonal skills ("I can keep people talking about themselves").

In spite of its brevity, the scale has reasonable test-retest reliability (.69 over a period of six weeks). Correlations with other personality measures were modest, but in the expected directions. For instance, scores on the Opener Scale correlate positively with a measure of empathy and negatively with a measure of shyness. Further evidence for the validity of the scale was obtained in a laboratory study of interactions between same-sex strangers. Subjects who scored high on the scale compared to those who scored low elicited more self-disclosure from people who weren't prone to engage in much disclosure.

Interpreting Your Score

Our norms are based on the original sample of 740 undergraduates studied by Miller, Berg, and Archer (1983). They found a small but statistically significant difference between males and females.

Norms

	Females	Males
High score:	35–40	33–40
Intermediate score:	26–34	23–32
Low score:	0–25	0–22

Source: From Miler, L. C., Berg, J. H., & Archer, R. L. (1983). Openers: individuals who elicit intimate self-disclosure. *Journal of Personality and Social Psychology, 44,* 1234–1244. Table 1, p. 1235 (adapted). Copyright © 1983 by the American Psychological Association. Adapted with permission of the publisher and R. L. Archer. No further reproduction or distribution is permitted without written permission from the American Psychological Association.

EXERCISE 8.2 *Self-Reflection:* How Do You Feel About Self-Disclosure?

This exercise is intended to make you think about your self-disclosure behavior. Begin by finishing the incomplete sentences below (adapted from Egan, 1977). Go through the sentences fairly quickly; do not ponder your responses too long. There are no right or wrong answers.

1. I dislike people who . . .

2. Those who really know me . . .

3. When I let someone know something I don't like about myself . . .

4. When I'm in a group of strangers . . .

5. I envy . . .

6. I get hurt when . . .

7. I daydream about . . .

8. Few people know that I . . .

9. One thing I really dislike about myself is . . .

10. When I share my values with someone . . .

Based on your responses to the incomplete sentences, do you feel you engage in the right amount of self-disclosure? Too little? Too much?

In general, what prevents you from engaging in self-disclosure?

Are there particular topics on which you find it difficult to be self-disclosing?

Are you the recipient of much self-disclosure from others, or do people have difficulty opening up to you?

CHAPTER 9 FRIENDSHIP AND LOVE

EXERCISE 9.1 *Self-Assessment:* **Social Avoidance and Distress Scale**

INSTRUCTIONS

The statements below inquire about your personal reactions to a variety of situations. Consider each statement carefully. Then indicate whether the statement is true or false in regard to your typical behavior. Record your responses (T or F) in the space provided on the left.

The Scale

_____ 1. I feel relaxed even in unfamiliar social situations.

_____ 2. I try to avoid situations that force me to be very sociable.

_____ 3. It is easy for me to relax when I am with strangers.

_____ 4. I have no particular desire to avoid people.

_____ 5. I often find social occasions upsetting.

_____ 6. I usually feel calm and comfortable at social occasions.

_____ 7. I am usually at ease when talking to someone of the opposite sex.

_____ 8. I try to avoid talking to people unless I know them well.

_____ 9. If the chance comes to meet new people, I often take it.

_____ 10. I often feel nervous or tense in casual get-togethers in which both sexes are present.

_____ 11. I am usually nervous with people unless I know them well.

_____ 12. I usually feel relaxed when I am with a group of people.

_____ 13. I often want to get away from people.

_____ 14. I usually feel uncomfortable when I am in a group of people I don't know.

_____ 15. I usually feel relaxed when I meet someone for the first time.

_____ 16. Being introduced to people makes me tense and nervous.

_____ 17. Even though a room is full of strangers, I may enter it anyway.

_____ 18. I would avoid walking up and joining a large group of people.

_____ 19. When my superiors want to talk with me, I talk willingly.

_____ 20. I often feel on edge when I am with a group of people.

_____ 21. I tend to withdraw from people.

_____ 22. I don't mind talking to people at parties or social gatherings.

_____ 23. I am seldom at ease in a large group of people.

_____ 24. I often think up excuses in order to avoid social engagements.

_____ 25. I sometimes take the responsibility for introducing people to each other.

_____ 26. I try to avoid formal social occasions.

_____ 27. I usually go to whatever social engagements I have.

_____ 28. I find it easy to relax with other people.

Scoring the Scale

The scoring key is reproduced below. Circle your true or false response each time it corresponds to the keyed response below. Add up the number of responses you circle, and this total is your score on the Social Avoidance and Distress (SAD) Scale. Record your score below.

1. False	8. True	15. False	22. False
2. True	9. False	16. True	23. True
3. False	10. True	17. False	24. True
4. False	11. True	18. True	25. False
5. True	12. False	19. False	26. True
6. False	13. True	20. True	27. False
7. False	14. True	21. True	28. False

My Score _____

What the Scale Measures

As its name implies, this scale measures avoidance and distress in social interactions. David Watson and Ronald Friend (1969) developed the scale to assess the extent to which individuals experience discomfort, fear, and anxiety in social situations and the extent to which they therefore try to evade many kinds of social encounters. To check the validity of the scale, they used it to predict subjects' social behavior in experimentally contrived situations. As projected, they found that people who scored high on the SAD Scale were less willing than low scorers to participate in a group discussion. The high scorers also reported anticipating more anxiety about their participation in the discussion than the low scorers. Additionally, Watson and Friend found a strong negative correlation (−.76) between the SAD and a measure of affiliation drive (the need to seek the company of others).

Interpreting Your Score

Our norms are based on data collected by Watson and Friend (1969) on over 200 university students.

Norms	
High score:	**16–28**
Intermediate score:	**6–15**
Low score:	**0–5**

Source: From Watson, D. L., & Friend, R. (1969). Measure of social-evaluative anxiety. *Journal of Consulting and Clinical Psychology, 33*, 448–457. Table 1, p. 450 (adapted). Copyright © 1969 by the American Psychological Association. Adapted with permission of the publisher and David Watson. No further reproduction or distribution is permitted without written permission from the American Psychological Association.

EXERCISE 9.2 *Self-Reflection:* How Do You Relate to Friends?

The following questions (adapted from Egan, 1977) are designed to help you think about how you deal with friendships.

1. Do you have many friends or very few?

2. Whether many or few, do you usually spend a lot of time with your friends?

3. What do you like in other people—that is, what makes you choose them as friends?

4. Are the people you hang out with like you or different from you? Or are they in some ways like you and in other ways different? How?

5. Do you like to control others, to get them to do things your way? Do you let others control you? Do you give in to others much of the time?

6. Are there ways in which your friendships are one-sided?

7. What would make your friendships more satisfying?

EXERCISE 10.1 *Self-Assessment:* Passionate Love Scale

INSTRUCTIONS

We would like to know how you feel (or once felt) about the person you love, or have loved, most passionately. Some common terms for passionate love are romantic love, infatuation, love sickness, or obsessive love. Please think of the person whom you love most passionately right now. If you are not in love, please think of the last person you loved. If you have never been in love, think of the person you came closest to caring for in that way.

Try to describe the way you felt when your feelings were most intense.

Whom are you thinking of?

_____ Someone I love right now.
_____ Someone I once loved.
_____ I have never been in love.

Your answers should range from (1) Not at all true to (9) Definitely true. Enter your responses in the blank spaces before each item.

1	2	3	4	5	6	7	8	9
Not at all true								Definitely true

The Scale

_____ 1. I would feel deep despair if _____ left me.

_____ 2. Sometimes I feel I can't control my thoughts; they are obsessively on _____.

_____ 3. I feel happy when I am doing something to make _____ happy.

_____ 4. I would rather be with _____ than anyone else.

_____ 5. I'd get jealous if I thought _____ was falling in love with someone else.

_____ 6. I yearn to know all about _____.

_____ 7. I want _____ physically, emotionally, and mentally.

_____ 8. I have an endless appetite for affection from _____.

_____ 9. For me, _____ is the perfect romantic partner.

_____ 10. I sense my body responding when _____ touches me.

_____ 11. _____ always seems to be on my mind.

_____ 12. I want _____ to know me—my thoughts, my fears, and my hopes.

_____ 13. I eagerly look for signs indicating _____'s desire for me.

_____ 14. I possess a powerful attraction for _____ .

_____ 15. I get extremely depressed when things don't go right in my relationship with _____.

Scoring the Scale

Scoring this scale is extremely simple. Just add up the numbers entered in the 15 blanks above. The total is your score on the Passionate Love Scale.

My Score _____

What the Scale Measures

Developed by Elaine Hatfield and Susan Sprecher (1986), this scale measures feelings of *passionate love,* which they define as a state of intense longing for union with another. *Cognitive features* of passionate love include preoccupation with the partner, idealization of the relationship, and desire to know the other person. *Emotional features* of passionate love include sexual attraction, physiological arousal, and longing for reciprocity. *Behavioral features* include maintaining physical closeness, trying to determine how the other person feels about you, and demonstrating your love to your partner. Evidence for validity of the scale mostly consists of data showing that the scale correlates with other measures in the way that one would expect. For example, robust positive correlations have been found between the scores on the scale and measures of relationship commitment, relationship trust, relationship satisfaction, and sexual satisfaction.

Interpreting Your Score

Our norms are based on data available at Elaine Hatfield's website.

Extremely passionate: 106–135 points
Wildly, even recklessly in love

Passionate: 86–105 points
Passionate, but less intense

Average: 66–85 points
Occasional bursts of passion

Cool: 45–65 points
Tepid or infrequent passion

Extremely cool: 15–44 points
No thrill, never was

Source: Reprinted from Hatfield, E., & Sprecher, S. (1986). Measuring passionate love in intimate relationships. *Journal of Adolescence 4*(9), p. 391, Figure 1. © 1986 with permission from Elsevier and Elaine Hatfield.

EXERCISE 10.2 *Self-Reflection:* Thinking Through Your Attitudes About Marriage and Cohabitation

1. Regardless of your current marital status, what are your ideal criteria for selecting a mate?

2. How do you know if you are really ready for marriage?

3. What areas of self-awareness or knowledge of self do you feel you need to explore before you make a long-term commitment to a relationship?

4. In what ways is cohabitation a realistic preparation for marriage, and in what ways is it not?

EXERCISE 11.1 *Self-Assessment:* **Personal Attributes Questionnaire (PAQ)**

INSTRUCTIONS

The items below inquire about what kind of a person you think you are. Each item consists of a pair of characteristics, with the letters A–E in between. For example:

Not at all artistic   A   B   C   D   E   Very artistic

Each pair describes contradictory characteristics—that is, you cannot be both at the same time, such as very artistic and not at all artistic.

The letters form a scale between the two extremes. You are to enter a letter that describes where you fall on the scale. For example, if you think you have no artistic ability, you would enter A. If you think you are pretty good, you might enter D. If you are only medium, you might enter C, and so forth.

The Scale

_____	1. Not at all aggressive	A	B	C	D	E	Very aggressive
_____	2. Not at all independent	A	B	C	D	E	Very independent
_____	3. Not at all emotional	A	B	C	D	E	Very emotional
_____	4. Very submissive	A	B	C	D	E	Very dominant
_____	5. Not at all excitable in a major crisis	A	B	C	D	E	Very excitable in a major crisis
_____	6. Very passive	A	B	C	D	E	Very active
_____	7. Not at all able to devote self completely to others	A	B	C	D	E	Able to devote self completely to others
_____	8. Very rough	A	B	C	D	E	Very gentle
_____	9. Not at all helpful to others	A	B	C	D	E	Very helpful to others
_____	10. Not at all competitive	A	B	C	D	E	Very competitive
_____	11. Very home oriented	A	B	C	D	E	Very worldly
_____	12. Not at all kind	A	B	C	D	E	Very kind
_____	13. Indifferent to others' approval	A	B	C	D	E	Highly needful of others' approval
_____	14. Feelings not easily hurt	A	B	C	D	E	Feelings easily hurt
_____	15. Not at all aware of feelings of others	A	B	C	D	E	Very aware of feelings of others
_____	16. Can make decisions easily	A	B	C	D	E	Have difficulty making decisions
_____	17. Give up very easily	A	B	C	D	E	Never give up easily
_____	18. Never cry	A	B	C	D	E	Cry very easily
_____	19. Not at all self-confident	A	B	C	D	E	Very self-confident
_____	20. Feel very inferior	A	B	C	D	E	Feel very superior
_____	21. Not at all understanding of others	A	B	C	D	E	Very understanding of others
_____	22. Very cold in relations with others	A	B	C	D	E	Very warm in relations with others
_____	23. Very little need for security	A	B	C	D	E	Very strong need for security
_____	24. Go to pieces under pressure	A	B	C	D	E	Stand up well under pressure

Scoring the Scale

The Personal Attributes Questionnaire (PAQ) is made up of three 8-item subscales, but we are only going to compute scores for two of these subscales, so the first step is to eliminate the 8 items from the unused subscale. Put an X in the spaces to the left of the items for the following items: 1, 4, 5, 11, 13, 14, 18, and 23. These items belong to the subscale that we won't be using, and they can be ignored. Of the remaining items, one (item 16) is reverse-scored as follows: If you circled A, enter 4 in the space to the left of the item if you circled B, enter 3; if you circled C, enter 2; if you circled D, enter 1; and if you circled E, enter 0. All the rest of the items are scored in the following manner: A = 0, B = 1, C = 2, D = 3, and E = 4. Based on the responses you circled, enter the appropriate numbers for the remaining items in the spaces to the left of the items.

The next step is to compute your scores on the femininity and masculinity subscales of the PAQ. To compute your score on the *femininity* subscale, add up the numbers next to items 3, 7, 8, 9, 12, 15, 21, and 22, and enter your score in the space below. To compute your score on the *masculinity* subscale, add up the numbers next to items 2, 6, 10, 16, 17, 19, 20, and 24, and enter your score in the space below.

My score on the femininity subscale _____

My score on the masculinity subscale _____

What the Scale Measures

Devised by Janet Spence and Robert Helmreich (1978), the PAQ assesses masculinity and femininity in terms of respondents' self-perceived possession of various personality traits that are stereotypically believed to differentiate the sexes. The authors emphasize that the PAQ taps only limited aspects of sex roles: certain self-assertive/instrumental traits traditionally associated with masculinity and certain interpersonal/expressive traits traditionally associated with femininity. Although the PAQ should not be viewed as a global measure of masculinity and femininity, it has been widely used in research to provide a rough classification of subjects in terms of their gender-role identity. As explained in your text, people who score high in both masculinity and femininity are said to be androgynous. People who score high in femininity and low in masculinity are said to be feminine sex-typed. Those who score high in masculinity and low in femininity are characterized as masculine sex-typed, and those who score low on both dimensions are said to be sex-role undifferentiated.

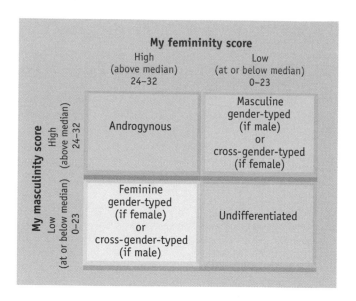

Interpreting Your Score

You can use the chart here to classify yourself in terms of gender-role identity. Our norms are based on a sample of 715 college students studied by Spence and Helmreich (1978). The cutoffs for "high" scores on the masculinity and femininity subscales are the medians for each scale. Obviously, these are arbitrary cutoffs, and results may be misleading for people who score very close to the median on either scale, as a difference of a point or two could change their classification. Hence, if either of your scores is within a couple of points of the median, you should view your gender-role classification as tentative. Also, keep in mind that the perception of some of these traits has changed over time. As mentioned in your text, some of the traditional masculine traits aren't viewed as strictly masculine today.

My classification _____

What percentage of subjects falls into each of the four gender-role categories? The exact breakdown will vary depending on the nature of the sample, but Spence and Helmreich (1978) reported the following distribution for their sample of 715 college students.

Category	Males	Females
Androgynous	25%	35%
Feminine	8%	32%
Masculine	44%	14%
Undifferentiated	23%	18%

Source: Adapted from Spence, J. T., & Helmreich, R. L. (1978). *Masculinity and femininity: Their psychological dimensions, correlates, and antecedents.* Austin: University of Texas Press. Copyright © 1978. By permission of the University of Texas Press.

EXERCISE 11.2 *Self-Reflection:* **How Do You Feel About Gender Roles?**

1. Can you recall any experiences that were particularly influential in shaping your attitudes about gender roles? If yes, give a couple of examples.

2. Have you ever engaged in cross-sex-typed behavior? Can you think of a couple of examples? How did people react?

3. Do you ever feel restricted by gender roles? If so, in what ways?

4. Have you ever been a victim of sex discrimination (sexism)? If so, describe the circumstances.

5. How do you think the transition in gender roles has affected you personally?

Source: © Cengage Learning

EXERCISE 12.1 *Self-Assessment:* Sexuality Scale

INSTRUCTIONS

For the 30 items that follow, indicate the extent of your agreement or disagreement with each statement, using the key shown below. Record your responses in the spaces to the left of the items.

+2	+1	0	−1	−2
Agree	Slightly Agree	Neither Agree nor Disagree	Slightly Disagree	Disagree

The Scale

_____ 1. I am a good sexual partner.
_____ 2. I am depressed about the sexual aspects of my life.
_____ 3. I think about sex all the time.
_____ 4. I would rate my sexual skill quite highly.
_____ 5. I feel good about my sexuality.
_____ 6. I think about sex more than anything else.
_____ 7. I am better at sex than most other people.
_____ 8. I am disappointed about the quality of my sex life.
_____ 9. I don't daydream about sexual situations.
_____ 10. I sometimes have doubts about my sexual competence.
_____ 11. Thinking about sex makes me happy.
_____ 12. I tend to be preoccupied with sex.
_____ 13. I am not very confident in sexual encounters.
_____ 14. I derive pleasure and enjoyment from sex.
_____ 15. I'm constantly thinking about having sex.
_____ 16. I think of myself as a very good sexual partner.
_____ 17. I feel down about my sex life.
_____ 18. I think about sex a great deal of the time.
_____ 19. I would rate myself low as a sexual partner.
_____ 20. I feel unhappy about my sexual relationships.
_____ 21. I seldom think about sex.
_____ 22. I am confident about myself as a sexual partner.
_____ 23. I feel pleased with my sex life.
_____ 24. I hardly ever fantasize about having sex.
_____ 25. I am not very confident about myself as a sexual partner.
_____ 26. I feel sad when I think about my sexual experiences.
_____ 27. I probably think about sex less often than most people.
_____ 28. I sometimes doubt my sexual competence.
_____ 29. I am not discouraged about sex.
_____ 30. I don't think about sex very often.

Sexual Esteem	Sexual Depression	Sexual Preoccupation
1. _____	2. _____	3. _____
4. _____	5. R _____	6. _____
7. _____	8. _____	9. R _____
10. R _____	11. R _____	12. _____
13. R _____	14. R _____	15. _____
16. _____	17. _____	18. _____
19. R _____	20. _____	21. R _____
22. _____	23. R _____	24. _____
25. R _____	26. _____	27. R _____
28. R _____	29. R _____	30. R _____
_____	_____	_____

My Scores

Scoring the Scale

To arrive at your scores on the three subscales of this questionnaire, transfer your responses into the spaces provided below. If an item number has an R next to it, this item is reverse-scored, so you should change the + or − sign in front of the number you recorded. After recording your responses, add up the numbers in each column, taking into account the algebraic sign in front of each number. The totals for each column are your scores on the three subscales of the Sexuality Scale. Record your scores at the bottom of each column.

What the Scale Measures

Developed by William Snell and Dennis Papini (1989), the Sexuality Scale measures three aspects of your sexual identity. The Sexual Esteem subscale measures your tendency to evaluate yourself in a positive way in terms of your capacity to relate sexually to others. The Sexual Depression subscale measures your tendency to feel saddened and discouraged by your ability to relate sexually to others. The Sexual Preoccupation subscale measures your tendency to become absorbed in thoughts about sex on a persistent basis.

Internal reliability is excellent. Thus far, the scale's validity has been examined through factor analysis, which can be used to evaluate the extent of overlap among the subscales. The factor analysis showed that the three subscales do measure independent aspects of one's sexuality.

Interpreting Your Score

Our norms are based on Snell and Papini's (1989) sample of 296 college students drawn from a small university in the Midwest. Significant gender differences were found only on the Sexual Preoccupation subscale, so we report separate norms for males and females only for this subscale.

Source: From Snell, W. E., & Papini, D. R. (1989). The sexuality scale: An instrument to measure sexual-esteem, sexual-depression, and sexual-preoccupation. *Journal of Sex Research, 26*(2), 256–263. Copyright © 1989 Society for Scientific Study of Sex. Reprinted with permission from Taylor & Francis and W. E. Snell.

Norms

	Sexual Esteem Both sexes	Sexual Depression Both sexes	Sexual Preoccupation Males	Sexual Preoccupation Females
High score:	+14 to +20	+1 to +20	+8 to +20	−1 to +20
Intermediate score:	0 to +13	−12 to 0	−2 to +7	−10 to −2
Low score:	−20 to −1	−20 to −13	−20 to −3	−20 to −11

1. Who do you feel was most important in shaping your attitudes regarding sexual behavior (parents, teachers, peers, early girlfriend or boyfriend, and so forth)?

2. What was the nature of their influence?

3. If the answer to the first question was not your parents, what kind of information did you get at home? Were your parents comfortable talking about sex?

4. In childhood, were you ever made to feel shameful, guilty, or fearful about sex? How?

5. Were your parents open or secretive about their own sex lives?

6. Do you feel comfortable with your sexuality today?

CHAPTER 13 CAREERS AND WORK

EXERCISE 13.1 *Self-Assessment:* Assertive Job-Hunting Survey

INSTRUCTIONS

This inventory is designed to provide information about the way in which you look for a job. Picture yourself in each of these job-hunting situations and indicate how likely it is that you would respond in the described manner. If you have never job-hunted before, answer according to how you would try to find a job. Please record your responses in the spaces to the left of the items. Use the following key for your responses:

1	2	3	4	5	6
Very Unlikely	Somewhat Unlikely	Slightly Unlikely	Slightly Likely	Somewhat Likely	Very Likely

The Scale

_____ 1. When asked to indicate my experiences for a position, I would mention only my paid work experience.

_____ 2. If I heard someone talking about an interesting job opening, I'd be reluctant to ask for more information unless I knew the person.

_____ 3. I would ask an employer who did not have an opening if he knew of other employers who might have job openings.

_____ 4. I downplay my qualifications so that an employer won't think I'm more qualified than I really am.

_____ 5. I would rather use an employment agency to find a job than apply to employers directly.

_____ 6. Before an interview, I would contact an employee of the organization to learn more about that organization.

_____ 7. I hesitate to ask questions when I'm being interviewed for a job.

_____ 8. I avoid contacting potential employers by phone or in person because I feel they are too busy to talk with me.

_____ 9. If an interviewer were very late for my interview, I would leave or arrange for another appointment.

_____ 10. I believe an experienced employment counselor would have a better idea of what jobs I should apply for than I would have.

_____ 11. If a secretary told me that a potential employer was too busy to see me, I would stop trying to contact that employer.

_____ 12. Getting the job I want is largely a matter of luck.

_____ 13. I'd directly contact the person for whom I would be working, rather than the personnel department of an organization.

_____ 14. I am reluctant to ask professors or supervisors to write letters of recommendation for me.

_____ 15. I would not apply for a job unless I had all the qualifications listed on the published job description.

_____ 16. I would ask an employer for a second interview if I felt the first one went poorly.

_____ 17. I am reluctant to contact an organization about employment unless I know there is a job opening.

_____ 18. If I didn't get a job, I would call the employer and ask how I could improve my chances for a similar position.

_____ 19. I feel uncomfortable asking friends for job leads.

_____ 20. With the job market as tight as it is, I had better take whatever job I can get.

_____ 21. If the personnel office refused to refer me for an interview, I would directly contact the person I wanted to work for, if I felt qualified for the position.

_____ 22. I would rather interview with recruiters who come to the college campus than contact employers directly.

_____ 23. If an interviewer says "I'll contact you if there are any openings," I figure there's nothing else I can do.

_____ 24. I'd check out available job openings before deciding what kind of job I'd like to have.

_____ 25. I am reluctant to contact someone I don't know for information about career fields in which I am interested.

Scoring the Scale

To score this scale, you have to begin by reversing your responses on 18 of the items. On these items, convert the response you entered as follows: 1 = 6, 2 = 5, 3 = 4, 4 = 3, 5 = 2, and 6 = 1. The items to be reversed are 1, 2, 4, 5, 7, 8, 10, 11, 12, 14, 15, 17, 19, 20, 22, 23, 24, and 25. After making your reversals, add up the numbers that you have recorded for the 25 items on the scale. This total is your score on the Assertive Job-Hunting Survey.

My Score _____

What the Scale Measures

Developed by Heather Becker, Susan Brown, Pat LaFitte, Mary Jo Magruder, Bob Murff, and Bill Phillips, this scale measures your job-seeking style (Becker, 1980). Some people conduct a job search in a relatively passive way—waiting for jobs to come to them. Others tend to seek jobs in a more vigorous, assertive manner. They act on their environment to procure needed information, obtain helpful contacts, and get their foot in the door at attractive companies. This scale measures your tendency to pursue jobs assertively.

Test-retest reliability for this scale is reasonable (.77 for an interval of two weeks). The scale's validity has been supported by demonstrations that subjects' scores increase as a result of training programs designed to enhance their job-hunting assertiveness. Also, those who have job-hunted before tend to score higher than those who have never job-hunted.

Interpreting Your Score

Our norms are based on a sample of college students who had applied to a university counseling center for career-planning assistance

Norms
High score:	117–150
Intermediate score:	95–116
Low score:	0–94

Source: Adapted from Becker, H., Brown, S., Lafitte, P., Magruder, M. J., Murff, B., & Phillips, B. (1980). Assertive job-hunting survey. *Measurement and Evaluation in Guidance, (13)*1, 43–48.

Important vocational decisions require information. Your assignment in this exercise is to pick a vocation and research it. You should begin by reading some occupational literature. Then you should interview someone in the field. Use the outline below to summarize your findings.

1. *The nature of the work.* What are the duties and responsibilities on a day-to-day basis?

2. *Working conditions.* Is the working environment pleasant or unpleasant, low-key or high-pressure?

3. *Job entry requirements.* What kind of education and training are required to break into this occupational area?

4. *Potential earnings.* What are entry-level salaries, and how much can you hope to earn if you're exceptionally successful?

5. *Opportunities for advancement.* How do you move up in this field? Are there adequate opportunities for promotion and advancement?

6. *Intrinsic job satisfactions.* What can you derive in the way of personal satisfaction from this job?

7. *Future outlook.* How is supply and demand projected to shape up in the future for this occupational area?

EXERCISE 14.1 *Self-Assessment:* Manifest Anxiety Scale

INSTRUCTIONS

The statements below inquire about your behavior and emotions. Consider each statement carefully. Then indicate whether the statement is generally true or false for you. Record your responses (T or F) in the spaces provided.

The Scale

_____ 1. I do not tire quickly.

_____ 2. I believe I am no more nervous than most others.

_____ 3. I have very few headaches.

_____ 4. I work under a great deal of tension.

_____ 5. I frequently notice my hand shakes when I try to do something.

_____ 6. I blush no more often than others.

_____ 7. I have diarrhea once a month or more.

_____ 8. I worry quite a bit over possible misfortunes.

_____ 9. I practically never blush.

_____ 10. I am often afraid that I am going to blush.

_____ 11. My hands and feet are usually warm enough.

_____ 12. I sweat very easily even on cool days.

_____ 13. Sometimes when embarrassed, I break out in a sweat that annoys me greatly.

_____ 14. I hardly ever notice my heart pounding, and I am seldom short of breath.

_____ 15. I feel hungry almost all the time.

_____ 16. I am very seldom troubled by constipation.

_____ 17. I have a great deal of stomach trouble.

_____ 18. I have had periods in which I lost sleep over worry.

_____ 19. I am easily embarrassed.

_____ 20. I am more sensitive than most other people.

_____ 21. I frequently find myself worrying about something.

_____ 22. I wish I could be as happy as others seem to be.

_____ 23. I am usually calm and not easily upset.

_____ 24. I feel anxiety about something or someone almost all the time.

_____ 25. I am happy most of the time.

_____ 26. It makes me nervous to have to wait.

_____ 27. Sometimes I become so excited that I find it hard to get to sleep.

_____ 28. I have sometimes felt that difficulties were piling up so high that I could not overcome them.

_____ 29. I must admit that I have at times been worried beyond reason over something that really did not matter.

_____ 30. I have very few fears compared to my friends.

_____ 31. I certainly feel useless at times.

_____ 32. I find it hard to keep my mind on a task or job.

_____ 33. I am unusually self-conscious.

_____ 34. I am inclined to take things hard.

_____ 35. At times I think I am no good at all.

_____ 36. I am certainly lacking in self-confidence.

_____ 37. I sometimes feel that I am about to go to pieces.

_____ 38. I am entirely self-confident.

Scoring the Scale

The scoring key is reproduced below. You should circle each of your true or false responses that correspond to the keyed responses. Add up the number of responses you circle, and this total is your score on the Manifest Anxiety Scale.

1. False	2. False	3. False	4. True
5. True	6. False	7. True	8. True
9. False	10. True	11. False	12. True
13. True	14. False	15. True	16. False
17. True	18. True	19. True	20. True
21. True	22. True	23. False	24. True
25. False	26. True	27. True	28. True
29. True	30. False	31. True	32. True
33. True	34. True	35. True	36. True
37. True	38. False		

My Score _____

What the Scale Measures

You just took a form of the Taylor Manifest Anxiety Scale (1953), as revised by Richard Suinn (1968). Suinn took the original 50-item scale and identified all items for which there was a social desirability bias (11) or a response set (1). He eliminated these 12 items and found that the scale's reliability and validity were not appreciably decreased. Essentially, the scale measures trait anxiety—that is, the tendency to experience anxiety in a wide variety of situations.

Hundreds of studies have been done on the various versions of the Taylor Manifest Anxiety Scale. The validity of the scale has been supported by demonstrations that various groups of psychiatric patients score higher than unselected groups of "normals" and by demonstrations that the scale correlates well with other measures of anxiety. Although the Manifest Anxiety Scale is no longer a "state of the art" measure of anxiety, it is an old classic that is relatively easy to score.

Interpreting Your Score

Our norms are based on data collected by Suinn (1968) on 89 undergraduates who responded to the scale anonymously.

Norms

High score:	16–38
Intermediate score:	6–15
Low score:	0–5

Source: From Taylor, J. A. (1953, April). A personality scale of manifest anxiety. *Journal of Abnormal and Social Psychology, 48*(2), 285–290. Table 1, p. 286 (adapted). Public Domain. Originally published by The American Psychological Association.

EXERCISE 14.2 *Self-Reflection:* What Are Your Attitudes on Mental Illness?

1. List seven adjectives that you associate with people who are diagnosed as mentally ill.

2. If you meet someone who was once diagnosed as mentally ill, what are your immediate reactions?

3. List some comments about people with psychological disorders that you heard when you were a child.

4. Have you had any actual interactions with "mentally ill" people that have supported or contradicted your expectations?

5. Do you agree with the idea that psychological disorders should be viewed as an illness or disease? Defend your position.

CHAPTER 15 PSYCHOTHERAPY

EXERCISE 15.1 *Self-Assessment:* Attitudes Toward Seeking Professional Psychological Help

INSTRUCTIONS

Read each statement carefully and indicate your agreement or disagreement, using the scale below. Please express your frank opinion in responding to each statement, answering as you honestly feel or believe.

0 = Disagreement
1 = Probable disagreement
2 = Probable agreement
3 = Agreement

The Scale

_____ 1. Although there are clinics for people with mental troubles, I would not have much faith in them.

_____ 2. If a good friend asked my advice about a mental health problem, I might recommend that he see a psychiatrist.

_____ 3. I would feel uneasy going to a psychiatrist because of what some people would think.

_____ 4. A person with a strong character can get over mental conflicts by himself, and would have little need of a psychiatrist.

_____ 5. There are times when I have felt completely lost and would have welcomed professional advice for a personal or emotional problem.

_____ 6. Considering the time and expense involved in psychotherapy, it would have doubtful value for a person like me.

_____ 7. I would willingly confide intimate matters to an appropriate person if I thought it might help me or a member of my family.

_____ 8. I would rather live with certain mental conflicts than go through the ordeal of getting psychiatric treatment.

_____ 9. Emotional difficulties, like many things, tend to work out by themselves.

_____ 10. There are certain problems that should not be discussed outside of one's immediate family.

_____ 11. A person with a serious emotional disturbance would probably feel most secure in a good mental hospital.

_____ 12. If I believed I was having a mental breakdown, my first inclination would be to get professional attention.

_____ 13. Keeping one's mind on a job is a good solution for avoiding personal worries and concerns.

_____ 14. Having been a psychiatric patient is a blot on a person's life.

_____ 15. I would rather be advised by a close friend than by a psychologist, even for an emotional problem.

_____ 16. A person with an emotional problem is not likely to solve it alone; he or she is likely to solve it with professional help.

_____ 17. I resent a person—professionally trained or not—who wants to know about my personal difficulties.

_____ 18. I would want to get psychiatric attention if I was worried or upset for a long period of time.

_____ 19. The idea of talking about problems with a psychologist strikes me as a poor way to get rid of emotional conflicts.

_____ 20. Having been mentally ill carries with it a burden of shame.

_____ 21. There are experiences in my life I would not discuss with anyone.

_____ 22. It is probably best not to know everything about oneself.

_____ 23. If I were experiencing a serious emotional crisis at this point in my life, I would be confident that I could find relief in psychotherapy.

_____ 24. There is something admirable in the attitude of a person who is willing to cope with his conflicts and fears without resorting to professional help.

_____ 25. At some future time I might want to have psychological counseling.

_____ 26. A person should work out his own problems; getting psychological counseling would be a last resort.

_____ 27. Had I received treatment in a mental hospital, I would not feel that it had to be "covered up."

_____ 28. If I thought I needed psychiatric help, I would get it no matter who knew about it.

_____ 29. It is difficult to talk about personal affairs with highly educated people such as doctors, teachers, and clergymen.

Scoring the Scale

Begin by reversing your response (0 = 3, 1 = 2, 2 = 1, 3 = 0) for items 1, 3, 4, 6, 8, 9, 10, 13, 14, 15, 17, 19, 20, 21, 22, 24, 26, and 29. Then add up the numbers for all 29 items on the scale. This total is your score. Record your score below.

My Score _____

What the Scale Measures

The scale assesses the degree to which you have favorable attitudes toward professional psychotherapy (Fischer & Turner, 1970). As discussed in your text, there are many negative stereotypes about therapy, and many people are reluctant to pursue therapy. This situation is unfortunate, because negative attitudes often prevent people from seeking therapy that could be beneficial to them.

Interpreting Your Score

Our norms are shown below. The higher your score, the more positive your attitudes about therapy.

Norms
High score: 64–87
Medium score: 50–63
Low score: 0–49

Source: From Fischer, E. H., & Turner, J. L. (1970). Orientation to seeking professional help: development and research utility of an attitude scale. *Journal of Consulting and Clinical Psychology, 35,* 82–83. Table 1 (adapted). Copyright © 1970 by the American Psychological Association. Adapted with permission of the publisher and Edward Fischer. No further reproduction or distribution is permitted without written permission from the American Psychological Association. For educational use only.

EXERCISE 15.2 *Self-Reflection:* What Are Your Feelings About Therapy?

1. What type of therapeutic approach do you think you would respond to best if you were seeking a therapist? In thinking about this question, consider not only theoretical approaches and professions, but whether you would prefer a male versus a female, individual therapy versus group therapy, and so on.

2. What personal traits would you look for in a therapist?

3. Do you have a sense of what your family beliefs are about psychotherapy and its use? If you had to articulate these beliefs in a few sentences, what would you say?

4. Before you read Chapter 15, what did you picture in your mind as happening in a therapy session? How accurate was that picture? What were some of your inaccurate perceptions about therapy?

5. Statistics show that more women seek psychotherapy than men. Why do you think this is so?

CHAPTER 16 POSITIVE PSYCHOLOGY

EXERCISE 16.1 *Self-Assessment:* What Is Your Happiness Profile?

INSTRUCTIONS

All of the questions below reflect statements that many people would find desirable, but answer only in terms of whether the statement describes how you actually live your life. Please be honest and accurate. Use the following scale to answer the questions:

5 = Very much like me
4 = Mostly like me
3 = Somewhat like me
2 = A little like me
1 = Not like me at all

The Scale

_____ 1. My life serves a higher purpose.

_____ 2. Life is too short to postpone the pleasures it can provide.

_____ 3. I seek out situations that challenge my skills and abilities.

_____ 4. I keep score at life.

_____ 5. Whether at work or play, I am usually "in a zone" and not conscious of myself.

_____ 6. I am always very absorbed in what I do.

_____ 7. I am rarely distracted by what is going on around me.

_____ 8. I have a responsibility to make the world a better place.

_____ 9. My life has a lasting meaning.

_____ 10. No matter what I am doing, it is important for me to win.

_____ 11. In choosing what to do, I always take into account whether it will be pleasurable.

_____ 12. What I do matters to society.

_____ 13. I want to accomplish more than other people.

_____ 14. I agree with this statement: "Life is short—eat dessert first."

_____ 15. I love to do things that excite my senses.

_____ 16. I love to compete.

Scoring the Scale

Your Orientation to Pleasure score is the sum of points for questions 2, 11, 14, and 15; your Orientation to Engagement score is the sum of points for questions 3, 5, 6, and 7; your Orientation to Meaning score is the sum of points for questions 1, 8, 9, and 12; your Orientation to Victory score is the sum of points for questions 4, 10, 13, and 16.

My Orientation to Pleasure Score _____

My Orientation to Engagement Score _____

My Orientation to Meaning Score _____

My Orientation to Victory Score _____

Interpreting Your Scores

The questionnaire measures four possible routes to happiness: through pleasure, engagement, meaning, and victory. What is your highest score of the four? This is your dominant orientation. And what is the configuration of your scores? That is, are you "high" (> 15) on all four orientations? If so, you are oriented toward a full life and are likely to be highly satisfied. Or are you "low" (< 9) on all four orientations? If so, you may have a more empty life and are likely to be dissatisfied. You might consider doing something different—anything!—in your life. And if you are high on one or two orientations, chances are that you are satisfied with life, although you might seek further opportunities for pursuing your signature way of being happy.

Source: Based on Peterson, C. (2006). *A primer in positive psychology.* New York: Oxford University Press; and Peterson, C., Park, N., & Seligman, M. E. P. (2005). Orientations to happiness and life satisfaction: The full life versus the empty life. *Journal of Happiness Studies, 6,* 25–41.

EXERCISE 16.2 *Self-Reflection:* Thinking About How You Construe Happiness

Imagine that medicine has developed a new "happiness" pill. If you take this pill everyday it will make you feel positive emotions more frequently. There are also no negative side effects, and it is inexpensive to buy. Would you take it? Why or why not?

Imagine that you have found the famous "Aladdin's Lamp" and the genie has granted you three wishes. What would you wish for? Sorry, you can't wish for more wishes.

1.

2.

3.

(a) What do your answers tell you about your idea of happiness or the good life?

(b) Are your answers based on any specific assumptions about human nature or the relationships between people and the societies they live in? What are those assumptions?

Source: Based on Compton, W. C. (2005). *An introduction to positive psychology.* Belmont, CA: Thompson/Wadsworth.